Fodor's **Road Guide USA**

Connecticut
Massachusetts
Rhode Island

First Edition

Fodor's Travel Publications
New York Toronto London Sydney Auckland
www.fodors.com

Fodor's Road Guide USA: Connecticut, Massachusetts, Rhode Island

Fodor's Travel Publications
President: Bonnie Ammer
Publisher: Kris Kliemann
Executive Managing Editor: Denise DeGennaro
Editorial Director: Karen Cure
Director of Marketing Development: Jeanne Kramer
Associate Managing Editor: Linda Schmidt
Senior Editor: Constance Jones
Director of Production and Manufacturing: Chuck Bloodgood
Creative Director: Fabrizio La Rocca

Contributors
Editor: Arabella Meyer
Additional Editing: Karen Deaver, Jennifer Kasoff, and Julie Stonberg
Writing: Michelle Bodak Acri (Connecticut), Ann Moan (Rhode Island restaurants), Jeff
Perk (Massachusetts), Valerie Russo (Massachusetts lodgings and events), and Kevin
Weaver (Rhode Island), with William Fox, Kimberly Grant, Rosalind Maringer, Ellen
McCurtin, Eric Reymond, Jordana Rosenberg, Valerie Russo, Peter Terzian, Margo Waite,
and Kirstin Weisenberger
Research: Kim Bacon, Jennifer Cohen, Helen Kasimis, Matthew Scheer, and Lindsey Sharp
Black-and-White Maps: Rebecca Baer, Robert Blake, David Lindroth, Todd Pasini
Production/Manufacturing: Robert B. Shields
Cover: Sara Gray/Stone, (background photo), Bart Nagle (photo, illustration)
Interior Photos: CT Office of Tourism/John Muldoon (Connecticut), Artville
(Massachusetts), Photodisc (Rhode Island)

Copyright
Copyright © 2001 by Fodors LLC

Color-map copyright © 2001 by Maps.com and Fodors LLC. All other maps copyright ©
2001 by Fodors LLC.

Fodor's is a registered trademark of Random House, Inc.

All rights reserved under International and Pan-American Copyright Conventions.
Published in the United States by Fodor's Travel Publications, a unit of Fodors LLC, a
subsidiary of Random House, Inc., and simultaneously in Canada by Random House of
Canada Limited, Toronto. Distributed by Random House, Inc., New York.

*No maps, illustrations, or other portions of this book may be reproduced in any form
without written permission from the publisher.*

First Edition
ISBN 0–679–00500–5
ISSN 1528–1442

Special Sales
Fodor's Travel Publications are available at special discounts for bulk purchases for sales promotions
or premiums. Special editions, including personalized covers, excerpts of existing guides, and
corporate imprints, can be created in large quantities for special needs. For more information,
contact your local bookseller or write to Special Markets, Fodor's Travel Publications, 280 Park
Avenue, New York, NY 10017. Inquiries from Canada should be directed to your local Canadian
bookseller or sent to Random House of Canada, Ltd., Marketing Department, 2775 Matheson
Boulevard East, Mississauga, Ontario L4W 4P7. Inquiries from the United Kingdom should be sent
to Fodor's Travel Publications, 20 Vauxhall Bridge Road, London SW1V 2SA, England.

PRINTED IN THE UNITED STATES OF AMERICA
10 9 8 7 6 5 4 3 2 1

CONTENTS

Great Road Trips

Of all the things that went wrong with Clark Griswold's vacation, one stands out: The theme park he had driven across the country to visit was closed when he got there. Clark, the suburban bumbler played by Chevy Chase in 1983's hilarious *National Lampoon's Vacation*, is fictional, of course. But his story is poignantly true. Although most Americans get only two precious weeks of vacation a year, many set off on their journeys with surprisingly little guidance. Many travelers find out about their destination from friends and family or wait to get travel information until they arrive in their hotel, where racks of brochures dispense the "facts," along with free city magazines. But it's hard to distinguish the truth from hype in these sources. And it makes no sense to spend priceless vacation time in a hotel room reading about a place when you could be out seeing it up close and personal.

Congratulate yourself on picking up this guide. Studying it—before you leave home—is the best possible first step toward making sure your vacation fulfills your every dream.

Inside you'll find all the tools you need to plan a perfect road trip. In the hundreds of towns we describe, you'll find thousands of places to explore. So you'll always know what's around the next bend. And with the practical information we provide, you can easily call to confirm the details that matter and study up on what you'll want to see and do, before you leave home.

By all means, when you plan your trip, allow yourself time to make a few detours. Because as wonderful as it is to visit sights you've read about, it's the serendipitous experiences that often prove the most memorable: the hole-in-the-wall diner that serves a transcendent tomato soup, the historical society gallery stuffed with dusty local curiosities of days gone by. As you whiz down the highway, use the book to find out more about the towns announced by roadside signs. Consider turning off at the next exit. And always remember: In this great country of ours, there's an adventure around every corner.

HOW TO USE THIS BOOK

Alphabetical organization should make it a snap to navigate through this book. Still, in putting it together, we've made certain decisions and used certain terms you need to know about.

LOCATIONS AND CATEGORIZATIONS

Color map coordinates are given for every town in the guide.

Attractions, restaurants, and lodging places are listed under the nearest town covered in the guide.

Parks and forests are sometimes listed under the main access point.

Exact street addresses are provided whenever possible; when they were not available or applicable, directions and/or cross-streets are indicated.

CITIES

For state capitals and larger cities, attractions are alphabetized by category. Shopping sections focus on good shopping areas where you'll find a concentration of interesting shops. We include malls only if they're unusual in some way and individual stores only when they're community institutions. Restaurants and hotels are grouped by price category then arranged alphabetically.

RESTAURANTS

All are air-conditioned unless otherwise noted, and all permit smoking unless they're identified as "no-smoking."

Dress: Assume that no jackets or ties are required for men unless otherwise noted.

Family-style service: Restaurants characterized this way serve food communally, out of serving dishes as you might at home.

Meals and hours: Assume that restaurants are open for lunch and dinner unless otherwise noted. We always specify days closed and meals not available.

Prices: The price ranges listed are for dinner entrées (or lunch entrées if no dinner is served).

Reservations: They are always a good idea. We don't mention them unless they're essential or are not accepted.

Fodor's Choice: Stars denote restaurants that are Fodor's Choices—our editors' picks of the state's very best in a given price category.

LODGINGS

All are air-conditioned unless otherwise noted, and all permit smoking unless they're identified as "no-smoking."

AP: This designation means that a hostelry operates on the American Plan (AP)—-that is, rates include all meals. AP may be an option or it may be the only meal plan available; be sure to find out.

Baths: You'll find private bathrooms with bathtubs unless noted otherwise.

Business services: If we tell you they're there, you can expect a variety on the premises.

Exercising: We note if there's "exercise equipment" even when there's no designated area; if you want a dedicated facility, look for "gym."

Facilities: We list what's available but don't note charges to use them. When pricing accommodations, always ask what's included.

Hot tub: This term denotes hot tubs, Jacuzzis, and whirlpools.

MAP: Rates at these properties include two meals.

No smoking: Properties with this designation prohibit smoking.

Opening and closing: Assume that hostelries are open year-round unless otherwise noted.

Pets: We note whether or not they're welcome and whether there's a charge.

Pools: Assume they're outdoors with fresh water; indoor pools are noted.

Prices: The price ranges listed are for a high-season double room for two, excluding tax and service charge.

Telephone and TV: Assume that you'll find them unless otherwise noted.

Fodor's Choice: Stars denote hostelries that are Fodor's Choices—our editors' picks of the state's very best in a given price category.

NATIONAL PARKS

National parks protect and preserve the treasures of America's heritage, and they're always worth visiting whenever you're in the area. Many are worth a long detour. If you will travel to many national parks, consider purchasing the National Parks Pass ($50), which gets you and your companions free admission to all parks for one year. (Camping and parking are extra.) A percentage of the proceeds from sales of the pass helps to fund important projects in the parks. Both the Golden Age Passport ($10), for those 62 and older, and the Golden Access Passport (free), for travelers with disabilities, entitle holders to free entry to all national parks, plus 50% off fees for the use of many park facilities and services. You must show proof of age and of U.S. citizenship or permanent residency (such as a U.S. passport, driver's license, or birth certificate) and, if requesting Golden Access, proof of your disability. You must get your Golden Access or Golden Age passport in person; the former is available at all federal recreation areas, the latter at federal recreation areas that charge fees. You may purchase the National Parks Pass by mail or through the Internet. For information, contact the National Park Service (Department of the Interior, 1849 C St. NW, Washington, DC 20240-0001, 202/208—4747, *www.nps.gov*). To buy the National Parks Pass, write to 27540 Ave. Mentry, Valencia, CA 91355, call 888/GO—PARKS, or visit www.national-parks.org.

IMPORTANT TIP

Although all prices, opening times, and other details in this book are based on information supplied to us at press time, changes occur all the time in the travel world, and Fodor's cannot accept responsibility for facts that become outdated or for inadvertent errors or omissions. So **always confirm information when it matters,** especially if you're making a detour to visit a specific place.

Let Us Hear from You

Keeping a travel guide fresh and up-to-date is a big job, and we welcome any and all comments. We'd love to have your thoughts on places we've listed, and we're interested in hearing about your own special finds, even the ones in your own back yard. Our guides are thoroughly updated for each new edition, and we're always adding new information, so your feedback is vital. Contact us via e-mail in care of roadnotes@fodors.com (specifying the name of the book on the subject line) or via snail mail in care of Road Guides at Fodor's, 280 Park Avenue, New York, NY 10017. We look forward to hearing from you. And in the meantime, have a wonderful road trip.

THE EDITORS

Important Numbers and On-Line Info

LODGINGS

Adam's Mark	800/444—2326	www.adamsmark.com
Baymont Inns	800/428—3438	www.baymontinns.com
Best Western	800/528—1234	www.bestwestern.com
	TDD 800/528—2222	
Budget Host	800/283—4678	www.budgethost.com
Clarion	800/252—7466	www.clarioninn.com
Comfort	800/228—5150	www.comfortinn.com
Courtyard by Marriott	800/321—2211	www.courtyard.com
Days Inn	800/325—2525	www.daysinn.com
Doubletree	800/222—8733	www.doubletreehotels.com
Drury Inns	800/325—8300	www.druryinn.com
Econo Lodge	800/555—2666	www.hotelchoice.com
Embassy Suites	800/362—2779	www.embassysuites.com
Exel Inns of America	800/356—8013	www.exelinns.com
Fairfield Inn by Marriott	800/228—2800	www.fairfieldinn.com
Fairmont Hotels	800/527—4727	www.fairmont.com
Forte	800/225—5843	www.forte-hotels.com
Four Seasons	800/332—3442	www.fourseasons.com
Friendship Inns	800/453—4511	www.hotelchoice.com
Hampton Inn	800/426—7866	www.hampton-inn.com
Hilton	800/445—8667	www.hilton.com
	TDD 800/368—1133	
Holiday Inn	800/465—4329	www.holiday-inn.com
	TDD 800/238—5544	
Howard Johnson	800/446—4656	www.hojo.com
	TDD 800/654—8442	
Hyatt & Resorts	800/233—1234	www.hyatt.com
Inns of America	800/826—0778	www.innsofamerica.com
Inter-Continental	800/327—0200	www.interconti.com
La Quinta	800/531—5900	www.laquinta.com
	TDD 800/426—3101	
Loews	800/235—6397	www.loewshotels.com
Marriott	800/228—9290	www.marriott.com
Master Hosts Inns	800/251—1962	www.reservahost.com
Le Meridien	800/225—5843	www.lemeridien.com
Motel 6	800/466—8356	www.motel6.com
Omni	800/843—6664	www.omnihotels.com
Quality Inn	800/228—5151	www.qualityinn.com
Radisson	800/333—3333	www.radisson.com
Ramada	800/228—2828	www.ramada.com
	TDD 800/533—6634	
Red Carpet/Scottish Inns	800/251—1962	www.reservahost.com
Red Lion	800/547—8010	www.redlion.com
Red Roof Inn	800/843—7663	www.redroof.com
Renaissance	800/468—3571	www.renaissancehotels.com
Residence Inn by Marriott	800/331—3131	www.residenceinn.com
Ritz-Carlton	800/241—3333	www.ritzcarlton.com
Rodeway	800/228—2000	www.rodeway.com

Sheraton	800/325—3535	www.sheraton.com
Shilo Inn	800/222—2244	www.shiloinns.com
Signature Inns	800/822—5252	www.signature-inns.com
Sleep Inn	800/221—2222	www.sleepinn.com
Super 8	800/848—8888	www.super8.com
Susse Chalet	800/258—1980	www.sussechalet.com
Travelodge/Viscount	800/255—3050	www.travelodge.com
Vagabond	800/522—1555	www.vagabondinns.com
Westin Hotels & Resorts	800/937—8461	www.westin.com
Wyndham Hotels & Resorts	800/996—3426	www.wyndham.com

AIRLINES

Air Canada	888/247—2262	www.aircanada.ca
Alaska	800/426—0333	www.alaska-air.com
American	800/433—7300	www.aa.com
America West	800/235—9292	www.americawest.com
British Airways	800/247—9297	www.british-airways.com
Canadian	800/426—7000	www.cdnair.ca
Continental Airlines	800/525—0280	www.continental.com
Delta	800/221—1212	www.delta.com
Midway Airlines	800/446—4392	www.midwayair.com
Northwest	800/225—2525	www.nwa.com
SkyWest	800/453—9417	www.delta.com
Southwest	800/435—9792	www.southwest.com
TWA	800/221—2000	www.twa.com
United	800/241—6522	www.ual.com
USAir	800/428—4322	www.usair.com

BUSES AND TRAINS

Amtrak	800/872—7245	www.amtrak.com
Greyhound	800/231—2222	www.greyhound.com
Trailways	800/343—9999	www.trailways.com

CAR RENTALS

Advantage	800/777—5500	www.arac.com
Alamo	800/327—9633	www.goalamo.com
Allstate	800/634—6186	www.bnm.com/as.htm
Avis	800/331—1212	www.avis.com
Budget	800/527—0700	www.budget.com
Dollar	800/800—4000	www.dollar.com
Enterprise	800/325—8007	www.pickenterprise.com
Hertz	800/654—3131	www.hertz.com
National	800/328—4567	www.nationalcar.com
Payless	800/237—2804	www.paylesscarrental.com
Rent-A-Wreck	800/535—1391	www.rent-a-wreck.com
Thrifty	800/367—2277	www.thrifty.com

Note: Area codes are changing all over the United States as this book goes to press. For the latest updates, check www.areacode-info.com.

Fodor's Road Guide USA

Connecticut
Massachusetts
Rhode Island

Connecticut

Connecticut may be the third-smallest state in the nation, but it is among the hard-est to define. Indeed, you can travel from any point in the Nutmeg State, as it is known, to any other in not much more than two hours, yet the land you travel—fewer than 60 mi top to bottom and 100 mi across—is incredibly varied. There are Connecticut's rivers, estuaries, and more than 100 mi of shoreline where salty sea air blows over beach communities like Old Lyme and Stonington. Patchwork hills and peaked mountains loom in the northwestern corner, and once-upon-a-time mill towns were founded along rivers with names like Housatonic and Naugatuck. Finally, there is seemingly endless farm-land in the northeast, where cows just might outnumber people (and definitely outnum-ber the traffic lights), as well as the chic bedroom communities of New York City like Greenwich and New Canaan, where boutique shopping bags seem to be the dominant accessory. Each section of the state is different, yet each defines Connecticut.

Just as diverse as the landscape are the state's residents, who numbered more than 3.25 million at last count. There really is no such thing as the definitive Connecticut Yankee, however. Few families can trace their roots back to Connecticut in the 1600s, when it was founded as one of the 13 original colonies, but the state motto is also "He who transplanted still sustains." And so the face of the Nutmegger is that of the family from Naples who tend pizza ovens in New Haven, the farmer in Norfolk whose land dates back five generations, the grandmother from New Britain who makes the state's best pierogies, and the lady from Westport who lunches, not to mention the celebrity nestled in the Litchfield Hills and the buzz-cut submariner from the Groton Naval Submarine Base.

A unifying characteristic of the Connecticut Yankee, however, is his or her propen-sity for inventiveness: You might say that the Nutmeggers have been setting trends

CAPITAL: HARTFORD	POPULATION: 3,274,069	AREA: 5,009 SQUARE MILES
BORDERS: MA, RI, NY	TIME ZONE: EASTERN	POSTAL ABBREVIATION: CT
WEB SITE: WWW.TOURISM.STATE.CT.US		

for centuries. They are historically known for both their intellectual abilities and their desire to have a little fun. As evidence of the former, consider that the nation's first public library was opened in New Haven in 1656 and its first state house built in Hartford in 1776; Tapping Reeve opened the first law school in Litchfield in 1784; and West Hartford's Noah Webster published the first dictionary in 1806. As proof of the latter, note that Lake Compounce in Bristol was the country's first amusement park, Bethel's P. T. Barnum staged the first three-ring circus, and the hamburger, the lollipop, the Frisbee, and the Erector Set were all invented within the state's 5,009 square mi. Most recently, Connecticut Yankees are putting this old-fashioned ingenuity to work at revitalizing the state's cities. Bridgeport, New Haven, Hartford, and Waterbury are each hard at work at reinventing themselves.

Not surprisingly, Nutmeggers have a healthy respect for their history. For decades, the Mystic Seaport museum, which traces the state's rich maritime past through living history exhibits, has been one of the premier tourist attractions. Today, however, slot machines in casinos in the southeastern woods of Connecticut are giving the sailing ships a run for their money. Foxwoods Casino near Ledyard, opened in 1992 and, run by the Mashantucket Pequots, is the world's largest casino—it draws over 55,000 visitors per day. The Mohegan Sun Casino in nearby Uncasville is working hard to catch up. Thanks in large part to the lure of these casinos, not to mention the state's rich cultural attractions, cutting-edge restaurants, shopping outlets, first-rate lodgings, and an abundance of natural beauty (including 93 state parks and 32 state forests), tourism is now the second leading industry in the state. Is it any wonder given all the state has to offer?

History

Connecticut takes its name from the Indian *Quinnetucket,* a reference to the "long, tidal river" that runs 45 mi through the center of the state.

The Native Americans, of course, lived off the bounty of Connecticut's land long before European settlers arrived. In 1620 there were at least 16 separate tribes in Connecticut, among them the Paugusetts in what is today Fairfield County, the Quinipiacs in New Haven, the Mohegans in the northeast, and the Pequots along the southeastern coast. In 1614 Adriaen Block sailed up the lower Connecticut River in search of trading possibilities with the Native Americans. The year 1633 saw the permanent arrival of the first Europeans, when a party of Dutch from New Netherlands successfully navigated that long tidal river and established the first European settlement—a trading post near what would eventually become the capital of the state of Connecticut, Hartford.

In 1636 the Rev. Thomas Hooker moved his congregation 100 mi from Cambridge, Massachusetts, to Hartford and with that, colonization began in earnest as settlers dug their roots deep into the land up and down the Connecticut River and the shoreline. Shortly thereafter, the towns of Windsor, Hartford, and Wethersfield banded

CT Timeline

1614	1620	1633	1636
Adriaen Block sails up the lower Connecticut River in search of trading possibilities with the Native Americans.	At least 16 separate Indian tribes exist in Connecticut.	The first Europeans, a party of Dutch from New Netherlands, establish the first European settlement—a trading post that would eventually become the capital of the state of Connecticut, Hartford.	Rev. Thomas Hooker moves his congregation 100 mi from Cambridge, Massachusetts to Hartford.

INTRODUCTION
HISTORY
REGIONS
WHEN TO VISIT
STATE'S GREATS
RULES OF THE ROAD
DRIVING TOURS

together to adopt the Fundamental Orders of Connecticut and organize themselves as the independent commonwealth known as the Connecticut Colony. These orders, which many regard as the world's first constitution, are the reason behind Connecticut's designation as "The Constitution State"—an appellation you will notice on state license plates.

The next significant date in early Connecticut history was 1662—the year that far-thinking Connecticut Gov. John Winthrop persuaded Charles II of England to grant the Connecticut Charter. The charter, considered extremely liberal for its time, granted the colony a great degree of self government and independence, which would provide Connecticut with a secure political framework for more than a century. In the period immediately following the Declaration of Independence, when most states were struggling to find legal justification for their actions, Connecticut simply dropped all references to Great Britain from its charter and continued on.

During the Revolutionary War, Connecticut earned yet another nickname, "The Provision State," for keeping Washington's troops fortified during the winter of 1777–78 at Valley Forge and in the winter of 1779–80 in Morristown, New Jersey. (In later wars Connecticut continued this tradition of key material support: The Colt Firearms factory in Hartford supplied the Union troops with rifles and revolvers in the Civil War. By the end of World War I it was estimated that Connecticut alone had produced 54% of the nation's munitions. And, in the 1940s, the state's specialized manufacturing industries, which by then included vital aircraft contractors such as Stratford's Sikorsky Aircraft, were key to the defense effort.)

No matter how plentiful Connecticut's provisions were, however, none could help the men of Connecticut who tried to defend Groton's Fort Griswold and New London against British troops led by traitorous Norwich resident Benedict Arnold. Connecticut Revolutionary War–era heroes, on the other hand, included Coventry's Nathan Hale, famed for his declaration, "I only regret that I have but one life to lose for my country"; General Israel Putnam of Pomfret, who admonished, "Don't fire until you see the white of their eyes"; and Roger Sherman of New Milford, who engineered the Connecticut Compromise, resulting in a House of Representatives and Senate as we know them today.

It is estimated that between 1780 and 1840 approximately 750,000 people left Connecticut because much of the state's fertile land had been exhausted. Historians attribute Connecticut's rapid industrial growth in the 1800s to the innovation and creativity of those who remained. In fact, a study by the Connecticut Historical Commission reveals that between 1790 and 1930 Connecticut regularly led all states in the number of patents granted and between 1870 and 1900 and the number of manufacturers in Connecticut jumped from 5,128 to over 9,000.

With this boom in industry and the manufacturing of everything from textiles in Manchester and hardware in New Britain to typewriters in Hartford and hats in Danbury, came an ever-increasing influx of immigrants. In 1870 native-born Americans

1639	**1662**	**1717**	**1764**	**1776**
Windsor, Hartford, and Wethersfield band together to adopt the Fundamental Orders of Connecticut and organize themselves as the independent commonwealth known as the Connecticut Colony.	Connecticut Gov. John Winthrop persuades Charles II of England to grant the Connecticut Charter.	The Collegiate School moves from Old Saybrook to New Haven and is renamed Yale a year later.	The *Connecticut Courant* is launched in Hartford. Today, it is called the *Hartford Courant* and is the oldest continuously operating newspaper in the country.	Samuel Huntington, Roger Sherman, William Williams, and Oliver Scott sign the Declaration of Independence.

made up 75% of Connecticut's population, but with the arrival of Irish, Italian, Polish, Russian, and Lithuanian immigrants this figure had fallen to 35% by World War II. It is a migration that continues today, thus the state motto: "He who transplanted still sustains."

Regions

1. SOUTHWESTERN CONNECTICUT

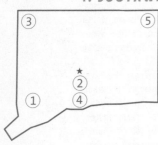

Southwestern Connecticut is a rich swirl of old New England and new New York. This region has the highest cost of living and most expensive homes of any community in the country, and its bedroom communities are home primarily to white-collar executives; some still make the nearly two-hour dash to and from "the city," while others enjoy a more civilized morning drive to Stamford. Strict zoning has preserved a certain privacy and rusticity uncommon in other such densely populated areas, and numerous celebrities—Paul Newman, David Letterman, Michael Bolton, Diana Ross, and Mel Gibson, among them—live in Fairfield County.

Venture away from the wealthy communities, and you'll discover cities in different stages of urban renewal: Stamford, Norwalk, Bridgeport, and Danbury. These four have some of the region's best cultural and shopping opportunities, but the economic disparity between Connecticut's upscale towns and troubled cities is perhaps nowhere more visible than in Fairfield County.

Towns listed: Bridgeport, Danbury, Fairfield, Greenwich, New Canaan, Norwalk, Ridgefield, Stamford, Stratford, and Westport.

2. THE CONNECTICUT RIVER VALLEY

Westward expansion in the New World began along the meandering Connecticut River. Dutch explorer Adriaen Block first explored the area in 1614, and in 1633 a trading post was set up in what is now Hartford. Within five years, throngs of restive Massachusetts Bay colonists had settled in this fertile valley. What followed was more than three centuries of shipbuilding, shad hauling, and river trading with ports as far away as the West Indies and the Mediterranean.

Less touristy than the coast and northwest hills, the Connecticut River Valley is a swath of small villages and uncrowded state parks punctuated by a few small cities and a large one: the capital city of Hartford. To the south of Hartford, with the exception of industrial Middletown, genuinely quaint hamlets vie for a share of Connecticut's tourist crop with antiques shops, scenic drives, and trendy restaurants.

1780-1840	1781	1790-1930	1807	1842
Three quarters of a million people leave Connecticut due to the fact that the state's limited supply of fertile land is exhausted.	Norwich resident Benedict Arnold leads British troops on an attack of Groton and New London.	Connecticut regularly leads all states in the number of patents granted.	The first major United States dictionary is published by Noah Webster.	Wadsworth Atheneum, the nation's first public art museum, is founded in Hartford.

INTRODUCTION
HISTORY
REGIONS
WHEN TO VISIT
STATE'S GREATS
RULES OF THE ROAD
DRIVING TOURS

Towns listed: Avon, Cheshire, Chester, East Haddam, Enfield, Essex, Farmington, Glastonbury, Hartford, Ivoryton, Manchester, Middletown, New Britain, Simsbury, Southington, Stafford Springs, West Hartford, Wethersfield, Windsor Locks

3. THE LITCHFIELD HILLS

Two highways, I–84 and Route 8, form the southern and eastern boundaries of the Litchfield Hills region. New York, to the west, and Massachusetts, to the north, complete the rectangle. Here in the foothills of the Berkshires is some of the most spectacular and unspoiled scenery in Connecticut. Grand old inns are plentiful, as are sophisticated eateries. Rolling farmlands abut thick forests, and trails—including a section of the Appalachian Trail—traverse the state parks and forests. Two rivers, the Housatonic and the Farmington, attract anglers and canoeing enthusiasts, and the state's three largest natural lakes, Waramaug, Bantam, and Twin, are here. Sweeping town greens and stately homes anchor Litchfield and New Milford. Kent, New Preston, and Woodbury draw avid antiquers, and Washington, Salisbury, and Norfolk provide a glimpse into New England village life as it might have existed two centuries ago.

Favorite roads for admiring fall foliage are U.S. 7, from New Milford through Kent and West Cornwall to Canaan; Routes 41 to 4 from Salisbury through Lakeville, Sharon, Cornwall Bridge, and Goshen to Torrington; and Route 47 to U.S. 202 to Route 45 from Woodbury through Washington, New Preston, and Warren.

Towns listed: Bristol, Cornwall, Kent, Lakeville, Litchfield, New Milford, New Preston, Norfolk, Riverton, Salisbury, Washington, Waterbury, Woodbury

4. NEW HAVEN AND THE SOUTHEASTERN COAST

As you drive northeast along I–95, culturally rich New Haven is the final urban obstacle between southwestern Connecticut's overdeveloped coast and southeastern Connecticut's quieter shoreline villages. The remainder of the jagged coast, which stretches all the way to the Rhode Island border, consists of small coastal villages, quiet hamlets, and undisturbed beaches. The only interruptions along this mostly undeveloped seashore are the industry and piers of New London and Groton. Mystic, Stonington, Old Saybrook, Clinton, and Guilford are havens for fans of antiques and boutiques. North of Groton, near the town of Ledyard, the Mashantucket Pequot Tribal Nation owns and operates Foxwoods Casino. The Mohegan Indians run the Mohegan Sun casino in Uncasville.

Towns listed: Branford, Clinton, Groton, Guilford, Ledyard, Madison, Milford, Mystic, New Haven, New London, Niantic, Norwich, Old Lyme, Old Saybrook, Stonington, Waterford

5. THE QUIET CORNER

Few visitors to Connecticut experience the old-fashioned ways of the state's "Quiet Corner," a vast patch of sparsely populated towns that seem a world away from the

1870-1900 The number of manufacturers in Connecticut jumps from 5,128 to more than 9,000.

1881 Storrs Agricultural College, the predecessor of the University of Connecticut, is founded.

1900 The first naval submarine is constructed.

1958 The Connecticut Turnpike is opened.

1974 Ella Grasso is the first woman elected governor.

rest of the state. The Quiet Corner has a reclusive allure: People used to leave New York City for the Litchfield Hills; now many are leaving for northeastern Connecticut, where the stretch of Route 169 from Brooklyn past Woodstock has been named a National Scenic Byway.

The cultural capital of the Quiet Corner is Putnam, a small mill city on the Quinebaug River whose formerly industrial town center has been transformed into a year-round antiques mart. Smaller jewels in and around the Putnam area are Brooklyn, Pomfret, and Woodstock—three towns where authentic Colonial homesteads still seem to outnumber the contemporary, charmless clones that are springing up all too rapidly across the state.

Towns listed: Brooklyn, Coventry, Pomfret, Putnam, Storrs, Woodstock

When to Visit

Connecticut is inviting year-round, but fall and spring are especially beautiful times to visit. An autumn drive along the Merritt Parkway, U.S. 7 in Litchfield County, or Route 169 in the Quiet Corner among leaves of scarlet, yellow, and orange is memorable indeed. Connecticut blossoms in springtime, too, with the yellow of daffodils and forsythia, the pink of dogwoods, and the scent of pale purple lilacs. If you visit in summer, chances are you will have a lot of company—especially along the shoreline. Yet, to be remembered is the fact that some of Connecticut's most indulgent pleasures are tied to the season of sun: enjoying a lobster roll oozing with butter at one of the shoreline's seafood shanties, taking in a band concert on an old New England green, and diving between the cool waves of the Long Island Sound on a hot July day.

The weather remains relatively equal around much of the state, with the exception of the northwestern hills, where the temperature is occasionally as much as 10°F lower than the rest of Connecticut. The state's record cold snap, in fact, was recorded in the hills of Falls Village, where it reached 32°F below zero in February 1943. The highest the thermometer ever reached was 105°F in Danbury in 1991. Approximately 44 inches of precipitation falls each year; in recent years it has mostly been in the form of rain.

CLIMATE CHART
Average High/Low Temperatures (°F) and Monthly Precipitations (in inches)

	JAN.	FEB.	MAR.	APR.	MAY	JUNE \
BRIDGEPORT	34/18	38/19	45/29	60/39	70/48	80/58
	15.4	14.2	12.8	4.9	3.8	3.6
	JULY	AUG.	SEPT.	OCT.	NOV.	DEC.
	84/61	81/60	74/52	65/40	50/31	39/20
	3.2	3.9	3.7	3.6	6	13.9
	JAN.	FEB.	MAR.	APR.	MAY	JUNE \
HARTFORD	38/21	39/22	45/30	58/40	67/50	75/60
	10.7	10.2	8.5	4.2	3.4	2.9
	JULY	AUG.	SEPT.	OCT.	NOV.	DEC.
	81/67	80/65	73/58	64/48	52/38	40/19
	3.5	3.7	3.3	3.3	4.4	8.3

ON THE STATE CALENDAR
WINTER

Mid-Nov.–early Jan. **Fantasy of Lights.** Lighthouse Point Park in New Haven is lit up with more than 45 spectacular lighting displays and you can sit in on a narrated drive-through. | 203/777–2000, ext. 603.

Dec. **Christmas Town Festival.** This weekend festival in Bethlehem features arts and crafts, hayrides, carolers, food booths, and the opportunity to get your Christmas cards postmarked in "Christmas town." | 203/266–5557.

First Night Hartford. This family-oriented celebration of the New Year takes place at various locations throughout Hartford on December 31. Continuous performances take place during the afternoon and evening, culminating in a fireworks display. | 860/728–3089.

Feb. **Connecticut Flower and Garden Show.** The Connecticut Expo Center in Hartford is transformed into an oasis of blooming gardens. You can attend educational seminars and purchase plants, flowers, and gardening supplies. | 860/529–2123.

Salisbury Invitational Ski Jump and U.S. Eastern Ski Jump Championships. Built in 1926, this is one of the oldest ski jumping program sites in the nation. The level of competition at this tournament is Olympic-caliber. | 860/435–9729.

SPRING

Apr. **Daffodil Festival.** More than 500,000 daffodils are abloom in Meriden's Hubbard Park during this festival. Highlights include include arts and crafts displays, live entertainment, fireworks, and amusement rides. | 203/630–4259.

Late Apr.–early May **Civil War Reenactment.** Union and Confederate military and civilian camps convene at Hammonasset Beach State Park in Madison. A simulated battle takes place each day. | 203/481–2393.

May **Dogwood Festival.** Thousands of dogwood trees color the Fairfield Green and its surroundings. Events include garden tours, arts and crafts, and live entertainment. | 203/255–1011.

Eastern Women's Intercollegiate Rowing Regatta Championships. Top competitors participate in this elite women's competition on scenic Lake Waramaug in New Preston. | 860/658–7776.

Lobsterfest. Mystic Seaport is the venue for this good old-fashioned lobster bake. | 860/572–5315.

Dodge Dealers Grand Prix. The best drivers from the International Motorsports Association and the Sports Car Club of America take part in this sports car race at Lime Rock Park in Lakeville. It is the largest race of this kind in North America. | 860/435–5000 or 800/RACE–LRP.

SUMMER

June **Farmington Antiques Weekend.** More than 600 dealers gather at the Farmington Polo Grounds for Connecticut's largest antiques event. | 508/839–9735.

June–Aug. **Eugene O'Neill Theater Center.** Students of the theater have been honing their skills at this center in Waterford for more than 40 years. All are invited to readings and performances of the National Playwrights Conference, the National Puppetry

	Conference, the National Music Theater Conference, and the Cabaret Symposium.	860/443–5378.
Mid-June–mid-Sept.	**Music Mountain Summer Music Festival.** Falls Village plays hosts to this summer chamber music festival. It is the country's oldest continuously operating festival of this nature.	860/824–7126.
Late June–early July	**International Festival of Arts and Ideas.** Performing and visual artists from around the globe gather on the New Haven Green and surroundings for theatrical performances, classical, jazz, and pop music, a street festival, children's activities, and more.	203/498–1212.
July	**Ancient Fife and Drum Corps Muster and Parade.** In Deep River, this is the oldest and largest muster of these spirited corps.	860/347–0028.
July–Aug.	**Norfolk Chamber Music Festival.** Performances by world-class talents take place in a historic concert hall on the grounds of the scenic Ellen Battell Stoeckel Estate. This is Connecticut's version of the famed Tanglewood festival which is held in Massachusetts.	860/542–3000.
	Canon Greater Hartford Open. One of the most successful tournaments on the PGA tour, this open attracts the top names in golf to Cromwell.	860/246–4GHO.
Aug.	**The Brooklyn Fair.** Held the weekend before Labor Day at the Brooklyn Fairgrounds, this is the oldest continuously operating agricultural fair in the state and it usually draws huge crowds. The carnival rides and petting zoo are major attractions.	860/779–0012.
	Greatest Bluefish Tournament on Earth. Although it covers the entire Long Island Sound, this fishathon is headquartered at Captain's Cove in Bridgewater. Prizes are awarded based on various criteria.	203/366–BLUE.
	The Pilot Pen Tennis Women's Championships. Held at the Connecticut Tennis Center at Yale University in New Haven, this tournament draws the world's top ranked women.	203/776–7331.

FALL

Sept.	**Durham Fair.** Known for attracting nationally acclaimed country-music performers, this is the state's largest agricultural fair.	860/349–9495.
	Norwalk International In-Water Boat Show. This is the largest power and sailboat show in the Northeast.	212/984–7011.
	Norwalk Oyster Festival. More than 200 crafters, vintage vessels, fireworks, and waterfront demonstrations gather to celebrate the history of the Long Island Sound at this waterfront festival.	203/838–9444.
Oct.	**Head of the Connecticut Regatta.** Harbor Park is the end point for this rowing regatta, which traditionally draws more than 600 boats and 3,000 competitors.	860/346–1042.

INTRODUCTION
HISTORY
REGIONS
WHEN TO VISIT
STATE'S GREATS
RULES OF THE ROAD
DRIVING TOURS

Witch's Dungeon Horror Museum. Authorized by Universal Studios, this seasonal museum is dedicated to the actors and makeup artists of classic horror films. | 860/583–8306.

Walking Weekend. Twenty-five towns in the northeastern corner of the state participate in a weekend of more than 50 guided walks. | 860/928–1228.

State's Greats

Connecticut's beauty lies in its diversity. From the chic splendor of Fairfield County's Gold Coast to the jeweled colors of Litchfield to the calming peace of the Quiet Corner there is a part of the state to suit every personality.

Beaches, Forests, and Parks

Connecticut has more than 100 mi of shoreline along the Long Island Sound, and it is here that its favored beaches lie. Many of these beaches, among them **Sherwood Island** in Westport, **Hammonasset** in Madison, and **Rocky Neck** in Niantic, are also state parks. **Lake Waramaug State Park** in New Preston has a sandy beach and one of the state's most serene lakes. **Kent Falls State Park** in Kent has a stunning waterfall. In all, Connecticut has a total of 93 state parks and 32 state forests. The state's largest private nature preserve is Litchfield's **White Memorial Conservation Center,** a 4,000-acre sanctuary that has the facilities for everything from hiking to fishing, birding to cross-country skiing.

Culture, History, and the Arts

Connecticut was one of the 13 original colonies and as such has a very strong sense of, and respect for, its history. Just about every town in the state has a historical society that oversees the preservation of one or more historic house-museums. Particularly exceptional are the sites maintained by Litchfield, Greenwich, and Wethersfield. The country's first public art museum is Hartford's **Wadsworth Atheneum.** Other outstanding monuments to the arts include the **Yale University Art Gallery** and the **Yale Center for British Art,** both in New Haven, the **New Britain Museum of American Art,** Waterbury's **Mattatuck Museum,** Ridgefield's **Aldrich Museum of Contemporary Art,** New London's **Lyman Allyn Art Museum,** and Old Lyme's **Florence Griswold Museum,** dedicated to the once-upon-a-time Old Lyme Art Colony. Literary arts are well respected in Hartford at the **Mark Twain House,** where the great author penned such literary classics as *Tom Sawyer* and *Huckleberry Finn,* and at the **Harriet Beecher Stowe House,** home of the author of *Uncle Tom's Cabin.* The performing arts, meanwhile, are well representing in New Haven at the **Shubert Performing Arts Center,** in Stamford at the **Stamford Center for the Arts,** and in Hartford at **The Bushnell.** Finally, various "theme" museums flourish in the state, from the new $120 million **Mashantucket Pequot Museum and Research Center** in Ledyard to the much smaller, but absolutely charming, **Carousel Museum of New England** in Bristol.

Sports

Pick a sport, any sport, and chances are you'll have the opportunity to enjoy it in Connecticut.

Downhill skiers have five mountains to choose from, including **Mohawk Mountain Ski Area** in Cornwall and **Powder Ridge Ski Area** in Middlefield. The Housatonic and Farmington rivers are happy hunting grounds for freshwater fishing enthusiasts, and there's always the shoreline for those who prefer their catch to be lightly salted. Golfers have dozens of opportunities to practice their chip shots, among them **Richter Park** in Danbury, which has been rated one of the top courses in the country by *Golf*

Digest, **Lyman Orchards** in Middlefield, which consists of two gems designed by and Gary Player and Robert Trent Jones. Hikers, meanwhile, particularly enjoy the portion of the **Appalachian Trail** that passes through the state in Kent and the view from atop Mount Tom in Litchfield. **North American Canoe Tours** in New Hartford supplies the tubes from which to explore the Farmington River.

As for spectator sports, Connecticut does not exactly have a corner on the big leagues of professional sports. Minor-league baseball is a favorite Connecticut spectator sport—there are three Double-A teams in the state: **the New Haven Ravens, the Norwich Navigators,** and **the New Britain Rock Cats.** Another team, **the Bridgeport Bluefish,** is not affiliated with the big leagues but is a major tourist draw. Luckily, excitement about baseball does not interfere with the state's true passion: rooting for the University of Connecticut's men's and women's basketball teams, perennial leaders of the Big East. The men's team won the NCAA title for the first time ever in 1999—the state is still celebrating.

Rules of the Road

License requirements: To drive in Connecticut you must be at least 16 years old and have a valid driver's license. Residents of other countries may drive with a valid driver's license from their home countries if it is issued in English or if they have an international permit from their own country.

Speed Limits: In 1998 Connecticut raised the speed limit from 55 mph to 65 mph on 334 mi of highway. Heavily traveled stretches of highway remain at 55 mph. Check posted speed limits carefully.

Right Turn on Red: You may make a right turn at a red light after coming to a full stop anywhere in the state unless a posted sign indicates otherwise.

Seat Belt and Helmet Laws: All drivers and front-seat passengers must wear seat belts. Children under the age of four must ride in a federally approved child-restraint system. Connecticut state law requires that anyone under the age of 12 wear a helmet while riding a bike.

For More Information: Contact the State Department of Motor Vehicles at 800/842–8222.

The Scenic Litchfield Hills Driving Tour
FROM NEW MILFORD TO WASHINGTON

Distance: Approximately 45 mi   Time: Half-day
Breaks: The inns and restaurants surrounding Lake Waramaug are an ideal stopping point, whether for a meal or to extend this half-day trip into an overnight.

This tour will take you through the hills and valleys of southern Litchfield County, past a covered bridge and a rambling river, past charming inns and sparkling waters. It is a spectacular drive to take in the fall.

❶ **New Milford** (I–84, Exit 7 to U.S. 7 and U.S. 202) is the largest town in Litchfield County and has one of the area's largest greens. Surrounding the green are beautifully restored 18th- and 19th-century homes and structures such as the town hall, which marks the site that was home to Roger Sherman—the only man to sign all four of the country's founding documents: the Articles of Association, the Declaration of Independence, the Articles of Confederation, and the Constitution.

❷ U.S. 7 to **Kent** runs parallel to the Housatonic River and is arguably the most scenic road in the state during fall-foliage season. **Bulls Bridge** is one of two covered bridges remaining of the 18 that once spanned the Housatonic and dates to 1842; it is still open to vehicular traffic.

❸ Farther up U.S. 7, downtown Kent is known for a handful of fine art galleries. The **Sloane-Stanley Museum** (U.S. 7) displays a collection of art by author and artist Eric Sloane as well as his unique—and quite extensive—collection of tools from the 17th to 19th

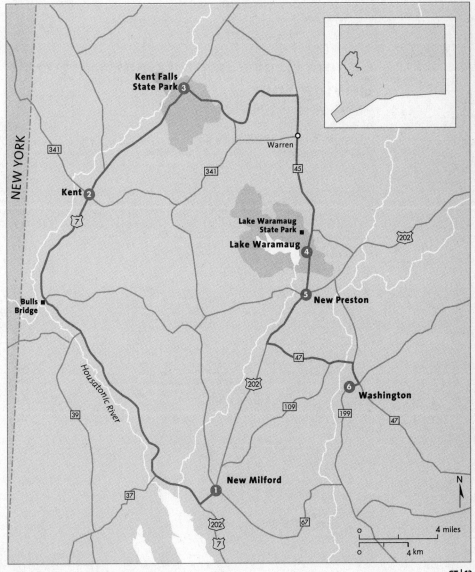

centuries. **Kent Falls State Park** (north of Kent on U.S. 7) comprises 295 acres and features one of the most impressive waterfalls in the state.

❹ Lake Waramaug (Route 45 south to New Preston) is Connecticut's second largest natural lake and is said to be reminiscent of Switzerland's Lake Lucerne. The **Lake Waramaug State Park** has a shaded picnic area and sandy beach. **Hopkins Vineyard** (Hopkins Rd.) is one of the state's most popular wineries and overlooks the lake.

❺ Farther down Route 45, the village of **New Preston,** perched above a 40-ft waterfall on the Aspetuck River, has a little town center that is packed with antique and specialty shops.

❻ **Washington** (Rte. 45 to U.S. 202 to Rte. 47 to Rte. 199) is one of the best-preserved colonial towns in Connecticut. The green, laid out in the 1740s, is surrounded by stately homes; the **Institute for American Indian Studies,** which details the history of the North-eastern Woodland Indians, is a fine place to wind up your tour.

Connecticut's Impressionist Art Trail Driving Tour

FROM GREENWICH TO NEW LONDON

Distance: Approximately 115 mi Time: Two days
Breaks: Try stopping overnight in Old Lyme. It is the town most closely identified with the Impressionist Art movement in the state and has two charming country inns. If hunger hits

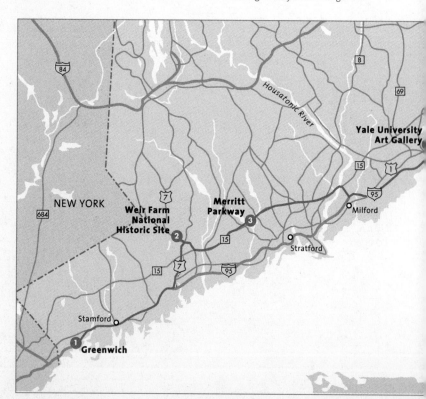

anywhere along the way, chances are that any exit off I–95 will help solve that dilemma. An especially pleasant detour is Exit 53 off I–95 to scenic Route 146 along the coast through Branford and Guilford.

This portion of Connecticut's Impressionist Art trail traces the state's undulating coastline. Connecticut's rich history as a haven for artists of the American Impressionist movement is explored in both visual and written detail.

INTRODUCTION
HISTORY
REGIONS
WHEN TO VISIT
STATE'S GREATS
RULES OF THE ROAD
DRIVING TOURS

❶ **Greenwich** (I–95, Exits 3 or 4), one of Connecticut's wealthiest communities, puts the gold into this region's designation as the Gold Coast. The **Bush-Holley Historic Site** (39 Strickland Rd.), run by the Historical Society of the Town of Greenwich, was the site of the first Connecticut art colony. The circa 1732 central-chimney saltbox once boarded painters John Twachtman, Childe Hassam, J. Alden Weir, and Elmer Livingstone MacRae. The **Bruce Museum** has a small, but worthwhile, collection of American Impressionist paintings as well.

❷ **Weir Farm National Historic Site** in Wilton (I–95, Exit 15 to U.S. 7 north) is the state's only National Historic Site and was once the home of American Impressionist J. Alden Weir. Though the park today encompasses 60 acres, Weir's original 153 wooded acres inspired countless paintings and sketches by Weir and visiting friends: Hassam, Twachtman, Albert Pinkham Ryder, and John Singer Sargent among them.

❸ Take the Merritt Parkway (U.S. 7 to Rte. 33 to Rte. 15, which is the Merritt Parkway) en route to your next stop. The Merritt is considered one of the country's most scenic highways.

Connecticut River

Lyman Allyn Art Museum

Florence Griswold Museum ❺
Old Lyme

New London ❻

Branford   Madison   Old Saybrook

Long Island Sound

N

0   10 miles
0   10 km

❹ Return to I–95 north in Milford to New Haven (I–95, Exit 47) and the **Yale University Art Gallery.** The gallery has an extensive collection of American art, including many works by American Impressionists.

❺ In Old Lyme (I–95, Exit 70), the **Florence Griswold Museum** was once a boardinghouse that served as the center of the Impressionist movement in Connecticut in the early 20th century. Prominent members of the Old Lyme Art Colony included Willard Metcalfe, Clark Voorhees, Childe Hassam, and Henry Ward Ranger. The artists painted for their hostess the row of panels in the dining room that now serve as the museum's centerpiece.

❻ In New London (I–95, Exit 83) the **Lyman Allyn Art Museum** has a noteworthy gallery devoted to the American Impressionists.

AVON

MAP 3, E3

(Nearby towns also listed: Farmington, Hartford, Simsbury, West Hartford)

Settled in the mid-1600s, the town that we now know as Avon was originally known as Nod and was part of Farmington. Some say this unusual appellation came from the Indian word *noadt*, meaning "a great way off." Given their means of transportation, Nod might have seemed a long way from the main part of town. Today, however, Avon is an easily accessible town in the rolling hills of the Farmington River Valley, just west of Hartford.

Information: Avon Chamber of Commerce | 250 Constitution Plaza, Hartford, 06103 | 860/527–9258, ext. 250 | fax 860/293–2592 | www.avonchamber.com. **Greater Hartford Tourism District** | 234 Murphy Rd., Hartford, 06114 | 860/244–8181 or 800/793–4480 | fax 860/244–8180 | ctfuntour@aol.com | www.enjoyhartford.com.

Attractions

Farmington River Tubing. You'll get an up-close-and-personal tour of the Farmington River via inner tube from this facility which is about 12 mi northwest of Avon. Tubes, life jackets, and return rides to the parking area are included. No kids under 10 or under 4 ft 5 inches tall. | Satan's Kingdom State Recreation Area, U.S. 44, New Hartford, | 860/693–6465 | fax 860/793–4470 | $12 | www.visitconnecticut.com/farmingtonrivertubing | Memorial Day–Labor Day, daily.

Farmington Valley Arts Center. Housed in a 19th-century brownstone, this studio complex showcases the work of nationally known artists whose mediums include ceramics, stone, wood, and watercolors. Arts and crafts are for sale in the gallery shop. | 25 Arts Center La. | 860/678–1867 | fax 860/674–1877 | Free | Jan.–Oct., Wed.–Sat. 11–5, Sun. noon–4; Nov.–Dec., Mon.–Sat. 10–5, Sun. noon–5.

The Pickin' Patch. This farm caters to those whose yen for pick-your-own produce goes far beyond strawberries. You can harvest everything from A (asparagus) to Z (zucchini). | Woodford Farm, Nod Rd. | 860/677–9552 | Free, pay per pound | Apr.–Oct., daily 8–6; Nov.–Dec., daily 8–5.

Roaring Brook Nature Center. Directly west of Avon, this 115-acre nature center has many Native American exhibits, including an Eastern Woodlands Indian longhouse, self-guided wooded trails, and nature displays for children. | 70 Gracey Rd., Canton | 860/693–0263 | fax 860/693–0264 | www.sciencecenterct.org | $3 | Sept.–June, Tues.–Sat. 10–5, Sun. 1–5; July–Aug., Mon.–Sat. 10–5, Sun. 1–5.

KODAK'S TIPS FOR TAKING GREAT PICTURES

Get Closer
· Fill the frame tightly for maximum impact
· Move closer physically or use a long lens
· Continually check the viewfinder for wasted space

Choosing a Format
· Add variety by mixing horizontal and vertical shots
· Choose the format that gives the subject greatest drama

The Rule of Thirds
· Mentally divide the frame into vertical and horizontal thirds
· Place important subjects at thirds' intersections
· Use thirds' divisions to place the horizon

Lines
· Take time to notice lines
· Let lines lead the eye to a main subject
· Use the shape of lines to establish mood

Taking Pictures Through Frames
· Use foreground frames to draw attention to a subject
· Look for frames that complement the subject
· Expose for the subject, and let the frame go dark

Patterns
· Find patterns in repeated shapes, colors, and lines
· Try close-ups or overviews
· Isolate patterns for maximum impact (use a telephoto lens)

Textures that Touch the Eyes
· Exploit the tangible qualities of subjects
· Use oblique lighting to heighten surface textures
· Compare a variety of textures within a shot

Dramatic Angles
· Try dramatic angles to make ordinary subjects exciting
· Use high angles to help organize chaos and uncover patterns, and low angles to exaggerate height

Silhouettes
· Silhouette bold shapes against bright backgrounds
· Meter and expose for the background illumination
· Don't let conflicting shapes converge

Abstract Composition
· Don't restrict yourself to realistic renderings
· Look for ideas in reflections, shapes, and colors
· Keep designs simple

Establishing Size
· Include objects of known size
· Use people for scale, where possible
· Experiment with false or misleading scale

Color
· Accentuate mood through color
· Highlight subjects or create designs through color contrasts
· Study the effects of weather and lighting

From *Kodak Guide to Shooting Great Travel Pictures* © 2000 by Fodor's Travel Publications

Ski Sundown. Overlooking the Litchfield Hills, this ski area is approximately 15 mi west of Avon and boasts a variety of trails, ranging from very difficult to easy. The vertical drop of 625 ft is the second largest in the state. | Ratlum Rd., New Hartford | 860/379–9851 or 860/379–7669 (snow conditions) | fax 860/379–1853 | www.skisundown.com | $24–$33 | Dec.–Mar., daily 9 AM–10 PM.

ON THE CALENDAR
SEPT.: *Avon Day.* The Town Green in the downtown area is filled with live music in the gazebo, a dining tent with Taste-of-Avon booths, rides, and games on the last Saturday of the month. | 860/409–4300.

Dining
Avon Old Farms Inn. Contemporary. Housed in a converted 1757 farmhouse, this eatery has four separate dining rooms. The Forge, the most romantic dining area, has field stone walls, horse stall booths, and a large country fireplace. The chef's signature dish is Grand Marnier chocolate mousse cake. Try the Thai shrimp or pan-seared sea bass. It has a hugely popular Sun. brunch. | 1 Nod Rd. | 860/677–2818 | No lunch Sun. | $18–$25 | AE, D, MC, V.

Dakota. American. With fieldstone fireplaces, bear rugs, wooden furniture, and Native American artifacts, this casual spot is reminiscent of an Adirondack mountain lodge. Try the teriyaki sirloin. Kid's menu. Sun. brunch. | 225 W. Main St. | 860/677–4311 | No lunch | $15–$18 | AE, D, DC, MC, V.

The Frog and The Peach. American. This intimate dining spot is in a Victorian-style cottage 4 mi west of Avon. It was fully renovated in 2000, has curved walls and is candlelit. The restaurant is known for nori-wrapped salmon with a wasabi red onion puree and Moroccan-spice-glazed double-cut pork chops. For dessert, try the warm pumpkin bread pudding with cream cheese caramel and chantilly cream. Sun. brunch. No smoking. | 160 Albany Tpke., Canton, | 860/693–6345 or 860/693–6352 | No dinner Sun. No lunch weekends | $12–$25 | AE, MC, V.

Lodging
Avon Old Farms Hotel. At the foot of Talcott Mountain and across the street from a golf course, this hotel is housed in a redbrick Colonial-style building. There is a garden gazebo and a wooden bridge on the grounds. Restaurant, bar, complimentary Continental breakfast, room service. In-room data ports, cable TV. Pool. Sauna. Gym. Laundry service. Business services. Pets allowed. | 279 Avon Mountain Rd. | 860/677–1651 or 800/836–4000 | fax 860/677–0364 | www.avonoldfarmshotel.com | 160 rooms | $170–$311 | AE, D, DC, MC, V.

Hillside Motel. Rooms at this quiet roadside motel have views of the countryside. It is 5 mi west of town. Cable TV. | 671 Albany Tpke., Canton | 860/693–4951 | 16 rooms | $42–$45 | MC, V, D, AE.

BRANFORD

MAP 3, E6

(Nearby towns also listed: Guilford, Madison, New Haven)

The town of Branford, founded in 1644, was a prosperous port and later the site of a saltworks that provided salt to preserve food for the Continental Army during the Revolutionary War. The small Branford Village of Stony Creek, with a few tackle and antiques shops, a general store, and a marina, is the departure point for cruises to the Thimble Islands. Legend has it that Captain Kidd buried pirate gold on one of the group of more than 90 tiny islands ranging in size from 20 acres to nothing more than rocky humps visible only at low tide. Branford Center is built around a verdant green bequeathed to the town in 1699 and is home to the requisite New England–style town hall and 19th-century churches. Today, the town covers almost 28 square miles, and is easily accessible from I–95, about 10 mi west of I–91. An active Branford land trust is buying up land and blazing trails for ecological conservation. Home to a growing biotechnolgy industry, many residents commute to New Haven.

Information: Branford Chamber of Commerce | 230 E. Main St., Branford, 06405 | 203/488–5500 | fax 203/488–5046 | jcushing@branfordct.com | www.branfordct.com. **Connecticut River Valley and Shoreline Visitors Council** | 393 Main St., Middletown, 06457 | 860/347–0028 or 800/486–3346 | fax 860/704–2340 | crvsvc@cttourism.org | www.cttourism.org.

Attractions

Harrison House and Museum. Built in 1724, this salt-box is home to the Branford Historical Society. Its center chimney and clapboard siding are typical of homes of the period. A herb garden and a barn, displaying a collection of farm implements and other artifacts, are also on the 2-acre property. | 124 Main St. | 203/488–4828 | Donation suggested | June–Sept., Fri.–Sat. 2–5, or by appointment.

Hilltop Orchards. This orchard and country store was established in 1867, and is legendary for its pies. Varieties are numerous and include apple, pumpkin, and thimbleberry (the berries for which the Branford islands were named). You may pick your own apples, peaches, or pumpkins, depending on the season, and visit Captain Kidd's Landing, a living-history pirate museum that is being built on the property. | 616 E. Main St. | 203/488–0779 | Daily 9:30–5:30.

Sea Mist II. On this boat you'll be treated to narrated cruises of Branford's Thimble islands. | Stony Creek Dock, Thimble Island Rd. | 203/488–8905 | $8 | May–mid-Oct. Wed.–Mon.

Stony Creek Puppet House Theater. Built as a silent movie house in the early 1900s, this small theater is the site of children's performances (among them clown, puppet, and magic shows) in the summer, as well as adult and teen performances and concerts throughout the year. It is also the home of the only performing Sicilian puppet theater in the nation. | 128 Thimble Island Rd. | 203/488–5752 | Call for ticket prices | Call for schedule.

Volsunga IV. You can take a narrated cruise of Branford's Thimble islands with this group. | Stony Creek Dock, Thimble Island Rd. | 203/488–9978 | May–mid-Oct. | $8 | www.thimbleislands.com.

ON THE CALENDAR
JUNE: *Branford Festival.* Every Father's Day Weekend, downtown fills with games, crafts booths, strawberry-inspired foods, and live music, culminating with the New Haven Symphony concert Sunday evening. | 203/488–5500.

Dining

★ **Le Petit Café Marketplace.** French. This eatery overlooks the Branford Green. Along with fresh meat, seafoods and cheeses, homemade breads, soups, and desserts, you can take out duck au cassoulet, roast rack of lamb, crispy apple tart, flourless chocolate cake, and chocolate upside souflée. The café is take-out only. | 225 Montowese St. | 203/483–9791 | Closed Sun. | $10–$15 | MC, V.

USS Chowder Pot III. American. A giant lobster adorns the roof of this casual eatery. Try the baked stuffed lobster or shrimp, chowder pot platter, or any one of the broiled seafood dishes. Kid's menu. | 560 E. Main St. | 203/481–2356 | $13–$24 | AE, DC, MC, V.

Lodging

Abigail's Bed Breakfast. This 1870s white Colonial home has a marble fireplace and three porches. One of the porches provides a view of the terraced gardens and is heated and furnished with a sofa. Complimentary Continental breakfast weekdays. TV in common area. No kids under 12. No smoking. | 85 Cherry Hill Rd., | 203/483–1612 | 2 rooms | $110–$150 | D, MC, V.

Days Inn and Conference Center. Rooms at this two-story hotel are decorated mostly in blues and have wood furniture. I-95 runs right behind the hotel. Complimentary Continental breakfast, room service. Some kitchenettes, cable TV. Pool. Gym. Laundry facilities. Business services. Pets allowed (fee). | 375 E. Main St., | 203/488–8314 | fax 203/483–6885 | 78 rooms, 3 suites | $130–$150; $175 suites | AE, D, DC, MC, V.

BRIDGEPORT

MAP 3, C6

(Nearby towns also listed: Fairfield, Milford, Stratford, Westport)

Bridgeport, a city with a less-than-stellar reputation, may not be the first place you think of to visit on the Connecticut shoreline, but it has a number of engaging attractions that make it well worth a detour. Chief among them: the state's only zoo, which encompasses 36 acres in the northeastern part of town; Captain's Cove Seaport on historic Black Rock Harbor, home port of the tall ship HMS *Rose* and the lightship *Nantucket*; and downtown Bridgeport's Barnum Museum, temple of P. T. Barnum, showman extraordinaire and former mayor of Bridgeport. Like many of Connecticut's major cities, Bridgeport is currently hard at work at revitalization. The first major evidence of such efforts is the new ballpark at Harbor Yard, home of the Bridgeport Bluefish, members of minor-league baseball's Atlantic League.

Information: **Bridgeport Regional Business Council** | 10 Middle St., 14th floor, Bridgeport, 06604 | 203/335–3800 | fax 203/366–0105 | info@brbc.org | www.brbc.org. **Coastal Fairfield County Convention and Visitor Bureau** | 297 West Ave., Gate Lodge-Mathews Park, Norwalk, 06850 | 203/899–2799 or 800/866–7925 | fax 203/853–7524 | info@www.coastalct.com | www.visitfairfieldco.org.

Attractions

The Barnum Museum. This grand Byzantine Romanesque–style museum is associated with past resident and former mayor P. T. Barnum. Exhibits depict the life and times of the great showman, who presented performers like General Tom Thumb and Jenny Lind, the Swedish Nightingale. You can also tour a scaled-down model of Barnum's legendary five-ring circus. | 820 Main St. | 203/331–1104 | fax 203/339–4341 | www.barnum-museum.org | $5 | Tues.–Sat. 10–4:30, Sun. noon–4:30.

Beardsley Zoological Gardens. More than 120 species are spread out over 36 acres at this zoo. The indoor walk-through South American rain forest alone justifies a visit. Also in the park are a carousel museum with a working carousel, a New England farmyard, and a variety of animals ranging from bison to timber wolves. | 1875 Noble Ave. | 203/394–6565 | fax 203/394–6566 | www.beardsleyzoo.org | $6 | Daily 9–4; Rain forest, daily 10–3:30.

Bridgeport Bluefish. A member of the Atlantic League of professional baseball, the Bluefish were league champions in 1999. | Harbor Yard, 500 Main St. | 203/345–4800 or 1 877/GO–BLUES (tickets) | fax 203/345–4830 | www.bridgeportbluefish.com | $5–$11 | Apr.–Sept.; call for game times.

Captain's Cove Seaport. You can come by land, sea, or air to this marina. In the summer this bustling port on historic Black Rock Harbor has a boardwalk with more than two dozen little shops, a casual seafood restaurant, band concerts on Sunday afternoons, and narrated harbor cruises. The harbor is home to the HMS *Rose*—a replica of a Revolutionary War–era 24-gun frigate and one of the largest wooden tall ships in action today—and the Lightship #112 *Nantucket*. | 1 Bostwick Ave. | 203/335–1433 | $2 to tour lightship, $5 to

ICE CREAM, YOU SCREAM

There are close to 70 ice-cream shops in Connecticut that make hundreds of flavors of homemade ice cream. That's right, homemade. Move over Haagen-Dazs, make way Ben and Jerry, Nutmeggers love their ice cream and there's no shortage of dedicated men and women in the state who are up at the crack of dawn churning out the sweet stuff for the state's residents and you, you lucky visitors. Here are some favorite stops:

Timothy's (2974 Fairfield Ave., Bridgeport, 203/366–7496) still makes ice cream using old-fashioned salt-and-ice makers stationed in the shop's front window. Favorite flavors here include chocolate chip, peach, (which owner Timothy Larkin says "he can hardly keep in the store"), and Black Rock (a tastly mix of French vanilla and chocolate-covered almonds).

Stosh's in Kent (38 N. Main St., 860/927–4485) shares space with an antiques dealer in the restored Kent Railroad Station. Try the Dippidopolus—16 scoops of ice cream, plus chocolate sauce, bananas, nuts, and all the trimmings. You can walk it off among Kent's downtown art galleries.

Dave Redente, owner of Peaches 'N Cream (U.S. 202, Litchfield, 860/496–7536), says he likes to "keep things as traditional as possible," at his shop, and that means using fresh, natural ingredients. His peach, blueberry, and red raspberry ice creams are top summer sellers.

Norman Rockwell would have loved Shady Glen in Manchester (Manchester Parkade, W. Middle Tpke., 860/643–0511 and 840 E. Middle Tpke., 860/649–4245). The waitresses here wear old-fashioned green uniforms with white aprons, the bus boys wear paper hats, and you can still order an ice cream soda to share at the counter, with two straws.

One of the most beloved attractions in Mystic is Mystic Drawbridge Ice Cream (2 W. Main St., 860/572–7978 or Rte. 27, 860/536–2223). The Main Street location, which has handsome wood floors and an antique soda fountain, has been the site of an ice-cream shop almost continuously since the 1700s. At least 30 flavors are available at each location daily—Mystic Mud is a favorite.

Ashley's (2100 Dixwell Ave., Hamden, 203/287–7566) has been a sweet-and-creamy tradition in Greater New Haven since 1973. Among the shops' repertoire of 150 flavors are sweet cream, coffee Oreo, and bittersweet chocolate. Ashley's sundae-to-end-all-sundaes, the Downside Watson, includes seven scoops, nine toppings, and two bananas served on a Frisbee. Ashley's has additional locations in Branford, and Guilford.

The University of Connecticut's Dairy Bar (Rte. 195, Storrs, 860/486–2634), part of the school of agriculture, has been a campus institution for more than 60 years. The Oreo cookie, chocolate chip, and Jonathan's supreme (named for the Husky mascot) are the flavors to try, either by themselves or sandwiched between the Dairy Bar's gigantic chocolate-chip cookies.

© Corbis

tour frigate when in port | www.captainscoveseaport.com | Memorial Day–Labor Day, call for hrs.

Discovery Museum and Wonder Workshop. A planetarium, several hands-on science exhibits, a computer-art exhibit, a virtual basketball game, and the *Challenger* learning center (which has a computer-simulated space flight), make up the Discovery Museum. The Wonder Workshop schedules story-telling, arts-and-crafts, science, and other programs. | 4450 Park Ave. | 203/372–3521 | fax 203/374–1929 | www.discoverymuseum.org | $7 | Sept.–June, Tues.–Sat. 10–5, Sun. noon–5; July–Aug., Mon.–Sat. 10–5, Sun. noon–5.

Ferry to Port Jefferson, L.I. This journey across the Long Island Sound lasts approximately 75 minutes. Many shops and restaurants are within walking distance of the ferry terminal in Port Jefferson. | Water St. Dock | 888/443–3779 | Daily.

Polka Dot Playhouse. Musicals as well as dramas are presented by this professional playhouse. It recently celebrated the opening of a new theater inside a turn-of-the-century building. | 177 State St. | 203/333–3666 | fax 203/332–7529 | $23–$30 | Year-round, call for performance times.

ON THE CALENDAR

MAY: *Greek Festival.* Mountains of Greek food and pastries are on sale at this annual event. There is also live musical entertainment and dancing. | 203/374–5561.
JUNE: *Olde Black Rock Lobster Festival.* Carnival rides, a parade, and scrumptious lobster cooked many different ways at this festival during the first weekend of the month. | 203/334–0293.
JUNE–JULY: *Barnum Festival.* Besides being known as the greatest showman on earth, P. T. Barnum was once mayor of Bridgeport. This festival serves as a tribute to Barnum; events include a parade, fireworks display, and car show. | 203/367–8495.
AUG.: *Greatest Bluefish Tournament on Earth.* Although it spans the entire Long Island Sound, this fishathon is headquartered at Captain's Cove in Bridgewater. Prizes are awarded based on various criteria. | 203/366–BLUE.

Dining

Black Rock Castle. Irish. With a crenellated roof line, towers, and Gothic arches, the building of this restaurant actually resembles a castle. The menu includes Irish whiskey steak, Kenmare mussel stew, broiled salmon with Dijon caper sauce, and bangers and mash. There is live musical entertainment Thurs.–Sun. evenings. | 2895 Fairfield Ave. | 203/336–3990 | $7–$20 | AE, D, MC, V.

Tony's Huntington Inn. Italian. Tony's has occupied this former gas station since 1937. You can eat on the patio overlooking the surrounding countryside, or in the sky-lighted dining room with its oak floors and mahogany tables. Try the lobster ravoli. | 437 Huntington Tpke., | 203/374–5541 | $10–$15 | V, MC, AE.

Lodging

Holiday Inn. Two blocks from the train and bus stations, this nine-floor hotel is in the center of Bridgeport. 2 restaurants, bar, room service. In-room data ports, cable TV. Indoor and outdoor pool. Gym. Laundry services. Business services. Small pets allowed. | 1070 Main St. | 203/334–1234 | fax 203/367–1985 | 234 rooms, 6 suites | $129–$139; $350 suites | AE, D, DC, MC, V.

Ramada Plaza Hotel. In the corporate section of Shelton, 10 mi north of Bridgeport, this seven-story hotel sees mostly business travelers and hosts many conferences and meetings. Restaurant, bar. Indoor pool, sauna, exercise equipment. | 780 Bridgeport Ave., Shelton | 203/929–1500 | 155 rooms | $99–$136 | AE, D, DC, MC, V.

Trumbull Marriott. This five-story hotel is approximately 7 mi from Bridgeport. 2 restaurants, bar, room service. In-room data ports, cable TV. Indoor and outdoor pools. Hot tub,

sauna. Gym. Laundry services. Business services. | 180 Hawley La., Trumbull | 203/378–1400
| fax 203/378–4958 | 324 rooms, 3 suites | $177–$199;, $300–$400 suites | AE, D, DC, MC, V.

BRISTOL

(Nearby towns also listed: Farmington, New Britain, Southington, Waterbury)

There were some 275 clock makers in and around Bristol during the late 1800s—it is
said that by the end of the 19th century just about every household in America told
time to a Connecticut clock. Eli Terry, for whom nearby Terryville is named, first mass-
produced clocks in the mid-19th century. Seth Thomas, for whom nearby Thomaston
is named, learned under Terry and carried on the tradition. Bristol's American Clock
and Watch Museum on Maple Street is the only museum of its kind in the country—
and an astounding place to be when the big hand hits the 12. Lake Compounce on the
Bristol-Southington line is the country's oldest continuously operating amusement
park.

Information: Greater Bristol Chamber of Commerce | 10 Main St., 1st Floor, Bristol, 06010-
6527 | 860/584–4718 | fax 860/584–4722 | info@bristol-chamber.org | www.bristol-cham-
ber.org. **Litchfield Hills Visitors Council** | Box 968, Litchfield, 06759 | 860/567–4506 |
fax 860/567–5214 | www.litchfieldhills.com.

Attractions

American Clock and Watch Museum. More than 3000 timepieces are on display in this
museum which is housed in an 1801 house. The collection of manufactured clocks is quite
extensive. | 100 Maple St. | 860/583–6070 | fax 860/583–1862 | $5 | Apr.–Nov., daily 10–5.

Burlington Trout Hatchery. More than 90,000 pounds of trout that are used to stock
state waters are raised annually at this hatchery. | 34 Belden Rd., Burlington | 860/673–2340
| Free | Daily 8–3:30.

H.C. Barnes Memorial Nature Center. Self-guided nature trails, a nature library and animal exhibits about local wildlife and live animals are among the many highlights at this
70-acre nature center. | 175 Shrub Rd. | 860/585–8886 | $2 | Center Wed.–Fri. 1–5, Sat. 10–4,
Sun. noon–4; Trails, daily dawn–dusk.

★ **Lake Compounce Theme Park.** Opened in 1846, this is the oldest amusement park in the
country. Rides and attractions at this sprawling 325-acre facility include an antique
carousel, a classic wooden roller coaster, and a white-water raft ride. The park also has pic-
nic areas, a beach, and a water park with slides and a wave pool. | 822 Lake Ave. | 860/583–
3300 | fax 860/589–7974 | www.lakecompounce.com | $6.95; $23.95 includes all-day rides
| Memorial Day–late Sept., call for hrs.

Lock Museum of America. More than 22,000 locks, keys, and other ornate hardware items
are displayed in eight rooms. Highlights include a cannon ball safe and a range of Euro-
pean locks dating back to the 1500s. | 230 Main St., Terryville | 860/589–6359 | fax 860/589–
6359 | www.lockmuseum.com | $3 | May–Oct., Tues.–Sun. 1:30–4:30.

★ **New England Carousel Museum.** Full-size pieces in the Coney Island, Country Fair, and
Philadelphia styles and many miniature carousels make up the collection at this museum.
Carousel art carving demonstrations are given in the replica antique carving shop. | 95
Riverside Ave. | 860/585–5411 | fax 860/314–0483 | $4 | Apr.–Nov., Mon.–Sat. 10–5, Sun. noon–
5; Dec.–Mar., Thurs.–Sat. 10–5, Sun. noon–5.

Tunxis Trail. The parking lot of Lake Compounce Theme Park is the access point for this
14.6 mi series of nine trails. Try the high-water challenging Cussgutter Junction trail, or
take Tookey's Trail for a slow incline. | 822 Lake Ave. | www.ctwoodlands.org | Daily.

ON THE CALENDAR

MAY: *Balloons over Bristol.* Held along Memorial Blvd., this is one of the largest hot-air balloon rallies in the Northeast. In addition to the balloon launches, there are also carnival rides, a crafts fair, food vendors, and live entertainment. | 860/584–4718 or 860/583–3053.

SEPT.–OCT.: *Chrysanthemum Festival.* Named in honor of the chrysanthemum flower, which grows abundantly in Bristol, this town-wide celebration lasts three weeks. Events include a parade, food festival and auto show. | 860/584–4718.

OCT.: *Witch's Dungeon Horror Museum.* Authorized by Universal Studios, this seasonal museum is dedicated to the actors and makeup artists of classic horror films. | 80 Battle St. | 860/583–8306.

Dining

Angelino's. Italian. You can try any imaginable pasta dish, or the ever-popular chicken Milanese in this bright, window-lined, plant-filled eatery about 1½ mi from downtown. | 650 Farmington Ave., | 860/589–0669 | $7–$16 | AE, D, DC, MC, V.

Lodging

Chimney Crest Manor. Rooms at this English Tudor manor in Bristol's historic district have impressive views of the Farmington Valley. Some of the suites have working fireplaces and the garden has a gargoyle fountain. There is a two-night minimum stay from Sept.–Oct. and on major holidays. Full breakfast. Cable TV, in-room VCRs. No smoking. | 5 Founders Dr. | 860/582–4219 | fax 860/584–5903 | 2 rooms, 4 suites | $105–$125; $145–$165 suites | AE, MC, V.

Radisson Inn. The large meeting facility at this seven-story hotel attracts many business travelers during the week. Downtown is 2 mi away. Restaurant, bar. Refrigerators, in-room VCRs. Indoor pool, sauna, hot tub. Business services. | 42 Century Dr. | 860/589–7766 | 120 rooms | $79–$149 | AE, D, DC, MC, V.

BROOKLYN

MAP 3, I3

(Nearby towns also listed: Pomfret, Putnam, Woodstock)

The village of Brooklyn bears no resemblance to the more famous borough of New York City of the same name. White picket fences and beautifully restored Colonial homes are the norm here. Built in 1771, the oldest Unitarian meeting house in the country is located at the junction of U.S. 6 and Route 169. Brooklyn is also the birthplace of Isreal Putnam, who exclaimed during the battle of Bunker Hill, "Don't fire till you see the whites of their eyes." The town's claim to fame is the Brooklyn Fair, which is one of the state's oldest fairs and is held the weekend before Labor Day. Primarily an agricultural area, Brooklyn is home to corn farms, dairy farms and, believe it or not, a buffalo farm.

Information: **Northeastern Connecticut Chamber of Commerce** | 3 Central St., Danielson, 06239 | 860/774–8001 | fax 860/774–4299 | elizabeth.kuszaj@snet.net. **Northeast Connecticut Visitors District** | Box 598, Putnam, 06260 | 860/928–1228 or 888/628–1228 | fax 860/928–4720 | quietcorner@snet.net | www.ctquietcorner.org.

Attractions

Creamery Brook Bison. The buffalo roam at this 120-acre working dairy farm. Its original purchase of five buffalo in 1990 has grown to a herd of more than 70. Wagon rides are given to the fields where the herd grazes. | 19 Purvis Rd. | 860/779–0837 | fax 860/779–0126 | $6 | Weekdays 2–6, Sat. 9–2; wagon rides July–Sept., weekends at 1:30.

Logee's Greenhouses. Founded in 1892, this family-run facility has seven greenhouses overflowing with more than 1,500 varieties of indoor plants. Begonias, of which the greenhouses boast more than 400 varieties, are a specialty. | 141 North St., Danielson | 860/774–8038 or 888/330–8038 | fax 888/774–9932 | www.logees.com | Free | Mid-Feb.–June, Mon.–Sat. 9–5, Sun. 11–5; July–mid-Feb., Mon.–Sat. 9–4, Sun. 11–4.

New England Center for Contemporary Art. An extensive collection of contemporary Chinese art is on display at this museum. The exhibitions include paintings and large sculptures on display outdoors, and are rotated annually. | 248 Pomfret Rd. | 860/774–8899 | www.museum-necca.org | Free | Tues.–Sun. noon–5.

Prudence Crandall House. Now a National Historic Landmark, this house was opened in 1883 as a boarding school expressly "for girls of color," the first school of its kind in New England. The site has changing exhibits that deal with black and women's history, period furnishings, and a research library. | Rtes. 14 and 169, Canterbury | 860/546–9916 | fax 860/546–7803 | $2.50 | Wed.–Sun. 10–4:30, or by appointment.

ON THE CALENDAR

JUNE: *Antique Truck Show & Flea Market.* A combination of more than 200 antique trucks and 100 flea-market vendors gather the Brooklyn Fairgrounds. | Rtes. 6 and 169 | 860/886–4621.

AUG.: *Brooklyn Fair.* Held the weekend before Labor Day at the Brooklyn Fairgrounds, this is the oldest continuously operating agricultural fair in the state and it usually draws huge crowds. The carnival rides and petting zoo are major attractions. | Rtes. 6 and 169 | 860/779–0012 or 860/774–8001.

Dining

★ **Golden Lamb Buttery.** Continental. This restaurant is housed in a barn in the middle of a thousand-acre farm 2 mi north of Brooklyn. Upon arrival, you will be served cocktails in the barn, taken on a hayride, and finally seated at your table. There are no printed menus, and absolutely no rush at this peaceful place, which is known for its roast duck, crab-stuffed smoked salmon, heaping plates of vegetables, dense chocolate pie, and pecan coffee tort. Jacket and tie are only required for dinner. | 499 Bush Hill Rd. | 860/774–4423 | Reservations essential | Jacket and tie | Closed Jan.–mid-Apr. No lunch Mon. No supper Sun.–Thurs. | Prix-fixe $65 | No credit cards.

Hank's Restaurant. American. The rooster-themed decorations on the walls of the dining room can be explained by the "Hank's Roost" sign which hangs outside and denotes the previous name of this casual spot. Try the prime rib, or one of the many chicken dishes. | 416 Providence Rd. | 860/774–6071 | $9–$17 | AE, D, DC, MC, V.

Lodging

Friendship Valley Inn. Rooms are decorated with antiques and named after previous owners of this 1795 yellow Colonial manor. The innkeeper also arranges group tours to Great Britain. Complimentary breakfast. No air-conditioning, no room phones, TV in common area. No pets. No kids under 7. No smoking. | 60 Pomfret Rd. | 860/779–9696 | friendship-valley@snet.net | www.friendshipvalleyinn.com | 5 rooms | $105–$155 | AE, MC, V.

CHESHIRE

MAP 3, E4

(Nearby towns also listed: New Britain, Southington, Waterbury)

Settled in 1694, Cheshire has a rich history of farming in central Connecticut. Bishop Farms, for example, is a working farm that was established prior to the Revolutionary War. The town is also home to Cheshire Academy, a private school that was once a Civil

War academy. Among the estimated 26,000 residents of Cheshire are Mickey, Minnie, the Lone Ranger, and Charlie McCarthy, who've taken up residence at the town's Barker Character, Comic, and Cartoon Museum.

Information: **Cheshire Chamber of Commerce** | 265 Highland Ave., 06410 | 203/272–2345 | fax 203/271–3044 | cheshire.chamber@snet.net | www.cheshirechamber.com. **Central Connecticut Tourism District** | 1 Grove St., Ste. 310, New Britain, 06053 | 860/225–3901 | fax 860/225–0218 | info@centralct.org | www.centralct.org.

Attractions

Barker Character, Comic, and Cartoon Museum. A comprehensive collection of comic strip, cartoon, western, TV, and advertising memorabilia are on display at this unique museum. Highlights include a rare "Yellow Kid" vending machine from 1899 and momentos from most major toy manufacturers. Also on the premises is the Barker Animation Gallery, which displays memorable drawings, cartoon strips, and the like. | 1188 Highland Ave. | 203/699–3822 | www.barkermuseum.com | Free | Museum: Tues.–Sat. 11–5; Barker Animation Art Gallery: Mon–Sat. 9:30–5:30.

Bishop Farms. You can pick your own apples or tour a fruit and grape winery at this 200-year-old working farm. There is also an antiques shop and bakery on the premises. | 500 S. Meriden Rd. | 203/272–8243 | July–Dec., daily 10–5 (call ahead).

Lock 12 Historical Park and Farmington Canal Linear Park. From 1828 to 1848, the Farmington Canal was a major freight and passenger route from New Haven to Northampton, Massachusetts. The Lock 12 Historical Park contains the only authentically restored section of the old canal, as well as a museum, gardens, blacksmith shop, and picnic area. Adjacent to the park is the 6 mi Farmington Canal Linear Park that is paved and follows part of the canal's route. | 487 Brooksvale Rd. | 203/272–2743 | Free | Mar.–Nov., daily 10–5.

ON THE CALENDAR

JUNE: *Strawberry Festival.* The Congregational Church runs this festival on their green. Strawberry shortcake, hamburgers and crafts are on sale. | 111 Church Dr. | 203/272–5323.

Dining

Watch Factory Restaurant. Austrian. You can sit in the romantic, candle-lighted, blond wood-accented dining room or outside in the courtyard of this turn-of-the-century watch factory building. Try the Wiener schnitzel, goulash, or a steak prepared with artichoke hearts and basil. | 122 Elm St. | 203/271–1717 | Closed Sun.–Mon. | $17–$21 | AE, MC, V.

Lodging

Academy Bed & Breakfast. There is an apple orchard on the grounds of this 1790 Federal-style home. Each room is decorated with the works of local artists that are available for purchase. Complimentary breakfast. In-room data ports, TV in common area. No smoking. | 376 Academy Rd. | 203/271–0754 | fax 203/272–2823 | www.academy-bb.com | 3 rooms | $95–$125 | AE, MC, V.

CHESTER

MAP 3, F5

(Nearby towns also listed: East Haddam, Essex, Ivoryton, Old Saybrook)

Chester has a quaint Main Street lined with upscale boutiques and artisans' studios. It is the home base for the National Theater of the Deaf and the starting point of the

Chester–Hadlyme Ferry, which crosses the Connecticut River in a grand total of five minutes.

Information: Middlesex County Chamber of Commerce | 393 Main St., Middletown, 06457 | 860/347–6924 | fax 860/346–1043 | info@middlesexchamber.com | www.middlesexchamber.com. **Connecticut River Valley and Shoreline Visitors Council** | 393 Main St., Middletown, 06457 | 860/347–0028 or 800/486–3346 | fax 860/704–2340 | crvsvc@cttourism.org | www.visitctrivershore.com.

Attractions

Connecticut River Artisans Cooperative. Founded in 1980, this crafts cooperative sells traditional and contemporary handcrafts, including pottery, jewelry, and folk art pieces. | 4 Water St. | 860/526–5575 | Free | www.ctartisans.com | Jan.–mid-Mar., Fri.–Sun. 10–5; mid-Mar.–Dec., Wed.–Sun. 10–5.

Chester Charter Inc. This charter service based at the Chester airport provides open-cockpit biplane rides over the lower Connecticut River Valley. | 61 Winthrop Rd. | 860/526–4321 or 800/752–6371 | $150–$1000 | Year-round; rides by reservation only.

Chester-Hadlyme Ferry. The *Selden III* is the second-oldest continually operating ferry in the country. It's only a five-minute trip across the Connecticut River, but there are nice views of the valley and Gillette Castle. | 148 Ferry Rd. | 860/526–2743 or 860/347–0028 | $.75 | Apr.–mid-Dec., daily 7–6:45, weekends 10:30–5:00.

ON THE CALENDAR

FEB.: *Winter Carnival.* An ice-carving competition, art gallery openings, horse and carriage rides, and various events held throughout downtown are included in this celebration of the season of snow. | 860/526–2077.
JUNE–JULY: *Hands Tell Stories.* Performed by the Chester-based National Theater of the Deaf in both sign language and spoken word, this family-oriented story-telling series lasts two weeks. | 860/724–5179.
AUG.: *Chester Fair.* The Chester Fairgrounds is the venue for this agricultural fair. Highlights include livestock/animal shows, arts and crafts displays, and baking contests. | Rte. 154 | 860/526–2402.

Dining

Fiddlers. Seafood. Blond bentwood chairs, lacy stenciling, and prints of famous schooners decorate this spot. Specialties include bouillabaisse and lobster in a peach reduction. | 4 Water St. | 860/526–3210 | Closed Mon. No lunch Sun. | $14–$20 | DC, MC, V.

The Inn at Chester American. This casual eatery is housed in a 1700s barn house. Try the rack of lamb or the seared duck breast and crème brûlée. The wine list is quite comprehensive. | 318 W. Main St. | 860/526–9541; 800/949–7829 | Reservations required weekends | $17–$26 | AE, DC, MC, V.

Restaurant du Village. French. Flowers and candlelight help set the romantic mood at this elegant spot. Best bets are the escargot in a puff pastry and filet mignon. | 59 Main St. | 860/526–5301 | Closed Mon.–Tues. No lunch | $26–$29 | AE, MC, V.

Lodging

The Inn at Chester This 18th century clapboard inn was once a farmhouse for a local family, the Parmalees. The rooms are furnished with Eldred Wheeler antique reproductions. There is a billiard room and on-site massages can be arranged. 2 restaurants, complimentary breakfast. Sauna. Tennis court. Gym. Library. Baby-sitting. Pets allowed (fee). | 318 W. Main St. | 860/526–9541 or 800/949–7829 | fax 860/526–4387 | www.innatchester.com | 41 rooms, 1 suite | $105–$215 | MC, V.

CLINTON

(Nearby towns also listed: Guilford, Madison, Old Saybrook)

Visitors to this shoreline town used to come primarily for its antiques: East and West Main streets in downtown Clinton are lined with antiques and collectibles shops. Today, however, these same visitors are as likely to come for something new they can pick up at Clinton Crossing, which offers the largest collection of premium outlets in the state.

Information: **Chamber of Commerce** | 50 E. Main St., Box 334, Clinton, 06413 | 860/669–3889 | fax 860/669–3889 | chamber@clintonct.com | www.clintonct.com. **Connecticut River Valley and Shoreline Visitors Council** | 393 Main St., Middletown, 06457 | 860/347–0028 or 800/486–3346 | fax 860/704–2340 | crvsvc@cttourism.org | www.visitctrivershore.com.

OUTLET BOUND

There are those for whom bargain shopping is not so much a necessity as it is a way of life. A calling. These are the shoppers who now flock to Clinton and Westbrook on the Connecticut shoreline. Yes, Donna Karan and Ralph Lauren have moved here. Even Kenneth Cole and Clifford & Wills. Indeed, these designers, and more than one hundred of their closest friends, have set up shop at Clinton Crossing Premium Outlets and Westbrook Factory Stores, which together boast close to 140 opportunities for premium bargain shopping. Hallelujah!

The vital statistics:

Name: Clinton Crossing Premium Outlets
Address: Rte. 81, Clinton
Directions: I–95, Exit 63
Phone: 860/664–0700
Web: www.chelseagca.com/location/clinton/clin.html
No. of stores: 70
Highlights: Isabel Ardee, Donna Karan, Lauren by Ralph Lauren, Jones New York Men, Barneys New York, Panasonic, Bose, WestPoint Stevens, Crate & Barrel, Kenneth Cole, Off 5th–Saks Fifth Avenue Outlet hours: Mon.–Sat. 10–9, Sun. 10–6 (Sun. until 8 from July–Labor Day). Call for winter hours.

Name: Westbrook Factory Stores
Address: 314 Flat Rock Place, Westbrook
Directions: I–95, Exit 65
Phone: 860/399–8656
Web: www.charter-oak.com/westbrook
No. of stores: 65
Highlights: Clifford & Wills, Starter, Woolrich, We're Entertainment, Nordic Track, Oneida, Easy Spirit, London Fog, Golf DayHours: Mon.–Sat. 10–9, Sun. 11–6. Call for winter hours.

Surveys say that manufacturers' retail outlets are the fastest growing segment of the retail industry. So, what are you waiting for? Ladies and gentlemen, start your wallets! (P.S. Both outlet centers have ATMs.)

© Corbis

Attractions

Chamard Vineyards. Established in 1983, this vineyard has more than 20 acres of vines. A tour of the property includes a visit the the underground wine cellar and barrel-aging rooms. | 115 Cow Hill Rd. | 860/664–0299 or 800/371–1609 | fax 860/664–0297 | www.chamard.com | Free | Wed.–Sat. 11–4.

Clinton Crossing Premium Outlets. Among the 70 big-name outlets to be found here are Off 5th-Saks Fifth Avenue, Donna Karan, Nautica, and Versace. | Rte. 81, off I–95 at Exit 63 | 860/664–0700 | fax 860/669–3033 | www.chelseagca.com | Mon.–Sat. 10–9, Sun. 10–6.

Stanton House. Built in 1789 by Adam Stanton, who operated a general store and salt distillery on the premises, this house-museum contains almost all the original furnishings and an excellent collection of Staffordshire and American dinnerware. | 63 E. Main St. | 860/669–2132 | Free | June–Sept., Tues.–Sun. 2–5.

Westbrook Factory Stores. Timberland, Haggar, Reebok, Bugle Boy, and J.Crew are some of the more than 65 stores represented at this outlet center. There's also a restored 1902 cruising yawl and steam engine on display. | 314 Flat Rock Pl. | 860/399–8656 | fax 860/399–8739 or 888/SHOP–333 | www.charter-oak.com/westbrook | Mon.–Sat. 10–9, Sun. 11–6.

ON THE CALENDAR

AUG.: *Bluefish Festival.* , Begun in 1974 as a simple fishing contest, this townwide celebration on the third weekend of the month. It includes crafts displays, a children's bicycle parade, carnival-type rides, and bluefish dinners. | 860/669–3889.

Dining

Aqua Restaurant. Contemporary. Every table in the dining room and on the outdoor deck has a view of the Long Island Sound. Try the gorgonzola-crusted sirloin steak in merlot sauce or one of the hand-cut fish steaks. | 34 Riverside Dr., | 860/664–3788 | Closed Oct.–Mar. and Mon.–Tues. Apr.–May | $11–$22 | AE, MC, V.

Harpoon Louie's. Seafood. Less than 1 mi from Clinton Beach, this eatery serves up a variety of seafood dishes, including lobster, stuffed or boiled, and a seafood paella that differs in grades of hotness. The dining room is lined with boat and lighthouse pictures and there is live music, predominantly folk singers, almost every night. | 1 Beach Park Rd. | 860/669–7743 | $11–$19 | AE, MC, V.

Marty's Seafood Restaurant. Seafood. The dining rooms of this shoreline spot are filled with more than 100 mounted fish and a full-size tugboat. Try the Maine lobster or New England clam chowder. On Wednesday there is an all-you-can-eat fish fry buffet and Thursday is an all-you-can-eat clam buffet. | 110 Boston Post Rd. | 860/669–1269 | Breakfast also available | $8–$14 | MC, V.

Lodging

Captain Stannard House. Antiques and dark wood furniture fill this 19th century sea captain's mansion turned inn. There is a piano in the dining room and the Long Island Sound is 1 block away. Complimentary breakfast. Cable TV in some rooms, no room phones, cable TV in common area. Bicycles. Business services. No smoking. | 138 S. Main St., Westbrook | 860/399–4634 | www.stannardhouse.com | 8 rooms | $95–$135 | MC, V.

Clinton Motel. Clinton Crossing Premium Outlets is 2.5 mi from this single-level motel. There is a restaurant three blocks away. Some microwaves, some refrigerators, cable TV. Pool. | 163 E. Main St. | 860/669–8850 | fax 860/669–3849 | 15 rooms | $52–$89 | AE, D, DC, MC, V.

Talcott House. All rooms at this 1890 cedar-shingle beach cottage on the Long Island Sound offer wonderful views of the sunset and the Sound. The first floor guest room has a private glass-enclosed veranada, while the second floor bedrooms are decorated with late 1800s French furniture. It is 3 mi south of Clinton. Complimentary Continental breakfast weekdays, complimentary breakfast weekends. No air-conditioning, no room phones, TV in common area. Beach. No kids under 10. No smoking. | 161 Seaside Ave., Westbrook | 860/399–5020 | 4 rooms | $150–$165 | AE, MC, V.

Water's Edge. On a bluff overlooking the Long Island Sound, this 15-acre resort is spread out over manicured lawns and fronted by a stretch of white sand beach. All rooms have two-poster beds and are done in soft colors. 2 restaurants, bar, room service. In-room data ports, some kitchenettes, cable TV. Indoor pool, outdoor pool. Hot tub, massage, sauna, spa. 2 tennis courts. Health club, beach. Children's activities. Laundry services. Business services. | 1525 Boston Post Rd., Westbrook | 860/399–5901 or 800/222–5901 | fax 860/399–8644 | www.watersedge-resort.com | 100 rooms, 66 villas | $175–$225; $250–$290 villas | AE, D, DC, MC, V.

Welcome Inn Bed & Breakfast. The innkeeper of this 1895 Victorian farmhouse has his cabinet shop on the property and has built or restored most of the furniture in the house. There is a 10-ft-long deacon's bench on the front porch. Complimentary breakfast. Cable TV, no room phones. No smoking. No kids under 10. | 433 Essex Rd., Westbrook | 860/399–2500 | fax 860/399–1840 | 4 rooms | $85–$145 | MC, V.

Westbrook Inn Bed & Breakfast. The beach is just one block away from this 1876 Victorian home. Rooms are filled with antiques and decorated with understated floral wallpaper. Complimentary breakfast. Some refrigerators, cable TV, no room phones. Fishing. | 976 Boston Post Rd. | 860/399–4777 | fax 860/399–8023 | 10 rooms, 1 cottage | $129–$149, $175–$245 cottage | D, MC, V.

CORNWALL

MAP 3, C2

(Nearby towns also listed: Kent, Lakeville, Litchfield, Norfolk, Salisbury)

Connecticut's Cornwalls can get confusing. There's Cornwall, Cornwall Bridge, West Cornwall, Cornwall Hollow, East Cornwall, and North Cornwall. What this quiet corner of the Litchfield Hills is primarily known for is its fantastic natural vistas and its red-covered bridge, which spans the Housatonic and is easily one of the most photographed spots in the state. For your information, the covered bridge is in West Cornwall, not Cornwall Bridge.

Information: Chamber of Commerce of Northwest Connecticut | 333 Kennedy Dr., Box 59, Ste. R101, Torrington, 06790 | 860/482–6586 | fax 860/489–8851 | dave@northwestchamber.org | www.northwestchamber.org. **Litchfield Hills Visitors Bureau** | Box 968, Litchfield, 06759 | 860/567–4506 | fax 860/567–5214 | www.litchfieldhills.com.

Attractions
Clarke Outdoors. You canoe, kayak, or raft along the Housatonic River. The drop-off is at Falls Village and the pick-up is at Housatonic Meadows Picnic Area, a state park. | 163 U.S. 7, West Cornwall | 860/672–6365 | fax 860/672–4268 | www.clarkeoutdoors.com | Apr.–Oct.

Housatonic Meadows State Park. Tall pine trees near the Housatonic River shade the campsites in this 451-acre park. Fly-fishers consider the 2-mi stretch of the river within the park to be among the best places in New England to test their skills against trout and bass. | U.S. 7, Sharon, | 860/927–3238 | Free | Daily 8–dusk.

Housatonic River Outfitters. A full service fly shop, guide services, and fly-fishing instruction are provided by this outfitter. Wade and drift-boat trips are among the various guided trips you can go on. | 24 Kent Rd., Cornwall Bridge | 860/672–1010 | www.dryflies.com | Daily 9–5.

Mohawk Mountain Ski Area. Mohawk's 23 trails, with a vertical drop of 640 ft, include plenty of intermediate terrain, with a few trails for beginners and a few steeper sections toward the top of the mountain. A small section of the mountain is devoted to snowboarders and there are facilities for ice-skating. | 46 Great Hollow Rd. | 860/672–6100 or 860/672–6464 (snow conditions) | fax 860/672–0117 | www.goski.com | Nov.–early Apr., Fri.–Sat. 8:30–10, Sun. 8:30–4.

Sharon Audubon Center. Many mammals and various species of birds make their home at this 758-acre sanctuary which is less than 5 mi west of Cornwall. If you want to hike, there are 11 mi of trails and nature walks. | 325 Cornwall Bridge Rd., Sharon | 860/364–0520 | fax 860/364–5792 | www.audubon.org/local/sanctuary/sharon | $3 | Visitor center and nature store, Mon.–Sat. 9–5, Sun. 1–5; Trails, daily dawn–dusk.

West Cornwall Covered Bridge. Built in 1841, this barn-red, covered bridge incorporates strut techniques that have been copied by bridge builders around the country. | U.S. 7 at Rte. 128 | Free | Daily.

ON THE CALENDAR

MAY: *Covered Bridge Dance.* Food vendors and live musical entertainment along the banks of the Housatonic River and dancing in the historic covered bridge on the Sunday of Memorial Day Weekend help Cornwall celebrate the coming of summer. | Main St., W. Cornwall | 860/672–4959.

Dining

Cafe by the Bridge. American/Casual. You will have a view of the Cornwall Bridge from this eatery which is housed in a century-old former horse stable. For dinner try the steak or stuffed shrimp. | 421 Sharon–Goshen Tpke., West Cornwall | 860/672–0178 | Breakfast also available. No supper Sun.–Wed. | $10–$14.

Lodging

Cornwall Inn. One of the two buildings that comprise this inn dates back to 1871. Some rooms have strip cedar bed frames and most of them are done in light pastel colors. Restaurant, complimentary Continental breakfast (weekends only). In-room hot tubs, no room phones, TV in common area. Pool. Pets allowed. | 270 Kent Rd. | 860/672–6884 or 800/786–6884 | fax 860/672–0352 | 14 rooms in 2 buildings | $89–$169 | AE, D, MC, V.

COVENTRY

MAP 3, G3

(Nearby towns also listed: Manchester, Storrs)

Historians will recognize Coventry as the birthplace of the Revolutionary War hero Capt. Nathan Hale, who was hanged as a spy by the British in 1776. It was Hale who spoke the immortal last words, "I only regret that I have but one life to lose for my country." Gardeners and herbalists, on the other hand, regard Coventry first and foremost as the home of Caprilands Herb Farm, which the late Adelma Grenier Simmons built into a center of worldwide renown.

Information: **Windham Region Chamber of Commerce** | 1010 Main St., Box 43, Willimantic, 06226 | 860/423–6389 | fax 860/423–8235. **Northeast Connecticut Visitors District** | Box 598, Putnam, 06260 | 860/928–1228 or 888/628–1228 | fax 860/928–4720 | quietcorner@snet.net | www.webtravels.com/quietcorner.

Attractions

Caprilands Herb Farm. This nationally renowned herb farm draws thousands of visitors annually to 38 gardens that hold more than 300 varieties of herbs. There's a 12-luncheon lecture program and high tea held on various weekends from May to December. There are Scottish Blackface Sheep on the grounds. Oil, potporri, seeds, teas, botanicals, wreaths, arrangements are for sale. | 534 Silver St. | 860/742–7244 | www.caprilands.com | Free | Daily 10–5.

Memory Lane Countryside Antique Center. The more than 50 dealers in this house and two barns specialize in everything from furniture to jewelry. Next door the owners have opened Memories Too, same hours, same kind of stuff. | 224 Boston Tpke | 860/742–0346 | Free | Wed.–Sun. 10–5.

Nathan Hale Homestead. This homestead was rebuilt in 1776 by Deacon Richard Hale, Nathan's father, although evidence suggests that Nathan never set foot in the house. It was constructed the year he died, and many of his other siblings had already grown to adulthood by the time their father relocated here. That said, family artifacts are on exhibit in the completely furnished home. The grounds include a corncrib and an 18th-century barn. | 2299 South St. | 860/742–6917 or 860/423–6389 | $4 | Mid-May–mid-Oct., daily 1–4.

ON THE CALENDAR

JULY: *Encampment & Muster.* A weekend historical encampment on the grounds of the Nathan Hale Homestead. On Saturday there is a revolutionary war battle—a reenactment of struggle between colonists and the British. Each year no one is sure which side will win. Sunday afternoon brings the Coventry Fife and Drum Corps, which hosts a muster (individual marchers play and then all join in on a stirring grand finale). Expect all sorts of demonstrations of colonial crafts as well as living-exhibits of Colonial life. | 2299 South St. | 860/742–6917 or 860/423–6389.

Dining

Bidwell Tavern. American. This 1822 tavern was once the town hall. The casual menu has anything from burgers and 26 varieties of chicken wings to prime rib. There's outdoor dining on the deck. Kid's menu. | 1260 Main St. | 860/742–6978 | $10–$16 | AE, D, DC, MC, V.

Dimitri's Pizza. Pizza. While this place began in 1972 as a mom-and-pop pizzeria, it now serves chicken and veal parmesan, steaks, and seafood dishes. You can feast on white Greek pizza with feta and calamata olives, vegetable-topped pizza, or standard pepperoni slices by the fire in the wood-floored dining room or outdoors on the patio. | 3444 Main St. | 860/742–7373 | Closed Mon. | $8–$15 | AE, MC, V.

Lodging

Special Joys Bed & Breakfast. Two of the guest rooms at this 1958 Victorian-inspired Cape on 2 acres have private entrances and private baths. One has a bay window, a brass bed, and an antique wedding gown displayed on a mannequin. There is a balcony overlooking the garden, and an antique doll and toy shop downstairs. Complimentary breakfast. Cable TV. No kids under 6. | 41 N. River Rd. | 860/742–6359 | 3 rooms | $62 | D, MC, V.

DANBURY

MAP 3, B5

(Nearby towns also listed: New Milford, Ridgefield)

Danbury was the hat-manufacturing capital of America for nearly 200 years—until the mid-1950s. Rumors persist that the term "mad as a hatter" originated here. Hat makers suffered widely from the injurious effects of mercury poisoning, a fact that is said to explain the resultant "madness" of veteran hatters. Today suburbs-ringed

Danbury is a manufacturing city, producing a variety of goods including optical equipment, ball bearings, pharmaceuticals, and machinery.

Information: Greater Danbury Chamber of Commerce | 39 West St., Danbury, 06810 | 203/743–5565 | fax 203/794–1439 | www.danburychamber.com. **Housatonic Valley Tourism District** | 30 Main St., Box 406, Danbury, 06810 | 203/743–0546 or 800/841–4488 | fax 203/790–6124 | hvtd@snet.net | www.housatonic.org.

Attractions

Danbury Fair Mall. One of the largest malls in New England, Danbury Fair has more than 225 shops and a huge working carousel in the food court. | I–84, Exit 3 | 203/743–3247 | Mon.–Sat. 10–9:30, Sun. 11–7.

Danbury Museum and Historical Society. Danbury was once known as the hat capital of America; the museum explores the history of this industry in the 1790 John Dodd Shop. The 1785 John and Mary Rider House has late 18th- and early 19th-century furnishings and changing exhibits, while the birthplace of Pulitzer Prize–winning composer Charles Ives contains memorabilia and late-19th-century furnishings. Due to extensive, long-term renovations, you should call ahead before visiting. | 43 Main St. | 203/743–5200 | www.danburyhistorical.org | Free; special exhibits: $3 | Call for hrs.

Danbury Railway Museum. A station built for the New Haven Railroad in 1903 houses this museum. In the train yard are 20 or so examples of freight and passenger railroad stock, including a restored 1944 caboose, a 1948 Alco locomotive, and an operating locomotive turntable. Museum exhibits include vintage American Flyer model trains. There are also rail excursion trips and hands-on railroad work. | 120 White St. | 203/778–8337 | www.danbury.org/drm | $3 | Jan.–Mar., Wed.–Sat. 10–4, Sun. noon–4; Apr.–Dec., Tues.–Sat. 10–5, Sun. noon–4.

Military Museum of Southern New England. This top-notch museum exhibits an elegant and impressive collection of U.S. and allied forces memorabilia from World War II, including 60 armored vehicles. The outdoor exhibit includes 19 tanks dating from WWII to the present. A computer allows access to the names on the Vietnam Veterans Memorial in Washington. | 125 Park Ave. | 203/790–9277 | fax 203/790–0420 | www.usmilitarymuseum.org | $4 | Oct.–Mar., Fri.–Sat. 10–5, Sun. noon–5; Apr.–Sept., Tues.–Sat. 10–5, Sun. noon–5.

Richter Park Golf Course. *Golf Digest* has rated this 18-hole, par-72 course one of the top 25 public courses in the country. Connecticut golfers voted it the number one public golf course in the state. | 100 Aunt Hack Rd. | 203/792–2550 | www.richterpark.com | $17–$48 | Mid-Apr.–mid-Nov.

Stew Leonard's. The self-proclaimed "Disneyland of Supermarkets," Stew Leonard's has a petting zoo, animated characters lining the aisles, scrumptious chocolate-chip cookies, and great soft ice cream. It is as much an experience as it is a supermarket. | 99 Federal Rd. | 203/790–8030 | www.stew-leonards.com | Daily 8 AM–10 PM.

ON THE CALENDAR

JUNE–SEPT.: *Ives Concert Park.* This 5,500-seat outdoor amphitheater includes everything from gentle symphonies to jazz soloists performances, rock shows to big name musicians. Located on the grounds of Western Connecticut State University. | 203/837–9226.

SEPT.: *Taste of Greater Danbury.* Area chefs showcase their goodies at this annual event. | 203/743–5565.

NOV.–DEC.: *Holiday Craft Exhibition and Sale.* Brookfield Craft Center hosts this exhibition and sale of fine American handicrafts designed by more than 300 artists from around the country. The mediums showcased include wood, glass, ceramics, jewelry, fiber, and baskets. | 203/775–4526.

Dining

Bella Italia. Italian. You can choose to eat in the pizzeria, the dining room with ceramic dishes lining the walls, or the candle-lit dining room with flowers on the tables. The owners are straight from Italy and serve changing daily specials including shrimp, chicken and veal dishes. | 2 Padanaram Rd. | 203/743–3828 | $10–$15 | AE, D, MC, V.

Emerald City Cafe. Contemporary. A storefront gussied up with Art Deco touches. The menu's choices range from burgers to Alaskan salmon, focaccia sandwiches to chicken Lyonnaise. Diners who order an entrée from the right side of the menu get a free movie for Bethel Cinemas next door, excludes Fri. and Sat., but good for 30 days. Sun. brunch. No smoking. | 269 Greenwood Ave., Bethel | 203/778–4100 | Closed Mon. No lunch. No dinner Sun. | $13–$19 | AE, MC, V.

Ondine. French. Drifts of fresh flowers, soft lighting, handwritten menus, and waiters in white jackets equal unadulterated romance at this formal spot. Try the venison, sweet breads, and soufflés. There's a five-course prix fixe menu. | 69 Pembroke Rd. | 203/746–4900 | Closed Mon. No lunch Tues.–Sat. | $45 | AE, D, DC, MC, V.

Lodging

Best Inn & Suites. This reliable, chain hotel is in downtown and near restaurants, banks, and other businesses. Complimentary Continental breakfast. Cable TV. Indoor pool. Some hot tubs. Exercise equipment. | 78 Federal Rd. | 203/743–6701 | 24 rooms, 24 suites | $80–$85, $95–$100 suites | AE, D, DC, MC, V.

Danbury Hilton and Towers. Danbury's most luxurious hotel opened in 1981 and is 3 mi from Danbury Airport, off I–84, and near I–684. Suites have kitchenettes and sitting area. There's a common room with pool table and a free local shuttle. Restaurant, bar, room service. In-room data ports, cable TV. Indoor pool. Saunas, hot tub. 2 tennis courts. Gym. Laundry facilities, laundry service. Business services. Pets allowed. | 18 Old Ridgebury Rd. | 203/794–0600 | fax 203/830–5188 | www.danburyhilton.com | 242 rooms | $109–$199 | AE, D, DC, MC, V.

Ethan Allen Inn. The Ethan Allen company headquarters are next door to this expansive, modern hostelry entirely furnished with Ethan Allen pieces. It is next door to Ives Center and 1 mi from the mall. Restaurant, bar, complimentary breakfast, room service. Cable TV. Pool. Sauna. Gym. Laundry facilities, laundry service. Business services. | 21 Lake Ave. | 203/744–1776 or 800/742–1776 | fax 203/791–9673 | ealleninn@aol.com | 61 rooms, 138 2-room suites | $87.50–$115 | AE, D, DC, MC, V.

Holiday Inn. The Danbury Railway museum and the Danbury Fair Mall are 5 mi from this four-story hotel. Rooms have wood furniture. Restaurant, bar, room service. In-room data ports, cable TV. Pool. Laundry service. Business services. Pets allowed. | 80 Newtown Rd. | 203/792–4000 | fax 203/797–0810 | 114 rooms | $100–$139 | AE, D, DC, MC, V.

Ramada Inn. The two-story main building and five-story tower at this hotel have traditional decor with earth tones. Suites include full size pullout sofabeds. The bus line, Danbury train station, and the downtown area are five minutes away. The hotel is one of the few in the country that boasts the Outback Steak House on its premises. Restaurant, bar, room service. In-room data ports, cable TV. Indoor pool. Laundry service. Business services. Pets allowed. | 116 Newtown Rd. | 203/792–3800 | fax 203/730–1899 | 171 rooms, 10 suites | $139–$175 | AE, D, DC, MC, V.

Radisson Hotel & Suites. This hotel with a 3-story atrium lobby is in a former office building near western Danbury corporate centers. It serves business travelers almost exclusively. Several extended-stay suites with kitchen facilities are available. Restaurant, bar. Some kitchenettes, cable TV. Some hot tubs. Exercise equipment. Business services. | 42 Lake Ave. Ext. | 203/791–2200 | 22 rooms, 65 suites | $159, $169–$219 suites | AE, D, DC, MC, V.

EAST HADDAM

(Nearby towns also listed: Chester, Essex, Ivoryton, Middletown, Old Lyme)

East Haddam is the only town in the state (with the exception of a slice of Wethersfield) that occupies both banks of the Connecticut River. Its two defining attractions on those banks cover opposite extremes of the architectural spectrum: Goodspeed Opera House, a white-wedding-cake Victorian known to be the birthplace of the American musical, and Gillette Castle built by the actor William Gillette.

Information: Middlesex County Chamber of Commerce | 393 Main St., Middletown, 06457 | 860/347–6924 | fax 860/346–1043 | info@middlesexchamber.com | www.middlesexchamber.com. **Connecticut River Valley and Shoreline Visitors Council** | 393 Main St., Middletown, 06457 | 860/347–0028 or 800/486–3346 | fax 860/704–2340 | crvsvc@cttourism.org | www.cttourism.org.

Attractions

Allegra Farm and The Horse Drawn Carriage & Sleigh Museum of New England. John and Kate Allegra not only offer sleigh, hay, and carriage rides using authentic vehicles right out of a Currier and Ives scene, they also have a 12,000-square-ft post-and-beam barn museum that houses an impressive collection of more than 30 restored antique carriages and sleighs. Children especially love the pony rides and the opportunity to visit the livery stable and its tenants—a donkey, llama, sheep, and 30 horses. | Rte. 82 and Petticoat La. | 860/873–9658 | www.allegrafarm.com | $2.50 | Weekends 11–5; call for weekday and winter hrs.

Camelot **Cruises, Inc.** Offers cruises on the Connecticut River, including fall foliage, Sunday brunch, Dixieland jazz, and murder mystery theme cruises. | 1 Marine Park | 860/345–8591 | fax 860/345–8478 | www.camelotcruises.com | Apr.–Dec.

Devil's Hopyard State Park. The highlight of this 860-acre park is Chapman Falls, whose waters cascade more than 60 ft. It is also an idyllic spot for picnicking, camping, fishing, and hiking. And the name? Legend has it that the numerous potholes at the base of the falls are the results of the devil hopping from ledge to ledge in order to avoid getting wet. | 366 Hopyard Rd. | 860/873–8566 | Free | Daily 8–dusk.

★ **Gillette Castle State Park.** An excellent spot for hiking and picnicking, this 200-acre property contains the state park system's most unusual structure—the outrageous 24-room oak-and-fieldstone hilltop castle, modeled after the medieval castles of the Rhineland and built by the eccentric Hartford-born actor and dramatist William Gillette. Designated a state park, tour the castle and hike on trails near the remains of the 3-mi private railroad that chugged about the property until the owner's death in 1937. | 67 River Rd. | 860/526–2336 | Castle $4; grounds free | Daily 8–sunset. Admission to the castle may be limited due to renovations, call for details.

★ **Goodspeed Opera House.** The upper floors of this 1876 Victorian gingerbread structure have served as a venue for theatrical performances for more than 100 years. In the 1960s the Goodspeed underwent a restoration that included the stage area, the Victorian bar, the sitting room, and the drinking parlor. More than 15 Goodspeed productions have gone on to Broadway, including *Annie, Man of La Mancha., Gentlemen Prefer Blondes* and *Shenandoah.* | Rte. 82 | 860/873–8668 | www.goodspeed.org | Apr.–Oct.

St. Stephen's Church and Nathan Hale Schoolhouse. This church, built in 1794 and moved to its present site in 1890, is listed in the *Guinness Book of World Records* as having the oldest bell in the United States. It was supposedly crafted in Spain in 815, but most historians think it was really made in the 1400s, and it is believed to have been taken by Napoléon from a monastery and used for ballast in a ship. East Haddam resident, Captain Andrews, discovered it in Florida and brought it back to his hometown, where it now sits in the belfry of St. Stephen's, a small stone Episcopal church with cedar shingles. Behind the church is the one-room schoolhouse where Nathan Hale is said to have taught from 1773 to 1774, after his graduation from Yale. | Main St. | 860/873–9547 | Free | Call for hrs.

Sundial Herb Gardens. The three formal gardens here—a knot garden of interlocking hedges, a typical 18th-century geometric garden with a central sundial, and a topiary garden—surround an 18th-century farmhouse. A Colonial barn serves as a formal tearoom and a shop where you'll find herbs, books, and rare and fine teas. Sunday afternoon teas and special programs take place throughout the year. | 59 Hidden Lake Rd., Higganum | 860/345–4290 | www.sundialgardens.com | $1 | Jan.–mid-Oct. and early Nov.–late Nov., weekends 10–5; late Nov.–Dec. 24, daily 10–5.

ON THE CALENDAR
SEPT.: *East Haddam Fair.* A community fair that has recently been revived since its demise in the early 1930s. Beside agricultural and local art exhibits, there are exhibits in "forgotten arts" like butter churning, and wool dying and spinning. Rides are no faster than ponys, hay mazes, and a do-si-do in a square dance. | 860/873–8878.

Dining
Gelston House. Continental. This restaurant is in a white clapboard Victorian inn and next door to the Goodspeed Opera House. A glass-enclosed dining room overlooks the Connecticut River. Try roast rack of veal, Atlantic salmon, or lobster risotto. Open-air dining in the beer garden. Sun. brunch. | 8 Main St. | 860/873–1411 | Closed Mon.–Tues. | $18–$22 | AE, MC, V.

Lodging
Bishopsgate Inn. A center-hall, Colonial-style inn that was built in 1818 and has a mix of antiques and collectibles. The rooms have four-poster beds and framed watercolor prints. Two of the inn's three-stories are open to guests and each has a sitting room. There are six fireplaces throughout the inn; four in the guest rooms. Complimentary breakfast. No room phones, no TV in rooms, cable TV in common area. No smoking. | 7 Norwich Rd. | 860/873–1677 | fax 860/873–3898 | www.bishopsgate.com | 5 rooms, 1 suite | $100–$125 rooms, $150 suite | D, MC, V.

Gelston House. The guest rooms in this 1853 Italianate Victorian are furnished with sleigh beds, Victorian secretaries, and floral curtains. Three of the five have views of the Connecticut River. Restaurant, complimentary Continental breakfast. Cable TV. | 8 Main St. | 860/873–1411 | 3 rooms, 2 suites | $100–$125, $225 suites | AE, MC, V.

ENFIELD

MAP 3, F2

(Nearby towns also listed: Stafford Springs, Windsor Locks)

Just off I–91 on the east bank of the Connecticut River, Enfield was once home to legendary Colonial preacher Jonathan Edwards. A marker on Enfield Street denotes the spot where in 1741 Edwards delivered his fiery sermon, "Sinners in the Hands of an Angry God," in the church where his father was pastor. Modern day Enfield has a population of nearly 45,000 and is home to the corporate headquarters of Lego and Hallmark's eastern distribution center. Tobacco as well as agricultural farms can be found along the outskirts of the city.

Information: North Central Connecticut Chamber of Commerce | 113 Elm St., Enfield, 06082 | 860/741–3838 | fax 860/741–3512 | chamber@ncccc.org. **Connecticut's North Central Tourism Bureau** | 111 Hazard Ave., Enfield, 06082 | 860/763–2578 or 800/248–8283 | fax 860/749–1822 | eileen@cnctb.org | www.cnctb.org.

Attractions

Easy Pickin's Orchard. Pick your own fresh fruits, vegetables, and flowers or take a wagon ride, paint a pumpkin, or make a scarecrow to celebrate fall at this orchard. | 46 Bailey Rd. | 860/763–3276 | Aug.–Oct., Mon.–Thurs. 9–noon, Fri.–Sat. 9–5.

Martha A. Parsons House. In an age where the average American moves once every seven years, it's refreshing to visit this house, built in 1782 and home to generations of the same family for more than 180 years before becoming a museum. A highlight of the house is the hallway papered in a rare George Washington memorial pattern from 1800. The wallpaper is said to exist in only one other house in the country. | 1387 Enfield St. | 860/745–6064 | Free | May–Oct., Sun. 2–4:30, or by appointment.

ON THE CALENDAR
JULY: *Fourth of July Town Celebration.* An old-fashioned celebration on the town green with events that include a road race, Taste of Enfield, entertainment, crafts, a parade, and fireworks. | 860/749–1820.

Dining

Figaro's. Italian. You can sit at a green marble table amid more than 2,000 plants to order from the menu of huge-portioned, Americanized Italian standards like chicken parmesan. This restaurant has been a local favorite for 25 years. | 90 Elm St. | 860/745–2414 | $10–$19 | AE, D, DC, MC, V.

Lodging

Benjamin Lord House. You can sip your morning coffee on the 45-ft porch that wraps around this 1876 Queen Anne Victorian house. The well-preserved interior includes five ornamental fireplaces with detailed carvings of birds and faces, Dioclesian windows, brick chimneys with corbelled tops, and 15 stained-glass windows. Complimentary Continental breakfast. Some in-room data ports, in-room VCRs. | 154 Pearl St. | 860/749–7005 | 3 rooms | $95 | AE, DC, MC, V.

Red Roof Inn. There are two two-story buildings that make up this modern, standard hotel. It is within walking distance of Enfield's shops and restaurants. In-room data ports. Pets allowed. | 5 Hazard Ave. | 860/741–2571 | fax 860/741–2576 | 108 rooms | $52–$96 | AE, D, DC, MC, V.

ESSEX

MAP 3, G5

(Nearby towns also listed: Chester, East Haddam, Ivoryton, Old Lyme, Old Saybrook)

Essex, often called one of the best small towns in America, looks much as it did in the mid-19th century, at the height of its shipbuilding prosperity. So important was Essex's boat manufacturing to a young America that the British burned more than 40 ships here during the War of 1812. Gone are the days of steady trade with the West Indies, when the aroma of imported rum, molasses, and spices hung in the air. Whitewashed houses—many the former roosts of sea captains—line Main Street, whose shops sell clothing, antiques, paintings and prints, and sweets.

Information: Middlesex County Chamber of Commerce | 393 Main St., Middletown, 06457 | 860/347–6924 | fax 860/346–1043 | info@middlesexchamber.com | www.middlesexchamber.com. **Connecticut River Valley and Shoreline Visitors Council** | 393 Main St., Middletown, 06457 | 860/347–0028 or 800/486–3346 | fax 860/704–2340 | crvsvc@cttourism.org | www.cttourism.org.

Attractions

Connecticut River Museum. Housed on the last remaining steamboat dock on the Connecticut river (built in 1878), this museum has a permanent exhibit on the river that includes ship building and steamboats. In addition, it has a full-size reproduction of the world's first submarine, the *American Turtle*; the original was built by David Bushnell in 1776. Boats are on display in the summer, when the museum hosts different shows featuring various antique boats. | Steamboat Dock, 67 Main St. | 860/767–8269 | fax 860/767–7028 | www.connix.com/~crm | $4 | Tues.–Sun. 10–5.

Essex Steam Train and Riverboat Ride. The steam train travels alongside the Connecticut River and through the lower valley on its hour-long round-trip journey. If you wish to continue, a riverboat can take you up the river, where you will pass sights such as Gillette Castle and the Goodspeed Opera House on your 2½ hour ride. | Valley Railroad, 1 Railroad Ave. | 860/767–0103 | www.valleyrr.com | May–Dec.

ON THE CALENDAR

JUNE: *Hot Steamed Music Festival.* Live performances of traditional jazz and Dixieland steams things up at Valley Railroad. | 800/348–0003.

JUNE: *Shad Bake.* This event at the Essex Elementary School has been a rite of spring for more than 40 years. The shad is cooked on planks over an open fire and there is live entertainment. | 860/767–8663.

Dining

Griswold Inn. American. Billed as America's oldest continuously operating inn (1776), this white clapboard building has plank flooring and a mix of antiques and collectibles. You can eat in one of the five individually named dining rooms (all serving the same menu) before going into the tap room for an after dinner drink. The tap room also serves lunch. Favorites on the changing dinner menu include prime rib, baked stuffed shrimp or fresh fish. Also, try the Sunday English Hunt breakfast with muffins, eggs, fresh cod, chipped beef, and more. Live music every night in the tap room. Sun. brunch. | 36 Main St. | 860/767–1776 | fax 860/767–0481 | www.griswoldinn.com | $16–$24 | AE, MC, V.

Steve's Centerbrook Café. Continental. A country Victorian house with latticework and gingerbread trim is home to this restaurant. Try the osso buco or rack of lamb with pesto bread pudding. Don't forget to save room for the desserts, including the marjolaine hazelnut four-tier meringue with fresh praline garnish. No smoking. | 78 Main St., Centerbrook | 860/767–1277 | Closed Mon. No lunch | $14–$19 | AE, MC, V.

Lodging

Griswold Inn. A 1776 inn with a mix of Colonial, Federal, and Victorian decor that is in downtown Essex, near the Connecticut River. The inn is a main hub of the town's social life. Some of the rooms have fireplaces and most are furnished with period antiques. Restaurant, bar, complimentary Continental breakfast. TV in common area. Some pets allowed (fee). No smoking. | 36 Main St. | 860/767–1776 | fax 860/767–0481 | www.griswoldinn.com | 16 rooms, 15 suites | $95–$125, $150–$200 suites | AE, MC, V.

Riverwind. A rose-beige clapboard Victorian with ivory gingerbread trim that overflows with antiques and collectibles. The individually decorated rooms have antique furnishings and stenciling. Some have four-poster beds and ceiling fans. There are numerous public sitting rooms and parlors, many with fireplaces. Two-night minimum stay on weekends from mid-April to early January. Complimentary breakfast. No room phones, TV in common area. No pets. No kids under 12. No smoking. | 209 Main St., Deep River | 860/526–2014 | fax 860/526–0875 | www.riverwindinn.com | 8 rooms, 1 suite | $95–$155 | AE, MC, V.

FAIRFIELD

(Nearby towns also listed: Bridgeport, Norwalk, Westport)

Founded in 1639, Fairfield actually preceded the famed Old Post Rd. Although it was known primarily as an agricultural community in its early days, Fairfield turned its attention to the shipping industry in order to recover after it was burned to the ground by the British in 1779. The Greenfield Hill section of town is home to thousands of century-old dogwood trees (and the popular Dogwood Festival honoring such each May). Southport has grand estates and panoramic views of the Long Island Sound, while downtown Fairfield is just the place to browse a bookstore and lick an ice-cream cone.

Information: **Chamber of Commerce** | 1597 Post Rd., Fairfield, 06430-5991 | 203/255–1011 | fax 203/256–9990 | info@fairfieldctchamber.com | www.fairfieldctchamber.com. **Coastal Fairfield County Convention and Visitor Bureau** | 297 West Ave., Gate Lodge-Mathews Park, Norwalk, 06850 | 203/899–2799 or 800/866–7925 | fax 203/853–7524 | info@visitfairfieldco.org | www.visitfairfieldco.org.

Attractions

Connecticut Audubon Birdcraft Museum and Sanctuary. The museum is located on the grounds of the sanctuary and was established in 1914 by the founder of the Connecticut Audubon society. The sanctuary was the first privately owned songbird facility in the nation and it has a hands-on children's activity corner, 5.2 acres of trails, and a pond known to attract a wide variety of waterfowl during spring and fall migration. | 314 Unquowa Rd. | 203/259–0416 | fax 203/259–1344 | www.ctaudubon.org | $2 | Tues.–Fri. 10–5, weekends noon–5.

Connecticut Audubon Center of Fairfield. This center maintains a 160-acre wildlife sanctuary that includes 6 mi of rugged hiking trails and special walks for people with visual impairments and mobility problems. You'll find woodlands, meadows, streams, marshes and ponds with raised boardwalks and bridges that provide access to the various habitats. | 2325 Burr St. | 203/259–6305 | fax 203/254–7673 | www.ctaudubon.org | $2 | Center Tues.–Sat. 9–4:30; grounds daily dawn–dusk.

Fairfield Historical Society Museum. This small museum, in a Georgian house near the Fairfield town green, has collections on life in Fairfield spanning 350 years. Artifacts include locally made furniture, costumes, paintings, decorative arts, and maps. Walking tours of the green and downtown are offered periodically; there is also a genealogical library and gift shop. | 636 Old Post Rd. | 203/259–1598 | fax 203/255–2716 | www.fairfieldhistoricalsoc.org | $3 | Tues.–Sat. 10–4:30, Sun. 1–4:30.

Fairfield University. A Jesuit University with approximately 4,000 students on 200 acres with 32 buildings. | 1073 N. Benson Rd. | 203/254–4000 | www.fairfield.edu.

   Quick Center for the Arts This theater and gallery complex is part of Fairfield University. Events include concerts, plays, and programs for children. | N. Benson Rd. | 203/254–4010 | fax 203/254–4113 | www.quickcenter.com | Children's events, $10; adult programs $24–$38 | Call for schedule.

Ogden House and Gardens. This 1750 saltbox was owned by the Ogden family for 125 years and has been restored and furnished with period artifacts. An 18th-century-style kitchen and wildflower gardens are also on the property. | 1520 Bronson Rd. | 203/259–1598 | $2 | Mid-May–mid-Oct., weekends 1–4:30.

MAY: *Garlicfest.* The folks at Notre Dame High School, sponsors of this event, are strong believers in the appeal of garlic. Area restaurants offer tastes of garlic-infused meals and desserts, yes, desserts. | 203/372–6521.

MAY: *Dogwood Festival.* Thousands of dogwood trees can be counted on to color the Fairfield Green and its surroundings. Events include garden tours, arts and crafts, and live entertainment. | 203/255–1011.

JUNE: *Fairfield County Irish Festival.* All things Irish are available under three tents, including continuous live entertainment, at this festival at Roger Ludlow Field. | 203/259–4025.

JULY: *Clambake.* Can you get more New England than a clambake? The folks in Fairfield don't think so. This one takes place on Jennings Beach and includes live entertainment and special activities for kids. | 203/255–1011.

JULY: *Pequot Library Book Sale.* Close to 100,000 books are collected for this sale each year. It benefits the Fairfield library. | 720 Pequot Ave. | 203/259–0346.

Dining

Paci. Italian. This 1874 former train depot has 30-ft ceilings, hardwood floors, exposed-brick walls, white-linen tablecloths, and views of passing trains. Try the fresh fish, fillet steak, free range duck or chicken, or the spinach ravioli. No smoking. | 96 Station St. | 203/259–9600 | Closed Sun.–Mon. No lunch | $17–$36 | AE, D, DC, MC, V.

Rawley's Hot Dogs. American/Casual. A drive-in where the hot dogs are deep-fried in vegetable oil and then grilled for just a few seconds—a recipe that dates to 1946. Martha Stewart is a regular, favoring a cheesedog with the works. If you're not in the mood for a hot dog, then try the hamburgers, tuna melt, or grilled cheese. | 1886 Post Rd. | 203/259–9023 | Closed Sun. | $2–$4 | No credit cards.

Voilà. French. This frame house on the green has stone fireplaces, lace curtains, and black-and-white-checked tablecloths. Try the salmon à la florentine, coquilles St-Jacques Provençal, *crevettes Voilà* (shrimp cooked in garlic, herbs, spices and white wine), or pasta dinner specials. There's open air dining in the front. No smoking. | 70 Reef Rd. | 203/254–2070 | No lunch Sun. | $16.50–$22.50 | AE, DC, MC, V.

Lodging

Fairfield Motor Inn. A two-story, upscale motor lodge. Restaurant, bar. In-room data ports, refrigerators, cable TV. Pool. Business services. Pets allowed(fee). | 417 Post Rd. | 203/255–0491 | fax 203/255–2073 | 80 rooms | $80–$100 | AE, D, DC, MC, V.

Seagrape Inn. Each of the suites in this three-story former apartment building has a theme—there is the celestial, with angels, moons, and stars galore, and the lighthouse, with an old sea chest. All have separated living, dining, and sleeping areas. Some have cathedral ceilings, skylights, and views of the Long Island Sound. Restaurant. Kitchenettes, cable TV. | 1160 Reef Rd. | 203/255–6808 | fax 203/256–3224 | 14 suites | $140–$325 | AE, MC, V.

FARMINGTON

MAP 3, E3

(Nearby towns also listed: Avon, Bristol, Hartford, New Britain, Simsbury, West Hartford)

Busy Farmington, incorporated in 1645, is a classic river town with lovely estates, a perfectly preserved Main Street, and the prestigious Miss Porter's School, the late Jacqueline Kennedy Onassis's alma mater. More than 100 houses in town, many along Main Street, date prior to 1835, and a great majority of the village has been declared a historic district. Antiques shops can be found near the intersection of Routes 4 and 10, along with some excellent house museums.

Information: Associated Chambers of Commerce | 250 Constitution Plaza, Hartford, 06103 | 860/527–9258 | fax 860/293–2592 | info@metrohartford.com | www.metro-hartford.com. **Greater Hartford Tourism District** | 234 Murphy Rd., Hartford, 06114 | 860/244–8181 or 800/793–4480 | fax 860/244–8180 | ctfuntour@aol.com | www.enjoy-hartford.com.

Attractions

★ **Hill-Stead Museum.** This Colonial Revival farmhouse is one of the Farmington Valley's greatest treasures. It was converted from a private home to a museum by its unusual owner, Theodate Pope Riddle, a turn-of-the-century architect, who also designed the elaborate sunken garden, now the colorful stage for poetry readings by nationally known writers every other weekend in summer. The museum contains a superb collection of Impressionist art. Paintings by Monet hang at each end of the drawing room, and Manet's *Guitar Player* hangs in the middle. | 35 Mountain Rd. | 860/677–4787 | fax 860/677–0174 | www.hill-stead.org | $7 | May–Oct., Tues.–Sun. 10–5; Nov.–Apr., Tues.–Sun. 11–4.

Stanley-Whitman House. A museum since the 1930s, the house was built in 1720 and has a massive central chimney, an overhanging second story, and superlative 18th-century furnishings. The story of two Farmington families—the Smiths and the Whitmans—are told through the artifacts in the house. | 37 High St. | 860/677–9222 | fax 860/677–7758 | www.stanleywhitman.org | $5 | May–Oct., Wed.–Sun. noon–4; Nov.–Apr., weekends noon–4.

Westfarms Mall. This upscale 140-shop mall includes Nordstrom, April Cornell, Williams-Sonoma, and Restoration Hardware. | I–84, Exit 40 | 860/561–3024 | Mon.–Sat. 10–9:30, Sun. 11–6.

ON THE CALENDAR

JUNE AND SEPT.: *Farmington Antiques Weekend.* More than 600 dealers gather for Connecticut's largest antiques event at the Farmington Polo Grounds. The shows take place over the second weekend of June and Labor Day weekend. | 508/839–9735.

JUNE–AUG.: *Sunken Garden Poetry Festival.* Local and nationally acclaimed poets read their works against the backdrop of the stunning sunken gardens at the Hill-Stead Museum. | 860/677–4787.

Dining

Apricot's. Continental. This white Colonial has windows overlooking the gardens and the Farmington River. Try the fried calamari, chicken potpie, filet mignon or roast rack of New Zealand lamb. There's a more casual pub downstairs and you can have your lunch outside on the patio. | 1593 Farmington Ave. | 860/673–5405 | Reservations essential | $18–$25 | AE, DC, MC, V.

The Silo. Continental. This dining room is in a former early-19th-century barn, which was converted into a restaurant 60 years ago and is still run by the same family which opened it. The wide-board pine paneling on the walls balances the dark mahogany booths and tables. Try the mushroom-crusted salmon in saffron-corn broth, or have steak Diane cooked by your table-side. There is a pianist Thursday, Friday, and Saturday evenings. | 330 Main St. | 860/677–0149 | Closed Sun. No lunch Sat. | $15–$24 | MC, V, AE.

Stonewell. Contemporary. The dining room's ceiling is high and the walls are lined with original oil paintings of tropical and New England scenes by the chef and owner at this restaurant. Try the lamb chops, or the Hawaiian delight—a ½ pineapple shell brimming with shrimps, scallops, and pineapple chunks. | 354 Colt Hwy. | 860/677–8855 | $12–$19 | AE, MC, DC, V.

Lodging

Centennial Inn. This all-suites inn is on 12 wooded acres and has large rooms decorated in a Colonial style. There's a playground on the property. Complimentary Continental breakfast. In-room data ports, kitchenettes, cable TV, in-room VCRs. Pool. Hot tub. Gym. Laundry facilities, laundry service. Business services. Pets allowed. No smoking. | 5 Spring La. | 860/677–4647 or 800/852–2052 | fax 860/676–0685 | www.centennialinn.com | 112 suites | $129–$219 | AE, DC, MC, V.

Farmington Inn. This local inn has paintings by local artists, fresh flowers, and a mix of antique and reproduction furnishings throughout. All the rooms have bathrooms with white, Italian carrera marble floors and the suites have complimentary bathrobes. Complimentary Continental breakfast, room service. In-room data ports, some refrigerators, cable TV, some in-room VCRs. Business services. | 827 Farmington Ave. | 860/269–2340 or 800/648–9804 | fax 860/677–8332 | www.farmingtoninn.com | 60 rooms, 12 suites | $129–$149, $139–$169 suites | AE, D, DC, MC, V.

Farmington Marriott. A five-story chain option that is in a suburban wooded spot, yet still near I–84 and 10 minutes southwest of Hartford. The standard rooms have desks and king or double beds, but in a quiet setting. The hotel's Proprietor's Lounge has live entertainment, dancing, over 30 microbrews. Restaurant, bar, room service. In-room data ports, cable TV. 2 pools (1 indoor). Hot tub. 2 tennis courts. Gym. Laundry facilities, laundry service. Business services. | 15 Farm Springs Rd. | 860/678–1000 | fax 860/677–8849 | $109–$179, $200–$500 suites | 381 rooms, 13 suites | AE, D, DC, MC, V.

Homewood Suites. At this hotel, less than 2 mi from I–84, every suite has a full kitchen, separate dining, living, and sleeping areas, attracts extended-stay business travelers. Complimentary Continental breakfast. In-room data ports, kitchenettes, cable TV, in-room VCRs. Indoor pool. Exercise equipment. Business services. | 2 Farm Glen Blvd. | 860/321–0000 | fax 860/321–0001 | 121 suites | $139–$169 | AE, D, DC, MC, V.

GLASTONBURY

MAP 3, F3

(Nearby towns also listed: Hartford, Manchester, Wethersfield)

The Glastonbury/Rocky Hill Ferry was not yet in service when a group of settlers from Farmington crossed the Connecticut in 1639 to purchase from the Wangunk Indians the land would eventually become Glastonbury. It wasn't much later, however, that the ferry, the nation's oldest in continuous operation, went into business in 1655. Today, Glastonbury is a white-collar suburb with a population of almost 29,000 and apple orchards along its outer fringes. Downtown Glastonbury is a corporate center and it is just 6 mi southeast of Hartford.

Information: Chamber of Commerce | 2400 Main St., Glastonbury, 06033 | 860/659–3587 | fax 860/659–0102 | generalinfo@glastonburychamber.org | www.glastonburychamber.org. **Greater Hartford Tourism District** | 234 Murphy Rd., Hartford, 06114 | 860/244–8181 or 800/793–4480 | fax 860/244–8180 | ctfuntour@aol.com | www.enjoyhartford.com.

Attractions

Connecticut Audubon Center at Glastonbury. This center, adjacent to 48-acre Earle Park and trail system, has exhibits on native flora, fauna, and the ecosystem of the Connecticut River, as well as a hands-on discovery room. There's also a butterfly garden, bird feeding station, and picnic area. | 1361 Main St. | 860/633–8402 | fax 860/659–9467 | www.ctaudubon.org | Discovery Room, $1; Audubon Center, free | Tues.–Fri. 1–5, Sat. 10–5, Sun. 1–4.

Glastonbury/Rocky Hill Ferry. This shuttle across the Connecticut River is the country's oldest continuously operating ferry service. | Rte. 160 | 860/563–9758 | May–Oct.

Museum on the Green. A museum in Glastonbury's original Town Hall (ca. 1840) that has exhibits relating to Native Americans, abolitionists, and life in the 19th century. | 1944 Main St. | 860/633–6890 | Free | Mon.–Thurs. 10–4, or by appointment.

ON THE CALENDAR
MAY: *Used Book Sale.* The Welles-Turner Memorial Library offers some 15,000 books for sale each year. | 860/652–7719.

Dining
Ambassador of India. Indian. This storefront eatery is the among the most popular Indian restaurants in the state. The menu offers a wide array of dishes representing the many regions of India. Try the goat, lamb, or crab. Live sitar music Wed. No smoking. | 2333 Main St. | 860/659–2529 | Closed Mon. No lunch Sat. | $18–$28 | AE, DC, MC, V.

J. Gilbert's. Steak. A comfortable, updated steak house featuring T-bone, center-cut fillet, tuna steak, some Southwestern dishes. Kid's menu. | 185 Glastonbury Blvd. | 860/659–0409 | No lunch | $10–$28 | AE, D, MC, V.

The Union. Contemporary. A modern restaurant that's a cross between a neighborhood pub and a chic dining establishment. The dining room's central focus is a huge circular bar set on a dais. The seasonally changing menu has included blackened pork tenderloin, shrimp and lobster tagliatelle, New Zealand rack of lamb, and grilled tuna. House-brewed beers are offered. Sun. brunch. | 2935 Main St. | 860/633–0880 | No lunch Sat. | $12–$24 | AE, D, DC, MC, V.

Lodging
Butternut Farm. Every guest room in this 1720 Colonial farmhouse has original brick fireplaces and pumpkin-pine floorboards. Complimentary breakfast. No TV. No smoking. | 1654 Main St. | 860/633–7197 | fax 860/659–1758 | 5 rooms | $79–$99 | AE.

GREENWICH

MAP 3, A7

(Nearby towns also listed: New Canaan, Norwalk, Stamford)

The area now known as Old Greenwich was purchased from the Siwanoy Indians by settlers from the New Haven Colony in 1640. The arrival of the railroad in 1848 accelerated the influx of new residents and set Greenwich on its way to becoming the wealthy suburb that it is. The median price of a houses in Greenwich is $525,000 and the average is over $800,000, with many selling well over $1 million. Glorious Greenwich has some of the state's chicest restaurants, ritziest car dealers, and poshest boutiques. In other words, bring your credit card. A great many of Greenwich's residents actually work and spend their free time in New York City, which is just 30 mi to the southwest.

Information: **Chamber of Commerce** | 21 W. Putnam Ave., Greenwich, 06830 | 203/869–3500 | fax 203/869–3502 | www.greenwichchamber.com. **Coastal Fairfield County Convention and Visitor Bureau** | 297 West Ave., Gate Lodge-Mathews Park, Norwalk, 06850 | 203/899–2799 or 800/866–7925 | fax 203/853–7524 | info@visitfairfieldco.org | www.visitfairfieldco.org.

Attractions
Audubon Center of Greenwich. More than 1,000 species of flora and fauna have been recorded at this center which is spread out over 600 acres. The exhibits survey the local environ-

ment and include ecology and bird-watching programs as well as hawk-watching in the fall. There are 8 mi of trails that meander through woods and fields where you might see deer, coyote, fox, and birds, including woodpeckers. | 613 Riversville Rd. | 203/869–5272 | fax 203/869–4437 | greenwich.center.audubon.org | $3 | Daily 9–5.

Bruce Museum. In 1993, Robert M. Bruce, a textile manufacturer bequeathed his Victorian stone mansion to town for museum, which has become a must-see for both children and adults. There's a section devoted to environmental history with a wigwam, a spectacular mineral collection, a marine touch tank, and a 16th-century-era woodland diorama. There's also a small but worthwhile collection of American Impressionist paintings. | 1 Museum Dr. | 203/869–0376 | fax 203/869–0963 | www.brucemuseum.com | $4, free on Tues. | Tues.–Sat. 10–5, Sun. 1–5.

Bush-Holley Historic Site. This site's central-chimney saltbox house (circa 1732) has a wide-ranging collection of artworks by sculptor John Rogers, potter Leon Volkmar, and painters Childe Hassam, Elmer Livingstone MacRae, and John Twachtman. It is run by the Historical Society of Greenwich and the visitor center, in the circa 1805 storehouse, holds exhibition galleries and a gift shop. The property also includes an old post office and a renovated barn. There are workshops and lectures throughout year. | 39 Strickland Rd. | 203/869–6899 | fax 203/861–9720 | hstg.org | $6; visitor center and gallery free | Jan.–Mar., Sat. 11–4, Sun. 1–4; Apr.–Dec., Wed.–Fri. noon–4, Sat. 11–4, Sun. 1–4.

Greenwich Avenue. Greenwich Avenue is one of the major shopping streets in lower Fairfield county, with handsome versions of the nation's most popular retailers. Numerous small specialty shops and restaurants are also part of the action.

Putnam Cottage Museum. The small, barn-red cottage was built in 1690 and served as Knapp's Tavern during the Revolutionary War. As such, it was a frequent meeting place of Revolutionary War hero General Israel Putnam. Today you may stroll through the herb garden and examine the cottage's Colonial furnishings and prominent fieldstone fireplaces. | 243 E. Putnam Ave. | 203/869–9697 | $5 | Apr.–Dec., Wed., Fri., and Sun. 1–4.

ON THE CALENDAR
APR.: *New England Regional Daffodil Show.* This show at Christ Church features over 1,000 daffodils in horticultural and artistic exhibits. | 203/661–6142.
MAY: *Bruce Museum Outdoor Crafts Festival.* A sale of fine crafts in wood, fiber, metal, glass, ceramics, jewelry and more. | 203/869–0376.

Dining
Dome. Eclectic. A colorful restaurant with murals, faux-leopard carpeting, and bright blue banquettes. The menu has shock appeal, with dishes such as sesame-peanut glass noodles and lacquered tuna. Also try the wide assortment of vegetarian risottos, napoleons, veggie roasts, and flatbreads. Kid's menu. Sun. brunch. No smoking. | 253 Greenwich Ave. | 203/661–3443 | $11–$26 | AE, DC, MC, V.

Le Figaro Bistro de Paris French. An elegant French bistro on Greenwich Avenue. Try the free-range chicken, veal paillard, lamb shank, or anglet steak. Save room for the chef's special apple tart. | 372 Greenwich Ave. | 203/622–0018 | No lunch Sun. | $16.95–$22.95 | AE, DC, MC, V.

Manero's American. This huge, bustling, family-style restaurant comprises three dining rooms, which can seat a total of 600. Steak, lamb chops, hamburgers, and lobster are the mainstays. Valet parking is available. | 559 Steamboat Rd. | 203/869–0049 | $18.95–$28.95 | AE, DC, MC, V.

Rebeccas. Contemporary. An open kitchen serves up-to-the-minute New American dishes at this chic restaurant. The extensive menu includes dover sole, shellfish, squab, duck, lamb and veal. | 265 Glenville Rd. | 203/532–9270 | Closed Mon. No lunch Fri. and weekends | $36–$54 | AE, MC, V.

★ **Restaurant Jean-Louis.** French. Opened in 1985, this elegant restaurant has a mirrored dining room with a pressed-tin ceiling and fresh flowers. The innovative cuisine has won numerous awards. Try the five-course tasting menu. One of the signature dishes is the endive salad with three American caviars. | 61 Lewis St. | 203/622–8450 | fax 203/622–5845 | www.restaurantjeanlouis.com | Reservations essential | Jacket required | Closed Sun. No lunch July–Aug. and Sat. | $34–$38 | AE, D, DC, MC, V.

Restaurant Thomas Henkelmann. French. This elegant restaurant is housed within the original building of the Homestead Inn. It has a large fireplace and antique furniture and the tables have fresh flowers and crisp napery. Special dishes on the seasonally changing menu include ravioli of assorted mushrooms with sautéed sweet breads, trio of Hudson Valley duck fois-gras, and crisp cherry purses filled with almond cream. The wine list is extensive. | 420 Field Point Rd. | 203/869–7500 | fax 203/869–7502 | Reservations essential | Jacket required | $30–$37 | AE, DC, MC, V.

64 Greenwich Avenue. Continental. This centrally located restaurant has three dining rooms on two floors, with a large working fireplace in the main dining room. The varied menu includes sesame-crusted tuna, peppercorn-seasoned New York sirloin with cognac cream, as well as hamburgers and a gratin of macaroni and cheese. The carmelized banana split is everyone's favorite. You can also dine at the bar. | 64 Greenwich Ave. | 203/861–6400 | Closed Sun. | $9.95–$21.95 | AE, DC, MC, V.

Thataway Cafe. American. A large, informal restaurant with an equally large bar that caters primarily to a young crowd and movie-goers. Local business people frequent this spot for a quick lunch. Try the grilled chicken sandwiches or cobb salad. There is live music on Sunday nights. | 409 Greenwich Ave. | 203/622–0947 | $11.95–19.95 | AE, DC, MC, V.

Lodging

Cos Cob Inn. In this late-18th-century white house, breakfast is served in the common room with a white marble fireplace and French doors. Each room is unique—there are brass, pewter, sleigh, panel, and four-poster beds, and views of the garden or the river. Complimentary Continental breakfast. In-room data ports, some kitchenettes, some in-room hot tubs, cable TV, in-room VCRs. No pets. No kids under 10. | 50 River Rd., Cos Cob | 203/661–5845 or 877/549–4063 | fax 203/661–2054 | 14 rooms | $119–$249 | AE, DC, MC, V.

★ **Homestead Inn.** An Italiante wood-frame house with a belvedere, ornate bracketed eaves, and an expansive front porch that was built in 1799 and converted into an inn in 1859. Half of the rooms here are in a pair of newer outbuildings, which are more spacious than the main house, but lack its character and history. Restaurant, bar. In-room data ports, cable TV. Business services. No smoking. | 420 Field Point Rd. | 203/869–7500 | fax 203/869–7502 | www.homesteadinn.com | 22 rooms, 6 suites | $150–$395 | AE, DC, MC, V.

Howard Johnson. This standard chain hotel is less than 1 mi from town in a residential area of Riverside. Restaurant. Cable TV. Outdoor pool. Pets allowed. | 1114 Post Rd., Riverside | 203/639–3691 | 104 rooms | $99 | AE, D, DC, MC, V.

Hyatt Regency Greenwich. A modern chain option in Old Greenwich. The lobby has a gazebo and babbling brook and outside there are English manor-style gardens with landscaped lawns. There's also a four-story tropical atrium. Restaurant, bar, room service. In-room data ports, cable TV. Indoor pool. Beauty salon, hot tub, sauna, spa, steam room. Health club. Laundry service. Business services. | 1800 E. Putnam Ave. | 203/637–1234 | fax 203/637–2940 | $264–$299 | AE, D, DC, MC, V.

Stanton House Inn. A Federal-style mansion built in 1840 and enlarged in 1899 under the supervision of renowned architect Stanford White. There is a mixture of antiques and reproductions throughout the inn. Two-night minimum stay on weekends. Complimentary Continental breakfast. Some refrigerators, some kitchenettes, cable TV. Pool. No smoking. | 76 Maple Ave. | 203/869–2110 | fax 203/629–2116 | 23 rooms, 2 suites | $129–$189, $215 suites | AE, D, DC, MC, V.

GREENWICH

INTRO
ATTRACTIONS
DINING
LODGING

GROTON

MAP 3, H6

(Nearby towns also listed: Ledyard, Mystic, New London, Niantic, Stonington, Waterford)

Home to the United States Naval Submarine base and the Electric Boat Division of General Dynamics, designer and manufacturer of nuclear submarines, Groton is often called the submarine capital of the world. The major draw at the Submarine Force Museum is The USS *Nautilus,* the world's first nuclear-powered submarine and a National Historic Landmark.

Information: Chamber of Commerce of Southeastern Connecticut | 105 Huntington St., New London, 06320 | 860/443–8332 | fax 860/444–1529 | chamberscct@juno.com | www.chambersect.org. **Southeastern Connecticut Tourism District** | 470 Bank St., Box 89, New London, 06320 | 860/444–2206 or 800/TO–ENJOY | fax 860/442–4257 | more2see@aol.com | www.mysticmore.com.

Attractions

Bluff Point Coastal Reserve. It's a 1½-mi hike from the parking lot to the rocky bluff for which this park is named. Here a mile-long stretch of sand and tidal salt marsh overlooks Mumford Cove, the Poquonnock River, and the Long Island Sound. Facilities are limited, but horseback riding, biking, snorkeling, hiking, and swimming are encouraged. | Depot Rd. | 860/445–1729 | Free | Daily 8–dusk.

Fort Griswold Battlefield State Park. This park contains the remnants of a Revolutionary War fort. Historic displays at the museum mark the site of the massacre of American defenders by Benedict Arnold's British troops in 1781. A sweeping view of the shoreline can be had from the top on the 135-ft-tall Groton monument. | Monument St. and Park Ave. | 860/445–1729 | Free | Park daily 8–dusk; museum and monument Memorial Day–Labor Day, daily 10–5.

Hel-Cat II. Striped bass and blues are the catch of the day on this 144-ft party fishing boat from June to October. Cod, pollock, mackerel, blackfish, and sea bass are the goals in winter and spring. There's a restaurant on board and your bait is included. | 181 Thames St. | 860/535–2066 or 860/445–5991 | $27–$42 | Jan.–May, weekends; June–Oct., daily.

Project Oceanology. The 55-ft *Enviro-Lab* leaves from the Avery Point Campus of the University of Connecticut on a 2½-hour cruise called Project Oceanology. Passengers become marine biologists onboard as they are are invited to assist the instructors (actual marine scientists) in measuring and recording data, learning about navigational instruments, and analyzing samples collected from the ocean floor. | 1084 Shennecossett Rd. | 800/364–8472 | fax 860/449–8008 | www.oceanology.org | $17 | Mid-June–Aug., daily 1–4.

Shennecosset Golf Course. A popular course with calming views of Long Island Sound, Shennecosset was first laid out in 1898 and reconfigured in 1926 by Donald Ross. It has a strong sense of history. | 93 Plant St. | 860/445–0262 | $29–$35 | Daily 6:30–dusk.

Submarine Force Museum. The world's first nuclear-powered submarine, the *Nautilus* was launched from Groton in 1954 and is permanently berthed at this museum. You are welcome to climb aboard and imagine yourself as a crew member during the boat's trip under the North Pole more than 40 years ago. The museum also charts submarine history with memorabilia, artifacts, and displays that include working periscopes and controls. The museum is outside the entrance to the submarine base. | 1 Crystal Lake Rd. | 860/694–3174 | www.ussnautilus.org | Free | Mid-May–mid-Oct., Wed.–Mon. 9–5, Tues. 1–5; late Oct.–early May, Wed.–Mon. 9–4.

ON THE CALENDAR

JULY: *Subfest.* A fireworks extravaganza, food, circus, live music and a carnival are among the events that take place on the U.S. Naval Submarine Base New London. | Rte. 12, Groton | 860/694–3238.

Lodging

Clarion Inn. A comfortable, family-oriented inn that is right across from Wal-Mart. The suites have a living room with pull-out couch. Restaurant, bar, room service. Cable TV. Indoor pool. Barber shop, beauty salon, hot tub. Gym. Laundry facilities. Business services. Pets allowed (deposit). | 156 Kings Hwy. | 860/446–0660 | fax 860/445–4082 | 69 rooms, 2 suites | $169–$209 | AE, D, MC, V.

Howard Johnson This two-story hotel is 2 mi from the New London sub base and 5 mi from the beach, the Groton submarine base, the Mystic Seaport and the Mystic Aquarium. Complimentary Continental breakfast. Exercise room. No pets. | 580 Poquonnock Rd. | 860/445–0220 or 800/406–1411 | fax 860/445–6184 | www.hojo.com | 48 rooms | $49–$59 | AE, D, DC, MC, V.

Quality Inn. A pleasant budget alternative near the U.S. Submarine Base, golf course, and beach. Restaurant, bar, complimentary Continental breakfast. In-room data ports, cable TV. Pool, wading pool. Gym. Laundry facilities. Business services. | 404 Bridge St. | 860/445–8141 | 110 rooms | $71–$175 | AE, D, DC, MC, V.

GUILFORD

MAP 3, F6

(Nearby towns also listed: Branford, Clinton, Madison, New Haven)

The group of English settlers who founded Guilford in 1639 was led by the Rev. Henry Whitfield, whose house today is the oldest in Connecticut and a state museum. The Guilford Green, crisscrossed by pathways, dotted with benches, and surrounded by historic homes and specialty shops, is considered by many the prettiest green in the state and is actually the third largest in the Northeast.

Information: Guilford Chamber of Commerce | 741 Boston Post Rd., Ste. 101, Guilford, 06437 | 203/453–9677 | fax 203/458–2508 | chamber@guilfordct.com | www.guilfordct.com. **Connecticut River Valley and Shoreline Visitors Council** | 393 Main St., Middletown, 06457 | 860/347–0028 or 800/486–3346 | fax 860/704–2340 | crvsvc@cttourism.org | www.cttourism.org.

Attractions

Bishop's Orchards. Is there anything more delicious than fruit you've picked fresh from the vine? Bishop's, established in 1871, is one of the most popular places in the area to do so. Here you'll have your choice of strawberries, blueberries, peaches, pears, raspberries, and apples, depending on the season. There's also a pumpkin patch, large farm market, and Christmas trees and wreaths when 'tis the season. | 1355 Boston Post Rd. | 203/453–2338 or 203/453–6424 for information on picking | www.bishopsorchards.com | Mon.–Sat. 8–6, Sun. 9–6.

Henry Whitfield State Museum. This museum focused on local and state history is in the oldest house in Connecticut and the oldest stone house in New England. It was built by the Rev. Henry Whitfield, an English minister who settled here in 1639. The furnishings in the medieval-style building were made between the 17th and 18th centuries. The visitor center contains two exhibition galleries, with changing exhibits, and a gift shop. | 248 Old Whitfield St. | 203/453–2457 | fax 203/453–7544 | $3.50 | Feb.–mid Dec., Wed.–Sun. 10–4:30; mid-Dec.–Jan. by appointment.

Hyland House. This clapboard saltbox (circa 1660) was the home of George Hyland and family. The historic home focuses on everyday family life in the decades before the American Revolution. | 84 Boston St. | 203/453–9477 | $2 | June–Aug., Tues.–Sun. 10–4; Sept.–mid-Oct., weekends 10–4.

JULY: *Guilford Handcrafts Festival.* One of the state's top outdoor shows takes place over the third weekend of the month. Highlights include more than 130 American craftspeople, food, music, storytelling, and crafts demonstrations on the Guilford Green. | 203/453–5947.

Dining
Cilantro American. A charming building houses this very friendly, casual restaurant on the green in Guilford. Sandwiches, salads, wraps and pastries are all home made. | 85 Whitfield St. | 203/458–2555 | Breakfast also available | $5.50 | AE, DC, MC, V.

★ **Quattro's.** Italian. A steady menu of Italian favorites (grinders, chicken Parmesan) in a soft, relaxing dining room with candles and flowers. Try the seafood—such as red snapper or halibut. No smoking. | 1300 Boston Post Rd. | 203/453–6575 | No lunch Sun. | $14–$21 | AE, DC, MC, V.

Lodging
Guilford Suites Hotel. A straightforward, comfortable, all-suites, two-story hotel. It's set up for families, with suites that include a living room, bedroom, king-size beds and pull-out sofas. Complimentary Continental breakfast. Kitchenettes, cable TV. | 2300 Boston Post Rd. | 203/453–0123 or 800/626–8604 | fax 203/458–1244 | 32 suites | $110–$120 | AE, D, DC, MC, V.

Tower Suites Motel. This single-story, all-suites motel was built in 1970. It has basic suites that are good for families. The beach is 3 mi away. Refrigerators, cable TV. | 320 Boston Post Rd. | 203/453–9069 | fax 203/458–2727 | 13 suites | $89–$99 | AE, D, MC, V.

HARTFORD

MAP 3, E3

(Nearby towns also listed: Avon, Farmington, Glastonbury, Manchester, New Britain, Simsbury, West Hartford, Wethersfield, Windsor Locks)

Hartford, the state capital, is also where one of Connecticut's first European settlement was founded in 1633. America's insurance industry was born in Hartford in 1810—largely in an effort to protect the Connecticut River Valley's tremendously important shipping interests. Throughout the 19th century, insurance companies expanded their coverage to include fires, accidents, life, and (in 1898) automobiles. Through the years, Hartford industries have included the inspection and packing of tobacco (a once-prominent industry in the northern river valley) and the manufacture of everything from bedsprings to artificial limbs, pool tables, and coffins. Like many of Connecticut's cities, Hartford is hard at work at revitalization.

Information: Greater Hartford Associated Chambers of Commerce | 250 Constitution Plaza, Hartford, 06103 | 860/525–4451 | fax 860/293–2592 | info@metrohartford.com | www.metrohartford.com. **Greater Hartford Tourism District** | 234 Murphy Rd., Hartford, 06114 | 860/244–8181 or 800/793–4480 | fax 860/244–8180 | ctfuntour@aol.com | www.enjoyhartford.com.

NEIGHBORHOODS

Blue Hills. In the northwest corner of the city, this is primarily a single-family residential area (its owner occupancy rate is 55%, the highest in the city) with well-maintained yards and houses. There is a large African-American and West Indian population here. St. Francis–Sinai Hospital is here, as is much of the University of Hartford, and there is a shopping district along Blue Hills Avenue.

North East. Bordered by Keney Park to the north and west, Spring Grove Cemetery to the south, and the railroad yards to the east, this neighborhood has been an area of both small businesses and as large-scale manufacturing since the late 19th century, and its architecture reflects the successive eras of the city's history as it grew from a riverside town to an industrial city.

North Meadows. The northeast section of the city is a business and industrial area that was developed in the 1980s. You'll find things like car dealerships and the Connecticut Transit Bus Garage. The Meadows Music Center is also here.

Clay Arsenal Just north of the downtown area is Clay Arsenal, whose central arteries are Main Street and Albany Ave. It was mainly farmland prior to 1847, when the Hartford–Springfield Railroad, which now forms the neighborhoods eastern border, was constructed. It has been home to successive immigrant populations, first Irish, then Jewish. It is now primarily a Puerto Rican and African American community.

Upper Albany. Most of this neighborhood was once occupied by family farms. Around the early 1880s, the railroads were expanded bringing industry soon followed. Most of the houses in the neighborhood were built between 1890 and 1920. It was successively inhabited by second-generation Irish families, middle-class Italian families, and Jewish families through World War II. After that the area became predominantly African American and today also has Puerto Ricans and other Caribbean groups. The main street for business and industry here is Albany Avenue.

The West End. A prestigious area that is known for its impressive architecture. Much of the neighborhood was built around the turn of the century and nearly three quarters of it is listed on the National Register of Historic Districts. There are estate-like homes in the northern section, large Victorians in the middle and southern sections, and older apartment buildings in the east, which is known as Clemens Place. The University of Connecticut School of Law and the Hartford Seminary are located here. The commercial district on Farmington Avenue, caters to the retail and service needs of the residents.

Asylum Hill. Sandwiched in between West and downtown, this has long been a residential and institutional neighborhood, though it is no longer the posh area it was 100 years ago. There are several large insurance companies, including the Aetna and ITT Hartford, as well as St. Francis Hospital. The Mark Twain House and the Harriet Beecher Stowe House are among the grand Victorian homes in the area once known as Nook Farm.

Downtown. The downtown area is the regional center for insurance and finance. People commute there for work but leave at the end of the day for their homes in the surrounding neighborhoods and suburbs. The city is working to increase the appeal of the downtown riverfront area as a destination beyond it identity as a job center, by promoting it as a venue for the arts and special events like First Night on New Year's Eve.

Parkville. A busy commercial area along Park Street with well-kept residential areas on the side streets. The industrial section is found by the railroad tracks. Primarily Puerto Rican and Portuguese, there is also a growing contingent of Asian business owners.

Frog Hollow. Just east of Parkville, this thriving Latino area was originally developed as housing for employees of the factories which lined Capitol Avenue. The residential section contained multi-family buildings to accommodate the mainly immigrant workers who lived there. Products like Columbia bicycles and Underwood and Olivetti typewriters were manufactured here. The neighborhood is also home to the Olmsted-designed Pope Park. Park Street, lined with restaurants and stores, is the major street here and Portuguese, Puerto Ricans and other Latin Americans come from throughout the city and the state to shop, eat, and worship. There is also a popular farmer's market here.

South Green. The city's smallest neighborhood borders downtown to the south. The commercial areas are Main and Park Streets. Along Congress Street there are well-maintained and attractive multi-family homes, apartments, and condominiums. Hartford Hospital, the city's largest general medical and surgical hospital, is here and many medical offices and clinics are located on side streets off the hospital campus.

Sheldon Charter Oak. Just outside downtown, this is a densely populated residential area with public housing, apartments, andcondominiums. It is historically important as it was site of the area's first colonial settlement in 1623, a Dutch trading post. The neighborhood owes its development to Samuel Colt, inventor of the automatic revolver, who built his factory complex there in 1855. The complex, with its landmark dome, housed an armory, worker's lodging, a social hall, a church, a parish house, a park, and Colt's own mansion, Armsmear. Colt willed the grounds of the estate to the city for use as a park, and Colt Park was opened to the public in 1905. Today the Colt factory complex also has studio space that has attracted local artists to live in the area.

Charter Oak-Zion. A primarily residential neighborhood in the southwestern part of the city with all types of housing from public housing apartments and two- and three- family dwellings to single-family homes. It also has two technical colleges: Albert I. Prince Technical School and Capital Community Technical College. Rocky Ridge is the neighborhood park.

Barry Square. This area was named for Father Michael Barry whose Irish Catholic church built St. Augustine in 1902. It is partly residential, with apartments and three-family homes on the north side and single- and two-family homes in the center and southwest parts, and partly institutional. Trinity College is there, as well as the Institute for Living, one of the nation's oldest psychiatric facilities.

The South West. A neat well-maintained middle class neighborhood. It had its start in the late 1800s with the newly established trolley lines and continued to develop in the housing booms that followed the two World Wars.

The South End. Established after World War I, when the land was subdivided and developed, this is primarily an Italian community that has well-kept residential areas. Franklin Avenue—with many restaurants, bakeries, retail shops, and clubs—is the major street. Goodwin Park (one of the city's seven parks), which includes a golf course, is a source of neighborhood pride.

The South Meadows. An industrial and commercial area next to the Connecticut River in the southeast part of the city. The Connecticut Resources Recovery Authority facility is here, as well as the Metropolitan District Commissions Yard, the water pollution control plant, and Brainard Airport.

TRANSPORTATION INFORMATION

Airport: Hartford and the surrounding areas are served by Bradley International Airport. I–91, exit 40 in Windsor Locks, about 10 mi north of Hartford. | 888/624–1533.

Amtrak Commuter rail system with links to Hartford in New Haven that runs out of Union Station. | 800/872–7245.

Connecticut Transit. Bus service for Hartford and surrounding towns. | 860/525–9181.

Driving Around Town: There is no reason, other than personal preference, not to drive into Hartford. Unlike Boston or New York where you might be better advised to leave the car and take public transportation, Hartford is not fraught with the same traffic congestion, Byzantine street patterns, or competition for parking spaces. For those who wish to go the public transportation route, Union Station in downtown Hartford, a turn-of- the-century brownstone building that has been restored, provides Amtrak service and nonstop bus transportation to every major Northeast city. Taxi and airport limousine service is also offered from the center. Once in the city, there are buses operated by CTTransit that traverse the city's neighborhoods and take you out as far as the surrounding suburbs for anywhere from $1 to $3.45 depending on how far you travel. There are also taxis or, if you're destination is downtown, it is most likely just a short walk away from Union Station.

Like any other city that is a regional job center, rush hour here is extremely slow going. Two interstate highways intersect on the east side of the city: north–south Interstate–91, and east–west Interstate–84. (It should also be noted that there is no beltway around the city so everyone going in or out of Hartford must use one of these routes.) To ease the crunch, there are controlled high-occupancy vehicle lanes designed to reduce the number of vehicles on the highways but if you can plan your trip to avoid these times, you should and you'll find traveling to Hartford quite painless. Once you've reached your destination, your choices will be either metered parking on the streets provided you don't mind keeping an eye on the allotted time or a garage (there are some 25 garages in Hartford where you can park for hours or days). Parking is relatively plentiful and it is safe to park on the street in most areas. It is a small city and most attractions, restaurants and hotels tend be concentrated in the downtown area or nearby it so parking the car and walking may be the most convenient. A word of caution: downtown Hartford can be deserted at night and while crime has been on the decline, exercise caution if visiting the city at night.

Attractions

ART AND ARCHITECTURE

The Bushnell. This grand theater with an Art Deco interior is a National Historic Landmark and presents more than 300 events a season, from Broadway blockbusters like *Phantom of the Opera* to symphonies and traditional operas. You may recognize it as the site of Hartford's 1996 presidential debate. | 166 Capitol Ave. | 860/987–3900 or 888/824–2874 | fax 860/987–6080 | www.bushnell.org | Call for performance schedule and ticket prices.

Harriet Beecher Stowe House. This Gothic Victorian cottage built in 1871 stands as a tribute to the author of one of 19th-century America's most popular and influential novels, *Uncle Tom's Cabin*. It was Stowe's last residence and inside are her writing table and effects, several of her paintings, a period pinewood kitchen, and a terrarium of native ferns, mosses, and wildflowers. | 77 Forest St. | 860/525–9358 | fax 860/922–9259 | www.hartnet.org/~stowe | $6.50, includes Katherine S. Day House | Memorial Day–mid-Oct. and Dec., Mon.–Sat. 9:30–4:30, Sun. noon–4:30; mid-Oct.–Nov. and Jan.–Memorial Day, Tues.–Sat. 9:30–4, Sun. noon–4:30.

Katherine S. Day House. Katherine Seymour Day was the grandniece of Harriet Beecher Stowe and benefactor of the Stowe Center. She purchased this building, built in 1884, in 1939 to help preserve what was then known as the Nook Farm area (of which the Mark Twain House is also a part). Today, the Day House offers a glimpse into the Victorian era with its grand interiors and changing exhibits, displaying the holdings of the Stowe Center and the Stowe-Day Library, a research collection of 19th-century literary history, including a major collection of Stowe's writings. | 71 Forest Ave. | 806/522–9258, ext. 517 | $6.50, includes Harriet Beecher Stowe House | Memorial Day–mid-Oct. and Dec., Mon.–Sat. 9:30–4:30, Sun. noon–4:30; mid-Oct.–Nov. and Jan.–Memorial Day, Tues.–Sat. 9:30–4, Sun. noon–4:30.

★ **Mark Twain House.** Nook Farm, a late-19th-century neighborhood, was home to several prominent families. Samuel Langhorne Clemens, better known as Mark Twain, had his Stick-style Victorian mansion built here in 1874. During his residency he published seven major novels, including *Tom Sawyer*, *Huckleberry Finn*, and *The Prince and the Pauper*. His personal memorabilia and original furnishings are on display and the one-hour guided tours of the house discuss its spectacular architecture and interiors as well as Twain's personal and family life. Renovations in 1998 restored the master bedroom and the drawing room, and also opened to the public for the first time the rooms of family butler, George Griffin, a prominent member of Hartford's African-American community. | 351 Farmington Ave. | 860/247–0998, ext. 26 | fax 860/278–8148 | www.hartnet.org/twain | $9 | May–Oct. and Dec., Mon.–Sat. 9:30–4, Sun. noon–4, last tour at 4; Nov. and Jan.–Apr., Mon., Wed.–Sat. 9:30–5, Sun. noon–5, last tour at 4.

Old State House. This building with an elaborate cupola and roof balustrade was designed by Charles Bulfinch, the architect who redesigned the U.S. Capitol after it was burned by the British in 1812. The Great Senate Room, where everyone from Abraham Lincoln to George Bush has spoken, contains a Gilbert Stuart portrait of George Washington that remains in its commissioned location. On a lighter note, and for a chance to see a two-headed calf, drop by the small but distinctive museum of oddities upstairs. At 12:15 every Tuesday, the trial of the Africans who mutinied on the *Amistad* in 1839—an event depicted in the 1997 Steven Spielberg movie of the same name—is re-enacted in the very court-room where it first took place. | 800 Main St. | 860/522–6766 | fax 860/522–2812 | Free | Weekdays 10–4, Sat. 11–4.

State Capitol. This grandiose capitol rises above Bushnell Park and is visible citywide. The colossal edifice is composed of wholly disparate architectural elements. Built in 1879 of marble and granite—to the tune of $2.5 million—this gilt-dome wonder is replete with crockets, finials, and pointed arches. It houses the governor's office and legislative chambers and displays historic statuary, flags, and furnishings. | 210 Capitol Ave. | 860/240–0222 | fax 860/240–8627 | www.cslib.org/lwv | Free | Weekdays 8–5; Tours: Year-round weekdays 9:15–1:15, Apr.–Oct. Sat. 10:15–2:15.

CULTURE, EDUCATION, AND HISTORY

Trinity College. This four-year liberal arts college on a beautiful 100-acre campus has a strong reputation. It has been on this site 1878. The chapel was completed in 1932 and designed by the architect of the National Cathedral in Washington, Phililp Frohman. | 300 Summit St. | 860/297–2000 | www.trincoll.edu | Free | Daily.

MUSEUMS

Connecticut Historical Society. This extensive historical society has an excellent collection of 18th- and 19th-century furniture, three galleries of Connecticut landscape paintings, and changing exhibits pertaining to—what else?—Connecticut history. The library is a leading resource for local history and genealogy. Various programs, lectures, and events are held throughout the year. | 1 Elizabeth St. | 860/236–5621 | fax 860/236–2664 | www.chs.org | $5 | Galleries Tues.–Sun. noon–5; library Tues.–Sat. 10–5.

Hartford Police Museum. The Hartford Police Museum is the first of its kind in the northeast. The collection includes photographs, artifacts and historical information on the Police Department, which was officially established in 1860 but actually dates back as far as 1636 when Samuel Wakeman was appointed Constable of "Herteford Towne" by the English and Dutch immigrants who settled in the area. Exhibits cover contemporary policing as well as information on women in the police force, police training, and a look into the daily life of a Hartford Police Officer. Kids will particularly enjoy the interactive exhibit where they sit behind the wheel of a police car and listen to actual police dispatches. Group tours can also be arranged. | 101 Pearl St. | 860/722–6152 | Free | Weekdays 9–4:30.

Museum of Connecticut History. An impressive museum exhibiting artifacts of Connecticut military, industrial, and political history, including the state's original Colonial charter. It holds a vast assemblage of Samuel Colt firearms; the so-called Arm of Law and Order was manufactured in Hartford. | Connecticut State Library, 231 Capitol Ave. | 860/757–6535 | Free | Weekdays 9–4, Sat. 10–4, Sun. noon–4.

★ **Wadsworth Atheneum.** With more than 50,000 works and artifacts spanning 5,000 years, the Wadsworth is the second largest public art museum in New England and the oldest in the nation, predating the Metropolitan Museum of Art by 35 years. Among the notable items to look for are five wall drawings by Connecticut's own Sol LeWitt, the well-known conceptual artist, as well as the first American acquisitions of works by Salvador Dalí and the Italian artist Caravaggio. Particularly impressive are the museum's collections of Baroque, Impressionist, and Hudson River School artists—including pieces by Frederic Church and Thomas Cole—as well as what some consider the world's finest collection of Pilgrim-era furnishings. The museum's café is a nice spot for lunch. | 600 Main St. | 860/278–2670 | fax 860/527–0803 | www.wadsworthatheneum.org | $7; free Sat. 11–noon and Thurs. | Tues.–Sun. 11–5.

PARKS

Bushnell Park. Designed by Jacob Weidenmann, this park fans out from the State Capitol building and was the first public space in the country with natural landscaping instead of a traditional village-green configuration. Amid the park's 40 acres are 150 varieties of trees as well as landmarks like a 1914 Stein and Goldstein carousel and the 100-ft-tall, 30-ft-wide medieval-style Soldiers and Sailors Memorial Arch, dedicated to Civil War soldiers. | Downtown, between Jewell, Elm, and Trinity Sts. | Free | Park daily; carousel Apr.–Sept., call for hrs.

Colt Park This large park near downtown Hartford offers ice-skating and hiking in winter and facilities for baseball, rugby, basketball, swimming, and running in summer. Free supervised lunch for all children is served at noon daily. | Wethersfield Ave. | 860/722–6539 (pool information).

Elizabeth Park Rose Gardens. These rose gardens, the first municipal such garden in the country, are a glorious sight to behold, especially in mid- to late June, when some 14,000 bushes representing more than 900 varieties of roses burst into bloom. | 150 Walbridge Rd. | 860/722–6541 | Free | Daily dawn–dusk.

RELIGION AND SPIRITUALITY

Center Church and Ancient Burying Ground. Built in 1807, Center Church is patterned after London's Church of St. Martin-in-the-Fields. The parish itself dates from 1632 and was started by Puritan clergyman Thomas Hooker (1586–1647), who established Hartford. Five of the stained-glass windows were created by Louis Tiffany. The Ancient Burying Ground in the churchyard is filled with granite and brownstone headstones, some dating from the 1600s. | 675 Main St. | 860/249–5631 | Free | Mid-Apr.–mid-Dec, Wed., Fri. 11–2, or by appointment.

SPORTS AND RECREATION

Hartford Wolf Pack. This hockey team, an AHL affiliate, plays at the Hartford Civic Center. | 1 Civic Center Plaza | 860/246–7825 | www.wolfpackhockey.com | Oct.–Apr.

SIGHTSEEING TOURS/TOUR COMPANIES

Lady Fenwick. Deep River Navigation offers cruises of the Connecticut River aboard this reproduction of an 1850s steam launch. | Charter Oak Landing | 860/526–4954 | fax 860/526–2322 | www.deeprivernavigation.com | Memorial Day–early Oct.

Heritage Trails Sightseeing Tours. This company offers a two-hour tour of the capital via minibus as well as various themed tours of Greater Hartford. Tours depart from various Hartford hotels; call for details. | Box 138, Farmington | 860/677–8867 | www.charteroak-tree.com | Daily.

ON THE CALENDAR

FEB.: *Connecticut Flower and Garden Show.* The Connecticut Expo Center is transformed into an oasis of blooming gardens, educational seminars, and plants, flowers, and gardening supplies for sale at this annual show. | 860/529–2123.
MAR.: *The Original Connecticut Home Show.* An annual event prodcued by the Homebuilder's Association of Hartford County since 1947 that showcases hundreds of products and services for the home at the Hartford Civic Center. | 860/563–4212.
JUNE: *Taste of Hartford.* One of the largest food festivals in New England, with samplings from the areas best chefs. | 860/728–3089.

JULY: *Mark Twain House Days.* This celebration of the author includes special tours of his home, concerts, a frog-jumping contest, and riverboat rides. | 860/247–0998.
JULY: *Riverfest.* A joint celebration by the towns of Hartford and East Hartford of the Connecticut River and our country's independence. Live entertainment, activities, food, and fireworks. | 860/713–3131.
DEC.: *Festival of Trees.* More than 200 adorned Christmas trees, wreaths, and holiday decorations deck the halls of the Wadsworth Atheneum. There are also special events, entertainment, and a holiday boutique. | 860/278–2670.
DEC.: *First Night Hartford.* A family-oriented celebration of the New Year at various locations in Hartford. Continuous performances take place throughout the afternoon and evening of the 31st, culminating in a fireworks display. | 860/728–3089.

WALKING TOUR

Start at the **Old State House** (800 Main St.) the oldest state house in the nation and site of the signing of the country's first written constitution. Detour off Main St. to 101 Pearl St. (about a quarter of a mile southwest) for a look at the history of Hartford's finest at the **Hartford Police Museum.** From there walk east on Pearl to get back to Main for a look at the **Center Church and Ancient Burying Ground.** Revolutionary soldiers and early settlers are buried here. Next stop, down the street is the **Wadsworth Atheneum,** one of the country's oldest art museums and home to more than 45,000 works of art. Where Main St. and Capitol Ave. meet, head west down Capitol. First stop is the Art Deco National Landmark **Bushnell** Theater, which presents some 300 events a year. Just north of the theater, in the shadow of the State Capitol building, is **Bushnell Park,** America's oldest public park. See the Soldiers and Sailors Memorial Arch honoring veterans of the Civil War, ride the antique carousel in season, and visit the Pump House Gallery. The Hartford Marathon, an annual October event, also finishes here. Returning to Capitol Ave., the next stop is the modern Gothic-style **State Capitol** designed by New York Architect Richard Upjohn and built in 1878, with interiors featuring polished granite columns and stained glass. Just steps down the block is the **Museum of Connecticut History,** which exhibits permanent and changing displays of original historic objects, images, and manuscripts that illustrate four hundred years— and counting—of Connecticut's political, economic and military history. Next stop is a bit farther (almost a mile to the northwest) so you might wish to break the tour into two parts starting here. The **Harriet Beecher Stowe House** (71 Forest Ave.) is just off Farmington Ave. The author lived here from 1871 to 1896. Next door is the lesser known **Katherine S. Day House.** The house, built in 1884, was purchased in 1939 by Day, who was Stowe's niece, to help preserve the 19th-century Nook Farm area where the houses stand. Farther down Farmington Avenue is the **Mark Twain House,** the author's 1874 19-room mansion with impressive interiors by Louis Comfort Tiffany and his home for seventeen years. From here make a right on to Woodland Ave and head north to Asylum Ave (this is about 4/10 of a mile). Make a left on Asylum and head west (for about 1/3 of a mile) to the **Connecticut Historical Society** to take in its multimedia exhibit on the *Amistad.* After that, you can reflect on all that you have absorbed of Connecticut's diverse and rich history—or just take a well-deserved rest and stop to smell the roses- literally—at the **Elizabeth Park Rose Gardens,** where'll you find America's first municipal rose garden with some 14,000 rose bushes representing 900 varieties of roses. A lovely park year-round, it is especially impressive in June when everything is in bloom.

Dining

INEXPENSIVE

First and Last Tavern. Italian. Old pictures of historic Hartford in the 1860's and local heros decorate the walls of this hallowed pizza hall. Neopolitan pizza, spinach scampi, stuffed eggplant, manicotti, cioppino, and veg. lasagna are all popular items. The tavern also sells its own marinara and spicier puttanesca sauces. | 939 Maple Ave. | 860/956–6000 | No lunch Sun. | $7–$15 | AE, D, DC, MC, V.

MODERATE

Black-Eyed Sally's Bar-B-Que & Blues. American. A jiving barbecue house with the feel of a Southern juke joint. Specialties include jambalaya, Louisiana-style hickory-smoked pork ribs, and panfried crab cakes with Cajun remoulade. Blues music Thurs.–Sat. nights. | 350 Asylum St. | 860/278–7427 | Closed Sun. No lunch | $10–$16 | AE, MC, V.

EXPENSIVE

Civic Café. Contemporary. A spacious, hip, and smartly designed restaurant. The nightly changing menu offers inventive preparations of chicken, seafood, and steak. On Wednesday nights there is a martini bar. | 150 Trumbull St. | 860/493–7412 | Closed Sun. No lunch Sat. | $23–$26 | AE, D, DC, MC, V.

★ **Max Downtown.** American. This spot is where it's happening in Hartford. The dining room has black leather booths and rich wood and is a favorite for business lunches. Try the steak, fresh fish, pork chops, chicken, or pasta. Cigar bar. | 185 Asylum St. | 860/522–2530 | Reservations essential | No lunch weekends | $17–$27 | AE, D, DC, MC, V.

Pastis. French. A Parisian-style brasserie featuring steak frites, coq au vin, and beef Bourguignon. There is also a wine bar. | 201 Ann St. | 860/278–8852 | Closed Sun. | $17–$25 | AE, DC, MC, V.

Peppercorn's Grill. Italian. A mainstay of Hartford's downtown scene, this restuarant's dining room has colorful murals on the walls and formal tables topped with white linen. Try the carpaccio of smoked Sicilian swordfish or the grilled and roasted fillet of veal. No smoking. Kid's menu. | 357 Main St. | 860/547–1714 | Closed Sun. | $18–$24 | AE, DC, MC, V.

VERY EXPENSIVE

★ **The Savannah.** Eclectic. A tale of two Savannahs: the one in Georgia, where one of the owners grew up, and the region in Africa, where her sister lives. The elaborate culinary creations are influenced by Southern and African flavors, as well as Spanish, French, and Asian. Try the tuna crusted with sesame seeds and topped with warm bananas and papaya. On Tuesday nights there's jazz. | 391 Main St. | 860/278–2020 | Closed Sun.–Mon. No lunch Sat. | $27–$49 | AE, MC, V.

Lodging

INEXPENSIVE

Grand Chalet Hartford. This four-story hotel was built in 1965 and completely revamped in 1998. It is 2½ mi from downtown Hartford's business and shopping districts, as well as the University of Connecticut's law school and Trinity College. For dining, there is a Hilltop Steakhouse adjacent to the hotel and a handful of other chain restaurants within one mile. Complimentary Continental breakfast. Outdoor pool. Exercise room. Laundry facilities. Business services. | 185 Brainard Rd. | 860/525–9306 | fax 860/525–2990 | $46–$90 | AE, D, DC, MC, V.

Holiday Inn. A chain option in East Hartford that is within five minutes of downtown Hartford. Restaurant, bar, room service. Cable TV. Indoor pool. Gym. Laundry facilities, laundry service. Business services. Pets allowed. | 363 Roberts St., East Hartford | 860/528–9611 | fax 860/289–0270 | 130 rooms | $100–$130 | AE, D, MC, V.

Ramada Inn-Capitol Hill. This glass-front chain hotel is in downtown Hartford and right across the street from Bushnell Park. Restaurant, bar, complimentary Continental breakfast. In-room data ports, cable TV. Business services. Pets allowed (fee). | 440 Asylum St. | 860/246–6591 | fax 860/728–1382 | 96 rooms | $87–$97 | AE, D, DC, MC, V.

MODERATE

Crowne Plaza Hartford Downtown. A chain option that is convenient to downtown attractions. Restaurant, bar, room service. In-room data ports, cable TV. Pool. Gym. Laundry service. Business services. Pets allowed. | 50 Morgan St. | 860/549–2400 | fax 860/527–2746 | 350 rooms, 4 suites | $109–$189 | AE, D, DC, MC, V.

Hastings Hotel & Conference Center. This large corporate hotel, with lots of windows and marble floors, is on meticulously landscaped grounds in downtown Hartford. It has eight floors, 56 meeting rooms, a business and computer center and two on-site restaurants. It is geared toward the business traveler and is a popular destination for corporate retreats. However, it is certainly not limited to that and with all the luxurious amenities under one roof and the polish of $6 million renovation, it is a tempting option for any traveler. Restaurant, bar, room service. In-room data ports, cable TV. Massage, sauna, spa. Basketball, volleyball. Laundry facilities. Business services. No pets. | 85 Sigourney St. | 860/727–4200 | fax 860/727–4215 | www.dolce.com/properties/hastings | 271 | $99–$139 | AE, D, DC, MC, V.

EXPENSIVE

★ **The Goodwin.** The facade of this grand city hotel—and registered historic landmark—dates back to 1881, but the rest of the building was completely rebuilt from top to bottom in the 1980s. Restaurant, bar, room service. In-room data ports, cable TV. Gym. Laundry service. Business services. Pets allowed. | 1 Haynes St. | 860/246–7500 or 800/922–5006 | fax 860/247–4576 | www.goodwinhotel.com | 111 rooms, 13 suites | $99–$239 | AE, D, DC, MC, V.

VERY EXPENSIVE

Hilton Hartford Hotel. Connected to the Civic Center by an enclosed bridge, this chain option has 22 modern floors as well as a casual bar and grill. 2 restaurants, room service. In-room data ports, cable TV. Indoor pool. Hot tub, sauna. Gym. Laundry service. Business services. | 315 Trumbull St. | 860/728–5151 | fax 860/240–7247 | 390 rooms, 12 suites | $250–$300 | AE, D, DC, MC, V.

IVORYTON

MAP 3, F5

(Nearby towns also listed: Chester, East Haddam, Essex, Old Lyme, Old Saybrook)

Ivoryton was named for its steady import of elephant tusks from Kenya and Zanzibar during the 19th century: piano keys were Ivoryton's leading export during this time. At one time, the Comstock-Cheney piano manufacturers processed so much ivory that Japan regularly purchased Ivoryton's surplus, using the scraps to make souvenirs. The Depression closed the lid on Ivoryton's pianos, and what remains today is a sleepy, shady hamlet.

Information: **Middlesex County Chamber of Commerce** | 393 Main St., Middletown, 06457 | 860/347–6924 | fax 860/346–1043 | info@middlesexchamber.com | www.middlesexchamber.com. **Connecticut River Valley and Shoreline Visitors Council** | 393 Main St., Middletown, 06457 | 860/347–0028 or 800/486–3346 | fax 860/704–2340 | crvsvc@cttourism.org | www.cttourism.org.

Attractions

Ivoryton Playhouse. The River Rep players walk the floorboards at this playhouse from June through September. Year-round events include children's performances, concerts, and dances. | 103 Main St. | 860/767–8348 or 860/767–7318 | Call for performance schedule and ticket prices.

Museum of Fife & Drum. This museum presents a visual and musical history of America on parade, from the Revolutionary War to the present. Displays include fifes and drums (of course), military swords, uniforms, medals, and photos. | 62 N. Main St. | 860/767–2237 or 860/399–6519 | www.fifedrum.com/thecompany | $2 | June–Aug., weekends 1–5.

ON THE CALENDAR
JULY: *Ancient Fife and Drum Corps Muster and Parade.* The oldest and largest muster of these spirited corps. | 860/347–0028.

Dining
Copper Beech Inn. French. There are four dining rooms here, each with its own character, from the peach Ivoryton Room, once the home's living room, with floral wall coverings and elegant Queen Anne–style chairs, to the Garden Porch, with only four tables, which has burgundy sponge-painted walls, 19th Century Audubon prints, and rattan chairs. Entrées include such specialties as the renowned seafood stew; a vegetable Napoléon with layers of crisp potato slices, spiced black beans, diced summer vegetables, and polenta on a bed of sautéed baby spinach; and herb-crusted roast lamb, and served with a warm salad of eggplant, fennel, tomato, and Provençal olives, and a lavender-scented lamb glaze. | 46 Main St. | 860/767–0330 or 888/809–2056 | No lunch | $23–$28 | AE, MC, V.

Lodging
Copper Beech Inn. This white clapboard inn is set on seven acres off Ivoryton's quiet Main Street. Four of the rooms are on the second floor of the main house and the other nine are in a converted two-floor carriage barn. The charming and elegant rooms, furnished with antiques and reproductions, are spacious and airy. Many have canopied beds and baths with clawed-foot tubs. Complimentary breakfast. No kids under 10. No smoking. | 46 Main St. | 860/767–0330 or 888/809–2056 | www.copperbeechinn.com | 13 rooms | $105–175 | AE, MC, V.

KENT

MAP 3, B3

(Nearby towns also listed: Cornwall, New Milford, New Preston, Washington)

Kent has the area's greatest concentration of art galleries, some nationally renowned, a tradition begun by the founding of the Kent Art Association in 1923 by a group of "runaway" New York artists. Most of these galleries are within a few blocks of each other on Kent's Main Street (U.S. 7). Home to a prep school of the same name, Kent once held many ironworks. The Schaghticoke Indian Reservation, one of the state's last remaining Native American reservations, is also here. During the Revolutionary War, Schaghticokes helped defend the Colonies: They transmitted messages of army intelligence from the Litchfield Hills to Long Island Sound, along the hilltops, by way of shouts and drumbeats.

Information: Chamber of Commerce | Box 124, Kent, 06757 | 860/927–1463 | fax 860/927–1463 | www.kentct.com. **Chamber of Commerce of Northwest Connecticut** | 333 Kennedy Dr., Box 59, Torrington, 06790-0059 | 860/482–6586 | fax 860/489–8851 | dave@northwestchamber.org | www.northwestchamber.org. **Litchfield Hills Visitors Bureau** | Box 968, Litchfield, 06759 | 860/567–4506 | fax 860/567–5214 | www.litchfieldhills.com.

Attractions
Appalachian Trail. The famous trail's longest riverwalk is the almost 5-mi hike from Rte. 31, west of Kent, to Cornwall Bridge along the Housatonic River. | Information: Appalachian Mountain Club, 5 Joy St., Boston, MA, 02108 | 617/523–0636 | www.ct-amc.org | Daily.

Bachelier-Cardonsky Gallery. This gallery primarily exhibits American contemporary artists, with an emphasis on figurative art. | 10 N. Main St., 2nd floor | 860/927–3129 | Free | Mid-Apr.–Dec., Fri.–Sun. 11–5, and by appointment.

Bulls Bridge. This bridge just off U.S. 7, south of Kent, is one of three covered bridges in Connecticut and is open to cars. Do be careful, however: George Washington's horse is said to have slipped on a rotted plank and tumbled into the roaring river. | U.S. 7 to Bulls Bridge Rd. | Free | Daily.

Kent Falls State Park. At this 295-acre state park you can hike a short way to one of the most impressive waterfalls in the state and picnic in the lush hemlock grove above the falls. | U.S. 7 | 860/927–3238 | Free | 8–dusk.

Macedonia Brook State Park. A 2,300-acre park with 13 mi of blazed hiking trails that is also ideal for cross-country skiing. Its highest accessible peak reaches 1,350 ft. | Macedonia Brook Rd. | 860/927–3238 | Free | 8–dusk.

Paris–New York–Kent Gallery. This gallery exhibits well-established 20th-century artists, as well as contemporary international and American artists. There are occasionally outdoor sculpture exhibitions. | Kent Station Sq., U.S. 7 | 860/927–4152 | Free | Mid-Apr.–Dec., Fri.–Sun. 11–5, and by appointment.

Sloane-Stanley Museum. Hardware-store buffs and vintage tool aficionados, not to mention Tim "The Tool Man" Taylor, will feel at right at home at this unusual museum. Artist and author Eric Sloane (1905–85) was fascinated by Early American woodworking tools and implements, and his collection on display ranges from the 17th to the 19th centuries. The museum, a re-creation of Sloane's last studio, also encompasses the ruins of a 19th-century iron furnace. Sloane's books and prints, which celebrate vanishing aspects of the American heritage from barns to covered bridges, are on sale here. | U.S. 7 | 860/927–3849 or 860/566–3005 | $3 | Mid-May–Oct., Wed.–Sun. 10–4.

ON THE CALENDAR
MAY–OCT.: *Farmers' Market.* Fresh is the word that applies to this market, which takes place on Saturdays at the Kent Green Shopping Village. | 860/927–1463.

Dining
Fife 'N Drum Restaurant and Inn. Continental. The main dining room of this inn has high ceilings, a fireplace, and brick walls with wood trim. The chef's selections are taken from a variety of cuisines and always include seasonal foods. Favorites are the roast duck, which is carved and flambéd table-side, steak au poivre, and rack of lamb. The wine list has won a *Wine Spectator* awards for many years. You can dine on the patio in nice weather. | 53 N. Main St. | 860/927–3509 | www.fifendrum.com | Closed Tues. | $13.95–$24.50 | AE, MC, V.

Stroble's Baking Company. American. A friendly, small restaurant that serves local residents and students from nearby boarding schools. There is a patio to accommodate diners. Try the home made selections and baked goods. | 14 N. Main St. | 860/927–4073 | $5.25–$8.50 | AE, DC, MC, V.

Lodging
Fife 'N Drum Restaurant and Inn. This family-owned and -operated inn is over a gift shop in the middle of town. It's within walking distance of Kent's attractions. The rooms are individually appointed—some have Ralph Lauren wallpaper and fabrics and some have four-poster beds. Restaurant, bar. Cable TV. Shop. No pets. No smoking. | 59 N. Main St. | 860/927–3509 | fax 860/927–4595 | www.fifendrum.com | 8 rooms | $95–$110 | AE, MC, V.

Rosewood Meadows. This white-clapboard Greek Revival was built in 1860. It is on 2 acres with a barn, a stream, and rose gardens. The common area includes a paneled sitting room with a fireplace and a living room with a beehive fireplace. The cozy guest rooms have antiques, plank floors, and quilts; two have fireplaces. Complimentary breakfast. No pets. No smoking. | 230 Kent Cornwall Rd., | 860/927–4334 or 800/600–4334 | 4 rooms, 1 cottage | $85–$105 | AE, MC, V.

LAKEVILLE

(Nearby towns also listed: Cornwall, Norfolk, Salisbury)

You can usually spot an original Colonial home in Lakeville by looking for the grapevine design cut into the frieze above the front door—the trademark of the builder of the town's first homes. The lake of Lakeville is Lake Wononskopomuc. As you drive along U.S. 44 or Route 41, you'll catch glimpses of the lake's sparkling waters—the closest you're likely to get because most of its shoreline is private property.

Information: **Chamber of Commerce of Northwest Connecticut** | 333 Kennedy Dr., Box 59, Torrington, 06790-0059 | 860/482–6586 | fax 860/489–8851 | dave@north-westchamber.org | www.northwestchamber.org. **Litchfield Hills Visitors Bureau** | Box 968, Litchfield, 06759 | 860/567–4506 | fax 860/567–5214 | www.litchfieldhills.com.

Attractions

Holley House Museum and Salisbury Cannon Museum. The holdings of this museum chronicle 18th- and 19th-century life. There are items from an ironmaster's home and an 1808 Classical Revival wing that contains family furnishings, Colonial portraits, and a Holley Manufacturing Co. pocketknife exhibit. "From Corsets to Freedom" is a popular hands-on exhibit, set in the 1870s, demonstrating the debate between women's rights versus "women's sphere" in the home. Admission includes the on-site Salisbury Cannon Museum, where hands-on exhibits and activities survey the contributions of area residents and the local iron industry to the American Revolution. | 15 Millerton Rd. | 860/435–2878 | fax 860/435–6469 | www.salisburyassociation.org/hhm | $3 | Mid-June–mid-Oct., weekends noon–5, or by appointment.

The Hotchkiss School. An elite college preparatory school that was founded in 1891 by Maria Harrison Bissell. At the encouragement of Timothy Dwight, then president of Yale University, Mrs. Hotchkiss established the school to prepare students to enroll at Yale. Known for its beauty, the 500-acre campus, with its dorms and school buildings, has two lakes and a 9-hole golf course. | Rte. 112 | 860/435–2591 | fax 860/435–0042 | www.hotchkiss.pvt.k12.ct.us | Free | Call to arrange a tour.

ON THE CALENDAR
MAY: *Dodge Dealers Grand Prix.* The largest sports car race in North America features top drivers from the International Motorsports Association and the Sports Car Club of America. It takes place at Lime Rock Park. | 860/435–5000 or 800/RACE–LRP.
JUNE–SEPT.: *Music Mountain Summer Music Festival.* The country's oldest continuously operating summer chamber music festival is in Falls Village's Gordon Hall. | 860/824–7126.
JUNE: *Grove Festival.* This lakeside international arts festival includes musicians, theatrical performers, and dancers from around the world. It takes place on the last Saturday of the month. | 860/435–0561.

Dining

The Boathouse at Lakeville. Contemporary. You know you're near a prep school here: crew oars from nearby Kent, Hotchkiss, and Berkshire cheerfully grace the dining room as do the cane-seat canoes that hang from the ceiling. This bistro-style restaurant caters to all tastes and those looking for sushi will be as happy as steak lovers. In winter, a fireplace makes it especially cozy. | 349 Main St. | 860/435–2111 | No lunch Sun.–Thurs. | $7–$18 | AE, MC, V.

Charlotte. Contemporary. This romantic antique-filled (the furnishings are for sale) bistro is set in a 1775 building that was once the home of the town's iron master. The food in the upstairs main dining room is sophisticated and draws on both French and Asian influences. Downstairs is the wine bar, a popular place to meet friends for a drink, where you can choose from over a dozen wines sold by the glass. | 223 Main St. | 860/435–3551 | $12–$22 | AE, MC, V.

West Main. Contemporary. Previously in a smaller space in Sharon, West Main is known for its eclectic mix of excellent American fare with Asian and Middle Eastern influences—among the most popular dishes are the Asian-grilled tuna and the seared shrimp with shandong noodles. There is outside dining on the deck. Take-out, delivery, and a prix-fixe menu are all available. | 8 Holley Rd. | 860/435–1450 | Closed Tues. | $7–$23 | AE, MC, V.

Lodging

1890 Colonial Bed & Breakfast. A late Colonial-style home built in 1890, this bed-and-breakfast is 5 mi southwest of Lakeville. The grounds cover 5 acres, 2½ of which have gardens. The rooms are large and have high ceilings, hard-wood floors and moldings. Each has its own sitting area or you can relax on the screened porch overlooking the gardens. Two-night minimum weekends. Complimentary breakfast. No air-conditioning, cable TV, no room phones. Pool. No pets. No kids under 12. | Rte. 41, Sharon | 860/364–0436 | colonial@mohawk.net | 3 rooms | $80–$125 | No credit cards.

Inne at Iron Masters. The grounds of this motel contain an English country gardens and several gazebos. In colder weather, you can warm yourself by the fireplace in the common area. Guest rooms are individually appointed and have sitting areas. Restaurant, bar, complimentary Continental breakfast. Cable TV. Pool. Pets allowed. | 229 Main St. | 860/435–9844 | fax 860/435–2254 | www.innatironmasters.com | 28 rooms | $75–$135 | AE, D, DC, MC, V.

Interlaken Inn. A conference and business retreat complex that is also appropriate for families. You have a choice of the main building, English Tudor house or Victorian-style building with wraparound porch. The rooms are modern American. Restaurant, room service. Cable TV. Pool, lake. Sauna. 2 tennis courts. Gym, beach, water sports. Fishing. Laundry service. Business services. Pets allowed (fee). | 74 Interlaken Rd. | 860/435–9878 | fax 860/435–2980 | www.interlakeninn.com | 73 rooms, 7 suites | $149–$189, $289–$319 suites | AE, MC, V.

Wake Robin Inn. This Georgian Colonial–Revival inn was built in 1898 as a girls school. Inside the rooms have period furnishings, some with fireplaces. Sharing the 12-acre site is a small motel with a more modern look. Complimentary Continental breakfast. Cable TV. Business services. Pets allowed (fee). | Rte. 41 | 860/435–2515 | fax 860/435–2000 | www.wakerobininn.com | 24 rooms in inn, 15 in motel | $95–$175, $225 suites | AE, D, MC, V.

LEDYARD

MAP 3, H5

(Nearby towns also listed: Groton, Mystic, New London, Norwich, Stonington)

There is no doubt that Ledyard, in the woods of southeastern Connecticut between Norwich and the coastline, is known first and foremost for the Mashantucket Pequot Tribal Nation's Foxwoods Resort Casino. It is the world's largest casino and draws more than 55,000 visitors daily. With the recent opening of the $120 million Mashantucket Pequot Museum and Research Center, however, the tribe has moved beyond gaming to educating the public about their history as well as that of other North American tribes.

Information: **Chamber of Commerce of Southeastern Connecticut** | 105 Huntington St., New London, 06320 | 860/443–8332 | fax 860/444–1529 | chambersectpres@snet.com | www.chambersect.org. **Southeastern Connecticut Tourism District** | 470 Bank St., Box 89, New London, 06320 | 860/444–2206 or 800/TO–ENJOY | fax 860/442–4257 | more2see@aol.com | www.mysticmore.com.

Attractions

Foxwoods Resort Casino. This casino on the Mashantucket Pequot Indian Reservation is the world's largest gambling operation. The skylit Colonial-style compound draws visitors to its 5,750 slot machines, 3,500-seat high-stakes bingo parlor, poker rooms, Keno station, smoke-free gaming area, theater and Race Book room. The complex includes more than 1,400 hotel rooms, as well as a retail concourse, a food court, and 25 restaurants. A large game room and arcade and a movie theater in-the-round keep the kids entertained, along with Turbu Ride, which has specially engineered seats that simulate takeoffs and G-force pressure. | Rte. 2 | 860/312–3000 or 800/752–9244 | www.foxwoods.com | Daily 24 hrs.

★ **Mashantucket Pequot Museum and Research Center.** Opened in 1998, this expansive complex across from Foxwoods Casino explores the history and culture of northeastern woodland tribes in general and the Pequots in particular. Highlights include a re-created glacial crevice, a caribou hunt from 11,000 years ago, a 17th-century fort, and a sprawling "immersion environment"—a re-creation of a 16th-century village with life-size figures and real smells and sounds. The research center, to which admission is free, holds thousands of books and artifacts. Native American cuisine is available at the restaurant, and the shop sells contemporary Native American arts and crafts. | 110 Pequot Trail | 860/396–6800 | fax 860/396–7013 | www.mashantucket.org | $12 | Memorial Day weekend–Labor Day, daily 10–7; Labor Day–Memorial Day weekend, Wed.–Mon. 10–6.

ON THE CALENDAR

SEPT.: *Ledyard Fair.* This annual weekend-long town fair is more than 50 years old and has everything from a garden tractor pull to a pie eating contest. There are lots of activities geared toward kids, including a Little Miss Ledyard Fair contest and a pet show. | 860/204–0533.

Dining

Cedars Steakhouse. Steak. Getting reservations here is always a challenge. The lure of the casino's entertainment and the consistently good all-American fare (think chops, lobsters, and grilled shish kebobs) has made this a popular destination, especially on weekends. | Foxwoods Resort Casino, Rte. 2 | 860/312–4252 | Reservations essential in the dining room | $18–$25 | AE, D, DC, MC, V.

★ **Stonecroft Country Inn.** Contemporary. The dining room of this 1807 Georgian Colonial inn is a converted barn with granite walls and pine floors. The menu, which changes with the season, draws on culinary influences from France to Thailand. Especially popular when its in season is the game. In cooler weather, the room is warmed by a fireplace and in the summer there is outdoor dining on terrace. | 515 Pumpkin Hill Rd. | 860/572–0771 | Reservations essential | $17–$33 | AE, MC, V.

Lodging

Abbey's Lantern Hill Inn. No two rooms here are alike and each has its own name (such as Downeast and Southwest) to reflect its personality. What the rooms share is warmth and coziness; each has polished wood floors with throw rugs, large beds with quilts, and outside sitting areas with views of the surrounding countryside. Two have fireplaces and one has its own private courtyard (they say this one is perfect for pets). Complimentary breakfast. Some in-room hot tubs. Pets allowed. | 780 Lantern Hill Rd. | 860/572–0483 | fax 860/572–0518 | www.abbeyslanternhill.com | 8 rooms | $79–$140 | AE, MC, V.

Applewood Farms Inn. This 1826 center-chimney, Colonial farmhouse is on the State and National Register of Historic Landmark properties. It has 33 acres (the inn shares a border with Nature Conservancy land as well) with paths to walk and great birdwatching. Guests can also practice their "short game" on a USGA chipping and putting green. The rooms have views of the surrounding countryside and are furnished with antiques; four have fireplaces. Complimentary breakfast. Hot tub. Putting green. Pets allowed. No kids under 10. | 528 Colonel Ledyard Hwy. | 860/536–2022 or 800/717–4262 | fax 860/536–6015 | www.visitmystic.com/applewoodfarmsinn | 6 rooms | $105–$290 | AE, MC.

Grand Pequot Tower. This luxury hotel with sunken piano in the lobby is above its own casino and is just down the concourse from the rest of the Foxwoods casinos. You can choose from a variety of rooms and suites, some of which can be combined to form two-bedroom apartments. Many of the rooms and all the suites have separate sitting areas and some even have dining tables. The suites are not always available on weekends. 4 restaurants, bar, room service. Some in-room safes, some in-room hot tubs, cable TV. Indoor pool. Barbershop, beauty salon, sauna, spa, steam room, hot tub. Gym. Baby-sitting, laundry service. Business services. | Rte. 2 | 860/312–3000 or 800/369–9663 | www.foxwoods.com | 824 units | $155–$375 | AE, D, DC, MC, V.

The Great Cedar. A huge fish tank with trout greets you as you enter the lobby of this Foxwoods Casino resort hotel. Rooms decorated in a Native American motif. Bar, room service. Cable TV. Indoor pool. Hot tub, sauna, steam room. Gym. Baby-sitting. Business services. | Rte. 2 | 860/312–3000 or 800/369–9663 | www.foxwoods.com | 264 rooms, 48 suites | $140–$210 | AE, D, DC, MC, V.

Stonecroft. An 1807 Georgian Colonial inn on 6½ acres of woodlands and meadows. The individually decorated rooms range from English country charm to romantic French canopy beds, some have fireplaces. Two-night minimum on weekends. Restaurant, complimentary Continental breakfast. Some in-room hot tubs, some room phones, no TV in rooms. No smoking. | 515 Pumpkin Hill Rd. | 860/572–0771 | fax 860/572–9161 | www.stonecroft.com | 10 rooms | $130–$250 | AE, D, MC, V.

Two Trees Inn. Foxwoods Casino's version of a New England Inn is directly across from the casino and has a free shuttle bus to the gaming action. The rooms have a Native American motif and some have a view of the woodland garden with gazebo. Restaurant, bar. Cable TV. Indoor pool. Hot tub. Gym. Baby-sitting, laundry service. | Rte. 2 | 860/312–3000 or 800/369–9663 | www.foxwoods.com | 280 units | $90–$175 | AE, D, DC, MC, V.

LITCHFIELD

MAP 3, C3

(Nearby towns also listed: Cornwall, New Preston, Washington)

Everything in Litchfield seems to exist on a larger scale than in neighboring burgs, especially the impressive Litchfield Green and the white Colonials that line the broad, elm-shaded streets. Harriet Beecher Stowe, author of *Uncle Tom's Cabin,* and Henry Ward were born and raised in Litchfield, and many famous Americans earned their law degrees at the Litchfield Law School.

Information: Chamber of Commerce of Northwest Connecticut | 333 Kennedy Dr., Box 59, Torrington, 06790-0059 | 860/482–6586 | fax 860/489–8851 | dave@northwestchamber.org | www.northwestchamber.org. **Litchfield Hills Visitors Council** | Box 968, Litchfield, 06759 | 860/567–4506 | fax 860/567–5214 | www.litchfieldhills.com.

Attractions

Haight Vineyard and Winery. Despite the area's severe climate, this winery flourishes. Stop in for vineyard walks, winery tours, and tastings. | 29 Chestnut Hill Rd. | 860/567–4045 | fax 860/567–1766 | www.ctwineries.com | Free | Mon.–Sat. 10:30–5, Sun. noon–5.

Litchfield History Museum. The well-organized galleries at this museum display paintings, furniture, clothing, and household objects from the 18th to 20th centuries. The extensive reference library has information about the town's many historic buildings, including the Sheldon Tavern (where old G. W. slept on several occasions) and the Litchfield Female Academy, where Sarah Pierce taught girls not just sewing and deportment but also mathematics and history. | 7 South St. | 860/567–4501 | fax 860/567–3565 | $5 (includes Tapping Reeve House and Litchfield Law School) | Mid-Apr.–Nov. Tues.–Sat. 10–5, Sun. 1–5.

★ **Tapping Reeve House and Litchfield Law School.** In 1773, Judge Tapping Reeve enrolled his first student, Aaron Burr, in what was to become the first law school in the country. (Before Judge Reeve, students studied the law as apprentices, not in formal classes.) This site is dedicated to Reeve's remarkable achievement and to the notable students who passed through its halls: Oliver Wolcott Jr., John C. Calhoun, Horace Mann, 3 U.S. Supreme Court justices, and 15 governors, not to mention innumerable senators, congressmen, and ambassadors. The 1998 renovations added an interactive multimedia exhibits, an excellent introductory film, and beautifully restored facilities. | 82 South St. | 860/567–4501 | fax 860/567–3565 | $5 | Mid-Apr.–Nov. Tues.–Sat. 11–5, Sun. 1–5.

Topsmead State Forest. The forest's chief attractions are a Tudor-style "cottage" designed by architect Richard Henry Dana Jr. and beautiful gardens and lawns. You'll also find picnic grounds, hiking trails, and cross-country skiing areas. | Buell Rd. | 860/567–5694 | Free | Forest daily 8–dusk; house tours June–Oct., 2nd and 4th weekends of the month noon–5.

White Flower Farm. You will find many ideas for your garden as you stroll through White Flower Farm's myriad gardens. The farm is the home base of a renowned mail-order operation that sells perennials and bulbs to gardeners throughout the United States. | Rte. 63 | 860/567–8789 | www.whiteflowerfarm.com | Nov.–Dec. and mid-Feb.–Mar., daily 10–5; Apr.–Oct., daily 9–6.

White Memorial Conservation Center. This is Connecticut's largest nature center and wildlife sanctuary. The 4,000-acre sanctuary contains fishing areas, bird-watching platforms, two self-guided nature trails, several boardwalks, and 35 mi of hiking, cross-country skiing, and horseback-riding trails. The main conservation center is home to a completely remodeled natural history museum, the best in the state, and a must-see for lovers of the outdoors. | U.S. 202 | 860/567–0857 | fax 860/567–2611 | www.litchfieldct.com | Grounds free, conservation center $4 | Grounds open daily; conservation center Mon.–Sat. 9–5, Sun. noon–5.

ON THE CALENDAR

JUNE: *Northwest Connecticut Balloon Festival & Craft Fair.* The Goshen Fairgrounds are the site of hot-air balloon rides, a juried crafts show, car show, fireworks, amusement rides, and more on the last weekend of the month. | 860/489–3378.

JULY: *Litchfield Open House Tour.* A self-guided tour of the village's historic homes and gardens, both private and public, takes place on the second Saturday of the month. | 860/567–9423.

Dining

The Bistro East. American. This restaurant at the Litchfield Inn has a seperate tavern, a popular bar-lounge frequented by guests of the hotel and the general public. All of the choices are farm-raised and all the desserts are homemade. Seasonal dishes are always offered, as is seafood. The raspberry Charlotte is the most popular dessert. | 432 Bantam Rd. | 860/567–4503 | No lunch Mon.–Tues. | $15–$21 | AE, DC, MC, V.

The Village Restaurant. Continental. This casual, classic restaurant was built in 1890 and has booths and wood floors. There is also a cheaper pub menu served in the tap room, which patrons in dining room may select from as well. There are excellent handmade pastas, and the classic village burger and the salmon crab cakes are good choices. Kid's menu. Sun. brunch. | 25 West St. | 860/567–8307 | $13–$21 | AE, MC, V.

★ **West Street Grill.** Continental. One of the best-known restaurants in the state has art on the walls and overlooks the village green. Fish, steak, poultry, lamb, and pasta are the staples. Try the pan-crusted diver sea scallops or the lemon-scented veal chop. | 43 West St. | 860/567–3885 | Reservations essential Fri.–Sat. | $17–$34 | AE, MC, V.

Lodging

Litchfield Inn. A Victorian-style, contemporary hotel with landscaped grounds bordered by trees, and close to hiking trails, shopping, and the historic district. Restaurant, bar, complimentary breakfast, room service. In-room data ports, cable TV. Laundry service. Business services. | 432 Bantam Rd. | 860/567–4503 or 800/499–3444 | fax 860/567–5358 | 32 rooms | $120–$200 | AE, DC, MC, V.

Yankee Pedlar Inn. The rooms in this 1891 inn 5 mi northwest of Litchfield have four-poster beds and stenciled walls. There is a fireplace and rough-hewn, exposed beams in the lobby and a wide, curved stair-case leading to the guest rooms. Restaurant, complimentary Continental breakfast. Cable TV. | 93 Main St., Torrington | 860/489–9226 or 800/777–1891 | fax 860/482–7851 | www.pedlarinn.com | 60 rooms | $89–$109 | AE, MC, V.

MADISON

MAP 3, F6

(Nearby towns also listed: Branford, Clinton, Guilford)

Madison, home to Hammonasset Beach State Park, the shoreline's most popular stretch of sand, is a particularly pleasant place to visit in summer. Downtown Madison has a historic tree-shaded green and is especially conducive to strolling. The small stretch of businesses along U.S. 1 includes one of the state's best independent bookstores and a sweets shop with scrumptious homemade ice cream. Farther down U.S. 1, Lenny and Joe's Fish Tale is a requisite stop for those who equate summer with sweet strips of fried clams. Take them outside to eat at a picnic table and be sure to purchase a Lenny and Joe's T-shirt to bring home—it's one of the state's more popular souvenirs.

Information: **Chamber of Commerce** | 22 Scotland Ave., Box 706, Madison, 06443 | 203/245–7394 | fax 203/318–0403 | chamber@madisonct.com | www.madisonct.com. **Connecticut River Valley and Shoreline Visitors Council** | 393 Main St., Middletown, 06457 | 860/347–0028 or 800/486–3346 | fax 860/704–2340 | crvsvc@cttourism.org | www.cttourism.org.

Attractions

Allis-Bushnell House and Museum. Built in 1785, this historic landmark is the home of the Madison Historical Society. Civil War buffs will particularly enjoy the society's collection of memorabilia relating to the USS *Monitor*: owner Cornelius Bushnell, founder of the Union Pacific Railroad, was chief backer of the ironclad ship. | 853 Boston Post Rd. | 203/245–4567 | Free | May–Sept., Wed., Fri., and Sat. 1–4.

Hammonasset Beach State Park. The largest of the state's shoreline sanctuaries, Hammonasset has 2 mi of white sandy beaches, a nature center, a wheelchair-accessible trail through a salt marsh, and a popular 541-site campground. | I–95, Exit 62 | 203/245–2785 | $5–$12 Apr.–Sept.; free at other times | Daily 8–8, or 8–dusk which ever comes first.

MAY: *Civil War Reenactment.* Union and Confederate military and civilian camps convene at Hammonasset Beach State Park during the first weekend of the month. Battles take place each day. | 203/481–2393.

MAY: *Sound Winds Kite Festival.* Hammonasset Beach State Park is alive with kite-flying demonstrations and lessons, kite-building workshops, and a kite museum. | 860/344–6200.

JUNE: *Shoreline Flea Market.* "One man's trash is another man's treasure" is an annual saying in Madison. This flea market in mid June has between 50 and 60 dealers in attendance | 860/245–8720.

AUG.: *Chesnut Hill Concerts.* This series of classical music concerts, held on four successive Friday evenings during the month, is a tradition more than 30 years old. There is picnicking on the historic village green and then a performance of chamber music, ranging from Beethoven to Dvorak to Debussy, at the First Congregational Church. | 203/245–5736.

Dining

Café Allegre. Italian. This restaurant in the Inn at Lafayette blends traditional old-world recipes with innovative new touches. Try the *lumanche al fungo and filetto di pomodoro*, escargots and wild mushrooms over angel-hair pasta or the *involtindi di melanzane*, eggplant stuffed with ricotta. | 725 Boston Post Rd. | 203/245–7773 | Closed Mon. No lunch Sun. | $22–$36 | AE, D, MC, V.

Lenny and Joe's Fish Tale. Seafood. Scrumptious fried clams, scallops, scrod, lobster, steamers, and more are served at this casual drive-in near Hammonasset Beach State Park. No need to change out of your swimsuit. | 1301 Boston Post Rd. | 203/245–7289 | $6.95–$11.95 | No credit cards.

Noodles Casual Cuisine. Continental. At this cozy neighborhood hangout try the Maryland crab cakes, pesto ravioli, or cioppino. | 508 Old Toll Rd. | 203/421–5606 | Closed Mon. No lunch | $10.99–$18.99 | AE, MC, V.

Lodging

Dolly Madison Inn & Restaurant. This white clapboard inn, built around the turn-of-the-century, is a well-known local watering hole. It's just a short walk to the beach. The rooms, which are on the second floor, are uneven in terms of renovation. If that is important, be sure to ask, but overall it is a fine place to stay for a night. Restaurant. | 73 W. Wharf Rd. | 203/245–7377 | 11 rooms | $50–$115 | AE, MC, V.

Inn at Lafayette. An impressive inn in a converted 19th-century church in the center of Madison. The inn has hand-woven rugs, grand murals and faux-textured walls. All of the rooms have marble bathrooms, complete with Egyptian cotton linens and bathrobes. Restaurant, complimentry Continental breakfast, room service. In-room dataports, cable TV. Business services. | 725 Boston Post Rd. | 203/245–7773 | fax 203/245–6256 | 5 rooms | $125–$175 | AE, D, DC, MC, V.

Madison Beach Hotel. This hotel overlooks Long Island Sound and has a lobby with white wicker furniture and a water view. Most of the rooms have wicker furniture and some have balconies. Two-night minimum stay on weekends. 2 restaurants, bar, complimentary Continental breakfast. Cable TV. Beach. Laundry service. Business services. Pets allowed (fee). | 944 W. Wharf Rd. | 203/245–1404 | fax 203/245–0410 | 29 rooms, 6 suites | $115–$225 | Closed Jan.–Feb. | AE, D, MC, V.

Madison Post Road Bed & Breakfast. An 1830 farmhouse with fireplaces in both the living dining rooms. The guest rooms are individually decorated and have been given names, such as the Garden Room, Red Room, etc. All have country furnishings and wood floors; one has a wrought-iron bed. Complimentary breakfast. Cable TV, in-room VCRs. Library. No pets. No smoking. | 318 Boston Post Rd. | 203/245–2866 | fax 203/245–4955 | www.madisonpost.com | 4 rooms | $70–$110 | AE, D, MC, V.

Tidewater Inn. Built in the late 1800s, the Tidewater used to be a stagecoach stop. Now adorned with Oriental accents and furniture dating from the 1930s and '40s, there are still antiques and fireplaces in some rooms. The 2-acre landscaped property has an English garden and is 1 mi from three different beaches. Two-night minimum stay on weekends, Memorial Day to Labor Day. Complimentary breakfast. Some in-room hot tubs, cable TV. No smoking. | 949 Boston Post Rd. | 203/245–8457 | fax 203/318–0265 | www.madisonct.com/tidewater | 8 rooms, 1 suite | $110–$185 | AE, MC, V.

MANCHESTER

MAP 3, F3

(Nearby towns also listed: Coventry, Glastonbury, Hartford)

Manchester, settled circa 1673, was known for many years as Cheneyville and Silktown for the world-famous Cheney Bros. Silk Manufacturing Co., which put it on the map beginning in 1838. The Cheneys were extremely civic-minded and along with their rows of silk, velvet, and yarn mills they built and maintained homes for their workers (who made up 25% of Manchester's workforce at the turn of the century), and schools for their workers' children. They also supplied water and electricity to the community, built a fire station, a public library, and even a cultural center for their workers' enjoyment. Although the business is long gone, having foundered in the Depression, the Cheneys' mark remains in Manchester today. Many of the old mills have been converted into attractive apartments, the workers' cottages have been gussied up and renovated, the old Cheney schoolhouse is now home to the local historical society, and the cultural center serves as a theater.

Information: **Greater Manchester Chamber of Commerce** | 20 Hartford Rd., Manchester, 06040-5973 | 860/646–2223 | fax 860/646–5871 | staff@manchesterchamber.com | www.manchesterchamber.com. **Greater Hartford Tourism District** | 234 Murphy Rd., Hartford, 06114 | 860/244–8181 or 800/793–4480 | fax 860/244–8180 | ctfuntour@aol.com | www.enjoyhartford.com.

Attractions

Cheney Homestead. Timothy Cheney was both a farmer and a clockmaker. His sons, however, opted not to go into the family business and instead launched the silk industry for which Manchester was renowned in the 1850s. This 1780 homestead features 18th- and 19th-century furnishings and paintings from both centuries, quilts made from Cheney silk, and a restored 18th-century schoolhouse on the grounds. | 106 Hartford Rd. | 860/643–5588 | $2 | Fri.–Sun. 10–3, or by appointment.

Fire Museum. A turn-of-the-century firehouse is home to this museum that features hand- and horse-pulled fire-fighting equipment, an 1860 steam fire engine, and other fire-fighting memorabilia. | 230 Pine St. | 860/649–9436 | Free | Mid-Apr.–mid-Nov., Fri.–Sat. 10–5, Sun. noon–5.

Little Theater of Manchester at Cheney Hall. The Little Theater community theater was founded in 1960 and produces at least three major works, such as *Driving Miss Daisy* and *Ain't Misbehavin'*, annually. The group rehearses and performs in Cheney Hall, an elegant Victorian structure that was built in 1866 as a theater and cultural community center. Poetry readings and other performance art are staged here as well. | 177 Hartford Rd. | 860/647–9824 or 860/645–6743 (box office) | www.cheneyhall.org | $25–$30 | Performances year-round.

Lutz Children's Museum. The key word at this museum is "hands-on." Exhibits and activities explore science, history, nature, and wildlife. | 247 S. Main St. | 860/643–0949 | $3 | Tues.–Wed. 2–5, Thurs.–Fri. 9:30–5, weekends noon–5.

Oak Grove Nature Center. This 53-acre park is operated by the town and has fields, nature trails, ponds, and streams that are yours for exploring. | Oak Grove St. | 860/647–3321 | Free | Daily dawn–dusk.

ON THE CALENDAR
NOV.: *Manchester Road Race.* This annual Thanksgiving Day, 5-mi event attracts a huge field, including some of the best runners in the country. It's held early enough— 10 AM—that you'll be home for dinner in plenty of time. | 860/649–6456.

Dining
Bugaboo Creek Steak House. Steak. The dining room replicates a Canadian hunting lodge, right down to the Royal Canadian mountie at the door, talking moose, stone fireplace, and twig furniture. The menu features sirloin, strip, prime rib, chicken, pasta, and fish. Kid's menu. | 1442 Pleasant Valley Rd. | 860/644–6100 | $4.99–$17.99 | AE, D, DC, MC, V.

Cavey's French Restaurant. French. This sophisticated restaurant has many fine antiques in its dining room. Try the filet of sea bass, which is poached in basil-infused olive oil and served with lemongrass sauce, or the rack of lamb, which is four little chops in a mustard crust and moistened with an enriched reduction of lamb jus. | 45 E. Center St. | 860/643–2751 | Reservations essential on Sat. | Closed Sun.–Mon. No lunch | $24–$32 | AE, MC, V.

Cavey's Italian Restaurant. Italian. This casual Northern Italian restaurant is warm and welcoming with tall tapered candles and white tablecloths. The seasonal menu features local produce, fresh herbs from the garden and homemade pastas. | 45 E. Center St. | 860/ 643–2751 | Reservations essential on Sat. | Closed Sun.–Mon. | $19–$25 | AE, MC, V.

Lodging
Clarion Suites Inn. This all-suites chain hotel is within easy commuting distance of Hartford (it's just off I–84) and is close to the University of Connecticut. The rooms are set up for long term stays, and relocations. Buffet dining room, bar, complimentary breakfast. In-room data ports, kitchenettes, cable TV. Pool. Hot tub, sauna. Tennis court. Gym. Laundry facilities, laundry service. Business services, airport shuttle. Pets allowed (fee). | 191 Spencer St. | 860/643–5811 or 800/992–4004 | 104 suites | $107–$161 | Dinner included Mon.–Thurs. | AE, D, DC, MC, V.

Connecticut Motor Lodge. A comfortable, refurbished motor lodge right off of I–84. Cable TV. | 400 Tolland Tpke | 860/643–1555 | fax 860/643–1881 | 32 rooms | $40–$65 | AE, MC, V.

Courtyard By Marriott. This three-story hotel is less than half mile from the Buckland Hills Mall and within 5 mi of several area business, including Gerber Scientific, United Technology and Pratt & Whitney, as well as numerous cultural attractions. The rooms are designed for business travelers (with two phone lines and data ports) and are furnished with contemporary looking furniture in neutral shades. Restaurant, room service. In-room data ports. Indoor pool. Exercise room. Laundry service. Business services. No pets. | 225 Slater Rd. | 860/ 533–8484 or 800/321–2211 | fax 860/644–2800 | www.marriott.com | 90 rooms | $99–$139 | AE, D, DC, MC, V.

MIDDLETOWN

MAP 3, F4

(Nearby towns also listed: East Haddam, New Britain, Wethersfield)

Middletown, once a bustling river city, was named for its location halfway between Hartford and the Long Island Sound (it's also about halfway between New York City and Boston). The wealthiest town in the state from about 1750 to 1800, Middletown had been in decline for more than a century before being chosen to take part in the National Trust for Historic Preservation's "Main Street Program." This multiyear rehabilitation project is intended to revitalize the downtown area. The imposing campus of Wesleyan University, founded here in 1831, is traversed by High Street, which Charles Dickens once called "the loveliest Main Street in America"—even though Middletown's actual Main Street runs parallel to it a few blocks east. High Street is an architecturally eclectic thoroughfare. Note the massive, fluted Corinthian columns of the Greek Revival Russell House (circa 1828), a private home at the corner of Washington Street, across from the pink Mediterranean-style Davison Arts Center, was was built just 15 years later; farther on are gingerbreads, towering brownstones, Tudors, and Queen Annes. A few hundred yards up on Church Street, which intersects High Street, is the Olin Library. The distinctive 1928 structure was designed by Henry Bacon, the architect of the Lincoln Memorial.

Information: **Middlesex County Chamber of Commerce** | 393 Main St., Middletown, 06457 | 860/347–6924 | fax 860/346–1043 | info@middlesexchamber.com | www.middlesexchamber.com. **Connecticut River Valley and Shoreline Visitors Council** | 393 Main St., Middletown, 06457 | 860/347–0028 or 800/486–3346 | fax 860/704–2340 | crvsvc@cttourism.org | www.cttourism.org.

Attractions

Lyman Orchards and Lyman Orchards Golf Club. There's something to make everyone happy at Lyman Orchards: a farm market with fresh fruits and vegetables, gourmet goodies, and a bake shop; acres of pick-your-own fruits like strawberries, peaches, and apples (open June–October); and two top-notch golf courses (open March–November), one designed by Robert Trent Jones, the other by Gary Player. It's 10 minutes' drive southwest of Middletown. | Rtes. 147 and 157, Middlefield | 860/349–1793 or 888/349–1566 | www.lymanorchards.com | Market open daily 9–7.

Powder Ridge Ski Area. Half of the 17 trails at this family ski area are designed for intermediate skiers, the others split between beginner trails and Black Diamonds (though they are not especially challenging); all trails are lit for night skiing. One quad lift, two doubles, and a handle tow cover the mountain. Special features include an immensely popular snowtubing area with its own tow, a snowboard park, an alpine park, a full-service restaurant, and ski instruction for children ages 4 and up. | 99 Powder Hill Rd., Middlefield | 860/349–3454 | www.powderridgect.com | Dec.–early Apr.

Wesleyan University. This four-year liberal arts university, founded in 1831, has a student body of approximately 2,700 full-time undergraduates. | 318 High St. | 860/685–2200 | www.wesleyan.edu | Daily.

Olin Memorial Library. One of the most architecturally significant buildings on Wesleyan's campus, Olin Library was designed by Henry Bacon and executed by McKim, Mead & White in the 1920s. | 252 Church St. | 860/685–3873 | www.wesleyan.edu/library.

ON THE CALENDAR
JULY–AUG.: *Canon Greater Hartford Open.* The GHO, one of the most successful tournaments on the PGA tour, attracts top names in golf to the Tournament Players Club at River Highlands in Cromwell. | 860/246–4GHO.

SEPT.: *Durham Fair.* The state's largest agricultural fair is known for its nationally acclaimed country-music performers. | 860/349–9495.

OCT.: *Head of the Connecticut Regatta.* Harbor Park is the end point for this rowing regatta, which traditionally draws more than 600 boats and 3,000 competitors. | 860/346–1042.

NOV.–DEC.: *Wesleyan Potters Exhibit and Sale.* A fine selection of pottery and handicrafts made by 300 artisans are for show and sale at this annual event that takes place during the two weeks following Thanksgiving. | 860/347–5925.

Dining

First and Last Tavern. Italian. This is the third and newest of the First and Lasts (the others are in Avon and Hartford), which are known for consistently good pizzas and pastas as well as tasty brick-oven breads. It has quickly gained favor with locals who like the old-fashioned Italian cooking and the friendly and efficient service. Take-out and delivery is available. | 220 Main St. | 860/347–2220 | $6–$15 | AE, MC, V.

Taj of India. Indian. At lunch this eatery attracts a work crowd looking for a quick and inexpensive bite. Dinner draws a loyal after-work crowd looking for good food in a quiet setting. The menu features all the classic dishes from *sag paneer* to *chicken vindaloo*. | 170 Main St. | 860/346–2050 | $6–$15 | AE, MC, V.

Tuscany Grille. Italian. This restaurant in the lobby of the former Middlesex Opera House, now a landmark building, has become a popular place for young professionals to meet for drinks and unwind after the workday. The menu is filled with classic northern Italian dishes and there is outside dining on the patio. Take-out and delivery is also available. | 120 College St. | 860/346–7096 | $10–$17 | AE, MC, V.

Lodging

Comfort Inn. A comfortable, central inn that is near I-84, I-91, and Routes 2, 3, and 9. It is also close to West Farm Malls, Wesleyan, Trinity, Goodspeed Opera House, and steamboat rides. It is 10 minutes' drive north of Middletown. Complimentary Continental breakfast. Cable TV. Pets allowed. | 111 Berlin Rd., Cromwell | 860/635–4100 | fax 860/632–9546 | 77 rooms | $79–$94 | AE, MC, V.

Holiday Inn. This three-story chain option has traditional furnishings. The rooms are done in navy and neutral colors and have corporate art and bright lighting. Restaurant, bar, room service. In-room data ports, refrigerators, in-room hot tubs, cable TV. Indoor pool. Sauna. Gym. Laundry service. Business services. Pets allowed. | 4 Sebethe Dr., Cromwell | 860/635–1001 | fax 860/635–0684 | 143 rooms, 2 suites | $139; $179 suites | AE, D, DC, MC, V.

Middletown Motor Inn. This is your basic no-frills motel that is comfortable and convenient. Service is friendly and the price makes its a good place to hang your hat for the night. Cable TV. Some pets allowed (fee). | 988 Washington St. | 860/346–9251 | 41 rooms | $50–$65 | AE, MC, V.

Radisson Hotel & Conference Center. This hotel between Hartford and New Haven caters to both business travelers and families. It is near Dinosaur State Park and 20 minutes from Lake Compounce Amusement Park. Restaurant, bar, room service. Cable TV. Indoor pool. Health club, hot tub, sauna. Laundry facilities, laundry service. | 100 Berlin Rd., Cromwell | 860/635–2000 | fax 860/635–6970 | $120–$350 | 211 rooms, 4 suites | AE, D, DC, MC, V.

Riverdale Motel. A white, two-story motel on a hill above the Connecticut River that was built in 1988 and is 3½ mi north of downtown Middletown. Golf (Portland has three courses) and boating are five minutes' drive away. Complimentary breakfast. Laundry facilities. | 1503 Portland Cobalt Rd., Portland | 860/342–3498 | 39 rooms | $54–$69 | AE, D, DC, MC, V.

MILFORD

MAP 3, D6

(Nearby towns also listed: Bridgeport, New Haven, Stratford)

Milford, established in 1639, is Connecticut's sixth-oldest municipality, and, despite the fact that it has more than 48,000 residents and has one of the most commercial stretches of the Boston Post Road running through its center, it retains the feel of a small-town coastal community. The town green, the second largest in the state, is at the heart of this community, and sparkles in winter with thousands upon thousands of tiny white lights strung in its many trees. The duck pond and waterfall behind city hall is a pleasant place to while away a spring afternoon and has served as a background for generations of wedding pictures, while the town's many beaches, open to the public for the price of parking, are inviting come summer.

Information: **Chamber of Commerce** | 5 N. Broad St., Box 389, Milford, 06460 | 203/878–0681 | fax 203/876–8517 | chamber@milfordct.com | www.milfordct.com. **Greater New Haven Convention and Visitors Bureau** | 59 Elm St., New Haven, 06510 | 203/777–8550 or 800/332–STAY | fax 203/782–7755 | mail@newhavencvb.org | www.newhavencvb.org.

Attractions

Connecticut Audubon Coastal Center at Milford Point. An 840-acre coastal reserve is where the Housatonic River meets the Long Island Sound. An observation tower provides a bird's-eye view of all the center has to offer: a pathway to a sandy beach for strolling (swimming is not allowed), observation platforms at the water's edge, an environmental education center, and the fabulous array of birds that inhabit the adjacent wildlife management area. Guided canoe trips through the salt marsh are especially popular from May through September. | 1 Milford Point Rd. | 203/878–7440 | fax 203/876–2813 | www.ctaudubon.org | Center $2, grounds free | Center Tues.–Sat. 10–4, Sun. noon–4; grounds dawn–dusk.

Milford Historical Society Wharf Lane Complex. This historical society oversees the preservation of three 18th-century homes close to Milford Harbor. The 1700 Eells-Stow House is said to be the oldest-surviving home in Milford. The Bryan-Downs House (circa 1785) has an excellent collection of Native American artifacts as well as a general store/gift shop. Finally, there's the 1780 Clark Stockade House, which served as the city's first hospital, in one of its various incarnations. Every even year there are candlelight tours with a Christmas theme on the first weekend of December. | 34 High St. | 203/874–2664 | Free | Memorial Day–Columbus Day weekends 2–4.

Milford Jai-Alai. One of the few remaining forums on the East Coast for the sport known as the world's fastest ball game. | 311 Old Gate La. | 203/877–4242 | fax 203/877–5192 | www.jaialai.com | $2, reserve seating Fri.–Sat. nights, $4–$5 | Mon. and Wed.–Sun., call for game times.

Milford Landing. If you're planning to travel to Connecticut over water, one of the nicest places in the state to tie up is this new complex for temporary docking at the head of Milford Harbor. The 40 slips available for vessels of up to 50 ft are city-owned and serviced by a top-notch staff. Overnight slips are available; there are also rest rooms, shower facilities, and a laundromat. Not to mention a stunning rose garden, ice cream parlor, adjacent picnic pavilion, tennis, and basketball courts. Several restaurants are within walking distance. | 37 Helwig St. | 203/874–1610 | fax 203/874–1619 | Apr.–Nov.

Silver Sands State Park. The state has recently completed the first phase of a multiyear renovation of this park with its signature beach and old-fashioned wooden boardwalk. At low tide, walk out to Charles Island—reputed to be one place that Captain Kidd buried his treasure. | 600 E. Broadway, off Meadowside Rd. | 860/424–3200 | Free | Daily.

ON THE CALENDAR

MAY: *Meet the Artists & Artisans.* An annual show of more than 200 top artists and crafters on the Milford Green. Only original work is on display and for sale. Prizes are awarded by juries. There is also live music, refreshments. | 203/874–5672.

AUG.: *Great American Sand Sculpture Competition.* Your imagination is the only limit at this annual sand-drenched competition on Walnut Beach. The categories for competition are: 10 and under, 11–16, 17 and over, families, friends, and clubs. Prizes include cash, trophies, and ribbons. | 203/878–6647.

AUG.: *Oyster Festival.* More than 200 arts and crafts dealers, entertainment, games, waterfront activities, and oysters galore are available at this annual event. | 203/878–5363.

Dining

Jeffrey's. Contemporary. New American cuisine is served in a casual and elegant spot. Try the hazelnut and coriander-crusted halibut served over saffron capellini with seasonal vegetables and pink grapefruit verjus vinagrette or the rock shrimp and crab cake with chili and horseradish aïoli. | 501 New Haven Ave. | 203/878–1910 | Closed Sun. No lunch Sat. | $17–$26 | AE, D, DC, MC, V.

Paul's Famous Hamburgers. American. A drive-in established in 1946. Try the fresh and juicy burgers, hot dogs on toasted buns, clam rolls, fries, Reubens, and milk shakes. | 829 Boston Post Rd. | 203/874–7586 | Closed Sun. | $5–$9.

Rainbow Gardens Inn. Continental. This country inn on the Milford Green is overflowing with flowered prints, family photos, antiques, and collectibles. Try the raspberry chicken explosion (salad with grilled chicken, fruits, and raspberry vinagrette), and heaven and earth (angel hair pasta with grilled chicken, mushrooms, and celestial sherry stroganoff sauce). There's open-air dining on the front porch. Beer and wine only. No smoking. | 117 N. Broad St. | 203/878–2500 | No lunch Sun. No dinner Mon. | $14–$25 | AE, MC, V.

Scribner's. Contemporary. The dining room has a post-and-beam construction with red oak and mahogany, which makes it resemble the interior of an old sailing ship. Try the red snapper with tangy rum sauce, the swordfish gorgonzola, or the Angus beef. Kid's menu. No smoking in the dining room. | 31 Village Rd. | 203/878–7019 | No lunch weekends | $15.95–$26 | AE, MC, V.

Lodging

Comfort Inn. This five-story hotel is right off I-95, 3 mi from downtown Milford, 2 mi from the ocean and 10 mi from New Haven and the Bridgeport Ferry. Bar, complimentary breakfast. In-room data ports. Hot tub. Laundry facilities. Laundry service. No pets. | 278 Old Gate La. | 203/877–9411 | fax 203/877–9411, ext. 101 | www.comfortinn.com | 119 rooms | $69–$175 | AE, D, DC, MC, V.

Hampton Inn. A chain hotel close to I-95 and area businesses, and just 1 mi from the beach. Complimentary Continental breakfast. Cable TV. Business services. | 129 Plains Rd. | 203/874–4400 | fax 203/874–5348 | $79–$95 | 148 rooms | AE, D, MC, V.

Rainbow Gardens. This historic Victorian country inn was built in 1855 and has original hardwood floors, carved wooden staircase, and stained-glass windows. It is overflowing with antiques and collectibles. The property overlooking Milford Green has a full perennial garden and a picket fence with rose gardens. It is a three-block walk to the beach. Restaurant, complimentary breakfast. No room phones, no TV in rooms. No smoking. | 117 N. Broad St. | 203/878–2500 | www.bbonline.com/ct/rainbow | 3 rooms (with shared bath) | $100–$125 | AE, MC, V.

MYSTIC

MAP 3, I5

(Nearby towns also listed: Groton, Ledyard, New London, Stonington)

The village of Mystic has tried with dedication to recapture the seafaring spirit of the 18th and 19th centuries—and succeeded. Some of the nation's fastest clipper ships were built here in the mid-19th century and today the town is home to Mystic Seaport, the country's largest maritime history museum, and Mystic Aquarium and Institute for Exploration. Downtown Mystic has a varied collection of boutiques, galleries, restaurants, and ice-cream shops within a few-block span of the Mystic River.

Information: Chamber of Commerce | 28 Cottrell St., Box 143, Mystic, 06355 | 860/572–9578 | fax 860/572–9273 | info@mysticchamber.org | www.mysticchamber.com. **South-**

eastern Connecticut Tourism District | 470 Bank St., Box 89, New London, 06320 | 860/
444–2206 or 800/TO–ENJOY | fax 860/442–4257 | more2see@aol.com | www.mystic-
more.com.

Attractions

Argia. A replica of a 19th-century Chesapeake Packet schooner, the *Argia* offers cruises of
Fishers Island Sound, two or three hour sails, and is available for large group charters. | 73
Steamboat Wharf | 860/536–0416 | $34–$36 | May–Oct.

Denison Pequotsepos Nature Center. More than 150 species of birds have been spotted
at this 125-acre nature preserve. There are also 7 mi of trails through woodlands and
meadows (including some ideal for cross-country skiing) and a natural history museum
with native wildlife exhibits and a gift shop. | 109 Pequotsepos Rd. | 860/536–1216 | fax 860/
536–2983 | $6 | Mon.–Sat. 9–5, Sun. 10–4; trails daily dawn–dusk.

★ **Mystic Aquarium/Institute for Exploration.** This aquarium has more than 4,500 speci-
mens and 50 exhibits of sea life, including a 2½-acre outdoor exhibit that shows off seals
and sea lions from around the world; the Marine Theater, where you'll find marine mam-
mal demonstrations; and the beloved Penguin Pavilion. The aquarium completed a massive expansion in the spring of 1999, adding new exhibits such as a re-creation of the
Alaskan coastline with the world's largest (750,000-gallon) outdoor beluga whale habitat. World-renowned ocean explorer Dr. Robert Ballard, the man who discovered the
Titanic, has moved his research headquarters here. His institute features, among many
other things, Ballard's discoveries from the ocean floor and uses high-tech exhibits to take
visitors on a simulated dive 3,000 ft below the ocean surface. | 55 Coogan Blvd. | 860/572–

© Corbis

MYSTIC AND MORE

It used to be mostly "Mystic" that drew visitors to southeastern Connecticut. It is,
indeed, now much more.

Mystic Seaport, the country's largest and most impressive maritime history
museum, and Mystic Aquarium, home to everyone's favorite dolphins, whales, and
penguins for decades, remain top draws in this part of the state. In fact, the aquarium recently completed a multimillion-dollar renovation and the addition of the
Institute for Exploration headed by renowned ocean explorer Dr. Robert Ballard (the
man who discovered the Titanic). The area's other recent additions include Foxwoods, the already legendary casino in Ledyard that draws more than 55,000 visitors a day; the Mashantucket Pequot Museum and Research Center in Ledyard,
which offers a comprehensive look Native American heritage; and the Mohegan
Sun Casino in Uncasville, which itself draws thousands per day to its slot machines.
Beyond these additions, the area has the art museums of Old Lyme (once home of
an Impressionist art colony), sleepy fishing villages like Noank—where you can eat
lobster-in-the-rough at a picnic table by the water, winding bike trails, a vineyard,
sandy beaches (though you'll have plenty of company in season), snuggly inns, and
schooners that can take you for a ride into the sunset.

And, of course, there's more, but you'll have to see for yourself.

Related towns: Groton, Ledyard, Mystic, Niantic, New London, Norwich, Old Lyme,
Stonington.

For more information contact Connecticut's Mystic and More/Southeastern
Connecticut Tourism Bureau at 860/444–2206, 800/TO-ENJOY, or www.mystic-
more.com.

5955 | fax 860/572–5969 | www.mysticaquarium.org | $16 | July–Aug., daily 9–6; Sept.–June, daily 9–5.

★ **Mystic Seaport.** The largest marine museum in the world, the Seaport encompasses 17 acres of indoor and outdoor exhibits that provide a fascinating look at the area's rich maritime heritage. In the narrow streets and historic buildings, craftspeople give demonstrations of open-hearth cooking, weaving, and other skills of yesteryear. With more than 480 vessels, Mystic Seaport has the largest collection of ships and boats in the world, including the *Charles W. Morgan,* the last wooden whaling ship afloat. You can climb aboard for a look or for sail-setting demonstrations and reenactments of whale hunts. There are also dozens of ship's figureheads, a tremendous collection of maritime art, cruises on 19th-century vessels, thousands of manuscripts and maps, and a tavern. | 75 Greenmanville Ave. | 860/572–0711 | www.mysticseaport.org | $16 | May–Oct., daily 9–5; Nov.–Apr., daily 9–4.

Mystic Whaler. This schooner offers overnight sailing trips and day as well as dinner cruises. The overnight trips run anywhere from 2 to 5 days. | 7 Holmes St. | 860/536–4218 | $250–$360 two–day trip, $375–$485 three–day trip, $625–$735 five–day trip | May–Oct.

Olde Mistick Village. This shopping village is styled in a re-creation of what an American village might have looked like in the 1700s. Stores here sell crafts, clothing, souvenirs, and food. | Coogan Blvd. and Rte. 27 | 860/536–1641 | Mon.–Sat. 10–6, Sun. noon–5, extended hrs. in the summer.

Williams Beach Park. The public beach here is just 100 yards long but is sheltered and inviting for families. There is also an indoor pool at the center, baseball fields, volleyball, tennis courts, picnic facilities, and a playground. | Mystic Community Center, off of Harry Austin Dr. | 860/536–3575 | Beach free; other activities $12 | Mid-June–Labor Day, daily 10–dusk.

ON THE CALENDAR

MAY: *Lobsterfest.* A good old-fashioned lobster bake at Mystic Seaport. | 860/572–5315.
JUNE: *Sea Music Festival.* A celebration of the music of the sea with live performances. | 860/572–5315.
JULY: *Antique & Classic Boat Rendezvous.* Pre-1950s wooden sail and motorboats gather at Mystic Seaport and for a parade on the Mystic River. | The Boat Shed at Mystic Seaport | 860/572–5315.
JULY–AUG.: *Melville Marathon.* You can't say they don't know how to throw a party at Mystic Seaport. Melville and Moby enthusiasts gather at the seaport for this 24-hour reading of *Moby Dick* in celebration of the author's birthday. | 888/9SEAPORT(973–7678).
AUG.: *Mystic Outdoor Art Festival.* About 300 juried artists, entertainment, and food in historic downtown Mystic. | 860/572–9578.
OCT.: *Chowderfest.* Whether you like your chowder clear or creamy, with clams or with corn, you'll find it at this annual Mystic Seaport festival. | 860/572–5315.

Dining

★ **Abbott's Lobster in the Rough.** Seafood. An unassuming seafood shack alongside the Mystic River, 3½ mi south of Mystic. Try the lobster, mussels, clams, and crab legs. There's open-air dining at picnic tables. | 117 Pearl St., Noank | 860/536–7719 | Closed Mon.–Thurs. Labor Day–Columbus Day | $3.95–$18 | AE, MC, V.

Flood Tide. Continental. The Inn at Mystic's restaurant was modeled after an old sea captain's home and has a view of the sea. Try the pan-seared halibut or the broiled salmon. There is open-air dining on a terrace. Sun. brunch. | U.S. 1 and Rte. 27 | 860/536–8140 | $22–$30 | AE, D, DC, MC, V.

★ **Go Fish.** Seafood. A sleek, bright, bustling eatery with sophisticated New American cuisine and traditionally prepared seafood. It also has a sushi bar. Kid's menu. | Olde Mistick Village | 860/536–2662 | $16–$24 | AE, D, DC, MC, V.

Mystic Pizza. Pizza. This popular pizza parlor was immortalized in the Julia Roberts film named for it. Besides pizza, it's known for pasta and grinders. Kid's menu. | 56 W. Main St. | 860/536–3737 | $3–$18 | D, MC, V.

Restaurant Bravo Bravo. Italian. This bistro in the Whaler's Inn in the heart of downtown Mystic overlooks the main street. Try the fettuccine with grilled scallops, roasted apples, sundried tomatoes, and gorgonzola cream sauce. | 20 E. Main St. | 860/536–1506 | $14.95–$25 | AE, MC, V.

Seamen's Inne. American. A restaurant in a Colonial-style building with wood furniture, a fireplace, and views of Mystic Seaport. You'll find traditional New England fare, including steak and seafood. Try the clambake dinners, lobster, Portuguese fisherman's stew, or the prime rib. Entertainment on weekends. Kid's menu. Sun. brunch. | 75 Greenmanville Ave. | 860/572–5303 | $14.25–$23.95 | AE, D, MC, V.

Lodging

Comfort Inn. This chain hotel is less than 1 mi from Mystic Aquarium and Seaport and offers shuttle service to Foxwoods. Complimentary Continental breakfast. Cable TV. Gym. Laundry service. Business services. | 48 Whitehall Ave. | 860/572–8531 | fax 860/572–9358 | 120 rooms | $59–$149 | AE, D, DC, MC, V.

Days Inn. The Mystic trolley stops in front of this chain hotel that is less than 1 mi from Mystic Aquarium and Seaport. There is also a shuttle to Foxwoods. Restaurant, room service. Some in–room hot tubs, cable TV. Pool. Playground. Laundry facilities, laundry service. Business services. | 55 Whitehall Ave. | 860/572–0574 | fax 860/572–1164 | www.whghotels.com/dimystic/ | 121 rooms, 2 suites | $149–$179 | AE, D, DC, MC, V.

House of 1833. This white clapboard Greek Revival house was built in 1833 (of course) and is on 3 acres. The large common rooms include a formal parlor with a Belgian marble fireplace, and a music room with a baby grand piano and 19th-century crystal chandelier. Guest rooms have both antiques and reproductions. Each is filled with floral patterns and romantic touches such as canopied beds with sheer curtains and fireplaces. At breakfast, guest are treated to live piano music. Complimentary breakfast. Outdoor pool. Tennis court. Bicycles. | 72 N. Stonington Rd. | 860/536–6325 or 800/367–1833 | www.visitmystic.com/1833 | 5 rooms | $99–$249 | MC, V.

★ **Inn at Mystic.** The three buildings here include a turn-of-the-century inn, a gatehouse, and a motor lodge spread over 15 hilltop acres that overlook the harbor, which include gardens and 1¼ mi of walking trails. All the rooms have antiques and period reproductions. Half of them also have fireplaces, canopy beds, private balconies or patios. Restaurant, bar, room service. In-room hot tubs, cable TV. Pool. Putting green, tennis court. Boating. Business services. Pets allowed. No smoking. | U.S. 1 and Rte. 27 | 860/536–9604 or 800/237–2415 | fax 860/572–1635 | www.innatmystic.com | 67 rooms | $125–$275 | AE, D, DC, MC, V.

Mystic Hilton. This chain option is across from Mystic Aquarium and close to the seaport, as well as to Mystic's shops and restaurants. Restaurant, bar, complimentary Continental breakfast, room service. In-room data ports, cable TV. Indoor pool. Gym. Playground. Laundry service. Business services. | 20 Coogan Blvd. | 860/572–0731 | fax 860/572–0328 | www.hiltons.com | 183 rooms | $189–$375 | AE, D, MC, V.

Mystic Howard Johnson Inn. This two-story, inn-style motel was built in 1965. The spacious, comfortably furnished rooms have been updated to look as contemporary as those of residential-hotel counterparts. It is an easy walk to the both the Mystic Aquarium and Mystic Seaport, and there is a Bickford's restaurant on the property and a Friendly's next door. Restaurant, bar. In-room data ports. Indoor pool. | 179 Greenmanville Ave. | 860/536–2654 or 800/406–1411 | fax 860/536–1950 | www.hojo.com | 77 rooms | $40–$190 | AE, D, DC, MC, V.

Old Mystic Inn. All the rooms in this former book shop, which was built in 1784, are named after New England authors. The house is furnished with antiques and reproductions, and the modern Victorian-style carriage house has four rooms with canopied beds. The grounds include perennial gardens, and a gazebo, and you can enjoy complimentary wine and cheese on Saturday evenings. Complimentary breakfast. Some in-room hot tubs, no room phones, no TV. No smoking. | 52 Main St. | 860/572–9422 | www.visitmystic.com/oldmysticinn | 8 rooms | $135–$165 | AE, MC, V.

Residence Inn Mystic. This three-story inn-style hotel is just ½ mi from the Mystic Aquarium and Olde Mistick Village and one mi from the Mystic Seaport. Rooms have sleek, contemporary furniture in neutral colors. Complimentary Continental breakfast. In-room data ports. Laundry facilities, laundry service. Business services. Pets allowed (charge may apply). | 40 Whitehall Ave. | 860/536–5150 or 800/331–3131 | fax 860/572–4724 | www.residenceinn.com | 128 suites | $110–$199 | AE, MC, V.

Steamboat Inn. A posh inn that is a foot from the Mystic River in the heart of downtown and its shops, restaurants, and attractions. All the rooms have water views and some have fireplaces. Two-night minimum on weekends. Complimentary Continental breakfast. Some in-room hot tubs, cable TV. No smoking. | 73 Steamboat Wharf | 860/536–8300 | visitmystic.com/steamboat | $120–$275 | 10 rooms | AE, D, MC, V.

The Whaler's Inn and Motor Court. This inn/motel is in the center of Mystic's Historic District and a ten-minute walk from Mystic Seaport. The rooms have four-poster and sleigh beds. Restaurant. Cable TV. | 20 E. Main St. | 860/536–1506 or 800/243–2588 | fax 860/572–1250 | whalersinn@riconnect.com | www.whalersinnmystic.com | 39 rooms, 2 suites | $105–$215 | AE, D, MC, V.

NEW BRITAIN

MAP 3, E4

(Nearby towns also listed: Bristol, Cheshire, Farmington, Hartford, Middletown, Southington, Waterbury, West Hartford, Wethersfield)

New Britain got its start as a manufacturing center producing sleigh bells. From these modest beginnings, it soon became known as "Hardware City," distributing builders' tools, ball bearings, locks, and other such items. No longer just a factory town, New Britain is also home to Central Connecticut State College and a first-rate museum of American art.

Information: **Chamber of Commerce** | 1 Court St., New Britain, 06051 | 860/229–1665 | fax 860/223–8341 | wfmillerik@aol.com | www.newbritainchamber.com. **Central Connecticut Tourism District** | 1 Grove St., Ste. 310, New Britain, 06053 | 860/225–3901 | fax 860/225–0218 | info@centralct.org | www.centralct.org.

Attractions

Connecticut Wolves. This United Soccer League team plays about 15 to 20 home games, ranging from A-league games to invitationals to cup matches, in Veteran's Stadium. The City of New Britain purchased the Connecticut Wolves in July 1999, making the Wolves the first American soccer team and the second American sports franchise to be owned by a municipality. | Veteran's Stadium, Willowbrook Park, 635 S. Main St. | 860/223–5425 | www.ct-wolves.com | Apr.–Sept., call for game times.

Copernican Observatory & Planetarium. This observatory and planetarium on the campus of Central Connecticut State University has one of the largest public telescopes in the nation and offers a variety of programs geared toward both children and adults. | 1615 Stanley St. | 860/832–3399 | $3.50 | Shows Fri.–Sat., call for times.

New Britain Museum of American Art. A museum in a turn-of-the-century house that has 19 galleries and more than 4,000 works of art, surveying the history of American art. Though the collection includes luminaries such as Thomas Cole, Georgia O'Keefe, and Thomas Hart Benton, it is the selection of Impressionist artists that deserves special note—Mary

Cassatt, William Merritt Chase, Childe Hassam, and John Henry Twachtman, among them. | 56 Lexington St. | 860/229–0257 | fax 860/229–3445 | www.nbmaa.org | $3, free Sat. 10–noon | Tues.–Fri. and Sun. noon–5, Sat. 10–5.

New Britain Rock Cats. The Rock Cats, the Double-A affiliate of the Minnesota Twins, play at New Britain Stadium. | Willow Brook Park, S. Main St. | 860/224–8383 | www.rockcats.com | Apr.–Sept., call for game times.

New Britain Youth Museum. This kids-oriented museum displays everything from circus miniatures to artifacts from other cultures. The displays can include dolls and musical instruments from around the world and many hands-on activities. | 30 High St. | 860/225–3020 | www.connecticutnow.com or www.nbyouthmuseum.tripod.com | Free | Sept.–June, Tues.–Fri. 1–5, Sat. 10–4; July–Aug., weekdays 1–5.

ON THE CALENDAR
JULY–AUG.: *Summer Music Festival.* Come and hear a wide range of music—rock, jazz, country, big band, Motown, polka, and more—at these summer concerts at the Darius Miller Bandshell in Walnut Hill Park. The concerts are co-sponsored by the *Hartford Courant.* | 860/826–3360.

Dining
Great Taste. Chinese. This place solves many problems such as: where to go when everything else is closed on Sunday, where to go if you're eating alone and don't want to feel awkward about it, and where to go if you want really good Chinese food at a good price. Some people balk at the fact that it looks a bit like a chain restaurant, but most cease to notice this once they experience the friendly, efficient service and huge plates of food. The menu is extensive and includes all the usual favorites (orange chicken, dragon and phoenix). | 597 W. Main St. | 860/826–8988 | $6–$15 | AE, MC, V.

Lodging
Ramada Inn. This four-story hotel was built in 1973. It is geared toward the business traveler—there are eight meeting rooms and it is near I-84 (15 minutes west of Hartford) and 28 mi from Bradley Airport. Guest rooms are comfortabe and done in neutral and dark colors. Restaurant, bar, room service. Outdoor pool. Laundry facilities, laundry services. Business services. Pets allowed (fee). | 400 New Britain Ave., Plainville | 860/747–6876 or 888/298–2054 | fax 860/747–9747 | www.ramada.com | 106 rooms | $60–$210 | AE, D, DC, MC, V.

NEW CANAAN

MAP 3, B7

(Nearby towns also listed: Greenwich, Norwalk, Stamford, Westport)

So rich and elegant is the landscape in New Canaan that you may want to pick up a local street map and spend the afternoon driving around the estate-studded countryside, which includes everything from a Frank Lloyd Wright house and Philip Johnson's Glass House to imposing Georgians and clapboard farmhouses. Or you might prefer lingering on Main Street, which is loaded with upscale shops.

Information: **Chamber of Commerce** | 111 Elm St., New Canaan, 06840 | 203/966–2004 | fax 203/966–3810 | www.newcanaanchamber.com. **Coastal Fairfield County Convention and Visitor Bureau** | 297 West Ave., Gate Lodge-Mathews Park, Norwalk, 06850 | 203/899–2799 or 800/866–7925 | fax 203/853–7524 | info@visitfairfieldco.org | www.visitfairfieldco.org.

Attractions

New Canaan Historical Society. A variety of buildings are run by this organization. The Town House contains a costume collection, 1845 pharmacy, and library of local history and genealogy. Other buildings on the premises include the 1764 Hanford-Silliman House, 1799 Rock schoolhouse, sculptor John Rogers 1878 studio, a tool museum, and a print shop. | 13 Oenoke Ridge Rd. | 203/966–1776 | www.nchistory.org | Free | Town House, Tues.–Sat. 9:30–12:30 and 2–4:30; other buildings, call for hrs.

New Canaan Nature Center. This nature center has more than 40 acres of woods and habitats. You can take part in the hands-on natural science exhibits at the Discovery Center in the main building or walk along its 4 mi of nature trails. Demonstrations take place at the cider house in fall and the maple sugar shed in spring (reservations required). There is also the Fall Fair in October and a Christmas Market in December. | 144 Oenoke Ridge Rd. | 203/966–9577 | fax 203/966–6536 | www.newcanaannature.com | Free | Mon.–Sat. 9–4; grounds daily dawn–dusk.

Weir Farm National Historic Site. The state's only National Park, 5 mi northeast of New Canaan, is dedicated to the legacy of painter J. Alden Weir (1852–1919), one of the earliest American Impressionists. The property's 60 wooded acres include hiking paths and a restored rose and perennial garden. There are tours of Weir's studio and sculptor Mahonri Young's studio, and you can take a self-guided walk past Weir's painting sites. | 735 Nod Hill Rd., Wilton | 203/834–1896 | www.nps.gov/wefa | Free | Wed.–Sun. 8:30–5; grounds daily dawn–dusk.

ON THE CALENDAR

APR.: *New Canaan Sewing Group Spring Sale.* This group, 170 strong, offers top quality handmade items for sale at St. Marks Episcopal Church. You'll find needle point, embroidery, painted items, and eighteen-inch dolls. The proceeds benefit charity. | 203/966–1171.

MAY–SEPT.: *Silvermine Chamber Music Series.* The Silvermine Guild Arts Center hosts this series of chamber-music concerts. | 203/966–9700.

Dining

Ching's Table. Pan-Asian. An elegant restaurant with a sophisticated menu that includes dishes native to China, Thailand, Malaysia, Vietnam, and Indonesia. You'll find various combinations of chicken, pork, beef, vegetables, tofu, and shellfish. No smoking. | 64 Main St. | 203/972–8550 | $12–$22 | AE, MC, V.

Sole Ristorante. Italian. This dining room has terra-cotta walls, barrel-vaulted ceilings with painted cherubs, and mosaic floors. The menu features sophisticated incarnations of pasta, fish, pizza, shellfish, chicken, and beef. Try the wood roasted chicken or the veal Milanaise. | 105 Elm St. | 203/972–8887 | Reservations essential | No lunch Sun. | $13–$30 | AE, MC, V.

Lodging

The Maples Inn. A 1908 yellow clapboard inn with 13 gables, most of which are veiled by a canopy of venerable maples. You'll find antiques and collectibles and a wraparound porch. Most of the rooms have canopied beds, and there is an inviting reception room with a fireplace. Complimentary Continental breakfast. Some kitchenettes, cable TV. No smoking. | 179 Oenoke Ridge Rd. | 203/966–2927 | fax 203/966–5003 | 10 rooms, 2 suites | $125–$145, $175 suites | AE, MC, V.

Roger Sherman Inn. This white clapboard house dates from 1740 and is in quiet surroundings. It is near a golf course and the nature center. Restaurant, bar, complimentary Continental breakfast. Cable TV. Laundry service. Business services. No smoking. | 195 Oenoke Ridge | 203/966–4541 | fax 203/966–0503 | www.rogershermaninn.com | 16 rooms, 1 suite | $130–$180, $300 suite | AE, DC, MC, V.

Village Inn of New Canaan. This three-story inn is in heart of New Canaan. It's an easy walk to village shops, restaurants and churches as well as the train to Manhattan (one hour). The inn was built in the 18th century and many of its rooms have fireplaces and old-fashioned touches like four-poster beds, yet all are up to speed technologically, with modems and voice mail. It is a popular venue for weddings and can accommodate families and groups by connecting guest rooms. Restaurant, bar, complimentary Continental breakfast. In-room data ports, some kitchens. Baby-sitting. Laundry service. Business services. No pets. | 122 Park St. | 203/966–8413 or 800/370–2224 | fax 203/966–8413 ext.53 | www.villageinnnc.com | 32 rooms | $100–$225 | AE, D, DC, MC, V.

NEW HAVEN

MAP 3, D6

(Nearby towns also listed: Branford, Guilford, Milford)

New Haven is a city of extremes. The historic district surrounding Yale University and the shops, museums, theaters, and restaurants on nearby Chapel Street prosper; away from the campus and the city common lie pockets of poverty. Nonetheless, it is an excellent city to visit: for its theaters, the Shubert, Long Wharf, and Yale Rep among them; its museums, including the Yale University Art Gallery and the Yale Center for British Art; its restaurants; its plethora of good bookstores; the list goes on. A good introduction is a tour of Yale University—stop by the Yale Visitors Center on Elm Street.

© Corbis

TAKE ME OUT TO THE BALL GAME

Connecticut has long been a state divided. Sandwiched between the Boston Red Sox to the north and the New York Yankees and Mets to the south, Nutmeggers had no baseball team to call their very own. That changed when the New Haven Ravens, Norwich Navigators, and New Britain Rock Cats came to town.

All three are Eastern League Double A affiliates of major-league baseball. The New Haven Ravens (Seattle Mariners) play at historic Yale Field, where George Bush, Lou Gehrig, and Ted Williams once stood behind home plate; the Navigators (New York Yankees) at Senator Thomas J. Dodd Memorial Stadium in Norwich; and the Rock Cats (Minnesota Twins) keep things groovin' in their new New Britain stadium. Connecticut fans couldn't be happier.

Part of this euphoria is propagated by the promotional efforts of the teams themselves. First, there are the mascots: Rally, the giant turquoise-and-black Raven; Tater, the bright green Gator; and Rocky, the cool-as-a-cucumber Rock Cat (check out his shades). They are on top of the dugout singing, chasing a fly ball gone astray, stopping in for a birthday party at the stadium. In short, they are every kid's best friend.

And then there are the promotions themselves. What would you like? A free hat? Gym bag? Beach towel? Bean-bag mascot? Just pick your night and get to the gates early. Some nights there are even fireworks. Fan cards earn you points toward free merchandise and tickets. Fans-turned-sumo-wrestlers bop stomachs on the field between innings. T-shirts that are shot into the stands.

All of this seems to make everyone feel right at home and, best of all, gives you an identity—a team to root for—not to mention a season full of peanuts and Crackerjacks.

Information: Greater New Haven Chamber of Commerce | 900 Chapel St., 10th Floor, Box 1445, New Haven, 06510 | 203/787–6735 | fax 203/782–4329 | anyone@gnhcc.com | www.newhavenchamber.com. **Greater New Haven Convention and Visitors Bureau** | 59 Elm St., New Haven, 06510 | 203/777–8550 or 800/332–STAY | fax 203/782–7755 | mail@newhavencvb.org | www.newhavencvb.org.

Attractions

Amistad Memorial. It was a New Haven jailhouse that held captive the Africans who seized control of the merchant ship *Amistad* that was illegally transporting the once-free Mendis to a life of slavery. President John Quincy Adams journeyed to New Haven to fight to restore the freedom of the men. A 14-ft bronze sculpture stands at the site of the original jail and portrays Senghe Pieh (Joseph Cinque, leader of the revolt). | City Hall, 165 Church St. | Free | Daily.

Black Rock Fort and Fort Nathan Hale. This structure was built in 1776 to protect the prosperous port of New Haven from the dastardly British. Fort Nathan Hale was built nearby in the early 1800s in preparation of the War of 1812 and rebuilt in 1863 in preparation for the Civil War (though the action of this war never reached these shores). Remnants of the military fortifications are still evident. | Woodward Ave. | 203/946–8027 | Free | Memorial Day–Labor Day, daily 10–4.

Grove Street Cemetery. This cemetery is a National Historic Landmark. The first burial took place in 1797. Here you will find the final resting place of Connecticut greats like Noah Webster, Eli Whitney, and Charles Goodyear. | 227 Grove St. | 203/787–1443 | Daily 8–3.

Lighthouse Point Park. A public beach, nature trails, concession stands, and stunning antique carousel in a turn-of-the-century beach pavilion are the attractions of this 82-acre park. | 2 Lighthouse Rd. | 203/946–8005 | $6 Memorial Day–Labor Day; free Labor Day–Memorial Day | Daily dawn–dusk.

Long Wharf Theatre. This revered theater presents works by new writers and imaginative revivals of neglected classics. | 222 Sargent Dr. | 203/787–4282 | www.longwharf.org | Call for schedule and ticket prices.

New Haven Colony Historical Society. This Colonial Revival beauty built in 1930 by J. Frederick Kelly has a skylit rotunda, marble staircases, and an elegant ballroom. The exhibits focus on the history of the New Haven Colony and the city as well as inventions by city forefathers. Here you will find Eli Whitney's cotton gin and Charles Goodyear's rubber inkwell. There's also an excellent research library and ongoing exhibit on the *Amistad*. | 114 Whitney Ave. | 203/562–4183 | $2 | Sept.–June, Tues.–Fri. 10–5, weekends 2–5; July–Aug., Tues.–Fri. 10–5, Sat. 2–5.

New Haven Green. This green, bordered on one side by the Yale campus, is a fine example of Colonial urban planning. As early as 1638, village elders set aside a 16-acre plot as a town common. Three early 19th-century churches—the Gothic-style Trinity Episcopal Church, the Georgian-style Center Congregational Church, and the predominantly Federal United Church—contribute to its present appeal. | Church and College Sts. | 203/946–8029 | Free | Daily.

New Haven Ravens. The Double-A affiliate of Major League baseball's Seattle Mariners play home games at historic Yale Field. | 252 Derby Ave. | 800/728–3671 | www.ravens.com | Apr.–Sept.

Peabody Museum of Natural History. This museum dates to 1876 and houses more than 9 million specimens and is the largest natural-history museum in Connecticut. In addition to exhibits on Andean, Mesoamerican, and Pacific cultures, the venerable museum has an excellent collection of birds, including a stuffed dodo and passenger pigeon. The main attractions for children and amateur paleontologists alike are some of the world's earliest reconstructions of dinosaur skeletons. | 170 Whitney Ave. | 203/432–5050 | www.peabody.yale.edu | $5 | Mon.–Sat. 10–5, Sun. noon–5.

Schooner Inc. Sea Adventure and sunset cruises are offered aboard the 91-ft gaff-rigged wooden schooner *Quinnipiack*. | 60 S. Water St. | 203/865–1737 | May–Oct.

Shore Line Trolley Museum. The oldest rapid-transit car and the world's first electric freight locomotive are among the classic trolleys on display at this family museum. Admission includes a 3-mi round-trip ride aboard a vintage trolley. | 17 River St., East Haven | 203/467–6927 | $5 | Memorial Day–Labor Day, daily 10:30–4; May, Sept.–Oct., and Dec., weekends 10:30–4; Apr. and Nov., Sun. 10:30–4.

Shubert Performing Arts Center. The grande dame of Connecticut theaters opened in 1914. Its stage has hosted the premieres of such legendary musicals as *My Fair Lady, Damn Yankees,* and, in 1999, *The Civil War.* And then there are the ballets and the operas, the comedies and the dramas that the recently refurbished theater stages from September through May. | 247 College St. | 203/562–5666 or 800/228–6622 | www.shubert.com | Call for schedule and ticket prices.

West Haven Board Walk. For the first half of the 20th century Savin Rock Amusement Center was *the* place to have a good time in Greater New Haven. Sad to say, the roller coaster, the Ferris wheel, the carousel, and the cotton candy are long gone. What remains, however, is a lovely boardwalk along the West Haven shore that is the perfect place for a stroll. Or a bike ride. Or a bit of rollerblading. You can bring Fido along (most people do), fly a kite, or a simply spend your time here watching a game of boccie—the competition gets pretty fierce. | Captain Thomas Blvd. | 203/937–3651 | Parking: $10 for non-residents | Daily dawn–dusk.

★ **Yale University.** New Haven may be a manufacturing center dating from the 19th century, but the city owes its fame to Elihu Yale. In 1718 Yale's contributions enabled the Collegiate School, founded in 1701, to settle in New Haven, where it changed its name to Yale University. This is one of the nation's great universities and its fourth oldest. The campus has some handsome neo-Gothic buildings and a number of noteworthy museums. The university's knowledgeable guides conduct one-hour walking tours that include Connecticut Hall in the Old Campus, which counts Nathan Hale, William Howard Taft, and Noah Webster among its past residents. | 149 Elm St. | 203/432–2300 | www.yale.edu | Tours weekdays at 10:30 and 2, weekends at 1:30.

Beinecke Rare Book and Manuscript Library. Included in this collection are a Gutenberg Bible, illuminated manuscripts, and original Audubon bird prints. However, the building itself is almost as much an attraction—the walls are made of marble cut so thin that the light shines through, making the interior a breathtaking sight on sunny days. | 121 Wall St. | 203/432–2977 | www.library.yale.edu/beinecke | Free | Weekdays 8:30–5; Exhibits: also Sat. 10–5 Sept.–July.

Harkness Tower. The most notable example of the Yale campus's neo-Gothic architecture is this tower, built between 1917 and 1921, which was modeled on St. Botolph's Tower in Boston, England. The university's famous motto, inscribed on Memorial Gate near the tower, is sometimes described as the world's greatest anticlimax, "For God, for country, and for Yale." A good time to visit is on a Friday evening in summer when the Yale Guild of Carilloneurs perform free concerts at 7 PM. Bring your own blanket or lawn chair and be prepared for a glorious chorus from the tower's 54 carillon bells. | High St. | 203/432–2309 | Free | Daily.

★ **Yale Center for British Art.** This collection of British art is the most comprehensive outside Britain itself. The center's skylit galleries, designed by Louis I. Kahn, contain works by Constable, Hogarth, Gainsborough, Reynolds, and Turner, to name but a few. Extensive renovations in 1998 spruced up its overall look considerably. | 1080 Chapel St. | 203/432–2800 | fax 203/432–9628 | www.yale.edu/ycba | Free | Tues.–Sat. 10–5, Sun. noon–5.

Yale Repertory Theatre. This theater, home stage for the Yale School of Drama, mounts world premieres as well as fresh interpretations of the classics. | 222 York St. | 203/432–1234 | www.yale.edu/yalerep | Call for schedule and ticket prices.

Yale University Art Gallery. Since its founding in 1832, this gallery has amassed more than 85,000 objects from around the world, dating from ancient Egypt to the present day.

Highlights include works by van Gogh, Manet, Monet, Picasso, Winslow Homer, and Thomas Eakins, as well as Etruscan and Greek vases, Chinese ceramics and bronzes, and early Italian paintings. The gallery's collection of American decorative arts is considered one of the finest in the world. Be certain not to miss the re-creation of a Mithraic shrine downstairs. | 1111 Chapel St. | 203/432–0600 | fax 203/432–7159 | www.yale.edu/artgallery | Free | Tues.–Sat. 10–5, Sun. 1–6.

ON THE CALENDAR

MAY: *Harbor Heritage Weekend.* This commemoration of the British invasion of New Haven opens the forts for the season and features a Revolutionary War encampment, period cooking, a parade, and military drill and skirmish. It takes place at Black Rock Fort and Fort Nathan Hale. | Woodward Ave. | 203/865–2000, ext. 183.

JUNE–JULY: *International Festival of Arts and Ideas.* Performing and visual artists from around the globe gather on the New Haven Green and surroundings for theatrical performances, classical, jazz, and pop music, a street festival, children's activities, and more. | 888/ARTIDEA (888/278–4332) | www.artidea.org.

AUG.: *Pilot Pen Tennis Women's Championships.* The Connecticut Tennis Center at Yale University hosts this Tier II women's tennis tournament. | 203/776–7331.

NOV.–DEC.: *Celebration of American Crafts.* The Creative Arts Workshop in New Haven's Audubon Arts District hosts this national juried and invitational exhibit and sale of more than 10,000 pieces from more than 400 artisans from around the country. | 203/562–4927.

NOV.–JAN.: *Fantasy of Lights.* A narrated drive-through tour of Lighthouse Point Park, which is lit up with more than 45 spectacular lighting displays. | 203/777–2000, ext. 603, ext. 262 for weather notification.

Dining

★ **Café Pika Tapas.** Spanish. This chic, colorful, and cosmopolitan café serves tapas from every region of Spain as well as a few salads and entrées. The paella is a standout. | 39 High St. | 203/865–1933 | Closed Mon. No lunch Sun. | $13.75–$17.75 | AE, DC, MC, V.

Caffé Adulis. Ethiopian. This restaurant has high ceilings and exposed brick. On the menu are vegetarian dishes, stews, and shellfish. Try the shrimp in tomato-basil sauce with unsweetened coconut, dates, Parmesan cheese, and cream and the seared tuna | 228 College St. | 203/777–5081 | No lunch | $8.95–$19.95 | AE, MC, V.

★ **Frank Pepe's Pizzeria.** Pizza. Pepe's has an international reputation for pizza–especially its white clam pie—so expect to wait awhile for a table. It's worth it. It first opened in 1925 and has retained the original green metal ceiling. The restaurant has hardwood floors and you can eat in one of the booths. On weekends it is populated by families while at lunch during the week, expect to run into local businesspeople. | 157 Wooster St. | 203/865–5762 | Closed Tues. No lunch Mon. and Wed.–Thurs. | $5–$20.

Louis' Lunch. American. An all-American luncheonette that is on the National Register of Historic Places. Legend has it that it is the birthplace of the hamburger in America. The first-rate burgers are cooked in an old-fashioned upright broiler. | 261–263 Crown St. | 203/562–5507 | Closed Sun.–Mon. No dinner Sun.–Wed. | $5.

Union League Café. French. This elegant restaurant has high ceilings, wood floors and tinted windows. The constantly changing menu of French country cuisine has in the past featured dishes such as walnut-crusted sea bass with saffron, leeks, and potatoes and roast duck breast with celeriac mousse and sauteed apples. Menu is prix fixe on Sunday. | 1032 Chapel St. | 203/562–4299 | No lunch weekends | $14–$20 | AE, DC, MC, V.

Lodging

The Colony. This hotel combines an old-fashioned look with modern amenities. It is downtown, adjacent to Yale's Old Campus, and within walking distance of Yale's theaters. Restaurant, bar, complimentary breakfast, room service. Cable TV. Laundry service. Business services. | 1157 Chapel St. | 203/776–1234 or 800/458–8810 | fax 203/772–3929 | 80 rooms, 6 suites | $83–$109 | AE, DC, MC, V.

The Historic Mansion Inn. An 1844 Greek Revivial mansion that was restored in 1998 and is five blocks from Yale University. It has a Library with 11-foot high arching doorways. Rooms are furnished with Queen Anne replicas, four-poster beds, and fireplaces. Complimentary breakfast. Cable TV. Library. | 600 Chapel St. | 203/865–8324 | www.thehistoricmansioninn.com | $129–$149 | 7 rooms | AE, D, DC, MC, V.

Holiday Inn. This chain option is in the heart of the Yale community. Restaurant, bar, room service. Cable TV. Pool. Gym. Laundry service. Business services. | 30 Whalley Ave. | 203/777–6221 | fax 203/772–1089 | www.holiday-inn.com | 160 rooms | $95–$119 | AE, D, DC, MC, V.

New Haven Grande Chalet. This eight-story chain hotel was renovated in 1998 and is just off I–95 at Exit 46. Many of the rooms have views of the New Haven Harbor. Complimentary Continental breakfast. In-room data ports, cable TV. Pool. Gym. Laundry service. Business services. Pets allowed. | 400 Sargent Dr. | 203/562–1111 | 153 rooms | $70–$90 | AE, D, DC, MC, V.

New Haven Hotel. Two blocks from Yale and close to the New Haven Coliseum and the Shubert and Palace Theaters. It has a spacious, elegant lobby. Most of the floors have common areas and all of the suites have balconies. Restaurant, bar, room service. Cable TV. 2 indoor pools. Laundry service. Business services. | 229 George St. | 203/498–3100 | fax 203/498–3190 | www.nhhotel.com | 88 rooms, 4 suites | $125, $185 suites | AE, D, DC, MC, V.

Omni New Haven Hotel. Downtown New Haven's newest hotel has an elegantly appointed interior with warm lighting, textured walls and hardwood furnishing fitted with plush velvet pillows. Rooftop restaurant, bar. In-room data ports, cable TV. Gym. Laundry service. Business services. | 155 Temple St. | 203/772–6664 | fax 203/974–6777 | 306 rooms | $119–$149 | AE, D, MC, V.

Residence Inn by Marriott. The only all-suite hotel in New Haven is off I–95 at Exit 46. It's close to the downtown area, and the water, and the summer port of the *Amistad* is just across the highway. Restaurant. Kitchenettes, cable TV. Pool. Hot tub. Laundry service. Business services. Pets allowed (fee). | 3 Long Wharf Dr. | 203/777–5337 | www.residence.com | 112 suites | $145–$180 | AE, D, MC, V.

Swan Cove Bed and Breakfast. This shingled inn in Oyster Point, a historic seaside section of New Haven on Long Island Sound, has water views from its guest rooms. Rooms have wrought-iron and whitewashed furniture, queen beds, feather pillows and down comforters. Complimentary breakfast. Cable TV. Business services. | 115 Sea St. | 203/776–3240 | $159–$199 | 5 suites | AE, D, DC, MC, V.

★ **Three Chimneys Inn.** A lovely 1870 Victorian mansion with Georgian furnishings and four-poster and canopy beds. Some rooms have ornamental fireplaces. Complimentary breakfast. Cable TV. Business services. | 1201 Chapel St. | 203/789–1201 | fax 203/776–7363 | www.threechimneysinn.com | 11 rooms | $180 | AE, D, MC, V.

NEW LONDON

MAP 3, H5

(Nearby towns also listed: Groton, Ledyard, Mystic, Niantic, Norwich, Stonington, Waterford; Block Island, RI)

New London, on the banks of the Thames River, has long had ties to the sea. In the mid-1800s, in fact, it was the second largest whaling port in the world. Appropriately, it is home to the United States Coast Guard Academy, which uses a 100-acre campus on the Thames to educate and train its cadets. Ocean Beach Park, an old-fashioned beach resort with a wooden boardwalk, is owned by the city and allows residents and visitors alike an up-close-and-personal view of New London's connection to the sea.

Information: Chamber of Commerce of Southeastern Connecticut | 105 Huntington St., New London, 06320 | 860/443–8332 | fax 860/444–1529 | chambersect@snet.net | www.chambersect.org. **Southeastern Connecticut Tourism District** | 470 Bank St., Box 89, New London, 06320 | 860/444–2206 or 800/TO–ENJOY | fax 860/442–4257 | more2see@aol.com | www.mysticmore.com.

Attractions

Connecticut College. Founded in 1911, Connecticut College is one of the Seven Sisters and was formerly a women's college. Today is a private, co-ed, liberal arts university with 1,600 students. | 270 Mohegan Ave. | 860/447–1911 | www.camel.conncoll.edu | Daily.

Connecticut College Arboretum. This expansive arboretum has 750 acres of natural ecosystems, native trees and shrubs, ponds, walkways, and hiking trails. | 270 Mohegan Ave. | 860/439–5020 | fax 860/439–5482 | www.conncoll.edu/ccrec/greennet/arbo/welcome.html | Free | Daily dawn–dusk; tours May–Oct., weekends at 2.

Lyman Allyn Art Museum. This museum at the southern end of the Connecticut College campus was named by its founder Harriet U. Allyn after her father, a whaling merchant. In a neoclassical building designed by Charles Platt are collections of American fine arts from the country's earliest years through present day. The galleries of Connecticut's decorative arts and American Impressionist paintings are also noteworthy. | 625 Williams St. | 860/443–2545 | $4, includes admission to Lyman Allyn Dolls and Toys | Tues.–Sat. 10–5, Sun. 1–5.

Ferry from New London to Block Island, Rhode Island This ferry operates from mid-June through mid-September. | 14 Eugene O'Neill Dr. | 860/442–7891 | Mid-June–mid-Sept.

Ferry from New London to Fishers Island, New York. Year-round ferry service across Fishers Island Sound. | State St. | 860/443–6851 (recorded information) or 860/442–0165 | Daily.

Ferry from New London to Orient Point, New York. You can take both traditional and high-speed ferry service to the tip of Long Island's North Fork. | 2 Ferry St. | 860/443–5281 | Daily.

Garde Arts Center. This 1926 theater is in the midst of a five-year, $19 million renovation and expansion that will restore it to its former gilded-age glory. The 1,500-seat theater presents live arts performances throughout the year, including Broadway, family, and comedy series. It is also the home base of the Eastern Connecticut Symphony Orchestra. | 325 State St. | 860/444–7373 | www.gardearts.org.

Hempsted Houses. These two houses in New London's historic district are among the few to survive the 1781 fires set by British troops under the command of Benedict Arnold. The 1678 Joshua Hempsted House is one of the earliest documented frame houses in New England, while the Nathaniel Hempsted House, built in the mid-1700s, is one of the most unusual, because it was built out of stone. | 11 Hempstead St. | 860/443–7949 or 860/247–8996 | www.hartnet.org/als | $4 | Mid-May–mid-Oct., Thurs.–Sun. noon–4.

Lyman Allyn Dolls and Toys. It's a toss-up as to who will enjoy this museum more, children or their parents, who can find toys of their youth here. A lovingly refurbished Victorian dollhouse, a hall of dolls, a construction site with classic toys, and a Lego playstation are just a few of the attractions here. Many galleries include interactive "playzones," where children young and old can play. | Harris Pl., 165 State St. | 860/437–1947 | $4, includes admission to the Lyman Allyn Art Museum | Tues.–Sat. 1–5.

Monte Cristo Cottage. This Registered National Landmark was the childhood home of Pulitzer and Nobel Prize-winning playwright Eugene O'Neill. Fans of *Long Day's Journey into Night* will appreciate the re-creation of the room that O'Neill describes in the play. His only comedy, *Ah, Wilderness* was also set in this cottage. | 325 Pequot Ave. | 860/443–0051 or 860/443–5378 | fax 860/443–9653 | $5 | Memorial Day–Labor Day, Tues.–Sat. 10–5, Sun. 1–5.

Ocean Beach Park. This popular beach is ½-mi long. There's also an Olympic-size outdoor pool, a miniature golf course, a video arcade, and a picnic area. | 1225 Ocean Ave. | 860/447–3031 | Free; parking $5–$8 | Memorial Day–Labor Day, daily 9 AM–10 PM.

Science Center of Eastern Connecticut. This science center devoted to children has more than 60 exhibits relating to the discovery of electricity, animals, light, sound, and more. You can explore the marine touch tank. There is also a theater, darkroom, and greenhouse. | 33 Gallows La. | 860/442–0391 | fax 860/442–5008 | $6 | Tues.–Sat. 10–6, Sun. 1–5.

U.S. Coast Guard Academy. This 100-acre cluster of redbrick buildings includes a museum and visitors' pavilion with a gift shop. You can board the three-masted training barque, the USCGC *Eagle,* when it's in port. Free concerts are staged periodically throughout the year. | 15 Mohegan Ave. | 860/444–8270 | www.uscg.mil | Free | Academy daily 9–5; museum weekdays 9–4:30, Sat. 10–4:30, Sun. noon–5.

ON THE CALENDAR

APR.–MAY: *Connecticut Storytelling Festival.* The Connecticut College campus is the setting for this weekend of storytelling workshops and presentations. | 860/439–2764. **JULY: *Sail Fest.*** This outdoor waterfront festival includes a street fair, live entertainment, a craft show, tall ships, and fireworks. | 860/444–1879.

Dining

Recovery Room. Italian. This white Colonial storefront restaurant across from the hospital specializes in pizza. | 445 Ocean Ave. | 860/443–2619 | No lunch weekends | $6–$14 | MC, V.

Modesto's. Eclectic. A unique blend of fine Italian and Mexican specialties from a menu of more than 40 entrées. Try the camarones Cancun, chile rellenos, fettuccine, or veal saltimbocca. Live guitar Sun. | 10 Rte. 32, Franklin | 860/887–7755 | $10.95–$25.95 | AE, D, MC, V.

Timothy's. Contemporary. This 1750s building houses one of the best restaurants in the region. The dining room has rich maroon with dark green tones and original terrazzo floor and window seating. There are also showcases of wine bottles. Try duck with raspberry framboise or wild mushroom pasta with lingonberry demi-glace. No smoking. | 181 Bank St. | 860/437–0526 | Closed Sun.–Mon. No lunch Sat. | $12.95–$24.95 | AE, D, DC, MC, V.

Lodging

Queen Anne Inn. This 1903 Queen Anne–style Victorian was fully remodeled in 1985 and rooms with period antiques, brass or canopy beds. Breakfast is served in a parlor. The reception area has a hand-carved mantle. Complimentary breakfast. Cable TV in some rooms. Hot tub. | 265 Williams St. | 860/447–2600 or 800/347–8818 | fax 860/443–0857 | www.queen-anne.com | 10 rooms | $95–$185 | AE, MC, V.

Radisson Hotel. This chain hotel right off I–95 (at Exit 83) is 15 minutes away from Foxwoods, Mohegan Sun, and Mystic. Restaurant, bar, complimentary breakfast, room service. In-room data ports, refrigerators, cable TV. Indoor pool. Laundry service. Business services. | 35 Governor Winthrop Blvd. | 860/443–7000 or 800/333–3333 | fax 860/443–1239 | $79–$129, $129–$159 suites | 116 rooms, 4 suites | AE, D, DC, MC, V.

Red Roof Inn. A good budget alternative, this hotel is 20 minutes from Foxwoods, 10 minutes from Mystic Seaport, and just eight minutes from Ocean Beach. It has grounds filled with flowers and trees. Picnic area. Some in-room data ports, cable TV. Pets allowed. | 707 Colman St. | 860/444–0001 | fax 860/443–7154 | www.redroof.com | 108 rooms in 2 buildings | $69–$99 | AE, D, DC, MC, V.

NEW MILFORD

MAP 3, B4

(Nearby towns also listed: Danbury, Kent, New Preston, Washington)

If you're approaching the Litchfield Hills from the south, New Milford is a practical starting point to begin your visit. It was also a starting point for a young cobbler named

Roger Sherman, who, in 1743, opened his shop where Main and Church streets meet. A Declaration of Independence signatory, Sherman also helped draft the Constitution and the Articles of Confederation. You'll find old shops, galleries, and eateries all within a short stroll of New Milford green—one of the longest in New England.

Information: Greater New Milford Chamber of Commerce | 11 Railroad St., New Milford, 06776 | 860/354–6080 | fax 860/354–8526 | nmchamb@mail2.nai.net | www.newmilford.com. **Litchfield Hills Visitors Council** | Box 968, Litchfield, 06759 | 860/567–4506 | fax 860/567–5214 | www.litchfieldhills.com.

Attractions

The Silo. This silo and barn is packed with objets de cookery, crafts, and an array of goodies and sauces. The founder and director of the New York Pops, Skitch Henderson and his wife, Ruth, own and operate this bazaar, where culinary superstars give a variety of cooking classes between March and December. | 44 Upland Rd. | 860/355–0300 | Apr.–Dec., daily 10–5; Jan.–Mar., Tues.–Sun. 10–5.

ON THE CALENDAR

MAR.–DEC.: *Elephant's Trunk Flea Market.* You can spend your Sunday treasure hunting at this local flea market. | 860/355–1448 | Sun.

JULY: *Village Fair Days.* The New Milford Village Green is dotted with more than 200 arts and crafts dealers, antiques, food, and live entertainment at this annual event. | 860/354–6080.

Dining

Adrienne. American. With the original hardwood floors and four working fireplaces, this 18th century house along the Housatonic River is a warm and cozy place to have a romantic dinner. The dining room has just 14 tables, antique mirrors and reproduction paintings on the walls. Try the venison and save room for the crème Brûlée. For outdoor dining, try the flagstone terrace with white wrought iron tables and chairs, overlooking the garden and the Housatonic River. | 218 Kent Rd. | 860/354–6001 | Closed Mon. No lunch | $15.25–$25.50 | AE, D, DC, MC, V.

The Bistro Café. Contemporary. Copper pots and vintage photos decorate this café in a redbrick building. Try the grilled New York strip steak with gorgonzola cheese crust or the sesame seared salmon with Japanese mustard miso sauce. | 31 Bank St. | 860/355–3266 | $15–$22 | AE, MC, V.

Clamps. American/Casual. This roadside stand has been a summertime ritual in Connecticut since 1939. Grilled burgers, clams, chicken strips, fries, onion rings. | U.S. 202 | No phone | Closed Nov.–Apr. | $5–$8.

Lodging

Barton House. This inn, one block from the Village Green, has fieldstone terraces and a front porch, as well as a piano in the living room. Rooms are decorated with ceiling fans, antique furniture—like brass beds and New Milford memorabilia—and are filled with fresh-cut flowers daily. Complimentary candle-lit breakfast. | 34 East St. | 860/354–3535 | 2 rooms | $85–$95 | AE, MC, V.

The Homestead Inn. This 1853 Victorian inn is furnished with country antiques, while the additional motel-style rooms next door are a bit simpler and have reproduction furniture. The landscaped grounds with perennial gardens are in the historic part of town, and within walking distance of restaurants, shops, a move theater, and the green. Complimentary Continental breakfast. Cable TV. No smoking. | 5 Elm St. | 860/354–4080 | fax 860/354–7046 | www.homesteadct.com | 14 rooms in 2 buildings | $85–$110 | AE, D, DC, MC, V.

NEW PRESTON

MAP 3, B3

(Nearby towns also listed: Kent, Litchfield, New Milford, Washington, Woodbury)

The crossroads village of New Preston, perched above a 40-ft waterfall on the Aspetuck River, has a little town center that's packed with antiques shops specializing in everything from 18th-century furnishings to out-of-print books. Lake Waramaug, north of New Preston on Route 45, is an area that reminds many of Austria and Switzerland. If you drive the 8-mi perimeter of the lake, named for Chief Waramaug, one of the most revered figures in Connecticut's Native American history, you'll see beautiful inns—many of which serve delicious food—and homes. The state park of the same name, at the northwest tip, is an idyllic 75-acre spread, great for picnicking and lakeside camping.

Information: **Chamber of Commerce of Northwest Connecticut** | 333 Kennedy Dr., Box 59, Torrington, 06790-0059 | 860/482–6586 | fax 860/489–8851 | dave@north-westchamber.org | www. northwestchamber.org. **Litchfield Hills Visitors Council** | Box 968, Litchfield, 06759 | 860/567–4506 | fax 860/567–5214 | www.litchfieldhills.com.

Attractions

Lake Waramaug State Park. This 680-acre lake begs for swimming. There's a nicely shaded picnic area, a sandy beach, and a lakeside campground. Biking around the lake is a favorite activity. | Lake Waramaug Rd. | 860/868–2592 | Memorial Day–Labor Day, weekends $5–$8; free weekdays and the rest of the year | Daily, 8–sunset.

Hopkins Vineyard. This popular winery overlooking Lake Waramaug has been producing more than 13 varieties of wine, from sparkling to dessert, since 1979. A weathered red barn houses a gift shop and tasting room; there's also a picnic area on the property. The wine bar serves a fine cheese and pâté board. | Hopkins Rd. | 860/868–7954 | fax 860/868–1168 | Free | Jan.–Feb., Fri.–Sat. 10–5, Sun. 11–5; Mar.–Apr., Thurs.–Sat. 10–5, Sun. 11–5; May–Dec., Mon.–Sat. 10–5, Sun. 11–5.

ON THE CALENDAR

MAY: *Eastern Women's Intercollegiate Rowing Regatta Championships.* An elite women's competition on scenic Lake Waramaug. | 860/658–7776.

Dining

The Birches Inn. Contemporary. This renovated inn has plants and picture windows overlooking Lake Waramaug and serves stylish New American cuisine with innovative French and Asian touches. Try the roasted red-beet tartar, Atlantic salmon, or grilled pork loin. No smoking. Open-air dining on porch. | 233 W. Shore Rd. | 860/868–1735 | Closed Jan.–Feb. and Tues.–Wed. No lunch | $17–$24 | AE, MC, V.

Boulders Inn. Contemporary. A grand turn-of-the-century inn that was once a summer home. The octagonal shaped dining room is all windows and overlooks Lake Waramaug. Try the steam savoy cabbage-wrapped halibut fillet with shiitake mushrooms and arugala kuinoa pilaf, dill, and infused broth. There's open-air dining on terraces overlooking the lake. No lunch. | E. Shore Rd. | 860/868–0541 | Reservations essential on Fri.–Sat. | Closed Tues.; closed Mon.–Wed. Jan.–Apr.; closed Mon. Nov.–Dec. No lunch Nov.–Apr., no lunch weekdays May–Oct. | $19–$28 | AE, MC, V.

Hopkins Inn. Continental. This 1847 Victorian inn is high on a hill overlooking Lake Waramaug. The restaurant emphasizes Swiss and Austrian specialties. Try roast duck à l'orange, sweetbreads, or Wiener schnitzel. Open-air dining on terrace. Kid's menu. | 22 Hopkins Rd. | 860/868–7295 | Closed Jan.–Mar. Closed Mon. | $28–$41 | AE, MC, V.

ONE LAST TRAVEL TIP:

Pack an easy way to reach the world.

Wherever you travel, the MCI WorldCom Card℠ is the easiest way to stay in touch. You can use it to call to and from more than 125 countries worldwide. And you can earn bonus miles every time you use your card. So go ahead, travel the world. MCI WorldCom℠ makes it even more rewarding. For additional access codes, visit **www.wcom.com/worldphone**.

EASY TO CALL WORLDWIDE

1. Just dial the WorldPhone® access number of the country you're calling from.
2. Dial or give the operator your MCI WorldCom Card number.
3. Dial or give the number you're calling.

Canada	1-800-888-8000
Mexico	01-800-021-8000
United States	1-800-888-8000

EARN FREQUENT FLIER MILES

Limit of one bonus program per customer. All airline program rules and conditions apply. © 2000 WorldCom, Inc. All Rights Reserved. The names, logos, and taglines identifying WorldCom's products and services are proprietary marks of WorldCom, Inc. or its subsidiaries. All third party marks are the proprietary marks of their respective owners.

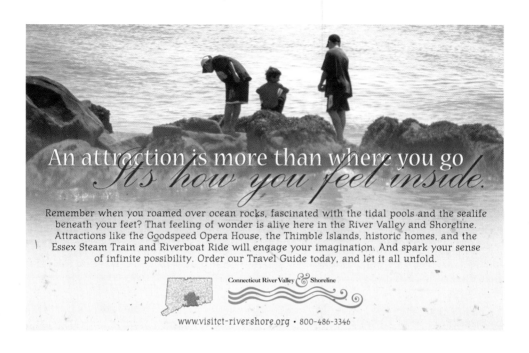

An attraction is more than where you go
It's how you feel inside.

Remember when you roamed over ocean rocks, fascinated with the tidal pools and the sealife beneath your feet? That feeling of wonder is alive here in the River Valley and Shoreline. Attractions like the Goodspeed Opera House, the Thimble Islands, historic homes, and the Essex Steam Train and Riverboat Ride will engage your imagination. And spark your sense of infinite possibility. Order our Travel Guide today, and let it all unfold.

Connecticut River Valley & Shoreline

www.visitct-rivershore.org • 800-486-3346

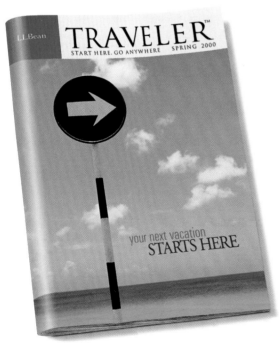

Free Catalog!

- Wrinkle-free clothes
- Great luggage
- Must-have accessories

Simply call L.L.Bean to order your free catalog today

800.552.9974

Shop on-line at llbean.com/traveler

Le Bon Coin. French. A charming restaurant in a little house on the side of a country road. Try the crêpes Suzette, lobster bisque, lamb shank, and frogs' legs. | 223 Litchfield Tpke | 860/868–7763 | Closed Tues.–Wed. No lunch Sun. | $16.95–$22.95 | MC, V.

Lodging

Apple Blossom Country Inn. This 1842 New England Colonial is surrounded by trees and well-manicured lawns. Rooms evoke the Colonial era with their wide plank floors, quilts, and numerous antiques. One room has a fireplace. Complimentary Continental breakfast. No room phones, TV in common area. No pets. No smoking. | 137 Litchfield Tpke | 860/868–9954 | nkopp@rcn.com | www.appleblossominn.com | 3 rooms | $70–$135 | AE, DC, D, MC, V.

Atha House. One mile south of New Preston, this Cape Cod cottage stands among many trees and landscaped lawns on three acres. You can lounge in the living room with the fireplace and grand piano, or relax on the patio watching horses graze in a pasture. Complimentary breakfast. No air-conditioning, TV in common area. Pets allowed. No smoking. | Wheaton Rd. | 860/355–7387 or 860/355–7307 | 2 rooms | $90–$110 | AE, DC, D, MC, V.

★ **The Birches Inn.** A turn-of-the-century, Adirondack-style inn with antiques and country furnishings that overlooks Lake Waramaug. Some of the rooms have lake views and some have private decks. Two-night minimum stay on weekends. Restaurant, complimentary Continental breakfast. Cable TV. Lake. Beach, water sports. Bicycles. No smoking. | 233 W. Shore Rd. | 860/868–1735 or 888/590–7945 | fax 860/868–1815 | www.thebirchesinn.com | 12 rooms | $95–$300 | AE, MC, V.

★ **Boulders Inn.** This posh country inn was built in 1895 and overlooks Lake Waramaug. There are fine antiques and country furnishings throughout and some rooms have fireplaces. Restaurant, complimentary breakfast. Some in-room hot tubs, no TVs in some room. Lake. Hiking, beach, boating, bicycles. Business services. | 387 E. Shore Rd. | 860/868–0541 or 800/552–6853 | fax 860/868–1925 | www.bouldersinn.com | 6 rooms in inn, 8 rooms in cottages, 3 rooms in carriage house | $260–$320 | AE, MC, V.

★ **Hopkins Inn.** A grand 1847 Victorian inn high on a hill overlooking Lake Waramaug that is one of the best bargains in the area. The inn's light and airy rooms are decorated with floral wallpapers and country antiques, and many overlook the lake. Restaurant, bar. No air-conditioning, no room phones, no TV in rooms. Lake. Beach. No smoking. | 22 Hopkins Rd. | 860/868–7295 | fax 860/868–7464 | www.thehopkinsinn.com | 11 rooms | $67–$84 | AE, D, MC, V.

7C Herb Garden Bed and Breakfast. This 1730s Colonial house on 4 acres sits beneath numerous maple trees and beside a large organic garden. The sandbox, swings, and many toys of this B&B make it a good for families, or anyone traveling with a child. A gift shop on site sells handmade crafts, organic herbs, jams, and other souvenirs. Complimentary breakfast. No air-conditioning, TV in common area. Shops. Playground. No pets. No smoking. | 210 Baldwin Hill Rd. | 860/868–7760 | 2 rooms | $75–$105 | No credit cards.

NIANTIC

MAP 3, H6

(Nearby towns also listed: Groton, New London, Old Lyme, Waterford)

Niantic, which is actually part of East Lyme—along the Connecticut coastline, really comes to life in the summer. Rocky Neck State Park is the center of much of this activity and offers saltwater fishing, a picnic area, campground, and crescent-shaped beach that seems the perfect spot to feel the salt air on your face.

Information: Chamber of Commerce of Southeastern Connecticut | 105 Huntington St., New London, 06320 | 860/443–8332 | fax 860/444–1529 | chambersect@snet.com

| www.chambersect.org. **Southeastern Connecticut Tourism District** | 470 Bank St., Box 89, New London, 06320 | 860/444–2206 or 800/TO–ENJOY | fax 860/442–4257 | more2see@aol.com | www.mysticmore.com.

Attractions

Children's Museum of Southeastern Connecticut. This excellent facility uses a hands-on approach to engage kids in the fields of science, math, and current events. | 409 Main St. | 860/691–1255 | fax 860/691–1194 | www.childmuseumsect.conncoll.edu | $4 | Labor Day–Memorial Day, Tues.–Thurs. and Sat. 9:30–4:30, Fri. 9:30–8, Sun. noon–4; Memorial Day–Labor Day Mon.–Thurs. and Sat. 9:30–4:30, Fri. 9:30–8, Sun. noon–4.

Rocky Neck State Park. Among the attributes of this state park are its picnic facilities, saltwater fishing, and historic stone and wood pavilion. The park's mile-long crescent-shape strand is one of the finest beaches on Long Island Sound. There is also a salt marsh observation deck and a fishing and crabbing area accessible to those with disabilities. | Rte. 156 | 860/739–5471 | Apr.–Sept. $5–12; free otherwise | Daily 8–sunset.

ON THE CALENDAR

AUG.: *Seaweed Festival.* You can taste a variety of local seaweeds while learning about the nutritional and environmental properties of indigenous marine plantlife at the Children's Museum's annual event. | 860/691–1111.

Dining

Constantine's. American. When you dine at this downtown Niantic eatery, you can watch boats and ships slipping in and out of Niantic Bay. The menu concentrates on steak and seafood dishes. Try the steamed lobster and grilled fish specials, which are particular favorites. | 252 Main St. | 860/739–2848 | $6–$20 | Closed Mon. | AE, D, MC, V.

Family Pizza. Italian. This famliy-owned restaurant was built in 1995. Over the years, it has established an excellent rapport with the families of the Niantic area. Windows overlooking Niantic Bay surround the dining room, which has a fireplace, warm oak wood panneling and delicate wallpaper. | 233 Main St. | 860/739–0466 | $5.95–$10.95 | No credit cards.

Lyme Tavern. American. This eatery at the northeastern tip of the Rocky Neck State Park is the place to go to watch the game–any game. With 17 TVs, it is a sports bar of the first order. Food is standard pub fare: sandwiches, burgers, wings and lots of beer. Complimentary appetizers at half time of football games. | 279 W. Main St. | 860/739–5631 | $6–$17 | AE, DC, D, MC, V.

Lodging

Days Inn Niantic. This chain hotel is 15 mi from Mohegan Sun and 30 mi from Foxwoods casinos. It is also 15 minutes from Mystic Seaport and Aquarium Restaurant. Cable TV. Business services. | 265 Flanders Rd. | 860/739–6921 | 93 rooms | $69–$149 | AE, D, DC, MC, V.

The Inn at Harbor Hill Marina. A three-story, 1870s residence on a hill with views of the marina, Niantic River, and Long Island Sound. All of the rooms have contemporary furnishings and views of the water. Picnic area, complimentary Continental breakfast. Some microwaves, some refrigerators, cable TV. Dock. No pets. No smoking. | 60 Grand St. | 860/739–0331 | fax 860/691–3078 | www.innharborhill.com | 9 rooms | $130–$195 | AE, D, MC, V.

Niantic Inn. This inn is across from the beach and within walking distance of shops, movies, restaurants, and the children's museum. Microwaves, refrigerators, cable TV. Beach. | 345 Main St. | 860/739–5451 | fax 860/739–2997 | 24 rooms | $60–$170 | AE, D, MC, V.

Ramada Inn and Suites. A chain option with a restaurant next door that is near the beach, to which the hotel provides passes. It is also 15–20 minutes from both Foxwoods and Mohegan Sun. Complimentary Continental breakfast. In-room data ports, some microwaves, some refrigerators, cable TV. Pool. Business services. | 248 Flanders Rd. | 860/

739–5485 or 800/942–8466 | fax 860/739–4877 | 38 rooms, 12 suites | $79–$139 | AE, D, DC, MC, V.

Starlight Motor Inn. This motel is 3 mi from the beach and close to shops, restaurants, movies, and the children's museum. Mohegan Sun is 12-15 mi away and Foxwoods is 25-30 mi away. Mystic is just a 20-minute drive. Restaurant. Cable TV. Pool. | 256 Flanders Rd. | 860/739–5462 | fax 860/739–0567 | 48 rooms | $46–$120 | AE, D, DC, MC, V.

NORFOLK

(Nearby towns also listed: Lakeville, Riverton, Salisbury)

Norfolk, thanks to its severe climate and terrain, is one of the best-preserved villages in the Northeast. Notable industrialists have been summering here for two centuries, and many enormous homesteads still exist. At the junction of Route 272 and U.S. 44 is the striking town green. At its southern corner is a fountain, designed by Augustus Saint-Gaudens and executed by Stanford White, which stands as a memorial to Joseph Battell, who turned Norfork into a major trading center.

Information: Chamber of Commerce of Northwest Connecticut | 333 Kennedy Dr., Box 59, Torrington, 06790-0059 | 860/482–6586 | fax 860/489–8851 | dave@northwestchamber.org | www.northwestchamber.org. **Litchfield Hills Visitors Council** | Box 968, Litchfield, 06759 | 860/567–4506 | fax 860/567–5214 | www.litchfieldhills.com.

Attractions

Campbell Falls. Fishing, hiking, and picnicking are popular activities at this state park, though the cascading falls are the prime attraction. | Rte. 272 | 860/482–1817 | Free | Daily 8–sunset.

Dennis Hill. Dr. Frederick Shepard Dennis lavishly entertained guests, among them President William Howard Taft and several Connecticut governors, in the stone pavilion of what is now this state park. From its 1,627-ft height you can see Haystack Mountain, Massachusetts, Vermont, and, it is said, on a clear day, New Haven Harbor, all the way across the state. You can hike or picnic on the park's 240-acre grounds. | Rte. 272 | 860/482–1817 | Free | Daily 8–sunset.

Haystack Mountain State Park. There is a spectacular vantage point atop this state park, with a challenging trail to the top for the brave, and a road halfway up for the rest of us. | Rte. 272 | 860/482–1817 | Free | Daily 8–sunset.

Loon Meadow Farm. A hayride followed by a bonfire and mulled cider? A horse-drawn carriage ride? A sleigh ride? Here, the choice is yours. | 41 Loon Meadow Dr. | 860/542–6085 | Year-round by appointment.

Norfolk Artisans Guild. This guild carries works by more than 60 local artisans—from hand-painted pillows to handcrafted baskets and weather vanes. | 24 Greenwoods Rd. E | 860/542–5487 | Wed.–Sun. 10–5.

ON THE CALENDAR

JULY–AUG.: *Norfolk Chamber Music Festival.* This festival is Connecticut's version of Tanglewood. There are performances by world-class talents in this historic concert hall on the grounds of the Ellen Battell Stoeckel Estate. | 860/542–3000.

Dining

Mizza's Pizza. Pizza. Though grinders, pastas, and salads are all menu options, New York–style pizza is the specialty at this local favorite with casual wood tables and chairs. | 20 John J. Curtis Rd. | 860/542–6848 | $2–$15 | AE, MC, V.

★ **The Pub.** American. This casual spot in a redbrick Victorian by the Norfolk green is where locals gather, whether for burgers or lamb curry. | Station Place, U.S. 44 | 860/542–5716 | Closed Mon. | $8.95–$18.95 | AE, MC, V.

Lodging

Angel Hill Bed & Breakfast. An 1880 Victorian inn on 8 acres. In summer, relax on the welcoming porches, in the Victorian gazebo, or the living room with fireplace. The rooms are individually appointed and have antiques. Many also have canopy beds and some have fireplaces. There is also a carriage house which is set up as an apartment. Complimentary breakfast. No cable TV in some rooms, no room phones, cable TV in common area. Library. Laundry services. No kids under 12. No pets. No smoking. | 54 Greenwoods Rd. E | 860/542–5920 | www.angel-hill.com | 4 rooms, 1 carriage house | $150–$160 rooms, $185 carriage house | No credit cards.

Blackberry River Inn. This 1763 inn—with carriage house and cottage—is on 27 acres and is listed on the National Register of Historic Places. Rooms have Colonial furnishings and four-poster beds. Some also have fireplaces. Complimentary breakfast. Cable TV in rooms, in-room VCRs, TV in common area. Pool. Tennis. Swimming, hiking, fishing. Library. No pets. No kids under 12. No smoking. | 538 Greenwood Rd. W | 860/542–5100 or 800/414–3636 | fax 860/542–1763 | www.blackberryriverinn.com | $115–$135 rooms, $165–$215 suites | 15 rooms, 4 suites | AE, D, MC, V.

★ **Greenwoods Gate Bed & Breakfast Inn.** This bed and breakfast has romantic turn-of-the-century suites, with rich native cherry and soft pastels and antique furnishings, canopied and brass iron beds, and fine linen appointments. Some rooms have thick oriental rugs, plush feather sofas and magnificant bay windows. Guests can partake of afternoon tea and refreshments in the beautifully decorated center hall library, spacious grounds or grand parlor by fireside. Two-night minimum stay on weekends. Complimentary breakfast. No room phones, no TV. Business center. No smoking. | 105 Greenwoods Rd. E | 860/542–5439 | fax 860/542–5897 | www.greenwoodsgate.com | 4 suites | $175–$250 | No credit cards.

★ **Manor House.** An 1898 Bavarian Tudor with period furniture, imported antique French beds and 20 stained-glass windows designed by Tiffany. Some rooms have fireplaces and all have ceiling fans. The house has plenty of common space—a living room, library, and sunporch. The grounds are landscaped and have perennial gardens. Two-night minimum stay on weekends. Complimentary breakfast. No air-conditioning, some in-room hot tubs, no room phones, no TV. No smoking. | 69 Maple Ave. | 860/542–5690 | www.manorhouse-norfolk.com | 8 rooms, 1 suite | $125–$225 | AE, MC, V.

Mountain View. An 1875 Victorian country inn on 3 acres near the Norfolk Green. It has period furnishings, brass and four-poster beds, a wraparound front porch, and fireplace. It is close to the Norfolk Chamber Music Festival, and Greenwoods Theater. | 7 rooms. Bar, complimentary breakfast. No room phones, no TV. | 67 Litchfield Rd. | 860/542–6991 | fax 860/542–5689 | www.mvinn.com | $75–$125 | D, MC, V.

NORWALK

MAP 3, B7

(Nearby towns also listed: Fairfield, Greenwich, New Canaan, Stamford, Westport)

In the 19th century, Norwalk became a major New England port and manufactured pottery, clocks, watches, shingle nails, and paper. It later fell into a state of neglect, in which it remained for much of the 20th century. During the past decade, however, Norwalk's coastal business district has been the focus of a major redevelopment project. Art galleries, restaurants, and trendy boutiques have blossomed on and around Washington Street; the stretch is now known as the SoNo (short for South Norwalk) commercial district. Norwalk is the home of Yankee Doodle Dandies: In 1756, Colonel

VACATION COUNTDOWN Your checklist for a perfect journey

Way Ahead

- ❑ Devise a trip budget.
- ❑ Write down the five things you want most from this trip. Keep this list handy before and during your trip.
- ❑ Book lodging and transportation.
- ❑ Arrange for pet care.
- ❑ Photocopy any important documentation (passport, driver's license, vehicle registration, and so on) you'll carry with you on your trip. Store the copies in a safe place at home.
- ❑ Review health and home-owners insurance policies to find out what they cover when you're away from home.

A Month Before

- ❑ Make restaurant reservations and buy theater and concert tickets. Visit fodors.com for links to local events and news.
- ❑ Familiarize yourself with the local language or lingo.
- ❑ Schedule a tune-up for your car.

Two Weeks Before

- ❑ Create your itinerary.
- ❑ Enjoy a book or movie set in your destination to get you in the mood.
- ❑ Prepare a packing list.
- ❑ Shop for missing essentials.
- ❑ Repair, launder, or dry-clean the clothes you will take with you.
- ❑ Replenish your supply of prescription drugs and contact lenses if necessary.

A Week Before

- ❑ Stop newspaper and mail deliveries.
- ❑ Pay bills.
- ❑ Stock up on film and batteries.
- ❑ Label your luggage.
- ❑ Finalize your packing list—always take less than you think you need.
- ❑ Pack a toiletries kit filled with travel-size essentials.
- ❑ Check tire treads.
- ❑ Write down your insurance agent's number and any other emergency numbers and take them with you.
- ❑ Get lots of sleep. You want to be well-rested and healthy for your impending trip.

A Day Before

- ❑ Collect passport, driver's license, insurance card, vehicle registration, and other documents.
- ❑ Check travel documents.
- ❑ Give a copy of your itinerary to a family member or friend.
- ❑ Check your car's fluids, lights, tire inflation, and wiper blades.
- ❑ Get packing!

During Your Trip

- ❑ Keep a journal/scrapbook as a personal souvenir.
- ❑ Spend time with locals.
- ❑ Take time to explore. Don't plan too much. Let yourself get lost and use your Fodor's guide to get back on track.

Thomas Fitch threw together a motley crew of Norwalk soldiers and led them off to fight at Fort Crailo, near Albany, New York. Supposedly, Norwalk's women gathered feathers for the men to wear as plumes in their caps in an effort to give them some appearance of military decorum. Upon the arrival of these foppish warriors, one of the British officers sarcastically dubbed them "macaronis" slang for dandies. The saying caught on, and so did the song.

Information: **Greater Norwalk Chamber of Commerce** | 101 East Ave., Box 668, Norwalk, 06852 | 203/866–2521 | fax 203/852–0583 | chamber@norwalk.ct.us | www.chamber.norwalk.ct.us. **Coastal Fairfield County Convention and Visitor Bureau** | 297 West Ave., Gate Lodge-Mathews Park, Norwalk, 06850 | 203/899–2799 or 800/866–7925 | fax 203/853–7524 | info@visitfairfieldco.org | www.visitfairfieldco.org.

Attractions

Lockwood-Mathews Mansion Museum. The architecture is the draw here. The house was designed by Detlef Lienau and it is one of the finest Second Empire style houses built in the nation. The museum has an audio tour, antique music box display, and a gift shop. | 295 West Ave. | 203/838–9799 | fax 203/838–1434 | www.lockwoodmathews.org | $5 | Mid-Mar.–Dec., Wed.–Sun. noon–5, Jan.–Mar.

★ **Maritime Aquarium at Norwalk.** The cornerstone of the SoNo historic district is this 5-acre waterfront center that brings to life the ecology and history of the Long Island Sound with exhibits of marine life, river otters, sharks, and seals. In addition to the expansive aquarium, there are marine-mammal cruises aboard the *Oceanic* and an IMAX theater. | 10 N. Water St. | 203/852–0700 | fax 203/838–5416 | www.maritimeaquarium.org | $8.25; IMAX theater $6.75; combined $12.50 | Labor Day–June, daily 10–5; July–Labor Day, daily 10–6.

Stew Leonard's. This self-proclaimed "Disneyland of Supermarkets," has a petting zoo, animated characters lining the aisles, scrumptious chocolate-chip cookies, and great soft ice cream. | 100 Westport Ave. | 203/847–7213 | Daily 7 AM–11 PM.

Sheffield Island Lighthouse. The 3-acre park at the base of this island lighthouse is a prime spot for a picnic. The 1868 lighthouse has four levels and 10 rooms to explore. | Hope Dock, Washington and N. Water Sts. | 203/838–9444 | Round-trip ferry service and lighthouse tour, $15; $4 for tour only if you arrive on your own boat | Call for hrs.

WPA Murals. These 1930s Works Progress Administration (WPA) murals brighten the halls of Norwalk City Hall. There are close to 20 restored paintings here, several of which feature scenes from local history. It is one of the largest collections of such murals in the country. | City Hall, 125 East Ave. | 203/866–0202 | Free | Weekdays 9–5.

ON THE CALENDAR
JULY: *Round Hill Scottish Games.* Bagpipe competitions, caber tossing, and clans clad in tartan descend on Cranbury Park. | 203/324–1094.
AUG.: *SoNo Arts Celebration.* An extravagant celebration of the arts throughout historic South Norwalk. Events include a juried arts and crafts show, a sculpture race, and children's activities. | 203/866–7916 or 203/866–2521.
SEPT.: *Norwalk International In-Water Boat Show.* The largest power and sailboat show in the Northeast. | Norwalk Cove Marina, Exit 16 off I–95 | 212/984–7011.
SEPT.: *Norwalk Oyster Festival.* A waterfront festival celebrating the history of Long Island Sound with more than 200 juried crafters, vintage vessels, fireworks, children's activities, entertainment, skydivers, and waterfront demonstrations. | Veterans Park | 203/838–9444.

Dining
Barcelona Restaurant and Wine Bar. Mediterranean. A contemporary restaurant in a restored mill. Try the ostrich fillet, or the chicken scarpiello. There's also a Tapas bar. | 63 N. Main St. | 203/899–0088 | No lunch | $16–$24 | AE, D, DC, MC, V.

Cote D'Azur. French. A neighborhood bistro with dining by candlelight and rustic furnishings. Try braised rabbit, red snapper, Provençal fish soup. | 86 Washington St. | 203/855–8900 | Closed Sun.–Mon. | $14–$25 | AE, MC, V.

Habana. Latin American. Ceiling fans, banana trees, and a high energy level characterize Habana. The contemporary Cuban cuisine has some Argentinean, Peruvian, Mexican, Puerto Rican, and Brazilian dishes thrown in for spice. Try the plantain coated Chilian sea bass. Live music Sun. | 70 N. Main St. | 203/852–9790 | No lunch weekends | $16–$24 | AE, DC, MC, V.

Meson Galicia. Spanish. This bright, festive restaurant has exposed red brick walls, still life on the walls, and plants in the green curtained windows through which sunlight streams. The windows look out onto the brick patio, which is surrounded by flowers and trees and has tables with umbrellas in the summer. Try the parrillada-grilled seafood—shrimp, clams, mussles, scallops, squid, white fish—with a little garlic broth served with vegetables and rice or anything for the popular Tapas menu. No smoking in dining room. | 10 Wall St. | 203/866–8800 | Reservations essential on Fri. and Sat. | Closed Mon. No lunch weekends | $20–$26 | AE, DC, MC, V.

Silvermine Tavern. American. This colonial dining room with American folk art is overflowing with antiques and has a menu of traditional New England favorites with some contemporary touches. Try the spice-marinated grilled shrimp with shrimp risotto. There is open-air dining on a deck overlooking the mill pond. Kid's menu. Sun. brunch. | 194 Perry Ave. | 203/847–4558 | Closed Tues. | $16–$28 | AE, DC, MC, V.

Lodging

Club Hotel by Doubletree. This 7-floor, cement, high-rise hotel, is 10-15 minutes away from downtown Norwalk and near many of the area's attractions. The rooms and interior are furnished with traditional wood furniture, conservative color schemes and corporate art. Restaurant, bar. Cable TV. Indoor pool. Exercise Room. Laundry service. Business services. | 789 Connecticut Ave. | 203/853–3477 | fax 203/855–9404 | 265 rooms | $89–$164 | AE, D, DC, MC, V.

Courtyard Norwalk. This four-story chain hotel caters to business travelers. It is just east of U.S. 7 and only 3 mi north of Norwalk's historic center. Restaurant (closed weekdays), bar, room service. In-room data ports, cable TV. Pool. Hot tub. Gym. Laundry facilities, laundry services. Business services. No pets. | 474 Main Ave. | 203/849–9111 | fax 203/849–8144 | 145 rooms | $50 | AE, D, DC, MC, V.

Four Points by Sheraton. Near I–95, the Merritt Parkway, and trains, this chain option is also close to the Maritime Center. Restaurant, bar, room service. Cable TV. Gym. Business services. | 426 Main Ave. | 203/849–9828 | fax 203/846–6925 | www.sheraton.com | 125 rooms, 2 suites | $99–$169, $249 suites | AE, D, DC, MC, V.

Norwalk Inn and Conference Center. Catering both to the leisure and business traveler, this two-story inn just a quarter mile north of I–95 (at Exit 16) is in a quiet, residential neighborhood. Rooms are appointed with a tasteful selection of oak cabinets and tables. Restaurant, bar, complimentary breakfast, room service. In-room data ports, refrigerators, cable TV. Pool. Gym. Laundry service. Business services. No pets. | 99 East Ave. | 203/838–5531 | fax 203/855–9722 | www.norwalkinn.com | 71 rooms | $100–$150 | AE, D, DC, MC, V.

Round Tree Inn. In these two, two-story buildings each room has two full-sized beds. Restaurant. Cable TV. | 469 Westport Ave. | 203/847–5827 | 48 rooms | $78–$135 | AE, MC, V.

Silvermine Tavern. An 18th-century country inn with antiques, paintings, and wood floors that overlooks a mill pond. Some rooms have canopy beds. It is close to the Lockwood-Mathews Mansion Museum, and the Maritime Aquarium. Restaurant, complimentary Continental breakfast. No room phones, no TV. Business services. No smoking. | 194 Perry Ave. | 203/847–4558 | fax 203/847–9171 | www.silverminetavern.com | 10 rooms, 1 suite | $100–$145, $185 suite | AE, DC, MC, V.

NORWICH

(Nearby towns also listed: Ledyard, New London)

Three of eastern Connecticut's major rivers—the Quinebaug, the Shetucket, and the Yantic—converge in Norwich; thus it should come as no surprise that this was once a thriving mill town. Outstanding architecture from this period still remains, from Georgians to Italianate Victorians. The Connecticut Trust for Historic Preservation and the city are hard at work restoring the town to its former glory—a distinct possibility given the rise in tourism that has resulted from the town's proximity to the state's two casinos.

Information: **Eastern Connecticut Chamber of Commerce** | 1 Thames Plaza, Suite 211, Norwich, 06360 | 860/887–1647 | fax 860/889–7615 | eccc@99main.com | www.ecc-chamber.org. **Southeastern Connecticut Tourism District** | 470 Bank St., Box 89, New London, 06320 | 860/444–2206 or 800/TO–ENJOY | fax 860/442–4257 | more2see@aol.com | www.mysticmore.com.

Attractions

Christopher Leffingwell House. This 1675 home of early industrialist and deputy commissary to the Continental army, Christopher Leffingwell, was a meeting place for patriots during the Revolutionary War. It has been restored and features period antiques. | 348 Washington St. | 860/889–9440 | $5 | mid-May–mid-Oct., Tues.–Sun. 1–4.

Mohegan Park and Memorial Rose Garden. The formal rose gardens here peak in late June. The park also has swimming and picnicking areas, fishing, and nature trails. | Judd Rd. | 860/823–3759 | Free | Daily 9–dusk.

Mohegan Sun. The Mohegan Indians, known as the Wolf People, operate this casino, 15 minutes west of Ledyard, that has more than 3,000 slot machines, 180 gaming tables, bingo, a theater, "Kids Quest" family entertainment complex, and, among 20 food-and-beverage suppliers, three fine-dining restaurants. For betting on the ponies, you'll find Race Book, a simulcast theater with NYRA (New York Racing Association) broadcasts. Free entertainment, including nationally known acts, is presented nightly in the Wolf Den. | Mohegan Sun Blvd., Uncasville | 888/226–7711 | fax 860/204–8328 | www.mohegansun.com | Daily 24 hrs.

Native American Burial Grounds. These grounds are the final resting place of Uncas, the Mohegan chief who gave the original land for the settlement of Norwich and aided its settlers in their battles against the fierce Pequots. | Sachem St., off Rte. 32 | Free | Daily.

Norwich Golf Course. This 1935 course was built as part of the Norwich Inn but is now nicely maintained by the town. | 685 New London Tpke | 860/889–6973 | Mar.–Nov.

Norwich Navigators. The 'Gators, the Double-A affiliate of baseball's New York Yankees, play at Senator Thomas J. Dodd Stadium. | 14 Stott Ave. | 800/644–2867 | fax 860/886–5996 | www.gators.com | Apr.–Sept.

Slater Memorial Museum & Converse Art Gallery. A museum on the grounds of the Norwich Free Academy that has the largest plaster-cast collection of classical statues in the country, including *Winged Victory, Venus de Milo,* and Michelangelo's *Pietà.* | 305 Broadway | 860/887–2505 | $2 | Sept.–June, Tues.–Fri. 9–4, weekends 1–4; July–Aug., Tues.–Sun. 1–4.

Tantaquidgeon Indian Museum. This small museum highlights Native American life and legend, with an emphasis on eastern Woodlands tribes. | 1819 Norwich–New London Tpke., Uncasville | 860/848–9145 | Donations suggested | May–Sept., Tues.–Sat. 10–3.

ON THE CALENDAR

MAY: *Chelsea Street Festival.* A day of arts and entertainment in the heart of downtown. | 860/887–2789.

AUG.: *Harbor Day.* A tribute to the last days of summer with a float and raft contest, food, and entertainment on the waterfront. | 860/886–4683.

SEPT.: *Historic Norwich Town Days.* Reenactments of Revolutionary War–era life including crafts demonstrations, lectures, and discussions take place on the Norwich Town Green. | 860/886–7845.

NOV.–DEC.: *Winter Festival.* A celebration of the winter season beginning with the illumination of city hall in late November and followed by a monthlong series of events, including a parade, carol sing, and house-decorating contest. | 860/889–0754.

Dining

Kensingtons. Contemporary. A restaurant in the Spa at Norwich Inn that offers regional New England and spa cuisine. The intimate dining room has a handpainted mural and candlelit tables. Try the five onion bisque, seafood scampi (lobster, crab, and gulf shrimp) with linguine, or the grilled breast of chicken with tomato, herbs, and mushrooms. There's open-air dining on the patio deck overlooking the golf course and reflecting pool. Sun. brunch. No smoking. | 607 W. Thames St. | 860/886–2401 | $25–$39 | AE, DC, MC, V.

Lodging

Comfort Suites Norwich. This five-story hotel is appropriate for business travelers as well as tourists. The hotel runs shuttles to nearby Mohegan Sun and Foxwoods casinos. Complimentary breakfast. Cable TV. Hot tub. | 275 Otrobondo Ave. | 860/892–9292 | 119 rooms | $89–$209 | AE, D, DC, MC, V.

Spa at Norwich Inn. A Georgian-style inn and villas on 38 acres along the Thames River that is the state's most luxurious spa. There are spring fed ponds on the tree-filled, landscaped grounds. Rooms have four-poster beds, country print quilts, and wide-wood plank floors. The main building has 45 rooms; the other accommodations are two-story townhouses with kitchens and living rooms. Restaurant, bar, room service. Some kitchenettes, cable TV. 3 pools (1 indoor). Beauty salon, sauna, spa, steam room. 2 tennis courts. Health club, hiking. Laundry service. Business services. | 607 W. Thames St. | 860/886–2401 or 800/ASK–4SPA | fax 860/886–9483 | www.norwichinnandspa.com | 45 rooms, 54 villas, 4 suites | $150–$350 rooms, $450–$900 suites | AE, DC, MC, V.

Ramada Hotel. A six-story hotel right off I–395 in a suburban neighborhood. The rooms are decorated in blue and mauve and are newly renovated. Even numbered rooms have balconies. Restaurant, bar, room service. In-room data ports, refrigerators, microwaves, cable TV. Indoor pool. Laundry services. Business services. | 10 Laura Blvd. | 860/889–5201 | fax 860/889–1767 | 127 rooms | $99–$165 | AE, D, DC, MC, V.

OLD LYME

MAP 3, G6

(Nearby towns also listed: East Haddam, Essex, Ivoryton, Niantic, Old Saybrook)

Old Lyme, on the other side of the Connecticut River from Old Saybrook, is renowned among art lovers for its history as America's foremost Impressionist art colony. Artists then and now have been drawn to the area for its lovely countryside and shoreline. While this small town only has two main streets, it is near four major area beaches.

Information: Chamber of Commerce of Southeastern Connecticut | 105 Huntington St., New London, 06320 | 860/443–8332 | fax 860/444–1529 | chambersect@snet.net | www.chambersect.org. **Southeastern Connecticut Tourism District** | 470 Bank St., Box

89, New London, 06320 | 860/444–2206 or 800/TO–ENJOY | fax 860/442–4257 | more2see@aol.com | www.mysticmore.com.

Attractions

★ **Florence Griswold Museum.** Central to Old Lyme's artistic reputation is this museum, a former boardinghouse that hosted members of the Old Lyme art colony, including Willard Metcalfe, Clark Voorhees, Childe Hassam, and Henry Ward Ranger, in the early 20th century. Griswold, the descendant of a well-known family, offered artists both encouragement and housing. The artists painted for their hostess the double row of panels in the dining room that now serve as the museum's centerpiece. Many of their other works are also on display in revolving exhibits, along with 19th-century furnishings and decorative items. The landscaped 11-acre estate is a perfect setting for the 1817 late-Georgian mansion. The museum is part of the Connecticut Impressionist Art Trail, a self-guided tour of 12 related sites across the state. | 96 Lyme St. | 860/434–5542 | fax 860/434–6259 | www.flogris.org | $4 | Jan.–Mar., Wed.–Sun. 1–5; Apr.–Dec., Tues.–Sat. 10–5, Sun. 1–5.

Lyme Academy of Fine Arts. This academy in an 1817 Federal home has a popular gallery with works by contemporary artists, including the academy's students and faculty. | 84 Lyme St. | 860/434–5232 | Donations suggested | Tues.–Sat. 10–4, Sun. 1–4.

Dining

★ **Bee and Thistle Inn.** American. A 1756 Colonial inn that is considered one of the state's most romantic dining spots: firelight, candlelight, and floral prints. The small dining room is surrounded by bay windows overlooking the property and has wicker baskets hanging from

KODAK'S TIPS FOR PHOTOGRAPHING PEOPLE

Friends' Faces
- Pose subjects informally to keep the mood relaxed
- Try to work in shady areas to avoid squints
- Let kids pick their own poses

Strangers' Faces
- In crowds, work from a distance with a telephoto lens
- Try posing cooperative subjects
- Stick with gentle lighting—it's most flattering to faces

Group Portraits
- Keep the mood informal
- Use soft, diffuse lighting
- Try using a panoramic camera

People at Work
- Capture destination-specific occupations
- Use tools for props
- Avoid flash if possible

Sports
- Fill the frame with action
- Include identifying background
- Use fast shutter speeds to stop action

Silly Pictures
- Look for or create light-hearted situations
- Don't be inhibited
- Try a funny prop

Parades and Ceremonies
- Stake out a shooting spot early
- Show distinctive costumes
- Isolate crowd reactions
- Be flexible: content first, technique second

From Kodak Guide to Shooting Great Travel Pictures © 2000 by Fodor's Travel Publications

the ceiling. Try the breast of duck with duck ravioli, roulade of chicken breast filled with duxelles of mushroom and parmesan, crab ravioli, or Thai green curry shrimp. Sun. brunch. | 100 Lyme St. | 860/434–1667 | www.beeandthistle.com | Breakfast also available. Closed first 3 weeks in Jan. and Tues. | $22–$30 | AE, D, DC, MC, V.

The Hideaway. American. This restaurant in the Old Lyme Shopping Center has bamboo chairs and oil lamps at each table in its two-story dining room overlooking the Lieutenant River. The menu touches all the bases: salads, burgers, sandwiches, seafoods, burritos, and steaks. Try the daily fish specials. | 19 Halls Rd. | 860/434–3335 or 860/434–2003 | fax 860/434–0702 | $5.95–$19.95 | AE, MC, V.

Old Lyme Inn. American. The inn's open and spacious dining room has chandeliers and white linen tablecloths. A handpainted mural of a ship on the sea graces one wall. Try the crab cakes or rack of lamb, which is slow-roasted and has a herb and citrus crust. Sun. brunch. | 85 Lyme St. | 860/434–2600 | $21–$32 | AE, D, DC, MC, V.

Lodging

★ **Bee and Thistle Inn.** A 1756 inn on 5½ acres with landscaped lawns that lead to the Lieutenant River, where you will find lounge chairs in which to relax. The property also has a sunken perennial garden and herb garden. Some of the antique-filled rooms have four-poster beds or canopy beds. All have wingback chairs, hardwood floors, Oriental rugs, Victorian-style wallpaper, and are adorned with plants and flowers from the garden. Restaurant. No TV in some rooms. No smoking. | 100 Lyme St. | 860/434–1667 or 800/622–4946 | fax 860/434–3402 | www.beeandthistleinn.com | 11 rooms; 1 cottage | $79–$159 | Closed 3 weeks in Jan. | AE, MC, V.

Old Lyme. This two-story, white clapboard 1850s inn is on 2 acres in Old Lyme's historic district. It's filled with Empire and Victorian furnishings and a maple spiral staircase leads to the rooms. Restaurant, bar, complimentary Continental breakfast. Cable TV. Business services. Pets allowed (as long as the pet is not in the room when guest is not there). | 85 Lyme St. | 860/434–2600 or 800/434–5352 | fax 860/434–5352 | www.oldlymeinn.com | 13 rooms | $99–$160 | AE, D, DC, MC, V.

OLD SAYBROOK

MAP 3, G6

(Nearby towns also listed: Clinton, Essex, Ivoryton, Old Lyme)

Old Saybrook, where the Connecticut River meets Long Island Sound, has much to offer. In July and August a trolley run by the Chamber of Commerce shows visitors the sights, from its restaurants to its antiques shops to the old-fashioned soda fountain where you can share a sundae with your sweetie. A series of year-round events ranges from arts and crafts festivals to a Christmas Torchlight Parade.

Information: Chamber of Commerce | 146 Main St., Box 625, Old Saybrook, 06475 | 860/388–3266 | fax 860/388–9433 | chamber@oldsaybrookct.com | www.oldsaybrookct.com. **Connecticut River Valley and Shoreline Visitors Council** | 393 Main St., Middletown, 06457 | 860/347–0028 or 800/486–3346 | fax 860/704–2340 | crvsvc@cttourism.org | www.cttourism.org.

Attractions

Essex-Saybrook Antiques Village. More than 120 antiques and collectibles dealers inhabit this three-story post-and-beam barn. | 345 Middlesex Tpke | 860/388–0689 | www.esavantiqs.com | Tues.–Sun. 11–5.

Fort Saybrook Monument Park. The monument in this 18-acre park marks the location of Yale College prior to its migration to New Haven, where it eventually became a full university. There are storyboards that depict the history of the Saybrook Colony, and views of the Connecticut River. | College St. | 860/395–3152 | Free | Daily dawn–dusk.

General Hart House. General William Hart led Patriot troops in the fight against the British in the American Revolution. Today his home, a fully-restored, center-hall Georgian built in 1767, is home to the Old Saybrook Historical Society. | 350 Main St. | 860/388–2622 | Free | May–mid-Sept., Fri.–Sun. 1–4.

James Gallery and Soda Fountain. This white clapboard landmark on the National Register of Historic Places was built as a general store and operated as a pharmacy and, later, a soda fountain from 1877 to 1994. The pharmacist for 50 years was Anna Louise James, the first black female pharmacist in Connecticut. Though the pharmacy has since closed, the soda fountain remains a cozy place for an ice-cream soda; a gallery, featuring oils, watercolors, prints, and pottery, has been added. | 2 Pennywise La. | 860/395–1406 | Memorial Day–Labor Day, daily noon–10; Labor Day–Memorial Day, Fri. 3–7, Sat. noon–10, Sun. noon–7.

Old Saybrook Trolley. If you're a summer visitor to Old Saybrook this is *the* way to travel. The tour loop includes such landmarks as Fort Saybrook Monument Park, downtown, town marinas, hotels, restaurants, even Amtrak. Pickup locations throughout town. | 860/395–0867 | Memorial Day–Labor Day, Fri.–Sun.

ON THE CALENDAR
JULY: *Arts & Crafts Show.* More than 200 artists and craftspeople gather on the town green for this event. | 860/388–3266.
DEC.: *Christmas Torchlight Parade.* This Colonial tradition ushers in the holidays with a torchlight parade and muster with more than 40 fife and drum corps. A carol sing follows on the green. | 860/388–3266.

Dining

★ **Aleia's.** Italian. This restaurant's dining room has high ceilings and stuccoed walls with silk leaves inside them and hand-painted marble tables. Try the veal chops with roasted garlic–mashed potatoes and sautéed greens or the penne Arabiata. | 1687 Boston Post Rd. | 860/399–5050 | Closed Mon. No lunch | $13–$26 | AE, MC, V.

★ **Café Routier.** French. A funky bistro with work from local artists on the walls. Try the grilled camp trout, Chinese five spice duck breast, or steak frites. Save room for one of the homemade desserts, such as the lavender or espresso crème brûlé. No smoking. | 1080 Boston Post Rd. | 860/388–6270 | Closed Mon. Sept.–May. No lunch | $15–$21 | AE, D, DC, MC, V.

Pat's Kountry Kitchen. American. An antiques-filled restaurant where an over-stuffed bear may dine with you in the candlelight. Try the clam hash, pork chops, or chicken marsala. | 70 Mill Rock Rd. E | 860/388–4784 | $9–$16 | AE, MC, V.

Lodging

The Comfort Inn. A business-oriented, three-story hotel in this historic seaside community that is representative of the chain. Restaurant, bar, room service. In-room data ports, some kitchenettes, some microwaves, some refrigerators, some in-room hot tubs, cable TV. Pool. Laundry facilities. No pets. | 100 Essex Rd. | 860/395–1414 | fax 860/388–9578 | www.comfortinn.com | 120 rooms | $55–$180 | AE, D, DC, MC, V.

Deacon Timothy Pratt Bed and Breakfast. This inn, built in 1746 and renovated in 1999, is on a gas-lit street in Old Saybrook's historic district and next door to an old-fashioned ice cream parlor. There are bicycling and jogging trails on the grounds. The period-style rooms have four-poster canopy beds and working fireplaces. Some rooms have sitting areas. Complimentary breakfast. Cable TV. Business facilities. | 325 Main St. | 860/395–1229 | 3 rooms | $110–$230 | AE, MC, V.

Heritage Motor Inn. A family-oriented, one-story motor inn that is connected to the owner's 1755 home. Rooms are decorated with Colonial Hitchcock furniture and have murals of either landscapes or waterscapes. All the rooms have a patio. Cable TV. Pool. | 1500 Boston Post Rd. | 860/388–3743 | 12 rooms, 1 suite | $65–$95; $140 suite | AE, D, MC, V.

Sandpiper Motor Inn. This three-story simple motel is ideal for families. The rooms have standard double beds and private baths. Complimentary Continental breakfast. Cable TV. Pool. Pets allowed. | 1750 Boston Post Rd. | 860/399–7973 or 800/323–7973 | fax 860/399–7387 | 44 rooms | $75–$135 | AE, D, DC, MC, V.

Saybrook Point Inn & Spa. This luxury inn is on the Connecticut River at the point where it enters Long Island Sound. It has panoramic views and rooms furnished with 18th-century replicas. All the rooms have either patios or balconies and some have fireplaces. You can dock your boat here and charter boat fishing is available. Restaurant, bar, room service. Refrigerators, cable TV. 2 pools (1 indoor). Hot tub, spa, steam room. Health club. Laundry service. Business services. | 2 Bridge St. | 860/395–2000 or 800/243–0212 | fax 860/388–1504 | www.saybrook.com | 50 rooms, 12 suites | $179–$295; $355–$485 suites | AE, D, DC, MC, V.

POMFRET

MAP 3, I2

(Nearby towns also listed: Brooklyn, Putnam, Woodstock)

Pomfret, one of the grandest towns in the region, was once known as the inland Newport. Today it is a quiet stopping off point along Route 169, designated one of the ten most scenic byways in the country. The hilltop campus of the Pomfret School offers some of Connecticut's loveliest views.

Information: Northeastern Connecticut Chamber of Commerce | 3 Central St., Danielson, 06239 | 860/774–8001 | fax 860/774–4299 | elizabeth.kuszaj@snet.net. **Northeast Connecticut Visitors District** | Box 598, Putnam, 06260 | 860/928–1228 or 888/628–1228 | fax 860/928–4720 | quietcorner@snet.net | www.webtravels.com/quietcorner.

Attractions

Martha's Herbary. A combination herb-themed gift shop, garden, and learning center in a 1780 home. Classes in the demonstration kitchen cover everything from cooking with herbs to making herbal facial masks. | 589 Pomfret St. | 860/928–0009 | www.marthasherbary.com | Labor Day–Mar., Tues.–Sun. 10–5; Apr.–Labor Day, daily 10–5.

Mashamoquet Brook State Park. The present 860-acre park was formed by combining Mashamoquet Brook, Wolf Den, and Saptree Run. It has an attractive trail system, as well as swimming, fishing, and camping facilities. | U.S. 44 | 860/928–6121 | Memorial Day–Labor Day $5–$8 on weekends | Daily 8–dusk.

Sharpe Hill Vineyard. One of the state's newest wineries is in an 18th-century-style barn on 100 acres in the hills of Pomfret. Its wine has already won awards from the Tasters Guild. Tours and tastings are given, and from May through October you can nibble on smoked salmon and fruit and cheese in the wine garden. | 108 Wade Rd. | 860/974–3549 | www.ctwineries.com | Free | Fri.–Sun. 11–5.

ON THE CALENDAR

MAY: *Getaway Gardens Weekend.* Tours, demonstrations, and lectures are hosted by garden shops, greenhouses, farms, nurseries at this annual event. Twenty one towns participate. All Free. | 888/628–1228 or 860/928–1228. .

Dining

Vanilla Bean Café. American. This restaurant in a 19th-century barn has high ceilings with exposed beams. You can also eat outside on the patio with bentwood chairs and umbrellas. Try the homemade soups, gumbo, fish cakes, or choose from the daily pasta specials.

| 450 Deerfield Rd. | 860/928–1562 | www.thevanillabean.com | Breakfast also available on weekends. No dinner Mon.–Tues. | $5–$16 | No credit cards.

Lodging

Celebrations Inn. This 100-year-old inn is furnished with antiques and was once part of Miss Vinton's School for Girls. Complimentary breakfast. TV in common area. Library. No pets. No smoking. | 330 Pomfret St., | 860/928–5492 | fax 860/928–3306 | 5 rooms | $95–$140 | AE, MC, V.

PUTNAM

MAP 3, I2

(Nearby towns also listed: Brooklyn, Pomfret, Woodstock)

Ambitious antiques dealers have reinvented Putnam, a mill town 30 mi west of Providence that became neglected after the Depression. In earlier days the textile industry was the town's main support and silk was manufactured here. Putnam's downtown, with more than 450 antiques dealers, is the heart of the Quiet Corner's antiques trade.

Information: **Northeastern Connecticut Chamber of Commerce** | 3 Central St., Danielson, 06239 | 860/774–8001 | fax 860/774–4299 | elizabeth.kuszaj@snet.net. **Northeast Connecticut Visitors District** | Box 598, Putnam, 06260 | 860/928–1228 or 888/628–1228 | fax 860/828–4720 | quietcorner@snet.net | www.webtravels.com/quietcorner.

Attractions

Antiques Marketplace. This three-level, 20,000-square-ft extravaganza houses nearly 200 dealers. | 109 Main St. | 860/928–0442 | Daily 10–5.

ON THE CALENDAR
OCT.: *Putnam Business Association Halloween Celebration.* All the local merchants in this historic town dress up for Halloween and give out candy at this annual event. | 860/928–1350.
NOV.: *Light Up Putnam.* Putnam gets dressed up in lights every year on the day after Thanksgiving. | Kennedy Dr. in Rotary Park | 860/774–8001.

Dining

The Vine Bistro. Contemporary. A stylish bistro in the heart of downtown with local artwork on the walls. Try the grilled salmon, rack of lamb, eggplant rollatini, or vodka rigatoni with shrimp. There's open-air dining on the sidewalk patio. No smoking. | 85 Main St. | 860/928–1660 | Closed Mon. | $7–$20 | AE, MC, V.

Lodging

The Colonnade. This 1860s Greek Revival inn has porches on both floors, as well as a screened-in circular porch surrounding the house. It overlooks 5 acres of pastures and barns. Complimentary breakfast. No room phones, no TVs. | 255 E. Putnam Rd. | 860/963–2569 | 2 rooms, 1 suite | $75–$95 room, $125 suite | V, MC.

King's Inn. A country inn overlooking a pond that is within walking distance of downtown. The rooms have either cream colored walls or floral wallpaper and all have wood furniture. Complimentary Continental breakfast. Cable TV. Pool. Business services. Pets allowed. | 5 Heritage Rd. | 860/928–7961 or 800/541–7304 | fax 860/963–2463 | 40 rooms, 1 suite | $60–$120 | AE, D, DC MC, V.

RIDGEFIELD

(Nearby town also listed: Danbury)

In Ridgefield, you'll find a rustic Connecticut atmosphere within an hour of Manhattan. The town center is a largely residential sweep of lawns and majestic Colonial and Victorian homes. Its two main tourist draws are a study in contrast: a Revolutionary War–era museum and a cutting-edge museum devoted to contemporary art.

Information: **Chamber of Commerce** | 9 Bailey Ave., Box 191, Ridgefield, 06877 | 203/438–5992 or 800/FUN–1708 | fax 203/438–9175 | chamber@ridgefield-ct.com | www.ridgefield.net. **Housatonic Valley Tourism District** | 30 Main St., Box 406, Danbury, 06810 | 203/743–0546 or 800/841–4488 | fax 203/790–6124 | hvtd@snet.net | www.housatonic.org.

Attractions

Aldrich Museum of Contemporary Art. The Aldrich presents changing exhibits of cutting-edge work rivaling that of any small collection in New York City. Some of the artists who have exhibited here recently are: Janine Antoni, Doug Aitkene, Petah Coyne, John Currin, Geanne Dunning, Olafur Eliasson, Karen Finley, Robert Gober, Ann Hamilton, and Matthew Ritchey. It also has an outstanding 2-acre sculpture garden. | 258 Main St. | 203/438–4519 | fax 203/438–0198 | www.alrich.org | $5 | Tues.–Thurs. and weekends noon–5, Fri. noon–8.

Keeler Tavern Museum. A British cannonball is lodged in a corner of this museum, which was a historic inn in the 18th century and the former home of noted architect Cass Gilbert (1859–1934). Furniture and Revolutionary War memorabilia fill the museum, where guides dressed in Colonial costumes conduct tours. The sunken garden is particularly lovely in spring. | 132 Main St. | 203/438–5485 | fax 203/438–9953 | $4 | Feb.–Dec., Wed. and weekends 1–4.

ON THE CALENDAR

MAY–OCT.: *Garden of Ideas.* Come to this demonstration-inspiration garden in the spring, when the marsh attracts waterfowl and redwing blackbirds. In the summer, you can observe organic vegetable and herb gardens in bloom. In the fall, you can enjoy the foliage and see wild rice growing in the marsh. Unusual perrenials, shrubs and small trees are sold. | 203/431–9914.

Dining

Bernard's Inn at Ridgefield. Continental. This dining room has a fireplace, yellow and sage walls, and candlelit tables with white linen tablecloths and flowers. Try the Black Angus steak (prepared tableside), vichyssoise, Dover sole, or rack of lamb. | 20 West La. | 203/438–8282 | Reservations essential Fri.–Sat. | No lunch Sun. | $20–$32 | AE, MC, V.

The Elms Restaurant and Tavern. Contemporary. This spot really holds two restaurants side-by-side. The more formal restaurant is divided into four sections and has hand stenciling of flowers and pineapples on the walls. The less formal pub is in a colonial-style bar and has wood tables with candles. In the restaurant, try the lamb two ways—a devil cut lamb chop with sliced loin of lamb served with an onion marmalade, summer squash, and garlic chive whipped potatoes. In the tavern, try the homemade organic chicken sausage or bangers and mash. Kid's menu. Sun. brunch. No smoking. | 500 Main St. | 203/438–2541 | Reservations are essential on holidays | Closed Mon.–Tues. | $22–$29 | AE, DC, MC, V.

Stonehenge. French. This elegant restaurant is in a white-clapboard inn on 10 acres of woodlands and gardens, overlooking a pond. Try the wild mushroom and herb pastries, goat cheese and eggplant gâteau with tomato coulis, or Dover sole with peppercorn sauce. Save rooms for the desserts, such as the pistachio and white chocolate soufflé and the white chocolate ice cream. Sun. brunch. | U.S. 7 | 203/438–6511 | Reservations essential Fri.–Sat. | Jacket required | Closed Mon. | $18–$34 | AE, D, MC, V.

Lodging

The Elms. Two buildings make up this hotel—the main inn built in the 1760s and a newer building next door. The common areas have fireplaces and the rooms are decorated in either a Victorian or country style. Rooms have homemade quilts and hard wood floors. Some rooms have four-poster beds and floral wallpaper. Restaurant, bar, complimentary Continental breakfast. No-smoking rooms, cable TV. Laundry service. Business services. | 500 Main St. | 203/438–2541 | fax 203/438–2541 | www.elmsinn.com | 20 rooms | $135–$200 | AE, DC, MC, V.

Ridgefield Motor Inn. A one-story exterior corridor motel just east of Ridgefield with well-maintained rooms, done in burgundies and mauves. The Sangeet Restaurant is on premises and serves traditional Indian fare. Restaurant, bar. In-room data ports, microwaves, refrigerators, some in-room hot tubs, cable TV. No pets. | 296 Ethan Allen Hwy. | 203/438–3781 | 25 rooms | $35–$90 | AE, D, DC MC, V.

Stonehenge Inn and Restaurant. A refined white clapboard inn overlooking a pond, manicured lawns, and woodlands. The rooms have carpets, floral wallpaper and dark-wood furniture. Some also have four-poster beds. Restaurant, bar, complimentary Continental breakfast, room service. Cable TV. Business services. | Stonehenge Rd. | 203/438–6511 | fax 203/438–2478 | 12 rooms; 4 suites | $90–$200 | AE, MC, V.

West Lane. A three-story Colonial from the 1800s. The inn has 19th-century period furnishings and individually decorated rooms. Two of the rooms have fireplaces. Complimentary Continental breakfast. In-room data ports, cable TV, in-room VCRs. Laundry service. | 22 West La. | 203/438–7323 | www.westlaneinn.com | 18 rooms | $125–$180 | AE, DC, MC, V.

RIVERTON

MAP 3, D2

(Nearby town also listed: Norfolk)

Almost every New Englander has sat in a Hitchcock chair. Riverton, formerly Hitchcockville, is where Lambert Hitchcock built the first one in 1826. The Farmington and Still rivers meet in this tiny hamlet. It's one of the more unspoiled regions in the hills, great for hiking and driving and Yankee pot roast at the Old Riverton Inn.

Information: Chamber of Commerce of Northwest Connecticut | 333 Kennedy Dr., Box 59, Torrington, 06790-0059 | 860/482–6586 | fax 860/489–8851 | dave@northwestchamber.org | www.northwestchamber.org. **Litchfield Hills Visitors Council** | Box 968, Litchfield, 06759 | 860/567–4506 | fax 860/567–5214 | www.litchfieldhills.com.

Attractions

Hitchcock Museum. A museum in an 1829 granite Union Church that is devoted to the work of Lambert Hitchcock, founder of the original Hitchcock Chair Co. Original hand-stenciled Hitchcock beauties are on display. Tours are arranged through the Hitchcock Factory Store. | Rte. 20 | 860/379–4826 | Free | By appointment.

American Legion and People's State Forests. These two state forests border the west bank and the east bank, respectively, of this west branch of the Farmington River—a stretch that has been designated a National Wild and Scenic River. The hiking, fishing, tubing, and canoeing here are superb. | West River and East River Rds | 860/379–2469 | Free | Daily 8–dusk.

APR.: *Riverton Fishing Derby.* A tradition since 1951, this derby is held on opening day of Connecticut's fishing season; prizes are awarded in adult and youth divisions. | 860/567–4506.

OCT.: *Riverton Fair.* The last fair of the fall season. | 860/567–4506.

Dining

Old Riverton Inn. American. From this inn's dining room you can look out at the Farmington River from under high, exposed-beam ceilings. Try the stuffed pork chops or prime rib. | Rte. 20 | 860/379–8678 or 800/378–1006 | Closed Mon.–Tues. | $12–$17 | AE, D, DC, MC, V.

Lodging

Heritage Inn. This converted tobacco warehouse has an 1870s tobacco press on its front porch. Rooms are furnished with Chippendale and Queen Anne reproductions and have ceiling fans. Complimentary breakfast. Cable TV. | 34 Bridge St. | 860/354–8883 | 20 rooms | $95–$125 | AE, D, DC, MC, V.

Old Riverton Inn. A historic 1796 inn overlooking the west branch of the Farmington River. Rooms are decorated in the colonial style and have Hitchcock furniture, some antiques and handmade quilts. Restaurant, bar, complimentary breakfast. Cable TV. | Rte. 20 | 860/379–8678 or 800/378–1006 | fax 860/379–1006 | $85–$195 | 11 rooms, 1 suite | AE, D, DC, MC, V.

SALISBURY

MAP 3, B2

(Nearby towns also listed: Cornwall, Lakeville, Norfolk)

Were it not for the obsolescence of its ironworks, Salisbury might be the largest city in Connecticut. Instead, it settles for having both the state's highest mountain, Bear Mountain (2,355 ft), and its highest point, the shoulder of Mt. Frissel (2,380 ft)—whose peak is in Massachusetts. There's a spot on Mt. Frissel where if the urge strikes you (as it does many) you can stretch your limbs across the Connecticut, Massachusetts, and New York borders. Iron was discovered in Salisbury in 1732, and for the next century, the slopes of Salisbury's Mt. Riga produced the finest iron in America. Swiss and Russian immigrants, and later Hessian deserters from the British army, worked the great furnaces. As the spread of rail transport opened up better and more accessible sources of ore, the region's lumber supply was eventually depleted, and the introduction of the Bessemer process of steel manufacturing—partially invented by Salisbury native Alexander Holley—reduced the demand for iron products. Most signs of cinder heaps and slag dumps are long gone, having been replaced by grand summer homes, gardens, and inns.

Information: **Chamber of Commerce** | Box 704, Salisbury, 06068 | 860/435–0740 | www.salisbury-chamber.org. **Chamber of Commerce of Northwest Connecticut** | 333 Kennedy Dr., Box 59, Torrington, 06790-0059 | 860/482–6586 | fax 860/489–8851 | dave@northwestchamber.org | www.northwestchamber.org. **Litchfield Hills Visitors Council** | Box 968, Litchfield, 06759 | 860/567–4506 | fax 860/567–5214 | www.litchfieldhills.com.

Attractions

Harney & Sons Fine Teas. Harney supplies its high-quality Darjeeling, Earl Gray, Keemun, and other blends to some of the world's best hotels and restaurants. At the tasting room you can sample some of the 100 varieties and browse the gift shop of tea-related items. If you call ahead you might even be able to schedule a tour, led by founder John Harney himself, of the factory where the tea is blended and packaged. | 11 Brook St. | 860/435–5050 | fax 860/435–5051 | Mon.–Sat. 10–5.

ON THE CALENDAR

FEB.: *Salisbury Invitational Ski Jump and U.S. Eastern Ski Jump Championships.* An olympic-caliber competition at the oldest ski jumping program site in the nation (Satre Ski Hill), built in 1926. | Off U.S. 44 | 860/435–9729.

Dining

The Riga Room. Contemporary. The main dining room of the White Hart Inn has Italian tapestries, chandeliers, and a fireplce. Try the Maine lobster and baked brie in phyllo pastry, or the grilled pork tenderloin with bourbon brown sugar marmalade and Peruvian potatoes. | Rte. 41 and U.S. 44 | 860/435–0030 | www.whitehartinn.com | $19–$27 | Breakfast also available on weekends. No dinner Sun.–Thurs. No lunch | AE, DC, MC, V.

The Tap Room. Contemporary. A historic tavern within the White Hart Inn that has a wooden bar, wide-plank wood floors, and candlelit tables. Try the spicy shrimp, artichoke and tomato on olive bread, or the beef tournedos with brie and potatoes. The adjacent enclosed patio is called the Garden Room and serves the same menu. | Rte. 41 and U.S. 44 | 860/435–0030 | www.whitehartinn.com | $13.95–$19.95 | Breakfast also available weekdays | AE, DC, MC, V.

Lodging

Earl Grey Bed & Breakfast. The inn is on a hill overlooking Salisbury's village center. One room has French doors opening onto a private terrace, the other has an 1850 sleigh bed. The owners put fresh fruit and flowers in the rooms daily. Complimentary breakfast. No room phones, no TV. | Box 177 | 860/435–1007 | fax 860/435–1007, ext. 53 | rboyle@discovernet.net | 2 rooms | $140–$160 | No credit cards.

Under Mountain Inn. An 18th-century clapboard farmhouse on 3 acres that overlooks a horse pasture, lake, and mountains. The rooms are decorated with Williamsburg colors—cranberry, Victorian rose, and Williamsburg blue. Many of the rooms have canopy beds, one has a four-poster, and another has a brass bed. All have wicker love seats and some have stuffed wing chairs or rockers. You can reach the Appalachian Trail from the property. Two-night minimum stay on weekends. Dinner, which is not open to the public, is served in an English pub. Bar, complimentary breakfast. No room phones, no TV in rooms. Hiking. No smoking. | 482 Under Mountain Rd. | 860/435–0242 | fax 860/435–2379 | 7 rooms | $175–$225 | MAP | MC, V.

White Hart Inn. This rambling country inn overlooks the Salisbury village green and has an expansive front porch. The rooms are filled with Thomasville furniture and Waverly wall coverings. Two-night minimum stay on weekends. 2 restaurants, bar. Cable TV. Laundry service. Business services. Pets allowed. | 15 Under Mountain Rd. | 860/435–0030 or 800/932–0041 | fax 860/435–0040 | www.whitehartinn.com | 26 rooms | $115–$235 | AE, D, DC, MC, V.

SIMSBURY

MAP 3, E2

(Nearby towns also listed: Avon, Farmington, Hartford, West Hartford)

With its colonial-style shopping centers, smattering of antiques shops, and proliferation of insurance-industry executives, Simsbury—though tucked into the Farmington River Valley—closely resembles the chic bedroom communities of Fairfield County. In fall, the view from Heublein Tower in Talcott Mountain State Park is unsurpassed in the valley.

Information: Chamber of Commerce | 749 Hopmeadow St., Box 224, Simsbury, 06070 | 860/651–7307 | fax 860/651–1933 | charity.p.folk@snet.com | www.simsburycoc.org. **Associated Chambers of Commerce** | 250 Constitution Plaza, Hartford, 06103 | 860/527–9258 | fax 860/293–2592 | info@metrohartford.com | www.metrohartford.com.

Greater Hartford Tourism District | 234 Murphy Rd., Hartford, 06114 | 860/244–8181 or 800/793–4480 | fax 860/244–8180 | ctfuntour@aol.com | www.enjoyhartford.com.

Attractions

International Skating Center of Connecticut. This world-class, twin-rink facility has been the home of such skating luminaries as Viktor Petrenko, Ekaterina Gordeeva, Scott Davis, Isabelle Brasseur, and Lloyd Eisler. Lessons, public skating sessions, and ice shows are held throughout the year. | 1375 Hopmeadow St. | 860/651–5400 | www.skatenation.com | Public skating $6, shows $29—$40 | Daily; call for hrs.

Massacoh Plantation. At this property owned by the Simsbury Historical Society you'll learn about the 300-year, largely agrarian history of Simsbury, which was settled in 1640 and incorporated in 1670. There is a Victorian carriage house (circa 1880), a 1795 cottage and herb garden, a 1740 schoolhouse, and, the highlight, a period-furnished 1771 home of sea captain Elijah Phelps. You can view the houses only on a tour, but the strollable grounds are accessible on your own. | 800 Hopmeadow St. | 860/658–2500 | $6 | May–Oct., Tues.–Sun. 1–4 (last tour at 2:30); grounds open year-round.

Simsbury Farms Golf Course. This course among the barns and orchards of Simsbury's recreational complex offers a nice mix of challenging and attainable holes. | 100 Old Farms Rd. | 860/658–6246 | 18 holes, with cart rental $40 | Apr.–Nov.

Talcott Mountain State Park. Hike 1½ mi from the parking lot to the 165-ft Heublein Tower, a former private home, and you'll be rewarded with views of four states. | Rte. 185 | 860/242–1158 | Free | Park, daily 8–dusk; tower late Apr.–Labor Day, Thurs.–Sun. 10–5; Labor Day–late Oct., daily 10–5.

ON THE CALENDAR

SEPT.: *Septemberfest.* Sample wares from local craftspeople, drink local Connecticut brew at this event. | 860/651–7307.

Dining

Simsbury 1820 House. Continental. A 19th-century inn on the National Register of Historic Places that is filled with antiques and reproductions is home to this restaurant. Try the veal scaloppine with slow-roasted Portebello mushroom slices in port wine enhanced demi glaze topped with warm gorgonzola. Other favorites include the filet mignon, seafood stew, and mushrooms risotto. | 731 Hopmeadow St. | 860/658–7658 | Closed Fri.–Sun. No lunch | $18–$24 | AE, D, DC, MC, V.

Lodging

Merrywood Bed and Breakfast. A Colonial Revival inn filled with American and Continental antiques. Breakfast is served with hand-made linens on antique English porcelain. Complimentary breakfast. Minibars. | 100 Hartford Rd. | 860/651–1785 | fax 860/651–8273 | 3 rooms | $140–$165 | AE, D, DC, MC, V.

Simsbury 1820 House. This 19th-century inn is filled with a mixture of antiques and modern furniture. It has original lead-glass windows and finely carved woodwork. In winter, you can relax by the fireplace in either the parlor or the hearth room. The rooms are decorated with period fabrics and antiques. Restaurant, complimentary Continental breakfast, room service. In-room data ports, cable TV. Laundry service. Business services, airport shuttle. | 731 Hopmeadow St. | 860/658–7658 or 800/879–1820 | fax 860/651–0724 | www.simsbury1820house.com | 31 rooms, 3 suites | $135–$195 | AE, D, DC, MC, V.

Simsbury Inn. An attractive full-service hotel that is decorated in a French country style. Some of the rooms have four-poster beds, others have canopy beds. All are done in pale blue and white. Restaurant, bar, complimentary Continental breakfast, room service. Refrigerators, cable TV. Indoor pool. Hot tub, sauna. Tennis court. Gym. Laundry service. Business services, airport shuttle. | 397 Hopmeadow St. | 860/651–5700 or 800/634–

2719 | fax 860/651–8024 | www.simsburyinn | 82 rooms; 16 suites | $250–$350; suites $450 | AE, D, MC, V.

SOUTHINGTON

MAP 3, E4

(Nearby towns also listed: Bristol, Cheshire, New Britain, Waterbury)

Southington, in the central portion of the state, is most often visited in the winter for its small family ski area, in the fall for its apple harvest festival, and in the late spring and summer for its drive-in theater—one of only three in the state.

Information: Greater Southington Chamber of Commerce | 51 N. Main St., Southington, 06489 | 860/628–8036 | fax 860/276–9696 | southingtoncoc@megahits | southingtoncoc.com. **Central Connecticut Tourism District** | 1 Grove St., Ste. 310, New Britain, 06053 | 860/225–3901 | fax 860/225–0218 | info@centralct.org | www.centralct.org.

Attractions

Barnes Museum. This 1836 landmark was home to a prominent local family for more than a century. It contains original furnishings and accessories as well as a historical and genealogical library. | 85 N. Main St. | 860/628–5426 | Free | Mon.–Wed. and Fri. 9–5., Thurs. 11–7.

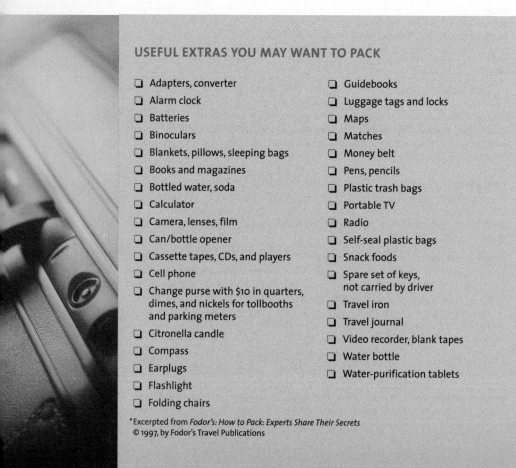

USEFUL EXTRAS YOU MAY WANT TO PACK

- ❑ Adapters, converter
- ❑ Alarm clock
- ❑ Batteries
- ❑ Binoculars
- ❑ Blankets, pillows, sleeping bags
- ❑ Books and magazines
- ❑ Bottled water, soda
- ❑ Calculator
- ❑ Camera, lenses, film
- ❑ Can/bottle opener
- ❑ Cassette tapes, CDs, and players
- ❑ Cell phone
- ❑ Change purse with $10 in quarters, dimes, and nickels for tollbooths and parking meters
- ❑ Citronella candle
- ❑ Compass
- ❑ Earplugs
- ❑ Flashlight
- ❑ Folding chairs

- ❑ Guidebooks
- ❑ Luggage tags and locks
- ❑ Maps
- ❑ Matches
- ❑ Money belt
- ❑ Pens, pencils
- ❑ Plastic trash bags
- ❑ Portable TV
- ❑ Radio
- ❑ Self-seal plastic bags
- ❑ Snack foods
- ❑ Spare set of keys, not carried by driver
- ❑ Travel iron
- ❑ Travel journal
- ❑ Video recorder, blank tapes
- ❑ Water bottle
- ❑ Water-purification tablets

*Excerpted from *Fodor's: How to Pack: Experts Share Their Secrets*
© 1997, by Fodor's Travel Publications

Mt. Southington Ski Area. This small mountain has 14 trails off the 425-ft vertical range, split equally between beginner, intermediate, and advanced. All trails are lit for night skiing and are serviced by a triple chairlift, one double, two T-bars, one J-bar, and a handle tow. There are also a halfpipe and terrain park for snowboarders. The ski school (with 150 instructors) includes a popular SKIwee program for kids from 4 to 12 years old. The Mountain Room provides respite for skiers and snowboarders alike. | 396 Mt. Vernon Rd. | 860/628-0954 or 800/982-6828 | www.mountsouthington.com | Dec.–Mar.

Plantsville General Store Antique Center. This antiques shop offers a step back in time via 25 dealers of antiques and collectibles. | 780 S. Main St., Plantsville | 860/621-5255 | www.pgsantiques.com | Wed.–Sat. 10–5, Sun. noon–5.

Southington Twin Drive-in. One of only three remaining drive-in movie theaters in the state. | 935 Meriden-Waterbury Tpke | 860/628-2205 | Mar.–Oct.

ON THE CALENDAR
APR.: *Daffodil Festival*. More than 500,000 flowers are abloom in Hubbard Park. Events at this festival include arts and crafts, live entertainment, fireworks, and amusement rides. | 203/630-4259.
OCT.: *Southington Apple Harvest Festival*. A street festival celebrating fall's favorite fruit—the apple—with apple foods and products, a carnival, arts and crafts, a parade, road race, and live entertainment. | 860/628-8036.

Dining
Brannigan's Restaurant. American. A casual family restaurant decorated with shamrocks, antiques, and old photographs. It also has a carousel. On Wednesdays and Sundays, it's all you can eat pork baby back ribs. Also try the fish fry. Kid's menu. Sun. brunch. | 176 Laning St. | 860/621-9311 | $7–$22 | AE, MC, V.

Cadillac Ranch Restaurant. American/Casual. This self-proclaimed Nashville showcase is fun and funky and has live country western music and two-step lessons. In keeping with the Nashville theme, the food is all-American (think burgers and fried chicken—filling but not fancy) with a Southern influence. | 45 Jude La., | 860/621-8805 | Closed Mon. No lunch | $5–$17.50 | AE, D, MC, V.

El Sombrero Restaurant & Cantina. Mexican. This place is easygoing and fun (good for families but has broader appeal as well) and the food is excellent. Try the shrimp sautéed with garlic, wine, and tomatoes or the chicken breast cooked in spicy mole sauce. Wings, nachos, and stuffed jalapeños are also on the menu. Wash it down with one of the potent margaritas. | 151 Queen St., | 860/621-9474 | $8–$14 | AE, MC, V.

Lodging
Chaffee's Bed and Breakfast. This ranch-style house, 2 mi south of Exit 32 off I–84, is on a ½ acre property in a quiet residential neighborhood, 1 mi northeast of downtown. The single room of this bed-and-breakfast is secluded from the rest of the house with its own private bath. The living room contains a working organ, many books, and a TV. And, if you're on a diet, you should be warned; the hostess bakes her very own pastries for breakfast. Complimentary breakfast. No room phones, TV in common area. No pets. No smoking. | 28 Reservoir Rd. | 860/628-2750 | 1 room | $50 | AE, MC, V.

Hampton Inn. This four-story chain option opened in 1986. The rooms have either one king-size bed or two double beds. All also have a table and chairs. The hotel is near both I–91 and the Merritt Parkway. Complimentary Continental breakfast. In-room data ports, cable TV. Laundry service. Business services. | 10 Bee St., Meriden | 203/235-5154 | fax 203/235-7139 | 124 rooms | $85–$95 | AE, D, MC, V.

Holiday Inn Express. A comfortable and straightforward chain option. The rooms have king-sized or double beds. Complimentary Continental breakfast. Cable TV. Pool. Gym. Business services. | 120 Laning St. | 860/276-0736 | fax 860/276-9405 | 122 rooms | $89-$99 | AE, D, DC, MC, V.

Ramada Inn. This representative of the chain is oriented toward business travelers and is 5 mi south of Southington. Restaurant, bar, complimentary Continental breakfast, room service. Cable TV. Indoor pool. Gym. Laundry Service. Business services. Pets allowed. | 275 Research Pkwy., Meriden | 203/238-2380 | fax 203/238-3172 | 150 rooms | $139-$149 | AE, D, DC, MC, V.

Susse Chalet Southington. This two-story hotel stands just off I-84 at exit 32, 2 mi north of downtown. Complimentary Continental breakfast. In-room data ports, cable TV. Pool. Laundry facilities. Business Services. No pets. | 426 Queen St. | 860/621-0181 | $55-$75 | 148 rooms | AE, D, DC, MC, V.

STAFFORD SPRINGS

MAP 3, G2

(Nearby towns also listed: Enfield, Windsor Locks)

Stafford Springs first gained fame for its mineral springs and then in the 1800s became known for its textile mills. Today, this town in the Quiet Corner of Connecticut has quaint mills, Victorian houses and rolling New England scenery. However, its not all peace and quiet; in the summer NASCAR racing at Stafford Motor Speedway is the biggest attraction in this part of the state.

Information: **Stafford Chamber of Commerce** | Box 75, Stafford Springs, 06076 | 860/872-0587 | info@connel.com | www.connel.com/stafford.coc. **Connecticut's North Central Tourism Bureau** | 111 Hazard Ave., Enfield, 06082 | 860/763-2578 or 800/248-8283 | fax 860/749-1822 | eileen@cnctb.org | www.cnctb.org.

Attractions

Civilian Conservation Corps Museum. A small museum dedicated to preserving Civilian Conservation Corps photographs and artifacts. | 166 Chestnut Hill Rd. | 860/684-3430 | Free | Memorial Day-Labor Day, daily noon-4.

Stafford Historical Museum. This small museum displays postcards, maps, pictures, and clothing manufactured in Stafford Springs since its incorporation. The displays, which go back to the 1880s, are in the old Railroad Station in Haymarket Square. | Haymarket Square. Rtes. 32 and 190 | 860/684-3646 | Free | Open the second Sunday of the month 2-4.

Stafford Motor Speedway. NASCAR auto racing takes place on the ½-mi oval track here. | Rte. 140 | 860/684-2783 | www.staffordspeedway.com | $12.50 | Apr.-Labor Day.

ON THE CALENDAR

AUG. *Stafford Motor Speedway Swap Meet.* Check out the Harley Davidson display and dog show at this motorcycle market during the third weekend of the month at the Stafford Springs Motor Speedway. | Rte. 140 | 860/445-9745.

Dining

Traveler Food and Books. American/Casual. An excellent place for a road-trip stop if you're looking for a good place to grab a quick, inexpensive bite but have had enough of fast-food chains. The menu has a little of everything, from soups and sandwiches to steak. The real draw, though, is that you can select a book from the shelves in the dining room and take it with you when you leave—free! You may have to look hard for something you really want to read (think garage sale), but that's part of the fun. There is a separate bookstore downstairs, if you're looking for something more serious. It's 4 mi east of Stafford Springs. | 1257 Buckley Hwy. (Exit 74 off I-84), Union | 860/684-4920 | Breakfast also available | $4.25-$10 | AE, D, MC, V. .

Lodging

The Pond House Bed & Breakfast. A peaceful retreat with country charm that is in the village of Stafford Springs. It has a private pond and is nestled into 4 wooded acres with a waterfall and crisscrossed by paths and brooks. The guest rooms are named for birds. The Blue Heron room, which overlooks the pond, has antiques, fabric walls, and a wood-beam ceiling. The Hummingbird room has its own porch, antiques, and a canopy bed. Complimentary breakfast. No smoking. | 19 Crystal Lake Rd. | 860/684–1644 | www.sturbridge.com/ph | 2 rooms | $75 | No credit cards. .

STAMFORD

MAP 3, A7

(Nearby towns also listed: Greenwich, New Canaan, Norwalk)

Glitzy office buildings, chain hotels, and major department stores are among the modern landmarks in revitalized Stamford, the most dynamic city on the southwestern shore. Restaurants, nightclubs, theaters, and shops line Atlantic and lower Summer streets, poised to harness the region's affluence and satisfy the desire of suburbanites to spend an exciting night on the town without having to travel to New York City.

Information: Chamber of Commerce | 733 Summer St., Stamford, 06901 | 203/359–4761 | fax 203/363–5069. **Southwestern Area Commerce & Industry Association** | 1 Landmark Sq., No. 230, Stamford, 06901 | 203/359–3220 | fax 203/967–8294. **Coastal Fairfield County Convention and Visitor Bureau** | 297 West Ave., Gate Lodge-Mathews Park, Norwalk, 06850 | 203/899–2799 or 800/866–7925 | fax 203/853–7524 | info@visitfairfieldco.org | www.visitfairfieldco.org.

STAMFORD

INTRO
ATTRACTIONS
DINING
LODGING

Attractions

Bartlett Arboretum. This 64-acre arboretum is owned by the University of Connecticut and holds natural woodlands, cultivated gardens, marked ecology trails, a swamp walk, and a pond. Spring is the ideal time to view the wildflower garden. In the spring and fall you can buy plants at the greenhouse. | 151 Brookdale Rd. | 203/322–6971 | Free | Grounds daily 8:30–dusk; visitor center weekdays 8:30–4.

First Presbyterian Church. One of the city's most unusual architectural attractions is this church shaped like a fish. Yes, a fish. Designed by Wallace K. Harrison, it also has the state's largest mechanical-action pipe organ and eye-catching stained-glass windows by Gabriel Loire of France. | 1101 Bedford St. | 203/324–9522 | Free | Sept.–June, weekdays 9–5; July–Aug., weekdays 9–3.

Stamford Center for the Arts. A popular center for the arts that presents everything from symphony performances and comedy shows to musicals and operas. | 307 Atlantic St. | 203/325–4466 | www.onlyatsca.com.

Stamford Museum and Nature Center. Oxen, sheep, pigs, and other animals roam this New England–style farmstead with many nature trails. The five gallery exhibits survey natural history, art, mines and minerals, Americana, and Native American life. Two enjoyable times to visit are during spring harvest and maple-sugaring season. There is a children's playground in which the equipment is shaped like animals. | 39 Scofieldtown Rd. | 203/322–1646 | www.stamfordmuseum.org | $5 | Grounds: Mon.–Sat. 9–5, Sun. 1–5; farm: daily 9–5; planetarium shows Sun. at 3; observatory Fri. 8 PM–10 PM.

Stamford Town Center. This upscale mall houses more than 130 stores including Saks Fifth Avenue, Talbots, a Pottery Barn superstore, and Tommy Hilfiger. | 100 Greyrock Pl | 203/356–9700 | Weekdays 10–9, weekends noon–6.

Sterling Farms Golf Course. This is one of the state's most popular 18-hole golf courses. It was designed by Geoffrey Cornish. | 1349 Newfield Ave. | 203/461–9090 | Mar.–Dec.

United House Wrecking. One man's trash is another man's treasure—United House Wrecking sells acres of architectural artifacts, decorative accessories, antiques, nautical memorabilia, lawn furnishings, and other collectibles. | 535 Hope St. | 203/348–5371 | fax 203/961–9472 | www.unitedantiques.com | Mon.–Sat. 9:30–5:30, Sun. noon–5.

Whitney Museum of American Art at Champion. The primary focus of this museum, affiliated with the Whitney Museum in New York City, is 20th-century American painting and photography. Past exhibits have included works by Edward Hopper, Alexander Calder, and Georgia O'Keefe. Free gallery talks are held on Tuesday, Thursday, and Saturday at 12:30. | 400 Atlantic St. | 203/358–7630 | Free | Tues.–Sat. 11–5.

ON THE CALENDAR
JAN.: *Winterfest.* Activities held at the Stamford Museum and Nature Center include horse-drawn hayrides, sled dogs, ice harvesting, and crafts. | 203/322–1646.
MAY: *Bartlett Arboretum Spring Garden Faire.* This show and sale typically features more than 10,000 plants. | 151 Brookdale Rd. | 203/322–6971.
JUNE: *Sail for the Sound Regatta.* A celebration of Long Island Sound with tall ships, yacht races, and live entertainment. | 203/967–8350.

Dining
★ **La Hacienda.** Mexican. Elaborate Spanish and Mexican oil paintings adorn this restaurant's walls. The two dining rooms have rod iron furniture and there's also a patio where you can eat in good weather. It's known for mole sauce, which is featured in many dishes. Try the Argentine steak or Chicken fajitas. Kid's menu. | 222 Summer St. | 203/324–0577 | No lunch Sun. | $13–$25 | AE, DC, MC, V.

Morton's of Chicago. Steak. An elegant, simple restaurant on the ground floor of the Swiss Bank building in the heart of downtown that has mahogony paneling and oil lamps. There's an open, brick kitchen so you can watch your steak being prepared. Try the filet mignon or porterhouse. Cigar bar. | 377 N. State St. | 203/324–3939 | No lunch | $20–$35 | AE, DC, MC, V.

Ocean 211. Seafood. The private tables at this spot are separated by drapery and lit by candles. Try the soft-shell crab, sole with carrot-ginger sauce, tilapia with Israeli couscous, or salmon with black bean sauce. | 211 Summer St. | 203/973–0494 | Closed Sun. No lunch Sat. | $20–$28 | AE, D, DC, MC, V.

Lodging
Budget Hospitality Inn. Rising seven stories above Stamford's business district, this hotel is north of I–95. The rooms are basic with floral patterned bedspreads and burgundy carpets. Some of the rooms have ocean views. Restaurant, room service, complimentary Continental breakfast. In-room data ports, cable TV. Pool. Gym. Laundry service. Business services, free parking. Pets allowed (fee). | 19 Clark's Hill Ave. | 203/327–4300 | www.budgethospitalityinn.com | 86 rooms | $60–$159 | AE, D, DC, MC, V.

Grand Chalet Stamford. This eight-story chain hotel stands just south of I–95 (at Exit 6) on Stamford's western edge and caters to the business traveler. Complimentary Continental breakfast. In-room data ports, cable TV. Pool. Gym. Laundry facilities. Free parking. Pets allowed. | 135 Harvard Ave. | 203/357–7100 | 158 rooms | $75–$95 | AE, MC, V.

Holiday Inn Select. A chain option in downtown Stamford. The rooms are lime green and maroon and have either king-size beds or two double beds. The rooms with king-size beds have sofas and all rooms have a desk and chairs. Restaurant, bar, room service. In-room data ports, cable TV. Indoor pool. Gym. Laundry service. Business services. Pets allowed. | 700 Main St. | 203/358–8400 | fax 203/358–8872 | www.holiday-inn.com | 383 rooms | $205–$215 | AE, D, DC, MC, V.

Stamford Marriott Hotel. A 16-floor chain option near downtown that was built in 1977. It is geared toward business travelers and all of the rooms have desks and chairs. Restaurant, bar, room service. In-room data ports, cable TV. 2 pools (1 indoor). Barbershop, beauty salon, hot tub, sauna, steam room. Basketball, health club, racquetball. Shops. Laundry service. Business services. | 2 Stamford Forum | 203/357–9555 | fax 203/324–6897 | 506 rooms, 6 suites | $119–$279; suites $399 | AE, D, DC, MC, V.

Sheraton Stamford Hotel. This five-story hotel has an atrium lobby. The hotel has spacious rooms and was recently renovated. Restaurant, bar, room service. Cable TV. Indoor pool. Sauna. Gym. Shops. Laundry service. Business services. | 2701 Summer St. | 203/359–1300 | fax 203/348–7937 | 445 rooms, 25 suites | $219–$230 | AE, D, DC, MC, V.

Stamford Suites. This all-suites hotel is within walking distance of downtown. The rooms have white walls with photographs and flowers. The hotel has some long-term, corporate renters. There is secure underground parking. Complimetary Continental breakfast. Kitchenettes, cable TV. Laundry service. | 720 Bedford St. | 203/359–7300 | fax 203/359–7304 | 42 suites | $125–$229 | AE, D, MC, V.

Westin Stamford. A full-service hotel catering to the business traveler. Select a room with a king-size bed or one with two double beds. Restaurant, bar, complimentary Continental breakfast, room service. In-room data ports, refrigerators, cable TV. Indoor pool. Hot tub. Tennis court. Gym. Laundry service. Business services. | 1 1st Stamford Pl | 203/967–2222 | fax 203/967–3475 | 470 rooms, 28 suites | $109–$199 | AE, D, DC, MC, V.

STONINGTON

MAP 3, I6

(Nearby towns also listed: Groton, Ledyard, Mystic, New London)

The memorable village of Stonington pokes into Fishers Island Sound. Today a quiet fishing community clustered around white-spired churches, Stonington is far less commercial than nearby Mystic. In the 19th century, though, this was a bustling whaling, sealing, and transportation center. Historic buildings line the town green and border both sides of Water Street up to the imposing Old Lighthouse Museum. You can tour the home of Capt. Nathaniel Palmer, who discovered Antarctica in 1820.

Information: Chamber of Commerce of Southeastern Connecticut | 105 Huntington St., New London, 06320 | 860/443–8332 | fax 860/444–1529 | chamberscct@juno.com | www.chamberscct.org. **Southeastern Connecticut Tourism District** | 470 Bank St., Box 89, New London, 06320 | 860/444–2206 or 800/TO–ENJOY | fax 860/442–4257 | more2see@aol.com | www.mysticmore.com.

Attractions

Captain Nathaniel B. Palmer House. The Victorian home of the man who discovered Antarctica in 1820. Exhibits focus on both his career and family. You can see a scale model of Palmer's ship, *The Hero*, in which he discovered Antarctica. | 40 Palmer St. | 860/535–8445 | $4 | May–Oct., Tues.–Sun. 10–4, last tour at 3.

Old Lighthouse Museum. The six rooms of this 1823 lighthouse depict life in a coastal town circa 1649, as well as the shipping and whaling industries. The top of the tower offers prime views of Long Island Sound and three states. | 7 Water St. | 860/535–1440 or 860/535–1492 | $4 | July–Aug., daily 10–5; May–June, Sept.–Oct., Tues.–Sun. 10–5, or by appointment.

Stonington Vineyards. Since 1987 this small coastal winery has grown premium vinifera, including chardonnay and French hybrid grape varieties. You can browse through the works of local artists in the small gallery or take a picnic lunch on the grounds. | 523 Taugwonk Rd. | 860/535–1222 | fax 860/535–2182 | www.stonigtonvineyards.com | Free | Daily 11–5; tours at 2.

JULY: *Blessing of the Fleet.* A celebration of the town's commercial fishing fleet, which includes a parade and clam and lobster bake. | 860/444–2206.

AUG.: *Stonington Fair.* You'll find arts and crafts, face painting, entertainment, a book fair, food, and fun for the whole family here. | 860/535–2476.

Dining

Boom. Contemporary. A candlelit restaurant on the water with bay windows on all sides that give you a view of the boatyard and Stonington Harbor. The seafood comes straight from the Patty Jo Fishing Company, a local fishery. Try the lightly battered, cornmeal-crusted oysters to start before moving onto the filet mignon with cognac peppercorn sauce and gorgonzola polenta or the native flounder with lump crab meat sauce and plum-tomato orzo. Kid's menu. Sun. brunch. | 194 Water St. | 860/535–2588 | No lunch Sun. | $10–$18 | AE, MC, V.

Randall's Ordinary. American. The waitstaff at this 17th-century inn 2 mi northeast of Stonington wears Colonial garb as they serve traditional New England fare prepared over an open hearth. All three dining rooms have antique tables and chairs and are lit by candles. Try the Yankee pot roast, chicken potpie, or steak. Prix-fixe dinner. | Rte. 2, North Stonington | 860/599–4540 | Breakfast also available | prix fixe $39 | AE, MC, V.

Lodging

★ **Antiques and Accommodations.** A Victorian country home built in the mid-1800s with British accents. Two-night minimum stay on weekends. Complimentary breakfast. Cable TV, no room phones. No smoking. | 32 Main St., North Stonington | 860/535–1736 or 800/554–7829 | fax 860/535–2613 | www.visitmystic.com/antiques | 4 rooms, 2 suites | $129–$289 | MC, V.

Lasbury's Guest House. This separate small red guest house faces the home of the mother-daughter proprietors across a small garden. Guest rooms overlook a salt-marsh inlet from Long Island Sound. No air-conditioning in some rooms, refrigerators, cable TV. No kids under 6. | 41 Orchard St. | 860/535–2681 | 3 rooms (2 with shared bath) | $95 | No credit cards.

Randall's Ordinary. The hotel is in two historic buildings on 250 wooded acres 2 mi northeast of Stonington. The newly refurbished rooms have stenciled walls, area rugs, and wooden wide plank floors; three have a stone patio. Two-night minimum on weekends. Restaurant, dining rooms. Some room phones, no TV in some rooms. Business services. No smoking. | Rte. 2, North Stonington | 860/599–4540 | fax 860/599–3308 | www.randall-sordinary.com | 14 rooms, 4 suites | $125–$350 | AE, MC, V.

STORRS

MAP 3, G3

(Nearby town also listed: Coventry)

The majority of the rolling hillside and farmland of Storrs are occupied by the 4,400 acres and 12,000 students of the main campus of the University of Connecticut. Many cultural programs, sporting events, and other happenings take place here. University Parking Services and the Student Union supply campus maps.

Information: **Windham Region Chamber of Commerce** | Box 43, Willimantic,¢ 06226 | 860/423–6389 | fax 860/423–8235. **Northeast Connecticut Visitors District** | Box 598, Putnam, 06260 | 860/928–1228 or 888/628–1228 | fax 860/928–4720 | quiet-corner@snet.net | www.CTquietcorner.org.

Attractions

Mansfield Drive-In and Eastern Connecticut Flea Market. With three big screens, this is one of the state's three remaining drive-in theaters. The Eastern Connecticut Flea Market, with 200 vendors, is held here on Sunday from the first weekend of spring until Thanksgiving weekend. | Rtes. 31 and 32 | 860/423–4441 (drive-in) or 860/456–2578 (flea market) | www.mansfieldi.hollywood.com | Drive-in Apr.–May, Sept., Fri.–Sun., June–Aug. nightly.

University of Connecticut. Established in 1881 as an agricultural school, the University of Connecticut is now a public university with more than 10,000 undergraduates. | Storrs Rd. (Rte. 195) | 860/486–2000 | www.uconn.edu | Daily.

Ballard Institute and Museum of Puppetry. Hand puppets, rod puppets, body puppets, shadow puppets, marionettes—this museum has more than 2,000 puppets in its extraordinary collection. Half were created by Frank Ballard, a master of puppetry who established the country's first complete undergraduate and graduate degree program in puppetry at UConn more than three decades ago. Exhibits change seasonally. If you're lucky you might even catch Oscar the Grouch from *Sesame Street* on display. | University of Connecticut Depot Campus, 6 Bourn Pl., U-212 | 860/486–4605 | $2 | Mid-Apr.–mid-Nov., Fri.–Sun. noon–5.

Connecticut State Museum of Natural History. From mollusks and fossils to sharks and wigwams, the exhibits at this state museum on the UConn campus cover our diverse natural history. | Campus of University of Connecticut, Rte. 195 | 860/486–4460 | Free | Thurs.–Mon. noon–4.

University of Connecticut Greenhouses. The UConn greenhouses are internationally acclaimed for their more than 3,000 different plants, from 900 varieties of exotic orchids to banana plants and a redwood tree. Organized tours are given weekends by advance appointment. | 75 N. Eagleville Rd. | 860/486–4460 | Free | Weekdays 8–4.

William Benton Museum of Art. This museum's permanent collection includes European and American paintings, drawings, prints, and sculptures from the 16th-century to the present. | 245 Glenbrook Rd. | 860/486–4520 | Free | Tues.–Fri. 10–4:30, weekends 1–4:30. Closed between exhibitions.

ON THE CALENDAR

APR.–NOV.: *Eastern Connecticut Flea Market.* Sundays are made for browsing at the Mansfield Drive-in Theater. | 860/456–2578.

Dining

Altnaveigh Inn & Restaurant. Continental. This historic inn and restaurant is in a rustic 1734 farmhouse. Here you'll dine in an open room with two working fireplaces. Known for bouillabaisse, rack of lamb, and beef Wellington. Open-air dining on patio. Sun. brunch. | 957 Storrs Rd. | 860/429–4490 | No lunch weekends | $18–$30 | AE, D, DC, MC, V.

Lodging

Still Waters Bed and Breakfast. This contemporary glass and fieldstone structure, inspired by the designs of Frank Lloyd Wright, is on 50 wooded acres. Rooms are appointed with an eclectic mix of antiques and modern furnishings. All rooms overlook the ponds; one has a fireplace, hot tub, and a private deck. Complimentary breakfast. Some in-room hot tubs, cable TV. Pond. Hiking, fishing. No pets. No smoking. | 129 Summit Rd. | 860/429–9798 | 4 rooms | $75 | No credit cards.

Storrs Farmhouse on the Hill. This popular B&B is 2 mi from the University of Connecticut. You'll find hiking paths and fishing five minutes away. Complimentary breakfast. No room phones. | 418 Gurleyville Rd. | 860/429–1400 | $70 | No credit cards.

STRATFORD

(Nearby towns also listed: Bridgeport, Milford)

Stratford, named after the English town Stratford-upon-Avon, has more than 150 historic homes, many of which are on Long Island Sound. The Academy Hill neighborhood, near the intersection of Main (Route 113) and Academy Hill streets, is a good area to stroll.

Information: **Bridgeport Regional Business Council** | 10 Middle St., Bridgeport, 06601 | 203/335–3800 | fax 203/366–0105 | info@brbc.org. **Coastal Fairfield County Convention and Visitor Bureau** | 297 West Ave., Gate Lodge-Mathews Park, Norwalk, 06850 | 203/899–2799 or 800/866–7925 | fax 203/853–7524 | info@visitfairfieldco.org | www.visitfairfieldco.org.

Attractions

Boothe Memorial Park and Museum. The unusual buildings on this 32-acre complex include a blacksmith shop, carriage and tool barns, and a museum that traces the history of the trolley. Also on the grounds is a beautiful rose garden, whose wedding section includes the roses Love, Honor, and Cherish, a sunken garden, and a children's playground. | Main St. | 203/381–2068 or 203/381–2046 | Free | Park daily dawn–dusk; museum June–Oct., Tues.–Fri. 11–1, weekends 1–4.

Catharine B. Mitchell Museum and Captain David Judson House. The Capt. David Judson House is a post-and-beam, center-chimney Colonial that was built circa 1750. Its exhibits include examples of locally made furniture. The Mitchell Museum displays the collections of the Stratford Historical Society. | 967 Academy Hill | 203/378–0630 | $2 | Mid-May–Oct., Wed. and weekends 11–4; genealogy library year-round, Tues.–Thurs. 9–2.

Stratford Antique Center. This cavernous shop showcases the wares of more than 200 different dealers. | 400 Honeyspot Rd. | 203/378–7754 | fax 203/380–2086 | www.stratfordantique.com | Daily 10–5.

ON THE CALENDAR

FEB.: *Stratford National Guard Armory Antiques Show.* More than 75 dealers of affordable antiques and collectibles gather to sell their wares here. | 63 Armory Rd. | 203/758–3880.

Dining

Marnick's. American/Casual. A family restaurant overlooking the beach that serves everything from burgers and club sandwiches to roast beef and swordfish dinners. Try the lobster rolls. Kid's menu. | 10 Washington Pkwy. | 203/377–6288 | Breakfast also available | $6–$19 | AE, D, DC, MC, V.

Lodging

Marnick's Motel. At this small, two-story oceanfront motel, you can choose a room with either double or king-size beds. All of the rooms have pictures of boats and the water; some have ocean views. Restaurant. Some microwaves, some refrigerators, cable TV. Beach. Fishing. | 10 Washington Pkwy. | 203/377–6288 | 29 rooms | $65–$95 | AE, D, DC, MC, V.

Nathan Booth House. An 1843 Federal Greek Revival farm house adjacent to Boothe Memorial Park is home to this hotel. The inn has wide-board chestnut floors, handmade doors, original hardware, and a separate carriage house barn and gazebo. There are fireplaces in the guest parlor and the dining room. Complimentary breakfast. In-room data ports, no room phones, no TV in rooms, cable TV in common area. No pets. No kids under 13. No smoking. | 6080 Main St., Putney | 203/378–6489 | 4 rooms | $100–$125 | AE, MC, V.

Ramada Inn. A chain option near I–95 that has clean, standard rooms. Restaurant, bar, room service. Indoor pool. Business services. Pets allowed. | 225 Lordship Blvd. | 203/375–8866 | fax 203/375–2482 | 145 rooms | $99–$109 | AE, D, MC, V.

WASHINGTON

(Nearby towns also listed: Kent, Litchfield, New Milford, New Preston, Woodbury)

The beautiful buildings of the Gunnery prep school mingle with stately Colonials and churches in Washington, one of the best-preserved Colonial towns in Connecticut. The Mayflower Inn, south of the Gunnery on Route 47, attracts an exclusive clientele. Washington was settled in 1734, and in 1779, became one of the first towns in the United States to be named for George Washington.

Information: Chamber of Commerce of Northwest Connecticut | 333 Kennedy Dr., Box 59, Torrington, 06790-0059 | 860/482–6586 | fax 860/489–8851 | dave@north-westchamber.org. **Litchfield Hills Visitors Council** | Box 968, Litchfield, 06759 | 860/567–4506 | fax 860/567–5214 | www.litchfieldhills.com.

Attractions

Gunn Memorial Library and Museum. The circa 1780 museum contains period furnishings, decorative arts, and antique clothing. The 1908 library includes the Connecticut Room, which has state, local, and genealogical books. | Wykeham Rd. and Rte. 47 | 860/868–7756 | Free | Museum Thurs.–Sun. noon–4; library Mon. and Fri. 9:30–5, Tues. 2–8, Thurs. 9:30–8, Sat. 9:30–3.

The Institute for American Indian Studies. This museum, 6 mi south of Washington, has an excellent and thoughtfully arranged collection of exhibits and displays that detail the history of the Northeastern Woodland Native Americans. Highlights include a replicated longhouse and nature trails. | 38 Curtis Rd., Southbury | 860/868–0518 | $4 | Jan.–Mar., Wed.–Sat. 10–5, Sun. noon–5; Apr.–Dec., Mon.–Sat. 10–5, Sun. noon–5.

ON THE CALENDAR
JUNE–AUG.: *The Institute for American Indian Studies.* The Institute runs a series of summer camps for children. Each camp is taught by a different expert in areas of Native American studies, such as Native American Legends and Lore or Native Lifeways. | 860/868–0518.

WHAT TO PACK IN THE TOY TOTE FOR KIDS

- ❑ Audiotapes
- ❑ Books
- ❑ Clipboard
- ❑ Coloring/activity books
- ❑ Doll with outfits
- ❑ Hand-held games
- ❑ Magnet games

- ❑ Notepad
- ❑ One-piece toys
- ❑ Pencils, colored pencils
- ❑ Portable stereo with earphones
- ❑ Sliding puzzles
- ❑ Travel toys

*Excerpted from *Fodor's: How to Pack: Experts Share Their Secrets*
© 1997, by Fodor's Travel Publications

Dining

G.W. Tavern. American. Both traditional and contemporary New England fare—fish-and-chips, meat loaf, chicken potpie—are served up in this rustic tavern, with a mural of surrounding countryside and hand-hewn beams. Kid's menu. Weekend brunch. | 20 Bee Brook Rd. | 860/868–6633 | $9–$25 | AE, MC, V.

The Mayflower Inn. Continental. This restaurant is in one of the state's most polished inns. The dining room overlooks the Shakespean Garden and the tables are adorned with fresh orchids. Try the house-smoked salmon, game sausage, or fish. There is outdoor dining on the patio. No smoking. | 118 Woodbury Rd. | 860/868–9466 | $19–$30 | AE, MC, V.

Lodging

Mayflower Inn. The main inn here is a three-story, clapboard-and-shingle building. The grounds cover 28 acres and have streams, stone walls, beautiful gardens, and hiking trails. The rooms have canopy beds, fireplaces, antiques and balconies. Two-night minimum stay on weekends. Restaurant, bar, room service. Cable TV, in-room VCRs. Pool. Sauna, spa, steam room. Tennis court. Health club. Laundry service. Business services. No smoking. | 118 Woodbury Rd. | 860/868–9466 | fax 860/868–1497 | www.mayflowerinn.com | 17 rooms, 8 suites | $380–$1200 | AE, MC, V.

Rocky River Motel. This motel is a good bet for budget-conscious travelers. It's just 2 minutes from downtown Washington. Cable TV. | 236 Kent St. | 860/355–3208 | 19 rooms | $55 | AE, D, MC, V.

WATERBURY

MAP 3, D4

(Nearby towns also listed: Bristol, Chesire, New Britain, Southington, Woodbury)

Waterbury, in the Naugatuck River Valley, was once known as Brass City for its role as the country's top producer of brass products. Evidence of the prosperity of the city's brass barons can still be seen in the city's hillside district northwest of downtown, where grand old Queen Annes, Greek and Georgian Revivals, and English Tudors remain, a few of which have been turned into bed-and-breakfasts.

Two musts in downtown are the Mattatuck Museum, which tells the story of the valley's industrial past and boasts an impressive collection of American art, and Howland-Hughes's Connecticut Store. This turn-of-the-century department store now sells only goods that are made in Connecticut, including everything from blankets to glass tableware.

Information: Greater Waterbury Chamber of Commerce | 83 Bank St., Box 1469, Waterbury, 06721 | 203/757–0701 | fax 203/756–3507 | wby.chamber@snet.net | www.waterburychamber.org. **Waterbury Region Convention and Visitors Bureau** | 21 Church St., Waterbury, 06702 | 203/597–9527 | fax 203/597–8452.

Attractions

Howland-Hughes' The Connecticut Store. A wide-ranging store stocked entirely with items made in Connecticut, from Wiffle balls to Pez candy, fine pottery to glassware. | 120 Bank St. | 203/753–4121 | fax 203/753–4128 | Tues.–Sat. 9:30–5.

Mattatuck Museum. This downtown Waterbury beauty was designed by architect Cesar Pelli (who also designed the renovations for New York's Museum of Modern Art). The museum is renowned not only for its exhibits on the history of the Greater Naugatuck River Valley, but also its collection of 18th-, 19th-, and 20th-century art. The collection includes portraits by John Trumbull and Ralph Earl, landscapes by Frederic Church and John

Twachtman, and contemporary pieces by Josef Albers and Alexander Calder. It also has a fine café. | 144 W. Main St. | 203/753–0381 | Free | Tues.–Sat. 10–5.

Quassy Amusement Park. This small amusement park on Lake Quassapaug, 3 mi west of Waterbury, is best suited for families with small children and has approximately 30 rides and games, a picnic grove, boat rides, and a beach. | Rte. 64, Middlebury | 203/758–2913 | General admission is free; additional cost per ride | Apr.–May and Sept.–Oct., weekends noon–6; Memorial Day–Labor Day, daily 11–9.

Seven Angels Theatre. This theater presents top-rate plays, musicals, children's performances, cabaret concerts, and youth programs. | Hamilton Park Pavilion, Plank Rd. | 203/757–4676 | fax 203/591–8223 | Call for ticket prices and performance schedule.

Dining

Bacco's. Italian. Established in 1930, this is *the* place to go for pizza in Waterbury. If you're not in the mood for one of the famous pizzas, try the chicken Florentine or veal Milano. Kid's menu. | 1230 Thomaston Ave. | 203/755–0635 | Closed Mon. No lunch weekends | $14–$27 | AE, DC, MC, V.

★ **Carmen Anthony Steak House.** Steak. Rich wood paneling, oil paintings on the walls, and white linen on the tables characterize this upscale steak house. Try the filet mignon, rib eye steak, or New York Angus beef. | 496 Chase Ave. | 203/757–3040 | No lunch weekends | $16–$27 | AE, D, DC, MC, V.

★ **Diorio Restaurant and Bar.** Italian. This restaurant has been a Waterbury tradition for more than 50 years. It has retained its original mahogany bankers booths, marble and brass bar, tin ceilings, and exposed brick. Pasta, veal, chicken, steak, seafood are the staples of the menu. Try the veal Monteleoni (sautéed veal with prosciutto, sage, and marsala sauce over garlic pasta). | 231 Bank St. | 203/754–5111 | Closed Sun. No lunch Sat. | $13.95–$28.95 | AE, D, DC, MC, V.

Lodging

Courtyard by Marriott. You'll have a view of the city or highway from this 11-story, standard chain option near I–84. All the rooms have a desk and chair. Cable TV. Indoor pool. Hot tub. Gym. Laundry service. Business services. | 63 Grand St. | 203/596–1000 or 800/321–2211 | fax 203/753–6276 | 199 rooms | $99–$119 | AE, D, DC, MC, V.

House on the Hill. An 1888, three-story Victorian mansion is home to this inn, which has an English-style garden in which 5,00 bulbs are planted. You can relax on the huge porch with wicker furniture or in the mahogany library or cherry wood parlor. The rooms are individually decorated, filled with antiques and have sitting areas. The beds are brass, iron, or pencil-post canopy and have handmade Ohio quilts. Some of the bathrooms have original bathtubs with marble surrounds and pedestal sinks. Two-night minimum stay on weekends. Complimentary breakfast. No air-conditioning in some rooms, cable TV. Pets allowed. No smoking. | 92 Woodlawn Terr | 203/757–9901 | 4 suites | $125–$175 | Closed mid-Dec.–mid-Jan. | AE, D, DC, MC, V.

Quality Inn Waterbury. This eight-story chain hotel is near Waterbury's Brass City Mall and a local gym, to which the hotel provides free passes. Complimentary Continental breakfast. Some in-room data ports, some refrigerators, some microwaves, cable TV, TV in common area. Outdoor pool. Business services. No pets. | 88 Union St. | 203/575–1500 | fax 203/753–9485 | 104 rooms | $80–$104 | AE, D, DC, MC, V.

Sheraton Waterbury. This standard chain hotel has rooms with either two double beds or a king-size bed. Restaurant, bar, room service. In-room data ports, cable TV. Indoor pool. Hot tub, sauna. Gym, racquetball. Laundry service. Business services. Pets allowed. | 3580 E. Main St. | 203/573–1000 | fax 203/573–1349 | 279 rooms | $115–$129 | AE, D, DC, MC, V.

Tucker Hill Inn. A New England Colonial-style inn built in 1923 that is close to downtown Middlebury, 3 mi west of Waterbury. The inn was originally a tearoom at a trolley stop on the way to Waterbury. The rooms have country-style antiques and furnishings. Complimentary breakfast. No air-conditioning in some rooms, cable TV, no room phones. Pets allowed (no fee). No smoking. | 96 Tucker Hill Rd., Middlebury | 203/758–8334 | fax 203/598–0652 | 4 rooms | $90–$140 | AE, MC, V.

WATERFORD

MAP 3, H6

(Nearby towns also listed: Groton, New London, Niantic)

One of the most exciting reasons to come to Waterford, a town of 17,000 shoreline residents, is to view a performance at the Eugene O'Neill Theater Center. In summer, the theater, a testing ground for students as well as masters of the arts, opens performances of the National Playwrights Conference, the National Puppetry Conference, the National Music Theater Conference, and the Cabaret Symposium to the public.

Information: Chamber of Commerce of Southeastern Connecticut | 105 Huntington St., New London, 06320 | 860/443–8332 | fax 860/444–1529 | chamberscct@juno.com | www.chamberscct.org. **Southeastern Connecticut Tourism District** | 470 Bank St., Box 89, New London, 06320 | 860/444–2206 or 800/TO–ENJOY | fax 860/442–4257 | more2see@aol.com | www.mysticmore.com.

Attractions

Captain John's Dock. Lighthouse cruises as well as sightseeing tours in search of whales, seals, and eagles, depending on the time of year, leave from Captain John's aboard the 100-ft-long *Sunbeam Express*. Naturalists from Mystic Aquarium accompany the boat. | 15 1st St. | 860/443–7259 | Various tours operate year-round; call for details.

Harkness Memorial State Park. The former summer estate of Edward Stephen Harkness, a silent partner in Standard Oil, encompasses formal gardens, picnic areas, a beach for strolling and fishing (though not swimming), and the 42-room Italian villa-style mansion Eolia. The first two stories of the mansion are on view and have furnished rooms filled with antiques. | 275 Great Neck Rd. | 860/443–5725 | Memorial Day–Labor Day $4–$8; free at all other times | Daily 8–dusk.

Parasail USA. It's a whole new way to view the shoreline—from 1,200 ft above Long Island Sound. Fear not, all takeoffs and landings are done from the platform of a boat. | 15 1st St., Capt. John's Dock | 860/444–7272 | Late May–mid-Oct.

ON THE CALENDAR
MAY: *Sheep to Shawl Day.* Demonstrations on sheep shearing, spinning, weaving, and dyeing wool take place at Jordan Green. This event has been a tradition for 25 years. | 860/442–2707.
JUNE–AUG.: *Eugene O'Neill Theater Center.* Students of the theater have been honing their skills at this center for more than 40 years. The center invites the public to readings and performances of the National Playwrights Conference, the National Puppetry Conference, the National Music Theater Conference, and the Cabaret Symposium. | 860/443–5378.
JULY–AUG.: *Summer Music at Harkness.* Two months of musical performances—from classical to pop—with cooling ocean breezes added in take place at Harkness Memorial State Park. | 860/442–9199.

Dining
Sunset Ribs. American. You'll witness wonderful sunsets on the Niantic River whether you eat outside on the patio or inside in the dining room of this restaurant. The ribs with smoked barbecue sauce are, of course, the specialty but the copious menu includes many other

options including pastas, hamburgers, chicken and seafood dishes. | 378 Rope Ferry Rd. | 860/443–7427 | $12–$18 | Closed end Dec–early Mar. | MC, V.

Lodging

Oakdell Motel. This two-story motel, 2 mi north of I–95, has been family-owned and operated since 1972. A gazebo crowns the broad lawns that encircle the pool; there is space to relax and enjoy what wildlife creeps from the woods. Two penthouse rooms have private balconies overlooking the pool. Complimentary Continental breakfast, picnic area. Some kitchenettes, microwaves, refrigerators, cable TV. Pool. Pets allowed. | 983 Rte. 85 | 860/442–9446 | www.oakdellmotel.com | 22 rooms | $55–$135 | AE, D, DC, MC, V.

WEST HARTFORD

(Nearby towns also listed: Avon, Farmington, Hartford, New Britain, Simsbury, Wethersfield)

More cosmopolitan than many of its suburban neighbors, West Hartford is alive with a sense of community. Gourmet food and ethnic grocery stores abound, as do unusual boutiques and shops. A stroll around West Hartford Center (Exit 42 off I–84) will reveal well-groomed streets busy with pedestrians and lined with coffee shops.

Information: Chamber of Commerce | 948 Farmington Ave., West Hartford, 06107 | 860/521–2300 | fax 860/521–1996 | whchamber@snet.net | www.whchamber.com. **Greater Hartford Tourism District** | 234 Murphy Rd., Hartford, 06114 | 860/244–8181 or 800/793–4480 | fax 860/244–8180 | ctfuntour@aol.com | www.enjoyhartford.com.

Attractions

Museum of American Political Life. The museum on the campus of the University of Hartford houses rare political materials and memorabilia—buttons, posters, bumper stickers, and pamphlets—from the campaigns of U.S. presidents starting with George Washington and going up to the present. A small section is devoted to memorabilia from the women's rights and temperance movements. | 200 Bloomfield Ave. | 860/768–4090 | Free | Sept.–May, Tues.–Fri. 11–4, weekends noon–4; June–Aug., Tues.–Fri. 11–4, Sat. noon–4.

Noah Webster House and Museum. This is the birthplace of the famed author (1758–1843) of the *American Dictionary*. The 18th-century farmhouse contains Webster memorabilia and period furnishings, which you can see on the guided tour. | 227 S. Main St. | 860/521–5362 | $5 | Sept.–June, daily 1–4; July–Aug., Mon.–Tues. and Thurs.–Fri. 10–4 weekends 1–4.

★ **Science Center of Connecticut.** This is the kind of museum that makes you glad you have kids to give you an excuse to visit it. A life-size walk-through replica of a 60-ft sperm whale greets patrons. Additional attractions include a wildlife sanctuary and a planetarium. The Kids Factory teaches about magnetics, motion, optics, sound, and light through colorful hands-on exhibits. Some "Mathmagical" toys in the lower exhibit hall are a giant bubble maker, a hands-on weather station, and a walk-in kaleidoscope. | 950 Trout Brook Dr. | 860/231–2824 | fax 860/232–0705 | www.sciencecenterct.org | $6; laser and planetarium shows $3 | Call for hrs.

ON THE CALENDAR
JUNE: ***Celebrate! West Hartford.*** Arts and crafts, entertainment, children's activities, food, sporting events, and more are on offer at this celebration. | 860/523–3159.

Dining

The Back Porch Bistro. Contemporary. This popular local favorite has open-air dining on the porch and a farmhouse interior. Try the steamed mussels with saffron and white wine sauce or the grilled salmon with citrus glaze. Save room for the hot apple crisp at dessert. | 971 Farmington Ave. | 860/231–1922 | Closed Sun. | $15–$21 | AE, MC, V.

Butterfly Chinese Restaurant. Chinese. The dining room of this restaurant is done is black and pink. It is one of the most popular Chinese restaurants in the state and serves Cantonese food. | 831 Farmington Ave. | 860/236–2816 | $6–$17 | AE, MC, V.

Lodging

West Hartford Inn. This modern, five-story brick hotel is family owned and has comfortable, spacious rooms. It is West Hartford's only hotel and is close to local attractions. Complimentary Contiental breakfast. Cable TV. Laundry service. No pets. | 900 Farmington Ave. | 860/236–3221 | fax 860/236–3445 | www.westhartfordinn.com | 53 rooms | $84 | AE, DC, MC, V.

WESTPORT

MAP 3, C7

(Nearby towns also listed: Bridgeport, Fairfield, New Canaan, Norwalk)

Westport, an artists' mecca since the turn of the century, continues to attract creative types. Despite commuters and corporations, Westport remains more arty and cultured than its neighbors: If the rest of Fairfield County is stylistically five years behind Manhattan, Westport lags by just five months. Paul Newman and Joanne Woodward have their main residence here. Greens Farms is the neighborhood by the water and Sherwood Island State Park has great beaches.

Information: Chamber of Commerce | Box 30, Westport, 06881 | 203/227–9234 | fax 203/454–4019 | wcc@webquill.com | www.bcnnews.com/westport/chamber. **Coastal Fairfield County Convention and Visitor Bureau** | 297 West Ave., Gate Lodge-Mathews Park, Norwalk, 06850 | 203/899–2799 or 800/866–7925 | fax 203/853–7524 | info@visitfairfieldco.org | www.visitfairfieldco.org.

Attractions

Nature Center for Environmental Activities. This 62-acre wildlife sanctuary has 3 mi of trails, including a swamp loop trail and a trail for the visually impaired. The center's museum has a marine touch tank, a wildlife rehabilitation center, and changing exhibits relating to the local environment. | 10 Woodside La. | 203/227–7253 | fax 203/227–8909 | $1 | Museum Mon.–Sat. 9–5, Sun. 1–4; sanctuary daily dawn–dusk.

Sherwood Island State Park. Summer visitors to Westport congregate at this state park, which has a 1½-mi sweep of sandy beach, two water's-edge picnic groves, an environmental-protection museum with artifacts from the parks and forestry divisions, and several food concessions. | I–95, Exit 18 | 203/226–6983 | $5–$12; free after Labor Day | Grounds daily dawn–dusk; museums and concessions Memorial Day–Labor Day daily.

ON THE CALENDAR

JUNE–AUG.: *Levitt Pavilion for the Performing Arts.* More than 60 free concerts are staged at this outdoor pavilion close to downtown Westport and the Saugatuck River. | 203/221–4422.

JUNE–SEPT.: *Westport Country Playhouse.* A revered summer stock professional theater in business for more than 70 years. | 25 Powers Ct | 203/227–4177.

JULY: *Outdoor Arts Festival.* You can choose your preferred art form: paintings, sculpture, photography, performing arts, or interactive arts at this annual festival. | Main St. | 203/226–4261.

AUG.: *White Barn Theatre.* Weekend performances of new works by both well-known and up-and-coming artists take place at this theater. | 452 Newtown Ave. | 203/227–3768.

Dining

Acqua. Mediterranean. Resembling a Tuscan villa, this restaurant has handpainted frescos on its ceiling and walls. The dining room has a wood-burning oven and tumbled marble on the floor. Try the wood-oven cooked pizzas, pasta, free range chicken, carpaccio of beef, lobster, or Dover sole, the most popular dish. Sun. brunch. No smoking (except in bar). | 43 Main St. | 203/222–8899 | No lunch Sun. | $11–$30 | AE, DC, MC, V.

Bridge Café. Contemporary. This restaurant on the west bank of the Saugatuck River has oriental rugs on its tile floor and contemporary oil paintings on its stucco wall. The menu features pasta, veal, shellfish, beef, tuna, and chicken. Open-air dining on the stone patio overlooking the river. Sun. brunch. No smoking. | 5 Riverside Ave. | 203/226–4800 | No lunch Sun. | $20–$32 | AE, DC, MC, V.

Cobb's Mill Inn. Continental. A Colonial-style, three-story restaurant with a view of the waterfall that is 3 mi north of Westport. It's known for foie gras, Fishers Island oysters, and domestic lamb. Sun. brunch. | 12 Old Mill Rd., Weston | 203/227–7221 | No lunch Mon. and Sat. | $17–$36 | AE, D, DC, MC, V.

Da Pietro's. Contemporary. The eight tables of this restaurant have fine china and are lit by candles. Handpainted silk scarfs adorn the walls. Try the roasted monkfish with curry-coconut sauce, lasagna of French snails, sautéed veal tenderloins, or roast rack of lamb with wine and garlic sauce. | 36 Riverside Ave. | 203/454–1213 | Closed Sun. No lunch | $17–$27 | AE, DC, MC, V.

Miramar. Contemporary. The walls of this sophisticated restaurant are either hand-rubbed, creating texture and color, or mahogany. The mahogany bar has a glowing alabaster top. Try the grilled sirloin over Tuscan bruschetta, yellowfin tuna tartar or the paella. Open-air dining on patio with river views. Sun. brunch. | 2 Post Rd. W | 203/222–2267 | $22–$29 | AE, D, DC, MC, V.

Splash. Pacific Rim. Cutting-edge cuisine is served in a white clapboard country inn at this eatery. Try the calamari salad with tossed greens and chile oil. Open-air dining on a veranda overlooking Long Island Sound. Sun. brunch. | 260 Compo Rd. S | 203/454–7798 | Closed Mon. from Sept.–May | $21–$38 | AE, D, MC, V.

★ **Tavern on Main.** American. A landmark 19th-century building in downtown serving sophisticated New American comfort food. Try the wild mushroom ravioli or potato-wrapped sea bass. Open-air dining under a canopy on the terrace overlooking Main Street. Sun. brunch. | 146 Main St. | 203/221–7222 | $12–$25 | AE, DC, MC, V.

The Three Bears. Contemporary. One of Westport's landmark restaurants is this spot with six fireplaces and an extensive menu. Start with the salmon pepper grilled aïoli with roasted eggplant purée or the grilled asparagus in tarragon oil before moving onto the giant pork chop with pickled red onion chutney in a port wine glaze. Kid's menu. Sun. brunch. | 333 Wilton Rd. | 203/227–7219 | Closed Mon. No lunch Sun. | $16–$26 | AE, DC, MC, V.

Lodging

The Inn at Longshore. This inn is furnished in Colonial-style colors and was recently refurbished. The rooms have chairs, a table and views of either the Sound or the golf course. Complimentary Continental breakfast. Cable TV. Pool. Driving range, 18-hole golf course, 9 tennis courts. Business services. | 260 S. Compo Rd. | 203/226–3316 | fax 203/226–5723 | 9 rooms, 3 suites | $125–$195 | AE, MC, V.

★ **Inn at National Hall.** A three-story building on the banks of the Saugatuck River that was built in 1873, but only became a hotel in 1993. Most of the individually decorated rooms have views of the river. All the rooms are named—e.g. the India Room, which has handpainted murals on the walls, the Watermelon Room, the Gold Star Room, etc. Most of the rooms have king or queen canopy beds. Restaurant, bar, complimentary Continental break-

fast, room service. Refrigerators, cable TV. Laundry service. Business services. No smoking.
| 2 Post Rd. W | 203/221–1351 or 800/628–4255 | fax 203/221–0276 | www.innatnationalhall.com
| 8 rooms, 7 suites | $255–$650 | AE, D, DC, MC, V.

Westport Inn. A full-service motor lodge with standard rooms. The two-story motel also
has balconies. Restaurant, bar, room service. Cable TV. Indoor pool. Hot tub, sauna. Gym.
Laundry service. Business services. | 1595 Post Rd. E | 203/259–5236 or 800/446–8997 | fax
203/254–8439 | 116 rooms | $124–$164 | AE, D, DC, MC, V.

WETHERSFIELD

MAP 3, E3

*(Nearby towns also listed: Glastonbury, Hartford, Middletown, New Britain, West
Hartford)*

Wethersfield, a vast Hartford suburb, dates from 1634. As was the case throughout
early Connecticut, some of the Native Americans indigenous to these lands fought
the arriving English with a vengeance; here their struggles culminated in the 1637
Wethersfield Massacre, when Pequot Indians killed nine settlers. Three years later, the
citizens held a public election, America's first defiance of British rule, for which they
were fined five British pounds.

Information: Associated Chambers of Commerce | 250 Constitution Plaza, Hartford,
06103 | 860/527–9258 | fax 860/293–2592 | info@metrohartford.com | www.metro-
hartford.com. **Greater Hartford Tourism District** | 234 Murphy Rd., Hartford, 06114 | 860/
244–8181 or 800/793–4480 | fax 860/244–8180 | ctfuntour@aol.com | www.enjoy-
hartford.com.

Attractions

Buttolph-Williams House. This turn-of-the-century landmark has a fine collection of
period furnishings. | 249 Broad St. | 860/529–0460 | Call for admission prices | May–Oct.,
Wed.–Mon. 10–4.

Comstock Ferre and Co. Founded in 1820, this is the country's oldest continuously operating seed company. It's in a chestnut post-and-beam building, a National Historic Landmark, that dates to the late 1700s. Comstock Ferre sells more than 800 varieties of seeds
and 3,000 varieties of perennials. | 263 Main St. | 860/571–6590 | Free | Wed.–Sun. 9–5.

Dinosaur State Park. What kids aren't fascinated by dinosaurs? They're sure to enjoy the
Jurassic-period dinosaur tracks that are housed under a geodesic dome at this state park,
3 mi south of Wethersfield. You can make plaster casts of the tracks to bring home (call
ahead for instructions on what materials to bring). There are dioramas depicting the
area in prehistoric times, a picnic area, museum shop, and nature trails. | 400 West St.,
Rocky Hill | 860/529–8423 | www.dinosaurstatepark.org | $2 | Park daily 9–4:30; center Tues.–
Sun. 9–4:30.

Webb-Deane-Stevens Museum. The Joseph Webb House, Silas Deane House, and Isaac Stevens
House, all built in the mid- to late 1700s, form one of the state's best historic house museums. The structures, well-preserved examples of Georgian architecture, reflect their owners' lifestyles as a merchant, a diplomat, and a tradesman, respectively. The Webb House,
a registered National Historic Landmark, was the site of the strategy conference between
George Washington and the French general Jean-Baptiste Rochambeau that led to the British
defeat at Yorktown. | 211 Main St. | 860/529–0612 | $8 | May–Oct., Wed.–Mon. daily 10–4;
Nov.–Apr., weekends 10–4.

ON THE CALENDAR

MAY: *Wethersfield Weekend Festival.* A weekend of activities that pay tribute to the town's maritime past, including special tours and museum exhibits and a re-created waterfront with costumed interpreters. | 860/721–2890.

Dining

Ruth's Chris Steak House. Steak. The place to go for serious steak is this eatery with leather-cushioned, high back booths that is 100 yards west of Wethersfield. Every steak is served sizzling hot and dripping with butter. Heat from a 1,800°F oven seals in the juices. | 2513 Berlin Tpke., Newington | 860/666–2202 | No lunch | $18–$26 | AE, D, DC, MC, V.

Lodging

Chester Bulkley House. This 1830 Greek Revival House in the heart of historic Old Wethersfield is only steps away from antique shops, museums, restaurants, and the river. Rooms evoke the 19th-century through the carefully selected assortment of period furnishings. An outdoor patio allows you to sun yourself when the weather permits. Complimentary breakfast. No room phones, no TV. No pets. No smoking. | 184 Main St. | 860/563–4236 | fax 860/257–8266 | 5 rooms | $85–$95 | AE, D, DC, MC, V.

Ramada Inn. This four-story, spacious chain option is near I–91 and has rooms with either king or double beds. Complimentary Continental breakfast, room service. Cable TV. Laundry service. Business services. Pets allowed. | 1330 Silas Deane Hwy. | 860/563–2311 | 111 rooms | $66–$89 | AE, D, DC, MC, V.

WINDSOR LOCKS

MAP 3, F2

(Nearby towns also listed: Enfield, Hartford, Stafford Springs)

Windsor Locks was named for the locks of a canal built in 1833 to bypass falls in the Connecticut River; the canal closed to make way for a railroad line. Most will recognize the town as the home of Bradley International Airport, the central transportation hub in the state. Along Route 20 to the airport you will see evidence of the reason behind the area's designation as Tobacco Valley—tobacco fields where broadleaf tobacco for cigar wrappers is still grown.

Information: North Central Connecticut Chamber of Commerce | 113 Elm St., Enfield, 06082-3719 | 860/741–3838 | fax 860/741–3512 | chamber@ncccc.org. **Connecticut's North Central Tourism Bureau** | 111 Hazard Ave., Enfield, 06082 | 860/763–2578 or 800/248–8283 | fax 860/749–1822 | eileen@cnctb.org | www.cnctb.org.

Attractions

Connecticut Fire Museum. This museum 2 mi east of Windsor Locks and on the same grounds as the Connecticut Trolley Museum covers 100 years of fire trucks (1850–1950) and also features models and memorabilia covering the history of this noble profession. | 58 North Rd., East Windsor | 860/623–4732 | $2 | July–Aug., weekdays 10–4, weekends noon–5; May–June and Sept.–Oct., weekends noon–5.

Connecticut Trolley Museum. Clang, clang, clang goes the antique trolley on the 3½-mi ride at this museum 2 mi east of Windsor Locks. Cars date from 1894 to 1949; there is also a visitor center with restored trolley cars and memorabilia, a gift shop, and a picnic area. | 58 North Rd., East Windsor | 860/627–6540 | fax 860/627–6510 | $6 | Memorial Day–Labor Day, Mon.–Sat. 10–5, Sun. noon–5; Labor Day–mid Oct. and Apr.–Memorial Day, Sat. 10–5, Sun. noon–5.

★ **New England Air Museum.** The more than 80 historic aircraft at this museum include flying machines that date from 1870. A World War II–era P-47 Thunderbolt and B-29 Superfortress are on display, along with other vintage fighters and bombers. Open cockpit on Sunday, held periodically, allows you a chance to climb aboard. | Rte. 75, at Bradley International Airport | 860/623–3305 | www.neam.org | $6.50 | Daily 10–5.

Old New-Gate Prison and Copper Mine. This was the country's first chartered copper mine (in 1707) and later (in 1773) Connecticut's first Colonial prison. Tours of the underground mine (where temperatures rarely top 55°F) are a great way to chill out in summer. It is 2 mi west of Windsor Locks | Newgate Rd., East Granby | 860/653–3563 or 860/566–3005 | $3 | Mid-May–Oct., Wed.–Sun. 10–4:30.

ON THE CALENDAR

MAY: *Arts and Crafts Festival.* The Windsor Town Green is the site of this annual festival, which features more than 100 craftspeople and artisans and is part of the town's celebration of the return of the shad to the waters of the Connecticut and Farmington rivers. | 860/688–5393.

JULY–AUG.: *Concert Under the Stars.* Each Thursday night for a 7 week period different bands perform on the town green. The bands range from reggae to youth ensembles. | 860/285–1990.

Dining

Albert's Restaurant and Cigar Bar. American. This restaurant has a separate cigar bar-lounge. Try the create-your-own-combo by mixing baby back ribs, shrimp scampi, clams casino, broiled pork chops. | 159 Ella Grasso Tpke | 860/292–6801 | $9–$18.95 | AE, D, DC, MC, V.

Concorde's Restaurant. Continental. Watch planes take off and land from the restaurant in the Sheraton Hotel. Try the grilled swordfish or the Black Angus prime rib. Live jazz on sundays. | 1 Bradley International Airport Rd. | 860/627–5311 | $14–$24 | AE, D, DC, MC, V.

The Mill on the River Restaurant. Continental. A 200-year-old grist mill is home to this restaurant with exposed wood beams. It's on the water and 3 mi south of Windsor Locks. There are thirty different fountains on the property and in the restaurant. Try the redfish nouvelle or pasta maison. Sun. brunch. No smoking. | 989 Ellington Rd., South Windsor | 860/289–7929 | No lunch weekends | $15–$20 | AE, D, DC, MC, V.

Lodging

Courtyard by Marriott. A two-story chain option 2 mi south of Windsor Locks and near I–91 that has standard rooms with your choice of king or double beds. Some of the rooms have balconies. Restaurant. In-room data ports, cable TV. Indoor pool. Gym. Video games. Laundry facilities, laundry service. Business services, airport shuttle. | 1 Day Hill Rd., Windsor | 860/683–0022 | fax 860/683–1072 | 149 rooms | $140–165 | AE, D, DC, MC, V.

Doubletree Bradley Airport. This five-story airport hotel is a mile from Bradley International Airport. A concierge-level guest lounge for business travelers was recently installed. You'll be offered chocolate chip cookies at check-in. Room service. In-room data ports. Gym. Laundry facilities, laundry services. Business services. | 16 Ella Grasso Tpke | 860/627–5171 | 198 rooms, 2 suites | $169–$199 | AE, D, DC, MC, V.

Fairfield Inn Hartford Airport. This three-story hotel is just a mile south of the airport. The Copper Hill Country Club is only 10 minutes away in Granby (5 mi to the northwest). Complimentary Continental breakfast. In-room data ports, cable TV. Pool. Laundry services. Business services, airport shuttle. No pets. | 2 Loten Dr. | 860/627–9333 | 135 rooms | $84 | AE, D, DC, MC, V. .

Homewood Suites. A three-story, all-suites hotel that is 1 mi from airport. It was refurbished in January 2000 and you can get a two-room suite with separate living room. Complimentary Continental breakfast. In-room data ports, kitchenettes, cable TV. Pool. Hot tub. Gym. Laundry facilities, laundry service. Business services, airport shuttle. | 65 Ella Grasso Tpke | 860/627–8463 | fax 860/627–9313 | 132 suites | $169–$249 | AE, D, DC, MC, V.

Residence Inn by Marriott. A chain option near both I–91 and the airport and 9 mi south of Windsor Locks. The rooms have two double beds, a table and chairs. Complimentary Continental breakfast. Cable TV. Pool. Hot tub. Business services, airport shuttle. Pets allowed. | 100 Dunfey La., Windsor | 860/688–7474 | 96 suites | $149–$179 | AE, D, DC, MC, V.

Sheraton Bradley Airport Hotel. This chain option is in Bradley International Airport and some of the rooms have views of the runway. It's just a five-minute walk to the terminals from here. Restaurant, bar, complimentary Continental breakfast, room service. Cable TV. Indoor pool. Sauna. Gym. Laundry service. Business services. | 1 Bradley International Airport | 860/627–5311 | fax 860/627–9348 | 237 rooms | $179–$219 | AE, D, DC, MC, V.

WOODBURY

MAP 3, C4

(Nearby towns also listed: New Preston, Washington, Waterbury)

There may very well be more antiques shops in the town of Woodbury than in all the towns in the Litchfield Hills combined. Five magnificent churches and the Greek Revival King Solomon's Temple, formerly a Masonic lodge, line U.S. 6; they represent some of the finest-preserved examples of Colonial religious architecture in New England.

SOMETHING OLD

Woodbury is known as the antiques capital of Connecticut. It's hard to argue with this self-proclaimed designation when there are more than 30 shops in this town of roughly 8,600 residents. What is especially enticing is the fact that the majority of the shops are along scenic U.S. 6, a pretty little winding road through the hills and valleys of Litchfield County.

British Country Antiques (203/263–5100) occupies 7,000 square ft of house and barn showrooms highlighting 18th- and 19th-century English pine and French fruitwood country furnishings. Hamrah's Oriental Rug Co. (203/266–4343) has a premium collection of Persian and European rugs and tapestries. Monique Shay Antiques (203/263–3186) specializes in French Canadian painted cupboards, armoires, tables, and accessories. Jennings & Rohn (203/263–3775) covers the centuries with European furniture, accessories, old master paintings, and drawings from the 16th to 20th centuries. Thomas Schwenke Antiques (203/266–0303), meanwhile, specializes in American Federal and English from 1780 to 1820.

And then there's Le Manoir Country French Antiques for Quimper faience, Nancy Fierberg for Americana, Wayne Pratt for 18th- and 19th-century furniture and custom copies of rare antiques . . .

For more information and a complete list of dealers, call the Litchfield Hills Travel Council at 860/567–4506.

Make a day of it. Make a weekend of it.

© Corbis

Information: **Greater Waterbury Chamber of Commerce** | 83 Bank St., Box 1469, Woodbury, 06721 | 203/757–0701 | fax 203/756–3507 | wby.chamber@snet.net | www.waterburychamber.org. **Litchfield Hills Visitors Council** | Box 968, Litchfield, 06759 | 860/567–4506 | fax 860/567–5214 | www.litchfieldhills.com.

Attractions

Abbey of Regina Laudis. The Benedictine nuns here were made famous by their best-selling CD *Women in Chant.* The nuns make and sell fine handicrafts, honey, cheese, herbs, beauty products, and more. An 18th-century Neopolitan crèche with 80 hand-painted Baroque porcelain figures is on view from March through December. It is 15 mi east of Woodbury. | Flanders Rd., Bethlehem | 203/266–7637 | Free | Mon.–Tues. and Thurs.–Sun. 10–4.

Flanders Nature Center/Land Trust. Van Vleck Farm and Whittemore sanctuaries are both a part of this scenic nature center nestled in Woodbury's rolling hills. A Christmas tree farm, hiking trails, and gardening programs are among the center's highlights. | Church Hill and Flanders Rds | 203/263–3711 | Free | Daily dawn–dusk.

Glebe House Museum and Gertrude Jekyll Garden. In this large gambrel-roof Colonial, Dr. Samuel Seabury was elected America's first Episcopal bishop in 1783. It holds an excellent collection of antiques. British horticulturist Gertrude Jekyll designed the historic garden—her only existing garden in the United States. | Hollow Rd. | 203/263–2855 | $4 | Apr.–Nov., Wed.–Sun. 1–4.

Woodbury Ski Area. This small, laid-back ski area with a 300-ft drop has 18 downhill trails of varying difficulty that are serviced by a double chairlift, three rope tows, a handle tow, and a T-bar. About half of the 9 mi of cross-country trails are groomed, and 1 mi is lighted and covered by snowmaking. There's a snowboard and alpine park, a skateboard and in-line skating park, an area for mountain biking in the snow, and a special area for sledding and tubing serviced by its own lifts and tows. Snow biking and snowshoeing are other options. Ski parties are held Friday and Saturday nights in the base lodge; lessons are given for ages 2 and up. | Rte. 47 | 203/263–2203 | fax 203/263–2823 | www.woodburyskiarea.com | Nov.–early Apr.

ON THE CALENDAR

APR.–NOV.: *Woodbury Flea Market.* Saturday is the day to visit this venerable market. | 203/263–2841.

DEC.: *Christmas Town Festival.* This weekend festival in Bethlehem features arts and crafts, hayrides, carolers, food booths, and the opportunity to get your Christmas cards postmarked in this "Christmas town." | 203/266–5557.

Dining

Carmen Anthony Fish House. Seafood. This upscale restaurant has oil paintings on the walls, teak and mahogany appointments, and a bronze statue of a mermaid. Try the 2- to 6-pound lobsters, Alaskan crab legs, oysters Rockefeller, or sautéed salmon. Live piano music weekends. Kid's menu. | 757 Main St. S | 203/266–0011 | No lunch Sun. | $16–$30 | AE, DC, V.

★ **Carole Peck's Good News Café.** Contemporary. A modern restaurant with changing artwork. The healthy, innovative, New American fare is prepared by one of the state's most revered chefs. Try the baked lobster macaroni, horseradish crusted halibut with beet relish, or the spicy pork tenderloin with coconut rice and mixed melon salsa. | 694 Main St. S | 203/266–4663 | Closed Tues. | $15–$28 | AE, DC, MC, V.

Curtis House. American. A 1736 inn at the foot of antiques row is home to this restaurant known for seafood, steak, and roasts. Kid's menu. | U.S. 6 | 203/263–2101 | No lunch Mon. | $15–$21 | AE, D, MC, V.

Lodging

Curtis House. This two-story, Colonial inn was built in 1736 and became a hotel in 1754. The rooms have antiques and canopy beds. You can relax in the gardens. Two-night minimum stay on weekends. Restaurant, bar. Cable TV in some rooms, no TV in some rooms. No smoking. | 506 Main St. S | 203/263–2101 | www.curtishouse.com | 18 rooms | $67–$123 | D, MC, V.

The Heritage. A conference resort that caters to business retreats. The rooms have flowered blankets and sheets along with carpeted floors. Some of the rooms in the three-story building 1 mi west of Woodbury have views of the golf course. Restaurant, bar, room service. Cable TV. 2 pools (1 indoor). Barbershop, hot tub, massage, sauna, steam room. 9-hole golf course, 2 tennis courts. Gym, racquetball. Fishing. Bicycles. Baby-sitting, laundry service. Business center. | 522 Heritage Rd., Southbury | 203/264–8200 or 800/932–3466 | fax 203/264–5035 | www.dolce.com | 158 rooms, 5 suites | $119–$169 | AE, D, DC, MC, V.

Hilton. A three-story, full-service hotel in a quiet setting and ½ mi south of Woodbury. The rooms are filled with Ethan Allan furniture and were renovated in 2000. Restaurant, bar, room service. Cable TV. Indoor pool. Hot tub, sauna. Gym. Laundry service. Business services. Pets allowed. | 1284 Strongtown Rd., Southbury | 203/598–7600 | fax 203/598–0837 | 198 rooms | $105–$155 | AE, D, DC, MC, V.

Hummingbird Hill. A red clapboard house in the middle of Woodbury's historic district, this inn provides terrycloth bathrobes in each room, as well as fresh chocolates, nightly. Complimentary breakfast. TV in common area. | 891 Main St. South | 203/ 263–3733 | 2 rooms | $90 | AE, MC, V.

WOODSTOCK

MAP 3, I2

(Nearby towns also listed: Brooklyn, Pomfret, Putnam)

The landscape of this enchanting town is splendid in every season—the gently rolling hills seem to stretch for miles. Roseland, Henry Bowen's spectacular Carpenter Gothic summer "cottage," now a property of the Society for the Preservation of New England Antiquities, is reason alone to visit.

Information: Northeastern Connecticut Chamber of Commerce | 3 Central St., Danielson, 06239 | 860/774–8001 | fax 860/774–4299 | elizabeth.kuszaj@snet.net. **Northeast Connecticut Visitors District** | Box 598, Putnam, 06260 | 860/928–1228 or 888/628–1228 | fax 860/928–4720 | quietcorner@snet.net | www.webtravels.com/quietcorner.

Attractions

Roseland Cottage. This pink board-and-batten Gothic Revival home, built in 1846 by New York publisher and merchant Henry Bowen, is likely the region's most notable historic home. All of the antiques are from the original owners, as are the Chinese wall coverings. Even the garden has the original box wood hedges that four presidents—Ulysses S. Grant, Rutherford B. Hayes, Benjamin Harrison, and William McKinley—have visited and Henry Bowen's original design for the flower gardens has been preserved. The original ice house, privy wood shed, garden house and carriage house remain. There's even an indoor bowling alley with the original pins and balls. | Rte. 169 | 860/928–4074 | $4 | June–mid-Oct., Wed.–Sun. 11–5. Tours on the hr; last tour at 4.

Scranton Shops. The site for these local artists and crafts shops was once an early New England blacksmith shop and is 1 mi south of Woodstock. Some 90 local artisans show work here. You'll find Fox Hunt Farms behind the shops. | 300 Rte. 169, South Woodstock | 860/ 928–3738 | Daily 11–5.

ON THE CALENDAR

MAY: *May Day Celebration.* Dancing around the May Pole and children's activities take place at Roseland Cottage. | 860/928–4074.

SEPT.: *Woodstock Fair.* The state's second oldest agricultural fair. | 860/928–3246.

OCT.: *Walking Weekend.* Woodstock is just one of 25 towns in the northeastern corner of the state that participates in this weekend of more than 50 guided walks. | 860/928–1228.

DEC.: *Christmas Carol Sing.* A holiday carol sing in the barn at Roseland Cottage. | 860/928–4074.

Dining

Fox Hunt Farms Gourmet and Café. American/Casual. A country café on 4 picturesque acres that serves sandwiches, salads, wraps, and soups. There are tables on the deck for outdoor dining. No smoking. | 292 Rte. 169 | 860/928–0714 | Closed Mon. | $7–$18 | No credit cards.

Inn at Woodstock Hill. Continental. Here you'll dine among chintz and reproduction antiques in a rambling white clapboard inn. Try the baked Dijon rack of lamb, grilled swordfish, or veal chops. No smoking. Kid's menu. Sun. brunch. | 94 Plaine Hill Rd. | 860/928–0528 | Closed Mon. | $16–$28 | D, MC, V.

Lodging

Inn at Woodstock Hill. The rooms in this white clapboard country inn have four-poster or canopy beds. All are decorated with Waverly chintz-style fabrics and some have fireplaces. Restaurant, complimentary Continental breakfast. In-room data ports, cable TV. Business services. | 94 Plaine Hill Rd. | 860/928–0528 | fax 860/928–3236 | www.webtravels.com/woodstockhill | 22 rooms | $90–$155 | D, MC, V.

B & B at Taylor's Corner This inn, built in 1795 and renovated in 1988, features eight working fireplaces. The rooms are furnished with antiques and reproductions and all have fireplaces. Many of the rooms overlook the herb and flower gardens in the back. Complimentary breakfast. Cable TV in some rooms, no TV in some rooms, some in-room VCRs, TV in common area. No pets. No kids under 12. No smoking. | 880 Rte. 171 | 860/974–0490 | 3 rooms, 1 suite | $80–$140; $195 suite | AE, D, DC, MC, V. .

TOP TIPS FOR TRAVELERS

Smart Sightseeings

Don't plan your visit in your hotel room. Don't wait until you pull into town to decide how to spend your days. It's inevitable that there will be much more to see and do than you'll have time for: choose sights in advance.

Organize your touring. Note the places that most interest you on a map, and visit places that are near each other during the same morning or afternoon.

Start the day well equipped. Leave your hotel in the morning with everything you need for the day—maps, medicines, extra film, your guidebook, rain gear, and another layer of clothing in case the weather turns cooler.

Tour museums early. If you're there when the doors open you'll have an intimate experience of the collection.

Easy does it. See museums in the mornings, when you're fresh, and visit sit-down attractions later on. Take breaks before you need them.

Strike up a conversation. Only curmudgeons don't respond to a smile and a polite request for information. Most people appreciate your interest in their home town. And your conversations may end up being your most vivid memories.

Get lost. When you do, you never know what you'll find—but you can count on it being memorable. Use your guidebook to help you get back on track. Build wandering-around time into every day.

Quit before you're tired. There's no point in seeing that one extra sight if you're too exhausted to enjoy it.

Take your mother's advice. Go to the bathroom when you have the chance. You never know what lies ahead.

Hotel How-Tos

How to get a deal. After you've chosen a likely candidate or two, phone them directly and price a room for your travel dates. Then call the hotel's toll-free number and ask the same questions. Also try consolidators and hotel-room discounters. You won't hear the same rates twice. On the spot, make a reservation as soon as you are quoted a price you want to pay.

Promises, promises. If you have special requests, make them when you reserve. Get written confirmation of any promises.

Settle in. Upon arriving, make sure everything works—lights and lamps, TV and radio, sink, tub, shower, and anything else that matters. Report any problems immediately. And don't wait until you need extra pillows or blankets or an ironing board to call housekeeping. Also check out the fire emergency instructions. Know where to find the fire exits, and make sure your companions do, too.

If you need to complain. Be polite but firm. Explain the problem to the person in charge. Suggest a course of action. If you aren't satisfied, repeat your requests to the manager. Document everything: Take pictures and keep a written record of who you've spoken with, when, and what was said. Contact your travel agent, if he made the reservations.

Know the score. When you go out, take your hotel's business cards (one for everyone in your party). If you have extras, you can give them out to new acquaintances who want to call you.

Tip up front. For special services, a tip or partial tip in advance can work wonders.

Use all the hotel resources A concierge can make difficult things easy. But a desk clerk, bellhop, or other hotel employee who's friendly, smart, and ambitious can often steer you straight as well. A gratuity is in order if the advice is helpful.

© Artville

Massachusetts

There's no hiding the fact that Massachusetts is little. It's the nation's sixth smallest state, diminutive enough to fit comfortably within Texas some 30 times over. Yet if ever a state offered a convincing case for good things coming in small packages, it's Massachusetts. From sandy beaches shaped by the Atlantic Ocean to mountaintops whose vistas encompass New York and Vermont, the state's diverse landscape has been attracting tourists since the days of stagecoaches and steam engines. So few miles lie between ocean surf and lofty pine-covered peaks that a determined traveler could enjoy a morning saltwater swim, spend the afternoon hiking at the opposite end of the state, and be back in time for a fresh seafood dinner overlooking the ocean. At the same time, it sometimes appears as if every square mile of Massachusetts has a museum, historic site, scenic view, nature trail, or other attraction inviting discovery. For maximum enjoyment, you'll want to decide at the outset whether to concentrate on one or two regions within the state, thoroughly soaking up the sights and activities, or whether to see and do a little bit of everything, knowing you'll have to pass over plenty of temptations vying for your attention along the way.

The state's principal magnet for tourists and residents alike is its vast coast. Although the overland distance between its northern and southern coastal neighbors barely exceeds 100 mi, wedged within this small span are nearly 2,000 mi of shoreline. Highlights include the great barrier beaches at the mouth of the Merrimack River, the rocky granite ledges surrounding Cape Ann, the score of park-protected islands in Boston Harbor, and the windswept dunes of the Cape Cod National Seashore. From decades-old artist colonies in weather-beaten former fishing communities to family beach resorts whose popularity predates the automobile, Massachusetts clearly lives up to its Bay State nickname with the fuss it makes over its waterfront.

CAPITAL: BOSTON		POPULATION: 6,041,123	AREA: 8,257 SQUARE MILES
BORDERS: RI; CT; NY; VT; NH; THE ATLANTIC OCEAN	TIME ZONE: EASTERN	POSTAL ABBREVIATION: MA	
WEB SITE: WWW.MAGNET.STATE.MA.US			

The lion's share of seaside tourism belongs to Cape Cod and its offshore islands of Nantucket and Martha's Vineyard. So much so, in fact, that their economies are almost wholly dependent on the "summer people" who fill beaches, shops, and seafood shacks for as long as the weather allows. Busy marinas attest to the appeal of what's offshore, as well, as local waters lure sailing and sportfishing enthusiasts from all over the East Coast.

As it happens, the state's single most popular coastal attraction isn't a beach or quaint fishing village at all, but rather New England's biggest city: Boston. Although much of its formerly industrial harborfront has been revitalized with the addition of public promenades and cruise boats, Boston's most bankable asset is its history. The city's 370-year evolution from Puritan colony in an uncharted New World to a thriving modern commercial center has given it more than its fair share of history-making people and events commemorated in museums and historic sites all over town. The Greater Boston metropolitan area is also home to half the state's population, all its major sports teams, scores of colleges and universities, and one of the nation's busiest international airports—all of which makes it easy to see why "the Hub" is true to its nickname as both the principal destination for more than 11 million business and leisure travelers every year and the gateway to the entire New England region.

If you can resist spending your whole vacation in the city or by the ocean, you may be pleasantly surprised to discover that Massachusetts has as much or more to offer visitors away from the coast as on it. Stroll battlefields on which Colonial Minutemen stood up to King George's finest regiments of Redcoats. Explore the Merrimack River mill towns that rose and fell with the Industrial Age, their great hydro-powered facto-

STATE SYMBOLS

Every state has its nickname and state flower, its state tree, bird, and song. But how many have a state cookie, bean, or polka? State emblems have grown a lot more interesting since you last wrote school reports on them. Nowadays kids in elementary grades are as apt to create the symbols as look them up in an encyclopedia. Class projects launched by Massachusetts schoolchildren over the past decade now vie with legislators' regional jingoism when it comes to expanding the state's list of official symbols. That state cookie, for instance, was nominated by third-graders. Of course it's chocolate chip, in honor of America's original chocolate-chip cookie, invented at Massachusetts's Toll House Restaurant in 1930. Schoolkids also had a hand in designating the state muffin (corn), the state dessert (Boston cream pie), the state berry (cranberry), and the state cat (the tabby). Other endearing expressions of local pride have resulted in the designation of the navy bean as Massachusetts's official state bean, for its starring role in Boston baked beans; Johnny Appleseed as the official folk hero of the Commonwealth, because he was born here; the Boston terrier as the state dog, since it was the first purebred species developed in America; and "Say Hello to Someone from Massachusetts" as the official state polka, because, well, it has the state's name in the title.

© Corbis

INTRODUCTION
HISTORY
REGIONS
WHEN TO VISIT
STATE'S GREATS
RULES OF THE ROAD
DRIVING TOURS

ries preserved in tribute to Yankee ingenuity and immigrant labor. Spend a morning shopping in arts-and-crafts-filled college towns, head for the hills in the afternoon to hike in the extensive forests crowning the rugged central and western highlands, and finish the day with fine fireside dining in a classic country inn. Leave room in your itinerary for chance encounters, too, for sprinkled throughout the state's interior are tidy little villages straight out of a Norman Rockwell calendar. With soaring church steeples, jumbled antiques shops, and old-fashioned general stores that are still the heart and soul of their tiny communities, such rural oases quickly make you forget that Massachusetts is, in fact, one of the most heavily urbanized states in the country.

Compact size makes it easy to mix and match attractions and activities, from the Cape Cod seashore to the Berkshire Hills along the New York border, but although it's tempting to equate short distances with short amounts of time, stepping out of the fast lane leaves a more lasting impression of this state than running laps around it. Since there are so many centuries of accumulated stories waiting to be retold and relived, you owe it to yourself to enjoy them at leisure.

History

Archaeologists have found evidence suggesting that Paleo-Indian hunters lived in Massachusetts at least 9,000 years ago. Stone implements, assorted pottery fragments, and remains of wooden fish weirs in several of the state's rivers prove that their descendants continued to occupy the region's coastlines and major waterways until historic times. On the eve of European discovery of the New World in the 15th century, tens of thousands of Native Americans lived in hundreds of villages throughout the future Bay State.

It is often suggested, even by some museum exhibits, that Norse Vikings led by Leif Eriksson made landfall in Massachusetts around AD 1000, but no conclusive evidence of this has yet been found. It is more widely accepted that the first Europeans to visit Massachusetts shores were Portuguese, French, and English fishermen who crossed the North Atlantic in the wake of explorer John Cabot's 1497 voyage to Newfoundland. Lured by his reports of unlimited quantities of codfish, these fishermen dried and salted their catch on New England's shores, occasionally trading tools and clothing with Native Americans.

Between 1524 and 1620, more than two dozen navigators (from Giovanni da Verrazano to Jamestown founder Capt. John Smith) representing England, France, and Holland passed through Massachusetts waters. Many never set foot ashore. Others specifically came to collect medicinal plants, animal pelts, and timber, or to assess the potential for establishing permanent settlements. Inevitably, the newcomers encountered coastal residents of the Wampanoag, Massachusetts, Patuxet, Nauset, and Pocasset tribes, among others. Despite cultural misunderstandings and occasional violence, relations were generally friendly, but in 1615 the Native Americans, defenseless against European diseases such as smallpox, fell victim to the first of many devastating epidemics.

MA Timeline

7000 BC	1497–98	1620	1628
Paleo-Indians settle along the coast.	John Cabot's voyage between the Hudson River and Nova Scotia establishes English claims to what is now Massachusetts.	Mayflower Pilgrims arrive in Provincetown, move to Plymouth; beginning of the Old Colony.	First Puritans arrive in Salem, the seed of what becomes the Massachusetts Bay Colony.

On the heels of the subsequent decline of the huge indigenous population came a series of English colonists, encouraged in their profit-seeking adventures by a king and parliament anxious to trump the New World empires then being established by Spain and France. For the English, success finally came with one of the least prepared groups to make the attempt: a small boatload of religious dissidents, entrepreneurs, and indentured servants now collectively known to history as the Pilgrims. After making landfall at the tip of Cape Cod in November 1620, the *Mayflower* passengers finally disembarked at Plymouth Rock, the site of an abandoned Patuxet village, its fields already cleared for cultivation. Nearly half the colony perished in the unforgiving winter that followed, almost ending the Colonial experiment before it began. But the survivors persevered, overcoming natural obstacles and their own shortcomings to eventually flourish and multiply.

Within a decade, the Pilgrim "Old Colony" acquired a new neighbor to the north: the Massachusetts Bay Colony, begun in 1628 under a royal charter granted to a group of so-called Puritans. Like some of the Pilgrims, the Puritans disagreed enough with the Church of England about religious doctrine to embrace the unknown hazards of emigration in their quest for a perfect society. Harvard University, Boston's public schools, and the state legislature are among the still-thriving institutions originally founded by the Puritans. Tens of thousands of disaffected fellow citizens followed the Puritans' lead, encouraged by reports that played up New England's natural assets and played down Colonial hardships. Rapidly expanding English settlement undermined relations with Native Americans, finally resulting in the 1675–76 war with a tribal alliance led by the Wampanoag sachem Metacom, known to the English as King Philip. Though Colonial victory drove all but a few Native Americans out of Massachusetts, the cost crippled the Colonial administrations, ending their autonomy from England. In the war's aftermath the English crown revoked both the Pilgrim and Puritan charters, and by the end of the 17th century took direct control over its most populous holdings in North America by combining them into the royally governed Province of Massachusetts.

Mother England proceeded to spend the 1700s draining its treasury with expensive wars against other European powers. Massachusetts merchants, particularly those in the provincial capital of Boston, grew prosperous on foreign trade, much of it illegal competition against domestic British firms. The cash-strapped king and his ministers, resenting the flagrant smuggling and perceiving a huge cost to the crown in defending the American frontier from French and Indian aggression, attempted to grab a slice of the traders' profits through a series of taxes, such as the 1764 Sugar Act, the 1765 Stamp Act, and the 1768 Townshend Acts. Chafing at having their liberties pruned back after decades of lax oversight, pugnacious Massachusetts led the Colonial resistance to the unpopular new levies, arguing that "taxation without representation is tyranny." The right to raise revenue, insisted the colonies, belonged to their own elected assemblies rather than to England's Parliament. In reply, Parliament dissolved the Massachusetts assembly, among others, and in 1768 sent soldiers to Boston to enforce the royal policies.

1675–76	1691	1764	1768	1770
King Philip's War between colonists and Native Americans cripples both sides, but ends in defeat for the Wampanoags and their allies.	England establishes the province of Massachusetts.	English Parliament passes the Sugar Act, first of a series of unwelcome taxes designed to defray the costs of protecting and administering the colonies.	British troops are quartered in Boston as local resistance to royal policies grows.	The Boston Massacre heightens tensions between colony and crown.

Hair-trigger passions on both sides of this constitutional debate were inflamed by such watershed events as the 1770 Boston Massacre, in which fearful British troops slew five members of a garbage-throwing mob, and the 1773 Boston Tea Party, in which colonists scuttled crates of tea in the harbor to protest a new set of import duties. Parliament retaliated with the 1774 Coercive Acts, which included closing Boston's port to all trade, but the move backfired. Instead of yoking his subjects to his will, King George III only ignited more Colonial anger with his inflexibility. And so on the afternoon of April 19, 1775, by a bridge on the Concord River, west of Boston, local militia shot back at startled English Redcoats—"the shot heard 'round the world" that plunged Massachusetts, and very soon all 12 of its Colonial neighbors, into a long and costly war of independence.

Massachusetts was at the vanguard of the Revolution, but after the morale-boosting Battle of Bunker Hill, in June 1775, and the British evacuation from Boston eight months later, the battlefields shifted permanently out of state. Massachusetts contributed as significantly to the new American republic's political framework after the war as it had to starting the conflict, which is why so many of the state's most popular historic sites—such as the homes of John Adams and Paul Revere, or landmarks along Boston's Freedom Trail—are national monuments. Modern preservation of luxurious Federal-style mansions and museums filled with collections begun by local merchant princes lent additional perspective on the spoils of war, as Massachusetts shipowners and traders, unfettered by royal restraints, amassed huge fortunes in overseas freight after the Revolution ended. But Thomas Jefferson's 1807 Embargo Act, halting all foreign trade, and "Mr. Madison's War" of 1812, which disrupted access to European markets, altogether torpedoed the state's reliance on maritime commerce and industry.

Fortunately for the state economy, in 1814 an inventive engineer named Francis Cabot Lowell replicated an English-style power loom on the banks of the Charles River in Waltham, just upstream from Boston. It was the final machine Lowell and his partners required to create the nation's first fully automated textile factory. With it, Lowell singlehandedly jump-started America's fledgling Industrial Revolution. By century's end Massachusetts had become home to dozens of giant "mill towns," planned industrial cities dedicated to churning out cloth, shoes, paper, furniture, toys, pianos, wire, rifles, shovels, and scores of other mass-produced products for a growing nation and the world.

Industrialization also brought tremendous social change. New transportation infrastructure like the Erie Canal enabled subsistence farmers to move to the more arable Ohio Valley, leaving their abandoned fields to become, 150 years later, some of the state's deepest forests. European and Canadian immigrants flocked to factory jobs in Massachusetts cities, adding ethnic foods and folkways to the state's melting pot. And a new breed of bootstrapped aristocracy arose, whose legacy partly survives in the civic institutions donated by proud citizens who made good with their inventions.

1773	1774	1775	1776	1814
Angry about new duties on imported tea, Bostonians empty a cargo of it into their harbor during what becomes known as the Boston Tea Party.	England closes Boston Harbor to all shipping to punish the colonists.	"The shot heard 'round the world" touches off the American Revolution at Concord. Two months later, American militias inflict severe casualties on the British at the Battle of Bunker Hill.	After an eight-month siege, British troops evacuate Boston without a shot. No further battles are fought on Massachusetts soil.	Francis Cabot Lowell imports England's Industrial Revolution to America, opening the nation's first bale-to-cloth textile mill in Waltham.

With social change came a bevy of writers, religious leaders, and reformers to critique the results and inspire efforts to do better. Whether opposing the complicity of northern textile makers in Southern slavery, exposing the injustice of child labor, or saving songbirds from extinction at the hands of women's hatmakers, some of the nation's earliest and most enduring social critics found 19th-century Massachusetts fertile soil for their reform movements.

The early years of the 20th century were marred by unrest, as Massachusetts industrialists fought a losing and sometimes violent battle against labor unions. The 1912 Bread and Roses Strike in Lawrence, with which organized labor first overcame ethnic and class rivalries previously exploited by mill owners, was but one of many steps on the long road to improving the state's working conditions. Some steps had unintended consequences: Calvin Coolidge was chosen to be Warren Harding's vice president in 1920 largely because of the reputation he acquired as the governor who broke the disastrous 1919 Boston Police Strike. The Great Depression ultimately shuttered many Massachusetts factories for good, and gave the state its first taste of declining population. World War II brought industrial prosperity back to Massachusetts, albeit too briefly to do more than postpone the continued flight of residents to the Sun Belt. In the decades following native son John F. Kennedy's victory in the 1960 election, Massachusetts has capitalized on its long tradition of education and invention, becoming a national leader in high technology, business consulting, and academic research.

Regions

1. GREATER BOSTON

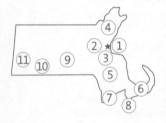

Boston bills itself as "America's Walking City," and rightly so. Inviting frequent comparison to Europe, Boston's compact downtown, narrow and irregular 17th-century streets, and old-world architecture make it a genuine pleasure to traipse around town on foot. Attractions not within easy walking distance of one another are readily accessible by public transit, including ferries that shuttle around the city's busy inner harbor.

Because of both its age and its willingness to preserve the past, the city is renowned for its historic sites, from Paul Revere's house to John F. Kennedy's birthplace. Boston's historic legacy is complemented by top-ranking art and science museums and a panoply of performing-arts institutions, including resident symphony, ballet, and theater companies. The metro region also has a superabundance of colleges, universities, and conservatories—more than 60 in all—many of which feature their own cultural attractions, from art galleries to concert halls. And in addition to the seasonal home games of local major-league hockey, baseball, and basketball teams, there are special annual sporting events, such as the Boston Marathon, held in mid-April, and the Head of the Charles Regatta,

1825	**1912**	**1923**	**1960**	**1892**
Opening of the Erie Canal spurs large numbers of Massachusetts farmers to abandon their small farms for more productive Midwestern land.	The Bread and Roses Strike shuts down woolen mills in Lawrence.	Calvin Coolidge, vice president and former Massachusetts governor, becomes president after the death of Warren Harding.	John F. Kennedy, senator from Massachusetts, is elected president.	The first successful gasoline-powered car is built by Charles and Frank Duryea in Springfield, Massachusetts.

at the end of October, which regularly draw hundreds of thousands of spectators from around the world.

The side effect of so much to see and do is that the city's high season for tourism runs from March through November, even though the most favorable weather doesn't arrive until May and ends by October. With demand for hotel rooms so high throughout most of the year, and supply much lower than in cities of comparable size, Boston routinely ranks as one of the nation's most expensive vacation destinations, second only to New York City. Casual visitors should be particularly careful to avoid arriving during graduation exercises at area universities, in late May and early June, when vacancies are scarcest and prices most exorbitant.

In addition to its namesake, Greater Boston comprises several dozen towns and cities in four different counties surrounding Boston Harbor. Route 128, the circumferential highway that rings Boston and its immediate neighbors, has traditionally defined the outer edge of the metropolitan area, but explosive economic growth in both the mid-1980s and late 1990s has spread city-style traffic, housing, and population well into the MetroWest and MetroSouth suburbs. The city of Boston, whose boundary is identical with Suffolk County, now accounts for less than 20% of the total metropolitan population. Economically, however, downtown Boston draws workers from about a 70-mi radius, including Rhode Island, southern New Hampshire, Cape Cod, and central Massachusetts.

Towns listed: Boston, Braintree, Brookline, Burlington, Cambridge, Dedham, Lexington, Lynn, Lynnfield, Newton, Quincy, Saugus, Somerville, Waltham, Wellesley

2. METROWEST

West of Boston, between Route 128 and the outer circumferential I–495, lies the increasingly urbanized arc of MetroWest bedroom communities, executive office parks, and shopping malls. Since most of the development follows arterial state roads such as Routes 3A, 2, 9, and 16, some towns have a dual personality, with one foot in the modern age of chain stores and divided highways and the other in century-old village streetscapes lined with small shops and historic homes. A few working farms remain, on back roads farthest from the busy highway interchanges, and visitors will find show gardens and wildlife sanctuaries in the area as well.

Towns listed: Bedford, Concord, Framingham, Natick, Sudbury

3. METROSOUTH

MetroSouth's suburbs are all within Norfolk County, which stretches between Rhode Island and Massachusetts Bay along Greater Boston's southern edge. It includes most of the Charles River watershed, and is crossed by major commuter rail lines and highways that radiate from Boston like spokes. Housing developments share the glacially flattened landscape with large retail shopping centers and suburban employers such as footwear manufacturer Reebok International, whose world headquarters is located

INTRODUCTION
HISTORY
REGIONS
WHEN TO VISIT
STATE'S GREATS
RULES OF THE ROAD
DRIVING TOURS

1961	1966	1974	1988	1998
The first nuclear-powered surface vessel, the USS Long Beach CG (N) 9, is launched at Quincy, Massachusetts.	Edward W. Brooke, From Massachusetts, becomes the first black man to be elected to the U.S. Senate by popular vote.	A federal judge initiates a program of court-ordered busing in Boston in order to achieve racial integration in Boston's public schools. The order sparks violent demonstrations and boycotts.	Massachusetts native George Bush beats Massachusetts Governor Michael Dukakis to become the forty-first president of the U.S.	Cambridge native Matt Damon wins the Oscar for Best Original Screenplay for *Good Will Hunting*, which was set in Boston.

here. Greater Boston's only museum devoted to whaling is found in the area, and visitors also come to watch the major-league sports teams that play in Foxboro Stadium, less than 30 mi from downtown Boston.

Towns listed: Foxborough, Sharon

4. NORTH OF BOSTON

North of Boston encompasses the diverse landscape of Essex County, whose coastal inlets and protected harbors were among the first town sites of the 17th-century Puritans, in the years before they founded Boston. The region's unparalleled number of surviving First Period dwellings has earned it recognition from the National Park Service as a National Heritage Area. Besides traditional fishing and boat-building towns along the shore, the region includes some of the nation's earliest planned industrial cities, built along the turbine-spinning falls of the Merrimack River. There are also small villages whose agricultural origins are preserved in appearance only, their rambling farmhouses and large pastures now strictly a suburban refuge from city life.

One of the largest unbroken tracts of undeveloped salt marsh north of Chesapeake Bay is found in this region, protected in part by the Parker River National Wildlife Refuge. The granite roots of the Appalachian Mountains a hundred miles inland expose themselves here and there along the shore with dramatic boulders on which the surf ceaselessly crashes. Where such outcroppings are broken by rivers, wide sand beaches have formed, including some of the finest—and most popular—in the state.

Towns listed: Amesbury, Andover and North Andover, Beverly, Danvers, Essex, Gloucester, Haverhill, Ipswich, Lawrence, Lowell, Marblehead, Newburyport, Rockport, Salem, Salisbury

5. SOUTHEASTERN MASSACHUSETTS

The southeastern corner of the state sits atop the great plain of glacial debris left behind at the end of the last Ice Age more than 10,000 years ago. Now the northern boundary of this region roughly matches the northernmost extent of the state's scrub-pine forests, which thrive on the dry, sandy soil deposited here during the retreat of those ancient melting glaciers. Coincidentally, the northern edge of the two counties that comprise southeastern Massachusetts was once the 17th-century dividing line between the Puritan and the Pilgrim colonies. Some of the state's earliest towns were established here; as a result, a number of prominent historical attractions remain. Most famous are those related to the Pilgrims, but the region enjoys a rich maritime legacy, rich enough to require several museums.

During the 19th century the region became highly industrialized, with large-scale production of shoes, shovels, nails, cotton cloth, whale oil, and jewelry transforming small towns into big manufacturing centers. Despite its factories, the region still contributes significantly to the state's agricultural revenues, particularly with cranberries, the signature crop of southeastern Massachusetts.

Seaside resorts and second-home vacation communities have long flourished here, thanks to the long, sandy beaches that line Cape Cod Bay. The region's second coastline, fronting Buzzards Bay, is better known for its yacht-filled marinas, although it, too, features a few spectacular public beaches. Year-round, visitors also come to shop for wholesale bargains at factory outlet centers found along the region's major interstate highways.

Towns listed: Brockton, Dartmouth, Duxbury, Fall River, New Bedford, Plymouth, Westport

6. CAPE COD AND THE ISLANDS

INTRODUCTION
HISTORY
REGIONS
WHEN TO VISIT
STATE'S GREATS
RULES OF THE ROAD
DRIVING TOURS

Cape Cod, known far and wide as simply "the Cape," is the king of New England summer resorts. Within its 15 towns, whose boundaries are nearly unchanged since they were drawn over 300 years ago, are well over a hundred beaches, each of which, like the towns themselves, has a character and loyal clientele of its very own. As if water sports and sunshine weren't enough, the Cape also enchants the millions of visitors who annually flock to its shores with art galleries, crafts shops, golf courses, and, of course, culinary traditions such as fried clams, fish-and-chips, and saltwater taffy.

Each town is subdivided into distinct villages, mostly vestiges of early settlements preserved now to aid postal delivery and confuse out-of-towners. As a general rule, those villages facing Nantucket Sound have the greatest concentration of contemporary beachside motels, roadside restaurants, and family amusements, while villages around the curving shore of Cape Cod Bay tend to have opted for historical preservation over commercial development. The Cape's interior, meanwhile, has grown positively suburban, largely because of an explosive increase in the number of year-round residents willing to commute great distances in order to enjoy the Cape's landscape and quality of life. Despite the pressures of growth, the Cape's wetlands and wildlife sanctuaries continue to be major stopping points on the Atlantic coastal flyway for migratory birds, and thus a major destination for dedicated New England bird-watchers.

Summer is the best season in which to enjoy the region's beaches, but it is also the busiest. Spring and fall are as good as summer for everything but comfortable swimming, and smaller crowds easily make up for the less predictable weather. Since tourism to the Cape and islands is so strongly seasonal, many businesses close for the winter, leaving off-season visitors with the least number of lodging, dining, and entertainment options, albeit at the best prices.

Cape Cod is geologically and culturally related to Martha's Vineyard and Nantucket, a pair of resort islands off its southern shore. The Elizabeth Islands, a chain of small islands west of Martha's Vineyard, are almost entirely under private ownership, with very limited access to visitors.

Towns listed: Barnstable Village, Bourne, Brewster, Centerville, Chatham, Dennis, Eastham, Falmouth, Harwich, Hyannis, Mashpee, Orleans, Provincetown, Sandwich, Truro, Wellfleet, Woods Hole, Yarmouth

7. MARTHA'S VINEYARD

Named in 1602 by a passing English navigator, Martha's Vineyard is the largest of Massachusetts's offshore islands. Although the personalities of its constituent towns and villages range from blue-collar rustic to country-club exclusive, the island as a whole deliberately cultivates a barefoot, roll-down-the-windows, easygoing style. Since the "Vineyard way" also includes utter respect for privacy, the island has long been favored by celebrities who value being treated with conscious anonymity.

Like nearby Cape Cod, to which it is linked by daily ferry and air service, the Vineyard is primarily for summer sun worshipers and beachgoers, although upland forests and meadows are worth the attention of hikers, bird-watchers, and other nature lovers. A thriving arts community, represented in boutiques and galleries all across the island, ensures that no visitor need leave empty-handed. A network of paved bike paths and seasonal shuttle buses helps eliminate the need for a car during the summer.

Towns listed: Aquinnah, Chilmark, Edgartown, Oak Bluffs, Vineyard Haven, West Tisbury

8. NANTUCKET ISLAND

Some 30 mi off Cape Cod's southern shore lies tiny Nantucket, nicknamed the "Gray Lady" for its enshrouding fogs and cedar-shingled homes weathered to a silvery shade of slate. Cobblestoned streets and carefully preserved architecture in the island's historic port are framed by sandy, windswept moors, a combination that's unique and unequivocally picturesque. Nantucket beaches range from intimate to vast, with water and wave conditions to suit every taste. And though water sports and historic sites may be the strongest magnet for visitors, those inland moors, which include most of the world's last remaining acres of a globally rare grassland ecosystem, are gradually becoming appreciated in their own right.

Nantucket shares in the regional swing between busy summers and slow, almost vacant winters, except during holidays. Bicycles are the preferred mode of transportation for visitors, a choice made easier by Nantucket's small size, its island-wide system of paved bike paths, bike rack–equipped shuttle vans, and intentionally prohibitive rates for ferrying cars from the mainland.

Town listed: Nantucket

9. CENTRAL MASSACHUSETTS

West of the almost sea-level basin occupied by Greater Boston is the undulating upland plateau of central Massachusetts. New England's second largest city, Worcester, is in this region. So is the nation's largest man-made supply of drinking water, Quabbin Reservoir, which fills the faucets and baths of half the state's residents. Most of this region was cleared for agricultural use by the early 19th century, and was then abandoned as farmers moved to more productive land west of the Appalachians. Over time, natural reforestation reclaimed the empty fields and pastures, making much of central Massachusetts as densely wooded today as it probably ever has been. But farms and orchards still can be found throughout the region; bushels of fresh produce at seasonal roadside stalls provide ample proof. Urban museums, state parks, an entire interpretive historic village in Sturbridge, and the Blackstone River Valley National Heritage Corridor are among the region's principal attractions for visitors.

Towns listed: Brimfield, Gardner, Grafton, Leominster, Sturbridge, Uxbridge, Worcester.

10. PIONEER VALLEY

The Pioneer Valley is Massachusetts's farm country. Here in the wide floodplain of the Connecticut River, New England's longest waterway, aeons of sediments have over time built up such fertile soil that the valley's farms are routinely ranked tops in the nation for productivity. But even within Massachusetts, the region is known less for its sweet corn and ripe summer berries than for its college towns. Of the nearly dozen institutions of higher education that dot the region, the most famous are the so-called Five Colleges—Amherst, Hampshire, Smith, Mt. Holyoke, and the University of Massachusetts—clustered in three adjacent towns at the Pioneer Valley's very center. The influence of mostly private liberal arts colleges is reflected in the regional wealth of small museums, arts-and-crafts galleries, used bookstores, and sporting-goods stores. It also extends to the pace of life itself, which is why many towns here run on the academic calendar, turning sleepy during summer months, staying active through the fall and spring semesters, and going absolutely crazy during back-to-back commencement weeks in late May.

The Holyoke Range, a modest little series of mountains, crosses the valley along a lazy diagonal, protected by a series of state forests and parks. The low peaks and open ledges of the range afford a number of fine vistas, some accessible even by car. Hiking trails also abound and are popular for both warm-weather walks and winter cross-country skiing.

Towns listed: Amherst, Chicopee, Deerfield, Greenfield, Hadley, Holyoke, Northampton, South Hadley, Springfield

11. THE BERKSHIRES

Some of Massachusetts's most extreme topography is found in its western end, where the Taconic Mountains crowd over the New York state line and face off against the Hoosac Range, foothills of Green Mountains in Vermont. Massachusetts's tallest peaks are among the lineup, while between the opposing sides are headwaters for two rivers: the Hoosic, a north-flowing tributary of the Hudson River, and the Housatonic, which flows south into Long Island Sound. Because Berkshire County encompasses this meeting place of mountains, the whole geological tumble is traditionally known as the Berkshire Hills, or simply the Berkshires for short.

A century ago, wealthy moguls and their retinues from around the country built palatial vacation homes here to enjoy the landscape and summer's beautiful weather. Today many of the surviving mansions have become fine inns or museums, or have had their grounds converted to outdoor venues for performing-arts groups such as the Boston Symphony Orchestra. This seasonal cornucopia of live music, dance, and theater has turned the region into the summer culture capital of New England, which is why area accommodations are able to command such high prices during performance-packed summer weekends. Autumn's palette of brightly colored foliage brings out the leaf peepers in droves, while winter's snow-covered peaks lure skiers from all the large cities within a couple of hours' driving distance.

Towns listed: Great Barrington, Lee, Lenox, North Adams, Pittsfield, Sheffield, Stockbridge, West Stockbridge, Williamstown

When to Visit

Humorists have poked fun at New England's notoriously fickle weather for generations, and rightly so. The influence of several major barometric phenomena, such as the Arctic and Bermuda high-pressure systems, the presence of both cold and warm ocean currents just offshore, and the intersection of tropical and polar air masses all contribute to the mighty unpredictability of Massachusetts's weather.

Despite the many exceptions, it is possible to list some general rules. Spring thaw, known in rural areas as mud season, comes in March and April throughout most of the state, although snowstorms are not unusual all the way into April. On Cape Cod and the islands, spring is a gradual, lingering season; on the mainland it is so short that wintry chill may spoil most weeks right through mid-May before suddenly being displaced by Memorial Day weekend's beach-going temperatures. Summer humidity averages well below that of the southern and midwestern United States, and heat waves in excess of 100°F are unusual.

Precipitation falls fairly uniformly throughout the year, but thunder and lightning storms are infrequent. The shorter days of fall bring cooler temperatures, and by October the first frosts inland. A week or two of Indian Summer, those perfectly warm, dry, sunny days reminiscent of mid-June, also arrive with October. The first fleeting snow flurries may fall as early as mid-November, but real winter snowstorms tend to hold off until mid-December. January and February are the coldest months, with temperatures often below freezing for days at a stretch. Winter is also hurricane season in the North Atlantic, but coastal Massachusetts is more often battered by winter gales, or "nor'easters," than by full-bore hurricanes.

Differences in weather from one end of the state to the other are determined mostly by elevation and proximity to the sea. Coastal areas tend to experience cooler summers and less snowy winters than inland, thanks to the fact that air over water warms and cools more slowly than air over land. Less snow along the shore doesn't make winter there any less bitter: although winter air is in fact warmer along the water, it won't feel that way when propelled by coat- and glove-piercing 50 mph gusts.

West of Boston, the most extreme high-elevation temperatures are found in the Berkshires, atop the Taconic Range. Despite being mere low bumps compared to western U.S. mountain ranges three times as high, there is scant protection from polar air sweeping down from the north, which is why Mt. Greylock and other auto-accessible peaks feel downright raw and wintry when the damp Canadian clouds roll in, even in the height of summer.

CLIMATE CHART
Average High/Low Temperatures (°F) and Monthly Precipitation (in inches)

	JAN.	FEB.	MAR.	APR.	MAY	JUNE
BOSTON	36/22	38/23	46/31	56/40	67/50	76/59
	3.6	3.6	3.7	3.6	3.3	3.1
	JULY	AUG.	SEPT.	OCT.	NOV.	DEC.
	82/65	80/64	73/57	63/47	52/38	40/27
	2.8	3.2	3.1	3.3	4.2	4.0
	JAN.	FEB.	MAR.	APR.	MAY	JUNE
WORCESTER	31/15	33/17	42/25	54/35	66/45	75/54
	3.7	3.5	4.0	3.9	4.3	3.9
	JULY	AUG.	SEPT.	OCT.	NOV.	DEC.
	79/60	77/59	70/50	60/41	47/31	35/20
	3.9	3.8	4.0	4.3	4.5	4.1

FESTIVALS AND SEASONAL EVENTS
WINTER

Dec. **Nantucket Noel and Christmas Stroll.** Nantucket's cobblestone streets are filled for one week with Yuletide cheer, as shops unveil holiday decorations and window displays, restaurants tempt visitors with special feasts, and inns keep their hearths alight. | 508/228–1700.

Shaker Christmas. In the Berkshires, a Shaker Christmas is celebrated in authentic style and dress at Hancock Shaker Village, on U.S. 20 west of Pittsfield. | 413/443–0188 or 800/817–1137.

First Night. Boston was the birthplace of First Night, the art- and performance-filled New Year's Eve phenomenon now celebrated in hundreds of cities worldwide. Some say the first is still the best; dress warmly and come see for yourself. | 617/542–1399.

Jan. **The Moby Dick Marathon.** This event in the old whaling port of New Bedford tests the endurance of readers rather than runners as author Herman Melville's birthday is marked by a weekend-long reading aloud of his most famous novel. Held at the New Bedford Whaling Museum atop downtown Johnny Cake Hill, surrounded by historic waterfront sights described in *Moby Dick* more than a century ago. | 508/997–0046.

SPRING

Apr. **Lexington Green Battle Reenactment.** Modern Lexington returns to its storied past with the Lexington Green Battle

Reenactment, which reawakens the town at daybreak on April 19, exactly as in 1775. | 781/862–1703.

Boston Marathon. On the third Monday of the month, thousands of long-distance runners compete in the famous Boston Marathon between Hopkinton and downtown Boston, arguably the toughest marathon course in the world. | 617/236–1652.

Daffodil Festival. Nantucket's festival heralds spring with a classic-car parade, tailgate picnics, and an estimated 3 million daffodils planted along island roads since 1974. | 508/228–1700.

May **Portuguese Festival.** Highlighted by the colorful Blessing of the Fleet, the festival celebrates the indelible influence of the Portuguese community on Provincetown, both past and present. | 508/487–3424.

SUMMER

July **Esplanade Concerts.** The free outdoor Esplanade Concerts in Boston are always a treat, but most memorable is the performance on the Fourth of July. Hundreds of thousands of happy listeners camp out all day on the riverbanks to save a spot from which to hear the venerable Boston Pops Orchestra play Tchaikovsky's *1812 Overture,* its climax accompanied by cannon, church bells, and fireworks. | 617/266–1492.

The Lowell Folk Festival. The nation's largest free folk-music festival, starring scores of international, national, and regional performers at outdoor stages throughout the Lowell National Historical Park in downtown Lowell. | 978/970–5000.

Aug. **Berkshire Craft Fair.** Contemporary artisans of every description reveal the infinite variety wrought by creative hands and minds at the Berkshire Craft Fair in Great Barrington. | 413/528–3346, ext. 28.

Sandcastle and Sculpture Contest. Contestants of all ages compete on Nantucket in the annual Sandcastle and Sculpture Contest. | 508/228–1700.

AUTUMN

Sept. **Eastern States Exposition.** West Springfield hosts New England's largest regional agricultural fair. Better known as The Big E, it runs for more than two weeks beginning after Labor Day. | 413/737–2443.

Oct. **Head of the Charles Regatta.** Harvard Sq., Cambridge, becomes the world's epicenter of competitive rowing during this regatta, which attracts racers and spectators from around the globe. | 617/864–8415.

Nov. **Thanksgiving.** Not surprisingly, the home of the first Pilgrim settlement, Plymouth, celebrates Thanksgiving week in style, with a parade, historic reenactments, and events at historic homes throughout town. | 508/747–7525 or 800/USA–1620.

State's Greats

Massachusetts's most prominent feature is surely its history, for so much of it is the story of the nation itself. Pilgrims and patriots, abolitionists and suffragists, Thoreau and Kerouac, Mary Baker Eddy and JFK: they all not only slept here, but lived, debated, wrote, and, in many cases, are buried here. It's a multifaceted heritage of Colonial settlement, politics, immigration, and invention, brought to life through museums, historic sites, and interpretive villages throughout the state.

The superlatives don't end with the legacies of Massachusetts's most illustrious sons and daughters. Wildlife sanctuaries, conservation areas, and state parks (here traditionally called reservations) all offer exceptional four-season activities, from birdwatching to snowshoeing. In particular, the state is justly famous for its unspoiled 30-mi shoreline along the outer reach of Cape Cod, and for the brilliant display of fall foliage throughout its central and western forests.

For anyone who prefers urban amenities to the great outdoors, there is Boston, self-styled hub of New England, with arts, music, dining, shopping, and sports enough to fill any vacation to overflowing. Best of all, Massachusetts is small enough so that one visit can include it all: city, country, and shore.

Beaches, Forests, and Parks

Every part of the Massachusetts coast has some stretch of sand that any knowing local will confidently inform you is arguably the state's best. By and large, they are all telling the truth; no matter which part of the shore you visit—north of Boston, south of Boston, **Cape Cod, Martha's Vineyard,** or **Nantucket**—a perfect beach awaits. Some have fine sand, others have coarse; some have heavy surf and strong undertow, others are as calm as a reflecting pool. Some have all of the above by turns, depending upon when you visit. Between June and September, crowds are inevitable on any day that promises no rain, but arrive early or after 4 PM on a weekday, and you may find all the elbow room you could want.

Massachusetts makes up for its lack of national forests with the sixth-largest state park system in the country, comprising more than 275,000 acres. The largest and wildest tracts are in **the Berkshires.** In every region of the state these holdings are complemented by privately owned but publicly accessible sanctuaries and conservation properties, such as those administered by the **Massachusetts Audubon Society** in Pittsfield, Lenox, Northampton, Falmouth, and Wellfleet, among others. **Boston's park system** is especially noted for the contributions of Frederick Law Olmsted, the grandfather of landscape architecture, who completed some of his finest work within the city.

Culture, History, and the Arts

By the sheer size of its population, Boston is the state's 500-pound gorilla in the arts, but cultural attractions are found throughout Massachusetts. Summer is an especially prolific season for performing arts outside the city. **Boston's symphony and ballet** take up seasonal residency in the Berkshires and on Cape Cod, and many other performers follow suit. **The Berkshires,** traditionally a retreat for New Yorkers escaping Manhattan's heat and humidity, have become a veritable Lincoln Center in the country, with summer-long music, dance, and theater festivals.

History buffs need only pick an era, and somewhere in Massachusetts there will be something that fits the bill, starting with the prehistoric artifacts of the **Peabody Foundation for Archaeology** in Andover, or the **Harvard Semitic Museum** in Cambridge. **Pilgrim Hall Museum and Plimoth Plantation,** both in Plymouth, will teach you about New England's first successful European settlers, the former with artifacts, the latter with interpretive reenactments of the Pilgrims' lives circa 1627.

INTRODUCTION
HISTORY
REGIONS
WHEN TO VISIT
STATE'S GREATS
RULES OF THE ROAD
DRIVING TOURS

Colonial life is also amply illustrated by a series of 17th-century dwellings, from the **Coffin House** outside of Newburyport to the **Hoxie House** in Sandwich, on Cape Cod. Boston's **Freedom Trail** will focus your attention on the events, people, and places important to the American Revolution, whose battlefields can be seen west of the city in Concord's **Minuteman National Historical Park.** Immerse yourself in the 19th century at sites across the state, from **Old Sturbridge Village,** a re-created 1830s rural community, to **Lowell National Historical Park,** whose exhibits on the Industrial Revolution span entire city blocks. Other facets of the 1800s are on display in scores of intimate museums and historic sights, such as the **Willard House and Clock Museum** in Grafton, the **Hadley Farm Museum** in the Pioneer Valley, and Salem's **Peabody Essex Institute,** whose vast galleries and historic homes are filled with artifacts procured during the rich heyday of the East India merchant trade.

Fans of American letters will find numerous landmarks to visit, such as Herman Melville's Pittsfield home, **Arrowhead,** his friend Nathaniel Hawthorne's famous **House of Seven Gables,** in Salem, and the **Emily Dickinson Homestead,** in Amherst. The legacies of utopian communities, both religious and philosophical, invite contemplation at the **Hancock Shaker Village,** in the Berkshires, and the **Fruitlands Museums,** in the rural farmland outside the central Massachusetts city of Leominster, where Louisa May Alcott's father Bronson attempted to plant the seeds of social idealism. Maritime trades are given their due in the **Essex Shipbuilding Museum,** as well as in three very distinct museums devoted to separate aspects of the whaling industry: the **Kendall Whaling Museum,** in Sharon, the **New Bedford Whaling Museum,** and the **Nantucket Whaling Museum.**

When you're ready to enter the modern age, consider visiting the **Gropius House** in bucolic Lincoln, designed by the founder of the Bauhaus, or Boston's **John F. Kennedy Library and Museum.** And if you're impatient to experience the next century, drop in on Boston's unique and highly interactive **Computer Museum.**

Sports

If the Massachusetts legislature ever debates selecting a state sport, the contenders would surely include sailing, fishing, and golfing. Children raised on Cape Cod, Martha's Vineyard, and Nantucket often seem to take to the sea as soon as they can walk, and busy marinas are found in every decent harbor in the state. Seaside communities are apt to have a handful of yacht clubs each—or, if they're like tiny Marblehead, half a dozen.

Learning to sail is as easy as enrolling in a week or two of classes from a community boating program in Boston, Fall River, or Nantucket, among other places. Adventuresome travelers without that much spare time may prefer to try a hand at **sea kayaking,** a sport that's taken Massachusetts by storm in the past few years. Equipment rental, sales, and lessons are already available from outfitters in Beverly and Essex on the coast north of Boston, in Plymouth and near New Bedford along the state's southeastern shores, and on Nantucket and Martha's Vineyard. More outfitters are opening up every year; look for them whenever you're near the coast.

Fishing for striped bass and bluefish is a serious summertime business on the Cape and the islands, where surfcasters line up shoulder-to-shoulder when schools of these saltwater prizefighters are reported to be biting. Charter boats are abundant, too, departing from 27 ports, including Falmouth, Hyannis, Provincetown, Nantucket, and Martha's Vineyard, for anglers who want to try their luck in deep water. Although the state's ocean sportfishing hogs the limelight, Berkshire and Central Massachusetts residents know that many of the state's mountain streams are a flycaster's dream. In fact, **trout fishing** in western Massachusetts along the Cold, Deerfield, and Green rivers is frequently compared by experts to the more famous streams of northern New England, which is why high-caliber handcrafted fly-rod manufacturer Thomas and Thomas is located near the Pioneer Valley town of Greenfield. Fishing is permitted in more than 2,000 ponds, lakes, and reservoirs across Massachusetts, many of which are routinely stocked by the state Division of Fisheries and Wildlife (800/ASK–FISH for suggested fishing spots and how to obtain a fishing license).

Massachusetts's first golf course, the thoroughly Scottish-style unmanicured **Highland Golf Links** in Truro, opened in 1890. It's still in use, as popular now as ever. It's been joined by scores of other public greens from Boston to the Berkshires. Cape Cod is particularly esteemed by amateur and pro golfers alike for the variety, quality, and quantity of its golf courses, many of which are open year-round.

Bicycling has been a Massachusetts pastime for longer than golf. Cyclists were the first constituency to lobby for paved roads, a century ago. More recently the state has joined the nationwide movement to create paved bike paths out of abandoned railroad corridors. Cyclists can now enjoy the 25-mi **Cape Cod Rail Trail** between Dennis and Wellfleet, the 11-mi **Minuteman Commuter Bikeway** between Cambridge and Greater Boston's western suburbs, and the 10-mi **Norwottuck Rail Trail** between Northampton and Amherst, the centerpiece of an expanding Pioneer Valley bikeway network.

Other Points of Interest

Perhaps Massachusetts's most prized wildlife viewing area is the one never shown on any map: the **Stellwagen Bank Marine Sanctuary,** under the nutrient-rich waters of Massachusetts Bay, off the northern tip of Cape Cod. Stellwagen is a prime feeding ground for humpback, finback, sei, blue, minke, and North Atlantic right whales, all endangered species. Between April and October, they raise their newborn young here before migrating south for the winter. **Whale-watching cruises** depart daily in summer from Boston, Gloucester, Newburyport, Plymouth, Barnstable Village, and Provincetown, and weekly from Nantucket.

Rules of the Road

License Requirements: Drivers in Massachusetts must be at least 18 years old and must have a valid driver's license from their home state or country.

Speed Limits: The maximum speed limit in Massachusetts, 65 mph, is only found along the interstates. On the more congested portions of the interstate system in and around Boston, the maximum is 50 to 55 mph. Numbered state highways have a maximum speed limit of 55 mph and are frequently posted much lower. Observe speed limits carefully, as speeding tickets are punitively expensive.

Right Turn on Red: Massachusetts allows right turns at red lights after coming to a complete stop and yielding to all pedestrians, unless otherwise posted. Note that most urban intersections, especially in Boston, are posted with NO RIGHT TURN ON RED signs, although not always conspicuously.

Seatbelt and Helmet Laws: Massachusetts law requires that everyone riding in a private passenger vehicle wear seatbelts. This applies to drivers and all passengers age 12 and over, in cars, vans, and small trucks. State law also requires that motorcyclists and their passengers wear helmets.

For More Information: Contact the Massachusetts Registry of Motor Vehicles at 617/351–4500, or visit its Web site, www.magnet.state.ma.us/rmv.

Historic Cape Cod Driving Tour
ALONG THE OLD KING'S HIGHWAY

INTRODUCTION
HISTORY
REGIONS
WHEN TO VISIT
STATE'S GREATS
RULES OF THE ROAD
DRIVING TOURS

Distance: 40 mi; 64 km   Time: 1 day

This tour follows an old Colonial thoroughfare known as the King's Highway, now Route 6A, from the Cape Cod Canal to Orleans, on the eastern side of Cape Cod. Preservation efforts by the towns along the way ensure that the view from your car window is largely free of anything discordantly modern; instead, you'll get an eyeful of old-fashioned architectural idioms, from the simple Cape cottage and its steep-roof salt-box cousin to the clapboard inns and Greek Revival civic buildings typically arrayed around neatly mown town greens. A handful of museums and similar attractions encourage tarrying along the way, and gentle Cape Cod Bay beaches are often just a turn away. Outside of summer many businesses cut back on hours of operation, some in anticipation of closing completely until next year, but spring and fall are less crowded.

① Begin the tour in **Bourne** (Sagamore Rotary, at Rte. 3S and U.S. 6E). Long, tall **Sagamore Bridge**, a big WPA-era span in the Art Deco style, carries U.S. 6 over the **Cape Cod Canal,** the world's widest. The first 8-mi canal was completed in 1914 as a private venture, but it proved too narrow for safe passage. The federal government bought out the first owners in 1928, doubling the width and adding the giant highway and railroad bridges that are Cape Cod's only ground transportation link to the rest of the world. Bluffs on both sides of the canal are surmounted by stretches of U.S. 6, and paved service roads that are open only to pedestrians, skaters, and cyclists run parallel, too, close enough

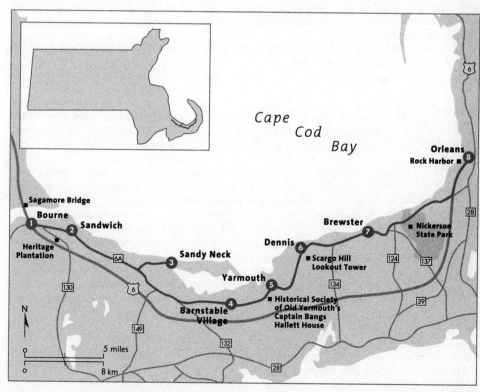

to the water to wave to boaters. Overlooks with parking on the north side of the canal (U.S. 6W, between Sagamore Rotary and Bournedale) provide access to these.

❷ Your first stop is **Sandwich** (exit 1 from U.S. 6, then 3 mi east on Rte. 6A to right at Tupper St., or follow signs for historic district). The old center of Sandwich, the Cape's oldest town, belongs in the dictionary under "quaint." Its needle-spired church, still-functioning 1640 gristmill, and other historic structures both real and reproduced present the perfect backdrop for a stroll, particularly before or after visiting the **Sandwich Glass Museum** or nearby Yesteryears Doll Museum, each of which exhibits exactly what you'd expect— antique, locally made glassware and thousands of dolls, respectively. Worth the 1-mi detour south of Town Hall is the **Heritage Plantation,** whose many acres of show gardens and buildings encompass more collectible Americana than you probably knew existed, from cigar-store carved totems and military miniatures to antique cars and a work-ing 1912 carousel.

❸ In **Sandy Neck** (Sandy Neck Rd., off Rte. 6A), Cape Cod's largest salt-marsh ecosystem and miles of barrier dunes provide hours of walking, bird-watching, and beachcomb-ing possibilities, and swimming, too. Don't forget sunblock or drinking water.

❹ The approach to **Barnstable Village** includes many homes designed in the old Cape style, 1½ stories with one or two windows flanking a side or central door. Older, larger, and set back from the road is the **Sturgis Library,** occupying a former parsonage built in 1644. Genealogical collections may be viewed inside. Turn north at the traffic light to admire the harbor, or to take a trip in search of the world's largest mammals with **Hyannis Whale Watcher Cruises.** Barnstable's 1855 brick **Customs House** (immedi-ately east of traffic light) attests to the tiny community's long-lost importance as a port of entry for foreign shipping. Now the building houses the historical maritime collections of the **Donald G. Trayser Memorial Museum.**

❺ As you cross from Barnstable into **Yarmouth,** look at the hedge on the right for the 17th-century granite boundary marker inscribed B-Y. Nearly opposite the Yarmouth Port village post office is the circa 1780 **Winslow Crocker House,** an affluent merchant's home moved here in 1936 and turned into the house-size display case for a private antiques collection, now open to weekend summer and fall tours. Next to the post office, facing the old village common, is the **Historical Society of Old Yarmouth's Captain Bangs Hallett House,** an 1840 residence also open to seasonal tours. Behind the house are 50 wooded acres with ponds and nature trails.

❻ Not far from the small village green in **Dennis** stands the **Scargo Hill Lookout Tower** (south on Old Bass River Rd., then left on Scargo Hill Rd., follow signs). On clear days the panoramic view from the stone parapet encompasses most of the shore of Cape Cod Bay, from Plymouth to Provincetown. Though mostly hidden from the tower by foliage, Dennis's half-dozen fine bayside beaches are easily accessible at the end of nearly every road that turns north from Route 6A. Some, such as Mayflower Beach and Corporation Beach, are equipped with both bathhouses and food concessions, and are signposted from the highway. Arts complement recreation at the **Cape Playhouse,** the nation's oldest professional summer theater. Sharing the grounds of the Playhouse are the **Cape Museum of Fine Arts,** showcasing the work of local artists past and present, and the barnlike 1930s **Cape Cinema,** where independent and foreign films are shown.

❼ In **Brewster** houses share the highway with undeveloped tracts of salt marsh as Route 6A skirts the shore of Cape Cod Bay, which is often visible across the treeless wetlands. The **Cape Cod Museum of Natural History** takes advantage of its marshy surroundings with interpretive trails that build on the lessons learned from the museum's indoor exhibits. More scenic walking is found on trails around the old **Stony Brook Mill** (at the village's flashing traffic light make a sharp southwest turn from Rte. 6A onto Stony Brook Rd. and proceed 1 mi), a functioning 1873 gristmill that anchored an area of town once known as Factory Village. **Nickerson State Park** has trails for cycling, horseback riding, and hiking, as well as ponds for swimming, boating, and fishing. Bicyclists are drawn to the park largely because of the 25-mi **Cape Cod Rail Trail,** which passes beneath Route 6A by the park entrance.

INTRODUCTION
HISTORY
REGIONS
WHEN TO VISIT
STATE'S GREATS
RULES OF THE ROAD
DRIVING TOURS

8 In **Orleans** during the War of 1812 a British landing party from ships anchored in the bay attempted to come ashore at **Rock Harbor** (turn northwest from Rte. 6A onto Main St. and proceed ⅔ mi), until persuaded to reconsider by fire from local militiamen's guns. A very different waterfront is found across town on the Atlantic shore at **Nauset Beach** (Main St. southeast from Rte. 6A to Beach Rd. to the end), where the brisk, long surf rolls up the wide sandy strand, and nothing stands between you and Portugal but endless waves. In summer, bathrooms and snacks are both available at Nauset.

Blackstone Valley Driving Tour

FROM WORCESTER TO THE BLACKSTONE GORGE

Distance: 50 mi; 80 km   Time: 1 day

This tour explores the many natural and historic features of the Blackstone River Valley National Heritage Corridor, in central Massachusetts. The tongue-twisting BRVNHC, a national model for alliances between federal, state, and private nonprofit preservation groups, celebrates the legacy of America's early evolution from an agrarian to an industrial society. Here are the remnants of some of New England's earliest factories, powered by the Blackstone River's steep descent to the sea. Here, too, are the ruins of the old Blackstone Canal, which ran beside the river, connecting central Massachusetts farmers to new markets up and down the Eastern Seaboard and speeding the growth of manufacturing away from the coast. As you drive through the area you'll also encounter farms and townscapes that have survived since the Colonial era, as well as vestiges of the Native Americans who have inhabited this part of Massachusetts since before the dawn of recorded history. Though the National Park Service doesn't own a single acre or building in the Corridor, it provides expert interpretive rangers and printed materials, and coordinates signage to make it easier to find your way from one sight to the next.

1 Begin the tour in **Worcester** (central Massachusetts; access from I–90 W, exit 10 A, or I–290, exits 12–19). The Blackstone River rises slightly north of Worcester, whose early industrial concerns were built along its banks and those of its tributaries. To appreciate the city's growth into a diversified manufacturing center and the Blackstone Canal's role in facilitating this growth, drop by the **Worcester Historical Museum.** As one of the National Heritage Corridor's many partners, the museum also stocks the clear and detailed BRVNHC road map and related interpretive brochures.

2 Head southeast on Route 122 into the town of **Grafton.** Before factory mass production became the Blackstone's way of life, individual handcrafted artisanry was the rule. The **Willard House and Clock Museum** illustrates the handiwork of three generations of clockmakers, beginning with timepieces crafted before the American Revolution, displayed amid period furnishings from the 18th and 19th centuries. Handsome **Grafton**

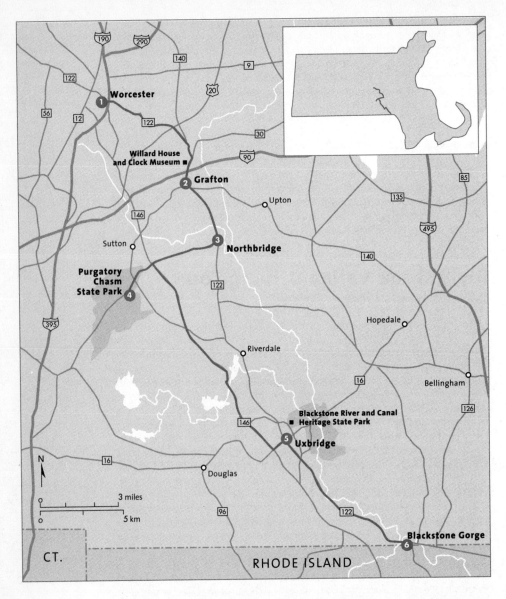

Common (South of the Willard House to Wesson St., west to North St., south to Rte. 140, 2 mi) has a historic marker commemorating the Native Americans who originally inhabited the area, but they haven't gone very far, as you'll see if you drop in on any of the public events held a mile away at the Nipmuc tribe's Hassanamisco Reservation.

❸ Continue south on Route 122, over the Blackstone River into Northbridge, turning west onto Sutton Street, which becomes Central Turnpike after crossing the Sutton town line. When the Willard brothers launched their clockmaking dynasty, most of their valley neighbors were farmers. Pastoral Waters Farm is a remarkably unaltered throwback to that era, with its genuine Colonial farmhouse and regular living history events.

④ Next comes Purgatory Chasm State Park. During the last Ice Age, some 14,000 years ago, runoff from the retreating 1-mi-thick continental ice sheet scoured a small gorge out of the solid granite slopes now flanking the Blackstone Valley. The boulder-strewn ¼-mi chasm, tucked within thick woods, is an ideal spot to stop for short, steep, rock-hopping hikes or picnics, or both.

⑤ Take Route 146 southeast, then head northeast on Route 16 to the town of **Uxbridge**. The best-preserved remnants of the short-lived Blackstone Canal, built in 1828 and bank-rupted 20 years later by railroad competition, are found at the **Blackstone River and Canal Heritage State Park.** Hike or bike along the old canal towpath, paddle through the canal itself by canoe, and enjoy sweeping vistas from King Philip's Rock, a tall ledge named after the 17th-century Wampanoag sachem.

⑥ Head southeast on Route 122 to the **Blackstone Gorge** (on southwest side of Rte. 122 in Blackstone, on the Rhode Island state line). Mill dams and their affiliated ponds have tamed the Blackstone River's rapids, but one section proved too difficult to bottle up with a dam. Stroll to the overlook above the gorge and its waterfall, or join a narrated river tour below the falls aboard the *Blackstone Valley Explorer.*

AMESBURY

MAP 6, I1

(Nearby towns also listed: Haverhill, Newburyport, Salisbury)

Amesbury is between New Hampshire and the Merrimack River, 43 mi north of Boston. When navigator Samuel de Champlain sailed up the Merrimack in 1605, its valley was occupied by the southernmost tribes of the Pennacook confederation. After Euro-peans settled the area in 1645, Amesbury's ferry became the major transit point on the lower Merrimack. During the 1800s, the town became a world-renowned carriage manufacturer after industrialists recognized the power potential in the steep drop of the narrow Powwow River, which still tumbles over rocky cascades behind down-town's Market Square. Now that the factories have vanished, Amesbury has returned to a more sedate country pace, abetted by working farms within its borders, some centuries old. Visitors will find Amesbury easy to reach, with interchanges from both I–95 and I–495 along the town's perimeter.

Information: **Alliance for Amesbury** | 5 Market Sq., Amesbury 01913 | 978/388–3178. **North of Boston State Visitor Center** | I–95 S, between New Hampshire state line and Exit 60 | alliance@shore.net.

Attractions
Amesbury Sports Park. This recreational facility offers four-season family fun. In warmer weather try the driving range, go-carts, water bumper cars, and miniature golf. In winter, you can experience the thrill of snow tubing. Snowmaking equipment guarantees a good ride even when nature doesn't provide one. When hunger strikes, visit the on-site restau-rant and cafeteria. | 12 Hunt Rd., exit 54 off I–495 | 978/388–5788 | Daily.

Bartlett Museum. This small historical museum in the oldest part of Amesbury is a veri-table Old Curiosity Shop of artifacts and memorabilia spanning Amesbury's early settle-ment and industrial history. The building itself is the former 1870 Ferry School, later named after a native son, Josiah Bartlett, one of the signers of the Declaration of Independence, whose birthplace was down the street. | 270 Main St. | 978/388–4528 | $2 | Memorial Day–early Sept., Fri. and Sun. 1–4, Sat. 10–4.

John Greenleaf Whittier Home. John Greenleaf Whittier, the "Quaker poet," was already on his way to becoming one of America's most beloved literary figures when he bought this house in 1836, then only a four-room cottage. Whittier was also a vigorous political activist, abolitionist, and roof-raising public speaker. He lived here until his death in 1892. | 86 Friend St., exit 54 off I-495 | 978/388–1337 | $3.50 | May–Oct., Tues.–Sat. 10–4; Nov.–Apr., by appointment.

Lowell's Boat Shop. Established in 1793, this is the oldest continuous boat-building operation in the nation, the birthplace of the fisherman's dory—a sturdy, seaworthy boat that was also used by the United States Life Saving Service—and one of the first mass production builders. Today it is a working museum and a training ground for boatbuilders and is listed on the National Register of Historic Places and has been designated a National Historic Landmark. | 459 Main St. | 978/388–0162 | www.lowellboatshop.org | Weekdays 10–4.

Rocky Hill Meetinghouse. This 1785 building was once used for church services and public meetings. You can still see its original 18th-century interior. It is on the National Register of Historic Places. | 4 Portsmouth Rd. | 978/462–2634 | www.spnea.org | By appointment.

ON THE CALENDAR

JUNE–JULY: *Amesbury Days.* A weeklong celebration where you can ride in an antique carriage (made in Amesbury, America's carriage capital), go on a trolley tour, join a walking tour, watch a road race, meet local authors at a book-signing, and enjoy musical entertainment and refreshments. Festivities end on July 4 with a fireworks display at Woodsom Farm. | Main St. | 978/388–3178.

Dining

Flatbread. American/Casual. Locals come here for pizzas made with organic ingredients and baked in a wood-fired clay oven. Try the "punctuated equilibrium" topped with red onions, oven-roasted sweet red peppers, rosemary, and kalamata olives. The colorful interior is decorated with art by Amesbury's school children, and there's outdoor dining at umbrella-shaded tables overlooking the Powwow River and the millyard (town common). | 5 Market Sq. | 978/834–9800 | www.flatbread.net | Closed Mon. No lunch | $10–$17 | MC, V.

Lodging

Susse Chalet. This hotel has a "100% satisfaction guaranteed" policy and a VIP program for frequent guests. Family restaurants, a movie theater, and a miniature-golf course are nearby; and Hampton and Salisbury Beaches are a 15-minute drive. Complimentary Continental breakfast. Cable TV. Pool. | 35 Clarke Rd. | 978/388–3400 or 800/5–CHALET | fax 978/388–9850 | www.sussechalet.com | 105 rooms | $80–$85 | AE, D, DC, MC, V.

AMHERST

MAP 6, D3

(Nearby towns also listed: Deerfield, Hadley, Northampton, South Hadley)

Home to Amherst College, Hampshire College, and University of Massachusetts–Amherst—the largest public university in New England—Amherst is the quintessential college town. Casual manners and cheap eats are the rule rather than the exception. It also means that unlike the state's coastal resorts, summer is the slow season, savored by residents who get to enjoy the area's lakes, hiking trails, and bookstores for themselves. Fall and spring are when most visitors descend on the tiny town, to use it as a base for leaf-peeping excursions on area backroads or to applaud sons and daughters receiving their diplomas. Amtrak rail service along the length of the Pioneer Valley connects Amherst with eastern Vermont, central Connecticut, and New York City.

Information: Amherst Area Chamber of Commerce | 409 Main St., Amherst 01002 | 413/253–0700 | chamber@amherstcommon.com | www.amherstcommon.com.

Attractions

Amherst College. Founded in 1821 by a group of gentlemen that included Noah Webster, Amherst College has evolved into a highly selective liberal arts institution enrolling slightly more than 1,500 undergraduates. The earliest structures at the center of the leafy 964-acre campus occupy a hill with spectacular southeastern views of the nearby Holyoke Range. The highlight of the original quadrangle is an exemplary Greek Revival chapel designed by the locally prolific Isaac Damon, one of the nation's earliest trained architects. | Rte. 116 (S. Pleasant St.) and Rte. 9 (College St.), exit 19 off I–91 | 413/542–2000 | www.amherst.edu | Free | Daily.

Pratt Museum of Natural History. This modest museum has two floors of exhibits, which emphasize paleontology, evolution, and the geological history of the Pioneer Valley. There's also an eye-catching Mineral Hall upstairs, whose collection of rocks and glittering crystals includes meteorites. Of special note is the large footprint of *Eubrontes giganteus,* a huge Mesozoic-era carnivore that once roamed the banks of the Connecticut River. | Off Rte. 116, near the main entrance of Amherst College | 413/542–2165 | fax 413/542–2713 | www.amherst.edu/~pratt | Free | Weekdays 9–3:30, Sat. 10–4, Sun. noon–5.

Amherst History Museum. The local historical society's museum is in the circa-1750 Strong House and has both period rooms and changing exhibits drawn from a permanent collection of decorative objects, household artifacts, and tools spanning three centuries of town life. It also sponsors special events, such as an annual summer garden tour. | 67 Amity St. | 413/256–0678 | $3 | Mid-May–Columbus Day, Wed.–Sat. 12:30–3:30; Columbus Day–mid-May, Fri.–Sat. 12:30–3:30.

Emily Dickinson Homestead. Emily Dickinson (1830–86) was born in this sturdy brick house built by her grandfather. She spent all but about 15 years of her life here. Guided tours illuminate her reclusive life. | 280 Main St. | 413/542–8161 | www.amherst.edu/~edhouse | $5 | Mar., Wed. and Sat. 1–4; Apr.–May, Wed.–Sat. 1–4; June–Aug., Wed.–Sun. 1–4; Sept.–Oct., Wed.–Sat. 1–4; Nov.–Dec. 9, Wed. and Sat 1–4.

Jones Library. This attractive Colonial Revival public library has several special collections that merit attention. One contains the papers and manuscripts of Robert Frost, who held a teaching position at Amherst College several times during his career. The other includes the papers and memorabilia of Emily Dickinson. | 43 Amity St. | 413/256–4090 | Free | Sept.–May, Mon., Wed., and Fri. 9–5:30, Tues. and Thurs. 9–9:30, Sun. 1–5; shorter hrs in the summer.

★ **National Yiddish Book Center.** The world's largest museum of Yiddish literature and culture is in a building that resembles a cluster of structures typical of a *shtetl.* Inside, you have access to 1.5 million Yiddish books, a fireside reading area and a visitors center with exhibits. There are also a theater, gardens, and an English-language bookstore. It is in the Harry and Jeanette Weinberg Building adjacent to Hampshire College. | 1021 West St. (Rte. 116) | 413/256–4900 or 800/535–3595 | www.yiddishbookcenter.org | Free | Sun.–Fri. 10–3:30. Closed Jewish holidays.

Norwottuck Rail Trail. This trail begins in Northampton and ends in Amherst. *See* Northampton.

Quabbin Reservoir. This site, 15 mi southeast of Amherst, supplies drinking water for the greater Boston area. It was created during the 1930s by flooding the Swift River valley, including four towns. Today two great dams hold back 412 billion gallons of water. The visitors center has pictures of the former villages, and you can hike, fish, and bird-watch on the grounds. | 485 Ware Rd., off Rte. 9, Belchertown | 413/323–7221 | fax 413/784–1751 | www.state.ma.us/mdc/quabfish.htm#season | Free | Visitor Center open daily 9–4:30; grounds open daily dawn–dusk.

University of Massachusetts. With more than 80 departments in 10 different schools and an enrollment of more than 20,000 students, UMass–Amherst sits at the apex of the state university system. Its sprawling, mostly contemporary campus is dominated by the university library, whose 28-story brick tower is one of the tallest buildings in town, visible from vantage points all across the Pioneer Valley. | Robsham Visitors Center, Massachusetts Ave., off Rte. 116 | 413/545–0111 | www.umass.edu | Free | Daily.

Fine Arts Center. A campus centerpiece, the Fine Arts Center includes a 2,000-seat concert venue, recital hall, and two theaters. It also houses the University Gallery, which specializes in exhibitions of contemporary art, sometimes drawing on the university's own collection of American 20th-century works. | 207 Hasbrouck Hall, off N. Pleasant St. | 413/546–3670 (gallery), 413/545–2511 (box office), or 800/999–UMAS | www.umass.edu/fac | Free | Gallery, Tues.–Fri. 11–4:30, weekends 2–5. Box office, weekdays 10–4.

© Corbis

PIONEER VALLEY ARCHITECTURE

Following the uncertain years of tight monetary credit after the end of the American Revolution, most Pioneer Valley towns entered an era of expansion, from the 1780s through the 1820s. Newfound prosperity from agriculture and small business enabled many residents to build homes and churches whose Federal-period architectural stylings now lend a defining visual character to their towns. At the time, the nation was only just beginning to value professional architecture, mostly through the work of Boston's Charles Bulfinch, who had trained in England. So the construction that resulted from the Pioneer Valley's growth depended primarily upon self-taught "housewrights." But several were so prolific, and their designs so accomplished, that they became as influential in their day as any formally trained architect.

One of these significant Valley builders was Isaac Damon, who moved to Northampton in 1812 from coastal Massachusetts and practiced his craft in the area for more than 20 years. His most accessible legacy is the original Amherst College campus; of particular note are Johnson Chapel and South Hall, a strikingly beautiful Greek Revival complex perched atop a hill. He also built a series of town meeting-houses, six of which still survive, including the First Church in Springfield and the Second Church in Hadley. Work by his apprentices, such as Deerfield's 1824 Unitarian Church, also demonstrates that Damon's effect on valley architecture was not limited to what he wrought with his own hands.

The other major influence on period construction was Asher Benjamin, who first came to the Pioneer Valley around 1796. Although he only worked in the region for a few years—the 1797 Leavitt-Hovey House, now used by the Greenfield Public Library, is one of his few local works that remain—his designs are widespread. This is because he authored seven pattern books that were widely used by local builders for some 50 years. In fact, Benjamin's *The American Builder's Companion* is considered the nation's first architectural textbook.

JUNE: *A Taste of Amherst.* Tables are set up on the common so you can sample what's available in local restaurants. There's also musical entertainment by national pop bands, children's activities, and a beer and wine tasting. | Rtes. 116 and 9 | 413/253–0700.

Dining

Antonio's. Pizza. There is no waitstaff here—you order your food and pick it up at the counter. Popular items include the fresh tomato and basil pizza and the black bean, chopped tomato, feta cheese, and avocado pizza. You can dine at one of nine marble tables here or take your food away with you. | 31 N. Pleasant St. | 413/253–0808 | $8–$15 | No credit cards.

Black Sheep. Café. Sandwiches are the specialty of this bakery/deli/coffeeshop/gourmet food store patronized by Amherst residents and students. Try the Black Sheep baguette (fresh mozzarella, basil pesto, sundried tomatoes, and balsamic vinegar served on a French baguette) or the valley girl (smoked turkey, brie, lettuce, tomato, and honey mustard on a baguette). | 79 Main St. | 413/253–3442 | fax 413/253–6544 | Breakfast also available | $3–$6 | MC, V.

Elijah Boltwood's Tavern at the Lord Jeffery Inn. American. Here you'll find family dining on traditional hearty New England fare in a neo-Colonial inn owned by Amherst College. It's best known for burgers, fish-and-chips, maple-glazed ribs, and New England pot roast. There's open-air dining on a garden patio. Kids' menu. Sun. brunch. No smoking. | 30 Boltwood Ave. | 413/253–2576 | Breakfast also available | $7–$20 | AE, DC, MC, V.

Judie's. American/Casual. For more than two decades, Amherst residents have been coming here for popovers the size of a small football. They're included with some of the dishes—like the seafood scampi in a popover—or they can be ordered à la carte. There are also exotic soups (like hot curried chicken carrot bisque), imaginative salads (such as the goat cheese–praline–walnut) and mouth-watering desserts. The bar is famous for martinis that are almost as big as the popovers. | 51 N. Pleasant St. | 413/253–3491 | $7–$15 | AE, D, MC, V.

La Cucina di Pinocchio. Italian. A northern Italian trattoria with subdued lighting and casual elegance that has some of the area's finest meals without pretension. Try the calamari salad, gamberi fra diavolo, linguine pescatore, filetto di Medici, and risotto with porcini mushrooms and grappa. No smoking. | 30 Boltwood Walk | 413/256–4110 | No lunch Sun. | $12.95–$21.95 | AE, DC, MC, V.

Pasta e Basta. Italian. One of Amherst's top inexpensive restaurants is this casual spot. The best deal on the menu is the grill and pasta—order your choice of pasta, sauce, vegetable, and grill (chicken, shrimp, tuna, swordfish, salmon) at the counter and then bring your plate to one of 20 tables or booths. | 26 Main St. | 413/256–3550 | $5.75–$8.50 | No credit cards.

Windowed Hearth at the Lord Jeffery Inn. Contemporary. You'll find formal but unpretentious dining amid views of the town common at this restaurant with a seasonally changing menu that highlights the distinctive regional flavors of New England fish, game, and produce. Known for pecan-crusted duck breast, Beaujolais-braised lamb, and beef tenderloin. No smoking. | 30 Boltwood Ave. | 413/253–2576 | Closed Sun.–Tues. No lunch | $24–27.50 | AE, DC, MC, V.

Lodging

★ **Allen House Inn.** A Victorian inn that was restored with great attention to detail in order to recapture the beauty of the era in which it was built. It won a Historic Preservation Award in 1991, and has authentic antiques, period furniture, art, and wall coverings. Complimentary breakfast. In-room data ports, TV in common area. No kids under 8. No smoking. | 599 Main St. | 413/253–5000 | fax 413/253–0846 | www.allenhouse.com | 7 rooms (5 with shower only) | $75–$155 | AE, D, MC, V.

The Black Walnut Inn. This 1821 brick, Federal-style house, 3 mi north of Amherst's common, is true to its name as there are 35 black walnut trees growing on its 1.5-acre grounds. The rooms have antiques and period reproductions including canopy and sleigh beds. There is a gas fireplace in the parlor and chandeliers in the hall and dining room. Locals frequently have breakfast at the inn with friends who are guests and, in the evening, tea, homemade cookies, and sherry are served. Complimentary breakfast. In-room data ports, cable TV. No pets. No smoking. | 1184 N. Pleasant St., North Amherst | 413/549–5649 | www.blackwalnutinn.com | 7 rooms | $98–$128 | AE.

Campus Center Hotel. You'll find spacious rooms with large windows that have views of the campus and countryside here. The walls are exposed cinderblock and the rooms have modern furnishings. Free local transportation. Cable TV. Barbershop. Health club. Shops, video games. Business services. | 918 Campus Center, UMass | 413/549–6000 | fax 413/545–1210 | www.aux.umass.edu/hotel | 116 rooms, 2 suites | $72–$105, $250 suite | AE, D, DC, MC, V.

Ivy House Bed and Breakfast. This restored 1750s Colonial Cape is on a residential street one block from the University of Massachusetts and within walking distance of the town center. Complimentary breakfast. No TV. No kids. No smoking. | 1 Sunset Ct | 413/549–7554 | 2 rooms | $90 | No credit cards.

Lord Jeffery Inn. This rambling neo-Colonial inn overlooking the town common is at the edge of the Amherst College campus. Some of its rooms face the town common, while others face historic churches nearby, and some have balconies that overlook a garden; all are decorated with darker New England colors. Restaurants, bar. In-room data ports, cable TV. Pets allowed (fee). | 30 Boltwood Ave. | 413/253–2576 | fax 413/256–6152 | www.pinnacle-inns.com/lordjefferyinn | 48 rooms, 8 suites | $99–$189, $149–$189 suites | AE, DC, MC, V.

University Lodge. This renovated motel next to the University of Massachusetts campus has comfortable and unpretentious colonial-style rooms. Cable TV. | 345 N. Pleasant St. | 413/256–8111 | hojohadley@aol.com | 20 rooms | $69–$99 | AE, D, DC, MC, V.

ANDOVER AND NORTH ANDOVER

MAP 6, I2

(Nearby towns also listed: Haverhill, Lawrence, Lowell)

North Andover and Andover were originally one town, settled in 1640 on land acquired from the Pentucket tribe, one of the southern allies of New Hampshire's Pennacook confederation. Split first into separate parishes, and finally, in 1855, into separate towns, the two Andovers have now become distinct from one another. Or so their residents would have you believe. Outwardly, both count among the state's more affluent communities, with well-preserved Colonial homes and strong public schools. But North Andover has shunned industrial development, preferring to be a rural bedroom community with large tracts of open space. Its neighbor, on the other hand, has embraced high-tech office development by such companies as Hewlett Packard, Raytheon, and Compaq/Digital. Andover is also the home of the prestigious Phillips Academy, a coeducational boarding school whose landscaped campus lends a collegiate air to one end of downtown.

Information: **Merrimack Valley Chamber of Commerce** | 264 Essex St., Lawrence 01840 | 978/686–0900 | www.merrimackvalleychamber.com.

Attractions

Andover Historical Society. Amos Blanchard, an Andover banker, built this late Federal-style house and English-style barn in 1819. Guides use his family's middle-class life and their household artifacts to personalize America's shift from an agrarian to a mercantile and industrial nation during the 1820s–40s. The AHS also maintains a library and archive on the premises, with extensive local genealogical records. | 97 Main St., Andover | 978/475–2236 | fax 978/470–2741 | www.ultranet.com/~andhists | $4 | Tues.–Fri. 9–5, Sat. 9–3.

Harold Parker State Forest. At this 3,000-acre park there are campsites and recreation for all seasons—guided nature walks, swimming, picnicking, hiking, canoeing, cross-country skiing, horseback, mountain biking, bird-watching, fishing, and seasonal hunting. | 1951 Turnpike Rd., North Andover | 978/686–3391 | www.state.mass.us | Free, parking $2 | Year-round.

Phillips Academy. Known to students and applicants simply as "Andover," this distinguished coeducational boarding school enjoys facilities and grounds similar to those of a small college. Founded in 1778, it is the quintessential New England prep school, with wide manicured lawns and stately, redbrick Georgian buildings. | 180 Main St., Andover | 978/749–4000 | www.andover.edu | Free | Daily.

Addison Gallery of American Art. The name of this museum belies the size of its collection, which covers three floors of exhibition space. It has an excellent and varied scope, including prints, paintings, and sculpture from throughout the past 300 years, plus novelties such as ship models. Its highlight is the outstanding photography collection, which spans the life and artistic possibilities of the medium, from early daguerreotypes to Man Ray's rayograms. | Chapel Ave., Andover | 978/749–4015 | fax 978/749–4025 | www.andover.edu/addison | Free | Labor Day–July, Tues.–Sat. 10–5, Sun. 1–5.

ANDOVER AND
NORTH ANDOVER

INTRO
ATTRACTIONS
DINING
LODGING

Robert S. Peabody Museum for Archaeology. A small museum dedicated to the ancient indigenous peoples of North and South America, with changing exhibits drawn largely from its own extensive collections. Highlights on long-term display include artifacts and dioramas related to New England's Native Americans, and ceramics from the Pecos Pueblo in New Mexico. The museum frequently complements its exhibits with presentations by noted professionals from the field. | 175 Main St., Andover | 978/749–4490 | fax 978/749–4495 | www.andover.edu/rspeabody | Free | Labor Day–July, Tues.–Sat. noon–5.

Stevens–Coolidge Place. This 90-acre estate was once the summer home of diplomat John Gardner Coolidge and his wife, Helen Stevens Coolidge, who knew it as Ashdale Farm. Over the course of some 30 years, the Coolidges remodeled the farmhouse along neo-Colonial lines, filled it with fine art, antiques, and Oriental rugs gathered from their globe-trotting travels, and planted acres of formal gardens. The landscaping includes a sunken rose garden inside an old stone barn foundation, perennial gardens, and specimen trees. | 137 Andover St., North Andover | 978/682–3580 | fax 978/356–2143 | www.thetrustees.org | Grounds: free; house: $4 | Grounds, daily. House tours, Mother's Day–Columbus Day, Sun. 1–5; June–Aug., Wed. 2–4, or by appointment.

ON THE CALENDAR

DEC.: *Brickstone Square Tree Lighting Ceremony.* There's a 100-ft evergreen tree, Santa's village, carousel, petting zoo, free cookies, apple cider, and hot chocolate on the Sunday after Thanksgiving. | Brickstone Sq., Andover | 978/749–3008.

Dining

Andover Inn. Continental. You'll dine elegantly at this classic inn on the campus of Phillips Academy, complete with black-tie waitstaff and classical music. It is known for filet mignon, roast duck, and the Sunday evening *rijstafel*. Live music nightly. Kids' menu. No smoking. | 1 Chapel Ave., Andover | 978/475–5903 | Reservations essential | Jacket and tie required | No lunch weekends | $23–$27 | AE, D, DC, MC, V.

China Blossom. Chinese. A well-appointed, spacious restaurant with efficient service and decorated in warm tones that won't distract you from your meal. Known for Szechuan beef and seafood dishes. Buffet. | 946 Osgood St., North Andover | 978/682–2242 | $6–$15 | AE, D, DC, MC, V.

Merrimax. American. Like the hotel in which it's located (the Wyndham Andover), this restaurant caters to the business traveler. To attract patrons on the weekends, a prime-rib or chicken buffet with salad bar, two vegetables, and dessert is available on Friday and Saturday evenings. | 123 Old River Rd., Andover | 978/975–3600 | fax 978/975–0383 | $15–$28 | AE, D, DC, MC, V.

Palmer's Restaurant and Tavern. Eclectic. This red clapboard former inn blends in with the residential neighborhood. There are three dining rooms and a large bar with entertainment on weekends. The menu changes with the seasons. A popular appetizer is crab cakes with remoulade sauce, which can be followed by grilled club sirloin with roasted peppers and potato pancake in a balsamic glaze or haddock fillet with shrimp roasted with creole sauce. Kids' menu. Sun. brunch. | 18 Elm St., Andover | 978/470–1606 | June–mid-Nov., no brunch Sun.; Mid-Nov.–May, no dinner Sun. | $17–$27 | AE, D, DC, MC, V.

Sweet Basil. Thai. At this understated yet comfortable restaurant within a strip mall, the cuisine leans toward the sweet rather than the hot and spicy side of the Asian spectrum. Try the duck choo chee, beef with macadamia nuts, and chicken satay. No smoking. | 209 North St. (Rte. 28), Andover | 978/470–8098 | $16–$21 | AE, D, DC, MC, V.

Lodging

Andover Inn. This elegant 1930s neo-Georgian, country-style inn is on the grounds of prestigious Phillips Academy. There are antiques in the lobby, while the rooms resemble more modern hotels. There's big-band dance music on Friday and Saturday evenings. Bar, dining room, room service. Beauty salon. Business services. | 4 Chapel Ave., Andover | 978/475–5903 or 800/242–5903 | fax 978/475–1053 | www.andoverinn.com | 23 rooms, 2 executive suites, 4 junior suites | $115, $150–$195 suites | AE, D, DC, MC, V.

Hawthorn Suites Andover. This extended-stay hotel caters to the business traveler with preferred pricing for 30-day stays and shuttle service to specific companies in Andover. Appetizers and fruit juices are served in the Hawthorn Room on Mondays through Thursdays. The property is just off exit 45 on Route 93. Complimentary breakfast. In-room data ports, kitchenettes, cable TV. Outdoor pool. Exercise room. Laundry facilities, laundry services. Business services. Pets allowed. | 4 Riverside Dr., Andover | 978/475–6000 or 800/527–1133 | fax 978/475–6639 | hawthorn.com | 84 rooms | $124–$159 studio, $134–$169 1–bedroom suite, $169–$209 2–bedroom suite | AE, D, DC, MC, V.

Holiday Inn Tewksbury/Andover. Near the intersection of I–93 and I–495 on the Tewksbury/Andover line, this hotel offers easy access to southern New Hampshire and Boston. It has Victorian-style decor, marble floors, and mahogany detail. Children up to 12 eat and stay free. Restaurant, bar with entertainment, room service. In-room data ports, some refrigerators, cable TV. Indoor pool. Hot tub. Gym. Business services. | 4 Highwood Dr., Tewksbury | 978/640–9000 or 800/HOLIDAY | fax 978/640–0623 | www.holiday-inn.com | 237 rooms, 6 suites | $94–$149, $119–$169 suites | AE, D, DC, MC, V.

Ramada Rolling Green Inn and Conference Center. This property has an attractive garden atrium and more than 20,000 square ft of conference space. The carpeted lobby has a wood front desk, a map of the town of Andover, and an entrance to the indoor courtyard, where you'll find one of the hotel's two pools. Restaurant, bar, room service. Cable TV. 2 pools (1 indoor). Hot tub. 9-hole par-3 golf, indoor tennis. Health club. Business services. | 311 Lowell St., Andover | 978/475–5400 or 800/2–RAMADA | fax 978/470–1108 | www.fine-hotels.com | 179 rooms, 10 suites | $149–$250 | AE, D, DC, MC, V.

Susse Chalet Inn of Tewksbury. Price and location are this hotel's best features. It's only 3 mi west of Andover and 2 mi from Lowell, a historic city with many sightseeing attractions and commuter rail connections to Boston. Complimentary Continental breakfast. Cable TV. Pool. Laundry facilities. | 1695 Andover St. (Rte. 133), Tewksbury | 978/640–0700 or 800/5–CHALET | fax 978/640–1175 | www.sussechalet.com | 133 rooms | $65–$105 | AE, D, DC, MC, V.

Tage Inn. This renovated chain inn has Queen Anne–style furnishings in every guest room. Guests are greeted by a fountain in the lobby, which is also decorated with three brass chandeliers, and there are large windows that provide a good deal of light. Restaurant, complimentary Continental breakfast. In-room data ports, cable TV. Indoor pool. Hot tub. Tennis. Gym. Video games. Business services. | 131 River Rd. | 978/685–6200 or 800/322–TAGE | fax 978/794–9626 | www.tageinn.com | 180 rooms | $79.95–$110.95 | AE, D, DC, MC, V.

Wyndham Andover. This hotel is off Route 93, near Canobie Lake Park and Rockingham Park in New Hampshire. It has a marble lobby and the rooms have oak desks, which are ideal business travelers. Behind the hotel there is a walking/bike trail. Restaurant, bar. In-room data ports, some refrigerators, cable TV. Indoor pool. Hot tub. Gym. Pets allowed. | 123 Old River Rd., Andover | 978/975–3600 or 800/WYNDHAM | fax 978/975–2664 | www.wyndham.com | 293 rooms | $79–$149 | AE, D, DC, MC, V.

AQUINNAH (MARTHA'S VINEYARD)

(Nearby towns also listed: Chilmark, West Tisbury)

Aquinnah is the most remote town on Martha's Vineyard. It no longer takes a full day to get here as it did in the days of horse-and-buggy travel. However, the town's character is still rooted in the self-reliance born of this isolation. Once known as Gay Head, the town changed its name in 1998 after voters petitioned the state legislature to let them return to the Algonquian word for "high land," an apt description of the town's prevailing topography. The new name is a reminder that Wampanoag sachems once ruled the Vineyard, and specifically reflects the fact that their descendants still comprise more than a third of the town's population. Aquinnah's most notable feature is its former namesake, the colorful Gay Head cliffs, a National Natural Landmark and part of the tribal lands. The redbrick lighthouse atop the cliffs, a welcome friend to mariners since 1856, is among the Vineyard's most photogenic sights.

Information: Martha's Vineyard Chamber of Commerce | Box 1698, Vineyard Haven 02568 | 508/693–0085. **Information Center** | Beach Rd., Vineyard Haven | 508/693–0085 | mvcc@vineyard.net | www.mvy.com.

Attractions

Aquinnah (Gay Head) Cliffs. These mile-long cliffs are a national landmark. The layers of sands, gravels, and clays of various hues, which the seas and glaciers have turned into waving bands of color, tell the story of a forested land that was destroyed by floods and covered with new growth. | Western end of state road and Moshup Trail | 508/645–2300 | Free | Daily.

Aquinnah Lighthouse. The redbrick light was built in 1844 to replace a wooden tower authorized by President John Quincy Adams. It is maintained by the Martha's Vineyard Historical Society under a 35-year lease with the U.S. Coast Guard. | Western end of state road and Moshup Trail | 508/627–4441 | $2 | Late June–mid-September, Fri.–Sun. about 1½ hr before sunset–½ hour after sunset.

Cranberry Lands. As you go along West Basin Road, you'll see the Vineyard Sound shore of Menemsha Light and an area of cranberry bogs gone wild that is a popular nesting site for birds. At the end of the road, with marshland on the right and low dunes and grasses on the left, there is a great view of the quiet fishing village of Menemsha across the water. | W. Basin Rd. | 508/645–2300 | Free | Daily.

Lobsterville Beach. This 2 mi, rocky, cold-water beach on Vineyard Sound is adjacent to the sand dunes along Lobsterville Road. It has a nesting area for seagulls and is a popular fishing spot. From the beach, there's a great view of Cuttyhunk and the Elizabeth Islands; on clear evenings, you can see the lights of New Bedford. No dogs allowed. | Lobsterville Rd. | 508/645–2300 | Free | Daily.

Moshup Beach. Aquinnah's public beach is a cold-water surf beach off Moshup Trail. Walk along the beach for a good view of Aquinnah Cliffs. | Moshup Trail | 508/645–2300 | Free, $15 parking in summer | Parking lot open 9 am–11 pm.

Quitsa Pond Lookout. You'll have a good view of the adjoining Menemsha and Nashaquitsa ponds, the woods and the ocean from this spot. | State Rd. | 508/645–2100 | Free.

MARTHA'S VINEYARD

Martha's Vineyard has been a favorite destination for New York celebrities for decades, but the First Family's annual visits during President Clinton's first three years in office have catapulted the island firmly into the international spotlight. Despite the problems that ride the coattails of popularity, such as crowds and sharp price hikes, the island is still a gem. That old Vineyard magic, deep relaxation, is still in abundant supply. The trick is simply knowing when to visit, and where to go.

Like Cape Cod, the Vineyard clings to its maritime roots with its simple split into two halves, up island and down island. The more easterly down-island towns—Vineyard Haven, Oak Bluffs, and Edgartown—are the only ones with ferry access to the mainland, and are thus most congested in July and August. The western, or up-island towns—West Tisbury, Chilmark, and Aquinnah—are predominately rural, with more scenic than commercial attractions. Since most visitors are bound for the beach, it's easy to avoid the crowds by spending the first half of the day exploring local wildlife sanctuaries and woodlands, then hitting the shore in the late afternoon, after sunburn and exhaustion have sent most people packing. Likewise, those in the know avoid paying dearly for the dubious and frustrating privilege of idling in traffic waiting to board the Woods Hole car ferry, and instead bring or rent a bicycle. Short distances and paved paths aren't the only incentive for taking up a two-wheeler: with a bike, you'll never have to hunt for parking.

Before Memorial Day weekend in late May or after Labor Day weekend in September, the island becomes blessedly free of gridlock, prices at many establishments drop a notch, and it no longer requires a three-month advance reservation to bring your car across by ferry. And though some shops and most up-island restaurants are strictly summer businesses, nature doesn't stop putting on a good show, from spring flowers to autumn sunsets. As for the weather, it's genuinely pleasant from mid-April until the clocks turn back to standard time in October. Just remember your sweater, and perhaps a windbreaker for extended beachcombing strolls, and don't plan on swimming without a wet suit.

Related towns: Aquinnah, Edgartown, Chilmark, Oak Bluffs, Vineyard Haven, West Tisbury

© Corbis

AUG.: *The Legends of Moshup Pageant.* On the third Saturday of the month the Wampanoag Tribal Council sponsors this event where you'll hear their creation story for the island of Martha's Vineyard (Noepe) with dancing, drumming, and narration. Bring a picnic, spread out your blanket, and watch a spectacular sunset before the pageant begins. | 20 Black Brook Rd. | 508/645–9265.

Dining

The Restaurant at Outermost Inn. Contemporary. There are always fresh lobster, fish, steak, and vegetarian entrées on the menu here. Try the grilled free-range duck breast with blueberry and balsamic vinegar or the grilled yellow-fin tuna with a fresh tomato vinaigrette. This casual spot has a fireplace, hardwood floors, and a glassed-in porch with a great view of the sunset. Dinner seatings are at 6 and 8 pm. | 171 Lighthouse Rd. | 508/645–3511 | fax 508/645–3514 | Reservations essential | Closed Mid-Oct.–May. No lunch | $60 prix–fixe | AE, D, MC, V.

Lodging

Duck Inn. The inn is named for the wild ducks that visit the 5½-acre property and also for the low spots in the house where you must duck to avoid bumping your head. The first floor of this 200-year-old farmhouse is built of granite; there's also a granite fireplace. Second-floor guest rooms have views of the ocean and Gay Head lighthouse. It's a short walk to the beach or to Gay Head cliff. Complimentary breakfast. No air-conditioning, cable TV in 1 room. Hot tub, massage. Pets allowed in 1 guest room. | 160 State Rd. | 508/645–9018 | fax 508/645–2790 | 5 rooms | $85–$200 | Closed Jan.–Mar. | MC, V.

Outermost Inn. This light, open, and airy Martha's Vineyard beachhouse has lots of windows, providing all rooms with water views. There are hardwood floors throughout, and each room has a different type of hardwood flooring. Guests have free access to the soft-drink bar, but it's a dry town, so BYOB. The beach is a 10-minute walk away. Dining room, complimentary breakfast. No air-conditioning. No kids under 12. No smoking. | Lighthouse Rd. | 508/645–3511 | fax 508/645–3514 | www.outermostinn.com | 7 rooms | $240–$320 | Closed mid-Oct.–Apr. | AE, D, MC, V.

BARNSTABLE VILLAGE (CAPE COD)

MAP 6, K6

(Nearby towns also listed: Centerville, Hyannis, Mashpee, Yarmouth)

Barnstable Village is one of seven villages within the town of Barnstable, and the judicial seat of Barnstable County, which covers the whole of Cape Cod. Scenic Route 6A traverses the village, on the southern rim of Cape Cod Bay. A few shops and historic sites lie along the narrow, heavily trafficked highway, but the focal point of the community is its harbor, which hums in summer with small boats, whale-watch cruises, and the conversations of dockside restaurant patrons.

Information: **Hyannis Area Chamber of Commerce** | 1481 Rte. 132, Hyannis 02601 | 508/362–5230 or 877/HYANNIS | www.hyannis.com.

Attractions

Cape Cod Art Association Gallery. This association of 500 local Cape Cod artists mounts monthly exhibitions, with juried awards and prizes, at their fine-art gallery, 1 mi east of Barnstable Village. All works are for sale. The association also holds classes, workshops, and demonstrations throughout the year. | 3480 Rte. 6A | 508/362–2909 | Free | Mon.–Sat. 10–4, Sun. noon–5.

Customs House. The U.S. government built this site in 1855–1856 to serve as both a customs house and post office. The second floor now houses maritime artifacts from Barnstable county. The post office, on the first floor, currently operates only during the Village Stroll in December. | Cobb's Hill (Rte. 6A) | 508/362–2092 | June 16–Oct. 12, Tues.–Sun. 1:30–4:40.

Donald G. Trayser Memorial Museum. The main theme of this town-owned museum is the sea and Barnstable's historical connection to it. Exhibits focus on the town's maritime past. The three-building complex includes Barnstable's Old Custom House, a carriage shed dominated by a large horse-drawn hearse, and the nation's oldest jail, built in 1690, whose walls still display graffiti from its Colonial prisoners. | Main St. (Rte. 6A) | 508/362–2092 | www.barnstablepatriot.com/trayser/museum | Fathers Day–mid-Oct., Tues.–Sun. 1:30–4:30.

Hyannis Whale Watcher Cruises. Off the tip of Cape Cod, just north of Provincetown, lies Stellwagen Bank National Marine Sanctuary, whose nutrient-rich waters attract a number of endangered whale species from spring through fall. This outfit offers 3½-hour excursions to Stellwagen, with colorful commentary by on-board naturalists. Their spacious, jet-powered vessel's three decks maximize space at the railings for passengers, and the absence of a propeller makes it safer for the whales, too. | Millway Marine Boatyard, Barnstable Harbor | 508/362–6088 or 800/287–0374 | fax 508/362–9739 | www.whales.net | $26 | May–Oct., daily.

Nickerson Memorial Room. A room at Cape Cod Community College that has an extensive non-circulating collection of books, periodicals, and manuscripts dealing with all aspects of the study of Cape Cod. | 2240 Iyanough Rd., off Rte. 132, West Barnstable | 508/362–2131, ext. 4445 | www.capecodhistory.org | Free | Mon., Wed., and Fri 8:30–4; Tues 8:30–3.

Olde Colonial Courthouse. Built in 1774, this was the colony's second courthouse. The King's Court was held here during the pre-revolutionary era and it was here that the famous Protest March of September 1774 was held. There's an annual lecture series at 7:30 PM on Tuesdays in July and August. | 3018 Main St. (Rte. 6A) | 508/362–8927 | By appointment.

© Corbis

THE CAPE VS. THE SEA

Slowly but steadily, Cape Cod is disappearing. Geologically quite young, the Cape is essentially a great big pile of debris left behind by melting Continental glaciers during the last Ice Age, 14,000 to 20,000 years ago. Without solid bedrock underpinnings like the rest of Massachusetts, the Cape is at the mercy of the surrounding sea. The steady pounding of the surf and powerful high tides known as storm surges chip away at the land, stealing away several feet each year. Even worse is the loss of coastal acreage to rising sea levels. Currently three times more real estate is quietly submerged each year than is lost to the highly visible forces of erosion, and global warming will only accelerate this. Although the Cape permanently loses an average of 80 acres annually, the entire process of reducing it to an underwater sandbar will still take up to 5,000 years. Nonetheless, there are already effects on residents and visitors: buildings and homes that have tumbled into the sea, traffic detours due to unanchored sand dunes migrating windward across roads, and increased risk of storm-related flooding in low-lying areas. If you want a front-row seat for the irresistible force of nature, come to Cape Cod: the show has already begun.

Sandy Neck Beach. This stretches 6 mi across a peninsula that ends at Sandy Neck Light. It is one of the most beautiful on Cape Cod with dunes, soft sand, and sea spread endlessly east, west, and north. The adjacent Great Salt Marsh used to be harvested for salt hay and is now a refuge for birds. The main beach has lifeguards, snack bar, restrooms, and showers. | 425 Sandy Neck Rd., West Barnstable | 508/362–8300 | Parking $10 Memorial Day–Labor Day | Daily 9–9, staffed 9–4.

Sandy Neck Light. This lighthouse dates from 1857 and has been out of commission since 1952. It is now privately owned and no longer accessible from the beach; the best view of it is from Barnstable harbor. | 425 Sandy Neck Rd., West Barnstable | 508/362–8300.

Sturgis Library. After this circa-1645 residence for Rev. John Lothrop was converted into a library in 1867, it acquired the distinction of being the oldest library building in the nation. Now one of Barnstable's seven public libraries, it has special collections including some of the region's leading genealogical resources, as well as small displays related to local history. | 3090 Main St. (Rte. 6A) | 508/362–6636 | www.capecod.net/sturgis | Free | Mon., Wed., and Fri. 10–5; Tues. and Thurs. 1–8; Sat. 10–4; Sun. 1–5 | Closed Sun. in July and Aug.

West Parish Meetinghouse. This 1717 structure, whose steeple is surmounted by a large golden rooster, is the oldest Congregational church in the United States. In its belfry is a genuine Revere bell, one of only 148 known church bells cast by the famous patriot and his sons. | 2049 Meetinghouse Way, West Barnstable | 508/362–4445 | Free | Late May–mid-Oct., daily 9–5; mid-Oct.–late May, weekdays 9–5.

ON THE CALENDAR

JULY: *4th of July Parade.* The 20-minute parade begins at 9:30 in Barnstable Village, proceeds down Main Street, winds around the cemetery and ends at the hollow. There are floats, antique cars, horses, and a color guard. Children can march in costume and decorate their bikes. At the conclusion, there is a flag raising ceremony and children's activities. | Main St. (Rte. 6A) | 508/362–2093.

DEC.: *Barnstable Village Christmas Stroll.* Merchants provide refreshments and Santa Claus puts in an appearance at the Barnstable Comedy Club while jugglers, bands, and choirs provide entertainment. There's also a tree lighting ceremony. | Main St. (Rte. 6A) | 508/362–5230.

Dining

Barnstable Tavern and Grille. Seafood. This traditional colonial tavern has been in operation since 1799, and is amid a cluster of shops in the historic district. Try the pistachio pan-fried sole, prime rib, or lobster. If the weather is nice, have lunch outside under an umbrella on the patio. Live music on Fridays 5–7. Kids' menu. No smoking in dining room. | 3176 Main St. | 508/362–2355 | $13.99–$21.95 | AE, D, DC, MC, V.

Dolphin Restaurant. Contemporary. As its name suggests, seafood is the specialty of this restaurant that has been owned and operated by the Smith family for more than 50 years. Try the chilean sea bass with a lobster–and–roasted corn salsa, or swordfish with a hazelnut crisp, or panfried soft-shell crab. Dishes use locally grown ingredients such as vine-ripened tomatoes and fresh basil. | 3250 Main St. (Rte. 6A) | 508/362–6610 | fax 508/362–1666 | No lunch Sun. | $15–$22 | AE, D, MC, V.

Harbor Point. Seafood. This eatery is on a secluded hillside overlooking Barnstable Harbor and Cape Cod Bay, 1 mi east of Barnstable. In the evenings there are exceptional sunset views. It's known for fresh seafood, sautéed lobster, and lamb chops. Try the lobster-stuffed filet mignon. Kid's menu. Sun. brunch. No smoking in main dining room. | Harbor Point Rd., Cummaquid | 508/362–2231 | Reservations essential | Closed Jan. 1–Apr. 1 | $16.95–$24.95 | MC, V.

Mattakeese Wharf. Seafood. The casual dining rooms and over-the-water decks, ¼ mi from Barnstable Village, provide exceptional views of boats, seagulls, and sunsets. Try the bouillabaisse, baked stuffed shrimp, and lobster. Open-air dining. Live music Wed.–Sun. Sun.

BARNSTABLE VILLAGE
(CAPE COD)

INTRO
ATTRACTIONS
DINING
LODGING

brunch. No smoking in dining room. | 271 Mill Way | 508/362–4511 | Closed Nov.–Apr. | $13–$28 | AE, D, MC, V.

Lodging

Acworth Inn. Romantic getaways are a specialty of this quiet, bright, and airy inn built in 1860 and 1½–2 mi east of Barnstable. Each room has a queen-size bed and is decorated in white and pastel colors. It's a 10-minute walk to the bay. Complimentary breakfast. Cable TV in some rooms, no room phones. No kids under 12. No smoking. | 4352 Old King's Hwy. (Rte. 6A), Cummaquid | 508/362–3330 or 800/362–6363 | fax 508/375–0304 | www.acworthinn.com | 5 rooms (2 with shower only), 1 suite | $115–$150, $185 suite | AE, D, MC, V.

Ashley Manor. This lovely old home has extensive grounds and guest rooms and suites furnished with antiques. Some rooms also have fireplaces. The manor is within walking distance of the beach. Complimentary breakfast. Some in-room hot tubs. Tennis. No kids under 14. | 3660 Olde Kings Hwy. (Rte. 6A) | 508/362–8044 or 888/535–2246 | fax 508/362–9927 | www.capecod.net/ashleymn | 6 rooms, 4 suites | $135–$195, $185–195 suites | AE, D, MC, V.

★ **Beechwood Inn.** A pretty Victorian inn with a wraparound porch and rooms with fireplaces or water views. There are king- and queen-size beds available, and all the furnishings are antiques. The harbor is within walking distance. A two-night minimum stay is required on weekends and in August. Complimentary breakfast. Refrigerators. No kids under 12. No smoking. | 2839 Main St. (Rte. 6A) | 508/362–6618 or 800/609–6618 | fax 508/362–0298 | www.beechwoodinn.com | 6 rooms | $95–$180 | AE, MC, V.

Cobb's Cove. The house was designed in saltbox colonial style by proprietor/owner Henri-Jean Chester, a retired civil engineer. The interior has huge wood beams, rough burlap walls, and a heavy wooden doors studded with nail heads. Guest rooms are large and filled with antiques and reproductions. Each has a dressing area and private bath with whirlpool tub and plush terrycloth robes. Dining room, complimentary breakfast. No air conditioning, in-room hot tubs, no room phones, no TV. Library. No pets. No smoking. | 31 Powder Hill Rd. | 508/362–9356 | fax 508/362–9356 | www.cobbscove.com | 6 rooms | $149–$189 | AE, D, MC, V.

Heaven on High. Nestled high on a hill overlooking dunes, Great Salt Marsh, and the Bay at Sandy Neck, this is a cross between a California beach house and Cape Cod comfort. The great room is filled with overstuffed chairs and couches, fireplace, and natural oak floors and a deck runs the full length of the house, offering panoramic views. Each room is named for the collection it houses—for example, the French Ivory room has Art Deco celluloid, clocks, bureau sets, and perfume bottles, as well as Victorian bamboo furniture. Dining room, complimentary breakfast. Refrigerators. Putting green. No pets. No smoking. | 70 High St., West Barnstable | 508/362–4441 or 800/362–4044 | fax 508/362–4465 | www.heavenonhigh.com | 3 rooms | $145–$165 | Nov.–Jan. | D, MC, V.

Honeysuckle Hill. This Queen Anne house, 5 mi west of Barnstable, is on the National Register of Historic Places. The guest rooms have feather beds and down comforters. The 1¼-acre property includes gardens, lawns, woods, a waterfall and fishpond, and a patio furnished with umbrellas and chairs. Bottled water, soft drinks, cookies, apples, chocolate, and sherry are available at no extra charge. Complimentary breakfast. Cable TV in some rooms, some in-room VCRS, no room phones. Kids over 12 only. No smoking. | 591 Main St. (Rte. 6A), West Barnstable | 508/362–8418 or 800/441–8418 | fax 508/362–8386 | www.honeysucklehill.com | 4 rooms, 1 suite | $100–$150, $180–200 suite | AE, D, MC, V.

BEDFORD

MAP 6, H3

(Nearby towns also listed: Boston, Burlington, Concord, Lexington)

Bedford's proximity to downtown Boston, 15 mi away, is enhanced by I–95 and U.S. 3, two of Boston's busiest commuter highways, which border the town on two sides.

The town is also at one end of the popular Minuteman Commuter Bikeway, which follows a scenic former railbed into Cambridge. Though Bedford's population is little more than 12,000, the town's various industrial and corporate offices employ twice that number. Bedford is also the location of Hanscom Field, a shared military and civil aviation facility that provides small-plane pilots with their safest point of entry into the Boston area.

Information: **North Suburban Chamber of Commerce** | 3 Baldwin Green Common, Suite 204, Woburn 01801 | 781/272–0207 | www.nsubcc.org.

Attractions
Minuteman Commuter Bikeway. This 10.5-mi, 12 ft-wide asphalt trail follows an abandoned railroad from Bedford to Lexington Center to Arlington. It has a slight incline and runs parallel to the route Paul Revere took on his famous ride. Nonmotorized activities such as biking, walking, jogging, roller-blading, and cross-country skiing are permitted. | South Rd. at Loomis St. | 781/275–8503 | Daily.

ON THE CALENDAR
SEPT.: *Bedford Day.* There's a parade featuring the Bedford Minutemen (an organization of historical re-enactors), Citizen of the Year, high school band, and chamber of commerce on the third Saturday of the month. After the parade, nonprofits and businesses operate booths in the town hall showcasing their products and there are a variety of small town activities. | 12 Mudge Way | 781/275–8100.

Dining
Bistro 44 Restaurant and Bar. American. Ceramic tile, marble, and wood, plus art, glass grills, and steel chandeliers, equals cool, casual dining in this bistro-style restaurant. It serves a lot of seafood, but pot roast and pork chops are on the menu too, and there is also an on-site bakery. Kids' menu. No smoking. | Renaissance Bedford Hotel, 44 Middlesex Tpke | 781/275–5500 | $13–$28 | AE, D, DC, MC, V.

Cafe Luigi's. Italian. This bustling eatery is a place where parents can enjoy a good Italian meal, order some wine, and know their kids will be happy, too, with chicken fingers, mozzarella sticks, and plain pasta. Try the frutti di mare—lobster, scallops, and shrimp served over fettuccine with alfredo sauce. | 152 Great Rd. | 781/271–0666 | $5.95–$12.95 | AE, D, MC, V.

Dalya's. Mediterranean. This restuarant resembles an old European farmhouse with wrought-iron chandeliers, working fireplace, high-backed chairs, and wooden tables with colorful napkins. Try the fresh Maine crab cakes, Boston scrod, Long Island duck, or bouillabaisse. The Mediterranean-style Yankee pot roast uses elements from both cuisines— roasted garlic, truffle oil, and feta cheese–mashed potatoes. | 20 North Rd. | 781/275–0700 | Closed Sun. No lunch Sat. | $9.50–$24 | AE, D, DC, MC, V.

Lodging
Bedford Motel. A motel-style building set back from the road. All rooms face a landscaped area with trees and have white modern furniture. The bathrooms contain a large shower with a seat. In the office there is a microwave available for guest use as well as free coffee and ice. Cable TV. | 30 North Rd. | 781/275–6300 | 44 rooms | $64–$89 | AE, D, MC, V.

Ramada Sovereign Hotel. This hotel is near high-technology companies and historic Concord and Lexington. The hotel's attractive central atrium contains a café and pool. All of the rooms look out on the pool. Restaurant, bar, complimentary breakfast. Pool. Gym. Business services. | 340 Great Rd. (Rte. 225) | 781/275–6700 or 800/2–RAMADA | fax 781/275–3011 | 99 rooms, 2 suites | $109–$119 | AE, D, DC, MC, V.

Renaissance Bedford Hotel. This comfortable hotel is on a property with a 2½-mi jogging trail. In 2000, it completed a $33 million renovation. The hotel is next to the Mitre Corporation and 2½ mi from the Burlington Mall. Restaurant, bar with entertainment, room service. In-room data ports, minibars, refrigerators, cable TV. Indoor pool. Hot tub. Tennis courts. Gym. Business services. | 44 Middlesex Tpke | 781/275–5500 | fax 781/275–8956 | www.renaissancehotels.com | 285 rooms, 13 suites | $180, $200 suites | AE, D, DC, MC, V.

Timothy Jones House. This 1775 Georgian-style mansion is one of two remaining houses designed by the famous architect Reuben Duren. It was the country home of Timothy Jones, who fought in the battle at Concord's Old North Bridge. Guest rooms are on the second floor and have nonworking fireplaces. The Shaker Room has a queen-size pencil-post bed crafted by a New Hampshire artisan, a 17th-century pine chest, handmade quilts, and braided rugs. The Rose Room has a four-poster double bed and writing table, original wide-pine floors, and lace curtains. Dining room, complimentary Continental breakfast. No room phones, some in-room VCRs, no TV in some rooms. Library. No pets. No kids under 8. No smoking. | 231 Concord Rd. (Rte. 62) | 781/275–8579 | fax 781/276–1741 | 3 rooms | $90–$120 | No credit cards.

Travelodge Bedford. A chain offering in the heart of Bedford that is within walking distance of many restaurants. The rooms have a basic decor and six of them have balconies. In-room data ports, cable TV. Pool. No pets. | 285 Great Rd. | 781/275–6120 | fax 781/275–0407 | www.travelodge.com | 41 rooms | $89–$110 | AE, D, DC, MC, V.

BEVERLY

MAP 8, I2

(Nearby towns also listed: Boston, Danvers, Essex, Marblehead, Salem)

The city of Beverly considers itself one of the oldest communities in the state, having been settled by English fishermen in 1626 as part of next-door Salem. For much of its early history the town's bread and butter came from its port, which shared in the lucrative late 18th-century East Indies trade, but little remains of those glory days. Nor are there many reminders of Beverly's heavy industrial period, when it was headquarters to the world's largest manufacturer of shoemaking machinery. By the late 19th century, the northern, pastoral end of Beverly became famous as Boston's "Gold Coast," a country refuge for the city's rich and famous. Many large mansions from that era remain, and continue to be the gilded lining on Beverly's current stature as a bedroom community for Boston, 18 mi to the south. Beverly's growth as a residential suburb has been abetted by having five stations on two separate commuter rail lines, but the community's location astride Route 128, the metro region's circumferential highway, also provides convenient access to points north and west.

Information: **Beverly Chamber of Commerce** | 28 Cabot St., Beverly 01915 | 978/232–9559 | fax 978/232–9372 | www.townonline.com/beverly/chamber.

Attractions

Beverly Historical Society. This private, professionally staffed organization maintains three historic local residences within the community, offering interpretive guided tours of each. | 117 Cabot St. | 978/922–1186 | fax 978/922–7387 | www.beverlyhistory.org | June–Oct., Tues.–Fri. 10–4, Sat. noon–4; Nov.–May, Wed.–Fri. 10–4, Sat. noon–4.

Balch House. John Balch was one of the first to settle in the area of Beverly, and also one of the first to recieve a "Thousand Acre Grant". In 1636, he built a house on his new land, which is now one of the nation's oldest documented wooden dwellings. | 448 Cabot St. | 978/922–1186 | fax 978/922–7387 | www.beverlyhistory.org | $4 | June–Oct., Tues.–Fri. 10–4, Sat. noon–4.

John Cabot House. John Cabot was an 18th-century merchant and privateer, which is a polite way of saying he was a licensed pirate who was given free reign by the young American republic to plunder the shipping of enemies at sea. This mansion, which he had built in 1781, has both period rooms and exhibits of personal and household effects, from costumes to children's toys. It also houses a research library whose collections are prized by both casual and serious genealogists tracing local roots. | 117 Cabot St. | 978/922–1186 | fax 978/922–7387 | www.beverlyhistory.org | $4 | June–Oct., Tues.–Fri. 10–4, Sat. noon–4; Nov.–May, Wed.–Fri. 10–4, Sat. noon–4.

John Hale House. Built in 1695, this house belonged to the Rev. John Hale, pastor of Christ Church in Beverly at the time of the Salem witchcraft trials and subsequent author of *A Modest Inquiry into the Nature of Witchcraft*, long held to be the definitive text on the subject. Remodeled in 1745 and furnished in the early 19th century, the home has period rooms spanning 200 years. Tours pay particular heed to the original owner's relationship to witchcraft, but also note the family ties to Nathan Hale, Connecticut's Revolutionary War hero. | 39 Hale St. | 978/922–1186 | fax 978/922–7387 | www.beverlyhistory.org | $4 | May 1–Oct. 1, by appointment only.

"Le Grand David and His Own Spectacular Magic Company." Marco the Magi began bedazzling audiences with Sunday afternoon magic shows featuring Le Grand David and Co. in 1975, taking over an old downtown movie house that had seen better days. To the delight and acclaim of thousands of young and old, some of whom have grown up with repeat visits over the years, the spectacle-filled shows have never ceased. In the meantime, the theater has been restored to its 1920s glory, the sets and costumes have become magnificent, and the magic has remained as fresh and exciting as ever. | Cabot Street Cinema Theatre, 286 Cabot St. | 978/927–3677 | $15 | Sun. at 3 PM.

Sedgwick Gardens at Long Hill. Built in the style of an 1800s Charleston, South Carolina, mansion, this was the summer residence of *Atlantic Monthly* editor Ellery Sedgwick. There are 5 acres of formal gardens, 100 acres of woodland with 2 mi of trails, an apple orchard, and a meadow. The house is headquarters for the Trustees of Reservations and is open occasionally for guided tours. | 572 Essex St. | 978/921–1944 | www.thetrustees.org | Free admission to gardens | Gardens open daily dawn–dusk.

Wenham Museum. This spacious historical museum's exhibits range from local memorabilia to the 1690 house it occupies, 3 mi north of Beverly. In general it attempts to illustrate how New England families have lived, worked, and played over three centuries. The collection is particularly strong in that "play" department, with antique toys, a model railroad room with six operating layouts, and more than 5,000 dolls, a thousand of which are on display at any given time. | 132 Main St. (Rte. 1A), Wenham | 978/468–2377 | fax 978/468–1763 | www.wenhammuseum.org | $5 | Tues.–Sun. 10–4.

ON THE CALENDAR

MAR.–DEC.: *North Shore Music Theatre.* This 1,800-seat theater-in-the-round hosts Broadway musicals, celebrity concerts, and children's shows. Every seat is a good one—within 50 ft of the stage. | 62 Dunham Rd., exit 19 off Rte. 128 | 978/232–7200 | www.nsmt.org.

JUNE: *Beverly in Bloom.* Beverly is known as the Garden City, because wealthy families built magnificent summer homes and gardens here. The focus on gardens continues to this day, culminating in this annual festival held over the last weekend in June. There are tours of private gardens, window-box and traffic-island contests, and floral exhibits. There are also demonstrations on floral arranging and designing container gardens, and a children's flower parade in which the "floats" are children's bikes, wagons, and carriages decorated with blossoms. | 978/232–9559 | www.beverlychamber.com.

JULY–AUG.: *Beverly Homecoming.* An old-fashioned Yankee homecoming that kicks off with a lobster festival in Lynch Park. There's also an arts and crafts show, nightly band concerts, road race, boat cruises, and tennis and golf tournaments. On the final evening, there is a fireworks display at Lynch Park. | Citywide | 978/232–9559.

Dining

Beverly Depot. Steak. Occupying two floors of an old-time train station, this restaurant has a railroad motif that gives it character. It also sports wood floors, and some stained-glass windows. Salad bar. Kid's menu. | 10 Park St. | 978/927–5402 | No lunch | $12.95–$25.95 | AE, D, DC, MC, V.

Chianti Tuscan Restaurant. Italian. The northern Italian fare at this upscale eatery includes pumpkin tortellini in a gorgonzola sauce and osso buco. The interior has brick walls, a tin ceiling, and an atrium area overlooking the patio, where you can sit under umbrella shaded tables in summer. On Thursday evenings, patrons are serenaded by a strolling violinist. | 285D Cabot St. | 978/921–2233 | No lunch weekends | $13–$25 | AE, D, MC, V.

Sian Delight. Thai. Popular dishes at this 40-seat, café-style restaurant include chicken fever (stir-fry chicken with pepper, pineapple, scallion, and cashews in a Thai chilli paste) and pad Thai. There are tablecloths and bamboo placemats on each oak table and Thai posters on the walls. | 150 Cabot St. | 978/922–8514 | No lunch Mon. | $6.95–$13.25 | AE, D, DC, MC, V.

Lodging

Beverly Farms Bed and Breakfast. This 1840 colonial-style house has wooden beams, fireplaces, shutters, and many antique period furnishings. It is in a residential area on the tip of Cape Ann between Manchester-by-the-Sea and Beverly. Complimentary Continental breakfast. No room phones, cable TV in common area. No kids under 12. No smoking. | 28 Hart St. | 978/922–6074 | www.virtualcities.com/ma/bevfarms.htm | 3 rooms | $90–$110 | No credit cards.

Bunny's Bed and Breakfast. There are wonderful views of the city from this 1940 colonial-style structure on the highest hill in Beverly. There are a few antiques and wood floors throughout. One of its rooms has a small sitting area while another has a Japanese rug and fireplace. The owner/innkeeper serves a lavish Continental breakfast and will accommodate special diets with advance notice. Complimentary Continental breakfast. No air-conditioning, no room phone, cable TV in common area. No kids under 14. No smoking. | 17 Kernwood Heights | 978/922–2392 | fax 978/922–2392 | www.virtualcities.com | 3 rooms (1 with private bath, 2 with shared bath) | $75–$135 | No credit cards.

Emmaus Rose B and B. Built into the side of a hill overlooking the Danvers River, this bed-and-breakfast is within walking distance of a quiet beach and park. The one-room studio apartment has a homey feel, private patio, queen-size mahogany-panel bed, and original oil paintings and antique mirrors on the walls. | 1 studio apt. Complimentary Continental breakfast. Kitchenette, no room phone, no TV. Library. No pets. No smoking. | $90 | 16 S. Terrace Rd. | 978/922–2313 | No credit cards.

Lakeview Motor Lodge. This renovated all-suite motel is across the street from the commuter rail. The larger suites have a furnished living room and walk-through kitchen with appliances. The smaller suites have a separate kitchen, but the bedroom and sitting rooms are combined. It's a 38-minute ride to Boston, even less to Salem. Complimentary Continental breakfast (in season). In-room data ports, cable TV. | 5 Lakeview Ave. | 978/922–7535 | fax 978/922–8403 | 21 suites | $83–$99 | AE, D, MC, V.

Vine and Ivy Bed and Breakfast. This Greek Revival Cape was once part of a turn-of-the-century equestrian estate. It has antique furnishings and fireplaces in the sitting rooms. The landscaped grounds include English gardens and a courtyard with an in-ground swimming pool. The property is 1 mi from the beach and from the commuter rail to Boston. Dining room, complimentary breakfast. Cable TV. Pool. Laundry service. No smoking. | 212 Hart St. | 978/927–2917 or 800/975–5516 | fax 978/927–4610 | www.vineandivy.com | 5 rooms, 1 suite | $135–$250 | AE, D, DC, MC, V.

BOSTON

(Suburbs also listed: Braintree, Brookline, Burlington, Cambridge, Dedham, Lexington, Lynn, Lynnfield, Newton, Quincy, Saugus, Sharon, Somerville, Waltham, Wellesley; nearby: Bedford, Beverly, Brockton, Concord, Danvers, Foxborough, Framingham, Marblehead, Natick, Salem, Sudbury)

Modern Boston today has a population of approximately 500,000 and sprawls around the tiny peninsula upon which it was founded in 1630. Its English Puritan founders were attracted to the land because it was originally surrounded on nearly all sides by water, making it easy to defend. A deepwater harbor at its front door and a river at its back also made the town a natural choice for the Colonial capital, since 17th-century transportation and communication were largely dependent on boats. For its first 150 years, Boston was the leading Colonial port in North America, its wharves crowded with sailing vessels bound to and from every continent on the globe. Although other neighbors along the Eastern Seaboard outgrew Boston by the end of the 18th century, the city continued to amass great wealth with maritime trade throughout the 1800s, and some of the world's finest shipbuilders continued to ply their craft in Boston until well after World War II. Now that the city's economy has shifted from manufacturing to high-tech, high finance, and higher education, the revitalized piers bustle with private yachts and harbor cruise boats, while seaport warehouses find new life as apartments and offices.

Information: Greater Boston Convention and Visitors Bureau | 2 Copley Pl., Suite 105, Boston 02116-6501 | 617/536–4100 or 888/SEE–BOSTON. **Boston Common Visitor Information Center** | 147 Tremont St. | 617/536–4100 or 800/888–5515 | www.bostonusa.com.

NEIGHBORHOODS

Allston. Once full of stockyards, slaughterhouses, and meatpacking plants, today Allston is largely populated by students (from nearby Boston College and Boston University) and young families. Quirky and inexpensive, the neighborhood has discount furniture stores, thrift shops, local bars, and small grocery stores lining the streets. It is connected to downtown Boston by streetcars on the Green line.

Back Bay. A tidal inlet called the Back Bay became stagnant and polluted when dams were erected to harness the tides. To eradicate the problem, the bay was filled in, starting at the foot of the Public Garden in 1857 and proceeding westward for the next 40 years. More than 450 acres of prime real estate were created and streets and buildings were erected in a Parisian boulevard–style design.

Today, Back Bay contains a mix of Victorian town houses, modern offices, and chic shops and restaurants. Its central street is Commonwealth Avenue, a tree-lined promenade that's part of the "Emerald Necklace" string of green connecting parks designed by Frederick Law Olmsted. Three of Boston's most famous buildings—the McKim building of the Boston Public Library, H. H. Richardson's Trinity Church, and the John Hancock Tower—are in Back Bay's Copley Square.

Beacon Hill. A delightful maze of cobblestoned streets with gas lanterns, redbrick sidewalks, and 18th- and 19th-century town houses, the hill was originally 60 ft higher than it is today. It came to be known as Beacon Hill after citizens erected a mast holding a bucket of tar which could be set afire to warn of enemy approach. The south slope overlooking Boston Common was settled by Boston's elite including John Hancock and Mayor Harrison Gray Otis. The north slope was home to Boston's free African American community and is part of the Black Heritage Trail. Today, Beacon Hill is one of the most desirable and expensive neighborhoods in Boston.

Brighton. Graduate students, young professionals, and families live in private residences and small apartment buildings here. It is a fairly quiet neighborhood, near Allston, and connected to downtown Boston by streetcars on the Green line.

Charlestown. Charlestown was settled in 1629, making it a year older than Boston. The neighborhood is now a mix of old brownstones and apartment buildings, many of which are being renovated and priced out of the reach of its working-class residents. Charlestown was once home to an active Navy Yard, which is now a National Historical Park, and to the oldest commissioned warship in the U.S. Navy, "Old Ironsides." Also in Charlestown is the Bunker Hill Monument, which commemorates one of the first major battles of the American Revolution.

Chinatown. First settled by Chinese immigrants who came to work on the railroads in the 19th century, today the densely packed, approximately 1-square-mi area is the third-largest Asian neighborhood in the country. Many of its 4,300 residents are recent

ICE-CREAM HEAVEN

Despite spending six months out of the year clad in wool coats and sweaters, New Englanders consume twice as much ice cream, on average, as residents of any other region of the United States. Ben Cohen, of Ben & Jerry's fame, has tried to account for this phenomenon by hypothesizing that since feeling warm is really only a matter of the difference between body temperature and air temperature, ice-cream consumption works wonders at staving off winter shivers, by narrowing that critical gap between your insides and New England's frozen outsides. But taste some local Massachusetts-made ice cream for yourself and you'll know in an instant why the record holds.

Boston is the natural heavyweight contender in the high-quality super-premium ice cream sweepstakes, with four home-grown chains—Emack & Bolio's, Herrell's, JP Licks, and Toscanini's—comfortably leading the pack, outdistancing out-of-town contenders such as Ben & Jerry's and Baskin-Robbins. Even in the middle of January, these local companies' scoop shops are as busy on a Friday night as a florist's on Valentine's Day. As soon as warm weather arrives, summer ice-cream stands open up for brisk business in seemingly every town east of the Connecticut River. Keep an eye out for Cherry Farms Ice Cream on Conant Street in Danvers; White Farms Ice Cream on Route 133 in Ipswich; Gary's Ice Cream on Route 3A south of Lowell; Erikson's Ice Cream on Route 62 about 7 mi west of Concord; Crescent Ridge Dairy Bar at 407 Bay Road in Sharon; Farfar's Danish Ice Cream Shop on Route 3A in Duxbury; and Four Seas Ice Cream on Main Street in Centerville, on Cape Cod.

As for what flavors to try, every store has its specialties, but in general Massachusetts's predilection for chocolate- and coffee-flavored desserts comes through strong in its ice cream. Every conceivable permutation of mocha, espresso, Kahlúa, fudge, chocolate pudding, and chocolate chips is therefore well represented, but fruit flavors made from locally grown berries are also a sure summertime bet. One final note: milk shakes in Massachusetts are only made with milk and flavored syrup, so if you want a milk shake made with ice cream, be sure to order a frappe (rhymes with trap).

© Corbis

immigrants. There are at least 50 restaurants and many shops selling jewelry, fabric, herbs and spices, live poultry, fresh produce, and packaged Asian grocery items. Come here for some of the best restaurant and shopping values in downtown Boston.

Dorchester. Boston's largest neighborhood and one of its oldest was founded in 1630. The neighborhood's historical diversity is exhibited in its architecture, from the old Victorian homes of wealthy Bostonians to the triple-deckers of immigrants. Along Dorchester's waterfront is the John F. Kennedy Library and Museum, the Commonwealth Museum and Massachusetts Archives, and the University of Massachusetts–Boston.

East Boston. Long before the airport was built, East Boston was famous for its shipping and transportation businesses. It was on the wharves of East Boston that Donald McKay built the world's fastest clipper ships. Today East Boston is dominated by the activities of Logan International Airport. Once a predominantly Italian neighborhood, the triple-decker and wood-frame houses are presently occupied by many ethnic groups, including recent immigrants. For a great view of the Boston skyline from East Boston, ride the water-shuttle to the airport.

Fenway. One of the first residents of the marshland known as the Back Bay Fens (or Fenway, as it's known today) was Isabella Stewart Gardner who erected a neo-Renaissance Italian villa here at the turn of the last century. Today the area is home to Fenway Park and the Boston Red Sox, the Victory Gardens (a community garden for Bostonians), the Museum of Fine Arts, Symphony Hall, Harvard Medical School, and several colleges. Olmsted's Emerald Necklace of connecting parks includes the Fens.

Financial District. Since the 18th century, Boston's financial district has been a birthplace of invention, innovation, and financial services. The Boston Stock Exchange, the third oldest in the country, was founded here in 1834; the nation's first mutual fund was developed in Boston in 1924. The district also contained the laboratories of Alexander Graham Bell and Thomas Edison, who invented the stock ticker in the late 1860s.

Hyde Park. There's a mixture of city and suburban life here, including the George Wright Golf Course. It's on the south end of the city, close to Dedham and I–95. It's home to Boston Mayor Tom Menino.

Jamaica Plain. There are several stories about how Jamaica Plain got its name. It might have been named for earlier inhabitants from the Jamico tribe; it might have been developed with profits from the Jamaican rum trade. In any case, "JP" is a diverse neighborhood with residents from every walk of life, sexual orientation, and ethnic group. Architecture includes Victorian-era buildings such as the Taylor House Bed and Breakfast, an 1855 Italianate Victorian house that was once owned by the Haffenreffer family of brewers. (The brewery, now called the Sam Adams Brewery, is about 1 mi away and is open for tours.) In or adjacent to Jamaica Plain are three Boston parks—Franklin Park, Arnold Arboretum, and Jamaica Pond. The pond, which is fed by natural springs, is the largest and purest body of water in Boston and the city's backup water supply. Nonmotorized boats are available for hire, and there's a jogging path around the pond's 1.5-mi perimeter.

Mattapan. Named for the Mattahunt Indians who lived here, this was once a mill center on the Neponset River. Like other Boston neighborhoods, it developed as the railroads and streetcars made the downtown accessible. Today, Mattapan is predominantly residential with single, two, and three-family homes.

North End. The North End is Boston's oldest residential neighborhood and is remembered for its most famous resident—Paul Revere—and the role Old North Church played in the American Revolution. Years later, it housed Irish, Jewish, and Italian immigrants in tightly packed tenements. Today, the neighborhood is most closely associated with its Italian connection. The streets are lined with Italian restaurants, cafés, and markets (where Italian is still spoken). In summer, processions and festivals are held in honor of saints. Families of Italian descent and many professionals live in North End apartments and condos.

Roslindale. Originally a streetcar suburb of Boston, today Roslindale is a section of West Roxbury and home to wide cross section of people—Lebanese, Irish, African Americans, Haitians, Italians, and Portuguese (to name a few). Roslindale Square is considered a good example of historic preservation and economic revitalization; it received a National Trust for Historic Preservation Main Street Award.

Roxbury. From the 18th century until the early 20th century, Boston's well-to-do residents owned country estates in Roxbury—a notable resident was Royal Governor William Shirley, who initiated the successful 1745 military expedition against the French garrison at Louisbourg, Nova Scotia. His home (the Shirley-Eustis House) is open to visitors. Today, Roxbury is the heart of Boston's African-American community. Its famous

MAKING LAND IN BOSTON

When Boston's Puritan founders first arrived, the peninsula on which they elected to build their capital city was a mere 750 acres in extent. Today the city occupies about 48 square mi, but Boston could not have begun to reach its present size if it had not taken the unusual step of making land out of water. As a result, most of the city's central neighborhoods are built atop old estuaries, bays, and tidal flats.

There is no historical record explaining what gave Bostonians the idea to start expanding into the water around them. The only related acts of engineering at the time were the dike-building activities of the Dutch, who displaced water through complicated systems of dams and drainage as opposed to raising submerged land above sea level. Wherever the inspiration came from, the first filling began modestly, in the late 17th century. All along the waterfront, from the Back Bay of the lower Charles River to the Town Cove facing the harbor, the boundary of the town steadily expanded. Although the shape of the city changed, its street alignments didn't, which is why downtown Boston has such a confusing web of odd angles and gratuitous curves, the asphalt and concrete forever preserving the irregularities of the city's original shoreline. A small example of the early shoreline is illustrated with a series of thin brass lines embedded in the plaza in front of historic Faneuil Hall, one of Boston's many landmarks built atop landfill.

These early undertakings drew from Boston's own hills, whose upper halves were carted down and dumped into the water lapping at their bases. Such "improvements" were mostly the work of private property speculators, and often pitted neighbor against neighbor in fractious lawsuits—particularly when someone's hillside property was literally undermined by their backyard abutter.

The most ambitious land-making project was undertaken by the state government in the 19th century, with the complete filling of Back Bay. This addition of some 580 acres to the city took 35 years to complete, with gravel and sand being freighted in from the suburbs around the clock. The fashionable neighborhood built atop the new acreage was such a resounding commercial success that future land-making largely became the province of public works. During the 20th century, the city continued to make land along the South Boston waterfront, expanding that district so far into the harbor that Castle Island is now a misnomer. The city's international airport, in East Boston, has also swallowed up several former islands beneath its jet-age runways and terminals. Even today, amid occasional controversy and worries about environmental impacts, Boston's expansion continues, with the ongoing conversion and enlargement of the Spectacle Island municipal dump into a showcase harbor recreational area. Where it will all end, only time will tell, but one fact seems certain: don't rely on last year's map of Boston. It's already out of date.

© Artville

citizens include abolitionist William Lloyd Garrison and the Black Muslim leader Malcolm X. The Museum of the National Center for Afro-American Artists is in Roxbury.

South Boston. Known as "Southie," this predominantly Irish part of Boston includes Carson Beach, the Seaport District, and Castle Island (now connected to the mainland). During the American Revolution, British prisoners of war were incarcerated on Castle Island where a pre–Civil War fort still stands and is open for tours in summer. The original fort was blown up by the Loyalists during the Revolution, and rebuilt in stone. South Boston is known for its triple-deckers and single-family town houses. It's the home of Boston's annual St. Patrick's Day Parade.

South End. The South End was initially a fashionable neighborhood and has become one once again. It was created by landfill in the mid-19th century and filled with bow-front town houses around English-style squares and parks. It was deserted by wealthy residents as the Back Bay became the chic place to live. For about 100 years, the South End was a community of rooming houses and lodgings for lower-middle-class renters. Today, gentrification has brought many young professionals to the area along with trendy restaurants and gay-popular bed-and-breakfasts and bars. Boston's African-American community also has a significant presence here.

Theater District. You'll find drama, comedy, ballet, opera, and Broadway shows in this neighborhood south of the Boylston Street side of the Common and Public Garden. There's the Colonial Theater (the oldest continuously operating theater in Boston and its most opulent), the Charles Playhouse (home of "Shear Madness," America's longest running play), and the Wang Center for the Performing Arts.

West End. The West End, separated from Beacon Hill by Cambridge Street, was once filled with narrow, twisted streets and tenements where Irish, Italian, Jewish, and Greek immigrants lived. In the 1960s era of urban renewal, the neighborhood was obliterated and replaced with skyscraper apartment buildings. Historic buildings worth a visit include the Harrison Gray Otis House (open for tours), Old West Church (a working United Methodist church where organ concerts are often held), and the Bulfinch building of Massachusetts General Hospital (which contains the ether dome, site of the first successful operation using anesthesia).

West Roxbury. West Roxbury, which borders Roslindale and Hyde Park, was once part of Roxbury but it formed its own government in 1851. It was annexed by Boston in 1874. Although it's part of a large city, its tree-lined streets and single-family homes give it a suburban feel.

TRANSPORTATION INFORMATION

Airport: Boston and the surrounding areas are served by Logan International Airport, in East Boston, off I–93. Call 800/235–6426.

Airport Transportation: The Water Shuttle runs between Logan and Rose Wharf, in downtown Boston's financial district. One-way tickets cost $10 ($17 round-trip), and there are special prices for seniors and children. Call 800/235–6426 or 617/439–3131 for schedules. You can also take the bus from Logan to South Station, in downtown Boston. Go to the lower level of any terminal at Logan and look for the bus with SOUTH STATION on the front windshield. Tickets cost $6 each way. Call 800/235–6426 for schedules. A third possibility is to take the free Massport shuttle bus (#22 or #33) to the subway station and then take the Blue Line subway to Boston. The fare is 85¢.

Amtrak serves the city from South Station. Call 617/345–7460 or 800/USA–RAIL for fares and schedules.

Bus Lines: Bonanza (800/556–3815), Greyhound (800/231–2222), and Peter Pan Trailways (800/343–9999) serve Boston at the South Station Terminal.

Intra-City Transit: Once in Boston, transportation options include city-owned buses, taxis, elevated trains, and the subway, which is run by the Massachusetts Bay Transportation Authority and is known informally as "the T." Call 617/722–3200 for information.

Driving Around Town Boston is called the "Walking City" because it's a pleasure to walk to historic sites in close proximity—and because it's a horror to drive. Aggressive drivers, one-way streets, never-ending construction, and detours (especially due to the Big Dig, a massive project that will replace a major elevated expressway with a layer underground highway) make driving a nightmare for visitors.

Once you've arrived, there's the problem of finding a vacant and legal parking space. On-street parking is either by meter space or resident parking permit. It is important to obey parking regulations as tickets and towing are carried out with speed and regularity. The least expensive ticket is $25 for parking in a space with an expired meter. After a series of tickets, the "Boston Boot" goes on—a steel clamp that is affixed to the wheel of your car. To get the boot removed, you have to pay all your outstanding parking tickets plus a fee to have the boot removed.

If your hotel is in downtown Boston, your best bet is to leave your car in a garage and sightsee on foot and by taking the subway (known as the "T"). Garage parking costs between $12 and $20 per day. Parking is available at all conference hotels. Major public lots are at Government Center and Faneuil Hall Marketplace, beneath Boston Common (entrance on Charles St.), beneath Post Office Sq., at the Prudential Center, Copley Place, and off Clarendon St. near the John Hancock Tower. Some hotels offer discounted parking to their guests. Free parking is available for guests of the Doubletree Club Hotel Boston/Bayside which borders South Boston and Dorchester (the hotel is less than one block from the T).

Attractions

ART AND ARCHITECTURE

Commonwealth Avenue Mall. This eight-block, tree-lined promenade down the middle of Commonwealth Avenue is a perfect window on the architectural charms of Boston's Back Bay. The neighborhood's block-by-block development from east to west over the latter half of the 19th century created a showcase of architectural styles, from stately 1850s brownstones at one end to Victorian excess at the other. | Commonwealth Ave. | 617/536–4100 | Free | Daily.

Harrison Gray Otis House. Built in 1796, this Federal-style house in Beacon Hill was designed by noted early American architect Charles Bulfinch for his friend Harrison Gray Otis, a wealthy local lawyer and real-estate speculator who served in Congress and eventually became mayor of Boston. Guided tours of the premises show off the opulent decorative style that prevailed among Boston's affluent at the turn of the 19th century. The house is also headquarters of the Society for the Preservation of New England Antiquities (SPNEA), whose research library and extensive historical archives are available by appointment. | 141 Cambridge St. | 617/227–3956 | fax 617/227–9204 | www.spnea.org | Tours $4; library and archives $5 | Wed.–Sun., tours on the hr 11–4.

Isaac Royall House. Isaac Royall made his fortune from his West Indies sugar plantations and the slave trade in the 18th century. Upon returning to Boston in 1737, he bought the 400-acre estate of early Colonial governor John Winthrop. Barely 1 acre of that property remains, but it includes Winthrop's house, expanded by Royall, as well as a large building that housed Royall's 37 slaves, the last surviving slave quarters north of the Mason-Dixon line. | 15 George St., Medford | 781/396–9032 | $3 | May–Oct., Wed.–Sun. 2–5.

Paul Revere House. The North End home of the famous midnight rider of the Revolution is also the only 17th-century building left in downtown Boston. Although extensively modified by successive owners, the house has been restored to reflect its years as the Revere family home, with interpretive staff on hand throughout the structure to educate and entertain. | 19 North Sq | 617/523–2338 | fax 617/523–1775 | www.paulreverehouse.org | $2.50 | Apr. 15–Oct., daily 9:30–5:15; Nov.–Dec. and Apr. 1–14, daily 9:30–4:15; Jan.–Mar., Tues.–Sun. 9:30–4:15.

Shirley–Eustis House. This large Georgian house in Roxbury has a prominent octagonal cupola and was designed by early American architect Peter Harrison in the mid-1700s for then Royal Governor William Shirley. Shirley was able to afford the luxurious estate thanks to royal gifts bestowed upon him for initiating the successful 1745 military expedition against the French garrison at Louisbourg, Nova Scotia. Restored nearly to its original finery, the property also includes an 1806 carriage house and period gardens. | 33 Shirley St. | 617/442–2275 | $5 | June–early Oct., Thurs.–Sun. noon–4.

State House. Under the bright golden dome of the State House reside the executive and legislative branches of Massachusetts's government. Designed by Charles Bulfinch, the original redbrick building, now much expanded, was completed in 1798. Tours include the Hall of Flags, with its collection of historically significant flags, and the Senate and House chambers of the Great and General Court, as the legislature is known. | Beacon St., at Boston Common | 617/727–3676 | Reservations essential on weekdays | Free | Tours weekdays and Sat. 10–3:30.

Statue of Benjamin Franklin. Before he gained fame as a Philadelphian, Benjamin Franklin was a Boston boy, born near the site of this statue. His father ran a ship chandlery near the North End, and young Ben used to go fishing as a child in the waters of the Back Bay, where the Public Garden is today. | 45 School St., in front of Old City Hall.

BEACHES, PARKS, AND NATURAL SIGHTS

Arnold Arboretum. Maintained by Harvard University on behalf of the city, this botanical park in Jamaica Plain has more than 14,000 trees, shrubs, and woody vines in its collection, spread over 265 hilly acres. In spring it's known for its outstanding lilacs, and in autumn its maples provide a brilliant dash of color. | 125 Arborway | 617/524–1718 | Free | Daily.

Blue Hills Trailside Museum. This museum is at the edge of the 6,500-acre Blue Hills Reservation, the largest public park in the Greater Boston area. Operated by the Massachusetts Audubon Society, it has interpretive displays on local ecology, as well as live animal exhibits that will introduce you to some of the Reservation's resident mammals and reptiles. Special programs are also offered throughout the year. | 1904 Canton Ave., Milton | 617/333–0690 | www.massaudubon.org | $3 | Tues.–Sun. 10–5.

Boston Common. Established in 1634, shortly after Boston itself was founded, the 48-acre Common was originally communal grazing land, used for military exercises and public executions. In the 19th century it acquired landscaping, and today it is the largest park downtown, filled with trees, commemorative monuments, and benches suitable for leisurely people-watching. City park rangers offer tours throughout the year, most often in summer. | Tremont, Boylston, Beacon, and Park Sts. | 617/635–3445 (Boston Parks and Recreation Department events line) | Free | Daily.

★ **Public Garden.** This formal English floral park at Boston Common was once tidal mudflats. What a difference landscaping makes: today the city-owned block, abortively begun as a private botanical garden, is a showcase for the skill of the city's gardeners. In addition to thousands of flowers rotated through the seasonally changing display beds, there are hundreds of trees representing more than 70 species, not to mention an abundance of public sculpture, from the classic to the contemporary. The park's pond has been famous since 1877 for its foot-pedaled Swan Boats, which make leisurely cruises in warm months. | Charles, Beacon, Boylston, and Arlington Sts. | 617/635–4505 | Free | Daily.

CULTURE, EDUCATION, AND HISTORY

★ **African Meeting House/Museum for Afro-American History.** Completed in 1806, this is the nation's oldest-surviving black church. It was also a recruitment center for the famous Massachusetts 54th Colored Infantry Regiment. Restored to its 1854 appearance, the Beacon Hill property, owned by the Museum of Afro-American History and managed by the Park Service, still hosts public functions, plus contemporary art exhibits in its small ground-floor gallery. | 8 Smith Ct., off Joy St. | 617/725–0022 | fax 617/739–1285 | www.afroammuseum.org | Free | Memorial Day–mid-Sept., daily 10–4; mid-Sept.–Memorial Day weekdays 10–4.

Black Heritage Trail. Self-guiding tour brochures for this walking trail, available from the Smith School or the African Meeting House, describe 15 sites around Beacon Hill that had some significance in the early 19th century, when this area was the center of the Boston free black community. Guided tours of the trail are offered year-round by the National Park Service. | Tours depart from the Robert Gould Shaw Memorial, at Park and Beacon Sts. | 617/742–5415 | www.afroammuseum.org | Free | Memorial Day–mid-Sept., daily at 10, noon, and 2; mid-Sept.–Memorial Day, by appointment.

Boston African American National Historic Site. The centerpiece here is the Abiel Smith School, built in 1834 as Boston's public school for African-American children. Exhibits within the restored Beacon Hill school delve into the history of Boston's black community on Beacon Hill, while programs include excellent ranger-guided tours of the Black Heritage Trail. | 46 Joy St. | 617/725–0022 | fax 617/720–0848 | www.nps.gov/boaf | $5 donation suggested | Memorial Day–mid-Sept., daily 10–4; mid-Sept.–Memorial Day, weekdays 10–4.

Boston Massacre Site. Both Bostonians and visitors frequently walk across this tiny pedestrian island in a busy downtown intersection without realizing what lies underfoot. The circular ring of cobblestones set into the pavement identifies where five colonists were slain on March 5, 1770, when British soldiers fired into an abusive mob. The victims are all buried in the Granary Burying Ground, a couple of blocks away on Tremont Street. | State and Devonshire Sts. on the traffic island | 617/720–3290 | Free | Daily.

Boston National Historical Park. Eight separate historic sites comprise the Boston National Historical Park, but only three are federally owned; the rest, including the Old State House, Old South Meeting House, Faneuil Hall, Paul Revere House, and Old North Church, are privately or municipally owned park affiliates. Park Service rangers offer many interpretive programs throughout the year, particularly abbreviated guided walking tours of the Freedom Trail, the famous 2½-mi route weaving together 16 historic sites around Boston. | 15 State St. | 617/242–5642 | www.nps.gov/bost | Varies; refer to specific site | Daily.

Boston Women's Heritage Trail. Self-guided walks in five parts of Boston—downtown, North End, Beacon Hill, Chinatown, and Back Bay—highlight the work of well-known Boston women and lesser-known leaders. The trail guide is available at the Women's Educational and Industrial Union, 356 Boylston Street in the Back Bay. | 617/576–3869.

Bunker Hill Monument. Work began on this tall granite obelisk in 1827, to commemorate the important Revolutionary War battle that took place on June 17, 1775. The monument, which as most schoolchildren know is really on Breed's Hill, like the misnamed battle itself, was finally completed in 1843. To get to the observation room you have to climb 294 steps to the top. | Monument Sq., Charlestown | 617/242–5641 | Free | Daily 9–5 (entrance closes at 4:30).

Charlestown Navy Yard. In 1799, when the young American republic decided it was in need of a navy, Boston was among the six cities selected to host the new naval operations. Although some warships were constructed over the yard's 174-year history, it was known primarily for repair work, supplying ships for duty, and, during the Cold War, modernizing the nation's aging World War II fleet. In addition to the U.S.S. *Constitution,* visitors can see dry docks, a ropewalk, and a World War II destroyer. | Charlestown Navy Yard, Charlestown | 617/242–5601 | www.nps.gov/bost | Free | Early Sept.–mid-June, daily 9–5; mid-June–early Sept., daily 9–6.

U.S.S. *Constitution.* Nicknamed "Old Ironsides" for the strength of its hard oak hull in battle, the *Constitution* is the world's oldest commissioned naval vessel. Launched in 1797, the ship's critical victories in the War of 1812 lifted the fledging American Navy into the ranks of world powers. | Charlestown Navy Yard, Charlestown | 617/242–2308 | ussconstitution.navy.mil | Free | Top deck daily 9:30–dusk; below-deck tours daily 9:30–3:50.

U.S.S. *Constitution* Museum. This two-story museum details the construction of the *Constitution,* its many voyages, plus the art and science of naval engagement by warships under sail. Numerous artifacts and engaging interactive exhibits make this a family favorite. | Charlestown Navy Yard, Charlestown | 617/426–1812 | www.ussconstitutionmuseum.org | Free | June–early Sept., daily 9–6; early Sept.–May, daily 9–5.

Dorchester Heights Monument. George Washington's first victory in the Revolutionary War was forcing the evacuation of British troops from Boston, a result achieved by the rebels' fortification of Dorchester Heights with cannon. This South Boston monument, a Georgian Revival white marble tower, was erected in commemoration of that morale-boosting turn of events in March 1776. | Thomas Park, off E. Broadway | 617/242–5675 | Free | Grounds open daily; tower mid-June–early Sept., Wed. 4–8, weekends 10–4.

Visitor Center. The main National Park Service Visitor Center is the departure point for most ranger-led walking tours. The helpful staff will answer your questions about the park, Boston, and many other unrelated topics as best they can. The center also has a well-stocked little bookstore filled with adult and children's titles related to Boston's history and the park's affiliated sites. | 15 State St. | 617/242–5642 | Free | Early Sept.–mid-June, daily 9–5; mid-June–early Sept., daily 9–6.

Boston Public Library. The Renaissance Revival main branch of the Boston Public Library was built in Copley Square in 1895. Behind its grand facade and giant bronze doors are ornate, vaulted-ceiling reading rooms, lots of polished marble, and a number of artworks, including allegorical murals by John Singer Sargent. | 700 Boylston St. | 617/536–5400 | www.bpl.org | Free | Mon.–Thurs. 9–9, Fri.–Sat. 9–5.

Boston Tea Party Ship and Museum. This is a reconstruction of the colonial brig *Beaver,* one of the three vessels whose cargo of East Indies tea was plundered by angry colonists on the night of December 16, 1773. Costumed guides explain the events leading up to this inflammatory act, and also describe what life was like for 17th-century merchant seamen. | Congress St. Bridge | 617/338–1773 | fax 617/338–1974 | www.historictours.com | $8 | Apr.–Nov., daily 9–5.

Boston University. One of the largest private universities in the Boston area, BU enrolls more than 29,000 students in a wide variety of undergraduate and graduate programs, including schools of medicine, engineering, and law. The main campus stretches along the bank of the Charles River west of Kenmore Square. | Commonwealth Ave. | 617/353–2169 | www.bu.edu | Free | Mar.–Memorial Day and Labor Day–Nov., weekdays 9–5; Memorial Day–Labor Day, weekdays 9–6.

Central Burying Ground. When this historic burying ground near Boston Common was established in 1756, it was at the fringes of the town. As befitted its remote location, it was primarily used for burials of people who couldn't qualify for a more prestigious eternal address in one of Boston's three downtown burying grounds. The most famous occupant is Gilbert Stuart, who is best remembered for his portraits of George Washington. | Boylston St. | 617/635–4505, ext. 6516 (Boston Parks and Recreation Department Historic Burying Grounds Initiative) | Free | Daily.

Copp's Hill Burying Ground. Originally called North Burying Ground when it was established in 1659, the North End's Copp's Hill was Boston's second cemetery. Numerous prominent Bostonians from the 17th to 19th centuries are interred here, including the Puritan ministerial clan of Increase Mather and his descendents; Robert Newman, who hung the warning lanterns atop Old North Church for Paul Revere; and Prince Hall, a black anti-slavery activist. Many other African-Americans who lived in early Boston's free black community on Beacon Hill are buried here, too, in unmarked graves. | Hull and Snow Hill Sts. | 617/635–4505, ext. 6516 (Boston Parks and Recreation Department Historic Burying Grounds Initiative) | Free | Daily.

Emerson Majestic Theatre. This well-preserved Beaux-Arts theater, opened in 1903, was one of three opera houses built by wealthy local opera-lover Eben Jordan. The Majestic's gilded interior, rich decorative plasterwork, and Maxfield Parrish–style lobby murals now greet patrons of, among others, Dance Umbrella, one of the nation's leading presenters of contemporary dance in all its varied forms. | 219 Tremont St. | 617/482–7570 (Dance Umbrella information) or 617/824–8000 (Majestic box office) | fax 617/824–8725 | www.danceumbrella.org | $20–$65 | Sept.–June; call for performance schedule.

★ **Faneuil Hall.** The original market building, donated to the city by merchant Peter Faneuil, was erected in 1742; the current inheritor of this name and location is the third building and was designed by Charles Bulfinch in the early 1800s. Ascend to the public auditorium on the second floor to see the space that earned the building its nickname as "the Cradle of Liberty" in the wake of the Revolution. National Park Service rangers posted at the site deliver talks summarizing the historically significant events that have taken place here. | Merchants Row, at the corner of Congress and North Sts. | 617/242–5642 | Free | Daily 9:30–4:30.

Granary Burying Ground. The city's third burying ground, was founded in downtown Boston in 1660 as South Burying Ground. Its current name came after 1737, when a grain storage building was moved next door. Many famous Bostonians rest here—including patriots and politicians such as Paul Revere, Sam Adams, and John Hancock—and Ben Franklin's parents, for whom the great Philadelphian erected the 25-ft obelisk with epitaph at the center of the site. | Tremont St. | 617/635–4505, ext. 6516 (Boston Parks and Recreation Department Historic Burying Grounds Initiative) | Free | Daily.

Hatch Shell. The Edward A. Hatch Memorial Concertorium, called the Hatch Shell, is Boston's most famous Art Deco structure. It's on the Esplanade, a grassy strip along the Boston side of the Charles River. The Hatch Shell is the site of many free open-air summer performances including the Boston Pops Orchestra Fourth of July concert, a tradition started more than 50 years ago by conductor Arthur Fiedler. | Storrow Dr. | 617/727–9547, ext 450 | Free | Call for performance schedule.

Huntington Theatre Company. This professional theater company, in residence at Boston University and across from Symphony Hall, offers a half-dozen productions each season. From the latest works by leading playwrights to honored classics of the American and European stage, the Huntington's productions generally garner plenty of critical praise. | 264 Huntington Ave. | 617/266–0800 | fax 617/421–9674 | www.bu.edu/huntington | $10–$52 | Sept.–June.

Jordan Hall. The gleaming wood and rich bronze decorations of this 1903 performance hall were restored to their former glory after an $8.2 million renovation in 1995. Jordan Hall, which is part of New England Conservatory, is a National Historic Landmark. | 30 Gainsborough St. | 617/536–2412 | Varies | Call for performance schedule.

King's Chapel Burying Ground. This downtown cemetery was established in 1630 and is the final resting place of John Winthrop, the first govenor of Massachusetts Bay Colony; William Dawes, who rode with Paul Revere on the famed midnight ride; Mary Chilton Winslow, the first woman to step off the *Mayflower;* and Elizabeth Pain, who is thought by some to be the model for Nathaniel Hawthorne's Hester Prynne. | Tremont St. | 617/635–4505, ext. 6516 (Boston Parks and Recreation Department Historic Burying Ground Initiative) | Free | Daily.

New England Holocaust Memorial. Each of the six glass towers that rise like chimneys—or candles—from linear Carmen Park represents one of the principal Nazi death camps in World War II. The six million numbers tattooed into the glass panes of the five-story towers symbolize the victims of those camps who died in the Holocaust. Inscriptions by soldiers, survivors, and others serve as reminders of what humanity must never forget, lest it be repeated. | Carmen Park, off of Congress St. | 617/859–5969 | Free | Daily.

Old South Meeting House. Built in 1729 as a place of worship for Boston's Puritans, Old South later became a genuine public meeting house, a role it upholds to this day, when its congregation moved to the Back Bay in 1872. Among the many controversial debates that have taken place within its walls was that which led to the Boston Tea Party on December 16, 1773. Exhibits in this Downtown Crossing site describe this and other historic events that have become part of the building's legacy. | 310 Washington St. | 617/482–6439 | fax 617/482–9621 | www.oldsouthmeetinghouse.org | $3 | Apr.–Oct., daily 9:30–5; Nov.–Mar., daily 10–4.

Site of the first U.S. public school. A plaque in the sidewalk at Old City Hall draws your attention to the fact that in 1635 the Puritan leaders of Boston established the Boston Latin School here, the first public school in the nation. Although it has moved to the Fenway neighborhood west of Back Bay, Boston Latin continues to thrive as one of two prestigious entrance-by-exam schools in the Boston public school system. | 45 School St. | Free | Daily.

Symphony Hall. Though its benefactors couldn't be troubled to acquire enough land to give this concert hall a fittingly grand entry, the interior is considered to have some of the finest acoustics anywhere. As the name suggests, it is home to the Boston Symphony Orchestra, as well as the Boston Pops Orchestra. Occasional touring solo artists are heard in concert here as well. | 301 Massachusetts Ave. | 617/266–1492 or 888/266–1200 (tickets) | www.bso.org | $13–$75 | Box office daily, main offices weekdays.

Wang Center for the Performing Arts. Though this former cinema in the Theater District appears to be unremarkable from the outside, the interior more than fulfills its original conceit of being a cathedral for popular entertainment, from the palatial marble lobby to the 3,700-seat auditorium awash in gold and velvet. The Wang is home to the Boston Ballet, the city's premier ballet company. When not in use by the ballet, the Wang's stage is host to major Broadway musicals, big-name dancers such as Mikhail Baryshnikov, and Mark Morris, to Riverdance, and even occasional screenings of classic films. | 270 Tremont St. | 617/482–9393 | fax 617/451–1436 | Boston Ballet $20–$69 | Box office Mon.–Sat. 10–6, Boston Ballet season Oct.–May.

MUSEUMS

Children's Museum. This museum, in a huge brick warehouse on Boston's formerly industrial waterfront, is one of the country's leading museums for children. There are hands-on exhibits for all ages, including a climbing maze for little ones, big puppetlike sea critters seemingly dredged from just outside the museum's door, a karaoke booth, building blocks and giant toys, plus an acclaimed exhibit on Tokyo for teens. | 300 Congress St., Museum Wharf | 617/426–8855 | fax 617/426–5466 | www.bostonkids.org | $7 | Sat.–Thurs. 10–5, Fri. 10–9.

Dreams of Freedom. This state-of-the-art permanent exhibit chronicles the experience of immigrants to the Boston area—from the earliest Puritans to recent arrivals—through a collection of artifacts, images, oral histories, interactive exhibits, and a multimedia show. Stop and listen to the stories of "virtual immigrants" (mannequins with video-projected faces) who explain what brought them to America and what sort of life they created for themselves in their new home. The site is across the street from Old South Meeting House on the Freedom Trail. | International Institute of Boston, 1 Milk St. | 617/695–9990 | www.dreamsoffreedom.org | $7.50 | Sun.–Fri. 9:30–6, every other Sat. 9–1.

Gibson House Museum. This Italian Renaissance Revival mansion, one of many elegant town houses in Back Bay, is dedicated to the Victorian Age. Its furnishings and seasonal programs, from afternoon high tea to holiday decorating, amply illustrate life in the Victorian era. | 137 Beacon St. | 617/267–6338 | fax 617/267–5121 | $5 | Tours on the hour May–Oct., Wed.–Sun. 1–3; Nov.–Apr., weekends 1–3.

Institute of Contemporary Art. This small three-story museum, in Copley Square/Back Bay, occupies a handsome Romanesque former police station. Besides changing exhibits of new and provocative work in many media, its intimate theater showcases the latest in experimental film and video. | 955 Boylston St. | 617/266–5152 | fax 617/266–4021 | www.ICA-Boston.org | $6 | Wed. and weekends noon–5, Thurs. noon–9, Fri. noon–7.

★ **Isabella Stewart Gardner Museum.** The plain facade of this Venetian-style palazzo belies the sumptuous interior within, whose skylit garden court is widely regarded as one of Boston's best public spaces. The exceptional collection of European (with a focus on the Italian Renaissance), Asian, and Islamic art was originally the private collection of "Mrs. Jack" Gardner, flamboyant wife of a turn-of-the-century Boston Brahmin, one of the city's social elite. A small café and gift shop are also on the premises. | 280 The Fenway | 617/566–1401 | fax 617/278–5167 | www.boston.com/gardner | $10 weekdays, $11 weekends | Tues.–Sun. 11–5.

John F. Kennedy Library and Museum. Multiple theaters and more than two dozen individual galleries present an affecting portrait of the last native son Massachusetts sent to the White House. Exhibits on JFK's political career make thorough use of TV clips, newspaper reports, and other media to create a strong impression of being an eyewitness who has stepped back in time. The museum's location at the edge of Dorchester Bay offers exceptional views of the Boston skyline. | Columbia Point, next to the University of Massachusetts Campus | 617/929–4547 | fax 617/929–4538 | www.cs.umb.edu/jfklibrary/museum.htm | $8 | Daily 9–5.

★ **Museum of Fine Arts.** The half-million objects in this sprawling, block-long museum in the Fenway neighborhood include galleries upon galleries of American and European painting, sculpture, and decorative arts, from medieval to modern. It also has outstanding offerings in Asian art and artifacts, from a Zen garden to a room full of Buddhas; the largest collection of Near Eastern artifacts outside of Egypt; and rare and antique musical instruments. Special programs, concerts, and an outstanding film series keep art lovers coming back for more. | 465 Huntington Ave. | 617/267–9300 | fax 617/236–0362 | www.mfa.org | $12 | Mon.–Tues. 10–4:45; Wed.–Fri. 10–9:45 (Thurs. and Fri. after 4:45, only West Wing is open), weekends 10–5:45.

Museum of Science. With more than 600 interactive exhibits on science and technology, this museum between Boston and Cambridge is filled with hours' worth of activities to engage hands and minds. Among the permanent highlights are galleries devoted to mathematics, physics, and electricity, the last of which includes the world's largest Van de Graaff generator, capable of producing indoor lightning. | 1 O'Brien Hwy. | 617/723–0100 | fax 617/589–0454 | www.mos.org | $10 | Sat.–Thurs. 9–5 (July 5–early Sept., Sat.–Thurs. 9–7), Fri. 9–9.

Charles Hayden Planetarium. In addition to the daily planetarium shows, there are laser light shows set to rock music on Thursday–Sunday evenings at this site in the Museum of Science. | 1 O'Brien Hwy. | 617/523–6664 | $7.50; discounted combination tickets including museum admission are available | Daily.

Mugar Omni Theater. The five-story domed screen and bone-rattling surround-sound ensure an unforgettable cinematic experience at this theater in the Museum of Science, which exclusively presents large-format OMNIMAX films. | 1 O'Brien Hwy. | 617/523–6664 | $7.50; discounted combination tickets including museum admission are available | Daily.

Nichols House Museum. The only mansion on Beacon Hill that's open to the public, this museum conveys some sense of high-society life in Boston before the Great Depression with the heirlooms of Rose Standish Nichols, its last owner. The original Federal design was done by Charles Bulfinch, and in 1804 the house was among the first built atop Beacon Hill, as part of the real-estate development that carved up the farm of painter John Singleton Copley. | 55 Mt. Vernon St. | 617/227–6993 | $5 | Tues.–Sat. 12:15–4:15.

Old State House Museum. Built in 1713, this downtown structure is Boston's oldest public building. The golden lion and unicorn on its gable are from its days as the seat of royal Colonial administration; the name refers to its use for state government after the Revolution. Currently maintained by the Bostonian Society—conservators of local history—the building now houses a museum whose always fascinating changing exhibits illuminate intriguing chapters from Boston's past. | 206 Washington St., at State St. | 617/720–3290 | fax 617/720–3289 | www.bostonhistory.org | $3 | Daily 9–5.

RELIGION AND SPIRITUALITY

First Church of Christ, Scientist. Better known as the Mother Church, this 14-acre Back Bay complex is the world headquarters of Christian Science and a Boston landmark. The original Romanesque church was completed in 1894 and in 1906 Byzantine and Italian Renaissance extensions were added. The plaza has a huge reflecting pool and is surrounded by administrative buildings, which were added in the early 1970s. | 175 Huntington Ave., at Massachusetss Ave. | 617/450–3790 | Free | Mon.–Sat. 10–5, Sun. 11–3.

King's Chapel. The current church in downtown Boston, completed in 1756, is considered one of the best examples of Georgian architecture in America. The 4-ft-thick granite walls were intended to support a steeple that was never completed for lack of funds. Before being converted into the country's first Unitarian church after the Revolution, it was the North American headquarters of the Church of England. | 58 Tremont St. | 617/227–2155 | Free | Tours, Mon. and Thurs.–Sat. 10–4, Tues–Wed. 1–4.

★ **Old North Church.** Built in 1723, this North End church is Boston's oldest, and its most famous. On the night of April 18, 1775, Paul Revere had the church sexton, Robert Newman, hang lanterns in the steeple as a signal to patriots in Charlestown that British troops were taking the water route to Cambridge on their long march into the countryside. The 175-ft steeple includes the nation's oldest church bells, which were cast in 1744. | 193 Salem St. | 617/523–6676 | fax 617/720–2854 | www.oldnorth.com | Free | Nov.–May, daily 9–5; June–Oct., Mon.–Fri. 9–6.

Park Street Church. This 1809 Congregational church stored gunpowder in its basement during the War of 1812, giving rise to the site's nickname, "Brimstone Corner." It was at this Boston Common site that the famed abolitionist William Lloyd Garrison, who founded the New England Anti-Slavery Society in 1832, gave his first public speech condemning slavery. | 1 Park St., near Boston Common | 617/523–3383 | www.parkstreet.org | Free | July–Aug., Tues.–Sat. 9:30–3:30; year-round Sun. services at 8:30, 11, 4:30, and 7.

Trinity Church. Built in the early 1870s, this landmark Copley Square building helped confirm the preeminent status of its architect, H. H. Richardson. The style, now known as Richardsonian Romanesque, has often been emulated, but never equaled. John LaFarge designed much of the stained glass, and Augustus Saint-Gaudens worked on some of the interior decorative sculpture. | 206 Clarden St. | 617/536–0944 | Free | Daily.

SHOPPING

Faneuil Hall Marketplace. The conversion of historic Faneuil Hall and adjacent Quincy Market into the city's top retail area in the 1970s is largely credited with sparking Boston's modern renaissance, and also with establishing the premier model for downtown revitalization in other cities across the country. Most Bostonians disingenuously claim never to set foot in the place, although they *always* bring out-of-town visitors to see it. Comprised primarily of Quincy Market's three long brick and granite buildings, once the city's raucous dockside wholesale market, today's Marketplace near the waterfront is filled with specialty food stalls, restaurants, and scores of shops selling all manner of gifts, fashions, and accessories. | 4 S. Market Bldg. | 617/523–1300 | www.faneuilhallmarketplace.com | Free | Daily.

Guild of Boston Artists. The guild was started in 1914, and among its first members were painters Edmund Tarbell and Frank Benson. Aiming to keep traditional arts before the public, the guild runs historical shows several times a year in its Back Bay home and has painting demonstrations. | 162 Newbury St. | 617/536–7660 | fax 617/437–6442 | Free | Sept.–July, Tues.–Fri. 9:30–4:30 and Sat. 10–5.

Shops at Prudential Center. Dozens of specialty shops line the spacious corridors of this Back Bay urban mall. It is at the base of the 52-story Prudential Tower, next door to the Copley Place Mall, and is anchored by Saks Fifth Avenue and Lord & Taylor department stores. Restaurants, a food court, and the Sheraton Boston Hotel are also part and parcel of the place, which opens into the Hynes Convention Center. | 800 Boylston St. | 617/266–0590 or 800/SHOP–PRU | www.prudentialcenter.com | Free | Mon.–Sat. 10–8, Sun. 11–6.

SPORTS AND RECREATION

Boston Red Sox. Experience major-league baseball in Fenway Park, the last of the old-fashioned venues. This open-air stadium, built in 1917, is famous for its endearing physical irregularities and intimidating leftfield wall, better known as the Green Monster. The stadium will be razed by 2005 and replaced with a new stadium at a different site. | 4 Yawkey Way | 617/267–1700 (tickets) or 617/267–9440 (front office) | redsox.com | $12–$35 | Apr.–Oct.

Boston Celtics. The Larry Bird era of the Celtics is long gone, but the championship flags still fly proudly from the rafters over the court, awaiting the day when they'll be joined by new ones. The team shares its new downtown home, the state-of-the-art FleetCenter, with the Boston Bruins hockey team, among others. | FleetCenter, Causeway St. | 617/523–3030 (tickets) or 617/523–6050 (front office) | www.nba.com/celtics | Nov.–Apr.

Boston Bruins. Fans from the South and Southwest are getting a taste for hockey through expansion teams and relocated franchises, but a night in the stands at a Bruins game in downtown Boston is the real McCoy. After the Zamboni machines have cleared the ice and the puck starts to fly, there's no mistaking the fact that you're in the heart of hockey fandom, where passions run deep but decorum doesn't. | FleetCenter, Causeway St. | 617/624–1000 (tickets) or 617/624–1050 (front office) | www.bostonbruins.com | Oct.–Apr.

SIGHTSEEING TOURS

Boston by Foot. Since 1976, this nonprofit organization's volunteer guides have helped visitors and residents appreciate Boston's history and architecture at a pedestrian's pace. On any given day, up to five different 90-minute walking tours are available, rain or shine. Special half- and full-day strolls are also offered on selected holidays. Departure times and days vary according to tour, so call for detailed information. | 77 N. Washington St. | 617/367–3766 (recorded information) or 617/367–2345 | www.bostonbyfoot.com | $8–$9 | May–Oct., daily.

Boston Duck Tours. The colorful Ducks, vintage World War II amphibious vehicles painted in bright primary colors and christened with names that pun on local landmarks and celebrities, are surely the most eye-catching vehicles on Boston's streets. They are also deservedly the most popular of the city's many narrated tour operators. To their overview of city history served up while driving around Boston proper, the Ducks add the unbeatable experience of sluicing straight into the Charles River for a duck's-eye view of Beacon Hill, Back Bay, and Cambridge. Tours depart from the Boylston Street side of the Prudential Center, in the Back Bay. | 790 Boylston St. | 617/723–3825 | $21 | Apr. 5–Nov. 28, daily 9–½ hr before dusk.

Boston Harbor Cruises. BHC is Boston's largest cruise company, with narrated sightseeing trips around Boston Harbor, summertime lunch cruises, and whale-watching excursions to Stellwagen National Marine Sanctuary across Massachusetts Bay. The company's fleet is modern, comfortable, and generally equipped with food and beverage service onboard. | 1 Long Wharf | 617/227–4321 | www.bostonharborcruises.com | $8–$15 sightseeing cruises, $28 whale-watching cruises | Call for hrs.

Brush Hill/Gray Line Tours. This company's fleet of red Beantown Trolleys provides narrated tours of Boston as they continuously loop through the city, making stops near all the major attractions in downtown, the North End, Charlestown, Beacon Hill, Back Bay, and the Fenway. For maximum convenience, ticket holders are allowed unlimited reboarding privileges throughout the day and may join the tours at any stop along their route. | 16 S. Charles St., in State Transportation Building | 617/236–2148 | $20; you can purchase tickets onboard trolleys | Daily.

Historic Boston Walks. Costumed historical interpreters portraying Benjamin Franklin, Abigail Adams, Calvin Coolidge, and Sophie Tucker show you Boston. Each three-hour program includes a walk, lunch, and gratuity. | International Institute of Boston, 1 Milk St., across from Old South Meetinghouse | 781/648–0628 | $39 | July–Labor Day, Tues. (Coolidge), Wed. (Franklin), Thurs. (Tucker), Fri. (Adams) at 9:30, reservations required.

Provincetown Ferry Service, Bay State Cruise Company. Bay State has the exclusive contract for the seasonal ferry service between Boston and Provincetown, at the tip of Cape Cod. The company offers a choice between a small, fast boat, the *Spray,* or a large, slow boat, *Provincetown II.* Both boats are suitable for day trips. The slow one, which is less expensive, includes onboard entertainment—a live DJ, karaoke, children's activities, dancing. | Commonwealth Pier, next to World Trade Center | 617/748–1428 | www.baystatecruisecompany.com | $18 one-way, $30 round-trip on the *Provincetown II,* $25 one-way, $40 round-trip on the *Spray.*

OTHER POINTS OF INTEREST

Copley Square. This landscaped plaza in the heart of Back Bay is surrounded by several of the city's more notable architectural landmarks, from Trinity Church and the Boston Public Library to the gleaming John Hancock Tower. In summer it becomes the particularly busy host of a twice-weekly farmers' market, but any time of year its benches are a good front-row seat for enjoying the ever-changing urban waltz. | Bordered by St. James Ave. and Boylston St., Clarendon and Dartmouth Sts. | Free | Daily.

Franklin Park Zoo. Behind the classical limestone statuary at the entrance gates lie more than the 70 animal-filled acres, including habitats made to resemble the Australian Outback, Serengeti savannah, and tropical forest of the African gorilla. An indoor Bird World with three different climates, a large, screened aviary, and a new Children's Zoo are also part of the grounds in Jamaica Plain. | 1 Franklin Park Rd. | 617/442–2002 or 617/541–LION | fax 617/989–2025 | $7 | weekdays 10–4, weekends 10–6.

John Hancock Observatory. Boston's Back Bay is the home to New England's tallest building, which provides the highest view in the region, accompanied by an informative audio-visual presentation on Boston's physical expansion down through the centuries. The vista from the 60th floor can extend as far as neighboring New Hampshire when the weather is clear. | 200 Clarendon St. | 617/247–1977 | fax 617/572–6497 | $6 | Daily 9 AM–10 PM.

★ **Louisburg Square.** A small Beacon Hill park enclosed in wrought-iron fencing, Louisburg Square is cooperatively owned by the residents of the impeccably restored 19th-century town houses that surround it and defines this narrow block-wide square. Louisa May Alcott and William Dean Howells are among the famous residents who have had a share in that tiny green space, and if their ghosts were to return they would find that little appears to have changed. | Between Mt. Vernon and Pinckney Sts. | Free | Daily.

★ **New England Aquarium.** Harbor seals and sea lions greet you to this venerable institution next to the Financial District, whose cavernous interior holds a giant ocean tank filled with sea turtles, tropical fish, sharks, and moray eels. Scores of smaller aquariums around the sides of the building illustrate marine ecosystems from the Amazon to the Maine coast, and penguins splash around a simulated rookery. The aquarium also has regularly changing exhibits. | Central Wharf | 617/973–5200 | www.neaq.org | $12.50 | Weekdays 9–5, weekends 9–6.

Prudential Skywalk View and Exhibit. This indoor observation deck, on the 50th-floor of Back Bay's Prudential Tower, provides one of the city's most spectacular panoramas, rivaling the Hancock Observatory a few blocks away. | 800 Boylston St., Back Bay | 617/859–0648 | fax 617/859–0056 | $5 | Daily 10–10.

ON THE CALENDAR

MAR.: *New England Spring Flower Show.* This show features acres of landscaped gardens and thousands of flowers and horticultural displays. | Bayside Exposition Center, 200 Mount Vernon St., Dorchester | 617/536–9280 | fax 617/262–8780.

APR.: *Boston Marathon.* The oldest annual marathon in the world, starts in Hopkinton and continues through eight communities before finishing in Copley Square, Boston. It is held on the third Monday in April. For a Spectator's Guide, route map, and registration requirements, see the Web site listed here. | 617/236–1652 (information) or 508/435–6905 (information and registration) | www.bostonmarathon.org.

APR.: *Lantern Celebration.* A ceremony in North End's Old North Church commemorates the hanging of the two lanterns on April 18, 1775, that alerted Paul Revere that British troops were crossing the Charles River en route to Lexington. The ceremony includes the reading of "Paul Revere's Ride" by one of Revere's descendents, the reading of Revere's own account of his ride by actor/historic reenactor David Connor, and the carrying of the lanterns to the steeple by a descendent of Robert Newman, the church's sexton. Music is provided by the First Michigan Fife and Drum Corps. | 193 Salem St. | 617/523–6676 | www.oldnorth.com | Third Sun. in Apr. at 8 PM.

MAY: *Annual Street Performers Festival.* Not just anyone can perform at Boston's Faneuil Hall Marketplace. Auditions take place during the Annual Street Performers Festival on Memorial Day weekend. Each act—clowns, jugglers, magicians, puppeteers, musicians, dancers, and storytellers—has 15 minutes to impress a panel of judges and the audience. | Faneuil Hall Marketplace | 617/523–1300 | www.faneuilhallmarketplace.com | Memorial Day weekend.

MAY: *Happy Birthday JFK.* The John F. Kennedy Library and Museum offers free admission every May 29 in celebration of President Kennedy's birthday. The museum's three theaters, period settings, and 25 dramatic multimedia exhibits enable visitors to step back into the re-created world of the Kennedy White House and experience the challenges faced by America during the 1960s. Parking is free; free shuttle service from the JFK subway stop on the Red line is provided. | Columbia Point, next to the University of Massachusetts campus | 617/929–4523 | www.cs.umb.edu/jfklibrary | May 29.

JUNE: *Bunker Hill Weekend.* On June 17, 1775, British regulars faced Colonial militiamen at the Battle of Bunker Hill. The British victory was hard-won: the Colonial militia proved worthy adversaries. This historic battle is commemorated with 18th-century manual of arms and musket firing demonstrations. The community celebrates this event with a three-hour parade that ends at the Bunker Hill Monument. For more information, see the National Park Service Web site listed here. | Charlestown Navy Yard, Charlestown | 617/242–5601 | www.nps.gov.

JUNE: *Neponset River Greenway Festival.* This one-day event features boat cruises on the Neponset and Charles rivers as well as arts and crafts and environmental exhibits, folk music, and the Milton Farmers' Market. Advance boat ticket purchase is recommended. | Milton Landing, Wharf St., in Lower Mills, on the Dorcester/Milton border | 617/822–4046 or 617/542–7696 | fax 617/542–0383.

JUNE–JULY: *Boston Harborfest.* This weeklong celebration of the city's waterfront, seafood, and maritime history attracts some two million people with more than 200 events. Highlights include a competition for the title to the city's best clam chowder, visits by naval vessels from around the world, historical reenactments, walking tours, free outdoor concerts, and fireworks. | 617/227–1528 | www.bostonharborfest.com | Late June–early July.

JUNE AND SEPT.: *Executive Etiquette and Social Savvy.* Could you use a little help polishing your business and social graces? In the Ritz-Carlton's Executive Etiquette dinner class, adults discuss the role of the host and learn about making reservations, ordering food and wine, seating arrangements, cultural protocol, office courtesies, the art of conversation, cell-phone etiquette, proposing toasts, smoking rules, alcohol awareness, when to discuss business, paying the bill, and more. There's also a special one-day program for children called "A Day of Social Savvy." | Ritz-Carlton Boston, 15 Arlington St. | 617/536–5700.

JULY: *Esplanade Concerts.* Boston's best-known Art Deco structure—the Hatch Shell—at the foot of Beacon Hill, is the site of the popular summer concert series started by Boston Pops conductor Arthur Fiedler in 1929. The tradition continues with a variety of performances throughout the summer, including the nationally televised Fourth of July Pops Concert and Fireworks featuring Tchaikovsky's *1812 Overture*. The weeklong series of Boston Pops concerts takes place in early summer with concerts by other performing ensembles scheduled for the remainder of the summer. The Hatch Shell is situated on the ribbon of green parkland along the Boston side of the Charles River. | Hatch Memorial Shell, Charles River Esplanade | 617/727–9547, ext. 450 (Hatch Shell events) or 617/266–1492 (Boston Pops information) | fax 617/727–8091 | www.state.ma.us/mdc.

JULY–OCT.: *Paul Revere Tonight.* David Conner plays Paul Revere at the Old North Church in North End. At this event, Revere tells the stories of his life in Boston before and during the revolution and talks about the Old North Church and his famous midnight ride. | Old North Church, 193 Salem St. | 617/523–6676 | www.oldnorth.com | $12 | Thurs. and Fri. at 8 PM.

DEC.: *First Night Boston.* This New Year's Eve celebration starts in the afternoon and runs to the wee hours. There's something for everyone—parades, ice sculpting, performance art, indoor concerts, laser shows, and fireworks—at scores of venues all over the city. The subway is free after 8 PM | 617/542–1399 | www.firstnight.org.

WALKING TOURS

Freedom Trail (approximately 4 hours)

Despite the labyrinthine quality to Boston's downtown streets, this walk is made easy: all you have to do is follow the red line, that is, the red bricks embedded in the pavement, which mark the route of the full Freedom Trail through the city. Begin at the corner of Beacon and Park streets, in front of the gold-domed **State House.** Follow the red line in the sidewalk down the hill along Park Street to the 1809 **Park Street Church,** at the corner of Tremont Street, a center for the 19th-century abolition movement. Designed by Peter Banner, the church is distinguished by a 217-ft-tall steeple, an imitation of the needle-spired London works by Banner's fellow English church architect Christopher Wren. On Tremont Street next to the church is the **Granary Burying Ground,** one of Boston's 16 historic cemeteries and the final resting place for such notable figures as Samuel Adams, John Hancock, James Otis, and Paul Revere. Most of the tombstones were rearranged during Victorian-era beautification efforts so as to permit the use of newly invented lawnmowers; the graves themselves are actually strewn haphazardly about. Continue down the block to the corner of Beacon Street, where **King's Chapel** stands diagonally across the intersection. Its architect, Peter Harrison, was a prolific Colonial designer of royal governors' mansions and houses of worship, including Newport's historic Truro Synagogue; his planned steeple was left unfinished owing to the church's difficulties in raising money. The red line takes a brief side trip to the chapel's burying ground, and then continues down School Street. Behind King's Chapel, in the first of School Street's two short blocks, is the ornate mansard-roof Old City Hall, in front of which stands a **statue of Benjamin Franklin.** Old Ben is commemorated here because he was born about a block away. On the sidewalk in front of him is a plaque honoring the **site of the first U.S. public school.** Although it has since moved elsewhere in the city, the 1635 Boston Latin School is still in operation as one of the most prestigious components of the Boston public school system. Resume walking down School Street to its intersection with Washington Street. There to the right is the attractive redbrick **Old South Meeting House,** built in 1729 and for many decades the largest building in Boston. Famous as the site of the heated assembly that precipitated the Boston Tea Party in 1773, Old South has continued to be a public forum for uncensored debate of politics and current affairs. Follow the red line down Washington Street to the 1713 **Old State House,** on State Street next to the National Park Service Visitor Center. As Boston's oldest public building, it has had a checkered history, much of which is documented within the excellent and often overlooked museum inside. Opposite the front of the building, on its east side, notice the slightly raised cobblestone ring on the small traffic island. This marks the **site of the Boston Massacre,** remembered now as one of the most incendiary events leading up to the American Revolution. Turn back to the Old State House and note the balcony on the second floor, from which the Declaration of Independence was given its first public reading to cheering Bostonians, an event repeated every July 18. Continue on the red line across the busy intersection and down New Congress Street to the "Cradle of Liberty," **Faneuil Hall,** behind the statue of Sam Adams. The present 1763 building, the third on the site since the original was built in 1742, has hosted many famous orators, from early patriots to John F. Kennedy. To appreciate how much of Boston now sits on landfill, notice the brass marks set into the plaza surface, outlining the city's original shoreline and later wharves. Leaving behind the colorful hubbub of Quincy Market's food courts and shops, behind Faneuil Hall, follow the red line past the evocative **Holocaust Memorial** and through the ever-changing landscape of Boston's massive "Big Dig" highway relocation project, until finally emerging in the historic North End. After a short stroll along restaurant-lined Hanover Street, turn right on Richmond Street and then left on North Street. On the left midway up the block facing cobbled North Square—actually a triangle—is the **Paul Revere House,** built around 1680. If the structure seems small now, consider how much smaller it would have been with a family of six children. Follow the red line back to Hanover Street, up three blocks, and left through the Paul Revere Mall, an irregular walled plaza better known to the neighborhood's Italian residents as the Prado. Towering over the back of the plaza is the famous **Old North Church,** whose role on the night before the outbreak of the American Revolution is immortalized in Longfellow's poem "Paul Revere's Ride." From the front of the church, head up Hull Street to **Copp's Hill Burying Ground,** the final resting place of many Colonial North End and Beacon Hill residents. Some of the old gravestones bear scars of musket balls, a reminder of the target practice by British soldiers garrisoned in Boston after the outbreak of the Revolution. Back on Hull Street, follow the red line downhill to Commercial Street and the Charlestown Bridge over the mouth of the Charles River. On the opposite side the line soon splits; turn left through City Square and the narrow Colonial streets of this historic neighborhood, zigzagging up the hill to the **Bunker Hill Monument.** The Revolutionary War battle commemorated by the monument was nominally a defeat for the rebellious patriot militia, but the victory cost the Redcoats nearly half their forces, the worst casualty rate in British military history. Continue back down to the waterfront, staying to the left when the red line splits at the former militia training field, now a small park. After passing beneath U.S. 1 and crossing Chelsea Street, enter the **Charlestown Navy Yard,** home to the world's oldest commissioned warship, the **USS *Constitution.*** In addition to its annual turn-around cruise of Boston Harbor, so the hull weathers evenly while docked, the 1797 frigate salutes the "striking of the colors" with a shot from her cannon in the late afternoon, when the flag is lowered. You can return to downtown by way of a short $1 harbor cruise aboard an MBTA commuter ferry from the Navy Yard's Pier 4. Choose between the ferry to Long Wharf and the New England Aquarium, or the ferry to Lovejoy Wharf, beside North Station.

Beacon Hill and Back Bay (approximately 4 hours)

Begin at the corner of Beacon and Park streets, in front of the gold-domed **State House.** Walk west down Beacon Street, turn right on Joy Street, and then turn left up at the top of the block, on Mt. Vernon Street. Ahead on the right at No. 55 is the **Nichols House Museum,** one of the first mansions built on Beacon Hill and one of the few open to the public. Continue downhill on Mt. Vernon Street past the stately Federal-era private homes whose elegant brick facades epitomize Old Boston. Soon on the right comes **Louisburg Square,** a private pocket-size park belonging to the town-house residents on either side. The park's deteriorating statues are of Columbus and Aristides the Just. Follow the sloping brick sidewalks down Mt. Vernon to busy Charles Street and turn left, resisting, if possible, two blocks of tempting restaurants and shops. At the corner of Beacon Street cross the intersection and enter the wrought-iron gate of the **Public Garden,** whose tree-filled grounds count as one of the city's loveliest oases for strolling, bench-sitting, and people-watching. Walk around the shallow duck lagoon or over its small footbridge, aiming for the larger-than-life-size bronze statue of George Washington astride his horse on the west side of the garden. Follow the general's gaze through the gates and across Arlington Street, which was once the edge of the tidal river basin behind the city, known as Back Bay. Enter the exclusive neighborhood built atop the bay's landfill via the **Commonwealth Avenue Mall,** the linear park that links the Public Garden to the so-called Emerald Necklace of urban green space, which together constitute the pride of the city's park system. After admiring Back Bay's stately 19th-century architecture for two blocks, turn left at Clarendon Street and proceed to **Trinity Church,** the unmistakable mountain of Romanesque masonry at the east end of Copley Square. Beyond the historic church, handsomely reflecting it in 62 stories of mirrored glass, is the John Hancock Tower, at the top of which is the **John Hancock Observatory,** offering the highest panoramic views in all New England. Facing Trinity Church from the west side of the square is the main branch of the **Boston Public Library,** a beautiful Italian Renaissance monument to public learning. Step through the huge bronze doors for a look at the ornate marble interior, with its stone regal lions seated by the grand staircase, and many fine allegorical murals upstairs. Back out on the street, turn left from the library steps and left again at the corner to continue westward along Boylston Street. Two blocks ahead on the left is the sprawling Prudential Center, whose 52-story centerpiece, familiarly known to locals as The Pru, dominates the skyline with its '60s-style International look. Enter the **Shops at Prudential Center** from the escalators on the Boylston Street side, and thread through the mall concourse toward the opposite entrance, stopping along the way, perhaps, to catch an express elevator to the **Prudential Skywalk View and Exhibit** on the 52nd floor. At the southwest exit, beside Restaurant Marché Mövenpick, take the escalators down and cross the street to the **First Church of Christ, Scientist,** whose modern concrete forms are better known to Bostonians as the Christian Science Center, or, most familiarly, as the Mother Church. Designed by I. M. Pei and Araldo Cossutta, the spacious complex is softened by the 670-ft reflecting pool that stretches nearly all the way to Massachusetts Avenue. There, at the west end of the plaza, are the original 19th-century church buildings, as well as the Christian Science Publishing Society. Turn left after exiting the Publishing Society and walk to the intersection of Huntington Avenue; at the corner is **Symphony Hall,** whose prim Italian Renaissance exterior and small lobby cannot begin to hint at the acoustic pleasures of a concert within this beloved cultural landmark. To return to downtown, ignore the subway station entrance immediately outside Symphony Hall and instead cross Huntington to either station entrance marked "Inbound Trains Only." Proceed through the unmanned turn-stiles, have exact fare or token ready, and board the first trolley that appears.

Dining

INEXPENSIVE

Addis Red Sea. Ethiopian. This South End restaurant incorporates bright fabrics, basketweave tables, hand-carved wooden seats, and other traditional artifacts from the Horn of Africa to provide the proper ambience for appreciating authentic Ethiopian/Eritrean dishes, all of which are eaten with the aid of the *injera* flatbread on which the food is served rather than with silverware. Try the *gomen wot* (collard greens), lamb in pepper sauce, and strips of beef sautéed with onions and spices. Weekend lunch. Beer and wine only. No smoking. | 544 Tremont St. | 617/426–8727 | No lunch | $5.95–$16.95 | AE, DC, MC, V.

Artú. Italian. Enter through the kitchen of this North End restaurant and savor the cheerfully controlled chaos of the line cooks preparing hearty portions of traditional Italian favorites for an appreciative crowd of families and others who value good food at a budget-friendly price. Try the sausage fusilli or quazzette *alla Donato,* which is shrimp, squid, mussels, and sole over linguine and red sauce. Beer and wine only. No smoking. | 6 Prince St. | 617/742–4336 | $6–$15 | AE, MC, V.

Bob the Chef's. Southern. Casual, stylish dining amid contemporary furnishings in Boston's South End. There are photos of jazz musicians from nearby Berklee College of Music on the walls. Try the fried chicken and ribs combo or the soul fish sandwich. Entertainment Thurs.–Sun. Sun. brunch. No smoking. | 604 Columbus Ave. | 617/536–6204 | Closed Mon. | $6.25–$15 | AE, D, DC, MC, V.

Cafe Marliave. Italian. This reliable 19th-century institution is hidden away in the center of a downtown block. The original artwork is still on the walls and dedicated regulars love the no-nonsense square meals. It is known for chicken Marsala, spaghetti, and beef. No smoking in dining room. | 10 Bosworth St. | 617/423–6340 | Closed Sun. | $7.95–$12.95 | AE, D, DC, MC, V.

Dixie Kitchen. Cajun. Paper napkins, Delta roots music in the background, and a wall-size map of Louisiana food festivals set the proper relaxed tone for dishing up authentic bayou comfort food in Boston's Back Bay. The menu ranges from from po' boys to catfish, oysters to fried alligator. Try the catfish Marguery and shrimp Louisianne. No alcohol. No smoking in dining room. | 182 Massachusetts Ave. | 617/536–3068 | $8–$12 | AE, MC, V.

Himalaya. Indian. Large streetside windows add to the openness of this understated Back Bay restaurant, whose expertly prepared cuisine is well balanced between North and South Indian selections. Try dosa, uttapam, lamb shashik, and lobster Malabar. Beer and wine only. No smoking. | 95 Massachusetts Ave. | 617/267–6644 | $7–$15 | AE, D, DC, MC, V.

Restaurant Marché of Boston Mövenpick. Eclectic. Back Bay's lively European version of a traditional cafeteria, with an array of freestanding cooking stations serving made-to-order dishes from pizza to sushi in a setting styled after a Mediterranean market plaza. Try the Swiss rösti, rotisserie chicken, and dessert crêpes. Beer and wine only. No smoking. | Prudential Center, 800 Boylston St. | 617/578–9700 | $5.99–$10.80 | AE, D, DC, MC, V.

White Star Tavern. American. This friendly neighborhood tavern in Copley Square offers seafood, green plates for vegetarians, sandwiches, and burgers. Try the tempura-battered fish-and-chips. It also has a good line of microbrews and a wide selection of half bottles of wine. | 565 Boylston St. | 617/536–4477 | No lunch Mon. | $8–$16 | AE, D, DC, MC, V.

Zuma's Tex Mex Cafe. Tex-Mex. This Faneuil Hall area spot is famous for its margaritas, but the inexpensive and filling south-of-the-border basics ensure a steady crowd of value-conscious diners. Try the enchiladas, burritos, or a grill. Kid's menu. No smoking in dining room. | 7 N. Market St. | 617/367–9114 | $8–$15 | AE, D, DC, MC, V.

MODERATE

Assaggio. Italian. Romance (and the aroma of good food) is in the air at this eatery in Boston's North End. The downstairs dining room has vine-entwined columns and linen tablecloths and candles on each table. Upstairs, star constellations twinkle on the ceiling and a Botticelli painting graces the wall. Popular entrées include the chicken or veal saltimbocca stuffed with prosciutto, smoked mozzarella, and sage and then sautéed in a sherry wine with shiitake mushrooms. The chef's specials change nightly and often feature fresh seafood with pasta and risotto. | 29 Prince St. | 617/227–7380 | www.assaggio.com | $10–$26 | AE, D, MC, V.

Bomboa. Brazilian. This Back Bay/South End restaurant attracts groups of repeat customers who share platters of French/Brazilian dishes and pitchers of sangria. Try the ceviche (fresh seafood cured in citrus) or steak frites with chimichuri sauce (garlic, parsley, and olive oil), and also the delicious breads and breadsticks. | 35 Stanhope St. | www.bomboa.com | 617/236–6363 | fax 617/236–6424 | No lunch | $16–$24 | AE, D, DC, MC, V.

★ **Brasserie Jo.** French. Paris comes to Boston, and stays in the Colonnade Hotel under the name of Brasserie Jo. With sun shining through the windows, and high ceilings, this restaurant can be very bright in the afternoon. Its walls are lined with posters from France, and there is a wine bottle display which complements its extensive wine list. Entrées include steak au poivre, rack of lamb, and fillet of skate. There is a raw bar, and two private dining rooms are also available. Weekend brunch. | Prudential Building, 120 Huntington Ave. | 617/425–3240 | $15.95–$25.95 | AE, D, DC, MC, V.

Bristol Lounge. American. This restaurant in Back Bay's Four Seasons Hotel offers a choice of clublike lounge seating for intimate socializing over food and drinks, a plush yet not overly formal dining room, or a lively bar. It is known for burgers, Caesar salad, and lobster. Live music. Sun. brunch. No smoking in dining area. Free parking weekdays at lunch, otherwise parking (fee). | 200 Boylston St. | 617/351–2054 | $12–$25 | AE, D, DC, MC, V.

Casa Romero. Mexican. Enter the Romero family's Back Bay home and you will find three dining rooms accented by authentic Mexican tilework and a lovely oasis of a patio garden. You will be transported south of the border by expertly prepared regional cuisine. Try the sautéed stuffed squid with tomato and chipotle sauce. Open-air dining in garden. No smoking. | 30 Gloucester St. | 617/536–4341 | No lunch | $12.50–$24 | D, MC, V.

Charley's Eating and Drinking Saloon. American. A boisterous, family-friendly, Back Bay beer-and-burger haven inside a renovated Victorian school. There's open-air dining on sidewalk. Kids' menu. Weekend brunch. No smoking. | 284 Newbury St. | 617/266–3000 | $12.99–$22 | AE, D, DC, MC, V.

Claremont Cafe. Contemporary. A small spot in the South End serving creative, seasonally changing dishes with global influences. It is known for crab cakes and the unusual combination salads, like the pear and prosciutto salad. Open-air dining on sidewalk. Weekend brunch. No smoking. | 535 Columbus Ave. | 617/247–9001 | Closed Mon. No dinner Sun. | $14.95–$25.95 | AE, MC, V.

Ciao Bella. Italian. A chic people-watchers' hotspot in the heart of Boston's trendiest shopping district. Half-size pasta dishes are available at dinner. There's a lot of seafood on the menu as well as traditional pasta dishes. Try the veal chop. Open-air dining on sidewalk. Sun. brunch. | 240A Newbury St. | 617/536–2626 | $10.95–$35.95 | AE, D, DC, MC, V.

Durgin Park. American. This timeless institution, established in 1826, in the Faneuil Hall area, dishes up square meals in a come-as-you-are atmosphere of long, communal tables and famously no-nonsense waitstaff. Try the pot roast, corned beef, or seafood. | 30 N. Market St. | 617/227–2038 | $6.95–$41.95 | AE, D, DC, MC, V.

The Exchange. Continental. The atmosphere of an exclusive club pervades this former bank building between the Financial Distric and Faneuil Hall, but the only prerequisite to enjoying the top-flight service and food is a good appetite. Try the fire-roasted breast of chicken, herb-crusted aged prime tenderloin, or cured North Atlantic salmon. | 148 State St. | 617/726–7600 | Closed Sun. No lunch Sat., no dinner Mon. | $11–$23. | AE, D, DC, MC, V.

Ginza. Japanese. Lovely kimono-clad waitresses, some of the city's top sushi chefs, and a kitchen that stays open until 4 AM most nights make this a popular spot in Chinatown. Try the sashimi, broiled seafood, and hot pots. Beer, wine, and Sake only. | 16 Hudson St. | 617/338–2261 | $14–$26 | AE, MC, V.

★ **Lala Rokh.** Middle Eastern. Persian calligraphic art and a bright, intimate dining room within a historic brick, Beacon Hill town home are the backdrop for exotic, fragrant, heartfelt cooking from the land of the shahs. Try the *torshi* (pickled chutneys), *ghormeh sabzi* (leg of lamb stew), *morgh polo* (slow-cooked chicken), *mahi-e-rouz* (grilled marinated fish), and *ferani* (rose custard). No smoking. | 97 Mt. Vernon St. | 617/720–5511 | No lunch | $14–$17.50 | AE, DC, MC, V.

Ristorante Lucia. Italian. Updated versions of Italian masterpieces are on the first floor and a G-rated Sistine Chapel ceiling replica is over the upstairs bar at this North End purveyor of authentic dishes from Abruzzi. Try the *abruzzo in fiore* (veal rolled and stuffed with prosciutto, cheeses, and spices) or the linguine Marco Polo (fresh shrimp, clams, mussels, and octopus over linguine). No smoking in dining room. Valet Parking after 5 (fee). | 415 Hanover St. | 617/367–2353 | No lunch Mon.–Thurs. | $8.50–$30 | AE, MC, V.

Skipjack's. Seafood. In a city full of restaurants that pride themselves on preparing good seafood, this modestly stylish Copley Square spot is a true star, serving whatever is fresh from the Pacific to the Atlantic, plus a few rivers in between, at reasonable prices. Known for clam chowder, fried calamari, and cioppino. Try mussels bianco and the mixed seafood kabob. Kid's menu. Early bird suppers. Sun. brunch. No smoking in dining room. | 199 Clarendon St. | 617/536–3500 | $15–$20 | AE, D, DC, MC, V.

Sonsie. Contemporary. A busy bistro/café atmosphere, with bar at the front and restaurant in the back. Its varied menu includes regional seafood as well as vegetarian dishes, steak, and duck. The menu keeps changing and has included dishes such as baked stuffed crab backs, charcoal duck breast with pears and vanilla, fried calamari, and brick-oven pizza. Parking (fee). | 327 Newbury St. | 617/351–2500 | Breakfast also available | $9–$24 | AE, D, DC, MC, V.

★ **Les Zygomates.** French. A friendly bistro that has an extensive wine list and offers a good-value prix-fixe lunch and dinner menu plus several à la carte dishes. Some favorites are the roasted duck breast marinated in balsamic vinaigrette with Lyonnaise potatoes; seared king salmon Napoleon with clams au vermouth; and flank steak with cumin. | 129 South St. | 617/542–5108 | Reservations essential | Closed Sun. No lunch Sat. | $14–$20 | AE, D, DC, MC, V.

EXPENSIVE

Anthony's Pier 4. Seafood. A tried-and-true old warhorse of a waterfront restaurant, with nautical decor and a highly prized city view. While known for its seafood, Anthony's also serves steak, chicken, and pasta. Try one of the warm popovers. The dining room opens up to the outside, so you can sit and look out over the water. Free parking. | 140 Northern Ave. | 617/482–6262 | Jacket required | $17.95–$50 | AE, D, DC, MC, V.

Black Crow Cafe. Contemporary. An informal neighborhood storefront in Jamaica Plain that is conducive to lingering alone or with friends belies the imaginatively upscale menu, laced with Caribbean and Asian accents. Try the catch of the day, chicken breast, and key lime pie. Weekend brunch. Beer and wine only. No smoking. | 2 Perkins St. | 617/983–9231 | Closed Mon. | $19–$25 | AE, D, MC, V.

Cafe Budapest. Hungarian. Czech, Bavarian, and French decorative themes set the old-world tone in this Back Bay institution. The unique decor is complemented by original paintings, cozy alcoves for couples, and a strolling violinist. Try the veal gulyas or Wiener schnitzel. Live music Tues.–Sat. Kids' menu. No smoking. Parking (fee). | 90 Exeter St. | 617/266–1979 | Reservations essential | $19.50–$32.50 | AE, D, DC, MC, V.

Cafe Louis. Italian. This small, contemporary, gourmet café—an offspring of Providence, Rhode Island's, most famous restaurant, Al Forno—is tucked inside one of Boston's most fashionable, upscale clothing stores in Copley Square. Try the native fish, clams al forno, thin-crust pizzas, and any of the dessert tarts for two. Open-air dining on patio. Beer and wine only. No smoking. Free parking. | 234 Berkeley St. | 617/266–4680 | Closed Sun. No dinner Mon. | $18–$22 | AE, D, DC, MC, V.

Davide. Italian. If Dean Martin's ghost came to Boston, he'd surely be found haunting this intimate, North End subterranean room, with its velvet trim, Rat Pack background music, and tuxedo-clad staff. Try the osso buco with saffron risotto or roasted rack of lamb. Parking (fee). | 326 Commercial St. | 617/227–5745 | No lunch July–Aug. and weekends | $18–$38 | AE, D, MC, V.

Davio's. Italian. Choose between formal dining downstairs or informal café atmosphere upstairs; both floors benefit from the same exquisite northern Italian preparations and attention to detail. This Back Bay eatery is known for its meat dishes and homemade sausage. Open-air dining on patio. Kid's menu. Valet parking (fee). | 269 Newbury St. | 617/262–4810 | Dining room: $14.95–$33.95; Café: $9.95–$18.95 | AE, D, DC, MC, V.

Filippo Ristorante. Italian. Mirrors, curtains, and celebrity photos line the walls of this reliable North End spot, whose second-floor dining room is frequently rented out for special occasions. A simpler lunch menu is served in the more casual setting downstairs. Crauccio—scallops, clams, mussels, calamari, shrimp, and lobster in a marinara sauce served over pasta—is a favorite. No smoking in dining room. | 283 Causeway St. | 617/742–4143 | Jacket and tie | $20–$35 | AE, MC, V.

The Hungry I. French. Elegance abounds in this Beacon Hill building, from the welcoming cornucopia of fresh produce and flowers to the attentive service and impeccable country French cuisine. You can choose from the rabbit baked in mustard sauce and in a crock to the venison au poivre, but make sure you save room for the homemade pastries. Open-air dining on garden patio. Sun. brunch. No smoking. | 71½ Charles St. | 617/227–3524 | No lunch | $22–$34 | AE, DC, MC, V.

Icarus. Contemporary. Soothing and romantic Arts and Crafts dining room in South End is filled with mission furniture. The menu changes frequently. Some of the recent favorites have been the grilled shimp with mango and jalapeño and the porcini-crusted halibut with spring vegetables and cabernet vinaigrette. Live music Fri. No smoking. Parking (fee). | 3 Appleton St. | 617/426–1790 | Reservations essential on Fri. and Sat. | Closed Sun. in July–Aug. No lunch | $21.50–$29.50 | AE, D, DC, MC, V.

Jimmy's Harborside. Seafood. There are other things on the menu, but seafood is king at this tried-and-true old standby overlooking Boston Harbor on the Historic Waterfront and amid the piers serving the city's commercial fishing fleet. Kids' menu. No smoking in dining room. Valet parking (fee) | 242 Northern Ave. | 617/423–1000 | $15–$50 | AE, D, DC, MC, V.

★ **Legal Sea Foods.** Seafood. Handsomely decorated in dark wood, this Back Bay member of the imperial dynasty of Boston seafood restaurants—part of a regional chain that has expanded across the city and suburbs since humble beginnings in the 1970s—excels at serving perfectly prepared fish, the simpler the better. Try clam chowder, smoked bluefish pâté, raw shellfish, Portuguese fisherman's stew, and the daily specials. Kids' menu. No smoking. | Prudential Center, 800 Boylston St. | 617/266–6800 | $13–$40 | AE, D, DC, MC, V.

Maison Robert. French. This Financial District restaurant provides elegant and formal dining—with only the slightest hint of French attitude in the service. Try the rack of lamb or smoked lobster and make sure you save room for the apple tart. No smoking. | 45 School St. | 617/227–3370 | Reservations essential | Jacket required in dining room | Closed July, Sun.–Mon. | Dining room: $19–$32; Café: $12–$25 | AE, DC, MC, V.

Mamma Maria. Italian. The flavorful dishes at this North End eatery showcase the diversity of Italian regional cuisine and thoroughly dispel the stereotypes about red sauce and pasta. Try the homemade handcut pasta in traditional Tuscan style with roasted-rabbit pancetta and rosemary or the wood-grilled bone-in beef tenderloin with roasted red and yellow Holland peppers and seabeans. No smoking. Parking (fee). | 3 North Sq | 617/523–0077 | No lunch | $19–$32 | AE, D, DC, MC, V.

Metropolis Café. Contemporary. You are crowded elbow-to-elbow in high-backed booths by the tiny bar at this South End restaurant with sophisticated food that gives a stylish American touch to the northern Italian and southern French standards. Try the duck confit, garlic-roasted chicken, prosciutto-wrapped cod, risotto of the day, or lemon gâteau. Weekend brunch. No smoking. Valet Parking (fee). | 584 Tremont St. | 617/247–2931 | Reservations essential | No lunch | $16–$22 | AE, MC, V.

Morton's of Chicago. Steak. No sedately murmuring dealmakers in this Back Bay restaurant, just crowds of well-dressed diners conversing eagerly over the heady mix of sumptuous food, sterling service, and well-appointed, contemporary decor. Try the shrimp Alexander or broiled sea scallops wrapped in bacon if you want something other than the wide offering of steak, including porterhouse, prime rib, and filet mignon. No smoking. Valet parking (fee). | 1 Exeter Plaza | 617/266–5858 | No lunch | $20–$33 | AE, DC, MC, V.

Oak Room. Steak. Lots of oak surround well-dressed guests with a measure of elegance matched by the food and service at this Back Bay restaurant in the Fairmont Copley Plaza Hotel. The New York strip steak, tenderloin, fresh New England seafood, lobster, and salmon are recommended. Raw bar. Live music Tues.–Sat. Kid's menu. No smoking. Valet parking (fee). | Fairmont Copley Plaza Hotel, 138 St. James Ave. | 617/267–5300 | No lunch | $17.95–$66 | AE, D, DC, MC, V.

★ **Olives.** Mediterranean. High ceilings, dark wood, and large streetside windows in Charlestown seem barely to contain the enthusiastic crowds that come to feast on some of the city's finest creative dining by chef Todd English. Try the wood-grilled steaks, house-cured duck prosciutto, any local fish dish, and the panache of seasonal sorbets. No smoking in dining room. Valet parking (fee). | 10 City Sq | 617/242–1999 | Closed Sun. No lunch | $20–$29.95 | AE, DC, MC, V.

Parker's Restaurant at the Omni Parker House. American. This restaurant in the longest continuously operating hotel in America has been an innovator in Boston cuisine. It was here that Parker House rolls and Boston Cream Pie (the official Massachusetts dessert) were created. The universally accepted term for the catch of the day—scrod—was coined here. You'll find traditional fare, like black Angus New York sirloin, Block Island swordfish, herb-charred salmon, and, of course, baked Boston scrod. | 60 School St. | 617/227–8600 | fax 617/227–2120 | www.omnihotels.com | Breakfast also available. Closed Sun. No lunch | $16–$27 | AE, D, DC, MC, V.

Pravda 116. Mediterranean. Chic nightclub atmosphere in the Theater District—there is a club on the lower level, in fact, that spills over into the restaurant after 10 PM—with a long bar, and an open kitchen. Try the Maine crab and noodle cake, grilled tuna, pistachio-crusted salmon, and lemon torte. Live music Thurs. nights during dinner. DJ Thurs.-Sat. nights. Valet or garage parking (fee) | 116 Boylston St. | 617/482–7799 | Closed Sun. and Mon., no lunch | $18–$29 | AE, DC, MC, V.

Ristorante Toscano. Italian. Italian pottery and art enliven this intimate and elegant Beacon Hill trattoria, where the menu concentrates on the cuisine of Florence. The chef concentrates on Tuscan food including the boneless leg of lamb and many veal dishes. No smoking in dining room. Valet parking (fee). | 47 Charles St. | 617/723–4090 | No lunch Sun. | $18–$45 | AE, MC, V.

Saffron Restaurant and Bar. Contemporary. This upscale Newbury Street eatery offers western food with Indian spices. Popular entrées include tandoori rack of lamb as well as tandoori chicken sliced in fine julienne, flavored with pepper, balsamic vinegar, and olive oil, and layered on Indian bread. The restaurant's two levels are connected by a circular staircase and it has paintings from India on the walls and floor-to-ceiling windows. There are outdoor patio-style tables which are perfect for people-watching as you dine. | 279A Newbury St. | 617/536–9766 | fax 617/536–9892 | $14–$29 | AE, D, DC, MC, V.

75 Chestnut. Contemporary. Brocade fabrics, dark wood, and oil paintings of old Boston help pamper the Beacon Hill neighborhood regulars almost as much as do the ample portions of richly sauced meat and seafood they come back for time and again. Known for wood-grilled beef, roast duck, and pasta with lobster. No smoking in dining room. Valet parking (fee), free garage parking. | 75 Chestnut St. | 617/227–2175 | No lunch | $19–$27 | AE, DC, MC, V.

711 Boylston. Continental. This Back Bay restaurant's fare has a Mediterranean influence. For appetizers, try the rock shrimp spring roll which is deep fried with julienne vegetables and served with mango chutney on the side before moving on to the seared sword-fish chop served with vegetables and potatoes. Save room for the house-made desserts. There's a full-service bar and an extensive wine list. The black velvet settees, leopard-trimmed bar stools, and granite bar with peach and mirror accents give this upscale eatery an Art Deco look. Soft jazz and blues (recorded) plays softly in the background. | 711 Boylston St. | 617/437–0002 | fax 617/262–2254 | Closed Sun.–Mon. No lunch | $14–$36 | AE, DC, MC, V.

Top of the Hub. Contemporary. The city looks stunning from this 52-story perch in Back Bay, and the inventive, Italian-influenced menu does its best to live up to equally lofty stan-dards. Known for clam chowder, osso buco, and seafood. Live music. Sun. brunch. No smok-ing in dining room. | 800 Boylston St. | 617/536–1775 | Reservations essential | $21–$45 | AE, D, DC, MC, V.

Turner Fisheries. Seafood. No noisy waterfront fish shack here, just spacious Back Bay din-ing with pleasantly understated decor and a noise level that allows normal conversations, complemented by food that more than holds its own against the high-profile harborside competition. Try the pan-seared sea scallops, nontraditional bouillabaisse, tuna sashimi, and the famed clam chowder. Live music Thurs.–Sat. Kids' menu. Sun. brunch. No smok-ing in dining room. Parking (fee) | Westin Hotel, Dartmouth and Stuart Sts. | 617/424–7425 | $19–$29 | AE, D, DC, MC, V.

Ye Olde Union Oyster House. Seafood. You can see that this Faneuil Hall area restaurant is old from the odd angles and low ceilings. Here you'll find crowds of tourists and a gen-erous helping of true-blue Boston accents and bluff hospitality. It is known for raw shell-fish, lobsters, shore dinners, and seafood platters. Raw bar. Kids' menu. Sun. brunch. No smoking. | 41 Union St. | 617/227–2750 | $16.95–$65 | AE, D, DC, MC, V.

VERY EXPENSIVE

Ambrosia on Huntington. Contemporary. This Back Bay restaurant has an artsy interior and exciting menu of French Provincial dishes with Asian kick. Try the lobster sashimi, St. Pierre fish steamed in bamboo, wood-roasted sirloin, and pan-seared venison. No smok-ing. Valet parking (fee). | 116 Huntington Ave. | 617/247–2400 | www.ambrosiaonhunting-ton.com | Reservations essential | No lunch Sat.–Sun. | $26–$37 | AE, D, DC, MC, V.

Aujourd'hui. Contemporary. This dining room in Back Bay's Four Seasons Hotel is one of the city's finest with a menu that changes—of course—with the seasons. Known for grilled tenderloin, roasted lobster, veal medallions, and chocolate soufflé. Kids' menu. Sun. brunch. No smoking. Valet parking (fee). | 200 Boylston St. | 617/351–2072 | Reservations essen-tial | Jacket and tie | $33–$45 | AE, D, DC, MC, V.

Bay Tower. French. You can enjoy candlelight dining with unrivaled downtown and har-bor views from atop one of the Financial District skyscrapers. In this restaurant, traditional Escoffier technique is improved upon by accents from around the globe. Try lobster bisque and Grand Marnier soufflé. Entertainment. No smoking. Parking (fee). | 60 State St., 33rd floor | 617/723–1666 | Closed Sun. No lunch | $23.50–$39 | AE, D, DC, MC, V.

★ **Biba.** Contemporary. The regularly changing menu in this Back Bay restaurant is critically acclaimed for its innovative dishes, dash of whimsy, and daring to include a category labeled "offal." The ground-floor bar is a popular spot for noshing on appetizers. Try lob-ster pizza, foie gras appetizers, and unique pastas and sausages. Sun. brunch. No smok-ing in dining room. Valet parking (fee). | 272 Boylston St. | 617/426–7878 | Reservations essential | $26–$45 | AE, D, DC, MC, V.

★ **The Federalist.** Continental. Part of the Fifteen Beacon Hotel, this restaurant evokes the stately tradition of a prestigious club. The menu includes classics such as a traditional New England clambake, beef Wellington, pan-roasted salmon, fresh Dungeness crab, and sautéed Dover sole. The restaurant's wine cellar has 1700 selections and can also be reserved as a private dining room. "The Fed," which is ½ block from the State House and ½ block from the financial district, caters to the legal and financial communities.

| 15 Beacon St. | 617/670–1500 | fax 617/670–1500 | Breakfast also available | $28–$44 | AE, D, DC, MC, V.

★ **L'Espalier.** French. This converted, Back Bay town house–restaurant prides itself on grace and elegance. The decor is supplemented by a huge staircase and wood paneling on the walls. Entrées include roasted rack of lamb in green olive tapenade, and grilled marinated Black Angus tenderloin with endive and spinach–black truffle–oxtail sauce. No smoking. Valet parking (fee). | 30 Gloucester St. | 617/262–3023 | Reservations essential | Jacket and tie | Closed Sun. No lunch | $65–$82. | AE, D, DC, MC, V.

Grill 23. Steak. Neoclassic details in the decor add a note of deluxe elegance to the high-ceiling dining room and open kitchen, which fill the former trading floor of the Art Deco Salada Tea building in Boston's Back Bay. Here you can have the slow-roasted tenderloin of beef, New York sirloin, or poppyseed-encrusted tuna with orange zest. Parking (fee). | 161 Berkeley St. | 617/542–2255 | Reservations essential | Jacket and tie | No lunch | $24.50–$30.75 | AE, D, DC, MC, V.

★ **Hamersley's Bistro.** Contemporary. High ceilings, cream tones, and country accents give this long, open dining room in Boston's South End a light, gracious elegance, matched by impeccable service and a bold, often-changing menu pairing local ingredients with French technique. While it is known for roast chicken, you may want to try the mushroom sandwich, special fish entrées, and lemon custard. Open-air dining on sidewalk plaza. No smoking. Parking (fee). | 553 Tremont St. | 617/423–2700 | No lunch | $24–$39 | AE, D, DC, MC, V.

Locke-Ober. Continental. This Downtown Crossing restaurant has been Boston's ultimate oasis of privilege since 1875, drawing the city's men of wealth and power with gold and leather, discreet service, and cuisine that's unswervingly faithful to time-honored European tradition. Women who can stand the Old Boy network ambience are welcome, too. Try the lobster Savannah or Black Angus sirloin. Valet parking (fee). | 3 Winter Pl | 617/542–1340 | Reservations essential | Jacket and tie | Closed Sun. No lunch Sat. | $23–$65 | AE, D, DC, MC, V.

No. 9 Park. Contemporary. One of Boston's most eagerly anticipated restaurants prior to its 1998 opening, this Beacon Hill eatery is presided over by chef-owner Barbara Lynch, whose innovative departures from the cuisine of Tuscany have earned her well-deserved national acclaim. It is known for its appetizers, crispy duck, and poached lobster. No smoking. Valet parking (fee). | 9 Park St. | 617/742–9991 | Reservations essential | Closed Sun. No lunch Sat. | $29–$36 | AE, D, DC, MC, V.

Pignoli. Italian. A stylish and welcoming decor, knowledgeable and efficient waitstaff, and an adventuresome menu starring the freshest seasonal fish and produce all add up to memorable dining. Not surprisingly, there are many regulars who treat the Back Bay's Pignoli as their home away from home. Try the polenta with wild mushrooms, the risottos, seared tuna and foie gras, and roasted duck. Open-air dining on sidewalk plaza. No smoking in dining room. Valet parking (fee) | 79 Park Plaza | 617/338–7500 | No lunch | $28–$36 | AE, D, DC, MC, V.

Plaza III Kansas City Steakhouse. Steak. Casual atmosphere and two floors of dining and bar areas—including a no-smoking floor—attract a chatty crowd of tourists and downtown office workers to this Faneuil Hall area restaurant. Try the Kansas City strip steak or filet mignon. Open-air dining on plaza. Kids' menu. Sun. brunch. Parking (fee). | 101 S. Market Bldg. | 617/720–5570 | $30–$40 | AE, D, DC, MC, V.

Ritz Carlton Dining Room. Continental. Crystal chandeliers, opulent fabrics, piano accompaniment, and lots of gold leaf set the perfect stage for the seasonally changing classic cuisine, prepared and served with all the panache expected from the Back Bay's Ritz. Try the duck confit, Dover sole, and chateaubriand. Live music. Kids' menu. Sun. brunch. On Fri. and Sat. there is dining and dancing on the roof. Parking (fee). | 15 Arlington St. | 617/536–5700, ext. 41 | Reservations essential | Jacket and tie | Closed Mon. | prix–fixe $61–$99 | AE, D, DC, MC, V.

Rowes Wharf Restaurant. Contemporary. Windows overlooking the Boston harbor scene, tapestry-style carpeting, and lustrous woodwork combine with the professional wait-staff to create an appropriately luxurious setting for attractively presented and perfectly prepared New England cuisine that changes daily. Kids' menu. Sun. brunch. No smoking in dining room. Parking (fee). | Boston Harbor Hotel, 70 Rowes Wharf | 617/439–3995 | Reservations essential | Jacket and tie | $28–$38 | AE, D, DC, MC, V.

Seasons Restaurant. Contemporary. At this Faneuil Hall restaurant you'll find dining with city views and seasonally changing, regional New England cuisine that has been a standard for Boston's gourmands throughout the '80s and '90s, accompanied by a stellar 14-page collection of American wines. Kids' menu. No smoking. Parking (fee). | Regal Bostonian Hotel, North and Blackstone Sts. | 617/523–3600 | Reservations essential | No lunch weekends. No dinner Sun. | $38–$64 | AE, D, DC, MC, V.

Lodging

INEXPENSIVE

Beacon Inns & Guesthouses. This four-story 19th-century brick town house is on Newbury Street, a pedestrian-friendly, people-watching thoroughfare of galleries, chic shops, and restaurants with outdoor cafés. Guest rooms are simply furnished; the property's best features are the prime Back Bay location and low rates. Kitchenettes, no TV. No pets. | 248 Newbury St. | 617/266–7142 | fax 617/266–7276 | 30 rooms | $109 | MC, V.

Best Western Boston—The Inn at Longwood Medical. Harvard Medical School and five hospitals are in the vicinity of this Medical District chain option. The hotel is within walking distance of Fenway Park and the Museum of Fine Arts, as well as several colleges and universities—Simmons, Emmanuel, Northeastern, and Wheelock. The rooms are big and have desks. Restaurant, bar, dining room, room service. In-room data ports, cable TV. Shops. Business services. | 342 Longwood Ave. | 617/731–4700 or 800/528–1234 | fax 617/731–6273 | www.bestwestern.com | 155 rooms, 5 suites | $109–$249, $239–$299 suites | AE, D, DC, MC, V.

Best Western Terrace Inn. This hotel is in Brighton, a residential neighborhood and home to St. Elizabeth's Hospital. The T to downtown Boston stops in front of the hotel. The rooms are decorated in a standard modern style. Complimentary Continental breakfast. Cable TV. Free parking. | 1650 Commonwealth Ave. | 617/566–6260 or 800/528–1234 | fax 617/731–3543 | www.bestwestern.com/terraceinn | 72 rooms, 6 suites | $109–$149, $150–200 suites | AE, D, DC, MC, V.

Boston Hotel Buckminster. In Kenmore Square, near Fenway Park and several nightclubs, this hotel has simply decorated rooms with newly renovated bathrooms. The front rooms on the fourth, fifth, and sixth floors have views of the Charles River, while the back rooms on the same floors have views of Fenway Park. Some kitchenettes, some refrigerators, cable TV. Laundry facilities. | 645 Beacon St. | 617/236–7050 or 800/727–2825 | fax 617/262–0068 | 95 rooms, 25 suites | $89–$209, $149–$289 suites | AE, D, DC, MC, V.

College Club. You can stay at a private club in Boston even if you don't know a member. The oldest women's college club in the country welcomes both male and female nonmember guests. Each guest room in this Back Bay Victorian brownstone has period antiques and five rooms have ornamental fireplaces. The club is on Boston's most elegant street, Commonwealth Avenue, and is just a short walk from the Public Garden and the exclusive shops and galleries of Newbury Street. Dining room, complimentary Continental breakfast. In-room data ports, no TV. Business services. No smoking. | 44 Commonwealth Ave. | 617/536–9510 | fax 617/247–8537 | www.thecollegeclubofboston.com | 11 rooms (6 with shared bath) | $80–$130 | MC, V.

Copley House. These apartments are in seven brownstone buildings within a five block radius—all near the Prudential Center in Boston's Back Bay. Furnishings are simple and local phone calls are free. The best features are the central location and low price. Kitchenettes, Cable TV. No pets. | 239 W. Newton St. | 617/236–8300 or 800/331–1318 | fax 617/424–1815 | www.copleyhouse.com | 65 rooms | $95–$175 | AE, D, DC, MC, V.

Copley Inn. This small, quaint, homey, and comfortable hotel occupies a late-19th-century Back Bay brownstone. Some rooms have ornamental fireplaces. It is two blocks from the subway. Kitchenettes, cable TV. No smoking. | 19 Garrison St., at St. Botolph St. | 617/236–0300 or 800/232–0306 | fax 617/536–0816 | www.copleyinn.com | 21 rooms (6 with shower only) | $125–$135 | AE, MC, V.

★ **John Jeffries House.** This small, turn-of-the-century inn was once a residence for nurses at the Massachusetts Eye and Ear Infirmary and is named for the founder of that institution. It has period furnishings, multipaned bay windows, original molding, and hardwood floors. The inn stands at the foot of Beacon Hill near the Longfellow Bridge and near the Charles Street subway station. Complimentary Continental breakfast. Some kitchenettes. No smoking. | 14 David G. Mugar Way | 617/367–1866 | fax 617/742–0313 | 23 rooms, 23 suites | $90–$175, $140–$155 suites | AE, D, DC, MC, V.

Milner Hotel. This strict brownstone is two blocks from the Common and the subway. The lobby of the hotel has high ceilings, pillars, and ornate molding and there is also some rich dark wood that harkens back to 1877 when the hotel was built. Complimentary Continental breakfast. Cable TV. | 78 Charles St. South | 617/426–6220 or 800/453–1731 | fax 617/350–0360 | mhboston@ix.netcom.com | www.milner-hotels.com | 64 rooms, 8 suites | $89–$189, $100–$212 suites | AE, D, DC, MC, V.

Taylor House Bed and Breakfast. This 1855 Italianate Victorian house was once owned by the Haffenreffer family of brewers. (Their brewery is now called the Sam Adams Brewery and is about 1 mi away.) The Jamaica Plain inn has custom-made wooden beds, a Victorian garden, and courtyard. It is only 100 yards from pristine Jamaica Pond and is also near restaurants, shops, and public transportation. Complimentary Continental breakfast. In-room data ports, in-room VCRs. Free parking. No smoking. | 50 Burroughs St. | 617/983–9334 or 888/228–2956 | fax 617/522–3852 | www.taylorhouse.com | 10 rooms (6 with private bath, 2 with shared bath), 2 suites | $85–$175 | AE, D, MC, V.

MODERATE

Chandler Inn. Built in early 1900s for the Coast Guard, this inn is on a cobblestone street in the South End, 2 blocks from Back Bay T. It is gay-friendly and has a gay bar. Rooms contain blonde furniture, entertainment armoires, and clothing armoires. Bar, complimentary Continental breakfast. Cable TV. No pets. | 26 Chandler St. | 617/482–3450 or 800/842–3450 | fax 617/542–3428 | www.chandlerinn.com | 56 rooms | $135–$145 | AE, D, DC, MC, V.

Constitution Charters. Even if you don't have time for a cruise, you can enjoy bed and breakfast aboard a luxury yacht or sailboat docked at Constitution Marina in the Charlestown neighborhood of Boston. The marina is home to the U.S.S. *Constitution*, the oldest commissioned warship in the U.S. Navy. It is on the Freedom trail in Boston's Inner Harbor, just a five-minute walk to the Fleet Center and public transportation. You can rent a motorboat, motoryacht, sailboat, or houseboat here. Complimentary Continental breakfast. Pool. Laundry facilities. | Constitution Marina, 28 Constitution Rd. | 617/241–9640 | fax 617/242–3013 | www.bostonharbor.com/cmhtm/ | $165–$200 | Closed Jan.–Apr. | D, MC, V.

Days Hotel. This renovated hotel (completed in 2000) is across the highway from Christian Herter Park on the Charles River in Brighton, 3 mi from downtown. The lobby opens to the dining room, and the rooms are decorated in earth tones. Restaurant, bar with entertainment. No-smoking floors, cable TV. Pool. Business services. Free parking. | 1234 Soldiers Field Rd. | 617/254–1234 or 800/DAYSINN | fax 617/254–1234 | 113 rooms, 6 suites | $159–$239, $250 suites | AE, D, DC, MC, V.

Doubletree Club Hotel Boston/Bayside. This corporate hotel has conservative furnishings and colors—dark wood, glass tables, blue/green hues. It borders South Boston and Dorchester and is next to Carson Beach and the Bayside Exposition Center. Free extras include chocolate-chip cookies at check-in, shuttle service within a 5-mi radius, and a pass to use the pool and exercise facilities of the University of Massachusetts–Boston, which is a 5-minute drive or 10-minute walk. In-room data ports, cable TV, in-room VCRs. Exercise room. Laundry service. Business services, airport shuttle, free parking. No pets. | 240 Mount Vernon St. | 617/822–3600 or 888/222–TREE | fax 617/822–2865 | www.doubletreehotels.com | 195 rooms, 2 suites | $149–$189 | AE, V, DC, D, MC.

Doubletree Guest Suites. This full-service, all-suite hotel is on the bank of the Charles River at the Boston/Cambridge border, 1 mi from Harvard Square. The suites, which sleep up to six, have a living room, bedroom, bathroom, minibar, two TVs, and three phones. Shuttle service in Boston and Cambridge is offered and Boston trolley tours pick up and drop off at the hotel. Restaurant, jazz club. In-room data ports, minibars, some microwaves, refrigerators, cable TV. Indoor pool. Hot tub. Gym. Laundry facilities. Business services. | 400 Soldiers Field Rd. | 617/783–0090 or 888/222–TREE | fax 617/783–0897 | www.doubletreehotels.com | 310 suites | $159–$259 suites | AE, D, DC, MC, V.

82 Chandler Street Bed & Breakfast. This 1863 redbrick town house is in a quiet residential neighborhood in the South End. B&B guests receive full breakfast—pancakes, French toast, eggs, sausage, fruit, beverages. Complimentary breakfast. Kitchenettes. No pets. No kids under 7. No smoking. | 82 Chandler St. | 617/482–0408 or 888/482–0408 | fax 617/482–0659 | www.channel1.com/82chandler | 3 rooms, 2 studios | $175, $160 studios | No credit cards.

★ **Harborside Inn.** A 19th-century warehouse was renovated to create this downtown inn. Its notable features include exposed brick walls, hardwood floors, Oriental rugs, original story-high windows, and an eight-floor skylit atrium. Restaurant, complimentary Continental breakfast, room service. In-room data ports, cable TV. Gym. | 185 State St. | 617/723–7500 | fax 617/670–2010 | www.hagopianhotels.com | 54 rooms, 2 suites | $165–$200, $245–$330 suites | AE, D, DC, MC, V.

Howard Johnson Hotel—Boston/Fenway. Next to Fenway Park, this hotel is ideal for baseball fans, and is close to Harvard Medical School and area colleges and universities. Rooms have queen- and king-size beds and some also have views of the ballpark. Restaurant, bar with entertainment. No-smoking rooms, cable TV. Pool. Business services. Free parking. Pets allowed. | 1271 Boylston St. | 617/267–8300 | fax 617/267–2763 | 94 rooms | $115–$199 | AE, D, DC, MC, V.

Howard Johnson Hotel—Boston/Kenmore. This central, Kenmore Square hotel is next to the Boston University campus, one block from the subway and two blocks from Fenway Park. Restaurant, 2 bars with entertainment. Cable TV. Indoor pool. Free parking. Pets allowed. | 575 Commonwealth Ave. | 617/267–3100 | fax 617/424–1045 | 179 rooms | $135–$235 | AE, D, DC, MC, V.

MidTown Hotel. This moderately priced Boston hotel has extra-large rooms, including 88 connecting rooms appropriate for families. It is in the Back Bay, across from the Christian Science "Mother Church," and The Prudential Center. Restaurant. In-room data ports, cable TV. Free parking. | 220 Huntington Ave. | 617/262–1000 or 800/343–1177 | fax 617/262–8739 | www.midtownhotel.com | 159 rooms | $119–$239 | AE, D, DC, MC, V.

Newbury Guest House. Back Bay's Newbury Street is Boston's fashion headquarters and gallery row. This guest house has three connecting brownstones built in the 1880s as private residences for affluent Bostonians. It has hardwood floors, Oriental rugs, a reproduction Victorian decor, and Rudy, the black-and-white cat. Complimentary Continental breakfast. In-room data ports, cable TV. | 261 Newbury St. | 617/437–7666 or 800/437–7668 | fax 617/262–4243 | www.hagopianhotels.com | 32 rooms | $125–$165 | AE, D, DC, MC, V.

EXPENSIVE

Boston Back Bay Hilton. A renovated hotel in Back Bay that is near Symphony Hall, Fenway Park, and one street over from Newbury Street, Boston's fashion and gallery row. The rooms overlook the downtown area, Fenway, or the Charles River. The hotel also has a sundeck. Restaurant, bar. In-room data ports, cable TV. Indoor pool. Gym. Business services. Some pets allowed. | 40 Dalton St. | 617/236–1100 or 800/HILTONS | fax 617/867–6104 | www.boston-backbay.hilton.com | 385 rooms, 9 suites | $215–$365, $450 suites, $1,000 3–bedroom suites | AE, D, DC, MC, V.

Boston Park Plaza Hotel and Towers. When President Clinton visits Boston, he stays at the Boston Park Plaza. Built in 1927, it was one of the first to offer in-room radios. Pamphlets outlining a self-guided walking tour are available. This hotel, near the Boston Common, is a member of Historic Hotels of America. Boston trolley tickets are sold in the lobby and the hotel is a trolley pickup/drop-off point. Restaurant, bar, room service. In-room data ports, refrigerators, cable TV. Barbershop, beauty salon. Gym. Shops and pharmacy. Business services. Parking (fee). | 64 Arlington St. | 617/426–2000 or 800/225–2008 | fax 617/426–5545 | www.bostonplaza.com | 960 rooms, 21 suites | $199–$249, $425 suites | AE, D, DC, MC, V.

Boston Wyndham Downtown. This corporate hotel was created out of the Batterymarch Building in 1999. Many original Art Deco details remain from the 14-story skyscraper, built in 1928: terra-cotta reliefs, marble, and polished brass, to name just a few. Each guest room has business-friendly amenities such as a workstation, two phone lines, and a daily newspaper. The property is in the Financial District, four blocks from the subway and the airport water shuttle. Restaurant, bar, room service. In-room data ports, minibars. Sauna. Gym. Library. Business services. Parking (fee). | 89 Broad St. | 617/556–0006 or 800/996–3426 | fax 617/556–0053 | www.wyndham.com | 362 rooms, 66 suites | $189–$380, $229–$440 suites | AE, D, DC, MC, V.

Colonnade Hotel. An independent European-style hotel in Back Bay with a modern decor and the only rooftop pool in Boston. Its restaurant, Brasserie Jo, is Boston's only authentic French-style brasserie. There is a subway stop near the hotel's front entrance. The hotel provides bathrobes and umbrellas to its guests. Restaurant, bar. In-room data ports, minibars, room service, cable TV. Pool (in season). Gym. Baby-sitting. Some pets allowed. | 120 Huntington Ave. | 617/424–7000 or 800/962–3030 | fax 617/424–1717 | www.colonnadehotel.com | 285 rooms, 12 suites | $225–$350, $450–$1,050 suites | AE, D, DC, MC, V.

★ **Gryphon House.** A brownstone with eight open-plan suites, each with a sitting area and gas-log fireplace and decorated in a different style (Italian, Victorian, neo-Gothic, Arts and Crafts). Some of the rooms have views of the Charles River. The house has murals painted by a local artist and original 1848 French (Zuber) wallpaper. It stands on a side street just off Kenmore Square in the Back Bay. Complimentary Continental breakfast. In-room data ports, refrigerators, cable TV, in-room VCRs. Business services. Free parking. No smoking. | 9 Bay State Rd. | 617/375–9003 or 877 877/375–9003 | www.innboston.com | 8 suites | $179–$275 suites | AE, D, DC, MC, V.

Holiday Inn–Express Boston. In South Boston, within walking distance of the subway. This standard chain option is 2 mi from downtown, shipping areas, and historic Boston. Complimentary Continental breakfast. In-room data ports, cable TV. Gym. Video games. Laundry facilities. Airport shuttle. Free parking. | 69 Boston St. | 617/288–3030 or 800/642–0303 | fax 617/265–6543 | www.hiexpress.com | 118 rooms, 8 suites | $159–$450, $225–$450 suites | AE, D, DC, MC, V.

Holiday Inn–Boston/Logan Airport. A renovated hotel in East Boston, 3 mi from downtown, with soundproof guest rooms that have large working desks. The lobby has mahogany trim, a marble front desk, and a grand piano. Restaurant, bar. In-room data ports, cable TV. Pool. Gym. Business services. Airport shuttle. | 225 McClellan Hwy. | 617/569–5250 or 800/HOLIDAY | fax 617/569–5159 | www.holiday-inn.com/bos-loganapt | 350 rooms | $190–$250 | AE, D, DC, MC, V.

Holiday Inn Select–Boston/Government Center. This West End hotel is one block from the subway, three blocks from Fleet Center, and four blocks from Faneuil Hall and Quincy Marketplace. It is within walking distance of Massachusetts General Hospital, the Charles River Esplanade, Beacon Hill, and Charles Street's antiques shops and restaurants. It has deluxe guest rooms decoated in neutral tones. Restaurant, bar. In-room data ports, cable

TV. Pool. Gym. Laundry facilities. Business services. | 5 Blossom St. | 617/742–7630 or 800/
HOLIDAY | fax 617/742–4192 | www.holiday-inn.com/bos-government | 303 rooms, 2 suites
| $229–$289, $450–$650 suites | AE, D, DC, MC, V.

Omni Parker House. Established in 1854, this is the longest continuously operating hotel
in America. From its kitchens came Parker House rolls and the catch-of-the-day called
scrod. It was the meeting place for literary groups such as the Saturday Club, which established the *Atlantic Monthly* magazine; the hotel is now featured on the Literary Trail of
Greater Boston. This downtown property was recently renovated and is across the street
from historic King's Chapel and close to the Common, the State House, and Faneuil Hall.
2 restaurants, bar with piano entertainment. In-room data ports, some minibars, cable
TV. Gym. Business services. | 60 School St. | 617/227–8600 or 800/THE-OMNI | fax 617/
742–5729 | www.omnihotels.com | 552 rooms, 21 suites | $159–$339, $279–$425 suites | AE,
D, DC, MC, V.

Radisson Hotel Boston. A central location in the heart of Boston's Theater District is this
hotel's distinguishing feature. There are two subway stops across the street. The hotel also
has its own 490-seat off-Broadway theater. The lobby is small, with marble floors, mahogany
tables, and a grandfather clock. The rooms are large, and each one has a balcony, as well
as a harbor or city view. 2 restaurants, bar, dining room. In-room data ports, cable TV.
Indoor pool. Gym. Laundry facilities. Business services. Parking (fee). | 200 Stuart St. | 617/
482–1800 or 800/333–3333 | fax 617/451–2750 | www.radisson.com | 356 rooms, 26 suites |
$199–$279, $229–$309 suites | AE, D, DC, MC, V.

VERY EXPENSIVE

Beacon Hill Bed & Breakfast. This 1869 brick Victorian rowhouse on Beacon Hill has large
guest rooms with high ceilings. There is an eclectic mixture of antiques including French
armoires and Oriental rugs. Each guest room has a sofabed in addition to a queen or a
double. The garden was designed by a leading 19th-century landscape architect, Arthur
Shurtleff, and has potted plants, shrubs, ivy-covered walls, and wisteria. Dining room,
complimentary breakfast. Cable TV, some room phones, some in-room VCRs. No pets. No
smoking. | 27 Brimmer St. | 617/523–7376 | 3 rooms | $275 | No credit cards.

★ **Boston Harbor Hotel.** An archway framing a view of Boston Harbor is this hotel's most striking feature. Each guest room has a city or harbor view. The public areas are embellished
by one of the nation's finest private antiquarian map collections. The hotel stands just in
front of the Logan Airport water shuttle in Boston Harbor, just two blocks from the subway, and within walking distance of attractions such as the New England Aquarium. A
chauffeured town car is offered to guests at no charge, based upon availability. 2 restaurants, bar with entertainment. In-room data ports, minibars, no-smoking floors, room
service, cable TV. Indoor pool. Beauty treatments, Hot tub, message, spa. Gym. Business ser-
vices. Parking (fee). Some pets allowed. | 70 Rowes Wharf | 617/439–7000 or 800/752–7077
| fax 617/345–6799 | www.bhh.com | 230 rooms, 26 suites | $405–$685, $495–$1,750 suites
| AE, D, DC, MC, V.

Boston Marriott Copley Place. The Marriott is connected to Copley Place, an upscale mul-
tifloor shopping mall in historic Copley Square. This hotel has oversized double or king-
size beds, and family packages. There is also a car rental desk, a business center, and the
Champion Sports Bar. Restaurant, bar with entertainment, room service. In-room data ports,
cable TV. Indoor pool. Hot tub, massage. Gym. Shops. Video games. Business services. | 110
Huntington Ave. | 617/236–5800 or 800/228–9290 | fax 617/236–5885 | www.marriott.com
| 1,147 rooms, 47 suites | $224–$354, $500–$1,800 suites | AE, D, DC, MC, V.

Boston Marriott Long Wharf Hotel. This hotel boasts one of the best locations in Boston.
It's next to the water shuttle to Logan Airport, Boston Harbor cruises, and the subway; it
is the closest hotel to Boston's Italian North End. Rooms have partial harbor views and overlook either Columbus Park or the New England Aquarium. Boston trolley tickets are sold
in the lobby; the hotel is a trolly pickup/drop-off point. The lobby has a nautical theme, as
well as drawings of historic boston and the long wharf area and paintings by local artists.

2 restaurants, bar. In-room data ports, cable TV. Indoor pool. Hot tub. Gym. Shops. Video games. Laundry facilities. Business services. | 296 State St. | 617/227–0800 or 800/228–9290 | fax 617/227–2867 | www.marriott.com | 400 rooms, 10 suites | $350, $400–$2,000 suites | AE, D, DC, MC, V.

Copley Square Hotel. This small European-style hotel is on Copley Square, two blocks from the subway. It was built in 1891 and the design of the interior was created by combining European and American styles, the net result being that no two rooms are exactly alike. The rooms have rich wood furnishings. Restaurants, bar. In-room data ports, cable TV. Business services. | 47 Huntington Ave. | 617/536–9000 or 800/225–7062 | fax 617/267–3547 | www.copleysquarehotel.com | 143 rooms, 6 suites | $285–$395, $345–$385 suites | AE, D, DC, MC, V.

Eliot Suite Hotel. This luxury all-suite property in Back Bay is on Boston's grandest street, Commonwealth Avenue. It has suites with marble baths and period furnishings as well as modern amenities including fax machines. Restaurant. In-room data ports, minibars, cable TV. Video games. Laundry services. Business services. Some pets allowed. Parking (fee). | 370 Commonwealth Ave. | 617/267–1607 or 800/44–ELIOT | fax 617/536–9114 | www.eliothotel.com | 16 rooms, 79 suites | $235–$295, $235–$395 suites | AE, DC, MC, V.

★ **Fairmont Copley Plaza.** This 1912 palatial hotel, in Boston's Back Bay, is a splendid example of French and Venetian Renaissance design. It has crystal chandeliers and mirrors, gilt coffered ceilings, and trompe l'oeil paintings. Every American president since William Taft has visited the hotel; more weddings have taken place in the Oval Room than in Trinity Church next door. The hotel is a member of Historic Hotels of America. Its neighbors in Copley Square include Hancock Tower, Trinity Church, and the Boston Public Library. Restaurant, bar with piano entertainment and jazz trio. In-room data ports, no-smoking floors, room service, cable TV. Barbershop, beauty salon. Gym. Shops. Business services. Some pets allowed. | 138 St. James Ave. | 617/267–5300 or 800/527–4727 | fax 617/247–6681 | boston@fairmont.com | www.fairmont.com | 379 rooms, 61 suites | $259–$349, $349–$1,500 suites | AE, DC, MC, V.

Fifteen Beacon. An elegant, luxury hotel in a 1903 ten-story Beaux Arts building on Beacon Hill. Each guest room has its own color scheme, furniture design, and commissioned artwork as well as a queen-size poster bed (some with canopies), gas fireplace, and CD stereo with CD library. Restaurant, bar, room service. In-room data ports, in-room safe, minibar, some in-room hot tubs, cable TV. Massage. Gym. Laundry service. Business services. No pets. | 15 Beacon St. | 617/670–1500 or 877/XV–BEACON | fax 617/670–2525 | www.xvbeacon.com | 61 rooms, 3 suites | $495–$1400 | AE, D, DC, MC, V.

★ **Four Seasons Hotel Boston.** The decor of this luxury hotel captures Boston's old-world charm; its location in the Back Bay across from the Public Garden makes it convenient to every historic entertainment and cultural attraction in the city. Guests are offered town-car transportation to all downtown locations and special services such as twice-daily housekeeping. 2 restaurants, bar with entertainment, complimentary Continental breakfast, room service. In-room data ports, in-room safes, minibars, cable TV. Indoor pool. Hot tub, massage, spa. Health club. Laundry service. Business services. Some pets allowed. Parking (fee). | 200 Boylston St. | 617/338–4400 | fax 617/423–0154 | www.fourseasons.com | 288 rooms, 72 suites | $465–$505, $645–$1,950 1–bedroom suites, $2,300–$3,600 2–bedroom suites | AE, D, DC, MC, V.

Hyatt Harborside Hotel at Boston's Logan International Airport. Guest rooms in this Airport chain offering are soundproof and many have outstanding views of the Boston skyline. The hotel lobby has a marble floor, domed ceiling, and a picture window that looks out onto the harbor. Restaurant, bar. In-room data ports, cable TV. Indoor pool. Hot tub, sauna. Gym. Business services, convention center. Airport shuttle. | 101 Harborside Dr. | 617/568–1234 | fax 617/567–8856 | www.boston.hyatt.com | 270 rooms, 11 suites | $300–$375; $895–$1,250 suites | AE, D, DC, MC, V.

Hilton Boston Logan Airport. This hotel offers shuttle service to airport terminals, the subway and the water shuttle. Restaurant, bar, snack bar, room service. In-room data ports, cable TV. Massage, sauna. Gym. Indoor pool. Shops. Business services. Airport shuttle. Pets allowed. | Logan Airport | 617/568–6700 | fax 617/568–6800 | www.hilton.com | 600 rooms, 4 suites | $380, $599 1–room suite, $750 2–room suite | AE, D, DC, MC, V.

★ **Le Meridien Boston.** This granite-and-limestone building is one of Boston's most unusual hotel properties. It was built in 1922 to house the Federal Reserve Bank of Boston and much of the original detail remains, particularly in the Julien Bar, the former reception room for the bank's governors. The room has high, gilt, coffered ceilings, carved doorways, motifs of cornucopias, and walls decorated by two N. C. Wyeth murals. The hotel is in the center of the Financial District and many rooms overlook the attractive park in Post Office Square. 2 restaurants, bar with pianist, room service. In-room data ports, minibars, cable TV. Indoor pool. Massage. Gym. Business services. | 250 Franklin St. | 617/451–1900 | fax 617/423–2844 | www.lemeridienboston.com | 326 rooms, 17 suites | $199–$485, $299–$915 suites | AE, D, DC, MC, V.

The Lenox. This Copley Square hotel was built in 1900 as Boston's answer to New York's Waldorf Astoria. Large rooms were designed to accommodate guests' huge steamer trunks. Today, this independent boutique property has both state-of-the-art amenities such as in-room Web TV romantic extras such as wood-burning fireplaces in some rooms. 2 restaurants, bars. In-room data ports, no-smoking floors, room service, cable TV. Gym. Laundry services. Business services. | 710 Boylston St. | 617/536–5300 or 800/225–7676 | fax 617/267–1237 | www.lenoxhotel.com | 212 rooms, 3 suites | $308–$348, $408–$598 suites | AE, D, DC, MC, V.

Regal Bostonian Hotel. This modern hotel in downtown, and across from Faneuil Hall, has specially appointed rooms containing make-up mirrors, Crabtree & Evelyn products, and fresh flowers. Many rooms have balconies overlooking Faneuil Hall Marketplace, and some have fireplaces. Some new guest rooms have glass-interior walls. Restaurant, bar with entertainment, room service. In-room data ports, minibars, some in-room hot tubs, cable TV. Gym. Business services. | Faneuil Hall Marketplace | 617/523–3600 | fax 617/523–2454 | www.regalhotel.com | 201 rooms, 12 suites, 4 buildings | $285–$375, $650–$800 suites | AE, D, DC, MC, V.

★ **The Ritz-Carlton, Boston.** A private club was originally planned for this Back Bay spot but the mayor persuaded the developer to build a deluxe hotel instead. Since its opening in 1927, this hotel has set the standard for elegance in Boston. Revered traditions include afternoon tea in the Lounge, gourmet cuisine in the original award-winning Dining Room, and dining and dancing to big band–era music on the Rooftop. New traditions include private dining in the Wine Cellar and Caviar Indulgence in the Lounge. Guest rooms have views of the Public Garden, Newbury Street, or Commonwealth Avenue. Suites have wood-burning fireplaces. 2 restaurants, bar, room service. In-room data ports, minibars, cable TV. Barbershop, massage, spa. Gym. Shops. Business services. Some pets allowed. | 15 Arlington St. | 617/536–5700 | fax 617/536–1335 | www.ritzcarlton.com | 275 rooms, 42 suites | $445, $545–$1,210 suites | AE, D, DC, MC, V.

Seaport Hotel and World Trade Center Boston. This Seaport District property sets the standard for corporate hotels. It offers en-route check-in with Boston Coach, T3 digital networking, mobile phones with "follow me" capability for trade-show attendees, and an in-house teleproduction studio. The hotel also has family packages and such unusual amenities as free swimming lessons and underwater music. Restaurant, bar, snack bar. In-room data ports, in-room safes, minibars, refrigerators, cable TV. Indoor pool. Massage, sauna, spa. Health club. Business services, convention center. Parking (fee). | 1 Seaport La. | 617/385–4000 or 877/SEAPORT | fax 617/385–4001 | www.seaporthotel.com | 426 rooms, 30 suites | $325, $375 suites | AE, D, DC, MC, V.

Sheraton Boston Hotel. With more than 360,000 square ft of meeting space, the Sheraton in Back Bay is Boston's largest convention hotel. It is attached to the Hynes Convention Center and Prudential Center shopping mall. Its rooms have views of the city, the Charles River, or the pool. Restaurant, bars with entertainment. In-room data ports, cable TV.

Indoor pool. Hot tub. Gym. Laundry service. Business services. Pets allowed. | 39 Dalton St. | 617/236–2000 | fax 617/236–1702 | www.sheraton.com | 1,071 rooms, 130 suites | $299–$349, $350–$1,800 suites | AE, D, DC, MC, V.

Swissôtel. Boston's only Swiss-owned hotel is in Downtown Crossing and has a traditional Boston look with fine art, antiques, crystal chandeliers, rich wood paneling, and marble accents throughout the property. There are Swiss touches, too, such as Swiss chocolates at check-in and muesli (cereal), Bundnerfleisch (air-dried beef), and a variety of Swiss wines served in the hotel restaurant. Restaurant, bar with entertainment. In-room data ports, no-smoking floors, room service, cable TV. Indoor pool. Hot tub, massage, sauna, steam room. Health club. Business services. Some pets allowed. | 1 Ave. de Lafayette | 617/451–2600 or 800/621–9200 | fax 617/451–2198 | www.swissotel.com | 501 rooms, 27 suites | $325–$425, $475–$2,200 suites | AE, D, DC, MC, V.

The Tremont Boston, a Wyndham Historic Hotel. A multimillion-dollar top-to-bottom upgrade has rejuvenated this old hotel in the Theater District, near the Wang Center for the Performing Arts and Tufts Medical Center. It was built in the 1920s and has been restored to its original beauty. It is decorated with sports vintage style furniture. Restaurant, bar with entertainment. In-room data ports, cable TV. Business services. | 275 Tremont St. | 617/426–1400 or 800 800/331–9998 | fax 617/482–6730 | www.wyndham.com | 322 rooms | $249–$349 | AE, D, MC, V.

BOURNE (CAPE COD)

MAP 6, J6

(Nearby towns also listed: Falmouth, Plymouth, Sandwich)

With its giant highway and railroad bridges, this gateway to Cape Cod served as the site of a Dutch trading post in the 1620s, became permanently settled by 1640, and was finally incorporated in 1884. Shortly after its incorporation, Bourne gained national attention when President Grover Cleveland chose the town for his summer White House. The coming of passenger rail service allowed tourists to follow the lead of the 22nd president and to enjoy Buzzards Bay fishing, boating, and beaches. A century after spearheading the transformation of Cape Cod from maritime industry to prime-time resort, Bourne's proximity to off-Cape interstates is turning it into a bedroom community for Boston and Providence, Rhode Island.

Information: Cape Cod Canal Region Chamber of Commerce | 70 Main St., Buzzards Bay, 02532 | 508/759–6000. **Visitor Center** (seasonal, late May–early Oct.) | 46 Sagamore Rotary, Sagamore | 508/888–7839 | canalreg@capecod.net | www.capecod-canalchamber.org.

Attractions

Adventure Isle. A multi-acre, honky-tonk amusement park 2 mi south of the Bourne Bridge on the town's commercial strip, with New England's largest go-cart track, bumper cars and bumper boats, miniature golf, batting cages, laser tag, and rides for small children. | 343 MacArthur Blvd. | 508/759–2636 or 800/535–2787 | fax 508/759–3512 | www.adventureisle.com | $11.95 | Mar.–Nov., daily 10 AM–11 PM.

Aptucxet Trading Post Museum. Aptucxet was originally an area where itinerant Dutch traders bartered for furs from Native Americans. In 1627, the local English built the original of this small replica to gain a foothold over the Dutch. Its diamond-paned windows and other ornamental features are holdovers from medieval architecture back home. Other historic structures moved to the site include a windmill and the depot used by President Grover Cleveland during his visits to the area. | 24 Aptucxet Rd. | 508/759–9487 | $3.50 | May–June and Sept.–Columbus Day, Tues.–Sat. 10–5, Sun. 2–5; July–Aug., Mon.–Sat. 10–5, Sun. 2–5.

Bourne Scenic Park. This campground on the bank of the Cape Cod Canal has 425 electric sites and 37 tent sites. | 370 Scenic Hwy. | 508/759–7873 | $23 for electric site, $20 for tent | Apr.–Oct., daily.

Cape Cod Canal Cruises. Take a cruise through what's often billed as the world's widest sea-level canal. Trips of variable length are available, and some feature onboard musical entertainment. | Onset Town Pier, Onset Ave. | 508/295–3883 | $12-$13 | Memorial Day–Oct., daily; May, weekends.

National Marine Life Center. This small oceanographic institute offers lectures and educational programs on the region's marine ecosystem. In 2001, the center will begin work on an expanded animal-care hospital and nursery for the rehabilitation of stranded whales, sea turtles, seals, and other marine animals. | 120 Main St., Buzzard's Bay | 508/759–8722 | fax 508/759–5477 | www.nmlc.org | Free | Memorial Day–Labor Day, Mon.–Sat. 10–6.

Pairpoint Crystal Co. Inside this nondescript metal warehouse is the oldest glass company in the country—it's been handcrafting traditional lead crystal since 1837. Visitors may observe glassblowers at work, in addition to purchasing their wares which are mostly expert reproductions of museum pieces. | 851 Sandwich Rd. | 508/888–2344 or 800/899–0953 | fax 508/888–3537 | www.pairpoint.com | Free | Shop May–Oct., weekdays 9–6, Sat. 10–6, Sun. 11–6; Nov.–Apr., Mon.–Sat. 10–5, Sun. 11–5. Glassblowing May.–Dec., weekdays 9–4:30.

Dining

The Bridge. American. Traditional New England fare mingles with Italian and Thai dining at this 1950s restaurant, where heaping portions and modest prices are the rule; stick to the basics for the best value, as the fanciest items reach too far. Known for Yankee pot roast and fresh scrod. Kids' menu. Early bird suppers weekdays. | 21 Rte. 6A, Sagamore | 508/888–8144 | $10–$18 | D, DC, MC, V.

The Lobster Trap. Seafood. Fish-and-chips, chowders, steamers, and, of course, lobster are served at this popular no-frills seafood house with an outdoor terrace overlooking Buzzard's Bay. A fish market, open year-round, is adjacent. | 290 Shore Rd. | 508/759–3992 | www.lobstertrap.com | Closed Oct.–May | $5–$16 | MC, V.

Stir Crazy. Pan-Asian. A welcome alternative to the nearby delis and chowder houses, Stir Crazy is known for its lively (and spicy) Cambodian-Thai-Vietnamese creations. The menu offers such pleasing entrées as *lock lack* (sirloin tips served on a bed of watercress) and an array of curry dishes. | 626 MacArthur Blvd., Pocasset | 508/564–6464 | Closed Mon. | $9–$13 | MC, V.

Lodging

Bay Motor Inn. This motel features landscaped grounds with gardens, fresh-cut flowers in guest rooms (in season), and senior discounts. The town center, Buzzards Bay, the Cape Cod Canal, and the bike trail are within walking distance. Picnic area. Some kitchenettes, cable TV. Pool. Some pets allowed (fee). | 223 Main St. | 508/759–3989 | fax 508/759–3199 | www.capecod.com/baymotorinn | 17 rooms | $79–$110 | Closed Nov.–Mar. | AE, D, MC, V.

Best Western Bridge–Bourne Hotel. This clean, modern motel is 100 ft from the Bourne Bridge, on the town's commercial Route 28. Many of the brightly decorated rooms have views of the bridge and Cape Cod Canal. Restaurant, bar, complimentary Continental breakfast weekends. In-room data ports, some kitchenettes, some microwaves, some refrigerators, some in-room hot tubs, cable TV. Pool. Hot tub. Video games. | 100 Trowbridge Rd. | 508/759–0800 or 800/675–0008 | fax 508/759–4575 | www.bestwesterncapecod.com | 43 rooms | $109–169 | AE, D, DC, MC, V.

Onset Pointe Inn. This turn-of-the-century Victorian mansion was built as the summer home of John Eastman (of Eastman Kodak). Guest rooms in the main inn have wonderful water views because the building sits on a narrow peninsula, surrounded on three sides by Onset Bay. The property also has two cottages and a gazebo. Kayak and paddleboat rentals

are available. Cape Cod Canal cruises depart from Onset Pier, a five-minute walk from the inn. Picnic area, complimentary Continental breakfast. Cable TV in common area. Boating. Business services. No kids under 13 in main inn. | 9 Eagle Way, Onset | 508/295–8442 or 800/35–ONSET | fax 508/295–5241 | 9 rooms and 5 suites in 3 buildings | $140–$250 | AE, D, MC, V.

BRAINTREE

(Nearby towns also listed: Boston, Brockton, Dedham, Quincy)

Braintree, a residential suburb 12 mi south of downtown Boston, benefits from that old saw about location, location, location. Intercity fixed-rail transit links Braintree to Boston and Cambridge. Express bus service connects the town directly to Logan International Airport. And interstate highways on Braintree's periphery give the town easy access to the rest of Massachusetts and southern New England. Although most of its citizens commute elsewhere to work, the town has a small business base among office parks along I–93, and is also home to the South Shore Plaza, one of Greater Boston's largest shopping malls.

Information: **South Shore Chamber of Commerce** | 36 Millerstyle Rd., Box 690625, Quincy, 02269 | 617/479–1111 | fax 617/479–9274 | www.southshorechamber.org.

Attractions

Braintree History Museum/General Sylvanus Thayer Birthplace. This 1720 home has been restored with authentic period furnishings to reflect life in the mid-18th century. Thayer, the superintendent of the military academy at West Point from 1817 to 1833, gave his hometown its first public library, and also founded a private academy for boys. In addition, the site includes 2 historic gardens, a research center, and a museum. | 786 Washington St. | 781/848–1640 | $2 | Mid-Apr.–mid-Oct., Sat.–Wed. 10:30–4:00.

F1 Boston. You can feel like a kid again at this sports complex with two indoor go-cart tracks, a virtual-reality video games room, and billiards. To operate a go-cart, you must have a valid driver's license and be wearing closed-toe shoes. Before 8 PM, you must be at least 18 years old; after 8 PM, you must be 21 or older. There's also a restaurant and bar. | 290 Wood Rd. | 781/848–2300 | fax 781/848–2310 | www.f1boston.com | $10 (additional fee for go-carts) | Mon.–Wed. 10 AM–11 PM, Thurs.–Fri. 10 AM–1 AM, Sat. 8 AM–1 AM, Sun. 8 AM–11 PM.

ON THE CALENDAR
JUNE–JULY: *Independence Day Celebration.* The festivities on the first Saturday of the month include an open-air flea market, pony and amusement rides, games, musical entertainment, police canine and public safety demonstrations, parachuting, wrestling and monster-wheel car-crush shows, lighting of the lake with 1,500 road flares, and a fireworks display. | 781/794–8901.

Dining
Caffè Bella. Italian. Mediterranean artifacts and a seasonally changing menu that emphasizes northern Italian cuisine can be found at this restaurant 4 mi southeast of Braintree. | 19 Warren St., Randolph | 781/961–7729 | Closed Sun. No lunch | $14–$19 | AE, DC, MC, V.

Campanale's Restaurant. Italian. This family-owned restaurant's dining room has oil lamps on each table, eucalyptus wreaths on the walls, sheer floral curtains, and borders around the windows that match the tablecloths. Try the seafood fra diavolo, chicken marsala, or veal piccata. There is a full service bar. | 88 Pearl St. | 781/843–6966 | $9–$19 | AE, DC, MC, V.

Giomatti Ristorante & Bar. Italian. Popular entrées at this family-owned restaurant include veal braccialettine, chicken parmesan, and chicken and veal marsala served with fresh pasta. The restuarant's walls are decorated with scenes from Italy. There are separate smoking and nonsmoking dining rooms. On weekends there is live jazz and R&B entertainment. | 462 Quincy Ave. | 781/380–8180 | $9–$14 | AE, D, DC, MC, V.

Lodging

Candlewood Suites. This burgundy-tone clapboard building contains suites with dining and living areas. Behind the building is a gazebo and barbecues. The property is on a quiet street near the Days Inn and office buildings and across the street from the F1 Boston complex. In-room data ports, kitchenettes, cable TV, in-room VCRs. Gym. Laundry facilites, laundry services. No pets. | 235 Wood Rd. | 781/849–7450 or 800/CANDLEWOOD | fax 781/849–7493 | www.candlewoodsuites.com | 101 studio apartments, 32 1-bedroom units | $149 studio, $169 one bedroom | AE, D, DC, MC, V.

Days Inn. The three-story property offers typical accommodations with neat and comfortable rooms. The real attraction is the location at I–93, leading to Boston, and Route 3 to Plymouth and Cape Cod. It's a five-minute drive to the subway. A Boston sightseeing trolley makes daily pickups/drop-offs. Complimentary Continental breakfast. In-room data ports, some microwaves, some refrigerators, cable TV. Gym. Laundry facilities. Business services. Some pets allowed (fee). | 190 Wood Rd. | 781/848–1260 or 800/DAYS–INN | fax 781/848–9799 | 104 rooms, 2 suites | $89–$119, $109–$119 business class, $199 suites | AE, D, DC, MC, V.

Holiday Inn Express. This hotel is within a 20-minute drive from Boston and Plymouth, and 10 minutes south of Braintree. Discounts available to guests at local restaurants and attractions. Complimentary Continental breakfast. In-room data ports, some microwaves, some refrigerators, cable TV. Laundry service. Business services. Pets allowed (fee). | 909 Hingham St., Rockland | 781/871–5660 | fax 781/871–7255 | www.holiday-inn.com | 76 rooms, 5 minisuites | $114, $135 minisuites | AE, D, DC, MC, V.

Holiday Inn–Randolph. This renovated four-story hotel is about 3 mi from downtown Braintree and 11 mi from Boston. There's complimentary shuttle service within a 5-mi radius, including subway and commuter rail stations, shopping malls, and restaurants. A Boston sightseeing trolley picks up and drops off passengers. The restaurant hosts comedy shows on Friday and Saturday evenings. Restaurant, bar, room service. In-room data ports, cable TV. Pool. Laundry facilities. Business services. | 1374 N. Main St., Randolph | 781/961–1000 or 800/HOLIDAY | fax 781/963–0089 | hirandolph@aol.com | www.holiday-inn.com | 158 rooms | $149 | AE, D, DC, MC, V.

Sheraton Braintree Hotel. This hotel, across the street from the South Shore Plaza in Braintree, is convenient for travel to Boston and other South Shore destinations. Popular with business travelers and families, the hotel offers a free shuttle to the subway. Restaurant, bar, room service. In-room data ports, cable TV. Indoor and outdoor pools. Hot tub, sauna. Gym. | 37 Forbes Rd. | 781/848–0600 | fax 781/843–9492 | www.sheratonhotels.com | 376 rooms, 18 suites | $159–$229, $279–$329 suites | AE, D, DC, MC, V.

BREWSTER (CAPE COD)

MAP 6, L6

(Nearby towns also listed: Chatham, Dennis, Harwich, Orleans)

Brewster faces Cape Cod Bay from inside the crook of Cape Cod's elbow. A small residential town filled with early 19th-century sea captain's homes, Brewster was founded in 1804 and is one of three Cape towns named after local clergymen. A third of the community is open space, including Nickerson State Park, a 2,000-acre forest that was once a private farm. Historic Route 6A, or Old King's Highway, links the town's east-

BREWSTER
(CAPE COD)

INTRO
ATTRACTIONS
DINING
LODGING

ern and western villages with those of its neighboring towns. The highway itself is one of the town's principal attractions, because of the many antiques shops, art galleries, and bed-and-breakfast inns found along it.

Information: **Brewster Visitor Information Center** | Box 1241, Brewster, 02631 | 508/896–3500 | fax 508/896–1086. **Town Hall** (staffed May–Oct., self-serve year-round) | 2198 Main St., 02631 | 508/896–3500 | infobrew@capecod.net | www.brewstercapecod.org.

Attractions

Brewster Historical Society Museum. Exhibits on local maritime history, a re-created early 20th-century barber shop and post office, a Victorian doll house, and a children's room highlight this local museum in an 1840s house. A short nature trail behind the property leads to Cape Cod Bay. | 3371 Main St. | 508/896–9521 | Free | June and early Sept., weekends 1–4; July–Aug., Tues.–Fri. 1–4.

Cape Cod Museum of Natural History. This modest museum is well suited for children, with its introduction to local ecology using salt- and freshwater aquariums, a working beehive, and other active displays. It takes advantage of its location at the edge of an 82-acre bayside preserve, with self-guided trails and staff-led educational programs. Adults may be particularly interested in the salt-marsh cruises, one of many field trips offered throughout the summer. | 869 Rte. 6A | 508/896–3867 | ccmnh.org | $5 | Mon.–Sat. 9:30–4:30, Sun. 1–4:30.

Harris–Black House. An impoverished family of 13 lived in this restored one-room house from 1795. | Drummer Boy Park, Rte. 6A | 508/896–9521 | Free | June and early Sept., weekends 1–4; July–Aug., Tues.–Fri. 1–4.

Higgins Farm Windmill. Built in 1795, Brewster's only remaining windmill—made of pine, with a roof shaped like an upturned boat—is often illuminated at night. | Drummer Boy Park, Rte. 6A | 508/896–9521 | Free | June and early Sept., weekends 1–4; July–Aug., Tues.–Fri. 1–4.

New England Fire and History Museum. This museum's cluster of buildings contains the world's largest collection of fire memorabilia, from a 1929 Mercedes Benz fire engine to a unique animated diorama of the Great Chicago Fire. Other exhibits include a blacksmith shop and an antique drugstore. | 1439 Main St. | 508/896–5711 | www.capecodhistory.org/firemuseum | $5 | Memorial Day–Columbus Day, weekdays 10–4, weekends noon–4, Sept.–May noon–4.

Nickerson State Park. Formerly a private estate, this is the largest state park on Cape Cod. Its nearly 2,000 pine-covered acres include several ponds suitable for swimming, fishing, and boating, numerous hiking trails, and a 418-site campground. The Cape Cod bike path also passes by the front entrance. | 3488 Main St. | 508/896–3491 | www.state.ma.us/dem/nick.htm | Camping $12–$15 | Park daily, campground mid-April–Columbus Day, daily.

Punkhorn Parklands. Once home to the Saquatuck Indians, these 800 acres of conservation land offer 45 mi of trails through lush pine forests and bogland. The short Eagle Point Trail, which begins to the right of the parking lot, leads to a scenic overlook on Upper Mill Pond. Trail maps are available at Brewster Town Hall. Off Stony Brook Rd. | End of Run Hill Rd. | Free | Daily.

Stony Brook Mill. Also known as the Old Grist Mill, this photogenic 1873 mill with its small waterwheel powered by namesake Stony Brook is only the latest incarnation to occupy this site. The first was erected here in 1663 and helped spawn a small factory village of water-driven local industry along the now-peaceful banks of the small brook. | Stony Brook Rd., West Brewster | 508/896–1734 | Free | July–Aug., Thurs.–Sat. afternoons.

APR.: *Brewster in Bloom.* A yearly celebration of the arrival of the town's daffodil blossoms is held on the last weekend of the month. It includes tours of Brewster's historic inns, a golf tournament, an arts and crafts show, an antiques fair, a 5-mile run, and a parade along Route 6A. | 508/896–3500.

Dining

Bramble Inn. Contemporary. This Greek Revival country inn built in 1861 serves classy four-course prix-fixe dinners with a "New World" flair, that is, American with a touch of French. Popular entrées include the rack of Colorado lamb, assorted seafood curry, and the boneless breast of chicken with lobster. No smoking. | 2019 Main St. | 508/896–7644 | No lunch | $43–$55 prix fixe | AE, D, MC, V.

Brewster Fish House. Seafood. After years of being a standard boiled lobster and broiled pollack kind of place, this local institution has caught the winds of culinary change, and now dishes up eclectic seafood dishes accented by Asian, Southwestern, and regional American flavors. Try pan-seared lobster with chipotle butter, and crème brûlée. No smoking in dining room. | 2208 Main St. | 508/896–7867 | $13–$24 | MC, V.

Brewster Inn and Chowder House. Seafood. Locals gather regularly at this small homey restaurant for broiled scrod, Yankee pot roast, and what some say is the best clam chowder on the Cape. | 1993 Main St. | 508/896–7771 | $8–$15 | AE, D, MC, V.

Cafe Alfresco. Contemporary. A quaint bakery café adjacent to the Lemon Tree Village shopping complex, serving homemade pastries and specialty sandwiches, including a hearty lobster club. Outdoor seating. | 1097 Main St. | 508/896–1741 | fax 508/896–2735 | $5–$16 | AE, D, DC, MC, V.

★ **Chillingsworth.** French. Classical music accompanies the almost achingly formal seven-course extravaganzas at this restaurant in a building from the 1700s but decorated with contemporary art. An à la carte bistro menu is available in a separate and more informal dining room. Open-air dining on the patio out front. Sun. brunch. | 2449 Main St. | 508/896–3640 | Reservations essential | Jacket required in main room | Call for hrs | $15–$23 | AE, DC, MC, V.

Cobie's. Seafood. The Cape's classic white-clapboard clam shack has been serving exceptional fried seafood and lobster rolls since 1948. It's a great place to stop for ice cream after a day at Nickerson State Park. | 3260 Main St. | 508/896–7021 | Closed mid-Sept.–mid-Apr. | $8–$12 | No credit cards.

★ **High Brewster Inn.** Contemporary. This old farmhouse has an intimacy exceeded only by the elegance of its four-course prix-fixe meals based on both traditional and updated New England cooking. Try classic American favorites, such as rack of lamb, cape seafood, and Wellfleet oysters. Beer and wine only. No smoking. | 964 Setucket Rd. | 800/203–2634 or 508/896–3636 | Reservations essential on summer weekends | Call for hrs | Prix–fixe $40–$60 | AE, MC, V.

Old Manse Inn. Contemporary. This restaurant is in an early 18th-century inn with period furnishings and has a menu of solid New England fare. Traditional dishes have been updated to reflect new trends in lighter sauces, fresh accompaniments, and attractive presentation. Entrées include the sautéed breast of duck, halibut, salmon, pork chops, and steak. No smoking. | 1861 Main St. | 508/896–3149 | Closed Mon. from Jan.–Mar. Closed Sun. from July–Aug. | $17–$30 | AE, D, DC, MC, V.

Lodging

Bramble Inn. This mid-19th-century inn has antique furnishings, a courtyard garden, and one of the top three restaurants on Cape Cod. It is in a historic district, within walking distance to the beach, antiques shops, and a tennis club. Restaurant, complimentary break-

BREWSTER
(CAPE COD)

INTRO
ATTRACTIONS
DINING
LODGING

fast. Cable TV, no room phones. No kids under 8. | 2019 Main St. | 508/896–7644 | fax 508/896–9332 | 8 rooms | $115–$165 | Closed Jan.–Apr. | AE, D, MC, V.

Brewster Farmhouse Inn. This upscale country inn consists of an 1846 Greek Revival main house and a cottage. Guest rooms have king-size canopy beds and working fireplaces. The property is within walking distance of Paine's Creek Beach and the Cape Cod Museum of Natural History. It is also close to the bike trail. Picnic area, complimentary breakfast. In-room data ports, in-room hot tubs, cable TV. Pool. Hot tubs. Bicycles. No kids under 16. No smoking. | 716 Main St. | 508/896–3910 or 800/892–3910 | fax 508/896–4232 | www.brewsterfarmhouseinn.com | bnbinn@capecod.net | 7 rooms (4 with shower only, 2 with shared bath), 1 suite | $115–$225 | AE, D, DC, MC, V.

Candleberry Inn. A mixture of vintage and contemporary furnishings fill this impressive 1750 Georgian house at Brewster's town center. The spacious carriage house suite has a shady verandah. The inn is surrounded by landscaped gardens and a pleasant outdoor sitting area. Complimentary breakfast. Some in-room hot tubs, cable TV, no room phones, no TV in some rooms. No kids under 10. No smoking. | 1882 Main St. | 508/896–3300 | www.candleberryinn.com | 9 rooms | $95–$195 | AE, MC, V.

★ **Captain Freeman Inn.** This mid-19th-century home has period furnishings and a wrap-around porch overlooking 2½ acres of gardens and lawns. The innkeepers offer personal services such as arranging private canoe and kayak trips and guided historical tours. A cooking school is held weekends during the off-season. It is within walking distance of the beach, restaurants, shops, and a bicycle trail. Complimentary breakfast. Cable TV in some rooms, some room phones, in-room VCRs and movies. Pool. Massage. Bicycles. Laundry facilities. Airport shuttle. No kids under 10. No smoking. | 15 Breakwater Rd. | 508/896–7481 or 800/843–4664 | fax 508/896–5618 | visitus@capecod.net | www.captfreemaninn.com | 14 rooms | $130–$250 | AE, MC, V.

Greylin House. This Greek Revival house built in 1837 contains period reproductions along with the genuine articles. Breakfast often includes pastries made with fruits and berries grown on the property. The house is within walking distance of the beach and several good restaurants. Picnic area, complimentary breakfast. Some pets allowed (fee). No kids under 8. No smoking. | 2311 Main St. | 508/896–0004 or 800/233–6662 | fax 508/896–0005 | www.capecodtravel.com/greylin | 5 rooms | $85–$125 | Closed Dec.–Mar. | AE, D, MC, V.

High Brewster Inn. This 3-acre property, 2 mi from the center of town, consists of a house built in the 18th century and four cottages. The main inn contains antique furnishings, overlooks Lower Mill Pond, and is next to an old gristmill and herring run. Each cottage has a private yard and deck, living room with fireplace, kitchen, bedroom, and bath. Restaurant, complimentary Continental breakfast, room service. Some room phones. Some pets allowed (fee). No smoking. | 964 Satucket Rd. | 508/896–3636 or 800/203–2634 | fax 508/896–3734 | 2 rooms in main house, 2 cottages, 2 houses | $95–$115, $165–$220 cottages ($1,000–$1,400/wk) | Closed Jan.–Mar. | AE, MC, V.

Isaiah Clark House. The inn sits on 5 landscaped acres containing flower gardens, fruit trees, berry patches, and a small ornamental pond. Three guest rooms have working fireplaces. The library has a concert grand piano; the screened porch has wicker furniture. Breakfast is served on the deck, in season. Complimentary breakfast. Some rooms phones, cable TV in some rooms. Business services, airport shuttle. No kids under 10. No smoking. | 1187 Main St. | 508/896–2223 or 800/822–4001 | fax 508/896–2138 | inkeeper@isaiahclark.com | www.isaiahclark.com | 7 rooms | $110–$140 | AE, D, MC, V.

Linger Longer by the Sea. This traditional colony of one- and two-story gray-shingled cottages—one of a fast-disappearing breed—is at the end of a quiet country road on Cape Cod Bay. Many of the spotless units have water views. (A smaller cluster of lesser-priced cottages is in a wooded grove a short walk from the beach.) The private beach is ideal for swimming and water sports. Picnic area. No air-conditioning in some rooms, kitchenettes, microwaves, refrigerators, cable TV. Beach. Laundry facilities. | 261 Linnell Landing Rd. | 508/896–3451 or 508/240–2211 | fax 508/896–8272 | linger@gis.net | www.capecod-travel.com/lingerlonger | 6 apartments, 7 cottages | $800–$1725/wk | Closed Dec.–Mar. | D, MC, V.

Michael's Cottages and Bed and Breakfast. Two rooms in a 1890s clapboard Cape house, four cottages, and a small house make up this peaceful colony set on 2 landscaped acres. The cottages are truly rustic, with knotty-pine walls, fireplaces, and screened-in porches. Complimentary Continental breakfast. Some kitchens, some refrigerators, some microwaves, cable TV. | 618 Main St. | 508/896–4025 or 800/399–2967 | fax 508/896–3158 | www.sun-sol.com/michaels | 2 rooms, 4 cottages, 1 2-bedroom house | $95–$115 for rooms; $625–$700/wk cottages; $1025/wk 2–bedroom house | AE, D, MC, V.

Ocean Edge Resort and Golf Club. This 388-acre waterfront resort offers extensive amenities for business and leisure travelers. There's a turn-of-the-century building with elaborate plasterwork, woodwork, paneling, and fireplaces, that contains meeting space. Three- and four-day golf and tennis schools and daily Children's programs are offered. 3 restaurants, bar with entertainment, room service. In-room data ports, microwaves, cable TV. 6 pools (2 indoor). Hot tub. Driving range, putting green, 18-hole golf course, tennis. Gym, hiking. Beach. Bicycles. Children's programs (ages 4–12), playground. Business services, airport shuttle. | 2907 Rte. 6A | 508/896–9000 or 800/343–6074 | fax 508/896–9123 | www.oceanedge.com | 90 rooms, 2 suites; 177 cottages | $275–$365, $425–$500 suites, $575–$925 villas | MAP | AE, D, DC, MC, V.

The Old Manse Inn. Each sunny room of this 1801 sea captain's home is tastefully decorated in rustic New England style; many have four-poster canopy beds and working fireplaces. A hearty breakfast is served on a screened-in sunporch. Restaurant, bar, picnic area, complimentary breakfast. Cable TV, no room phones, no TV in some rooms. No kids under 8. No smoking. | 1861 Main St. | 508/896–3149 | fax 508/896–1546 | www.oldmanseinn.com | 8 rooms | $105–$125 | Closed Jan.–Mar. | AE, D, MC, V.

Old Sea Pines Inn. Once a private girls' school, this inn on 3 ½ acres features colorful gardens, a wraparound porch, and period furniture. It is popular for the Sunday evening dinner theater performances by the Cape Cod Repertory Theater Company, which are held in the dining room from mid-June through mid-September. The inn is ½ mi from bay beaches and ¼ mi from a bicycle trail. Complimentary breakfast, room service. No air-conditioning in some rooms, no room phones. Kids under 8 in family suite only. Business services. No smoking. | 2553 Main St. | 508/896–6114 | fax 508/896–7387 | seapines@c4.net | www.old-seapinesinn.com | 23 rooms (6 with shared bath), 4 suites | $65–$125, $110–$155 suites | AE, D, DC, MC, V.

Pepper House Inn. Built in 1793 in the Federal style, this former sea captain's home contains antique and reproduction furniture, four-poster and canopy beds, and a screened porch. A full breakfast is served with china and silver on an outdoor deck. The inn is within walking distance of Cape Cod Bay beaches, restaurants, antiques shops, and galleries. It is close to a bicycle trail. Picnic area, complimentary breakfast. Cable TV, no room phones. No kids under 10. No smoking. | 2062 Main St. | 508/896–4389 | fax 508/896–5012 | pepper@capecod.net | www.pepperhouseinn.com | 4 rooms (1 with shower only) | $109–$139 | AE, MC, V.

Ruddy Turnstone Bed and Breakfast. This B&B, built in the early 1800s, is on 3 acres of land overlooking the marsh and the bay. There are three rooms in the main house and two in the carriage house, a restored barn brought over from Nantucket. Picnic area, complimentary breakfast. No room phones, no TV in some rooms. No kids under 10. No smoking. | 463 Main St. | 508/385–9871 or 800/654–1995 | fax 508/385–5696 | www.sunsol.com/ruddyturnstone | 5 rooms (1 with shower only), 1 suite | $100–$130, $160 suite | Closed Dec.–Jan. | MC, V.

BREWSTER
(CAPE COD)

INTRO
ATTRACTIONS
DINING
LODGING

BRIMFIELD

(Nearby town also listed: Sturbridge)

Rural Brimfield appears to have changed little since it was founded in 1731. The irregularly shaped town common is still flanked by the original town hall, clapboard Colonial homes, and the First Congregational Church atop its small hill, a relative newcomer from 1823. Before construction of I–90 bypassed Brimfield to the north, the town fed and refueled travelers on U.S. 20, the old federal highway connecting Boston and Albany, New York. Now the town's claim to fame is its summertime flea markets, where three times a year empty fields along the highway are transformed into a massive mart of antiques and collectibles with hundreds of dealers and thousands of buyers. The impact of the Brimfield Fleas on regional accommodations is nothing short of overwhelming, so expect high prices and few vacancies throughout south-central Massachusetts during these events.

Information: **Tri-Community Chamber of Commerce** | 380 Main St., Sturbridge, 01566-1057 | 508/347–7594 or 800/628–8379 | fax 508/347–5218 | chamber@hey.net | www.sturbridge.org.

Attractions

Brimfield State Forest. This 3,200-acre property preserves land at the source of two waterways, one flowing west to the Connecticut River, the other flowing east toward the Thames. There are multiuse trails for hiking, mountain biking, horseback riding, and cross-country skiing. The most popular feature is Dean Pond, with swimming, and fishing. | Dean Pond Rd. | 413/267–9687 | www.state.ma.us/dem | $2 | Memorial Day–Labor Day, daily.

ON THE CALENDAR

MAY, JULY, AND SEPT.: *Brimfield Outdoor Antiques Show.* These internationally renowned antiques shows feature the merchandise of more than 4,000 dealers. The six-day (Tuesday–Sunday) shows take place along a 1-mi stretch of U.S. 20. | 413/283–6149 or 800/628–8379.

Dining

Francesco's Italian Restaurant. Italian. One of Brimfield's only restaurants is this no-frills family-operated Italian diner, serving generous pasta dishes. | 45 Palmer Rd. | 413/245–4640 | fax 413/245–3906 | $8–$14 | AE, D, MC, V.

Lodging

New England Motel. This country motel is in the wide valley that accommodates the thrice-yearly flea markets. The simple, yellow-sided structure has decent rooms decorated with antiques. Refrigerators, cable TV, no room phones. | 30 Palmer Rd., | 413/245–3348 | fax 413/245–7024 | www.antiques-brimfield.com | 9 rooms | $45 | Closed Nov.–Apr. and flea market weekends | AE, D, MC, V.

BROCKTON

(Nearby towns also listed: Boston, Braintree, Sharon)

Brockton calls itself the "City of Champions," in honor of Rocky Marciano and Marvelous Marvin Hagler, two local boys turned boxing stars. The city was itself a champion, too, until the nation's shoe industry fled to lower-wage, nonunion states and overseas. Between the start of the War of 1812 and the end of World War II, shoemaking was Brockton's economic lifeblood, employing more than 30,000 residents at the industry's peak in the 1920s. Greater Boston's robust economy has lifted Brockton's suburban commuters, but the urban core faces challenges common to many old industrial centers.

Information: **Metro South Chamber of Commerce** | 60 School St., Brockton, 02301-4087 | 508/586–0500 | fax 508/587–1340 | info@metrosouthchamber.com | www.metrosouthchamber.com.

Attractions

Brockton Historical Society. Brockton's history is celebrated with halls devoted to hometown pugilist Rocky Marciano, a tribute to the town's fire-fighting history, a gallery of celebrity and presidential footwear, and a 300-piece mortar and pestle collection. Many exhibits are housed in the Homestead, a former shoemaker's house and one-time tavern. | 216 N. Pearl St. | 508/583–1039 | www.brocktonma.com | $2 | Sun. 2–4.

Fuller Museum of Art. The diverse modern and cross-cultural exhibits presented by this spacious suburban museum are much like the building itself: a mixture of inviting and surprising. The site makes creative use of the adjacent pond, incorporating it into an open courtyard. | 455 Oak St. | 508/588–6000 | fax 508/587–6191 | www.fullermuseumofart.org | $5 | Tues.–Sun. noon–5.

ON THE CALENDAR
JUNE: *Irish Festival.* Attractions at this three-day festival at Stonehill College include more than 500 musicians and entertainers, step-dancing demonstrations, horse show-jumping, Gaelic games, as well as cultural exhibits and Irish products. It is a fundraiser for the Irish Cultural Centre in Canton. | 888/GO–IRISH.
JULY: *Brockton Fair.* This 11-day fair, begun in 1874, features a spectacular midway full of rides and games, magic shows, agricultural shows, a petting zoo, comedy vaudeville, performances by local bands, fireworks, and a demolition derby. | 508/586–8000.

Dining

Christo's. Greek. Locals swear by this family-owned restaurant with four colorful, bustling dining rooms. Specialties include such Greek standards as baked rack of lamb and shish kebab. The Greek salads here are near-legendary; bottles of Christo's homemade Greek dressing are available to take home. | 782 Crescent St. | 508/588–4200 | $10–$14 | D, DC, MC, V.

Lodging

Best Western Carlton House. This renovated hotel is a good choice for travelers trying to cover a lot of ground and businesspeople seeking a meeting place that is easily accessible. About 3 mi from town on Rte. 24, near the Westgate Shopping Mall. Restaurant, bar with entertainment/dancing, room service. In-room data ports, some in-room hot tubs, cable TV. Pool. Business services. | 1005 Belmont St. | 508/588–3333 | fax 508/588–3333 | 65 rooms | $99 | AE, D, DC, MC, V.

Holiday Inn Metro South. This standard chain hotel off Rte. 24 is next to a shopping mall and a cinema, and about 15 minutes from the center of town. Restaurant, bar, room service. In-room data ports, in-room safes, some kitchenettes, some microwaves, some refrigerators, cable TV. Pool. Hot tub, sauna. Gym. Laundry services. Business services. | 195 Westgate Dr. | 508/588–6300 or 800/HOLIDAY | fax 508/580–4384 | www.holiday-inn.com | 186 rooms, 3 suites | $119–$139, $179 suites | AE, D, DC, MC, V.

BROCKTON

INTRO
ATTRACTIONS
DINING
LODGING

BROOKLINE

MAP 6, I4

(Nearby towns also listed: Boston, Cambridge, Dedham, Newton)

Boxed in by Boston on three sides, Brookline is a residential island within the larger city. Named for the boundary-marking brooks that emptied into the tidal Back Bay mudflats behind Boston's peninsula, the town was mostly farmland when it was incorporated in 1705. The brooks now flow underground, and the farms have all been replaced by handsome detached homes and apartment blocks built on wide boulevards, Parisian style. Today Brookline is known within the Greater Boston region for the excellence of its public schools, the size of its Russian and Jewish communities, and the beauty of its neighborhoods. Since the town is thoroughly integrated into the larger metropolitan transit system, its accommodations, shops, and restaurants are all easily accessible from Boston and Cambridge. Nonsmokers may particularly appreciate Brookline's tough smoking ban, which includes all restaurants and bars.

Information: **Brookline Chamber of Commerce** | 1330 Beacon St., Ste. 347, Brookline, 02446 | 617/739–1330 | info@brooklinechamber.com | www.brooklinechamber.com.

Attractions

Frederick Law Olmsted National Historic Site. Frederick Law Olmsted is considered the grandfather of American landscape architecture. After creating New York's Central Park, Olmsted moved to this suburban estate to establish his professional practice while designing much of Boston's city park system. In addition to designing thousands of national, state, and local parks, Olmsted wrote the mission statement for the founding of the National Park Service itself. | 99 Warren St. | 617/566–1689 | www.nps.gov/frla | Free | Fri.–Sun. 10–4:30; interior tours every half hour 10:30–3:30.

John F. Kennedy Birthplace National Historic Site. The nation's 35th president was born in this three-story house on a quiet residential street on May 17, 1917. The family moved away when John was only 4, but in 1966 his mother helped refurnish the house to its appearance during those brief years. | 83 Beals St. | 617/566–7937 | www.nps.gov/jofi | $2 | Apr.–Nov., Wed.–Sun. 10–4:30.

Puppet Showplace Theater. Because New England is home to such a large number of professional puppeteers, this intimate little performance space is able to devote itself exclusively to the art of puppetry. Although the different shows staged each week are most often intended for kids 5 and older, the theater has a series for preschoolers and also helps produce "puppet slams" aimed strictly at adults. | 32 Station St. | 617/731–6400 | www.puppetshowplace.org | $8 | Call for hrs.

ON THE CALENDAR

NOV.: *First Light.* Brookline welcomes the holiday season with a weekend-long nondenominational celebration that commences with the lighting of the snowflakes hanging from the town's streetlamps. Shops and restaurants in Coolidge Corner, Washington Square, Brookline Village, and lower Beacon Street offer free musical performances, costumed cartoon characters, children's craft workshops, cooking demonstrations, and store windows elaborately decorated by local artists. | 617/730–2050.

Dining

Five Seasons. Contemporary. Enjoy an upscale menu emphasizing organic foods, including vegetarian and even macrobiotic selections, in a bright and airy split-level dining room with a stylish bar. Known for organic meats and wine, vegetarian dishes, and fresh fish. Kids' menu. Weekend brunch. No smoking. | 1634 Beacon St. | 617/731–2500 | $12–$18 | AE, D, DC, MC, V.

Rubin's Kosher Delicatessen and Restaurant. Kosher. Rubin's has been serving traditional kosher breakfasts and deli favorites since 1927, from extra-lean corned beef and hot Romanian pastrami to homemade chopped liver and chicken soup, plus Eastern European dishes such as kasha varnishkas, latkes, and blintzes, not to mention contemporary additions such as chicken piccata, Portobello mushroom burgers, and vegetarian stir-fry. Kids' menu. Early bird suppers Mon.–Thurs. Beer and wine only. No smoking. | 500 Harvard St. | 617/731–8787 | Breakfast also available. Closed Sat. No dinner Fri. | $10–$20 | AE, D, MC, V.

Zaftigs Eatery. American. Imagine culinary school grads opening up a deli restaurant and you'll have an idea of what to expect from this family-friendly neighborhood place, where stylish artwork complements the well-prepared square meals. Known for beef brisket, burgers, and desserts. Try the Reuben and baked meat loaf. Beer and wine only. Kids' menu. Sun. brunch. No smoking. | 335 Harvard St. | 617/975–0075 | $7–$14 | AE, D, DC, MC, V.

Lodging

Bertram Inn. This restored turn-of-the-century merchant's home features oak and cherry paneling, antiques, and fireplaces in two rooms. It has complimentary beverage and snack service. Dining room, complimentary Continental breakfast. In-room data ports, cable TV, in-room VCRs and movies. Free parking. Some pets allowed. No smoking. | 92 Sewall Ave. | 617/566–2234 or 800/295–3822 | fax 617/277–1887 | www.bertraminn.com | $169–$239 | 14 rooms | AE, MC, V.

Brookline Manor Inn. This four-story Victorian mansion is in Coolidge Corner, a quaint shopping neighborhood. The inn's dark woodwork, modern furniture, and austere tile bathrooms make it more spartan than most bed and breakfasts, if no less comfortable. Complimentary breakfast. Some kitchenettes, some microwaves, some refrigerators, cable TV. No smoking. | 32 Centre St. | 800/535–5325 | fax 617/734–5815 | www.brookline-manorinn.com | 35 rooms | $89–$155 | AE, MC, V.

Holiday Inn–Brookline. This upscale chain is close to downtown Boston (4 mi) and across the street from streetcar transit to Boston. Also nearby is Coolidge Corner, which is home to many shops. The hotel features an atrium, and is in the heart of historic Brookline. Some suites have French doors. Restaurant, bar, snack bar. In-room data ports, some kitchenettes, cable TV. Pool. Hot tub. Gym. Business services. | 1200 Beacon St. | 617/277–1200 or 800/HOLIDAY | fax 617/734–6991 | www.holidayinn.com | 225 rooms, 23 suites | $189–$220 | AE, D, DC, MC, V.

BURLINGTON

MAP 8, C2

(Nearby towns also listed: Bedford, Boston, Lexington, Lynnfield)

For more than 150 years after its founding in 1799, Burlington was primarily a farm town. Boston's breweries relied on its hops and rye, and Boston's abattoirs sent their hams to Burlington for curing. Then in the 1950s the highway came: Route 128, now also designated I–95. In the decade that followed, Burlington became the biggest boomtown in Massachusetts, with industry, offices, and housing drawn to its cheap and available land. Today Burlington is a prosperous satellite city to Boston, a blend of suburb and business center, with some of the region's largest shopping malls clustered around its interstate off-ramps.

Information: **North Suburban Chamber of Commerce** | 3 Baldwin Green Common, Ste. 204, Woburn, 01801 | 781/933–3499 | fax 781/933–1071 | www.nsubcc.org.

Attractions

Burlington Mall. Burlington's largest tourist draw is this shopper's paradise with more than 150 stores at exit 32B off Route 128. Filene's, Lord & Taylor, Macy's, Crate & Barrel, Eddie Bauer, Coach, Sephora, and Victoria's Secret all have sizable outposts here. | 75 Middlesex Tpke. | 781/272–8667 | fax 781/229–0420 | www.shopsimon.com | Mon.–Sat. 10–10, Sun 11–6.

Dining

Cafe Escadrille. Continental. Named after a WWI French Air Service squadron, this elegant (if pricey) restaurant serves such fine-dining standbys as Chateaubriand and steak au poivre. A spacious downstairs café has a menu of light dishes; the upstairs "gourmet room" has table-side cooking. | 26 Cambridge St. | 781/273–1916 | www.cafeescadrille.com | Closed Sun. | $18–$28 | AE, DC, MC, V.

Dandelion Green. Continental. Enjoy reliable surf-and-turf dining in an informal spot designed like a greenhouse. Known for fresh seafood and steak. Salad bar. Kids' menu. No smoking. | 90 Mall Rd. | 781/273–1616 | $16–$29 | AE, D, DC, MC, V.

Legal Sea Foods. Seafood. This Burlington Mall outpost of the venerable Boston institution brings the freshest seafood imaginable to this land-locked suburban town. Start with the always-great clam chowder, then move on to grilled fish or steamed lobster. | 1131 Middlesex Tpke. | 781/270–9700 | $15–$27 | AE, D, DC, MC, V.

Outback Steakhouse. Steakhouse. Steaks at this chain restaurant come in a range of sizes, from Victoria's filet (a 9-ounce tenderloin) to the Melbourne (a 20-ounce porterhouse). Try the drover's platter, chicken and ribs cooked "on the barbie" with chips, and cinnamon apples. | 34 Cambridge St. | 781/270–9300 | www.outbacksteakhouse.com | No lunch | $8–$18 | AE, D, DC, MC, V.

Lodging

Boston Marriott Burlington. Easy access to Boston and the whole of the technology belt is this hotel's main selling point. There are more than 90 rooms specially equipped for business travelers, plus rooms on an executive floor. Also close to the Burlington Mall. Restaurant, bar with entertainment, room service. In-room data ports, cable TV. 2 pools (1 indoor). Hot tub. Gym. Video games. Laundry facilities. Local shuttle. Business services. | 1 Mall Rd. | 781/229–6565 | fax 781/229–7973 | www.marriott.com | 419 rooms, 4 suites | $119–$199, $200–$350 suites | AE, D, DC, MC, V.

Crowne Plaza Boston/Woburn. Convenient to the sights of Boston, Salem, Lexington, and Concord, as well as corporate offices along Route 128/I–95, this hotel is popular with both leisure and business travelers. Modern in design and geometrically shaped with lots of glass, the hotel has rooms on seven floors. Executive suites have a living room, wet bar, and conference table. Restaurant, bar. In-room data ports, some minibars, cable TV. Pool. Hot tub. Gym. Laundry service. Business services. Local shuttle. | 2 Forbes Rd., Woburn | 781/932–0999 or 800/2–CROWNE | fax 781/932–0903 | www.crowneplaza | 345 rooms | $169–$189, $189–$209 executive floor | AE, D, DC, MC, V.

Four Points Barcelo Hotel. This full-service business hotel is adjacent to the Burlington Mall. Restaurant, bar, room service. In-room data ports, cable TV. Pool. Laundry service. | 30 Wheeler Rd. | 781/272–8800 | fax 781/221–4605 | www.starwoodlodging.com | 180 rooms | $200–$300 | AE, D, DC, MC, V.

Hampton Inn. This business-oriented hotel is about 5 mi east of town and is less expensive than comparable properties in Boston. It's about 10 mi from downtown Boston and the technology belt around the city; the hotel is also close to Woburn Mall. Restaurant, bar, complimentary Continental breakfast. In-room data ports, some refrigerators, cable TV. Laundry service. Business services. Kids under 18 stay free. | 315 Mishawum Rd., Woburn | 781/935–7666 | fax 781/933–6899 | www.hamptoninn.com | 99 rooms | $149 | AE, D, DC, MC, V.

Homestead Village Guest Studios. This budget-priced hotel for extended-stay visitors provides larger-than-average studio rooms without unnecessary frills. Each room has a fully stocked kitchen, including cookware and a coffeemaker. In-room data ports, kitchenettes, microwaves, refrigerators, cable TV. Laundry facilities, laundry service. Pets allowed (fee). | 40 South Ave. | 781/359–9099 | fax 781/359–9044 | www.stdyhsd.com | 140 rooms | $109 1–6 nights; $89 7–29 nights; $69 30 or more nights | AE, D, DC, MC, V.

Ramada Inn. You'll find clean, basic accommodations convenient to the sights of Boston, Salem, Lexington, and Concord, as well as corporate offices along Route 128. Restaurant, bar with entertainment. In-room data ports, cable TV. Pool. Gym. Business services. Local shuttle. Pets allowed. | 15 Middlesex Canal Park Rd., Woburn | 781/935–8760 or 800/2–RAMADA | fax 781/938–1790 | www.ramadawo.com | 195 rooms, 24 suites | $149–$169, $169–$189 executive room, $229–$259 suites | AE, D, DC, MC, V.

Red Roof Inn. This motel with two floors is about 2–3 mi from downtown Burlington and near to the attractions of Boston and its northern suburbs. It's also close to a small shopping mall as well as the commuter rail. Complimentary Continental breakfast. In-room data ports, cable TV, in-room movies. Indoor pool. Hot tub. Laundry facilities. Business services. | 19 Commerce Way, Woburn | 781/935–7110 or 800/843–7663 | fax 781/932–0657 | io238@redroof.com | www.redroof.com | 159 rooms, 5 suites | $90–$150, $130–$160 suites | AE, D, DC, MC, V.

Susse Chalet Inn of Woburn. This hotel with a glass-enclosed foyer is next to the Logan Express airport bus, near the commuter rail to Boston, and 3 mi from the Burlington Mall and downtown Burlington. Complimentary Continental breakfast. In-room data ports, cable TV. Pool. Business services. | 285 Mishawum Rd., Woburn | 781/938–7575 | fax 781/937–0623 | 129 rooms | $109–$119 | AE, D, DC, MC, V.

CAMBRIDGE

MAP 8, E5

(Nearby towns also listed: Boston, Brookline, Lexington, Newton, Somerville, Waltham)

Cambridge was settled in 1631 during the first outward expansion of the Puritan "Old Planters" from Boston, established a year earlier across the Charles River. The most enduring legacy of those early Cantabrigians, as residents are called, is the college they founded, the first in North America. Today, more than three and a half centuries later, that college has grown into one of the most recognizable names in higher education: Harvard University. Between Harvard and the Massachusetts Institute of Technology, the other major university within the city limits, Cambridge has become a world-famous educational powerhouse. Although a large proportion of its residents either go to school or are employed by one, Cambridge is also a center for biomedical research, business consulting, and high-tech industrial firms. Its restaurants, shops, and performing arts would be the envy of cities twice its size, and its architectural landscape transforms even aimless strolling into a fruitful pastime.

Although the physical distance between Cambridge and Boston is negligible enough to be all but ignored by visitors, politically and culturally the two rarely meet eye to eye. In recent years, however, rampant gentrification has begun to undermine Cambridge's racial and economic diversity, pitting its liberal and inclusive self-image against a hyperactive real-estate market.

Information: Cambridge Office for Tourism | 14 Brattle St., Ste. 208, Cambridge, 02138-3728 | 617/441–2884 or 800/862–5678 | fax 617/441–7736. **Visitor Information Booth** | 0 Harvard Sq, Cambridge | 617/497–1630 | info@cambridge-usa.org | www.cambridge-usa.org.

Attractions

American Repertory Theatre. This professional theater company affiliated with Harvard University presents a handful of full-scale productions each year in repertory, often including the holiday family favorite *King Stag*. The company's season usually features premieres of new works by American playwrights as well as novel stagings of Greek, Shakespearean, and European classics. | 64 Brattle St. | 617/547–8300 | fax 617/495–1705 | www.amrep.org | $22–$55 | Oct.–May.

Blacksmith House. Once the home of Dexter Pratt, the village blacksmith immortalized in a poem written by his neighbor up the street, Henry Wadsworth Longfellow, this clapboard structure is now shared by the Cambridge Center for Adult Education and a bakery. A granite marker identifies the site of the spreading chestnut tree under which Pratt labored, and metal inlaid artwork in the outer wall of an adjacent building captures its spirit. | 56 Brattle St. | 617/354–3036 | Free | Call for hrs.

KODAK'S TIPS FOR PHOTOGRAPHING THE CITY

Streets
- Take a bus or walking tour to get acclimated
- Explore markets, streets, and parks
- Travel light so you can shoot quickly

City Vistas
- Find high vantage points to reveal city views
- Shoot early or late in the day, for best light
- At twilight, use fast films and bracket exposures

Formal Gardens
- Exploit high angles to show garden design
- Use wide-angle lenses to exaggerate depth and distance
- Arrive early to beat crowds

Landmarks and Monuments
- Review postcard racks for traditional views
- Seek out distant or unusual views
- Look for interesting vignettes or details

Museums
- Call in advance regarding photo restrictions
- Match film to light source when color is critical
- Bring several lenses or a zoom

Houses of Worship
- Shoot exteriors from nearby with a wide-angle lens
- Move away and include surroundings
- Switch to a very fast film indoors

Stained-Glass Windows
- Bright indirect sunlight yields saturated colors
- Expose for the glass not the surroundings
- Switch off flash to avoid glare

Architectural Details
- Move close to isolate details
- For distant vignettes, use a telephoto lens
- Use side light to accent form and texture

In the Marketplace
- Get up early to catch peak activity
- Search out colorful displays and colorful characters
- Don't scrimp on film

Stage Shows and Events
- Never use flash
- Shoot with fast (ISO 400 to 1000) film
- Use telephoto lenses
- Focus manually if necessary

From *Kodak Guide to Shooting Great Travel Pictures* © 2000 by Fodor's Travel Publications

Christ Church. The oldest church in Cambridge was built in 1760 by Anglicans loyal to the English crown. It was designed by Peter Harrison, architect of Boston's Anglican Church, King's Chapel. After the Tory congregation was chased out of town in the months leading up to the Revolution, Christ Church was used to house patriot soldiers and then reopened for holiday services in 1775, with George and Martha Washington in attendance. | O Garden St. | 617/876–0200 | Free | Daily 9–5.

Harvard Square. The hub of Cambridge is this peninsula at the intersection of Massachusetts Avenue and JFK Street across from Harvard Yard, a lively meeting place for students, hippies, musicians, and friendly punk rockers. The Out-of-Town Newsstand, a local landmark, has a comprehensive selection of magazines and newspapers from all over the world. The adjacent Cambridge Visitor Information Booth (617/497–1630) stocks maps and brochures of Cambridge. | www.harvardsquare.com | Daily.

Harvard University. Chartered in 1636 to "advance Learning and perpetuate it to Posterity," and named two years later in honor of a local Puritan minister who bequeathed his library to the young school, Harvard is the oldest institution of higher education in the country. From its humble beginnings next to a cow yard, Harvard has grown to include more than 18,000 students and nearly 3,000 faculty in a dozen undergraduate, graduate, and professional schools in Cambridge and Boston. At the university's heart is Harvard Yard, with its tree-filled quadrangles of dorms, classrooms, and administrative offices. | Harvard Sq | 617/495–1573 | www.harvard.edu | Daily.

Arthur M. Sackler Museum. Inside the unusual postmodern facade of the Sackler are the university's Asian and Islamic art collections, selections of which are displayed in regularly changing exhibits. The museum's top floor features Harvard's Greek and Roman antiquities. | 485 Broadway | 617/495–9400 | www.artmuseums.harvard.edu | $5, includes the Fogg Art Museum | Mon.–Sat. 10–5, Sun. 1–5.

★ **Fogg Art Museum.** Harvard's collections of Western art are housed in this museum, ranging from the Middle Ages to the 20th century. Also within the Fogg is the entrance to the Busch-Reisinger Museum, built off the back of the Fogg, which holds the university's art from the Germanic countries of central and northern Europe. | 32 Quincy St. | 617/495–9400 | www.artmuseums.harvard.edu | $5, includes the Arthur M. Sackler Museum | Mon.–Sat. 9–5, Sun. 1–5.

Harvard Houses. Student residential life after freshman year is centered on 13 Harvard Houses, each of which is essentially a mini-college of living quarters, dining facilities, and seminar rooms presided over by a live-in faculty house master. The earliest, built in 1930–31, are the seven River Houses on the banks of the Charles, whose towers, courtyards, and impressive Georgian symmetry are possibly the most photographed backdrop for films set in Boston. | Various locations; River Houses principally along Memorial Dr. | 617/495–1573 | Daily.

Harvard Information Office. This office stocks publications related to the university, including descriptive self-guided tour brochures for historic Harvard Yard, campus maps, and illustrated guides to the university museums. Free public tours are also offered here, departing every day the office is open. | Holyoke Center Arcade, 1350 Massachusetts Ave. | 617/495–1573 | www.harvard.edu | June–Aug., daily; Sept.–May, Mon.–Sat. 9–5.

Harvard Museum of Cultural and Natural History. This museum is actually four in one. Its many interconnected galleries include such highlights as the famous "glass flowers" collection from the Botanical Museum; the birthstone gems and meteorite gallery of the Mineralogical and Geological Museum; the vast cases of stuffed mammals in the Museum of Comparative Zoology; and the beautiful artwork of Native Americans in the Peabody Museum of Archaeology and Ethnology. | 26 Oxford St. | 617/495–3045 | www.hmnh.harvard.edu | $5 | Mon.–Sat. 9–5, Sun. 1–5.

Harvard Semitic Museum. This small museum exhibits artifacts from its lengthy history of sponsorship of Near Eastern and Middle Eastern archaeological digs. Among its highlights are cuneiform tablets, ceramics, and 19th-century photos of the Middle East. | 6 Divinity Ave. | 617/495–4631 | fax 617/496–8904 | www.fas.harvard.edu/~semitic | Free | Mon.–Sat. 10–4, Sun. 1–4.

Massachusetts Hall. This brick building is Harvard's oldest, built in 1720. It has always housed students, and during the Revolutionary War it served as a barracks for Continental Army soldiers. Today, in addition to the freshmen living on the top floor, Massachusetts Hall houses the offices of Harvard's president, vice presidents, and treasurer. It is not open to the public. | Harvard Yard by Johnston Gate | 617/495–1573 | Daily.

Radcliffe Institute for Advanced Study. Opened in 1879 as the Society for the Collegiate Instruction of Women, Radcliffe College merged with Harvard in 1999 to become the Radcliffe Institute for Advanced Study Research and Graduate Center. A walk through the small, peaceful campus should include a visit to Schlessinger Library's exhibits on women's history, the small Agassiz Theater, and McKim, Mead, and White's graceful gymnasium. | 10 Garden St. | 617/495–8601 | fax 617/496–0255 | www.radcliffe.edu | Free | Daily.

University Hall. Completed in 1815, this is one of two buildings in Harvard Yard designed by Charles Bulfinch, America's first professional architect and a Harvard graduate. A prime example of the Federal style begun by Bulfinch, the granite University Hall was originally filled with classrooms, a dining hall, and a chapel; now it holds administrative offices. | Harvard Yard | 617/495–1573 | Daily.

Widener Memorial Library. This hulking brick building, donated in memory of a graduate who died in the sinking of the *Titanic,* is the centerpiece of Harvard's library system. The Widener's stacks are off-limits to the public, but there are interesting historical dioramas below the main staircase. | Harvard Yard | 617/495–2411 | Mon.–Thurs., 9 AM–10 PM; Fri., 9–7; Sat., 9–5; Sun., 12–8.

Longfellow National Historic Site. This mid-Georgian house was Washington's Revolutionary headquarters before becoming the great American poet's domicile between 1837 and 1882. It contains a stellar collection of period decorative arts and 19th-century European and American paintings by Gilbert Stuart, Albert Bierstadt, and Jean-Baptiste Corot. The house will reopen in spring 2002 after a two-year restoration; special programs and neighborhood walking tours are available in season. In the meantime, the secluded gardens and serene landscaped grounds are worth a visit. | 105 Brattle St. | 617/876–4491 | fax 617/497–8718 | www.nps.gov/long | $2.

Massachusetts Institute of Technology. Better known as MIT, this university first opened its doors in 1865, addressing the needs of Industrial Age learning with laboratories as classrooms. Today the institute is a national leader in generating new patents and starting up new businesses. Its mile-long campus on the bank of the Charles River includes many outdoor works of art and buildings by such noted architects as I. M. Pei and Eero Saarinen. | 77 Massachusetts Ave. | 617/253–4795 | www.mit.edu | Daily; tours weekdays 10 and 2.

Hart Nautical Galleries. These galleries feature 40 ship models, originally part of MIT's Department of Naval Architecture and Marine Engineering. The models represent 1,000 years of shipbuilding, from the ancient Vikings to modern supertankers. Ongoing exhibits also illustrate deep-sea exploration and World War II shipbuilding. | 77 Massachusetts Ave. | 617/253–4444 | fax 617/253–8994 | www.mit.edu/museum | Free | Daily 9–8.

List Visual Arts Center at MIT. In addition to being the custodian of MIT's permanent art collection, exhibited all over the campus, the List offers changing exhibits of contemporary work by artists from around the world. Notice that the building is itself an oversize modern artwork, with a commissioned piece using colored tiles integrated into its facade. | Wiesner Bldg., 20 Ames St. | 617/253–4680 | $5 | Feb.–June and Nov.–Dec., Tues.–Thurs., Sat., and Sun. noon–6, Fri. 12–8.

MIT Museum. Filling the second floor of an otherwise nondescript building a couple of blocks off campus, this museum's changing exhibits reveal the overlap between art and science. You'll find sculptures that "come alive" through technology or simple physics, artworks that reveal the beauty of geometry, and works from the museum's holography collection. The gift shop is great for both kids and adults. | 265 Massachusetts Ave. | 617/253–4444 | fax 617/253–8994 | www.mit.edu/museum | $5 | Tues.–Fri. 10–5, weekends noon–5.

Mt. Auburn Cemetery. The first garden cemetery in America is the final resting place of Henry Wadsworth Longfellow, Charles Bulfinch, Mary Baker Eddy, Winslow Homer, Oliver Wendell Holmes, Isabella Stewart Gardner, Fanny Farmer, and Bernard Malamud, among

88,000 others. The stunningly landscaped 174 acres are an ideal spot for a morning picnic brunch, as well as haven for birders. | 580 Mt. Auburn St. | 617/547–7105 | Free | Apr.–Oct., Daily 8–6; Nov.–Mar., Daily 8–5.

Peabody Museum of Archaeology and Ethnology. One of the country's earliest ethnology museums in a Victorian-era building. Its exhibits are devoted to North American Indians and native cultures of Mesoamerica. There is also space for changing exhibits. The Pacific Island exhibit halls were left in their original Victorian-era incarnation, but other parts of the building have been modernized. | 11 Divinity Ave. | 617/496–1027 | fax 617/495–7535 | www.peabody.harvard.edu | $6.50; free Sun. 9–noon and Wed., 3–5 May and June | Daily, 9–5.

ON THE CALENDAR

MAY: *Harvard Square Book Festival.* Cambridge, one of the world leaders in bookstores per capita, hosts a weeklong book fair featuring author's luncheons, poetry readings, and book signings. It culminates in an outdoor book fair on Sunday. Proceeds benefit the literacy programs of the Cambridge School Volunteers. | 617/499–2082.

JUNE: *Hong Kong Dragon Boat Festival.* The main event, a two-day series of boat races, celebrates the life and death of Qu Yuan, China's first famous poet. The hand-carved teak boats made in Hong Kong feature elaborately carved dragon heads and tails. Each crew consists of 16 paddlers, a drummer, and a steersman. Festivities along the banks of the Charles include musical, dance, and martial arts performances and booths offering Asian cuisine. | 617/426–6500, ext. 778.

OCT.: *Head of the Charles Regatta.* This weekend event attracts more than 250,000 spectators and 4,500 participants from around the world. With three bends and seven bridges on this 3-mi stretch of the Charles, it is considered the most challenging "head" in the world. | 617/868–6200.

Dining

Arrow Street Crepes. French. This small side-street eatery is an improved, indoor rendition of those ubiquitous Parisian street vendors who dish up a mouthwatering array of sweet and savory crêpes on demand. Try the merguez (spicy North African lamb sausage), spiced pear and blue cheese, and chocolate ganache with fresh strawberries. No alcohol. No smoking. | 1 Arrow St. | 617/661–2737 | Closed Mon. | $5–$8 | MC, V.

Blue Room. Contemporary. The attractive, warm-toned design is matched by exceptionally creative multicultural dishes prepared amid the choreographed flurry of the open kitchen. Known for roast chicken. Try the No. 1 tuna, the grilled skirt steak, and the warm chocolate cake with cinnamon cream. Open-air dining on patio. Live music Sun. afternoons. Sun. brunch. | 1 Kendall Sq | 617/494–9034 | No lunch | $19–$26 | AE, D, DC, MC, V.

Bombay Club. Indian. A contemporary second-floor space overlooking the busy edge of Harvard Square that predominantly focuses on the cuisine of Northern India, with a sprinkling of favorites from other central and southern regions of the subcontinent. Known for lamb vindaloo, vegetarian dishes, and nan breads. Try prawn saag. Lunch buffet. Sun. brunch. No smoking. | 57 JFK St. | 617/661–8100 | $12–$14 | AE, DC, MC, V.

Casablanca Restaurant. Mediterranean. Dominated by a large mural depicting characters from its cinematic namesake, this one-time grubby student haunt was transformed in the mid-'90s to a chic French colonial restaurant with an inspired menu. Sample from a plate of North African bread spreads or dig into a grilled lamb steak with braised artichokes and fava beans. | 40 Brattle St. | 617/876–0999 | www.casablancaharvardsq.com | $17–$23 | AE, DC, MC, V.

Chez Henri. Eclectic. Stylish and loud, with an inventive menu blending French and Cuban influences with an upscale approach to presentation and use of fresh local ingredients. Try the steak frites, crispy cod cakes over black-bean salsa, and paella Cubana. No smoking in dining room. | 1 Shepard St. | 617/354–8980 | No lunch | $17–$27 | AE, DC, MC, V.

Cottonwood Cafe. Southwestern. Fiery Southwestern colors create a warm and welcoming environment in which to enjoy the richly flavored border-straddling cuisine. A simpler, lower-priced pub menu is available in the adjoining cantina. Try the mesquite-grilled lamb, shrimp and chicken *barbacoa*, and grilled chile sausage and smoked shrimp on pepper fettuccine. Open-air dining on sidewalk. Weekend brunch. No smoking in dining room. | 1815 Massachusetts Ave. | 617/661–7440 | $13–$19 | AE, D, DC, MC, V.

East Coast Grill and Raw Bar. Eclectic. The bright and funky decor perfectly suits the monster portions of bold, chili-accented equatorial cuisine, ranging from creative Caribbean, Asian, and African-influenced seafood dishes to serious Southern barbecue. All dishes are served with upscale accompaniments and are aided by a mean lineup of tropical cocktails. Try a "martini from hell." Raw bar. No smoking in dining room. Sunday brunch. | 1271 Cambridge St. | 617/491–6568 | No lunch | $14–$22 | AE, D, MC, V.

Elephant Walk. Eclectic. This spacious contemporary restaurant on a busy avenue at the edge of one of Cambridge's older residential neighborhoods serves upscale renditions of both Cambodian and French cuisine. No smoking in dining room. | 2067 Massachusetts Ave. | 617/492–6900 | No lunch Sun. No lunch Sat. in summer | $10–$25 | AE, D, DC, MC, V.

Giannino. Italian. Nestled in the modern courtyard of the Charles Hotel, this homey dining room serves the cuisine of the Abruzzi region of Northern Italy. Braised and roasted meats, like a rich osso buco, are required eating. | 5 Bennett St. | 617/576–0605 | $12–$20 | AE, D, DC, MC, V.

Harvest. Contemporary. New ownership has returned this local pioneer of American regional cuisine to top form, with inventive dishes that pair the freshest local ingredients with wild mushrooms, Himalayan red rice, spicy aïoli, black-bean mango salsa, and other intriguing exotica. Known for seafood, game, and lamb dishes. Open-air dining on garden terrace. Kids' menu. Sun. brunch. No smoking in dining room. | 44 Brattle St. | 617/868–2255 | $19–$29 | AE, D, DC, MC, V.

Helmand. Afghan. This elegant, somewhat sunny Mediterranean eatery incorporates Afghani brassware, textiles, and musical instruments, complementing the authentic ethnic cuisine at this East Coast sister of the well-known San Francisco restaurant of the same name. Try the *aushak* (leek-filled ravioli), *kaddo* (panfried and baked bay pumpkin), and any of the lamb dishes. No smoking. | 143 First St. | 617/492–4646 | No lunch | $10–$16 | AE, MC, V.

Henrietta's Table. Contemporary. You'll feel like you're in a country inn at this restuarant with a produce market at its entrance. The creatively updated traditional New England fare has decidedly winning results. Try Maine rock crab cakes, grilled venison sausage, smoked pork chops, roasted duck, local microbrewed beers, and farmer's custard. Open-air dining on courtyard patio. Kids' menu. Sun. brunch. No smoking. | Charles Hotel, 1 Bennett St. | 617/661–5005 | $15–$20 | AE, DC, MC, V.

La Groceria Ristorante and Pizzeria. Italian. A longstanding neighborhood favorite, this corner storefront offers generous portions of northern Italian pasta, meat, and seafood. Known for antipasto, veal dishes, and baked pasta. Kids' menu. | 853 Main St. | 617/876–4162 | $10–$17 | AE, D, DC, MC, V.

Pho Pasteur. Vietnamese. An attractive outpost of a local ethnic chain that is favored by students, local business owners, and shoppers passing through the Garage mini-mall. It is suitable for both solitary dining and lingering over sweet Vietnamese coffee with a group of friends. Try the beef and chicken noodle soup, shrimp with lemongrass, and seafood fire pot. Beer and wine only. No smoking. | The Garage, 36 JFK St. | 617/864–4100 | $6–$11 | AE, MC, V.

Rialto. Contemporary. Hotel dining reaches new heights of sophistication with the French- and Italian-influenced cuisine of Jody Adams, one of the region's top chefs. Try the Tuscan-style sirloin steak with Portobello mushrooms and arugula salad or the slow-roasted

Long Island duck with braised escarole. | Charles Hotel, 1 Bennett St. | 617/661–5050 | Reservations essential | No lunch | $19–$36 | AE, DC, MC, V.

Rhythm and Spice. Caribbean. The bright, airy dining room festooned with Caribbean flags perfectly matches the hearty, spicy island fare and cooling cocktails. Try the gundy, jerk pork, curried goat, and vegetarian rôti. Live music Fri. and Sat. nights. No smoking in dining room. | 315 Massachusetts Ave. | 617/497–0977 | $9–$15 | AE, MC, V.

★ **Sandrine's Bistro.** French. This gaily colored bistro brings the flavors of Alsace to Harvard Square. *Flammenkuche,* an Alsatian pizza served with a variety of toppings (try the traditional, with bacon, carmelized onions, and fromage blanc), is a surefire crowd pleaser. Carnivores won't want to pass on meatier entrées like choucroute au riesling, served with a pork chop, bacon, bratwurst, and bauernwurst. | 8 Holyoke St. | 617/497–5300 | www.sandrines.com | No lunch Sun.–Mon. | $17–$32 | AE, MC, V.

Upstairs at the Pudding. Contemporary. The top floor of Harvard's famous theatrical Hasty Pudding Club sets the stage for crowd-pleasing, seasonally changing contemporary cuisine, attractively presented amid centuries-old theater posters and a delightful rooftop herb garden. Known for rack of lamb, risotto, fresh seafood, and homemade pasta. Open-air dining on roof patio. Sun. brunch. No smoking. | 10 Holyoke St. | 617/864–1933 | $19–$35 | AE, DC, MC, V.

Lodging

Best Western Homestead. This North Cambridge hotel is ½ mi from the subway, just minutes from Harvard Square and downtown Boston. Also nearby is Fresh Pond. Rooms are tastefully decorated with rich colors and wood furniture, and include terry cloth bathrobes. Kids under 18 stay free. Restaurant, bar, complimentary Continental breakfast. In-room data ports, cable TV. Indoor pool. Hot tub. Laundry service. Business services, airport shuttle, free parking. | 220 Alewife Brook Pkwy. | 617/491–8000 or 800/491–4914 | fax 617/491–4932 | www.bestwestern.com | 69 rooms | $159–$249 | AE, D, DC, MC, V.

Boston Marriott Cambridge. This 26-story high-rise is at the heart of Cambridge's Kendall Square business district and adjacent to MIT's main campus. 2 restaurants, bar, room service. In-room data ports, cable TV. Hot tub, sauna. Gym. Video games. Laundry facilites, laundry services. Business services. | 2 Cambridge Center | 617/494–6600 | fax 617/494–0036 | www.marriotthotels/boscb | 431 rooms | $309–$399 | AE, D, DC, MC, V.

Cambridge Bed and Muffin. A garden path off a secluded street leads to this 1886 New England wood-frame house two blocks from the bustling banks of the Charles River. The three rooms are awash in lace trimmings, pink and periwinkle linens, and handmade quilts. Complimentary breakfast. | 267 Putnam Ave. | 617/576–3166 | www.bedandmuffin.com | 3 rooms | $40–$60 | AE, MC, V.

A Cambridge House. This 1892 house contains antique furnishings and four-poster canopy beds. Guests are offered a complimentary breakfast, beverages, baked goods, and fresh fruit any time of the day, and hors d'oeuvres and pasta in the evening. There are working fireplaces in most guest rooms, as well as in the library and the parlor. Complimentary breakfast. In-room data ports, cable TV. Business services, free parking. | 2218 Massachusetts Ave. | 617/491–6300 or 800/232–9989 | fax 617/868–2848 | innach@aol.com | www.acambridgehouse.com | 15 rooms | $189–$270 | AE, D, DC, MC, V.

★ **Charles Hotel in Harvard Square.** This hotel features simple Shaker-style furniture. There are views of the Charles River, Harvard Square, and the Boston skyline from the top floor. The Regattabar features top jazz performers most evenings. 2 restaurants, bar with entertainment, room service. In-room data ports, minibars, cable TV. Indoor pool. Barbershop, beauty salon, hot tub, massage, spa. Gym. Shops. Laundry service. Business services, parking (fee). Some pets allowed. | 1 Bennett St. | 617/864–1200 or 800/882–1818 | fax 617/864–5715 | 296 rooms, 45 suites | $239–$439, $539 suites | AE, DC, MC, V.

A Friendly Inn at Harvard Square. A comfortable inn, tucked away in a secluded part of Cambridge, within walking distance of Harvard Yard. Complimentary Continental breakfast. Laundry service. No smoking. | 1673 Cambridge St. | 617/547–7851 | fax 617/547–7851 | www.afinow.com | 20 rooms | $107–$137 | AE, D, DC, MC, V.

Harvard Square Hotel. This hotel is one block from the Harvard Square subway stop. Guests have dining privileges at the Harvard University Faculty Club and The Inn at Harvard. Snack bar. In-room data ports, in-room safes, refrigerators, cable TV. Laundry service. | 110 Mt. Auburn St. | 617/864–5200 or 800/458–5886 | fax 617/864–2409 | www.doubletreehotels.com | 73 rooms | $209–$229 | AE, D, DC, MC, V.

Holiday Inn Express Hotel and Suites. This hotel, offering six different room styles, is 1 mi from downtown Boston and convenient to the subway and the Galleria Mall, the embarkation point for Charles River cruises. Breakfast is served in the Great Room. Popular with business travelers. Complimentary Continental breakfast. In-room data ports, refrigerators, cable TV. Laundry service. | 250 Monsignor O'Brien Hwy. | 617/577–7600 | fax 617/354–1313 | 112 rooms, 21 suites | $89–$199, $199–$249 suites | AE, D, DC, MC, V.

Howard Johnson Cambridge. This moderately priced hotel is on the Charles River between Harvard and MIT, 3 mi from downtown Boston and a 10-minute walk to the subway. Inside this 16-story hotel are a Greek Restaurant and a Japanese steak house. 2 restaurants, bar. In-room data ports, some refrigerators, cable TV. Indoor pool. Baby-sitting. Business services, free parking. Local shuttle. Pets allowed. | 777 Memorial Dr. | 617/492–7777 | fax 617/492–6038 | 205 rooms | $135–$245 | AE, D, DC, MC, V.

Hyatt Regency Cambridge. Guests may enjoy views of the Boston skyline from the hotel's indoor lap pool with retractable roof and sundeck, and also from the area's only revolving rooftop restaurant and lounge. It is along the Charles River, and many of the guest rooms have private patios or balconies. Restaurant, bar, room service. In-room data ports, cable TV. Indoor pool. Hot tub, sauna, steam room. Gym. Shops. Laundry service. Business services. Local shuttle. Valet parking. | 575 Memorial Dr. | 617/492–1234 or 800/233–1234 | fax 617/491–6906 | www.cambridge.hyatt.com | 469 rooms, 10 suites | $169–$354, $650–$875 suites | AE, D, DC, MC, V.

★ **Inn at Harvard.** Just a block east of Harvard Square at the corner of Harvard Yard, this luxury European-style inn is owned by Harvard University and managed by Doubletree. Rooms overlook a central courtyard decorated with statues and murals. Restaurant, bar. In-room data ports, cable TV. Business services, parking (fee). | 1201 Massachusetts Ave., | 617/491–2222 or 800/458–5886 | fax 617/491–6520 | www.theinnatharvard.com | 113 rooms, 1 suite | $249–$329, $400–$850 suite | AE, D, DC, MC, V.

Isaac Harding House. This guest house, a newly remodeled 1860s Victorian, is on a quiet side street only a seven-minute walk to the subway. The building contains a mixture of antique and contemporary decor, and is accessible for travelers with disabilities. Dining room, complimentary Continental breakfast. No smoking. | 288 Harvard St. | 617/876–2888 or 877/489–2888 | fax 617/497–0953 | www.irvinghouse.com | 14 rooms (2 with shared bath) | $99–$270 | AE, D, DC, MC, V.

Mary Prentiss Inn. This neoclassic Greek Revival style mansion is on a shady residential street outside Harvard Square. Two rooms have two-story lofts; others have private hot tubs and fireplaces, as well as seperate entrances onto a backyard terrace. Dining room, complimentary breakfast. Some kitchenettes, some minibars, some microwaves, some refrigerators, some in-room hot tubs, cable TV. No smoking. | 6 Prentiss St. | 617/661–2929 | fax 617/661–5989 | www.maryprentissinn.com | 20 rooms | $169–$269 | AE, D, MC, V.

Residence Inn by Marriott. This property is designed for guests wishing to stay five nights or longer. It contains studio units and one- and two-bedroom suites with fully equipped kitchens, living rooms, bedrooms, and bathrooms; some have fireplaces. Complimentary Continental breakfast. In-room data ports, kitchenettes, cable TV. Indoor pool. Hot tub. Gym. Laundry facilities. Business services. Pets allowed (fee). | 6 Cambridge Center | 617/349–0700 or 800/331–3131 | fax 617/547–8504 | www.residenceinn.com | 221 suites | $169 | AE, D, DC, MC, V.

Royal Sonesta Hotel. This renovated modern hotel is on the bank of the Charles River near the Museum of Science and the Cambridge Side Galleria shopping mall, the departure point for cruises on the Charles River. Most rooms have river views and original contemporary art. During Summerfest, free ice cream, free use of bicycles, and free boat rides on the Charles River are provided. 2 restaurants, bar, room service. In-room data ports, mini-bars, cable TV. Indoor and outdoor pools. Massage. Gym. Business services, local shuttle, parking (fee). | 5 Cambridge Pkwy., | 617/806–4200 or 800/SONESTA | fax 617/806–4232 | www.sonesta.com | 400 rooms, 23 suites | $239–$389, suites $329–950 | AE, D, DC, MC, V.

Sheraton Commander. This boutique hotel in historic Harvard Square is a five-minute walk from the subway. Open since 1927, it was in this hotel's ballroom that John F. Kennedy announced his candidacy for Congress. Some guest rooms have four-poster beds. 14 deluxe suites, and 9 executive kings are available. Restaurant, bar, room service. In-room data ports, some refrigerators, cable TV. Gym. Video games. Business services, free parking. | 16 Garden St. | 617/547–4800 or 800/535–5007 | fax 617/868–8322 | www.sheratoncommander.com | 175 rooms, 24 suites | $179–$324 | AE, D, DC, MC, V.

Susse Chalet Inn. This small, economical hotel is a 10-minute drive from Harvard Square and Cambridge's main attractions. Complimentary Continental breakfast. Cable TV. Laundry service. Business services. | 221 Concord Tpke. | 617/661–7800 or 800/524–2538 | fax 617/868–8153 | www.sussechalet.com | 78 rooms | $107 | AE, D, DC, MC, V.

University Park Hotel at MIT. The public areas of this MIT-affiliated hotel are decorated with student art. The circuit-board designs in the armoire are also a reminder that a leading technical institute is right next door. Guest rooms contain work desks and specially designed ergonomic chairs. Located in Cambridge's University Park, the hotel also features a roof garden and a library. Restaurant, bar, room service. In-room data ports, cable TV. Gym. Business services. | 20 Sidney St. | 617/577–0200 or 800/222–8733 | fax 617/494–8366 | www.univparkhotel.com | 210 rooms, 27 suites | $179–$229, $249–$329 suites | AE, D, DC, MC, V.

CAPE COD

See Barnstable Village, Bourne, Brewster, Centerville, Chatham, Dennis, Eastham, Falmouth, Harwich, Hyannis, Mashpee, Orleans, Provincetown, Sandwich, Truro, Wellfleet, Woods Hole, and Yarmouth.

CENTERVILLE (CAPE COD)

MAP 6, K7

(Nearby towns also listed: Barnstable Village, Hyannis, Mashpee)

Centerville, one of the seven villages of Barnstable, is most notable for what it's not. It's not a bustling commercial hub, like big sister Hyannis. Nor is it a historic tableau of Colonial architecture, like Barnstable Village. Rather, Centerville is primarily a residential area of fairly average complexion by the region's standards, which is to say, a mix of young middle-class families and affluent retirees. It's also beside the beach. And therein lies its charm for visitors and residents alike, especially those seeking a place apart from the hubbub of the more heavily trafficked parts of Cape Cod.

Information: Hyannis Area Chamber of Commerce | 1481 Rte. 132, Hyannis, 02601 | 508/362–5230 or 877/HYANNIS | fax 508/362–9499 | www.hyannischamber.com.

CENTERVILLE
(CAPE COD)

INTRO
ATTRACTIONS
DINING
LODGING

Attractions

Centerville Historical Society Museum. Cape Cod history is the broad subject on display at this modest museum. Displays range from Victorian period rooms to military artifacts, antique gowns to samples of local 19th-century industrial products. These are accompanied by special exhibits on differing themes that change every few weeks throughout the season. | 513 Main St. | 508/775–0331 | fax 508/862–9211 | www.capecodhistory.org/centerville | $2.50 | Mid-June–mid-Sept., Wed.–Sun. 1:30–4:30.

Craigville Beach. This wide arc of sandy shore facing Centerville Harbor is considered by many to be the best beach in town. Needless to say, such high regard means that crowds are more the rule than the exception throughout summer. The beach has bathhouses and snack bars in season. | Craigville Beach Rd., Craigville | Seasonal parking $9 | Daily 9–9.

Osterville Historical Society Museum. Housed in an 1824 sea captain's home in one of Cape Cod's quaintest villages, this museum's exhibits include furnishings, dolls, and displays related to village history, including a complete boat shop. The adjacent 18th-century Cammett House is also part of the museum. | 155 West Bay Rd., Osterville | 508/428–5861 | Mid-June–Sept., Thurs.–Sun. 1:30–4:30.

ON THE CALENDAR

AUG.: *Centerville Old Home Week.* Every year since 1904, residents celebrate town pride with a 5K road race, an auction, musical performances, a make-your-own-sundae party at Four Seas Ice Cream, and exhibits and lectures on local history at the Centerville Historical Society Museum and the town library. | 508/771–0650.

Dining

Regatta of Cotuit. Contemporary. Enjoy updated Continental fare enlivened by sophisticated use of regional ingredients and some spicy Asian touches in a restored Federal mansion with antiques, Oriental rugs, and fireplaces in each of the eight dining rooms. There's a lighter menu available during early evening hours. Try wild mushroom strudel, loin of lamb, and lemon and strawberry tiramisu. Early bird suppers. No smoking in dining rooms. | 4631 Falmouth Rd., Cotuit | 508/428–5715 | $23–$29 | AE, MC, V.

Wimpy's Seafood Cafe. Seafood. This Cape standby occupies an cozy 1821 tavern and its recent additions. The menu is predominantly fried seafood, but stick to Wimpy's more imaginative specials or a simple bowl of chowder. | 752 Main St., Osterville | 508/428–6300 or 508/428–3474 | $10–$20 | AE, DC, MC, V.

Lodging

Adam's Terrace Gardens Inn. This 19th-century inn is on historic Captain's Row and two doors down from the Centerville Historical Society Museum. A French bistro–style breakfast of quiche, crêpes, and French toast is served on the screened porch overlooking the garden. Bicycles, beach chairs, umbrellas, and afternoon tea are provided at no extra charge. It's a 10-minute walk to Craigville Beach. Complimentary breakfast. No air-conditioning, cable TV, no room phones. No smoking. | 539 Main St. | 508/775–4707 | fax 508/775–4707 | www.bedandbreakfast.com | 8 rooms (3 with shared bath) | $90–$115 | D, MC, V.

Centerville Corners Motor Lodge. In the heart of Centerville Village, across the street from Four Seas Ice Cream Shop and a seven-minute walk from Craigville Beach. Guest rooms are decorated in typical Cape Cod fashion, with lots of blues and boats. Picnic area, complimentary Continental breakfast (in season). Cable TV. Indoor pool. Sauna. Pets allowed (fee). | 1338 Craigville Rd. | 508/775–7223 or 800/242–1137 | fax 508/775–4147 | www.centervillecorners.com | 48 rooms | $105–$140 | Closed Oct.–mid-Apr. | AE, D, MC, V.

Inn at Fernbrook. This shingle-style Queen Anne 1881 house was once owned by Dr. Herbert Kalmus, the man who invented Technicolor and who frequently entertained such illustrious guests as Walt Disney and Gloria Swanson. The grounds—including a sunken rose garden—are part of a larger acreage designed by Frederic Law Olmsted. Complimentary breakfast. No air-conditioning in some rooms, some kitchenettes, some refrigerators, no room phones, no TV in rooms, TV in common area. Library. Laundry facilities. No kids under 12. No smoking. | 481 Main St. | 508/775–4334 | 6 rooms, 1 cottage | $110–$150 | Closed Nov.–May | No credit cards.

Ocean View Motel. A modern two-story motel with contemporary furnishings that's 100 ft from Craigville Beach. Refrigerators, cable TV. No smoking. | Craigville Beach Rd. | 508/775–1962 or 800/981–2313 | fax 508/775–1962 | www.capecodoceanviewmotel.com | 9 rooms | $100–$120 | Closed Nov.–Mar. | AE, MC, V.

Trade Winds Inn. This mid-Cape inn is set upon 5 acres in the village of Craigville, 2 mi south of Hyannis. It overlooks Lake Elizabeth, where President Kennedy learned to sail. It is the only hotel in the area with a private beach. Some rooms have ocean views and patios or balconies. Complimentary Continental breakfast (in season). Cable TV. Putting green. Beach. | 780 Craigville Beach Rd. | 508/775–0365 or 877/444–7966 | www.twicapecod.com | 46 rooms, 3 buildings | $109–$225 | Closed Nov.–Apr. | AE, MC, V.

CHATHAM (CAPE COD)

MAP 6, L6

CHATHAM
(CAPE COD)

INTRO
ATTRACTIONS
DINING
LODGING

(Nearby towns also listed: Brewster, Harwich, Orleans)

Chatham is one of Cape Cod's most attractive towns, with many fine 19th-century captain's homes along its streets. Norman Rockwell couldn't conceive a more post-card-perfect downtown, lined with small shops and galleries, presided over by the tall church steeple, and serenaded on select summer evenings by concerts at the town bandstand. Unlike most of its neighbors, Chatham still hosts a small commercial fishing fleet, whose fresh catch of the day turns the Town Pier into a colorful wholesale market catering to locals and tourists alike. Chatham's shores have always been in a state of flux, particularly since a 1987 winter storm punched an ever-expanding channel through the barrier beach protecting its eastern side.

Information: Chatham Chamber of Commerce | Box 793, Chatham, 02633-0793 | 508/945–5199 or 800/715–5567. **Information Booth** | 533 Main St., Chatham | 508/945–5199 or 800/715–5567 | www.chathamcapecod.org.

Attractions

Atwood House. This gray-shingle 1752 house, one of Chatham's oldest, is now occupied by the Chatham Historical Society, whose collections run the gamut from shells and tools to maritime art and antique toys. Also on the property are a fishing camp from the 1940s and the old Chatham Railroad freight shed, which contains a trio of well-known murals by Alice Stalknecht Wright of a church supper with clearly identifiable depictions of more than 130 townsfolk. | 347 Stage Harbor Rd. | 508/945–2493 | www.atwoodhouse.org | $3 | Mid-June–Sept., Tues.–Fri. 1–4.

Chatham Light. A majestic view of Chatham's harbor and the Atlantic Ocean attracts crowds to the base of this famous beacon. The U. S. Coast Guard Auxiliary offers tours of the light on the first and third Wednesdays of every month between April and October, barring inclement weather. | Main St., near Bridge St. | 508/945–0719 | Free | Apr.–Oct., 1st and 3rd Wed. of each month, 1–4 PM.

Fish Pier. Chatham's fishing fleet returns here to unload the daily catch between 3 and 4 in the afternoon, an event that draws both locals and tourists. | Shore Rd. and Barcliff Ave. | 508/945–5186 | Free | Observation deck open daily.

Old Grist Mill. One of the Cape's many windmills, built in 1797, holds frequent demonstrations of its original wheat- and corn-grinding mechanism. | Near Chase Park off Shattuck Pl. | Free | July–Aug., weekdays 10–3.

Monomoy National Wildlife Refuge. This 2,750-acre refuge consists primarily of Monomoy Island, now actually two islands once linked to Chatham by a finger of land that washed away decades ago. The refuge also encompasses estuarial salt-marsh and freshwater ponds on Chatham's shore. The refuge is home to almost 300 species of birds, a growing year-round colony of gray seals, and a large winter population of harbor seals. | Wikis Way, on Morris Island | 508/945–0594 or 508/443–4661 | Free | Summer, daily 8–4.

Play-a-round. This elaborate wooden playground was designed by architect Robert Leathers with the assistance of local children. Swinging rope bridges, castle turretts, jungle gyms, and tubular slides—as well as a section for people with disabilities—make up the popular children's attraction. | Depot Rd. near Veteran's Field | Free | Daily.

Railroad Museum. After more than 50 years of faithful service as the Chatham Railroad Company's passenger station, this 1887 Victorian depot was turned into a museum chock-full of railroad memorabilia, including signs, artifacts, photos, models, and a detailed diorama of the Chatham rail yards circa 1915. Out front is a 1910 wooden caboose from the New York Central Railroad, restored and open for inspection. | Depot Rd. | 508/945–2809 | Free | Mid-June–mid-Sept., Tues.–Sat. 10–4.

Rip Ryder Monomoy Island Ferry. The Rip Ryder, a speedy passenger vessel, takes regular shuttle trips to Monomoy Island, as well as fishing excursions and harbor seal cruises. | 508/945–5450 | www.monomoyislandferry.com | $10; seal excursions $15 | Daily 8–4.

ON THE CALENDAR

JUNE–AUG.: *Monomoy Theatre*. Monomoy Theatre has been training Ohio University's graduate and undergraduate students in all aspects of theater for 42 years. Every summer, the students put on eight productions—a musical, several dramas and comedies, and a Shakespeare play. | 508/945–1589.

JULY–SEPT.: *Band Concerts*. Local bands perform in Kate Gould Park every Friday at 8 PM during the summer. Bring chairs and blankets. | 508/945–5199.

OCT.: *Seafest Weekend*. Tours of Chatham Lighthouse, open houses on local fishing boats, and demonstrations of such maritime arts as rigging, boating, and net mending round out this celebration of Chatham's seafaring history. | 508/945–5199.

Dining

Andiamo Restaurant. Italian. Andiamo—which means "let's go" in Italian—is a bustling dinner spot. Specialties include a rich lobster ravioli and veal scallopini. | 2653 Main St., South Chatham | 508/432–1807 | Reservations essential | Closed Nov.–Apr. No lunch | $10–$23 | MC, V.

Carmine's Pizza. Pizza. In the Gallery shopping complex, Carmine's serves what many consider to be the best pizza on Cape Cod. | 595 Main St. | 508/945–5300 | $10–$16 | AE, D, MC, V.

Chatham Inn. Seafood. The elegant main dining room of the great oceanfront resort prepares such New England coastal standards as sweet Chatham lobster or swordfish steak. The inn's Tavern serves seafood and grilled entrées in a less formal setting. | 297 Shore Rd. | 508/945–0096 or 800/527–4884 | fax 508/945–4978 | www.chathambarsinn.com | Reservations essential | Jacket required | Main dining room $22–$37, Tavern $18–25 | AE, DC, MC, V.

Chatham Seafood House and Isobar. Seafood. A homey, family-owned chowder house with an adjacent tavern serving lobster, shellfish, and fried fish. | 2175 Main St. | 508/432–9060 | www.seafoodhouse.com | No lunch weekdays | $15–$22 | AE, DC, MC, V.

Chatham Squire. Seafood. The nautical decor inside matches the weather-beaten drinking-hole look of the outside, but this belies the creative touches that have crept into the recipes. Known for oysters, calamari, and fresh local fish. In addition to seafood, the kitchen aslo serves up favorites such as steak, chicken, and pasta dishes. Raw bar. Kids' menu. No smoking. | 487 Main St. | 508/945–0945 | $16–$22 | AE, D, MC, V.

Chatham Wayside Inn. Contemporary. The restaurant in this 1860s sea captain's home specializes in fresh local seafood. Sit in the fireside dining room or on the patio and dip into a spicy cioppino—shellfish in a tangy tomato sauce served over pasta—or sample "the short stack" of swordfish medallions and filet mignon served over mashed potatoes and vegetables. | 512 Main St. | 508/945–5550 | fax 508/945–3407 | www.waysideinn.com | $13–$24 | D, MC, V.

Christian's. Contemporary. Two different dining styles in one early 19th-century house: new American–tinged Continental fare downstairs, and a more casual burger-and-pizza menu upstairs. Downstairs features a nautical theme, while the upstairs is decorated with old books and movie posters. Both menus share a number of regional and seafood favorites. In the upstairs piano bar, there's live music nightly in summer, Fri. and Sat. nights the rest of the year. No smoking. | 443 Main St. | 508/945–3362 | No lunch | $9–$23 upstairs, $11–$26 downstairs | D, MC, V.

Impudent Oyster. Seafood. Classical music and white linens complement the hearty portions of local fruits of the sea dished up in predominantly Mediterranean styles or grilled plain and simple. Try the *moules na cataplana* (Portuguese mussels), barbecued tuna, and pesca fra diavolo. Kids' menu. No smoking. | 15 Chatham Bars Ave. | 508/945–3545 | Reservations essential in summer | $17–$24 | AE, MC, V.

Pate's Restaurant. Contemporary. This tried-and-true Cape establishment has been in business for more than 30 years. The warm, woody dining room turns out a prime rib that locals rave about, as well as a near-legendary Caesar salad. | 1260 Main St. | 508/945–9777 | No lunch. Closed Jan.–Apr. | $15–$22 | AE, DC, MC, V.

Le Petit Cafe. French. This intimate mom-and-pop bistro is decorated with impressionist paintings, mustard jars, and earthenware pitchers. Try such imaginative dishes as pheasant sausage served with parmesan–mashed potatoes or stick with solid standbys, like the rich bouillabaisse. | 155 Crowell Rd. | 508/945–0028 | fax 508/945–3354 | Closed Mon. | $15–$22 | AE, MC, V.

The Sou'wester Almost by the Sea. American/Casual. A rock 'n' roll nightclub with live entertainment that serves steaks, seafood, and pub fare. | 1549 Main St. | 508/945–4424 | www.souwester.com | No lunch | $5–$16 | AE, D, MC, V.

★ **Vining's Bistro.** Continental. This airy, high-ceilinged restaurant has large windows overlooking Chatham's Main Street, making it an ideal spot for people-watching. Start with the unusual lobster taco appetizer, then move on to Vining's wood-grilled meats and seafood dishes, like a skillet-roasted "Portuguese style" scrod. | 595 Main St. | 508/945–5033 | fax 508/945–1944 | Closed mid-Jan.–Apr. | $17–$21 | AE, D, MC, V.

Lodging

Bradford of Chatham. This village-within-a-village comprises seven historic houses and two newer buildings on 2 acres of landscaped grounds and gardens. Rooms are quiet, and many feature private hot tubs, balconies or decks, four-poster beds, and fireplaces. Complimentary Continental breakfast. Cable TV. Pool. No kids under 12. | 26 Cross St. | 508/945–1030 or 800/562–4667 | fax 508/945–9652 | bradfordinn@bradford.com | www.bradfordinn.com | 42 rooms, 9 buildings | $185–$425 | AE, DC, MC, V.

Captain's House Inn. This British-owned and -staffed inn consists of four buildings—an 1839 Greek Revival mansion, the attached carriage house, the "stables," and a 200-year-old cottage. Most guest rooms have canopied four-poster beds, sitting areas, and fireplaces. The property with its 2½ acres of lawns and gardens is ½ mi from the beach. Picnic area, complimentary breakfast. Some in-room hot tubs, cable TV in some rooms. Massage. Bicycles. No kids under 11. No smoking. | 369–377 Old Harbor Rd. | 508/945–0127 or 800/315–0728 | fax 508/945–0866 | info@captainshouseinn.com | www.captainshouse-

CHATHAM
(CAPE COD)

INTRO
ATTRACTIONS
DINING
LODGING

inn.com | 19 rooms (3 with shower only), 6 suites, 4 buildings | $125–$225, $250–$375 suites | AE, D, MC, V.

Carriage House Inn. A comfortably modest residence with spacious guest rooms decorated with simple country furniture. A hearty morning meal is served under a crystal chandelier in the main dining room. The carriage-house guest rooms have access to private outdoor sitting areas. Complimentary breakfast. No kids under 14. No smoking. | 407 Old Harbor Rd. | 508/945–4688 or 800/355–8868 | www.capecodtravel.com/carriagehouse | 6 rooms | $170–$195 | AE, D, MC, V.

Chatham Bars Inn. A member of Historic Hotels of America, this onetime hunting lodge is the premier oceanfront resort on Cape Cod. Open since 1914, the inn features beautifully landscaped grounds on 22 acres of oceanfront property, including a formal tea garden and a ¼ mi-long private beach. Many rooms have balconies and fireplaces, as well as ocean views. Sunday night, a Grand Buffet is served in the main dining room. Extensive recreational activities are offered for the whole family. 3 restaurants, bar with entertainment, room service. Air-conditioning in some rooms, in-room data ports, some refrigerators, cable TV. Pool. Hot tub. Putting green, tennis. Gym. Beach. Children's programs (ages 4–12). Business services. | 297 Shore Rd. | 508/945–0096 or 800/527–4884 | fax 508/945–5491 | www.chathambarsinn.com | 40 rooms in inn; 30 cottages with 165 individual rooms | $190–$400, $405–$1,200 suites | AE, DC, MC, V.

Chatham Highlander. Attractive front gardens welcome visitors to this property in Chatham Village. Notice the square-shape yew bushes—the handiwork of the innkeeper, an amateur English gardener. Picnic area. Some kitchenettes, refrigerators, cable TV. 2 pools. | 946 Main St. | 508/945–9038 | fax 508/945–5731 | www.realmass.com/highlander | 27 rooms, 1 suite, 2 buildings | $104–$134, $198 suite | Closed Dec.–Mar. | AE, D, MC, V.

Chatham Motel. Secluded and quiet, this motel is in a pine grove set back from the highway, and is about 1½ mi from Chatham Village. The motel consists of three buildings, one a renovated schoolhouse, and there are facilities for outdoor cooking and grilling. Picnic area. Refrigerators, cable TV. Pool. Playground. | 1487 Main St. | 508/945–2630 or 800/770–5545 | www.chathammotel.com | 32 rooms | $115–$165 | Closed Nov.–Apr. | MC, V.

Chatham Tides Waterfront Motel. This motel is right on a private beach and all guest rooms have sundecks and views of the ocean and Nantucket Sound. It is in a quiet residential area of summer homes and is a five-minute drive from Chatham Village. No air-conditioning in some rooms, some kitchenettes, some microwaves, cable TV. | 394 Pleasant St., South Chatham | 508/432–0379 | fax 508/432–4289 | www.allcapecod.com/chathamtides | 24 rooms, 24 town houses | $150–$275, $1,300–$1,800/wk for town houses | MC, V.

Chatham Town House Inn. The inn's five buildings (including two private cottages) are clustered in a minivillage on 2 landscaped acres. The main inn was built in 1881 for Captain Daniel Webster Nickerson, one of the founders of Chatham. It has been owned and operated by the Peterson family for 25 years. David Peterson, executive chef, is a graduate of the Culinary Institute of America. Russell Jr., who has a Coast Guard captain's license, takes guests sportfishing. Mrs. Peterson's specialty is breakfast, often including dishes from her native country, such as oven-baked Finnish pancakes with fresh-fruit mélange. Restaurant, bar, picnic area, complimentary breakfast. Some refrigerators, cable TV. Pool. Hot tub, massage. Laundry facilities (cottages). No smoking. | 11 Library La. | 508/945–2180 or 800/242–2180 | fax 508/945–3990 | reservations@capecod.net | www.chathamtownhouse.com | 25 rooms, 2 suites, 2 cottages | $155–$395, $425 suites, $475 cottages | AE, D, DC, MC, V.

Chatham Wayside Inn. Built in 1860 for a sea captain, this inn is next to Kate Gould Park in the village of Chatham and within walking distance of shops, restaurants, and the beach. Many rooms have patios or balconies, fireplaces, and canopy or four-poster beds. Restaurant. Cable TV. Pool. Some hot tubs. Shop. | 512 Main St. | 508/945–5550 or 800/391–5734 | fax 508/945–3407 | wayside@waysideinn.com | www.waysideinn.com | 56 rooms, 2 buildings | $165–$365 | DC, MC, V.

Cranberry Inn. Open since 1830, this inn is furnished with antiques and period reproductions. Some guest rooms have fireplaces or balconies. A full country breakfast is prepared by a Johnson and Wales–trained chef. At the back of the property there's a nature trail leading to the Mill Pond. The beach and village are within walking distance. Complimentary breakfast. Cable TV. Library. No kids under 8. No smoking. | 359 Main St. | 508/945–9232 or 800/332–4667 | fax 508/945–3769 | www.cranberryinn.com | 18 rooms, 2 suites | $170–$260, $230–$350 suites | AE, D, MC, V.

Cyrus Kent House. This romantic 1877 sea captain's house is just off Chatham's main commercial street. Picnic area, complimentary breakfast. Cable TV. No smoking. | 63 Cross St. | 508/945–9104 or 800/338–5368 | www.capecodtravel.com/cyruskent | 7 rooms | $155–$290 | AE, MC, V.

Dolphin of Chatham. This 1805 inn is surrounded by 3 acres of well-kept grounds and beautiful gardens. A "honeymoon windmill" cottage is available. It's a 10-minute walk from shops and the beach, and is convenient to whale-watching on George's Bank. Restaurant (serving breakfast), picnic area. Some kitchenettes, some refrigerators, some in-room hot tubs, cable TV. Pool. Business services. | 352 Main St. | 508/945–0070 or 800/688–5900 | fax 508/945–5945 | romance@dolphininn.com | www.dolphininn.com | 38 rooms | $149–$210, $210–$275 suites, $1,700/wk cottages | AE, D, MC, V.

The Hawthorne. This waterfront property has been family-owned and -operated for 40 years. The rooms are clean and quiet, and offer views of Chatham Harbor, Pleasant Bay, and the Atlantic Ocean. While its private beach attracts many windsurfers, others opt for a game at the public 9-hole golf course next door or for a trek at the nearby bicycle trails. Some kitchenettes, microwaves, refrigerators, cable TV. | 196 Shore Rd. | 508/945–0372 | www.thehawthorne.com | 26 rooms, 1 cottage | $145–$165, $300 cottage | Closed mid-Oct.–mid-May | AE, MC, V.

Mary Rockwell Stuart House. This grand, 1823 inn is within walking distance of Chatham's shopping district and beaches and has rooms outfitted with gas fireplaces and private bathrooms. Complimentary breakfast. No kids under 14. No smoking. | 314 Main St. | 508/945–4634 | fax 508/945–4634 | www.axs.com/mrshouse | 6 rooms | $195–$275 | Closed Jan.–Mar. | AE, D, MC, V.

The Moorings. The ocean is visible from many of the windows of this 1864 building with adjoining carriage houses, situated on 1 acre of beautifully gardened grounds. Complimentary breakfast. Some kitchenettes, some microwaves, refrigerators, some in-room hot tubs, cable TV, some in-room VCRs. Bicycles. | 326 Main St. | 508/945–0848 or 800/320–0848 | fax 508/945–1577 | www.mooringscapecod.com | 15 rooms | $138–$225 | Closed Jan.–mid-Feb. | AE, D, MC, V.

★ **Moses Nickerson House Inn.** In the 1800s, this was the home of a sea captain and his eight children. Today the house is surrounded by gardens, making it one of the most photographed bed-and-breakfasts in Chatham. It is within walking distance of village shops, restaurants, and a fishing pier. Complimentary breakfast. Cable TV. No kids under 12. No smoking. | 364 Old Harbor Rd. | 508/945–5859 or 800/628–6972 | fax 508/945–7087 | tmnhi@capecod.net | www.capecodtravel.com/mosesnickersonhouse | 7 rooms | $139–$189 | AE, D, MC, V.

Nantucket House of Chatham. This Greek Revival clapboard house was floated over from Nantucket in 1870 on a barge. Have your morning coffee under the large linden tree in the backyard. Complimentary breakfast. Some refrigerators, no room phones, no TV. No smoking. | 2647 Main St., S. Chatham | 508/432–5641 | fax 508/430–2711 | www.capecod.net/nhbnb | 5 rooms | $120–$175, suites $265 | MC, V.

Old Harbor Inn. This inn, the former residence of a doctor, features rooms with cathedral ceilings, gas-log fireplaces, English country–style decor, and an outside deck. It's around the corner from historic Chatham Village and a short walk from Oyster Pond as well as the pier, where fishing boats come in with their catch between 3 and 4 in the afternoon.

Complimentary buffet breakfast. Cable TV, some VCRs, no room phones. No kids under 14. No smoking. | 22 Old Harbor Rd. | 508/945–4434 or 800/942–4434 | fax 508/945–7665 | www.chathamoldharborinn.com | $139–$219 | 8 rooms | MC, V.

Pleasant Bay Village Resort. About 3 mi north of Chatham, this 6-acre resort features peaceful Chinese gardens, five waterfalls, and an ornamental pond. Original art is on display both inside and throughout the grounds. It's a five-minute walk to Pleasant Bay. Restaurant, room service. In-room data ports, some kitchenettes, refrigerators, cable TV. Pool. Playground. Business services. No smoking. | 1191 Orleans Rd. | 508/945–1133 or 800/547–1011 | fax 508/945–9701 | www.pleasantbayvillage.com | 58 rooms, 10 suites | $165–$255, $355–$455 suites | Closed Nov.–Apr. | AE, MC, V.

Port Fortune Inn. This renovated 1910 inn is across the street from the beach, and some rooms have ocean views. It's a five-minute walk to Chatham lighthouse and a 10-minute walk to shops and restaurants. Rooms are decorated with antiques and quality reproductions, and most have four-poster beds. A patio overlooks a lovely perennial garden. Beach towels and chairs available for guests. Complimentary Continental breakfast. No kids under 12. No smoking. | 201 Main St. | 508/945–0792 or 800/750–0792 | www.capecod.net/portfortune | 13 rooms (3 with shower only), 2 buildings | $135–$190 | AE, MC, V.

Queen Anne Inn. This old inn is decorated with antiques and handmade quilts and many rooms have fireplaces. The restaurant, open for dinner, is known for local fresh seafood and contemporary American cuisine. Restaurant, dining room, complimentary Continental breakfast. Some in-room hot tubs, cable TV. Pool. Hot tubs, massage. 3 tennis courts. Business services. No smoking. | 70 Queen Anne Rd. | 508/945–0394 or 800/545–4667 | fax 508/945–4884 | www.queenanneinn.com | 31 rooms | $187–$327 | Closed Jan. | AE, D, MC, V.

Seafarer of Chatham. This motel has a large garden and rooms with hand-stenciled walls. The property is within walking distance of Ridgevale Beach. Some kitchenettes, cable TV. No smoking. | 2079 Main St. | 508/432–1739 or 800/766–2772 | fax 508/432–1739 | www.seafarerofchatham.com | 20 rooms | $122–$150 | AE, MC, V.

Surfside Motor Inn. A clean, basic motel across from Chatham Light and the beach. Complimentary Continental breakfast. No air-conditioning, some kitchenettes, some refrigerators, cable TV. | 25 Holway St. | 508/945–9757 | fax 508/945–2614 | www.capecodtravel.com/surfsideinn | 20 rooms | $90–$120 | Closed mid-Oct.–May | No credit cards.

★ **Wequassett Inn Resort and Golf Club.** This resort with gardens is on 23 acres. Many rooms have fireplaces, private decks, and water views. Dining room, room service. In-room data ports, minibars, cable TV, in-room VCRs. Pool. Massage. Tennis. Gym, beach, water sports, boating. Children's programs (ages infant–12). Business services, airport shuttle. | Rte. 28 | 508/432–5400 or 800/225–7125 | fax 508/432–5032 | info@wequassett.com | www.wequassett.com | 104 rooms, 6 suites, 20 buildings | $295–$500, $500 and $795 suites, $550 Rose Cottage | Closed mid-Nov.–mid-Apr. | AE, D, DC, MC, V.

CHICOPEE

MAP 6, D4

(Nearby towns also listed: Holyoke, South Hadley, Springfield)

A diverse city of about 60,000 residents, Chicopee is near the confluence of the Chicopee and Connecticut rivers, 92 mi west of Boston, and less than 3 mi north of Springfield. Prior to settlement by European colonists, the area was historically the junction of two principal Native American trade routes, one following a north–south path alongside the Connecticut River, the other following an east–west path between Boston Harbor and New York's Hudson River valley. The latter route forded the Connecticut River at Chicopee Falls, a now-vanished cascade that also provided excellent fishing before industrial dams ruined the river's mighty salmon runs. Today the city continues to stand at a strategic modern crossroads, those aboriginal paths having been replaced by I–91 and I–90. Westover Air Force Base, home to the 439th Military Airlift Wing, is the city's major employer, but Chicopee has a diverse industrial sector, producing such varied products as sporting goods, office supplies, and the eastern edition of the *Wall Street Journal*.

Information Chicopee Chamber of Commerce | 264 Exchange St., Chicopee, 01013 | 413/594–2101 | fax 413/594–2103 | gseklecki@map.com | www.chicopeechamber.org.

Attractions
Chicopee Memorial State Park. These 575 acres of state parkland include two 25-acre ponds ideal for swimming and fishing, 2½ mi of paved bike trails, and paths for mountain bikes. | 570 Burnett Rd. | 413/594–9416 | Free | Daily.

Dining
Hu Ke Lau Chinese Restaurant and Dinner Theater. Chinese. This Pioneer Valley institution is more than a restaurant; it's an experience. Hu Ke Lau's dining room seats more than 1,000 people and features a near-legendary Chinese-Polynesian-American buffet. The main stage hosts a Hawaiian musical show complete with fire-eating Thursday through Sunday, and the adjoining comedy club has attracted such future stars as Rosie O'Donnell and Chris Rock. | 705 Memorial Dr. | 413/593–5222 | fax 413/593–6293 | $9–$25 | AE, D, MC, V.

Lodging
Comfort Inn Parwick Center. This full-service chain is just a short distance from exit 5 of the Massachusetts Turnpike. Restaurant, bar with entertainment, complimentary Continental breakfast. Cable TV. Barbershop, beauty salon. Gym. Video games. Laundry facilities, laundry service. Business services. Pets allowed. | 450 Memorial Dr. | 413/739–7311 or 800/221–2222 | fax 413/594–5005 | www.bestlodging.com | 100 rooms | $49–$109 | AE, D, DC, MC, V.

Ramada Inn. This standard chain hotel is in Chicopee, near I–91 and I–90. Restaurant, bar. In-room data ports, cable TV. Pool. Playground. | 357 Burnett Rd. | 413/592–9101 or 800/228–2828 | fax 413/594–8333 | 122 rooms | $85–$90 | AE, D, DC, MC, V.

Super 8 Chicopee Motor Lodge. This economic option is near I–91 and I–90. There's 24-hour coffee in the lobby. Complimentary Continental breakfast. Cable TV. Pool. Pets allowed. | 463 Memorial Dr. | 413/592–6171 | fax 413/598–8351 | 106 rooms | $52–$70 | AE, D, MC, V.

CHILMARK (MARTHA'S VINEYARD)

MAP 6, J8

(Nearby towns also listed: Aquinnah, West Tisbury)

Like its next-door neighbors on the western end of Martha's Vineyard, sparsely populated Chilmark is primarily a rural and agricultural community. The town center is little more than an intersection of quiet country roads, quaintly nicknamed Beetlebung Corner, around which the library, town hall, and local general store have gathered to keep each other company. Most summer visitors rent or own vacation homes hidden down unmarked sandy lanes that disappear into the up-island forests. The liveliest part of town is the fishing village of Menemsha, whose boats bring in the fresh catch of the day featured on menus all across the Vineyard. Menemsha's boat basin, popular with visiting yachts in summer, is also home to the island's Coast Guard station.

CHILMARK
(MARTHA'S
VINEYARD)

INTRO
ATTRACTIONS
DINING
LODGING

Information: Martha's Vineyard Chamber of Commerce | Box 1698, Vineyard Haven, 02568 | 508/693–0085 | fax 508/693–9589. **Information Center** | Beach Rd., Vineyard Haven | 508/693–0085 | mvcc@vineyard.net | www.mvy.com.

Attractions

Chilmark Cemetery. Lillian Hellman and John Belushi are two notables who are buried in this small graveyard. | South Rd. | Free | Daily.

Fulling Mill Brook. Walking trails bordered by blueberry and huckleberry bushes on this small, peaceful conservation land lead to the lowlands around the famous trout stream. The main parking lot is at the Middle Road entrance and there's additional parking available near the South Road entrance. | Middle Rd. | Free | Daily.

Menemsha Hills Reservation. More than 5 mi of trails loop around this conservation property in an irregular figure eight, traversing oak woodlands grown up on former grazing land, and leading down to an isolated rock- and boulder-strewn beach on Vineyard Sound. The reservation also includes Prospect Hill, one of Martha's Vineyard's highest points, and a windblown lookout platform at the top of the 150-ft cliff above the beach. Besides the deer, hawks, and songbirds drawn to the woodland's berry shrubs, the rocky shore sometimes attracts seals. | North Rd. | 508/693–3678 | www.thetrustees.org | Free | Daily dawn–dusk.

Waskosim's Rock Reservation. Waskosim's Rock—one of the highest points on the Vineyard, offering a panoramic view of the surrounding countryside—is the primary landmark of these 185 acres of woodlands and rolling green hills. A 3-mile hike begins at the trailhead off North Road; look for the ruins of an 18th-century homestead. | North Rd. | 508/627–7141 | Free | Daily dawn–dusk.

Dining

Beach Plum Inn. Contemporary. At this secluded ocean-view restaurant, island-grown produce, organic ingredients, and creative accompaniments jazz up the classic French-inspired cuisine, lightened for modern palates. The menu changes daily, and offers à la carte selections as well as prix-fixe dinners. Try the beef Wellington and fresh fish dishes. Open-air dining on deck. BYOB. No smoking. | 50 Beach Plum La., Menemsha | 508/645–9454 | Reservations required | No lunch | $25–$40 | AE, D, MC, V.

★ **Feast of Chilmark.** Contemporary. The tastes of local produce and imaginatively prepared seafood predominate this quiet, casual dining room. Sample the oven-seared scallops or sautéed shrimp with tomato and cheese in a puff pastry. | State Rd. | 508/645–3553 | Closed Oct.–May | $17–$38 | AE, MC, V.

Home Port. Seafood. Striking sunset and harbor views accompany the tried-and-true baked, broiled, and fried seafood served up to busloads of tourists; knowing locals get takeout from the kitchen door and enjoy it on nearby Menemsha Beach. Try the clam chowder. Open-air dining. Raw bar. BYOB. No smoking. | End of North Rd., Menemsha | 508/645–2679 | Reservations essential | Closed mid-Oct.–mid-Apr. No lunch | $25–45 | MC, V.

Lodging

Beach Plum Inn and Restaurant. Each room of this remodeled inn is individually decorated. Accommodations in the main house are elegant, while cottages are more country in style. Many rooms have ocean views. Guest passes to private beaches and health club are available. Restaurant, picnic area, complimentary breakfast. In-room data ports, refrigerators, some in-room hot tubs, cable TV, in-room VCRs and movies. Tennis. Business services. | 50 Beach Plum La., Menemsha | 508/645–9454 | fax 508/645–2801 | www.beachpluminn.com | 11 rooms | $250–$400 | Closed Jan.–Mar. | AE, D, DC, MC, V.

The Inn at Blueberry Hill. Set on 56 acres of rural Vineyard property, this high-end Cape-style cedar shingle house and its three cottages provide a secluded haven far from the island's more commercial sites. Guest rooms are outfitted with simple Shaker-inspired furniture;

many have access to private terraces and patios. Theo's Restaurant serves local produce and seafood. Children under 12 are allowed in the inn's separate cottages, when available. Restaurant, complimentary breakfast. Some refrigerators, cable TV, TV in common area. Pool. Outdoor hot tub, massage, spa. Tennis. Gym. Library. No smoking. | 74 North Rd. | 508/645–3322 or 800/356–3322 | fax 508/645–3799 | www.blueberryinn.com | 25 rooms | $220–$260, suites $300–$700 | Closed Nov.–Apr. | AE, MC, V.

Menemsha Inn and Cottages. This inn is aptly named Menemsha, a Wampanoag word that means "point of observation." From the extensive grounds there are views of Vineyard Sound and Gay Head Lighthouse. A stone wall-enclosed garden slopes down to the water. The property is 1 mi from Lucy Stone Beach. Cottages have wood-burning fireplaces. Free shuttle and passes to the beach are offered. Complimentary Continental breakfast. In-room data ports, some kitchenettes, no air-conditioning, no room phones, in-room VCRs. Gym. Tennis. | North Rd., Menemsha | 508/645–2521 | www.menemshainn.com | 9 rooms in main building, 6 suites in carriage house; 12 cottages | $175–$215, $275 suites, $1,800–$2,200/wk cottages | Closed Nov.–Apr. | No credit cards.

CONCORD

(Nearby towns also listed: Bedford, Boston, Lexington, Sudbury, Waltham)

Historic Concord is deeply engraved in the national memory due to its almost accidental role at the outset of the American Revolution. Because of the shots that were fired there on the morning of April 19, 1775, the small wooden bridge over the placid Concord River on the north side of town is one of the cornerstones of American history. Colonial buildings that witnessed the events of that day still stand around the town green, lending Concord a pleasantly timeless quality. Two generations after the Revolution, Concord earned itself a permanent place in American letters thanks to the prolixity of its authors, including Thoreau, Emerson, Hawthorne, and Alcott. The town's stiff resistance to capitalizing on its legacy with souvenir shops, theme motels, or related commercial ventures reinforces its 19th-century character, but it is mostly a desire not to encourage more tourism that motivates such apparent consideration.

Information: **Concord Chamber of Commerce** | 2 Lexington Rd., Concord, 01742 | 978/369–3120 | fax 978/369–1515. **Visitor Kiosk** | Heywood St. | 978/369–3120 | conchamber@ma.ultranet.com | www.concordmachamber.org.

Attractions

Codman House. Now owned and maintained by the Society for the Preservation of New England Antiquities, this house was originally the rural 18th-century Georgian-style estate known as "the Grange." Changes to the house and grounds over five generations of Codmans have endowed the place with a rich variety of architectural and decorative features, inside and out. The 16-acre grounds include a turn-of-the-century Italianate garden and a formal English country garden. | The Grange, Codman Rd., Lincoln | 781/259–8843 | www.spnea.org | $4 | June–mid-Oct., tours on the hour Wed.–Sun. 11–4.

Concord Free Public Library. Among this library's special collections are original editions of books by such local literary figures as Thoreau, Emerson, Hawthorne, and Alcott. There are also artifacts related to Thoreau, including one of the pencils his family produced, and sculptures by Concord resident Daniel Chester French, including a life-size statue of Emerson done posthumously. | 129 Main St. | 978/318–3300 | www.ultranet.com/~cfpl | Free | Call for hrs.

Concord Museum. This spacious museum profiles local history from before European contact up through Concord's era of literary splendor. Emerson's study is on display; so are artifacts from Thoreau's cabin at Walden Pond. | 200 Lexington Rd. | 978/369–9609 | www.concordmuseum.org | $7 | Mon.–Sat. 9–5, Sun. noon–5.

DeCordova Museum and Sculpture Park. Opened in 1950 on the country estate of a Boston entrepreneur, the DeCordova has become arguably the region's leading showcase for New England artists, with changing exhibits. The main galleries cascade down a hillside amid landscaped grounds filled with modern sculpture. | 51 Sandy Pond Rd., Lincoln | 781/259–8355 | fax 781/259–3650 | www.decordova.org | Museum $6; sculpture park free | Museum Tues.–Sun. 11–5; sculpture park daily dawn–dusk.

Drumlin Farm Education Center and Wildlife Sanctuary. This educational farm's 180 acres cover a variety of habitats, from pastures to ponds to woodlands. Besides the property's self-guiding trails, there are live farm animals in the barns and a nature center with exhibits of local wild animals. Befitting the headquarters of the Massachusetts Audubon Society, the farm hosts numerous special programs for all ages throughout the year. | 208

LITERARY CONCORD

The first wholly American literary movement was born in Concord, the tiny town west of Boston that, quite coincidentally, also witnessed the beginning of the American Revolution. Under the influence of essayist and poet Ralph Waldo Emerson, a group eventually known as the Transcendental Club (but called the Hedges Club at the time) assembled regularly in Emerson's Concord home. Henry David Thoreau, a fellow townsman and famous proponent of self-reliance, was an integral club member, along with others such as pioneering feminist Margaret Fuller and poet Ellery Channing, who were drawn to Concord simply because of Emerson's presence. These are names that have become indelible bylines in high school anthologies and college syllabi, but Concord also produced beloved children's book authors such as Louisa May Alcott and Harriet Lothrop, pseudonymously known as Margaret Sydney. Even Nathaniel Hawthorne, whose various places of temporary residence around Massachusetts constitute a literary trail all on their own, made his home in Concord during both the early and late periods of his career.

The cumulative inkwells of these authors have bestowed upon Concord a literary legacy unique in the United States, both for its influence on literature in general and for the quantity of related sights packed within such a small radius. From Alcott's Orchard House to Hawthorne's Old Manse, nearly all their houses remain standing, well preserved and open for tours. The Thoreau Institute, within walking distance of a reconstruction of Thoreau's famous cabin in the woods at Walden Pond, is a repository of his papers and original editions. Emerson's study sits in the Concord Museum, across the street from his house. Modern copies of their works may be perused in the Concord Free Public Library. Even their final resting places are here, on Authors Ridge in Sleepy Hollow Cemetery, a few short blocks from the town common.

Once each month a trolley tour originating in Boston makes the rounds of all of Concord's literary landmarks; inquire at the Concord Chamber of Commerce visitors kiosk on Heywood Street for details (978/369–3120).

© Artville

S. Great Rd., Lincoln | 781/259–9807 or 800/AUDUBON | www.massaudubon.org | $6 | Mar.–Oct., Tues.–Sun. 9–5, Nov.–Feb. Tues.–Sun. 9–4.

Grapevine Cottage. The original Concord grapevine, the grape made legendary by Welch's jams and jellies, still grows in the garden of this privately owned house. A plaque tells the history of the Concord grape. | 491 Lexington Rd. | Closed to the public.

Great Meadows National Wildlife Refuge. Concord's portion of this 3,000-acre refuge includes the meadows that give the property its name. The large wetlands and open ponds that constitute most of the refuge are home to numerous migratory waterfowl, examples of which may generally be seen from this parcel's bike trail. | Monsen Rd., off Rte. 62 | 978/443–4661 | Free | Daily.

Gropius House. Completed in 1938, this is the home that Bauhaus founder Walter Gropius designed for his family upon moving to the United States to teach at Harvard. Gropius helped launch modern architecture in America, and his house was the first step. Personal effects and family furnishings give the impression that Gropius has only left briefly, to return soon. | 68 Baker Bridge Rd., Lincoln | 781/259–8098 | www.spnea.org | $5 | June–mid-Oct., tours on the hour Wed.–Sun. 11–4; mid-Oct.–May, tours on the hour weekends 11–4.

Jonathan Ball House. The Concord Art Association is housed in this 1753 building, once a station on the Underground Railroad. | 37 Lexington Rd. | 978/369–2578 | Free | Tues.–Sat. 10–4:30.

Minute Man National Historical Park. On April 19, 1775, British troops marched from Boston to Concord to seize a suspected cache of rebel arms. Turned back by the "shot heard 'round the world" at Concord's North Bridge, the British retreated under continual fire along what is today known as Battle Road. This national park encompasses both the bridge and a major section of that road, with year-round and seasonal visitor centers to help make sense of that memorable day's events. | 174 Liberty St. | 978/369–6993 | www.nps.gov/mima | Free | Daily.

Old North Bridge. The "shot heard 'round the world" was fired at this pastoral wooden bridge, ½ mi from Concord Center, when American Minutemen turned the tables on British Redcoats on the morning of April 19, 1775. Daniel Chester French's famous statue The Minuteman commemorates the battle at the foot of the bridge. | Off Monument St. | Free | Daily.

Orchard House. In 1858, the 26-year-old Louisa May Alcott moved into this house with her sisters and parents. The house, actually two 18th-century farmhouses joined together by Alcott's father, was immortalized in Alcott's *Little Women*. Here is also where her perpetually dreamy father, Bronson, founded the Concord School of Philosophy, which still has its home behind Orchard House. | 399 Lexington Rd. | 978/369–4118 | www.louisamayalcott.org | $6 | Apr.–Oct., Mon.–Sat. 10–4:30, Sun. 1–4:30; Nov.–Dec. and mid-Jan.–Mar., weekdays 11–3, Sat. 10–4:30, Sun. 1–4:30.

Ralph Waldo Emerson House. From 1835 until his death in 1882, author Ralph Waldo Emerson lived in this house on the edge of Concord's center. Although his study and portions of his library are elsewhere, the property still features enough personal effects to give the place an air of authenticity. | 28 Cambridge Tpke., at Rte. 2A | 978/369–2236 | $5 | Mid-Apr.–Oct., Thurs.–Sat. 10–4:30, Sun. 2–4:30.

Sleepy Hollow Cemetery. At the back of this cemetery stands Authors Ridge, the final resting place for all of Concord's most famous writers, including Thoreau, Hawthorne, Alcott, and Emerson. Daniel Chester French, sculptor of the statue of Lincoln in the Lincoln Memorial in Washington, D.C., is also buried here. One of his many commissions for a memorial to those who died in war, *Mourning Victory*, stands by the cemetery's west side. | Bedford St. | Free | Daily.

Old Manse. Rev. William Emerson, who built this house in 1770, watched the opening battle of the American Revolution spill over onto his fields from the North Bridge. Decades later, his grandson, Ralph Waldo Emerson, moved in for a year before buying a house on the other side of town. But the most notable occupant was Nathaniel Hawthorne, who rented the house with his wife and wrote the stories that gave the property its name. | 269 Monument St. | 978/369–3909 | www.thetrustees.org | $6 | Mid-Apr.–Oct., Mon.–Sat. 10–5:30, Sun. noon–5.

Walden Pond State Reservation. Thanks to the book written by Henry David Thoreau, who spent two years living in a tiny cabin in the surrounding woods, this may be the most famous pond in the country. Locals appreciate its fine swimming to such an extent that on most summer days the pond has crowds to rival the most popular ocean beach. Literary pilgrims looking for Thoreauvian serenity most of the year should stick to the late afternoon hours or to hikes along wooded trails away from the pond. | 915 Walden St. | 978/369–3254 | Parking $2 from May–Oct. | Daily, 7–6:30.

The Wayside. This house was owned briefly by Bronson Alcott in the 1840s, before he and his family, including the adolescent Louisa May, moved to Boston. Nathaniel Hawthorne bought the property from Alcott and fixed it up; it was to be the only house he would ever own. Although a third Concord author, Harriet Lothrop, eventually lived in the house, too, Hawthorne's apt name has been the one that has stuck. | 455 Lexington Rd. | 978/369–6975 | www.nps.gov/mima/wayside | $4 | Tours May–Oct., daily.

ON THE CALENDAR

APR.: *North Bridge Battle Commemorations.* On the Saturday before Patriots' Day, militia and British Redcoats reenact the skirmish that sent the British retreating to their Boston garrison, marking the beginning of the Revolutionary War. The Patriots' Day Parade takes place on Monday, Patriots' Day. | 978/369–6993.

Dining

Colonial Inn. American. Traditional stick-to-your-ribs Yankee fare is served up in the neo-Colonial dining rooms of this late 18th-century inn fashioned out of three houses. One of the two tap rooms still has its original fittings. Known for fresh seafood, roast prime rib, and afternoon high tea. Open-air dining on patio. Live music nightly. Kids' menu. Sun. brunch. No smoking in dining room. | 48 Monument Sq | 978/369–2373 | $17–$27 | AE, D, DC, MC, V.

Papa Razzi. Italian. One of a popular minichain of chic Boston-based northern Italian restaurants, decorated with Italian movie posters and photos of celebrities. The comprehensive menu offers brick-oven pizzas and such popular pasta dishes as *rigatoni con luganega* (ground italian sausage in tomato cream sauce). Sun. brunch. | 768 Elm St. | 978/371–0030 | fax 978/371–9586 | $9–$24 | AE, D, DC, MC, V.

Walden Grille. Contemporary. An upscale bistro in a converted firehouse, this eatery serves such eclectic fare as salmon risotto and marinated lamb kebabs. Save room for the restaurant's decadent chocolate torte. | 24 Walden St. | 978/371–2233 | fax 978/371–8285 | $13–$30 | AE, D, MC, V.

Lodging

Best Western at Historic Concord. Some rooms in this renovated, moderately priced hotel overlook the pool and the landscaped grounds and gardens. It's a 10- to 15-minute walk to historic Concord center. Complimentary Continental breakfast. In-room data ports, cable TV. Pool. Hot tub. Gym. Laundry facilities. Business services. Pets allowed (fee). | 740 Elm St. | 978/369–6100 | fax 978/371–1656 | 106 rooms | $104–$119 | AE, D, DC, MC, V.

Colonial Inn. Guests here step back to the era of Concord's literary greats. Sunday brunch includes improvisational performances by actresses portraying Louisa May Alcott, Mrs. Emerson, and Mrs. Hawthorne. Rooms in the 1716 main inn are uniquely furnished and have exposed-beam ceilings, decorative fireplaces, and four-poster beds. From the inn it is a five-minute walk to Concord's top sights. Restaurant, bar with entertainment. Cable TV. Business services. | 48 Monument Sq | 978/369–9200 or 800/370–9200 | fax 978/371–1533 | www.concordscolonialinn.com | 15 rooms in main building, 32 rooms in Prescott wing, 6 suites in Rebecca's House, 2 suites in cottage | $159–$225, $295–$475 suites | AE, D, DC, MC, V.

The Concordian Motel. This clean, classic New England roadside motel is 1 mi from Concord's town center. Complimentary Continental breakfast. Some microwaves, some refrigerators, cable TV. | 71 Hosmer St., Acton | 978/263–7765 | fax 978/263–5232 | 45 rooms | $59–$75 | AE, D, DC, MC, V.

Hawthorne Inn. Several literary families—the Alcotts, Emersons, and Hawthornes—owned land on this property, but Hawthorne was the only one who actually ever lived in the house. Henry Thoreau surveyed the land. The 1870 building contains antiques and original paintings by Norman Rockwell. On the grounds are gardens, a sitting area, a fountain, and a European larch brought from England by Nathaniel Hawthorne and planted by Bronson Alcott. Complimentary Continental breakfast. No smoking. | 462 Lexington Rd. | 978/369–5610 | fax 978/287–4949 | www.concordmass.com | 7 rooms | $195–$215 | AE, D, MC, V.

Holiday Inn–Boxborough Woods. This hotel is approximately a 15-minute drive from Concord, and about one-hour from Boston. Some of the rooms face an indoor tropical courtyard. Restaurant, bar, picnic area, room service. In-room data ports, cable TV. Indoor pool. Sauna. Gym. Business services. | 242 Adams Pl., Boxborough | 978/263–8701 or 800/HOLIDAY | fax 978/263–0518 | www.holidayinn.com | 143 rooms, 7 suites | $149–$179, $225–$275 suites | AE, D, DC, MC, V.

North Bridge Inn. This three-story gray-clapboard house at Concord's town center has suites equipped with kitchens, sitting areas, and work spaces. The family-friendly inn welcomes both children and pets. Complimentary breakfast. In-room data ports, kitchenettes, microwaves, refrigerators, cable TV, in-room VCRs. Pets allowed. No smoking. | 21 Monument St. | 978/371–0014 or 888/530–0007 | fax 978/371–6460 | www.northbridgeinn.com | 6 suites | $125–$250 | AE, MC, V.

DANVERS

MAP 6, I2

(Nearby towns also listed: Beverly, Boston, Lynnfield, Salem)

Danvers, established in 1630, was one of Massachusetts's earliest Puritan settlements. In those days it was known as Salem Village, part of what was a very large Salem township. The infamous 1692 Salem witchcraft trials took place here, in fact, despite impressions to the contrary cultivated by modern Salem. Now Danvers all but disowns the legacy of the witchcraft hysteria and has instead established itself as the retail shopping center for Greater Boston's northern suburbs. Its proximity to Boston—17 mi away—firmly places Danvers within that city's sphere of economic influence, but I–95 also gives resident commuters convenient access to the suburban office parks and high-tech firms on the metro region's outer edge.

Information: **North of Boston Convention and Visitors Bureau** | 17 Peabody Sq, Peabody, 01960 | 978/977–7760 or 800/742–5306 | fax 978/977–7758 | www.northofboston.org.

Attractions
Connor's Farm. A family farm established in 1904, with 140 acres and eight greenhouses of corn, peaches, tomatoes, and other local crops. Pick-your-own strawberries, raspberries, and sweet peas are available in the summer, apples and pumpkins in the fall. Don't forget to take home a bag of hot apple cider doughnuts. | 30 Valley Rd. | 978/777–1245 | fax 978/774–6250 | www.connorsfarm.com | Free | Apr.–Oct., daily 9–6.

Glen Magna Farms. Owned by the Danvers Historical Society, this attractive country estate was once an expansive working farm, albeit a "gentleman's seat," purchased explicitly to provide wealthy Salem merchant Joseph Peabody and his family with sanctuary from the War of 1812. The property, which stayed in the family for 144 years, now includes an 1890s Colonial Revival mansion, several styles of ornamental gardens, and a unique 1793 summer "teahouse." | Ingersoll St. (Endicott Park entrance) | 978/777–1666 | fax 978/777–5681 | www.glennmagnafarms.org | House and garden tour $5, grounds $1.50 | June–Sept., Tues. and Thurs. 10–4. House tours Wed. at 10 and 2, garden tour at 11.

Rebecca Nurse Homestead. Rebecca Nurse was a respected elder in 17th-century Salem Village, until, that is, some young girls accused her of witchcraft. This First Period saltbox house was her home, and tours stick to facts rather than conjecture when it comes to describing the witch hysteria's local impact. The farm, surrounded by fields and a family burying ground at the rear of the property, includes a replica of the 1672 village meetinghouse created for a movie set. | 149 Pine St. | 978/774–8799 | $4 | Mid-June–mid-Sept., Tues.–Sun. 1–4:30; mid-Sept.–Oct., weekends 1–4:30.

Witchcraft Victims' Memorial. This modern outdoor memorial sits in a small open lot across the street from the location of the original Salem Village Meetinghouse, which was used during the 1692 Salem witch hysteria for pretrial hearings. The pale granite memorial honors the 19 village residents executed during the hysteria that began in the home of Reverend Parris, which once stood about 1 mi west. | 176 Hobart St. | Free | Daily.

ON THE CALENDAR

JUNE–JULY: *Danvers Family Festival.* This weeklong festival offers a champagne celebration at a 19th-century estate (Glen Magna Farms), a bicycle safety rodeo, Colonial reenactment skits, a crafts fair, a strawberry shortcake sampling, a pancake breakfast, a picnic, a spaghetti supper, a Polish block party, Irish music, band concerts, '50s music, a tennis tournament, a fishing derby, story-telling, pony rides, a dog show, children's train rides, puppet shows, fireworks, a fly-over and parachute exhibition, and the traditional "horrible parade." | 978/777–0001.

OCT.: *Topsfield Fair.* This 10-day fair at Topsfield Fairgrounds was started in 1818, making it the oldest agricultural fair in the country. It features an opening-day parade and giant pumpkin contest; flower, livestock, draft horse, and poultry shows; horse and oxen pulling; the Hallamore eight-horse Clydesdale Hitch; 4-H displays; Grange exhibits; barn tours; a petting farm; a farm and fair museum; amusement rides; and fireworks. | 207 Boston St., Topsfield | 978/887–5000 | www.topsfieldfair.org.

Dining

Fantasy Island. Chinese. This restaurant doesn't look like much on the outside, but the interior is funky and ultra-modern. Adventuresome eaters will want to try the fantasy island volcano, a combination of lobster, shrimp, beef, roasted pork, and chicken mixed with vegetables. | 175 Water St. | 978/777–8085 | www.fisland.net | $5–$17 | AE, D, DC, MC, V.

The Hardcover. American. Its name refers to the many books that define the gracious decor for dining on reliable surf-and-turf standards. Favorites include the onion soup, and for dinner, the combo platter and the baked shrimp with prime rib. About 3 mi from downtown Danvers. Salad bar. Kids' menu. No smoking in dining room. | 15A Newbury St. | 978/774–1223 | No lunch | $17–$28 | AE, D, DC, MC, V.

Jake's Grill. American. The comprehensive menu of this local favorite has something for everyone, including barbecue, burgers, pasta, seafood, fajitas, and Greek dishes. | 80 Newbury St. | 978/774–3300 | fax 978/774–0816 | $6–$16 | AE, MC, V.

Legal Sea Foods. Seafood. One of a growing number of suburban outlets of the Boston area's most famous name in seafood, where freshness and quality have always mattered more than trendy preparations. Known for clam chowder, lobsters, and shellfish. About 2–3 mi from Downtown Danvers. Raw bar. Kid's menu. No smoking. | 210 Andover St., Northshore Shopping Center, Peabody | 978/532–4500 | $15–$35 | AE, D, DC, MC, V.

Ponte Vecchio. Italian. This rustic eatery in a strip mall serves what many consider to be the best veal chop north of Boston; other popular dishes include baked oysters with mascarpone cheese and creamy risotto specials. An adjacent trattoria serves lighter fare. | 435 Newbury St. | 978/777–9188 | $14–$22 | AE, D, DC, MC, V.

Lodging

Comfort Inn North Shore. This large, spacious branch of the chain hotel is at the junction of U.S.1 and Route 128/I–95. Complimentary Continental breakfast. In-room data ports, some microwaves, some refrigerators, cable TV. Indoor-outdoor pool. Gym. Laundry facilities, laundry service. Business services. No pets. | 50 Dayton St. | 978/777–1700 | fax 978/777–4647 | www.comfortinn.com | 140 rooms | $70–$169 | AE, D, DC, MC, VI.

Courtyard by Marriott. Built in 1986, this business-oriented hotel is a three-story, brick, colonial-style building about ½ mi from downtown Danvers, just off Route 128/I–95 behind the Liberty Tree Mall. 2 restaurants, bar. In-room data ports, cable TV. Pool. Gym. Laundry facilities, laundry service. Business services. | 275 Independence Way | 978/777–8630 or 800/321–2211 | fax 978/777–7341 | www.courtyard.com | 121 rooms, 2 suites | $115–$130 | AE, D, DC, MC, V.

Days Inn Salem/Boston. This two-building property, just off Route 128/I–95 and 2 mi south of downtown Danvers, is near historic Salem. Off-season rates drop by about half. Picnic area, complimentary Continental breakfast. In-room data ports, cable TV. Pool. Laundry facilities. Business services. | 152 Endicott St. | 978/777–1030 or 800/329–7466 | fax 978/777–0264 | 129 rooms, 2 buildings | $89–$109 | AE, D, DC, MC, V.

Quality Inn King's Grant Inn. This two-story inn has an Old English–style decor and a tropical garden and sitting area by the pool, complete with live birds flying about. It's about 10 minutes' drive from downtown Danvers. Restaurant, bar with entertainment, complimentary Continental breakfast, room service. In-room data ports, cable TV. Indoor pool. Hot tub. Business services. | Rte. 128 at Trask La. | 978/774–6800 | fax 978/774–6502 | 125 rooms, 2 suites | $119–$150, $250 suites | AE, D, DC, MC, V.

Residence Inn by Marriott. This inn is a home away from home. Grocery-shopping services, daily newspapers, and summer barbecues on Wednesday evenings are included. The two-bedroom suites have living rooms with fireplaces, two bathrooms, and two TVs. Complimentary Continental breakfast, picnic area. In-room data ports, kitchenettes, microwaves, refrigerators, cable TV. Pool. Tennis courts. Gym. Laundry facilities, laundry service. Business services, free parking. Some pets allowed (fee). | 51 Newbury St. | 978/777–7171 or 800/331–3131 | fax 978/774–7195 | www.residenceinn.com | 72 1-bedroom suites, 24 2-bedroom suites | $119–$149 1–bedroom suites, $159–$179 2–bedroom suites | AE, D, DC, MC, V.

Sheraton Ferncroft Resort. This resort has an 18-hole golf course designed by Robert Trent Jones that's been awarded four-stars (out of a possible five) by *Golf Digest*. The eight-story building lies on more than 700 acres. Rooms are decorated with wood furniture and dark colors. It's about half hour from downtown Boston. Restaurant, bar with entertainment. In-room data ports, refrigerators, cable TV. 2 pools (1 indoor). Hot tub, sauna, steam room. Driving range, 18-hole and 9-hole par-3 golf courses, putting green, tennis courts. Health club. Cross-country skiing. Business services. | 50 Ferncroft Rd. | 978/777–2500 | fax 978/750–7959 | www.sheraton.com | 367 rooms, 19 suites | $179–$225, $250–$500 suites | AE, D, DC, MC, V.

Super 8 Motel. This two-building motel features large rooms in a quiet country setting. The property is 2 mi from Sandy Beach and 6 mi from Salem. Restaurant, bar with entertainment, complimentary Continental breakfast. Pool. Business services. | 225 Newbury St. | 978/774–6500 | fax 978/762–649 | 78 rooms, 2 suites in 2 buildings | $75–$90, $99–$129 suites | AE, D, DC, MC, V.

DARTMOUTH

MAP 6, I7

(Nearby towns also listed: Fall River, New Bedford, Westport)

Dartmouth is a coastal community little known outside its region. For most of its history, Dartmouth has been an agricultural town, a legacy upheld by the handful of working farms that still remain. Over the past century Dartmouth has become a prominent vacation resort, too, its attractive beaches and scenic yacht anchorages so appealing that summer cottage colonies and, more recently, trophy-sized second homes have become a distinct feature of the town's coast. In recent decades the construction of the state university campus now known as UMass–Dartmouth has spearheaded the community's suburbanization, a process that continues today. The town still contains remarkably rural landscapes outlined with 18th-century drystone walls and rambling Federal-style farmhouses, but Dartmouth's increasingly mall-lined roadways suggest such anachronisms are seriously endangered, if not already well on the way to extinction.

Information: **New Bedford Office of Tourism** | 52 Fisherman's Wharf, New Bedford, 02740-6398 | 508/979–1745 or 800/508–5353 | fax 508/070–1763 | amotta@www.ci.new-bedford.ma.us | www.ci.new-bedford.ma.us.

Attractions

Children's Museum. This modern, highly hands-on museum, housed in what was once a dairy barn, engages its young audience not just with giant Legos and environments to explore, such as a big fishing boat, but also with workshops, demonstrations, celebrations, and a summer camp. | 276 Gulf Rd., South Dartmouth | 508/993–3361 | fax 508/993–3332 | $3.75 | Weekdays 10–5, Sat. 10–4.

Demarest Lloyd State Park. This small state park is known for its family-friendly beach facing the wide mouth of the Slocum River. Sandbars create pockets of shallow water ideal for small swimmers, and even at high tide there's no undertow or strong waves. Although there are no food stands other than the occasional itinerant ice-cream truck, there are picnic grills for do-it-yourselfers. Bathhouses with full showers and an attractive wooded setting are added benefits. | Barneys Joy Rd. | 508/636–8816 | $2 parking | Memorial Day–Labor Day, weekdays 10–6, weekends 8–6.

Dining

Bridge Street Cafe. Contemporary. This popular, family-owned restaurant in an old gas station with a second-story outdoor deck bridges the gap between the mundane and the much-too-fancy. The soft-shell crabs are a favorite among the locals. | 10A Bridge St., Tadanarama Village, South Dartmouth, | 508/994–7200 | fax 508/979–8187 | No lunch Sun.–Mon. | $13–$26 | AE, MC, V.

Lodging

Comfort Inn North Dartmouth. A clean, no-frills motel off exit 12 off I–195 and a 10-minute drive to the seaside. Restaurant, complimentary Continental breakfast. In-room data ports, cable TV. Pool. Laundry service. | 171 Faunce Corner Rd., North Dartmouth | 508/996–0800 | fax 508/996–0800 | www.comfortinndartmouth.com | 85 rooms | $80–$139 | AE, D, DC, MC, V.

DEDHAM

MAP 6, H4

(Nearby towns also listed: Boston, Braintree, Brookline, Newton, Quincy, Sharon, Wellesley)

Dedham is approximately 20 mi southwest of downtown Boston, next to circumferential Route 128/I–95. Within a few years after being established in 1636 the town put its waterways to work powering gristmills and fueling mills. One of the historical firsts to which Dedham lays claim is the nation's first canal, built to ensure adequate water supply for these early industries. The nation's oldest frame house, erected in 1636, also survives within the town's boundaries. Over the centuries, Dedham's attractiveness to industry continued to grow, aided in the 1800s by a local pool of wealthy investors, and in the 1900s by strong transportation links to Boston and the rest of southern New England. Since the end of World War II, manufacturing has been supplanted by corporate office parks along the interstate and by large retail shopping plazas that attract both city and suburban neighbors.

Information: Neponset Valley Chamber of Commerce | 190 Vanderbilt Ave., Norwood, 02062 | 781/769–1126 | fax 781/769–0805 | www.nvcc.com.

Attractions

Dedham Historical Society Museum. Founded in 1859, this society has collected such items as important furniture—including the 1652 Metcalf chair, which is the oldest dated American chair—paintings by artists such as John Constable, the silver collection of American silversmith Katherine Pratt, and 19th-century photographs of Dedham. | 612 High St. | 781/326–1385 | www.dedhamhistorical.org | $2 | Tues.–Fri., noon–4.

Fairbanks House. This 1636 dwelling is the oldest surviving wood-frame house in America, now maintained by a family association descended from its first owner, yeoman farmer Jonathan Fairbanks. Guided tours describe the house and the lives of its occupants, amid furnishings from the 18th to the early 20th centuries. There is also an archive available to researchers by appointment. | 511 East St. | 781/326–1170 | fax 781/326–2147 | www.fairbankshouse.com | $5 | May–Oct., tours on the hour Tues.–Sat. 10–5, Sun. 1–5.

ON THE CALENDAR
DEC.: *Dedham Choral Society Holiday Concert.* This highly regarded choral society, founded in 1955, has an impressive repertoire which includes the Requiems of Mozart, Brahms, Verdi, Fauré, and Duruflé, as well as Elgar's Dream of Gerontius. Every December they hold a concert at St. Mary's Church in Dedham and St. Paul's Episcopal Cathedral, Boston Common, in Boston. | 781/326–1520.

Dining

Finian's Pub. American/Casual. The best bet here is the all-you-can-eat Sunday brunch; be sure to arrive hungry. You can get just about anything you can think of but favorites include the smoked ham, sausage, fried potatoes, barbecue chicken, crêpes, pastries, and quiche. If that sounds too heavy, there is also plenty of salad and fresh fruit, and the chefs make a point of ensuring that the buffet table is constantly refilled throughout the meal. Sun. brunch. | 910 Washington St. | 617/329–0097 | $5–$10 | AE, MC, V.

Isabella. Contemporary. This cozy, sophisticated restaurant has garnered rave reviews for its consistently great food (and generous servings). Especially good are the short ribs and the paella. There is a small bar which serves wine and beer and framed prints line three of the walls—the fourth is a mural. The service is polished and attentive. | 566 High St. | 781/461–8485 | No lunch weekends | $10–$28 | AE, MC, V.

Vinny Testa's. Italian. Carbo-loaders take note: this casual, comfortable restaurant is famous for dishing up mammoth portions of tasty pasta at relatively low prices; fortunately, *piccolo* portions—as well as human-size pizzas—are also available for anyone lacking a sumo wrestler's appetite. Known for pasta. Try the farfalle con pollo. | 233 Elm St. | 781/320–8999 | $7–$20 | AE, D, DC, MC, V.

Lodging

Boston–Dedham Holiday Inn. The hotel at the junction of Route 1A and I–95 offers free local transportation. Some of the penthouse rooms have private balconies with views of the Blue Hills and the Neponset Valley. In the game room you'll find Ping-Pong, video games, and board games, and all guest rooms have Nintendo. The indoor pool is equipped with rainbow lighting and an underwater sound system, as well as small waterfalls. Restaurant, room service. In-room data ports, cable TV. Indoor pool. Gym. Video games. Business services. Laundry service. | 55 Ariadne Rd. | 781/329–1000 or 800/HOLIDAY | fax 781/329–0903 | www.holiday-inn.com | 203 rooms | $129, $160 penthouse | AE, D, DC, MC, V.

Comfort Inn. This 3-story hotel about 3 mi from downtown Dedham features nicely land-scaped grounds. Just off Route 128/I–95. Restaurant, bar, complimentary Continental breakfast. In-room data ports, cable TV. Pool. Gym. | 235 Elm St. | 781/326–6700 or 800/244–8181 | fax 781/326–9264 | 158 rooms, 8 suites | $99–$129, $149–$200 suites | AE, D, DC, MC, V.

Courtyard by Marriott. A three-story hotel 5 mi southwest of Dedham where everything is under one roof. In addition to the restaurant and bar, there are also a US Airlines desk and an Enterprise car rental desk. Boston is 20 mi away and Foxboro Stadium is 7 mi. Several area businesses including Compaq, Analog, and Bayer are all within 4 mi. Rooms, furnished with the business traveler in mind, are spacious and comfortable. Restaurant, bar, room service. In-room data ports. Indoor pool. Hot tub. Gym. Laundry facilities, laundry service. Business services. | 300 River Ridge Dr., Norwood | 781/762–4700 or 800/321–2211 | fax 781/762–9459 | www.marriott.com | 148 rooms, 109 suites | $100–$170 | AE, D, DC, MC, V.

Hilton Dedham Place. In a quiet area next to conservation land, the hotel is about 4 mi from downtown Dedham and within walking distance of the commuter rail. Suites have balconies, hot tubs, refrigerators, and sofa beds. Restaurant, bar with piano entertainment. In-room data ports, cable TV. Indoor pool. Hot tub, sauna. 2 tennis courts. Gym. Laundry facilities. Business services. | 25 Allied Dr. | 781/329–7900 or 800/HILTONS | fax 781/329–5552 | www.hilton.com | 250 rooms, 6 suites | $99–$225 | AE, D, DC, MC, V.

Ramada Inn and Resort. This resort hotel 4 mi southwest of Dedham caters primarily to business travelers (and often corporate retreats). There's a business class and executive suites for long term stays. Other travelers will find a lot to like here, though, especially golfers. In addition to the 18-hole golf course, there is also a driving range where you can practive your swing. Boston is a 20-minute drive and Foxboro Stadium is 10 minutes. Rooms are spacious and luxuriously comfortable in a corporate hotel kind of way. Restaurant, bar. In-room data ports, some kitchenettes. Indoor pool. Hot tub, sauna. 18-hole golf course, tennis court. Health club. Laundry service. Business services. | 434 Providence Hwy., Norwood | 781/769–7000 or 888/298–2054 | fax 781/762–6638 | www.ramada.com | 150 rooms | $59–$150 | AE, D, DC, MC, V.

Residence Inn by Marriott–Dedham. You'll find one-bedroom suites that accommodate up to three people here. Each suite has a living room and bedroom; some also have fire-places. Housekeeping, grocery shopping, daily newspaper, weekday evening hors d'oeu-vres, and dinner on Wednesday evenings are included. This hotel is just off Route 128/I–95. It's a three-minute walk to the commuter rail to Boston. Complimentary Continental breakfast. In-room data ports, kitchenettes, cable TV. Pool. Hot tub. Tennis. Basketball, gym, volleyball. Laundry facilities, laundry service. | 259 Elm St. | 781/407–0999 or 800/331–3131 | fax 781/407–0752 | www.residenceinn.com | 81 suites | $135–$165 | AE, D, DC, MC, V.

DEERFIELD

MAP 6, D3

(Nearby towns also listed: Amherst, Greenfield, Hadley, Northampton)

When families came in the 1670s to homestead the fertile lands between the Deer-field and Connecticut rivers, this was the edge of the frontier. The first Deerfield settlers, vanguards of an English colony, became unwitting pawns in the deadly wars between England and France. Local Native American tribes, on their own anti-Colonial initiative and later as proxies for the French, repeatedly destroyed the town during its infancy, most famously in the so-called Deerfield Massacre of 1704. Today the town comprises two distinct halves: South Deerfield, the administrative center, and Old Deerfield, home to the three private elementary and secondary schools for which the town is regionally known. Old Deerfield is also virtually synonymous with Historic Deerfield, a private preservation organization that maintains much of the village as a walk-through interpretive museum of Colonial and post-Colonial life. As a result of Historic Deerfield's pioneering restoration efforts, Deerfield's main thoroughfare, simply known as "The Street," is one of the finest Colonial townscapes in America.

Information: **Franklin County Chamber of Commerce** | 395 Main St., Greenfield, 01302 | 413/773–5463 | fax 413/773–7008 | fccc@crocker.com | www.co.franklin.ma.us.

Attractions

★ **Historic Deerfield.** This nonprofit organization is all but synonymous with the 17th-century country village it has helped to preserve. With more than 50 structures and 25,000 antiques to its name, Historic Deerfield is rightfully regarded as one of the nation's premier repositories of Colonial Americana. Fourteen of its historic homes are open for guided tours, and a large Collections Center displays some of the many treasures not on view in its houses. | 321 Old Main St. | 413/774–5581 | fax 413/773–7220 | www.historic-deerfield.org | Individual houses or the Collections Center $6. Combined admission to all of Historic Deerfield and Memorial Hall Museum $12 (ticket good for 2 consecutive days) | Daily 9:30–4:30.

Memorial Hall Museum. Founded in 1870, this museum is dedicated to preserving the area's history through extensive collections of furnishings, tools, costumes, quilts, kitchen wares, toys, and assorted other artifacts of daily life in early rural America. There is also an excellent Indian Room, whose exhibits not only describe regional Native American history but explain the errors in how the museum's Indian artifacts were interpreted in the past. The museum is famous for hosting a spring and fall invitational crafts fair. | 8 Memorial St. | 413/774–3768 | www.deerfield-ma.org | $6, combined admission with Historic Deerfield $12 | May–Oct., daily 9:30–4:30.

Yankee Candle. The flagship store of this company is the second-largest tourist destination in Massachusetts, with more than 2.5 million visitors annually. In addition to 90,000 square ft to explore and 160 candle fragrances to smell, there is also a car museum, historic candlemaking demonstrations, a "dip your candle" area that kids and adults can enjoy, and a restaurant. | U.S. 5 and Rte. 10, South Deerfield | 413/665–0004 or 877/636–7707 | Free | 9:30–6.

ON THE CALENDAR
FEB.–APR.: *Maple sugaring.* Farmers in nearly every hill town in the state gather sap from sugar maple trees and boil it down to pure maple syrup. Visitors can request a pamphlet from the Massachusetts Maple Producers Association that contains information on the maple sugar process and a listing of sugar houses open to the public. | 413/628–3912.

Dining

Chandlers Restaurant. Continental. This restaurant on the nicely landscaped grounds of Yankee Candle has as much going on as the rest of the complex. There is an all-you-can-eat barbecue on the patio, live folk music in the wine cellar lounge on Tuesday nights, and jazz in the main dining room on Thursday nights. The food is hearty, all-American fare; naturally, in the evenings, you dine by candlelight. | U.S. 5 and Rte. 10, South Deerfield | 413/665–1277 | $6–$15 | AE, D, DC, MC, V.

★ **Deerfield Inn.** Contemporary. Deerfield's historic Colonial streetscape is distilled in the ambience of this inn, and the elegance is carried through to a menu of regional American cuisine that's expertly prepared and artistically presented. Afternoon tea is held 4–5. The menu changes seasonally, and only the freshest local ingredients are used. Featuring organic and heart-smart specialties. Kids' menu. No smoking. | 81 Old Main St. | 413/774–5587 | $18–$30 | AE, DC, MC, V.

Lodging
★ **Deerfield Inn.** Part of historic Deerfield, the house is an 1884 Colonial, originally a stagecoach stop, that features tall white pillars and a large porch. It's in the Pioneer Valley, close to biking and hiking trails. Restaurant, bar, picnic area, complimentary breakfast. In-room data ports, cable TV. No smoking. | 81 Old Main St. | 413/774–5587 or 800/926–3865 (outside MA) | fax 413/775–7221 | www.deerfieldinn.com | 23 rooms | $255 | AE, DC, MC, V.

Deerfield's Yellow Gabled House. This yellow house with white trim and black shutters was built on the site of the Bloody Brook Massacre, where settlers and militiamen were killed by Native Americans in 1675. Guest rooms are individually decorated with period pieces and antiques. There's also a garden with seating for guests and a library with books about Historic Deerfield. Ten minutes from Historic Deerfield and three minutes from the Yankee Candle. Complimentary breakfast. Cable TV in some rooms. Library. No kids under 12. No smoking. | 111 N. Main St. | 413/665–4922 | 3 rooms (2 with shared bath), 1 suite | $110–$140 | No credit cards.

Motel 6. This economical motel, just off I–91, is 4 mi south of Deerfield, 5 mi from Deerfield Academy, and 10 mi from Amherst. Kids stay free, pets are allowed, there's free morning coffee, and no charge for local calls or HBO. Indoor pool. Laundry facilities. Some pets allowed. | 8 Greenfield Rd., South Deerfield | 413/665–7161 or 800/466–8356 | fax 413/665–7437 | www.motel6.com | 123 rooms | $54 | AE, MC, V.

DENNIS (CAPE COD)

MAP 6, K6

(Nearby towns also listed: Brewster, Harwich, Yarmouth)

Dennis straddles the center of Cape Cod. It's roughly equidistant from either end and stretches across the full width of the Cape, between the bay to the north and Nantucket Sound to the south. Dennis occupies a demographic center ground, too, balanced between white-collar affluence and a blue-collar work force. It resembles the rest of its Cape Cod neighbors in its heavy economic reliance on tourism, and in the fact that well over a fourth of its year-round population is retired. Route 134, the town's commercial strip laden with shopping plazas and traffic, contrasts sharply with the seaside sections of town, where historic 19th-century homes preside.

Information: Dennis Chamber of Commerce | Box 275, South Dennis, 02660 | 508/398–3568 or 800/243–9920. **Information Center** | 242 Swan River Rd., West Dennis | 508/398–3568 or 800/243–9920 | www.dennischamber.com.

Attractions
Cape Museum of Fine Arts. The significant role that Cape Cod and the surrounding Islands have played in American art is evident in this museum's collection, which has works that date from 1899 to the present. Some of the artists in the museum's collection are Charles Hawthorne, Oliver Chafee, Jan Selman, Hans Hofmann, and Red Grooms. In addition to its exhibitions, the museum also has lectures, tours, films, art discovery trips, and other programs. It is on the grounds of the Cape Playhouse Center for the Arts. | 820 Rte. 6A | 508/385–4477 | www.cmfa.org | $5 | Mid-May–mid-Oct., Mon.–Sat. 10–5, Sun. 1–5; mid-Oct.–mid-May, Tues.–Sat. 10–5, Sun. 1–5.

Jericho Historical Center. The 1801 Jericho House is a fine example of a "full Cape," a simple, symmetrical, residential design that originated on Cape Cod in Colonial times and has since spread across the country. Period furnishings are displayed inside. In the barn are exhibits related to local trades from cranberry growing to ice cutting, plus the charming Driftwood Zoo. | Old Main St., West Dennis | 508/398–6736 | Free | Late Jun.–Aug., Wed. 2–4, Fri. 10–noon; 1st 3 Sun. in Sept. 2–4.

Josiah Dennis Manse. This is the 1736 home of the town's namesake, a favorite local minister. The saltbox-style house features an exhibit on shipbuilding, which was briefly a local industry. A one-room 1770 schoolhouse shares the grounds. | 77 Nobscusset Rd. | 508/385–3528 | Free | Late Jun.–Sept., Tues. 10–noon, Thurs. 2–4; 1st 3 Sat. in Sept. 2–4.

ON THE CALENDAR
JUNE–SEPT.: *Cape Playhouse.* America's oldest professional summer theater has brought a variety of plays, comedies, mysteries, and musicals to Cape Cod for more than 70 years. Evening performances are Monday through Saturday at 8 PM; matinees Wednesday and Thursday at 2 PM; children's theater Friday mornings in July and August only. | 508/385–3911 or 877–385–3911.
AUG.: *Festival Days.* This five-day festival begins on a Saturday with a fireworks display. Other featured events are an arts and crafts show, an antique auto motorcade, sand-castle sculpting and kite flying contests, canoe races, and cruises on the Bass River. | 508/398–3568 or 800/243–9920.
DEC. *Visions of Christmas—"A Stroll Through the Villages of Dennis."* This annual event includes bed & breakfast open houses, tree lightings, Santa sightings, and more. | 508/398–3568.

Dining
Christine's. Eclectic. Comfortable and modern, with standard red-sauce Italian favorites complemented by a number of traditional Lebanese dishes. A 300-seat nightclub is attached. Try pasta with homemade sausage, and the Lebanese combination platter. Entertainment. Kids' menu. Early bird suppers. Sun. brunch. | 581 Main St., West Dennis | 508/394–7333 | No lunch | $9–$22 | AE, D, DC, MC, V.

The Devon Tea Room. Café. In addition to the many teas and delicious scones served here, you'll also find a full lunch with such hearty dishes as shepherd's pie and Irish stew with brown bread. Sandwiches, soups, salads, and a quiche of the day round out the offerings. The tables are set with bone china, linen, and dried flower arrangements, and there's jazz music playing in the background. | 294 Main St., West Dennis | 508/394–6068 or 800/394–0670 | Closed mid.-Dec.–Mar. | $3–$10 | AE, MC, V.

Ebb Tide Restaurant. Seafood. There are six cozy Colonial-style dining rooms at this oceanside restaurant. The emphasis is on fresh seafood (and lots of it), but steak lovers will find plenty to love, too. The McCormick family opened this restaurant in 1959 in a small captain's cottage, where they run it today. All the recipes here originated with the family. | 94 Chase Ave., Dennisport | 508/398–8733 | No lunch | $6–$16 | AE, MC, V.

★ **Gina's by the Sea.** Italian. This little hole in the dune may look unpromising from outside, but inside is another story: fine northern Italian meals are dished up in a cozy room and kept toasty warm in the chilly off-season by fireplaces. Known for seafood and pasta. Try the scampi à la Gina's or the chicken Gizmundo. | 134 Taunton Ave. | 508/385–3213 | Closed Dec.–Mar. No lunch | $9–$25 | AE, MC, V.

The Marshside. American. Casual, down-home eatery with a dependable diner-like menu available morning, noon, and night. Known for fried clams. Kids' menu. No smoking. | 28 Bridge St., East Dennis | 508/385–4010 | Breakfast also available | $11–$16 | AE, D, DC, MC, V.

Michael Patrick's Publick House. American. Owned and run by the MacDonald family, this restaurant is reminiscent of a real Irish pub with its genuinely friendly staff and absolute lack of pretension. There are cushioned booths in the wood-paneled dining room as well as a lounge with large screen TVs for watching sports. A good bet is the all-you-can-eat Sunday brunch. Other signature dishes are the fish-and-chips and the Paddy O'Burger with bacon, cheese, mushrooms, and onions. There's live entertainment, with both jazz and Irish singalongs. | 435 Main St., Dennisport | 508/398–1620 | $5–$12 | AE, MC, V.

Red Pheasant Inn. Contemporary. An antiques-filled country inn from the late 18th-century that offers robust, creative, and elaborately prepared American-French cuisine drawing on the finest local ingredients wherever possible. Known for salmon and rack of lamb. Try the baked stuffed lobster or the roast duckling. No smoking. | 905 Main St. | 508/385–2133 | Closed Mar. No lunch | $17–$29 | D, MC, V.

Royal Palace. Chinese. Comfortable alternative to the ubiquity of fried seafood and Continental cuisine. The only potential drawback is the lack of desserts. | 369 Main St., West Dennis | 508/398–6145 | No lunch | $7–$20 | AE, D, MC, V.

Scargo Café. Contemporary. Pleasant and informal, with a hint of neo-Colonial decor and a menu that has a little bit of everything, including pasta, steak, seafood, salads, and light fare. The kitchen stays open late enough to serve summer's after-theater crowd. Try ultimate surf-and-turf. In the heart of Dennis Village. Kids' menu. Early bird suppers Sept.–June. No smoking. | 799 Main St. | 508/385–8200 | $12–$18 | AE, D, MC, V.

Sundae School. Café. There are three Sundae Schools (the others in Harwich Port and East Orleans), and all have developed loyal followings because of the homemade ice cream and tasty concoctions like frappes and banana splits (topped with a bing cherry in season). Try the Bass River Mud ice cream (coffee ice cream with roasted almonds, chocolate chunks, and a fudge stripe)—a local favorite. There are benches set up outside where you can sit with your cone and watch the world go by. | 381 Lower County Rd., Dennisport | 508/394–9122 | $2–$6 | AE, MC, V.

Swan River Restaurant. Seafood. If the attached fish market doesn't give it away, the menu will: seafood is the story here, told in all its flavorful variations, from simple to creative, framed by views of the eponymous Swan River estuary and the ocean. Try the bouillabaisse, seafood Creole, and shrimp and littlenecks on linguine. Raw bar. Live music midweek evenings. Kids' menu. | 5 Lower County Rd., Dennisport | 508/394–4466 | Closed mid-Sept.–late May | $11–$20 | AE, D, MC, V.

Lodging

Breakers Motel. You'll find standard rooms at this two-story motel that has its own private beach on Nantucket Sound. It's within walking distance of restaurants and a 10-minute drive to downtown Dennis Village. Complimentary Continental breakfast. Some kitchenettes, some microwaves, refrigerators, cable TV. Pool. Beach. Pets allowed. | 61 Chase Ave., Dennisport | 508/398–6905 or 800/540–6905 (in MA) | fax 508/398–7360 | www.capecod-travel.com/breakers | 40 rooms, 3 suites | $100–$200, $210–$350 suites | Closed mid-Oct.–mid-Apr. | AE, MC, V.

"By the Sea" Guests. This property is near golf, tennis, and bike trails, and has a small stretch of private beach. The three-story building has conventional rooms plus suites, which can be rented weekly—the latter have balconies, views, fireplaces, and kitchenettes. Picnic area, complimentary Continental breakfast. No air-conditioning in some rooms, refrigerators, cable TV, no room phones. Beach. Business services. No smoking. | 57 Chase Ave., Dennisport | 508/398–8685 or 800/447–9202 | fax 508/398–0334 | bythesea@capecod.net | www.bytheseaguests.com | 12 rooms, 5 suites | $93–$150, $1,800–$2,500/wk suites | Closed Dec.–Apr. | AE, DC, MC, V.

Captain Nickerson Inn. The inn was built in 1828 as a Cape half-house, then later remodeled to its present Queen Anne Victorian style by Captain Nickerson in 1879. It's in a quiet, residential neighborhood and only 2 mi from West Dennis Beach, as well as also close to conservation land. The inn has stained-glass windows, parquet floors, antique fireplaces, and rocking chairs on the front porch. All of the guest rooms are on the second floor. About 5 ½ mi south of Dennis Village. Picnic area, complimentary breakfast. No room phones, cable TV and VCR in common area. Bicycles. No smoking. | 333 Main St., South Dennis | 508/398–5966 or 800/282–1619 | fax 508/398–5966 | www.bbonline.com/ma/captnick | 6 rooms (2 with shared bath, 4 with shower only), 1 suite | $87–$117, $150 suite | Closed Jan.–Feb. | D, MC, V.

Colonial Village. This seasonal property of motel units and cottages on 5 landscaped acres (with hundreds of rosebushes) has been family-owned and -operated for 40 years. It's 1½ blocks from beaches. No air-conditioning some rooms, some kitchenettes, cable TV. Indoor and outdoor pools. Hot tub, sauna. Beach. | 426 Lower County Rd., Dennisport | 508/398–2071 or 800/287–2071 | fax 508/398–2071 | www.sunsol.com/colonialvillage | 49 rooms, 10 4-room cottages | $105–$115, $775/wk cottages | Closed mid-Oct.–mid-May | D, MC, V.

Corsair and Cross Rip Ocean Front. The two hotels that make up this resort sit side by side on 3 acres and include a private beach. Geared towards families, you'll find children's programs in summer and golf, tennis, and fishing nearby. The on-site game room features air hockey, Ping-Pong, and table soccer, as well as a toddlers room. Picnic area, complimentary Continental breakfast (off-season). Some kitchenettes, cable TV. 3 pools (1 indoor). Hot tub. Beach. Children's programs (ages 5–14), playground. Laundry facilities. | 33–41 Chase Ave., Dennisport | 508/398–2279 or 800/201–1082 | www.corsaircrossrip.com | 47 rooms, 39 suites, 3 buildings | $165–$235, $195–$255 suites | Closed Nov.–Mar. | AE, MC, V.

Edgewater Beach Resort. This two-story, U-shape hotel has a beach, and many rooms have ocean views. Some kitchens, some microwaves, refrigerators, cable TV, some in-room VCRs and movies. Pool. Hot tub. Putting green. Gym. Beach. | 95 Chase Ave., Dennisport | 508/398–6922 | fax 508/760–3447 | $100–$210, $135–$200 suites | 86 rooms, 68 suites | Closed mid-Nov.–early Mar. | AE, D, MC, V.

The English Garden B & B. The guest rooms here are classically New England, but updated with polished plank floors, armoires, quilts, and French doors. Some have balconies and overlook the water. The colorful breakfast room has ocean views and is set up like a little café with tables for two. There's complimentary afternoon tea. Complimentary breakfast. No kids under 10. No pets. No smoking. | 32 Inman St., Dennisport | 508/398–2915 or 888/788–1908 | fax 508/398–2852 | www.theenlighgardenbandb.com | 8 rooms | $65–$129 | MC, V.

★ **Four Chimneys Inn.** This 1881 Victorian-era house, a former sea captain's home, is across the street from Scargo Lake. The property features extensive gardens and wooded areas, and rooms have high ceilings and antiques as well as reproductions; three have marble fireplaces. You're close to golf, tennis, and bike trails, and a 15-minute walk away from the beach and the Cape Cod Playhouse. Complimentary Continental breakfast. No air-conditioning in some rooms, no room phones, cable TV in common area. No kids under 8. No smoking. | 946 Main St. | 508/385–6317 or 800/874–5502 | fax 508/385–6285 | www.virtualcapecod.com/fourchimneys | 8 rooms | $90–$145 | Closed late Nov.–mid-Feb. | AE, MC, V.

The Garlands. A comfortable motel on the beach front where all the rooms have ocean views. The building is made up of eight wings, with rooms on two floors, and you'll find lots of light and bright colors. It's convenient to bike trails and several excellent restaurants, and is about five minutes north of Dennis Village. No air-conditioning, kitchenettes, cable TV. Beach. No kids under 5. | 117 Old Wharf Rd., Dennisport | 508/398–6987 | 20 rooms | $115–$143 | Closed mid-Oct.–mid-Apr. | No credit cards.

Gaslight Motel. This two-story motel is just across the street from the ocean. The guest rooms are simply but comfortably and prettily furnished. Morning coffee is complimentary and the price is one of the best you'll find on the Cape. Refrigerators. No pets. | 82 Chase Ave., Dennisport | 508/398–8831 or 877/398–8831 | www.gaslightmotel.com | Columbus Day–Memorial Day | 23 rooms | $60–$90 | MC, V.

Huntsman Motor Lodge. This unpretentious motel is in a quiet residential neighborhood. The swimming pool is very private, set back from the road in a pine hollow. The motel is close to the Cape Cod bike trail and beaches. Picnic area. Some kitchenettes, cable TV. Pool.

| 829 Main St., West Dennis | 508/394–5415 or 800/628–0498 | fax 508/398–7852 | 26 rooms | $79–$89 | MC, V.

★ **Isaiah Hall Bed and Breakfast Inn.** This B & B in an 1857 converted farmhouse is decorated with quilts and Oriental rugs and has an English country garden. It's on a quiet side street, a five-minute walk from the oldest summer playhouse in the United States and a 15-minute walk from the beach. Picnic area, complimentary Continental breakfast. Cable TV, in-room VCRs and movies. Library. No kids under 7. No smoking. | 152 Whig St. | 508/385–9928 or 800/736–0160 | fax 508/385–5879 | www.isaiahhallinn.com | 10 rooms, 1 suite | $96–$134, $163 suites | Closed mid-Oct.–mid-Apr. | AE, MC, V.

Joy House. This B&B is in a charming white clapboard house surrounded by a picket fence and a lovely landscaped garden with brick walkways. Pastel-colored guest rooms are subtly elegant, yet cozy, with colorful quilts. Two have fireplaces and one has its own sitting room. Complimentary breakfast. TV in common area. | 181 Depot St., Dennisport | 877/569–4687 | www.joyhousecapecod.com | 3 rooms | $90–$150 | MC, V.

Lighthouse Inn. This inn is a real lighthouse on a large, private 9-acre beach. The 1850 keeper's house has been owned and operated by the Stone family for 62 years. Lodging is available in the inn, motel, cottages, and the lightkeeper's house. Cottages have fireplaces. Restaurant, bar with entertainment, complimentary breakfast, room service. No air-conditioning in some rooms, in-room data ports, in-room safes, refrigerators, cable TV. Pool. Miniature golf, tennis. Beach. Children's programs (ages 3–10), playground. Business services. | 1 Lighthouse Inn Rd., West Dennis | 508/398–2244 | fax 508/398–5658 | www.lighthouseinn.com | $98–$150 | 65 rooms | Closed mid-Oct.–mid-May | MAP | MC, V.

Olde Wistaria House. A shingled Cape house built circa 1775 for Captain Atherton Bake is home to this B&B. It is on an acre of what is still known among the older townspeople as Christian Hill, overlooking the Bass River. Rooms are furnished with antiques, and there's floral-patterned fabric throughout. Afternoon refreshments are served in the parlor, or in nice weather, on the porch with antique wicker furniture. Complimentary breakfast. No kids under 12. No pets. | 44 Cove Rd., West Dennis | 508/398–3189 or 800/563–1551 | fax 508/398–3189 | www.oldewistariahouse.com | 3 rooms | $105–$125 | MC, V.

The Rose Petal Bed & Breakfast. This yellow clapboard farmhouse was built in 1872 for Almond Wixon, a member of a local seafaring family who was lost at sea in 1918. The guest rooms have antiques, brass beds, and quilts that are in keeping with the time period. There is a cozy parlor where you can watch TV, play the piano, or curl up with a good book from the house library. A guest refrigerator is stocked with complimentary beverages. Complimentary breakfast. No smoking. | 152 Sea St., Dennisport | 508/398–8470 | www.rosepetalof-dennis.com | 3 rooms | $72–$109 | MC, V.

Sea Lord Resort Motel. Across from Chase Avenue Beach, the three-story motel has many rooms with porches overlooking Nantucket Sound and the ocean, or with views of the pool. About 1–2 mi from Dennis Village. Children under 12 stay free. Some kitchenettes, some refrigerators, cable TV, no room phones. Pool. | 56 Chase Ave., Dennisport | 508/398–6900 | fax 508/760–1901 | www.sunsol.com/sealord | $95–$129 | 28 rooms | Closed mid-Oct.–mid-Apr. | D, MC, V.

Sea Shell Motel. Some of the rooms in this downtown Dennisport motel overlook its private beach. During the summer, breakfast is served on the deck. Close to several antiques shops. Complimentary Continental breakfast (seasonal). No air-conditioning in some rooms, some kitchenettes, some microwaves, refrigerators, cable TV. Beach. | 45 Chase Ave., Dennisport | 508/398–8965 or 800/698–8965 | fax 508/394–1237 | ssmotel@flashnet.net | 17 rooms, 1 suite | $85–$140, $220 2–bedroom suites | AE, D, DC, MC, V.

Soundings Seaside Resort. This resort is in a residential area and has well-kept lawns and a 365-ft private beach. Most rooms have views. The indoor pool has a hot tub in its center, and there's another pool right on the beach. Snack bar. In-room data ports, some kitchenettes, refrigerators, cable TV. Indoor and outdoor pools. Hot tub, sauna. Putting green.

Beach. Business services. | 79 Chase Ave., Dennisport | 508/394–6561 | fax 508/394–7537 | www.thesoundings.com | 102 rooms | $135–$295 | Closed mid-Oct.–mid-Apr. | MC, V.

Three Seasons Motor Lodge. This small, two-story motel on Nantucket Sound boasts ocean or pool views from every room. The room are cheerfully and comfortably furnished with wall-to-wall carpet and floral bedspreads. Many have private balconies or patios with picture windows. Restaurant. Refrigerators. Outdoor pool. Beach. | 421 Old Wharf Rd., Dennisport | 508/398–6091 | www.threeseasonsmotel.com | 61 rooms | $70–$175 | MC, V.

West Dennis Beach Motor Lodge. This two-story motel in a quiet village is close to golf and 1 mi from the beach and bike trails. The pool has an adjoining patio, and is nestled in a wooded area. Cable TV. Pool. | 691 Main St., West Dennis | 508/394–7434 | fax 508/394–1672 | www.sunsol.com/denniswest | 22 rooms | $65–$85 | AE, D, MC, V.

DUXBURY

MAP 6, J5

(Nearby town also listed: Plymouth)

Duxbury was originally settled by Pilgrims extending beyond the confines of their original plantation in neighboring Plymouth. Myles Standish, the Pilgrim's military commander, was among those early settlers, which is why the town features a towering monument in his honor. Shipbuilding became Duxbury's leading industry in the 18th century, but a too-shallow harbor forced local shipwrights to move elsewhere when demand grew for larger vessels. Until suburban flight struck Boston after World War II, the town remained predominantly rural, with a small historic village center on its waterfront. Now Duxbury, only 33 mi south of Boston, has become a bedroom community for Boston-bound commuters, albeit one of the most affluent, filled with fine historic homes and carefully wrought modern imitations.

Information: Destination Plymouth | 170 Water St., Ste. 10C, Plymouth, 02360–4056 | 508/747–7533 or 800/872–1620. **Plymouth Information Center** | 130 Water St., Plymouth, 02360 | 508/747–7525 | bak57@aol.com | www.visit-plymouth.com.

Attractions

Art Complex Museum. This intimate museum grew out of the private collection of Carl Weyerhaeuser, whose passion for prints, American paintings, Asian art, and Shaker furniture continues to be reflected in the permanent collection. The museum also exhibits works by contemporary regional artists. Befitting Weyerhaeuser's family ties to the lumber business, the building is itself an abstract artwork utilizing as much wood as possible, set in a beautifully forested dell. There are public tea services in summer at 2 and concerts on Sunday afternoons year-round. | 189 Alden St. | 781/934–6634 | fax 781/934–5117 | Free | Wed.–Sun. 1–4.

John Alden House. This 1653 building was the last home of the Mayflower Pilgrims, John and Priscilla Alden. It is managed by the Alden Kindred of America, Inc., an organization of descendents of John and Priscilla Alden. | 105 Alden St. 02331 | 781/934–9092 | www.alden.org | $2.50 | Mid-May–mid-Oct., Mon.–Sat. 10–5 and Sun. noon–5.

King Caesar House. This Federal mansion was built in 1808 for Ezra Weston II and his wife, Jerusha Bradford Weston. Mr. Weston was known as King Caesar for his worldwide pre-eminence in shipbuilding. | King Caesar Rd. | 781/934–6106 | $4.

Major John Bradford House. This 1674 shingled house was once the home of Major John Bradford, grandson of Mayflower Pilgrim William Bradford. John Bradford donated land for the building of the First Church, which led to Kingston's separation from Plymouth. The house—half 17th-century original and half 18th-century addition—contains period

DUXBURY

INTRO
ATTRACTIONS
DINING
LODGING

furnishings. Come for Sunday brunch and then tour the house and 17th-century period gardens. | Maple St. and Landing Rd., Kingston | 781/585–6300 | Donation requested for tours; brunch $8 | July–Aug., Sun. 9–noon.

ON THE CALENDAR

DEC.: *Christmas at the King Caesar House.* Local decorators transform the stately rooms of the King Caesar House into scenes of holiday activities with the types of decorations used in the first half of the 19th century. There's also an antiques gallery with items for sale from South Shore antique dealers. | 781/934–6106.

Dining

Sun Tavern. Contemporary. This 1741 former farmhouse contains wide-plank floors, original beams, a working wood-burning fireplace, a main dining room, and several smaller rooms. One of the tavern's specialties is the black diamond steak marinated for several days in honey, soy, ginger, garlic, and a touch of brown sugar and tomato juice. | 500 Congress St., | 781/837–4100 | fax 781/837–1212 | No lunch | $12–$23 | AE, D, MC, V.

Winsor House Restaurant. Contemporary. At this former sea captain's house, everything is made in the kitchen—including the bread, spring rolls, and desserts. Try the crab cakes, rack of lamb, Thai duck, or one of the many varieties of fresh fish. | 390 Washington St. | 781/934–0991 | No lunch | $16–$26 | AE, D, MC, V.

Lodging

Winsor House. This 1803 sea captain's home has an English-style pub, lounge, and restaurant. The spacious guest rooms are furnished with a mixture of antiques and period reproductions. One room has a queen-size canopy bed, another has two single-canopy beds. Paintings by local artists and photographs of Duxbury scenes adorn the walls. Restaurant, 2 bars. No air-conditioning in some rooms, no TV. No pets. No smoking. | 390 Washington St. | 781/934–0991 | fax 781/934–5955 | 4 rooms | $137–$221 | AE, D, MC, V.

EASTHAM (CAPE COD)

MAP 6, L6

(Nearby towns also listed: Orleans, Wellfleet)

Eastham was founded by Pilgrims sent to look for a new place to move their Colonial government, then seated at Plymouth. The shift in capitals never came about, but the location scouts so liked what they found on the outer shores of Cape Cod that they settled there themselves. From its infancy the town's agriculture overshadowed its maritime ventures, in part because the town lacked an adequate harbor. Now Eastham is the gateway to the Cape Cod National Seashore, whose main visitors center stands beside U.S. 6 in the center of town. Eastham's fields of grain long since gave way to housing, but the National Seashore ensures large oceanfront tracts will remain undeveloped. In addition to popular beaches fronting both the Cape Cod Bay and the Atlantic Ocean, Eastham contains the ecologically important Nauset Marsh, whose mix of navigable waters, salt-grass islands, and barrier beaches is favored by bird-watchers, kayakers, and surfcasters.

Information: Eastham Chamber of Commerce | Box 1329, Eastham, 02642 | 508/240–7211. **Eastham Visitor Information** | U.S. 6 | www.easthamchamber.com.

Attractions

Eastham Windmill. Of the half-dozen remaining windmills on Cape Cod, this one is the oldest. It was built in 1680 in Plymouth and subsequently moved here in 1793. | U.S. 6 | Late June–early Sept., Mon.–Sat. 10–5, Sun. 1–5.

Schoolhouse Museum. Owned by the Eastham Historical Society, this 1869 one-room structure holds school memorabilia and personal effects of townsfolk from generations past. | Nauset Rd. off U.S. 6 | 508/255–0788 | Free | July–Aug., weekdays 1–4; Sept., Sat. 1–4.

Swift-Daley House. This 1741 full Cape house offers a glimpse back into Colonial life with its antique textiles and period furnishings. The grounds also include a tool museum filled with implements from Eastham's past as a center for salt production and agriculture. | U.S. 6 | 508/255–0788 | July–Aug., weekdays 1–4; Sept., Sat. 1–4.

Three Sisters Lights. The history of these three Gothic Revival lighthouses dates back to 1837. Once known as the Three Sisters of Nauset, they guided mariners safely along the coastline. Over the past century and half, they have been separated and moved inland (and back out) and even sold off, but in 1990, the National Parks Service reunited (and renovated) them once and for all. The grounds are open to the public and tours of the lighthouses are given. | Nauset Light Beach Parking Lot, Ocean View Dr. | 508/240–2612 or 508/255–3421 (for tours) | Free | Year-round.

ON THE CALENDAR
SEPT.: *Windmill Weekend.* Events include a sand-art competition, road race, band concerts, an arts and crafts show, a tricycle race, and a square dance. The annual Antique & Classic Car Show is also held over the weekend. Excitement peaks with Sunday's parade | 508/240–7211.

Dining
Black Skillet Café. American/Casual. This place serves one meal—breakfast—but it's worth getting up early for. The pancakes (raspberry, blueberry, and apple-cinnammon) are cooked to order and have earned a loyal following, as has the raisin bread French toast. Arrive before noon to get your order in before closing. | 5960 Rte. 6A | 508/240–3525 | Breakfast also available. No lunch or dinner. Closed Columbus Day–May | $4–$9 | AE, MC, V.

Box Lunch. Fast food. The most popular item here is the rollwich, a combination of your choosing of meats, cheeses, salads, and spreads (and numerous choices for each) on pita bread, which is then rolled up to make for easy eating on the road. You can call your order in ahead of time. Other Box Lunches are in Brewster, Wellfleet, and Provincetown. | Seatoller Shops, U.S. 6 | 508/255–0799 | $4–$9 | AE, MC, V.

Eastham Lobster Pool. Seafood. You can get steaks and burgers here, but the main thing is, of course, lobster, and you can get it cooked any way you can dream of: fried, grilled, baked, or poached are among the most popular alternatives to boiled. In nice weather you can eat outside or else inside at communal wooden tables. | 4380 U.S. 6 | 508/255–9706 | Late Oct.–Apr. | $5–$15 | AE, MC, V.

Eastham Superette. Delicatessen. If it's a nice day, you can hit the deli counter here and order one of the signature overstuffed subs and head across the road to Windmill Green for a picnic. There's also fresh fruit, vegetables, and all the staples stocked by small grocery store. | U.S. 6, across from Windmill Green | 508/255–0530 | $4–$10 | AE, MC, V.

The Fairway Restaurant & Pizzeria. American/casual. This family-owned and -run restaurant 1½ mi north of Eastham is in a single-story, shingled building right on the main drag. Favorite dishes include the barbecue chicken pizza and the orange tequila shrimp and scallops. There are also lots of sandwiches, soups, and burgers. Kids' menu. | 1495 Rte. 6A | 508/255–3893 | $5–$15 | AE, MC, V.

Hole in One Donut Shop. Café. This is a great place to grab a cup of coffee and one of their hand-cut doughnuts or fresh muffins or bagels. You can sit at the counter on a swivel stool under stained-glass hanging lamps and while away the morning with the paper. | 1495 Rte. 6A, North Eastham | 508/255–9446 | $1–$6 | AE, MC, V.

Mitchel's Bistro. Contemporary. While you can get breakfast and lunch here, loyal diners especially praise the dinners. The tables are set with linen and candlelight and local produce is used. Two menu favorites are the grilled salmon with fresh orange and chili-butter sauce and the curried crab cakes. For a finishing culinary touch, there is a special cheesecake prepared every night. | Main St. Mercantile, U.S. 6 | 508/255–4803 | Breakfast also available | $6–$18 | AE, MC, V.

Lodging

Blue Dolphin Inn. This inn is centered on a narrow peninsula, 1 mi from ocean and bay beaches. Each room has a patio facing the woods of this 7-acre property. Two- and three-night whale-watching packages are available. Restaurant, picnic area. Refrigerators, cable TV. Pool. | 5950 U.S. 6, Box 1888, North Eastham | 508/255–1159 or 800/654–0504 | fax 508/240–3676 | www.capecod.net/bluedolphin.com | 49 rooms | $99–$109 | Closed Nov.–Mar. | AE, MC, V.

Captain's Quarters Motel and Conference Center. This motel has been family-owned and -operated for 15 years. The motel units are set far back from the road. The 6 acres of manicured grounds contain perennial and rock gardens, oak and pine trees. The property is next to the Cape Cod Bike Trail and 1 mi from Nauset Light Beach. Picnic area, complimentary Continental breakfast. Refrigerators, cable TV. Pool. Tennis. Bicycles. Business services. Beach shuttle (seasonal). | U.S. 6, North Eastham | 508/255–5686 or 800/327–7769 | fax 508/240–0280 | www.captains-quarters.com | 75 rooms | $99–$140 | Closed Dec.–Mar. | AE, D, DC, MC, V.

Cranberry Cottages. These Cape Cod cottages are in a shady grove close to National Seashore beaches and bicycle and nature trails. The property has been owned and operated by the Grant family for 40 years. It is beautifully landscaped, and there is also a blueberry patch where guests can pick their own in season. No air-conditioning in some rooms, some kitchenettes, refrigerators, cable TV. | 785 State Hwy. | 508/255–0602 or 800/292–6631 | www.sunsol.com/cranberrycottages | 14 cottages | $85–$90 1–bedroom cottages, $675–$775/wk 2–bedroom cottages | D, MC, V.

Eagle Wing Motel. A quiet motel with landscaped grounds and private decks that overlook protected wetlands. The owners describe it as having the size of a motel, with the amenities of a guest house. Rooms are very clean, and most have king-size beds. For adults and couples only. Refrigerators, cable TV. Pool. No smoking. | 960 State Hwy. | 508/240–5656 or 800/278–5656 | fax 508/240–5657 | www.eaglewingmotel.com | 19 rooms | $89–119 | Closed Oct.–May | D, MC, V.

Eastham Ocean View Motel. This family-oriented motel with a very distant ocean view is next to town hall, and also close to a windmill. Refrigerators, cable TV. Pool. | 2470 U.S. 6 | 508/255–1600 or 800/742–4133 | fax 508/240–7104 | 31 rooms | $85–$129 | Closed late Oct.–mid-Mar. | AE, D, DC, MC, V.

Eastham Windmill Bed & Breakfast. A front-end gabled inn built in 1898 for Chester Horton, a well-known Eastham resident. It was remodeled in 1999 and is on the National Registry of Historic Places. The Windmill View Room overlooks Windmill Park (the inn is across from the Eastham Windmill) and has its own sitting room. The Horton Room in the rear and has a smaller sitting room and a view of the grape arbor and the garden. Bus service is within walking distance. Complimentary Continental breakfast. No pets. No kids under 14. No smoking. | 55 Samoset Rd. | 508/240–1882 | fax 508/240–3111 | www.windmill-gallery.com | 2 rooms | $95–$125 | AE, MC, V.

Four Points Sheraton–National Seashore. This hotel is at the gateway to National Seashore Park beaches and salt marshes. An Audubon Society wildlife sanctuary and walking trails are nearby. Restaurant, bar with entertainment, complimentary Continental breakfast (in season), room service. In-room data ports, some refrigerators, cable TV. Indoor and outdoor pools. Hot tub. Tennis. Gym. Business services. Laundry service. | U.S. 6 | 508/255–5000 | fax 508/240–1870 | www.fourpoints-eastham.com | 107 rooms | $199–$219 | AE, D, DC, MC, V.

Midway Motel and Cottages. This motel is in a parklike setting with 3 landscaped acres in a pine and oak grove next to bicycle trails. Cottages have cathedral ceilings and one has a fireplace. You'll find picnic tables and grills, as well as shuffleboard, badminton, horse-shoes, and volleyball. Picnic area. Microwaves, refrigerators, cable TV, phone in common room. Bicycles. Playground. | 5460 U.S. 6, North Eastham | 508/255–3117 or 800/755–3117 | fax 508/255–4235 | www.midwaymotel.com | 11 motel rooms and cottages | $90–$146, $775–$875/wk cottages | AE, D, DC, MC, V.

Natasha's Dacha. This B&B is in woods filled with birds and between the National Seashore and First Encounter Beach on Cape Cod Bay. The Dacha is around the corner from Great Pond and down the road from a bicycle rental shop and the Cape Cod Rail Trail. Rooms are cheerful and homey with all the basic comforts. It is 3 mi to the Wellfleet Audubon Bird Sanctuary and 4 mi to Orleans for shopping and restaurants. Complimentary breakfast. | 585 Locust Rd. | 508/240–7826 | www.capecod.net/natashasdacha | 2 rooms | $65–$85 | No credit cards.

Over Look Inn. A carefully restored Victorian inn with brass beds, clawfoot tubs, and pedestal sinks. The innkeepers are Scottish and serve a full breakfast with specialties from their native country. During afternoon tea, which is served on the wraparound porch, the innkeeper dresses in full piper regalia and plays a tune for his guests. The inn also has a unique library of Winston Churchill photos, books, and prints and an Ernest Heming-way billiards room. Picnic area, complimentary breakfast. No room phones. Billiards. Library. No smoking. | 3085 County Rd. | 508/255–1886 | fax 508/240–0345 | stay@over-lookinn.com | www.overlookinn.com | 10 rooms | $135–$175 | AE, D, DC, MC, V.

Penny House Inn. This former sea captain's home is one of the oldest buildings in East-ham (1700). A friendly ghost—perhaps onetime owner Isaiah Horton, IV—is seen occasionally. Bike trails and a bird sanctuary are nearby. Complimentary breakfast. Some refrigerators, cable TV in some rooms, VCR in common area. Business services. No kids under 8. No smoking. | 4885 County Rd. | 508/255–6632 or 800/554–1751 | fax 508/255–4893 | www.pen-nyhouseinn.com | 11 rooms | $120–$205 | AE, D, MC, V.

Town Crier Motel. This motel on U.S. 6 offers direct access to the Cape Cod Rail Trail as well as the national seashore. Breakfast is served in the restaurant by the pool. The game room features a pool table, video games, and a pinball machine. Rooms are clean and spacious. Restaurant (breakfast only). Refrigerators, cable TV. Pool (indoor). | U.S. 6 | 508/255–4000 or 800/932–1434 | fax 508/255–7491 | www.towncriermotel.com | 36 rooms | $69–$109 | AE, D, DC, MC, V.

Viking Shores Motor Lodge. Surrounded by 7 acres of landscaped grounds, this one-story motel is also close to the national seashore on right on the Cape Cod Rail Trail. Picnic area, complimentary Continental breakfast. Refrigerators, cable TV. Pool. Tennis. Bicycles. | 5200 U.S. 6, North Eastham | 508/255–3200 or 800/242–2131 | fax 508/240–0205 | www.vsp.cape.com/~viking | 40 rooms | $95–$110 | Closed end of Oct.–Apr. | AE, MC, V.

The Whalewalk Inn. An 1830s Federal inn on 3 acres of lawns, meadows, and gardens. The rooms, which are divided among five buildings, are airy and elegant with antique and repro-duction furniture like four-poster beds and subtle color schemes. It is just 10 minutes from Cape Cod National Seashore and even closer, behind the inn, is the Cape Cod Rail Trail. After-noon hors d'oeuvres are served on the patio. Complimentary breakfast. Some refregiera-tors, no TV in some rooms, some in-room VCRs. Bicycles. No kids under 12. | 220 Bridge Rd. | 508/255–0617 | fax 508/240–0017 | www.whalewalkinn.com | 16 rooms | $135–$275 | MC, V.

Wheel In Cottages. These cottage are on 3 wooded acres and share a border with the National Seashore Park. There are flowering shrubs and well kept planters of sedum. A narrow path through the woods, just a stroll away, leads to a bike trail and beaches. All the cottages are completely furnished, have fully stocked kitchens, and are equipped with blankets and pillows as well. One cottage has a sun porch and the other two have spacious decks. Each house has a picnic table, outdoor chairs, and a grill. Kitchenettes, microwaves, in-room VCRs. No pets. | Box 114, North Eastham (off Rte. 6) | 508/255–2588 | www.wheelincottages.com | 3 cottages | $500–$900 per week | No credit cards.

EDGARTOWN (MARTHA'S VINEYARD)

(Nearby towns also listed: Oak Bluffs, Vineyard Haven, West Tisbury)

Edgartown is the site of the first European settlement on Martha's Vineyard, in 1642. Its physical appearance bears the strong imprint of its history as a whaling center throughout the first half of the 19th century, with lovingly restored Greek Revival captain's and merchant's mansions lining narrow downtown streets. The abundance of white-columned facades imparts a classical note that's echoed in the town's character, which tends to be more conservative than its island neighbors. So if you wish to don a jacket for dinner, Edgartown is the place to do so. Edgartown's beaches are almost uniformly superlative and enormously popular with families, surfcasters, parading teens, windsurfers, and everyone else. But the town's traditional passion has always been sailing—so much so that Edgartown Harbor is world famous in yachting circles simply because of the local mindset, although it doesn't hurt that the boat anchorage enjoys a panoramic view of one of the prettiest port towns in the world.

Information: **Martha's Vineyard Chamber of Commerce** | Box 1698, Vineyard Haven, 02568 | 508/693-0085 | fax 508/693-7589. **Edgartown Visitor Center** | Church St., Edgartown | no phone | mvcc@vineyard.net | www.mvy.com.

Attractions

Falmouth–Edgartown Ferry. The twin-deck *Pied Piper* provides seasonal ferry service between Edgartown and Falmouth, on Cape Cod, an hour away. Four to six daily departures are available through the summer, and advance reservations are encouraged. | Memorial Wharf, Dock St., Edgartown Harbor | 508/548-9400 | $24 round-trip | Memorial Day–mid-June and Oct., weekends and Mon. holidays; mid-June–Sept., daily.

East Beach. This miles-long barrier beach is part of the Cape Poge Wildlife Refuge, one of two large Trustees of Reservations properties along the remote outer shore of Chappaquiddick, the rural, sparsely populated part of Edgartown a few minutes' ferry ride across the harbor. Backed by high dunes and faced with seemingly limitless ocean, East Beach is beautiful enough for it not to matter if heavy surf sometimes makes it better for sunbathing and beachcombing than for swimming. There are portable toilets at the beach entrance, but no food concessions. | End of Dike Rd., Chappaquiddick | 508/693-7662 | www.thetrustees.org | $3 June–Sept. Free but limited parking | Daily.

★ **Felix Neck Wildlife Sanctuary.** Owned by the Massachusetts Audubon Society, this refuge protects a mixed habitat of forest and meadows around the shores of a large saltwater pond. A bird blind beside a smaller freshwater pond permits viewing of the waterfowl that frequent the property. Two miles of walking trails, a small nature center, and gift shop are also on site. | Vineyard Haven Rd. | 508/627-4850 | www.massaudubon.org | $3 | June–Sept., daily 8–4; Oct.–May, Tues.–Sun. 8–4.

Historic area. The oldest town on Martha's Vineyard has plenty of stories to tell about its past. Some of the more prominent tales are self-evident in the buildings along its historic harborfront, where the stout classical architecture speaks volumes about the wealth that accrued to the town's leading citizens over the decades following the American Revolution. Adjacent streets exhibit a range of other architectural idioms that each had their vogue during some part of the town's history. | School, Summer, Winter, and Water Sts. | 508/627-6145 | Free | Daily.

Joseph Sylvia State Beach. This wide, gentle arc of a beach is a family favorite, with the warmest, calmest water of any beach on Martha's Vineyard and 2 mi of sand on which to

KODAK'S TIPS FOR PHOTOGRAPHING LANDSCAPES AND SCENERY

Landscape
- Tell a story
- Isolate the essence of a place
- Exploit mood, weather, and lighting

Panoramas
- Use panoramic cameras for sweeping vistas
- Don't restrict yourself to horizontal shots
- Keep the horizon level

Panorama Assemblage
- Use a wide-angle or normal lens
- Let edges of pictures overlap
- Keep exposure even
- Use a tripod

Placing the Horizon
- Use low horizon placement to accent sky or clouds
- Use high placement to emphasize distance and accent foreground elements
- Try eliminating the horizon

Mountain Scenery: Scale
- Include objects of known size
- Frame distant peaks with nearby objects
- Compress space with long lenses

Mountain Scenery: Lighting
- Shoot early or late; avoid midday
- Watch for dramatic color changes
- Use exposure compensation

Tropical Beaches
- Capture expansive views
- Don't let bright sand fool your meter
- Include people

Rocky Shorelines
- Vary shutter speeds to freeze or blur wave action
- Don't overlook sea life in tidal pools
- Protect your gear from sand and sea

In the Desert
- Look for shapes and textures
- Try visiting during peak bloom periods
- Don't forget safety

Canyons
- Research the natural and social history of a locale
- Focus on a theme or geologic feature
- Budget your shooting time

Rain Forests and the Tropics
- Go for mystique with close-ups and detail shots
- Battle low light with fast films and camera supports
- Protect cameras and film from moisture and humidity

Rivers and Waterfalls
- Use slow film and long shutter speeds to blur water
- When needed, use a neutral-density filter over the lens
- Shoot from water level to heighten drama

Autumn Colors
- Plan trips for peak foliage periods
- Mix wide and close views for visual variety
- Use lighting that accents colors or creates moods

Moonlit Landscapes
- Include the moon or use only its illumination
- Exaggerate the moon's relative size with long telephoto lenses
- Expose landscapes several seconds or longer

Close-Ups
- Look for interesting details
- Use macro lenses or close-up filters
- Minimize camera shake with fast films and high shutter speeds

Caves and Caverns
- Shoot with ISO 1000+ films
- Use existing light in tourist caves
- Paint with flash in wilderness caves

From *Kodak Guide to Shooting Great Travel Pictures* © 2000 by Fodor's Travel Publications

enjoy it. Although there is plenty of free parking and the beach is right on one of the island's bike paths, there are no rest rooms. | Beach Rd. | 508/627–6145 | Free | Daily.

South Beach. Miles of sand facing the Atlantic make this public beach—also known as Katama Beach—one of the most popular on Martha's Vineyard. Due to strong surf and occasional riptides, it isn't the best choice for small children, but bodysurfers and Boogie boarders will appreciate the ocean breakers. There are portable toilets, changing areas, and shuttle buses to town in season, but no food concessions. | Katama Rd. | 508/627–6145 | Free | Daily.

Vincent House. The oldest house on Martha's Vineyard was built in 1672. An example of the full Cape style, it contains many original elements, from woodwork to fixtures. The Martha's Vineyard Preservation Trust, its owner, also uses it for displays related to island life. | 96 Main St. | 508/627–8619 (house and tours) | fax 508/627–8088 | www.vineyard.net/org/mvpt | $3. Combined tour of Trust-owned properties $7 | May–June 14 and early Sept.–Oct. 15, daily noon–3; June 15–early Sept., daily 10–3.

Old Whaling Church. The grand Greek Revival facade on this 1842 Methodist church is perhaps the most distinctive architectural landmark on Martha's Vineyard. Its nine-story steeple is a landmark of the more traditional sort, used for reference by sailors in local waters. In addition to regular Sunday services, the church doubles as a performing arts center, since its 500-seat capacity makes it the largest auditorium on the island. | 89 Main St. | 508/627–8619 | www.vineyard.net/org/mvpt | Church services free; performance prices vary. Guided tour of Whaling Church and other Preservation Trust properties $7 | Services and performances year-round. Tours May–mid-Oct., daily 11–2, starting from the Vincent House.

Vineyard Museum. This museum's several buildings are filled with permanent and changing exhibits drawn from the collections of the Martha's Vineyard Historical Society, custodian of the island's memorabilia and lore. Artifacts and tools from the island's whaling days, antique costumes and furnishings, local fine arts and crafts, and, most arrestingly, the giant Fresnel lens from an island lighthouse are among the museum's holdings. A research library with a number of genealogical resources is also available. | 59 School St. | 508/627–4441 | fax 508/627–4436 | www.vineyard.net/org/mvhs | $6 | Mid-June–Columbus Day, Tues.–Sat. 10–5; Columbus Day–mid-June, Wed.–Fri. 1–4, Sat. 10–4.

★ **Wasque Reservation.** This conservation property of the Trustees of Reservations occupies the far southeast corner of Martha's Vineyard, where the Atlantic Ocean and Nantucket Sound wrestle one another with pounding waves and dangerous riptides. Excellent birdwatching and surfcasting are the reservation's most popular attractions, although strong swimmers and bodysurfers are also attracted to the south-facing Wasque Beach, about ½ mi west of hazardous Wasque Point. Drinking water and portable toilets are found at the parking lot. | Wasque Rd. | 508/693–7662 | www.thetrustees.org | $3 June–Sept. Parking an additional $3 per vehicle June–Sept. | Daily dawn–dusk.

ON THE CALENDAR

APR: *Osprey Festival.* Celebrate the return of the osprey from their winter in South America with a day of craft projects, an obstacle course, and pony rides the first weekend of the month at Felix Neck Wildlife Sanctuary. | 508/627–4850.

SEPT.–OCT.: *Striped Bass and Bluefish Derby.* This is one of the oldest fishing derbies in the country, currently in its 55th year. Men, women, children, and seniors compete for prizes with their catches of striped bass, bluefish, benito, and albacore. The fish is filleted daily and donated to senior-citizens programs on the island. Advance registration is required. | Box 2101 | 508/939–9341.

Dining

Coach House. Continental. This comfortable dining room in a large historic 1891 hotel overlooking Edgartown Lighthouse offers not only attractive views but a broad menu of fine dishes. Try sirloin with capers, fresh shellfish, the catch of the day, and lamb. Kids' menu.

Sun. brunch. No smoking. | Harbor View Hotel, 131 N. Water St. | 508/627–3761 | $24–$36 |
AE, DC, MC, V.

David Ryan's. Contemporary. You can eat in the upstairs restaurant with slick, blond-wood booths and tables or in the downstairs café with high glass tables, and bright, buffed, backed modern metal bar stools. The menu is the same—local seafood preparations ranging from fish-and-chips to salmon with cilantro-yogurt sauce, or filet mignon with mushrooms and a balsamic glaze. The café becomes a hot night-spot later in the evening. | 11 N. Water St. | 508/627–4100 | $14–$31 | MC, V.

La Cucina. Contemporary. You can sit in the light breakfast room with tile floor, on the stone patio with oak umbrellas, or in the dining room with its landscapes by a local artist in this restaurant in the Tuscany Inn. The menu changes often, based on availability of fresh ingredients, but you can expect inventive Italian preparations such as braised pork with figs, and frisée salad with warm bacon and gorgonzola vinaigrette. | 22 N. Water St. | 508/627–8161 | Reservations essential | Closed Nov.–Apr. and Tues. | $29–$36 | AE, MC, V.

★ **L'Etoile.** French. Old-school English charm and decorative finery presage classic yet creative prix-fixe meals of unrestrained luxury, widely regarded as an unforgettable experience for those who don't blanch at the prices. Try the étuvé of native lobster and native seafood. Open-air dining on patio. No smoking. | Charlotte Inn, 27 S. Summer St. | 508/627–5187 | Reservations essential | Jacket requested | Closed Jan.–mid-Feb. No lunch | $62–$72 | AE, MC, V.

Newes from America. American. A triple-crown winner: good and hearty pastas, burgers, and seafood, all reasonably priced, and accompanied by an excellent lineup of draft microbrew beers. Try the onion soup and the big burger. Kids' menu. No smoking. | 23 Kelley St. | 508/627–4397 | $9–$20 | AE, DC, MC, V.

★ **Savoir Faire.** Contemporary. Small and intimate, with soft lighting and white linens lending a touch of elegance, and an upscale menu that makes food-lovers swoon. The menu features updated dishes with an Italian influence. For an appetizer, try the grilled sashimi tuna with asparagus puree; for dinner, the grilled breaded quail is a favorite. Open-air dining on the patio. Raw bar (outdoor). Beer and wine only. No smoking. | 14 Church St. | 508/627–9864 | Closed late Oct.–Apr. No lunch | $25–$32 | AE, MC, V.

Square Rigger. American. The restaurant is casual and the menu is basic with surf-and-turf favorites at a good price. Known for steak, lobster, and swordfish. Kids' menu. No smoking. | 225 Upper Main St. | 508/627–9968 | Closed Mon.–Wed. in Feb.–Mar. No lunch | $15–$30 | AE, MC, V.

Restaurant Atria. Contemporary. A trendy new restaurant with a martini bar and lounge downstairs. The menu changes daily. Try the crispy coconut soft-shell crab for an appetizer, and the jambalaya risotto with spiced prawns or the grilled 24-ounce T-bone and rib-eye with roasted garlic potatoes for the main course. Open-air dining in the rose garden. Raw bar (outdoor). No smoking in dining room. Sunday brunch. | 137 Upper Main St. | 508/627–5850 | Call for hrs. No lunch | $23–$40 | AE, MC, V.

Wharf Restaurant. American. Fine harbor views are the prime reason to consider dining in this relaxed local hangout, but affordability is a close second. Heavy on the seafood, especially local lobster. Popular entrées include the fisherman's platter, lobster ravioli, and filet mignon. Kids' menu. No smoking in dining room. | 3 Lower Main St. | 508/627–9966 | $13–$25 | AE, D, DC, MC, V.

Lodging

Arbor Inn. You'll find rocking chairs on the front porch and hand-painted murals decorating the breakfast room at this inn. Wisteria- and rose-covered arbors lead to the gardens where you can relax in a hammock. The back of the property abuts a bike path. The cottage has a kitchen, living room, and screened porch. Complimentary Continental breakfast. No TV in rooms, no room phones. No kids under 12. No smoking. | 222 Upper Main St.

EDGARTOWN
(MARTHA'S
VINEYARD)

INTRO
ATTRACTIONS
DINING
LODGING

| 508/627–8137 | www.mvy.com/arborinn | 10 rooms (2 with shared bath); 1 cottage | $135–$185, $1,000/wk cottages | Closed end of Oct.–Apr. | MC, V.

Ashley Inn. Formerly a sea captain's home built in the 1800s, this inn is right in downtown Edgartown. The rooms have antique furnishings and there are hammocks and apple trees in the backyard. Suites in the carriage house have hot tubs, fireplaces, and a full kitchen. Most rooms have canopy or four-poster beds. Picnic area, complimentary Continental breakfast. Some refrigerators, some in-room hot tubs, cable TV. No kids over 10 only. No smoking. | 129 Main St. | 508/627–9655 or 800/477–9655 | fax 508/627–6629 | www.ashleyinnmv.com | 10 rooms, 2 suites in carriage house | $145–$275; $475 suites | MC, V.

Captain Dexter House. This traditional white-clapboard house was built in 1840 by a prominent merchant family. Guest rooms feature queen-size canopy beds and antique pieces. The house is on a quiet street, across from the cemetery where sea captains rest, 1½ blocks from the historic Whaling Church. Picnic area, complimentary Continental breakfast. No smoking, no room phones. | 35 Pease's Point Way, Edgartown, | 508/627–7289 | fax 508/627–3328 | www.mvy.com/captdexter | 11 rooms | $150–$300 | Closed Nov.–mid-Apr. | AE, MC, V.

Colonial Inn of Martha's Vineyard. This renovated inn has a viewing deck that overlooks the harbor in Edgartown's historic district. Every employee is concierge-trained to ensure a high level of customer service. It's two blocks from the bus station, and about five minutes from the nearest beach. Restaurant, complimentary Continental breakfast. In-room data ports, some refrigerators, cable TV. Beauty salon. Shops. Business services. | 38 N. Water St. | 508/627–4711 or 800/627–4701 | fax 508/627–5904 | www.colonialinnmvy.com | 43 rooms | $160–$300 | Closed Jan.–Feb. | AE, MC, V.

★ **Daggett House.** This historic inn on the waterfront has a secret door dating back to the 17th century, when the building was a tavern. Noteworthy interior features include an open hearth and antiques; exterior amenities include a garden and private pier. Restaurant. Cable TV. No smoking. | 59 N. Water St. | 508/627–4600 or 800/946–3400 | fax 508/627–4611 | www.mvweb.com/daggett | 31 rooms in 4 buildings, 10 suites | $170–$265, $265–$575 suites | AE, D, MC, V.

Edgartown Inn. An inn built in 1798 for Captain Thomas Worth, whose son was a hero in the Mexican–American War, and later had the town of Fort Worth, Texas, named for him. This pretty place has French country furnishings and antiques. Some rooms in the main house have harbor views and balconies. There are also accommodations in the garden house and a converted barn. The property is one block from the harbor and two blocks from Main Street. No air-conditioning, no room phones, TV in some rooms and common area. No kids under 8. | 56 N. Water St. | 508/627–4794 | fax 508/627–9420 | www.edgartowninn.com | 20 rooms (4 with shared bath) in 3 buildings | $95–$210, $240 suite | Closed Nov.–early Apr. | No credit cards.

Harbor View Hotel. This member of Historic Hotels of America is the largest full-service hotel with meeting and banquet facilities on Martha's Vineyard. The property features a verandah with rocking chairs that overlooks the harbor and is across the street from the beach, but there is no swimming. Restaurant, bar. In-room safes, some kitchenettes, refrigerators, cable TV. Pool. Tennis. Business services. | 131 N. Water St. | 508/627–7000 or 800/225–6005 | fax 508/627–8417 | www.harbor-view.com | 124 rooms, 10 suites in 3 buildings | $300–$460, $510–$725 suites | AE, DC, MC, V.

Hob Knob Inn. A 19th-century Gothic Revival home whose rooms have antiques and fresh flowers while a cow motif gives the impression of a cheerful country spot. Services offered include private fishing charters and bike rentals (fees charged) and complimentary port wine served in the garden room. The inn is four blocks from the harbor and two blocks from the town center. Complimentary breakfast, dining room. No air-conditioning in some rooms, in-room data ports, cable TV. Massage, sauna. Gym. Fishing. Bicycles. Business services. No kids under 12. No smoking. | 128 Main St. | 508/627–9510 or 800/696–2723 | fax 508/627–4560 | www.hobknob.com | 20 rooms (2 with shared bath), 5 suites, 2 buildings | $200–$295; $375–$500 suites | AE, MC, V.

The Inn at 148 Main St. Built in the 1840s by a prominent whaling captain, this cross-gabled inn is a downtown landmark. The guest rooms, some of which have fireplaces, are distributed between the main house, a cottage, and the carriage house, which contains the largest of the rooms. It has a private entrance and a sleigh bed. Complimentary Continental breakfast. Cable TV. Outdoor pool. Hot tub. No kids under 12. No smoking. | 148 Main St. | 508/627–7248 | fax 508/627–9505 | www.theinnat148mainstreet.com | 8 rooms | $250–$400 | AE, MC, V, DC.

Jonathan Munroe House. The dignified, wraparound porch and attic windows peeking through the roof greet you at this two-story 18th-century house across from Old Whaling Church and 2½ blocks from the harbor. Every room is filled with antiques, and has a private bath. Complimentary breakfast. No TV. | 100 Main St. | 508/627–5536, 877/468–6763 | www.jonathanmunroe.com | 6 rooms | $185–$250 | MC, V.

Kelley House. This inn is in the gallery and shopping area of downtown Edgartown, near the waterfront. Opened in 1742 as a tavern, the property includes a pub serving regional micro-beers. Some suites have balconies and kitchettes. Bar, complimentary Continental breakfast. Refrigerators, cable TV. Pool. Business services. | 23 Kelly St. | 508/627–7900 or 800/225–6005 | fax 508/627–8142 | www.kelley-house.com | 53 rooms, 8 suites | $245–$315, $340–$685 suites | Closed last week of Oct.–mid-May | AE, DC, MC, V.

Point Way Inn. Built in 1851, the former sea captain's home has a porch overlooking main street, and a sculpture garden. Rooms have French doors, fireplaces, and balconies or terraces. Here you're within walking distance of the harbor and downtown. To reach other parts of the island, you can ride the island shuttle bus that stops across the street or use the inn's courtesy vehicle. Complimentary breakfast. Cable TV. Local shuttle. Some pets allowed. No smoking. | 104 Main St. | 508/627–8633 or 888/711–6633 | fax 508/627–3338 | pointwayinn@vineyard.net | www.pointway.com | 12 rooms | $225–$375 | AE, MC, V.

Shiretown Inn. This 18th-century home of a whaling captain is on the National Register of Historic Places. It is in downtown and within walking distance of shops, restaurants, and pubs. Restaurant, bar, complimentary Continental breakfast. Cable TV. Business services. No smoking. | 44 N. Water St. | 508/627–3353 or 800/541–0090 | fax 508/627–8478 | paradise@shiretowninn.com | 34 rooms in 4 buildings, 1 cottage | $169–$449 | D, MC, V.

The Tuscany Inn. You can partake of many of the joys of Tuscany in this white Italianate Victorian kept by Tuscan-born Laura Sbrana—try a cappuccino and biscotti in the floral gardens, or register for the cooking weekend and learn traditional preparations of *risotto con porcini, polenta e coniglio,* and other Tuscan favorites. Most guest rooms have canopy beds, white linens, and have either harbor or a garden view. Restaurant, complimentary breakfast June 1–Sept. 15. No rooms phones, TV in common area. | 22 N. Water St. | 508/627–5999 | fax 508/627–6605 | www.tuscanyinn.com | 8 rooms | $200–$395 | Closed Feb. | AE, MC, DC, V.

The Victorian Inn. This former whaling captain's home on the National Register of Historic Places has been one of the "Best Bed and Breakfasts" according to *Cape Cod Life* each year since 1996. Most guest rooms have four-poster canopy beds, some have a balcony overlooking the harbor, and all have freshly cut flowers and a decanter of sherry. Complimentary breakfast. No air-conditioning in some rooms, no TV, no room phones. No smoking. | 24 S. Water St. | 508/627–4784 | www.thevic.com | 14 rooms | $165–$350 | MC, V.

ESSEX

MAP 6, J2

(Nearby towns also listed: Beverly, Gloucester, Ipswich, Rockport)

Antiques, boats, and clams are highlights of Essex, a small coastal town of fewer than 4,000 residents about 25 mi north of Boston. During the 19th century, hundreds of wooden boats were built and launched here on the banks of the Essex River, predominantly schooners for the North Atlantic cod fisheries. Some of the boatyards still exist and continue to build fine handcrafted vessels for discerning sailors. After the heyday of wooden boats slipped away, the town might have fallen into obscurity but for the handiwork of a local cook, whose experiments with local shellfish back in 1916 produced one of the state's most beloved culinary inventions: the fried clam. The latest feather in the town's cap is its gold mine of antiques shops: more than three dozen line Routes 133 and 22 through the center of town, most conveniently within walking distance of one another.

Information: **Cape Ann Chamber of Commerce** | 33 Commercial St., Gloucester, 01930 | 978/283–1601 or 800/321–0133 | cacc@shore.net | www.cape-ann.com/cacc.

Attractions
Cogswell's Grant. In the 1930s, this circa 1730 farmhouse became the summer home of Bertram K. and Nina Fletcher Little, who eventually amassed one of the nation's foremost collections of American decorative arts. Bequeathed to the Society for the Preservation of New England Antiquities, it is positively overflowing with the Littles' extensive folk arts collection, from primitive paintings and painted furniture to Shaker furnishings and duck decoys. In addition to the visual feast inside, the farmhouse, barn, and grounds are themselves quite beautiful to behold. | Spring St. off Rte. 133 | 978/768–3632 | www.spnea.org | $6 | June–mid-Oct., tours on the hour Wed.–Sun. 11–4.

Essex River Cruises. On this narrated tour, you'll see several beautiful New England scenes—a barrier beach, salt marshes, little rivers, Hog Island, and the Cogswell Grant farm (a folk art museum open to the public). The captain will point out some of the 180 species of birds that nest or live along the river, and he'll explain the history of the shipbuilding, clamming, and salt-marsh-haying industries of Essex. Reservations are strongly recommended. | Essex Marina, 35 Dodge St. | 978/768–6981 or 800/748–3706 | www.essex-cruises.com | $20 for 1½ hour afternoon cruise; $22 for 2-hour weekend morning cruise | May–Oct., daily.

Essex Shipbuilding Museum. After launching its boatbuilding industry in 1668, Essex became an internationally recognized boatbuilding center by the late 19th century. This small historical museum, partly housed in the town's 1835 schoolhouse, explores this legacy with a unique combination of artifacts and actual practice. In addition to its historical exhibits, the museum owns and operates the Story Shipyard, founded in 1813, where wooden boats may often be observed under construction a stone's throw from the looming hull of a 1927 Essex-built fishing schooner. | 28 and 66 Main St. | 978/768–7541 | www.essexshipbuildingmuseum.com | $4 | June–Sept., Wed.–Mon. noon–4; Oct.–May, weekends noon–4.

ON THE CALENDAR
SEPT.: *Essex Clam Festival.* This fall festival in Martin Park includes arts and crafts, games, musical entertainment, seafood booths serving Essex clams in various recipes, and a chowder competition. | Behind Town Hall, off Martin St. | 978/283–1601.

Dining
Jan's Encore. Eclectic. A split personality presides here, but both sides are as true to themselves as could be: an upscale gourmet dinner menu is served in the informal and colorful dining room, while a hearty tavern menu of burgers, ribs, and beer is presented in the bar beneath the glow of ESPN. Try the mesquite-rubbed Black Angus steak, twin tournedos with Creole mustard sauce, soy-lacquered duck breast, roasted garlic gnocchi, and smoked ribs. Sun. brunch mid-Oct.–late May. No smoking in dining room. | 233 Western Ave. | 978/768–0000 | No lunch weekends | $13–$19 | AE, D, DC, MC, V.

Jerry Pelonzi's Hearthside. American. This 300-year-old converted farmhouse has five dining rooms with beamed ceilings, rough panel walls, and small windows; two dining rooms also have fireplaces. Lobster is the specialty—boiled, broiled, baked stuffed with lobster or crabmeat, or lobster pie. The restaurant also has a lighter-fare menu, a children's menu, and full bar service. It's popular with locals and tourists. | 109 Eastern Ave. | 978/768–6002 or 978/768–6003 | Closed Jan.–Mar. and Mon. | $11–$19 | AE, MC, V.

Periwinkles. Seafood. This restaurant has table-to-ceiling windows offering a panoramic view of the Essex River. You can also eat on the heated outdoor deck on the water. The menu contains the town's famous fried and steamed clams as well as other seasonal items—fresh halibut (spring), soft-shell crabs (early summer), striped bass from the Essex River (summer), pumpkin ravioli (fall), and warm winter salad. There's a large wine menu and microbrews. Piano entertainment on weekends. Kids' menu. | 74 Main St. | 978/768–6320 | $7–$23 | AE, D, DC, MC, V.

Regatta at Battleship Cove. American. You can sit on the deck with a view of the batttle-ship and order from a menu of burger and chicken sandwiches, or you can sit inside, under suspended 60-ft racing hulls, and feast on steak or sautéed fresh seafood. | 192 Davol St. | 508/679–4115 | No lunch Mon.–Thurs. in Nov.–Apr. | $10–$15 | AE, D, MC, V.

★ **Woodman's.** Seafood. Nothing could be simpler: choose chowder, fish, or shellfish; order at the register; wait for the matching number to be called; pause at the condiment counter for ketchup, tartar sauce, and utensils; return to your indoor booth or outdoor picnic table, and dig in. Nothing could be tastier, either. The restaurant bills itself as the "home of the fried clam." Raw bar. | 121 Main St. | 978/768–6451 | $5–$30 | No credit cards.

Lodging

Essex River House Motel. This 1950s-style motel is patronized by families who come back year after year. Its riverbank location offers views of the many egrets, cranes, and herons who fish in the salt marsh and of the setting sun behind the little steepled church. The motel is across the street from Woodman's restaurant and a five-minute walk to other seafood restaurants, antiques shops, and Story's boatyard and shipbuilding museum. Cable TV. Pets allowed. | 132 Main St. | 978/768–6800 | 15 rooms | $94 | Closed Nov.–mid-Apr. | D, MC, V.

George Fuller House. This Federal-style house built in 1830 by Essex shipwrights contains original wood carvings and paneling. Guest rooms have working fireplaces and many also have canopy beds. The property overlooks the salt marsh and river and is within walking distance of the Essex Shipbuilding Museum and Cogswell's Grant house museum. It's a five-minute drive to Crane's Beach. Picnic area, complimentary breakfast. In-room data ports, cable TV. No smoking. | 148 Main St., Essex | 978/768–7766 or 800/477–0148 | fax 978/768–6178 | www.cape-ann.com/fuller-house | 7 rooms (6 with shower only) | $115–$175 | AE, D, DC, MC, V.

FALL RIVER

MAP 6, H6

(Nearby towns also listed: Dartmouth, New Bedford, Westport; Tiverton, RI)

Settled in the late 17th century after Colonial militia displaced local Native Americans at the end of King Philip's War in 1676, Fall River has had a long and checkered history. Capitalizing on the import-export capabilities of its portside location on Mt. Hope Bay, the city skyrocketed to fame and fortune during the Industrial Revolution, becoming one of the world's leading cotton textile producers, second only to Manchester, England. When the city lost this moneymaking industry shortly before the Great Depression, it fell into a decade of bankruptcy. World War II's supply needs pulled it out of state receivership, and Fall River has slowly succeeded in resurrecting and diversifying its industrial base. A proud blue-collar city, Fall River is physically and culturally very much a product of its mill years, with hillsides of triple-decker housing built for textile workers, huge brick-mill complexes adapted for new uses, and a multicultural identity acquired through waves of immigration by aspiring mill hands from Ireland, Germany, Syria, Québec, and Portugal. In addition to being a factory-outlet discount-shopping capital, Fall River also has a notable collection of naval warships and several fine historical museums.

Information: **Fall River Area Chamber of Commerce and Industry** | 200 Pocasset St., Fall River, 02721 | 508/676–8226 | fax 508/675–5932 | ceo@fallriverchamber.com | www.fallriverchamber.com.

Attractions

Battleship Cove. Here where the wide Taunton River rolls out into the head of Mt. Hope Bay sits a collection of vintage warships from Japan, Russia, and the United States. The centerpiece is the mammoth battleship *Massachusetts,* known affectionately as "Big Mamie" to her former crew. A submarine, destroyer, PT boats, a Russian missile corvette, and Japanese suicide boats round out the World War II–era fleet. It's beneath the I–195 Braga Bridge. | 1 Central St. | 508/678–1100 or 800/533–3194 | fax 508/674–5597 | www.battleshipcove.com | $9 | Daily 9–5.

Factory Outlet District. What began as employee-discount counters in the city's textile mills has over time blossomed into a major retailing phenomenon: the outlet store. Although most of the factories are gone, their outlets remain, joined by many other discount apparel, houseware, jewelry, furniture, and candy retailers within the giant brick 19th-century mill buildings, which are clustered around Quequechan and Quarry streets, beside I–195. | I–195, between exits 7 and 8A | 508/675–5519 or 800/424–5519 (Tower Outlet Mill and Quality Factory Outlets); 508/678–5242 (Wampanoag Mill Factory Outlet Center); 508/674–2200 (Durfee Union Mills) | Free | Mon.–Thurs. 9–6; Fri. 9–8, Sat. 9–5, Sun. noon–6.

Fall River Carousel. This 1920s carousel has 48 horses and two chariots and is housed in a Victorian pavilion. It is the oldest functioning carousel in the country. | 1 Central St. | 508/324–4300 | $1 | Apr.–May and Sept.–Oct., weekends 12–4; June, daily 11–6; July–Aug. daily 11–7.

Fall River Heritage State Park and Museum. This spacious museum at the center of a park on the riverbank overlooking Battleship Cove devotes its cavernous exhibition hall to Fall River's industrial history. The city's brief tenure as one of the nation's largest textile producers is recalled with machinery, artifacts, and photographs, which unflinchingly record the terrible human toll incurred by use of child labor in the mills. A summer outdoor concert series has helped establish the park as a destination for local residents, too. | Davol St. off Rte. 79 | 508/675–5759 | www.state.ma.us/dem | Free | Sept.–June, daily 10–4; Jul.–Aug., daily 10–6.

Fall River Historical Society. This fine historical museum is near the crest of the aptly named Highlands district, the mansion-filled neighborhood once predominantly occupied by the city's great mill owners and other well-to-do citizens. Inside are richly decorated rooms depicting Fall River life during those affluent years, but exhibits also encompass other episodes from local history, including the infamous 1892 trial of alleged ax murderer Lizzie Borden. Visitors may browse or join an hourly house tour. | 451 Rock St. | 508/679–1071 | www.lizzieborden.org | $5 | Call for hrs.

Lizzie Borden Museum. You can visit this home where Lizzie Borden allegedly murdered her parents over a century ago and listen to a guide tell the story as you move through the rooms restored to appear as they did at the time of the Borden residence. | 92 2nd St. | 508/675–7333 | $7.50 | June–Sept., daily 11–2:30, Oct.–May, weekends only.

Marine Museum at Fall River. The 1-ton, 28-ft model of the *Titanic* is but one of many ship models on display at this large warehouse-like museum. One of the largest collections of artifacts from the famous sunken White Star liner is also on view, along with memorabilia from the Fall River Line of luxurious intercoastal passenger steamers that plied the route between New York City and Fall River. | 70 Water St. | 508/674–3533 | www.marine-museum.org | $4 | Weekdays 9–5, Sat. noon–5, Sun. and holidays noon–4.

St. Anne's Church and Shrine. Built in 1869, this large church houses many statues of saints and is a shrine to St. Anne, patron saint of homemakers and pregnant women. | S. Main St. | 508/674–5651 | Free | Daily.

ON THE CALENDAR

AUG: *Fall River Celebrates America.* For five days in mid-August, downtown and Heritage State Park fill with live music, international food stands, children's activities, and an arts, crafts, and collectibles fair. | 508/676–8226.

Dining

The Eagle Restaurant. American/Casual. You can order pasta in a 1- or 2-pound portion with one of 14 sauces at this downtown spot where the dining room is filled with mid-20th-century nostalgic pictures of ships. If pasta isn't your pleasure, you can get fish-and-chips or Portuguese steak. Alternative rock bands play Thursday–Saturday evenings. | 35 N. Main St. | 508/677–3788 | $6–$18 | AE, D, MC, V.

Estoril. Portuguese. Hearty and flavorful food is served with just enough formality to complement the elegantly appointed dining room. Try shrimp Mozambique (cooked in garlic and beer) or pork and littlenecks with potatoes (cooked in a white wine and garlic sauce). Live music Sat. nights. | 1577 Pleasant St. | 508/677–1200 | Closed Mon. | $8–$15 | D, MC, V.

The T.A. Restaurant. Portuguese. You can tuck into traditional dishes like pork *alentagana* (with potatoes in a garlic-white wine sauce) in one of the three dining rooms lined with pictures of the Azore Islands in this enormous downtown place. | 408 S. Main St. | 508/673–5890 | $8–$16 | MC, V, AE, D.

Waterstreet Cafe. Eclectic. The personalities of the Italian and Middle Eastern co-owners come through in the colorful design, art, eye-catching furnishings, and the daily-changing menu, which jazzes up meats, poultry, and local seafood in the quintessential California style. Known for roast duck and grilled sirloin. Try the veggie lasagna and Middle Eastern dishes. Local art exhibits. Live music Sat. Kids' menu. Outdoor dining in garden café. Sun. brunch. No smoking. | 36 Water St. | 508/672–8748 | Closed Mon. No dinner Sun.–Wed. | $12–$18 | AE, D, MC, V.

Lodging

Best Western Fall River. Hub-and-spoke travelers stay at reasonably priced properties such as this one and make day trips. Boston, Providence, Newport, and Cape Cod are all a 30- to 60-minute drive from Fall River. The three-story building features nicely landscaped grounds. Near Battleship Cove. Complimentary Continental breakfast. Cable TV. Indoor pool. Sauna, hot tub. Gym. | 360 Airport Rd. | 508/672–0011 | fax 508/676–6251 | 82 rooms | $64–$109 | AE, D, DC, MC, V.

1873 House Bed & Breakfast. This Greek Revival with stained-glass windows, in the Corky Row District, is a former convent. The guest rooms are simple, each with a unique bed, a fluffy comforter, and a whirlpool tub. Complimentary breakfast. No room phones, TV in common area. Sauna. No pets. No kids. No smoking. | 621 2nd St. | 508/679–8990 | 10 rooms | $75–$125 | D, MC, V.

Hampton Inn. This inn is convenient to Newport, Providence, and Cape Cod. It is near Fall River's Battleship Cove and factory outlets and Westport River's Winery. Rooms are on four floors, and guests can choose between a king or two doubles. Some rooms overlook the water. Complimentary Continental breakfast. In-room data ports, some refrigerators, cable TV. Hot tub, sauna. Tennis courts. Basketball, gym. Business services. | 53 Old Bedford Rd., Westport | 508/675–8500 | fax 508/675–0075 | www.lafrancehospitality.com | 133 rooms | $79–$124 | AE, D, DC, MC, V.

Historic Jacob Hill Farm Bed and Breakfast. This 1722 farm was a hunt club for the rich and famous from 1924 to 1943. Today, it is a quiet spot for a romantic getaway. The main house and carriage house are on a hill overlooking conservation land. Rooms are furnished with antiques and Oriental rugs, tapestries, hunting prints, fireplaces, canopy, and four-poster beds. An antique carriage, a gazebo, and a hammock hanging beneath old oak trees are also found on the property. Complimentary breakfast. No air-conditioning in cottage. Some in-room hot tubs, cable TV, some VCRs. Pool. Tennis court. No smoking. | 120 Jacob St., Seekonk | 508/336–9165 or 888/336–9165 | fax 508/336–0951 | host@inn-providence-ri.com | www.inn-providence-ri.com | 5 rooms, 2 suites, 1 cottage, 2 buildings | $120–229, $170–$190 suites, $140–$240 cottage | AE, D, MC, V.

Lizzie Borden Bed and Breakfast. This house has been restored to 1892, the year in which the infamous murders of Mr. and Mrs. Borden took place. Their daughter Lizzie was accused and acquitted, but the community never believed in her innocence. Guests are given an extended tour of the house and are served johnny cakes and sugar cookies, two foods the Bordens had for breakfast on their last day. You'll find complimentary evening snacks. Complimentary breakfast. No room phones, TV and VCR in common area. No kids under 12. No smoking. | 92 2nd St. | 508/675–7333 | fax 508/675–7333 | www.lizzie–borden.com | 4 rooms, 2 suites (5 shared bath) | $150–$200 | AE, D, MC, V.

Quality Inn–Somerset. Equidistant from Fall River, Providence, and Newport, this inn makes an ideal base for day trips to those popular destinations. Many rooms have water views. Fishing enthusiasts can drop a line into a saltwater inlet next to the hotel grounds. There's also a driving range and miniature golf nearby. About 10 minutes from Fall River. Complimentary Continental breakfast. In-room data ports, some in-room hot tubs, cable TV. Indoor pool. Gym, volleyball. Laundry facilities. Business services. Pets allowed. | 1878 Wilbur Ave., Somerset | 508/678–4545 | fax 508/678–9352 | qualityinn@meganet.net | 106 rooms, 2 suites | $94–$119, $170–$180 suites | AE, D, DC, MC, V.

YOUR FIRST-AID TRAVEL KIT

- ❏ Allergy medication
- ❏ Antacid tablets
- ❏ Antibacterial soap
- ❏ Antiseptic cream
- ❏ Aspirin or acetaminophen
- ❏ Assorted adhesive bandages
- ❏ Athletic or elastic bandages for sprains
- ❏ Bug repellent
- ❏ Face cloth

- ❏ First-aid book
- ❏ Gauze pads and tape
- ❏ Needle and tweezers for splinters or removing ticks
- ❏ Petroleum jelly
- ❏ Prescription drugs
- ❏ Suntan lotion with an SPF rating of at least 15
- ❏ Thermometer

*Excerpted from *Fodor's: How to Pack: Experts Share Their Secrets*
© 1997, by Fodor's Travel Publications

FALMOUTH (CAPE COD)

(Nearby towns also listed: Bourne, Mashpee, Oak Bluffs, Sandwich, Vineyard Haven, Woods Hole)

Falmouth, settled by Europeans around 1660, was one of the first Cape Cod towns to cash in on tourism. The arrival of passenger rail service in the 1880s inspired the construction of grand Victorian hotels along its waterfront to cater to vacationers who arrived by the "dude train" from Boston, on their way to the Martha's Vineyard and Nantucket steamship. Those old hotels are long gone, replaced by seaside neighborhoods of vacation cottages. The East Falmouth end of Route 28, which makes a dogleg pass through town, is lined with shopping malls, but the historic downtown remains a walkable retail area with many shops and restaurants.

Information: Falmouth Chamber of Commerce | 20 Academy La., Falmouth, 02540 | 508/548–8500 or 800/526–8532 | fax 508/548–8521. **Information Center** (May 15– Sept. 15) | 322 Palmer Ave., Falmouth, 02540 | falmouth@capecod.net | www.falmouth-capecod.com.

FALMOUTH
(CAPE COD)

INTRO
ATTRACTIONS
DINING
LODGING

Attractions

Ashumet Holly Wildlife Sanctuary. This small 45-acre Massachusetts Audubon Society sanctuary was once owned by a horticulturist famous during the first half of the 20th century for his work in propagating holly trees. One of the property's two trails is a self-guided exercise in identifying the fruits of his personal collection, which includes 8 species and 65 varieties of holly from around the globe. | 286 Ashumet Rd., East Falmouth | 508/563-6390 | www.massaudubon.org | $3 | Nature Center, Tues.–Sat. 9–4; trails, daily dawn–dusk.

Falmouth Historical Society Museums and Colonial Garden. The Julia Wood House, one of the large, square, Federal-style homes surrounding the 1747 village green, is now maintained by the local historical society as part of its museum devoted to the decorative tastes of Falmouth's citizenry during its first two centuries. The adjacent 1850 barn and circa-1730 Conant House are also part of the museum, housing exhibits on poet Kathy Lee Bates, the town militia's role in the American Revolution and the War of 1812, and an intimate look at the lives of local whaling families. Outside is a Colonial boxwood garden in which summer afternoon teas are held (call for schedule). | 55–65 Palmer Ave. | 508/548-4857 | fax 508/540–0968 | $3 | Mid-June–mid-Sept., Mon.–Thurs. 10–4, Sun. 1–4.

Passenger ferry service. Two companies offer seasonal passenger ferry service to Martha's Vineyard from opposite sides of Falmouth Harbor. Both allow bicycles to be carried aboard for a small extra charge and provide paid parking adjacent to or within a short walk of their respective piers.

Falmouth–Edgartown Ferry. The twin-deck *Pied Piper* makes the journey from the west side of Falmouth Harbor to Edgartown in exactly one hour. Four to six daily departures are available in summer, and reservations are encouraged. | Pier 37, 278 Scranton Ave. | 508/548–9400 | $24 round-trip | Memorial Day–mid-June and Oct., weekends; mid-June–Sept., daily.

Island Queen. This three-deck vessel shuttles between the east side of Falmouth Harbor and Oak Bluffs. The 40-minute trip is made at least twice daily in late spring and early fall, and up to eight times a day on summer weekends. Advance reservations are not accepted. | Pier 45, Falmouth Heights Rd. | 508/548–4800 | www.islandqueen.com | $10 round-trip | Memorial Day–Columbus Day, daily.

ON THE CALENDAR

JUNE–SEPT.: *College Light Opera Co. at Highfield Theatre.* This nonprofit educational summer-stock theater features the country's top collegiate musical theater performers in a variety of classic Broadway musicals. | 508/548–0668 (June 15–Sept.).

JULY: *Barnstable County Fair.* This nine-day fair features vegetable and flower judging; dog and horse shows; horse-, oxen-, and pony-pulling contests; blacksmithing demonstrations; amusement rides and games; children's programs; and major entertainers. | 508/563–3200.

JULY: *Cape Cod Theatre Project.* The mission of this theater project is to develop new American plays through a series of fully staged readings with extensive interaction between audience, actors, playwrights, and directors. Writers featured in recent seasons have included Jeff Daniels, Lanford Wilson, Paula Vogel, and Joe De Pietro. Many reputable film and TV actors have appeared. Readings take place at the Woods Hole Community Hall and Falmouth Academy. | 508/457–4242.

DEC.: *A Dickens of a Christmas.* Take a trip back in time with hot apple cider, roasted chestnuts, and sounds of the season sung by village carolers. Shop at the farmers' market for seasonal food treats. Vendors are dressed as characters in Dickens's novels. | 800/526–8532.

Dining

★ **Coonamessett Inn.** Seafood. A large pond and tranquil, garden-filled surroundings make this 1796 inn a hugely popular wedding spot, but guests don't have to exchange vows to enjoy the reliable Yankee fare served amid the work of local folk artist Ralph Cahoon. Known for seafood stew, clam chowder, and steak. Live music Fri. and Sat. nights. Kids' menu. Sun. brunch. No smoking. | 311 Gifford St. | 508/548–2300 | $13–$34 | AE, MC, V.

Flying Bridge. American. A gregarious, beer-and-batter-fried hot spot overlooking Falmouth Harbor next to transient boat slips that may be booked through the local harbormaster. Known for burgers and seafood. Open-air dining on deck. Kids' menu. No smoking. | 220A Scranton Ave. | 508/548–2700 | Closed mid-Oct.–Mar. | $16–$47 | AE, DC, MC, V.

Golden Sails. Chinese. The lengthy menu running to scores of dishes will be as familiar as the simple, unfussy setting; in addition to the large portions—some dishes comfortably feed two or three people—there's weekend karaoke. Try the General Tso's chicken. Entertainment Fri. and Sat. nights. | 143 Main St. | 508/548–3521 | $8–$16 | AE, D, MC, V.

Hearth 'n' Kettle Restaurant. American. This is the original of eight like-named restaurants in Massachusetts owned by chef Richard Catania, who prides himself on his "Cape Cod fare," such as all-natural lobster and clam chowders, strictly fresh local fish, and hearty breakfasts of corned-beef hash and steak and eggs. The fireplace with pewter kettles and a musket above the mantelpiece anchors the two dining rooms, where you can order a popular Thanksgiving turkey special, complete with leftover turkey sandwiches to go. | 874 Main St. | 508/548–6111 | Breakfast also available | $10–$16 | AE, D, MC, V.

Iguana's. Tex-Mex. You'll have to choose from the enormous menu of burgers, steaks, and Mexican standards like quesadillas, burritos, tacos, and fajitas, as well as from 50 microbrews. If the decision seems daunting, just ask the advice of the resident iguana—he's tried everything. | 31 Teaticket Hwy., East Falmouth | 508/548–6000 | $6–$14 | AE, MC, V.

Laureen's. Middle Eastern. This deli, directly across from the Town Hall Square in the Historic District, is a great place to pick up a lunch picnic. Warm feta cheese pizzas, baba ganoush, hummus, tabouleh, and hot entrées of the day are among the selections. | 170 Main St. | 508/540–9104 | Closed Sun. No dinner | $3–$10 | AE, D, MC, V.

Liam Maguire's Irish Pub. Irish. The nightly live entertainment in this welcoming nook is always traditional Irish folk music, excepting Thursday evenings, and sometimes includes songs sung by the Ireland-born owner, Liam, himself. The menu covers burgers, steaks, and salads, as well as traditional Irish dishes like shepherd's pie, corned beef and cabbage, and fish-and-chips (fresh local scrod in an ale batter). | 273 Main St. | 508/548–0285 | $5–$15 | AE, D, DC, MC, V.

Oysters Too. Seafood. You can dig into oysters on the half shell, escargot en croûte, seafood alfredo, or steak in this homey dining room with wooden chairs and tables reminiscent of country-style kitchen sets, and a stone fireplace. | 876 E. Falmouth Hwy., East Falmouth | 508/548–9191 | Closed Tues. No lunch | $9–$20 | AE, D, MC, V.

★ **Regatta of Falmouth-by-the-Sea.** Contemporary. This restaurant has a stellar view overlooking the water, with top-notch food to match. Classic cuisine gets a thorough makeover with local fish, meat and produce, plus a dash of Asian heat for good measure. Try the sautéed shellfish sampler. Early bird suppers. Dock space. No smoking in dining rooms. | 217 Clinton Ave. | 508/548–5400 | Closed Oct.–Memorial Day. No lunch | $23–$35 | AE, MC, V.

Lodging

Admiralty Inn. This year-round, family-friendly motel outside Falmouth Center has beach access and offers discount tickets to Martha's Vineyard. Poolside and hot-tub rooms and suites are available in the main building, and deluxe rooms are offered in an adjacent building. Suites have lofted king-size beds. Restaurant, bar with entertainment. Refrigerators, some microwaves, some in-room hot tubs, cable TV, some in-room VCRs. Indoor and outdoor pools. Hot tub. Children's programs (ages 5–12). Playground. Business services. | 51 Teaticket Hwy. | 508/548–4240 or 800/341–5700 | fax 508/457–0535 | motels@capecod.net | www.vacationinnproperties.com | 98 rooms, 28 suites | $120–$170, $155–$180 2–bedroom suites | AE, D, DC, MC, V.

Beach House. This property features unique theme rooms, individually decorated with hand-painted murals. Creative furnishings and bright colors accent the inn, which is just steps from the beach. The furniture throughout the inn was handcrafted in Maine, and there is a fireplace in the living room. The cottage has cathedral ceilings with skylights. It is on a quiet residential street a half block from the beach and a five-minute walk from the ferry. Picnic area, complimentary Continental breakfast. No room phones. Pool. No kids under 12. No smoking. | 10 Worcester Ct., Falmouth Heights | 508/457–0310 or 800/351–3426 | fax 508/548–7895 | www.capecodbeachhouse.com | 8 rooms (5 with shower only), 1 studio cottage | $169, $189 cottage | Closed Nov.–Apr. | MC, V.

Best Western Marina Tradewinds. This property overlooks Falmouth Harbor, and is within walking distance of the Martha's Vineyard ferry. Some rooms in the two-story building have views of the water. Complimentary Continental breakfast. Some kitchenettes, refrigerators, cable TV. Pool. Business services. | 26 Robbins Rd. | 508/548–4300 or 800/341–5700 | fax 508/548–6787 | motels@capecod.net | www.vacationinnproperties.com | 63 rooms, 18 suites | $150–$165, $180–$225 suites | Closed Nov.–Mar. | AE, D, DC, MC, V.

Capt. Tom Lawrence House. A former whaling captain's home, the inn is shaded by two huge maple trees, and features hardwood floors, high ceilings, and a circular staircase. Rooms are decorated in soft colors and large corner rooms have four-poster or canopy beds. It's a short distance from the beach, the village, a bike trail, the ferry shuttle, and the bus station for Boston- and Providence-bound buses. Complimentary breakfast. Refrigerators, cable TV, no room phones. No kids under 11 in main house. No smoking. | 75 Locust St. | 508/540–1445 or 800/266–8139 | fax 508/457–1790 | capttomhouse@aol.com | www.sunsol.com/captaintom | $125–$165, $150–$220 apartment | 8 rooms, 2 buildings, 1 apartment | Closed Jan. | AE, MC, V.

Carleton Circle Motel. At this simply furnished place some rooms have blond paneling on the walls, some have wood-frame beds, and many have green floral comforters. It may be one of the best values on the Cape and it's only ½ mi from the Cape Cod Winery. Microwaves, refrigerators, cable TV. Outdoor pool. | 579 Sandwich Rd., East Falmouth | 508/548–0025, 800/434–8150 | fax 508/548–0025, ext. 247 | www.carletoncircle.com | 38 rooms | $49–$99 | MC, V, AE, D.

Copper Beach Inn. This two-story home on the National Register of Historic Places was built in 1800, but the exterior was refinished shingle-style in 1881. The Queen Anne windows some antiques-filled rooms look out to the inn's namesake, a huge copper beech tree in the side yard. Two-night minimum weekends in summer. Complimentary breakfast. Cable TV, in-room VCRs. | 105 Locust St. | 508/540–5588 or 877/540–5588 | 3 rooms, 2 suites | $120–$165, 2–room suite $190 | AE, D, MC, V.

FALMOUTH
(CAPE COD)

INTRO
ATTRACTIONS
DINING
LODGING

Elm Arch Inn. The dining room wall of this early 19th-century inn still shows a cannonball scar from the War of 1812. Small and quiet, the Colonial inn is decorated in a country style, and has antiques and four-poster beds. The inn sits in the center of the village, less than 1 mi from the beach. No air-conditioning in some rooms, cable TV in some rooms and in common room, no room phones. Pool. | 26 Elm Arch Way | 508/548–0133 | 24 rooms (12 with shared bath), 3 buildings | $80–$100, $125 annex (sleeps 5) | Closed Nov.–Mar. | No credit cards.

Grafton Inn. This Victorian-style inn on Falmouth Heights overlooks Nantucket Sound and Martha's Vineyard and boasts a private beach. Restaurants and the Martha's Vineyard ferry dock are within walking distance. Picnic area, complimentary breakfast. Cable TV, no room phones. No kids under 16. No smoking. | 261 Grand Ave. S | 508/540–8688 or 800/642–4069 | fax 508/540–1861 | www.graftoninn.com | 11 rooms | $159–$210 | Closed end of Nov.–mid-Mar. | AE, MC, V.

Green Harbor Waterfront Motor Lodge. Every room in this motel has a sliding glass door that leads to the waterfront, plain white walls, and beds with blond, wooden headboards. Paddle and rowboats are available free of charge. Microwaves, refrigerators, cable TV. Outdoor pool. Dock, boating. | 134 Acapesket Rd., East Falmouth | 508/548–4747 or 800/548–5556 | fax 508/540–1652 | 40 rooms, 1 cottage | $98–$130, cottage $243 (7–night minimum) | AE, D, DC, MC, V.

Inn on the Sound. Set high upon a bluff with a view of Martha's Vineyard, this renovated 1875 inn offers panoramic ocean views; upscale, eclectic decor; and private decks. It is in a residential area within walking distance of the ferry, 1½ mi from Falmouth Village, and close to biking and hiking trails and whale-watching. Complimentary breakfast. No air-conditioning, cable TV, no room phones. No kids under 16. No smoking. | 313 Grand Ave. | 508/457–9666 or 800/564–9668 | fax 508/457–9631 | www.innonthesound.com | 10 rooms | $95–$195 | AE, D, MC, V.

Mariner Motel. This traditional motel has all ground-level rooms. It has flower gardens in the front and picnic tables and a field to the rear. It is less than ½ mi from the island ferry and village shopping. Children under 18 stay free. Picnic area. Refrigerators, cable TV. Pool. Some pets allowed (fee). No smoking. | 555 Main St. | 508/548–1331 or 800/233–2939 | fax 508/547–9470 | info@marinermotel.com | www.marinermotel.com | 30 rooms | $89–$129 | AE, D, DC, MC, V.

★ **La Maison Cappellari at Mostly Hall.** Constructed in 1849 by Captain Nye as a wedding gift, the structure has a widow's walk. A change in ownership now gives the inn a more European in feel and has mural paintings. It has pretty parklike grounds and is on the village green in Falmouth's historic district and around the corner from the free shuttle bus to the Martha's Vineyard ferry. Picnic area, complimentary breakfast. No room phones. No kids under 16. No smoking. | 27 Main St. | 508/548–3786 | fax 508/548–5778 | www.mostly-hall.com | 6 rooms (shower only) | $195–$240 | Closed for winter, call for schedule | AE, D, MC, V.

Palmer House Inn. This turn-of-the-century inn on the village green is on the National Register of Historic Places. Rooms are in the Queen Anne–style main house and in an adjacent cottage. The house is furnished with antiques and lots of lace. Some rooms have fireplaces. Complimentary breakfast. Refrigerators in some rooms, some in-room hot tubs, cable TV. Bicycles. Business services. No smoking. | 81 Palmer Ave. | 508/548–1230 or 800/472–2632 | fax 508/540–1878 | innkeepers@palmerhouseinn.com | www.palmerhouse-inn.com | 16 rooms (7 with shower only), 1 cottage suite | $105–$199; $225–$260 suite | AE, D, DC, MC, V.

Red Horse Inn. You can relax on the patio and enjoy the award-winning flower gardens or use the inn's complimentary itinerary-planning services and do some sightseeing. Rooms are individually decorated in different colors, and have plush carpeting, silk flowers, and high cathedral ceilings. It's a three-minute walk from the Martha's Vineyard ferry. In-room data ports, some refrigerators, cable TV. Pool. No kids under 10. | 28 Falmouth Heights

Rd. | 508/548–0053 or 800/628–3811 | www.redhorseinn.com | 22 rooms | $140–$175 | Closed Nov.–Apr. | AE, D, MC, V.

The Scallop Shell Inn. The guest rooms in this turn-of-the-century bed-and-breakfast have oversized-beds with many down pillows, some have mahogany balconies with panoramic views of Martha's Vineyard, and some have gas fireplaces with whirlpool tubs. You can choose an evening video from the inn's large collection. Complimentary breakfast. Some in-room hot tubs, cable TV, no rooms phones, in-rooms VCRs. | 14 Massachusetts Ave. | 508/495–4900, 800/249–4587 | fax 508/495–4600 | 7 rooms | $205–$280 | AE, MC, V.

Sea Crest Resort and Conference Center. This casual oceanfront resort on Old Silver Beach, one of Cape Cod's finest beaches, offers free recreational activities. Some rooms have sundecks, balconies, or patios; fireplaces; and views of the water. Private beach. Restaurant, bar with entertainment, picnic area, room service. In-room data ports, refrigerators, cable TV. Indoor and outdoor pools. Hot tub, sauna. Tennis courts. Gym. Beach. Children's programs (over age 3), playground. Business services, shuttle service. | 350 Quaker Rd., North Falmouth | 508/540–9400 or 800/225–3110 | fax 508/540–7710 | www.seacrest-resort.com | 266 rooms | $175–$260 | AE, D, DC, MC, V.

The Village Green. This Federal-cum-Victorian 1804 bed and breakfast overlooks the Village Green (hence the name). Lounge on one of this inn's two large porches with white wicker furniture and geraniums, as you sip complimentary sherry or nibble on a freshly baked cookie. Two of the guest rooms have working fireplaces, and the 75-ft bathroom attached to the Long Room has the original pressed-tin ceiling. Cable TV. No pets. No kids under 12. No smoking. | 40 Main St. | 508/5621 or 800/237–1119 | fax 508/457–5051 | 5 rooms | $150–$225 | AE, MC, V.

★ **Wildflower Inn.** You can enjoy award-winning breakfasts containing edible flowers and herbs at this Victorian-era inn. All ingredients are grown in the inn's gardens and sunrooms. Rooms are individually decorated and named after flowers. The cottage has a kitchen, living room, and lofted bed. Picnic area, complimentary breakfast. Some in-room hot tubs, no room phones, cable TV in common room. No kids under 11. No smoking. | 167 Palmer Ave. | 508/548–9524 or 800/294–5459 | fax 508/548–9524 | www.wildflower-inn.com | 5 rooms, 1 cottage | $125–$215 | MC, V.

FOXBOROUGH

MAP 6, H5

(Nearby towns also listed: Boston, Sharon)

Near the junction of I–95 and I–495, Foxborough is a modest town of some 15,000. With an unprepossessing mix of local businesses and rural open space, Foxborough would possibly be only one of Massachusetts's many unheralded small towns were it not for the fact that it is also home to the NFL's New England Patriots and the National Soccer League's New England Revolution. Both teams currently play in Foxboro Stadium, built in 1972. The town also has a unique attraction in its New England Harness Raceway, the only venue for harness horse-racing in all New England.

Information: **Neponset Valley Chamber of Commerce** | 190 Vanderbilt Ave., Norwood, 02062 | 781/769–1126 | fax 781/769–0808 | www.nvcc.com.

Attractions

The New England Patriots. Come watch the Pats heat up the gridiron in New England's crisp autumn weather at their open-air home between Boston and Providence. In addition to being easily accessible from the region's interstates, the stadium is also conveniently served by rail service from Boston. | Foxboro Stadium | 508/543–8200 (front office) or 800/543–1776 (tickets) | www.patriots.com | Aug.–Dec.

Tweeter Center for the Performing Arts. This outdoor amphitheater seats 19,900—8,000 in a covered pavilion and the rest on bleachers and the lawn. The venue at the junction of I–495 and Route 140 draws huge acts like Phish throughout the summer. | 888 S. Main St., Mansfield | 508/339–2333 | www.tweetercenter.com | May–Sept.

ON THE CALENDAR
NOV.–DEC.: *Festival of Lights.* With about a quarter of a million lights at Lasalette Shrine, this is one of the largest religious Christmas lighting displays in the East. The lights are turned on daily at 5 PM from Thanksgiving to New Year's. The public is also welcome to attend daily concerts and services. | 508/222–5410.

Dining

Funway Café. American/Casual. "No work, all play" is the motto at this place ½ mi from Foxboro Stadium. The walls are filled with jerseys and nostalgic sports-team photos, and the bar has 20 TVs showing the game. The eats range from grilled-chicken pesto pizza, to the Reuben and other sandwiches, to grilled swordfish steak with your choice of honey mustard, Cajun, or pan-blackened spices. | 2 Washington St. | 508/668–5505 | $6–$17 | AE, DC, MC, V.

Lafayette House. Continental. The oldest part of this historic Colonial tavern dates back to 1784. It has been expanded repeatedly over the years, but retains the charm and decorative theme of the original, serving a solid meat-and-potatoes menu. Kid's menu. No smoking. | 109 Washington St. | 508/543–5344 | $16–$29 | AE, D, DC, MC, V.

The Odessa. Continental. The large dining and banquet rooms feature a broad European menu, including many authentic Russian specialties. A sandwich, burger, and lighter-fare menu is also available in the bistro/bar. Try the hot and cold *zakuski* (appetizers), *chalahach with tkemali sous* (lamb chops with plum sauce), and *shashlyk* (a shish kabob with lamb, chicken, and pork). Salad bar (lunch). Entertainment on Fri. No smoking in dining rooms. | 108 Washington St. | 508/698–1727 | No dinner Mon.–Tues. | $7–$12 | AE, D, DC, MC, V.

Lodging

Colonel Blackinton Inn. Built in 1850 by a local entrepreneur as a double house for his two sons, the building is now an inn offering business amenities without losing its country charm. Rooms have four-poster beds and some overlook the Bungay River. A separate carriage house is available for meeting and receptions. The inn is on the main street of Attleboro, 15 minutes from Foxborough, a 35-minute drive from Providence, and an hour from Boston. Restaurant, bar, complimentary breakfast. In-room data ports, cable TV. Business services. | 203 N. Main St., Attleboro | 508/222–6022 or 800/734–2487 | fax 508/222–6888 | www.blackintoninn.com | 12 rooms | $89–$129 | AE, D, DC, MC, V.

Comfort Inn. This three-story hotel with a Victorian-style lobby accented by floral sofas is about 2 mi from the Tweeter Center and 5 mi from Foxboro Stadium. It was built a decade ago. Complimentary Continental breakfast. Cable TV. Gym. | 4 Fisher St. | 508/543–1000 | fax 508/543–2914 | www.comfortinn.com | 127 rooms | $118–$179 | MC, V, AE, D, DC.

Courtyard by Marriott. This moderately priced three-story business hotel is close to Foxboro Stadium and the Tweeter Center for the Performing Arts. It has a courtyard in the middle of the building. Rooms have king-size beds and pull-out couches. Restaurant, bar. In-room data ports, cable TV. Indoor pool. Hot tub. Gym. Laundry facilities. Business services. | 35 Foxborough Blvd. | 508/543–5222 | fax 508/543–0445 | www.courtyard.com | 149 rooms, 12 suites | $116–$139, $159 suites | AE, D, DC, MC, V.

Holiday Inn Mansfield. Catering to business travelers, this hotel is near the Tweeter Center and Foxboro Stadium. Noteworthy features include a tropical atrium with trees and waterfalls, a grand ballroom with a stage, and an amphitheater. It's a five-minute drive from Foxborough. Restaurant, bar, room service. In-room data ports, some in-room hot tubs, cable TV. Indoor pool. Hot tub, saunas. Tennis. Basketball, health club, racquetball, volleyball. Laundry services. Business services. | 31 Hampshire St., Mansfield | 508/339–2200 or 800/HOLIDAY | fax 508/339–1040 | www.holiday-inn.com | 202 rooms, 20 suites | $129–$169, $150–$200 suites | AE, D, DC, MC, V.

Residence Inn by Marriott. Popcorn awaits you in your suite at this extended-stay hotel at the junction of Route 140 and I–95. Monday through Thursday there is an evening hospitality reception with nibbles ranging from hors d'oeuvres to full barbecue. Complimentary Continental breakfast. Kitchenettes. Outdoor pool. Hot tub. Exercise equipment. Tennis. Basketball. | 250 Foxborough Blvd. | 508/698–2800 | 108 suites | $129–$159 | AE, D, DC, MC, V.

FRAMINGHAM

(Nearby towns also listed: Boston, Natick, Sudbury)

Ever since America's first shopping mall was built in Framingham in the early 1950s, the town has been defined by retailing. Although outwardly dominated by the heavily commercialized Route 9 strip, which Framingham shares with adjacent Natick, the town has a second, more old-fashioned side, centered around its pre-war downtown. Its busy malls and sizable population belie the fact that Framingham is in many respects a small town at heart, from its peaceful residential neighborhoods to its community sports leagues. Only 19 mi west of downtown Boston, Framingham is well connected to its metropolitan neighbor via commuter rail, express bus service, and I–90. As the center of the ever-expanding MetroWest region, Framingham is also becoming a dining and entertainment destination in its own right, for those seeking city quality and diversity with suburban convenience.

Information: MetroWest Chamber of Commerce | 1671 Worcester Rd., Suite 201, Framingham, 01701 | 508/879–5600 | fax 508/875–9325 | chamber@metrowest.org | www.metrowest.org.

Attractions

Danforth Museum of Art. The Danforth's permanent collection includes 19th- and 20th-century American and European prints, painting, photography, and sculpture. The museum is also known for hosting contemporary traveling exhibits and modern art installations, as well as for promoting arts appreciation among children with its junior galleries. | 123 Union Ave., off Rte. 126 | 508/620–0050 | $3 | Wed.–Sun. noon–5.

Garden in the Woods. Home to the New England Wild Flower Society, which is the founder and administrator of the New England Plant Conservation Program. It is the largest wildflower nursery in New England, with more than 1,700 plant varieties in a series of separate habitats on 45 acres. A couple of acres are also devoted to rare and endangered New England species, scores of which are not only indigenous but unique to the area. A gift shop sells books and plants. | 180 Hemenway Rd., off U.S. 20, North Framingham | 508/877–6574 | fax 508/877–3658 | www.newfs.org | $6 | Call for hrs.

ON THE CALENDAR

MAY AND SEPT.: *Greyhound Friends Open House.* This weekend event at the Greyhound Friends Kennel in Hopkinton serves as a get-together for retired racing greyhounds and their new owners and a means of increasing community awareness and support for the greyhound adoption program. Open-house activities include kennel tours and just-for-fun contests—the longest tail, the biggest smile, the best costume—which are held on the kennel grounds. It's about 20 minutes south of Framingham. | 508/435–5969.

JUNE: *New England's Largest Sale of Wildflowers.* The New England Wild Flower Society's 45-acre botanical garden offers more than 200 varieties of wildflowers and other garden perennials at this one-day sale. Special events include handouts, demonstrations, a plant auction, and a children's table. Free admission to the sale; regular admission to the garden. | 508/877–7630, ext. 3001.

Dining

John Harvard's Brew House. American. Spacious and well-lit, this popular brew pub blends the classic dark-wood interior and cheery hubbub of an old English tavern with above-average food and a broad menu of freshly made beers. Known for nachos and burgers. Try smoked ribs, tandoori chicken salad, and apple crisp. Kids' menu. Sun. brunch. | Shopper's World, 1 Worcester Rd. | 508/875–2337 | $9–$17 | AE, D, DC, MC, V.

Lodging

Red Roof Inn Boston/Framingham. On the northeast edge of Framingham, the two-story chain sits just off I–90 at exit 13, ½ mi from the Framingham Shoppers Mall. In-room data ports, cable TV. Pets allowed. | 650 Cochituate Rd. | 508/872–4499 | fax 508/872–2579 | 170 rooms | $72–$105 | AE, D, MC, V.

Sheraton Framingham. This six-story hotel is midway between Boston and Worcester, just off I–90, about five minutes from a shopping mall. Check out the club lounge. Restaurant, bar, room service. In-room data ports, cable TV. Indoor and outdoor pools. Hot tub. Gym. Business services. | 1657 Worcester Rd. | 508/879–7200 | fax 508/875–7593 | www.sheraton.com | 373 rooms | $159–$219 | AE, D, DC, MC, V.

GARDNER

MAP 6, F2

(Nearby town also listed: Leominster)

Gardner, a city of about 20,000 residents 60 mi northwest of Boston, has been a center of furniture-manufacturing for nearly its entire existence. Woodworking shops gravitated to what was then a rural farming community in the decades after Gardner was settled in 1764, and a cottage industry in chairs began in 1805. By the middle of the 19th century it became known as "Chair City" for the huge volume of wooden chairs produced here for markets around the world, a legacy celebrated by downtown's Gardner Heritage State Park. Today the city has diversified its industrial base, but small furniture companies remain part of the mix.

Information:Gardner Chamber of Commerce | 210 Main St., Gardner, 01440 | 978/632–1780 | www.gardnerma.com.

Attractions

Gardner Heritage State Park. This state park celebrates Gardner's legacy of fine furniture manufacturing, which gave rise to its 19th-century nickname "Chair City." At its peak, this industry produced 4 million chairs annually, examples of which are on display at the park visitors center, along with videos on the chair-making process, exhibits on the immigrant groups that worked the factories, and examples of other industrial products from the area. | 26 Lake St. | 978/630–1497 | www.state.ma.us/dem | Free | Tues.–Sat. 9–4, Sun.–Mon. noon–4.

ON THE CALENDAR

AUG.: *Summer Celebration.* Held on the first Saturday of the month at the Mount Wachusett Community College, this local celebration includes fireworks, food vendors, arts and crafts, and musical performances. | 444 Green St. | 978/632–1780.

Dining

Abigail's. American/Casual. This family restaurant in the Colonial Hotel and Conference Center serves up a wide assortment of dishes. For starters, try one of the "Abbyteasers" like coconut shrimp or baked seafood in mushroom caps. Salads, pizzas, sandwiches, burgers, steaks, pastas, and chicken dishes round out the menu. Dinner entrées also include such items as the herb-crusted swordfish and shrimp *czarina* (shrimp sautéed with julienne veggies on rice with a cayenne cream sauce). | 625 Betty Spring Rd. | 978/630–2500 | Breakfast also available | $6–$18 | AE, D, MC, V.

Lodging

Colonial Hotel and Conference Center. Just north of Route 2, on Gardner's eastern side, this two-story hotel sits on over 20 acres of forested land, insuring a tranquil and restful stay. Restaurant, bar, room service. Some refrigerators, some in-room hot tubs, cable TV. Pool. Hot tub. Laundry service. Business services. Pets allowed (fee). | 625 Betty Spring Rd. | 888/214–4991 or 978/630–2500 | fax 978/632–0913 | 112 rooms | $55–$250 | AE, D, MC, V.

GLOUCESTER

MAP 6, J2

(Nearby towns also listed: Essex, Rockport)

Gloucester is the codfish capital of the state. Massachusetts has other commercial fishing ports, and other nations have exploited cod, but none has piqued the literary imagination like Gloucester, which has been featured in such diverse works as Rudyard Kipling's *Captains Courageous,* Sebastian Junger's *The Perfect Storm,* and poetry by Longfellow, T. S. Eliot, and Charles Olson. The city's working waterfront, wooded surroundings, scenic harbor, and picturesque lighthouses have also inspired numerous painters, from Fitz Hugh Lane, Winslow Homer, and Marsden Hartley to contemporary residents of Rocky Neck, the nation's oldest artist colony. The city's prosperity has always been tied inextricably to the health of the North Atlantic fisheries, which is why plummeting stocks of cod and other species once thought inexhaustible now have Gloucester economically on the ropes. But the city's arts community continues to thrive, its restaurants continue to feature the freshest fish, and the pleasures of the ocean continue to fill Gloucester's classic seaside motels and inns with crowds of summer visitors.

Information: Gloucester Visitor Welcoming Center | Stage Fort Park, Gloucester, 01930 | 978/281–8865 | www.gloucesterma.com. **Cape Ann Chamber of Commerce** | 33 Commercial St., Gloucester, 01930 | 978/283–1601 or 800/321–0133 | cacc@shore.net | www.cape-ann.com/cacc.

Attractions

Beauport, the Sleeper-McCann House. This is the dream house of interior designer Henry Davis Sleeper, who decorated its warren of rooms and crannies with an eye toward both professional display and personal enjoyment. Some of his signature arrangements will be quite familiar, having been widely imitated both during and after Sleeper's ownership. Built in the early 1900s in the self-consciously rustic shingle style then favored by affluent vacation homeowners, Beauport overlooks Gloucester Harbor from a neighborhood full of similarly grandiose homes. | 75 Eastern Point Blvd. | 978/283–0800 | www.spnea.org | $6 | Mid-May–mid-Sept., tours on the hour weekdays 10–4; mid-Sept.–Columbus Day, tours on the hour daily 10–4.

Cape Ann Historical Museum. Maritime artifacts, Colonial silverware, Chinese porcelain, and antique furnishings—particularly from the Federal period—are the highlights of this community museum. Possibly the most remarkable segment of its collections is the art: paintings, drawings, and sculpture by local artists such as Winslow Homer and Milton Avery. Pride of place in the collection goes to the ascending star of 19th-century seascapes, Fitz Hugh Lane; the museum owns the largest number of his paintings. | 27 Pleasant St. | 978/283–0455 | fax 978/283–4141 | www.cape-ann.com/historical-museum | $4 | Mar.–Jan., Tues.–Sat. 10–5.

The Fisherman. Gloucester's most recognizable icon is this patina-covered bronze statue of a schooner fisherman at the helm of his storm-driven ship. Also known as *The Man at the Wheel,* the heroic larger-than-life figure was commissioned from sculptor Leonard Craske as the town's tricentennial memorial to those, as the base reads, "that go down to the sea in ships." | Western Ave. | Free | Daily.

Hammond Castle Museum. This imposing stone manor complete with dry moat was the home of John Hays Hammond, a multitalented inventor and engineer who accumulated hundreds of patents for his ingenuity. Set in the wooded western section of Gloucester overlooking Norman's Woe, a set of shoals celebrated in Longfellow's "Wreck of the Hesperus," the art-filled castle also features a giant pipe organ that's put to good use in special concerts, most popularly on Halloween. | 80 Hesperus Ave. | 978/283–2081 | www1.shore.net/~hammond | $6.50 | June–Aug., daily, call for hrs., Sept.–May, weekends 10–4.

Rocky Neck. This peninsula contains the first-settled artists' colony in the country. Famous artists-in-residence have included Winslow Homer, Maurice Prendergast, Jane Peter, and Cecilia Beaux. The area contains a mixture of private homes, restaurants, and galleries. Leave your car in the parking lot on Rocky Neck Avenue at the entrance to the neck and explore on foot. It takes from 30 minutes to one hour to walk the perimeter of the peninsula. | Rocky Neck Ave. | 978/283–1601 or 800/321–0133 | Daily.

Sargent House Museum. This 18th-century Georgian house was home to Judith Sargent Murray (1751–1820), a patriot and feminist who wrote many tracts and essays arguing the case for equal rights and education for women. The house features period furnishings. | 49 Middle St. | 978/281–2432 | Memorial Day–Columbus Day, Fri.–Mon. noon–4.

Wingaersheek Beach. This well-protected cove of white sand and dunes has rest rooms, a snack bar, and a lifeguard (on duty 10–5). From the beach you can see Annisquam Lighthouse in the bay. | Atlantic St. | 978/283–1601 or 800/321–0133 | Free; parking Memorial Day–Labor Day $10 weekdays, $15 weekends | Daily.

ON THE CALENDAR

MAY–OCT.: *Whale-Watching.* Five companies offer whale-watching cruises from Gloucester Harbor. | 978/283–1601.

JUNE: *Cape Ann Artisans Spring Studio Tour.* Meet artists in their studios and see their newest works. Maps are available from the Cape Ann Chamber of Commerce and the Gloucester Visitor Welcoming Center. | 978/281–3347.

JUNE: *St. Peter's Fiesta.* This four-day festival includes religious activities, music, food, sporting events, and a parade, and ends with the Blessing of the Fishing Fleet from the Boulevard (near the fisherman's statue) on Sunday afternoon. | 978/283–1601.

AUG.: *Waterfront Festival.* Enjoy a pancake breakfast, Yankee lobster bake, arts-and-crafts show, and entertainment at this weekend festival. | 978/283–1601.

SEPT.: *Gloucester Schooner Festival.* This four-day festival features the Mayor's Race for 100-ft schooners and races for other classes. Other events are a parade of sail, deck tours, public sails, a fish fry, and a boat-light parade starting from Lobster Cove, heading down the Annisquam River to Gloucester Harbor, followed by a grand fireworks display. | 978/283–1601.

Dining

Gloucester House. Seafood. This large wharf-side restaurant overlooks the water and serves all the fruits of the sea that you'd expect. It also has a museum-quality anchor collection. Known for lobsters and clambakes. Open-air dining on deck. Occasional live music.

Kids' menu. No smoking in dining room. | 63 Rogers St. | 978/283–1812 | $12–$30 | AE, D, DC, MC, V.

Jalapeños. Mexican. The comfortable, casual storefront location goes with the Mexican-themed decor and tasty south-of-the-border dishes that go beyond tacos and burritos—although those are available, too. Try the tamales, enchiladas, and shrimp combination plates. | 86 Main St. | 978/283–8228 | $10–$16 | AE, D, DC, MC, V.

L'Amante. Italian. The chef/owner of this eatery received culinary training in Italy. Try one of his northern Italian specialties, such as the potato-crusted Chilean sea bass served on sautéed spinach in a citrus beurre blanc or a risotto accompanied by a Tuscan or Piedmont wine. The restaurant, which is in a turn-of-the-century building in East Gloucester Square, has candle-lit tables and earth-toned walls sprinkled with gold dust and adorned with still-life photos of luscious vegetables and fruits. | 197 East Main St., East Gloucester | 978/282–4426 | fax 978/282–4496 | Reservations essential | Closed Jan. and Mon. No lunch | $17–$22 | AE, D, DC, MC, V.

The Rudder. Seafood. This restaurant is in a century-old building that originally was a fish-packing plant. Try the mussels or the Latin seafood bouillabaisse. Gloucester's oldest seasonal restaurant has a low ceiling decorated with greenery and little white lights, wide pine floors, a corner fireplace, and wharf-side deck seating. There's live entertainment many nights. | 73 Rocky Neck Ave. | 978/283–7967 | Closed Nov.–mid-May. No lunch | $14–$23 | D, MC, V.

Two Sisters Coffee Shop. . The owner/cook and staff prepare all dishes to order—everything from corned-beef hash, fresh veggie omelettes, fruit pancakes, haddock sandwiches, fish cakes, fish chowder, and a creation called eggs Valentine with lobster, spinach, and Hollandaise sauce. The 300-year-old building has a tin ceiling, handmade pine and cedar tables, and local photos and paintings. | 27 Washington St. | 978/281–3378 | Breakfast also available. No dinner; no lunch on weekends | $3–$8 | No credit cards.

★ **White Rainbow.** Continental. This restaurant in a historic 1833 building was constructed after an 1830 downtown fire. You can enjoy fine candlelight dining on pasta and fresh seafood in the lower level, or choose from a lighter menu in the café section. No smoking Sat. | 65 Main St. | 978/281–0017 | Closed Mon. No lunch | $27–$39 | AE, D, DC, MC, V.

Lodging

Atlantis Ocean Front Motor Inn. This motor inn on a 2-mi stretch of rocky coast offers a view of the ocean and the twin lighthouses on Thacher Island. The three-story property also has nice gardens. Discount passes are provided for whale-watch cruises and beach parking. Restaurant (breakfast only). No air-conditioning, cable TV. Pool. | 125 Atlantic Rd. | 978/283–0014 or 800/732–6313 | fax 978/281–8994 | 40 rooms | $130–$150 | Closed end of Oct.–Apr. | AE, MC, V.

Best Western Bass Rocks Ocean Inn. All of the large, oversize rooms have views of the ocean and Gloucester's rocky coastline, with sliding glass doors that open onto a patio or balcony. Outside, take time to smell the flowers in the hotel's spectacular gardens. There is also a billiards room. Near the Rocky Neck Art Colony. The motel is ¼ mi from a sandy beach and next to the 18-hole Bass Rocks Golf Club. Kids under 12 stay free. Complimentary Continental breakfast. Cable TV. Pool. Bicycles. Library. | 107 Atlantic Rd. | 978/283–7600 | fax 978/281–6489 | www.bestwestern.com | 48 rooms | $165–$250 | Closed Nov.–Apr. | AE, D, DC, MC, V.

Cape Ann's Marina Resort. Every room has a water view at this contemporary, shingled, multi-level motel in the center of a 300-slip marina and boatyard. Standard rooms on upper floors share a common balcony; those on the first floor have kitchenettes. There are outdoor grills and complimentary summer sunset cruises. A seasonal restaurant and whale-watch boat and deep-sea fishing excursions operate from the premises. Transient boat slips are often available. Restaurant. Some kitchenettes, cable TV, some in-room VCRs. Indoor pool. Hot tub. Laundry facilities, laundry service. Business services. No pets. | 75 Essex Ave. | 978/283–2112 or 800/626–7660 outside MA | fax 978/283–2116 | www.capeannmarina.com | 53 rooms | $90–$100 standard, $110–$120 deluxe, $170–$180 penthouse | AE, D, DC, MC, V.

Cape Ann Motor Inn. The best feature of this wood-shingle three-story motel is its location—right on Long Beach. Rooms have balconies and views over the beach, sea, and twin lights of Thacher Island—plus double bed, sofa bed, ceiling fans, and sliding-glass doors that open onto a common deck leading to the beach. Complimentary coffee in the lobby. Complimentary Continental breakfast. No air-conditioning, some kitchenettes, cable TV. Beach. Pets allowed. | 33 Rockport Rd., | 978/281–2900 or 800/464–8439 | fax 978/281–1359 | www.capeannmotorinn.com | 29 rooms, 1 suite | $115–$130, $200 suite | AE, D, MC, V.

Captain's Lodge. This single-story motel is on a quiet street in downtown Gloucester, less than ½ mi from Good Harbor Beach. The motel has a coffee shop, and some guest rooms have hot tubs. Some kitchenettes, cable TV. Pool. Tennis. | 237 Eastern Ave. | 978/281–2420 | fax 978/283–1608 | 47 rooms | $125–$150 | AE, D, DC, MC, V.

Manor Inn. This newly renovated inn on 5 landscaped acres gives you the feeling of seclusion, even though it's within walking distance of downtown Gloucester. Some rooms overlook the Anisquam River and salt marshes. Complimentary Continental breakfast. Cable TV. Pets allowed (fee). | 141 Essex Ave. | 978/283–0614 | 10 rooms in manor, 16 motel rooms | $89–$139 | AE, D, MC, V.

Ocean View Inn and Resort. This eight-building resort is on 5½ landscaped and garden-filled acres on Gloucester's rocky coastline. Most rooms have ocean views; some have wood-burning fireplaces and antiques. The oldest building is a 1907 English Tudor-style manor. There are also motel-style units and a Queen Anne–style cottage. Restaurants. Cable TV. 2 pools. Business services. Pets allowed. | 171 Atlantic Rd. | 978/283–6200 or 800/315–7557 | fax 978/283–1852 | oviar@shore.net | www.oceanviewinnandresort.com | 62 rooms in 6 buildings | $79–$265, $275 suites | AE, D, DC, MC, V.

Vista Motel. This renovated motel on 4 acres is two blocks from Good Harbor Beach. You can choose from standard or deluxe rooms, and efficiencies; all have ocean views. Some kitchenettes, refrigerators, cable TV. Pool. | 22 Thacher Rd. | 978/281–3410 | fax 978/283–7335 | www.vistamotel.com | 40 rooms in 3 buildings | $110–$130 | AE, D, MC, V.

The White House. This 1880 Victorian house on 2 acres has been a guest house since 1948. Rooms in the three-story main house and two-story wing are large, and each is uniquely furnished with antiques and family heirlooms, brass beds, and some ornamental fireplaces. Each guest room in the wing has a private entrance and outside sitting area. Guests have access to the private beach a block away at the bottom of the hill and receive complimentary passes to other Gloucester beaches. It is in the Magnolia section of Gloucester, in the southern part of town. Complimentary Continental breakfast. No air-conditioning in some rooms. No pets. No smoking. | 18 Norman Ave. | 978/525–3642 | 16 rooms | $85–$135 | AE, D, MC, V.

GRAFTON

MAP 6, G4

(Nearby towns also listed: Uxbridge, Worcester)

Some 30 mi west of Boston at the edge of the Blackstone River valley, Grafton is a small community with clear agrarian roots. Old farms continue to be prominent features of the local landscape, although next-door Worcester and growing economic activity along nearby I–495 are putting pressure on the town's open space. Historic sites around Grafton, including its large town common fringed with hulking clapboard homes and renovated 19th-century commercial buildings, are the principal attractions for casual visitors, while the possibility of living the life of a country squire not far from an interstate off-ramp is a powerful attraction for home buyers.

Information: Blackstone Valley Chamber of Commerce | 110 Church St., Whitinsville, 01588 | 508/234–9090 or 800/841–0919 | fax 508/234–5152 | www.blackstonevalley.org.

Attractions

Grafton Common. The town common has a gazebo in its center and is fringed with large clapboard homes, churches, and renovated 19th-century commercial buildings containing an antiques shop, country store, women's clothing boutique, and a restaurant. | Rte. 140 and Central Sq | 508/234–9090 or 800/841–0919 | Daily.

Willard House and Clock Museum. This museum includes the original 1718 one-room house of Joseph Willard, the earliest white farmer to settle in the area, expanded over the 18th century to accommodate his growing family. In addition to furnishings that reflect the growing comfort of the Willard clan, the house and barn are also filled with timepieces made by Willard's four grandsons, who dominated the region's clockmaking industry for 70 years. | 11 Willard St., North Grafton | 508/839–3500 | $5 | Tues.–Sat. 10–4, Sun. 1–5.

ON THE CALENDAR

SEPT.: *Harvest Fair and Apple Pie Social.* Grafton's town common is the site of an annual fair sponsored by the Evangelical Congregational Church of Grafton. It's held the last Sunday of the month and has live bluegrass or jazz entertainment, puppet shows, pony rides and other children's activities, an auction, an attic treasures sale, homemade apple pies, and delicious corn chowder made with a special recipe. | 508/839–4826.

Dining

The Olde Post Office Pub Restaurant. American. This restaurant emphasizes its former life with antique mail trucks, brass mailboxes, a postal-worker mannequin, and a carved Uncle Sam figure. There are three dining rooms and a sports bar. The menu has something for everyone—seafood, prime rib, deli sandwiches, and home-baked desserts. There's a kid's menu and entertainment by a magician on Thursday evenings. Sun. brunch. | Rte. 140 and Ray St., North Grafton | 508/839–6106 | fax 508/839–6329 | Breakfast also available Sat. | $5–$17 | AE, D, DC, MC, V.

Lodging

The Captain Slocomb House. This 1860 Italianate Victorian's antiques-furnished guest rooms are on the second floor and have ceiling fans. One room has twin beds, one has a queen-size bed, one has a queen-size canopy bed. Breakfast is served in the formal dining room or on the three-season porch. The property includes 4 acres of manicured lawns, flower gardens, and woods. Dining room, complimentary breakfast. No air-conditioning, no in-room TVs, no room phones, cable TV in common area. Pool. No pets. No smoking. | 6 South St. | 508/839–3133 | fax 508/839–3133 | judycsh@aol.com | 3 | $75–$100 | MC, V.

GREAT BARRINGTON

MAP 6, A4

(Nearby towns also listed: Sheffield, Stockbridge, West Stockbridge)

Great Barrington is closer to Manhattan than to Boston, and it shows. Vacationers and second-home owners from New York are the economic engine of the Berkshires in general, and Great Barrington is no exception, which is why the *New York Times* is found more widely on local coffee-shop counters than the *Boston Globe*. Although it's the largest town in the region's southern half, Great Barrington's population is less than 8,000; nevertheless, it possesses a busier, more cosmopolitan atmosphere than that number would suggest, in part because its stores, restaurants, and services are more typical of towns three or four times its size. Further highlights include a large arts community, whose works are often on display at one of the numerous galleries in the area, and proximity to a full four-season roster of recreational activities, from hiking to skiing.

Information: Southern Berkshires Chamber of Commerce | 362 Main St., Great Barrington, 01230-1804 | 413/528–1510 | vcenter@bcn.net | www.greatbarrington.org.

Attractions

Beartown State Forest. This forest's 11,000 acres of mixed hardwoods are a riot of color come autumn, but any time of year there's activity worth pursuing here, from cross-country skiing in winter to swimming at Benedict Pond in summer. A dozen primitive campsites offer proximity to the pond, but no showers or flush toilets. | 69 Blue Hill Rd., off Rte. 23 | 413/528–0904 | www.state.ma.us/dem | $2; fees for camping | Daily. Campground mid-May–Columbus Day.

Berkshire County Massachusetts Antiques Dealers Association. This area has the greatest concentration of antiques stores in the Berkshires. For a listing and map of more than 60 antiques and collectible shops, send an SASE to the Berkshire County Massachusetts Antiques Dealers Association. | Box 95, Sheffield | 413/229–2716 | weissjas@vgernet.net | Shops open year-round.

Monument Mountain Reservation. One of a small series of hills breaking up the broad expanse of the Housatonic River valley, this mountain's exposed rock ledges at its 1,735-ft peak provide exceptional views over the meandering river, the forested ranges on either side of the valley, and the scattered farms below. A single trail loops around the base, with a spur to the top. The mountain has literary associations, too: Nathaniel Hawthorne and Herman Melville met here on a picnic in 1850. It's about 5 mi from downton. | U.S. 7 | 413/298–3239 | www.thetrustees.org | Free | Daily 9–5.

Mt. Washington State Forest. This 400-acre state park is in the southwest corner of Massachusetts, 16 mi southwest of Great Barrington and on the New York border. The main attraction is Bish Bash Falls, which cascades 50 ft into a clear natural pool. To reach the falls, you have to hike down a steep trail into a gorge. Nearby is a free but primitive camping area open year-round. | East St. off Rte. 41 | 413/528–0330 | www.magnet.state.ma.us/dem | free | daily.

U.S. 7: ANTIQUES ALLEY

The southwest corner of Massachusetts is known far and wide for its numerous antiques dealers, most of whom are found along U.S. 7 between Great Barrington and the Connecticut state line. Decorators, collectors, and casual browsers will all find something to catch their fancy among the dozens of shops along this route, whose wares cover just about every style and period imaginable. Porcelains, clocks, quilts, and wicker; music boxes, rocking horses, and collectibles; English, American, and French country and formal furnishings and accessories—the inventory of treasures awaiting discovery would fill a book.

For a complete listing with addresses and a handy map, look for the free Berkshire County Antiques Dealers Association brochure, available at info booths and member shops throughout the region.

Related towns: Great Barrington, Sheffield

© Corbis

© 2000 Visa U.S.A. Inc.

When it Comes to Getting Cash at an ATM, Same Thing.

Whether you're in Yosemite or Yemen, using your Visa® card or ATM card with the PLUS symbol is the easiest and most convenient way to get cash. Even if your bank is in Minneapolis and you're in Miami, Visa/PLUS ATMs make getting cash so easy, you'll feel right at home. After all, Visa/PLUS ATMs are open 24 hours a day, 7 days a week, rain or shine. And if you need help finding one of Visa's 627,000 ATMs in 127 countries worldwide, visit **visa.com/pd/atm**. We'll make finding an ATM as easy as finding the Eiffel Tower, the Pyramids or even the Grand Canyon.

It's Everywhere You Want To Be®

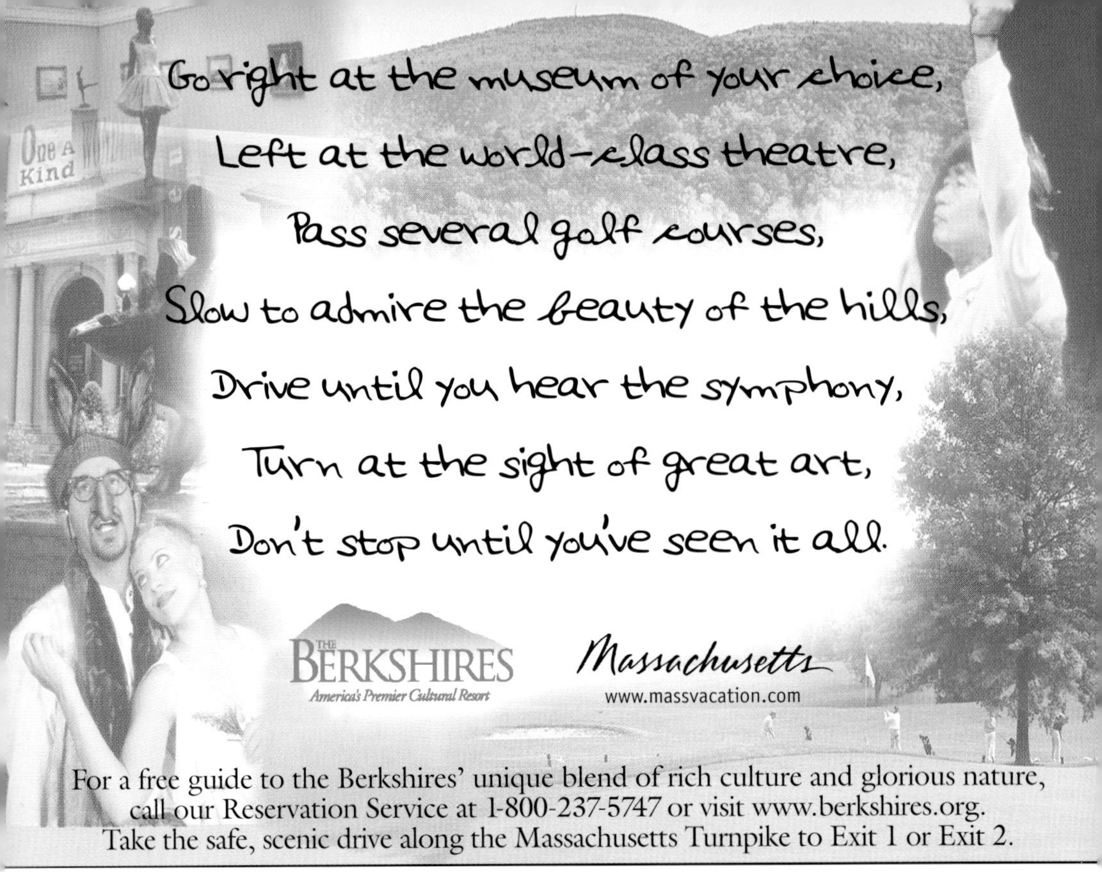

Go right at the museum of your choice,

Left at the world-class theatre,

Pass several golf courses,

Slow to admire the beauty of the hills,

Drive until you hear the symphony,

Turn at the sight of great art,

Don't stop until you've seen it all.

THE BERKSHIRES
America's Premier Cultural Resort

Massachusetts
www.massvacation.com

For a free guide to the Berkshires' unique blend of rich culture and glorious nature,
call our Reservation Service at 1-800-237-5747 or visit www.berkshires.org.
Take the safe, scenic drive along the Massachusetts Turnpike to Exit 1 or Exit 2.

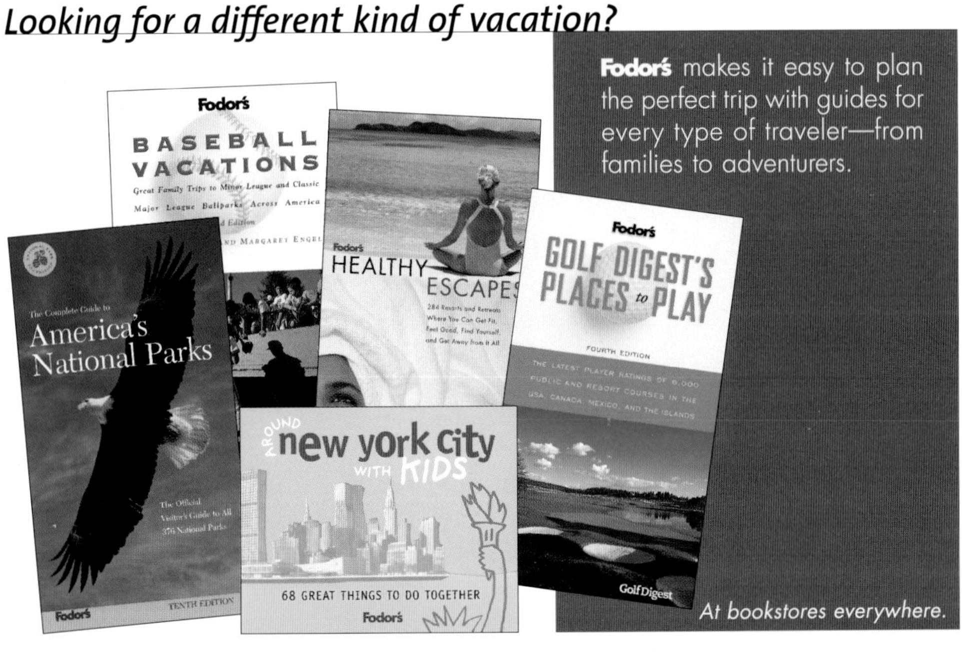

Looking for a different kind of vacation?

Fodor's makes it easy to plan the perfect trip with guides for every type of traveler—from families to adventurers.

Fodor's
BASEBALL VACATIONS
Great Family Trips to Minor League and Classic Major League Ballparks Across America
AND MARGARET ENGEL

The Complete Guide to
America's National Parks
The Official Visitor's Guide to All 375 National Parks
Fodor's   TENTH EDITION

Fodor's
HEALTHY ESCAPES
284 Resorts and Retreats Where You Can Get Fit, Feel Good, Find Yourself and Get Away from It All

Fodor's
GOLF DIGEST'S PLACES to PLAY
FOURTH EDITION
THE LATEST PLAYER RATINGS OF 6,000 PUBLIC AND RESORT COURSES IN THE USA, CANADA, MEXICO, AND THE ISLANDS
GolfDigest

AROUND
new york city
WITH KIDS
68 GREAT THINGS TO DO TOGETHER
Fodor's

At bookstores everywhere.

© 2000 Visa U.S.A. Inc.

When it Comes to Getting Cash at an ATM,

Same Thing.

Whether you're in Yosemite or Yemen, using your Visa® card or ATM card with the PLUS symbol is the easiest and most convenient way to get cash. Even if your bank is in Minneapolis and you're in Miami, Visa/PLUS ATMs make getting cash so easy, you'll feel right at home. After all, Visa/PLUS ATMs are open 24 hours a day, 7 days a week, rain or shine. And if you need help finding one of Visa's 627,000 ATMs in 127 countries worldwide, visit **visa.com/pd/atm**. We'll make finding an ATM as easy as finding the Eiffel Tower, the Pyramids or even the Grand Canyon.

It's Everywhere You Want To Be®

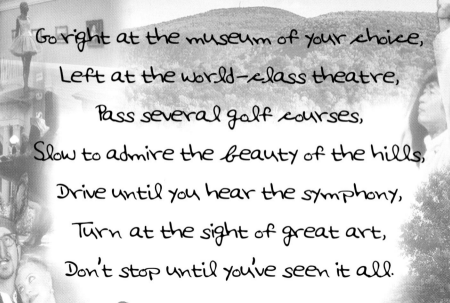

Go right at the museum of your choice,

Left at the world-class theatre,

Pass several golf courses,

Slow to admire the beauty of the hills,

Drive until you hear the symphony,

Turn at the sight of great art,

Don't stop until you've seen it all.

THE BERKSHIRES
America's Premier Cultural Resort

Massachusetts
www.massvacation.com

For a free guide to the Berkshires' unique blend of rich culture and glorious nature,
call our Reservation Service at 1-800-237-5747 or visit www.berkshires.org.
Take the safe, scenic drive along the Massachusetts Turnpike to Exit 1 or Exit 2.

Looking for a different kind of vacation?

Fodor's
BASEBALL VACATIONS
Great Family Trips to Minor League and Classic
Major League Ballparks Across America

The Complete Guide to
America's National Parks
The Official
Visitor's Guide to All
376 National Parks
Fodor's
TENTH EDITION

Fodor's
HEALTHY ESCAPES

AROUND
new york city
WITH KIDS
68 GREAT THINGS TO DO TOGETHER
Fodor's

Fodor's
GOLF DIGEST'S
PLACES to PLAY
FOURTH EDITION
GolfDigest

Fodor's makes it easy to plan
the perfect trip with guides for
every type of traveler—from
families to adventurers.

At bookstores everywhere.

Skiing. The high ridges of the Taconic and Hoosac ranges bordering Berkshire County give it the best downhill skiing in southern New England. Within a short radius of Great Barrington are three ski areas whose range of terrain will suit skiers and snowboarders of all skill levels. All offer equipment rentals on-site.

Butternut Basin. Butternut makes use of a 1,000-ft drop on the side of East Mountain, part of a large state park, which is why it doesn't have condos, restaurants, or shopping around its base lodge. Instead it offers undistracted daylight skiing, complete with multiple chairlifts, full snowmaking, ski school, and racing program. With more than half of its 22 trails designed for intermediate skiers, Butternut is known for its beautiful cruising runs and warm welcome to snowboarders. | Rte. 23 | 413/528–2000 or 800/438–SNOW | www.butternutbasin.com | Lift ticket $30–$39 per day | Dec.–Mar. daily.

Catamount. The two-dozen trails here are almost evenly split among beginner, intermediate, and expert runs, with some truly vertical double black diamond terrain for the fearless. Half the trails are open for night skiing, most are covered by snowmaking, and a handful of lifts ensure lines stay short. Repairs, racing, and all-day children's programs are also available. The mountain is along the New York border, and the ski trails cross into both states. | Rte. 23, South Egremont | 413/528–1262 or 800/342–1840 | fax 518/325–3155 | www.catamountski.com | $19–$40 | Dec.–Apr., daily.

Otis Ridge. This small ski area about 15 mi east of Great Barrington offers about a dozen runs across all skill levels, serviced by chairlifts and snowmaking. Half are open for night skiing. Restaurant, ski repairs, and weekend ski camp are also available. | 159 Monterey Rd., Otis | 413/269–4444 | www.otisridge.com | $15–$20 | Dec.–Mar., daily.

GREAT BARRINGTON

INTRO
ATTRACTIONS
DINING
LODGING

ON THE CALENDAR

JULY–AUG.: *Aston Magna Festival.* At this festival you'll hear early chamber music as the composer imagined it. The group has been recognized internationally for its contribution to the popularization of early music performed using historically accurate instruments and performance practices. The annual festival takes place on five successive Saturdays in St. James Church. | 413/528–3595 or 800/875–7156.

AUG.: *Berkshire Crafts Fair.* This juried retail crafts show at the Monument Mountain Regional High School, now in its 28th year, features the works of 95 exhibitors. It has been voted one of the top shows in the country by Harris Poll. | 413/528–3346, ext. 28.

Dining

Castle Street Café. Contemporary. Exposed brick, hand-blown glass lighting, original art, and William Gottlieb's famous photos of jazz legends add up to urbane contemporary elegance, which appropriately foreshadows the sophisticated menu and acclaimed wine list. A lighter menu is served in the bar, usually accompanied by a pianist performing on Nat "King" Cole's baby grand. Live music nightly late May–mid-Oct., live music Fri. and Sat. mid-Oct.–late May. No smoking. | 10 Castle St. | 413/528–5244 | Closed Tues. No lunch | $10–$22 | AE, D, MC, V.

Egremont Inn. Contemporary. This 1780 colonial inn 3 mi west of Great Barrington has both a formal dining room with an elaborate menu and a casual tavern with lighter fare. Both rooms have fireplaces and darkwood paneling; the dining room has two walls of windows with views of Karner Brook. There's also wraparound porch for summer dining. Try the boneless breast of chicken stuffed with arugula and mozzarella, filet mignon with a shallot vermouth sauces or shrimp sautéed with white wine and garlic. The wine list is extensive, with 200 different selections. | 10 Old Sheffield Rd. South Egremont | 413/528–2111 | www.egremontinn.com | Reservations essential | Closed Mon.–Tues. No lunch | $10–$16 tavern, $16–$28 dining room | AE, D, MC, V.

Helsinki Cafe. Eastern European. This establishment doubles as a teahouse and restaurant. The emphasis is on Finnish, Russian, and Jewish cuisine—gravlax and hot or cold borscht, for instance. The drink of choice is tea (although the café has a full liquor license). The booths and small tables have cushioned chairs, fringed draperies, photos and paintings by local artists, and teapots on the walls. Sun. brunch. | 284 Main St. | 413/528–3394 | $13–$19 | D, DC, MC, V.

Jodi's Country Cookery. Eclectic. Country antiques and furnishings combine for a kind of yeoman comfort. The menu ranges from rustic northern Italian dishes to Continental stand-bys like steaks and chops, mixed with other ethnic styles and flavors according to the chef's fancy. Known for draft microbrews and hearty from-scratch breakfasts. Open-air dining on porch and lawn. Entertainment (occasional). Kids' menu. No smoking in dining rooms. | 327 Stockbridge Rd. | 413/528–6064 | Closed Tues. Jan.–Apr. | $10–$20. | AE, D, DC, MC, V.

John Andrew's. Contemporary. Outwardly a large old house in the country 7 mi west of Great Barrington; inwardly a stylishly decorated chef-owned restaurant offering intimate dining with a beautifully prepared and presented menu that pairs the region's freshest ingredients with eclectic Asian and Mediterranean influences. Open-air dining on garden terrace. No smoking in dining room. | Rte. 23 at Blunt Rd., South Egremont | 413/528–3469 | Closed Wed. Sept.–June. No lunch | $16–$27 | MC, V.

Martin's Restaurant. American. A cheerful, breezy place with a diner menu that is slanted toward a food-savvy clientele; rock-bottom prices. Known for omelets, soups, vegetarian selections, and all-day breakfasts. Kids' menu. No smoking. | 49 Railroad St. | 413/528–5455 | No dinner | $4–$7 | No credit cards.

Painted Lady. Continental. An attractively maintained Victorian house lends decorative finery to this traditional European-American cuisine. Known for fresh seafood, pasta, and veal. Kids' menu. No smoking in dining rooms. | 785 S. Main St. | 413/528–1662 | No lunch | $13–$23 | D, MC, V.

Stagecoach Hill Inn. American. As the name suggests, this 1765 inn 10 mi south of Great Barrington once served stagecoach passengers. The dark-paneled, beamed, candle-lit din-ing room has white linen service and a fireplace. Its regional menu changes seasonally and dinners include salad and fresh herb bicuits. There is full bar service. | 854 S. Under-mountain Rd., Sheffield | 413/229–8585 | No lunch | $14–$24 | AE, MC, V.

Union Bar and Grill. Contemporary. This ultramodern eatery serves an eclectic, globally influenced American cuisine, from quesadillas and barbecued ribs to pan-roasted halibut, grilled salmon, and other selections finished with truffles, wild mushrooms, and other fancy ingredients. Known for pastas, pizza, nightly specials, and martinis. Kids' menu. Sun. jazz brunch. | 293 Main St. | 413/528–6228 | No lunch Tues.–Thurs. in summer, no lunch week-days in winter | $15–$19 | MC, V.

Lodging

Barrington Court Motel. All rooms in this two-story motel have new wallpaper and cherry furniture. Outside, the motel has nicely landscaped grounds and gardens, and is within walking distance of shops and restaurants. Complimentary Continental breakfast. Some kitchenettes, refrigerators, cable TV. Pool. Playground. Pets allowed (fee). | 400 Stockbridge Rd. | 413/528–2340 | 22 rooms, 3 suites | $125–$135, $225–$250 suites | AE, D, MC, V.

Briarcliff Motor Lodge. Approximately 1 mi north of the town center, this one-story motor inn is close to Tanglewood and the summer theaters, as well as to many of the area's antiques shops. Refrigerators, cable TV. Pets allowed. | 506 Stockbridge Rd. | 415/528–3000 | 16 rooms | $45–$175 | AE, D, DC, MC, V.

Coffing-Bostwick House. This Greek Revival inn has a wraparound porch and porte cochère. The inn and the 3½-acre property of lawns, gardens, and woods once belonged to the Coff-ing family, owners of the company that produced siding for the first iron-clad ships in the Civil War. Complimentary breakfast. No air-conditioning, cable TV, no room phones. No smok-ing. | 98 Division St. | 413/528–4511 | fax 413/528–9054 | cbhbnb@bcn.net | 6 rooms (with shared bath) | $80–$100 | No credit cards.

Egremont Inn. Rooms in this classic New England Colonial building have sitting rooms with fireplaces. There is also a wraparound front porch on the first floor and a restaurant serving gourmet country cuisine and offering live jazz. Weekend packages including some meals are available. About 3 mi west of Great Barrington. There's golf nearby. Restaurant, bar with entertainment, complimentary Continental breakfast (weekdays). TV in common area. Pool, tennis. Business services. | 10 Old Sheffield Rd., South Egremont | 413/528–2111 or 800/859–1780 | fax 413/528–3284 | egremontinn@taconicnet.com | www.egremontinn.com | 18 rooms, 1 suite | $140–$180, $190 suite | AE, D, MC, V.

1898 House. This bed-and-breakfast inn in the heart of the Berkshires has turn-of-the-century antique furnishings. It's within walking distance of downtown restaurants and antiques shops and a short drive to Tanglewood and the Norman Rockwell Museum. Complimentary breakfast. No room phones. No smoking. | 89 Taconic Ave. | 413/528–1315 | fax 413/528–2631 | 1898house@aol.com | pretzelcity.com/1898house | 3 rooms | $100–$120 | MC, V.

Great Barrington Days Inn. This two-story, exterior-corridor motel is in the center of town and close to the many restaurants and shops. Complimentary Continental breakfast. Refrigerators, cable TV. Pool. No pets. | 372 Main St. | 413/528–3150 | fax 413/528–3150 | 63 rooms | $79–$169 | AE, D, DC, MC, V.

Lantern House Motel. The rooms of this one-story motel are done in natural wood, with knotty-pine paneling. There's a three-night minimum stay on weekends in peak season and holidays. The Catherine Chocolates Shop and Butternut ski resort are nearby. In-room data ports, refrigerators, cable TV. Pool. | 254 Stockbridge Rd. | 413/528–2350 or 800/959–2350 | fax 413/528–0435 | 14 rooms | $75–$100 | D, MC, V.

Monument Mountain Motel. This L-shape motel with simple, clean rooms is surrounded by flower and vegetable gardens and 20 acres of landscaped grounds. Picnic area. Cable TV. Pool. Tennis. Playground. Business services. | 249 Stockbridge Rd. | 413/528–3272 | fax 413/528–3132 | 18 rooms | $100–$125 | AE, D, DC, MC, V.

Mountain View Motel. Set back from the road 300 ft, this motel is surrounded by trees and boasts mountain views. Completely renovated in 2000, all rooms have new furnishings. The suite has a hot tub and a small kitchen. Refrigerators, cable TV. | 304 State Rd. | 413/528–0250 | fax 413/528–0137 | 17 rooms, 1 suite | $90–$100, $200 suite | AE, D, DC, MC, V.

Race Brook Lodge. This 200-year-old New England barn 12 mi south of Great Barrington has been converted into a family-friendly lodge. Common rooms and guest suites have wood-beam ceilings and stenciled walls. Also in the lodge is the Horshoe Wine Bar. A brook flows through the grounds, and hiking trails lead to the summit of Mt. Everett (the state's second-highest peak) and Mt. Race, as well as to Race Brook Falls. It's at the base of the Taconic Mountain Range. Many antiques shops are nearby. Complimentary breakfast. No room phones, cable TV in common area. Some pets allowed (fee). No smoking. | 864 S. Under Mountain Rd., Sheffield | 413/229–2916 or 888/725–6343 | fax 413/229–6629 | info@rblodge.com | www.rblodge.com | 21 rooms (some with shower only) | $125–$175, $225 Brook House (sleeps 6) | AE, MC, V.

Seekonk Pines Inn. Named after a Native American word meaning "wild goose," the 1830s home has 4 acres of wooded land and is surrounded by another 325 acres of property— perfect for hikers or skiiers. Rooms are individually appointed; the Horace Church room, for instance, has yellow walls and white quilts that bring out the glowing hues of the maple bed frames. Complimentary breakfast, picnic area. No room phones, TV in common area. Hiking, bicycles. Cross-country skiing. No pets. No smoking. | 142 Seekonk Cross Rd. | 413/528–4192 or 800/292–4192 | www.seekonkpines.com | 6 rooms | $115–$175 | AE, MC, V.

Stagecoach Hill Inn. A 1765 redbrick inn 10 mi south of Great Barrington that has been welcoming travelers since 1829. Rooms in both the main building and cottage have an eclectic mix of family heirlooms, antiques, and period reproductions. The inn is popular with visitors to nearby private schools and antique collectors. Restaurant, bar, complimentary breakfast. No TV. Pool. Library. No pets. No kids under 10. No smoking. | 854 S. Undermountain Rd., Sheffield | 413/229–8585 | fax 413/229–8584 | 7 rooms, 2 with shared bath in main building; 4 rooms in cottage | $50–$145, $95–$125 cottage units | AE, MC, V.

Thornewood Inn. This turn-of-the-century Dutch colonial inn consists of a main inn and a carriage house, each furnished with antiques and mahogany pieces. Some rooms have fireplaces, French doors, and balconies. There are views of fields, the river, and mountains from the property. In summer the inn offers Sunday brunch on the porch with live jazz—the owner sitting in with the musicians. Dining room, complimentary breakfast. Cable TV. Pool. Cross-country skiing, downhill skiing. Business services. No kids under 12. No smoking. | 453 Stockbridge Rd. | 413/528–3828 or 800/854–1008 | fax 413/528–3307 | www.thornewood.com | 12 rooms | $115–$225 | AE, D, MC, V.

Turningpoint Inn. The six second-floor bedrooms are simply decorated at this 200-year-old inn, which was once a stagecoach stop. The two-bedroom cottage has a living room/kitchen and heated sun porch. The owner/chefs place as much emphasis on food as on accommodations—changing the breakfast menu daily and serving dinners to guests on weekends. Dining room, complimentary breakfast. No air-conditioning in some rooms, no cable TV in some rooms, no room phones. Some pets allowed. No smoking. | 3 Lake Buel Rd. | 413/528–4777 | 6 rooms (2 with shared bath), 1 two-bedroom cottage | $90–$150, $230 cottage | No credit cards.

Wainwright Inn. This inn, built by a captain in the Revolutionary War, was originally a tavern and stagecoach stop. Its most famous guest was Thomas Edison. There are wraparound porches, and some rooms have fireplaces. It's about a 15-minute drive from Tanglewood, the Norman Rockwell Museum, and ski resorts. Complimentary breakfast. Cable TV in some rooms, no room phones. No smoking. | 518 S. Main St. | 413/528–2062 | fax 413/528–9896 | www.wainwrightinn.com | 8 rooms | $125–$175 | MC, V.

Weathervane Inn. Originally a farmhouse, this 1785 inn on 10 landscaped acres has guest rooms with period furnishings and large sitting rooms. The former carriage house contains one suite and two guest rooms. A full breakfast is served in the sunroom overlooking the gardens. Home-baked cookies and cakes are served at afternoon tea. Complimentary breakfast. In-room data ports, no TV in some rooms, TV in common area. Outdoor pool. No pets. No smoking. | Rte. 23, South Egremont | 413/528–9580 or 800/528–9580 | fax 413/528–1713 | www.weathervaneinn.com | 8 rooms, 2 suites | $125–$175, $225–$250 suites | AE, MC, V.

Windflower Inn. This 1850s inn has antiques, a large screened porch with wicker furniture, and fireplaces in six guest rooms. Vegetables and herbs from the garden enhance the full breakfast. Home-baked, gluten-free items are also offered. Across the street from the inn and its 10 acres of landscaped grounds is a public country club with an 18-hole golf course. Complimentary breakfast. Cable TV, no room phones. Pool. Business services. | 684 S. Egremont Rd. | 413/528–2720 or 800/992–1993 | fax 413/528–5147 | www.windflowerinn.com | 13 rooms | $100–$200 | AE.

GREENFIELD

MAP 6, D2

(Nearby town also listed: Deerfield)

Greenfield is the kind of community that proves America's idealized small town is not a myth. Once a center for industrial tool-and-dye manufacturing, Greenfield's modern incarnation mixes community-college academe with light industry, and homegrown shops with truck-garden agriculture. No big neighbor has turned Greenfield into a suburb, no single employer has turned it into a company town, and no big-box national retailer has obliterated its downtown. Greenfield's location at I–91 and Route 2, better known as the scenic Mohawk Trail, ensures that its civic charm is readily available to travelers exploring the Pioneer Valley or merely passing through.

Information: **Franklin County Chamber of Commerce** | Box 898, Greenfield, 01302 | 413/
773–5463. **Visitor Center** | 395 Main St. | 413/773–5463 | fax 413/773–7008 | fccc@crocker.com
| www.co.franklin.ma.us.

Attractions

Northfield Mountain Recreation and Environmental Center. Owned by Northeast Utili-
ties, whose hydropower facility and reservoir take up part of the acreage, this mountain
offers miles of trails for year-round use by hikers, mountain bikers, and cross-country ski-
iers (rentals and lessons available in season). There are also tours of the powerhouse and
a small center with exhibits on local ecology and history. | 99 Millers Falls Rd., Northfield
| 413/659–3714 or 800/859–2960 | Free, except fees for cross-country skiing, river-boat
rentals, etc | Call for hrs.

Quinnetuket II Boat Cruises. These riverboat cruises on the Connecticut River offer beautiful scenery complemented by commentary on river-related history, geology, and ecology.
The 90-minute trips head downstream to the Turners Falls dam, passing through the storied French King gorge beneath Route 2's giant Art Deco highway bridge. If you're lucky,
you'll get glimpses of nesting bald eagles. | Riverview Landing, Northfield | 413/659–3714
or 800/859–2960 | $8 | Mid-June–Columbus Day, daily departures at 11, 1:15, and 3.

ON THE CALENDAR
JULY: *Green River Festival.* This two-day festival at Greenfield Community College
offers free dance lessons on Friday and performances by rock, folk, swing, and country
bands on Saturday. There are also hot-air balloons, fireworks, crafts, children's activities,
and American and ethnic foods. | 413/773–5463.
SEPT.: *Franklin County Fair.* This agricultural fair is one of the oldest in the country.
Events include horse and oxen draws, sheep and cattle shows, entertainment, midway
rides, and games. | 413/774–4282.

Dining

Andiamo. Italian. In dining rooms with glorious views out over the Pioneer Valley 15 mi
north of Greenfield, you can enjoy a menu of Tuscan-inspired dishes professionally prepared and attractively presented. Known for beef and pasta. Try trio del mare. Live music
Sun. Entertainment Fri. and Sat. | 199 Huckle Hill Rd., Bernardston | 413/648–9107 | No lunch
| $14–$23 | AE, D, DC, MC, V.

Famous Bill's. American. A downtown fixture that looks and feels as timeless as the tried-
and-true American standards that fill the bill of fare. Try the baked stuffed lobster, steak,
or pork tripe. Kids' menu. | 30 Federal St. | 413/773–9230 | No lunch Mon.–Sat. | $10–$23 |
MC, V.

Herm's. American. The traditional family restaurant you would expect to find behind the
unprepossessing storefront is here with all its familiar standbys, but peppery Cajun notes
have crept onto the menu, too, lending a nice flavorful surprise to several dishes. Known
for Cajun-style dishes and thick New York sirloin. Kids' menu. No smoking in dining rooms.
| 91 Main St. | 413/772–6300 | Closed Sun. | $10–$17 | AE, D, MC, V.

People's Pint. Eclectic. This relaxed, spacious local tavern brews its own exceptional beers
and sodas, dishes up plenty of vegetarian fare along with the kielbasa and barbecue, and
sponsors local music as diverse as its menu, including Celtic, jazz, blues, and rock. Known
for veggie burgers. Try tung noodles and pulled-pork barbecue. Live music Wed. and week-
ends. Beer and wine only. No smoking. | 24 Federal St. | 413/773–0333 | Closed Mon. Jun.–
Sept. No lunch | $5–$16 | No credit cards.

Lodging

★ **Brandt House.** This turn-of-the-century Colonial Revival house is on a quiet residential street
a five-minute walk from downtown. The house contains antiques and feather beds as well
as fireplaces and skylights in some rooms. There's a porch with a swing, a terrace, and 3½

acres of manicured lawns and gardens. The apartment has a full kitchen, hot tub, and loft bedroom, and is geared toward extended stays. Complimentary breakfast (Continental on weekdays). In-room data ports, some in-room hot tubs, cable TV, some in-room VCRs. Business services. Some pets allowed (fee). No smoking. | 29 Highland Ave. | 413/774–3329 or 800/235–3329 | fax 413/772–2908 | info@brandthouse.com | www.brandthouse.com | 8 rooms (2 with shared bath), 1 apartment | $125–$205; $300 apartment | AE, D, MC, V.

Candlelight Motor Inn. This one-story motel-style inn on the Mohawk Trail is near several private schools as well as scenic Shelburne Falls. There's golf and tennis nearby. Cable TV. Pool. Pets allowed (fee). | 208 Mohawk Tr | 413/772–0101 or 888/262–0520 | fax 413/773–0886 | 56 rooms | $84–$96 | AE, D, DC, MC, V.

Hitchcock House Bed and Breakfast. This three-story, sand-colored Victorian house with dark green shutters and turret was built in 1881 by Edward P. Hitchcock and designed by F.C.Currier, a renowned Springfield architect. The house, in a residential area, has a front porch, sun porch, deck, and gardens. There are two adjoining rooms with one double bed, twin beds, and a daybed—these are good for families. Dining room, complimentary breakfast. No TV in rooms, cable TV in common area. No pets. No smoking. | 15 Congress St. | 413/774–7452 | 4 rooms | $90–$110 | No credit cards.

Howard Johnson Inn. This hotel is convenient for visitors to the Lunt Design Center as well as five nearby colleges and preparatory schools. Clean, comfortable rooms. Restaurant, bar. Cable TV. Pool. | 125 Mohawk Tr | 413/774–2211 or 888/244–2211 | fax 413/772–2637 | 100 rooms | $94–$115 | AE, D, DC, MC, V.

Johnson Homestead. This 80-acre property nestled in the hills of Hog Hollow contains flower, vegetable, and herb gardens, woodlands, a brook, and open fields edged with stone walls. Rooms are furnished with antiques. The property's most distinguishing feature is the outdoor fireplace, where guests swap stories and toast marshmallows on summer evenings. The attractions of Shelburne Falls—the famous Bridge of Flowers, glacial pot holes, and artisan shops—are a six-minute drive. It's about 13 mi west of Greenfield. Complimentary breakfast. No air-conditioning, no room phones, cable TV and VCR in common area. No kids under 11. No smoking. | 79 E. Buckland Rd., Shelburne Falls | 413/625–6603 | 3 rooms (with shared bath) | $75 | No credit cards.

Old Tavern Farm. This inn—which was a stagecoach stop on the Post Road to Bennington, Vermont—has a Georgian Colonial center chimney, five Rumford fireplaces, and an 18th-century set-kettle in the kitchen (one of the earliers sinks). There's also a unique period ballroom with spring floor, vaulted ceiling, candle-lit chandeliers, and oil lamps. Pieces from the owner's extensive collection of Americana are on display, and there are two large formal parlor guest rooms with working wood-burning fireplaces, one with a reproduction queen-size, Queen Anne, four-poster bed and the other with a double-size four-poster canopy bed. Dining room, complimentary breakfast. No air-conditioning in some rooms, no room phones, no cable TV in some rooms, cable TV in common area. Some pets allowed. No smoking. | 817 Colrain Rd. | 413/772–0474 | fax 413/773–0377 | www.oldtavern-farm.com | 3 rooms | $110 | MC, V.

HADLEY

(Nearby towns also listed: Amherst, Deerfield, Northampton, South Hadley)

As the town with the largest acreage under cultivation in the Pioneer Valley, Hadley ranks as one of Massachusetts's top farming communities, though it numbers fewer than 5,000 people. English colonists who came upriver from Connecticut began raising crops on the fertile floodplain of the Connecticut River in 1659. Although Hadley is the only town in the five-college area without a college or university, it single-handedly hosts all of the area's shopping malls, which line Route 9 alongside the rich farmland. Attractions range from historical museums in the village of Hadley Center to many recreational opportunities, including the Norwottuck Rail Trail for cyclists and the Mt. Holyoke Range in Skinner State Park for hikers.

Information: Amherst Area Chamber of Commerce | 409 Main St., Amherst, 01002 | 413/253–0700 | fax 413/256–0771 | chamber@amherstcommon.com | www.amherst-common.com.

Attractions

Hadley Farm Museum. Occupying a barn built in 1782, this museum contains an extensive collection of agricultural implements and other equipment common to the rural America of yesteryear, from sleighs, wagons, and a spoke-wheeled stagecoach to plows, bean shellers, spinning wheels, and innumerable other examples of farm technology. Some items date back to the 17th century. | 147 Russell St. | 413/584–8279 | Free | May–Columbus Day, Tues.–Sat. 10–4:30, Sun. 1:30–4:30.

Porter-Phelps-Huntington Museum. Ten generations of farmers have occupied this 1752 house, the first to be built outside the stockaded town of Hadley. All the wives of the farm's owners kept diaries, which provide the basis for this museum's richly narrative interpretation of early American farm life. | 130 River Dr. | 413/584–4699 | $4 | Mid-May–mid-Oct., Sat.–Wed. 1–4:30.

ON THE CALENDAR

JUNE: *Amherst/Hadley Garden Tour.* This self-guided tour of eight gardens in Amherst and Hadley is organized by the Amherst Historical Society. The gardens are of many types—perennial, shade, cutting, English country, rock, vegetable, herb, unusual landscaping, borders, water features, and miniature boxwoods. | 413/256–0678.

JUNE–JULY: *Wednesday Folk Traditions.* International folk-music concerts are held on Wednesday evenings on the grounds of the Porter-Phelps-Huntington Museum. Picnickers are welcome. | 413/584–4699.

JULY–AUG.: *A Perfect Spot of Tea.* A revival of the colonial custom of afternoon tea takes place on the back veranda of the Porter-Phelps-Huntington Museum. There's musical entertainment as tea and pastries are served. | 413/584–4699.

Dining

Casa Antonio. Italian. Everything from pizza to steak and fish to eggplant parmesan are served at this family-run eatery. There are tables and booths and unusual decor including a fountain with frogs and goldfish and a gas-lit fireplace. Big picture windows offer views of cornfields. | 206 Russell St. | 413/586–3880 | fax 413/587–9957 | Closed Mon. | $6–$15 | AE, D, MC, V.

Lodging

Econo Lodge. This renovated property is a five-minute drive from Amherst College and the University of Massachusetts. Smith, Hampshire, and Mount Holyoke colleges are nearby. Standard motel rooms, clean. Complimentary Continental breakfast. Some refrigerators, cable TV. Pool. Basketball. Laundry facilities. | 237 Russell St. | 413/584–9816 | fax 413/586–7512 | 70 rooms | $79–$89 | AE, D, DC, MC, V.

Howard Johnson Inn. Within a few miles of this hotel are the campuses of the University of Massachusetts and Hampshire College. Yankee Candle is 13 mi north. Rooms have private balconies or patios, and suites have hot tubs. Kids under 16 stay free. Complimentary Continental breakfast. In-room data ports, some in-room hot tubs, cable TV. Pool. Gym. Laundry facilities. Business services. Pets allowed. | 401 Russell St. | 413/586–0114 or 800/654–2000 | fax 413/584–7163 | www.thhg.com | 100 rooms, 3 suites | $69–$129, $89–$149 suites | AE, D, DC, MC, V.

Norwottuck Inn. One wing of this family-owned and -operated L-shape motel has parking in front, and the other has an inside corridor. Guest rooms are large and have one or two queen-size beds and cherry furniture. Guests get complimentary health-club passes. Restaurant, bar, complimentary Continental breakfast. Some in-room data ports, cable TV. Outdoor pool. Bicycles. No pets. | 208 Russell St. | 413/587–9866 | fax 413/587–9957 | www.norwottuckinn.com | 21 rooms, 1 suite | $65–$119 | AE, D, MC, V.

HARWICH (CAPE COD)

MAP 6, L6

(Nearby towns also listed: Brewster, Chatham, Dennis, Orleans)

Harwich is the only Cape Cod town to have retained any significant agricultural base, in this case raising cranberries. In previous centuries the town was also a significant fishing port with scores of vessels unloading their catch at the town docks, but once its shallow harbor could no longer accommodate the larger-draft boats that came into use by the early 1900s, the fishing business fizzled. In its place Harwich turned, like the rest of its neighbors, to tourism, building its first resort hotel in 1880. These days the town's south shore along Route 28 is blanketed by motels, inns, and bed-and-breakfasts, and everywhere there is development pressure on open, buildable land; however, inland areas still convey the rural quality of life that continues to underpin the town's character.

Information: **Harwich Chamber of Commerce** | Box 34, Harwich Port, 02646 | 508/432–1600 or 800/441–3199. **Visitor Center** | 550 Main St. | 508/432–1600 | fax 508/430–2105 | harwichc@capecod.net | www.harwichcc.com.

Attractions

Brooks Free Library. This two-story building, part of the town library system, is well worth a visit to view the permanent collection of John Rogers figurines. | 739 Main St. | 508/430–7562 | www.vsg.cape.com/~brooks/ | Free | Mon., Wed. 10–6, Tues. noon–8, Thur.–Sat. 10–4.

Harwich Historical Society/Brooks Academy Museum. This 1844 building at the village center was built as a seminary and now contains exhibits related to local and regional history, from displays of old hand tools, toys, costumes, Indian artifacts, and antique glass, to a restored outhouse. The museum also features extensive exhibits on Harwich's cranberry industry. | 80 Parallel St., Harwich Center | 508/432–8089 | www.capecodhistory.org | Free | Mid-June–early Sept., Tues.–Fri. 1–4; Sept.–Oct., Thurs.–Fri. 1–4; and by appointment.

Harwich Junior Theatre. The mission of this group is to bring quality live theater to young people and their families. It offers a full curriculum of classes, preschool through young adult, and presents 12 shows a year. Casts and production crews are drawn from the classes and workshops, with adult roles played by actors from the theater community. | 105 Division St., West Harwich | 508/432–2002 | www.capecod.net/hjt.

Passenger ferry service. Freedom Cruise Line. Ferries depart three times daily for Nantucket from picturesque Saquatucket Harbor. The 90-minute crossings are scheduled to allow day-trippers to enjoy up to five hours ashore. | 702 Main St., Harwich Port | 508/432–8999 | www.capecod.net/freedom | $39 round-trip | May–Columbus Day, daily.

ON THE CALENDAR

SEPT.: *Cranberry Harvest Festival.* This mid-month four-day festival consists of hundreds of events including arts-and-crafts displays, fireworks, and the biggest small-town parade in the country. The parade follows a 2-mi route from Route 28 at Saquatucket Harbor to Doan Road. Families set up barbecues along the roadside as they watch the drum and bugle corps and local floats pass by. | 508/430–2811.

Dining

Bishop's Terrace. Continental. This family-owned and -operated restaurant was established in 1942. It has a tavern and three candle-lit dining rooms—an indoor glassed gazebo with a central garden and fountain, a glass terrace room, and a regatta room with boat models and a fireplace. Popular dishes on the dining room menu include rack of lamb, double-cut prime veal chop, roast Long Island duckling, and Chatham haddock. In addition there is a simpler tavern menu and a children's menu. There is live piano music Thurs.–Sun. in summer and Fri.–Sat. in spring and fall. Sun. brunch. | 108 Main St., West Harwich | 508/432–0253 | No lunch | $13–$21 | AE, MC, V.

The Cape Sea Grille. Seafood. Patrons drive for miles to dine at this spot, an old sea captain's house built in the late 1860s. The house specialty is the Sea Grille mixed grill: roasted lobster, smoked bacon-wrapped swordfish mignon, salmon with herb butter, and barbecued shrimp. There are candle-lit tables with white-linen napkins and burgundy tablecloths with white overlays. | 31 Sea St., Harwich Port | 508/432–4745 | Closed Labor Day–June. No lunch | $16–$25 | AE, MC, V.

Carriage House at the Gingerbread House. Eastern European. This restaurant specializes in pierogi, stuffed cabbage, specialty cakes, blintzes, sauerbraten, and homemade soups such as borscht, sorrel, and cold fruit soup. | 141 Division St., West Harwich | 508/432–1901 or 800/788–1901 | Breakfast also available. Closed Jan.–Apr. and Mon.–Wed. No dinner | $5–$12.

Country Inn. Contemporary. A 1780 inn surrounded by 6 acres of fields and woods. The menu features creative New England fare such as duck stuffed with apricots, barley, bacon, and Riesling wine sauce, and Basque-style braised lamb shanks. There's a main dining room, a tavern, and a small private dining room. The restaurant and tavern have four wood-burning fireplaces between them. Entertainment on weekends. | 86 Sisson Rd., Harwich Port | 508/432–2769 or 800/231–1722 | Closed Mon.–Thurs. in Jan.–Mar. No lunch | $15–$22 | AE, MC, V.

400 East. American/Casual. This restaurant serves salads, fresh-ground charbroiled burgers, grilled gourmet pizzas, pastas, steaks, barbecued baby back ribs, and fresh seafood. There's a broad mix of local patrons—families, senior citizens, and business people—and booth, table, and bar seating. | 1421 Rte. 39 | 508/432–1800 | $8–$16 | AE, D, MC, V.

L'Alouette. French. At this formal restaurant classic technique is evidenced by every dish. Try the duck à l'orange, filet mignon au poivre, veal medallions, and country pâté. Early bird suppers in fall and winter. | 787 Main St., Harwich Port | 508/430–0405 | Reservations essential | Closed Mon., also Tues. in winter. No lunch | $15–$28 | AE, D, MC, V.

The Stewed Tomato. Café. It's like an old-fashioned ice-cream parlor with red-and-white checked curtains. As the name suggests, stewed tomatoes are a specialty side dish. On weekdays, homemade soups and desserts are served; on Sundays, eggs Benedict is a special. Children are invited to color placemats while they wait for their food; their artwork adorns the walls. | 707 Main St., Harwich center | 508/432–2214 | Reservations not accepted | Breakfast also available. No dinner | $3–$5 | MC, V.

Lodging

★ **Augustus Snow House.** This turn-of-the-century house in the village of Harwich Port was owned by one of Cape Cod's first bankers and is filled with antiques. Every guest room has a fireplace. The property has a private beach one block away. The Brooks Academy Museum is 1 mi away. Complimentary breakfast. Some in-room hot tubs, cable TV. Beach. No kids under 12. No smoking. | 528 Main St., Harwich Port | 508/430–0528 or 800/320–0528 | fax 508/432–6638 | www.augustussnow.com | 5 rooms | $160–$190 | AE, D, MC, V.

Barnaby Inn. This 200-year-old house is set back 150 ft from the road. It contains large wallpapered guest rooms with wall-to-wall carpeting and some four-poster beds. The two deluxe rooms have wood-burning fireplaces. Breakfast is delivered to each guest room. Complimentary Continental breakfast. Refrigerators, some in-room hot tubs, cable TV, no room phones. Some pets allowed. No smoking. | 36 Rte. 28, West Harwich | 508/432–6789 or 800/439–4764 | fax 508/430–1938 | www.barnabyinn.com | 4 standard rooms, 2 deluxe rooms, 1 cottage | $100 standard, $140 deluxe | MC, V.

Cape Cod Claddagh Inn. This inn resembles a small Irish manor, with lace curtains, Oriental rugs, crystal and china, and Irish art. A newer building with three guest rooms is decorated in a Colonial style and the main house is Victorian. There's Irish entertainment in the pub and a lobster bake by the pool on Sun. afternoons, with Irish and Caribbean music. Dining room, bar with entertainment, picnic area, bar, complimentary breakfast. Refrigerators, cable TV. Pool. Some pets allowed. | 77 Main St., West Harwich | 508/432–9628 or 800/356–9628 | fax 508/432–6039 | www.capecodcladdaghinn.com | 11 rooms, 4 suites | $95–$150 | AE, MC, V.

Captain's Quarters. This 19th-century Queen Anne house has Victorian elements and a wraparound porch with wicker furniture overlooking the colorful perennial gardens. It's a three-minute walk to the (sandy) Harwich Port public beach and village. Complimentary Continental breakfast. Cable TV, no room phones. No pets. No smoking. | 85 Bank St., Harwich Port | 508/432–1991 or 800/992–6550 | www.cqbb.com | 5 rooms | $129 | Closed mid-Oct.–mid-May | AE, D, MC, V.

Coachman Motor Inn. This inn is next door to public tennis courts, in front of cranberry bogs, 1,000 yards from the ferry dock, and ½ mi from the beach. All rooms face the swimming pool. The innkeeper speaks German. Kids under 14 stay free. Restaurant. Refrigerators, cable TV. Pool. | 774 Main St., Harwich Port | 508/432–0707 or 800/524–4265 | fax 508/432–7951 | www.coachmanmotorinn.com | $115, $185 suite, $850/wk apartment | 26 rooms, 1 suite, 1 apartment | Closed Nov.–Apr. | AE, DC, MC, V.

Country Inn. This 18th-century inn is owned and managed by an award-winning chef who presents his creations in the full-service restaurant and tavern. Some guest rooms have fireplaces. Restaurant, bar with entertainment, complimentary Continental breakfast. Cable TV, no room phones. Pool. Beach. | 86 Sisson Rd., Harwich Port | 508/432–2769 or 800/231–1722 | fax 508/430–1455 | www.countryinncapecod.com | 6 rooms | $80–$120 | AE, MC, V.

Dunscroft by the Sea Bed and Breakfast Inn. This inn in a quiet residential area between two harbors has a private beach. Some guest rooms have canopy and four-poster beds, fireplaces, and limited water views. The library opens onto a large porch overlooking the gardens. Shops, restaurants, and galleries are within walking distance. Picnic area, complimentary breakfast. Some in-room hot tubs, cable TV in some rooms. Beach. Library. No kids under 12. No smoking. | 24 Pilgrim Rd., Harwich Port | 508/432–0810 or 800/432–4345 | fax 508/432–5134 | www.dunscroftbythesea.com | 9 rooms, 1 cottage | $165–$235, $265 cottage | AE, MC, V.

Gingerbread House. Gingerbread cutouts along the roof give this 1883 Queen Anne Victorian its name. Trees screen the house from the road and the 2 acres of landscaped grounds and old English cottage garden make it feel like it's miles away from civilization. The guest rooms are on the second floor and contain period reproduction furniture. There's also a front porch with open and screened areas with wicker furniture. Restaurant, complimentary breakfast. No room phones. No pets. No smoking. | 141 Division St., West Harwich | 508/432–1901 or 800/788–1901 | www.gingerbreadhousecapecod.com | 5 rooms | $85–$125 | MC, V.

Handkerchief Shoals Motel. This 3-acre property is in a quiet area, ½ mi from a public beach. The one-story motel has rooms decorated in bright colors, each with a desk and a sitting area. No air-conditioning, microwaves, refrigerators, cable TV. Pool. | Rte. 28, South Harwich | 508/432–2200 | www.sunsol.com/handkerchief | 26 rooms | $72–$85 | Closed mid-Oct.–mid-May | D, MC, V.

Harbor Breeze Bed and Breakfast. This building seems to say "Cape Cod" with its weathered cedarshake shingles. The 10-room guest wing surrounds a garden courtyard. Each room has a private entrance and some have decks or fireplaces. There are two two-room suites, and two rooms with floral decor and individual decks. Complimentary Continental breakfast. Refrigerators, some in-room hot tubs, cable TV, no room phones. Outdoor pool. No pets. No smoking. | 326 Lower County Rd., Harwich Port | 508/432–0337 or 800/455–0247 | www.harborbreezeinn.com | 9 rooms, 1 suite | $99–$145, $175 for suite | AE, D, MC, V.

Lion's Head Inn. This 200-year-old sea captain's house in a residential neighborhood off the highway has furnishings that are a mixture of modern and antique. One room has a queen-size canopy bed and an outdoor deck. There's a fireplaced living room, a parlor, and a terrace common area with a guest refrigerator and microwave. Complimentary beach passes. Complimentary afternoon snack and beverage. Complimentary Continental breakfast. No room phones. Outdoor pool. No pets. No smoking. | 186 Belmont Rd., West Harwich | 508/432–7766 or 800/321–3155 | www.capecodinns.com | 6 rooms, 2 cottages | $95–$125 standard, $125–$150 premium, $750/wk 1–bedroom cottage, $850/wk 2–bedroom cottage | D, MC, V.

Sea Heather Inn at Harwich Port. This property has two buildings. One is a former sea captain's home with a wraparound verandah, and the other is a balconied 12-unit motel. They are both 200 yards from the beach and 150 yards from town. Half of the rooms have views of Nantucket Sound. Complimentary Continental breakfast. Some microwaves, some refrigerators, cable TV. No kids under 10. No smoking. | 28 Sea St., Harwich Port | 508/432–1275 or 800/789–7809 | fax 508/432–1275 | www.seaheather.com | 20 rooms, 2 suites, 2 buildings | $105–$200, $200–$350 suites | AE, MC, V.

Seadar Inn by the Sea. There are three buildings on this property, one of which dates from the 18th century. Since the beach is just 100 ft away, many of the accommodations overlook the water. The Colonial-style guest rooms, as well as the dining room, are done in wood paneling. Some also have wood beam ceilings or porthole windows. Picnic area, complimentary Continental breakfast. In-room data ports, some refrigerators, cable TV, some in-room VCRs. Business services. | 1 Braddock La., Harwich Port | 508/432–0264 or 800/888–5250 | fax 508/430–1916 | www.seadarinn.com | 23 rooms, 3 suites, 3 buildings | $100–$205, $150–$275 suites | Closed mid-Oct.–mid-May | MC, V.

Winstead Inn and Beach Resort. This is one of the few resorts right on the beach in Harwich Port. Chairs, beach towels, and umbrellas are provided free. Guest rooms are furnished with a mix of antiques and period reproductions. Dining room, complimentary Continental breakfast. Refrigerators, some in-room hot tubs, cable TV. Beach. No pets. No smoking. | 4 Braddock La., Harwich Port | 508/432–4444 or 800/870–4405 | fax 508/432–9152 | www.winsteadinn.com | 14 rooms | $195–$325 | MC, V.

Wychmere Village. Four Cape Cod-style buildings (including one cottage) on 3 landscaped acres of pine trees and gardens comprise this property. The cottage has a living room, kitchen, and two bedrooms. Volleyball, shuffleboard, and horseshoes on the lawn. Nantucket ferry service is 300 yards away. Harbors, beaches, shops, and restaurants are within walking distance. Picnic area. Some kitchenettes, refrigerators, cable TV. Pool. Playground. No smoking. | 767 Main St., Harwich Port | 508/432–1434 or 800/432–1434 | fax 508/432–8904 | info@wychmere.com | www.wychmere.com | 24 rooms in 3 buildings, 1 cottage | $99–$149, $899/wk cottage | Closed mid-Dec.–mid-Mar. | AE, D, MC, V.

HAVERHILL

MAP 6, I2

(Nearby towns also listed: Amesbury, Andover and North Andover, Lawrence)

On the banks of the mighty Merrimack River, Haverhill is a former industrial city that rose from rural obscurity to national prominence on the prodigious output of its shoe factories, which specialized in women's footwear. The shoemaking has all been exported out of state or out of the country, but the city is still dominated by its old brick industrial buildings. Although Haverhill has recovered from the low point hit after the departure of its major employer, and former factories are finding new uses, "for lease" signs are not rare. Its downtown continues to await full occupancy; Haverhill's position between the thriving high-tech industries of southern New Hampshire and greater Boston has given local residents plenty of alternative employment opportunities. Parts of the town are unusually rural, particularly in the vicinity of the foremost local attraction, poet John Greenleaf Whittier's 19th-century farm.

Information: Greater Haverhill Chamber of Commerce | 87 Winter St., Haverhill, 01830-5759 | 978/373–5663 | fax 978/373–8060 | www.chamber.mva.net.

Attractions

Haverhill Historical Society. This society's headquarters on a hill above the Merrimack River contains several historic structures, including homes from the 18th and 19th centuries and a small Civil War–era shoemaker's shop. The society preserves a range of artifacts from several centuries of Haverhill life, lending its main exhibit room the air of a giant attic full of the city's cast-off and forgotten past. | 240 Water St. | 978/374–4626 | fax 978/521–9176 | $5 | Daily 10–5.

John Greenleaf Whittier Birthplace. One of 19th-century America's leading literary figures, eventually known as the Quaker Poet, was born in this small farmhouse in 1807. "The beauty of outward nature early impressed me," Whittier wrote of his childhood on the farm, where he lived with his parents and three siblings. Whittier sold the farm in 1836, after his father died, and moved his entire family to nearby Amesbury. | 305 Whittier Rd. | 978/373–3979 | $2 | May–Oct., Tues.–Sat. 10–5, Sun. 1–5; Nov.–Apr., Tues.–Fri. and Sun. 1–5, Sat. 10–5.

Winnekenni Castle and Park. Winnekenni (which means "very beautiful" in Algonquin) is an appropriate name for this, a favorite local picnic spot. The castle was built in 1873 by Dr. James R. Nichols, who wanted a summer house that looked like a castle. The city of Haverhill bought the property in 1895 and turned it into a city park. At the top of the hill is the castle, at the bottom is a playground, tennis courts, and walking trails around Kenoza Lake, one of the city reservoirs. The castle is the site of summer music and story-telling programs for families. The (empty) castle is locked unless there is an event. | Kenoza Ave. | 978/521–1686 | Free | Open for events Apr.–Dec. 1.

ON THE CALENDAR

APR.: *The Greater Haverhill Chamber of Commerce Business Expo.* On the second Thursday of the month, 150 business vendors display their products at the Cedardale Health and Fitness Center. The expo is followed by a reception. | 978/373–5663.
JULY: *Winnekenni Pancake Breakfast.* Celebrate the Fourth of July with a breakfast at Winnekenni Castle. The flapjacks are cooked on an outside griddle; you can dine at tables inside the castle or spread out a blanket in the park. | 978/521–1686.

Dining

99 Restaurant and Pub. American. This restaurant—which has both booth and bar seating—is popular with families because of its large portions, good prices, variety of entrée selections, and children's menu. | 786 River St. | 978/372–8303 | $5–$11 | AE, D, DC, MC, V.

Lodging

Best Western–Merrimack Valley. This recently renovated hotel is convenient to major highways and is close to the New Hampshire border. Executive and deluxe rooms are available with king-size beds, VCRs, microwaves, and refrigerators. Adjacent restaurant and lounge. Kids under 18 stay free. Complimentary Continental breakfast. In-room data ports, cable TV. Indoor pool. Hot tub. Gym. Laundry services. Business services. | 401 Lowell Ave. | 978/373–1511 | fax 978/373–1517 | bstwstmvl@aol.com | www.bestwestern.com | 127 rooms | $79–$149 | AE, D, DC, MC, V.

Comfort Suites–Haverhill. This hotel has two types of suites—one with two full-size beds and a couch, the other with a king-size bed with a full-size pull-out sofa. Customers tend to be business travelers and leisure travelers enroute to points north or south. Complimentary Continental breakfast. In-room data ports, refrigerator. Hot tub. Gym. Laundry facilities, laundry services. Business services. No pets. | 106 Bank Rd. | 978/374–7755 or 800/228–5150 | fax 978/521–1894 | www.hotelchoice.com | 131 suites | $125–$139, $115 single | AE, D, DC, MC, V.

HOLYOKE

MAP 6, D4

(Nearby towns also listed: Chicopee, Northampton, South Hadley, Springfield)

The decline in large-scale manufacturing across Massachusetts in the mid-20th century left many of the state's old industrial cities struggling to find some new use for their giant, outdated factory complexes. Holyoke is a prime example: during the 19th century it was hailed as the "Paper City," with 25 companies churning out more tons of writing paper than any other place in the world. Today only one paper mill survives; of the rest, all that remains are their brick skeletons, lining mile after mile of hand-dug hydropower canals. Artists are among the most visible newcomers to have recognized the beauty of the vast abandoned mills, and businesses are gradually following suit. The state has also contributed to the downtown revitalization effort with the creation of its Holyoke Heritage State Park, celebrating the city's industrial past. The Volleyball Hall of Fame, authentic steam-era train rides, and Wistariahurst—a historic mansion belonging to one of the city's early business moguls—are among the city's other attractions.

Information: Greater Holyoke Chamber of Commerce | 177 High St., Holyoke, 01040-6504 | 413/534–3376 | fax 413/534–3385 | holycham@exit3.com | www.holycham.com.

Attractions

Children's Museum. This museum engages its young visitors with things to touch, things to make, things to explore, and plenty of encouragement to try it all (under adult supervision, of course). In addition to all the hands-on activities and exhibits, there's a gift shop with crafts and novelty items. | 444 Dwight St. | 413/536–KIDS | $4 | Tues.–Sat. 9:30–4:30, Sun. noon–5.

Dinosaur Footprints Reservation. During the Mesozoic Era, 200 million years ago, a 20-ft *Eubrontes giganteus* took a walk through some mud, leaving behind footprints that resemble giant turkey tracks. Several of the shallow but unmistakable impressions, along with smaller tracks from a pair of other creatures, are to be seen here on a slab of sedimentary rock on the west bank of the Connecticut River. | U.S. 5 | 413/684–0148 | www.thetrustees.org | Free | Apr.–Nov., daily dawn–dusk.

Holyoke Heritage State Park. Holyoke was at one time the world's leading producer of fine writing paper. This state park's visitors center contains exhibits detailing the papermaking process, the silk industry that also thrived here, the lives of immigrant workers in the mills, and the construction of Holyoke's network of power canals. | 221 Appleton St. | 413/534–1723 | fax 413/534–1723 | www.state.ma.us/dem | Free | Tues.–Sun. noon–4:30.

Holyoke Merry-Go-Round. The 48 colorful wooden horses and two dazzling chariots on this beautiful antique carousel, restored to pristine condition complete with mechanical band organ, delight young riders and simply the young at heart. Built by the Philadelphia Toboggan Company in 1929, it has stood in a mountainside amusement park on Holyoke's outskirts for nearly 60 years. It is now one of fewer than 100 grand carousels still in existence. | 221 Appleton St. | 413/538–9838 | $1 | July–early Sept., Tues.–Sun. 10:30–4:30; mid-Sept.–June, weekends noon–4.

Mt. Tom Ski Area and Summer Slide. In winter this mountainside park turns on the snow-making and opens up its 17 trails to downhill skiing and snowboarding. In summer the rental skis are stowed away and the faucet is turned on for the water park, which includes a 400-ft slide, tube rides, and a wave pool. | U.S. 5 | 413/536–0416 or 800/545–7163 | www.mttom.com.

Volleyball Hall of Fame. This sports museum, located in Holyoke Heritage State Park, features interactive exhibits and other displays on the stars and great moments of volleyball history. The sport was invented in Holyoke in 1895, and officially became an Olympic event in 1964. The museum holds its annual induction ceremony every October. A gift shop is located onsite. | 444 Dwight St. | 413/536–0926 | www.volleyball.org | $3.50 | Tue.–Sat., 9:30–4;30; Sun., 12–4:30.

Wistariahurst Museum. William Skinner, a prominent silk manufacturer, moved into this grand Second Empire mansion in 1874, when he relocated his factory to Holyoke. Over the

THE TRUSTEES OF RESERVATIONS

Conserving private land expressly on behalf of public enjoyment has deep roots in Massachusetts, and is a direct result of the squalid, overcrowded conditions of its 19th-century Industrial Age cities. Urban problems attracted many social reformers in the decades following America's 1876 centennial, among them Frederick Law Olmsted, considered the grandfather of landscape architecture in this country. Olmsted and others felt that the lack of exposure to nature was one of the greatest ills facing city dwellers. Countrylike parks, it was believed, could be an antidote to the corrosive effects of city life on both physical and mental health. Besides the obvious need for bringing nature back into cities, it was also clear that existing natural spaces outside cities needed protection from eventual development. Uncommonly beautiful parcels of land, it was proposed, should be collected "just as the public library holds books and the art museum pictures for the use and enjoyment of the public." From these high ideals was founded in 1891 by Olmsted disciple and business partner Charles Eliot, who was also instrumental in the creation of a regional park commission for the Greater Boston area, the nation's first land preservation organization, the Trustees of Reservations.

To date the Trustees have amassed more than 80 publicly accessible properties across the state. True to the organization's mission statement, each one is a beauty, and their diversity reflects Massachusetts's ecological and cultural richness. Highlights are many. Some of the state's finest beaches are administered by the Trustees, from Wasque on Martha's Vineyard to Crane Beach in Ipswich. Holdings include dramatic coastal granite ledges in Rockport; dinosaur footprints in Holyoke; panoramic Monument Mountain in Great Barrington; and Bartholomew's Cobble, a botanically exceptional National Natural Landmark in Sheffield. The Trustees also conserve historically significant homes, from Hawthorne's Old Manse, in Concord, to Gilded Age mansions with formal display gardens, such as Naumkeag in Stockbridge. Most of the houses are open seasonally for guided tours and charge admission to nonmembers. Otherwise, except for their beaches, all Trustees properties are free and open to the public year-round. For more information about house tours, member programs, or to order a complete property guide, contact the Trustees of Reservations, 572 Essex St., Beverly, MA 01915-1530 (978/524–1858; www.ttor.org).

© Artville

next half century, no expense was spared in the creation of luxurious interiors. Now, in addition to offering a view of the decorative arts and tastes of the late Victorian era, the museum has a carriage house that offers exhibits on local natural and Native American history. | 238 Cabot St. | 413/534–2216 | www.holyoke.org | $5 | Mar.–mid-Aug. and Sept.–Oct., Wed. and weekends 1–5; Nov.–Feb., Wed. and weekends noon–4.

ON THE CALENDAR

MAR.: *St. Patrick's Day Parade.* Holyoke has the second-largest St. Patrick's Day parade in the country. The tradition was started in 1952 by Irish-American policemen and fire-fighters from Holyoke. Today, this three-hour televised event on the Sunday after St. Patrick's Day has about 40 floats and 35 bands, attracting 300,000 spectators to a city of 44,000. | 413/533–1700.

Dining

Delaney House. Contemporary. Elaborately prepared regional American cuisine and a 300-bottle wine list are the restaurant's undisputed stars, but the picturesque rural setting and understated colonial elegance play major supporting roles as well. Known for fresh seafood and game. Entertainment Fri. and Sat. Kids' menu. No smoking. | U.S. 5 | 413/532–1800 | Reservations essential | No lunch | $17–$24 | AE, D, DC, MC, V.

Yankee Pedlar Inn. American/Casual. Casual dining in a rambling inn fashioned from a 19th-century Victorian mansion. Known for pasta, veal, beef, and champagne brunch. Open-air dining on porch. Live music Fri.–Sun. Sun. brunch. | 1866 Northampton St. | 413/532–9494 | Closed Mon. | $15–$24 | AE, DC, MC, V.

Lodging

Holiday Inn Holyoke Holidome and Conference Center. This hotel is just off I–91, the north–south artery through western-central Massachusetts. The Volleyball Hall of Fame is nearby and Holyoke Mall, western New England's premier shopping destination, is adjacent. Restaurant, bar with entertainment, room service. In-room data ports, cable TV. Indoor pool. Hot tub. Gym. Video games. | 245 Whiting Farms Rd. | 413/534–3311 or 800/465–4329 | fax 413/533–8443 | www.holiday-inn.com | 219 rooms, 1 suite | $89–$144 | AE, D, DC, MC, V.

Super 8 Motel. Extras at this budget motel include complimentary doughnuts, coffee, and juice; free local calls; and use of the refrigerator and microwave at the front desk. The building has exterior corridors. Complimentary Continental breakfast. In-room data ports, cable TV. Outdoor pool. No pets. | 1515 Northampton St. | 413/536–1980 | fax 413/533–2775 | 52 rooms | $90–$98 | AE, D, DC, MC, V.

Yankee Pedlar Inn. The most unusual feature of this 1875 Victorian-style inn is a banquet hall (built to resemble an opera house) containing wall-paneling from Holyoke mansions, 25-ft-tall mirrors from England, and a chandelier from the Metropolitan Opera House in New York City. The antiques-furnished inn also has an excellent restaurant. Restaurant, bar with entertainment, complimentary Continental breakfast. In-room data ports, some kitchenettes, cable TV. | 1866 Northampton St. | 413/532–9494 | fax 413/536–8877 | info@yankeepedlar.com | www.yankeepedlar.com | 21 rooms in 4 houses, 5 apartments | $75–$150, $130 apartments | AE, DC, MC, V.

HYANNIS (CAPE COD)

MAP 6, K6

(Nearby towns also listed: Barnstable Village, Centerville, Mashpee, Nantucket, Yarmouth)

Hyannis is the business and commercial capital of Cape Cod. Although technically only a village within the town of Barnstable, Hyannis has a full fifth of the Cape's 200,000 year-round residents. Summer is undeniably its busiest season, but Hyannis has many shops, restaurants, and motels that operate year-round, and it holds a near monopoly on mid-Cape nightlife. It's well connected to the rest of Massachusetts by bus and airlines, and has seasonal Amtrak service from New York City. In summer the approaches to Hyannis Harbor routinely suffer gridlock as island-bound passengers flock to the two ferry companies serving Nantucket and Martha's Vineyard. Off-season, Hyannis maintains the only year-round boat service to Nantucket. The town is perhaps best known as the primary summer destination for the late President John F. Kennedy and his family. However, its famous oceanfront vacation estates (most built before the Great Depression brought an end to the Roaring '20s) also remind visitors that there is more to life in Hyannis than long lines at the ice-cream shop and endless traffic at the malls.

Information: Hyannis Area Chamber of Commerce | 1481 Rte. 132, Hyannis, 02601 | 508/362–5230 or 877/HYANNIS | www.hyannischamber.com.

Attractions

Car/passenger ferry service. Two companies provide year-round ferry connections to Nantucket from Hyannis Harbor, one for passengers only, the other for passengers and cars. Summer passenger service to Martha's Vineyard is also available. Bicycles are permitted on all vessels for an added charge, and advance passenger reservations are only accepted on select high-speed boats. Vehicle reservations are recommended but not required.

Hy-Line Cruises. Year-round passenger service to Nantucket aboard a swift and smooth water-jet catamaran, which makes the crossing in one hour. Slower, less expensive passenger service to both Nantucket and Martha's Vineyard is also provided in summer aboard regular single-hull vessels, which complete their respective runs in slightly under two hours. Prepaid passenger reservations are accepted only for the high-speed service. | Ocean St. Dock | 508/778–2600 or 888/778–1132 (in MA); 800/492–8082 (high–speed Nantucket ferry tickets, also in MA only) | www.hy-linecruises.com | $25 round-trip for regular service to Nantucket or Martha's Vineyard, $55 round-trip for high-speed Nantucket ferry | To Nantucket: high-speed ferry daily; regular service May–Oct., daily. To Martha's Vineyard: early Oct.–Memorial Day, weekends; Memorial Day–Oct., daily.

Steamship Authority. The Steamship Authority connects Hyannis and Nantucket with year-round service by car-carrying ferries, as well as seasonal service by high-speed passenger-only catamaran. Passenger reservations are accepted only on the high-speed boat, and are strongly recommended. Vehicle reservations are also recommended, but not required, for the regular service. | South Street Dock | 508/477–8600 or 508/495–FAST (high–speed ferry reservations) | www.islandferry.com | Passengers $24 round-trip via regular service or $46 round-trip via high-speed service. Vehicles $200–$300 round-trip | Daily.

John F. Kennedy Hyannis Museum. This museum in the former town hall consists of photographic and video displays about JFK's summers on Cape Cod. Tracing his life from adolescence to the presidency, the exhibits create a 29-year album of Jack, his friends, and the fabled Kennedy clan. | 397 Main St. | 508/790–3077 | $3 | Mid-Feb.–mid-Dec., Wed.–Sat. 10–4.

John F. Kennedy Memorial. Next to popular Veteran's Beach, this large, open memorial plaza honors the slain 35th president of the United States with a bronze relief facing the water on which he loved to sail and benches from which to admire the views of boat-filled Lewis Bay. | Ocean St. | 508/362–5230 | Free | Daily.

ON THE CALENDAR

JUNE: *Father's Day Car Show*. This show on Main Street features all kinds of exotic cars—antique, sports, classic, hot rods, custom, sports, muscle cars, kit cars, pickup trucks, four-by-fours, and race cars. | 508/775–2201.

JUNE–SEPT.: *Cape Cod Melody Tent*. Established in 1950, this is one of the oldest tent music theaters in the country. Music, theater, and comedy are showcased in this 2,300-seat theater-in-the-round where every seat is within 50 ft of the stage. | 508/775–9100.

AUG.: *Pops by the Sea.* The Boston Pops Orchestra leaves its usual performance venue on the Charles River Esplanade in Boston to give a Sunday afternoon performance on the Hyannis town green. Bring blankets or chairs. | 508/362–0066.

DEC.: *Village and Harbor of Lights.* This weekend event includes a Christmas tree lighting ceremony, a carol sing-along, and a bayberry candle lighting ceremony—a tradition that was started many years ago by the founder of Colonial Candle of Cape Cod. There's a boat parade in the harbor and Santa arrives by boat or duckmobile. During the day, merchants offer complimentary samplings of local fare and the John F. Kennedy Hyannis Museum has free admission admission. | 508/775–2201.

Dining

Barbyann's. American. A family favorite, with pizza, burgers, fried seafood, lots of appetizers, and even some Yankee-Mexican choices, served amid a playful decor. Open-air dining on patio. Kids' menu. Sun. brunch. | 120 Airport Rd. | 508/775–9795 | $10–$17 | AE, D, DC, MC, V.

Baxter's Fish N' Chips. Seafood. This restaurant on Hyannis harbor is a favorite with boaters and bathers. Takeout patrons sit at picnic tables on a deck overlooking the harbor. An over-21 crowd seeking table service is welcome in the dining room. Try the fried clams cooked to order and served with french fries and homemade tartar sauce or the lobster rolls, burgers, grilled fish, and shrimp. | 177 Pleasant St. | 508/775–4490 | Closed Columbus Day–Apr. and Mon. in Labor Day–Columbus Day | $9–$15 | AE, MC, V.

Fazio's Trattoria. Italian. This trattoria, owned and operated by Tom and Eileen Fazio, is in a refurbished bakery with wood floors, high ceilings, a deli case full of fresh pasta, breads and cheeses, and an espresso and cappuccino bar. The original brick oven is used to bake bread and pizza and the exhibition-style kitchen anchors the dining room. Try the homemade spinach fettuccine tossed with grilled vegetables, garlic, and olive oil or the veal scallopini. There's a wide selection of beers and wines, particularly Italian and California vintages. | 294 Main St. | 508/775–9400 | No lunch | $11–$17 | AE, D, MC, V.

Harry's. Cajun/Creole. The saints come marchin' in for New Orleans–style sandwiches, barbecued dishes, Cajun mussels, and blackened local fish with jambalaya. Families come for lunch and dinner and an over-21 crowd arrives later to hear live blues every evening in summer and on weekends in winter. | 700 Main St. | 508/778–4188 | $9–$19 | AE, D, DC, MC, V.

Original Gourmet Brunch. American. A casual breakfast, lunch, and brunch spot acclaimed by locals, with more than enough variety in its offerings to satisfy the choosiest diner. Known for chowder, chili, omelets, and French toast. Beer and wine only. Sun. brunch. No smoking. | 517 Main St. | 508/771–2558 | Breakfast also available. No dinner | $4–$7 | No credit cards.

★ The Paddock. Contemporary. One of the area's favorite dining experiences has a creative menu of updated Continental and New England dishes including steaks, fresh seafood, and such. Two of the dining rooms have the feel of an English pub, while the third room is more upscale and modern. There's a fine wine list with some 300 bottles. Try the 2-pound lobster, peppercorn steak, or the duck. Live music Fri.–Sun. Kids' menu. No smoking in dining room. | W. Main St. rotary | 508/775–7677 | Closed mid-Nov.–Apr. 1 | $16–$24 | AE, D, DC, MC, V.

Penguins Sea Grill. Seafood. Contemporary exposed brick and light-wood provide a comfortable venue for local and exotic seafood prepared simply on a wood fire or elaborately with Asian-, Mediterranean-, or Caribbean-inspired sauces and accompaniments. Known for wide fresh-fish selections. Try baked stuffed lobster and local mussels and clams, as well as the fabulous homebaked breads and desserts. Early bird suppers. Kids' menu. No smoking in dining room. | 331 Main St. | 508/775–2023 | Closed Jan.–mid-Feb. and Sun. and Mon. in mid-Feb.–May. No lunch | $15–$25 | AE, D, DC, MC, V.

Ristorante Barolo. Italian. It's classic Italian from the background music and decor to the hearty pasta, meat, and seafood dishes. Open-air dining in courtyard. | 297 North St. | 508/778–2878 | No lunch | $20–$32 | AE, DC, MC, V.

Roadhouse Cafe. Italian. Behind the yellow clapboards and black awning is an elegant series of dining rooms graced with Oriental rugs, antiques, candlelight, and a couple of fireplaces. Featured are seafood, pasta, and steaks prepared with subtle sophistication. A lighter sandwich and pizza menu is offered in the Backdoor Bistro, along with live jazz. Good wines by the glass. Try the codfish chowder or the chicken homard with lobster and Swiss cheese. Live music Mon., plus piano bar Fri. and Sat. (Wed.–Sun. in July–early Sept.). Early bird suppers. Free valet parking. | 488 South St. | 508/775–2386 | No lunch | $16–$23 | AE, D, DC, MC, V.

Roo Bar City Bistro. Contemporary. This sophisticated restaurant offers a a taste of the Big Apple on old Cape Cod—good music, dim lighting, and a crowded hip bar scene. From the wood-fired oven in the back wall come pizzas such as scallop and prosciutto with asparagus and goat cheese. Other popular dishes include pastas, grilled salmon with roasted-corn salsa, and grilled tenderloin with parsnip roll and garlic-sage jam. | 586 Main St. | 508/778–6515 | Reservations essential | No lunch | $15–$21 | AE, MC, V.

Sam Diego's. Mexican. A cheerful, almost cheesy Mexican dining room, a wildly popular bar, all-you-can-eat make-your-own tacos, and a menu with plenty of appealing choices for kids and adults. Open-air dining on patio. Kids' menu. | 950 Iyanough Rd. | 508/771–8816 | $9–$25 | AE, D, MC, V.

Starbuck's. American. Not the Seattle espresso chain, but a casual bar-eatery with whimsical design recalling Fibber McGee's closet and an equally eclectic menu of pub grub, salads, pasta, burgers, fajitas, stir-fry, and "buckwiches." Open-air dining on porch. Entertainment nightly. Kids' menu. | 645 Iyanough Rd. | 508/778–6767 | $7–$16 | AE, D, DC, MC, V.

Thai House Restaurant. Thai. Plain decor notwithstanding, the prompt, polite service and well-prepared dishes match the best Thai dining available in the big cities, all at prices that don't prey on tourists. Try fresh spring rolls, *tod mun* (shrimp and fish cakes), spicy string beans, crispy whole fish, and chicken lemongrass. No alcohol. No smoking. | 304 Main St. | 508/862–1616 | $7–$15 | AE, MC, V.

Lodging

★ **The Breakwaters.** These privately owned, weathered, gray-shingled cottages range in size from one to three bedrooms. Each unit contains a fully equipped kitchen, linens, and towels and has a deck or patio with a grill and picnic table. There is Mon.–Sat. maid service, free local calls, and an outdoor heated pool. The manager speaks French and English. Most units have a water view. Kitchenettes, cable TV. Outdoor pool. Beach. Baby-sitting. No pets. No smoking. | 432 Sea St. | 508/775–6831 | fax 508/775–6831 | www.capecod.com/breakwaters | $1,000/wk 1–bedroom units, $1,450/wk 2–bedroom units, $2,000/wk 3–bedroom units | 18 cottages | Closed mid-Oct.–Apr. | No credit cards.

Budget Host Inn Hyannis Motel. A year-round property with landscaped grounds is within walking distance of shops, restaurants, and theaters in downtown Hyannis. It is 1½ mi from the ferry. Rooms are clean and comfortable. There are also some efficiencies with kitchens. Kids under 17 stay free. In-room data ports, some kitchenettes, refrigerators, cable TV. Pool. | 614 Rte. 132 | 508/775–8910 or 800/322–3354 | fax 508/775–6476 | www.capecodtravel.com/hyannismotel | 35 rooms, 8 efficiencies | $69–$95 | AE, D, DC, MC, V.

Captain Gosnold Village. The 18 Cape Cod–style houses of the village contain multiple units, each with a private entrance and deck with gas grill. There are limited cooking facilities in the one-room studios but full kitchens in the one-, two-, and three-bedroom units. The property is landscaped with trees, flowers, and window boxes. Kitchenettes. Outdoor pool. No pets. | 230 Gosnold St. | 508/775–9111 | www.captaingosnold.com | 49 units | $105 studio, $170 1–bedroom unit, $240 2–bedroom unit, $280 3–bedroom unit | Closed mid-Nov.–mid-Apr. | MC, V.

Comfort Inn Hyannis. This renovated property is close to U.S. 6 but set back far enough from the road among the trees to be quiet. The three-story structure is on the side of a hill, and there are a couple of ponds nearby. Complimentary Continental breakfast. In-room data ports, cable TV. Indoor pool. Hot tub, sauna. Gym. Business services. Pets allowed (deposit). | 1470 Rte. 132 | 508/771–4804 | fax 508/790–2336 | www.comfortinn-hyannis.com | 104 rooms | $119–$169 | AE, D, DC, MC, V.

Country Lake. This family-oriented lakefront lodge is on 3 acres of landscaped grounds and about 3 mi from downtown Hyannis. It has a private dock with rowboats for guest use. Some efficiencies available. Kids under 13 stay free. Picnic area. Some kitchenettes, cable TV. Pool. Dock, boating. Library. | 1545 Iyanough Rd. | 508/362–6455 | www.sunsol.com/countrylake | 20 rooms | $59–$99 | Closed Dec.–Mar. | AE, D, MC, V.

Days Inn Hyannis. This property is adjacent to the Cape Cod Mall, just 3 mi from beaches and ferries. Rooms are on two floors, and are attractively furnished. Complimentary Continental breakfast. In-room data ports, cable TV. Indoor and outdoor pools. Hot tub. Gym. | 867 Rte. 132 | 508/771–6100 | fax 508/775–3011 | www.sunsol.com/daysinn | 99 rooms | $95–$200 | Closed Dec.–Jan. | AE, D, DC, MC, V.

Four Points Sheraton. A chain option near downtown Hyannis and beaches, 1 mi from Barnstable Airport. There's meeting space and a ballroom available for mid-size groups. Restaurant, bar with entertainment, room service. In-room data ports, cable TV. Indoor and outdoor pools. Hot tub. Tennis. Gym, volleyball. Business services, airport shuttle. | 1225 Bearses Way | 508/771–3000 or 800/325–3535 | fax 508/771–6564 | $89–$219 | Closed mid-Nov. 15–Apr. | AE, D, DC, MC, V.

Heritage House Hotel. This hotel is across from the Cape Cod train station and the bus station (which has service to Boston, Providence, and New York) and is a five-minute walk from the sights of downtown Hyannis. Dinner train, whale-watch, and golf packages are available. Restaurant, complimentary Continental breakfast (winter only). Refrigerators, cable TV. Indoor and outdoor pools. Hot tub, sauna. | 259 Main St. | 508/775–7000 or 800/352–7189 | fax 508/778–5687 | www.heritagehousehotel.com | 143 rooms | $85–$159 | AE, D, DC, MC, V.

Howard Johnson's. In downtown Hyannis, near shops, restaurants, and the harbor, this two-story motel-style property has typical chain-style rooms. Restaurant, bar, complimentary Continental breakfast. In-room data ports, cable TV. Indoor pool. Business services, free parking. | 447 Main St. | 508/775–3000 or 800/446–4656 | fax 508/771–1457 | 39 rooms | $119–$199 | AE, D, MC, V.

Hyannis Inn Motel. The second oldest motel in Hyannis was built almost a half-century ago by the current owner's grandfather. There is a main building and a 1981 wing. The main building served as press headquarters during John F. Kennedy's presidential campaign. The motel is set back from the road with a manicured lawn in front and pink roses growing along the white rail fence. Restaurant. In-room data ports, some refrigerators, some in-room hot tubs, cable TV. Heated indoor pool. 2 saunas. No pets. | 473 Main St. | 508/775–0255 or 800/922–8993 | fax 508/771–0456 | www.hyannisinn.com | 77 rooms | $98–$145 | Closed Dec.–Jan. | AE, D, MC, V.

Inn on Sea Street. This 1849 inn on 2 acres of manicured grounds has a main house, a mansard-roof Victorian house across the street, and a cottage. Guest rooms have antique furnishings including canopy beds and claw-foot tubs. The two-person white clapboard cottage is furnished with simple wicker and white-painted furniture. Beach chairs and towels are available; the beach is two blocks. Tee times at a private golf club can be arranged. Complimentary breakfast. Cable TV. No pets. No smoking. | 358 Sea St. | 508/775–8030 | fax 508/771–0878 | www.capecod.net/innonsea | 9 rooms (2 with shared bath), 1 cottage | $85–$130, $140 cottage | Closed Nov.–late Apr. | AE, D, MC, V.

International Inn. This hotel is known for its "Cuddle and Bubble" packages. These two-night marriage-survival getaways include a five-course gourmet dinner, two buffet breakfasts, and a room with a hot tub. The inn is ½ mi from the harbor and beach. Restaurant, bar. In-room data ports, in-room hot tubs, cable TV, some in-room VCRs. Indoor and out-

door pools. Sauna. Business services. | 662 Main St. | 508/775–5600 | fax 508/775–3933 | www.cuddles.com | 141 rooms | $110–$356 | D, DC, MC, V.

Ramada Inn Regency. You'll find standard guest rooms here, as well as loft suites, some of them efficiency units. Wood-beam ceilings and wood furniture accent the rooms and common areas. Close to downtown Hyannis, the Melody Tent, and the ferry dock. Restaurant, bar. Some kitchenettes, cable TV. Indoor pool. Hot tub. Business services. | 1127 Rte. 132 | 508/775–1153 or 800/676–0000 | fax 508/775–1169 | www.ccrh.com | 196 rooms, 20 suites | $139–$199, $169–$239 suites | AE, D, DC, MC, V.

Salt Winds Bed and Breakfast Guesthouse. The property includes the 1880 main house and the former carriage house, which now contains an apartment and some guest rooms. Accommodations have Ethan Allen furniture, some canopy beds, and hardwood floors covered with Berber rugs. The innkeeper/owner gives a complimentary 20-minute mini-van tour of Hyannis. Complimentary breakfast. Refrigerator, cable TV, no room phones, some in-room VCRS. Outdoor heated pool. Airport shuttle. No pets. No smoking. | 319 Sea St. | 508/775–2038 | www.oncapecod.net/saltwindsbb | 6 rooms, 1 efficiency, 1 2-bedroom apartment | $110, $155 efficiency, $175 2–bedroom apartment | Closed mid-Oct.–mid-May | AE, D, DC, MC, V.

Sea Breeze Bed and Breakfast by the Beach. This bed-and-breakfast has guest rooms in the main building plus two cottages, one featuring a rose garden and fireplace, the other with a hot tub. Some rooms have canopy beds, antiques, and water views. Breakfast is served in the garden gazebo, or the roof-top widow's walk, with a nice view of the sound. You're a two-minute walk from the beach. Picnic area, complimentary Continental breakfast. Cable TV. | 270 Ocean Ave. | 508/771–7213 | fax 508/862–0663 | www.seabreezeinn.com | 14 rooms; 2 cottages | $80–$140, $1,000–$1,800/wk cottages | AE, D, MC, V.

Sheraton Hyannis Resort. This full-service resort has many guest rooms with private patios and balconies. Restaurant, bar, dining rooms, picnic area, room service. In-room data ports, cable TV. Indoor and outdoor pool. Hot tub, spa. 18-hole par-3 golf course, putting green, tennis. Health club, volleyball. Children's programs (ages 4–13), playground. Business services, airport shuttle (seasonal). | 35 Scudder Ave. | 508/775–7775 or 800/325–3535 | fax 508/778–6423 | www.sheraton.com | 224 rooms | $169–$189 | AE, D, DC, MC, V.

Simmons Homestead Inn. A 10-room main house, along with a restored barn with guest rooms and a two-bedroom suite, occupy 2 acres in a residential area about ½ mi from town and the beach. Each guest room has a different animal theme; some rooms have canopy beds and fireplaces. Abutting the property is a pond with a dock for fishing. Ten-speed mountain bikes, fishing poles, beach chairs, and towels are complimentary. Informal itinerary-planning services are offered during the evening social hour on the wraparound porch. Complimentary breakfast. No room phones, cable TV in common area. Fishing. Bicycles. Business services. Pets allowed (fee). | 288 Scudder Ave., Hyannis Port | 508/778–4999 or 800/637–1649 | fax 508/790–1342 | www.capecodtravel.com/simmonsinn | 14 rooms and 1 suite in 2 buildings | $160–$200, $300 suite | AE, D, MC, V.

IPSWICH

MAP 6, J2

(Nearby towns also listed: Essex, Newburyport)

Founded in 1633, this coastal community 28 mi north of Boston is one of the oldest towns in America, home to the aptly named Castle Hill mansion and a notable district of 17th-century houses. Now famous for its clams, Ipswich also takes pride in its beaches and orchards.

Information: **Ipswich Business Association** | Box 94, Ipswich, 01938 | 978/356–4400 | www.ipswichma.com.

Attractions

Crane Memorial Reservation. This extensive oceanfront property of the Trustees of Reservations boasts a Gilded Age mansion and a lovely barrier beach. Special events scheduled throughout the year include concerts, high teas, holiday decorating, an end-of-summer sand-castle competition, and an autumn vintage-sports-car rally. | Argilla Rd. off Rte. 133, | 978/356–4351 | www.thetrustees.org | See specific sites below.

Castle Hill. Commonly known as the Great House, this 59-room Stuart-style mansion was built in 1927 by Chicago industrialist Richard T. Crane, Jr. The views of Ipswich Bay from the Grand Allee and the estate's landscaping are nearly as impressive as the grand house itself. | $7 | Grounds daily 8–dusk, house tours Memorial Day–early Oct., Wed.–Thurs. 9–5:30.

Crane Beach. This barrier beach enclosing much of Essex Bay is noted for soft white sand that stretches for miles. Granite-based Cape Ann to the east intercepts the Atlantic's roughest swells, making Crane ideal for young swimmers. Bathrooms, outdoor showers, a refreshment stand, and a shaded picnic area are maintained in summer. | $15 per car, $2 pedestrians and bicycles | Daily 8–dusk.

Crane Islands Tours. You can join seasonal excursions by boat, foot, and hay wagon to two islands that are part of Crane Wildlife Refuge. One of the two, Hog Island, affords views of three states and was the movie double for 17th-century Salem in the 1996 film *The Crucible.* | $12 | Memorial Day–early Oct., Fri.–Mon. at 10 and 2.

Ipswich Historical Society Museums. Ipswich has the greatest number of First Period houses in the country, most identified by markers. You can visit two houses maintained by the town's historical society (report to the society first). The organization's staff can also help suggest walking tours through the town's four historical districts. | 54 S. Main St. | 978/356–2811 | $7 for one or both houses | May–Columbus Day, tours on the hour Wed.–Sat. 10–4, Sun. 1–4.

John Heard House. This stately Federal home was built in the 1790s for a ship's captain whose West Indies trade established a mercantile dynasty. Five generations of Heards occupied the house, furnishing it with decorative art and work by local artist Arthur Wesley Dow. Also of interest are the collections of nautical instruments, children's toys, and carriages. | 40 S. Main St. | 978/356–2641 | $7 | May–Columbus Day, tours on the hour Wed.–Sat. 10–4, Sun. 1–4.

John Whipple House. Built around 1655, this First Period house reflects the personal tastes of six generations of Whipples. The collection of early handmade bobbin lace is a highlight. The grounds include a Colonial "housewife's garden" and antique shrub roses. | 53 S. Main St. | 978/356–2811 | $7 | May–Columbus Day, tours on the hour Wed.–Sat. 10–4, Sun. 1–4.

Ipswich River Wildlife Sanctuary. You might encounter otter, deer, herons, and egrets amid the meadows and wetlands of this 2,000-acre expanse 8 mi west of Ipswich. Nature walks, bird-watching, and guided canoe trips on the Ipswich River are offered. | 87 Perkins Row | 978/887–9264 | www.massaudubon.org | $3 | Tues.–Sun., Mon. holidays dawn–dusk.

Russell Orchards. These lovely orchards extend over 123 acres. Pick your own apples and berries in season, savor cider doughnuts and homemade pies at the store, or sample the hard cider or one of 21 fruit wines at the winery. Wine tastings on weekends. | 143 Argilla Rd. | 978/356–5366 | www.russellorchardsma.com | Free | May–first Sun. after Thanksgiving.

Wolf Hollow. This nonprofit organization conducts educational lectures and tours of its pack of 14 timber wolves on weekends, weather permitting. You'll even get to howl along with the wolves at the end of the tour! An informal tour is offered on Friday and group reservations are available weekdays. | 114 Essex Rd. | 978/356–0216 | fax 978/356–0724 | www.wolfhollowipswich.org | $4.50 | Nov.–Feb., weekends 1:30, Fri. 2; Mar.–Oct. weekends 1:30 and 3:30, Fri. 2.

ON THE CALENDAR

JULY: *Old Ipswich Days.* This three-day festival features the work of 60 artisans in its arts-and-crafts show. | 978/356–0115.

IPSWICH

INTRO
ATTRACTIONS
DINING
LODGING

MA | 299

JULY: *Logganiko Picnic.* More than a thousand people attend this celebration of Greek food and music at the Hellenic Community Center—it's been held annually since 1919. Many of Ipswich's Greek immigrants originally came from the remote village that lends its name to the picnic. | 978/356–4742.

Dining

Chipper's River Café. Contemporary. This casual dining room of blond wood and tile partially overlooks the narrow Ipswich River. The creative menu favors vegetables and spices over heavy sauces. Try the daily pasta special, the catch of the day, grilled chicken, and salads. Open-air dining on deck. Kids' menu. Weekend brunch. No smoking. | 1–3 Market St. | 978/356–7956 | $5.50–$15.25 | MC, V.

Clam Box of Ipswich. Seafood. An Ipswich landmark since 1938, this self-service diner is shaped like an open clam box. Head to the nautically themed dining room for large portions of the popular fried clams and lobster rolls. Deck seating is available. | 246 High St. | 978/356–9707 | Closed Dec.–Feb.; also Mar.–Memorial Day and Labor Day–Feb., Tues. | $9–$16 | No credit cards.

1640 Hart House. Continental. One of the oldest buildings in the country (it was built in 1640), the Hart House retains its Early American touches such as original hand-carved beams and floorboards and five working fireplaces. Try the grilled salmon with either lemon butter or horseradish dijonnaise, or filet mignon with beranaise sauce. Blues, folk, and Irish music is featured on weekends, and reservations are recommended. | 51 Linebrook Rd. | 978/356–9411 | $13–$19 | AE, D, MC, V.

Stone Soup Cafe. Continental. The dinner menu changes each night, but you can expect dishes like grilled tenderloin or seared salmon. Wood-paneling and paintings by local artists enhance the café, which seats 20. Reservations are recommended weeks in advance for the two dinner seatings per night, at 6 and 8:30. | 20 Mitchell Rd. | 978/356–4222 | Reservations essential | Breakfast also available. No dinner Sun.–Wed. | $11–$22 | No credit cards.

Lodging

★ **Miles River Country Inn.** A 100-year-old formal secret garden, a 2-acre pond garden, and more than 170 species of birds roam the grounds of this 18th-century inn. The pastries served at breakfast are made with fresh fruit from the gardens, eggs from the inn's chickens, and honey from its bees. The innkeeper speaks Spanish and French. Complimentary breakfast. No room phones, cable TV in common area. Pets allowed. No smoking. | 823 Bay Rd., Hamilton | 978/468–7206 | fax 978/468–3999 | www.milesriver.com | 10 rooms in summer, 8 rooms in winter (4 with shared bath) | $95–$175 | AE, MC, V.

Town Hill Bed and Breakfast. This 1845 Greek Revival home in one of Ipswich's historical districts is furnished with antiques and brass beds. It's close to one of the oldest stone arch bridges in the country. Complimentary breakfast. No room phones, TV in common area. No pets. No smoking. | 16 N. Main St. | 978/356–8000 or 800/457–7799 | fax 978/356–8000 | www.townhill.com | 10 rooms, 1 suite (2 with shared baths) | $85–$160 | AE, MC, V.

LAWRENCE

MAP 6, H2

(Nearby towns also listed: Andover and North Andover, Haverhill, Lowell)

Lawrence was built between 1845 and 1848 as a state-of-the-art industrial city. Unhealthy and exploitative working conditions, however, ultimately led to the Bread and Roses Strike of 1912. The conflict ended in a major victory for workers, giving them the right to unionize and compelling congressional investigations into unfair labor practices. The strikers' win was short-lived, though. Lawrence's aging textile mills grew increasingly obsolete, sending the town into a slump from which it has never recovered.

Now, despite its population of 70,000, Lawrence is unusually quiet, a place where parking is never a problem and rush hour is unknown. The city's past is its main attraction, especially when viewed through the excellent interpretive lens of downtown's Lawrence Heritage State Park.

Information: Merrimack Valley Chamber of Commerce | 264 Essex St., Lawrence, 01840-1516 | 978/686–0900 | www.merrimackvalleychamber.com.

Attractions

The Malden Mills Retail Store. This is the larger of two Malden Mills factory stores. Malden Mills is the maker of Polartec ® and Polarfleece ® fabrics. | 530 Broadway Ave. | 978/685–6341 or 800/252–6688 | www.maldenmillsstore.com and www.polartec.com.

Lawrence Heritage State Park. Lawrence attracted so many different ethnic groups to work in its giant textile mills along the Merrimack River that it was christened "Immigrant City." Through exhibits and ranger-guided tours, this state park presents the city's industrial and melting-pot legacies. | 1 Jackson St. | 978/794–1655 | www.state.ma.us/dem | Free | Daily 9–4.

Dining

Bishop's. American. A Lawrence institution for more than a half century, Bishop's has a traditional menu of mostly American fare—shrimp cocktail, lobster, oysters Rockefeller, roast beef—but also includes hummus, lamb, and other Middle Eastern dishes for which it has long been famous. | 99 Hampshire St. | 978/683–7143 | No lunch weekends | $15.95–$52 | AE, D, DC, MC, V.

Cedar Crest Restaurant. Italian. Veal parmigiana and baked stuffed shrimp are two of the favorites here, and each dinner is four courses. The restaurant retains the cedar walls and tables that date back to the restaurant's 1936 opening. The attached diner serves all day long. | 187 Broadway Ave. | 978/685–5722 | Breakfast also available | $12–$18 | No credit cards.

Lodging

Hampton Inn Boston/North Andover. On the Lawrence–North Andover border, this hotel is close to I-495, major businesses, and restaurants. The commuter rail station is 3 mi away; the trip to Boston takes 50 minutes. Single, double, and king-size beds are available. Complimentary Continental breakfast. In-room data ports, cable TV. Gym. Some pets allowed. | 224 Winthrop Ave. | 978/975–4050 | fax 978/687–7122 | www.hamptoninn.com | 126 rooms | $89–$99 | AE, D, DC, MC, V.

LEE

MAP 6, B4

(Nearby towns also listed: Lenox, Stockbridge)

Named after General Charles Lee, George Washington's second-in-command, this town of some 6,000 residents was founded in 1777. Since then, it has been home to diverse industries, from paper manufacturing to quarrying. Lee's white marble, reputed to be among the world's hardest, graces the U.S. Capitol and New York's St. Patrick's Cathedral. Even though Lee doesn't rely as heavily on tourism as the rest of its southern Berkshire neighbors, you will still find it a welcoming small town with an attractive main street. Since one of the two Berkshires exits on the Massachusetts Turnpike (I-90) is in Lee, the town also abounds with travel services from chain motels to family restaurants.

Information: **Lee Chamber of Commerce** | Box 345, Lee, 01238-0345 | 413/243-0852 | fax 413/243-4533 | info@leechamber.org | www.leechamber.org.

Attractions

Beartown State Forest. Seven miles west of Lee on Rte. 102 is this 11,000-acre park with beaver ponds, extensive trails, and Mount Wilcox rising to 2,150 ft. Here you can enjoy camping, hiking, horseback riding, snowmobiling, cross-country skiing, and fishing. | 69 Bluehill Rd., Monterey | 413/528-0904 | $2, camping $6.

October Mountain State Forest. The state's largest park has more than 17,000 acres of deep forest in the center of the Berkshires. Snowmobiling and hunting are popular, but outside of deer season, the forest is an ideal place for experienced hikers to commune with nature. The 546-site campground has full bathhouses and a dumping station for RVs. | Center St. | 413/243-1778 or 877/422-6762 (for reservations) | Reservations essential | www.magnet.state.ma.us/dem/parks/octm.htm | Free, camping $12 | Daily, campground mid-May–Columbus Day.

Santarella Museum and Gardens. Off Rte. 102 is the 1930s replica of an English thatched cottage that originally served as home and studio for Sir Henry Hudson Kitson, the sculptor best known for his statue of the Lexington Minuteman. Today it houses a museum dedicated to Kitson and galleries displaying contemporary artwork. After you stroll through the 4-acre sculpture park on the grounds, you can check out the gift shop. | 75 Main Rd., Tyringham | 413/243-0654 | $4 | May–Oct., daily 10–5.

ON THE CALENDAR

JUNE–AUG.: *Jacob's Pillow Dance Festival.* In the 1930s Ted Shawn, a pioneer in men's modern dance, purchased a farm in Becket to serve as a dance school. Now it hosts the oldest dance festival in America, offering ballet, jazz, and modern dance performances. Works in progress on the outdoor stage, talks, and Saturday lectures are free. | 413/243-0745.
OCT.: *Lee Founders Weekend.* Vintage cars, swing bands, Italian food, a Latino festival, and a parade all mark this annual celebration throughout Lee on the first weekend of the month. Other highlights include antiques and crafts sales, Revolutionary and Civil War displays, and a re-creation of a vintage baseball game. | 413/243-0852.

Dining

Cork 'N Hearth. Continental. Dine by Laurel Lake on house specialties such as pan-roasted seafood medley, Maine crab cakes, roasted duckling, or scampi. Exposed wooden beams and antique brassware add charm to the dining rooms. Kids' menu. No smoking. | U.S. 20, Lee-Lenox border | 413/243-0535 | Closed Mon. No lunch | $15.95–$19.95 | AE, MC, V.

51 Park Street. Italian. Here you'll find wood-fired pizzas such as those topped with hot wings or barbecue chicken. Can't miss your favorite TV program? Each booth has its own cable TV. | 51 Park St. | 413/243-2153 | No lunch Mon. | $6–$13 | MC, V.

Morgan House Inn. Contemporary. Don't be misled by the homey Colonial decor of this 1817 stagecoach inn. The regional American menu is decidedly upscale. Filet mignon, New York strip steak, and lamb tournedos are among the house specialties. Kids' menu. | 33 Main St. | 413/243-3661 | $12.95–$26 | AE, DC, MC, V.

Sullivan Station. American. This converted depot, appropriately decked out with railroad memorabilia, has freshened a traditional menu by serving mesclun salads, whole-grain bread, and ample vegetables. Best bets are the burgers, mixed grill, seafood platter, veal Parmesan, turkey club, and vegetarian pasta. Open-air dining on deck. Kids' menu. No smoking. | Railroad St. | 413/243-2082 | $6.95–$18.95 | AE, D, MC, V.

Lodging

Applegate Inn. This inn presides over 6 parklike acres with manicured lawns, flower beds, and views of the Berkshires. Across the street are a public tennis court and golf course.

The Godiva chocolates set out in each room are a nice touch. Complimentary Continental breakfast. Some in-room data ports, no room phones, cable TV in common area. Pool. No kids under 12. No smoking. | 279 W. Park St. | 413/243–4451 or 800/691–9012 | fax 413/243–9832 | www.applegateinn.com | 6 rooms, 1 suite, 1 2-bedroom carriage house | $145–$245, $330 suites | AE, MC, V.

Ashley Inn. This 1876 Classic Revival home showcases a large collection of clocks and other antiques. The bed-and-breakfast is in a residential neighborhood, less than ¼ mi from downtown. Complimentary breakfast. No room phones, TV in common area. No pets. No kids under 16. No smoking. | 182 W. Park St. | 413/243–2746 | fax 413/243–2489 | www.ashleyinn.com | 4 rooms | $110–$135 | AE, D, MC, V.

Chambery Inn. A lovely, old school-turned-inn, the Chambery prides itself on peace and quiet, the noise of its classrooms long forgotten. Each room in the 1885 home has a gas-fueled fireplace and antique furnishings. Room service. Some in-room hot tubs, cable TV. No kids under 15. No smoking. | 199 Main St. | 413/243–2221 or 800/537–4321 | fax 413/243–0039 | www.berkshireinns.com | 3 rooms, 6 suites | $99–$160, $135–$259 suites | AE, D, MC, V.

Crabtree Cottage. The "extras" distinguish this bed-and-breakfast: hand-crafted furniture, fresh flowers in every room, and port wine served in the afternoon. The 1862 Greek Revival building is one block from the historic downtown. Complimentary breakfast. Cable TV, in-room VCRs (and movies), no room phones. Outdoor pool. No pets. No kids under 12. No smoking. | 65 Franklin St. | 413/243–1780 | fax 413/243–3272 | www.crabtreecottage.com | 4 rooms | $150 | No credit cards.

Devonfield. Fine period furnishings and 26 acres of grounds distinguish this Federal-era manor house. It is near restaurants, Jacob's Pillow, Tanglewood, and the Norman Rockwell Museum. Picnic area, complimentary breakfast. No cable TV in some rooms. Pool. Tennis. Business services. No kids under 10. No smoking. | 85 Stockbridge Rd. | 413/243–3298 or 800/664–0880 | fax 413/243–1360 | www.devonfield.com | 7 rooms, 3 suites | $110–$275 | AE, D, MC, V.

Federal House Inn. Federal and Greek Revival styles are combined in this historic 1824 masterpiece. The beautifully restored inn has pine flooring and antiques throughout. It is nestled among pine and copper beech trees 4 mi from downtown Lee, ½ mi from the Berkshire Theater Festival, and 1½ mi from the Norman Rockwell Museum. Complimentary breakfast. No cable TV in some rooms, no room phones. No kids under 6. No smoking. | 1560 Pleasant St., South Lee | 413/243–1824 or 800/243–1824 | www.federalhouseinn.com | 10 rooms | $145–$225 | AE, D, MC, V.

★ **Historic Merrell Inn.** This former stagecoach stop is now an inn adorned with antiques and period reproductions. It's the only inn to be included in the Historic American Buildings Survey. Walk down the sweeping lawn to the screened gazebo for a view of the Housatonic River. Complimentary breakfast. Cable TV. No smoking. | 1565 Pleasant St., South Lee | 413/243–1794 or 800/243–1794 | fax 413/243–2669 | www.merrell-inn.com | 9 rooms, 1 suite | $95–175, $145–$245 suite | MC, V.

Parsonage on the Green. This center-hall Colonial house, furnished with family heirlooms, is on the village green in Lee's historic downtown. The covered porch affords a clear view of the First Congregational Church, with New England's highest steeple. Complimentary breakfast. No room phones, TV in common area. No pets. No kids under 12. No smoking. | 20 Park Pl. | 413/243–4364 | fax 413/243–2732 | www.bbhost.com/parsonage | 4 rooms | $130 (3–day minimum stay in summer) | No credit cards.

Pilgrim Inn. This inn is ¼ mi from the Massachusetts Turnpike, 5 mi from Tanglewood and the Norman Rockwell Museum, and close to five restaurants. The pool and shady picnic area are pleasant. Discounts for senior citizens are available. Picnic area, complimentary Continental breakfast. Cable TV. Pool. Laundry facilities. Business services. | 165 Housatonic St. | 413/243–1328 or 888/537–5476 | fax 413/243–2339 | Pilgriminn@aol.com | www.pilgriminn-berkshires.com | 35 rooms, 1 suite | $95–$195, $160–$225 suite | AE, D, DC, MC, V.

LENOX

MAP 6, B3

(Nearby towns also listed: Lee, Pittsfield, Stockbridge, West Stockbridge)

Despite being little more than a village, Lenox is the bed-and-breakfast capital of the Berkshires. Half a million visitors descend on the town every summer, drawn to the nightly performances at Tanglewood, the Boston Symphony Orchestra's summer home. Among Lenox's grand old houses that take in guests are most of the region's surviving summer "cottages" built in the late 19th century by wealthy industrialists. If its performing arts, architecture, and upscale dining were not enough to recommend it, Lenox also enjoys deeply wooded, parklike surroundings with miles of hiking trails and scenic back roads.

Information: **Lenox Chamber of Commerce** | The Curtis, 5 Walker St., Lenox, 02140 | 413/637–3646 | info@lenox.org | www.lenox.org.

Attractions

Berkshire Scenic Railway Museum. This museum in Lenox's half-timber 1903 station displays vintage locomotives, model railroads, and antique equipment. Don't miss the 15-minute ride on the time-honored diesel locomotive. | Willow Creek Rd. | 413/637–2210 | fax 518/392–2225 | www.regionnet.com/colberk/berkshirerailway.html | Free, train ride $2.50 | Memorial Day–Oct., weekends and holidays 10–4.

★ **The Mount/Edith Wharton Restoration.** Edith Wharton, author of the classic novel *The Age of Innocence* and the first woman to win a Pulitzer Prize, was also an expert interior decorator. She designed this 1902 mansion as her summer residence, putting into practice many of the ideas she popularized in her influential books on home decorating. Tours are conducted of the home and grounds. | Plunkett St. and U.S. 7 | 413/637–1899 or 888/637–1902 | www.edithwharton.org | $6 | Memorial Day–Oct., daily 9–2.

Pleasant Valley Wildlife Sanctuary. Covering more than 1,000 acres in the valley of Yokun Brook and on the surrounding slopes of Lenox Mountain, this sanctuary run by the Massachusetts Audubon Society is the picture of tranquility. It includes a hemlock gorge, a lime-

© Corbis

LENOX COTTAGES

During the waning years of the 19th century, some of America's wealthiest families began to take up summer residence in and around Lenox, drawn by the Berkshires' refreshing climate. The influx of Carnegies, Westinghouses, and Vanderbilts quickly turned the area into an "inland Newport," replete with mansions as luxurious as any in that seaside resort. Tycoons threw open their checkbooks and poured vast sums into constructing, furnishing, and landscaping scores of these magnificent, misleadingly named "cottages." Whole summers were devoted to endless socializing, the grand roundelay of lawn and dinner parties, amateur theatricals and amusements, tennis, tea, and gossip. Ultimately, the curtain came down on this Gilded Age, as Mark Twain so aptly called it, with the introduction of the federal income tax, the Great War, and the Crash of 1929. Fire, abandonment, and demolition have all taken their toll, but a few dozen cottages still remain. Some have been refurbished as luxury condominiums or private homes, or converted to school, convent, or other institutional use. Others, such as Blantyre, Cranwell, and Wheatleigh, have become exclusive resorts and hotels. And two are seasonally open to the public: The Mount, in Lenox, and Naumkeag, in neighboring Stockbridge.

stone cobble, a hummingbird garden, and precisely mapped walking trails. | 472 W. Mountain Rd. | 413/637–0320 | www.massaudubon.org | $3 | Nov.–mid-June, Tues.–Sun. dawn–dusk; late June–Oct. daily.

Tanglewood. For more than 60 years the Boston Symphony Orchestra has made its summer home at this scenic hilltop estate named after a series of stories by Nathaniel Hawthorne. In addition to the orchestral concerts, the nine-week Tanglewood season includes chamber-music, vocal, and jazz performances and a few evenings of pop and rock, with both indoor reserved and outdoor lawn seating. | 297 West St. (Rte. 183) | 617/638–9230 | www.bso.org/newdesign/education/tmc/htm | Concert tickets $12–$18 outdoors, $15–$79 indoors | Daily.

Chamber Music Hall and Formal Gardens. Designed by Eliel Saarinen, the Chamber Music Hall is used for master classes and student rehearsals. Nearby are the original formal gardens of the Tanglewood estate.

Koussevitzky Music Shed. Built in 1938, this 5,000-seat open-sided structure was designed by Eliel Saarinen. The noted architect's original plans were altered to suit financial constraints. Given the packed dirt underfoot and hard wooden seats, the word "shed" is more appropriate than you might imagine. Up to 10,000 listeners opt to enjoy shed concerts from their own chairs and blankets on the lawn outside, a Berkshire tradition that's hard to beat.

Hawthorne Cottage. This music classroom building is a 1940s reconstruction of the so-called Little Red Shanty on the Tappan farm that Nathaniel and Sophie Hawthorne rented in 1850–51. It was Caroline Tappan's friendship with Sophie that brought the Hawthornes to the area. While here, Nathaniel wrote part of his famous *House of Seven Gables,* as well as *Tanglewood Tales.*

Highwood Manor House. Now used for classes, offices, and private dining, this house was the physical inspiration for Hawthorne's *Tanglewood Tales.* Originally the neighboring estate to the Tappan family property, Highwood was acquired and integrated into the Tanglewood complex in 1987.

Seiji Ozawa Concert Hall. Completed in 1994, this intimate concert hall is notable for its all-wood contemporary design by William Rawn. The hall is used for Tanglewood's professional chamber and solo performances. As is the case with the Music Shed, there is more seating on the hillside at the back of the hall than inside.

Tanglewood Manor House. This is the summer house built in the mid-19th century by William and Caroline Tappan, whose descendents donated it to the Boston Symphony in the 1930s for a summer music school. The first floor holds a small visitors center with exhibits related to the history of Tanglewood.

ON THE CALENDAR

MAY–NOV.: *Shakespeare and Co.* This theater company performs Shakespearean comedy at the Mainstage open-air theater, in July and August. At Wharton Theatre, in Edith Wharton's home—The Mount—stories by Wharton and Henry James are adapted for the stage. Shakespeare's plays and others are also performed at the Stables Theater (indoor), the Oxford Court Theater (open-air), and the Duffin Theatre, a new 500-seat air-conditioned venue in Lenox Memorial High School. | 413/637–3353 (tickets).

JULY–AUG.: *Tanglewood Music Festival.* The Tanglewood Institute was founded by Serge Koussevitzky in 1938 as a summer school for talented young composers and conductors. Today, the 500-acre property is one of the world's premier cultural centers, presenting many styles of music, from orchestral to contemporary jazz. | 413/638–9230 or 617/266–1200 (tickets) or 888/266–1200.

SEPT.: *Apple Squeeze Festival.* This event cheerfully ushers in autumn and the first apple pressing for cider. For one weekend, Lenox Village is transformed into a country fair with great sidewalk sales, singers, bands, crafts demonstrations, face painting, a giant pumpkin weigh-off, pony rides, and lots and lots of apples! | 413/637–3646.

SEPT.: *Tub Parade.* A charming procession of horse-drawn carriages that re-creates the parades of decorated "tubs" (pony carts) begun by the "cottagers" of the 1890s to celebrate the end of summer. More than two dozen elaborately decorated antique wagons are pulled by driving and draft horses like those used more than a century ago. Inn tours and Victorian-age entertainment are scheduled after the parade. | 413/637–3646.

Dining

Apple Tree Inn. Continental. A gracious restaurant with views of the Stockbridge Bowl and the main gates of Tanglewood. Good choices are the five-onion soup or fresh pasta from the fine menu of French- and Italian-influenced dishes. Open-air dining on porch. Sun. brunch. No smoking. | 10 Richmond Mountain Rd. | 413/637–1477 | www.appletree-inn.com | Closed Sept.–June, Mon.–Wed. No lunch | $8–$28 | AE, D, DC, MC, V.

Bistro Zampano's. Eclectic. The emphasis in on food and not decor at this casual bistro. The fare is healthful and the choices wide-ranging, from lamb and salmon to the Portobello cheese steak. Enclosed patio seating available. | 395 Pittsfield Rd. | 413/448–8600 | No dinner Mon.–Tues. | $12–$18 | MC, V.

★ **Blantyre.** French. Indulge in an elaborate prix-fixe dinner in the formal restaurant of this luxury hotel. Tables are set with silver and fresh flowers. Cocktails are served in two sitting rooms and on the garden terrace, while after-dinner drinks are offered in the Main Hall amid the soothing strains of classical harp music. Recommended dishes include lobster risotto with zucchini, pan-roasted saddle of rabbit with Oregon truffles, and scallion gnocchi. | 16 Blantyre Rd. | 413/637–3556 | www.blantyre.com | Reservations essential | Jacket and tie | Closed Nov.–Apr. and Mon. No lunch Sept.–June | Prix–fixe $75 | AE, DC, MC, V.

Cafe Lucia. Italian. This former art gallery offers intimate inside dining and outside seating on a large covered deck. A seasonally changing menu pairs fresh local ingredients with top-quality meat, poultry, and seafood. No smoking. | 80 Church St. | 413/637–2640 | Closed Mon. and Nov.–May, Sun. No lunch | $14–$32 | AE, D, DC, MC, V.

Carol's. American. A bright, down-home place, open morning till afternoon, where everyone is made to feel like a regular. Kids' menu. | 8 Franklin St. | 413/637–8948 | Call for off-season hrs. No dinner | $2–$7 | No credit cards.

Church Street Cafe. Contemporary. This bistro-style café showcases local art while serving an eclectic lineup of regional American dishes. In summer, the outdoor deck might be the most sought-after spot in town. Try the Maine crab cakes and, for dessert, the chocolate-caramel duo. No smoking. | 65 Church St. | 413/637–2745 | Closed mid-Oct.–June, Sun.–Mon. | $16.95–$26.95 | MC, V.

Gateways Inn. Contemporary. Eighteenth-century Italian and French artwork from the owners' private collection graces the walls. The seasonally changing menu makes good use of locally grown produce. Vegetarian dishes and the rack of lamb remain popular. Open-air dining on terrace. No smoking. | 51 Walker St. | 413/637–2532 or 888/492–9466 | Closed Mon. No lunch late Oct.–May and on summer weekdays | $16–$27 | AE, D, DC, MC, V.

Lenox House Restaurant. Continental. The unpretentious candlelit dining room and separate lounge with fireplace add to this restaurant's welcoming atmosphere off-season. Among the house specialties are chicken almondine and baked scrod. Kids' menu. No smoking. | 55 Pittsfield-Lenox Rd. | 413/637–1341 | $12–$20 | AE, D, DC, MC, V.

Lenox 218. Italian. Vaulted ceilings, skylights, and hanging plants help to keep this eatery cheery. The northern Italian menu is sprinkled with a few regional American dishes such as Cajun-grilled fish and Idaho rainbow trout. Try the polenta and grilled eggplant. Kids' menu. No smoking. | 218 Main St. | 413/637–4218 | $13.95–$23.95 | AE, D, MC, V.

Panda House. Chinese. When you need a break from Continental and standard New England fare, this spacious restaurant is the ticket with its efficient service and lengthy menu of Mandarin, Hunan, and Cantonese dishes. Try General Tso's chicken or vegetarian paradise. Sun. brunch. No smoking. | 664 Pittsfield-Lenox Rd. | 413/499–0660 | $5.95–$32 | AE, D, MC, V.

★ **Trattoria Il Vesuvio.** Italian. You can enjoy *linguine vongole* or *arrosto di vitello* amid the traditional checkered tablecloths and photographs of Pompeii. Reservations are a good idea during the Tanglewood season. | 242 Pittsfield Rd. | 413/637–4904 | No lunch weekends | $11–$21 | AE, D, MC, V.

The Village Inn. American. The menu changes by season, but favorite dishes include Shaker pot roast and sautéed shrimp over angel-hair pasta. The restaurant in a 1771 inn features antiques, a working fireplace, and a garden view. Late-night dining. | 16 Church St. | 413/637–0021 | fax 413/637–9756 | No lunch | $18–$27 | AE, D, DC, MC, V.

Wheatleigh. French. Antique Waterford crystal chandeliers, Chippendale chairs, and an ornate fireplace with candelabras distinguish this Italian palazzo–inspired mansion, perfectly matched to the luxurious four-course prix-fixe menu that changes daily. Pre-theater (three-course), low-fat, grande degustation, and vegetarian menus are also available. Known for its menu's uniform excellence. Sun. brunch. No smoking. | Hawthorne Rd. | 413/637–0610 | www.wheatleigh.com | Reservations essential | $82, $105 (four courses) | AE, DC, MC, V.

Wyndhurst Restaurant. Contemporary. Part of the Cranwell Resort, Wyndhurst retains the Victorian elegance of this late-19th-century home-turned-inn. Note the ornately carved fireplace just outside the dining room and the elaborate menu of Asian-accented Continental cuisine. The elegant dining room is known for baby rack of lamb and hand-cut Black Angus steaks. Kids' menu. Sun. brunch. No smoking. | 55 Lee Rd. | 413/637–1364 | www.cranwell.com | $22–$29 | AE, D, DC, MC, V.

Lodging

Apple Tree Inn. This inn across the street from Tanglewood presides over 22 acres of landscaped lawns, gardens, and walking trails. From the pool there's a great view of the Berkshires. In summer the full-service tavern serves meals on a canopied deck. Restaurant, bar, picnic area, complimentary Continental breakfast. Cable TV. Outdoor pool. Tennis. | 10 Richmond Mountain Rd. | 413/637–1477 | fax 413/637–2528 | innkeeper@appletree-inn.com | www.appletree-inn.com | 34 rooms (3 with shared bath), 2 suites | $170–$375, $330–$375 suites | AE, D, DC, MC, V.

Birchwood Inn. Built in 1767, this large white Colonial Revival inn is on the National Register of Historic Places. Period antiques, eight working fireplaces, a sunken living room and library, and a walled-in manicured garden all contribute to its charm. Complimentary breakfast, afternoon tea. No air-conditioning, no cable TV in some rooms. Business services. No kids under 12. No smoking. | 7 Hubbard St. | 413/637–2600 or 800/524–1646 | fax 413/637–4604 | www.birchwood-inn.com | 12 rooms (2 with shared bath) | $100–$225 | AE, D, DC, MC, V.

Blantyre. Built in 1902, the Main House of this luxury hotel was designed in a Tudor Baronial style and is now filled with antiques dating to 1760. The carriage house contains both suites and rooms, and there are three cottages on the 100-acre property. Restaurant, complimentary Continental breakfast, room service. In-room data ports, cable TV. Pool. Hot tub, massage, sauna. Tennis courts. Laundry service. Business services. No kids under 12. No smoking. | 16 Blantyre Rd. | 413/637–3556 | fax 413/637–4282 | hide@blantyre.com | www.blantyre.com | 23 rooms, 3 suites, 3 cottages | $300–$575, $375–$700 suites, $475–$600 cottages | Closed Nov.–Apr. | AE, DC, MC, V.

Brook Farm Inn. This 1870s Victorian and its gardens are tucked away in a beautiful wooded glen. All rooms have period antiques and sitting areas and some also have canopy beds and fireplaces. On Saturday, poetry is read at afternoon tea. Picnic area, complimentary breakfast. Pool. Library. Business services. No kids under 15. No smoking. | 15 Hawthorne St. | 413/637–3013 or 800/285–7638 | fax 413/637–4751 | innkeeper@brook-farm.com | www.brookfarm.com | 12 rooms | $125–$210 | D, MC, V.

Candlelight Inn. This antiques-filled Victorian inn in Lenox Village offers dining in the courtyard in summer and before a warming fireplace in winter. Bar, dining room, complimentary Continental breakfast. No room phones, TV in common area. | 35 Walker St. | 413/637–1555 | innkeeper@candlelightinn-lenox.com | www.candlelightinn-lenox.com | 8 rooms | $155–$185 | AE, D, MC, V.

Canyon Ranch in the Berkshires. A dizzying array of healthful and rejuvenative activities are offered at this state-of-the-art resort and world-class spa. You can easily traverse the property via the indoor walkways that connect all the buildings. Rates include a $105 healing and health credit and 2 spa or sport services. Dining room. In-room data ports, cable TV, in-room VCRs. Indoor and outdoor pools. Beauty salon, hot tubs, massage, saunas, steam room. Tennis. Basketball, exercise equipment, hiking, racquetball, squash, volleyball, water sports, boating, bicycles. Cross-country skiing. Shops, library. Laundry facilities, laundry service. No pets. No kids under 14. No smoking. | 165 Kemble St. | 413/637–4100 or 800/742–9000 | fax 413/637–0057 | www.canyonranch.com | 102 rooms, 24 suites | $627–$893(3–day minimum stay) | AP | AE, D, DC, MC, V.

The Cliffwood Inn. The main floor of this Greek Revival home, done in a Stanford White style, features the original 1888 details, including parquet wood floors. The public areas are spacious, especially the 800-square-ft verandah. Most rooms have working fireplaces. Complimentary breakfast. Some in-rooms VCRs, no room phones, no TV in some rooms. Indoor and outdoor pools. No pets. No kids under 11. No smoking. | 25 Cliffwood St. | 413/637–3330 or 800/789–3331 | fax 413/637–0221 | www.cliffwood.com | 6 rooms, 1 suite | $146–$240 | No credit cards.

The Cornell Inn. Three separate buildings—one Victorian, one Colonial, and one "country-primitive"—are furnished with antiques and reproduction furniture. The grounds, which have a Japanese garden and waterfall, adjoin the 600-acre Kennedy Park with extensive trails. Bar. In-room data ports, cable TV. No pets. No kids under 13. No smoking. | 203 Main St. | 413/637–0927 or 800/637–0562 | fax 413/637–0927 | www.cornellinn.com | 27 rooms, 3 suites | $150–$300 (3–day minimum weekend stay) | AE, D, DC, MC, V.

Cranwell Resort and Golf Club. This mansion was originally Wyndhurst, one of the Lenox "cottages" built at the turn of the 20th century. Now Cranwell is a full-service resort on 380 acres with seven buildings that show a contemporary country style. Some of the guest rooms have fireplaces. 3 restaurants, bar with entertainment, picnic area. In-room data ports, some kitchenettes, some in-room hot tubs, cable TV. Pool. Driving range, 18-hole golf course, putting green, 4 tennis courts. Gym. Mountain bikes. Shops. Business services. | 55 Lee Rd. | 413/637–1364 or 800/272–6935 | fax 413/637–4364 | info@cranwell.com | www.cranwell.com | 105 rooms, 26 suites | $199–$449, $349–$449 suites | AE, D, DC, MC, V.

Eastover Resort. The emphasis at this recreational resort is on activities rather than on guest rooms, which are rustic. The main building is a Georgian mansion, and another houses a large Civil War museum. Certain weeks and weekends are reserved for families, couples, and singles. Bar with entertainment, dining room. Some room phones, no TV in some rooms. Indoor and outdoor pools. Driving range, putting green, tennis. Basketball, hiking, horseback riding, volleyball. Cross-country skiing, tobogganing. Kids' programs, playground. Business services. No pets. No smoking. | 430 East St. | 413/637–0625 or 800/822–2386 | fax 413/637–0625 | www.eastover.com | 138 rooms, 2 suites | $99–$132 | Closed Apr., Dec. 1–26 | AP | AE, D, MC, V.

Gables Inn. Built in 1885, this large in-town "cottage" is a former residence of author Edith Wharton. The inn has period furnishings, including an 1860 Renaissance bed. Outside, relax on the sunning patio or at the indoor pool in the garden. Picnic area, complimentary breakfast. Cable TV, in-room VCRs and movies. Indoor pool. Tennis. Library. No kids under 12. No smoking. | 81 Walker St. | 413/637–3416 or 800/382–9401 | fax 413/637–3416 | www.gableslenox.com | 18 rooms, 4 suites | $90–$225, $225 suites | D, MC, V.

Garden Gables. This 18th-century house in the downtown historic district is appointed with vintage English furnishings and 19th-century Dutch watercolors. You'll find hiking trails behind the 5-acre property. Picnic area, complimentary breakfast. Cable TV in cottages and common area. Pool. Business services. No kids under 12. No smoking. | 135 Main St. | 413/637–0193 | fax 413/637–4554 | gardeninn@aol.com | www.lenoxinn.com | 18 rooms | $145–$250 | AE, MC, V.

Gateways Inn and Restaurant. At this white clapboard inn with antique furnishings you can enjoy lunch on the canopied terrace, a drink at the boutique bar, or dinner at the restaurant. Public tennis courts are behind the property. The innkeeper speaks Italian and Spanish. Restaurant, bar, complimentary Continental breakfast. In-room data ports, room service. Cable TV. Business services. No kids under 12 except on request. | 51 Walker St. | 413/637–2532 or 888/492–9466 | fax 413/637–1432 | gateways@berkshire.net | www.gatewaysinn.com | 11 rooms, 1 suite | $100–$260, $275–$400 suite | AE, D, DC, MC, V.

Hampton Terrace. This 1882 Georgian Colonial home has operated as an inn since 1937. Oriental rugs, ornate molding, and photographs of the original owners grace the interior. The grounds include longstanding hedges and a grass tennis court. Complimentary breakfast. Some in-room hot tubs, some in-room VCRs, no room phones, no TV in some rooms. Tennis court. No pets. No kids under 10. No smoking. | 91 Walker St. | 413/637–1773 or 800/203–0656 | www.hamptonterrace.com | 11 rooms, 1 suite | $150–$195 | AE, D, DC, MC, V.

Harrison House. This Victorian-style inn faces Kennedy Park and stands across from the White Church on the Hill in Lenox Village. The spacious rooms have canopy and sleigh beds and wood-burning fireplaces embellished with European tiles. Rocking chairs await you on the wraparound porch. Complimentary breakfast. Cable TV, no room phones. No kids under 12. No smoking. | 174 Main St. | 413/637–1746 | www.harrison-house.com | $175–$240, $340 suite | AE, MC, V.

Howard Johnson. This chain hotel is 2 mi from Tanglewood and close to the Norman Rockwell Museum, Shaker Village, and The Mount. Complimentary Continental breakfast. Some microwaves, refrigerators, cable TV. Pool. Business services. | 462 Pittsfield Rd. | 413/442–4000 | fax 413/443–7954 | www.hojo.com | 38 rooms, 6 suites | $89–$185, $195 suites | AE, D, DC, MC, V.

Lilac Inn. If you like flowers, you're likely to appreciate this 1836 Italian Revival inn. The wallpaper and bedding have floral themes, and the building is next to Lilac Park, known for its profusion of lilacs, tiger lilies, and other blossoms. Complimentary breakfast. Some kitchenettes, some in-room VCRs, some room phones, no TV in some rooms. | 33 Main St. | 413/637–2172 | fax 413/637–2172 | www.berkshireweb.com | 5 rooms, 1 apartment | $195, $300 apartment | No credit cards.

The Ponds at Foxhollow. These sunny modern condominiums have one or two bedrooms, cathedral ceilings, and contemporary furnishings. You'll find the 200-acre wooded grounds 7 mi east of Lenox, off I–90. In-room data ports, kitchenettes, microwaves, refrigerators, in-room hot tubs, cable TV. Indoor and outdoor pools. Pond. Hot tub, sauna. 4 tennis courts. Gym. Plaground. Laundry facilities. No pets. | U.S. 7 | 413/637–1469 | fax 413/637–4181 | www.pondsatfoxhollow.com | 48 apartments | $1,200–$1,600 (weekly, 7–day minimum) | D, MC, V.

Rookwood Inn. While secluded, this lovely Queen Anne Victorian lies just one block from Lenox center and 1 mi from Tanglewood. Families are welcome, and afternoon refreshments are served. The innkeeper speaks Spanish. Complimentary breakfast. In-room data ports, some cable TV in rooms, cable TV in common area. Baby-sitting. No smoking. | 11 Old Stockbridge Rd. | 413/637–9750 or 800/223–9750 | fax 413/637–1352 | innkeeper@rookwood-inn.com | www.rookwoodinn.com | 20 rooms, 5 suites | $135–$225, $225–$300 suites | AE, D, DC, MC, V.

Summer White House. Chester A. Arthur, the 21st U.S. president, used to stay here. This house boasts a grand piano in the library, original American art in the parlor, and a $19,000 custom-designed bed. Outside, note the unusual porches, formal gardens, and fishpond. Complimentary Continental breakfast. Cable TV. No kids under 16. No smoking. | 17 Main St. | 413/637–4489 | fax 413/637–4489 | 6 rooms | $195 | D, MC, V.

Village Inn. This 18th-century property in the middle of town is furnished in the Colonial style. Some rooms have four-poster canopy beds; others have fireplaces. Restaurant, bar, complimentary breakfast. Some in-room hot tubs. No kids under 6. No smoking. | 16 Church St. | 413/637–0020 or 800/253–0917 | fax 413/637–9756 | www.villageinn-lenox.com | 32 rooms | $130–$260 | AE, D, DC, MC, V.

Walker House. This family-owned inn is on 3 landscaped and wooded acres in Lenox Village. Each guest room is named for a composer, there's a piano in the parlor, and films are shown on a 12-ft screen in the library. The country-home appeal and spacious common areas of Walker House make it a good choice for small reunions. Dining room, complimentary Continental breakfast. No room phones, TV in common area. Library. No kids under 12. Business services. Some pets allowed. No smoking. | 64 Walker St. | 413/637–1271 or 800/235–3098 | fax 413/637–2387 | phoudek@vgernet.net | www.walkerhouse.com | 8 rooms | $80–$200 | No credit cards.

Wheatleigh. This Gilded Age "summer cottage," with its columns, carved mantels, and Tiffany windows, was designed by the firm of Peabody and Stearns, based on a 16th-century Florentine palazzo. The 22-acre grounds were landscaped by Frederick Law Olmsted, designer of New York's Central Park. Many rooms have fireplaces and views. The hotel staff speak many languages, and the restaurant is internationally renowned. Next to Tanglewood. Restaurant, room service. In-room data ports, cable TV, in-room VCRs. Pool. Tennis. Gym. Business services. No kids under 9. No smoking. | Hawthorne Rd. | 413/637–0610 | fax 413/637–4507 | www.wheatleigh.com | 11 rooms, 8 suites | $365–$595, $725–$965 suites | AE, DC, MC, V.

★ **Whistler's Inn.** Built by a railroad tycoon during the Gilded Age, this inn has stunning displays of antiques and original art. The house once belonged to the family of the painter James Abbott McNeill Whistler; hence the name Whistler's Inn. The 7-acre wooded property is just across from Kennedy Park and two blocks from the town center. Picnic area, complimentary breakfast. No air-conditioning some rooms, cable TV. Business services. No smoking. | 5 Greenwood St. | 413/637–0975 | fax 413/637–2190 | rmears3246@aol.com | www.whistlersinnlenox.com | 14 rooms, 3 suites | $90–$190, $190–$275 suites | AE, MC, V.

The Yankee. This large, family-friendly motel has a western theme: The buildings and parking lots spread in a wide arc around the recreation area like wagons circled around a campfire. Some rooms have canopy beds and fireplaces. Picnic area, complimentary Continental breakfast. In-room data ports, some refrigerators, some in-room hot tubs, cable TV. 2 pools. Gym. Business services. | 461 Pittsfield/Lenox Rd. | 413/499–3700 or 800/835–2364 | fax 413/499–3634 | www.berkshireinns.com | 96 rooms, 7 suites | $85–$220, $179–$260 suites | AE, D, DC, MC, V.

LEOMINSTER

MAP 6, F3

(Nearby town also listed: Gardner)

At the junction of I–190 and Route 2, you'll find Leominster, a medium-size industrial city of about 40,000. Shopping malls abound, mixing local businesses and national retailers. Nearly every plastic pink flamingo and lawn ornament found across the country comes from Leominster's plastics industry, but today the city is trying to diversify its manufacturing base and tap into Massachusetts's most recent industrial breadwinner, biotechnology.

Information: **Johnny Appleseed Trail Association** | 110 Erdman Way, Leominster, 01453-1819 | 978/534–2302. **Johnny Appleseed Visitor Center** | Rte. 2W, between exits 34 and 35 | 978/534–2302 | johnny@appleseed.org | www.appleseed.org.

Attractions

Fruitlands Museum. Fruitlands was the name that utopian dreamer Bronson Alcott (the father of Louisa May Alcott) gave to his ultimately failed commune begun in 1843. The farmhouse is one of four attractions in the contemporary Fruitlands complex, the others being a Shaker museum, a North American Indian museum, and a gallery that exhibits both early American folk painting and American landscapes. It is 19 mi east of Leominster. | 102 Prospect Hill Rd., Harvard | 978/456–9028 | www.fruitlands.org | $8 | Mid May–Oct., daily 10–5.

ON THE CALENDAR

SEPT.: *Johnny Appleseed Parade.* At least 70 entries—including floats, fife-and-drum corps, and high-school bands—march in this annual event. The parade continues for 1½ mi along Rte. 12 and takes place the weekend nearest the September 26th birthday of Johnny Appleseed (John Chapman), more than 200 years ago. | 978/534–7500.

Dining

Rob's Country Kitchen Family. American. The interior of this family-oriented eatery is unpretentious, with white walls covered with pencil-and-ink illustrations of the countryside. The roast-turkey dinner is the hands-down favorite here, but barbecue ribs are also popular. Kids' meals. | 23 Sack Blvd. | 978/534–9878 | $5–$12 | AE, D, MC, V.

Lodging

Four Points Hotel. A hotel on the Johnny Appleseed Trail that offers full-service accommodations for weddings, proms, and corporate business. Restaurant, bar, complimentary Continental breakfast. In-room data ports, some refrigerators, cable TV. Indoor pool. Hot tub. Business services. | 99 Erdman Way | 978/534–9000 or 800/325–3535 | fax 978/534–0891 | www.sheraton.com | 187 rooms, 22 suites | $106–$155, $115–$180 suites | AE, D, DC, MC, V.

Groton Stagecoach Inn and Tavern. This Colonial-style inn built in 1678 has a carriage house that serves as a function hall. The canopy beds in the rooms were handmade by the innkeeper himself. Next door is the largest antiques dealer in New England, and golf and canoeing are a mile away. Restaurant, bar. Cable TV in common area. Pool. No smoking. | 128 Main St., Groton | 978/448–5614 or 877/782–4346 | fax 978/448–0016 | www.Groton-hotel-intel.com | 17 rooms, 2 suites | $75, 110 suites | AE, D, DC, MC, V.

Motel 6. Reliable and economical, this budget motel is modestly furnished and has standard amenities. Kids under 17 stay free. In-room data ports, cable TV. Outdoor pool. | 48 Commercial Rd. | 978/537–8161 | fax 978/537–2082 | 115 rooms | $56 | AE, D, DC, MC, V.

Super 8. You'll find good value and simple, modern furnishings in this four-story chain motel. Complimentary Continental breakfast. Cable TV. Video games. No pets. | 482 N. Main St. | 978/537–2800 | fax 978/840–4367 | www.super8.com | 101 rooms | $49–$79 | AE, D, DC, MC, V.

Wachusett Village Inn. Seven miles from Leominster off Rte. 2 is this year-round inn that not only welcomes tourists but also hosts corporate outings and conferences. Cross-country and downhill skiing is 4 mi away at Wachusett Mountain ski area. Restauant. Cable TV. 2 pools (1 indoor). Tennis courts. Health club. Ice-skating, sleigh rides, snowshoeing. Playground. | 9 Village Inn Rd., Westminster | 978/874–2000 or 800/342–1905 | fax 978/874–1753 | wvi@net1plus.com | www.wachusettvillageinn.com | 24 rooms, 18 suites, 8 cottages | $129–$179, $199–$289 suites, $109–$149 cottages | AE, D, DC, MC, V.

LEXINGTON

MAP 6, H3

(Nearby towns also listed: Bedford, Boston, Burlington, Cambridge, Concord, Somerville, Waltham)

Lexington, now an affluent suburb close to Boston, is best known for its starring role in the opening skirmishes of the American Revolution, an honor annually reprised with the help of costumed militiamen and redcoats during the town's annual Patriot's Day celebration. Modern Lexington has preserved many of the historical buildings that played bit parts in the events of that fateful spring morning in 1775.

The town is well connected to neighboring communities in the greater Boston area via public buses and is also one of four communities served by the popular Minuteman Commuter Bikeway.

Information: **Lexington Chamber of Commerce** | 1875 Massachusetts Ave., Lexington, 02421 | 781/862–1450. **Visitors Center** | 1875 Massachusetts Ave. | 781/862–1450 | www.lexingtonchamber.org.

Attractions

Battle Green. Once a simple town common, this patch of land was forever transformed at sunrise on the morning of April 19, 1775, when rider Paul Revere roused local militiamen, who were fired upon by British regulars on their way to seize a suspected rebel cache of arms. At one corner of the Battle Green, H. H. Kitson's idealized statue *The Minuteman* strikes a defiant pose in tribute to those 18th-century patriots. | Massachusetts Ave. | Free | Daily.

Lexington Historical Society. This historical society was among the earliest organizations in the United States to actively promote saving historic properties. The group preserves and conducts tours of three Lexington buildings associated with the American Revolution. | 1332 Massachusetts Ave. | 781/862–1703 | $4 per house, $10 for all 3 houses | Mid-Apr.–Oct., Mon.–Sat. 10–5, Sun. 1–5.

Buckman Tavern. This 1709 tavern has been restored to look much the way it did on the night of April 18, 1775, when local militiamen gathered inside to discuss facing British troops on the march from Boston. Later that night, in the predawn hours, Paul Revere and fellow alarm rider William Dawes refreshed themselves here after confirming the approach of the British. | 1 Bedford St. | 781/862–5598 | $4 | Mid-Apr.–Oct., Mon.–Sat. 10–5, Sun. 1–5.

Hancock-Clarke House. Two revolutionary leaders, Samuel Adams and John Hancock, were staying at this 17th-century parsonage on the night of April 18, 1775, when Paul Revere warned them that the British were marching out of Boston. The house contains artifacts from the revolution, as well as household items from the clerical families who lived here over the years. | 36 Hancock St. | 781/861–0928 | $4 | Mid-Apr.–Oct., Mon.–Sat. 10–5, Sun. 1–5.

Munroe Tavern. At this 1695 tavern British forces stopped to treat their wounded as they retreated from their confrontation with local militia in Concord on the morning of April 19, 1775. The building also serves as home to the Lexington Historical Society. | 1332 Massachusetts Ave. | 781/862–1703 | $4 | Mid-Apr.–Oct., Mon.–Sat. 10–5, Sun. 1–5.

Lexington Visitor's Center. Check out the diorama showing the confrontation between British regulars and the minutemen on Lexington Green. Free tours of Battle Green are offered in spring, summer, and fall. | 1875 Masachusetts Ave. | 781/862–1450 | fax 781/862–5995 | www.lexingtonchamber.org | free | Daily 9–5.

Museum of Our National Heritage. Throughout the year, this sizable museum presents changing exhibits of American history and culture. Exhibition themes range from Navajo weaving to Civil War photographs to the furniture of Frank Lloyd Wright. Ticketed concerts and other live entertainment are staged here on occasion. | 33 Marrett Rd. | 781/861–9638 | Free | Mon.–Sat. 10–5, Sun. 1–5.

APR.: *Lexington Green Battle Reenactment.* Thousands of people gather each year in downtown Lexington's chilly darkness to witness the reenactment of the 1775 confrontation between British soldiers and defiant Lexington militiamen, a spectacle complete with cannons, horses, and full regalia. You should arrive at Battle Green by 4:30 AM to claim a viewing spot for the battle at 5:30 AM on Patriot's Day. | Massachusetts Ave. (Rte. 225) | 781/862–1703.

OCT.: *Arts and Crafts Festival.* New England craft artists display and sell their works on the lawn of the Lexington Visitor's Center. | 1875 Massachusetts Ave. | 781/862–1450 | www.lexingtonchamber.org | Free.

Dining

Bertucci's. Italian. This chain pizzeria is known for its fresh salads and its thin-crust pizza and calzones direct from the wood-fired brick oven. Kids' menu. No smoking. | 1777 Massachusetts Ave. | 781/860–9000 | $8–$15 | AE, D, MC, V.

Carolinas. American/Casual. This eatery specializes in Angus beef burgers and ribs that weight in at 1¾ pounds *after* being cooked. Seating includes booths and tables inside and umbrella tables on the patio. | 1709 Massachusetts Ave. | 781/862–9797 | $6–$18 | AE, D, MC, V.

Lemon Grass. Thai. Warm colors and Thai art add to the pleasant tone of this storefront spot. The soups, curries, and noodle dishes go easy on the chilis in deference to American palates. No smoking. | 1710 Massachusetts Ave. | 781/862–3530 | No lunch Sun. | $6.15–$13.95 | AE, D, DC, MC, V.

Lodging

Desiderata Bed and Breakfast. This Victorian farmhouse has a formal living room with baby grand piano and a deck. The guest rooms are equipped with queen-size beds, and each has a different motif—Italian, French, or Irish. The property lies ½ mi from Minute Man National Historical Park and on the busline to the Alewife T station on Boston's Red line. Dining room, complimentary breakfast. Microwave, refrigerator, cable TV in common area, no room phones. Library. No pets. No smoking. | 189 Wood St. | 781/862–2824 | fax 781/862–8358 | lexleary@erols.com | 3 rooms | $85 | No credit cards.

Fireside B&B of Lexington. This Colonial garrison next to conservation land has a quiet, 1-acre backyard with a heated pool and apple trees. In the leisure room you can play board games on the pub table by a woodburning stove. Public transportation is a two-minute walk away. Dining room, complimentary Continental breakfast. No air-conditioning, no room phones, cable TV in common area. Outdoor pool. Business services. No pets. No kids under 16. No smoking. | 24 Eldred St. | 781/862–2053 | fax 781/861–7706 | innkeeper@firesidebb.com | www.firesidebb.com | 3 | $125–$175 | AE, MC, V.

Holiday Inn Express. This hotel, which caters to the business traveler, is in the high-tech district outside Boston. Complimentary Continental breakfast. In-room data ports, cable TV. Pool. Hot tub. Laundry facilities. Business services. Pets allowed (deposit). | 440 Bedford St. | 781/861–0850 or 800/HOLIDAY | fax 781/861–0821 | www.holiday-inn.com | 204 rooms, 28 suites | $129–$159, $149–$159 suites | AE, D, DC, MC, V.

Sheraton Lexington Hotel. This colonial-style inn is on the road where the Battle of Lexington and Concord took place in 1775, and it's also close to the Minute Man National Historical Park. The restaurant has floor-to-ceiling windows with views of the woods surrounding the property. Restaurant, bar with entertainment, picnic area. In-room data ports, cable TV. Pool. Gym. Business services. | 727 Marrett Rd. | 781/862–8700 or 888/627–7185 | fax 781/863–0404 | www.sheraton.com | 119 rooms, 2 suites | $179–$309 | AE, D, DC, MC, V.

Wyndham Billerica. Geared toward corporate travelers, this hotel built in 1999 offers work desks and conference rooms. The rooms also contain recliners and upscale bedding. It is 10 mi south of Lexington. Children under 18 stay free. In-room data ports, cable TV. Indoor pool. Exercise equipment. Business services. No pets. | 270 Concord Rd., Billerica |

978/670–7500 or 800/995–3426 (800/Wyndham) | fax 978/670–8898 | www.wyndham.com | 196 rooms, 14 suites | $179–$199 | AE, D, DC, MC, V.

LOWELL

MAP 6, H2

(Nearby towns also listed: Andover and North Andover, Lawrence)

In 1821 a group of business speculators began building the nation's first planned industrial city on the banks of the Merrimack River. They named the city after their founder, Francis Cabot Lowell, who revolutionized cloth manufacturing by designing the first American power loom. Eventually, dozens of mills employing tens of thousands of immigrant workers were in full swing, but the prosperity didn't last. As Lowell's textile industry began to collapse in the 1920s, mills were abandoned and urban decay set in. Today, thanks largely to the National Park Service, Lowell's downtown mills and extensive network of hydropower locks and canals are part of the sprawling Lowell National Historical Park. Other attractions such as the Sports Museum of New England, the New England Quilt Museum, and the American Textile History Museum continue to draw tourists to the city.

Information: **Greater Merrimack Valley Convention and Visitors Bureau** | 9 Central St., Ste. 201, Lowell, 01852-1836 | 978/459–6150 or 800/443–3332. **Merrimack Valley Visitor Center** | I–495 between exits 32 and 33, Chelmsford, 01824 | 978/250–9704 | www.lowell.org.

Attractions

American Textile History Museum. A block-long museum in a restored mill building that tells the story of textile production in America, from hand-spinning to mass production. The museum's ample space allows for scores of exhibits, from antique costumes to replicas of a piece-worker's log cabin and an 1870s factory floor with operating looms. A café, a gift shop, and a research library are also on-site. | 491 Dutton St. | 978/441–0400 | $5 | Tues.–Fri. 9–4, weekends 10–5.

Lowell National Historical Park. You can learn all about Lowell's legacy as the nation's first planned industrial community through guided walking, canal-boat, and bicycle tours; exhibits within several restored mills; the vintage trolleys; and a fine visitors center that should be your first stop. | 246 Market St. | 978/970–5000 | www.nps.gov/lowe | Free, canal tours $4–$6, Boott Cotton Mills Museum $4 | Visitors center daily 8:30–6.
Boott Cotton Mills Museum. This museum occupies several floors of the giant Boott Mill #6, stretching alongside the city's Eastern Canal. The primary exhibit, the weave room, is filled with the cacophony of working power looms from the 1920s. | 400 Foot of John St. | 978/970–5000 | $4 | Daily 9:30–4:30.
New England Folklife Center. This small center on the fifth floor of Boott Mill #6 showcases both traditional and contemporary folkways of the immigrant groups that have worked in Lowell. It also produces brochures for self-guided walking tours of the city's diverse ethnic communities. | 400 Foot of John St. | 978/970–5193 | Free | Weekdays 9–4, closed between exhibits.

Patrick J. Mogan Cultural Center. This large brick boardinghouse built in 1837 is now home to a permanent exhibit on mill girls, the young women recruited to labor in the mills, and the immigrants who eventually replaced them. It also hosts regularly changing exhibits on Lowell's more recent workers. | 40 French St. | 978/970–5000 | Free | Memorial Day–Columbus Day, daily 1–5; Columbus Day–Memorial Day, weekends 1–5.

New England Quilt Museum. From the traditional to the contemporary, if it has to do with quilting, it's here. The permanent collection of quilts illustrates the art and evolution of the craft, while changing exhibits demonstrate its continued vitality. Lectures and workshops are also offered. | 18 Shattuck St. | 978/452–4207 | fax 978/452–5405 | $4 | May–Nov., Tues.–Sat. 10–4, Sun. noon–4; Dec.–Apr., Tues.–Sat. 10–4.

Sports Museum of New England. The wonderful world of professional and amateur sports is the subject of this museum. The building, formerly a stove-maker's shop, is made conspicuous by a statue of the Portuguese soccer star Eusebio. Plenty of interactive displays give you the chance to be more than a spectator. | 25 Shattuck St. | 978/452–6775 | www.townline.com | $3 | Thurs.–Sat. 10–5.

University of Massachusetts–Lowell. This branch of the state university system enrolls over 9,000 undergraduate and graduate students each year in degree programs that range from the general arts and sciences to education, engineering, and management. | 1 University Ave. | 978/934–4000 | www.uml.edu | Free | Daily.

Whistler House Museum of Art. The American artist James Abbott McNeill Whistler was born in this simple clapboard house in 1834. Although the family moved away three years later and Whistler never returned, the museum honors Lowell's famous expatriate with family memorabilia and examples of his lesser-known artwork. Changing exhibits focus on contemporary artists with ties to Lowell. | 243 Worthen St. | 978/452–7641 | $4 | Mar.–Dec., Wed.–Sat. 11–4, Sun. 1–4.

ON THE CALENDAR

JULY: *Lowell Folk Festival.* One of the largest free folk festivals in the country is three days jam-packed with music, dancing, and food. There's something for everyone, from Cajun fiddling, blues, bluegrass, or gospel to puppet shows, story-telling, and crafts exhibits. The festival takes place on stages and in parks throughout the downtown area during the last full weekend in July. | Downtown Lowell | 978/970–5000.

AUG.: *Canal Heritage Day.* One Saturday in the month, costumed guides navigate boats through the locks and gatehouses of the Pawtucket Canal (built in 1796) and onto the Merrimack River. Check in at the Lowell National Park Visitor's Center. | 246 Market St. | 978/970–5000.

SEPT.: *Banjo and Fiddle Contests.* The sounds of bluegrass, Dixieland, and old-time mountain picking can be heard at this one-day annual event at Boarding House Park during the weekend after Labor Day. Banjo, fiddle, and dulcimer workshops begin at 10 AM. Banjo and fiddle contests start at noon and continue until 6. | Corner of French and John Sts. | 978/970–5000.

OCT.: *Lowell Celebrates Kerouac.* Beat Generation spokesman and author Jack Kerouac was born and raised in Lowell and worked as a journalist at the *Lowell Sun*. This annual literary festival celebrates his work. A brochure from the Lowell National Historical Park outlines a downtown walking tour of Kerouac's Lowell. | 978/970–5000.

Dining

La Boniche. French. French provincial describes the dining room and the seasonally changing menu that usually offers pasta, fish, veal, chicken, duck, pork, and steak, in addition to the short list of first courses. Live music Sat. | 143 Merrimack St. | 978/458–9473 | Closed Sun.–Mon. No lunch Sat. | $16–$28 | AE, MC, V.

Southeast Asian Restaurant. Pan-Asian. What this simple one-room storefront lacks in appeal it more than makes up for with its fragrant and flavorful Laotian, Thai, Cambodian, and Vietnamese dishes. Try the Thai curries, any Cambodian selection, or the Laotian noodles and seafood. | 343 Market St. | 978/452–3182 | $4.95–$10.95 | AE, D, MC, V.

The Brewhouse Café and Grill. American. Enjoy fresh ale or lager at any of several bars spread among three stories, or dine on entrées such as lobster or prime rib. The exposed wooden beams are a reminder of the building's past life as a mill. | 201 Cabot St. | 978/937–2690 | $5.95–$19.95 | AE, MC, V.

Lodging

Best Western Chelmsford Inn. This hotel off I–495 is geared to the business traveler. Lowell is 4 mi away; Lexington and Concord are 9 mi. Executive room rates include full breakfast for two. Restaurant. In-room data ports, minibars, cable TV. Pool. Hot tub. Gym. Business services. | 187 Chelmsford St., Chelmsford | 978/256–7511 or 888/770–9992 | fax 978/250–1401 | 120 rooms | $89–$99 | AE, D, DC, MC, V.

Courtyard by Marriott. This hotel that caters to corporate clients has work desks in each room and hosts a complimentary shuttle to local businesses on weekdays. It's off I–495. Restaurant, room service. In-room data ports, cable TV. Pool. Gym. Laundry facilities, laundry service. Business services. | 30 Industrial Ave. E | 978/458–7575 | fax 978/458–1302 | www.courtyard.com | 120 rooms, 12 suites | $119, $129–$139 suites | AE, D, DC, MC, V.

Doubletree Riverfront Hotel Lowell. This hotel in the heart of Lowell's National Historical Park is across from Lowell Memorial Auditorium and a five-minute walk to museums. Some rooms have a view of the Merrimack River. Restaurant, bar, room service. In-room data ports, cable TV. Indoor pool, wading pool. Hot tub. Gym. Laundry facilities. Business services. | 50 Warren St. | 978/452–1200 or 800/876–4586 | fax 978/453–4674 | www.doubletree.com | 252 rooms, 4 suites | $99–$189, $200–$300 suites | AE, D, DC, MC, V.

Hawthorne Suites. The suites here are larger than standard hotel rooms, and the modern furnishings were singled out for their excellence by the *Boston Globe*. It is 5 mi northeast of Lexington and 2 mi east of Lowell. Complimentary breakfast. In-room data ports, kitchenettes, microwaves, refrigerators, cable TV. Outdoor pool. Exercise equipment. Shop. Laundry facilities, laundry services. | 25 Research Pl., North Chelmsford | 978/256–5151 | fax 978/256–6633 | www.princetonproperties.com | 105 suites | $149–$159 | AE, D, DC, MC, V.

Radisson Heritage Hotels and Suites. This full-service hotel off I–495 and about 4 mi from Lowell primarily serves business travelers in the Chelmsford–Lowell area. Restaurant, bar, room service. In-room data ports, some microwaves, some refrigerators, cable TV, some in-room VCRs. Indoor pool. Gym. Business services. | 10 Independence Dr., Chelmsford | 978/256–0800 | fax 978/256–0750 | www.radisson.com | 132 rooms, 82 suites | $119–$159, $139–$179 suites | AE, D, DC, MC, V.

Westford Regency Inn and Conference Center. Geared to the business traveler, this hotel close to Lowell has a bilevel convention center. The spacious rooms each include a sitting area and a work area with desk. Take exit 32 off I–495. 3 restaurants, bar with entertainment, room service. In-room data ports, some refrigerators, cable TV. Indoor pool. Beauty salon, hot tub, sauna, steam room. Health club, racquetball. Business services. Pets allowed (deposit). | 219 Littleton Rd., Westford | 978/692–8200 or 800/543–7801 | fax 978/692–7403 | www.westfordregency.com | 193 rooms, 15 suites | $89–$125, $135–$239 suites | AE, D, DC, MC, V.

LYNN

MAP 6, I3

(Nearby towns also listed: Boston, Lynnfield, Marblehead, Salem, Saugus)

Lynn's 81,000 residents make it the most populous coastal community north of Boston, and the two cities are close enough to be well connected by rail and bus. In the 19th century, Lynn became a center for leather and shoe manufacturing. In fact, the Yankee Division marched into World War I with shoes from Lynn's factories. Now the city's main industry is building aircraft engines for military and commercial use, and its leading attraction is its Diamond District, an area of architecturally notable mansions next to the city's beach promenade.

Information: **Lynn Area Chamber of Commerce** | 23 Central Ave., Lynn, 01901 | 781/592–2900 | www.lynnchamber.com.

Attractions

Gannon Golf Course. This 18-hole semi-private course operates strictly on a first-come, first-served basis for non-members during the week; no reservations are accepted. On weekends, play is restricted to members until 3 PM, and membership is only granted to Lynn area residents. | 40 Great Woods Rd. | 781/592–8238 | Mar.–Nov. daily.

Lynn Heritage State Park. The park's visitor center occupies a renovated brick shoe factory, one of many that made Lynn a world leader in women's shoes a century ago. Photos, tools, machines, and artifacts on display illustrate the transformation of the local shoe business from a cottage craft to major industry. The park includes an oceanfront promenade where outdoor events are staged in summer. | Washington and Union Sts. | 781/598–1974 | fax 781/596–7161 | www.state.ma.us/dem | Free | Wed.–Sun. 9:30–4:30.

Lynn Historical Society Museum/Library. This trim 1836 clapboard house near downtown preserves the museum's vast permanent collection of hand tools used in the shoe industry and provides space for changing exhibits on Lynn's history. | 125 Green St. | 781/592–2465 | $4 | Museum, weekdays 9–4; tours, Mon.–Sat. 1–4.

Lynn Woods Reservation. The rolling woodlands here provided raw timber for shipbuilding in the 18th century. The reservation is one of the largest city parks in the nation. Within its 2,200 acres are a public 18-hole golf course and miles of trails for hiking, mountain biking, and cross-country skiing. | Lynnfield St. | 781/477–7123 | Free | Daily dawn–dusk.

ON THE CALENDAR

AUG.: *Lynn Harbor Monster Day.* At this children's festival held annually at the Heritage State Park Waterfront Park on the second Saturday of the month everything but the food is free: games, crafts, drawing contests, musical entertainment, puppet shows, traveling museum exhibits, and prizes for everyone. | 781/598–1974.

Dining

Porthole Restaurant and Pub. American. This casual restaurant with a nautical theme serves up large portions of fried clams, lobster, and liver and onions, making it popular with families. The upstairs and downstairs dining rooms have ocean views. Find the restaurant at the marina, accessible by boat or car. | 98 Lynnway | 781/595–7733 | www.portholerestaurant.com | $5–$15 | AE, D, DC, MC, V.

Lodging

Diamond District Inn. This 1911 Georgian Revival inn is on the National Register of Historic Places. Rooms are furnished with antiques, and two suites have working fireplaces and private decks. The property is 300 ft from a sandy beach. Complimentary breakfast. In-room data ports, in-room hot tubs. Business services. Some pets allowed (fee). No smoking. | 142 Ocean St. | 781/599–4470 or 800/666–3076 | fax 781/595–2200 | diamonddistrict@msn.com | www.diamonddistrictinn.com | 11 rooms, 3 suites | $145–$200, $225–$260 suites | AE, D, DC, MC, V.

Ocean View Bed and Breakfast. This Queen Anne Victorian has a wraparound porch, antique furnishings, and fireplaces in the foyer and dining room. The ocean view is a bonus, and it's an easy walk to the beach and the commuter rail station. Dining room, complimentary Continental breakfast. Cable TV, no room phones. No pets. No smoking. | 11 Ocean St. | 781/598–6388 | www.oceanviewbandb.com | $100–$125 | No credit cards.

LYNNFIELD

MAP 6, I3

(Nearby towns also listed: Boston, Burlington, Danvers, Lynn, Salem, Saugus)

Lynnfield, a suburb 15 mi north of Boston, is one of the most affluent communities in the state. Some of the structures surrounding its attractive common date back to the early 18th century, but being essentially a bedroom community, the town has no museums or historical sites open to the public.

Information: **North of Boston Convention and Visitors Bureau** | 17 Peabody Sq, Peabody, 01960 | 978/977–7760 or 800/742–5306 | info@northofboston.org | www.northof-boston.org.

ON THE CALENDAR

JULY: *Concerts on the Common.* Jazz, pop, and oldies concerts sponsored by the Friends of the Library are held on Wednesdays at the Lynnfield Common. | South Common and Main St. | 781/334–5411.

Dining

Kernwood. American. Colonial trappings, open-hearth cooking, and live piano music set the stage here for relaxed dining. Traditional fare is served, from hefty steaks to fresh seafood. Music Mon.–Sat. nights. Kids' menu. Early-bird suppers Mon.–Sat. No smoking. | 55 Salem St. | 781/245–4011 | $12.95–$25 | AE, D, DC, MC, V.

99 Restaurant and Pub. American/Casual. The moderate prices and large portions at this New England restaurant chain make it popular with families. The menu is wide-ranging, from baked scrod to sirloin tips to pasta, Kids' menu. Free refills on soda and coffee. | 317 Salem St. | 781/599–8119 | $6–$10 | AE, D, DC, MC, V.

MARBLEHEAD

MAP 6, I3

(Nearby towns also listed: Beverly, Boston, Lynn, Salem)

Long before its volunteers rowed George Washington across the Delaware, Marblehead had an uncommon devotion to boats and sailing, a passion that continues to this day. Although it has fewer than 20,000 residents, the town has six yacht clubs, whose members, friends, and fellow enthusiasts fill the harbor with thousands of sails each summer. Marblehead is almost easier to approach by sea than by land, but visitors who successfully navigate through the surrounding communities will find a small treasure of a town, with appealing shops and eateries and attractive Colonial homes lining the narrow, irregular streets.

Information: **Marblehead Chamber of Commerce** | 62 Pleasant St., Marblehead, 01945 | 781/631–2868. **Visitor Information Booth** | Pleasant and Essex Sts. | info@marble-headchamber.org | www.marbleheadchamber.org.

Attractions

Abbot Hall. What makes this brick Victorian town hall special is its exhibit room filled with historical documents and artwork. The highlight of the collection is Archibald Willard's famous painting *The Spirit of '76*, commissioned for the nation's centennial in 1876. | 188 Washington St. | 781/631–0000 | Free | June–Oct., weekdays 8–5, Sat. 9–6, Sun. 11–6; Nov.–May, Sat. 9–6, Sun. 11–6.

Crocker Park. This public park offers a panoramic view of Marblehead Harbor. Summer concerts are held here, and rest rooms are open Memorial Day to Labor Day. | Front St. | 781/631–2868 | Free | Daily.

Devereux Beach. Just before the causeway to Marblehead Neck lies Devereux Beach, once the site of an Indian encampment and now the town's most popular beach. Partly sandy and partly pebbled, the beach also has a playground, a restaurant with outdoor seating, and lifeguards in summer. | Ocean Ave. | 781/631–2868 | www.marbleheadchamber.org | Free, parking $5 July 4–Labor Day | Daily.

J. O. J. Frost Folk Art Gallery. This nonprofit gallery run by the Marblehead Historical Society displays delightful paintings of 1920s life on land and at sea by local folk artist J. O. J. Frost. Permanent and changing exhibits are shown here. | 170 Washington St. | 781/631–1768 | fax 781/631–0917 | www.marbleheadchamber.com | Donation suggested | Tues.–Sat. 10–4, Sun. 1–4.

Jeremiah Lee Mansion. Built in 1768 by a wealthy shipowner, this mansion is the epitome of Colonial luxury, from the architectural detailing on the facade to the sumptuous interior decorations. The drawing room's hand-painted English wallpaper alone is worth the price of admission. The Marblehead Historical Society also presents changing exhibits on local history here. | 161 Washington St. | 781/631–1069 | $4 | Mid-May–Columbus Day, weekdays 10–4, weekends 1–4.

King Hooper Mansion. This Georgian mansion is named after its original wealthy owner, who earned his unofficial title through his benevolence to the town. Now owned by the Marblehead Arts Association, the elegant house is used as an art gallery. | 8 Hooper St. | 781/631–2608 | Free | Mon.–Sat. 10–4, Sun. 1–5.

Old Town House. This circa 1727 building with identical front and back entrances is the second oldest municipal building in America. Marblehead town meetings were held here in the 18th and 19th centuries. A Civil War Museum occupies the 2nd floor. | Market Sq., Washington and State Sts. | 781/631–1768 | Free | Memorial Day–first weekend Dec.; Civil War Museum open by appointment.

ON THE CALENDAR
JULY: *Festival of Arts.* This festival, which takes place July 4th weekend, includes a street festival, children's activities, art exhibits and sales, and musical entertainment at Crocker Park. | 781/639–ARTS.
DEC.: *Marblehead Christmas Walk.* This two-day event, held the first weekend of December, is chock-full of holiday activities: a window-decorating contest, music and caroling, a tree lighting, a chorale at the Old North Church, crafts fairs, and the arrival of Santa and Mrs. Claus by lobster boat. Stores offer complimentary refreshments and there is free admission to the Jeremiah Lee Mansion and Civil War Museum. | 781/631–2868.

Dining
King's Rook. Café. This cozy wine bar and café is in Marblehead's historical district. Built in 1747, the building has low-beamed ceilings and pink terra-cotta walls adorned with prints and a mural that pays homage to the building's former owner, folk artist J. O. J. Frost. Popular menu items include thin-crust pizzas and the owner's homemade desserts: chocolate pot de crème and bread pudding with espresso, Kahlua, and chocolate. | 12 State St. | 781/631–9838 | No dinner Mon. | $5–$10 | D, MC, V.

The Landing. Seafood. The views of Marblehead Neck, the causeway, and the town's busy yacht anchorage ensure maximum crowds here throughout the warmer months. So attractive is the location that it's able to infuse the standard seafood-and-pasta menu with a cachet it would otherwise lack. Kids' menu. No smoking. | Clark Landing, 81 Front St. | 781/631–1878 | $13.95–$26.95 | AE, DC, MC, V.

Maddie's Sail Loft. Seafood. This bustling restaurant popular with the boating crowd is just 100 yards from the dock. You can sample fresh haddock, clams, shrimp, and oysters either upstairs (21 tables) or downstairs (10 tables). Nautical artifacts adorn the walls of both dining rooms. | 15 State St. | 781/631–9824 | No dinner Sun. | $9–$17 | No credit cards.

Trattoria Il Panino. Italian. This informal North Shore outpost of a Boston-based Italian chain is a local favorite. Try the saffron linguine with scallops and shrimp, shrimp and artichoke ravioli, lobster risotto, or zuppa di pesce. Open-air dining on the patio. No smoking. | 126 Washington St. | 781/631–3900 | No lunch | $9–$23 | AE, D, DC, MC, V.

Truffles. Café. Decorated with a pig motif, this café is known for its truffle-scented potatoes made during the holidays. The rest of the year, you can choose from many low-fat and vegetarian dishes such as pad Thai, made with fresh ingredients from Boston's Chinatown. Sit-down, take-out, and delivery service is available. | 114 Washington St. | 781/639–1104 | $5–$10 | AE, MC, V.

Lodging

Harbor Light Inn. This upscale North Shore inn is filled with 18th-century English antiques and Oriental rugs. Many rooms have working fireplaces; four have private sundecks. Outside, you'll find fountains surrounded by gardens, a heated swimming pool, and umbrella tables in a courtyard. The inn is in the historic harbor district, close to house museums, art galleries, antique shops, and restaurants. Dining room, complimentary Continental breakfast. In-room data ports, some in-room hot tubs, cable TV, in-room VCRs. Pool. Business services. No smoking. | 58 Washington St. | 781/631–2186 | fax 781/631–2216 | hli@shore.net | www.harborlightinn.com | 23 rooms, 3 suites | $115–$195, $245–$275 suites | AE, MC, V.

Harborside House. This white Georgian house, built by a ship's carpenter in 1850, is on a quiet one-way street and overlooks the water. The beautiful gardens, front porch, deck, and patio complement the house. The two guest rooms have wide-board floors, Oriental rugs, and period wallpaper; guest robes are provided. The house is close to historical sites, restaurants, and shops. Afternoon tea is available. Dining room, complimentary Continental breakfast. TV in common area. No pets. No kids under 8. No smoking. | 23 Gregory St. | 781/631–1032 | swliving@shore.net | www.shore.net/~swliving | 2 rooms with shared bath | $75–$95 | No credit cards.

Marblehead Inn. This 1872 three-story Victorian mansion is in a residential area on the main road between Marblehead and Salem. The house is surrounded by manicured grounds. All suites are furnished with antiques, two have patios, and one has a wood-burning fireplace. Ample parking is available. Complimentary Continental breakfast. Kitchenettes, some in-room hot tubs, cable TV, some in-room VCRs. No pets. No smoking. | 264 Pleasant St. | 781/639–9999 or 800/399–5843 | fax 781/639–9996 | www.marbleheadinn.com | 10 suites | $169–$199 | AE, MC, V.

Seagull Inn. What a view! This blue-with-white-trim Colonial inn is on Marblehead Neck, less than a block from the ocean and 2½ blocks from the lighthouse. The house has four decks and a beautiful yard with swings, Adirondack chairs, and croquet. Bicycles and kayaks are available at no extra charge. The Lighthouse Suite has a private entrance, full kitchen, bedroom, living room, two TVs, two VCRs, and two decks, one with a hammock, chairs, and a panoramic view of the ocean. Complimentary Continental breakfast. In-room data ports, refrigerators, cable TV, in-room VCRs and movies. Bicycles. Pets allowed. No smoking. | 106 Harbor Ave. | 781/631–1893 | fax 781/631–3535 | host@seagullinn.com | www.seagullinn.com | 3 suites | $100–$200 | MC, V.

Spray Cliff on the Ocean. This bed-and-breakfast is on a cliff overlooking the ocean, one block from Marblehead's main street. The rooms have been distinctively furnished by the innkeeper, a professional decorator. Five rooms have ocean views, three have fireplaces, and two have garden views. Beach chairs are available at no extra charge. Complimentary Continental breakfast. No air-conditioning, no TV, no room phones. Bicycles. No kids under 14. | 25 Spray Ave. | 781/631–6789 or 800/626–1530 | fax 781/639–4563 | spraycliff@aol.com | www.spraycliff.com | 7 rooms (4 with shower only) | $180–$225 | AE, MC, V.

MARTHA'S VINEYARD
(*see* Aquinnah, Chilmark, Edgartown, Oak Bluffs, Vineyard Haven, and West Tisbury)

MASHPEE (CAPE COD)

(Nearby towns also listed: Barnstable Village, Centerville, Falmouth, Hyannis, Sandwich)

Mashpee is among only a handful of towns in Massachusetts with a discernible Native American presence. The Mashpee, for whom this town is named, are part of the Wampanoag nation. Over the years, the community here has shown dedication to open-space preservation, with several privately maintained sanctuaries set aside for public enjoyment, a state-run marine reserve established in Waquoit Bay, and 2,000 acres designated to eventually become a National Wildlife Refuge. However, the town of Mashpee, situated in the upper portion of Cape Cod, has seen explosive growth in the past 20 years, more than doubling in population during the 1980s and maintaining double-digit growth throughout the 1990s. As a result, Mashpee now has its share of new seaside condominiums, vacation homes, and commercialization along Route 28.

Information: Mashpee Chamber of Commerce | Box 1245, Mashpee, 02649 | 508/477–0792 or 800/423–6274. **Information center** | Cape Cod Five Cents Savings Bank, Mashpee Commons | info@mashpeechamber.com | www.mashpeechamber.com.

Attractions

Cape Cod Children's Museum. When it's raining or the kids need something more stimulating than a trampoline, this spacious facility is the right choice. The most popular exhibit is a fabricated 30-ft pirate ship, but future techies like the planetarium and science exhibits. | 577 Great Neck Rd. S | 508/539–8788 | cccm@gis.net | www.capecodchildrensmuseum.pair.com | $3.50 | Mon.–Sat. 10–5, Sun. noon–5.

Cape Symphony Orchestra. In addition to performing outdoors at the Mashpee Commons in late July, the 90-member orchestra offers a monthly classical or pops concert at the Barnstable High School Performing Arts Center in Hyannis. | Mashpee Commons, Rte. 151; Arts Center, W. Main St., Hayannis | 508/362–1111 | Tickets $20–$50.

Lowell Holly Reservation. The American holly reaches the northern edge of its natural range in coastal Massachusetts, and this property of the Trustees of Reservations includes large stands of holly. What makes this peninsula between Mashpee and Wakeby ponds so unusual is that, unlike most of the land in New England, it has never been logged or farmed. | South Sandwich Rd., off Rte. 130S | 781/821–2977 | www.ttor.org | Seasonal parking $6, Memorial Day–Columbus Day, daily year-round parking, free | Daily 9–5.

Mashpee River Woodlands. More than 8 mi of trails and nearly 400 acres of conservation land run alongside the Mashpee River—perfect for birding, fishing, and canoeing. | Mashpee Neck Rd. | Free | Daily.

Old Indian Meeting House. The oldest church still standing on Cape Cod (built in 1684 but moved to this site later) is used by the local Wampanoag Indian tribe for meetings and worship services. | Meeting House Rd. | 508/477–0208 | Free | July–Aug., Wed. and Fri. 10–2.

Wampanoag Indian Museum. Historical baskets, weapons, and tools used by the local Wampanoags make up this small collection that testifies to the legacy of the local tribe. In the spring, a herring run in the river on the premises swarms with shiny fish making their way home to spawn. | 416 Rte. 130 | 508/477–1536 | Donation suggested | Mon.–Sat. 10–2; call to confirm.

ON THE CALENDAR

OCT.: *Octoberfest.* Held on Mashpee Common, the festival includes a beer garden, German music, and carnival rides for the kids. | 508/477–0792 or 800/423–6274.

Dining

Contrast at The Commons. Contemporary. Fancy sandwiches, individual pizzas, and bistro food with a flair share the menu, so everyone in your party will find something to suit his or her palate. Hand-painted tables, bold colors, and modern sculpture give the room a contemporary but warm feel. | Mashpee Commons, Rte. 151 | 508/477–1299 | $8–$24 | AE, MC, V.

The Flume. American. Wampanoag elder and chef Earl Mills pairs New England tastes with Native American tradition. Indian pudding is done to perfection, as is Yankee pot roast. Also try the chowder and cod cakes. | Lake Ave. | 508/477–1456 | Closed Dec.–Mar. No lunch | $10–$26 | MC, V.

Gone Tomatoes. Italian. A spacious and contemporary trattoria, with lofty ceilings and an always-crowded second-floor bar, this eatery is known for prompt, friendly service and huge portions of Sicilian and Tuscan food. Try the focaccia pizza, *calamari fra diavolo,* or *frutti di mare.* Kids' menu. Sun. brunch. | 11 Steeple St. | 508/477–8100 | $11–$18 | MC, V.

VINEYARD LIGHTHOUSES

Seafaring trade and maritime industry have been cornerstones of the Massachusetts economy throughout most of its history. The state also has some of the most treacherous shoals along the entire Eastern Seaboard. Because of the threat such offshore hazards have always posed to its economic lifeblood, the state has traditionally placed a high value on anything that could improve marine navigation, such as lighthouses. The oldest lighthouse in the nation has guided sailors to Boston Harbor's entrance since 1783, and lighted beacons have marked the spot since at least 1679. Up and down the Massachusetts coast, lighthouses flash in welcome or in warning, or both. Except for the unlucky few that have had to be replaced after being destroyed by storms—as happened to Nantucket's Great Point Light in 1984—all 42 Massachusetts lighthouses are 18th- or 19th-century historic landmarks. Not surprisingly, most are highly photogenic.

Martha's Vineyard alone has five, all still in use as fully automated lights, and, given the island's small size, you can make a day's tour out of visiting the whole collection. The oldest is Gay Head Light, atop the 130-ft-high scarp at the island's isolated southwestern tip, in the town of Aquinnah. The present brick tower dates back to 1856, when it replaced the 1799 original. East and West Chop, the opposing flanks of Vineyard Haven's harbor, are each marked with century-old lighthouses of the tall, white, conical variety. Somewhat unusually, the original East Chop light was built at private expense; the current incarnation, however, is standard government-issue, circa 1878. You'll find the final two in Edgartown, but only one, at the mouth of the harbor, is easily accessible. The other is at Cape Poge, on the far northeastern tip of Chappaquiddick's slowly migrating shoreline, a 6-mi round-trip hike from the nearest parking through a coastal wildlife refuge. The sand beneath the lighthouse foundation has shifted so much that it has had to be relocated away from the eroding beach seven times since its construction in 1893.

© Artville

Popponesset Inn. Continental. The inn's location overlooking Nantucket Sound makes it a popular spot for weddings. Best bets on the menu are traditional offerings such as baked stuffed lobster, grilled swordfish, and steak. It's 3 mi south of Mashpee. | Shore Dr., New Seabury | 508/477–1100 | Closed Jan.–Mar. Closed Mon. No lunch or dinner Nov.–Dec. and Apr.–May | $8–$30 | AE, MC, V.

Lodging

★ **New Seabury Resort and Conference Center.** This resort, on a whopping 2,300-acre peninsula surrounded by Nantucket Sound, is self-contained and has all the recreational facilities you'd ever want. Modern cottages set along narrow, crushed-seashell lanes contain the amenities you'd have at home; you won't have to leave the property unless you want to. 2 restaurants. 2 pools. 2 golf courses, miniature golf, 16 tennis courts. Health club, beach, water sports, boating, bicycles. No pets. No smoking. | Great Neck Rd. | 508/477–9400 or 800/999–9033 | fax 508/477–9790 | www.newseabury.com | 167 1- and 2-bedroom condos | $215–$275, $310–$385 2–bedroom units | AE, DC, MC, V.

NANTUCKET

MAP 6, L8

(Nearby towns also listed: Hyannis, Oak Bluffs)

Officially, the town, island, and county of Nantucket all share the same boundaries, but Nantucket Town—or just "town" for short—usually means the harborside village of shops, architecture, and whaling history that is one of the state's most famous—and expensive—tourist destinations. The whole island has been designated a National Historic Landmark, but the town's central historic district is so scrupulously protected from change that Herman Melville's ghost would no doubt feel right at home if he were to pay a visit. Outside the town at opposite ends of the island are the tiny residential villages Siasconset ('Sconset to locals) and Miacomet. Nantucket's airline connections to the mainland are frequent enough in summer to make its airport the busiest in all of New England. Islanders also enjoy daily ferry service to Cape Cod.

Information: **Nantucket Island Chamber of Commerce** | 48 Main St., Nantucket, 02554-3595 | 508/228–1700. **Visitor Services and Information Bureau** | 25 Federal St. | 508/228–0925 | www.nantucketchamber.org.

Attractions

African Meeting House. Of the nine sites on the island's African-American Heritage Trail tour, the only surviving building is this former school and church built in the early 19th century. Lectures, concerts, and readings illuminate the experiences of Cape Verdeans and African-Americans on Nantucket. | 29 York St. | 508/228–9833 | Free | July–Aug., Tues.–Sat. 11–3, Sun. 1–3.

Brant Point Lighthouse. This 1902 lighthouse at the head of the harbor stands 26 ft tall and shines a beacon visible 10 mi out to sea. You can reach the lighthouse via a small boardwalk. | Easton St. | Free | Daily.

Car/passenger ferry service. Several companies provide ferry service to Nantucket, but if you choose to bring a car, you narrow your options down to one. All the ferries accept bicycles for an additional charge.

Freedom Cruise Line. This company provides up to three daily departures from picturesque Saquatucket Harbor in Harwich Port, on the eastern side of Cape Cod. The 90-minute crossings are scheduled roundtrip daily during summer season with overnight parking available for $12 per night. | Straight Wharf, end of Main St. | 508/432–8999 | $39 round-trip | May–Columbus Day, daily.

Hy-Line Cruises. Hy-Line offers year-round passenger service from Hyannis aboard a swift and smooth water-jet catamaran that makes the crossing in one hour. Slower, less expensive passenger service from both Cape Cod and Martha's Vineyard (Oak Bluffs) is also provided in summer aboard single-hull vessels, which complete their runs in slightly under two hours. Prepaid passenger reservations are accepted only for the regular sevice. | Straight Wharf, end of Main St. | 508/778–2600 or 888/778–1132 (in MA), 800/492–8082 (regular–speed ferry tickets, in MA) | www.hy-linecruises.com | $25 round-trip for regular service, $55 round-trip for high-speed service | Hyannis: high-speed service daily, regular service May–Oct., daily. Oak Bluffs: May–Oct., daily.

Steamship Authority. The Steamship Authority runs car-carrying ferries between Nantucket and Hyannis year-round. It also offers seasonally high-speed, passenger-only service by catamaran. Reservations are accepted only on the high-speed boat and are strongly recommended. Vehicle reservations are required in advance for the regular service. | Steamship Wharf, end of Broad St. | 508/477–8600 or 508/495–FAST (high–speed ferry reservations

NANTUCKET'S ECOLOGICAL TREASURE

Many ages ago, before New England's southern coast was blanketed by industrial ports, homes with an ocean view, and beach resorts, much of this land beside the sea was sandy-soiled, quick-draining plain, grown over with grasses and wildflowers. Because of coastal development, these sand-plain grasslands have been in rapid decline wherever they used to exist. Today, these visually unarresting yet biologically rich meadows are so rare that nearly all the planet's remaining acreage is found in Massachusetts—90% on Nantucket alone.

Ecologically, sand-plain grasslands resemble Midwestern prairies, and serve the same vital role in preventing soil erosion and nutrient loss. In coastal areas, such erosion can severely degrade neighboring wetlands, which are themselves vital as nurseries to numerous fish species and other marine organisms. Where prairies depend on annual drought to kill off invasive shrubs and trees, sand-plain grasslands have counted on the withering effects of salt air. Grasslands are also important habitat for ground-nesting bird species, which in New England include the marsh hawk, the short-eared owl, and the grasshopper sparrow. Beetles, butterflies, and moths also inhabit these grasslands, which are of course part of a wider food chain extending far beyond the meadow's edge.

Where sand-plain grasses have survived, it is often as a result of human activity, such as coastal farming, which clears land of trees and shrubs. When Nantucket's early settlers cleared its forests, for example, first for fuel and housing and later for grazing sheep, the sand-plain grasslands spread through the island's interior. Now that coastal home-construction over the past century has wiped out most of the shoreline grasslands, these inland tracts are up against an unaccustomed threat. Not from human development—much of Nantucket's interior has been set aside as open land—but from other plants, such as fast-spreading shrubs, which sand-plain grasslands have never had to compete against along the shore. Using carefully controlled fires, several Nantucket conservation groups have tackled the challenge of perpetuating sand-plain grasslands where nature never intended them to be, but the odds are against long-term success.

© Artville

only) | www.islandferry.com | Passengers $24 round-trip for regular service, $42 round-trip for high-speed service; vehicles $118–$366 round-trip | Daily.

Coatue–Coskata–Great Point. This 1,400-acre wildlife preserve boasts 18 mi of scalloped barrier beaches that protect the harbor and provide a refuge for migrating birds, so bring your binoculars. Great Point Lighthouse is a dramatic sight for surf-casting fishermen, scallopers, and picnickers. Swimming is dangerous. | End of Wauwinet Rd. | 508/228–0006 | Free, four-wheel-drive vehicle permits required | Daily dawn–dusk.

Eel Point. This long spit of sand about 6 mi from town is one of the island's many unspoiled conservation areas. Because Eel Point is so well suited to bird watching, the Maria Mitchell Association leads popular birding trips and nature walks here. | Eel Point Rd. | 508/228–5387 (Maria Mitchell Association) | Free | Daily.

★ **First Congregational Church.** Climb to the top of this church's elegant steeple (120 ft or 92 steps up) for stunning 360-degree views of the island and town. Highlights within the church itself are a restored trompe l'oeil ceiling and an 1831 Appleton organ. | 62 Centre St. | 508/228–0950 | $2.50 | Mid-June–mid-Oct., Mon.–Sat. 10–4.

Gail's Tours, Inc. Gail Nickerson Johnson comes from a long line of Nantucketers, and it shows. Her guided tours, conducted in her air-conditioned red van, are rich in anecdote and history. She often ventures places no bus can go, makes stops for photographs, and tailors her tours to the interests of her passengers. Tours for day-trippers begin at the Nantucket Visitors Center on Federal Street. If you stay overnight, you will be picked up at your guest house. Reservations are recommended at least 24 hours in advance. | Box 3270 | 508/257–6557 | Reservations essential | $13 | Apr.–early Nov., daily 10, 1, and 3; mid-Nov.–Mar., by appointment.

Greater Light. Still under renovation, this former barn was converted in the 1930s into a whimsical summer house by two Philadelphia sisters, one an actress, the other an artist. It's undergoing renovation until 2002, so you can just see it from the outside. | 8 Howard St. | 508/228–1894.

Lily Pond Park. This mere 5 acres perched on the edge of town is good for bird-watching, in-season berry picking (blackberries, grapes, and raspberries), and plain old relaxing. You're likely to see deer and ducks, too. | N. Liberty St. | Free | Daily.

The Maria Mitchell Association. This organization, named for America's first female professor of astronomy, was established to increase public awareness and knowledge of the universe and the natural world. It maintains a number of attractions on Nantucket—from an aquarium to two observatories to several historic homes filled with artifacts—and runs a variety of programs. | 2 Vestal St. | 508/228–9198 | www.mmo.org.

The Aquarium. Past the flower-filled window planters on this tiny waterfront shack are fish tanks brimming with examples of local marine life. The association's volunteers are on hand to answer your questions about marine ecology. Specimen-gathering trips are also available. | 28 Washington St. | 508/228–5387 | $3 | mid-June–mid-Aug., Tues.–Sat. 10–4; Sept.–Oct., Fri.–Sat. 10–4.

Hinchman House. This 19th-century house is filled with natural-history exhibits ranging from live local reptiles to a century-old wildflower collection. You can learn about Nantucket's ecology and visit the Maria Mitchell Association's gift shop, too. | 7 Milk St. | 508/228–0898 | $3 | Mid-June–early Oct., Tues.–Sat. 10–4.

Loines Observatory. As an alternative to turning in early at night, wander over here for stargazing with the aid of powerful telescopes. Informative daytime tours are also available. | Milk St. Ext. | 508/228–9273 | www.mmo.org | $10 | Stargazing mid-June–mid-Sept., Mon., Wed., Fri. 9 PM–11 PM; mid-Sept.–mid-June, Mon. 8 PM–10 PM.

Maria Mitchell Science Library. Maria Mitchell, discovered a new comet in 1847 from the rooftop of her father's Nantucket bank. This library honoring her maintains collections of periodicals, naturalist field guides, science books, and volumes on local history and gardening. | 2 Vestal St. | 508/228–9219 | www.mmo.org | $3 | Mid-June–mid-Sept., Tues.–Sat. 10–4; mid-Sept.–mid-June, Wed.–Fri. 2–5, Sat. 9–noon.

Mitchell House. Maria Mitchell was born and raised in this house, which still retains the family's furnishings. Of special interest here are Mitchell's brass telescope and the only public roof walk in Nantucket. | 1 Vestal St. | 508/228–2896 | $3 | June–early Oct., Tues.–Sat. 10–4.

Vestal Street Observatory. The Maria Mitchell Association operates two observatories on Nantucket. The Vestal Street Observatory, known for its research and educational programs, focuses on daytime observations of sunspots. Note the outdoor scale model of the solar system. | 3 Vestal St. | 508/228–9273 | $3 | Tues.–Sat. 10–4.

★ **Milestone Bog.** This was the world's largest natural cranberry bog until it was slashed in half in 1959. It still spans over 200 acres and yields a spectacular harvest from late September through October. The rest of the year, the bog and its surrounding moors are hauntingly desolate and beautiful. | Milestone Rd. | Free | Daily.

Nantucket Life Saving Museum. This fascinating museum off Polpis Road displays artifacts recovered from the shipwrecked *Andrea Doria*, as well as equipment used in daring ocean rescues. The collection is housed within a re-created 1874 life saving service station. | Fulling Hill Rd. | 508/228–1885 | $4 | Mid-June–mid-Oct., daily 9:30–4.

Nantucket Historical Association. With more than two dozen properties under its care, the Nantucket Historical Association leads Nantucket's preservation efforts. The properties, half of which are accessible to the public, range from a small plot of former grazing land to the island's large and quite popular Whaling Museum. The NHA also hosts lectures, after-school programs, and an annual fund-raising antiques auction. | 15 Broad La. | 508/228–1894 | fax 508/228–5618 | www.nha.org | Visitors pass to all public NHA properties $10.

Fair Street Museum. Next door to the Quaker Meeting House, this spacious 1904 building hosts regularly changing exhibits that draw on the NHA's vast collection of artifacts, historical photos, and memorabilia. | 7 Fair St. | 508/228–1894 | $3 | Memorial Day–Columbus Day, daily 10–5.

Fire Hose–Cart House. This 1886 structure was one of several built after the 1846 Great Fire nearly destroyed the town. Scattered throughout residential neighborhoods, each held a manually operated fire cart in readiness for emergencies. This last remaining example contains the old hand-pumper known as Cataract #6. | 8 Gardner St. | 508/228–1894 | Free | Memorial Day–Columbus Day, daily 10–5; Columbus Day–early Dec., Fri.–Sun. 10–3.

Foulger-Franklin Memorial Fountain, Boulder, and Bench. Benjamin Franklin's mother, Abiah Foulger, was a Nantucket woman born and bred. This fountain near where her home once stood is dedicated to her memory. The boulder and bench to the north across the field commemorate the land grant Nantucket's first European settlers made to Abiah's father, Peter Foulger, in 1663. | Madaket Rd. | Free | Daily.

Hadwen House. William Hadwen, a wealthy whale-oil merchant, built this beautiful Greek Revival mansion in 1845. Its exceptional detailing both inside and out hint at the affluence Nantucket gained from the whaling industry, a fact reinforced by the home's 19th-century neighbors, which are among the island's finest houses. | 96 Main St. | 508/228–1894 | $4 | Memorial Day–Columbus Day, daily 10–5; Columbus Day–early Dec., Fri.–Sun. 10–3.

Macy-Christian House. This 1745 house built by the successful island merchant Nathaniel Macy contains rooms furnished with fine 18th- and 19th-century antiques. | 12 Liberty St. | 508/228–1894 | $2 | Memorial Day–Columbus Day, daily 10–5; Columbus Day–early Dec., Fri.–Sun. 10–3.

Old Gaol. So much heavy timber and iron was used in constructing this 1805 jailhouse that it cost as much as a whaling ship. Used until 1933, the building had to be modified periodically to foil repeated escapes (one young prisoner was able to climb out the chimney before the flue was reduced). | 15 Vestal St. | 508/228–1894 | Free | Memorial Day–Columbus Day, daily 10–5; Columbus Day–early Dec., Fri.–Sun. 10–3.

Old Mill. Built in 1746, this gristmill is the last surviving mill from these heights. When the weather cooperates, the mill still operates, grinding about a ton of corn into meal each summer. | Prospect St. | 508/228–1894 | $2 | Memorial Day–Columbus Day, daily 10–5; Columbus Day–early Dec., Fri.–Sun. 10–3.

Oldest House. Also known as the Jethro Coffin House, this simple 1686 saltbox was built as a wedding present for Jethro Coffin and his bride, Mary Gardner Coffin, by their fathers. Extensively renovated in the late 19th century, the house and its property provide a glimpse of how the island settlement looked in its first century. | Sunset Hill La. | 508/228–1894 | $3 | Memorial Day–Columbus Day, daily 10–5; Columbus Day–early Dec., Fri.–Sun. 10–3.

Peter Foulger Museum. The most modern of the NHA's museums, the Foulger contains the Stackpole Library and Research Center, whose books, dairies, nautical charts, documents, and image collections may be accessed for a daily fee. The NHA also hosts exhibits on the premises. | 15 Broad St. | 508/228–1894 (museum) or 508/228–1655 (library) | $5 | Call for hrs.

★ **Whaling Museum.** This former whale-oil candle factory is now a museum that explains the island's role as a leading 19th-century whaling town. Tools of the trade, captains' portraits, a 43-ft whale skeleton, and an unsurpassed collection of scrimshaw are just some of the objects on display. Lively gallery talks recount the tedium, excitement, hardship, and danger of whaling, and there's a well-stocked museum shop. | Broad St. | 508/228–1894 | $5 | Call for hrs.

Sankaty Head Lighthouse. Erected in 1849, this red-and-white striped lighthouse is precariously close to the edge of a 90-ft cliff. Since the mid-1920s, erosion has claimed more than 200 ft of shoreline and now seriously threatens the lighthouse. | Polpis Rd. | Free | Closed to the public.

★ **Siasconset.** Seven miles west of Nantucket town, "'Sconset," as it is affectionately known, is a picture-perfect village of small weathered cottages nestled together. The charming residences, covered top to bottom in climbing roses, line narrow lanes of crushed seashells. | Free | Daily.

ON THE CALENDAR

APR.: *Daffodil Festival.* Spring has sprung on Nantucket when more than 3 million daffodils bloom across the island. The three-day festival on the last full weekend of the month includes an indoor display of daffodil varieties, an antique-car parade, a tailgate picnic, and a tour of guest houses in the historic downtown district. | 508/228–1700.

JUNE: *Nantucket Film Festival.* Begun in 1996, this festival focuses attention on the art of screenwriting. Independent film showings, readings, and discussions take place throughout the town for the five days of the festival. | 508/325–6274.

AUG.: *Sandcastle and Sculpture Contest.* Singles, families, and teams build their best sand castles and sculptures during the second weekend of the month, for which ribbons are awarded in different categories. | 508/228–1700.

NOV.–DEC.: *Nantucket Noel and Christmas Stroll.* The month-long celebration begins the day after Thanksgiving with the Christmas-tree lighting and continues through New Year's Eve with holiday performances, concerts, and exhibitions. The early-December, three-day Christmas Stroll features more than 200 decorated Christmas trees, a window-decorating contest, carolers, an appearance by Santa Claus, and a special candlelight ecumenical service. | 508/228–1700.

Dining

★ **American Seasons.** Contemporary. Country artifacts, hand-painted murals, and game-board tables contribute to the appeal of this restaurant. The menu impresses with its sophisticated, creative approach to regional American favorites. Try the fresh seafood, lamb, or pork chops. Open-air dining on patio. No smoking. | 80 Centre St. | 508/228–7111 | Closed mid-Dec.–early Apr. No lunch | $25–$28 | AE, MC, V.

Atlantic Cafe. American. Ship models and nautical art enhance the pubby mood of this café. The eclectic menu of bar food, pastas, sandwiches, and salads is family-friendly. Try the codfish cakes. Kids' menu. | 15 S. Water St. | 508/228–0570 | $9–$21 | AE, D, DC, MC, V.

Boarding House. Contemporary. Soft candlelight casts a glow upon the intimate dining room where Mediterranean-influenced American dishes are prepared and presented with flair. Try the lobster tails, grilled marinated sea scallops, and the roast Szechuan quail. Open-air dining on patio. | 12 Federal St. | 508/228–9622 | Reservations essential June–Sept. | Patio closed Dec.–Apr. No lunch | $22–$30 | AE, MC, V.

Cap'n Tobey's Chowder House. Seafood. This rustic, shanty-style restaurant is well established, having had the same owner since the 1950s. The bouillabaisse and scampi are always good, and Cap'n Tobey's is known for traditional New England desserts. | Straight Wharf, end of Main St. | 508/228–0836 | Closed mid-Oct.–mid-May | $15.50–$19.95 | AE, D, DC, MC, V.

Center Street Bistro. Contemporary. This little restaurant has only about 20 seats crammed together, but if you're lucky, there will be a sidewalk table available. You'll find dishes like a smoked salmon and potato "taco" with capers and cream cheese on the eclectic and contemporary bistro menu. | 29 Centre St. | 508/228–8470 | Breakfast also available weekends | $6–$24 | No credit cards.

★ **Chanticleer.** French. The elegance of the four dining rooms and the views of the flower and herb gardens foreshadow the culinary enjoyment to come at this classic restaurant in Siasconset. An extensive wine list includes 25 selections by the glass. Seafood entrées are favorites. Open-air dining in the rose garden. | 9 New St., Siasconset | 508/257–6231 | Reservations essential | Jacket required | Closed Mon. and mid-Oct.–mid-May | prix–fixe $70, à la carte $35–$70 | AE, DC, MC, V.

Cioppino's. Continental. The intimate restaurant and cozy basement bar work well with the attractive yet unfussy preparations on the Italian-influenced menu. The wine list has some 400 selections. Try the cioppino, tournedos of beef with lobster topping, and tiger prawns over pesto pasta. Open-air dining on patio. Early bird suppers. No smoking. | 20 Broad St. | 508/228–4622 | Reservations essential | Closed Nov.–early May. No lunch weekends | $19.50–$28 | D, DC, MC, V.

Claudette's. Delicatessen. Who can resist a picnic on the beach at 'Sconset? If you didn't plan ahead before leaving town, stop in here to fill your picnic basket. | Post Office Sq., Siasconset | 508/257–6622 | Closed mid-Oct.–mid-May. No dinner | $6–$7 | No credit cards.

Club Car. Continental. This comfortable space with windows that look out onto Main Street accommodates both large and small parties. The historic bar is an actual railroad car. Try the scampi Dijonnaise, rack of lamb, or the roasted almond–and–walnut crusted swordfish. No smoking. | 1 Main St. | 508/228–1101 | Closed Oct.–late May. No lunch | $26–$40 | MC, V.

Company of the Cauldron. Contemporary. With just one set menu and one seating time per night, this tavern-like bistro often feels like a private dining room. The kitchen turns out consistently excellent food, such as the white gazpacho with sliced lobster meat and basil. | 7 India St. | 508/228–4016 | www.companyofthecauldron.com | Reservations essential | Closed Nov.–late May. No lunch | Prix–fixe $50 | MC, V.

DeMarco. Italian. Northern Italian cuisine is highlighted here, such as poached veal with a tuna-caper-anchovy sauce and fresh pasta with wild mushrooms, prosciutto, sage, and mascarpone. Upstairs is a bit louder than downstairs, but the downstairs bar is fun. | 9 India St. | 508/228–1836 | Closed mid-Oct.–mid-May. No lunch | $20–$38 | AE, MC, V.

Espresso Café. Café. Resembling a turn-of-the-20th-century ice-cream parlor, complete with tin ceiling, this bustling café serves killer espresso drinks, pastries, and healthful luncheon specials. Take-out available. | 40 Main St. | 508/228–6930 | Breakfast also available. No dinner early Sept.–late May | $4–$12 | No credit cards.

India House. Eclectic. This Colonial Quaker house, circa 1755, is now an inn with several cozy dining rooms that serve a tantalizing menu of Caribbean, Thai, French, and new American dishes. The wine prices are among the best values on the island. The basil-and-mint-crusted noisettes and the swordfish caponata are recommended. Open-air dining on the garden patio. No smoking. | 37 India St. | 508/228–9043 | Reservations essential | Closed Jan.–Mar. | $22–$34 | AE, D, MC, V.

Jared's. Continental. In the formal main dining room of one of the island's best-known inns, the menu favors traditionally prepared meats and fresh fish. There's also a wildly popular seafood buffet on Wednesdays and Sundays. No smoking. | Jared Coffin House, 29 Broad St. | 508/228–2400 | No lunch. No dinner Oct.–Apr. | $23–$35 | AE, D, DC, MC, V.

Le Languedoc Inn. Continental. This inn's intimate, candlelit dining rooms behind its early-19th-century facade have been synonymous with haute cuisine since 1976. The regularly changing menu offers creative American adaptations of classic French and Mediterranean dishes. The formal dining room requires reservations, while the separate café is less expensive and accepts walk-ins only. | 24 Broad St. | 508/228–2552 | Reservations essential in dining room | Closed mid-Dec.–mid-May and Sun. | $22–$38 (dining room), $12–$22 (café) | AE, MC, V.

Nantucket Tapas. Eclectic. Two popular dining options are available here: pull up a seat at the family-style tables set on big old barrels, or head to a white-cloth-covered table set for couples. Although most of the 33 tapas treats are Asian, you can choose dishes from all over the world. | 15 S. Beach St. | 508/228–2033 | www.nantuckettapas.com | $8.50–$11.50 | AE, MC, V.

The Pearl. Contemporary. If you're looking for sublime, elegant creations like salmon tartare with cucumber noodles and roasted beet oil, this is the place. The translucent white onyx bar and huge fish tank set a tranquil tone, and the dining room offers intimacy. | 12 Federal St. | 508/228–9701 | Reservations essential | Closed Jan. | $32–$42 | AE, MC, V.

Rope Walk. Seafood. This breezy harborside restaurant serves plenty of fresh seafood to match the view. There's a bit of everything else on the menu—chicken, pasta, grilled sirloin, lamb—in case you're not in the mood for fish. Open-air dining on the patio overlooking the water. Raw bar. Kids' menu. | 1 Straight Wharf | 508/228–8886 | Closed Oct.–May | $22–$28 | MC, V.

Rose and Crown. American. College kids love this cavernous place hung with old restaurant signs and hula hoops. Nachos, french fries from unpeeled potatoes, and pesto–and–goat cheese pizzas are the rule here. Live entertainment keeps the place hopping late into the night. | 23 S. Water St. | 508/228–2595 | www.theroseandcrown.com | Closed late Oct.–mid-Apr. | $10–$20 | AE, MC, V.

Schooner's. American. Old wooden floors and dark beams hung with ship's flags lend this sidewalk café a nautical flavor that doesn't carry over to the menu offerings. Chicken tenders, Caesar salads, tenderloin tips, and fajitas are favorites. The upstairs dining room overlooks the wharf. | 31 Easy St. | 508/228–5824 | Closed early Dec.–mid-Apr. | $8–$33 | AE, MC, V.

★ **Sconset Café.** Contemporary. This popular eatery in the heart of Siasconset is known for creatively prepared local fish, although you can order sandwiches and salads, too. When there's a wait, the staff gives you a beeper and sends you to the beach until a table is ready. | Post Office Sq., Siasconset | 508/257–4008 | www.sconsetcafe.com | Breakfast also available mid-June–early Sept. Closed mid-Oct.–mid-May | $20–$30 | No credit cards.

Sea Grille. Seafood. Here you'll find seafood, seafood, and more seafood—every imaginable kind, fixed in every imaginable way. Dishes are moderately priced, well prepared, and served in attractive surroundings. | 45 Sparks Ave. | 508/325–5700 | www.theseagrille.com | No lunch Sun. | $8–$27 | AE, MC, V.

Something Natural. Delicatessen. There are plenty of places to grab a take-out sandwich and dessert, but this is one of the best, partly because of the picnic area on the premises. | 50 Cliff Rd. | 508/228–0504 | Breakfast also available. No dinner. Closed late Oct.–mid-May | $4–$6 | AE, MC, V.

Straight Wharf. Contemporary. This long-time standby is still a favorite. While the indoor dining room is lovely, the covered deck on the water is the place to be. | 6 Harbor Sq., Straight Wharf | 508/228–4499 | Reservations essential | Closed late Sept.–late June and Mondays. No lunch | $32–$42 | AE, MC, V.

Summer House. Seafood. The jury is out from season to season on this modern restaurant. For some, the live piano music and location outweigh the uneven seasonal menu and fussy service. Ask around about the kitchen's current status. Lunch is served by the pool, surrounded by beach grass and ocean waves. | Ocean Ave., Siasconset | 508/257–9976 | Reservations essential | Closed early Sept.–early June | $38–$52 | AE, MC, V.

Tap Room. American. This eatery on the garden level of a dignified old inn is informal, popular, and budget-priced (for Nantucket). The selections on the menu range from "lite bites" to hearty New England dinners. Try the prime rib, pasta, or fried seafood. Open-air dining on the patio. | Jared Coffin House, 29 Broad St. | 508/228–2400 | $15–$25 | AE, D, DC, MC, V.

Tavern at Harbor Square. Seafood. Having your meal here with the view of the marina is almost like dining at sea—and you can see the catch of the day coming off the boat and right to the back door. The restaurant is known for locally raised oysters, fresh fish, and the fried fisherman's platter. Open-air dining in the gazebo. Kids' menu. | Straight Wharf, end of Main St. | 508/228–1266 | $11.95–$20.95 | AE, MC, V.

Topper's. Contemporary. You'll find a refined informality at this bayside restaurant in Nantucket's most luxurious—and secluded—country inn. The dining room serves an updated American menu and boasts an 20,000-bottle wine cellar plus the best single-malt Scotch collection on the island. Open-air dining on the patio. Sun. brunch. No smoking. | 120 Wauwinet Rd. | 508/228–8768 | Reservations essential | Closed Nov.–early May | $39–$56 | AE, DC, MC, V.

★ **21 Federal.** Contemporary. Expect both new and traditional American dishes at this establishment in a beautifully maintained Greek Revival house with 19th-century furnishings. The seared tuna with warm Asian salad and tamari beurre blanc is recommended. Open-air dining on the patio. | 21 Federal St. | 508/228–2121 | Reservations essential June–Sept. | Closed mid-Dec.–early Apr. No lunch | $24–$36 | AE, MC, V.

Vincent's. American. Pizza, calzones, and simple pasta dishes reign at this island standby, a best bet since it opened in 1954. Eat in or take out. | 21 S. Water St. | 508/228–0189 | Breakfast also available weekends. Closed Nov.–mid-Apr. | $8–$23 | MC, V.

White Elephant. Continental. The grill within the venerable White Elephant hotel prides itself on excellent harborside views and generous portions of fresh seafood. Classic New England favorites like lobster and steak are prepared without too much fuss, and the raw-bar offerings couldn't get any fresher. Al fresco dining is available on the terrace. | Easton St. | 508/325–1320 | Closed late-Oct.–mid-Apr. | $24–$38 | AE, D, DC, MC, V.

Lodging

Beachside at Nantucket. Halfway between the center of town and Jetties beach is this stylish two-story motel. Wicker and florals predominate, and some rooms have French doors opening onto decks with views of the pool. A great choice for families. Complimentary Continental breakfast. Refrigerators. Pool. No pets. No smoking. | 30 N. Beach St. | 508/228–2241 or 800/322–4433 | fax 508/228–8901 | info@thebeachside.com | www.thebeachside.com | 90 rooms, 3 2-bedroom suites | $225–$270, $340–$510 suites | Closed Dec.–Mar. | AE, D, DC, MC, V.

Carlisle House. Built in 1765, this inn has working fireplaces, wide pine floors, antique furnishings, and canopy beds. It is on a cobblestone street, close to the ferry and the beach. To get around Nantucket, you can hop on the shuttle bus that stops by the inn in summer. Complimentary Continental breakfast. No air-conditioning in some rooms, no room phones, no cable TV in some rooms. No kids under 10 without prior arrangement. No smoking. | 26 N. Water St. | 508/228–0720 | hli@shore.net | www.carlisle-house.com | 14 rooms (5 with shared bath), 2 suites (double occupancy only) | $75–$185, $285–$325 suites | AE, MC, V.

Carriage House. This charming converted carriage house is on a quiet lane of crushed scallop shells in the heart of the Old Historic District. Surrounded by trees and a flowered terrace, the inn contains an interesting Nantucket history and nature library. Complimentary Continental breakfast. No air-conditioning, no room phones, cable TV in common area. Library. No smoking. | 5 Ray's Court | 508/228–0326 | 7 rooms | $140–$170 | No credit cards.

★ **Centerboard Guest House.** This 19th-century inn is in the historic district and within walking distance of shops, restaurants, museums, galleries, the beach, and the ferry. The guest rooms come with amenities such as bathrobes and beach towels. Complimentary Continental breakfast. Some kitchenettes, refrigerators, cable TV. No smoking. | 8 Chester St. | 508/228–9696 | centerbo@nantucket.net | www.nantucket.net/lodging/centerboard | 7 rooms, 1 suite | $200–$255, 350 suites | Closed Jan.–Feb. | MC, V.

Centre Street Inn. The innkeeper has distinctively furnished each room here with antiques, English pine, and wicker furniture. Some rooms have working fireplaces and brass, white iron, or canopy beds. Relax on the garden patio in season. Complimentary Continental breakfast. No room phones. No kids under 8. No smoking. | 78 Centre St. | 508/228–0199 or 800/298–0199 | fax 508/228–8676 | inn@nantucket.net | www.centrestreetinn.com | 13 rooms (6 with shared bath), 7 suites | $125–$245, $175–$245 suites | Closed mid-Dec.–mid-Apr. | AE, D, MC, V.

Century House. Built in 1833, this homey Federal-style sea captain's house is furnished with antiques and reproductions. Request a room according to the bed style: sleigh, canopy, or spool. The front porch, set with rockers, sees a lot of action. Complimentary breakfast. No pets. No smoking. | 10 Cliff Rd. | 508/228–0530 | www.centuryhouse.com | 14 rooms | $125–$225 | Closed Jan.–Mar. | MC, V.

Chestnut House. This unpretentious inn is embellished with hooked rugs, Tiffany-style lamps, and distinctive paintings, all made by the creative innkeepers. The cheery, spacious cottage has its own deck. Complimentary breakfast voucher. No pets. No smoking. | 3 Chestnut St. | 508/228–0049 | fax 508/228–9521 | www.chestnuthouse.com | 1 room, 4 suites, 1 cottage | $150, $195 suite, $300 cottage | AE, MC, V.

Cliff Lodge. An 18th-century house that is a short stroll from downtown. It has spacious rooms with period molding and wainscoting. A tasteful country aesthetic prevails: paint-spattered floors, hooked rugs, and country curtains. You're welcome to use the roof walk, living room, sunporch, and garden patio. No pets. No kids under 12. No smoking. | 9 Cliff Rd. | 508/228–9480 | fax 508/228–6308 | 11 rooms, 1 apartment | $155–$205, $375 apartment | MC, V.

Cliffside Beach Club. About 1 mi from town on Cliffside Beach is this exclusive 1920s complex that began as a private club. Today it's open to anyone who can afford it. Within the low-rise cedar buildings are tasteful contemporary interiors with natural wood furnishings and white walls displaying local art. Some units have private decks, fireplaces, and wet bars. Restaurant, bar with entertainment, complimentary Continental breakfast. Some kitchenettes. Health club, beach. Playground. No pets. No smoking. | 46 Jefferson Ave. | 508/228–0618 | fax 508/325–4735 | www.cliffsidebeachclub.com | 27 rooms, 2 suites, 1 apartment, 1 cottage | $335–$535; $655–$1,310 suites, apartment, and cottage | Closed mid-Oct.–late May | AE.

Cobblestone Inn. This 1729 inn with simple furnishings is on a quiet cobblestone street in the historic district. Help yourself to complimentary sodas, cookies, coffee, and tea in the guest pantry. Vouchers are provided for full breakfast at restaurants in town. Complimentary breakfast. Cable TV. No smoking. | 5 Ash St. | 508/228–1987 | fax 508/228–6698 | cobble@nantucket.net | www.nantucket.net/lodging/cobblestoneinn | 5 rooms, 1 suite | $175–$225, $250–$275 suite | MC, V.

18 Gardner Street. A 19th-century guest house with comfortable rooms. Many of the rooms have handmade quilts, a fireplace, and assorted antiques. Complimentary Continental breakfast. Refrigerators. Bicycles. No pets. No smoking. | 18 Gardner St. | 508/228–1155 or 800/435–1450 | fax 508/325–0181 | www.bandbnantucket.com | 10 rooms, 2 suites | $165–$205, $200–$425 suites | AE, MC, V.

★ **Harbor House.** Flower-filled courtyards surround the 1886 main inn and adjacent town houses, which are just steps from the bustling town center. The inn rooms are dressed with floral and English-country style fabrics. The larger town-house rooms have pastel color schemes and upscale pine furniture. Restaurant, bar. Children's programs. No pets. | S. Beach St. | 508/228–1500 or 800/475–2637 | fax 508/228–7639 | www.harborhouseack.com | 104 rooms | $310–$425 | Closed Jan. | AE, D, DC, MC, V.

Hawthorn House. The small but cozy guest rooms in this 1850 house have stained-glass lamps, hooked rugs, and handmade quilts. The cottage is dark, but you can't beat the in-town location. Complimentary breakfast voucher. No pets. No smoking. | 2 Chestnut St. | 508/228–1468 | fax 508/228–1468 | hhguests@nantucket.net | www.hawthornhouse.com | 9 rooms (2 with shared bath), 1 cottage | $145–$175, $175 cottage | MC, V.

Jared Coffin House. Built for the shipowner Jared Coffin in 1845, the house became an inn the following year. The rooms spread throughout six buildings are furnished with antiques and reproductions. 2 restaurants, bar. No air-conditioning in some rooms, in-room data ports, some refrigerators, cable TV. Library. Business services. No pets. | 29 Broad St. | 508/228–2400 or 800/248–2405 | fax 508/228–8549 | www.jaredcoffinhouse.com | 60 rooms in 6 buildings | $150–$325 | AE, D, DC, MC, V.

Lyon Street Inn. This completely remodeled house impresses with its period touches and details. Note the variable-width floorboards, Colonial mantels, and oak ceiling beams. White walls and blond woodwork set off Oriental rugs, fine antiques, floral fabrics, and down comforters perfectly. On a quiet lane, the inn is a five-minute walk from the center of town. Complimentary Continental breakfast. No pets. No smoking. | 10 Lyon St. | 508/228–5040 | lyon@nantucket.net | 7 rooms | $190–$275 | Closed mid-Dec.–mid-Apr. | AE, MC, V.

Manor House. Spacious guest rooms, many with reproduction king canopy beds and working fireplaces, are the order of the day here. The screened-in and open porches are perfect for an afternoon retreat. The adjacent two-bedroom cottage is nicely appointed with wicker and chintz. Complimentary Continental breakfast. No pets. No smoking. | 31 Centre St. | 508/228–0600 or 800/872–6841 | fax 508/325–4046 | rhinn@aol.com | www.robertshouseinn.com | 15 rooms, 1 cottage | $215–$325, $475 cottage | AE, D, MC, V.

Martin House. This friendly 1804 hostelry boasts generous rooms, several with writing tables and couches. Many have a four-poster canopy bed; all have lovely linens and cut flowers. Even the inexpensive rooms tucked under the eaves on the third floor are still bright and sunny. Complimentary Continental breakfast. No pets. No kids under 11. No smoking. | 61 Centre St. | 508/228–0678 | fax 508/325–4798 | martinn@nantucket.net | 11 rooms (4 with shared bath), 2 suites | $150–$225, $275–$325 suites | MC, V.

Nantucket Inn. The price of your room in the heart of the island includes many amenities, from recreation to airport shuttle service. Guest rooms, many of which have cathedral ceilings and fireplaces, overlook three landscaped courtyards. Restaurant, 2 bars, room service. Refrigerators, cable TV. 2 pools (1 indoor). Hot tub. Tennis courts. Health club. Laundry facilities. Business services, airport shuttle. No pets allowed. | 27 Macy's La. | 508/228–6900 or 800/321–8484 | fax 508/228–9861 | ackinn@nantucket.net | www.nantucket.net/lodging/nantucketinn | 100 rooms | $205–$225 | Closed late Oct.–mid-Apr. | AE, D, DC, MC, V.

Nesbitt Inn. This family-operated inn is a bargain and a much-loved anomaly. Its backyard for children's activities, Victorian marble-top dressers and lace curtains, in-room wash basins, and a bygone sense of hospitality all contribute to its appeal. Refrigerators. No pets. No smoking. | 21 Broad St. | 508/228–0156 | fax 508/228–2446 | 12 rooms (all with shared bath) | $85 | Closed mid-Dec.–Mar. | MC, V.

Periwinkle Guest House. This inn is in the heart of town and within walking distance of the ferry. Many rooms are equipped with king or queen four-poster beds. Complimentary Continental breakfast. No pets. No smoking. | 11 India St. | 508/228–9267 or 800/872–6841 | fax 508/325–4046 | rhinn@aol.com | www.robertshouseinn.com | 16 rooms (2 with shared bath) | $125–$195 | Closed mid-Dec.–mid-Apr. | AE, D, MC, V.

Pineapple Inn. The memorable touches in this 1838 Greek Revival house are the goose-down quilts on the four-poster beds and the white marble bathrooms. Breakfast is noteworthy, too. Complimentary breakfast. In-room data ports. No pets. No smoking. | 10 Hussey St. | 508/228–9992 | fax 508/325–6051 | info@pineappleinn.com | www.pineappleinn.com | 12 rooms | $175–$310 | Closed mid-Dec.–late Apr. | AE, MC, V.

Roberts House. Established as an inn more than a century ago, this property offers comfortable four-poster canopy beds, wicker furniture on the porches, and lovely gardens. Off-season packages are available. Complimentary Continental breakfast. Cable TV. No smoking. | 11 India St. | 508/325–0750 or 800/992–2899 | fax 508/325–4046 | rhinn@aol.com | www.robertshouseinn.com | 42 rooms (4 with shared bath), 1 suite, 1 cottage | $175–$325, $270–$350 suite. $375–$475 cottage | D, MC, V.

Seven Sea Street Inn. This red post-and-beam inn on a peaceful side street is close to the ferry, beach, and historic downtown area. You can see the harbor from the roof deck. Most rooms contain Colonial fishnet canopy beds, and suites are equipped with gas-stove fireplaces. Picnic area, complimentary Continental breakfast. One in-room hot tub, cable TV. Business services. No kids under 5. No smoking. | 7 Sea St. | 508/228–3577 | fax 508/228–3578 | seast7@nantucket.net | www.sevenseasstreetinn.com | 9 rooms, 2 suites | $175–$225, $265–$295 suites | AE, D, MC, V.

★ **76 Main Street.** Oriental rugs, a blend of antiques and reproductions, richly carved woodwork, and handmade quilts fill this 1883 sea captain's house. The period inn rooms are lovely for couples, while the motel-like rooms in the rear annex, set around a flagstone patio and gardens, are better suited to families. Complimentary Continental breakfast. Refrigerators. No pets. No smoking. | 76 Main St. | 508/228–2533 | fax 508/228–2533 | 18 rooms | $150–$175 | Closed Jan.–Mar. | AE, D, MC, V.

Sherburne Inn. Originally built as the Atlantic Silk Factory, this Greek Revival building was once owned by Quakers hoping to provide an alternative to the cotton harvested by southern slaves. It has original yellow-pine floors, 13-ft ceilings, and two parlors with fireplaces and antiques. Complimentary Continental breakfast. In-room data ports, cable TV on request. No kids under 6. No smoking. | 10 Gay St. | 508/228–4425 | fax 508/228–8114 | sherinn@nantucket.net | www.sherburneinn.com | 8 rooms (6 with shower only) | $165–$295 | AE, D, MC, V.

Ships Inn. Built in 1831 by whaling captain Obed Starbuck, this downtown inn has guest rooms named after the ships he commanded. Furnished with period reproductions, the inn also is the birthplace of abolitionist and women's rights activist Lucretia Mott. Restaurant, bar, complimentary Continental breakfast. No air-conditioning in some rooms, refrigerators, cable TV. No smoking. | 13 Fair St. | 508/228–0040 | fax 508/228–6524 | www.shipsinn.com | 13 rooms (2 with shared bath) | $195–$210 | Closed Dec.–Apr. | AE, MC, V.

Summer House. Across from 'Sconset Beach, this collection of rose-covered cottages are snugly clustered around a flower-filled courtyard. The interiors are done in a simple English country style, with stripped antique pine furniture, white eyelet bedspreads, and trompe l'oeil borders on whitewashed walls. Some have a fireplace or kitchen. 2 restaurants, bar, bar with entertainment, complimentary Continental breakfast. Pool. No pets. No smoking. | 17 Ocean Ave., Siasconset | 508/257–4577 | fax 508/257–4590 | www.the-summerhouse.com | 9 cottages | $575–$900 | Closed Nov.–Apr. | AE, MC, V.

Tuckernuck Inn. Gaze at the panoramic harbor view from the widow's walk or enjoy an unusual game of chess with the oversized lawn chess set. The homey country inn is four blocks from Main Street and one block from the harbor. Restaurant, picnic area, complimentary Continental breakfast. In-room data ports, cable TV, in-room VCRs. Library. Laundry facilities. Business services. No smoking. | 60 Union St. | 508/228–4886 or 800/228–4886 | fax 508/228–4890 | www.tuckernuckinn.com | 19 rooms, 2 suites | $189–$250, $250 1–bedroom luxury suite, $295 2–bedroom suite | AE, MC, V.

Wade Cottages. This family-owned complex surrounding a central lawn provides an expansive ocean vista. Accommodations vary considerably, but most have a beach-worn style, some antiques, and fine views. Refrigerators. Beach. Laundry facilities. No pets. No smoking. | Shell St., Siasconset | 508/257–6308 or 212/989–6423 (off–season) | fax 508/257–4602 | seamail@wadecottages.com | www.wadecottages.com | 6 rooms (3 with shared bath), 1 suite, 6 apartments, 3 cottages | $345–$720, $945–$1,130 suite, $1,950–$2,700 apartments, $5,800 (2 weeks) cottages | Closed mid-Oct.–late May | AE, MC, V.

★ **The Wauwinet.** This 1876 inn's next-door neighbor is the Great Point Wildlife Refuge on the northeast tip of the island, 8 mi northeast of town. On the inn's property are two private beaches (oceanside and bayside) and gentle dunes, as well as lawns and gardens. The cheerful rooms have been designed with pine furnishings, country antiques, and art. Four-wheel-drive natural-history excursions and afternoon cheese and sherry are included in the room tariff. Restaurant, complimentary breakfast, room service. In-room data ports, cable TV, in-room VCRs and movies. Tennis courts. Beach, boating, bicycles. Library. Business services. Local shuttle. No kids under 12. No smoking. | Wauwinet Rd. | 508/228–0145 or 800/426–8718 | fax 508/228–6712 | www.wauwinet.com | 35 rooms, 5 cottages | $500–$700, $540–$1,010 cottages | Closed Nov.–Apr. | AE, DC, MC, V.

★ **Westmoor Inn.** One mile from town, just off the popular Madaket bike path, you'll find this former Vanderbilt summer mansion. The peaceful grounds and secluded garden patio offer a welcome respite from in-town crowds. Most guest rooms have a French-country style, with stenciled walls and floral fabrics. Complimentary Continental breakfast. Bicycles. No pets. No kids under 12. No smoking. | Cliff Rd. | 508/228–0877 or 888/236–7310 | fax 508/228–5763 | thewestmoor@nantucket.net | www.westmoor.com | 14 rooms | $195–$350 | Closed early Dec.–mid-Apr. | AE, MC, V.

Wharf Cottages. These weathered, wharf-side cottages are perfect for sailors who tie up at the marina or couples searching for a romantic getaway. Each has a little garden and deck, a full kitchen, and water views. Kitchenettes. Dock. No pets. No smoking. | New Whale St. | 508/228–4620 or 800/475–2637 | fax 508/325–1173 | www.nantucketislandresorts.com | 25 cottages | $410–$975 | Closed late Oct.–late Apr. | AE, D, DC, MC, V.

White Elephant. This hotel on the water's edge is the epitome of high style and service. The spacious guest rooms have rattan chairs, leather seats and headboards, crisp white linens, and marble vanities. Restaurant, bar, complimentary breakfast, room service. In-room data ports. Dock. No pets. No smoking. | 50 Easton St. | 508/228–2500 or 800/475–2637 | fax 508/325–1195 | www.whiteelephanthotel.com | 24 rooms, 30 suites, 12 cottages | $450–$690, $465–$750 suites, $395–$1,160 cottages | Closed late Oct.–mid-Apr. | AE, D, DC, MC, V.

NATICK

MAP 6, H4

(Nearby towns also listed: Boston, Framingham, Sudbury, Wellesley)

Formerly a shoe-manufacturing town, Natick in modern times has become a retailing center, known for the mall-lined strip of Route 9 it shares with next-door neighbor Framingham. What hotels along this highway lack in character, they more than make up for in convenience, with interstate, commuter rail, and express bus service all rapidly bridging the 18 mi between Natick and downtown Boston.

Information: **MetroWest Chamber of Commerce** | 1671 Worcester Rd. (Rte. 9), Framingham, 01701 | 508/879–5600 | chamber@metrowest.org | www.metrowest.org.

Attractions

Broadmore Wildlife Society. The 624 acres here include Indian Brook, marshes, forests, and a quarter-mile "All Persons" boardwalk that is handicapped accessible. Along the 9 mi of walking trails, you may encounter some of the resident beaver, mink, foxes, coyotes, and 150 species of birds. A Nature Center offers books, maps, and educational programs. | 280 Eliot St. | 508/655–2296 | www.massaudubon.org | $3 | Tues.–Sun. dawn–dusk.

ON THE CALENDAR
JULY: *Fourth of July.* The Sunday before Independence Day, Natick celebrates with fireworks, concerts, and a pancake breakfast, followed by a parade on the Fourth itself. | 508/647–6520.

Dining

Dolphin Seafood Too. Seafood. The two dining rooms on the main floor display photographs of old Natick, images of dolphins, and lots of flowers. A second floor with three dining rooms opens for special functions. The most popular dishes are seafood, pasta, and the spicy *salsa diablo*. | 12 Washington St. | 508/655–0669 | Reservations essential | Closed Sun. | $13–$19 | MC, V.

Johnny Rockets. American. This retro California import revives the nostalgic soda fountain of days gone by. From the all-day menu choose the No. 12 burger, chili fries, the Streamliner, or the malts. No alcohol. No smoking. | Natick Mall, Rte. 9 | 508/651–3546 | No dinner Sun. | $2.65–$5.85 | AE, D, MC, V.

Sherborn Inn. Continental. This historical Colonial home 10 mi south of Natick has been converted into a graceful country inn. The dining rooms serve traditional New England fare; the tavern offers sandwiches and snacks. Kids' menu. Sun. brunch. No smoking in dining rooms. | 33 N. Main St., Sherborn | 508/655–9521 | Closed Mon. | $17–$26 | AE, MC, V.

Lodging

Crowne Plaza. This classy hotel on Route 9 is close to I–495, Route 128/I–95, and I–90. Just across the street from the Natick Mall, it also provides a 24-hour courtesy shuttle to other businesses within a 2-mi radius. Restaurant, bar. In-room data ports, cable TV. Gym. Business services. Local shuttle. | 1360 Worcester Rd. | 508/653–8800 or 800/2CROWNE | fax 508/653–1708 | www.crowneplaza.com | 251 rooms, 2 suites | $189–$220, $600 suites | AE, D, DC, MC, V.

Hampton Inn Boston–Natick. This chain hotel 17 mi west of Boston at Rte. 9 caters to corporate overnighters, and you can easily catch the commuter rail from Natick into the city. Within 1 mi of the hotel are four shopping malls and lots of restaurants. Complimentary Continental breakfast. In-room data ports, cable TV. Gym. Business services. | 319 Speen St. | 508/653–5000 | fax 508/651–9733 | www.hampton-inn.com | 190 rooms | $115–$125 | AE, D, DC, MC, V.

Sherborn Inn. Just 10 mi south of Natick on Rte. 27 is this historical Colonial inn known for its restaurant and tavern. Guest rooms come with four-poster canopy beds. Restaurant, bar, complimentary Continental breakfast. | 33 N. Main St., Sherborn | 508/655–9521 or 800/552–9742 | fax 508/655–5325 | www.sherborninn.com | 4 rooms | $130–$150 | AE, MC, V.

Travelodge. Near major highways in the MetroWest area, this chain establishment offers economical lodging with standard furnishings for tourist and business travelers alike. Complimentary Continental breakfast. In-room data ports, in-room safes, cable TV. Business services. | 1350 Worcester Rd. | 508/655–2222 | fax 508/655–7953 | sleepbr@banet.net | 68 rooms | $114–$155 | AE, D, DC, MC, V.

NEW BEDFORD

(Nearby towns also listed: Dartmouth, Fall River, Westport)

New Bedford was once at the fore of the world's whaling fleet, sending more ships in search of the great sea mammals than all other American ports combined. Luckily for whales, the discovery of Pennsylvania oil ruined the market for whale oil, compelling New Bedford to trade in its harpoons for fishnets and shellfish traps. Less well known is the fact that the town also produced fine cotton cloth. The old textile mills hulking beside I–195 remain a prominent part of the cityscape.

Today, having weathered economic hard times, New Bedford attracts visitors to its picturesque working harbor and first-rate historical attractions. Don't miss the outstanding whaling museum, the adjacent Whaling National Historical Park, and the downtown historic district straight from the pages of *Moby-Dick*.

Information: New Bedford Office of Tourism | Pier 3, New Bedford, 02740-6398 | 508/979–1745 or 800/508–5353 | amotta@www.ci.new-bedford.ma.us | www.ci.new-bedford.ma.us.

Attractions

Buttonwood Park and Zoo. This 97-acre city park has a playground and facilities for tennis, basketball, and baseball. The modest zoo shows local fauna in their native habitat, but it also houses animals not found in Massachusetts, including two Asian elephants. A gift shop and a restaurant are on the zoo premises. | Rockdale Ave. | 508/991–6175 or 508/991–6178 (zoo) | Park free; zoo $4 | Park daily–dusk, zoo daily 10–5.

Fort Phoenix State Reservation. This state park off U.S. 6 has a small swimming beach facing New Bedford's outer harbor, within view of the massive hurricane barrier that stretches across the harbor's mouth. Some stone ramparts atop rock outcroppings above the beach and the huge iron cannon mounted behind them are all that remain of the Revolutionary War fortification that gives the park its name. | Green St., Fairhaven | 508/992–4524 | Free | July–Aug., daily 8–6; Sept.–June, daily 8–4.

New Bedford Art Museum. This 1918 former bank building hosts changing art exhibits that show the region's diversity, from paintings by 19th-century New Bedford resident Albert Bierstadt to work by contemporary artists. | 608 Pleasant St. | 508/961–3072 | $3 | Memorial Day–Labor Day, Sat.–Wed. 10–5, Thurs. and Fri. 10–7; Labor day–Memorial Day, Wed. and Fri.–Sun. noon–5, Thurs. noon–7.

★ **New Bedford Whaling Museum.** This museum preserves the nation's largest collection of whaling-related artifacts, from fanciful carved ship's figureheads and intricate scrimshaw to tools, photos, paintings, and whaler's souvenirs from faraway lands. A fully rigged 89-ft model of a whaling vessel (at half scale) and a skeleton of a blue whale are among the highlights. The museum schedules many special events, including an annual marathon reading of *Moby-Dick*. | 18 Johnny Cake Hill | 508/997–0046 | www.whalingmuseum.org | $4.50 | Daily 9–5.

New Bedford Whaling National Historical Park. Part of the national park system since 1996, the park embraces the entire Waterfront Historic District—34 acres and 70 historical buildings associated with New Bedford's boom years in the whaling industry. Stop at the visitor center for information on self-guided and volunteer-led walks through the district—and discover why another part of the park is in Barrow, Alaska. | 33 William St. | 508/996–4095 | www.nps.gov/nebe | Free | Daily 9–4.

FRUITS OF THE SEA

Great piles of empty clam shells found amid prehistoric remains of Native American encampments prove that seafood has been a favorite menu item in Massachusetts for more than 4,000 years. These days the state actually has to import a growing percentage of its seafood from elsewhere, since New England's commercial stocks have been all but ruined by overfishing, pollution, and other factors still subject to debate. Although overnight freight has erased most of the distinction between what's local and what's not, purists who will only dine on what's truly native to the region needn't worry about going hungry: you may have to pay a slight premium, but genuine fresh-off-the-boat seafood can still be had throughout the state.

Lobsters, for starters. The state's hatcheries help raise some half million of the critters every year just so you get to try some during your visit. You may not think that it matters whether the boiled lobster on your plate originally came from the waters of Maine or Massachusetts, but consider sampling at least one of each just for the sake of comparison. Remind yourself as you do so that science requires many sacrifices, including having to help yourself to seconds.

Stars on the local shellfish front include Wellfleet oysters, Chappaquiddick scallops, and Essex clams. Like lobsters, live shellfish are generally local, or at least from New England, so an order for anything raw on the half shell will almost guarantee you a taste of our most prized regional delicacies. Note that clams, in particular, masquerade under a variety of aliases—littlenecks, cherrystones, quahogs (KOH-hogs), and steamers, to name several—but they are as delectable by one name as another. So tasty, in fact, that the addition of a few to a pot of simmered milk produces something close to ambrosia—which we call chowder. There are as many chowder recipes as there are cooks in Massachusetts, but the best are never thickened with flour, so if yours wobbles like gelatin, send it back to the kitchen. On the subject of clams, please note that it is a little-known fact that failure to consume at least a quart of that Massachusetts miracle, the fried clam, can result in suspension of your visitors permit. The finest, some say, are served in Essex, whence they originated, but worthy contenders are found across the length and breadth of Cape Cod.

When it comes to fish, several local denizens are consistent favorites with cooks who know how to do more than drop battered fillets into hot oil. Monkfish is a firm, white-fleshed species whose ugliness when alive is exceeded only by its clear, almost sweet taste when served. Bluefish is an oily sort like salmon that, depending on the cut, cooks up as a dense fillet, like tuna or swordfish, but with a strong flavor all its own. Some folks consider it an acquired taste, but it is generally irresistible when paired with strong spices. Striper, or striped bass, is a prized game fish that chefs do their best to let stand alone, as its taste needs no accompaniment. Portuguese cooks make a mighty convincing case, though, that striped bass should be served stuffed with shellfish or baked in tomato-wine sauce. Mackerel isn't as common on local menus as it was a century ago, but its oily, sweet flesh is perfectly suited to grilling and broiling, and well worth trying if you have the chance. Cod, haddock, and flounder, all flaky and lean, are indispensable standards on traditional menus across the state, either fried, baked with herbed bread crumbs or sliced almonds, or broiled and served plain with lemon. All three species are nearing commercial extinction in Massachusetts waters, so more often than not these fish come from out of state. Or, the dish will be made from local scrod. Which isn't actually a single type of fish—it's a wholesaler's catch-all term for any of several lean whitefish species under 2.5 lbs in weight.

© Artville

Passenger ferry service. New Bedford is a gateway to Martha's Vineyard and the Elizabeth Islands, with passenger ferry service daily to both in summer and service at least twice-weekly to the Elizabeths other times of the year.

Cape Island Express Lines. The passenger-only *Schamonchi* is the ferry of choice for island-bound visitors seeking to avoid Cape Cod traffic and parking woes. Park across the street from the ferry pier on New Bedford's outer harbor, then enjoy the scenic 90-minute cruise across Buzzards Bay and through the Elizabeth Islands to Vineyard Haven, on the north side of Martha's Vineyard. | Billy Wood's Wharf | 508/997–1688 | www.mvferry.com | $17–$19 round-trip; parking $8 | Mid-May–Columbus Day, daily.

New Bedford–Cuttyhunk Ferry. Cuttyhunk is the only Elizabeth Island open to the general public. Access is provided by the small ferry *Alert II*, which makes the one-hour trip year-round, most frequently in summer. Bicycles welcome for a fee. | Fisherman's Wharf, Pier 3 | 508/992–1432 | www.cuttyhunk.com | $17.50 round-trip | Call for hrs.

Rotch-Jones-Duff House and Garden Museum. This 1834 mansion with its Greek Revival facade is a perfect example of the luxury to which New Bedford's whale-oil merchants once aspired. The lavish interior is rivaled only by the formal gardens outside, which span the entire block. | 396 County St. | 508/997–1401 | fax 508/997–6846 | House tours $4, gardens free | June–early Sept., daily 10–4; early Sept.–May, Tues.–Sun. 10–4.

Seamen's Bethel. This chapel for sailors and fishermen remains almost exactly as Melville described it in *Moby-Dick,* from the pulpit to the cenotaphs along the walls for those lost at sea. It is still in use, so don't be disappointed if it's closed to the public during weddings, funerals, or other services. | 15 Johnny Cake Hill | 508/992–3295 | Free | Memorial Day–mid-Sept., weekdays 10–4; mid-Sept.–Memorial Day, by appointment.

ON THE CALENDAR

JAN.: *Moby-Dick Marathon.* The complete text of Herman Melville's classic novel is read aloud annually to commemorate his departure from New Bedford on the Fairhaven whaling ship *Acushnet.* The nonstop reading starts at noon on January 3 and ends mid-afternoon on January 4. To participate, reserve your 10-minute reading spot in advance. | 508/997–0046, ext. 14 (reservations).

JULY: *Buzzards Bay Musicfest.* This four-day festival consists of four concerts—chamber music on Friday and Saturday and full orchestra on Thursday and Sunday—at the Fireman Performing Arts Center, at Tabor Academy in Marion. Concerts begin at 8 PM (except for the Sunday program, which starts at 2 PM). Admission is free; no reservations necessary. | 508/748–1266.

AUG.: *Feast of the Blessed Sacrament.* More than 300,000 people attend this annual four-day event whose crowning glory is the largest Portuguese feast in America. Held since 1915, the festival takes place around the first weekend of August and includes entertainment, a giant midway, and a rousing parade. | 508/992–6911.

DEC.: *First Night New Bedford.* New Bedford citizens plan projects to transform under-utilized parts of their city for this event. They've created a downtown skating pond decorated with Christmas trees and ice sculptures and also built an atrium garden in a downtown office building. Other First Night traditions include church bells, boat horns, a fireworks display at midnight, and a children's "countdown" that celebrates the new year in another time zone. | 508/979–1768.

Dining

Antonio's. Portuguese. You can really unwind at this inviting spot, which has lots of ceramic tile and a knotty-pine bar. The hands-down favorite dish, which feeds two, is the marinated pork with littlenecks. | 260 Coggeshall St. | 508/990–3636 | $7–$14 | No credit cards.

Davey's Locker. Seafood. You can watch the Martha's Vineyard ferry dock while eating shrimp Diane or Key West garlic shrimp. The inside dining area has a nautical theme. Open-air dining on the patio. | 1480 E. Rodney French Blvd. | 508/992–7359 | $9–$21 | AE, D, DC, MC, V.

Freestone's. American. A mix of marble, mahogany, and flea-market treasures sets the tone here. The menu offers a broad range of pasta, burgers, barbecue, and seafood. Try the fresh local seafood or the Black Angus sirloin. Kids' menu. No smoking. | 41 William St. | 508/993–7477 | $11.95–$19.95 | AE, DC, MC, V.

Lodging

Bedford Hill Inn. This restored 1888 Victorian includes Eastlake furniture, reproduction gas lights, and Oriental rugs. Rooms provide views of New Bedford Harbor and Martha's Vineyard. Complimentary Continental breakfast. Some kitchenettes, some microwaves, some refrigerators, cable TV, some room phones. No pets. No smoking. | 413 County St. | 508/991–8610 | gnewton@prodigy.net | 3 rooms (2 with shared bath) | $75–$115 | AE, MC, V.

Comfort Inn. This inn, close to the North Dartmouth Mall, is just 3 mi west of New Bedford. It's also a good choice for travelers visiting either Hyannis or Newport, Rhode Island, which are less than an hour's drive away. Complimentary Continental breakfast. In-room data ports, cable TV. Pool. Business services. | 171 Faunce Corner Rd., North Dartmouth | 508/996–0800 or 800/228–5150 | comfort@ultranet.com | www.choicehotels.com | 85 rooms | $80–$120 | AE, D, DC, MC, V.

New Bedford Inn. This economical hotel is across the street from a golf course and a short drive from New Bedford's historic waterfront, where ferries depart for Martha's Vineyard. Like other Quality Inn propeties, this hotel offers functional, economical, and convenient lodging for business or leisure travelers. Restaurant, bar with entertainment, room service. In-room data ports, cable TV. Indoor pool. Laundry facilities. Business services. | 500 Hathaway Rd. | 508/997–1231 or 800/DAYS–INN | fax 508/984–7977 | 153 rooms | $90–$110 | AE, D, DC, MC, V.

Edgewater Bed and Breakfast. This house dating to 1760 was part of the original settlement of Fairhaven, 2 mi east of New Bedford. It's right around the corner from the Joshua Slocum Memorial and a Pilgrim burial site. Some rooms have harbor views, working fireplaces, and period furnishings. Complimentary Continental breakfast. No air-conditioning, cable TV. No kids under 4. No smoking. | 2 Oxford St., Fairhaven | 508/997–5512 | fax 508/997–5784 | kprof@aol.com | www.rixsan.com/edgewater | 6 rooms, 3 suites | $80–$90, $110–$125 suites | AE, D, MC, V.

Orchard Street Manor. This Georgian Revival manor, built in 1845, retains original period accents such as anaglyphic wallpaper, brass chandeliers, and leaded-glass windows. It's a few blocks from the National Historical park and 3 mi from the ferry. Bar, complimentary breakfast. Some in-room hot tubs, no room phones, no TV in some rooms. | 139 Orchard St. | 508/984–3475 | www.ultranet.com/~mannad | 3 rooms, 1 suite | $95–$135 | MC, V.

Pineywood Farm Bed and Breakfast. This 1815 Cape Cod house and converted dairy barn on 3 acres is 10 mi east of New Bedford. A country style prevails throughout, and some guest rooms have cathedral ceilings, sundecks, antiques, and iron beds. Breakfast is served on the large porch overlooking the gardens. Ask about passes for the beach 1 mi away. Complimentary Continental breakfast. Cable TV, no room phones. Pool. No kids under 12. | 599 Front St., Marion | 508/748–3925 or 800/858–8084 | fax 508/748–2448 | www.virtualcities.com | 5 rooms (2 with shared bath) | $100–$125 | AE, MC, V.

NEWBURYPORT

MAP 6, I1

(Nearby towns also listed: Amesbury, Ipswich, Salisbury)

Founded in 1635 by the mouth of the Merrimack River, Newburyport grew to prominence in the 18th century through shipbuilding and the industrious trade of its merchant ships. The fortunes amassed by local traders built the many fine Federal-style mansions that, now preserved, give the city its distinctive character. Newbury-port currently thrives on a blend of tourism, small-scale local industry, and its pool of commuters, who shuttle the 30 mi between Newburyport and Boston each day via the interstate or rail service.

Information: **Greater Newburyport Chamber of Commerce and Industry** | 29 State St., Newburyport | 978/462–6680. **Visitors Information Booth** | Market Sq | 978/463–6614 | www.newburyportchamber.org | Summer daily 10–5.

Attractions

Coffin House. Originally a simple two-room dwelling when built in 1654, this home expanded over the centuries as several generations of the Coffin family opted to live under one roof. A good example of First Period architecture, it clearly shows how domestic needs and tastes changed from the 17th to 19th centuries. | 14 High Rd. | 978/462–2634 | www.spnea.org | $4 | June–mid-Oct., weekends 11–4 (tours hourly).

Spencer-Peirce-Little Farm. This imposing, stone-and-brick 1690 manor house still stands on this 230-acre working farm that's south of town off Rte. 1A. A great example of First Period architecture, the manor has rooms that reflect other periods, such as the 1807 Federal parlor and the 1930s kitchen. | 5 Little's La. | 978/462–2634 | www.spnea.org | $4 | June 1–Oct. 15, Wed.–Sun. 11–4 (tours hourly).

Cushing House Museum. The 21 rooms of this three-story 1808 Federal brick mansion offer you a glimpse into the life of 19th-century Newburyport. The house has an exceptional collection of silverware, paintings, locally made furniture, and formal period gardens. Exhibits devoted to the decorative arts and a research library are also housed here. | 98 High St. | 978/462–2681 | fax 978/462–0134 | $4 | May–Oct., Tues.–Fri. 10–4, Sat. by appointment; Nov.–Apr., weekdays by appointment.

Custom House Maritime Museum. Two giant steel buoys greet you at this museum, once the city's custom house and now a reminder of Newburyport's past glory as an international port. Captains' memorabilia, nautical instruments, ship models, and artifacts of the boatbuilding business are displayed, and there's also a well-appointed library of works by author J. P. Marquand, a regular summer visitor to the town. | 25 Water St. | 978/462–8681 | fax 978/462–8740 | $3 | Apr.–Dec., Mon.–Sat. 10–4, Sun. 1–4.

Market Square Historic District. Most of the buildings in the four-square-block district were built after an 1811 fire. Here you'll also find plenty of shops and the Custom House Maritime Museum. | Market Sq | Free | Daily.

Maudslay State Park. This 480-acre park 3 mi west of downtown has easy walking trails and access to the Merrimack River. You can bike, canoe, kayak, picnic, or enjoy the concert series organized by the Maudslay Arts Center. | Curzon Mill Rd. | 978/465–7223 | Free | Daily 8–sunset.

Parker River National Wildlife Refuge. This refuge, which extends over 4,600 acres of barrier beach and salt marsh, is one of the rarest ecosystems on the eastern seaboard. The main draw in summer is the swimming beach, and in spring and fall the bird watching. The refuge limits the number of cars admitted, so don't be surprised if the gates are closed on any given day. | Off Plum Island Tpke | 978/465–5753 | Cars $5, pedestrians and bicyclists $2 | Daily dawn–dusk.

Waterfront Park and Promenade. The park's green spaces and boardwalk along the Merrimack River are a stroll away from Market Square. | Free | Daily.

ON THE CALENDAR

MAY: *Spring Arts and Flower Festival.* This festival of crafts and entertainment showcases local visual and performing artists over Memorial Day weekend. | 978/462–6680.
JULY–AUG.: *Yankee Homecoming.* Waterfront concerts, house tours, entertainment, a

crafts fair, sidewalk sales, an antique-car parade, a 10K road race, a lobsterfest, fireworks, and children's activities are all part of this eight-day celebration. | 978/462–6680.

JULY–SEPT.: _Waterfront Park Concert Series._ You can lounge on the grass or stretch your legs on the boardwalk while enjoying jazz, blues, or chamber music. Concerts are held every Sunday from July to September. | 978/462–6680.

OCT.: _Fall Harvest Festival._ Hayrides, food, crafts, and entertainment kick off this event held annually on Columbus Day weekend since 1975. | 978/462–6680.

Dining

The Bayou. Southern. Dine on wild game, fresh seafood, or jambalaya here. You can dine on the first floor, a casual area with brickwork and French doors, or on the second floor, an elegant room with table linens and portraits of jazz musicians. | 50 State St. | 978/499–0428 | No lunch Mon. | $13–$25 | AE, D, MC, V.

David's. Eclectic. This cozy, publike restaurant downstairs from The Rim has a broad menu of simple but creative dishes. Try the broiled fish. Of special note is the separate children's room (ages 18 months and up), complete with baby-sitting, games, videos, and food service. Live entertainment Fri. and Sat. | 11 Brown Sq | 978/462–8077 | Reservations essential for children's room | No lunch | $6.95–$24 | AE, D, MC, V.

The Grog. Eclectic. This friendly tavern popular with the college crowd serves up better-than-average pub food and ethnic dishes. The clam chowder and Caesar salad are recommended. Live music Thurs.–Sun. nights. Kids' menu. | 13 Middle St. | 978/465–8008 | $6.95–$23.95 | AE, D, MC, V.

Jacob Marley's. American. This bright, family-friendly restaurant has lots of windows and a dining area in its solarium. Menu choices include salads, burgers, and pasta, but try the pan-seared haddock or the crab cakes. Live music Tues. and Fri.–Sun. Kids' menu. | 23 Pleasant St. | 978/465–5598 | $7.95–$14.95 | AE, D, DC, MC, V.

Nasturtiums. Eclectic. You can savor duck, quail, filet mignon, or one of several vegetarian dishes from the wide-ranging, adventurous menu. The restaurant is simply charming, with a brick wall, dried flower arrangements, love seats, and a welcoming staff. | 27 State St. | 978/463–4040 | Closed Mon. | $10–$26 | AE, D, MC, V.

The Rim. Contemporary. Upstairs from David's, The Rim has wood-burning fireplaces and red walls that give the dining room an Asian look. American and Pacific Rim influences yield a menu ranging from sushi to rack of lamb. The special children's room (ages 18 months and up), has baby-sitting, games, videos, and food service. | 11 Brown Sq | 978/462–8077 | Reservations essential for children's room | $17.50–$24.50 | AE, D, MC, V.

★ **Scandia.** Contemporary. This storefront's white linen and cut flowers create an upscale tone for dining on Italian- and French-influenced cuisine. Try the steak Diane or the blue-cheese tenderloin. Sun. brunch. Kids' menu. No smoking. | 25 State St. | 978/462–6271 | $15.95–$19.95 | AE, D, DC, MC, V.

Ten Center Street. Continental. Choose either restaurant here. The formal dining room upstairs serves smoked salmon, chicken parmigiana, pastas, and rich French sauces. Molly's Pub downstairs, with its exposed brick wall and fireplace, serves a more modest bar menu. Open-air dining on deck. Sun. brunch. | 10 Center St. | 978/462–6652 | $16.95–$22 | AE, D, DC, MC, V.

Lodging

★ **Clark Currier Inn.** A meticulously restored 1803 captain's mansion with a grand central staircase, period furnishings, and an award-winning Federal-style garden that has English roses and formal boxwood hedging. The property is within walking distance of the harbor and a short drive from Maudslay State Park. Complimentary breakfast. TV in common area. No smoking. | 45 Green St. | 978/465–8363 | www.clarkcurrier.com | 8 rooms | $105–$155 | AE, D, MC, V.

Country Garden Motel. The rooms in this 1901 farmhouse-turned-inn show country decorating touches throughout, such as floral bedding and dried-flower arrangements. The 4-acre property, 7 mi south of town on Rte. 1A, includes gardens and gazebos. Some kitchenettes, some in-room hot tubs, cable TV. Indoor pool. Spa. No pets. | 101 Main St. | 978/948–7773 or 800/287–7773 | fax 978/948–7947 | www.countrygardenmotel.com | 15 rooms, 4 suites | $85–$165 | AE, D, MC, V.

Essex Street Inn. This early 19th-century inn is downtown, close to shops and the waterfront. Some rooms have fireplaces and antique furnishings. Some in-room hot tubs. Parking (no fee). No smoking. | 7 Essex St. | 978/465–3148 | fax 978/462–1907 | www.org.newburyport.com | 18 rooms, 3 suites | $95–$205 | AE, D, DC, MC, V.

Garrison Inn. This four-story, 19th-century brick building faces Brown Square Park downtown and is close to shops and the waterfront. The elegant rooms are furnished with period pieces, and the loft suites are equipped with fireplaces. Restaurant, bar with entertainment. In-room data ports, cable TV. Business services. | 11 Brown Sq | fax 978/499–8555 | 16 rooms, 8 suites | $109, $149–$169 suites | AE, MC, V.

Morrill Place Inn. Period furnishings and four-poster canopy beds grace the guest rooms of this 23-room estate built in 1806. The lovely public rooms include an elegant dining room, the music room, winter and summer porches, and a terrace. Maudslay Park is nearby. Complimentary Continental breakfast. No air-conditioning, cable TV in common room. Pets allowed. | 209 High St. | 978/462–2808 or 888/594–4667 | fax 978/462–9966 | morrillpl@aol.com | 9 rooms (4 with shared bath) | $66–$125 | No credit cards.

Walton's Ocean Front. This inn on Plum Island, 3 mi from downtown and close to one of the top bird-watching spots in the United States, has modern rooms with wall-to-wall carpeting and ocean views. Kitchenettes, microwaves, some in-room hot tubs, cable TV, in-room VCRs. | Fordham Way | 978/465–7171 | fax 978/463–7679 | 2 rooms, 10 suites | $70–$225 | AE, MC, V.

The Windsor House in Newburyport. This 18th-century Federal mansion, complete with courtyard outside and a foot-thick firewall inside, was a wedding present for Jane Perkins and Lieutenant Aaron Pardee in 1786. Their master bedroom is now the bridal suite. Nearby is the Parker River Wildlife Refuge, and special birding packages are offered by the inn. There's also complimentary afternoon tea. Complimentary breakfast. In-room data ports, TV and VCR in common area. Business services. Some pets allowed. No kids under 8 (call for exceptions). No smoking. | 38 Federal St. | 978/462–3778 or 888–735–2969 | fax 978/465–3443 | windsorinn@earthlink.net | www.bbhost.com/windsorhouse | 4 rooms | $135 | AE, D, MC, V.

NEWTON

MAP 8, C6

(Nearby towns also listed: Boston, Brookline, Cambridge, Dedham, Waltham, Wellesley)

Newton, a town of 14 separate villages, is Boston's most affluent suburb. With large homes, landscaped streets, and municipal parks, Newton well earns its nickname as the "Garden City." Its superior public school system, nationally recognized municipal recycling program, and state-of-the-art public library all contribute to Newton's highly touted quality of life.

Information: Newton–Needham Chamber of Commerce | 199 Wells Ave., Suite 208, Newton, 02159 | 617/244–5300 | www.nnchamber.com.

Attractions

Boston College (BC). Founded in 1863, Boston College is one of the nation's oldest Jesuit universities. Its two campuses serve more than 13,000 undergraduate and graduate stu-

6 "I'm thirsty"s, 9 "Are we there yet"s, 3 "I don't feel good"s,

1 car class upgrade.

At least something's going your way.

Hertz rents Fords and other fine cars. ® REG. U.S. PAT. OFF. © HERTZ SYSTEM INC., 2000/005-00

Make your next road trip more comfortable with a free one-class upgrade from Hertz.

Let's face it, a long road trip isn't always sunshine and roses. But with Hertz, you get a free one car class upgrade to make things a little more bearable. You'll also choose from a variety of vehicles with child seats, Optional Protection Plans, 24-Hour Emergency Roadside Assistance, and the convenience of NeverLost,® the in-car navigation system that provides visual and audio prompts to give you turn-by-turn guidance to your destination. In a word: it's everything you need for your next road trip. Call your travel agent or Hertz at **1-800-654-2210** and mention PC# **906404** or check us out at **hertz.com** or AOL Keyword: **hertz**. Peace of mind. Another reason nobody does it exactly like Hertz.

Hertz

exactly.®

Offer available on standard and leisure daily, weekend and weekly rentals at participating locations through March 31, 2003. Upgrade subject to larger car availability at time of rental. Upgrades apply to car classes B-F (compact 4-door through full-size). Max. upgrade to class G (premium). Offer cannot be combined with any other offer, discount or promotion. Minimum rental age for this offer is 25. Blackout periods apply. Standard rental qualifications, rental period and return restrictions must be met. Advance reservations are required.

Find America *with a Compass*

  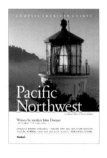 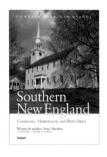

Written by local authors and illustrated throughout with images from regional photographers, Compass American Guides reveal the character and culture of America's most spectacular destinations. Covering more than 35 states and regions across the country, Compass guides are perfect for residents who want to explore their own backyards, and for visitors seeking an insider's perspective on all there is to see and do.

Fodor's Compass American Guides

At bookstores everywhere.

dents each year. Despite its name, the college's property lies altogether in Newton. | Chestnut Hill | 617/552–8000 | www.bc.edu | Free | Daily.

John J. Burns Library. BC's college library houses rare books and manuscripts, including its prestigious Irish collection. Two public display rooms host changing exhibits of the library's holdings, including the papers of William Butler Yeats, Samuel Beckett, and Graham Greene. The library itself is one of the finest examples of English Gothic architecture in America. | Bapst Building | 617/552–3282 | fax 617/552–2465 | www.bc.edu | Free | Weekdays 9–5.

McMullen Museum of Art. Though small, this two-floor museum presents striking exhibits that reach beyond its own permanent collection of European old masters and 19th-century American paintings. | Devlin Hall | 617/552–8100 | www.bc.edu/artmuseum | Free | Sept.–May, weekdays 11–4, weekends noon–5; June–Aug., weekdays 11–3, Sun. noon–5.

Jackson Homestead. Before the Civil War, this 1809 house was a station on the Underground Railroad, helping escaped slaves to freedom in the north. Now it hosts ongoing exhibits about the abolition movement and local history. | 527 Washington St. | 617/552–7238 | $2 | Sept.–June, Mon.–Thurs. noon–5, Sun. 2–5; July–Aug. Mon.–Thurs. noon–5.

New Repertory Theatre. This award-winning theater presents Boston and New England premieres of comedy, drama, and musicals. The 153-seat theater is equipped for the handicapped and the hearing impaired. | 54 Lincoln St., Newton Highlands | 617/332–1646 | www.newrep.org | Ticket prices vary | Sept.–June, Wed.–Sun. evening performances, Wed. and weekend matinees.

ON THE CALENDAR

JULY: *Fireworks on the Fourth of July.* The Independence Day celebration at Albemarle Field includes an open-air market with food vendors, a band concert. rides for kids, and the essential fireworks. | 617/244–5300.

Dining

Capital Grille. Contemporary. Dine amid leather furnishings and mahogany on grilled Norwegian salmon, lamb chops, boiled lobster, or dry aged steaks, the house specialty. The extensive wine list has more than 300 selections. | 250 Boylston St. | 617/928–1400 | No lunch | $16–$29 | AE, D, DC, MC, V.

Legal Sea Foods. Seafood. Huge and always crowded, this nautically themed restaurant in the Chestnut Hill Shopping Center perfectly prepares fresh seafood day in and day out. Splurge on the lobster or the cioppino. Kids' menu. No smoking. | 43 Boylston St. | 617/277–7300 | $12.95–$29.95 | AE, D, DC, MC, V.

O'Hara's Food and Spirits. American/Casual. Just around the corner from the New Repertory Theater, this busy, family-run pub has a loyal following, especially for the generous-sized lunch specials priced between $4 and $5. Popular entrées include baked stuffed haddock and chicken potpie. | 1185 Walnut St., Newton Highlands | 617/965–6785 | www.oharas-pub.com | Closed Sun. | $7–$13 | No credit cards.

Yerardi's. Italian. This family-owned restaurant in the Italian section of Newton has a wood-burning fireplace and family photos on the walls. In summer, there's alfresco dining on the patio by the bocce court. Popular dishes include fried calamari tossed in a spicy pepper sauce and Sicilian surf and turf—steak tips and shrimp on linguine. | 418 Watertown St. | 617/965–8310 | Closed Sun. | $8–$15 | AE, MC, V.

Lodging

Boston Marriott Newton. This renovated hotel is an affordable alternative to Boston's more expensive properties. It's next to the Charles River at I–90 and Route 128/I–95, a 15-minute drive from downtown Boston. 3 restaurants, bar with entertainment, picnic area, room service. In-room data ports, cable TV. Outdoor and indoor pools. Barbershop, hot tub. Gym. Playground. Laundry facilities. Business services. Some pets allowed. | 2345 Commonwealth Ave. | 617/969–1000 | fax 617/527–6914 | www.marriott.com | 430 rooms, 4 suites | $159–$245, $350 suites | AE, D, DC, MC, V.

Four Seasons Bed and Breakfast. This modern colonial-style house is on a quiet cul-de-sac next to conservation land. It has hardwood floors and a deck overlooking the garden. It's furnished with antiques, paintings, and the owner's handmade quilts. The kitchen is kosher. It's a five-minute walk to the Newton T stop on the Riverside Green Line. Complimentary Continental breakfast. No room phones, TV in common area. No pets. No kids under 12. | 15 Madoc St., Newton Center | 617/928–1128 | fax 617/928–1128 | 3 rooms (2 with shared bath) | $85, 2–night minimum | No credit cards.

Holiday Inn. Location is this dependable chain hotel's best feature. Catering to business travelers, the inn is off Route 128/I–95, next to MBTA Green Line service to Boston. Restaurant, bar, room service. In-room data ports, cable TV. Pool. Gym. Laundry service. Business services. Free parking. | 399 Grove St. | 617/969–5300 or 800/HOLIDAY | fax 617/965–4280 | www.holiday-inn.com | 192 rooms | $179 | AE, D, DC, MC, V.

Park Lane B and B. This residence blending colonial and Tudor styles has antiques, hardwood floors, and Victorian furnishings. It's on a quiet tree-lined street close to walking trails. The owners sell visitor T passes and have pickup/drop-off service for car rentals. Complimentary Continental breakfast. In-room data ports, cable TV, no phones. Exercise room. No pets. No smoking. | 11 Park La., Newton Center | 617/964–1666 or 800/772–6759 | fax 617/964–8588 | pranpran@juno.com | www.bostonbandb.com | 3 rooms (2 with shared bath) | $85 | AE, D, MC, V.

Sheraton Needham Hotel. This Needham hotel is near both Route 128/I–95 and I–90. It's less than 1/2 mi west of Newton. It boasts an entire executive floor, a sports bar, and room service for weary travelers. Restaurant, bar, room service. In-room data ports, cable TV. Indoor pool. Gym. Business services. | 100 Cabot St., Needham | 781/444–1110 | fax 781/449–3945 | knason@starlodge.com | www.sheratoneedham.com | 247 rooms, 16 suites | $279–$300 | AE, D, DC, MC, V.

Sheraton Newton Hotel. This suburban hotel offers some rooms with views of the Boston skyline. It's 6 mi from Logan Airport, 2 mi from Boston College, and within walking distance of restaurants and a park. An express bus to downtown Boston stops across the street. Restaurant, bar. In-room data ports, cable TV. Indoor pool. Sauna. Gym. Business services. | 320 Washington St. | 617/969–3010 or 800/325–3535 | fax 617/244–5894 | www.sheraton.com | 272 rooms | $109–$229 | AE, D, DC, MC, V.

Susse Chalet Inn of Newton. This inn is just across the street from two major malls, 8 mi from Boston, 6 mi from Fenway Park, and 2 mi from Boston College. Complimentary Continental breakfast. In-room data ports, cable TV. Pool. Barbershop, beauty salon. Shops. | 160 Boylston St. | 617/527–9000 or 800/524–2538 | fax 617/527–4994 | www.sussechalet.com | 144 rooms | $90–$125 | AE, D, DC, MC, V.

NORTH ADAMS

MAP 6, B2

(Nearby town also listed: Williamstown)

Nestled in the steep terrain of the northern Berkshires, North Adams was an isolated community until construction of the Hoosac Tunnel began in 1852. When it was completed in 1875, the 4.7-mile tunnel—then the world's longest—established a direct rail link with eastern Massachusetts. The Hoosac engineering triumph and the story of North Adams are recounted at Western Gateway Heritage State Park, one of the town's main attractions. In addition to its status as a railway boomtown, North Adams has long served as a gateway to several western Massachusetts state parks and forests. Now the town also takes pride in being home to the nation's largest art museum, the stunning Massachusetts Museum of Contemporary Art, which opened here in May 1999 in a renovated 19th-century mill complex.

Information: Northern Berkshire Chamber of Commerce | 57 Main St., North Adams, 01247 | 413/663–3735. **Tourist Information Booth** (June–mid-Oct.) | Union St., North Adams | 413/663–9204 | nbcc@bcn.net | www.nberkshirechamber.com.

Attractions

★ **Massachusetts Museum of Contemporary Art.** One of the largest museums in the world, MASS MoCA occupies 13 renovated buildings of a sprawling 19th-century industrial complex. Capitalizing on its sheer size, with one 40-ft-high gallery and another the size of a football field, the museum displays large-scale works that have rarely, if ever, been viewed publicly. The complex also encompasses theaters, rehearsal studios, and outdoor performance spaces for video, film, dance, and music. | 87 Marshall St. | 413/662–2111 | fax 413/663–8548 | www.massmoca.org | $8 | June–Oct., daily 10–6, Nov.–May, Wed.–Mon. 11–5.

Mohawk Trail State Forest. Occupying the remote mountainous reaches of the upper Deer-field River valley, this state forest is noted for its exceptional catch-and-release trout fishing, rough trails enjoyed by orienteers, and fire roads favored by snowmobilers. The park is 18 mi east of North Adams on Rte. 2. | Rte. 2, Charlemont | 413/339–5504 | www.state.ma.us/dem | $2, camping $10–$12 | Park daily, campground May–Columbus Day, daily.

Natural Bridge State Park. Though its span across Hudson Brook is but 30 ft, this natural bridge is the only one in the country that's carved out of marble. Some of the names and dates engraved in the stone are graffiti from the 19th century. A picnic area and rest rooms are maintained. | 1 mi north of the North Adams Visitors Center on Rte. 8 | 413/663–6312 | www.state.ma.us/dem | $2 | Daily.

Savoy Mountain State Forest. This state forest includes more than 11,000 acres of deeply wooded, flat-topped foothills. There are two cold swimming ponds, more than 60 mi of trails and fire roads, and a 45-site campground with showers, rest rooms, and four cabins. Visitors should take Rte. 2 east to Florida, then turn south on Central Shaft Rd. and follow the signs. | Central Shaft Rd., Florida | 413/663–8469 | www.state.ma.us/dem | $2 per car, camping $10–$12, cabins $25 | Park daily, campground Memorial Day–Columbus Day, daily.

Western Gateway Heritage State Park. This state park commemorates the tremendous impact of the Hoosac Tunnel on the northern Berkshires. Artifacts, photos, and interactive displays tell the story of the 4.7-mile-long tunnel, completed at great cost in 1875. | 9 Furnace St. Bypass, Bldg. 4 | 413/663–6312 | fax 413/663–6003 | www.state.ma.us/dem | Free | Daily 10–5.

ON THE CALENDAR
JULY: *Susan B. Anthony Celebration.* You can take part in a biathlon, a lawn party, and a cemetery tour as part of the five-day celebration that begins the Saturday before the first full weekend in August. | 413/663–3735.
OCT.: *Fall Foliage Festival.* This nine-day festival early in the month offers children's events, a pet show, a car show, bazaars, community suppers, a parade, and the Mount Greylock Ramble, a hike to the top of the highest peak in the state. | 413/663–3735.

Dining
Due Baci. Italian. This casual restaurant lets you enjoy classical music while feasting on well-prepared northern Italian dishes. Best bets are the veal, poultry, pasta, and steak Firenze. Kids' menu. | Holiday Inn Berkshires, 40 Main St. | 413/664–6581 | $6.95–$15.95 | AE, D, MC, V.

Lodging
★ **Blackinton Manor Bed and Breakfast.** You can't miss the 11-ft ceilings and wrought-iron balconies of this elegant 1830s Federal home. Furnished with antiques and 2 pianos, the inn has lovely gardens and a mountain view. Complimentary breakfast. Some in-room hot tubs, no TV in some rooms. Outdoor pool. No pets. No kids under 7. No smoking. | 1391 Massa-

chusetts Ave. | 413/663–5795 | fax 413/663–3121 | www.blackinton-manor.com | 4 rooms, 1 suite | $110–$210, $250 suite | MC, V.

Holiday Inn Berkshires. From the hotel, it's just one block to the Massachusetts Museum of Contemporary Art, a 10-minute drive to Mount Greylock, and a half-hour drive to whitewater rafting. Restaurant. In-room data ports, cable TV. Indoor pool. Hot tub, sauna, steam room. Health club. | 40 Main St. | 413/663–6500 or 800/HOLIDAY | fax 413/663–6380 | www.holiday-inn.com | 86 rooms | $109 | AE, D, DC, MC, V.

NORTHAMPTON

MAP 6, C4

(Nearby towns also listed: Amherst, Deerfield, Hadley, Holyoke, South Hadley)

With 30,000 residents, Northampton is Hampshire County's shire town, or judicial seat. Calvin Coolidge practiced law here before becoming the 30th U.S. president. At one end of downtown is the stately Victorian architecture and leafy campus of Smith College, a private women's college ranked among the nation's finest institutions of higher learning. The rest of downtown has thriving retail shops and good eateries aplenty, from ethnic fast-food priced for student budgets to upscale dining in an old stagecoach inn. The extension of two intercity bike paths through downtown is turning Northampton into a poster city for cycling, but I–91 still provides easy access for drivers.

Information: **Northampton Chamber of Commerce** | 99 Pleasant St., Northampton, 01060 | 413/584–1900 | north@valinet.com | www.northhamptonuncommon.com.

Attractions

Arcadia Wildlife Sanctuary. This 700-acre property of the Massachusetts Audubon Society protects waterfowl and wildflowers in the floodplain of the Connecticut River. The ecological habitats, which range from marsh to upland forest, are traversed by 5 mi of trails. No dogs. | 127 Combs Rd. | 413/584–3009 | www.massaudubon.org | $3 | Daily dawn–dusk.

Forbes Library. The city's public library is a magnificent Romanesque structure with an unmistakable 19th-century elegance. Inside, the Calvin Coolidge Memorial Room preserves portraits, photos, letters, and other documents related to the former president, who retired here after his White House years. | 20 West St. | 413/587–1011 | Free | Mon.–Wed. 11–3 and by appointment.

Historic Northampton. The local historical society maintains three homes whose architecture and furnishings reflect the Colonial and Federal periods. The organization also sponsors changing exhibits and special events and makes its archives available to researchers by appointment. | 46 Bridge St. | 413/584–6011 | www.historic-northampton.org | Donation suggested for the museum only; $3 for a tour of 3 houses | Museum: Tues.–Fri. 10–4, weekends noon–4; tours: weekends noon–4.
Damon House. Built by Isaac Damon for his family in 1813, this Federal house now hosts the historical society's changing exhibits. | 46 Bridge St. | 413/584–6011 | $3 for tour of three houses | Tours weekends noon–4.
Parsons House. This Colonial house was built circa 1658 and is one of only two remaining 17th-century structures in the Pioneer Valley. Although a remodeling around 1730 gave the house a very different look inside, its architecture remains significant. | 58 Bridge St. | 413/584–6011 | $3 for tour of three houses | Tours weekends noon–4.
Shepherd House. Two generations of Shepherds lived in this 1796 house, whose rooms are filled with period furnishings and mementos of their world travels. | 66 Bridge St. | 413/584–6011 | $3 for tour of three houses | Tours weekends noon–4.

Look Park. This 200-acre municipal park 2 mi west of Northampton is a community favorite. Open to the public are tennis courts, a wading pool, picnic grounds, a small lake with paddleboats, and a petting zoo with a miniature railroad. The park is linked to downtown via a paved bike path. | 300 N. Main St., Florence | 413/584–5457 | www.lookpark.org | $3 per vehicle, pedestrians and bicyclists free | Park daily 7–dusk; zoo May–Sept., daily 11–7.

Norwottuck Rail Trail. See Amherst.

Smith College. Founded in 1875, Smith is the largest private women's college in the United States. The campus is rich in Victorian architecture, particularly the college's earliest buildings along West Street. Also check out the Plant House, a building with a simulated forest. | Elm St. | 413/584–2700 | www.smith.edu | Free | Daily.
Smith College Botanic Garden/Lyman Conservatory. You can view plant species from around the world at the college's 12 connecting Victorian greenhouses and on the 125 acres of botanical gardens. Free tours are available to nonprofit groups. | College La. | 413/585–2740 | www.smith.edu/garden | Free | Daily 8:30–4.

ON THE CALENDAR
MAR. AND NOV.: *Smith College Botanic Garden Flower Show.* The staff of the botanic garden organize two annual plant exhibitions with accompanying lectures. The Spring Bulb Show runs for two weeks, starting the first Saturday in March; the Chrysanthemum Show is the first two weeks of November. | 413/585–2740.
MAY–JUN. AND OCT.: *Paradise City Arts Festival.* The juried show and sale of contemporary crafts and art draws more than 200 exhibitors from nearly 50 states. There are also craft demonstrations, live jazz, and food prepared by local chefs. The spring event takes place the last weekend in May or the first weekend in June; the fall event is held Columbus Day weekend. | 413/527–8994.
JULY: *New England Morgan Horse Show.* The Morgan was the first breed of horse developed in the United States. At this event at the Three-County Fairgrounds during the last week of the month, you can see 1,000 of the country's finest Morgan horses compete for prizes in 300 classes, including carriage driving, dressage, and English and Western pleasure. | 413/665–1165 | nemorganhs@aol.com.
SEPT.: *Three-County Fair.* Oxen and horse pulls, horticulture displays, arts and crafts, a farm museum, thoroughbred racing, and other entertainment all come together at this five-day fair held annually since 1818. The fair always ends on Labor Day. | Bridge St. | 413/584–2237 | www.3countyfair.com.

Dining
Eastside Grill. Eclectic. Consistently ranked among the area's best restaurants, the Eastside shows its New Orleans bent in the Cajun-influenced menu of pasta, seafood, and prime meats. Try the seafood pasta, gumbo, or pan-blackened fish. No smoking. | 19 Strong Ave. | 413/586–3347 | No lunch | $10.95–$15.95 | AE, D, DC, MC, V.

Hunan Gourmet. Chinese. Everything about this restaurant is elegant, from the radish-rose garnishes to the Chinese art to the black-lacquered tables with white tablecloths. The extensive menu includes Cantonese entrées and diet selections. Try the seafood hot-and-sour soup or gourmet chicken. Full bar service. | 261 King St. | 413/585–0202 or 413/585–0203 | $7–$15 | AE, MC, V.

Jake's. Café. This casual eatery with tables and counter space is a favorite with regulars. The most popular dish is the "no frills special"—home fries, scrambled eggs, meat, and cheese. Jake's is just across from the courthouse. | 17 King St. | 413/584–9613 | Breakfast also available. No dinner | $2–$5 | No credit cards.

La Cazuela. Mexican. Stylish Mexican and Southwestern motifs enliven this restaurant as much as the chilis enliven the inspired food. Vegetarians will find many choices on the menu. Recommended dishes include *camarones en adobo, chilis en nogada,* and Kahlúa mousse. Kids' menu. No smoking. | 7 Old South St. | 413/586–0400 | No lunch | $5.95–$13.95 | AE, D, MC, V.

Montana's Steakhouse at the Inn at Northampton. Steak. Specialties include Danish baby back ribs and prime rib—both slow-smoked on the premises—and a 24-ounce porterhouse steak. Dark wood paneling, old-style mirrors, red-glass lanterns on the tables, and music from the player piano lend a distinct western air to the dining room. | 1 Atwood Dr. | 413/586–1211 or 800/582–2929 | No lunch | $10–$23 | AE, D, DC, MC, V.

Northampton Brewery. American/Casual. This microbrewery serves exotic home brews and creative pub food such as Portobello marsala with fettuccine, sirloin steak Anthony, and vegetarian specials. There's open-air dining in the roof-top garden. | 11 Brewster Ct | 413/584–9903 | $11–$17 | AE, D, MC, V.

Paul and Elizabeth's. Vegetarian. The menu in this well-lit, relaxed eatery emphasizes organic ingredients, whole foods, and from-scratch preparations. Known for its flavorful soups, pastas, and vegetarian dishes, it also prepares some seafood dishes, such as tempura. Kids' menu. Sun. brunch. No smoking. | Thorne's Market, 150 Main St. | 413/584–4832 | $7.95–$13.95 | AE, MC, V.

Sylvester's Bakery and Restaurant. American. This was once the home of Dr. Sylvester Graham, for whom the graham cracker is named. Today, the downtown eatery serves nutritious homemade soups, sandwiches, and baked goods. It's popular with the arty crowd, and artwork adorns the walls of the two dining rooms. | 111 Pleasant St. | 413/586–5343 | Breakfast also available. No dinner | $4–$6 | MC, V.

Wiggins Tavern Restaurant at Hotel Northampton. Contemporary. Sophisticated fare is served in this 1786 Colonial tavern with hand-hewn beams, high ceilings, antiques, and three fireplaces. The tavern is justly proud of its colorful history and has welcomed many dignitaries over the years, from Eleanor Roosevelt to John F. Kennedy. Best bets are the macadamia-encrusted salmon, fire-roasted Long Island duck, and fresh seafood. Full bar and extensive wine list. Sun. brunch. | 36 King St. | 413/584–3100 | Closed Mon. No lunch | $14–$24 | AE, D, DC, MC, V.

Lodging

Autumn Inn. This colonial-style inn is in a quiet residential area across from Smith College. Fine art hangs on the walls, and the rooms have tasteful Colonial furnishings. Restaurant, picnic area. Some refrigerators, cable TV. Pool. | 259 Elm St. | 413/584–7660 | fax 413/586–4808 | www.autumninn.com | 28 rooms, 2 suites | $110, $145 suites | AE, DC, MC, V.

Hotel Northampton. This downtown, Victorian brick hotel is registered with the Historic Hotels of America. A glass-enclosed atrium adjacent to the lobby displays local art. Rooms are distinctively appointed with cherry furniture, and bathrooms have attractive imported tile. 2 restaurants, 1 bar, complimentary Continental breakfast, room service. In-room data ports, some kitchenettes, cable tv, some in-room hot tubs, in-room VCRs. Exercise equipment. Baby-sitting. Laundry service. Business services. No pets. | 36 King St. | 413/584–3100 or 800/547–3529 | fax 413/584–9455 | www.hotelnorthampton.com | 87 rooms, 12 suites | $125–$295, $155–$325 suite with 1 bath, $250–$550 2–bedroom suite with 2 baths | AE, D, DC, MC, V.

Inn at Northampton. This comfortable motel has cherry furniture, coffeemakers, hair dryers, and irons in every guest room. Gas-lit fireplaces glow in the sitting area of each of the three wings. It's 1 mi from downtown, off Route 5. Restaurant, bar, complimentary Continental breakfast weekdays. Cable TV. 2 pools (1 indoor), wading pool. Hot tub. Tennis courts, volleyball. Video games. | 1 Atwood Dr. | 413/586–1211 or 800/582–2929 | fax 413/586–0630 | innoho@javanet.com | www.thhg.com | 121 rooms, 3 suites | $109–$149, $159 suites | AE, D, MC, V.

Knoll Bed and Breakfast. A sweeping front lawn leads to this peaceful retreat 3 mi from Smith College and a 3-minute walk from Look Park. The 1910 English Tudor-style home on 17 acres of farmland and forest is filled with Oriental rugs and eclectic furnishings. Dining room, complimentary breakfast. No air conditioning, no room phones, TV in common area. No pets. No kids under 12. No smoking. | 230 N. Main St., Florence | 413/584–8164 | the-knoll@crocker.com | www.crocker.com/~theknoll | 4 rooms with 2 shared baths | $65–$70 | No credit cards.

Twin Maples Bed and Breakfast. Open pasture and woods surround this 200-year-old Colonial farmhouse 7 mi northwest of Northampton. The innkeeper raises Hereford cattle and produces maple syrup. Guest rooms contain antique Victorian and country furnishings, and a full country breakfast is served. Picnic area, complimentary breakfast. No room phones, TV in common area. No pets. No smoking. | 106 South St., Williamsburg | 413/268–7925 | fax 413/268–7243 | berkbb33@javanet.com | www.hamphillsbandb.com/twinmaples | 3 rooms with shared bath | $65–$75 | AE, MC, V.

OAK BLUFFS (MARTHA'S VINEYARD)

MAP 6, J7

(Nearby towns also listed: Edgartown, Falmouth, Nantucket, Vineyard Haven, West Tisbury, Woods Hole)

Oak Bluffs is a creation of religion and tourism. It's an unusual offspring: what began in 1835 as the annual gathering place for a Methodist revival meeting has, over time, become the most youth-oriented and nightlife-filled town on Martha's Vineyard. Granted, the Methodists merely got the ball rolling; resort developers seeking to cash in on the camp meetings' family values are ultimately behind the big push toward today's party atmosphere. The dance clubs, arcades, fast-food, and cinemas may be most appealing to the young, but a fringe benefit to being in a community that targets families is the prevailing affordability of both lodgings and restaurants—a particularly elusive trait on the Vineyard in the summer. In high season, Oak Bluffs also has the most ferry connections of any island town, to Woods Hole, Falmouth, Hyannis, and Nantucket.

Information: Martha's Vineyard Chamber of Commerce | Box 1698, Vineyard Haven, 02568 | 508/693–0085. **Oak Bluffs Information Booth** | Circuit Ave., Oak Bluffs | mvcc@vineyard.net | www.mvy.com.

Attractions

Car/passenger ferry service. A trio of companies provide ferry services between Oak Bluffs and Cape Cod and Nantucket from late spring to early fall. All vessels take bicycles for an added fee. Advance reservations for passengers are not accepted by any of the companies, but vehicle reservations are, where indicated.

Hy-Line Cruises. This company provides passenger-only service between Oak Bluffs and Hyannis, in the mid-Cape area, as well as between Oak Bluffs and Nantucket. The 1¾-hour Hyannis trip is made up to four times daily at the height of summer and once a day in late spring and early fall. The trip to Nantucket, made five times daily, takes about two hours each way. | Oak Bluffs Harbor, Circuit Ave. Ext | 508/778–2600 or 888/778–1132 in MA | www.hy-linecruises.com | $25 round-trip to Hyannis or Nantucket | Early May–Memorial Day, weekends; Memorial Day–Oct., daily. To Nantucket: June–mid-Sept., daily.

Island Queen. This three-deck vessel provides passenger-only service between Oak Bluffs and Falmouth Harbor, almost straight across Vineyard Sound. The 35-minute trip is made at least twice daily in late spring and early fall, and up to eight times on summer weekends. You can't bring your car, but you can bring your bicycle for an additional fee. | Oak Bluffs Harbor, Circuit Ave. Ext | 508/548–4800 | www.islandqueen.com | $10 round-trip | Memorial Day–Columbus Day.

Steamship Authority. The community-governed Steamship Authority links Oak Bluffs with Woods Hole on Cape Cod, a 45-minute journey away. Their large, lumbering vessels, the only ones able to transport vehicles, are also the least expensive for passengers. Vehicle fares do not include the driver or passengers. There are multiple daily departures. | Seaview Ave. | 508/477–8600 | www.islandferry.com. | Passengers: $10 round-trip; vehicles: $62–$194 round-trip | Daily.

Cottage Museum. This two-story museum in a whimsical 1868 cottage like the ones to which it's dedicated, shows off furnishings typical of the community's mid-19th century heyday. | 1 Trinity Park | 508/693–7784 | $1 donation | Mid-June–early Oct., Mon.–Sat. 10–4.

East Chop Lighthouse. Atop a high bluff overlooking Nantucket Sound, this 1876 cast-iron light replaced one that burned in 1828 and was used to signal Boston. | E. Chop Dr. | 508/627–4441 | $2. | Late June–early Oct., ½ hr before sunset–½ hr after sunset.

Flying Horses Carousel. This National Historic Landmark is the country's oldest merry-go-round in continuous operation. The handmade 1876 horses have real horse hair for their manes and glass eyes. | Oak Bluffs Ave. | 508/693–9481 | $1 | Late May–late June, weekends 11–5; July–mid-Oct. daily 10–10.

Ocean Park. Facing the sea, this large town green hosts band concerts throughout the summer and a fireworks display in August. | Sea View Ave. | Free | Daily.

Dining

Amity Café. American. A *Jaws* motif asserts itself through a giant shark mural and dishes like a "Benchley breakfast Burrito." Hungry? Don't miss the all-American "shark attack" consisting of three eggs, bacon, pancakes, French toast, home fries, and coffee. | 1 Park Ave. | 508/696–9922 | Breakfast also available. Closed mid-Oct.–mid-May. No lunch. No dinner | $8–$14 | No credit cards.

Jimmy Sea's. Italian. Sautéed garlic laces practically every classic Italian dish that comes from this popular kitchen. Patrons line up early and often for the generous portions of *vongole* (whole littleneck clams) marinara and linguine *puttanesca*. | 32 Kennebec Ave. | 508/696–8550 | No lunch | $15–$25 | MC, V.

Lola's. Southern. Gargantuan portions—leftovers are all but guaranteed, and a three-course meal is impossible to finish—and genuine Southern hospitality make for an exceptional value by Vineyard standards. Not suprisingly, the ribs and jambalaya are popular. Live music nightly late May–early Sept., four nights a week rest of the year. Open-air bar. Sun. brunch. No smoking in main dining room. | Beach Rd. | 508/693–5007 | No lunch | $9–$27 | DC, MC, V.

Offshore Ale Company. American/Casual. A handsome and dark barnlike dining room with shiny copper vats draws in crowds who like throwing shelled peanuts on the floor and sipping nutty microbrews. Burgers and wood-fired oven pizzas are the order of the day. | 30 Kennebec Ave. | 508/693–2626 | $7–$14 | AE, MC, V.

Season's Eatery & Pub. American/Casual. Irish theme nights and karaoke ratchet the sound and pace up a notch, but come on a night when neither is on tap and you'll find the food acceptable. A dozen TVs are constantly blaring over the bar, but the burgers, nachos, pastas, and fried calamari still taste good. | 19 Circuit Ave. | 508/693–7129 | $10–$17 | AE, D, DC, MC, V.

Smoke 'n Bones. Southern. The island's only dedicated rib joint serves plates of barbecued lobster, buckets of dried pork ribs, and buffalo wings and other BBQ favorites. Cords of wood are stacked up around the property next to buckets holding discarded bones. As the menu says: "Bone appetit." | 20 Oakland Rd. | 508/696–7427 | Breakfast also available. Closed mid-Oct.–late May. No lunch weekends | $8–$20 | MC, V.

★ **Sweet Life Café.** Contemporary. Sophisticated cuisine, soft lighting, and warm tones make this an easy island favorite. Outdoor candlelight dining doesn't hurt either. Look for ever-changing preparations such as lobster stuffed in artichoke or crispy sweetbread salad with Portobello mushrooms. Desserts are a phenomenon. | 63 Upper Circuit Ave. | 508/696–0200 | Closed Jan.–Mar. | $22–$36 | AE, D, MC, V.

Zapotec Café. Mexican. One of the island's least pretentious places is ensconced in a small Gingerbread-style house. Enjoy both Southwestern and Mexican-American fare such as *tacos de pescado*, barbecued swordfish with a yogurt sauce in a soft flour tortilla. The restaurant is crowded but cheerful and colorful. | 14 Kennebec Ave. | 508/693–6800 | Closed Nov.–late Apr. No lunch Sept.–mid-June | $12–$18 | AE, DC, MC, V.

Lodging

Admiral Benbow Inn. A few blocks from the Oak Bluffs harbor, on the busy road to Vineyard Haven, this small turn-of-the-20th-century B & B is a mishmash of comfortable antiques. With its stunning fireplace, the Victorian parlor may be where you choose to spend most of your time. Dining room, complimentary Continental breakfast. Refrigerators. No pets. No smoking. | 81 New York Ave. | 508/693–6825 | fax 508/696–6191 | cybern@cape.com | www.bedandbreakfast.com | 6 rooms | $75–$175 | Closed Jan.–Mar. | AE, D, MC, V.

Attleboro House. This classic 1874 Methodist Association campground house, complete with the requisite Gingerbread detailing, is directly across from the harbor and has plenty of front-porch rockers from which to take in all the action. Guest rooms are simple, with white curtains, and some have sinks. Shared bathrooms are even simpler. Staying at this charming throwback will certainly give you a rarified glimpse into an earlier time in Oak Bluffs history. Complimentary Continental breakfast. No pets. No smoking. | 42 Lake Ave. | 508/693–4346 | $75–$95. | 9 rooms (with shared bath) | Closed Oct.–mid-May | AE, D, MC, V.

Beach House. Light and airy, with an ocean view from the pretty front porch, Beach House is appropriately named. This turn-of-the-20th-century private summer home on a ½-mi-long public beach is just what a beach house should be. A five-minute walk from the ferry and downtown. Complimentary Continental breakfast. Cable TV, no room phones, in-room VCRs. No kids under 10. | 83 Seaview Ave. | 508/693–3955 | www.beachhousemv.com | 9 rooms | $150–$175. | AE, D, DC, MC, V.

Dockside Inn. This candy-colored, Victorian-style inn combines modern conveniences and luxuries with late-19th-century beauty. Some of the rooms have harbor views, and all are reached via the two-floor front porch. Enjoy the location on Oak Bluffs Harbor and the garden out back. Complimentary Continental breakfast. Some kitchenettes, some refrigerators, cable TV. Business services. No smoking. | Circuit Ave. Ext. | 508/693–2966 or 800/245–5979 | fax 508/696–7293 | www.vineyard.net/inns | 17 rooms, 5 suites | $150–$200 | Closed Nov.–Mar. | AE, D, MC, V.

Island Inn. On 7½ acres of landscaped grounds overlooking Nantucket Sound and a golf course, the inn offers the choice of a one- or two-bedroom suite, a condominium suite, or a cottage. Some units have water views. A bike path runs alongside the inn. There's a beach right next door and another 5 mi away. Picnic area. Kitchenettes, cable TV. Pool. 3 tennis courts. Playground. Laundry facilities. Business services. Pets allowed before Memorial Day and after Labor Day. | Beach Rd. | 508/693–2002 or 800/462–0269 | fax 508/693–7911 | innkeeper@islandinn.com | www.islandinn.com | 51 units | $85–$345 | Closed Dec.–Mar. | AE, D, DC, MC, V.

Martha's Vineyard Surfside Motel. Although the mid-town location makes for some noisy summer nights, this motel has spacious and bright rooms and fresh furnishings, albeit motel-style ones. Restaurant. Refrigerators, some in-room hot tubs, cable TV. Pets allowed (fee). | Oak Bluffs Ave. | 508/693–2500 or 800/537–3007 | fax 508/693–7343 | www.mvsurfside.com | 34 rooms, 4 suites | $140–$150 | AE, D, MC, V.

★ **Oak House Inn.** Built in 1872 across from the beach and named for the oak paneling throughout, the Oak House is a traditional Victorian inn with antiques, wood floors, and area rugs. There is a wraparound porch, and afternoon tea is served. Dining room, complimentary Continental breakfast. Cable TV. No kids under 10. No smoking. | Seaview Ave. | 508/693–4187 or 800/245–5979 | fax 508/696–7293 | www.vineyard.net/inns | 10 rooms | $190–$280 | Closed Nov.–Apr. | AE, D, MC, V.

OAK BLUFFS
(MARTHA'S
VINEYARD)

INTRO
ATTRACTIONS
DINING
LODGING

Pequot Hotel. A five-minute walk from the bustle of Oak Bluffs center, this Carpenter Gothic house on the edge of the Methodist Association camp grounds won't win any decorating contests. But you'll undoubtedly spend most of your time in the wide porch's rockers. Complimentary Continental breakfast. No cable TV in some rooms. No pets. No smoking. | 19 Pequot Ave. | 508/693–5087 or 800/947–8704 | www.pequothotel.com | 29 rooms, 1 3-bedroom apartment | $205–$225, $250–$300 apartment | Closed late Oct.–mid-May | AE, D, MC, V.

★ **Sea Spray Inn.** On the quiet edge of a big park and within walking distance of the town beach, this Victorian-era B&B has a wide wraparound porch. Guest rooms feature king-size, four-poster feather beds. Complimentary Continental breakfast. No pets. No kids under 12. No smoking. | 2 Naumkeag Ave. | 508/693–9388 | fax 508/696–7765 | seasprayinn@msn.com | 6 rooms, 1 suite | $150–$200 | Closed Dec.–Apr. | MC, V.

The Ship's Inn. The rooms at this B&B afford considerable privacy—all have separate entrances, and they are comfortable, with an upbeat decor. The lobby has a fireplace and the inn is close to public transportation. No pets. No smoking. | 18 Kennebec Ave. | 508/693–2760 | www.theshipsinn.com | $135–$175 | 15 rooms (2 with shared bath) | Closed Dec.–Mar. | AE, MC, V.

ORLEANS (CAPE COD)

MAP 6, L6

(Nearby towns also listed: Brewster, Chatham, Eastham, Harwich)

The only Massachusetts town with a French name, Orleans is outer Cape Cod's market town. The English settlers who purchased the land in 1642 from local Native Americans were primarily interested in agriculture. As the community expanded over the next century, commercial fishing became increasingly important. By the 1800s, the people of Orleans were primarily engaged in cod and mackerel fishing. As tourism increased in the early years of the 20th century, Orleans turned away from the sea and toward servicing its summer visitors, with retail trade and vacation-home construction. These days Orleans is popular among retirees; nearly a third of the town's 6,000 residents are 65 or older. Beaches, boating, biking, and restaurants are among the town's biggest attractions. Abundant lodging options and a location conveniently between the outer Cape's extremes make Orleans a good base for travelers.

Information: **Orleans Chamber of Commerce** | Box 153, Orleans, 02653 | 508/255–1386 or 800/865–1386 | info@capecod-orleans.com | www.capecod-orleans.com.

Attractions

Academy of Performing Arts. Formerly the town hall, this handsome 1873 building now hosts theater, music, and dance performances year-round, particularly in summer. | 120 Main St. | 508/255–1963 | fax 508/255–3075, but call first | www.apa1.org | June–mid-Sept., $14–$16; mid-Sept.–May, $12–$14 | June–mid-Sept., Tues.–Sun.; mid-Sept.–May, Thurs.–Sun. Call for performance times.

French Cable Station Museum. Between 1891 and 1959 this building was the American terminal for transatlantic communications via undersea cables between Cape Cod and France. Now the structure contains the original handmade equipment, preserved as it was last left, along with modest displays explaining the technology and the station's role in an earlier telecommunications age. | 41 S. Orleans Rd. | 508/240–1735 | Free | July–Aug., Mon.–Sat. 1–4, June and Sept., Fri.–Sun. 1–4.

Jonathan Young Windmill. For a demonstration of how saltwater was turned into salt—an early local industry—stop by this educational landmark mill. | Rte. 6A and Town Cove | Free | July–Aug., daily 11–4; late May–June and Sept.–early Oct., weekends 11–4.

Nauset Beach. Miles of tawny sand stretch south from the huge parking lot at this beach facing the Atlantic, ensuring plenty of elbow room for anyone willing to walk far enough. In summer, there are bathhouses with showers and a fried-seafood shack that also rents beach chairs and umbrellas. The nearby Nauset Lighthouse was moved from its precarious clifftop position to a safer site, in a notable feat of engineering. | Beach Rd. | Memorial Day–early Sept. $8; mid-Sept.–Memorial Day $5.

Rock Harbor. Today it hosts a charter fishing fleet and is a nice place to watch the sun set, but this harbor has a storied past. The former packet boat landing was the site of a War of 1812 episode in which the Orleans militia kept a British warship from coming ashore. | Rock Harbor Rd. | Free | Daily.

ON THE CALENDAR
SEPT.: *Fall for Orleans.* Celebrate the coming of fall at this festival at the end of the month. A parade down Main Street leads to Eldridge Park where numerous vendors, bands, and kids' activities await the crowds. | 508/255–1386 or 800/865–1386.

Dining
Barley Neck Inn. French. This stately country inn is marked by a large green lawn and an impressive flower and herb garden. Inside the house, fireplaces and imposing art liven up the mix of casual and serious dining options. Try the lamb shank. No smoking. | 5 Beach Rd., East Orleans | 508/255–0212 | Reservations essential | No lunch | $10–$23 | AE, DC, MC, V.

Captain Linnell House. Continental. Come to this Greek Revival home for an intimate dinner of traditional, perfectly prepared meats and fish. Try the rack of lamb with an herb-mustard crust, or the veal Milanese. There's open-air dining on the patio. No smoking. | 137 Skaket Beach Rd. | 508/255–3400 | Closed Mar. and Mon.–Tues. in Dec.–Feb. and Apr.–May. No lunch | $20–$30 | AE, MC, V.

Double Dragon. Chinese. Even with saltwater views on the town cove, this standard Chinese restaurant provides a pleasant break from Ye Olde Cape Cod, as does the menu of southern Chinese cuisine with some spicier Hunan and Mandarin dishes mixed in. No smoking. | 59 Cranberry Hwy. | 508/255–4100 | $6.25–$16.95 | AE, D, DC, MC, V.

Kadee's Lobster & Clam Bar. Seafood. This summer landmark excels at fish-and-chips, clams, and steamers, as well as more unusual seafood stews and Portuguese kale soup. But the prices can can really add up. Clean-cut college students wait on indoor and outdoor tables. | 212 Main St. | 508/255–6184 | Closed early Sept.–mid-May and weekdays in early June | $5.50–$24.50 | MC, V.

Land Ho! American. At the corner of Cove Road, this boisterous, fun tavern is decked out with dozens of wooden signs hanging from the rafters. Local gather for lively conversation and staples like burgers and sea-clam pie. | Rte. 6A | 508/255–5165 | $9–$17 | AE, MC, V.

Lobster Claw. Seafood. This family restaurant is filled with fishing nets, brightly painted tables, and happy customers digging into giant portions of inexpensive local seafood. Try the lobster club sandwich, surf-and-turf platter, and mud ice-cream pie. Kids' menu. Early-bird suppers. No smoking. | 42 Rte. 6A | 508/255–1800 | Closed Nov.–Mar. | $9.95–$15.95 | AE, D, DC, MC, V.

Mahoney's Atlantic Bar & Grill. Contemporary. The creative cuisine here—try grilled vegetables and polenta or drunken littlenecks steamed in ale—matches the fantastic location. The long bar is a nice place to hang out, too. | 28 Main St. | 508/255–5505 | Closed Jan.–Mar. | $12–$21 | AE, MC, V.

★ **Nauset Beach Club.** Italian. Flowers and table linens set the bistro-like tone in the small dining room of this residential-looking Cape cottage. And the food is as contemporary and sophisticated as the selective imported beer and wine list. Try one of the more than 20 wines by the glass while tucking into rack of lamb, seared scallops, or crab cakes. Desserts are an event. | 222 E. Main St. | 508/255–8547 | Closed Sun.–Mon. in mid-Oct.–late May. No lunch | $18–$23 | AE, D, DC, MC, V.

Old Jailhouse Tavern. Eclectic. Stop by this spacious restaurant for pizza, mushroom burgers, steaks, vegetable stir-fry, and, of course, pure New England seafood. The glass-walled, conservatory-style airiness provides a modern setting. Kids' menu. Sun. brunch. No smoking. | 28 West Rd. | 508/255–5245 | $13–$22 | AE, D, MC, V.

Rosina's Café. Italian. This former mom-and-pop place has expanded from its humble Italian roots, but with a little help ordering, you'll do quite well here. Try the pasta primavera, stuffed halibut, and the signature puttanesca. | 15 Cove Rd. | 508/240–5513 | Closed mid-Oct.–mid-Apr. and Mon. No lunch | $11–$26 | AE, DC, MC, V.

Sir Cricket's Fish and Chips. Seafood. A tiny hole-in-the-wall attached to the Nauset Lobster Pool, this no-frills, fried-seafood joint has just a few tables and a soda machine. | Rte. 6A | 508/255–4453 | $7–$15 | No credit cards.

The Yardarm. American/Casual. This place has a roadhouse feel to it (even with no smoking allowed), thanks to the pool tables and TV blaring sporting events. The large portions are a good value; try baked sole, barbecued ribs, or pot roast. Burgers and beers are also big. No smoking. | 48 Rte. 28 | 508/255–4840 | $8–$17 | AE, DC, MC, V.

Lodging

Barley Neck Inn. A bilevel motel on the road toward Nauset Beach, the Barley Neck has large rooms with standard motel-style furnishings—neither surprising nor disappointing. 2 restaurants. Refrigerators. Pool. No pets. | 5 Beach Rd., East Orleans | 508/255–0212 | fax 508/255–3626 | www.barleyneck.com | 18 rooms | $130–$160 | Closed late Nov.–Mar. | AE, MC, V.

The Cove. This motel near the Nauset and Skaket Beaches has landscaped terraces, a gazebo, dock, heated pool, and patio areas. Many of the rooms have private decks and waterviews. Guests at the only waterfront motel in Orleans receive complimentary, narrated harbor cruises. A conference room is also available. Picnic area. In-room data ports, microwaves, refrigerators, cable TV, in-room VCRs. Pool. Business services. | 13 Rte. 28 | 508/255–1203 or 800/343–2233 | fax 508/255–7736 | www.thecoveorleans.com | $109–$189 | 39 rooms, 8 suites in 5 buildings | AE, D, DC, MC, V.

★ **Kadee's Gray Elephant.** A mile from Nauset Beach, these small studio and one-bedroom units are carved from an early 19th-century sea captain's house. They've been flamboyantly painted and decorated with bright colors and intentionally mismatched florals and plaids—that somehow works as a light-headed seaside getaway. Restaurant. Kitchenettes. Mini golf. No pets. No smoking. | 216 Main St., East Orleans | 508/255–7608 | $140 | 6 apartments | Closed Dec.–Jan. | MC, V.

Nauset House Inn. A family-operated B & B whose owners pay great attention to detail and comfort. Guest rooms have stenciling, quilts, hand-painted furniture, antiques, and stained glass. The common spaces are equally appealing. Head to the orchard, lush conservatory, or lounge-worthy parlor. Nauset Beach is only a ½ mi away. The inn has loaner beach chairs and towels. Complimentary breakfast. No pets. No kids under 12. No smoking. | 143 Beach Rd., East Orleans | 508/255–2195 | fax 508/240–6276 | www.nausethouse-inn.com | 14 rooms (6 with shared bath) | $75–$140 | Closed Nov.–Mar. | D, MC, V.

Nauset Knoll Motor Lodge. High on a grassy hill, this seaside motel is in a quiet area. Every room has a commanding view of the ocean. The lodgings resemble Cape Cod cottages of 50 years ago, and the large rooms have views of the ocean. No air-conditioning, cable TV, no room phones. | 237 Beach Rd., East Orleans | 508/255–2364 | 12 rooms | $140 | Closed mid-Oct.–mid-Apr. | MC, V.

Olde Tavern Motel and Inn. This 18th-century sea captain's inn is close to the ocean and bay beaches and public tennis courts. On 3 acres, it is set back from the road and surrounded by woodland, yet it's only a five-minute walk to restaurants and shops. The main building is an 18th-century Colonial, the remaining portion of Higgins Tavern, a stagecoach stop Henry Thoreau wrote about in 1849. There are beam ceilings, hardwood floors, a fireplace, period furniture, and antiques in the lobby. A few rooms are in the original tavern, but most, furnished in a Colonial style, are in another building. Complimentary Continental breakfast. Refrigerators, cable TV. Pool. | 151 Rte. 6A | 508/255-1565 or 800/544-7705 | www.capecodtravel.com/oldetavern | 29 rooms | $79-$110 | Closed Dec.-Mar. | AE, D, MC, V.

Parsonage Inn. This Cape Cod–style house was built in 1770 and became a parsonage in 1848. It has wide pine floors, country antiques, artifacts from Kenya, and a grand piano (guests are invited to play). The inn is in a residential area and within walking distance of restaurants. It's near bike trails and Nauset Beach. Complimentary breakfast. No room phones. No kids under 6. No smoking. | 202 Main St., East Orleans | 508/255-8217 or 888/422-8217 | fax 508/255-8216 | 8 rooms | $110-$135 | Closed Jan. | AE, MC, V.

Ridgewood Motel and Cottages. This 3-acre property is in a rural/residential area on a dead-end street, 1 mi from the beach at Pleasant Bay and 3 mi from Orleans. The cottages (with full kitchens) are set in a pine grove. Picnic area, complimentary Continental breakfast for motel guests. No air-conditioning in cottages, some kitchenettes, refrigerators, cable TV, no room phones. Pool. Playground. No smoking. | 10 Quanset Rd., South Orleans | 508/255-0473 | www.ridgewoodmotel.com | 18 rooms, 6 cottages | $71-$82, $520-$630/wk cottages | MC, V.

Seashore Park Inn. This horseshoe-shaped inn—a popular family resort—has two floors of deluxe rooms, some of which come with a patio, deck, or balcony. A glass-and-brick building houses the indoor pool, and seal-watch tour packages are available. Complimentary Continental breakfast. Some kitchenettes, cable TV. Indoor and outdoor pools. Hot tub, sauna. Business services. No smoking. | 24 Canal Rd. | 508/255-2500 or 800/772-6453 | fax 508/255-9400 | info@seashoreparkinn.com | www.seashoreparkinn.com | 62 rooms | $99-$139 | Closed end of Oct.–mid-Apr. | AE, D, MC, V.

Ship's Knees Inn. This inn is a 200-year-old sea captain's house, filled with antiques and paintings. The house on this lush, 3-acre waterfront property is a four-minute walk from the beach. Picnic area, complimentary Continental breakfast. No air-conditioning in some rooms, cable TV in some rooms, no room phones. Pool. Tennis court. No kids under 12. No smoking. | 186 Beach Rd., East Orleans | 508/255-1312 | fax 508/240-1351 | www.ship-skneesinn.com | 19 rooms (8 with private bath), 2 cottages | $135, $875-$950/wk cottages | MC, V.

Skaket Beach Motel. This motel's five buildings are on 3 acres of wooded and landscaped grounds with gardens and a patio area that looks off into the woods. Breakfast includes blueberry and cranberry muffins made fresh every morning from the innkeeper's special recipe. Picnic area, complimentary Continental breakfast. Some in-room data ports, some kitchenettes, some microwaves, refrigerators, cable TV. Pool. Laundry facilities. | 203 Cranberry Hwy. | 508/255-1020 or 800/835-0298 | fax 508/255-6487 | www.skaketbeachmotel.com | 46 rooms | $99-$164 | Closed end Nov.–Mar. | AE, D, DC, MC, V.

PITTSFIELD

MAP 6, B3

(Nearby town also listed: Lenox)

Pittsfield, gratefully named after English parliamentarian and patriot sympathizer William Pitt, is the Berkshires' largest and most commercial community. It became a significant manufacturing center during the 19th and early 20th centuries, especially after inventor William Stanley moved his electric-generator factory to Pittsfield in the late 1800s. Stanley's company eventually became General Electric, whose plant for the testing and manufacture of transformers, electrical components, and industrial plastics dominates the east side of the city. Corporate downsizing has sharply soured Pittsfield's good fortunes in recent years. But the Berkshire Museum, the Berkshire Opera Company, and Herman Melville's home—Arrowhead—make Pittsfield worth adding to your itinerary.

Information: Berkshire Visitors Bureau | Berkshire Common, plaza level, 01201 | 413/443–9186 or 800/237–5747 | bvb@berkshires.org | www.berkshires.org.

Attractions

Arrowhead. From 1850 to 1863, Herman Melville and his family called this 40-acre farm home. Here Melville wrote *Moby-Dick* and other works; his study appears as if he might shortly return to pick up his pen. As headquarters to the Berkshire County Historical Society, the property also offers excellent changing exhibits on local history in the barn. | 780 Holmes Rd. | 413/442–1793 | fax 413/443–1449 | www.berkshireweb.com/arrowhead | $5 | Memorial Day–Oct., daily 9:30–5, house tours on the hr 10–4; Nov.–May, by appointment.

Berkshire Museum. Art, natural science, and history are encompassed under one roof here. Highlights range from the luminous Hudson River School landscapes in its painting collection to a hands-on display of aquatic creatures. There are regular changing and traveling exhibits from the museum's own vast collection or elsewhere, and a full schedule of lectures, workshops, films, and children's programs. | 39 South St. | 413/443–7171 | fax 413/443–2135 | www.berkshiremuseum.org | $6 | Sept.–June, Tues.–Sat. 10–5, Sun. noon–5; July–Aug., Mon.–Sat. 10–5, Sun. noon–5.

Berkshire Opera. This professional opera company utilizes performers from the Metropolitan Opera, New York City Opera, and other notable companies. The repertoire leans towards bel canto and contemporary, intimate works, rather than grandiose spectacles. Performances are given at the Koussevitzky Arts Center on the grounds of Berkshire Community College. | 1350 West St. | 413/443–1234 | fax 413/443–3030 | www.berkop.org | $20–$60 | Call for schedule.

Canoe Meadows Wildlife Sanctuary. The three branches of the Housatonic River converge just north of this Massachusetts Audubon Society property. A pair of small brooks join the river here, too, as it flows through wetlands bordered by woods and fields. A few miles of trails help provide access to the sanctuary's different habitats that provide refuge for a sizable amount of wildlife. | Holmes Rd. | 413/637–0320 | www.massaudubon.org | $2 | Tues.–Sun., 7–dusk.

Crane Museum. This museum 5 mi east of Pittsfield details the history and art of fine papermaking, from within an attractive stone mill once used for that same purpose. Since the museum's owner, Crane & Co., supplies all the paper for U.S. currency, there's a display of banknotes from around the world as well. | Pioneer Mill, off Housatonic St., Dalton | 413/684–2600 | Free | June–Columbus Day, weekdays 2–5.

★ **Hancock Shaker Village.** This was the third of thirteen communities founded in the nation by the United Society of Believers in Christ's Second Appearing, or Shakers, as they have come to be known. After 170 years, the whole village was converted into a museum dedicated to interpreting this religious order's agrarian lifestyle, domestic industry, and enduring design skills. Professional artisans demonstrate Shaker crafts, and the results are sold in the village museum shop. It's 5 mi west of downtown Pittsfield. | U.S. 20 | 413/443–0188 or 800/817–1137 | fax 413/447–9357 | www.hancockshakervillage.org | $13.50 (good for 10 consecutive days) | Self-guided tours, mid-May–late Oct., daily 9:30–5; guided tours, late Oct.–mid-May, daily 10–3.

Herman Melville Memorial Room at the Berkshire Athenaeum. Melville buffs will discover a wealth of primary research materials, family memorabilia such as the author's customs house badge, and the earliest portrait of Melville. The admirable collection is maintained by the Berkshire Public Library. | 1 Wendell Ave. | 413/499–9486 | Free | Labor Day–Independence Day, Mon.–Thurs. 9–9, Fri. 9–5, Sat. 10–5; July–Aug., Mon., Wed. 9–5, Tues., Thurs. 9–9, Fri. 9–5, Sat. 10–5.

Skiing. The generous snowfall and scenic slopes of the Taconic Range make for fine skiing conditions despite the modest height of its peaks. The section of the range near Pittsfield is where that snowfall is at its highest.

Bousquet Ski Area. This ski area has more than 20 trails, running the gamut from beginner to black diamond. Though the peak vertical drop is only 750 ft, Bousquet has a strong local following for its low-key attitude, youth-oriented atmosphere, and budget rates. | Dan Fox Dr. off U.S. 7 | 413/442–8316 | fax 413/445–4534 | www.bousquet.com | $20 | Dec.–Mar., daily.

Brodie Mountain. Calling itself the "Irish Alps," Brodie's 1,250-ft vertical drop is the region's highest. Most of its 28 trails are for advanced intermediates. There's also has a cross-country ski center with more than 15 mi of trails. In addition to full snowmaking, lift service, and ski programs for kids, the resort offers hotel and condo accommodations, year-round camping, and an indoor racquet club. It's 8 mi north of Pittsfield. | U.S. 7, New Ashford | 413/443–4752 or 413/443–4751 (recorded ski conditions) | www.skibrodie.com | $30–$38 | Dec.–Mar., daily.

Jiminy Peak. This is a full-scale resort 10 mi northwest of Pittsfield with slopeside condos, an inn, dining, weekend entertainment, a conference center, a health club, and a range of family ski programs. Complete snowmaking and chairlift coverage keep its 40 trails busy, and over half are open for night skiing, too. The 1,140-ft vertical drop provides some challenging expert runs, but two-thirds of the terrain is for beginning and intermediate skiers, with strong emphasis on the comfortable middle range. | 37 Corey Rd., Hancock | 413/738–5500 or 800/882–8859 (outside MA) | fax 413/738–5729 | www.jiminypeak.com | $42 | Late Nov.–Apr., daily.

REMEMBER ONE WORD: PLASTICS

The Berkshires are probably not the first place that would come to mind if you had to imagine the early history of plastics manufacturing in the United States. But Pittsfield and its northern neighbors are indeed the birthplace of many plastics-related innovations. The first man-made plastic substances were introduced in England in the 1860s, and were shortly followed by the invention of celluloid in nearby Albany, New York. Reacting to the commercial appeal of the new, inexpensive ivory substitute, a Berkshire investor bought the licensing rights to manufacture one of celluloid's English competitors. Levi Brown's American Zylonite Company, based outside North Adams, is thought to have become the nation's leading plastics producer in the early 1880s, before patent disputes with the Albany manufacturer forced the company to close. After the 1909 invention of high-performance thermoset plastics, which retain their shape even in high heat, Pittsfield-based General Electric Company launched research and development into industrial plastics. The company became a leader in custom injection molds and molding machinery, and in finding applications for the new polymer plastics being synthesized throughout the pre-war years. After World War II, General Electric concentrated on innovation, creating compounds now taken for granted in your eyewear, car, and home. At the same time, some 50 other plastics-related companies grew up in and around Pittsfield to capitalize on products coming out of GE's labs. The plastics industry continues to be one of the Berkshires' largest employers.

© Corbis

ON THE CALENDAR

MAY: *Massachusetts Sheep and Woolcraft Fair.* This annual fair at the Cummington Fairgrounds (25 mi. East of Pittsfield off Rte. 9 in Cummington) includes sheep and fleece judging, sheep-dog trials, workshops on spinning, dyeing wool, felting, and weaving, spinning contests, and a crafts fair. | 413/624–5562.

SEPT.–OCT.: *South Mountain Concerts.* Chamber music concerts are held in the historic Temple of Music built in 1918. | 413/442–2106.

DEC.: *Community Christmas of Hancock Shaker Village.* This annual event has become a holiday tradition for many families. Activities include sleigh rides or wagon rides and children's crafts. The 19th-century brick main house and roundstone barn housing sheep and cows are open. | 413/443–0188 or 800/817–1137.

Dining

Brewery at 34 Depot Street. American/Casual. Casual, family-friendly dining in a spacious, airy, and well-ventilated eatery separated by glass walls from the region's first microbrewery. Try the fine line of ales, lagers, and stouts while eating your burgers, veggie burrito, slab of ribs, or specialty salad. Kids' menu. | 34 Depot St. | 413/442–2072 | $5–$13 | AE, DC, MC, V.

Dakota Restaurant. American. As befits a rustic hunting lodge, with mounted moose and elk heads and canoes slung from the rafters, the menu here features strapping portions of hearty meats and seafood. Known for hand-cut aged prime beef, mesquite-broiled meats and fish, and a giant brunch buffet. Salad bar. Kids' menu. Early bird suppers. Sunday brunch. No smoking. | 1035 South St. | 413/499–7900 | No lunch | $12–$25 | AE, D, DC, MC, V.

South Mountain Grill. American. Hardwood abounds in this 225-seat, family-friendly restaurant. Prime rib, steak neptune, and lobster are the most popular dishes. All the booths provide views of the landscaped grounds. | 1015 South St. | 413/499–2075 | $14–$27 | AE, MC, V.

Lodging

The Berkshire Inn. This one-story inn, while offering nothing fancy, was renovated in 1998, so all the rooms are modern and feature wall-to-wall carpeting. Complimentary Continental breakfast. Cable TV. Outdoor pool. No pets. | 150 W. Housatonic St. | 413/443–3000 or 800/443–0633 | fax 413/443–3549 | 38 rooms | $89–$139 | AE, MC, V.

Comfort Inn. Built in 1998, this three-story modern motel is 2 mi south of downtown Pittsfield. Continental breakfast. In-room data ports, cable TV. Gym. Business services. No pets. | 1055 South St. | 413/443–4714 | fax 413/445–7400 | www.comfortinn.com | 58 rooms | $179–$199 | AE, D, DC, MC, V.

Crowne Plaza Hotel Pittsfield Berkshires. Inside, there's oak paneling, wood trim, and iron chandeliers with crystal prisms. Outside are the Berkshire mountains, which can be seen from every room. There is dining by the indoor pool under the domed glass ceiling, or outside on the patio. 3 restaurants, bar. In-room data ports, cable TV. Indoor pool. Beauty salon, hot tub, sauna. Gym. Business services. | 1 West St. | 413/499–2000 or 800/2–CROWNE | fax 413/442–0449 | www.crowneplaza.com | 177 rooms, 2 suites | $149–$269 | AE, D, DC, MC, V.

Heart of the Berkshires Motel. This basic motel is quiet and set back from the road. Just 2 mi from Hancock Shaker Village and a 15-minute drive from Tanglewood, it's also close to movie theaters. Cable TV. Some pets allowed. | 970 W. Housatonic St. | 413/443–1255 | 17 rooms | $199 | AE, D, MC, V.

Jiminy Peak. The hotel is located at the bottom of the slopes, and has a mountain-side view. In summer, trout fishing mini-golf, and a 3,000-ft alpine slide are major attractions. Downhill skiing is the main winter event. Packages are available year-round. Restaurant, bar with entertainment. Cable TV. 4 pools. 2 hot tubs. Tennis. Gym, hiking, fishing. Downhill skiing. Video games. Baby-sitting, children's programs (age 4–12). Laundry facilities. Business services. | Corey Rd., Hancock | 413/738–5500 or 800/882–8859 | fax 413/738–5513 | www.jiminypeak.com | 96 1-bedroom suites, 34 condos | $149–$339 | AE, D, DC, MC, V.

PLYMOUTH

(Nearby towns also listed: Bourne, Duxbury, Sandwich)

Shortly before the end of 1620, a small, leaky, crowded sailing vessel from Bristol, England, dropped anchor in Plymouth Harbor and altered the history of the continent. A smattering of Colonial settlements had already been started in North America, from the Spanish in Florida to the French in Nova Scotia, but none has resonated so strongly through the ages as the *Mayflower* Pilgrims' arrival at Plymouth Rock that cold December day. Pilgrim history is this town's trump card, and Plymouth plays it at every turn. The Plimoth Plantation is alone worth a detour from almost anywhere in the state. But there are many other attractions as well, from historic homes to whale-watch cruises. An hour south of Boston by road or commuter rail, Plymouth is also less than 15 mi from Cape Cod, and in summer just a 90-minute boat ride from Province-town, at the tip of the Cape.

Information: **Destination Plymouth** | 170 Water St. Ste. 10C, Plymouth, 02360 | 508/747–7533 or 800/872–1620. **Plymouth Information Center** | 130 Water St., Plymouth, 02360 | 508/747–7525 | bak57@aol.com | www.visit-plymouth.com.

Attractions

Burial Hill. This hilltop burying ground behind the First Church in Town Square contains the earliest marked graves of the Pilgrim settlers. It also offers a fine view over the center of town. | School St. | Free | Daily.

Cape Cod Cruises. Try the express ferry to Provincetown for a stress-free alternative to driving the length of Cape Cod—and make the trip across the bay in about 90 minutes. The vessel has a counter-service galley for food and drinks. | State Pier, Water St. | 508/747–2400 or 800/242–2469 | fax 508/746–7472 | www.captjohn.com | $26.50 round-trip; $2 extra for bikes | June 17–Sept. 4, daily, May 27–Sept. 4, weekends, Sept. 4–end of Sept., Tues., Wed., weekends.

Cole's Hill. This hill, with its strategic view of the harbor and proximity to a nearby stream, became the site of the Pilgrims' first settlement. A sarcophagus tells the story of those early days. Nearby stands a statue of Massasoit, the local Pokanoket sachem whose alliance and material aid was critical to the white settlers' survival. | Water St. across from Plymouth rock | Free | Daily.

Cranberry World. Operated by Ocean Spray, the growers' cooperative known for its cranberry juices, this center tells the history of cranberry cultivation. In addition to photos and farm implements, the center maintains a demonstration kitchen where cranberry products may be sampled. | 158 Water St. | 508/747–2350 | fax 508/746–8232 | www.oceanspray.com | Free | May–Nov., daily 9:30–5.

Howland House. The only Pilgrim home still standing on its original site, this late 1660s house was built by Jacob Mitchell, a housewright (carpenter) who came on the next ship to arrive in Plymouth after the *Mayflower*. It was later bought by Jabez Howland, who lived in it with his aged parents, both of whom were *Mayflower* passengers. The original one-bay house was expanded twice, including the addition of the two left-side rooms in 1750, and now contains period furnishings spanning the structure's first century, including many Howland family possessions. | 33 Sandwich St. | 508/746–9590 | fax 508/866–5056 | $3.50 | Memorial Day–Columbus Day, daily 10–4:30; Thanksgiving week (Thurs.–Sat.) 10–4:30.

Mayflower Society Museum. This museum is furnished to reflect the era of its construction in 1754. A formal 18th-century garden is also on the property. The house was once owned by Edward Winslow, whose great-grandfather came over on the *Mayflower*, and has been owned by the Mayflower Society since 1941. The house is known for its flying staircase. | 4

Winslow St. | 508/746–2590 | July–Labor Day, daily 10–4; Memorial Day–June, early Sept.–Oct., Fri.–Sun. 10–4.

Myles Standish State Forest. At more than 14,600 acres, this is the state's second-largest park. Its dry, sandy landscape of pitch pine is laced with fire roads and trails well suited for horseback riding, mountain biking, and cross-country skiing. Several ponds attract boaters, swimmers, and anglers, and the 475-site campground is among the most popular in the state. Boats must be nongasoline powered. No off roading, no dirt bikes, no four-wheelers. | Cranberry Rd., South Carver | 508/866–2526 or 877/422–6762 for camping reservations | www.state.ma.us/dem | $2; $10–$12 per camp site | Daily; campground mid-Apr.–Columbus Day.

National Monument to the Forefathers. This grandiose tower was erected in 1889. The 81-ft-tall solid granite monument is adorned with allegorical figures honoring early Plymouth's English settlers for possessing the virtues of liberty, law, education, faith, and

© Artville

THEY'RE STILL HERE

It is commonly assumed that Native Americans are no longer found in Massachusetts, having been forced out or killed centuries ago, leaving nothing but what their adversaries kept of their poetic place-names. Although it is true that tens of thousands of indigenous people lost their lives to epidemics, displacement, and armed conflict with land-hungry European settlers by the end of the 17th century, they have by no means vanished. When the Pilgrims arrived in 1620, the future state was home to the Massachusetts, Wampanoag, Pawtucket, Nipmuc, Pocumtuck, Wappinger, and Mahican tribes. Each of these was essentially a nation of smaller bands, which in turn comprised unions of village-based clans further divisible into extended family groups. A half-dozen of the Wampanoag tribe's original 50-plus bands remain within Massachusetts, although only one, the Aquinnah of Martha's Vineyard, has been accorded federal recognition. The Hassanamisco and Chaubunagungamaug bands of the Nipmuc are here, too, in south-central Massachusetts; descendants of the Pawtucket continue to live in the Merrimack Valley, their ancestral home; and members of Rhode Island's Narragansett tribe now live in southeastern Massachusetts. There are no Indian reservations per se in the state, but some of these surviving bands own their property, including a small chunk of Nipmuc territory that was, remarkably, never deeded to any white man.

Surprisingly few museums in Massachusetts provide accurate information about these original New Englanders, but there are some exceptions, most notably Deerfield's Memorial Hall Museum, the Fruitlands Museum in the rural countryside east of Leominster, and Plymouth's Pilgrim Hall Museum. Also in Plymouth is the must-see interpretive 1627 village, Plimoth Plantation, part of which is devoted to re-creating the homesite of a Wampanoag family known to have been neighbors with the Pilgrims. Contemporary Native American powwows, typically including music and dance, storytelling, kids' games, and crafts, are held in scattered locations throughout the state from spring through fall. Most welcome all comers. A handful are sponsored by the Massachusetts Center for Native American Awareness (617/884–4227); contact them for details.

morality—those believed to be needed to "civilize" the continent. | Allerton St. | 508/746–1620 | Free | Daily dawn–dusk.

Pilgrim Hall Museum. The largest collection of Pilgrim-related artifacts in existence is this museum's principal claim to fame. It occupies two floors of an imposing Greek Revival building in the heart of Plymouth. The only portrait of a *Mayflower* passenger is among its prized possessions, but the museum also makes an effort to shed light on the lives of the Native Americans who were here when the Pilgrim migration began and are still here today. | 75 Court St. | 508/746–1620 | fax 508/747–4228 | www.pilgrimhall.org | $5 | Feb.–Dec., Daily 9:30–4:30.

★ **Plimoth Plantation.** This living history museum reconstructs the English settlement at Plymouth as it appeared in 1627, in addition to interpreting life aboard the *Mayflower* with the aid of a full-scale replica in the town harbor. There are also exhibition galleries, a replica of a contemporary Native American homesite, and regular demonstrations of early 17th-century English crafts by artisans whose work is available for sale. Special programs are offered, among them a Colonial Thanksgiving dinner. | Rte. 3A | 508/746–1622 | fax 508/746–4978 | www.plimoth.com | $17–$19 | Apr.–Nov., daily 9–5.

Visitor Center. See a few exhibits here while also availing yourself of the food service, well-stocked bookstore, gift shop, and rest rooms.

Carriage House Craft Center. This 19th-century carriage house, part of the Plimoth Plantation, is staffed by shoemakers, basketmakers, potters, and joiners. The artisans do not wear period costumes, but do use period tools. | Warren Ave. | 508/746–1622.

Hobbamock's (Wampanoag Indian) Homesite. Hobbamock, an advisor to Massasoit, lived with his extended family near the original Plymouth settlement. This homesite provides an example of the typical 17th-century dwellings used by the local Indians. Costumed interpreters are on hand to explain and answer questions about Pokanoket Wampanoag culture, theology, and interactions with the English settlers.

Mayflower II. The crew and passengers who greet visitors to this replica of the most renowned ship in American history are stuck in the year 1621. From this historical vantage point they describe their voyage across the Atlantic and the events that precipitated that trip. They are fully able to discourse about their own particular circumstances, too, or gossip about their fellow passengers, if prompted. | State Pier, Water St. | 508/746–1622 | $7 | Apr.–Nov., daily 9–5.

Nye Barn. On the grounds of the Plimoth Plantation, the barn houses some rare breeds of livestock, including Kerry cows—a hardy Celtic strain—and Dorset horned sheep.

1627 Village. The heart of the plantation is this stockaded compound of thatch-roofed houses, gardens, and stock pens in which a large cast of costumed interpreters enact the daily lives of some 30 of the original Plymouth settlers, all without ever betraying knowledge of any event later than 1627. As they tend to farm animals, gardens, and chores—conversing with visitors all the while in 17th-century dialect—the villagers reveal a storehouse of information about their Colonial characters, from politics and religious beliefs to the chronology of their arrival in their new homeland.

Plymouth Antiquarian Society. The organization maintains three historic houses for public tours, which collectively provide a window on the lives of local residents from the earliest English Colonial settlement to the mid-20th century. | 508/746–0012 | fax 508/746–7908 | Combined admission to all properties $6 | June–early-Oct., Thurs.–Sat. 10–4.

Harlow Old Fort House. This circa 1677 house derives its name from the fact that its timbers were recycled from the fort built on Burial Hill by the *Mayflower* settlers in 1622. A 1920s "restoration" of the house made it more representative of the Colonial Revival movement than the real Colonial era, as the tour guides readily explain. | 119 Sandwich St. | 508/746–0012 | $4 | July–Aug., Fri. 10–4.

Hedge House. Built in 1809 by a well-to-do seafaring family, this rambling mansion was originally on Court Street and only moved to its current idyllic waterfront setting after World War I, when industrial use of the wharves was in decline. Period rooms representing the mid-19th century fill most of the house. There are also changing exhibits of domestic objects and personal effects, including regular displays drawn from the Antiquarian Society's extraordinary 19th-century costume collection. | 126 Water St. | 508/746–0012 | $4 | June–early Oct., Thurs.–Sat. 10–4.

1749 Spooner House. After its construction in the late 1740s, this cozy structure became home to five generations of the Spooner family. Nothing, it seems, was ever thrown out in those 200 years. Furnishings and decorations acquired over the generations, sometimes side-by-side with whatever they were meant to replace, are mixed and matched for aesthetic rather than historical interest, lending a warm, lived-in quality to the place. Selected rooms are also used as changing showcases for antiques drawn from the family's well-stocked attic. | 27 North St. | 508/746–0012 | $4 | June–early Oct., Thurs.–Sat. 10–4.

Plymouth Colony Winery. Fruit wines, in particular cranberry wines, are the specialty of this establishment, whose tasting room and shop occupies a renovated late-19th century cranberry screening house. In addition to free samples, visitors are given a tour of the production area. | Pinewood Rd. off U.S. 44 | 508/747–3334 | Free | Apr.–Dec., daily; Feb. and Mar., weekends.

Plymouth National Wax Museum. The story of the Pilgrims' journey from England to this very hill on which the museum stands is told with life-size wax dioramas. | 16 Carver St. | 508/746–6468 | fax 508/746–8245 | $6 | Mar.–May and Nov., daily 9–5; June and Sept.–Oct., daily 9–7; July–Aug., daily 9–9.

Plymouth Rock. This surprisingly diminutive stone may seem overwhelmed by the classical open-sided temple that has been built around it, but the touchstone of English settlement in the New World need not pretend to be humble. The rock was identified 125 years after the fact by Elder Faunce, who told the story as it was passed down to him by his forefathers. | Water St. | Free | Daily.

Richard Sparrow House. Dating back to 1640, this is the oldest-surviving house in Plymouth. The lean-to at the rear was added later; originally the structure was a two-room design two stories tall, with an attic space. It's furnished to the period, including a notable collection of 17th-century pottery. | 42 Summer St. | 508/747–1240 | $2 | Thurs.–Tues. 10–5, Sat. 10–8.

Site of First Houses. Short, steep Leyden Street, running up Cole's Hill from the harbor, is a vestige of the early Colonial settlement. The Pilgrims' first houses were built on it, and the private homes that stand here today each have historic plaques affixed to them identifying those original predecessors, now long vanished. | Leyden St. | Free | Daily.

Supersports Family Fun Park. This year-round amusement park 10 mi west of Plymouth has rides, miniature golf, arcade games, and a driving range. In winter, only the arcade and snack bar remain open. | 108 N Main St., Carver | 508/866–9655 | fax 508/866–9795 | Rides and activities priced individually | Call for hrs.

Whale-watch cruise. Capt. John Boats. This outfit offers four-hour trips to Stellwagen Bank National Marine Sanctuary at the eastern edge of Massachusetts Bay. Stellwagen is a prime summer feeding ground for such rare and endangered species as the humpback, sei, fin, and northern right whale. | Town Pier, Water St. | 508/747–2400 or 800/242–2469 | fax 508/746–7472 | www.captjohn.com | 26.50 | Apr.–May and Oct., weekends; June–Sept., daily.

ON THE CALENDAR

AUG., NOV.: *Pilgrims' Progress.* The 51 costumed marchers in this procession represent the survivors of the Pilgrim's first winter in Plymouth. The procession begins at 6 PM every Friday in August and November at the Mayflower Society House. | 508/747–7525.

SEPT.–OCT.: *King Richard's Faire.* This is a re-created 16th-century English marketplace at festival time. Minstrels sing, knights engage in jousting matches, and King Richard's chefs prepare Renaissance fare. | 508/866–5391.

OCT.: *Massachusetts Cranberry Harvest Festival.* Indulge your passion for cranberries over Columbus Day weekend with harvesting demonstrations, cooking contests, food, live country music, crafts exhibits, children's activities, hayrides, and helicopter rides. (Helicopters are used in the harvesting and maintenance of cranberries.) | 508/295–5799 or 508/295–4895.

OCT.–NOV.: *Autumnal Feasting.* Four types of dining events are available at Plimoth Plantation. At "Out of the Ordinarie" visitors can taste dishes that were familiar to the Wampanoag people and Plymouth's first English settlers. The fall menu includes seasonal roasted fowl, fish, harvest vegetables, and 17th-century cheesecake. For 1620 theme dining, visitors can sample foods from 17th-century Plymouth, England—roast beef, rice pudding, and cream-apple tart, to name a few. There's also a Victorian Thanksgiving dinner, complete with period entertainment, and a New England Thanksgiving buffet with everything from soup to nuts. Reservations are required. | 508/746–1622.

NOV.: *Thanksgiving Week.* Festivities begin with the Thanksgiving Parade through downtown and along the historic waterfront in the place where the first Thanksgiving was celebrated in 1621. The parade features many of the finest marching and musical units in the country, including the "Commandant's Own" U.S. Marine Drum and Bugle Corps and the famous "Mummers" from Philadelphia. Other events include the National Senior Drum and Bugle Corps Reunion, the Thanksgiving Concert Series, and a reenactment of the 1621 harvest feast at Plimoth Plantation. | 508/747–7525 or 800/USA–1620.

Dining

Bert's Cove. Continental. Macadamia-encrusted salmon, chicken sautéed with wild mushrooms, and pumpkin ravioli are a few of the offerings here. The restaurant is on Plymouth Beach, and the interior is full of weathered paneling that resembles driftwood. | 140 Warren Ave. | 508/746–3330 | fax 508/746–0455 | Closed Mon. Labor Day–Memorial Day | $9–$16 | AE, D, MC, V.

Colonial Restaurant. American. This restaurant has been in operation since the 1950s—and still retains a bit of the classic diner vibe with stools lining a counter and numerous booths. Among the homecooked meals, fried haddock and sirloin steak are favorites. | 39 Main St. | 508/746–0838 | Closed Thurs. | $7–$12 | D, MC, V.

East Bay Grill. Seafood. Views of Plymouth Harbor, the *Mayflower II*, and Cape Cod Bay are the prime attractions here. The traditional menu of surf-and-turf favorites holds no surprises. Kids' menu. No smoking in dining room. | 173 Water St, Town Wharf | 508/746–9751 | $13–$25 | AE, D, DC, MC, V.

Hearth and Kettle. American. Neo-Colonial decor and servers in Colonial attire place this restaurant within a hair's breadth of being a theme park. The menu offers a range of sandwiches, pasta, and full dinners, with many heart-healthy selections for the diet conscious. Known for fresh seafood. Kids' menu. Early bird suppers. No smoking in dining room. | John Carver Inn, 25 Summer St. | 508/747–7405 | $5–$16 | AE, D, DC, MC, V.

Iguana's Restaurant. Tex–Mex. Terra-cotta walls, an outdoor deck, and sombreros add festive touches to Iguana's. Enjoy burritos, enchiladas, and babyback ribs. | 170 Water St. | 508/747–4000 | fax 508/747–4001 | $10–$15 | AE, MC, V.

Isaac's Restaurant. American. Delight in the view of Plymouth Harbor while chowing down on sautéed jumbo shrimp or fettuccine with chicken. | 114 Water St. | 508/830–0001 | fax 508/746–7556 | $11–$17 | AE, D, DC, MC, V.

Mayflower Café. American. Firecracker salmon is a good choice here if you like spicy fare, and the boiled lobster is always a good bet. Paintings by local artists adorn the walls. | 300 Commercial St. | 508/487–0121 | Closed Nov.–Apr. | $5–$15 | No credit cards.

The Weathervane. Seafood. This booming 300-seat restaurant provides a topnotch view of the ocean. Try the fried-seafood combo or the lazyman's lobster (meat is removed from the shell so you can dig right in). The theme is nautical. | 6 Town Wharf | 508/746–4195 | $7–$13 | AE, MC, V.

Lodging

Blue Spruce Motel and Townhouses. This renovated property offers motel accommodations and town houses. On 6½ acres of landscaped grounds, it's close to the beach and 6½ mi south of Plymouth's historic center. In-room data ports, refrigerators, cable TV. Pool. Business services. | 710 State Rd. | 508/224–3990 or 800/370–7080 | fax 508/224–2279 | www.bluspruce-motel.com | 32 rooms, 4 town houses | $64–$88, $165–$187 town houses | AE, D, DC, MC, V.

Brewster House. This restored 1908 Colonial Revival house is full of original details, including a coffered-wood ceiling, sliding pocket doors, crown moldings, brass hardware, and arched entryways. Each guest room has a different theme—Colonial, Federal, and Harbor View—and all have floral arrangements, antiques, and canopy beds. A collection of Civil War memorabilia is on display in the innkeeper's study. The property is in Plymouth's historic district, a half block from the harbor. Complimentary breakfast. No room phones, no TV. No kids under 11. | 15 Brewster St. | 508/830–1913 or 888/426–8966 | 3 rooms | $85–$110 | MC, V.

Cold Spring Motel. This motel is one block from the harbor and harbor beach and has lawns, flowers, and pine trees. Complimentary Continental breakfast. Refrigerators, cable TV. | 188 Court St. | 508/746–2222 or 800/678–8667 | fax 508/746–2744 | 58 rooms, 3 suites, 2 cottages | $79–$119, $109–$139 cottages | Closed Dec.–Mar. | AE, D, MC, V.

Foxglove Cottage. All the rooms in this restored 1820 structure feature queen- or king-size beds with Laura Ashley details. Expect to see foxes or coyotes from the deck of this pastoral, 4-acre property. Complimentary breakfast. No room phones, TV in common area. | 101 Sandwich Rd. | 508/747–6576 | fax 508/747–7622 | www.foxglove-cottage.com | 3 rooms | $90–$95 | No credit cards.

Governor Bradford on the Harbour. This renovated hotel is on the Plymouth waterfront, within walking distance of major attractions, restaurants, and shops. The hotel's three floors are surrounded by landscaped grounds with flowers. Refrigerators, cable TV. Pool. | 98 Water St. | 508/746–6200 or 800/332–1620 | fax 508/747–3032 | www.governorbradford.com | 94 rooms | $103–$149 | AE, D, DC, MC, V.

John Carver Inn. This family resort in Plymouth's historic district has a Pilgrim Cove theme pool with a water-slide replica of the *Mayflower* and a 10-person hot tub in the center of the pool, which is decorated with hand-painted murals. Restaurant, bar, room service. Cable TV, some in-room hot tubs. Indoor pool. Hot tub. Health club. Laundry service. Business services. | 25 Summer St. | 508/746–7100 or 800/274–1620 | fax 508/746–8299 | www.john-carverinn.com | 79 rooms, 6 suites | $119–$139 | AE, D, DC, MC, V.

Mabbett House. Built around 1900 for the owner of a Plymouth wool mill, this Colonial Revival's guest rooms have high ceilings, working fireplaces, canopy and Eastlake four-poster beds, and other antique furnishings. Breakfast is served on a screened porch overlooking the garden. It's a five-minute walk to the harbor and downtown. Two-night minimum stay in high season. Complimentary breakfast. No room phones, TV in common area. No kids under 12. No smoking. | 7 Cushman St. | 508/830–1911 or 800/572–STAY | fax 508/830–9775 | www.mabbetthouse.com | 3 rooms, 1 suite | $139 | AE, MC, V.

Pilgrim Sands Motel. This motel is across the street from Plimoth Plantation. Half the rooms have a water view, half a plantation view. A Plymouth sightseeing trolley stops here. Some refrigerators, cable TV. 2 pools. Hot tub. | 150 Warren Ave. | 508/747–0900 or 800/729–SAND | fax 508/746–8066 | www.pilgrimsands.com | 64 rooms, 2 suites | $105–$140 | AE, D, DC, MC, V.

Sconehedge. You'll find poplar beams, copper and glass lighting fixtures, and numerous decorative touches faithful to the Arts and Crafts movement here. The 1910 mansion is filled with custom-crafted wallpaper, carpets, and handpainted furniture. Complimentary breakfast. No room phones, TV in common area. | 280 Sandwich St. | 508/746–1847 | fax 508/746–3736 | www.burrows.com/scone.html | 3 rooms, 1 suite | $135 | MC, V.

Sheraton Inn Plymouth at Village Landing. Expect typical chain rooms at this hotel in the historic center of town near a cluster of shops selling crafts and Plymouth-made wines. Restaurant, bar with entertainment. In-room data ports, cable TV. Indoor pool. Gym. Business services. | 180 Water St. | 508/747–4900 | fax 508/746–2609 | sheraton@tiac.net | www.sheratonplymouth.com | 175 rooms | $160–$225 | AE, D, DC, MC, V.

Steeple View Bed and Breakfast. Built in 1890, this farmhouse is 2½ mi south of Plymouth Rock, across from Plimoth Plantation. The house is furnished with antiques, Oriental rugs, and original art by the owner, a member of the Plymouth Art Guild and South Shore Art Association. The 1½-acre property has terraced gardens and a patio. Dining room, complimentary breakfast. No room phones. Pool. No kids under 12. No smoking. | 69 Cliff St. | 508/747–0823 | fax 508/747–4194 | www.steeple-view.com | 3 rooms | $85–$100 | No credit cards.

Whispering Oaks Motel. In operation since 1950, this motel offers basic, inexpensive service. It's 7 mi south of Plymouth. Cable TV. Pool. No pets. | 517 State Rd. | 508/224–2500 | fax 508/224–2909 | 22 rooms | $68–$80 | Closed Dec.–Mar. | AE, D, MC, V.

The Whitfield House. You'll be but a stone's throw from Plymouth Rock when you stay at this 1782 home. Asian rugs and paintings, velvet-upholstered furniture, and a teddy bear collection round out the decorations. The blue room features a four-poster, lace canopy bed. Complimentary breakfast. No room phones, no TV. No pets. No kids under 12. No smoking. | 26 North St. | 508/747–6735 or 800/884–2889 | fax 508/747–2722 | www.plymouthmassbandb.com/jackson.htm | 3 rooms | $95–$180 | No credit cards.

PROVINCETOWN (CAPE COD)

MAP 6, K5

(Nearby towns also listed: Truro, Wellfleet)

★ On a clear day, Provincetown is visible from the whole rim of Cape Cod Bay, thanks to the 252-ft-tall Pilgrim Monument erected atop its highest hill. The tower commemorates the landfall of the *Mayflower* Pilgrims, but P-town, as it's popularly called, banished the prim ghosts of those self-professed saints long ago. For much of the past century the community ethos has been devoutly tolerant of artists, iconoclasts, and gays, lending it a hedonistic and flamboyant edge found nowhere else in Massachusetts. If feather-waving cross-dressers, openly affectionate bare-chested male couples, and women holding hands somehow affront your sensibilities, Provincetown may not be your cup of tea. But if you can embrace, admire, or otherwise respect the local color, you'll discover a lovely little town chock-a-block with clapboard cottages, cozy inns, exceptional restaurants, eye-catching galleries, and long waterfront streets that fill from sidewalk to sidewalk with a happy parade of strolling pedestrians throughout the summer.

Information: **Provincetown Chamber of Commerce** | 307 Commercial St., Provincetown, 02657 | 508/487–3424 | info@ptownchamber.com | www.ptownchamber.com.

Attractions

Expedition *Whydah* Sea Lab and Learning Center. The *Whydah* is the world's only authenticated pirate wreck whose recovered remains are on public display. After foundering in a storm off the coast of Cape Cod in 1717, the ship eluded treasure hunters until 1983. This small exhibition center has numerous artifacts recovered by ongoing salvage operations, from weapons and gold coins to a pirate's leather shoe. | 16 MacMillan Wharf | 508/487–8899 | www.whydah.com | $5 | Call for hrs.

Old Harbor Station. This former U.S. Life Saving Service building, floated by barge from Chatham when erosion threatened, houses life-saving equipment used 100 years ago to rescue stranded sailors from these treacherous waters. On Thursday evenings the stren-

PROVINCETOWN
(CAPE COD)

INTRO
ATTRACTIONS
DINING
LODGING

uous and primitive rescue procedures are reenacted. | Race Point Beach | 508/487–1256 | Donation requested; Thurs. night reenactment: $3 | July–Aug., Fri.–Wed. 3–5, Thurs. reenactment.: 6–7; late May–June and early Sept.–mid-Oct., daily 1:30–2:30.

Pilgrim Monument and Provincetown Museum. Visitors to the Pilgrim Monument first pass through the museum at its base, which contains a diverse group of historical exhibits on the Pilgrims and maritime history. You'll find displays on local Arctic explorer Donald MacMillan and Provincetown Playhouse founder Eugene O'Neill, and very dated depictions of the events that befell the *Mayflower* Pilgrims upon their arrival here at Provincetown in November 1620. | High Pole Hill | 508/487–1310 | fax 508/487–4702 | www.pilgrim-monument.org | $6 | Apr.–June and Sept.–Nov., daily 9–5; July–Aug., daily 9–7. Last admission 45 min before closing.

Pilgrim Monument. Built to resemble an Italian campanile, this 252-ft granite tower offers an unrivaled panorama from the observation deck at the top, with views of nearly the entire Cape Cod Bay shoreline in clear weather. It stands in recognition of the first New World landfall of the *Mayflower* in the town harbor a month before it proceeded across the bay to Plymouth Rock. There is no elevator, only stairs.

Province Lands Visitor Center. This National Park Service center, a must-stop on any Outer Cape itinerary, is filled to the brim with exhibits about life in the dunes and information on guided walks, birding trips, bonfires, and other current programs. Admire the lovely 360-degree view from the observation deck. | Race Point Rd. | 508/487–1256 | Free | Early Apr.–late Nov., daily 9–5.

Provincetown Art Association and Museum. Provincetown has been known as an artists' haven since the start of the 20th century. Consequently, this small regional museum's permanent collection, selections of which are always on display, encompasses nearly a century of art with a local connection. Special exhibits and juried shows of contemporary works are also featured. | 460 Commercial St. | 508/487–1750 | fax 508/487–4372 | www.capecodaccess.com/gallery/paam.html | $3 | Call for hrs.

Town Wharf (MacMillan Wharf). This long wharf jutting out into the protected anchorage that once harbored the *Mayflower* now bustles with the commercial activity of the local fishing fleet and cruise boats, as well as the work of yacht owners preparing their boats for the next outing into Cape Cod Bay.

Whale-watching. Dolphin Fleet of Provincetown. At the southern tip of the offshore Stellwagen National Marine Sanctuary, Provincetown has a front-row seat on one of the planet's prime whale-feeding grounds. Although it isn't unusual to spy the great ocean mammals out on the watery horizon even from shore, the Dolphin Fleet brings visitors eye-to-eye with the whales. | Chamber of Commerce Building, Lopes Sq. | 508/349–1900 or 800/826–9300 | fax 508/349–1789 | www.whalewatch.com | $19 | Apr.–Oct., daily.

Whale-watching. *Portuguese Princess* Whale-watch. Hop aboard this vessel and within a short time you, too, can be out among the humpbacks and northern right whales that frequent the nutrient-rich waters offshore. Sperm, sei, fin, and minke whales are among the other rare and endangered cetacean species that may be spotted. | 70 Shankpainter Rd. | 508/487–2651 or 800/442–3188 | fax 508/487–6458 | www.princesswhalewatch.com | $16–$20 | Apr.–Oct., daily.

ON THE CALENDAR

JUNE: *Portuguese Festival.* This four-day festival celebrates the Portuguese contribution to Provincetown's past and present. Past events have included children's activities such as face painting and a fishing derby, a swing band concert at Pilgrim Monument, the homecoming clam dinner and dance, a cookout, a food court offering Portuguese cuisine, a demonstration of Portuguese dancing, a festival parade, and mass at St. Peter's Church followed by the Blessing of the Fleet. | 508/487–3424.

AUG.: *Grand Carnival.* Beginning on the third Wednesday of the month and continuing for a week, this festival includes parades (on Thursday), rides, and an assortment of food and crafts vendors. | 888/637–8010.

Dining

Bubala's by the Bay. Eclectic. This funky and campy seaside eatery, complete with outdoor seating and great people-watching, has a varied menu. Fishermen drop their catch off daily at the back door, and the kitchen whips up Jamaican fish stew, Cuban cod and beans, and burgers. | 183 Commercial St. | 508/487–0773 | Breakfast also available. Closed Nov.–late Apr. | $14–$26 | AE, D, MC, V.

★ **Cafe Edwige.** Contemporary. Impossibly small, but the cheerful staff, cathedral ceilings, large windows overlooking the street below, and a menu of upscale, passionately flavorful food make this spot feel like a secret shared by a happy and lucky few. Try the crab cakes. Open-air dining on deck. No smoking. | 333 Commercial St. | 508/487–2008 | Closed mid-Oct.–mid-May | $19–$25 | MC, V.

Carreiro's Tips for Tops'n Restaurant. American/Casual. A decidedly low-brow family restaurant that serves standard diner fare like bacon and eggs, but also fish dishes with a Portuguese twist. | 31 Bradford St. | 508/487–1811 | Closed mid-Nov.–mid-Mar. | $9–$14 | MC, V.

Chester. Contemporary. Memorable, beautifully presented, and artfully prepared contemporary dishes such as asparagus and fiddlehead risotto or lamb with cranberry sauce are highlighted here. The Greek Revival sea captain's house has just an understated and elegant dining room. | 404 Commercial St. | 508/487–8200 | Closed Jan.–mid-May. No lunch | $19–$32 | AE, MC, V.

The Commons. Continental. This bistro has a seasonal, innovative menu that might feature seared halibut with lobster risotto. Outdoor dining and people watching are popular. | 386 Commercial St. | 508/487–7800 | Closed Jan.–Mar. | $12–$25 | AE, MC, V.

CAPE COD NATIONAL SEASHORE

Cape Cod National Seashore is sometimes characterized as one of John F. Kennedy's lasting legacies. The longtime Hyannis Port summer resident pushed for the creation of this, New England's only national seashore, the year he entered the White House. It includes the entire 40-mi-long Atlantic coast, from the barrier beaches protecting Chatham Harbor to the marshes and sand dunes surrounding Provincetown. Its 44,000 acres encompass some of the finest examples of the Cape's three crown jewels: history, recreation, and scenery. The first landing place of the Mayflower Pilgrims is here, in Provincetown. Old timber and metal from countless shipwrecks occasionally rise out of their sandy graves along the isolated beaches of Truro and Wellfleet. Eroding bluffs have exposed prehistoric artifacts, too, but otherwise the most accessible evidence of the Nauset tribe that lived here prior to the Pilgrims is the boulder they once used for sharpening stone tools, now found atop Fort Hill in Eastham. Bike paths zigzag through the Provincetown dunes, hiking trails loop through the refreshing shade of a mature beech forest, and boardwalks cross an old Truro cranberry bog. Lighthouses stand on the great heights of the backside bluffs, their foghorns and bright beacons still warning ships away from dangerous shoals offshore. Endangered piping plovers build nests on the beaches, herons stalk through the salt marshes looking for a fishy snack, deer browse through the woods, and gray seals frolic in the waters off Chatham. For information on ranger-guided walks, campfire talks, self-guiding tours, and other programs, be sure to visit the National Seashore visitors centers in Eastham and Provincetown.

Related towns: Chatham, Orleans, Eastham, Wellfleet, Truro, Provincetown

© Artville

Dancing Lobster. Italian. The large, rustic harborside dining room seems barely able to contain the exuberant menu of lusty Sicilian dishes, with hints of North Africa and southern France, all prepared with sophistication but presented with simplicity. No smoking. | 463 Commercial St. | 508/487–0900 | Reservations essential | Closed Dec.–early May and Mon. | $18–$40 | MC, V.

★ **Front Street.** Contemporary. This casual, always-crowded bistro has local art on display and a huge primarily Italian menu, which also incorporates upscale Mediterranean and French dishes, tropical fruits, and even such intriguing flavors as black tea. Try the corn and crab chowder, herb-crusted rack of lamb, and the tea-smoked duck. There is also an extensive wine list. | 230 Commercial St. | 508/487–9715 | Reservations essential | $23–$40 | AE, D, MC, V.

Lobster Pot. Portuguese. Fragrant, richly flavorful, and belt-stretchingly large stews and seafood dishes ensure most patrons will have to be happily rolled out—though not before enjoying the harbor views. Try the *sopa do mar*—a bouillabaisse-type soup made from scallops, clams, oysters, mussels, shrimp, calamari, and fish poached in a provincial-style stock—or the *shellfish cataplana*—mussels, shrimp, and scallops simmered with Portuguese sausage, mushrooms, scallions, red potatoes, marinara sauce, and fish—or baked, stuffed fish Portuguese-style. No smoking in dining rooms. | 321 Commercial St. | 508/487–0842 | www.ptownlobsterpot.com | Closed mid-Dec.–early Feb. | $18–$35 | AE, D, DC, MC, V.

Lorraine's. Mexican. Local seafood influences the home-style, Mexican-inspired dishes at this robust and festive seaside eatery. Frequent entertainment and a lively bar clientele keep the place hopping. Nightly specials are always a good bet, but so are slow-cooked pork tenderloin with guacamole and steamed clams in a cilantro citrus broth. | 463 Commercial St. | 508/487–6074 | Closed Jan.–Mar. No lunch | $15–$24 | MC, V.

Martin House. Contemporary. New England food jazzed up by world influences inspires palates here night after night. The menu changes seasonally but you may find roasted lamb rib eye with mint chutney and quinoa–wild rice tabbouleh. The small romantic dining rooms, many with a fireplace, date to 1850. | 157 Commercial St. | 508/487–1327 | Closed Jan.–Mar., Tues.–Wed. No lunch | $16–$32 | AE, D, DC, MC, V.

The Mews. Contemporary. This longtime waterfront favorite, with soft romantic lighting and sublime service, reigns with seafood accented by cross-cultural influences. Popular entrées include spicy scallops and shrimp-and-crab mousse in a wonton on grilled filet mignon. The upstairs dining room is less formal, with a piano bar and lighter offerings from the same kitchen. | 429 Commercial St. | 508/487–1500 | No lunch mid-Oct.–mid-May, Mon.–Sat. | $10–$26 | AE, D, DC, MC, V.

★ **Mojo's.** Fast Food. A local institution since the early 1970s, this seasonal seafood shack has everything you'd expect (fried clams and french fries), but also the unexpected (hummus, tacos, and tofu burgers). Don't leave town without stopping here once. | 5 Ryder St. Ext. | 508/487–3140 | Closed mid-Oct.–early May | $2–$10 | No credit cards.

The Moors. Portuguese. Fishing nets, boating gear, and driftwood walls add an appropriately sea-salted ambience to this local institution. Hearty Portuguese fare, redolent of the sea, dominates the menu. Live music Wed.–Mon. late May–Sept., weekends rest of season. Kids' menu. Early bird suppers Sun.–Fri. No smoking in dining room. | 5 Bradford St. W | 508/487–0840 | Closed Nov.–Apr. | $13–$21 | AE, MC, V.

★ **Napi's.** Eclectic. A large collection of art, including paintings, sculpture, stained glass, graphics, ceramics, and crafts, creates an unusual setting that matches the multinational, polyglot menu ranging from Thai chicken to Brazilian steak, Greek shrimp to Italian pasta, with extensive vegetarian selections as well. Free parking, too, a Provincetown rarity. Kids' menu. Early bird suppers. No smoking. | 7 Freeman St. | 508/487–1145 | No lunch June–early Sept. | $13–$27 | AE, D, DC, MC, V.

Red Inn. Continental. The elegant dining rooms in this restored 1805 captain's mansion have Federal-era antiques, watery vistas through multipaned windows, and off-season warmth from a country fireplace. There's plenty of seafood and steak on the menu. Try the lobster stew or steak au poivre. No smoking. | 15 Commercial St. | 508/487–0050 | Reservations essential | Closed Mon.–Thurs. Dec.–Apr. No lunch | $29–$34 | AE, MC, V.

Sal's Place. Italian. From the moment you walk into this historic building, you'll sense the Italian slant of the restaurant. Chianti bottles are suspended from the ceiling in the front room, while in the back room you can dine overlooking the water. The portions are big, the flavors bold, and the mood is invitingly cozy. Try the steak Pizzaiola, a rib-eye steak in a marinara sauce that has olives and mushrooms. Open-air dining on deck. Beer and wine only. | 99 Commercial St. | 508/487–1279 | Closed Nov.–Apr. Closed Tues.–Thurs. in May and Sept.–Oct. No lunch | $12–$25 | MC, V.

Spiritus. Pizzeria. A wildly popular pizza joint by day and night, this place really gets going when the bars close at 1 AM and everyone who is still awake runs over here. Spiritus also serves strong coffee and croissants to the same crowd the next morning. | 190 Commercial St. | 508/487–2808 | Closed Nov.–Mar. | $2–$2.75 | No credit cards.

Lodging

Beaconlight Guesthouse. Close enough to the action for fun but far enough away for quiet, this elegant B&B has English overtones, designer wallpapers, antiques, and luxurious little extras such as six pillows on each bed. Outside, there are three decks from which to take in the town and harbor. It has a mostly gay clientele. Complimentary Continental breakfast. In-room data ports, refrigerators, cable TV. Outdoor hot tub. No pets. No smoking. | 12 Winthrop St. | 508/487–9603 or 800/696–9603 | fax 508/487–9603 | www.capecod.net/beaconlight | 7 rooms, 3 suites | $115–$175 | AE, D, MC, V.

Best Western Chateau Motor Inn. Landscaped grounds and gardens raise this basic motel property to a slightly higher level. It's a 15-minute walk from the commercial area, close to tennis courts and beaches, and some rooms have water views. Complimentary Continental breakfast. In-room data ports, some refrigerators, cable TV. Pool. Business services. | 105 Bradford St. W | 508/487–1286 | fax 508/487–3557 | chateau@bwprovincetown.com | www.bwprovincetown.com | 54 rooms | $159–$189 | Closed mid-Oct.–Apr. | AE, D, DC, MC, V.

Best Western Tides Beachfront. This family-oriented property has a 600-ft beach that is groomed every morning. The motel is in the east end, bordering Truro, 1½ mi from the bustle of downtown Provincetown. Restaurant. In-room data ports, refrigerators, cable TV. Pool. Beach. Laundry facilities. Business services. | 837 Commercial St. | 508/487–1045 | fax 508/487–1621 | tides@bwprovincetown.com | www.bwprovincetown.com | 64 rooms | $139–$219 | Closed mid-Oct.–Apr. | AE, D, DC, MC, V.

Blue Sea Motor Inn. Look here for a basic family-owned and -operated motel 1½ mi from the commercial center. There's a view of Provincetown from the private beach and from some guest rooms. Picnic area. In-room data ports, refrigerators, TV. Indoor pool. Hot tub. Beach. Laundry facilities. | 696 Shore Rd. | 508/487–1041 | www.blueseamotorinn.com | 32 rooms, 11 suites | $137–$172 | Closed mid-Oct.–Apr. | MC, V.

Bradford-Carver House. This carefully restored house has stylish rooms with antiques, ceiling fans, in-room CD players, and hundreds of videos for the VCRs. Rooms with gas fireplaces rent quickly. Complimentary Continental breakfast. In-room data ports, refrigerators, cable TV. No kids. No pets. No smoking. | 70 Bradford St. | 508/487–4966 or 800/826–9083 | fax 508/487–7213 | www.capecod.net/bradfordcarver | 5 rooms | $49–$199 | Closed Jan. | AE, D, MC, V.

Bradford Gardens Inn. This multiple-building inn is popular with lesbians; however, all are welcome to stay and enjoy the inn's beautiful decor, including, pine floors, antiques, and artwork. On the grounds are lush, extensive gardens. Many rooms have fireplaces. It's three blocks from the center of town and one block from the beach. Complimentary breakfast. Some microwaves, refrigerators, cable TV, in-room VCRs and movies. Some pets allowed. | 178 Bradford St. | 508/487–1616 or 800/432–2334 | fax 508/487–5596 | www.brad-fordgardens.com | 8 rooms, 3 cottages, 2 town houses, 1 penthouse | $85–$155 | AE, MC, V.

Bradford House and Motel. This motel and Victorian guest house property has a cherry four-poster bed in every room. It's in the west end, a five-minute walk from the center and the bay—close to beaches and bike rentals. Complimentary Continental breakfast (in season). Refrigerators, cable TV, no room phones. | 41 Bradford St. | 508/487–0173 | fax 508/487–0173 | www.bradfordhousemotel.com | 19 rooms | $135–$175 | MC, V.

★ **Brass Key.** When this hotel opened its doors in 1992, a whole new standard for P-lodging emerged. Completely restored from a 1830 sea captain's home, this luxurious inn and its adjacent buildings form a private enclave. Chic and oh-so-tasteful guest rooms feature scads of antiques paired with ultra-modern amenities like Bose stereos; some have fireplaces. The staff pampers guests, who enjoy being close to shops and restaurants but also getting away from them. The clientele is mostly gay and lesbian. There is complimentary wine and snacks at night. Complimentary Continental breakfast. In-room safes, some in-room hot tubs, cable TV, in-room VCRs. Pool. No pets. No smoking. | 67 Bradford St. | 508/487–9005 or 800/842–9858 | fax 508/487–9020 | www.brasskey.com | 36 rooms | $225–$425 | Closed early Nov.–mid-Apr. | AE, D, MC, V.

Cape Colony Inn. These motel rooms have standard-issue furnishings and are about a 20-minute walk from the center of town. Free movies. Refrigerators. Outdoor pool. Volleyball. No pets. | 280 Bradford St. | 508/487–1755 | www.capecolonyinn.com | 57 rooms | $105–$108 | Closed mid-Oct.–Apr. | D, MC, V.

The Captain and His Ship. A short walk from the center of town, these immaculate and spacious rooms are filled with period antiques and Oriental carpets. The 1887 sea captain's house, a Victorian with mansard roof, has harbor-view rooms. Complimentary Continental breakfast. No pets. No smoking. | 164 Commercial St. | 508/487–1850 or 800/400–2278 | www.captainandhisship.com | 9 rooms (2 with shared bath) | $85–$185 | Closed Nov.–Apr. | AE, MC, V.

The Commons. Right in the middle of town, this inn has comfortable and tasteful rooms, with wide-board floors, antiques, Oriental carpets, and marble baths. Some have bay-view balconies. Restaurant, bar, complimentary breakfast. | 386 Commercial St. | 508/487–7800 or 800/487–0784 | fax 508/487–6114 | www.capecod.net/commons | 14 rooms | $110–$165 | Closed Jan.–mid-Apr. | AE, MC, V.

Fairbanks Inn. The integrity of this historic 1776 inn in the center of town has been maintained, including its wide-plank pine floors and some original fireplaces. The inn has antique furnishings, a courtyard garden, and a sundeck. All but three rooms have a four-poster bed and working fireplace. Complimentary Continental breakfast. Cable TV. No kids under 15. No smoking. | 90 Bradford St. | 508/487–0386 or 800/324–7265 | fax 508/487–3540 | www.fairbanksinn.com | 14 rooms (2 with shared bath) | $110–$225 | AE, MC, V.

Land's End Inn. At the western end of town, about a 20-minute walk to the center, this quirky hilltop inn is filled to the brim with collections of Art Deco and Art Nouveau treasures, stained glass, wood carvings, and plants. Guest rooms are works of art and many have private decks and panoramic views of the harbor. Complimentary Continental breakfast. Some in-room hot tubs, some kitchenettes, no cable TV in some rooms. No pets. No smoking. | 22 Commercial St. | 508/487–0706 | fax 508/487–0706 | 14 rooms, 3 apartments | $85–$210 | MC, V.

Masthead Motel and Cottages. For a traditional Cape Cod cottage–style lodging on a 450-ft private beach, look no further than this quiet west end property. All apartments, suites, and cottages have ocean views. Picnic area. Some kitchenettes, refrigerators, cable TV, some in-room VCRs. Beach. | 31–41 Commercial St. | 508/487–0523 or 800/395–5095 | fax 508/487–9251 | www.capecodtravel.com/masthead | 9 rooms (2 with shared bath), 2 suites, 4 cottages, 7 apartments | $81–$197 | AE, D, DC, MC, V.

The Meadows. These motel-style rooms, between the center of town and the beach, are a good value and are popular with families. They're clean and bright, with standard motel furnishings. Refrigerators, cable TV. No pets. | 122 Bradford St. Ext. | 508/487–0880 or 888/675–0880 | fax 508/487–4691 | 20 rooms | $70–$80 | Closed Nov.–Mar. | MC, V.

Provincetown Inn. In summer, kids 12 and under stay and eat free at this family-friendly resort. This property—surrounded by water on three sides—has a private beach that adjoins the Cape Cod National Seashore and breakwater. There's nightly theater during the summer. Guests can leave their cars in the inn parking lot and take the public shuttle to town and other beaches. Restaurant, bar, picnic area, complimentary Continental breakfast. Cable TV. Pool. Beach. Business services. | 1 Commercial St. | 508/487–9500 or 800/942–5388 (in New England) | fax 508/487–2911 | www.provincetowninn.com | 100 rooms, 2 suites | $119–$184 | AE, MC, V.

Ship's Bell Inn. This beach-front inn is in the quiet east end, a 20-minute walk from the commercial center. It has a pretty front lawn and private patio. Picnic area. No air-conditioning, some kitchenettes, some microwaves, cable TV. Beach. | 586 Commercial St. | 508/487–1674 | fax 508/487–1675 | nancy@shipsbell.com | www.shipsbellinn.com | 8 rooms, 2 apartments, 6 studios, 1 suite | $89–$150 | Closed mid-Nov.–Apr. | AE, D, MC, V.

Somerset House Inn. Each room of this Victorian inn is decorated with antiques and period reproductions. The property is in the east end of town, near many galleries. Between May and September the inn has a mostly gay/lesbian clientele. Complimentary Continental breakfast. In-room data ports, refrigerators, cable TV. No smoking. | 378 Commercial St. | 508/487–0383 or 800/575–1850 | fax 508/487–4237 | www.somersethouseinn.com | 13 rooms (3 with shared bath), 1 apartment | $125–$200 | AE, MC, V.

Surfside Inn. Within walking distance of the center of town, this modern motel is right on the beach. Half the standard-issue rooms face the water; the others overlook the pool and Commercial Street. Pool. Pets allowed (fee). | 543 Commercial St. | 508/487–172 | fax 508/487–2087 | www.surfsideinn.cc | 84 rooms | $129–$189 | Closed late Oct.–mid-Mar. | D, MC, V.

Watermark Inn. From the street, the east end inn looks like a traditional Cape Cod house (though historically it's not), but the interior, designed by the owner-architect, is contemporary. The house is built on a seawall jutting out over the water, offering panoramic views of the bay. Some rooms have private decks and some have 13-ft ceilings and glass gables. The property is ½ mi from the commercial center and has a private beach. Kitchenettes, microwaves, cable TV. Beach. | 603 Commercial St. | 508/487–0165 | fax 508/487–2383 | www.watermark-inn.com | 10 suites | $150–$315 | AE, MC, V.

Watership Inn. This 1820 sea captain's house is now a rustic inn with spacious common rooms and antiques throughout that primarily caters to gay and lesbian guests. Relax in the gardens or yard—or play volleyball and croquet. The property is also one block from the harbor. Picnic area, complimentary Continental breakfast. No air-conditioning in some rooms, cable TV, no room phones. Volleyball. | 7 Winthrop St. | 508/487–0094 or 800/330–9413 | www.capecod.net/watershipinn | 15 rooms, 2 2-bedroom apartments | $90–$140 | AE, D, MC, V.

White Wind Inn. This large white Victorian inn is a Provincetown landmark at the start of the west end. The front porch is ideal for people-watching. Public rooms are decorated with antiques, chandeliers, art, and stained glass. The large guest rooms have high ceilings and four-poster beds; several rooms have water views and fireplaces. During the summer, the guests are mostly gay and lesbian. Picnic area, complimentary Continental breakfast. In-room data ports, refrigerators, cable TV. Some pets allowed. | 174 Commercial St. | 508/487–1526 or 888/449–WIND | fax 508/487–4792 | www.whitewindinn.com | 12 rooms (7 with shower only), 1 apartment | $120–$225 | AE, MC, V.

PROVINCETOWN

INTRO
ATTRACTIONS
DINING
LODGING

QUINCY

(Nearby towns also listed: Boston, Braintree, Dedham)

Settled by English traders in 1625, Quincy is best known as the home of two presidents, John Adams and John Quincy Adams. In addition to sending its native sons to serve the nation, the city provided high-quality paving and building stone from its granite quarries for more than 200 years, and its shipyards have been almost continuously active in one form or another since the 1700s. If Quincy's hopes for building supertankers materialize, it will be able to lay claim to virtually the last heavy industry in Massachusetts. Separated from Boston by no more than a river and linked to it by mass transit, Quincy and its hotels are close enough to provide a convenient and affordable alternative to downtown Boston. And remember to pronounce the name the way the locals do: "Quin-zee."

Information: South Shore Chamber of Commerce | Box 690625, Quincy, 02269 | 617/479–1111 | www.southshorechamber.org.

Attractions

Abigail Adams House. Abigail Smith (1744–1818), daughter of a Weymouth clergyman, has attained a lasting place in history as the wife of America's second president, John Adams, and mother of the sixth, John Quincy Adams. Biographers, meanwhile, have shown that she deserves attention on her own merits as political advisor, diarist, and correspondent. The 1685 farmhouse in which she was born has been restored to its mid-1700s appearance. | 180 Norton St., Weymouth | 781/335–7065 | $1 | July–early Sept., Tues.–Sun.

Adams National Historical Park. Administered by the National Park Service, these historic sites encompass five generations (1720–1927) of the illustrious Adams family, including two presidents and first ladies, three ministers, historians, and writers. | 1250 Hancock St. | 617/770–1175 | fax 617/472–7562 | www.nps.gov/adam | $2 | Mid-Apr.–mid-Nov., daily 9–5, last tour at 3:50; mid-Nov.–mid-Apr., Tues.–Fri. 10–4, no tours.
John Adams and John Quincy Adams Birthplaces. These two saltbox houses date from the seventeenth century. The elder Adams was born and raised at 133 Franklin Street; his son at 141 Franklin Street. Guided tours are available.
United First Parish Church. This is the only church in the United States where two former presidents (and their wives) are buried: John Adams and John Quincy Adams. Tours of the church are offered separately from the park tour. | 1306 Hancock St. | 617/773–1290 | $2.

Granite Railway Quarry-to-Wharf tours. Quincy is also the birthplace of large-scale granite quarrying (1825) and the first commercial railway (1826) in the nation. Quincy granite was valued for its hardness, dark color, and ability to take a high polish. Until the last quarry closed in 1963, Quincy granite was used in the construction of many buildings and monuments—including the Bunker Hill monument in Charlestown and the customs houses in Boston, Savannah, New Orleans, and San Francisco. Tours trace the route of granite from the quarries of West Quincy to the wharf on the Neponset River in North Quincy where the stone was loaded onto boats. | 617/822–4046 | Call for hrs. Reservations required.

Josiah Quincy House. This fine Georgian house was the home of the Quincy family. It is furnished with period wall paneling, fireplaces surrounded by English tile, and family heirlooms. | 20 Muirhead St. | 617/227–3956 | $2 | June–Oct. 15, tours on the hr weekends 11–4.

U.S. Naval Shipbuilding Museum. This museum is aboard the U.S.S. *Salem*, the 717-ft flagship of the U.S. Navy's sixth fleet. On a guided tour, you can see one of the engine rooms, visit the ship's bridge, and go below deck where more than 1,600 officers and sailors lived and worked. Step inside one of the three 8-inch gun turrets that once fired 260-pound shells almost 18 miles. | 739 Washington St. | 617/479–7900 | fax 617/479–8792 | www.uss-salem.org | $6 | Oct.–Apr., weekends 10–4; May–Sept., daily 10–4.

Quincy Historical Society. Occupying a former boy's school donated to the town by John Adams, this historical museum is located on the site where John Hancock, Revolutionary War–era president of the Continental Congress, was born. Exhibits detail Quincy's evolution from country retreat to industrial city, illustrated by artifacts, photos, and ephemera from the society's collections. There is also a research library. | Adams Academy Building, 8 Adams St. | 617/773–1144 | fax 617/472–4990 | Free | Weekdays 9–4, 1st Sat. of each month 1–4.

Quincy Homestead. Four generations of Quincys lived here, including Dorothy Quincy, who became the wife of John Hancock. Two of the rooms were built in 1686, the others in the 18th century. Admire period furnishings and the herb garden. | 1010 Hancock St. | 617/472–5117 | $3 | May–Oct., Wed.–Sun. noon–5.

ON THE CALENDAR
JUNE: *Blues Festival.* Regional and national blues performers are featured at this annual festival at Veteran's Memorial Stadium on the last Saturday of the month. | 617/472–9383.
JUNE–SEPT.: *South Shore Music Circus.* This 2,300-seat theater-in-the-round—15 mi south of Quincy—hosts celebrity concerts, country, blues, oldies, comedy, and children's shows. Every seat in the tent is within 50 ft of the stage. | 781/383–1400.
OCT.: *Birthday of John Adams.* This ceremony at United First Parish Church honors the life and public service of our nation's second president, John Adams. | 617/770–1175.
OCT.: *Spirits of Quincy's Past.* Behind the iron gates of the Hancock Cemetery, park rangers and volunteers take visitors on a candlelight tour of one of New England's oldest burying grounds. Historic figures "come back to life" to talk about what they did to help their community and their nation prosper. Refreshments of cider and angel or devil's food cake are served. | 617/770–1175.
NOV.: *City of Quincy Christmas Parade.* A weeklong series of holiday festivities begins with the annual Christmas Parade, which includes more than 20 bands, 24 floats, many specialty units, and a well-known honored guest—Santa Claus. | 617/376–1392.

Dining

Restaurant at The Red Lion Inn. Contemporary. This 1704 seaside inn, 6 mi south of Quincy, has an old-world flavor with low ceilings, antique beams, wide-plank floorboards, old handmade pine tables, and a wood-burning fireplace in each of the four dining rooms. The fresh seafood dishes are standouts on the menu. Try the charred rare tuna with glass-noodle salad or the Atlantic halibut in potato crust. Watch the preparations in the open kitchen. Outdoor seating available. | 71 S. Main St., Cohasset | 781/383–1704 | fax 781/383–9231 | www.theredlioninn1704.com | Closed Mon. No lunch | $14–$23 | AE, MC, V.

Siros. Contemporary. This waterside restaurant offers a view of boating activity at Marina Bay, on the Squantum peninsula in Quincy. There's inside seating for 120 people and, in summer, umbrella tables for 120 diners on the pier. Try the lobster-and-asparagus ravioli with orange-saffron cream sauce or the tuna puttanesca served over spaghetti. | 307 Victory Rd., Marina Bay | 617/472–4500 | Mid-Oct.–mid-May, closed Mon. | $16–$25 | AE, D, DC, MC, V.

X and O European Trattoria. Mediterranean. Old world meets new in this 184-seat trattoria in the center of Quincy. This eatery has stucco walls in rich gold and green hues, hardwood floors, marble-inlaid tables, and a long polished bar. Try one of the Italian or Greek specialties. Watch the pizzas bake in the colorfully tiled brick oven. Don't miss the baklava. | 1388 Hancock St. | 617/479–1900 | fax 617/328–7620 | www.xoeuropeantrattoria.com | No lunch weekends | $6–$22 | AE, D, DC, MV, V.

Lodging

Allen House. The inside of this 1905 shingle-style Colonial 20 mi south of Quincy has been restored with soft colors in a light and airy country style. The honeymoon room (complete with hot tub, fireplace, solarium area, and patio) is on its own floor surrounded by gardens. Breakfast might include baked-raspberry French toast, apple pancakes, and fruit scones. Complimentary breakfast. Some in-room hot tubs, no room phones. No kids under 12. No smoking. | 18 Allen Pl., Scituate | 781/545–8221 | fax 781/544–3192 | www.allenhousebnb.com | 6 rooms | $109–$199 | AE, MC, V.

Best Western Adams Inn. This inn features a boardwalk and gazebo over the Neponset River; some rooms have water views. The property is a pickup/drop-off point for Boston trolley sightseeing tours. Bar, complimentary Continental breakfast. Some in-room data ports, some refrigerators, cable TV. Pool. Business services, airport shuttle. | 29 Hancock St. | 617/328–1500 | fax 617/328–3067 | www.bwadamsinn.com | 100 rooms | $129–$159 | AE, D, DC, MC, V.

Clipper Ship Lodge. This gray New England–style clapboard building with white trim is at the east end of town. The large rooms have harbor views. The property is across the street from charter boating and fishing, within walking distance of shops and antiques stores, and a 20-minute drive from the commuter boat to Boston. Beach passes are provided. Restaurant, bar. Refrigerators, cable TV. Indoor pool. No pets. | 7 Beaver Dam Rd., Scituate | 781/545–5550 or 800/368–3818 | fax 781/545–9271 | www.cippershiplodge.com | 28 rooms, 1 suite | $109–$167 | AE, D, DC, MC, V.

Presidents' City Inn. This 1950s-style motel has a one-story wing (where you can park in front of your room) and a two-story wing. All guest rooms have double beds, cherry furniture, and ceramic showers—but no tubs. The café, which opens at 5:30 AM, serves breakfast and lunch. The motel is on a busy street across from Merrymount Park and the municipal stadium. It's a 5-minute walk to the Wollaston T stop. Restaurant. Cable TV. No pets. | 845 Hancock St. | 617/479–6500 | fax 617/479–6500 | 36 rooms | $102–$108 | AE, MC, V.

The Red Lion Inn. The guest rooms of this 1704 seaside inn in Cohasset Village have antique furnishings and working wood-burning or gas-lit fireplaces; most have four-poster beds, some have canopy beds. Original paintings and reproductions of scenes from old Cohasset postcards adorn the walls. On display in public areas of the inn are old coins and papers from 1745 to 1900 found on the property. Restaurant, bar. In-room data ports, some in-room hot tubs, cable TV, in-room VCRs. No pets. No smoking. | 71 South Main St., Cohasset | 781/383–1704 | fax 781/383–9231 | www.theredlioninn1704.com | 15 rooms | $185–$375 | AE, MC, V.

ROCKPORT

MAP 6, J2

(Nearby towns also listed: Essex, Gloucester)

More shore than town, tiny Rockport juts out into the Atlantic at the end of Cape Ann. With ocean on three sides and woods at its back, Rockport is a village of small picturesque harbors and classic seaside inns and motels. Like neighboring Gloucester, it's home to a vibrant artists' community, and you'll find plenty of art galleries full of seascapes and other local scenes. Thanks to the rail connection to Boston, many of Rockport's 8,000 residents commute. In summer the town's population nearly triples, as vacationers flock here for the shops, beaches, and scenic views.

Information: **Rockport Chamber of Commerce** | 3 Main St., Rockport, 01966 | 978/546–6575 or 888/726–3922. **Information Booth** (mid-May–mid-Oct.) | Upper Main St., Rockport | info@rockportusa.com | www.rockportusa.com.

Attractions

Bearskin Neck. Enjoy one of the best ocean views in town from this section of Sandy Beach. Bearskin Neck is named after a legendary skirmish between man and beast, in which a menacing bear was slain and skinned with a knife. To get to Bearskin Neck, take Rte. 127A

(Broadway) East to its end, take a left at Dock Square, and the Bearskin Neck Pennisula will be on the right. || Daily.

Halibut Point State Park. This park on steep granite cliffs that descend into tidal pools is filled with wildflowers and wildlife, especially birds. Time your visit to catch a granite-cutting demonstration or a guided wildflower walk. Recently an observation tower was converted into a visitors center with exhibits about the natural history of the land. The park is 3 mi north of downtown Rockport, off Rte. 127. | Gott Ave. | 978/546–2997 | Free | Daily, sunrise–sunset.

Rockport Art Association. Since 1920, the Rockport Art Association is one of the oldest organizations of its kind in the country. Its gallery displays the work of 250 living artists. | 12 Main St. | 978/546–6604 | Free | May–Sept., daily 10–5; Oct.–Apr., Tues.–Sun. 10–4.

Twin Lights. On Thacher Island, about ½ mi off the coast, you'll see two 165-ft lighthouses dating from the mid-1800s, one of which is still in operation. Commercial tours are not offered, but private boats can access the island, and rumor has it that if you ask the lightkeeper, he'll let you peek around inside. | Thacher Island | 978/546–7697 | www.shore.net/~gfisher/tia | Free.

ON THE CALENDAR
JUNE: *Rockport Chamber Music Festival.* This festival, which takes place for four weekends in June (starting on Thursdays), features chamber ensembles and soloists of international reputation. Concerts are held in the Rockport Art Association's Hibbard Gallery. | 978/546–7391.

Dining
Brackett's Oceanview Restaurant. American. Stop here and dine in front of picture windows overlooking the shore. The broad menu includes burgers, pasta, fried seafood, shrimp scampi, London broil, and other basic favorites. Kids' menu. BYOB. No smoking in dining room. | 29 Main St. | 978/546–2797 | Closed Nov.–Mar. | $8.95–$19.95 | AE, D, DC, MC, V.

Cafe Natura. Cafés. Healthy vegetarian sandwiches and soups make up the menu. Favorites include mozzarella, tomato, and basil on a baguette, and the Portobello mushroom sandwich. Local artists are prominently displayed. | 32 Bearskin Neck | 978/546–5200 | $5–$7 | No credit cards.

Ellen's Harborside. Seafood. No-nonsense seafood is the featured cuisine, and the walls are festooned with fishermen's implements. Try the fried clams and broiled haddock, and enjoy a lovely harbor view. | 1 T Wharf | 978/546–2512 | Closed Nov.–Apr. | $7–$20 | MC, V.

Emerson Inn by the Sea. Continental. One hundred yards from the sea, this inn has fantastic views, especially from the verandah. Try the Rockport bouillabaisse, or the grilled scallop and lobster fettuccine. | 1 Cathedral Ave. | 978/546–6321 or 800/964–5550 | Reservations essential | Closed Jan.–March and Mon.–Tues. No lunch | $18–$35 | AE, D, DC, MC, V.

The Greenery. Contemporary. An interesting view and traditional seafood dishes draw crowds to this restaurant. Try the grilled catch of the day or the bouillabaisse linguine. | 15 Dock St. | 978/546–9593 | Closed Jan.–Apr. | $10–$22 | D, DC, MC, V.

Helmut's Strudel. Café. You can get a sandwich here but the focus is definitely on the homemade fruit strudels. Eat one while enjoying a harbor view. | 49 Bearskin Neck | 978/546–2824 | Breakfast also available | $3–$10 | No credit cards.

My Place By the Sea. Seafood. You'll find it hard to choose which is better, the food or the views, at this lovely spot featuring adventurous dishes and a French design. Try the Szechuan salmon or the caramelized sea scallops. | 68 South Rd. | 978/546–9667 | fax 978/546–2033 | Reservations essential | Closed Nov.–Apr. | $17–$25 | AE, D, DC, MC, V.

Peg Leg Inn and Restaurant. American. Ocean views, a friendly staff, and casual decorations create a welcome feeling. An extensive menu of well-prepared classics includes lobster Thermidor, chicken pot pie, and baked stuffed shrimp. Open-air dining in greenhouse. Kids' menu. BYOB. | 18 Beach St. | 978/546–3038 | Closed Nov.–mid-Apr. | $9.95–$25.95 | AE, DC, MC, V.

Portside Chowder. Seafood. Chowders and grilled fish make up the menu at this nautical-themed spot. | 2 Doyle's Cove Rd. | 978/546–7045 | No dinner Oct.–Apr., no dinner Mon.–Thurs. May–June and Sept. | $10–$20 | No credit cards.

Seagarden Restaurant. Continental. Dine in one of three rooms here: the Rose Room, which has a New England feel and ocean views; the Brick Room, with ocean views and a brick floor; and the Mahogany Room, which resembles an old English library. Try the pan-seared breast of duck with pomegranate glaze or the filet mignon with wild mushrooms. | 44 Marmion Way | 978/546–3471 | Closed Nov.–mid-Apr. Closed Mon. No lunch | $16–$26 | AE, D, DC, MC, V.

Veranda at the Yankee Clipper Inn. Contemporary. This upscale restaurant is on the enclosed porch of a classic New England seaside inn with gorgeous ocean views. Try the cranberry balsamic duck breast or the shrimp and lobster fettucine. Kids' menu. BYOB. No smoking. | 96 Granite St. | 978/546–7795 | Reservations essential | Apr.–Sept., closed Mon. Oct.–early Dec., closed weekdays. Closed mid-Dec.–Mar. | $16–$36 | AE, D, MC, V.

Lodging

★ **Addison Choate Inn.** This 1851 Greek Revival inn has period furnishings, pinewood floors, some canopy beds, and beautiful gardens. It's two blocks from the harbor. Complimentary Continental breakfast. Cable TV, no room phones. Business services. No smoking. | 49 Broadway | 978/546–7543 or 800/245–7543 | fax 978/546–7638 | www.addisonchoate.com | 6 rooms (3 with shower only), 2 suites | $115–$195 | AE, D, DC, MC, V.

Beach Knoll Inn. You'll find original details such as pine floors and beamed ceilings in this 1740 building, along with lovely views of Back Beach in Sandy Bay today. Complimentary Continental breakfast. Kitchenettes, microwaves, refrigerators, cable TV, some room phones. No pets. No smoking. | 30 Beach St. | 978/546–6939 | fax 978/546–3529 | www.tiac.net/users/janef/beknolli.htm | 5 rooms, 5 suites | $72–$102 | No credit cards.

The Blueberry. Feel a part of the Hogan family as they share their home with you at this tiny bed-and-breakfast. Handmade quilts grace each room, and Mrs. Hogan's muffins have blueberries she picked herself. The Blueberry is in a residential area, but the yard adjoins woods with hiking trails. Guest rooms share a bath. Complimentary breakfast. Cable TV, no room phones. Pets allowed. No smoking. | 50 Stockholm Ave. | 978/546–2838 | members.aol.com/rockportBB | 2 rooms | $75 | No credit cards.

Captain's Bounty Motor Inn. This motel is right on the water in the harbor area, and all rooms have ocean views. It's also less than a five-minute walk from the train station. No air-conditioning, some kitchenettes, some microwaves, cable TV. | 1 Beach St. | 978/546–9557 | www.cape-ann.com | 24 rooms | $110–$140 | Closed Nov.–Apr. | D, MC, V.

Eagle House Motel. You'll find this white-clapboard motel on a residential side street across from the beach and close to town. It has gardens and a patio, and most of the rooms have tables and chairs outside. Some kitchenettes, refrigerators, cable TV. | 8 Cleaves St. | 978/546–6292 | fax 978/546–1136 | www.rockportusa.com/eaglehouse | 15 rooms | $89–$94 | Closed mid-Oct.–Apr. | AE, D, MC, V.

Emerson Inn by the Sea. Ralph Waldo Emerson summered here, penning a few works while seated on the rocky shore in front. The original structure, built in 1840, has a columned front porch and a 140-ft verandah overlooking the ocean. A 1913 addition has beautiful moldings, high ceilings, and an elegant grand parlor and dining room. The inn's lawn, which slopes down to the shore, has a rock garden in the middle, and there's also an antique perennial garden on the grounds. Complimentary breakfast. In-room data ports, cable TV in common area. Outdoor pool. Hot tub, massage, sauna. No smoking. | 1 Cathedral Ave., Pigeon

Cove | 978/546–6321 or 800/964–5550 | fax 978/546–7043 | www.emersoninnbythesea.com | 35 rooms, 2 suites | $125–$235 | Closed mid-Jan.–Feb. | AE, D, DC, MC, V.

Eden Pines Inn. This "inn" is actually a cedar-shingle summer cottage, with a small garden, a huge porch, and two sunbathing patios. The six guest rooms have cherry and wicker furniture, and magnificent ocean views. Complimentary Continental breakfast. Cable TV, no room phones. No pets. No kids under 13. No smoking. | 48 Eden Rd. | 978/546–2505 | fax 978/546–1157 | www.rockportusa.com/edenpinesinn | 6 rooms | $150–$175 | Closed Oct.–May | MC, V.

Inn on Cove Hill. Built in 1791, this antiques-filled inn has wide-plank pine floors and a Federal-style spiral staircase with a hand-carved wooden bannister. The third-floor porch has a panoramic view of the harbor, and most rooms have canopy beds. A Continental breakfast is served in the garden, or can be brought to your room. The inn is in a quiet residential neighborhood on the edge of downtown, five-minutes by foot from the beach. Complimentary Continental breakfast. Cable TV, no room phones. No smoking. | 37 Mt. Pleasant St. | 978/546–2701 or 888/546–2701 | www.cape-ann.com/covehill | 11 rooms (2 with shared bath) | $49–$123 | Closed mid-Oct.–mid-Apr. | MC, V.

Linden Tree Inn. Named for the huge linden tree that graces its front lawn, this antiques-filled inn is on a quiet street in town, about 800 ft from Front Beach. There's a lovely garden on the property, and the front porch overlooks the harbor. Picnic area, complimentary Continental breakfast. No air-conditioning in some rooms, some kitchenettes, no room phones. No smoking. | 26 King St. | 978/546–2494 or 800/865–2122 | fax 978/546–3297. | www.lindentree.com | 19 rooms (2 with shower only), 1 suite | $100–$150 | Closed 2 wks in Jan. | MC, V.

Peg Leg Inn. This "inn" is actually a cluster of five New England Colonial homes, some right on the water and some across the street. The buildings are furnished with period pieces and the property is full of gardens. It's three minutes on foot to Rockport Village. Restaurant, complimentary Continental breakfast. No air-conditioning. No smoking. | 2 King St. | 978/546–2352 or 800/346–2352 | www.cape-ann.com | 33 rooms | $90–$145 | Closed Nov.–mid-Apr. | AE, MC, V.

Pleasant Street Inn. Quirky and charming features abound in this 1893 inn, including a turret room, a room with a tin ceiling, and a tree swing in the yard. Complimentary Continental breakfast. Some kitchenettes, some refrigerators, some in-room hot tubs, no room phones, no TV in some rooms. No pets. No smoking. | 17 Pleasant St. | 978/546–3915 or 800/541–3915 | www.cape-ann.com/pleasant-street-inn | 8 rooms, 1 carriage house | $95–110, $1,000/wk carriage house (7–day minimum stay) | MC, V.

Rocky Shores Inn and Cottages. Once the summer home of a Texas oilman, this property includes a 1905 Victorian house surrounded by gardens and Cape Cod–style cottages. Guest rooms have antiques and fireplaces, and many boast views of the twin lighthouses of Thacher Island. While the main house is beautifully decorated with period pieces, the cottages feel a bit more rustic. The inn is 2 mi from Rockport Village and within walking distance of beaches. Complimentary breakfast. No air-conditioning, cable TV, no room phones. No smoking. | 65 Eden Rd. | 978/546–2823 or 800/348–4003 | www.rockportusa.com/rockyshores | 9 rooms; 11 cottages | $92–135, $900–$1,100/wk cottages | Closed Nov.–Apr. | AE, MC, V.

★ **The Sally Webster Inn.** This 1832 inn still has the original moldings and floor boards, and has been carefully decorated with period antiques. Several of the rooms have canopy beds; others have interesting cloud paintings. Complimentary Continental breakfast. No room phones, TV in common area. No pets. No kids under 12. No smoking. | 34 Mt. Pleasant St. | 978/546–9251 or 877/546–9251 | www.sallywebster.com | 8 rooms | $80–$95 | Closed Jan. | MC, V.

Seacrest Manor. Built in 1911, this English-style country home is on a hill amidst 2 acres of landscaped grounds. The house harbors a renowned art collection that includes works that have been in the manor since it was built along with pieces by contemporary local artists.

The John Kieran Nature Preserve is across the street. Rockport Village and beaches are less than a mile away. Complimentary breakfast. No air-conditioning, cable TV. Bicycles. No kids under 12. No smoking. | 99 Marmion Way | 978/546–2211 | www.seacrestmanor.com | 8 rooms (2 with shared bath) | $106–$152 | Closed Dec.–Mar. | No credit cards.

Seafarer Inn. The oldest of Rockport's small inns, the Seafarer (built in 1890) is an unpretentious home with gray shingles, black shutters, and white trim. The airy guest rooms are filled with wicker and brass furniture, and all have ocean views. You can see Gap and Gully coves from the sunroom, in which breakfast and afternoon tea are served. Complimentary Continental breakfast. No air-conditioning, cable TV, no room phones. No smoking. | 50 Marmion Way | 978/546–6248 or 800/394–9394 | www.seafarer-inn.com | 5 rooms, 2 suites | $105–$225 | MC, V.

Seaward Inn on the Atlantic. The nine colonial-style cottages and three main buildings that make up the Seaward Inn sit in a 2-acre nature preserve with marked trails. You can relax on the enclosed porch and watch lobstermen tend their pots. All rooms have ocean views. The Seagarden Restaurant is on the premises. Restaurant, complimentary breakfast. No air-conditioning, refrigerators, cable TV. Pond. | 44 Marmion Way | 978/546–3471 or 877/4SEAWARD | fax 978/546–7661 | info@seawardinn.com | www.seawardinn.com | 28 rooms; 9 cottages | $139–$249; $945–$2,000/wk cottages (7–night minimum) | Closed Nov.–mid-Apr. | AE, D, DC, MC, V.

Tuck Inn. Built in 1790, this Colonial inn is within walking distance of Rockport Village, three beaches, and the commuter rail station. Guest rooms have homemade quilts, pumpkin pine floors, mahogany furniture, and works by local artists. Complimentary Continental breakfast. Cable TV, no room phones. Pool. No smoking. | 17 High St. | 978/546–7260 or 800/789–7260 | www.rockportusa.com/tuckinn | 13 rooms (6 with shower only), 1 suite, 2 apartments | $79–$129, $114/night and $925/wk apartments (7 night minimum stay in Aug. and July) | MC, V.

Turks Head Motor Inn. This two story motel is in a quiet residential area 1½ mi from Rockport Village and ½ mi from the beach. It has a solarium with an indoor pool and an indoor/outdoor patio with lounge chairs. Cable TV. Indoor pool. | 151 South St. | 978/546–3436 | info@turksheadinn.com | www.turksheadinn.com | 28 rooms, 1 1-bedroom apartment | $105–$159 | Closed mid-Oct-Apr. | AE, D, MC, V.

★ **Yankee Clipper Inn.** Four buildings make up this inn—the Inn, the Quaterdeck, the Bulfinch House, and a three-bedroom villa called The Captain's Quarters. Some rooms have canopy beds, sundecks, or glass enclosed porches. The inn is ¼ mi from the beach and 1 mi from the village and train station. Two buildings are on the water; one is across the street. Terraced gardens on the property overlook the ocean. The villa is only available between June and September. Some in-room hot tubs, cable TV. Saltwater pool. Business services. No smoking. | 96 Granite St., Pigeon Cove | 978/546–3407 or 800/545–3699 | fax 978/546–9730 | www.yankeeclipperinn.com | 26 rooms, 1 3-bedroom villa | $109–$289, $2,500–$2,800/wk villa (7 night minimum) | Closed mid-Dec.–mid-Mar. | AE, D, MC, V.

SALEM

MAP 6, I3

(Nearby towns also listed: Beverly, Boston, Danvers, Lynn, Lynnfield, Marblehead)

★ Salem is a small city 16 mi north of Boston and rich in history. Its most infamous event, the Salem witch trials of 1692, actually occurred outside modern-day Salem in what is now neighboring Danvers. But this inconvenient little fact hasn't prevented a large number of Salem's shops from masquerading as witch-themed "museums," displaying small doses of historical facts or artifacts and selling every imaginable kind of Halloweenlike merchandise. More serious looks into Salem's past await visitors to the city's legitimate historical attractions, including the fascinating Peabody and Essex Museum, the Salem Maritime National Historic Site, and the 17th-century House of Seven Gables, which inspired Salem-born Nathaniel Hawthorne's novel of the same name. Although Salem suffers from a shortage of accommodations, its commuter rail and highway connections make it a convenient destination for day trips from elsewhere in the Greater Boston area.

Information: Salem Office of Tourism and Cultural Affairs | 59 Wharf St. Ste. C, Salem, 01970 | 978/741–3252 or 800/725–3662 | www.salem.org.

Attractions

Chestnut Street. Chestnut Street is considered one of the most architecturally distinguished streets in the United States. Stop into the Hamilton Mansion (No. 9,) or 34 Chestnut Street; both are open to the public. | Chestnut St. | 877/SALEM–MA | Free | Daily.

★ **House of Seven Gables.** This exquisite wooden mansion dating from 1668 is said to be one of the oldest in New England, but it's probably most famous for inspiring the Nathaniel Hawthorne book *The House of the Seven Gables.* Hawthorne himself was born nearby in 1804, and tours of the house he was born in are included in the price of tours of the House of Seven Gables. | 54 Turner St. | 978/744–0991 | $8 | Mid-Jan.–Dec., Mon.–Sat. 10–5, Sun. noon–5.

National Park Service Regional Visitor Center. In recognition of its many historic sites, the whole of Essex County, of which Salem is a part, has been designated a National Heritage Area. In this visitors center, which serves as the gateway to the region, you'll find an introductory film, brochures that map out the area's sights, helpful rangers to answer questions, and a well-stocked gift shop and bookstore. | 2 New Liberty St. | 978/740–1650 | fax 978/740–1655 | www.nps.gov/sama | Free | Daily 9–5.

★ **Peabody and Essex Museum.** Salem's seafaring past is brought to life at this 200-year-old museum, with exhibits of scrimshaw, a whale's jaw, boat models, and more. The East India Hall Galleries (on Liberty St.) showcase maritime treasures ranging from 16th-century Chinese blue porcelain to Indian colonial silver. | E. India Sq | 978/745–9500 or 800/745–4054 | fax 978/744–6776 | www.pem.org | $10 | Apr. 1–Oct. 31, Mon.–Sat. 10–5, Sun. noon–5; Nov. 1–Mar. 31, Tues.–Sat. 10–5, Sun. noon–5.

Crowninshield–Bentley House. In one half of this 1720s Georgian home, Hannah Crowninshield ran a basic boardinghouse. In the more opulent other half lived her wealthy merchant son, Benjamin. The restoration of the building emphasizes this dichotomy. Noted diarist and thinker Rev. William Bentley lodged with Mrs. Crowninshield. | 132 Essex St. | 978/745–9500 | www.pem.org | $10 | Apr. 1–Oct. 31, Mon.–Sat. 10–5, Sun. noon–5; Nov. 1–Mar. 31, Tues.–Sat. 10–5, Sun. noon–5.

Gardner–Pingree House. Built in 1804 by famous architect and woodcarver Samuel McIntire, this three-story Georgian Federal house is a fine example of that era's style. It's been restored to circa 1815, when it was inhabited by local merchant John Gardner. | 128 Essex St. | 978/745–9500 | www.pem.org | $10 | Apr. 1–Oct. 31, Mon.–Sat. 10–5, Sun. noon–5; Nov. 1–Mar. 31, Tues.–Sat. 10–5, Sun. noon–5.

John Ward House. Farmer and tanner John Ward had front row seats for the horrifying events of 1692—he lived with his family opposite the gaol used in the witch trials. The house was built around 1684. | Brown St. | 978/745–9500 | $10 | Apr. 1–Oct. 31, Mon.–Sat. 10–5, Sun. noon–5; Nov. 1–Mar. 31, Tues.–Sat. 10–5, Sun. noon–5.

Pickering Wharf. If you need a break from Salem's restored historic sites, come to this lively harborside village of shops and restaurants. You'll find elegant gifts from around the world and high-end fashion boutiques, along with Boris Karloff's Museum of Witches, Salem's Museum of Myths and Monsters, five eateries, and more. | Pickering Wharf | 978/740–6990 | Free; fee for museums and attractions | Daily 10–8.

Pioneer Village: Salem in 1630. Step back in time to when Salem was the capital of the Massachusetts Bay colony. You'll find thatched-roof cottages, period gardens, costumed interpreters, and live animals. One of America's oldest living history museums, this re-created 17th-century fishing village was established in 1930 to commemorate the 300th anniversary of Salem's original settlement. | Forest River Park, off West St. | 978/744–0991 | $7 | Mid-Apr.–Thanksgiving, Mon.–Sat. 10–5, Sun. noon–5.

Salem Maritime National Historic Site. The nation's first National Historic Site documents the development of shipping in the New England colonies from the settlement era through the Revolutionary War and beyond. | 193 Derby St. | 978/740–1660 | fax 978/746–1685 | www.nps.gov/sama | Free. Tour of the buildings: $3 | Daily 9–5.

Custom House. Nathaniel Hawthorne fans won't want to miss the restored offices of the 1819 Custom House, made famous in *The Scarlet Letter*. | Derby St. | Daily 9–5; July–Aug. 9–6.

Derby House. Built in 1762, this house belonged to maritime merchant Elias Hasket Derby, the country's first millionaire. | Derby St.

Narbonne House. Built in 1672, this is the oldest frame house of its type in Massachusetts. Over the years, it was home to craftsmen, seamen, and longshoremen. Its last inhabitants, seamstress sisters Sarah and Marie Narbonne, left behind many artifacts (currently on display) relating to their work and lives. | 170 Essex St.

Salem Trolley. Salem Trolley includes a one-hour narrated tour and unlimited all-day shuttle service to Salem's attractions. The route includes the historic downtown district, the waterfront, Winter Island, Salem Willows, and the McIntire Historic District. | 8 Central St. | 978/744–5469 | fax 978/745–7715 | $10 | Apr.–Oct., daily 10–5; Mar. and Nov., weekends 10–5.

Salem Wax Museum of Witches and Seafarers. A multimedia presentation immerses you in the sights and sounds of Salem's tragedies and triumphs, including the witch trials of 1692. You can get a combination pass which offers discounted admission to both the Wax Museum and Salem Witch Village. | 288 Derby St. | 800/298–2929 | www.salemwaxmuseum.com | $4.95 | Call for hrs.

KODAK'S TIPS FOR NIGHT PHOTOGRAPHY

Lights at Night
- Move in close on neon signs
- Capture lights from unusual vantage points

Fireworks
- Shoot individual bursts using a handheld camera
- Capture several explosions with a time exposure
- Include an interesting foreground

Fill-In Flash
- Set the fill-in light a stop darker than the ambient light

Around the Campfire
- Keep flames out of the frame when reading the meter
- For portraits, take spot readings of faces
- Use a tripod, or rest your camera on something solid

Using Flash
- Stay within the recommended distance range
- Buy a flash with the red-eye reduction mode

From *Kodak Guide to Shooting Great Travel Pictures* © 2000 by Fodor's Travel Publications

Salem Witch Museum. This museum presents an overview of Salem's 1692 witch trials. A newly opened exhibit explores the evolving perception of witches. | 19½ Washington Sq | 978/744–1692 | $6 | Sept.–June, daily 10–5; July–Aug., daily 10–7.

Salem Witch Village. Discover the myths and the facts surrounding witches and their craft on this guided tour | 800/298–2929 | fax 978/740–2839 | www.salemwitchvillage.com | $4.95 | Call for hrs.

Stephen Phillips Memorial Trust House. This Federal house is now a museum housing the collections of five generations of the Phillips family. In it you'll see antique furniture, Oriental rugs, porcelain, carriages, two Pierce Arrow automobiles, and a Model A Ford. | 34 Chestnut St. | 978/744–0440 | $3 | Late May–Oct., Mon–Sat. 10–4:30, last tour at 4.

West India Goods Store. Purveyors of coffee, teas, spices, and other goods. | 164 Derby St. | Free | Daily 9–5.

Witch Dungeon Museum. Observe a live reenactment of a witch trial, taken from the transcripts of 1692. Then tour a re-created dungeon. | 16 Lynde St. | 978/741–3570 | $5 | Apr.–Nov., daily 10–5.

Witch House. Join a narrative tour of the historic home of Jonathan Corwin, the judge who presided over the Salem witch trials. More than 200 accused witches were questioned on this site. | 310½ Essex St. | 978/744–0180. | $5 | Mid-Mar.–June and Sept.–Nov. 30, daily 10–4:30; July–Aug., daily 10–6.

ON THE CALENDAR

JULY: *Maritime Festival.* Learn how to cane a chair, watch shipwrights create masts and rigging to re-create a 1797 tall ship, and participate in other interactive demonstrations of historical trades at this event. | 978/744–3663 or 887/SALEMMA.

AUG.: *Heritage Days Celebration.* This weeklong community festival in the middle of the month begins with a road race and includes a chowder festival, outdoor concerts, sidewalk sales, and fireworks. The event concludes with a grand parade showcasing Salem's history. | 978/744–3663 or 887/SALEMMA.

OCT.: *Haunted Happenings.* This three-week extravaganza is the biggest Halloween festival in the world. It includes a Grand Opening Parade, "witch trials," psychic fairs, haunted houses, treasure hunts, and candlelight tours of historic homes. Nine museums and four haunted houses offer special activities and free concerts, and local hotels and restaurants host costume balls. The second Saturday is Children's Day; the second Sunday is Costumed Pet Day. | 978/744–0013.

Dining

Chase House. Eclectic. This wharfside restaurant features lots of super-fresh seafood along with interesting flavors and excellent steak. Try the Asian-spiced fish, the Mediterranean seafood platter, the prime rib, or the lobster linguine. Dine outside on a deck overlooking the wharf. Entertainment Thurs.–Sun. Kids' menu. Sun. brunch. | Pickering Wharf | 978/744–0000 | $12.95–19.95 | AE, D, DC, MC, V.

The Grapevine. Contemporary. This upscale bistro serves American food with an Italian flair. The menu changes every three months, but always includes pastas, risottos, and vegetarian dishes. There's a high ceiling, candles on each of the 26 linen-clothed tables, and colorful abstract paintings on the walls. In summer, umbrella tables are set up outside on the patio. | 26 Congress St. | 978/745–9335 | fax 978/744–9335 | www.grapevinesalem.com. | No lunch | $14–$22 | AE, D, DC, MC, V.

Lyceum Bar and Grill. Eclectic. This popular eatery looks out onto the Salem Green and offers dining on a glassed-in terrace. The menu mixes Mediterranean and Asian influences with upscale contemporary American cuisine, offering lots of excellent grilled dishes. Try the lobster and leek-stuffed crêpes, or the filet mignon. A note to history buffs: the restaurant is in the building where Alexander Graham Bell dialed out for the first time. Sun. brunch. | 43 Church St. | 978/745–7665 | No lunch Sat. | $16.95–$31.95 | AE, D, MC, V.

Nathaniel's Restaurant at the Hawthorne Hotel. Contemporary. Brass chandeliers illuminate this elegant dining room, which has fresh flowers on each table. Seafood is the specialty: try bouillabaisse or the seared sea scallops with three-caviar cream. There's live piano music on Thurs.–Sat. evenings and jazz for Sunday brunch. | 18 Washington Sq. W | 978/744–4080 or 800/SAY–STAY | fax 978/745–9842 | Breakfast also available | $16–$24 | AE, D, DC, MC, V.

Roosevelt's Restaurant and Saloon. American. The saloon is downstairs and the Victorian-style post-and-beam dining room is upstairs. In keeping with the theme, there are photographs of Teddy Roosevelt all over and a 6-ft statue of the former president in the dining room. All meats and fish are sautéed and grilled, and there's a soup and salad bar included with every entrée. Try chicken Christine: chicken tenders sautéed with brown sugar, wine, and pecans, and served over rice pilaf topped with scallions. The dining room also has a dance floor, and you can boogie to jazz music on weekend nights. | 300 Derby St. | 978/745–9608 | fax 978/745–3033 | Breakfast also available on Sun. No lunch | $8–$19 | AE, D, DC, MC, V.

Lodging

Amelia Payson House. This antiques-furnished 1845 Greek Revival house was built on land where the home of an accused witch once stood. It's on a residential street, about five-minutes (by foot) to Salem center. There is coffee and tea service any time, and a data port in the sitting room. Dining room, complimentary Continental breakfast. No room phones. No kids under 12. No smoking. | 16 Winter St. | 978/744–8304 | www.ameliapaysonhouse.com | 4 rooms | $85–$130 | Closed Jan.–Feb. | AE, D, MC, V.

Clipper Ship Inn. Guest rooms in the two buildings of this two-story brick motel have oak furniture and pastel walls. You can access your room from the outside. Picnic area. Cable TV. | 40 Bridge St. | 978/745–8022 | www.go.boston.com/clippershipinn | 45 rooms, 15 suites | $95–$135 | AE, D, MC, V.

Coach House Inn. Once a sea captain's home, this 1879 Victorian mansion is in Salem's historic district. Inside, wicker, and painted furniture abound, and most guest rooms have ornamental fireplaces and four-poster beds. Outside, you'll find landscaped lawns, perennial gardens, and a Victorian carriage house. Complimentary Continental breakfast. No room phones. No smoking. | 284 Lafayette St. | 978/744–4092 or 800/688–8689 | fax 978/745–8031 | www.coachhousesalem.com | 11 rooms (2 with shared bath) | $95–$180 | Closed Jan.–Feb. | AE, D, MC, V.

Hawthorne Hotel. This Federal-style brick building next to Salem Common features local history exhibits. Restaurant, bar with entertainment, room service. In-room data ports, cable TV. Gym. Laundry service. Business services. Pets allowed (fee). | 18 Washington Sq. W | 978/744–4080 or 800/729–7829 | fax 978/745–9842 | www.hawthornehotel.com | 89 rooms, 6 suites | $132–$189, $295 suites | AE, D, DC, MC, V.

Holiday Inn. This newly renovated hotel is on U.S. 1, at the junction of Route 128 and I-95. It's about 15-minutes by car from Salem and 20-minutes from Boston. Restaurant. In-room data ports, cable TV. Indoor Pool. Gym. Laundry facilities, laundry service. Business services. | 1 Newbury St., Peabody | 978/535–4600 | fax 978/535–8238 | www.holiday-inn.com/hotels/bosp | 200 rooms | $115–$145 | AE, D, DC, MC, V.

Inn at Seven Winter Street. There's a roof deck and a backyard garden at this three-story Victorian inn, which is a block from Salem's historical district. Some guest rooms have working fireplaces, some have Jacuzzis, and some have canopy beds. Sherry is served free every evening in the parlor. Dining room, complimentary Continental breakfast. Cable TV. No pets. No kids under 12. No smoking. | 7 Winter St. | 978/745–9520 | fax 978/745–0523 | www.inn7winter.com | 10 rooms | $150–$225 | AE, MC, V.

The Inn on Washington Square. This 1850 Greek revival inn overlooks Salem Common, a 9-acre park in the center of the city. Each guest room is different: one has a large private deck; another has a small kitchen. All have down comforters, coffeemakers, and antiques. The large honeymoon room has a king-sized canopy bed, a wood-burning fireplace, and a two-person Jacuzzi. Dining room, complimentary Continental breakfast. Refrigerators, some in-room hot tubs, cable TV, in-room VCRs and movies. No pets. No smoking. | 53 Washington Sq. N | 978/741–4997 or 888/697–3100 | fax 978/741–3874 | www.washingtonsquareinn.com | 5 rooms | $125–$195 | Closed Nov.–Mar. 15 | AE, D, DC, MC, V.

Joan's Bed and Breakfast. This homey mom-and-pop-style bed-and-breakfast is in residential South Peabody, about 10 mi from Salem. It's down the street from a pond with a walking trail and near a small family restaurant and ice-cream shop. Guests are served a full breakfast of pancakes or French toast, with homemade jam, breads, and pastries. Complimentary breakfast. No room phones, TV in common area. Pool. Laundry facilities. No smoking. | 210R Lynn St., Peabody | 978/532–0191 | 3 rooms (2 with shared bath) | $65–$80 | No credit cards.

Salem Inn. There are three historic buildings here—the West House, built in 1834; the 1854 Curwen House; and the Peabody House (1874). Each has been gracefully restored, and furnished with antiques and period details. Enjoy breakfast on a brick patio in a rose garden. Complimentary Continental breakfast. Some kitchenettes, some in-room hot tubs, cable TV. Some pets allowed. | 7 Summer St. | 978/741–0680 or 800/446–2995 | fax 978/744–8924 | www.saleminnma.com | 28 rooms, 11 suites | $149–$219 suites | AE, D, DC, MC, V.

SALISBURY

MAP 6, I1

(Nearby towns also listed: Amesbury, Newburyport)

Salisbury, which occupies the flat wetland plain between the mouth of the Merrimack River and the New Hampshire state line, is a small town with a big beach. Known as "Salisbury by the Sea," it's an old-fashioned family resort, full of game arcades, cotton candy, the scent of frying batter, and beachfront cottages crowded against each other along the shore. The junction of I–95 and I–495 at the southwest corner of town ensures that Salisbury is an easy drive from most of New England.

Information: Salisbury Chamber of Commerce | Box 1000, Salisbury, 01952 | 978/465–3581 or 800/779–1771. **North of Boston State Visitor Center** | I–95 between the New Hampshire state line and exit 60 | www.northshoreusa.com/salisbury.

Attractions
Joe's Playland. You'll find more than 200 arcade games, many state of the art, at Joe's. The facility prides itself on including games that challenge kids' minds while providing amusement. Directly across the street is Pirate's Park, with twenty rides geared towards the under 14 set. | 10 Broadway | 978/465–8311 | Free; game fees vary | Apr.–Sept., daily 10–midnight; Sept.–Mar., weekends 10–midnight.

ON THE CALENDAR
OCT.: *Old Fashioned Days.* As many as 80 craft-makers display their wares in this annual event, held the second or third weekend after Labor Day. | 978/465–3581.

Dining
Striper's Grille. Seafood. Known for fresh seafood, New England clambake, ribs, and homemade pies, this restaurant has an open-air dining deck on the water with a fantastic view. Try the Italian fish stew. Kids' menu. Salad bar. No smoking in dining rooms. | 175 Bridge Rd., Rings Island | 978/499–0400 | $12.95–$25 | AE, D, DC, MC, V.

Lodging
Beachway Motel. Since you'll most likely spend your time in Salisbury on the beach, this nuts-and-bolts motel will serve you just fine. Rooms are carpeted and furnished with the

basics, including desks. Cable TV. Outdoor pool. No pets. | 110 Beach Rd. | 978/465–0336 | 30 rooms | $89 | Closed Oct.–Nov. | AE, D, MC, V.

SANDWICH (CAPE COD)

MAP 6, K6

(Nearby towns also listed: Bourne, Falmouth, Mashpee, Plymouth)

Founded in 1640, Sandwich is the oldest town on Cape Cod. It's near the east end of the Cape Cod Canal, about 60 mi south of Boston, and was once known throughout the country for its glassware. The town's pioneering role in turning a rare and expensive import item into an affordable, widely available domestic commodity is documented at the Sandwich Glass Museum, one of several historical museums in the community. In addition to its cultural attractions, Sandwich is exceptionally blessed with period architecture, from Early Colonial to Victorian. A cluster of bed-and-breakfast homes and proximity to U.S. 6, make Sandwich a good base from which to explore the rest of Cape Cod.

Information: **Cape Cod Canal Region Chamber of Commerce** | 70 Main St., Buzzards Bay, 02532 | 508/759–6000. **Visitor Center** (seasonal, late May–early Oct.) | Rte. 130, Sandwich | 508/833–1632 | canalreg@capecod.net | www.capecodcanalchamber.org.

Attractions

★ **Heritage Plantation.** A stop here satisfies varied interests, as the plantation has three separate museums: one displaying antique cars; another devoted to military history; and a third with works of art. There's also a working carousel from 1912, and lovely gardens. | 67 Grove St. | 508/888–3300 | $9 | Mid-May–mid-Oct., daily 10–5.

Hoxie House and Dexter Gristmill. Dating to the 1630s, the Hoxie House is supposedly the oldest house on Cape Cod. Today it's a museum, complete with 17th-century furnishings. In the adjacent Dexter Mill (1654), you can watch live milling demonstrations. | Water St. | 508/888–1173 | House $2, house and gristmill $3 | Mid-June–mid-Oct., Mon–Sat. 10–5, Sun. 1–5.

Sandwich Boardwalk. This boardwalk, which crosses a salt marsh, a creek, and low dunes, was almost totally destroyed by a devastating double punch from a nor'easter and Hurricane Bob. To rebuild it, townspeople contributed new planks inscribed with messages, and volunteers installed them. | Town Neck Beach | Free | Daily.

Sandwich Fish Hatchery. More than 200,000 trout are raised here, to be dispatched to state ponds and caught by tax-paying anglers. Kids enjoy feeding the fish, who become crazed by the special food pellets. | 164 Rte. 6A | 508/888–0080. | Free | Daily 9–3.

Sandwich Glass Museum. The main industry in 19th-century Sandwich was producing vividly colored glass. This museum contains relics of the town's early history, as well as examples of blown and pressed glass. Glassmaking demonstrations are held in summer. | 129 Main St. | 508/888–0251 | $3.50 | Apr.–Dec., daily 9:30–5; Nov. and Feb.–Mar., Wed.–Sun. 9:30–4.

Scusset Beach State Reservation. A swimming beach and a fishing pier are among the attractions here. You can also camp overnight. It's at the east end of Cape Cod Canal. Although you can camp year-round, there's no water service or dumpsters from Columbus Day to early April. | Rte. 3 and U.S. 6 | 508/888–0859 or 877/422–6762 | www.state.ma.us/dem | $2; camping $8 | Daily.

Shawme-Crowell State Forest. This 2,700-acre forest has 285 wooded tent and RV campsites. Campers have free access to Scusset Beach. | Rte. 130, off U.S. 6 | 508/888–0351 | www.state.ma.us/dem | Free; camping $10–$12 ($10 for MA residents.) | Daily. Campground Apr.–Dec. 1.

Thornton W. Burgess Museum. This charming museum is dedicated to the life and characters of children's author Thornton Burgess, famous for his tales of Peter Rabbit, Reddy Fox, and other assorted animal friends. There's story-telling in July and August, featuring whatever live animal is the subject of the story. | 4 Water St. | 508/888–4668 | www.thorntonburgess.org | Donation requested | Apr.–Oct., Mon.–Sat. 10–4, Sun. 1–4.

ON THE CALENDAR

DEC.: *Christmas in Sandwich.* Museums, merchants, schools, and bed-and-breakfasts welcome visitors with open houses, exhibits, demonstrations, and holiday celebrations. The events take place over ten days in early December. | 508/759–6000.

Dining

Aqua Grille. Contemporary. A lively bar scene keeps the atmosphere upbeat in this airy dining room that's more Miami Beach than classic Cape Cod. Fittingly, the wide-ranging menu has more sass than many in the area, from soba noodles with spicy Thai sauce to chipotle aïoli or Cajun remoulade served with fish. Try the tuna sashimi, salads, and grilled fish specials, and wash them down with specialty martinis and margaritas. Open-air dining on porch. Kids' menu. | 14 Gallo Rd. | 508/888–8889 | Closed Nov.–Mar. | $8.95–$18.95 | AE, MC, V.

The Beehive Tavern. American. This Colonial-style, family-friendly roadside tavern serves pasta, soups, and seafood. Try the lobster pie or the baked scrod. | 406 Rte. 6A | 508/833–1184 | Breakfast available Sun. | $8–$19 | MC, V.

Belfry Inne and Bistro. Contemporary. Enjoy sophisticated dining in a converted brick church, with a regularly changing menu that might include lobster-scallop-leek phyllo strudel, filet mignon, crab-stuffed gray sole, or Thai chicken. Unique combinations include lots of fresh vegetables. Open-air dining on patio. Kids' menu. Early bird suppers. No smoking. | 8 Jarves St. | 508/888–8550 or 800/844–4542 | Reservations essential in summer | Closed Sun.–Mon. No lunch | $19–$25 | AE, MC, V.

Bobby Byrne's Pub. American. An offshoot of the popular Bobby Byrne's in nearby Mashpee, this spot also has a relaxed pub atmosphere, jukebox tunes, and traditional steak, seafood, and pasta. Try the Scott steak sandwich or the chicken fajitas. Kids' menu. No smoking in dining room. | Stop 'n' Shop Plaza Shopping Center, Rte. 6A | 508/888–6088 | $7.95–$11.95 | AE, D, MC, V.

Dan'l Webster Inn. Contemporary. Although not authentic, this restaurant looks like a genuine 18th-century tavern, with Colonial touches throughout the intimate dining rooms, some of which have fireplaces. The menu, however, leans toward the modern, with tropical fruit sauces and Pacific Rim influences on seasonings and side dishes. Don't skip the lobster chowder. Kids' menu. Early bird suppers. Sun. brunch. No smoking in dining rooms. | 149 Main St. | 508/888–3623 | $6.50–$28 | AE, D, DC, MC, V.

Dunbar Tea Shop. Scottish. The front of this little house is filled with tea accessories and collectibles. In the back, you can order afternoon high tea and ploughman's lunches. | 1 Water St. | 508/833–2485 | No dinner | $5–$10 | D, MC, V.

Horizons on Cape Cod Bay. Seafood. Shrimp, clams, scallops, scrod, and salmon come broiled, fried, or baked at this waterfront restaurant. You'll also find the traditional alternatives of steak and chicken. Every table, whether inside or outside on the deck, has a panoramic view of the bay. | 98 Town Neck Rd. | 508/888–6166 | Closed late Nov.–Mar. | $6–$17 | AE, D, DC, MC, V.

Marshland Restaurant. American. This no-frills coffee shop serves a mean Italian omelet with sausage, fresh veggies, and cheese. Other than that, the specials are a good bet. Try a chicken club sandwich, a turkey Reuben, or the prime rib dinner. | 109 Rte. 6A | 508/888–9824 | Breakfast also available. No lunch or dinner Sun., no dinner Mon. | $5–$15 | No credit cards.

SANDWICH
(CAPE COD)

INTRO
ATTRACTIONS
DINING
LODGING

Seafood Sam's. Seafood. Even with its odd location—near the power plant and Coast Guard Station—Sam's thrives on its reputation for fast, high-quality fried seafood. Order at the counter, take a number, and wait in the casual dining room. | 6 Coast Guard Rd. | 508/888–4629 | Closed Nov.–Mar. | $1.50–$12 | D, MC, V.

Lodging

Bay Beach Bed and Breakfast. This upscale bed-and-breakfast has its own beach and boardwalk, and every room has a private deck. Most rooms have ocean views; some have fireplaces. The back of the property overlooks a salt marsh. Dining room, complimentary breakfast. Refrigerators, some in-room hot tubs, cable TV. Exercise equipment. No kids under 16. No smoking. | 1–3 Bay Beach La. | 508/888–8813 or 800/475–6398 | fax 508/888–5416 | www.baybeach.com | 7 rooms | $195–$345 | Closed Nov.–mid-May | MC, V.

Belfry Inne and Bistro. Two buildings make up this property: a late 19th-century rectory with six guest rooms and a restaurant; and the more contemporary Drew House. All rooms have balconies and skylights, and the grounds have lovely gardens with benches. It's right in historic Sandwich Village, about 10-minutes by foot to the beach. Restaurant, room service. In-room data ports, some in-room hot tubs. Business services. No kids under 10. No smoking. | 8 Jarves St. | 508/888–8550 or 800/844–4542 | fax 508/888–3922 | www.belfryinn.com | 14 rooms (3 with shower only) in 2 buildings | $95–$165 | AE, MC, V.

Captain Ezra Nye House. Welcome to the home of an 1829 captain of the sea. It's in the village of Sandwich, ½ mi from the beach and within walking distance of museums, art galleries, and shops. Inside, you'll find antiques and art, and a delicious gourmet breakfast. Outside, you can relax on lawn chairs amidst flowers and trees. Dining room, complimentary breakfast. No room phones. No kids under 10. Business services. | 152 Main St. | 508/888–6142 or 800/388–2278 | fax 508/833–2897 | www.captainezranyehouse.com | 6 rooms | $105–$120 | AE, D, MC, V.

Country Acres. This quiet, "Old Cape" motel on seven wooded acres has a gazebo and an in-ground pool. Relax on the porch, which runs the length of the building. Sandwich Village and the beach are both about a mile away. Refrigerators, cable TV. Pool. | 187 Rte. 6A | 508/888–2878 or 888/860–8650 | fax 508/888–8511 | cntryacrs@aol.com | www.sunsol.com/countryacres | 17 rooms; 1 cottage | $79–$99; $560/wk cottages (7–day minimum stay) | AE, D, DC, MC, V.

Dan'l Webster Inn. This boutique hotel with four different dining rooms and a tavern is a popular local special occasion spot. A new wing has eight large rooms with four-poster beds, sitting areas, working fireplaces, and two-person showers. The property includes English gardens. Restaurants, bar, dining room, room service. Some in-room hot tubs, cable TV. Pool. Business services. | 149 Main St. | 800/444–3566 | fax 508/888–5156 | www.danlwebsterinn.com | 46 rooms; 8 suites | $149–$349 | AE, D, DC, MC, V.

Earl of Sandwich Motel. These Tudor-style buildings surround a duck pond and wooded lawn. Many rooms are rather dark, with ceiling beams, paneled walls, and quarry-tile floors, but they're spacious and have large windows. Pool. Pets allowed. | 378 Rte. 6A, East Sandwich, | 508/888–1415 or 800/442–3275 | fax 508/833–1039 | www.earlofsandwich.com | 24 rooms | $85–$109 | AE, D, DC, MC, V.

Inn at Sandwich Center. Across from the Sandwich Glass Museum in the center of town, this elegant inn features Laura Ashley bedding, handmade chocolates on the pillows at night, and some rooms with fireplaces. Ask for the Blue Room—it has a private deck overlooking lush gardens. Complimentary breakfast. No pets. No kids under 12. No smoking. | 118 Tupper Rd. | 508/888–6958 or 800/249–6949 | fax 508/888–2746 | www.innatsandwich.com | 5 rooms | $100–$135 | AE, MC, V.

Isaiah Jones Homestead. This mid-19th century house in Sandwich Village has seven guest rooms, five with fireplaces, and all with queen-size beds. You can relax on the front porch or on chairs in the garden. The Sandwich Glass Museum, the Doll Museum, Hoxie

House, and Shawme Pond are within walking distance. Picnic area, complimentary breakfast. No air-conditioning, some in-room hot tubs, no room phones. No kids under 16. No smoking. | 165 Main St. | 508/888–9115 or 800/526–1625 | fax 508/888–9648 | www.isaiahjones.com | 7 rooms (2 with shower only) | $95–$175 | AE, D, DC, MC, V.

Old Colony Motel. This motel in a residential neighborhood off Route 6A has colonial-style rooms with beamed ceilings and pine paneling. The building is surrounded by trees, and there's a cranberry bog around the corner. Picnic area, complimentary Continental breakfast. Refrigerators, cable TV. Pool. | 436 Rte. 6A, East Sandwich | 508/888–9716 or 800/786–9716 | www.sunsol.com/oldcolony | 10 rooms | $79–$89 | Closed Dec.–Feb. | AE, D, DC, MC, V.

Sandwich Motor Lodge. Families are more than welcome at this quiet Route 6A motel about 1½ mi from the beach. Complimentary Continental breakfast. Some kitchenettes, some refrigerators, cable TV. 2 pools (1 indoor). Hot tub. Laundry facilities. Some pets allowed. | 54 Rte. 6A | 508/888–2275 or 800/282–5353 | fax 508/888–8102 | www.sandwichlodge.com | 34 rooms, 33 suites | $116–$170 suites. | AE, D, DC, MC, V.

Sandy Neck Motel. You'll find typical Cape Cod–style rooms here, furnished with wicker and cherry furniture. The motel sits on 3 acres of landscaped grounds next to the Sandy Neck Beach entrance. Picnic area. Refrigerators, cable TV. | 669 Rte. 6A, East Sandwich | 508/362–3992 or 800/564–3992 | fax 508/362–5170 | snmotel@capecod.net | www.sandyneck.com | 12 rooms | $89–$99 | Closed Nov.–Mar. | AE, D, DC, MC, V.

Seth Pope House 1699 Bed and Breakfast. Amid many trees on 1 acre of property overlooking a salt marsh, this home was originally built in 1699 by one of Sandwich's early entrepreneurs. Antiques, wood headboards, four-poster beds, and armoires mesh with the exposed beams and wood details to produce a warm, cozy feel in the rooms, all of which have private baths. Complimentary breakfast. No room phones, TV in common area. No pets. No kids under 10. No smoking. | 110 Tupper Rd. | 508/888–5916 or 888/996–SETH | www.sethpope.com | 3 rooms | $85–$100 | Closed Apr. 15–Nov. 1 | MC, V.

Spring Hill Motor Lodge. This motel off Route 6A is convenient to golf, museums, beaches, restaurants, and shops. Picnic area. Some kitchenettes, refrigerators, cable TV. Pool. Tennis courts. No smoking. | 351 Rte. 6A, East Sandwich | 508/888–1456 or 800/647–2514 | fax 508/833–1556 | wwwsunsol.com/springhill | 24 rooms; 4 cottages | $89–$125, $180–$275/night, $1,100–$1,400/wk cottages (7–day minimum stay in June–Aug) | Closed Nov.–mid-Mar. | AE, D, DC, MC, V.

The Summer House. Steps away from Sandwich's center, this 1835 Greek Revival home is nestled amid many lovely gardens, insuring peace and quiet. Hardwood floors, antiques, handmade quilts, and numerous windows are some of the details that evoke the summers of eras long gone. Every room except one has a working fireplace. Delectable breakfasts are served in what was once the parlor and afternoon tea with fresh baked treats is served on the sunporch. Complimentary breakfast. No TV, no room phones. No pets. No kids under 6. No smoking. | 158 Main St. 02563 | 508/888–4991 or 800/241–3609 | www.capecod.net/summerhouse | 5 rooms | $85–$105 | AE, D, MC, V.

Village Inn. From March to November, this Sandwich Village inn hosts artists who teach two-, three-, and five-day workshops on oil and watercolor painting, pastels, monoprints, etching, and tile making. Built in 1830, the building features handmade furniture, American country antiques, a wraparound porch, and lovely gardens. It's within walking distance of shops, restaurants, museums, and the beach. Complimentary breakfast. No air-conditioning, no room phones. No kids under 8. No smoking. | 4 Jarves St. | 508/833–0363 or 800/922–9989 | fax 508/833–2063 | www.capecodinn.com | 8 rooms (2 with shared bath) | $85–$120 | AE, D, MC, V.

Wingscorton Farm. Tucked away on a dirt road off busy Route 6A, this farmhouse was once a stop on the Underground Railroad. Since it's still a working farm, you'll see plenty of four-legged friends. Guest accommodations include three elegant suites with wide-planked floor boards and Oriental rugs, as well as a detached cottage and a fully-equipped stone

SANDWICH
(CAPE COD)

INTRO
ATTRACTIONS
DINING
LODGING

carriage house. Complimentary Continental breakfast. Beach. Library. Pets allowed. No smoking. | 11 Wing Blvd, East Sandwich | 508/888–0534 | fax 508/888–0545 | 3 suites, 1 carriage house | $135; $175 carriage house | AE, MC, V.

SAUGUS

MAP 8, F3

(Nearby towns also listed: Boston, Lynn, Lynnfield)

The town of Saugus, just 9 mi from downtown Boston, is known within the region primarily for the Saugus Strip, or U.S. 1, which runs through the community like a pulsing commercial jugular. The oversize thematic architecture along the Strip includes some of greater Boston's most recognizable roadside icons: for example the Leaning Tower of Pizza; Chinese restaurants built to resemble the Forbidden City; and a life-size herd of plastic cattle grazing at the famous Hilltop Steak House. Historically, the town was home to the nation's earliest iron-making industry, the remnants of which are preserved at the Saugus Iron Works National Historic Site.

Information: **Saugus Chamber of Commerce** | 335 Central St., Saugus, 01906 | 781/233–8407 | director@sauguschamber.com | www.sauguschamber.com.

Attractions

Breakheart Reservation. These 655 wooded acres contain dirt trails for hiking and paved trails for biking and rollerblading. A sandy beach on Pierce Lake has lifeguards 10–6 in summer. There are picnic sites with grills, rest rooms, and free parking. Boating and camping are not permitted. | 177 Forest St. | 781/233–0834 | www.ma.us/mdc | Free. | Daily dawn–dusk.

Saugus Iron Works National Historic Site. Situated beside the Saugus River, this site is a replica of the original furnace and forge that began producing iron products in 1646, launching the iron industry in the American colonies. You can explore the iron works yourself, but tours are highly recommended. | 244 Central St. | 781/233–0050 | www.nps.gov/sair | Free | Grounds open Apr.–Oct., daily 9–5; Nov.–Mar., daily 9–4. Tours every 90 mins Apr.–Oct., daily 9:45–3:45.

ON THE CALENDAR

SEPT.: *Founder's Day Road Race.* This four-mile run starts at Highland Ave. and finishes at the high school. It's held on a Saturday, rain or shine. | 781/233–8407.

Dining

Hilltop Steak House. Steak. This local institution is hard to miss, due to the life-size herd of plastic cattle and giant cactus sign outside. Its earned a Texas-size reputation for serving every kind of steak cut imaginable, in portions that start big and get bigger, at remarkably modest prices. There's a butcher shop on the premises. Kids' menu. No smoking in dining room. | 855 Broadway | 781/233–7700 | $9–$32 | AE, D, DC, MC, V.

Saki Restaurant. Japanese. Popular dishes at this traditional Japanese restaurant include sushi, broiled meat or seafood with teriyaki sauce, seafood or meat sautéed with tepanyaki sauce, and tempura. You can eat at a table, the sushi bar, or sitting on the floor in a tatami room. | 670 Broadway | 781/233–3858 | $12–$25 | AE, D, DC, MC, V.

Lodging

Colonial Traveler Motor Court. Family-owned and -operated, this brick motel has a one-story wing with parking outside the rooms, and a two-story wing with a parking lot. Breakfast is served in the coffee shop and there are nightclubs across the street. A bus to the T stops directly in front of the building. Restaurant, complimentary Continental breakfast. In-room data ports, some refrigerators, cable TV. Laundry facilities. Pets allowed. | 1753

Broadway | 781/233–6700 or 800/323–2731 | fax 781/231–8067 | www.roomsaver.com | 24 rooms | $89–$129 | AE, D, MC, V.

Days Inn. Rooms are green and mauve at this four-story chain hotel, and they come equipped with movies and Nintendo. If you show the nearby gym your key, you can work out for free. Complimentary Continental breakfast. Cable TV. Laundry service. Airport shuttle. No pets. | 999 Broadway | 781/233–1800 | fax 781/233–1814 | www.daysinn.com | 150 rooms | $129 | AE, D, DC, MC, V.

SHARON

MAP 6, H4

(Nearby towns also listed: Boston, Brockton, Dedham, Foxborough)

An affluent community about 19 mi southwest of Boston, Sharon has taken care not to let rapid growth obliterate its green spaces and leafy, tree-filled neighborhoods. Although mostly residential, it's home to such attractions as the Kendall Whaling Museum and Borderland State Park. Commuter rail and I–95 provide Sharon with rapid connections to both downtown Boston and Providence, Rhode Island.

Information: Neponset Valley Chamber of Commerce | 190 Vanderbilt Ave., Norwood, 02062 | 781/769–1126 | www.nvcc.com.

Attractions

Borderland State Park. Once the home of artist/inventor Blanche Ames and her botanist husband Oakes, this is now a state park. You can tour the Ameses' English-style stone mansion, which was designed by Ames and built in 1910, on the third Friday (if you make a reservation) and Sunday of the month from Apr. through Nov. The 20 rooms contain many of the family's furnishings as well as Blanche's paintings and political cartoons. You can also picnic, hike, ride horses, fish, and canoe in the park's 1,570 acres. In winter you can go sledding and cross country skiing. | Massapoag Ave., North Easton | 508/238–6566 | fax 508/230–7193 | www.cr.nps.gov/nr/travel/pwwmh/ma72.html | Free | Memorial Day–Labor Day, 8–8; Labor Day–Oct. and May–Memorial Day, 8–6:30; Nov.–Apr., 8–4:30.

Kendall Whaling Museum. Though small, this museum has a wide-ranging collection of art, tools, and artifacts related to the history of the whaling industry. There are also displays about ongoing efforts to protect endangered whales. | 27 Everett St. | 781/784–5642 | $4 | Tues.–Sat. 10–5, Sun. 1–5.

Massachusetts Audubon Society Visual Arts Center and Trails. This center 5 mi north of Sharon is in the former home of wildlife painter and filmmaker Mildred Morse Allen, who bequeathed her house and 138-acre property (which she considered a bird sanctuary) to the Massachusetts Audubon Society. You'll find changing exhibits from the center's extensive collection of natural history art and photography. The Visual Arts Center and trails are open to the public. | 963 Washington St., Canton | 781/821–8853 | fax 781/821–8733 | www.massaudubon.org | $3 | Gallery Thurs.–Sat. 1–5, trails Tues.–Sun. 9–5.

ON THE CALENDAR

FEB.–MAR.: *Maple sugaring.* Learn how maple sap is harvested and processed at six Massachusetts Audubon properties: Moose Hill in Sharon, Arcadia in Easthampton, Blue Hills Trailside Museum in Milton, Drumlin Farm in Lincoln, Habitat in Belmont, and Ipswich River in Topsfield. Preregistration is required for the 1½-hour outdoor programs. | 800/AUDUBON.

Dining

La Cucina Italiana. Italian. Grape arbors, wine barrels, and candles on burlap-covered tables give this upscale trattoria, 6 mi northwest of Sharon, a rustic feel. Fish is a specialty—try the wild striped bass with puttanesca vinaigrette. All desserts, including the not-to-be-missed chocolate truffle torte, are prepared by the pastry chef. If you'd like to watch the cook/owner in action, reserve the chef's table in front of the open kitchen. | 960 Main St. (Rte. 109), Walpole | 508/660–VINO | Reservations essential | No lunch | $18–$28 | AE, D, DC, MC, V.

Lodging

Four Points Sheraton Hotel and Conference Center. This hotel 6 mi north of Sharon and geared toward business travelers is a short drive from the commuter rail station and Foxboro Stadium. Restaurant, bar. Cable TV. Pool. Gym. Business services. | 1151 Boston–Providence Tpke., Norwood | 781/769–7900 | fax 781/551–3552 | www.sheraton.com | 123 rooms, 3 suites | $119–$169 | AE, D, DC, MC, V.

Sharon Inn. Guest rooms in the three buildings of this family-owned and -operated motel have modern oak furniture, large desks, and coffeemakers. In summer, it's a popular pickup/drop-off point for Boston tours. Guests get a discount at the adjacent Bickford's restaurant. The property is 3 mi from Foxboro Stadium. In-room data ports, cable TV, in-room VCRs and movies. Outdoor pool. Laundry service. Business services. No pets. | 775 Providence Hwy. | 781/784–5800 or 800/879–5432 | fax 781/784–4862 | www.sharoninn.com | 53 rooms in 3 buildings | $99–$109 | AE, D, DC, MC, V.

SHEFFIELD

MAP 6, B4

(Nearby town also listed: Great Barrington)

Perched on the Connecticut state line in the southwestern corner of Massachusetts, Sheffield is a sparsely populated, two-village town known for its large number of antiques dealers. Agriculture has been one of the community's cornerstones, and it is still a major element of the town's landscape. Sheffield also occupies a footnote in history. It was the site of the last battle in Shays' Rebellion, the post-Revolutionary uprising by farmers looking for debt relief.

Information: **Southern Berkshires Chamber of Commerce** | 362 Main St., Great Barrington, 01230 | 413/528–1510 | vcenter@bcn.net | www.greatbarrington.org.

Attractions

Bartholomew's Cobble. This unusual landscape is filled with hundreds of plant species, including more than 50 ferns, all within this over 300-acre park 5 mi south of Sheffield. The plant diversity creates a rich habitat for wildlife, too, making the cobble a prime spot for bird-watching. Several miles of walking trails take you through woods, riverbanks, and open fields. The visitors center includes a one-room natural history museum with displays of skulls, mounted birds, and mammals. | Weatogue Rd., Ashley Falls | 413/229–8600 | www.ttor.org | $3 | visitors center and museum: daily 8:30–4:30; Trails: daily, dawn–dusk.

Colonel Ashley House. One of the area's oldest homes, the 1735 Ashley House was built by a young lawyer/surveyor in anticipation of his wedding. The furnishings and personal effects reflect the styles of the era, and the house itself is a fine example of 18th-century craftsmanship. In 1781, Colonel Ashley's slave was the first to sue for her freedom under the Massachusetts constitution of 1780, which outlawed slavery. It is 5 mi south of Sheffield. | Cooper Hill Rd., Ashley Falls | 413/229–8600 | www.ttor.org | $5 | Memorial Day–Columbus Day, weekends and Mon. holidays 10–5.

ON THE CALENDAR

AUG.: *Old Parish Church Antique Show; Berkshire Antiquarian Book Fair.* Browse for antique furniture and collectible books at Mt. Everett High School on the first weekend of the month. Nearly 30 antique and 20 book dealers participate. | 413/229–2129.

Dining

Limey's. English. Fish-and-chips and shepherd's pie are some of the traditional British favorites here. Walls are adorned with photos of historic scenes, and booths and soft lighting contribute to a relaxed atmosphere. | 650 N. Main St. | 413/229–9000. | $13–$22 | AE, D, MC, V.

Lodging

Ivanhoe Country House. This 1780 Colonial home sits amidst 20 primarily wooded acres adjoining the Appalachian Trail. Rooms have some antiques, including old rag rugs. The owners deliver breakfast to your door, so you can crawl back under the covers to eat. Complimentary Continental breakfast. Some kitchenettes, some refrigerators, no room phones, no TV in some rooms. Outdoor pool. Some pets allowed (fee). No smoking. | 254 S. Undermountain Rd. | 413/229–2143. | 7 rooms, 2 suites | $110–$125 | No credit cards.

Racebrook Lodge. Originally a barn, this 1784 building has stenciled walls and a cathedral ceiling. Complimentary breakfast. No room phones, TV in common area. Pets allowed (fee). No smoking. | 864 S. Undermountain Rd. | 413/229–2916 | www.rblodge.com. | 19 rooms, 3 suites | $125–$225. | AE, MC, V.

SOMERVILLE

(Nearby towns also listed: Boston, Cambridge, Lexington)

Somerville is one of the most rapidly changing communities in the greater Boston area. Once a major brickmaking center, with a heavy concentration of industry after the 1850s, the city was for generations a working-class "streetcar suburb" at the periphery of Boston and Cambridge. But now, with students, artists, and twentysomethings being priced out of Cambridge due to accelerating gentrification, Somerville is becoming the next best thing. Areas of town with good metro and bus access, such as Davis Square, are turning into dining and entertainment meccas, full of quirky cafés, music-filled bars, affordable restaurants, and other urban amenities in demand by the city's new bohemians.

Information: **Somerville Chamber of Commerce** | 2 Alpine St., Somerville, 02144 | 617/776–4100 | info@somervillechamber.org | www.somervillechamber.org.

Attractions

Somerville Museum. Specializing in local culture, diversity, and art, this museum hosts concerts on Sunday afternoons and lectures related to exhibits. | 1 Westwood Rd. | 617/666–9810 | Donation requested | Feb.–June and Sept.–Dec., Thurs. 2–7, Fri. 2–5, Sat. noon–5.

Somerville Theater. This five-screen theater hosts films, plays, concerts, and lectures. The 900-seat main auditorium has been restored to its original look as a 1914 vaudeville theater. It's right next to the Davis Sq. T stop on the Red Line. | 55 Davis Sq | 617/625–5700 recorded events, 617/354–4466 box office | Varies | Daily.

ON THE CALENDAR

JULY: *Artbeat*. The City Arts Council showcases Somerville's thriving resident creative talent with a three-day festival featuring live music on outdoor stages, food stands representing local restaurants, artist-created window displays in local shops, children's games, and other activites. | 617/625–6600, ext. 2985.

Dining

Bertucci's Pizza. Pizza. Unlike other Bertucci's, which serve pasta, this link in the chain serves only pizza, appetizers (including bruschetta and three-cheese focaccia bread), and desserts. Choose from about 20 specialty pizzas on the menu or create your own. The margherita (tomato, fresh mozzarella, and basil) is a favorite. It's worth the trip for the rolls alone—they're made from fresh pizza dough. | 197 Elm St. | 617/776–9241 | $10–$17 | AE, D, MC, V.

Dali Restaurant. Spanish. You'll think you're in Spain, with the cured hams, garlic, dried cod, and peppers hanging over the bar, the Spanish tiles and music, and the bullfight posters on the walls. Popular dishes include the garlic shrimp and the pork tenderloin with goat cheese and mushrooms. | 415 Washington St. | 617/661–3254 | fax 671/661–2813 | No lunch | $18–$24 | AE, DC, MC, V.

Gargoyles on the Square. Contemporary. Beautiful presentations incorporate snapping-fresh local seafood and produce at this neighborhood gem. Try the grilled duckling or the beef medallions, which are prepared differently at different times throughout the year. A jazz band plays on Sunday. | 219 Elm St. | 617/776–5300 | Closed Mon. No lunch | $14–$20 | AE, D, DC, MC, V.

Redbones. Barbecue. This friendly neighborhood roadhouse serves blue-ribbon barbecue with all the fixins, complemented by one of the best microbrew draft beer menus in greater Boston. It's known for ribs, pulled-pork sandwiches, and pecan pie. Try a monster margarita. | 55 Chester St. | 617/628–2200 | $8–$18 | No credit cards.

Rosebud Diner. American/Casual. The Rosebud is a 1941 Worcester dining car that's listed on the National Register of Historic Places. About 99% of the structure is original, including a porcelain floor, stained-glass windows, and the wooden booths. The menu has a little of everything, from omelettes, sandwiches, burgers, and salads, to seafood, meat loaf, and Italian dishes such as fettuccine puttanesca. There's also a full bar. | 381 Summer St. | 617/666–6015 | Breakfast also available | $2–$13 | AE, MC, V.

Lodging

Amerisuites Boston/Medford. Six miles from downtown Boston, this hotel has two-room suites that accommodate up to six people. It's in Medford, which borders Somerville. Complimetary Continental breakfast. In-room data ports, cable TV. Indoor pool. Health club. Business services. | 116 Riverside Ave. NE, Medford | 781/395–8500 | fax 781/395–0077 | www.amerisuites.com | 158 suites | $99–$199 | AE, D, DC, MC, V.

Holiday Inn–Boston/Somerville. This chain hotel is within walking distance of the subway and close to esteemed Boston-area universities, including MIT, Tufts, and Harvard. There's a solarium and a sundeck, and children eat and stay free. Restaurant, bar, room service. In-room data ports, cable TV. Indoor pool. Hot tub, sauna. Gym. Laundry facilities, laundry service. Business services. Free parking. | 30 Washington St. | 617/628–1000 or 800/HOLI-DAY | fax 617/628–0143 | www.holiday-inn.com | 184 rooms, 7 suites | $199–$250; $355 suites | AE, D, DC, MC, V.

Tage Inn. The hotel's New Mexico–style exterior is a distinctive contrast to other Somerville buildings. Guest rooms are either blue and cream or orange and cream, with cherry furniture. There's a free shuttle to area restaurants and public transportation. The Inn is ½ mi from the Wellington T stop on the Orange Line and 10 minutes by car from downtown Boston. Complimentary Continental breakfast. In-room data ports, refrigerators, cable TV. Health club. Business services. No pets. | 23 Cummings St. | 617/625–5300 or 800/322–TAGE | fax 617/625–5930 | www.tageinn.com | 148 rooms, 24 suites | $114–$145 | AE, D, DC, MC, V.

SOUTH HADLEY

MAP 6, D4

(Nearby towns also listed: Amherst, Chicopee, Hadley, Holyoke, Northampton)

South Hadley, a community of fewer than 17,000 residents, is home to Mount Holyoke College, the nation's oldest college for women, and still one of the most prestigious. Although much of the town is undeveloped land, its southern end looks more like a typical suburb, and many residents commute into nearby Springfield. South Hadley is also the southern gateway to Skinner State Park and Holyoke Range State Park, two extremely popular destinations for day hikers.

Information: **Amherst Area Chamber of Commerce** | 409 Main St., Amherst, 01002 | 413/253–0700 | chamber@www.amherstcommon.com | www.amherstcommon.com.

Attractions
Mount Holyoke College. Founded in 1837, this prestigious liberal arts institution is the nation's oldest women's college. The campus, designed in part by the noted landscape architect Frederick Law Olmsted, is graced with numerous examples of Victorian architecture, including some outstanding Gothic Revival buildings along Route 116. | College St. | 413/538–2000 | www.mtholyoke.edu | Free | Daily.

Joseph Allen Skinner Museum. The museum's three structures house a diverse collection, from Native American artifacts and 19th-century farm tools to medieval armor and stuffed birds. The principal building, built in the 1840s as a Congregational church, has a story to tell, too, having been relocated from one of the six Pioneer Valley towns erased from the map in order to make way for a giant reservoir. | 35 Woodbridge St. | 413/538–2085 | Free | May–Oct., Wed. and Sun. 2–5.

Mount Holyoke College Art Museum. Behind the modern concrete-and-glass facade of this museum is an abundant selection of ancient, medieval, American, European, and Asian art. There are also collections of photography, prints, and drawings, and changing displays in the main gallery. | Lower Lake Rd., off Rte. 116 | 413/538–2245 | fax 413/538–2144 | www.mtholyoke.edu/offices/artmuseum | Free | Tues.–Fri. 11–5, weekends 1–5.

Mt. Holyoke College Botanic Garden. There's a lot of flower power at Mt. Holyoke College. The campus contains a 6,500-square-ft greenhouse complex with temperate, tropical, aquatic, and desert plants and flowers. Scattered throughout the grounds are rock/alpine gardens, shade gardens, rhododendrons, perennials, and borders. | 50 College St. | 413/538–2116 | www.mtholyoke.edu/offices/botan | Free | Greenhouse open weekdays 9–4, weekends 1–4.

Talcott Greenhouse. This late-19th-century Victorian greenhouse contains both tropical plants, including succulents and cacti, and perennials. A rock garden and perennial beds surround it, and each spring there are popular bulb and perennials sales. | Lower Lake Rd., off Rte. 116 | 413/538–2116 | fax 413/538–2070 | www.mtholyoke.edu (search under Buildings and Gardens) | Free | Weekdays 9–4, weekends 1–4.

ON THE CALENDAR
MAR.: *Mt. Holyoke College Botanic Gardens Flower Show.* For the first two weeks of the month, the greenhouse staff of Mt. Holyoke puts on a spectacular flower show for the college and local community. | 413/538–2116.

Dining
Woodbridge's. American. This casual college-town eatery serves chicken, pasta, and fresh seafood. The 300-year-old building used to be the old town meeting house. Kids' menu. Early bird suppers. No smoking in dining room. | 3 Hadley St., on the common | 413/536–7341 | $10.95–$17.95 | AE, D, DC, MC, V.

Lodging
Grandmary's Bed and Breakfast. The three guest rooms in this Victorian house have lace curtains, period furnishings, and quilts. One room has a queen-size four-poster bed, another has a double bed, and the third has twin beds. The guest house is adjacent to the movie theaters, shops, and restaurants of South Hadley Commons. It's three minutes by foot to Mt. Holyoke College. Dining room, complimentary breakfast (Continental on weekdays). Cable TV. No pets. No kids under nine. No smoking. | 11 Hadley St. | 413/533–7381 | grandmarys@hotmail.com | 3 rooms (2 with shared bath) | $75–$110 | No credit cards.

SPRINGFIELD

MAP 6, D5

(Nearby towns also listed: Chicopee, Holyoke)

Springfield is Massachusetts's third-largest city and a place with a rich past. It was settled in the 17th century by William Pynchon, a deeply religious man whose disagreements with Puritans on fine points of church doctrine caused his writings to be considered heretical and publicly burned by Boston's executioner. Out of these contentious beginnings arose one of the state's most prosperous cities. By the early 20th century, Springfield had become a diverse industrial center, manufacturing guns, bicycles, cars, airplanes, and dictionaries. But by the 1960s its fortunes had waned, as one after another of its industrial employers moved elsewhere. Insurance and banking has filled the economic breach to some degree, but mergers and other factors beyond local control have taken their toll on these businesses as well. Yet the city's cultural institutions remain as much of an attraction now as they ever were, from the Springfield Armory National Historic Site (and adjacent quartet of museums around the pocket-size downtown Quadrangle), to the local symphony and theater. A steady resurgence in downtown dining and nightlife over the past few years also offers hope that the city's long-awaited renaissance may finally be under way.

Information: Greater Springfield Convention and Visitors Bureau | 1441 Main St., Springfield, 01103 | 413/787–1548 or 800/723–1548 | info@valleyvisitor.com | www.valleyvisitor.com.

NEIGHBORHOODS

Mattoon Street. This historic district just north of State Street's Quadrangle area has many lovely stone Victorian town houses, the majority of which were built between 1870 and 1890, on tree-lined streets. Most of the houses are residences, many of whose owners have restored them to their original state. There is an annual art festival here in September that attracts many visitors.

McKnight Historic District. This area has a cache of Victorian gingerbread architecture. Centered about Worthington Avenue, about a mile east of downtown, the area, which encompasses 306.5 acres, includes some 900 late Victorian wood-frame houses and the region's first planned residential area. Most of the 2½ or three-story homes were built between 1880 and 1900, about half of them by John and William McKnight, two former dry-goods dealers. St. James Avenue forms the eastern border, Armory and Federal

CAR RENTAL TIPS

- ❏ Review auto insurance policy to find out what it covers when you're away from home.
- ❏ Know the local traffic laws.
- ❏ Jot down make, model, color, and license plate number of rental car and carry the information with you.
- ❏ Locate gas tank—make sure gas cap is on and can be opened.
- ❏ Check trunk for spare and jack.
- ❏ Test the ignition—make sure you know how to remove the key.
- ❏ Test the horn, headlights, blinkers, and windshield wipers.

*Excerpted from *Fodor's: How to Pack: Experts Share Their Secrets*
© 1997, by Fodor's Travel Publications

Streets the western side, State Street lies South, and the Boston & Albany Railroad is north.

Forest Park At the southwest corner of the city, this neighborhood takes its name from the 735-acre park within it borders. There is the Forest Park Zoo on Sumner Avenue as well. There are many Victorian houses, but the architectural landscape is quite diverse and includes modern houses as well as apartment buildings and small postwar bungalows. There is an active civic organization here that works hard to preserve the neighborhood and protect the rights of its residents.

Maple Hill. Just east of downtown (Maple Street parallels Main Street), Maple Hill has houses that date from the 1820s to the 1920s. Dr. Seuss fans may want to visit Mulberry Street, which sits at the foot of the district. (Theodore Seuss Geisel, aka Dr. Seuss, spent his childhood in Springfield and the name of his first book was "And to Think That I Saw it on Mulberry Street.")

South End. A primarily Italian area on the western edge of the city that is sandwiched between downtown and Forest Park. It is the smallest of city's neighborhoods.

Indian Orchards. A large neighborhood in the northwest corner of the city that was once a plum orchard that belonged to the Caughmanyput Indians of the area. You will note that the street signs in the area are plum-colored in honor of its Native American heritage. The local Branch Library is the oldest in the city and there is an active civic organization. The *Titanic* Historical Society and Museum is here, at 208 Main Street. (Several of the streets in Indian Orchards are duplicates of street names in Springfield. This has to do with the fact the Indian Orchards was formerly the Village of Indian Orchards and developed at the same time as the downtown area of Springfield.)

TRANSPORTATION INFORMATION

Airport: Springfield is served by two airports: **Westover Metropolitan Airport** | 255 Padgette St, # 2, Chicopee | 413/593–5543. **Barnes Municipal Airport** | 110 Airport Rd, Westfield | 413/572–6275.

Transportation: Amtrak serves the city from 66 Lyman Street. Call 413/785–4230, 413/785–4264, or 800/USA–RAIL for fares and schedules.

Bus Lines: Peter Pan Bus Lines (413/781–3320) and **Pioneer Valley Transit** (413/732–6248) operate out of the bus station at 1776 Main Street.

Driving Around Town. With the exception of rush hour which, according to residents, is actually not all that bad anyway, Springfield is an easy city to drive to and around in. Highway access is good: the city is at the point where I–90 crosses I–91. The majority of traffic at rush hour is commuters traveling north-south between Connecticut and Massachusetts, to and from the large employment centers of Hartford and Springfield.

Getting into the city should not be a headache and once there, negotiating the streets should be equally painless. The main streets of the city are two-way, but many of the narrower streets and most of the side streets are one-way. This should not pose a problem for driving or changing direction since they basically follow an alternating pattern and street signage is clearly marked and consistent.

There are parking garages downtown (State Bliss Garage Co. at 16 Bliss St. and Tower Square Parking Garage at 1500 Main St. are two convenient ones) as well as lots near the exits for I–91 and I–90 where you can leave your car for long periods (from hours to days). Parking on the streets is also an option and space is rarely hard to find (and you can feel confident that your car will be safe: vandalism and theft are not big problems in the city). However, most of the parking is metered.

Attractions

ART AND ARCHITECTURE

Municipal Group. This collection of civic structures, built 1909-13, resulted from a national design competition. City Hall and Symphony Hall, a matched pair of giant Greek Revival buildings, dominate the group with their impressive line of Corinthian columns and elaborately decorated pediments. In between stands the 300 ft campanile, whose carillon bells can be heard throughout downtown. | Court St. | 413/263–6800 | www.quadrangle.org | Free | Daily.

BEACHES, PARKS, AND NATURAL SIGHTS

Forest Park. A true oasis, this 19th-century city park has enough trees to keep all visible signs of the metropolis at bay. Within the park's 735 acres you'll find miles of winding paths, a pond with paddleboats, tennis courts, playgrounds, swimming pools, an ice-skating rink, and a small zoo. | Sumner Ave. | 413/787–6461 (park) or 413/733–2251 (zoo) | $4 per car weekdays; $5 per car on weekends | Daily 8–dusk.

The Zoo in Forest Park. Springfield native Theodore Geisel, better known as Dr. Seuss, is said to have been inspired by his childhood visits here. (His father was the city's park commissioner.) More than 200 animals from different environments call this zoo home. | Sumner Ave. | 413/733–2251 | $3.50 | Mid-Apr.–mid-Nov., Mon.–Wed. and Fri.–Sat. 10–5, Thurs. 10–8, Sun. 10–6; mid-Nov.–Dec. and Feb.–mid-Apr., weekends 10–5.

Granville State Forest. More than 2,300 acres of deep woods along the Connecticut state line are protected by this state forest. There's a 22-site streamside campground with flush-toilets, hot showers, and drinking water. | West Hartland Rd. | 413/357–6611 or 877/422–6762 | www.state.ma.us/dem | Free; camping $10–12 | Daily; campground May–Columbus Day.

Laughing Brook Education Center and Wildlife Sanctuary. A major magnet for schoolchildren, this spot 8 mi east of Springfield has exhibits of local wildlife and numerous family-oriented natural history programs. There are also several miles of well-marked trails through woods, meadows, and a red maple swamp. The property includes the former home of children's author Thornton Burgess, who wrote about animals. | 793 Main St., Hampden | 413/566–8034 | www.massaudubon.org | $3 | Tues.–Sun. (and Mon. holidays) dawn–dusk.

CULTURE, EDUCATION, AND HISTORY

Springfield Armory National Historic Site. During the American Revolution, General George Washington built an arsenal here on a piece of high ground midway between New York and Boston. After the war it became one of the new nation's two federal armories. Now it features the largest display of U.S. small arms in the world, as well as 19th-century firearms-production machinery and extensive videos on firearms technology and the peole who produced them. | 1 Armory Sq., Federal and State Sts. | 413/734–8551 | www.nps.gov/spar | Free | Tues.–Sun. 10–4:30.

MUSEUMS

Indian Motorcycle Museum. In 1901, bicycle racers George Hendee and Oscar Hedstrom pooled resources to build a new type of bicycle equipped with a small gasoline-powered motor, and so began production of the nation's first motocycle. They named their brand Indian, and examples of early models fill this museum, set in what was once the manufacturing headquarters of the company. | 33 Hendee St. | 413/737–2624 | $3 | Daily 10–4.

★ **Springfield Library and Museums–The Quadrangle.** One ticket price grants admission to four architecturally diverse museums arranged around a small courtyard behind the stately 19th-century city library building. | The Quadrangle, 220 State St. | 413/263–6800 | www.spfldlibmus.org | $4 | Wed.–Sun. noon–4.

Connecticut Valley Historical Museum. Built in 1927, this Colonial Revival building presents exhibits on local history, often drawn from the Springfield library's vast collection of furnishings and household effects spanning more than three centuries. | The Quadrangle, 220 State St. | 413/263–6800 | www.quadrangle.org. | $6 (combined ticket to all Quadrangle museums) | Wed.–Fri. noon–4, weekends 11–4.

George Walter Vincent Smith Art Museum. The collection within this golden-brick building is as distinctive as its facade. There are casts of classical sculpture and assorted 19th-century American paintings, but the most significant holdings are from the Far East: an exceptional (and vast) collection of Chinese cloisonné, Islamic rugs, and Japanese artifacts such as lacquerware, samurai armor, and Noh costumes. | The Quadrangle, 220 State St. | 413/263–6800 | www.spfldlibmus.org | $6 (combined ticket to all Quadrangle museums) | Wed.–Fri. noon–4, weekends 11–4.

Museum of Fine Arts. This Art Deco building houses a mixed collection of American and European art, including Italian Baroque, old Dutch and Flemish masters, French Impressionists, Georgia O'Keeffe, and Alexander Calder. Particularly arresting is the giant wall-size painting by the singular Erastus Salisbury Field, *Historical Monument of the American Republic*. | The Quadrangle, 220 State St. | 413/263–6800 | www.spfldlibmus.org | $6 (combined ticket to all Quadrangle museums) | Wed.–Fri. noon–4, weekends 11–4.

Springfield Science Museum. The natural and physical sciences are the focus of most of this museum's exhibit halls, from its life-size *Tyrannosaurus rex* model and collections of minerals and mounted animals to its planetarium shows and children's Exploration Center. But the museum also includes fascinating exhibits on technology pioneered in Springfield. | The Quadrangle, 220 State St. | 413/263–6800 | www.spfldlibmus.org | $6 (combined ticket to all Quadrangle museums) | Wed.–Fri. noon–4, weekends 11–4.

SPORTS AND RECREATION

★ **Basketball Hall of Fame.** In the city that gave birth to basketball, this shrine to the sport covers its every incarnation, from academic to professional, historic to modern. Interactive exhibits pit visitors against the pros in jump shots, free throws, defensive play, and other maneuvers. Players inducted into the Hall of Fame are given their due in the Honor Court. | 1150 W. Columbus Ave. | 413/781–6500 | www.hoophall.com | 9$ | daily 9:30–5:30.

Storrowton Village. Within the Exposition grounds, this "village" is composed of 18th- and 19th-century buildings gathered from all over New England and placed around a traditional-looking village green. The assemblage includes a tavern, a meetinghouse, a school, a blacksmith shop, a law office, and homes. | 1305 Memorial Ave., West Springfield | 413/787–0136 | www.thebige.com | Guided tours mid-June–Labor Day, Mon.–Sat. 11–3:30, or by appointment.

★ **Six Flags New England.** Six Flags is New England's largest amusement park, with more than 130 rides and attractions. Highlights include a water park, the Superman Ride of Steel, and one of the steepest wooden roller coasters in the country, modeled after the famous Coney Island Cyclone. | 1623 Main St., Agawam | 877/474–9352 | $36.99 | Call for hrs.

ON THE CALENDAR

MAY: *World's Largest Pancake Breakfast.* A 1,200-ft table is set up on Main Street and more than 40,000 people enjoy 142,000 buttermilk pancakes with a variety of toppings, along with coffee, juice, and milk. The annual breakfast is a birthday party for Springfield. While diners add calories, entertainers (dance and aerobics performers) burn them. | 413/733–3800.

JUNE: *Taste of Springfield.* More than 30 of the region's finest restaurants offer samples of their specialties during this five-day festival. Bands provide live entertainment. | 413/733–3800.

JULY: *Glasgow Lands Scottish Festival.* This festival, which takes place the third Saturday of the month, celebrates Scottish/Celtic culture with live entertainment, traditional athletic competitions, Highland dance and pipe band competitions, and traditional Scottish food. | 413/848–2816.

JULY: *Indian Day.* Pay homage to the world's first motorcycle brand, which was invented and manufactured in Springfield. Indian Motocycle owners and riders gather in the last building that the company owned, which is now a museum. | 413/737–2624.

JULY: *Star Spangled Springfield.* This July 4 event features a ceremonial swearing-in of new citizens along with a military band concert and fireworks. | 413/748–6190.

SPRINGFIELD

INTRO
ATTRACTIONS
DINING
LODGING

SEPT.: *Eastern States Exposition (The Big E).* This 17-day event features major exhibits such as the Avenue of States and the Storrowton Village Museum, along with animals, entertainment, amusement rides, and products from around the world. | 413/737–2443.
NOV.: *Hall of Fame Tip-off Classic.* This is the opening game of the college basketball season. | 413/732–9585.
NOV.–JAN.: *Bright Nights at Forest Park.* Take a 2½-mi drive through Forest Park to see New England's largest lighting display. More than 350,000 bulbs illuminate holiday scenes such as Seussland, Winter Woods, and the North Pole Village. | 413/748–6190.

WALKING TOURS

The Quadrangle and South End (approximately 2 hours)
Start at the **Quadrangle,** signposted off State Street at the corner of Chestnut, behind the Springfield Library. Here, four of the city's museums face one another around a small lawn. The most architecturally eye-catching is almost certainly the 1895 **George Walter Vincent Smith Art Museum,** whose facade has a variety of ornamental flourishes executed in dark ruddy brick. Little is known about the life of the museum's namesake and principal benefactor, since he destroyed all his personal papers to ensure his privacy survived his death. Next door is the modern **Springfield Science Museum,** known for its dinosaur exhibit and planetarium. At the end of the quad is the **Connecticut Valley Historical Museum.** The final member of the assembly, the **Museum of Fine Arts,** announces its forward-looking outlook on art with its emblematic Art Deco design, once the cutting edge of modernism. From here, stroll out to Chestnut Street, turn right, and walk a short block and a half to Mattoon Street, on the right immediately after Harrison Avenue. This single block, with its tidy Victorian row houses, brick sidewalks, and gas lamps, is an example of elegant middle-class urban living from the late 1800's. Backtrack to Chestnut Street and turn down Harrison Avenue to Main Street. This intersection is clearly the heart of downtown, with corporate skyscrapers rising all around. Turn left on Main and proceed past the bank building to Court Street and adjacent Court Square Park, opposite the giant Civic Center. Down the block to the right, facing the park from the north side of Court Street, is the **Municipal Group.** This trio includes the grand pair of Parthenons, City Hall and Symphony Hall, and the towering 30-story Campanile in between. Continue south on Main Street four blocks, to Union Street. This is the edge of the South End, Springfield's Italian neighborhood, whose next five blocks on Main contain several colorful little deli markets and bakeries—a great place to stop for lunch. Then, turn west on Union Street, toward elevated I–91 and the Connecticut River. After passing beneath the interstate, Union dead-ends at the southern extremity of Riverfront Park. Turn left on West Columbus Avenue and end the tour at the city's leading attraction and international shrine to the heroes of hoop dreams everywhere, the **Basketball Hall of Fame.**

Dining

INEXPENSIVE

Sitar. Indian. This small storefront restaurant specializes in Punjabi dishes from Northern India in a spot that evokes a visit to the Far East. Try the lamb dishes, the saag paneer, and anything vindaloo. No smoking. | 1688 Main St. | 413/732–8011 | No lunch Sun. | $7.95–$14.25 | AE, MC, V.

Spaghetti Warehouse. Italian. In what used to be the American Linen Supply Co., this spot serves heaping portions of traditional pasta dishes with rich, flavorful sauces. Kids' menu. | 60 Congress St. | 413/737–5454 | $7.79–$13.99 | AE, D, DC, MC, V.

Theodore's. Barbecue. The focus here is ribs, served with Theodore's secret-recipe sauce. The blackened chicken is also popular. The heart of the restaurant is the old bar; antique pictures adorn the walls. | 201 Worthington St. | 413/736–6000 | No lunch weekends | $6–$15 | AE, MC, V.

MODERATE

Old Storrowton Tavern. American. This authentic country tavern in a replica Colonial village serves traditional Yankee fare, from potpies to prime rib. Open-air dining on patio in summer. No smoking. | Eastern States Exposition Grounds, 1305 Memorial Ave., West Springfield | 413/732–4188 | Reservations essential | Closed Sun. | $14–$23 | AE, D, MC, V.

Pioneer Valley Brew Pub. Eclectic. Stylish New American dishes with creative sauces and well-prepared seasonal vegetables add a gourmet flair to what could otherwise pass for a casual neighborhood eatery. The beer, brewed on the premises, meets the high expectations set by the food. Known for grilled meats, fresh seafood, and specialty salads. Try the vegetarian stir-fry. Kids' menu. | 51–59 Taylor St. | 413/732–2739 | Closed Sun.–Mon. No lunch Sat. | $16–$20 | AE, D, DC, MC, V.

Student Prince and Fort. German. A local favorite with a sturdy German meat-and-potatoes menu, this casual eatery has an adjoining bar filled with over 2,000 beer steins, some centuries old. Try Jägerschnitzel and sauerbraten. Kids' menu. No smoking in dining rooms. | 8 Fort St. | 413/734–7475 | $8.50–$20 | AE, D, DC, MC, V.

Wild Apples Café. American. Don't let the phrase "café" fool you: this is a booming restaurant. Folks have been coming for years for the old-fashioned chicken potpie. Others favor the pan-seared sea bass. Paintings of the French countryside mingle on the walls with quilts. | 60 Shaker Rd. | 413/525–4444 | Reservations essential | Closed Sun. | $12–$24 | AE, D, DC, MC, V.

EXPENSIVE

Caffeines Downtown. Contemporary. The sophisticated city cousin of a popular eatery in neighboring town of West Springfield. Known for grilled meats and seafood, it boasts an imaginative menu with Mediterranean, Asian, and American Southwest influences. Try the wild mushroom pasta and spicy shrimp with cilantro and tequila. | 254 Worthington St. | 413/788–6646 | Closed Sun. No lunch. | $14–$40 | AE, D, MC, V.

Hofbrauhaus. Continental. Antiques, murals of Bavaria, and a menu heavy with German, French, and Swiss traditional dishes lend a certain formality to this local institution. At the same time, tableside cooking plus daring menu options such as bear, alligator, venison, and buffalo, add some excitement. Kids' menu. Sun. brunch Oct.–Apr. No smoking in dining rooms. | 1105 Main St., West Springfield | 413/737–4905 | Reservations essential on weekends and holidays | No lunch Sat.–Thurs. from Jan.–Nov., no lunch weekends in Dec. | $13–$40 | AE, D, DC, MC, V.

Lodging

INEXPENSIVE

Dave's Inn. This 1898 home, in the historic Crescent Hill section, is staffed by students from the Crescent Hill School of the Arts, who prepare meals. There is also a modern recording studio available, and professional musicians often rent the inn while recording albums. Complimentary breakfast. Some in-room hot tubs, cable TV, no room phones. Pets allowed (fee). | 346 Maple St. | 413/747–8059 | fax 413/747–7609 | 6 rooms, 2 suites | $89–$13 | AE, D, MC, V.

Econo Lodge. This hotel is near Six Flags New England, The Basketball Hall of Fame, a movie theater and restaurant, and I–90 and I–91. Complimentary Continental breakfast. In-room data ports, cable TV. Business services. | 1533 Elm St., West Springfield | 413/734–8278 or 800/553–2666 | fax 413/736–7690 | 58 rooms | $58–$95 | AE, D, DC, MC, V.

Hampton Inn. This hotel, near the shopping centers in West Springfield, caters to business travelers. It's 6 mi from the Basketball Hall of Fame and 12 mi from Six Flags New England. Complimentary Continental breakfast. In-room data ports, cable TV. Pool. Business services. | 1011 Riverdale St., West Springfield | 413/732–1300 | fax 413/732–9883 | www.hampton-inn.com | 126 rooms | $109–$119 | AE, D, DC, MC, V.

Howard Johnson Express. HoJo's are of course instantly recognizable, and this is a classic, built in the 1950s. Complimentary Continental breakfast. In-room data ports, cable TV. Outdoor pool. No pets. | 1356 Boston Rd. | 413/783–2111 or 800/446–4656 | fax 413/783–7750 | 101 rooms | $60–$80 | AE, D, DC, MC, V.

Quality Inn. This property, near I–90 at I–91, is 7 mi from the Basketball Hall of Fame and 15 mi from Six Flags New England. Complimentary Continental breakfast. In-room data ports, cable TV. Pool. | 1150 Riverdale St., West Springfield | 413/739–7261 or 800/228–5151 | fax 413/737–8410 | jmeng@banet.net | www.qualityinn.com | 114 rooms | $75–$125 | AE, D, DC, MC, V.

Ramada Inn. This two-story chain was built in 1991, and has your basic modern motel conveniences. Complimentary Continental breakfast. In-room data ports, some in-room hot tubs, cable TV. Exercise equipment. Baby-sitting. Laundry service. Free parking. Pets allowed (fee). | 21 Baldwin St. | 413/781–2300 or 888/298–2054 | fax 413/732–1231 | 44 rooms, 4 suites | $59–$64; $120–$140 suites | AE, D, DC, V.

Red Roof Inn. You'll find this inn with basic accommodations 4 mi from The Big E state fair, and close to Six Flags New England, The Basketball Hall of Fame, I–90, and I–91. In-room data ports, cable TV. | 1254 Riverdale St., West Springfield | 800/733–7663 | fax 413/731–1009 | www.redroof.com | 111 rooms | $60–$94 | AE, D, DC, MC, V.

Super 8 Motel. Near the intersection of I–90 and I–91, this chain is also convenient to Six Flags New England and the Basketball Hall of Fame. There's a restaurant next door. Complimentary Continental breakfast. In-room data ports, some in-room hot tubs, cable TV. | 1500 Riverdale St., West Springfield | 413/736–8080 or 800/800–8000 | fax 413/747–9214 | 60 rooms, 2 suites | $89–$99 suites | AE, D, DC, MC, V.

MODERATE

Best Western Sovereign Hotel and Conference Center. The indoor tropical courtyard is one of this hotel's most noteworthy features. It's 5 mi from the Basketball Hall of Fame, 8 mi from Six Flags New England, and close to I–90, and I–91. Restaurant, bar, complimentary breakfast. In-room data ports, cable TV. Indoor pool. Hot tub, sauna. Gym. Laundry facilities. Business services. | 1080 Riverdale St., West Springfield | 413/781–8750 | fax 413/733–8652 | www.bestwestern.com | 262 rooms, 10 suites | $159–$200 | AE, D, DC, MC, V.

Comfort Inn. Wall paper with sponge prints and pictures of the countryside add warmth to this chain hotel. Many of the suites have kitchens. Complimentary Continental breakfast. In-room data ports, some kitchenettes, some in-room hot tubs, cable TV. Exercise equipment. No pets. | 106 Capital Dr. | 413/736–5000 or 800/228–5150 | fax 413/731–5379 | 53 rooms, 22 suites | $70–$250 suites | AE, D, DC, MC, V.

Holiday Inn Springfield. This hotel is 2 mi from the Basketball Hall of Fame and 7 mi from Six Flags New England, with easy access to I–90 and I–91. There's a Friendly's Express in the lobby, views of Springfield from the rooms, and an indoor pool under a solarium. Restaurant, bar. Some refrigerators, cable TV. Indoor pool. Gym. Laundry facilities. | 711 Dwight St. | 413/781–0900 or 800/465–4329 | fax 413/785–1410 | www.holiday-inn.com | 244 rooms, 13 suites | $99–$159, $159–$199 suites | AE, D, DC, MC, V.

Sheraton Springfield Monarch Place. This atrium-style hotel has the largest health club in Springfield and offers packages that include admission to the Basketball Hall of Fame (less than 1 mi) and Six Flags New England (5 mi). Some rooms overlook the river. Restaurants, bar. Cable TV. Indoor pool. Hot tub, massage, sauna. Basketball, health club, racquetball. Shops. Business services. | 1 Monarch Pl. | 413/781–1010 or 800/426–9004 | fax 413/734–3249 | www.sheraton-springfield.com | 325 rooms, 6 suites | $79–$204 | AE, D, DC, MC, V.

EXPENSIVE

Marriott Springfield. This chain option in the heart of downtown Springfield is within walking distance of the Basketball Hall of Fame. It's got an indoor pool under a solarium and an deck with lounge chairs. Rooms have views of the city or the river. Restaurant, 2 bars with entertainment. In-room data ports, cable TV. Indoor pool. Barbershop, beauty salon, hot tub. Health club. Shops. Business services. | Boland Way and E. Columbus Ave. | 413/781–7111 | fax 413/731–8932 | www.marriott.com | 261 rooms, 4 suites | $145, $300–$350 suites | AE, D, DC, MC, V.

STOCKBRIDGE

(Nearby towns also listed: Great Barrington, Lee, Lenox, West Stockbridge)

Stockbridge's Main Street often evokes visions of Norman Rockwell paintings. In fact, America's most famous illustrator spent his last 25 years in Stockbridge, turning its New England charm into images that have come to epitomize small-town America. The long verandah on its stout old stage-coach inn, Gilded Age "cottages" amid leafy back-road estates, museums dedicated to Rockwell and sculptor Daniel Chester French, vividly hued botanical gardens, and historic homes from the 18th century onward are among the many attractions. Even when overrun with summer throngs, Stockbridge keeps its composure, neither contrived nor overly commercial, and with it the reassuring promise that there truly is a place where Rockwell's art seems to dwell in life.

Information: Stockbridge Chamber of Commerce | 6 Elm St., Stockbridge, 01262 | 413/298–5200. **Stockbridge Visitors Center** | 41 Main St. | 413/298–4662 | www.stockbridgechamber.org.

Attractions

Berkshire Botanical Garden. Perennial and annual beds highlight the 15 landscaped acres here. Of note are a flower-fringed pond, a terraced herb garden, and floral display gardens of plants that thrive in the Berkshires. Plant sales, flower shows, and a harvest festival are among seasonal special events held annually. | Rtes. 102 and 183 | 413/298–3926 | www.berkshirebotanical.org | $5 | May–Oct., daily 10–5.

Cat and Dog Fountain. This fountain erected in 1862 depicts a frolicking cat and dog. It's in a triangular park next to the Red Lion Inn, and is ringed with pretty flowers in spring and summer. | Main St.

★ **Chesterwood.** This attractively landscaped estate was the summer home of Daniel Chester French, one of America's most acclaimed sculptors during the late 1800s and early 1900s. Tours take in both the house and studio, where you can view a scaled-down version of his portrait of Lincoln in the Lincoln Memorial, his most recognizable work. From Independence Day through Columbus Day, contemporary outdoor sculptures dot the grounds, which contain a delightful woodland walk. | 4 Williamsville Rd. | 413/298–3579 | www.chesterwood.org | $8.50 | May–Oct., daily 10–5.

Children's Chime Tower. A tower near the site of the 18th-century missionary settlement of Christian Indians that was dedicated in 1878 to the memory of Rev. Dudley Field, a Stockbridge resident and father of U.S. Supreme Court Justice Stephen Field. Following the donor's wishes, the chimes are rung every evening from "apple blossom time until frost." | Main St.

Merwin House "Tranquility." This 1820s Federal-style brick home was among the earliest in the area to be turned into a summer vacation house, after the newly built railroads of the late 19th century opened up the bucolic Berkshires to tranquility-seeking New Yorkers. The furnishings reflect the eclectic tastes of the well-traveled owners, and hint at the leisure they enjoyed during the growth of the local resort community. | 14 Main St. | 413/298–4703 | www.spnea.org | $4 | June–mid-Oct.; weekend tours on the hour, 11–4.

Mission House. The Rev. John Sergeant, an early settler who aimed to convert the local Native Americans to Christianity, built this house in 1739. It was also briefly the residence of the stern Calvinist preacher Jonathan Edwards. The meticulously restored home may alter a few preconceptions about Colonial aesthetics, with its bright palette of interior colors and elaborately scrolled Connecticut Valley doorway out front; it also contains the area's best exhibit on local Indian history. | Main St. and Rte. 102 | 413/298–3239 | www.thetrustees.org | $5 | Memorial Day–Columbus Day, daily 10–5.

National Shrine of The Divine Mercy. Run by the Marians of the Immaculate Conception, this shrine devoted to St. Faustina Kowalska attracts 35,000 pilgrims annually. The main shrine was built during the 1950s, and includes wooden statues carved in Italy and Stations of the Cross from Spain. The shrine is on a 350-acre tract, which aslo has outdoor shrines, a candle shrine, and a well-stocked gift shop. | Eden Hill, 2 Prospect Rd. | 413/298–3931 | www.marian.org | Daily 7–dusk.

★ **Naumkeag.** Deceptively characterized as a "cottage" by its owners, this large and luxurious 1885 mansion exemplifies the style to which Berkshire society became accustomed during the industrial boom at the end of the 19th century. Stanford White designed this house for Joseph H. Choate, a politically well-connected lawyer and onetime ambassador to the Court of St. James. The landscaping was conceived largely by Fletcher Steele, and is stunning enough to warrant a visit all on its own. | Prospect Hill Rd. | 413/298–3239 | www.ttor.org | House and garden $8, garden only $6 | Memorial Day–Columbus Day, daily 10–5 (last tour 4:15).

★ **Norman Rockwell Museum.** The largest public collection of the beloved artist's and long-time local's work is on display in this spacious and sunlit museum. A generous portion of the artwork is kept on permanent display, while the rest is drawn upon for changing exhibits. The 36-acre grounds, which welcome picnickers, also contain Rockwell's free-standing studio, moved here from its original location in town. | Rte. 183 | 413/298–4100 | fax 413/298–4142 | www.nrm.org | $9 | Nov.-Apr. Mon-Fri, 10am-4pm, weekends 10–5. May-Oct. daily, 10am-5pm.

ON THE CALENDAR

JUNE–SEPT.: *Berkshire Theatre Festival.* The second oldest summer theater in the nation inhabits the Berkshire Playhouse, an 1887 building designed by McKim, Mead & White as a casino. In 1927, it was moved to its present location and became home to this annual festival. Four shows are produced here each season, many of them new works. Among the stars who have graced the stage are Katharine Hepburn, Joanne Woodward, Gene Hackman, Dustin Hoffman, and Al Pacino. | 413/298–5576.

OCT.: *Berkshire Botanical Garden Harvest Festival.* Arts and crafts and flower bulbs are on sale at this two-day event where pony rides, miniature golf, a petting zoo, cherry-picker rides, children's crafts workshops, musical entertainment, an auction, and a giant tag sale will keep you and the kids entertained. | Rtes. 102 and 183 | 413/298–3926.

DEC.: *Stockbridge Main Street at Christmas.* A weekend festival early in the month that kicks off on Saturday with house tours, a reading by actors from the Berkshire Theater Festival, a cabaret tribute to Frank Sinatra, and caroling in front of the Red Lion Inn, followed by a candlelight walk to the holiday concert. On Sunday, Main Street gets spruced up to look as it did in Norman Rockwell's famous painting. There are also horse-drawn rides, ice sculptures, and an appearance by Santa Claus. | 413/298–5200.

Dining

Michael's. Continental. This is a relaxed and family-friendly traditional restaurant just off the main street where house specialties such as chicken marsala, chicken Dijon, grilled eggplant and feta, and shrimp scampi are diverse enough to satisfy most cravings but unsurprising enough not to intimidate. Kids' menu. | 5 Elm St. | 413/298–3530 | $12.95–$17.95 | AE, MC, V.

Once Upon a Table. Contemporary. A simply decorated, bistro-style restaurant with seasonal menus that might include baby roast rack of lamb and Maine crab cakes with horse-radish cream sauce. Its location, on an alley called The Mews, and its 30-seat capacity, give the place an intimate feel. | 36 Main St. | 413/298–3870 | Reservations essential | Closed Tues. | $14–$22 | AE, MC, V.

Red Lion Inn. Continental. The formal, antiques- and pewter-filled dining room of the region's most famous inn, a giant and rambling clapboard 1773 building, serves expertly prepared New England cuisine that is at once both deeply traditional yet thoroughly contemporary in its use of (and respect for) fresh top-quality ingredients. Try the skillet-seared sea scallops. Open-air dining in courtyard. Pianist Fri.–Sun. Kids' menu. No smoking. | 30 Main St. | 413/298–5545 | Reservations essential summer weekends | Jacket required | Breakfast also available | $21–$29 | AE, D, DC, MC, V.

Lodging

The Inn at Brookside. Velvet-upholstered antique chairs and sofas fill this 1805 home. Surrounding the inn are more than 5 acres of grounds complete with fruit trees and a brook. The property adjoins the Berkshire Botanical Garden, whose acreage was donated by the inn's original owner. Complimentary breakfast. No room phones, no TV. No pets. No kids under 18. No smoking. | 1 Interlaken Rd. | 413/298–3099 | fax 413/298–3399 | www.innat-brookside.com | 4 rooms | $180–$200 | Closed Nov.–May | AE, D, MC, V.

Inn at Stockbridge. Both the Georgian-style 1906 main house, with a gable roof and some original antiques, and the new cottage house contain all the expected amenities plus some extras—down comforters, fresh flowers, CD players, and sherry in each guest room. The rooms have been fashioned after various themes: Out of Africa, St. Andrews, and Provence. The 12-acre property is 1½ mi north of Stockbridge Village, 2 mi from the Norman Rockwell Museum, 2½ mi from Chesterwood, and 3 mi from Tanglewood. Dining room, complimentary breakfast. Some in-room hot tubs, TV in some rooms. Pool. Business services. No kids under 13. No smoking. | U.S. 7 | 413/298–3337 or 888/466–7865 | fax 413/298–3406 | www.stockbridgeinn.com | 12 rooms | $125–$275 | AE, D, MC, V.

Red Lion Inn. Established in 1773 as a stagecoach stop on the Boston–Albany route, this inn has been owned and operated by the Fitzpatrick family since 1968. There's an impressive collection of antiques and china inside and a sweeping front porch ideal for cocktails and people-watching. 1 restaurant, bars with entertainment, room service. Some microwaves, some refrigerators, cable TV, some in-room VCRs. 1 pool. Massage. Gym. Shops. Baby-sitting. Laundry service. Business services. | 30 Main St. | 413/298–5545 | fax 413/298–5130 | innkeeper@redlioninn.com | www.redlioninn.com | 77 rooms (20 with shared bath), 26 suites, 7 guest houses | $165–$187, $247–$400 suites | AE, D, DC, MC, V.

STURBRIDGE

MAP 6, F5

(Nearby town also listed: Brimfield)

Founded in 1738, Sturbridge followed the trajectory of many central Massachusetts towns, evolving from a purely agrarian community to one that depended to a large extent on the earnings of water-powered mills built along the Quinebaug River. After the various local industries followed suppliers, buyers, or profits out of the region, the town shrank, losing more than a third of its population between the 1860s and the 1920s. When U.S. 20 was built through town, it began providing amenities for travelers, a line of work that has greatly expanded now that it sits at the junction of I–84 and the Massachusetts Turnpike (I–90). But Sturbridge is far more than a bunch of motels and restaurants at the end of an off-ramp: it's most famous for being home to Old Sturbridge Village, a simulated 1830s rural American town composed of authentic structures gathered from around New England and peopled with costumed interpreters who re-create life in the early 19th century.

Information: **Tri-Community Chamber of Commerce** | 380 Main St., Sturbridge, 01566 | 508/347–7594 or 800/628–8379 | chamber@hey.net | www.sturbridge.com.

Attractions

★ **Old Sturbridge Village.** About 40 historic structures from around New England have been collected here on 200 acres beside the gentle Quinebaug River to create a small but complete 1830s-era village. Costumed interpreters describe and demonstrate different occupations typically found in a rural New England community, from farmer and millwright to shopkeeper, printer, and lawyer. The village also has a sizable museum of artifacts from the early 19th century, including an outstanding collection of antique clocks. | 1 Old Sturbridge Village Rd. | 508/347–3362 or 800/733–1830 | fax 508/347–5383 | www.osv.org | $18 (valid for 2 consecutive days) | Apr.–Oct., daily 9–5; Nov.–Mar., daily 10–4; Jan.–mid-Feb., weekends 10–4.

St. Anne's Shrine. You may not expect to find eighty Russian icons in a Roman Catholic Church, but St. Anne's is filled with them. Some of these inspirational works date from the 18th century and were collected between 1934 until the fall of the Soviet Empire, when they were whisked away for safekeeping. | 16 Church St. | 508/347–7461 | Free | Weekdays 10–4, weekends 10–6.

ON THE CALENDAR

OCT.: *Harvest Festival.* Thirty crafts vendors and a dozen chefs offer samplings of their creations during this celebration of autumn held on the first weekend after Columbus Day. | The Commons in Old Sturbridge | 508/347–7594.

NOV.: *New England Thanksgiving.* Stroll through village homes and attend meetinghouse services to see how families celebrated this holiday more than 150 years ago. Reservations are required for dinner served in Bullard Tavern. | Old Sturbridge Village | 508/347–3362, ext. 325, or 508/347–5383.

Dining

Oxhead Tavern. American. Built in 1876, this restaurant was originally a church, then a shoe factory. Wood floors, walls, and ceilings and antique farm equipment hanging on the walls help you go back in time. Roast turkey and fish-and-chips are typical dishes. | 366 Main St. | 508/347–7393 | $7–$12 | AE, D, DC, MC, V.

P. Bella's Trattoria. Italian. Extra decorative touches at this restaurant in the Sturbridge Host Hotel delight the eye and relax the nerves: black ceilings covered in Christmas lights, chandeliers that provide low lighting, and burlap tablecloths. Italian music in the foreground and the scent of garlic complete the effect. The best dishes are *vitello alla saltimbocca* and *bisteca alla gorgonzola*. | 366 Main St. | 508/347–7393 | No lunch | $11–$19 | AE, D, DC, MC, V.

Picadilly Pub. American. From the floorboards to the rustic carvings of lighthouses, wood abounds here. You can expect simple fare such as steaks and fish and chips. | 362 Main St. | 508/347–8189 | $8–$12 | AE, D, DC, MC, V.

★ **Publick House.** Continental. The original Colonial structure of this New England–style restaurant is enhanced inside by cathedral ceilings, exposed-wood rafters and beams, an open hearth, and a large period weather vane suspended from the rafters. Ebenezer's Tavern (in the Publick House) serves the same traditional dinner menu, plus a lighter pub menu. Lobster pie, prime rib, or the turkey dinner are always quality choices. Kids' menu. Early bird suppers weekdays. No smoking in dining room. | 295 Main St., on the Common | 508/347–3313 | $18.95–$28.95 | AE, DC, MC, V.

Rom's. Italian. Originally a small dairy shop, now grown to encompass six dining rooms seating hundreds, this local institution serves a mix of Italian and American standards, from pasta to roast beef, amid simple early American decor. Try the veal parmigiana. Kids' menu. | 171 Main St. | 508/347–3349 | $5.95–$18.95 | AE, D, DC, MC, V.

The Thomas Henry Hearthstone Inn. Continental. The restaurant, built in 1999, shares the same country colonial touches as the inn where it's found, including Shaker and Windsor furniture crafted by the owners. Baked scrod and filet mignon are favorites. | 453 Main St. | 508/347–2224 or 888/781–7775 | Closed Sun. No lunch | $15–$22 | AE, D, MC, V.

Whistling Swan. Continental. This meticulously restored 1855 inn has several intimate dining rooms serving French-Italian cuisine, from escargots to pasta, along with slightly more contemporary preparations such as New York sirloin with Kentucky bourbon sauce. A less elaborate tavern menu is available in the barn's more casual Ugly Duckling Loft. Kids' menu. No smoking. | 502 Main St. | 508/347–2321 | Closed Mon. | $16–$30 | AE, D, DC, MC, V.

Lodging

Colonel Ebenezer Crafts Inn. A Colonial farmhouse built around 1786 that is run by the Publick House Historic Inn, where you check in. There is period, antique, and reproduction furniture within, and you'll find perennial flower gardens, where you may take your afternoon tea, on the grounds. Complimentary Continental breakfast. No room phones, TV in common area. Pool. Cross-country skiing. Business services. No smoking. | Fiske Hill Rd. | 508/347–3313 or 800/782–5425 | fax 508/347–5073 | www.publickhouse.com | 8 rooms | $115–$155 | AE, D, DC, MC, V.

Comfort Inn and Suites. This hotel was built in 1999, but despite its modernity, details like contemporary Victorian floral borders on guest-room walls make for a homey place to rest your head. It's 1 mi east of Old Sturbridge. Kids under 18 stay free. Bar, complimentary Continental breakfast. In-room data ports, some microwaves, some refrigerators. 1 indoor pool. | 215 Charlton Rd. | 508/347–3306 | fax 508/347–3514 | www.sturbridgecomfortinn.com | 40 rooms, 30 suites | $100–$155 | AE, D, DC, MC, V.

Commonwealth Cottage. Set in the woods on a dead-end street, this 1873 Queen Anne Victorian is quiet and secluded. Each room is named for a family member or friend and includes heirlooms prized by the namesakes. Complimentary breakfast. No room phones, no TV. No pets. No smoking. | 11 Summit Ave. | 508/347–7708 | fax 508/347–1958 | www.commonwealthcottage.com | 4 rooms | $110 | No credit cards.

Econo Lodge. Two miles west of Old Sturbridge Village and 40 minutes from Six Flags New England, this landscaped property with gardens and a playground is also easily accessible: 2 mi west of the junction of I–84 and I–90. This chain hotel is clean and comfortable. Some refrigerators, cable TV. Pool. Playground. Laundry facilities. No pets. | 682 Main St. | 508/347–2324 | fax 508/347–7320 | 52 rooms | $60–$100 | AE, D, MC, V.

Old Sturbridge Village Lodges and Oliver Wight House. This property is owned by and next to Old Sturbridge Village. Guest rooms in the 1789 Oliver Wight House have canopy beds, antiques, and period furnishings. Note the hand-painted foyer downstairs. Packages including museum admission are available. Cable TV. Pool. | U.S. 20 | 508/347–3327 | fax 508/347–3018 | www.osv.org | 59 rooms, 2 suites | $85–$130, $105–$130 suites | AE, D, MC, V.

Publick House Historic Inn. Combining the best of two worlds, this 1771 inn on Sturbridge Common retains its Colonial beauty with period furnishings and gardens on the grounds while offering modern amenities and conveniences. Restaurant, bar. Cable TV. Tennis. Playground. Business services. No smoking. | Rte. 131 | 508/347–3313 or 800/782–5425 | fax 508/347–5073 | www.publickhouse.com | 15 rooms, 2 suites | $95–$140, $140–$160 suites | AE, DC, MC, V.

Sturbridge Coach Motor Lodge. A motel among birch and fruit trees and flowering shrubs that is across the street from Old Sturbridge Village. It's convenient with standard rooms. Cable TV. Pool. | 408 Main St. | 508/347–7327 | fax 508/347–2954 | 52 rooms, 2 suites | $75–$100, $100–$125 suites | AE, MC, V.

Sturbridge Country Inn. The glass of champagne waiting for you and the single queen-size bed in every room make this spot a cozy getaway for couples. Several of the rooms in this 1840s Greek Revival farmhouse have exposed beams, vaulted ceilings, and porches.

The house is decorated with reproduction Victorian and Colonial antiques. Complimentary Continental breakfast. Cable TV. Hot tubs. No pets. | 530 Main St. | 508/347–5503 | fax 508/347–5319 | www.sturbridgecountryinn.com | 8 rooms, 1 suite | $99–$179 | AE, D, MC, V.

Sturbridge Host Hotel and Conference Center. This hotel is right off I–90 at exit 9 and across the street from Old Sturbridge Village. Some rooms have fireplaces and views of Cedar Lake. The property includes 9 acres of manicured lawns, wildflowers, and a private lake beach with paddleboats and a pontoon boat. The lovely P. Bella's Trattoria is here. 3 restaurants, bar with entertainment, room service. Cable TV. Indoor pool. Hot tub. Miniature golf, tennis. Health club. Beach. Boating. Business services. | 366 Main St. | 508/347–7393 or 800/582–3232 | fax 508/347–3944 | www.fine-hotels.com | 237 rooms, 4 suites | $179–$225, $400 suites | AE, D, DC, MC, V.

Super 8 Motel. This straightforward motel is on Cedar Lake, 300 yards from Old Sturbridge Village. Some rooms have a view of the lake. Complimentary Continental breakfast. Cable TV. Pool. Pets allowed (fee). | 358 Main St. | 508/347–9000 or 800/800–8000 | fax 508/347–5658 | 58 rooms | $69–$120 | AE, D, DC, MC, V.

The Thomas Henry Hearthstone Inn. Although this structure was built in 1999, it is full of country Colonial charm, with lots of dried flowers and Shaker and Windsor furniture built next door by the owners. The showcase attraction is the two-story fireplace in the Great Hall. Restaurant, complimentary Continental breakfast. Some in-room hot tubs, cable TV. No pets. No smoking. | 453 Main St. | 508/347–2224 or 888/781–7775 | fax 508/347–2860 | www.hearthstonestur.com | 12 rooms | $130–$330 | AE, D, MC, V.

SUDBURY

MAP 6, G3

(Nearby towns also listed: Boston, Concord, Framingham, Natick, Waltham)

A growing suburb of Greater Boston, Sudbury is fast filling up its open space with contemporary homes and shopping plazas with names intended to evoke the landscape they are replacing. Yet there will always be one corner of town that will forever evoke the past, thanks to the foresight of Henry Ford. Ford's interest in preserving Americana led him to the threshold of Sudbury's Wayside Inn, a 1716 stagecoach inn immortalized by poet Henry Wadsworth Longfellow. Today the inn and its restaurant are Sudbury's star attractions, along with other structures gathered by Ford and reassembled around the inn, among them the original schoolhouse where Mary had a little lamb, an old gristmill, and a chapel designed to look like a classic New England Congregational church.

Information: **MetroWest Chamber of Commerce** | 1671 Worcester Rd., Framingham, 01701 | 508/879–5600 | chamber@metrowest.org | www.metrowest.org.

Attractions
Great Meadows National Wildlife Refuge. These 3,600 acres of freshwater wetlands are home to more than 200 species of birds. Nature trails, a wildlife education center, and a visitors' center are on the property. | Weir Hill Rd., off Lincoln Rd. | 978/443–4661 | Free | Daily 8–4:30.

Hosmer House. Once a post office, this 18th-century house in the town center retains a few of the features from its postal service days, such as sorting boxes, but it has been restored to its earlier domestic specifications. | Concorde Rd. and Old Sudbury Rd. | 978/443–8891 | Free | Weekends 10–dusk.

Longfellow's Wayside Inn. This late-17th–early-18th-century historical and literary shrine is America's oldest operating inn. It's decorated with period furnishings, and now operates as a restaurant. | 76 Wayside Inn Rd., off U.S. 20 | 978/443–1776 | Daily.

Gristmill. The waterwheel here continues to turn the stones that grind wheat and corn for the inn's bakery. | Apr.–Nov., Wed.–Sun. 9–5; Mon.–Tues., by appointment.

Martha Mary Chapel. A nondenominational, nonsectarian chapel built and dedicated by Henry Ford in 1940. Today it is used primarily for weddings and private services. | By appointment only.

Redstone School. A 1798 schoolhouse that is the very little red schoolhouse immortalized in "Mary Had a Little Lamb." | May–Oct., Wed.–Sun. by appointment.

ON THE CALENDAR

APR.: *Reenactment of March of Sudbury Minutemen to Concord on April 19, 1775.* When the sleeping townfolk of Sudbury were roused from on April 19, 1775, many proceeded to North Bridge in Concord to fight the Redcoats. Today this event is commemorated by a historical group, the Sudbury Companies of Militia and Minute, who assemble at 3:45 AM at the First Parish Church in Wayland to read the original roll call by the light of an 18th-century lantern. They march to the music of the Sudbury Fife and Drum Corps, arriving in Concord by mid-morning. | 978/369–6993.

JULY: *Fourth of July Parade.* This annual Independence Day event departs from Boston Post Road and follows a 2-mi route that winds up at town center. Approximately 40 floats and as many as 10 bands and fife and drum corps march. | 978/579–0000.

SEPT.: *Annual Muster of Fife and Drum.* Step back into the 18th century on the last Saturday of September for this muster featuring 18th-century military encampments as well as children's games, crafts, and contra dancing of the period. The most popular event is the parade of fife and drum companies from all over New England. | 978/443–1776.

Dining

Bulfinch's Restaurant. Continental. Wood paneling and white linen give this restaurant an elegant look. Rack of lamb or black and blue filet—a filet mignon with blue cheese—are some of the exquisite offerings. | 730 Boston Post Rd. | 978/443–4094 | Reservations essential | No lunch | $13–$26 | AE, D, MC, V.

....

Longfellow's Wayside Inn. Continental. Although added to the historic 18th-century stagecoach inn in 1929 (and restored in the 1950s after a disastrous fire), the main dining room upholds the classic New England style of this literary landmark. The fare—from seafood to prime rib—is prepared with time-honored simplicity. Try the Watside lobster casserole or the scrod. Kids' menu. No smoking. | Old Boston Post Rd. | 978/443–1776 | $15.95–$22.95 | AE, D, DC, MC, V.

Lodging

The Arabian Horse Inn. The grounds of this 1870 Victorian house share 9 acres with woods, meadows, streams, gardens, and a duck pond. Inside, you'll find antiques and period furnishings, and one suite with a fireplace. Guests are welcome to feed the owner's five Arabian horses and to see the antique-car collection. Complimentary breakfast. In-room data ports, some in room hot tubs, cable TV. Cross-country skiing. No smoking. | 277 Old Sudbury Rd. | 978/443–7400 or 800/272–2426 | fax 978/443–0234 | 3 suites | $179–$319 | MC, V.

Clarion Carriage House Inn. Rooms at this boutique country inn in the historic Wayside Inn district have sleigh or four-poster beds with comfortable underquilts and tranquil-sound machines. Rooms for business travelers also have fax machines and large desks. The inn provides complimentary extras, such as homemade chocolate-chip cookies, coffee, and cappuccino. Complimentary breakfast. In-room data ports, cable TV. Laundry service. Business services. | 738 Boston Post Rd. | 978/443–2223 or 800/637–0113 | fax 978/443–5830 | 34 rooms, 5 suites | $159–$179, $179 suites | MAP Mon.–Thurs. | AE, D, DC, MC, V.

Hunt House Inn. Each bedroom in this 1850 Italianate house in the King Philip historic district has a special touch, from brass or wrought-iron beds to heirloom 1930s maple furniture and hand-sponged and -stenciled walls. Complimentary breakfast. Some refrigerators, some room phones, no TV in some rooms. No pets. No smoking. | 330 Boston Post Rd. | 978/440–9525 | fax 978/440–9082 | www.hunthouseinn.com | 3 rooms | $105–$115 | AE, MC, V.

Longfellow's Wayside Inn. In operation since 1716, this inn was a stop on the Underground Railroad and was once owned by Henry Ford. The interior is furnished with antiques and period pieces. Be sure to visit the Ford Room, where the illustrious magnate entertained guests such as Calvin Coolidge and Thomas Edison. On the grounds are the Wayside Gristmill, the Martha Mary Chapel (built in memory of Ford's mother and mother-in-law), and the Redstone School (Mary of "Mary Had a Little Lamb" fame attended this school); Henry Ford had the building moved here from Sterling, Massachusetts. The inn has been designated a National Historic Site. Restaurant, bar, complimentary breakfast. No TV. No smoking. | 76 Wayside Inn Rd. | 978/443–1776 or 800/339–1776 | fax 978/443–8041 | www.wayside.org | 10 rooms | $96–$146 | AE, D, DC, MC, V.

Radisson Inn. This property is near I–495, the semicircular western beltway around the Greater Boston area. It has a standard hotel look, is in a high-technology town, and isn't near anything fun. There are also landscaped grounds. Restaurant, bar, room service. In-room data ports, cable TV. Indoor pool. Hot tub. Health club, racquetball. Business services. | 75 Felton St., Marlborough | 508/480–0015 or 800/333–3333 | fax 508/485–2242 | www.radisson.com | 206 rooms, 2 suites | $169, $229 suites | AE, D, DC, MC, V.

Sudbury Bed and Breakfast. The family who owns this 1956 Colonial-style home just blocks from town center welcomes you to read books from the family's library and curl up in front of the fireplace. Complimentary breakfast. TV in common area. Outdoor pool. Tennis. | 3 Drum La. | 978/443–2860 | fax 978/443–0070 | 3 rooms, some with shared baths | $75 | No credit cards.

TRURO (CAPE COD)

MAP 6, L5

(Nearby towns also listed: Provincetown, Wellfleet)

Truro is Cape Cod's most rural town, a windswept piece of the Outer Cape whose primary business these days is accommodating summer visitors in rustic cabins in the woods and in plain cottages along the shore. Edward Hopper may have been the town's most famous resident. Like Hopper, many artists continue to be attracted to Truro's elemental landscape of sky, land, and water. The principal attractions in town are mostly historic or scenic points within the Cape Cod National Seashore, in particular Highland Light, whose piercing beam is the first thing in America visible to ships arriving from Europe.

Information: Truro Chamber of Commerce | Box 26, N. Truro, 02652 | 508/487–1288. **Visitor Information** (seasonal) | Rte. 6A at Head of the Meadow Rd. and U.S. 6 | truro-coc@capecod.net | www.virtualcapecod.com/chambers/truro.html.

Attractions

Head of the Meadow Beach. This is a fine, relatively uncrowded town beach. There are lifeguards and temporary rest rooms in summer. | U.S. 6 | $5/car, from 9–4 | Daily.

Highland Golf Links. Perched on the edge of the Atlantic Ocean and overlooking Highland Light, this 9-hole public course has more in common with Scottish links courses than American ones. The windswept, natural terrain can be quite challenging. | Lighthouse Rd. | 508/487–9201 | $20 | Daily.

Highland Light. Spectacularly perched 117 ft above the sea, Highland Light (also known as Cape Cod Light) is the Cape's oldest lighthouse. | Off S. Highland Rd. | $3 | Mid-June–Sept., daily 10–8.

Pamet Harbor. Come at low tide so you can venture far out onto the salt marsh flats. For those less versed in the plants and animals that thrive in such conditions, there are identifying plaques to enrich your adventure. | Depot Rd. | Free | Daily.

Pilgrim Heights Area. This National Seashore area's claim to fame is a short trail that leads to the spot where the Pilgrims supposedly drank their first New England water. An adjacent bicycle trail connects this spot to Head of the Meadow Beach. | U.S. 6 | Free | Daily.

Truro Center for the Arts at Castle Hill. Offering more than 50 courses to a transient summer population, this popular center is housed in a converted 19th-century barn. Notable artists teach courses and classes of varying lengths in crafts, writing, photography, and painting. | 10 Meeting House Rd. | 508/349–7511 | www.castlehill.org | Prices vary | July–Aug.

Truro Historical Museum. Once a former summer hotel that hosted naturalist Henry David Thoreau, this charming museum now houses early Colonial artifacts, furnishings, whaling implements, scrimshaw, and ship models. | 6 Highland Light Rd. | 508/487–3397 | www.capecod.net/ths | $3; $5 combination ticket with lighthouse | June–Sept., daily 10–4:30.

Dining

Adrian's. Italian. Expansive hilltop views from this casual restaurant in the Outer Reach Resort encompass Provincetown, Pilgrim Lake, and Cape Cod Bay; the equally inclusive menu ranges from pizza and pasta to daily seafood specials, all executed with inventiveness. A house specialty is *sogliole in sapore* (sautéed flounder or sole marinated with caramelized onions, raisins, pine nuts, and vinegar, served with grilled polenta). Open-air dining under a canopy is available. Kids' menu. No smoking. | 535 U.S. 6 | 508/487–4360 | Closed mid-Oct.–mid-May. No lunch | $7–$24 | AE, MC, V.

Blacksmith Shop. Contemporary. Favorite entrées here include fillet of haddock in a mustard cream sauce and poached sole in white wine, Italian green sauce (made with olive oil and italian spices), and lemon juice. For dessert try the tiramasu and apricot soufflé. On Wednesday there is a special pasta menu. Kids' menu. No smoking. | 17 Truro Center Rd. | 508/349–6554 | Closed Mon.–Tues. from mid-Sept.–Apr. No lunch | $11–$15 | MC, V.

Montano's. Italian. Although there's a prevalence of seafood on the menu, a theme underscored in the casual nautical design, this restaurant's catch is otherwise rich in tried-and-true Italian dishes. Popular is steak *Umbriago*—a sirloin smothered with onions, roasted peppers, garlic, mushrooms, and wine. Kids' menu. Early bird dinner. No smoking. | 481 U.S. 6 | 508/487–2026 | No lunch | $10–$20 | AE, D, MC, V.

Paparazzi. American/Casual. This family-friendly, bayside spot with water views serves a mix of simple Italian and American dishes, all accompanied by soup and salad bar. Try the prime rib, chicken parmigiana, or the surf-and-turf platter. Salad bar. Kids' menu. No smoking. | 518 Shore Rd. | 508/487–7272 | Closed Mon.–Thurs. in mid-Oct.–May. No lunch | $10–$25 | AE, D, MC, V.

Terra Luna. Contemporary. The barn-board dining room here is small and decorated with modern art. The cuisine continues the trend of blending the rustic with the innovative. Try an ample portion of grilled striped bass or spicy stuffed lamb chops. | 104 Shore Rd. | 508/487–1019 | Closed mid-Oct.–mid-May | $16–$20 | AE, MC, V.

The Whitman House Restaurant. American. Thoroughly Colonial in decor, this old-fashioned restaurant has an extensive American menu that ranges from lobster to prime rib to baked, stuffed sole. It's an early bird-special kind of place. | Great Hollow Rd. | 508/487–1740 | Closed Dec.–Mar. No lunch | $15–$25 | AE, D, DC, MC, V.

Lodging

East Harbour Motel and Cottages. Landscaped grounds, gardens, a private beach, and a large sundeck with umbrellas and gas grills are among the amenities at this property near whale-watching, golf, tennis, and fishing. Rooms have four large windows facing the

water. Picnic area. No air-conditioning, microwaves, refrigerators, cable TV. Beach. Laundry facilities. | 618 Shore Rd. | 508/487–0505 | fax 508/487–6693 | www.eastharbour.com | 9 rooms, 1 apartment, 7 cottages | $84–$120; $900–$1000/wk cottages, $925 apartment | Closed end of Oct.–mid-Apr. | AE, D, MC, V.

Harbor View Village. The buildings here are in the traditional Cape Cod style and overlook a private beach with Provincetown visible in the distance. Some of the efficiencies and all of the cottages have private decks, and most rooms have water views. Whale-watching package deals are offered off-season. No air-conditioning, some kitchenettes, refrigerators, no room phones, TV. Beach. No kids under 7. | 168 Shore Rd. | 508/487–1087 | fax 508/487–6269 | www.capecod.net/hbrview | 8 motel rooms, 6 efficiencies, 3 cottages | $70–$80; $600/wk for two people, $75 per extra person in cottages | Closed Nov.–Apr. | MC, V.

Kalmar Village. This resort has been family-owned and -operated since 1968. Designed for families, it has landscaped grounds dotted with fully equipped Cape Cod cottages (with housekeeping) and proximity to the national seashore. Picnic area. No air-conditioning, kitchenettes, some microwaves, cable TV. Pool. Beach. Laundry facilities. | 674 Shore Rd. | 508/487–0585 | fax 508/487–5827 | www.kalmarvillage.com | 42 cottages, 8 efficiencies | $100–$125/night and $1,000–$2,000/wk for cottages (7 night minimum June–Aug.), $125/night efficiencies | Closed end of Oct.–mid-May | D, MC, V.

Moorlands Inn. Since the innkeepers are musicians and artists, you can expect lots of lovely images and sounds throughout this Victorian B&B. On a quiet back road, this peaceful place has uncluttered guest rooms that are bright and filled with antiques and natural wood accents. Complimentary Continental breakfast. Outdoor hot tubs. No pets. No smoking. | 11 Hughes Rd. | 508/487–0663 | www.moorlands.homepage.com | 5 rooms, 1 apartment, 3 cottages | $109–$149; $99/night, $775–$995/wk cottages (7–night minimum July–Aug.); $800 for apartment | MC, V.

Topmast Motel. The efficiency units here all have standard motel-style furniture and decks and are great for families. Kitchenettes, refrigerators, TV. Pool. No pets. | 209 Shore Rd. | 508/487–1189 | fax 508/487–6863 | www.capecodtravel.com/topmast | 33 rooms | $80 | Closed mid-Oct.–Apr. | MC, V.

Truro Vineyards of Cape Cod Inn. This 5-acre working vineyard has a renovated 1836 farmhouse within earshot of U.S. 6. Rooms and public areas are decorated with a nod toward the vinifera theme, with claret and deep-green hues as well as antique casks and presses. There's a large deck overlooking the rows and rows of grapes. Complimentary Continental breakfast. Some hot tubs. No pets. No smoking. | 11 Shore Rd. | 508/487–6200 | fax 508/487–6200 | 5 rooms (1 with shared bath) | $99–$129 | Closed Jan.–Apr. | MC, V.

UXBRIDGE

MAP 6, G5

(Nearby town also listed: Grafton)

The Blackstone Valley town of Uxbridge lies midway between Worcester and Providence, Rhode Island, a fact that abetted its growth back when the Blackstone Canal carried a significant volume of shipping between central Massachusetts and Rhode Island's seaport. Well before the canal opened in 1828, the confluence of several fast-flowing Blackstone tributaries had made Uxbridge a center for early Colonial industry, with an iron forge, sawmill, gristmill, and distillery among those benefitting from local water for power or processing. Textile mills, which arrived in 1810, made woolen manufacture the town's leading business for well over a century, although market agriculture never entirely disappeared from the upland farms and orchards surrounding the town's center. After the last textile manufacturer left in 1983, Uxbridge's giant mill buildings have been slowly finding new residential and commercial tenants. Since some of the best-preserved remnants of the long-abandoned Blackstone Canal are in Uxbridge, the town has become host to the Blackstone River and Canal Heritage Stage Park, whose visitors center and interpretive trails are also a shared centerpiece of the larger regional Blackstone River Valley National Heritage Corridor.

Information: Blackstone Valley Chamber of Commerce | 110 Church St., Whitinsville, 01588 | 508/234–9090 or 800/841–0919. **Riverbend Farm Visitors Center** | 287 Oak St., Uxbridge | 508/278–7604 | www.blackstonevalley.org.

Attractions

Blackstone Gorge. This quarter-mile gorge framed by 100-ft cliffs is in the Blackstone River Valley National Heritage Corridor. This is a great spot for hikers to pause and take in the view. To find the gorge from Route 122 in Blackstone, drive to the end of County Street. | | Free | Daily dawn–dusk.

Blackstone River and Canal Heritage State Park. Hiking, canoeing, kayaking, picnicking, bicycling, and bird-watching are enjoyed by many in this park, which was designed to commemorate the role that canals played in New England's early industrial development. There is cross-country skiing in the winter. | 287 Oak St. | 508/278–6486 | www.state.ma.us/dem | Free | Daily.

Blackstone Valley Explorer. This 49-passenger riverboat takes you on educational and scenic tours of the Blackstone River. The boat departs from several ports, but it's best to pick it up at the Blackstone Valley Visitor's Center in Pawtucket, Rhode Island, where you can see a 20-minute documentary about the National Heritage Corridor. The riverboat makes four trips per day on weekends, and is available by charter during the week. | 175 Main St., Pawtucket, RI | 401/724–2200 | www.tourblackstone.com | $5 | Apr.–Nov., weekends.

ON THE CALENDAR

JUNE–SEPT.: *Concerts at the Canal.* Free summer concerts are given Sunday afternoons from 3:30 to 5 at River Bend Farm Visitor Center in Blackstone River and Canal Heritage State Park. Many types of musical groups are showcased, a different one each week: swing bands, ethnic bands, folk ensembles, Native American flutes, and fife and drum corps. Bring a blanket or chair. | 508/278–7604.

Dining

Andimo's Italian Restaurant. Italian. You can snuggle with your sweetie or have a quiet family conversation in the privacy of one of the many booths here. Pictures of Italy hang throughout the restaurant. The best dishes are any of the Alfredos, and the veal parmigiana. | 31 S. Main St. | Closed Mon.–Tues. No lunch | $10–$16 | AE, D, MC, V.

Cocke and Kettle. Continental. The dining room in this 1780 mansion has retained some of its colonial features, with its fireplace and copper pots. Baked-stuffed lobster, shrimp, and king-cut prime rib are some of the better bets. | 240 S. Main St. | 508/278–5517 | Closed Mon. No lunch | $13–$21 | AE, D, MC, V.

Oyster Cabin. Contemporary. Rustic exterior and knotty-wood furnishings completely belie the urban sophistication of the third-generation chef-owner, whose accomplished bistro cuisine makes excellent use of the freshest regional produce, meats, and seafood and is matched with fine wines and generous desserts. Try the grilled tuna with blood orange and a beet and dill broth, pistachio and andouille sausage stuffed quail with black mission fig and juniper berry, grilled vegetable lasagna, roast duckling, and chilled crème brûlée. No smoking in dining room. | Rte. 146A | 508/278–4440 | Closed Mon.–Tues. No lunch | $17–$30 | AE, MC, V.

Lodging

Country Side Motel. If you're on a budget, this bare-bones motel about 14 mi west of Uxbridge center off Route 122 may be the ticket. It's as plain as white bread, with the expected bed, desk, and table, but you can't beat the price. Cable TV. | 115 Mechanic St. | 508/966–0440 | 19 rooms | $50 | AE, MC, V.

Courtyard by Marriott. This business-oriented hotel has easy access to I–495, I–90, and I–95, and Wrentham's discount outlets. You can expect predictable business-hotel decor—tasteful but impersonal. Restaurant, bar, limited room service. In-room data ports, cable TV. Indoor pool. Hot tub. Gym. Business services. | 10 Fortune Blvd., Milford | 508/634–9500 | fax 508/634–9694 | www.courtyard.com | 142 rooms, 10 suites | $119–$129, $149 suites | AE, D, DC, MC, V.

Quaker Inn and Conference Center. This motel in the Blackstone Valley, with its quiet country look, is from the classic road-trip era, and has been modernized for the contemporary traveler. It's a 20-minute drive from Worcester and Providence. Complimentary Continental breakfast. Some in-room data ports, cable TV. Pool. Gym. Business services. | 442 Quaker Hwy. | 508/278–2445 | fax 508/278–7083 | www.quakermotorlodge.com | 38 rooms | $55–$70 | AE, MC, V.

Radisson Hotel Milford. Close to the scenic Blackstone Valley and the retail outlets, restaurants, and movie theaters in Worcester and Wrentham, this hotel is also near I–495, I–90, and I–95. The concierge floor offers extra amenities such as Continental breakfast, hors d'oeuvres, and cocktails. Restaurant, bar with entertainment. In-room data ports, cable TV. Indoor pool. Sauna. Health club. Business services. | 11 Beaver St., Milford | 508/478–7010 or 800/333–3333 | fax 508/478–5600 | www.radisson.com | 166 rooms, 8 suites | $179–$199, $144–$214 suites | AE, D, DC, MC, V.

VINEYARD HAVEN (MARTHA'S VINEYARD)

MAP 6, J7

(Nearby towns also listed: Edgartown, Falmouth, Oak Bluffs, West Tisbury, Woods Hole)

Because of its monopoly on ferry service to the mainland, Vineyard Haven is the principal point of entry for Martha's Vineyard. It was originally the portside village within the larger town of Tisbury, but now that Vineyard Haven has become the island's leading residential and commercial community, nobody speaks of Tisbury anymore outside of Town Hall. By off-island standards, the place is still a locket-size miniature, with a year-round population of about 4,500, but come summer it blossoms into a busy resort, linked to its neighboring towns by shuttle buses and ever-popular bike paths. Visitors stepping off the ferry are greeted by a small, easily strollable downtown filled with shops and eateries, set against a historic backdrop of elegant old captains' mansions. Within walking distance of the yacht-filled harbor are numerous bed-and-breakfast inns, each as distinctive as its owner. Just don't bother looking for a liquor store, as Vineyard Haven is a dry town.

Information: Information Center | Beach Rd. | 508/693–0085 | mvcc@vineyard.net | www.mvy.com. **Martha's Vineyard Chamber of Commerce** | Box 1698, Vineyard Haven, 02568 | 508/693–0085.

Attractions

Car/passenger ferry service. Vineyard Haven is the only town on Martha's Vineyard with year-round ferry service to the mainland. It also benefits from seasonal passenger-only ferries from Connecticut, southeastern Massachusetts, and Cape Cod. All vessels allow bicycles to be brought along for a fee.

Cape Island Express Lines. The passenger-only *Schamonchi* is the ferry of choice for island-bound visitors seeking to avoid Cape Cod traffic and parking woes. After taking advantage of the inexpensive and plentiful parking across the street from the ferry pier on New Bedford's outer harbor, passengers enjoy a scenic 90-minute cruise across Buzzards Bay and through the Elizabeth Islands to Vineyard Haven. | Beach Rd., Tisbury Wharf | 508/997–1688 | www.mvferry.com | $17–$19 round-trip | Mid-May–Columbus Day, daily.

Fox Navigation. Seasonal weekend high-speed passenger service to Vineyard Haven from both New York Harbor and New London, Connecticut. The big, smooth-sailing, all-enclosed catamarans complete the Connecticut trip in 2½ hours and the passage from Liberty Landing, New Jersey (a quick hop by public transit from the Manhattan's World Trade Center) in five hours. The vessel offers two classes of service; the higher price buys more elbow room and better views. | Pier 44 | 860/437–6930 or 888/SAIL–FOX | www.foxnavigation.com | From CT $59–$89 round-trip; from NJ $169–$199 round-trip | Memorial Day–Columbus Day, Fri.–Sun. | Closed Mon.–Thurs.

Steamship Authority. The big car-carrying ferries of the Steamship Authority are Vineyard Haven's year-round lifeline to the mainland. The 45-minute journey is made at least eight times daily in winter and up to more than a dozen times daily on peak summer weekends. Reservations are required for your vehicle. | Steamship Terminal, Water St. | 508/477–8600 | www.islandferry.com | Passengers $10 round-trip; vehicles $62–$104 round-trip | Daily.

Centre Street Cemetery. This quiet plot between William and Franklin Streets, with its grave markers dating back to 1817, stands as a reminder of the folks who built this town and farmed this island. | Centre St. | Free | Daily.

Historic District. Although the Great Fire of 1883 destroyed much of Vineyard Haven's original Main Street commercial district, the quiet, residential blocks along parallel William Street were spared. The 50-odd 19th-century houses within this designated National Historic District clearly evoke the prosperity of the town's past, both in size and architectural detail. The neighborhood's buildings are also worth admiring, from the 1833 Methodist meetinghouse, now a theater, to the town hall. | William St. | Free | Daily.

Owen Park. On a grassy knoll sloping down to a little public beach and overlooking a fine harbor filled with wooden boats, this park is a nice place to escape the crowds and enjoy a picnic. | Owen Park Rd. | Free | Daily.

Tisbury Town Hall. Also known as Association Hall, town business is conducted on the first floor, while matters of art transpire above: the second floor of this classical 1844 building houses a theater where plays, concerts, and dances are performed beneath murals depicting island scenes of whaling and Native American gatherings. | 51 Spring St. | 508/696–4200 | Free | Daily.

Vineyard Playhouse. This year-round community and professional ensemble produces excellent drama, classics, and comedies; Shakespeare is presented at a nearby outdoor amphitheater in summer. Bring a pillow to sit on and mosquito repellent to the latter venue; the playhouse is air-conditioned. There is also a children's program. | 24 Church St. | 508/693–6450 | www.vineyardplayhouse.org | $17.50–$27.50.

West Chop & West Chop Lighthouse. About 2 mi from the center of town, the exclusive neighborhood of West Chop is home to some of the island's most notable residents. The brick lighthouse, built in 1838, has been moved twice to escape eroding cliffs. Walk beyond the light to a scenic harbor overlook with benches. | West Chop Rd. | Interior closed to the public.

ON THE CALENDAR

JULY: *Tisbury Street Fair.* Main street is closed down for this day-long festival when entertainers, arts and crafts booths, and food vendors fill the small town. | 508/693–0085.

Dining

Black Dog Tavern. American. One of the better-known restaurants in New England, this phenomenon has a life of its own now, albeit one that some would like to strangle. The waterfront tavern is so crowded that locals won't go there anymore, but visitors still descend on the place in droves. The American food is fine but pricey; you'll find cod, pasta, and the like. The menu changes daily but favorite items such as the garlic crusted fresh bluefish with tomato vinaigrette appear with some frequency. | 1 Beach St. Ext. | 508/693–9223 | www.theblackdog.com | Breakfast also available | $14–$28 | AE, D, MC, V.

Café Moxie. Contemporary. Fancy pizzas and salads predominate at lunch, but the kitchen gets more creative as night falls. Look for intriguing salmon, scallops, steak, and chicken preparations. The contemporary cuisine is as stylish as the interior design. During the summer, visiting chefs from Boston come in and cook for a night. | 48 Main St. | 508/693–1484 | www.cafemoxie.com | Mid-Sept.–Memorial Day, closed Sun.–Wed. | $20–$32 | D, MC, V.

Le Grenier. French. Traditional and authentic French dishes like frogs' legs, sweetbreads, and calves' brains have kept loyal patrons salivating since the late 1970s. The second-floor dining room isn't elegant, but it's candlelit and comfortable. | 96 Main St. | 508/693–4906 | No lunch | $22–$32 | AE, D, DC, MC, V.

Lodging

Crocker House Inn. On a quiet dead-end street within steps of a public beach, this lovely B&B has a wide variety of rooms, from a large loft with a balcony and harbor views to a lace-bedecked purple room with a brass bed. Some of the rooms have fireplaces. Complimentary Continental breakfast. Some in-room hot tubs, cable TV. Beach. No pets. No kids under 12. No smoking. | 12 Crocker Ave. | 508/693–1151 or 800/772–0206 | fax 508/693–1123 | www.crockerhouseinn.com | 8 rooms | $195–$365 | AE, MC, V.

Greenwood House. A 1906 Mission-style California bungalow with an Arts and Crafts look. It's on a quiet street two blocks from the beach, restaurants, and shops; four blocks from the ferry; and ½ mi from golf and tennis. Its rooms include a formal Colonial with a lace canopy bed, a country Colonial with a pencil-post bed and pine furniture, and a penthouse suite with antique and wicker furniture. Wicker furniture also provides cozy lounging on the porch, and there's a garage with a bike rack, and ample parking. Help yourself to beach towels and chairs for a day in the sun. Complimentary breakfast. In-room data ports, refrigerators, cable TV. Business services. No smoking. | 40 Greenwood Ave. | 508/693–6150 or 800/525–9466 | fax 508/696–8113 | www.greenwoodhouse.com | 2 rooms, 3 suites | $179–$269 | AE, DC, MC, V.

Hanover House. This 1906 Victorian with enclosed porch, patio, and gardens has period furnishings. The 1984 Victorian-style addition is a renovated carriage house made into three suites. Some of the rooms have private entrances from the porch. The property is next to a bike path; it's a five-minute walk from Main Street and 10 minutes from the beach. Complimentary Continental breakfast. Some kitchenettes, cable TV. Business services. No smoking. | 28 Edgartown Rd. | 508/693–1066 or 800/339–1066 | fax 508/696–6099 | www.hanoverhouseinn.com | 12 rooms (4 with shower only), 3 suites | $155–$225, $230–$305 suites | AE, D, MC, V.

The Look Inn. On a quiet street within walking distance of the town center, this small 1806 farmhouse has comfortable and homey rooms. Complimentary Continental breakfast. Cable TV. Hot tub, massage. Library. No pets. No kids under 12. No smoking. | 13 Look St. | 508/693–6893 | 3 rooms (with shared bath) | $125 | MC, V.

Martha's Place. After a complete makeover in the late 1990s, it's wonderfully obvious that this sophisticated 1840s Greek Revival has been attended to by a professional interior decorator (who happens to be one of the hospitable owners). Furnishings tend toward chandeliers and Oriental rugs; luxurious amenities include robes and fine Egyptian cotton linens. Some of the rooms have water views and fireplaces. The B&B is just three blocks from the ferry landing. Complimentary breakfast. In-room data ports, some in-room hot tubs, cable TV. Bicycles. No pets. No smoking. | 114 Main St. | 508/693–0253 | www.marthasplace.com | 6 rooms | $175–$395 | AE, D, MC, V.

★ **Thorncroft Inn.** Hidden behind trees on 3½ acres of landscaped grounds about 1 mi from downtown, this inn is made up of three buildings. Most of the formal, Colonial-style rooms have canopied four-poster beds and antiques dating from 1785 to 1840; many have working wood-burning fireplaces. Extensive concierge services are provided, including dinner reservations and printed directions to island restaurants. Dining room, complimentary breakfast. In-room data ports, some in-room hot tubs, cable TV, VCRs. Business services. No smoking. | 460 Main St. | 508/693–3333 or 800/332–1236 | fax 508/693–5419 | www.thornecroft.com | 14 rooms | $240–$500 | AE, D, DC, MC, V.

Tisbury Inn. This 1794 hotel, a mere block from the ferry landing, is smack in the center of town. While most rooms are small, those facing Main Street have the additional burden of being noisy. But the simple rooms are pleasant enough, are decorated in pastels and floral fabrics, and have firm mattresses. Restaurant, complimentary Continental breakfast. Indoor pool. Sauna, hot tub. Health club. No pets. No smoking. | 9 Main St. | 508/693–2200 or 800/332–4112 | fax 508/693–4095 | www.tisburyinn.com | 28 rooms, 4 suites | $195–$213, $269–$295 suites | AE, D, DC, MC, V.

Vineyard Harbor Motel. Just two blocks from the ferry landing and with access to the private harbor beach that overshadows this motel's uninspired, standard furnishings. Some kitchenettes. No pets. | 60 Beach Rd. | 508/693–3334 | fax 508/693–0320 | www.mvy.com/vharbor | 40 rooms | $160–$190 | D, MC, V.

WALTHAM

MAP 6, H3

(Nearby towns also listed: Boston, Cambridge, Concord, Lexington, Newton, Sudbury, Wellesley)

Waltham, a small city of about 60,000 residents and home to Brandeis University, straddles the Charles River a few miles upstream from Boston. The nation's first consolidated textile mill, combining all the steps of cloth manufacturing under one roof, was established in 1814 in Waltham, where the river was harnessed for power. Among the industries that followed were manufacturers of fine watches, and soon Waltham came to be known as "Watch City." This industrial legacy, celebrated by a museum inside the oldest of the riverside textile factories, has been completely supplanted by high tech. Renovated 19th-century brick mills along the Charles, filled by new tenants such as Lycos (the Internet portal), and acres of gleaming corporate headquarters strung along circumferential Route 128/I–95 have together made Waltham the second-largest office market in the metro area. At its heart Waltham still retains a small-town feeling, thanks to the many local retailers that continue to fill its downtown.

Information: Waltham–West Suburban Chamber of Commerce | 84 South St., Waltham, 02453-3537 | 781/894–4700 | wwscc@walthamchamber.com | www.walthamchamber.com.

Attractions
Brandeis University. Founded in 1948, Brandeis has rapidly become one of the nation's top-ranked private liberal arts institutions, with a combined undergraduate and graduate enrollment of approximately 4,000. The large campus, whose architectural modernism stands in marked contrast to most of its New England peers, covers an entire hill rising above the so-called Lake District of the Charles River. | 415 South St. | 781/736–4300 | www.brandeis.edu | Free | Daily. Tours Sept.–May, Tues.–Sun.
Rose Art Museum. On the lower end of campus next to the Spingold Theater, this museum's modern facade foreshadows the changing shows of modern and contemporary art exhibited within. The building seems small from the outside yet is surprisingly spacious inside—

there is much more here than first meets the eye. | 415 South St. | 781/736–3434 | www.brandeis.edu/rose | Free | Sept. 5–mid-June, Tues.–Wed. and Fri.–Sun. noon–5; Thurs. noon–9.

Charles River Museum of Industry. Here on the banks of the Charles River in 1814 a group of investors launched the nation's first fully integrated textile factory, capable of taking raw cotton and producing finished fabric. The renovated old mill in which this landmark achievement in industrialization occurred is now filled with a fascinating yard-sale jumble of displays, photos, and artifacts that highlight local manufacturing history, from textiles to cars, watches, and electronics. | 154 Moody St. | 781/893–5410 | fax 781/891–4536 | www.crmi.org | $4 | Mon.–Sat. 10–5.

Gore Place. Just off U.S. Route 20 (Main Street), this 1806 Federal-style mansion—once the home of the seventh governor of Massachusetts, Christopher Gore—occupies a 45-acre garden estate, which is still maintained as an example of a country estate, grazing livestock and all. In addition to the annual Sheepshearing Festival in spring, there are regular tours of the main house's 22 antiques-filled rooms, resplendent with American, European, and Asian furnishings. | 52 Gore St. | 781/894–2798 | www.goreplace.org | $7 | Mid-Apr.–mid-Nov., tours on the hour Tues.–Sat. 11–5, Sun. 1–4.

Lyman Estate, "The Vale." Built in 1793 by noted Salem architect Samuel McIntire, one of the leading practitioners of the Federal style, this estate is best known for its fine English country gardens. The property's historic greenhouses, a testament to the leisure pursuits of Boston's early aristocrats, are filled with camellias, grapevines, orchids, herbs, and other plants, many of which are on sale. Now maintained by the Society for the Preservation of New England Antiquities, the house is open only for rentals and special functions. | 185 Lyman St. | 781/891–4882 (greenhouses) or 781/893–7232 (house) | fax 781/893–7832 | www.spnea.org | Free | Greenhouses Mon.–Sat. 9:30–4; grounds daily 9–5, unless reserved for special events.

ON THE CALENDAR

APR.: *Sheepshearing Festival.* Sheepshearing and herding, spinning, weaving, and wool-dyeing are demonstrated at this annual spring event held at Gore Place, just off U.S. 20 (Main Street), on the last Saturday of the month. There's a tent for children's activities, a large crafts fair, wagon rides, puppeteers, Morris dancers and musical entertainment, historic demonstrators, and farm animals. | 781/894–2798.

SEPT.: *Harvest Fair.* This town festival held on the Common, next to city hall, consists of a crafts show, food vendors, police and fire department demonstrations, and other family activities. | 781/893–4040.

Dining

Absolutely Asia. Chinese. The clientele at this Asian-flavors restaurant is primarily corporate, of the high-tech breed. Black-and-white photographs of global scenes hang on the walls and the dining area has soft peach colors and white maple furniture. Chinese dishes reign, but other parts of Asia are also represented—Thailand, Malaysia, and Vietnam. Popular appetizers include fried calamari and crab Rangoon; General Tso's chicken and grilled sirloin steak with peppercorn sauce are recommended entrées. Full bar service. | 864 Main St. | 781/891–1700 | www.absolutelyasia.com | $5–$28 | AE, D, DC, MC, V.

Carambola. Cambodian. This 85-seat restaurant decorated with photographs of Cambodia is known for its delicious spring rolls. Try those made of pork, peanuts, and carrots wrapped with lettuce, mint, basil, and bean sprouts and served with *tuk trey* (fish) sauce. Also available are vegetarian spring rolls with wood-ear and shiitake mushrooms. Chicken lemongrass and *soupe Phnom-Penh,* which consists of rice noodles, sliced pork, and fried garlic, are also popular. | 663 Main St. | 781/899–2244 | www.carambola.com | No lunch weekends | $7–$20 | AE, D, DC, MC, V.

Grille at Hobbs Brook. Contemporary. Spacious, elegantly modern dining rooms at this Doubletree Guest Suites restaurant offer views of the chef's herb and vegetable gardens, a lovely place to peruse the broad menu of prime meats, fresh seafood, and pasta. Of note are a full salad bar and live music Monday through Saturday nights and on Sunday morning, during brunch. Kids' menu. Early bird suppers. Sun. brunch. | 550 Winter St. | 781/487–4263 | $17–$25 | AE, D, DC, MC, V.

Il Capriccio. Italian. Come to this intimate restaurant and feast on northern Italian cuisine, from Tuscan to Piedmontese, selectively presented on a regularly changing menu that emphasizes local farm produce and seafood; hundreds of Italian wine selections are an enticing accompaniment. Try the porcini mushroom soufflé, grilled veal, duck, seafood, and pasta specials. No smoking. | 888 Main St. | 781/894–2234 | Reservations essential | Closed Sun. No lunch | $23–$34 | AE, D, DC, MC, V.

Tuscan Grill. Italian. Quaint and rustic, this restaurant combines classic Italian style, an urban sensibility, and a cosmopolitan menu of contemporary northern Italian cuisine, robust yet refined, with upscale accompaniments and presentation. The spit-roasted loin of pork or any of the homemade pastas of the day are suggested. There's also a popular bar. No smoking in dining room. | 361 Moody St. | 781/891–5486 | $11.95–$18.50 | D, MC, V.

Lodging

Best Western TLC. This renovated business-oriented hotel is in the high-tech area, 10 mi from Boston. It is close to major highways I–90 and I–95. Restaurant, bar, room service. In-room data ports, cable TV. Indoor pool. Gym. Business services. | 477 Totten Pond Rd. | 781/890–7800 or 877/852–4683 | fax 781/890–4937 | 100 rooms | $159–$179 | AE, D, DC, MC, V.

Doubletree Guest Suites. High-tech workers frequent this all-suite hotel conveniently close to I–90 and I–95 and a 20-minute drive from Boston. A complimentary shuttle transports guests to businesses within a 5-mi radius. Restaurant, bar, complimentary breakfast (weekends). In-room data ports, cable TV. Indoor pool. Hot tub. Gym. Video games. Laundry facilities. Business services. | 550 Winter St. | 781/890–6767 | fax 781/890–8917 | www.doubletreehotels.com | $129–$244 | AE, D, DC, MC, V.

Four Points Sheraton. The look of this efficient and modern hotel reveals its focus on business travelers. It's close to local businesses and has a shuttle that operates within a 2-mi radius. Restaurant, Bar, room service. In-room data ports, cable TV. Indoor pool. Gym. Laundry service. Business services. | 420 Totten Pond Rd. | 781/890–0100 or 888/627–8165 | fax 781/890–4777 | www.starwoodhotels.com | 148 rooms | $89–$219 | AE, D, DC, MC, V.

Home Suites Inn. The owner is on-site to ensure that the inn lives up to its motto: "comfortable and connected." A fireplace, lounge, and complimentary coffee, tea, and lemonade add to the homey feeling. The exterior of the inn is done in a Spanish style, and there are gardens on the grounds. A shuttle bus is available to some locations. Every room has T1 lines for fast data transmission. Extended-stay rates are available. Restaurant, bar, picnic area, complimentary breakfast. In-room data ports, microwaves, refrigerators, cable TV, in-room VCRs. Pool. Gym. Laundry facilities, laundry service. Business services. | 455 Totten Pond Rd. | 781/890–3000 or 800/424–4021 | fax 781/890–0233 | www.homesuitesinn.com | 100 rooms, 13 suites | $169, $219 1–bedroom suites, $249 2–bedroom suites | AE, D, DC, MC, V.

Homestead Village Guest Studios. This new, extended-stay property has modern-looking studios with generic outdoor landscaping. Studios come with the latest business conveniences. In-room data ports, kitchenettes, cable TV. Laundry facilities. Pets allowed (fee). | 52 4th Ave. | 781/890–1333 or 888/STAYHSD | fax 781/890–1901 | www.stayhsd.com | 140 studios with bath | $99–$109 | AE, D, DC, MC, V.

Sierra Suites Hotel. The units at this all-suites hotel contain generic modern furnishings. Its convenience, located behind the Waltham Westin at the intersection of I–95, Route 128, and Totten Pond Road, is a draw, as are the coffee bar and 24-hour business center. In-room data ports, cable TV. Outdoor pool. Health club. Business services. No pets. | 32 4th Ave. | 781/622–1900 | www.sierrasuites.com | 135 studio suites | $159–$209 | AE, D, DC, MC, V.

Summerfield Suites by Wyndham. This tan stucco building encircles its heated outdoor pool. Each suite has a complete kitchen and cooking utensils, living room with pull-out sofa, bedroom(s) with king-size bed, and private bath(s) and vanity area. The front desk, on-site convenience store, and gym are open 24 hours. Complimentary breakfast. In-room data ports, kitchenettes, microwaves, refrigerators, cable TV, in-room VCRs. Outdoor pool. Hot tub. Gym. Laundry facilities, laundry service. Business services. Pets allowed. | 54 4th Ave. | 781/290–0026 | fax 781/290–0037 | www.summerfieldsuites.com | 85 1-bedroom suites, 51 2-bedroom suites | $239–$289 | AE, D, DC, MC, V.

Susse Chalet Waltham. The price/value leader in the high-tech belt around Boston, this renovated hotel is close to I–90 and I–95, with quick access to Technology Drive. Restaurant, bar, complimentary Continental breakfast. Cable TV. Business services. | 385 Winter St. | 781/890–2800 or 800/5CHALET | fax 781/890–1021 | 157 rooms, 2 suites | $96–$130, $161 suites | AE, D, DC, MC, V.

The Westin Waltham–Boston. The business traveler will benefit from this hotel's proximity and convenient shuttle to many area businesses. It's also close to both Bentley and Brandeis. Restaurant, bar, room service. In-room data ports, cable TV. Indoor pool. Hot tub, sauna. Gym. Business services. Pets allowed. | 70 3rd Ave. | 781/290–5600 | fax 781/290–5626 | www.westin.com | 316 rooms, 30 suites | $249, $289 suites | AE, D, DC, MC, V.

WELLESLEY

MAP 6, H4

(Nearby towns also listed: Boston, Dedham, Natick, Newton, Waltham)

One of Boston's wealthiest suburbs, Wellesley is also a college town, home to three institutions of higher learning, including Wellesley College, the alma mater of Hillary Rodham Clinton. Wellesley is also the midpoint along the route of the famous Boston Marathon. A crisscrossing of heavily commercial highways, including Routes 9 and 135, contributes an incongruously large quantity of traffic to the well-landscaped community. A mix of upscale boutiques and family-oriented shops fill downtown, along with some of the best dining in the vicinity, but the major attractions, such as the Davis Museum and Cultural Center, are all found on the local college campuses.

Information: **Wellesley Chamber of Commerce** | 1 Hollis St., Ste. 111, Wellesley, 02482 | 781/235–2446 | jl.wcc@worldnet.att.net | www.wellesleyweb.com.

Attractions

Babson World Globe. This giant hollow-steel globe on the campus of Babson College was once the largest revolving globe in the world. In need of repair, the globe remains stationary for the time being. When it was erected in 1955 it portrayed the world's political divisions. A good barometer of how times have changed is its transformation in the mid-1990s to a geographical representation, with a colorful rendering of Earth's oceans and continents. | Forest St., near Colman Hall | 781/239–6428 | www.babson.edu/archives | Free | Daily dawn–dusk.

Wellesley College. Founded in 1870, this undergraduate women's college is also one of the nation's top-ranking liberal arts institutions. Its hilly 500-acre campus, many of its trees tagged as if in a large arboretum, includes exceptional examples of collegiate Gothic architecture, the most prominent of which is the landmark tower over Green Hall, home to the admissions office. Tours are available by appointment. | 106 Central St. | 781/283–1000 | www.wellesley.edu | Free | Daily.

Davis Museum and Cultural Center. Appropriately for an educational institution, this museum's diverse collection runs the gamut of art history, from African, South American, and Asian antiquities to Cézanne, Calder, and Warhol, not to mention regular exhibitions of new contemporary art. The works are further complemented by the dramatic interior of the building itself, designed by the Spanish postmodernist José Rafael Moneo. | College Rd. | 781/283–2051 | fax 781/283–2064 | www.wellesley.edu/davismuseum | Free | Labor

Day–mid-June, Tues. and Fri.–Sat. 11–5 and Wed.–Thurs. 11–8.; mid-June–Labor Day, Tues.–Sat. 11–5 and Sun. 1–5.

ON THE CALENDAR

NOV.: *Wellesley Marketplace Craft Festival.* On the Saturday before Thanksgiving you can see over 90 exhibitors from all over Massachusetts showing their wares. Items on display include: baskets, pottery, glass, clothing, jewelry, toys and more. This event at the Wellesley High School is sponsored by the Wellesley Junior Women's Club and the proceeds go to local charities. Tickets can be puchased at the door. | 50 Rice St. | 781/431–2445.

Dining

Amarin of Thailand II. Thai. The spacious dining room here looks out on a side street near the heart of the downtown shopping district, but given the attractively presented and aromatic meals, few diners have a chance to be distracted by anything beyond the rim of their plates. Try the chicken coconut soup, beef penang, and seafood and curry dishes. Beer and wine only. No smoking. | 27 Grove St. | 781/239–1350 | No lunch Sun. | $7.25–$14.75 | AE, DC, MC, V.

Blue Ginger. Pan-Asian. Sculptural fixtures and a sleek, neutral design provide a soothing framework for an extraordinary melding of Asian and Western cuisine by nationally known chef-owner Ming Tsai. Try the foie gras and shiitake shumai, Indonesian curry pasta, and sake-miso-marinated sea bass. No smoking. | 583 Washington St. | 781/283–5790 | Closed Sun. No lunch weekends | $19–$28 | AE, MC, V.

Figs. Mediterranean. In a spacious, airy storefront with upscale contemporary decor, one of a metro-area quartet of gourmet pizzerias dishes up more than just its trademark paper-thin wood-fired brick-oven pizza. Try the house special—fig and prosciutto pizza—the salads, and the antipasto. | 92 Central St. | 781/237–5788 | $20–$29 | AE, DC, MC, V.

Lodging

Wellesley Inn on the Square. The inn is a block away from the commuter rail line to Boston and close to three colleges: Babson, Wellesley, and Massachusetts Bay Community College. It exudes tradition with everything from its White House–like construction to its tasteful flower arrangements. There are two different sections to the building; the older one was built in the 1850s. 2 restaurants, bar. Cable TV. Business services. | 576 Washington St. | 781/235–0180 | fax 781/235–5263 | www.wellesleyinn.com | 65 rooms, 5 suites | $129–$139, $110–$180 suites | AE, D, DC, MC, V.

Wellesley Travel Inn. Five miles from I–95 off exit 20B, this inn contains two motel-style brick buildings of two and three stories, both with elevators. Guest rooms are mauve and green and have dark-wood furniture. Complimentary morning coffee is available in the lobby; complimentary Continental breakfast is available on weekends. There is an on-site car rental agency. Cable TV, microwaves, refrigerators. Laundry facilities. Business services. No pets. | 978 Worcester St. | 781/235–8555 | fax 781/235–3318 | 61 rooms, 3 suites | $79–$109 | AE, D, MC, V.

WELLFLEET (CAPE COD)

MAP 6, L5

(Nearby towns also listed: Eastham, Provincetown, Truro)

Oysters, artists, and remote windswept beaches are among the attractions in Wellfleet, at the heart of the Cape Cod National Seashore. Its tasty bivalves, once the town's main export, are prized at raw bars and seafood restaurants throughout the Northeast, and its harbor is still one of the Cape's few with more fishing boats than yachts. Wellfleet's

WELLFLEET
(CAPE COD)

INTRO
ATTRACTIONS
DINING
LODGING

center lies west of busy U.S. 6, and many are the drivers who pass it by without a glance, never realizing how close they are to experiencing Cape Cod as it used to be prior to the arrival of the malls. What the town lacks in sportswear shops and beach-side motels it more than makes up for with its landscape, which ranges from great tracts of estuarial salt marsh to pine-forested bluffs standing sentinel over the Atlantic. Because Wellfleet is at the northern end of the ever-popular Cape Cod Rail Trail, its numerous art galleries and varied eateries make it a good destination for cyclists.

Information: Information Booth (May–Oct.) | U.S. 6, South, Wellfleet, 02663 | 508/349–2510 | wellfleet@capecod.net | www.capecod.net/wellfleetcc. **Wellfleet Chamber of Commerce** | Box 571, Wellfleet, 02667-0571 | 508/349–2510.

Attractions

Cape Cod Rail Trail. Utilizing the former bed of the old Penn Central Railroad laid in the late 1800s, this dedicated bike trail is one of the most popular attractions on the Cape. From South Dennis to South Wellfleet, this predominately flat 25-mi trail provides a leisurely way to take in the Cape's natural contours and geography. You'll pass kettle ponds, pine forests, marshes, and beaches. There are bikes and in-line skates for rent. The Wellfleet trailhead is at the U.S. Post Office on U.S. 6. | U.S. 6 .

First Congregational Church. This handsome 1850 Greek Revival church boasts the only clock in the world to strike its bells on ship's time. (It's alright to peek at your watch to confirm the time after hearing a series of bells.) The interior is lovely and has a 1873 organ used during summer concerts. | 200 Main St. | 508/349–6877 | Free | July–Aug.; concerts, Sun. 8.

Great Island. Administered by the national seashore, this island, really a 7-mi-long peninsula, makes a pleasant getaway during the height of summer. Soft sand makes for tough trekking, and tree cover is sparse, so bring plenty of sunscreen and water. During the 17th century animals were pastured on Great Island, and a tavern supplied sustenance to whalers and fishermen. | Chequesset Neck Rd. | Free | Daily.

Marconi Station. The first wireless communication, made possible by Italian radio and wireless pioneer Guglielmo Marconi, was sent between England and the United States from a station built on this inauspicious spot in 1903. Because of erosion, not much remains except the tower bases on the cliffs below. | Marconi Site Rd., South Wellfleet | Free | Daily.

★ **Massachusetts Audubon Society's Wellfleet Bay Wildlife Sanctuary.** These 1,000 acres are home to more than 250 species of birds. Enjoy excellent hiking and birding here, with views of the salt marshes and the bay. | 291 U.S. 6 | 508/349–2615 | $3 | Daily 8–dusk.

Skateboard Park and Playground. Opened in 2000, this park of ramps and levels provides a place for skate enthusiasts to show what they're made of. A next-door playground is perfect for kids under 10. | Kendrick Ave. | 508/349–2510.

Wellfleet Drive-In Theatre and Flea Market. By night, the old-fashioned tradition of outdoor double features lives on. A snack bar and miniature golf provide even more diversion. By day, the giant parking lot is transformed into a sprawling flea market. | U.S. 6, South Wellfleet | 508/349–2520 | $6.50 | Drive-in, late May–mid-Sept; flea market, July–Aug., Wed. and Thurs., weekends.

Wellfleet Pier. Bobbing with fishing boats, yachts, charters, sailboats, and party boats at high tide, this pleasure harbor is also lively at low tide when raking for oysters, clams, and quahogs on the tidal flats takes over. | Commercial St. | 508/349–9818, shellfish permits | Free | Daily.

ON THE CALENDAR

JULY–AUG.: *Square Dancing on the Pier.* Each Wednesday night square-dancing fans head for the pier. Line dancing like the Popcorn, the Hokey Pokey, and the Virginia Reel are called by an experienced octogenarian. | 508/349–2510.

Dining

★ **Aesop's Tables.** Contemporary. A handful of intimate dining rooms in an 1805 former sea captain's mansion with ship timbers from the 18th century provides a serene spot for creative Mediterranean-inspired new American cuisine, accompanied by some 75 wine selections from around the world. Try the chicken Rosalita (sautéed chicken breast with prosciutto, spinach, fontina gratinée, finished with truffle oil) or *bella notte* (fresh lobster meat with mushrooms, leeks, artichoke hearts, and sundried tomatoes in garlic herb butter.) You can also dine on the patio. Kids' menu. No smoking. | 316 Main St. | 508/349–6450 | $16–$27 | AE, DC, MC, V.

Bookstore & Restaurant. Seafood. There aren't any books lining the walls of the restaurant, but there are more oysters than you could ever catalog. They're grown in flats in front of the harborfront eatery and just don't get any fresher. | 50 Kendrick Ave. | 508/349–3154 | Breakfast also available. Closed Jan. | $12–$19 | AE, D, MC, V.

Captain Higgins. Seafood. Across from the town pier and adjacent to a picturesque marsh, this casual seafood restaurant has outdoor decks from which to take in the view. Wellfleet oysters, marinated calamari, and boiled lobster are popular, but so is bluefish with a sweet mustard glaze. If you've ever wondered what an ostrich burger tastes like, try one here. | Town pier | 508/349–6027 | Closed mid-Sept.–mid-June | $15–$20 | MC, V.

Duck Creek Tavern. Seafood. This Colonial country tavern at the Inn at Duck Creek is decorated with such local touches as lobster buoys. It's a chummy meet 'n' greet, where fresh seafood, along with a few concessions to those who don't eat fish—such as quiche, burgers, salads, and steak—provide fuel for the fire. Try the lobster bisque, chowder, fresh shellfish, kettle of fish, and seafood pie. There's live jazz music on Thursday through Sunday. Kids' menu. No smoking. | 70 Main St. | 508/349–7369 | No lunch | $7.95–$19 | AE, MC, V.

★ **Finely JP's.** Italian. It's an unassuming little roadside shack, loyal patrons love its consistency. Fish and pasta dishes are dressed simply with traditional Italian herbs and sauces, some with just olive oil and lemon. The Wellfleet paella is particularly noteworthy. | U.S. 6, South Wellfleet | 508/349–7500 | Closed mid-Dec.–mid-Jan.; call for hrs spring and fall. No lunch | $13–$16 | D, MC, V.

Flying Fish Café. Café. Breakfast devotees line up for fruit pancakes, three-egg omelets, and baked goods, but the party gets started with internationally influenced dishes like spicy jerk chicken and mussels in a Mexican tomato and garlic sauce. It's a casual place with an exposed kitchen. | Briar La. | 508/349–3100 | Breakfast also available. Closed mid-Oct.–mid-Apr. No lunch | $12–$19 | MC, V.

Lighthouse Restaurant. American/Casual. This homey, no-frills place really packs 'em in. Customers appreciate the inherent value of bacon-and-egg breakfasts and a plate of steamers and a beer at lunchtime. Dinner veers toward burgers and more beer. | 317 Main St. | 508/349–3681 | Breakfast also available. Closed Mar. | $10–$16 | D, MC, V.

Moby Dick's. Seafood. This rough-hewn fish shack is on the edge of a salt marsh, boasts friendly table service after you've ordered from the blackboard, and puts out the freshest fried seafood in the area. What more could you want? The deep-fried outer Cape onion is a specialty. | U.S. 6 | 508/349–9795 | Closed mid-Oct.–Apr. | $8–20 | No credit cards.

Painter's. Contemporary. This uneven chef-owned restaurant either soars or sinks with 10 to 15 seafood offerings. Dishes range from traditional Portuguese fare like hearty clam stew to pan-seared tuna with sesame and mustard seeds. The restaurant has a fresh feel, a small bar, and killer homemade desserts, such as flourless chocolate fig cake. | 50 Main St. | 508/349–3003 | Closed Nov.–early May. No lunch | $17–$31 | AE, MC, V.

PJ's Family Restaurant. Seafood. Not to be confused with Finely JPs, this Wellfleet tradition serves up heaps of fried seafood, steamers, traditional clam chowder, and soft-serve ice-cream cones. Place your order, take a seat in the knotty-pine dining area, watch the bustling open kitchen, and wait for your order, served in Styrofoam bowls, paper plates, and with plastic forks. | U.S. 6 | 508/349–2126 | Closed mid-Oct.–mid-Apr. | $8–$31 | MC, V.

WELLFLEET
(CAPE COD)

INTRO
ATTRACTIONS
DINING
LODGING

Serena's. Italian. Most of the easy-to-sell Italian blackboard specials are smothered in red sauce at this family place that caters to kids. Specialties include *fra diavolo*, a spicy fish stew. | U.S. 6, South Wellfleet | 508/349–9370 | Closed Dec.–Mar. No lunch | $14–$22 | AE, MC, V.

Sweet Seasons Café Restaurant. Contemporary. This gracious dining room at the Inn at Duck Creek overlooks a pond and has an inventive menu emphasizing fresh local fare from farm and ocean, along with good vegetarian selections. It's known for its fresh seafood and home-roasted coffee. No smoking. | 70 Main St. | 508/349–6535 | Closed mid-Sept.–end of June. No lunch | $16.95–$22.95 | AE, MC, V.

Van Rensselaer's. Seafood. A few dining areas make for a casual family eating and service that stays cheerful even when the place gets packed, which is most of the time. You can choose from the dinner menu or a bistro menu, for lighter fare. Besides seafood in all its possible permutations, menus include steak, poultry, and pasta. Try the mixed seafood grill, steak au poivre, lobster ravioli, lobster cake, baked-stuffed lobster, seafood fettuccine, and Wellfleet mud pie with homemade fudge sauce. There's also open-air dining on a screened deck, and breakfast in season and on weekends off-season. Kids' menu. Early bird suppers. No smoking. | 1019 U.S. 6, South Wellfleet | 508/349–2127 | Closed Dec.–Mar. No lunch | $13.95–$21.95 | AE, D, DC, MC, V.

Lodging

Even'tide Motel. This motel is on 11 acres of woodland abutting a bike and hiking trail through the woods to the beach. It provides trail maps, and bike rentals are available nearby. Aside from the motel, there are also Cape-style and A-frame cottages, most of which have decks, wood stoves, and ceiling fans. All of the cottages have picnic tables and a barbecue; some have maid service. Picnic area. Some kitchenettes, refrigerators, cable TV. Indoor pool. Playground. Laundry facilities. | 650 U.S. 6, South Wellfleet | 508/349–3410 or 800/368–0007 in MA | www.eventidemotel.com | 19 rooms, 8 suites, 4 efficiencies | $89–$107, $102–$120 suites, $122–$149 efficiencies, $700–$925/wk cottages | Closed Nov.–Mar. | AE, D, DC, MC, V.

Inn at Duck Creek. This 1815 sea captain's home on 5 acres is furnished with period antiques. Porches overlook a salt marsh, and there's a duck pond behind its two restaurants. It's a five-minute walk from Wellfleet center and a 10-minute walk from the harbor and beach. 2 restaurants, bar with entertainment, complimentary Continental breakfast. No air-conditioning in some rooms, no room phones, no TV. | 70 Main St. | 508/349–9333 | fax 508/349–0234 | www.capecod.net/duckinn | 25 rooms (8 rooms with shared bath) | $70–$95 | Closed Nov.–Apr. | AE, MC, V.

★ **Surf Side Colony Cottages.** Scattered throughout a stand of scrub pine trees, some between the ocean and road, these 1950s-style cottages are a two-minute walk to Le Count Hollow Beach. The exterior of the units are retro Florida, but the interiors are Cape Cod classic, complete with knotty pine. Some have roof decks; all have fireplaces, indoor and outdoor showers, screened porches, and rattan furnishings. Picnic area. Kitchenettes. Laundry facilities. Pets allowed off-season (fee). No smoking. | Ocean View Dr. | 508/349–3959 | fax 508/349–3959 | www.capecod.net/surfside | 18 cottages | $750–$1350/wk (7-night minimum) | Closed Nov.–Mar. | MC, V.

Wellfleet Motel and Lodge. Handy to the Cape Cod bike trail and across the street from the Audubon Society Center and hiking trails, this motel is also about 2 mi from national seashore beaches. The units all have a balcony or patio that overlooks the open and landscaped courtyard. Restaurant (seasonal), bar, picnic area. Refrigerators, cable TV. Indoor and outdoor pools. Hot tub. | 170 U.S. 6, South Wellfleet | 508/349–3535 or 800/852–2900 | fax 508/349–1192 | www.wellfleetmotel.com | 57 rooms, 8 suites | $71–$150, $225 suites | AE, MC, V.

Winterwood B&B. A former barn turned cozy B&B on a quiet side road, this place is filled with antiques and exposed beams. The Garden Suite is particularly nice, with a cathedral ceiling and whirlpool. Complimentary Continental breakfast. Refrigerators. Hot tub. No pets. No smoking. | Long Pond Rd. | 508/349–6737 | 3 rooms (2 with shared bath) | $100–$115 | Closed Jan.–Apr. | No credit cards.

WEST STOCKBRIDGE

MAP 6, A3

(Nearby towns also listed: Great Barrington, Lenox, Stockbridge)

West Stockbridge is the western gateway to Massachusetts. Situated 100 mi north of New York City and 142 mi west of Boston, the town straddles the first interstate exit on the Massachusetts Turnpike (I–90). In contrast to many of its Berkshire neighbors, West Stockbridge was for many decades more industrial than agricultural, deriving much of its wealth during the 18th and 19th centuries from marble quarries, lime kilns, and freight shipped on the Hudson and Berkshire Railroad, of which West Stockbridge was the eastern terminus. One of the principal commodities carried by rail was iron ore from Richmond, West Stockbridge's immediate northern neighbor. Since the demise of the local iron industry in 1923, West Stockbridge has become a rural community with fewer than 2,000 year-round inhabitants and a large colony of summer vacation homeowners. Although the small village center has art galleries, fancy restaurants, and other businesses catering to seasonal visitors, its hardware store, market, and other local shops seem to suggest that it is not about to become a boutique-laden tourist trap.

Information: Southern Berkshires Chamber of Commerce | 362 Main St., Great Barrington, 01230-1804 | 413/528–1510 | vcenter@bcn.net | www.greatbarrington.org.

Attractions
Berkshire Ice Cream Co. Ginger! Coconut almond! Vanilla caramel! Take your pick: for $1.50 you get a heaping scoop of "super-premium" deluxe ice cream with 16% butter fat. The owners claim the flavor is unbeatable because the milk comes from the company's own cows and the ice cream is made daily. | 2 Albany Rd. | 413/232–4111 | Weekdays noon–9, weekends noon–10.

ON THE CALENDAR
OCT.: *Scarecrow-making Contest.* Cider is served while attendees craft scarecrows. Tots start the day off, and adults wrap things up. Usually about 80 scarecrows are made, and the results are displayed all over town until Thanksgiving. | 413/528–1510.

Dining
Card Lake Inn. Continental. Chicken with grilled vegetables and pork chops are among the better dishes here. The restaurant, like the 1805 inn itself, is filled with antiques. | 29 Main St. | 413/232–0272 | fax 413/232–0272 | Reservations essential | Closed Mon.–Tues. | $8–$17 | MC, V.

Truc Orient Express. Vietnamese. White-linen elegance, a formal note not often associated with Vietnamese restaurants in the Northeast, suits the level of cooking here, which seems more appropriate to an imperial household than to a small Berkshire village. Try the happy pancake, duck, fried whole fish, and vegetarian selections. You can dine on deck in the open air during the summer. No smoking. | 3 Harris St. | 413/232–4204 | Closed Sept.–June and Tues. No lunch | $12–$18.50 | AE, D, MC, V.

Williamsville Inn. Contemporary. This intimate 1797 farmhouse with early American furnishings and handsome fireplaces in both candlelit dining rooms, boasts a varied menu that borrows from the French countryside and then tours the globe, picking up plenty of intriguing flavors and preparations along the way. Try the wild mushroom and leek-stuffed chicken with roasted garlic sauce, roasted pepper ravioli stuffed with fresh spinach and creamy ricotta, apricot-glazed rack of lamb, the fresh seafood specials, and all the desserts. | Rte. 41 | 413/274–6118 | Closed Mon.–Wed. No lunch | $15–$23 | AE, MC, V.

Lodging

Card Lake Inn. Originally a stage coach stop, this inn has brass beds with quilts, Colonial furniture, and original 1805 floorboards. There is also an outdoor deck café where you can relax and sip coffee. Restaurant, complimentary Continental breakfast. No room phones. TV in common area. No pets. No smoking. | 29 Main St. | 413/232–0272 | fax 413/232–0294 | www.cardlakeinn.com | 10 rooms | $150 | MC, V.

Williamsville Inn. Each room in this 1797 farmhouse is unique, though all are furnished with antiques. From May through October, the works of internationally renowned sculptors are displayed in the gardens of the 10-acre property. Restaurant, bar, complimentary breakfast. No room phones, no TV. Pool. Tennis. | Rte. 41 | 413/274–6118 | fax 413/274–3539 | www.williamsvilleinn.com | 15 rooms, 1 suite | $140–$150, $195 suites | AE, MC, V.

WEST TISBURY (MARTHA'S VINEYARD)

MAP 6, J8

(Nearby towns also listed: Aquinnah, Chilmark, Edgartown, Oak Bluffs, Vineyard Haven)

Bucolic West Tisbury is the vegetable patch, so to speak, of Martha's Vineyard. Its farms and truck gardens supply produce, often raised organically, and dairy products to many island restaurants. Its twice-weekly summer farmer's market is an island-wide institution, and its autumn livestock show and fair is among the most popular events of the year. A disproportionate number of the Vineyard's resident artists and writers live in West Tisbury, drawn, perhaps, by the absence of all but scenic and culinary distractions. Unprecedented growth in housing construction threatens the town's rural character, but residents seem determined not to lose the open space that makes West Tisbury such a desirable address.

Information: **Information Center** | Beach Rd., Vineyard Haven, 02568 | 508/693–0085 | mvcc@vineyard.net | www.mvy.com. **Martha's Vineyard Chamber of Commerce** | Box 1698, Vineyard Haven, 02568 | 508/693–0085.

Attractions

Cedar Tree Neck Wildlife Sanctuary. From a sphagnum bog to a pond, from wooded trails to a secluded beach, and from azaleas to pygmy beech trees, this 300-acre preserve is a study in contrasting environments. A hilly and unspoiled tract, Cedar Tree is off State Road, with access via a sometimes steep and rocky dirt road. | Indian Hill Rd. | 508/693–5207 | Free | Daily 8:30–5:30.

Chicama Vineyards Winery. It seems only fitting that this island would have a vineyard, but it didn't until 1971. Today, nearly 100,000 bottles of Chenin Blanc, merlot, and a cranberry dessert wine are produced from just a few acres of chardonnay and cabernet grape vines. You can also buy vinegars, mustards, and jellies, and attend tastings year-round. | Stoney Hill Rd. | 508/693–0309 | www.chicamavineyards.com | Free | Late May–mid-Oct., Mon.–Sat. 11–5, Sun. 1–5; call for off-season hours.

Field Gallery. Large white sculptures, posing and dancing out on an expansive lawn, cause many a passerby to come to a screeching halt. Tom Maley's fanciful creations aren't for sale, but the gallery hosts changing summer exhibits of island artists who do hope to sell their work. | State Rd. | 508/693–5595 | Free | June–Aug. daily; May, Sept.–Dec. weekends.

Long Point. This enormous 633-acre preserve has a quiet beauty to it, encompassing Long Cove (a saltwater inlet), Tisbury Great Pond, and lots of other little ponds, including the freshwater Homer's Pond. Swimming and bird-watching are prime activities. There are different entrances during the summer and off-season. In summer, turn left onto the unmarked dirt road (look for the mailboxes) ³⁄₁₀ of a mile west of the airport on Edgartown–West Tisbury Rd. | Waldron's Bottom Rd. | 508/693–3678 | $3 ($7 vehicles) mid-June–mid-Sept; free off-season | Mid-June–mid-Sept. 9–5; mid-Sept.–mid-June dawn–dusk.

★ **Manuel F. Correllus State Forest.** Laced with hiking and biking trails, a 2-mi nature walk, and horseback trails, this state forest is a much needed dam against the rising tide of development. Smack in the middle of the island, and surrounding the airport, the park is easily accessible no matter where you are staying. | Barnes Rd. | 508/693–2540 | Free | Daily dawn–dusk.

Martha's Vineyard Glassworks. "Artisans at work" aptly describes the scene here, where visitors watch the fascinating craft of creating fragile, colorful objets d'art from sand. The resident master glassblowers have their pieces in the collection of the Museum of Fine Arts in Boston. Of course, you can purchase a whole range of creations at the glassworks store. | 683 State Rd. | 508/693–6026 | Free | May–Oct. daily, Nov.–Apr. weekends.

Mayhew Chapel and Indian Burial Ground. Off State Road, this tiny 1829 chapel supplants an earlier one memorializing Thomas Mayhew, Jr., an original island colonist who converted the native Wampanoags to Christianity. Nearby, rough stones mark Native American graves, and a wooded loop trail leads to a lookout tower. | Indian Hill Rd. | Free | Daily.

Mill Pond. This small, tranquil roadside pond, a popular resting spot for graceful swans, is a charming place to picnic on your way up-island from Edgartown. The former 1847 grist mill across the street used to make wool for coats. | Edgartown–West Tisbury Rd. | Free | Daily.

Polly Hill Arboretum. On an old sheep farm laced with quiet walking trails, this delightful arboretum is home to more than 2,000 species of plants, almost 100 of which were developed by Polly Hill, an avid horticulturist. There are guided tours, lectures, and a visitor center. | 809 State Rd. | 508/693–9426 | www.pollyhillarboretum.org | $5 | Late May–mid-Oct., Thurs.–Tues. 7–7; mid-Oct.–late May, Thurs.–Tues. dawn–dusk; visitors center late May–mid-Oct, Thurs.–Tues. 9:30–4.

Ripley's Field Preserve. About ²⁄₃ mi from State Road, off Lambert's Cove Road, this 56-acre preserve will give you a great idea of what the island looked like 200 years ago. The meadows and woodlands are untouched. | John Hoft Rd. | Free | Daily.

Sepiessa Point Reservation. This Land Bank–Nature Conservancy property wraps around the 164-acre Tisbury Great Pond with walking trails, and as such, it's a haven for bird-watching. There are saltwater marshes, swimming, ocean views, and a boat launch, too. The point is located off West Tisbury Road. | New La. | 508/627–7141 | Free | Daily dawn–dusk.

Tisbury Meadow Preserve. A half mile south of the Tashmoo Overlook, this 83-acre preserve is open meadow toward the front of the property and woodland in the rear, where you'll find an 18th-century cart path. | State Rd. | Free | Daily.

Wompesket Preserve. This small 18-acre preserve, with a wet meadow and ponds, is nice for bird-watching. The best way to reach it is from marked trails from Ripley's Field or Tisbury Meadow Preserve. | Red Coat Hill Rd. | Free | Daily.

ON THE CALDENDAR

AUG.: *West Tisbury Agricultural Fair.* Held annualy since 1861, this old-fashioned fair includes arts and crafts vendors, a livestock competition, and plenty of games for the kids. | 508/693–0085.

WEST TISBURY
(MARTHA'S
VINEYARD)

INTRO
ATTRACTIONS
DINING
LODGING

Dining

Lambert's Cove Country Inn. Continental. A popular destination for a special celebration, this countrified dining room serves very good meals by candlelight. Local produce and seafood are prominently featured in delicate but refined preparations. Try the soft-shell appetizer and grilled Muscovy duck breast on caramelized onions. | Lambert's Cove Rd. | 508/693–2298 | Reservations essential | Closed Jan.–late June weekdays. No lunch | $22–$32 | AE, MC, V.

Lodging

The Bayberry. About a five-minute drive on a quiet country road from Vineyard Haven, this homey B&B welcomes you with its comfy living room filled with the innkeeper's pewter, majolica, and basket collections. A fireplace is often used in the winter, as is a piano. There is a breakfast room with a brick patio. In summer, beach passes are issued upon request. Complimentary breakfast. No air-conditioning in some rooms, no TV in rooms, cable TV in common area. No pets. No kids under 12. No smoking. | 49 Old Courthouse Rd. | 508/693–1984 | fax 508/693–4505 | mvbayberry@vineyard.net | www.mvbayberry.vineyard.net | 5 rooms (2 with shared bath) | $125–$175 | Closed Jan.–Feb. | MC, V.

Lambert's Cove Country Inn. This secluded 1790 farmhouse has an early American country interior, with handmade quilts on the beds, antiques, individually decorated rooms, and oriental rugs. The inn shares seven acres of grounds with gardens and an apple orchard. It is ¾ mi from Lambert's Cove Beach. Dining room, picnic area, complimentary breakfast. No room phones, TV in common area. Tennis court. No smoking. | Lambert's Cove Rd. | 508/693–2298 | fax 508/693–7890 | www.vineyard.net/biz/lambertscoveinn | 15 rooms | $185–$250 | Closed Jan. | AE, MC, V.

WESTPORT

MAP 6, I7

(Nearby towns also listed: Dartmouth, Fall River, New Bedford)

Westport, on the coast of Buzzards Bay, is the center of Massachusetts wine country. Ocean-moderated weather and sandy, well-drained soils provide conditions similar to the Bordeaux region of France, which is why Westport and its neighbors are home to some half-dozen vineyards. A centuries-old legacy of seaside agriculture is seen in local farms as well, whose products supply the kitchens of all the best area restaurants, and whose drystone-walled fields lend pastoral charm to any accidental straying from Route 88, the main highway through town. Westport is also deservedly proud of its large public beach, one of the state's best.

Information: **New Bedford Office of Tourism** | Pier 3, New Bedford, 02740 | 508/979–1745 or 800/508–5353 | amotta@www.ci.new-bedford.ma.us | www.ci.new-bedford.ma.us.

Attractions

Horseneck Beach State Reservation. All the necessary ingredients for the perfect beach are right here at Horseneck: a couple of miles of wide, beautiful sand with large, even waves rolling in from the open Atlantic. Food concessions, bathhouses with hot showers, and cheap parking are added pluses. The only drawback is that the beach is well known to every city dweller within a ½ hour drive, but avoid weekends and holidays and you won't be disappointed. | John Reed Rd. | 508/636–8816 | Beach $2; camping $12–$15 | Beach daily; campground mid-Apr.–mid-Oct., daily.

ON THE CALENDAR

JULY: *Agricultural Fair.* Nearly 10,000 people attend this five-day event that features livestock judging, a carnival, tractor pulls, and antique farm equipment demonstrations. The fair takes place from Wednesday to Sunday after the second weekend of the month and is held at the Westport Fairground downtown. | 401/624–6091.

Dining

Back Eddy. Seafood. Enjoy fine views of the Westport harbor from this new restaurant near Horseneck Beach. Try the Eddie spaghetti—mussels and sausage over pasta in an "angry" (i.e., spicy) tomato sauce—or the grilled peppered tuna over Asian salad. | 1 Bridge Rd. | 508/636–6500 | Closed Labor Day–mid-Oct and Mon. (call for hrs Columbus Day–Memorial Day). No lunch weekdays | $18–$24 | AE, D, MC, V.

Bittersweet Farm. Contemporary. The exposed beams of this converted barn on a 70-acre farm contrast pleasantly with the upscale dishes made with fresh local ingredients. A lighter burger-and-appetizer-oriented menu is offered in the downstairs tavern, along with live bands on weekends. The farm is known for its fresh seafood, rack of lamb, and veal chops. Try baked stuffed lobster and tournedos. Live music Fri. and Sat. Kids' menu. Early bird suppers. Sun. brunch. No smoking in dining room. | 438 Main Rd. | 508/636–0085 | No dinner Mon. No lunch Sat.–Tues. | $13.95–$22.95 | AE, D, DC, MC, V.

Priscilla Dining Room. Steak/Seafood. A nautical theme provides the backdrop for a menu rich in traditional American fare, from clams casino and chicken with penne to Jell-O and cheesecake. It's known for lobster salad, steak, and deluxe seafood platters. There is a bar and lounge, kids' menu, and early bird suppers on weeknights. | 66 State Rd. | 508/675–7185 | www.lafrancehospitality.com | $8.95–$16.50 | AE, D, DC, MC, V.

Lodging

Hampton Inn. While the styling of the rooms is rather generic, the hotel compensates by offering a choice of having either a reclining chair or a sofa in your room. There is a bar and restaurant, and some rooms afford a view of Wataputta Pond. Kids under 18 stay free. Restaurant, bar. In-room data ports, cable TV. Hot tub. No pets. | 53 Old Bedford Rd. | 508/675–8500 | fax 508/675–0075 | www.hamptoninn.com | 133 rooms | $124 | AE, D, DC, MC, V.

WILLIAMSTOWN

MAP 6, B2

(Nearby town also listed: North Adams)

Williamstown is the home of Williams College, a highly regarded liberal arts institution founded with a bequest from the 18th-century commander of Fort Massachusetts, the westernmost garrison built along the Massachusetts Colonial frontier. It's an arresting college town, with ivy-covered campus architecture and faculty residences integrated into the downtown to such a degree that it is all but impossible to distinguish where the college ends and the town begins. Williamstown's location at the end of the Mohawk Trail (Route 2), in the far northwest corner of the state, makes it a gateway to southern Vermont, whose Green Mountains crowd the horizon north of town. College alumni, famous in higher education for their loyalty, are always returning to Williamstown for one event or another, keeping the town's many small motels and inns more booked up than you would expect in such a remote locale. Many visitors also come specifically to seek out the town's two exceptional art collections, at the Sterling and Francine Clark Art Institute and the Williams College Museum of Art.

Information: Information Booth | Rte. 2 at U.S. 7 | 413/458–4922 | commerce@williamstown.net | www.williamstownchamber.com. **Williamstown Chamber of Commerce** | Box 357, Williamstown, 01267 | 413/458–9077 or 800/214–3799.

Attractions

Chapin Library of Rare Books and Manuscripts. This broad collection attempts to document civilization, and includes a book from the era of Charlemagne, examples of 16th-century printing, and Americana dating back to Columbus's day. The collection holds 50,000 volumes and 50,000 prints, letters, and assorted documents. | 26 Hopkins Hall Dr. | 413/597–2462.

Mt. Greylock State Reservation. Mt. Greylock is the highest point in Massachusetts, with an elevation of 3,491 ft and a 100-mi view from atop the 105-ft War Memorial Tower at its summit. As the name suggests, however, the peak is buried in clouds more often than not, and it's cooler and windier than its base. More than 50 mi of hiking trails run through the reservation's 12,500 acres, and there is a choice of rustic bunk rooms in the summit lodge or primitive camping on its western flank. The park goes through six different towns, including Williamstown. The office is 13 mi east of Williamstown. | Rockwell Rd., Lanesborough | 413/499–4262, 413/499–4263 | www.state.ma.us/dem | Free; camping $5 for Mass. residents, $6 for non-residents | Daily; campground Memorial Day–Columbus Day. Summit roads closed after first snowfall.

★ **Sterling and Francine Clark Art Institute.** This museum is most famous for its collection of Impressionist works, including more than 30 paintings by Renoir. But the Clark's exceptional collection includes much more, from the European Baroque to Winslow Homer, with sidelines in American silver and old master prints and drawings. Its art history library and conservation laboratory are considered to be among the nation's finest. | 225 South St. | 413/458–9545 | fax 413/458–5962 | www.clark.williams.edu | $5 July–Labor Day; free Labor Day–June | July–Labor Day, daily 10–5; Labor Day–June, Tues.–Sun. 10–5.

Williams College. This small liberal arts institution shares its campus and its origin with the town, both having been named after the same generous 18th-century militia colonel who commanded a frontier garrison a few miles to the east. The highly selective school, known for the dedicated loyalty of its alumni, has a picturebook campus full of graceful 19th-century architecture. | 880 Main St. | 413/597–3131 | www.williams.edu | Free | Daily.

Williams College Museum of Art. Befitting a school with a highly respected art history department, this collegiate museum has a broad collection spanning centuries, but its real strengths are in modern art, both American and non-Western. Changing exhibits and site-specific installations of contemporary work across a wide spectrum of styles, mediums, and themes are another hallmark. | Main St. | 413/597–2429 | fax 413/458–9017 | www.williams.edu/wcma | Free | Tues.–Sat. 10–5, Sun. 1–5.

ON THE CALENDAR

APR.: *Jazztown*. You might encounter improvisational luminaries such as Billy Taylor and Wynton Marsalis, as well as students from Williams College. Swing and hip-hop dance classes are also offered during this week-long festival. Performances and classes take place all over town, but most events are at the Clark Art Institute or Williams College. | 800/214–3799.

JUNE–AUG.: *Williamstown Theatre Festival*. Some of America's finest actors appear on the Main Stage at the Williamstown Playhouse each summer, where five productions are mounted; experimental works-in-progress are performed on the smaller Nikos Stage. | 413/597–3399 (information) or 413/597–3400 (box office).

Dining

Cozy Corner. Eclectic. Your taste buds might experience a pleasant bout of schizophrenia here, as you can sample dishes ranging from fish-and-chips to Greek pizza to shrimp Santorini. Aside from some photos of Greece, there aren't many decorative touches that distinguish this little spot, but you get some mighty generous portions for the price. | 850 Simonds Rd. | $7–$14 | AE, MC, V.

Le Jardin. French. This old home became a small inn and restaurant in 1972. It's a comfortable spot for the impeccable menu, which epitomizes the classic traditions of haute cuisine.

Known for salmon and rack of lamb. Try crisp Long Island duck. No smoking in dining room. | 777 Cold Spring Rd. | 413/458–8032 | Reservations essential July–Aug. weekends | Closed mid-Nov.–Apr. and Mon.–Wed. No lunch | $17–$24 | AE, D, DC, MC, V.

★ **Main Street Café.** Italian. The colors of the custom sponge-painted walls complement the exposed brick walls at this café, where shrimp Toscana and grilled swordfish compete for your attention. | 16 Water St. | 413/458–3210 | $16–$24 | AE, DC, MC, V.

Mezze Bistro. Eclectic. The menu here is in constant flux, but don't be surprised if you encounter sashimi tuna with watercress or filet mignon with roasted root vegetables, two regular favorites. The room design incorporates crisp blond birchwood with hanging tapestries and a thoughtful lighting scheme. Although reservations are not required, this place is happening, so you might want to play it safe and book ahead. Brunch is served on Sundays. | 84 Water St. | 413/458–0123 | No lunch | $17–$22 | AE, MC, V.

Water Street Grill. Eclectic. Bare wood floors and ceiling lend a rustic note to what is otherwise a contemporary college-town eatery with broad appeal as both a hip tavern and a high-energy place for affordable dining on everything from barbecue to vegetarian pasta and seafood. Try the steak or fajitas. There's a buffet at lunchtime on weekdays and live music on Friday and Saturday nights. Kids' menu. | 123 Water St. | 413/458–2175 | $7–$15 | AE, MC, V.

Wild Amber Grill. Contemporary. Good food that expertly straddles the boundary between classic Continental cuisine and more creative new American cuisine with an Asian touch is served in an informal Colonial-style. Try the filet mignon, rack of lamb, sesame-seared tuna, and sautéed Thai shrimp. When warm enough, there is open-air dining on a screened porch. A bar and lounge serves meals from a simpler menu. Kids' menu. No smoking in dining room. | 101 North St. | 413/458–4000 | Closed Sept.–June. No lunch | $15–$28 | AE, MC, V.

Yasmine's Restaurant. Continental. In one of the town's top hotels, The Orchards, with views of surrounding deeply wooded mountains, this restaurant tantalizes with a new American menu with strong French, Italian, and Asian influences. Dishes like whole lobster on arugula risotto and salmon spring rolls with shiitake mushrooms change hands with other innovative fare on a regular basis. Open-air dining on a patio is available is warm weather, and on Sundays brunch is offered. Kids' menu. No smoking in dining room. | 222 Adams Rd. | 413/458–9611 | $22–$30 | AE, DC, MC, V.

PACKING IDEAS FOR COLD WEATHER

- ❏ Driving gloves
- ❏ Earmuffs
- ❏ Fanny pack
- ❏ Fleece neck gaiter
- ❏ Fleece parka
- ❏ Hats
- ❏ Lip balm
- ❏ Long underwear
- ❏ Scarf
- ❏ Shoes to wear indoors
- ❏ Ski gloves or mittens

- ❏ Ski hat
- ❏ Ski parka
- ❏ Snow boots
- ❏ Snow goggles
- ❏ Snow pants
- ❏ Sweaters
- ❏ Thermal socks
- ❏ Tissues, handkerchief
- ❏ Turtlenecks
- ❏ Wool or corduroy pants

*Excerpted from *Fodor's: How to Pack: Experts Share Their Secrets*
© 1997, by Fodor's Travel Publications

Lodging

Berkshire Hills Motel. At this New England–style country motel guests are lulled to sleep by the sound of Hemlock Brook. Wooded grounds and flower gardens are appealing, and there is a fireplace in both the lobby and the breakfast room, which also has a deck for dining. A natural-spring swimming hole is across the street. Picnic area, complimentary breakfast. In-room data ports, cable TV. Pool. | 1146 Cold Spring Rd. | 413/458–3950 or 800/388–9677 | fax 413/458–5878 | bhmotel@bcn.net | 21 rooms | $109–$139 | AE, D, MC, V.

Buxton Brook Farm Bed and Breakfast. This 1800 Federal home is set on 70 acres of woods and gardens, furnished with period antiques, and with a wonderful view of Mount Greylock from the terrace. It's run by an enthusiastic hostess. Complimentary breakfast. TV in common area. Outdoor pool. No pets. No kids under 10. No smoking. | 91 Northwest Hill Rd. | 413/458–3621 | fax 413/458–3640 | 4 rooms, 1 suite | $110–$135 rooms; $160 suite | AE, D, MC, V.

Econo Lodge at the Springs. This generic motel is ideally situated to take advantage of this area's wealth of activities, any time of year. It's midway between Lenox and Williamstown, with its two art museums, and nearby skiing (book way ahead if you plan a stay during ski season): Brody Mountain is across the street, Jiminy Peak is 3 mi away. Other attractions within a short drive are the hiking trails on Mt. Greylock, golf courses, and Tanglewood. Restaurant, bar with entertainment. Refrigerators in some rooms, cable TV. Pool. Tennis court. Exercise equipment. | 94 State Rd., New Ashford | 413/458–5945 or 800/277–0001 | fax 413/458–5945 | www.econolodge.com | 44 rooms, 4 cottages | $125, $250 cottages | AE, D, DC, MC, V.

1896 House–Brookside and Pondside. Brookside and Pondside are the two small inns that make up 1896 House. They reside on 17 acres with a brook, a spring-fed duck pond, and gardens. There are two fishing holes on the brook. Brookside is hidden from the road on parklike grounds and features a front porch with rocking chairs, gardens with a gazebo, an outdoor dining patio, and a picnic area with Adirondack chairs. Pondside is a newly renovated Cape Cod classic. Picnic area. In-room data ports, cable TV. Pool. Fishing. | 910 Cold Spring Rd. | 413/458–8125 or 888/666–1896 | www.1896house.com | 31 rooms, 2 suites | $98–$125, $125–$175 suites | AE, D, DC, MC, V.

★ **Field Farm Guest House.** This is not your stereotypical lace-curtains, bursting-with-antiques bed-and-breakfast. This stunning 1948 home is the archetype of space-age design and is filled with a superb collection of modern Scandinavian and American furniture. The grounds sprawl across 300 acres and include an outstanding sculpture garden and a 1967 modern shingle guest house, which is known on the house-tours circuit. All in all, this is as iconoclastic an inn as you will find. Complimentary breakfast. Outdoor pool. Tennis. Hiking. No pets. No smoking. | 554 Sloan Rd. | 413/458–3144 | fax 413/458–3135 | www.thetrustees.org | 5 rooms | $145–$165 | D, MC, V.

Four Acres Motel. Quiet surroundings and a walking path through the gardens are high points at this motel 1 mi from Williams College. Picnic area, complimentary Continental breakfast. In-room data ports, cable TV. 1 pool. Hot tub. | 213 Main St. | 413/458–8158 | www.fouracresmotel.com | 31 rooms | $75–$125 | AE, D, DC, MC, V.

Orchards Hotel. The hotel was built around an interior courtyard with a garden and a fishpond. Rooms are furnished with antique reproductions and four-poster beds, and some have fireplaces. Restaurant, bar, room service. In-room data ports, some refrigerators, cable TV, in-room VCRs. Pool. Hot tub. Gym. Library. Business services. | 222 Adams Rd. | 413/458–9611 or 800/225–1517 | fax 413/458–3273 | www.orchardshotel.com | 49 rooms | $175–$275 | AE, DC, MC, V.

River Bend Farm. Center chimneys distinguish this 1770 Georgian Revival furnished with complete period authenticity. The 5-acre property contains flower and vegetable gardens and a fine view of the mountains. For the final touch, the jams and jellies served with breakfast are made by the owners. Complimentary breakfast. No room phones, no TV. No pets.

No smoking. | 643 Simonds Rd. | 413/458–5504 | 4 rooms (with shared bath) | $90 | Closed Nov.–Mar. | No credit cards.

Williams Inn. The owners manage this inn on the grounds of Williams College, and it's staffed by knowledgeable, longtime employees who help guests plan day trips. Bus tickets to Boston and New York are sold at the front desk; the bus stops out front. The lobby and living room with fireplace, herb and vegetable gardens, and bird feeders give the inn a country feeling. 2 restaurants, bar with entertainment, picnic area, room service. Cable TV. 1 indoor pool. Hot tub, sauna. Shop. Business services. Some pets allowed (fee). | Village Green, at U.S. 7 and Rte. 2 | 413/458–9371 or 800/828–0133 | fax 413/458–2767 | www.williamsinn.com | 103 rooms | $130–$180, $175–$200 suites | AE, D, DC, MC, V.

WOODS HOLE (CAPE COD)

MAP 6, J7

(Nearby towns also listed: Falmouth, Oak Bluffs, Vineyard Haven)

Woods Hole is actually a village in the town of Falmouth, but it has forged a strong separate identity for itself. Better, a strong double identity: not only is Woods Hole home to several of the nation's premier scientific educational institutions specializing in oceanography, but it's also the prime gateway for passengers and drivers heading to Martha's Vineyard by ferry.

Information: Falmouth Chamber of Commerce | 20 Academy La., Falmouth, 02540 | 508/548–8500 or 800/526–8532 | falmouth@capecod.net | www.falmouth-capecod.com.

Attractions

Car/passenger ferry service. Steamship Authority. The community-governed Steamship Authority links Woods Hole with both Vineyard Haven and Oak Bluffs on Martha's Vineyard, a 45-minute journey away. The large, lumbering vessels, the only ones able to transport vehicles, are also the least expensive for passengers. Summer passengers intent on leaving their vehicles parked on the Cape side before crossing should heed the electronic signboards on Route 28 approaching Falmouth, which advise when to use off-site parking lots (connected to the ferry dock by free shuttle van). | Steamship Authority Pier, off Rte. 28 | 508/477–8600 | www.islandferry.com | Passengers: $10 round-trip; vehicles: $62–$194 round-trip | Daily.

Nobska Light. Built in 1876, this 42-ft-tall cast-iron beauty helps guide ships through the dangerous waters between the Cape and Vineyard Sound. It also makes a nice place for a sunset picnic as dozens and dozens of sailboats pass by. | Church St. | Interior not open to the public.

OceanQuest. Marine science has never been so fun or interesting. These 90-minute educational trips aboard the 60-ft *Tiger Shark*, great for adults and kids alike, explore the bounty offered up by the sea. Water is sampled and traps are pulled from the harbor. | Water St. | 508/457–0508 or 800/376–2326 | $19 | July–Aug., four trips weekdays.

Woods Hole Historical Museum. Inside the Bradley House is an eclectic mix of historical objects, displays, and local memorabilia, including an 1895 scale model of the village. The 19th-century barn beside the house contains the museum's small-crafts collection, celebrating Cape Cod's history of producing fine small wooden boats for leisure and work. The Yale Shop, a building from the 1870s, an 1854 map of the area, and tools used to build ships can also be viewed. | 573 Woods Hole Rd. | 508/548–7270 | Free | Mid-June–Sept., Tues.–Sat. 10–4.

Woods Hole Oceanographic Institution Exhibit Center. This former Methodist church is an attractive clapboard building that contains two floors of vivid exhibits on marine science, from videos of hydrothermal vents to displays on the life cycles of various ocean creatures. Nearly everything on view is derived in one way or another from the work of the exhibit center's parent, WHOI, a private nonprofit research and educational organization best known for the discoveries of its pioneering deep-sea submersible *Alvin.* | 15 School St. | 508/289–2252 | $2 donation.

Marine Biological Laboratory/Woods Hole Oceanographic Institution Library. One of the best collections of biological, ecological, and oceanographic literature in the world is in tiny Woods Hole. Scientists from all over the world descend on this place to work on big problems like Alzheimer's, with the aid of secrets yielded from the deep sea. Nonresearchers gain access to the library only on a (popular) tour. | 100 Water St. | 508/289–7623 or 508/548–3705 | www.mbl.edu | Free | Tours mid-June–Aug., weekdays 1, 2, and 3.

Woods Hole Science Aquarium. The saltwater tanks in this simple government-issue building brim with marine life collected locally as a by-product of the research on fisheries populations and health conducted by the NMFS from its labs here in Woods Hole. The most popular residents are the playful seals seen in the outdoor pool in front of the building, most of which are recuperating from accident or illness. | Albatross St., at end of Water St. | 508/495–2001 | Free | Mid-June–early Sept., daily 10–4; mid-Sept.–early June, weekdays 10–4.

ON THE CALENDAR
JUNE: *Illumination Weekend.* Candles in bags line the streets for this festival, held on the first weekend of the month. Live performances of bluegrass and jazz on the streets of downtown are the high point. | 508/540–8500 | www.woodshole.com.

Dining
The Dome. Continental. If you've ever wanted to dine in a truly unique place, try the prime rib and scallops Provençal in this geodesic sphere designed in 1953 by Buckminster Fuller and still decorated in a '60s style. The dining room looks rather like a cruise-ship ballroom. | 533 Woods Hole Rd. | 508/548–0800 | Closed mid-Sept.–mid-May | $15–$20 | AE, D, MC, V.

★ **Fish Monger's Café.** Eclectic. The best eatery for all three daily meals in this tiny town overlooks the harbor, bustles, and expects big things from its kitchen. It delivers. The inventive daily seafood specials are always a good, creative bet and might pair grilled fish with a tropical fruit sauce or glaze. The lightly fried calamari comes with a hot-pepper sauce. | 25 Water St. | 508/540–5376 | Breakfast also available. Closed Dec.–late Feb. and Tues. Nov.–Mar. | $12–$23 | AE, MC, V.

Landfall. Seafood. This salty dockside spot has a menu that leans more than just a little toward the bounty of the deep. Try the lobster and the landfall pasta. Open-air dining is de rigueur in summer. Kids' menu. No smoking. | 2 Luscombe Ave. | 508/548–1758 | $17–$37 | AE, MC, V.

Leeside Bar and Grill. American. Featuring both casual dining upstairs and characterful noshing and drinking downstairs, this early 1900s rough-hewn local spot is not so much decorated as saddled with boating and fishing paraphernalia. The menu runs from chicken tenders, burgers, and sandwiches to steaks and fresh seafood. Try the marinated steak tips or the seafood nachos. No smoking in dining room. | 29 Railroad Ave., at Luscombe Ave. | 508/548–9744 | $6–$24 | AE, MC, V.

Lodging
Marlborough Bed and Breakfast. This bed-and-breakfast is open year-round, including holidays (reservations are essential during high season). The large traditional Cape Cod house is on a well-treed piece of property, with landscaped gardens and off-street lighted parking. Personalized trip-planning assistance and transportation to/from the Martha's Vineyard ferry are provided at no extra charge. An English paddle tennis court is on the property. Complimentary breakfast. In-room data ports, no in-room phones, TV in common area and cottage. Pool. No kids under 2. No smoking. | 320 Woods Hole Rd. | 508/548–

6218 or 800/320–2322 | fax 508/457–7519 | 5 rooms, 1 cottage | $125–$155, $175 cottage | AE, MC, V.

Nautilus Motor Inn. This motel made up of three buildings is across the street from the harbor. Some rooms have harbor views. It is a five-minute walk to the Martha's Vineyard ferry and the Woods Hole Oceanographic Institution. In-room data ports, cable TV. Pool. Tennis. Business services. | 539 Woods Hole Rd. | 508/548–1525 or 800/654–2333 in MA | fax 508/457–9674 | www.nautilusinn.com | 54 rooms | $98–$158 | Closed mid-Oct.–mid-Apr. | AE, D, DC, MC, V.

Sands of Time Motor Inn and Harbor House. Harbor House, built in 1875 as a sea captain's house, features rooms with four-poster beds and some fireplaces. All motel rooms have a private patio or balcony overlooking the water. Noted gardens surround the place. Newspapers and parking passes for a nearby private beach are available. The property is a short walk from the ferry dock and the Woods Hole Oceanographic Museum and Aquarium. Complimentary Continental breakfast. In-room data ports, cable TV. Pool. Business services. | 549 Woods Hole Rd. | 508/548–6300 or 800/841–0114 | fax 508/457–0160 | www.sandsoftime.com | 29 rooms; 2 apartments | $140–$170 | Closed end Oct.–mid-Apr. | AE, D, DC, MC, V.

Sleepy Hollow Motor Inn. Set back, private and hard to see from the road, this motel is a short walk to the beach and the Martha's Vineyard ferry. Nearby are the Woods Hole Oceanographic Institution, the Woods Hole Science Aquarium, and the Marine Biological Lab (with changing exhibits). The rooms are comfortable. Cable TV. Pool. | 527 Woods Hole Rd. | 508/548–1986 | fax 508/548–5932 | www.capecod.net/shmotel | 24 rooms | $95–$125 | Closed Nov.–mid-Apr. | AE, DC, MC, V.

Woods Hole Passage. This turn-of-the-20th-century house and barn has been transformed into a romantic getaway. In addition to comfortable and tasteful guest rooms, the large living room with overstuffed furniture serves as a focal point for conversation. If you're catching an early ferry, the innkeepers will pack breakfast to take away. Complimentary breakfast. Bicycles. No pets. No smoking. | 186 Woods Hole Rd. | 508/548–9575 or 800/790–8976 | fax 508/540–4771 | www.woodsholepassage.com | 5 rooms | $80–$120 | AE, D, DC, MC, V.

WORCESTER

MAP 6, F4

WORCESTER

INTRO
ATTRACTIONS
DINING
LODGING

(Nearby town also listed: Grafton)

Worcester is New England's second-largest city, with a population of 170,000. Its diversified industrial economy has helped it avoid the precipitous nose-dives that have hit other industry towns throughout the Northeast, although large-scale assembly-line manufacturing has virtually disappeared, having been replaced by smaller specialty industries and, most recently, a growing biotechnology sector. Forty miles west of Boston, Worcester is the only major New England city without a waterfront, but efforts are underway to rehabilitate the Blackstone River and its associated 19th-century canal, which once ran uncovered through downtown. Worcester is home to half a dozen colleges and universities, including Worcester Polytechnic Institute, Clark University, College of the Holy Cross, and the state university's medical school, but its large size prohibits it from feeling like a college town. Given the post-war flight of shops and residents from the downtown area, Worcester lacks a certain urban vitality as well, appearing to visitors mostly as a large assemblage of residential neighborhoods tethered to the monolithic downtown convention centers purely by the accident of geography. But despite appearances, Worcester indeed possesses a number of cultural attractions, including an outstanding art museum, the unique Higgins Armory Museum, and the acoustically superb Mechanics Hall concert space.

Information: **Central Massachusetts Tourist Council** | 33 Waldo St., Worcester, 01608 | 508/753–2920 or 800/231–7557. **Visitor Center** | Worcester Common Outlets, 100 Front St. | 508/754–0305 | bkenney@worcester.org | www.worcester.org.

Attractions

American Antiquarian Society. This research library houses the largest collection of source materials pertaining to early American history. The library specializes in works published before 1877, and has in its collection ⅔ of all the works known to have been published in the United States between 1640 and 1821. | 185 Salisbury St. | 508/755–5221 | Free | Weekdays 9–5.

Higgins Armory Museum. Arms and armor from the Middle Ages, the Renaissance, and feudal Japan are displayed, along with paintings, tapestries, and stained glass. Armor demonstrations and try-ons are sometimes held. | 100 Barber Ave. | 508/853–6015 | $5.75 | Tues.–Sat. 10–4, Sun. noon–4.

Purgatory Chasm State Park. Tucked deep in the woods, the ¼-mi chasm has granite slopes. | Purgatory Rd., Sutton | 508/234–3733 | Free | Daily.

Worcester Art Museum. A wide array of paintings, sculpture, decorative arts, prints, drawings, and photographs, from ancient Egypt to modern America, are displayed in changing exhibits. | 55 Salisbury St. | 508/799–4406 | $8; free Sat. 10–noon | Wed.–Fri. and Sun. 11–5; Sat. 10–5.

Worcester Common Outlets. Off I–90's exit 18, this indoor mall has nearly 100 outlet stores, including Esprit, Ann Taylor, Filene's Basement, and Off Fifth (Saks). | 100 Front St. | 508/798–2581 | Free | Mon.–Sat. 10–9, Sun. noon–6.

Worcester Historical Museum. The industrial and ethnically diverse history of Worcester (did you know that it was the birthplace of barbed wire, the monkey wrench, the smiley face, and the space suit?) is illustrated in this museum's galleries, which have permanent and changing exhibits, audiovisual displays, artifacts, and photographs. There is also a research library. | 30 Elm St. | 508/753–8278 | www.worcesterhistory.org | $3; $5 combined ticket with Salisbury Mansion | Tues.–Sat. 10–4, Sun. 1–4.

Salisbury Mansion. Built in 1772, this home belonged to leading businessman and philanthropist Stephen Salisbury. Guided tours will take you through the house, which has been restored to its 18th-century appearance. | 40 Highland St. | 508/753–8278 | $3; $5 combined ticket with historical museum | Thurs.–Sun. noon–4.

ON THE CALENDAR

JAN.: *Sleigh Rally.* Watch horse-drawn sleighs and wagons compete in a variety of events and then hop on for a ride. The rally takes place on a Sunday in mid-January. | 508/865–0101.

OCT.: *Waters Farm Days.* Celebrate living history at one of Blackstone Valley's oldest farms (1757) at this annual event that takes place the first weekend of the month. Highlights include hayrides, draft horses, blacksmithing, shingle mill and saw mill demonstrations, a lumberjack contest, crafts exhibits, antique tractor displays, a reconstructed Algonquin village, a petting zoo, a dog show, crafts, historical reenactments, and live music. One of the most popular food items served at the festival is hot apple crisp, made at Sutton Farm with Sutton Beauty apples. | 508/865–0101.

OCT.–APR.: *Music Worcester.* Music Worcester consists of three concurrent festivals. The Worcester Music Festival includes performances by touring international orchestras and Worcester's community chorus. The International Artist Series features chamber music. The Massachusetts Jazz Festival showcases some of the finest jazz ensembles in the country. Most performances take place in Mechanics Hall, thought to be the finest remaining pre–Civil War concert hall in the country. | 508/754–3231.

DEC.: *Christmas in Historic Sutton.* On the first Saturday in December, it's Christmas open house in Sutton, the quintessential New England town 13 mi east of Worcester. Twelve free-admission "trolleys" traveling three different routes transport visitors to many different sites. You can watch the village smithy at work at the Sherman Blacksmith Shop, or take a horse-drawn hayride or sleigh ride at Waters Farm. Learn about changes made in dairy farming and sip farm-fresh eggnog at Whittier Farms. Sample Eaton Farm confectioners' chocolate bark candy. Enjoy an historic wassail and Christmas concert at Vaillancourt Folk Art, the world's largest Santa Claus studio. Have your photo taken with Santa in an antique sleigh. End the day with a delicious Christmas dinner and the Festival of Lights Ball. | 508/865–9183.

Dining

Castle. Continental. This 1933 reproduction of a castle in Havana has two dining rooms. The Camelot Room features formal white-tablecloth Escoffier culinary classicism, while the Crusader Room has a family atmosphere and a more contemporary menu ranging from club sandwiches, pizza, and pasta to New York sirloin. As the self-professed "last bastion of chivalry or chauvinism," the restaurant presents a fresh rose to women guests, and only men are given menus with prices. Try steak au poivre, chateaubriand flamed tableside, and daily game specials. There's open-air dining on a patio. It's 6 mi west of Worcester. Kids' menu. No smoking. | 1230 Main St., Leicester | 508/892–9090 | Closed Mon., and Tues.–Thurs. mid-July–early Aug. No lunch Sun. | Reservations essential on weekends | $21–$34 | AE, D, DC, MC, V.

Restaurant at Tatnuck Bookseller Marketplace. Eclectic. This lively and engaging restaurant is in a booming bookstore housed in a converted turn-of-the-century spring factory that retains much of the original machinery. Custom shadowbox tables contain books and historic artifacts. You can choose everything from burgers to medallions of veal and shrimp to grilled marlin, and savor homemade root beer or orange soda. You can even eat outdoors next to a waterfall. | 335 Chandler St. | 508/756–7644 | fax 508/756–9425 | Breakfast also available | $6–$17 | AE, D, MC, V.

Shorah's Ristorante. Italian. Come here for casual corner-storefront dining, or sit at the bar, and order from a consistently high-quality menu of Italian favorites, including pizza, calzones, carpaccio, shrimp primavera, and veal saltimbocca. It's known for its fresh fish, veal, homemade Mediterranean salads, and pasta. No smoking in dining room. | 27 Foster St. | 508/797–0007 | No lunch Sun. in summer | $18–$27 | AE, D, DC, MC, V.

Sole Proprietor. Seafood. Seafood this good is ordinarily associated with waterfront dining. The surrounding university neighborhood may not match harbor views, but the comfortable, contemporary decor and cheerful environment help, as does the kitchen's proficiency with tastes ranging from Asian to Mediterranean. Try the smoked seafood, steamed mussels, salmon specialties, blackened tuna sashimi, mesquite-grilled catch of the day, and sushi appetizer. There's also a raw bar. Kids' menu. | 118 Highland St. | 508/798–3474 | No lunch Sat. Memorial Day–Labor Day | $17–$22 | AE, D, MC, V.

Lodging

Beechwood Hotel. This boutique hotel is in a landscaped biotech park next to the University of Massachusetts Medical School, ½ mi from downtown and a five-minute drive from Worcester's outlet mall. The hotel's 200-square-ft ballroom has a turn-of-the-century nondenominational chapel (moved from a hospital), with beautiful stained glass, carved wood, and frescoed walls. Restaurant, room service. Cable TV. Business services. | 363 Plantation St. | 508/754–5789 or 800/344–2589 | fax 508/752–2060 | www.beechwoodhotel.com | 50 rooms, 23 suites | $109–$179, $129–219 suites | AE, D, MC, V.

Crowne Plaza Hotel. This centrally located hotel is within walking distance of the Centrum, Mechanics Hall, the art museum, and outlets. Executive suites offer extra amenities. Restaurant, bar, room service. Cable TV. Indoor and outdoor pools. Hot tub. Gym. Airport shuttle. | 10 Lincoln Sq. | 508/791–1600 or 800/628–4240 | fax 508/791–1796 | 243 rooms, 7 suites | $134, $249–$299 suites | AE, D, DC, MC, V.

Hampton Inn. Your stay at Hampton Inn is "100% satisfaction guaranteed." This downtown hotel is one block from the Centrum and close to Mechanics Hall, Worcester Com-

mon Outlets, and across the street from the new Medical City. Complimentary breakfast. In-room data ports, some kitchenettes, some refrigerators, cable TV. Business services. | 110 Summer St. | 508/757–0400 | fax 508/831–9839 | www.hamptoninn.com | 99 rooms | $89–$119 | AE, D, DC, MC, V.

Holiday Inn. You'll find a wide-range of amenities and conveniences here. The rooms have a pleasant green and burgundy color scheme. Kids under 12 receive a complimentary dinner when an accompanying adult orders a meal. Restaurant, bar. In-room data ports, cable TV. Indoor pool. Hot tub, sauna. Fitness club. No pets. | 500 Lincoln St. | 508/852–4000 | fax 508/852–8521 | 140 rooms, 2 suites | $130–$160 | AE, D, DC, MC, V.

Worcester Courtyard by Marriott. Built in 2000, this hotel features wide-ranging amenities. All the rooms feature cherry-colored wood and forest green paint. All rooms have either a king- or two queen-size beds. Bar. In-room data ports, cable TV. Indoor pool. Hot tub. Exercise equipment. No pets. | 72 Grove St. | 508/363–0300 | fax 508/363–3563 | 126 rooms, 4 suites | $119 | AE, D, DC, MC, V.

YARMOUTH (CAPE COD)

MAP 6, K6

(Nearby towns also listed: Barnstable Village, Dennis, Hyannis)

Perched in the central portion of Cape Cod, Yarmouth is the Cape's third-largest town, with more than 22,000 residents, nearly a third of whom are retirees. Its southern side

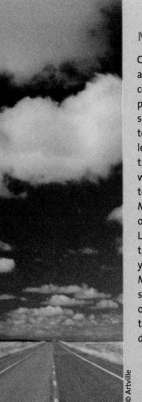

© Artville

NAVIGATING THE CAPE

Cape Cod is Massachusetts's most prominent feature, immediately recognizable on any map of the United States, jutting out into the Atlantic like a giant bent arm, complete with shoulder, elbow, and fist. This glacially formed appendage hits every point on the compass as it curls around Cape Cod Bay, mocking the fixed "north–south" designations on its state highway signs. To better orient yourself, as well as to understand what locals are saying when they give you directions, it's essential to learn the Cape's private lingo of navigational words and phrases. The basic directions are up and down. They're holdovers from sailing days: on a sea chart, heading west was called "climbing up the latitudes." Similarly, a return voyage from America to England required going "down east." So the shoulder part of Cape Cod, from Mashpee west to Buzzards Bay, is the Upper Cape, while everything east and north of Brewster and Harwich belongs to the Lower Cape. (The narrowest portion of the Lower Cape is also called the Outer Cape.) What's in between is mid-Cape. The farther down-Cape you go, the closer you get to Provincetown, and if someone tells you to go up-Cape, you're being pointed toward the Cape Cod Canal and the rest of Massachusetts, which is off-Cape. The shorelines, too, have their own names. The side of the Lower Cape that faces the Atlantic Ocean is known as the backside, as opposed to the bayside, which fronts Cape Cod Bay. Lastly, the coast along Nantucket Sound, from which all the ferries to Nantucket and Martha's Vineyard depart, is the south shore.

epitomizes the Coney Island aspect of the present-day Cape, with a jumble of fast-food outlets, vintage motels, timeshare condos, garish gift shops, miniature golf, and other amusements crowding the shoulders of Route 28. Yet Yarmouth also has some of Cape Cod's most charming historic residential districts on its quaint north side, along the Old King's Highway, Route 6A. As it embraces all the features of both old and new Cape Cod, Yarmouth can truly be said to offer something for everyone. Most of all, it provides access to that most prized Cape asset, the ocean: between Cape Cod Bay and Nantucket Sound, Yarmouth has 15 saltwater beaches.

Information: Visitor Information (May–Oct.) | U.S. 6, between exits 6 and 7 | 508/362–9796 | yarmouth@capecod.net | www.yarmouthcapecod.com. **Yarmouth Area Chamber of Commerce** | 657 Rte. 28, West Yarmouth, 02673 | 508/778–1008 or 800/732–1008.

Attractions

Bass Hole Boardwalk. Perhaps the lovliest spot in town, this boardwalk extends over a creek and marsh to Gray's Beach, a safe spit of sand for children. In addition, 2 mi of nature trails, tidal flats, and westward-facing benches make it an easy place to spend a few hours. | Center St., Yarmouth Port | Free | Daily.

Baxter Grist Mill. This is the Cape's only mill powered by a water turbine. (The rest use wind or paddle wheels.) Built in 1710, the mill is on the National Register of Historic Places. | Rte. 28, W. Yarmouth | Free | July–Aug., weekends 10–2.

Botanical Trails of the Historical Society of Old Yarmouth. Although there are more than 50 acres of woodlands and a pond on this property, there are only 2 mi of nature trails. But they're dense: you'll see lady's slippers, rhododendrons, hollies, blueberries, and more. | 231 Main St., Yarmouth Port | 508/362–3021 | $1 donation | Gatehouse July–Aug., daily 1–4; trails daily.

Captain Bangs Hallet House. This 1840 sea captain's home is the headquarters of the Historical Society of Old Yarmouth, which provides tours of the antiques-filled house. Behind the property are herb gardens and nature trails through 50 acres of woods and around a small pond. | 11 Strawberry La., Yarmouth Port | 508/362–3021 | $3 | June–Oct., tours on the hr Sun. 1–3.

Winslow Crocker House. Originally the home of a successful Colonial trader and land speculator, this 18th-century house was acquired in the 1930s by an antiques collector and relocated to its present spot. The collector, Mary Thacher, turned the house into a showcase for her early American furnishings, from Jacobean family heirlooms and Chippendale museum pieces to hooked rugs and folk-art ceramics. The property is now owned by the Society for the Preservation of New England Antiquities. | 250 Rte. 6A, Yarmouth Port | 508/362–4385 | www.spnea.org | $4 | June–Columbus Day, tours on the hr weekends 11–4.

ZooQuarium. Both entertaining and educational, this combination zoo and aquarium has a petting area with hoofed creatures, sea-lion shows, wandering peacocks, pony rides, and changing exhibits like "Zoo Nutrition," in which kids prepare meals for their webbed friends. | 674 Main St., West Yarmouth | 508/775–8883 | $8 | Feb.–late June and early Sept.–late Nov., daily 9:30–5; late June–early Sept., daily 9:30–6.

ON THE CALENDAR

OCT.: *Seaside Festival.* Held on Columbus Day weekend, the celebration includes over 150 arts and crafts vendors, parades, fireworks, and pie-eating contests. Most events take place across from the Yarmouth town office on Route 28. | 508/778–1008.

Dining

Abbicci. Italian. A yellow Colonial facade on this 1755 Cape Cod conceals a sleek, contemporary interior. Discerning regulars return for the exceptional and regularly changing northern Italian cuisine with Mediterranean, Provençal, and North African influences. Note the

---

prodigious dessert menu and outstanding wine list. This last is adjusted a couple of times a week with uncommon selections from California, Italy, and France, a dozen of which are served by the glass. Known for local seafood, braised rabbit, summer pasta dishes, and desserts. Early bird suppers (three-course prix-fixe). No smoking. | 43 Main St., Yarmouth Port | 508/362–3501 | Reservations essential | $17–$29 | AE, DC, MC, V.

Ardeo. Contemporary. Bright and airy, the dining room is defined by the numerous windows that enclose it. The innovative fare includes such items as the white bean and radicchio salad, the smoked chicken and goat cheese salad, pizzas, wraps, panini sandwiches, steaks, and pastas. Entrées include the salmon Provençale—grilled salmon over spinach, tomatoes, caramelized onions, and sprinkled with a balsamic sauce—or the scallop and monkfish kabob. | 23 V Whites Path, Union Station Plaza, South Yarmouth | 508/760–1500 | $6–$16 | AE, D, MC, V.

Black Rock Grille. Steak. Beef is the specialty here, certified Angus Beef; porterhouses, fillets, sirloins, and prime ribs fill the menu. The restaurant is also known for its lobster dishes. The three dining rooms are decorated with an equestrian theme: jockey caps, pictures of horses, and other antiques. On weekends live jazz is performed. | 633 Rte. 28 | 508/771–1001 | No lunch | $12–$32 | AE, MC, V.

Captain Parker's. Seafood. This casual seafood restaurant attracts families with its children's menu. | 668 Main St., West Yarmouth | 508/771–4266 | $6–$20 | AE, MC, V.

Clancy's. American. Depending on what time you dine here, you'll find entertainment at the bar or families enjoying fish-and-chips. | 175 Main St., West Yarmouth | 508/775–3332 | $7–$25 | AE, MC, V.

Colonial House Inn. American. This historic inn has three dining rooms: the Oak Room, the Colonial Room, and the Common Room, each with its own personality. The Oak Room has polished oak tables and details, the Colonial Room contains a large fireplace, and the Common Room is a glass-enclosed porch. Fresh seafood is the specialty, complemented by a variety of beef and chicken options. | 277 Main St. | 508/362–4348 | $15–$22 | D, MC, V.

Hearth 'N Kettle. American. This chain of family-owned Cape Cod eateries serves a wide variety of seafood (lobster, baked salmon, fried clams) as well as chicken and steak dishes. Sandwiches are available round the clock, including some innovative new comers like the lobster roll. Desserts and breads are homemade. The dining room overlooks a pond in the backyard. | 1196 Main St. | 508/394–2252 | Breakfast also available | $8–$15 | AE, D, MC, V.

★ **Inaho.** Japanese. Japanese-style design, service, and sushi bar transport diners half a world away, at the same time offering a unique (for Cape Cod) chance to experience seafood at its elemental best, whether raw or cooked. Known for tempura, teriyaki, and sushi. No smoking. | 157 Main St., Yarmouth Port | 508/362–5522 | Closed Sun.–Mon. in winter. No lunch | $20–$41 | MC, V.

Jack's Outback. American. A local hangout that lives up to its motto of "good food, lousy service," this serve-yourself joint features Yankee pot roast, homemade soups, and burgers for lunch. Breakfasts are solid and bountiful. | 161 Main St., Yarmouth Port | 508/362–6690 | No dinner | $2.50–$5 | No credit cards.

Oliver's Restaurant. Seafood. Opened in 1983, Oliver's serves fresh seafood including scrod, haddock, salmon, swordfish, and striped bass prepared in traditional ways like blackened, poached, broiled, and fried. More innovative approaches are also taken: for instance, the sea scallops baked in a rum and coconut sauce over angel hair pasta. In addition, there are a wide assortment of other menu choices, such as Long Island duck, steaks, and chicken courses. | Rte. 6A | 508/362–6062 | $11–$19 | AE, D, DC, MC, V.

Skipper Restaurant and Lookout Lounge. Seafood. The nautical design and scenic view of Nantucket Sound, best enjoyed from the seating over the water, complement an uncommonly eclectic menu in which traditional surf-and-turf is supplemented by flavorful Asian influences. Try the scrod zingarella, Thai seafood stew, fish specials, and New York sirloin. There's open-air dining on deck, a kids' menu, and early bird suppers. | 152 South Shore Dr. | 508/394–7406 | Closed Nov.–Mar. | $13.95–$23.95 | AE, D, MC, V.

Yarmouth House. Continental. You can dine in any of several rooms decorated to evoke Old Cape Cod, including a working waterwheel. The menu keeps in time with Cape seafood favorites and a range of alternatives, from meats and poultry to a few vegetarian selections. Known for seafood, beef, chicken, sautées, and stir-fry. Kids' menus and early bird suppers are offered. | 335 Main St., West Yarmouth | 508/771–5154 | $19–$34 | AE, D, DC, MC, V.

Lodging

All Seasons Motor Inn. Lawns, flowers, and shrubs landscape the grounds of this motel, in a quiet area at the end of Route 28, close to beaches and summer activities like boating and mini-golf. Boat rentals are also nearby. Restaurant (breakfast), picnic area. Refrigerators, cable TV, in-room VCRs. Indoor and outdoor pools. Hot tub. Gym. Video games. Playground. Laundry facilities. Business services. No smoking. | 1199 Main St. | 508/394–7600 or 800/527–0359 | fax 508/398–7160 | www.allseasons.com | 114 rooms | $99–$125 | AE, D, DC, MC, V.

Americana Holiday Motel. This family-operated strip motel has simple rooms. Try to get one in the back of the complex, overlooking a pine grove. Refrigerators. Indoor and 2 outdoor pools. Hot tub, sauna. Putting green. Video games. Playground. No pets. | 99 Main St., West Yarmouth | 508/775–5511 or 800/445–4497 | fax 508/790–0597 | www.americanaholiday.com | 149 rooms, 4 suites | $75–$79, $120 suites | Closed Nov.–Mar. | AE, D, DC, MC, V.

Bass River Motel. This motel is close to shops, restaurants, nightclubs, and the beach. It's about 7 mi from Hyannis. The motel's buildings and rooms are predictable Cape style; the grounds are landscaped and have horseshoe pits and shuffle board. There is a shuttle bus that stops just outside. Picnic area, complimentary Continental breakfast (weekends). Some kitchenettes, refrigerators, cable TV. Pool. | 891 Main St., South Yarmouth | 508/398–2488 | fax 508/394–4461 | bassriver@capecod.net | 20 rooms | $60–$85 | MC, V.

Beach 'n' Towne Motel. On a few acres of landscaped grounds, with flowers and gardens, this motel is three blocks from the Bass River and from deep-sea fishing. Four golf courses are within a 1-mi radius. Picnic area. Refrigerators, cable TV. Pool. Library. Playground. | 1261 Rte. 28, South Yarmouth | 508/398–2311 or 800/987–8556 | www.sunsol.com/beachntowne | 21 rooms | $61–$68 | Closed Dec.–Jan. | AE, D, MC, V.

Belvedere B&B. A Federal-style 1820s sea captain's house, the Belvedere has romantic and frilly rooms decorated with wicker, pink velvet chairs, rose-colored quilts, and lacy curtains. Breakfast is offered in the formal dining room or screened-in porch. Complimentary Continental breakfast. No pets. No kids under 12. No smoking. | 167 Old Main St., South Yarmouth | 508/398–6674 or 800/288–4080 | www.belvederebb.com | 5 rooms (2 with shared bath) | $100–$175 | AE, D, MC, V.

Best Western Blue Rock Motor Inn. All the guest rooms at this motel have a patio or deck that overlooks either the Blue Rock Golf Course, a swimming pool, or gardens and landscaped grounds. From here it's a short drive to Hyannis and about 3 mi to the beach. Restaurant, bar. Refrigerators, cable TV. Pool. 18-hole golf course, putting green, tennis court. Business services. | 39 Todd Rd. | 508/398–6962 or 800/237–8887 | fax 508/398–1830 | www.redjacketinns.com/bluerock | 45 rooms | $115–$165 | Closed Nov.–Mar. | AE, D, DC, MC, V.

Best Western Blue Water Resort. A 300-ft private ocean beach, a variety of family activities, and programs for kids are this resort's strongest selling points. There are also monthly theme weekends, and the resort is close to ferries. Most of the rooms have a balcony, patio, or terrace. Restaurant, bar with entertainment. Some in-room data ports. Some hot tubs, sauna. Putting green, tennis. Children's programs (ages 8–12). Business services. | 291 S. Shore Dr., South Yarmouth | 508/398–2288 or 800/367–9393 | fax 508/398–1010 | www.redjacketinns.com/bluewater | 97 rooms, 16 suites | $190–$270 | Closed Nov.–Mar. | AE, D, DC, MC, V.

Captain Farris House. Built in 1845 by Captain Allen Farris, this Greek Revival in South Yarmouth's historic district is on the National Register of Historic Places. It was refurbished in 1993; window treatments and antiques are appointed throughout. Most rooms have working gas fireplaces and hot tubs. You are encouraged to enjoy the dining room, with its Waterford chandelier; the open interior garden courtyard; a complimentary glass of sherry in the parlor; afternoon tea; and fresh baked goods. Picnic area, complimentary breakfast. In-room data ports, cable TV, in-room VCRs. Some hot tubs. Business services. No kids under 11. | 308 Old Main St., South Yarmouth | 508/760–2818 or 800/350–9477 | fax 508/398–1262 | www.captainfarris.com | 10 rooms (1 with shower only), 4 suites | $105–$150, $160–$210 suites | AE, D, MC, V.

Captain Jonathan Motel. A gazebo, playground, and picnic area with grills on 2 acres of landscaped grounds make this motel a good choice for families. Curbside public trolley service to the beach is available. Restaurants, shops, and the scenic Bass River Bridge are all within walking distance. Picnic areas, complimentary Continental breakfast. Microwaves, refrigerators, cable TV. Pool. Playground. | 1237 Main St. (Rte. 28) | 508/398–3480 or 800/342–3480 | fax 508/398–3480 | www.sunsol.com/captainjonathan | 21 rooms, 1 cottage | $65–$85; cottage $125/day | AE, D, DC, MC, V.

Cavalier Motor Lodge and Resort. This motel is less than a mile from the beach, within walking distance of restaurants and shops, and 6 mi from ferries. It features 4½ acres of landscaped grounds, where guests can play shuffleboard, volleyball, and bocce ball. There are also full kitchens in the cottages and family-friendly amenities. Some microwaves, refrigerators, cable TV. Indoor and outdoor pools. Hot tub, sauna. Putting green. Video games. Playground. Some pets allowed (fee). | 881 Main St. South Yarmouth | 508/394–6575 or 800/545–3536 | fax 508/394–6578 | 43 rooms, 22 cottages | $59–$99; cottages $650–$1050/wk | AE, D, DC, MC, V.

Colonial House Inn. This 1730s sea captain's mansion features many antiques and handmade afghans. It's 1 mi from a private beach and a 10-minute drive from Hyannis. Bar, 3 dining rooms, complimentary Continental breakfast. Cable TV. Indoor pool. Hot tub, massage. Business services. Some pets allowed (fee). | 277 Main St. (Rte. 6A), Yarmouth Port | 508/362–4348 or 800/999–3416 | fax 508/362–8034 | www.colonialhousecapecod.com | 21 rooms | $95–$125 | AE, D, MC, V.

Green Harbor on the Ocean. This resort on Lewis Bay has its own ocean beach and miniature golf course. Every unit has an outdoor space with a charcoal grill, and many rooms have water views. Refrigerators, cable TV. Pool. Miniature golf. Beach. Boating. | 182 Baxter Ave., West Yarmouth | 508/771–1126 or 800/547–4733 | fax 508/771–0701 | www.redjacketinns.com/greenharbor | 50 rooms, villas, and suites | $190; $1,650–$2,800/wk villas and suites | Closed end of Oct.–mid-May | MC, V.

Gull Wing Suites. Yarmouth's only all-suite property is near restaurants, local attractions, and the beach. The rooms are the perfect size for families, and they even have pull-out couches. There is also an outdoor pool set in the interior courtyard. Refrigerators, cable TV. Indoor and outdoor pools. Hot tub, saunas. Video games. Business services. | 822 Main St., South Yarmouth | 508/394–9300 or 800/676–0000 | fax 508/394–1190 | www.ccrh.com | 136 suites | $89–$129 | AE, D, DC, MC, V.

Hunters Green. The most popular amenities here are an indoor/outdoor pool and giant indoor whirlpool bath. The motel is within walking distance of restaurants and a shopping plaza. Picnic area. Cable TV. Indoor/outdoor pool. Hot tub. | 553 Main St., West Yarmouth | 508/771–1169 or 800/334–3220 | 74 rooms | $60–$75 | Closed Oct.–Apr. | AE, D, MC, V.

The Inn at Cape Cod. A stately Greek Revival with imposing columns, tucked back off Route 6A, this B&B has an unusually eclectic assortment of furnishings: from Victorian antiques and Oriental rugs to Italian armoires and Chinese curios. Room sizes vary, too, from very large to very small. Complimentary Continental breakfast. Cable TV. Business services. No pets. No kids under 8. No smoking. | 4 Summer St., Yarmouth Port | 508/375–

0590 or 800/850–7301 | fax 508/362–9520 | www.capecodtravel.com/innatcapecod | 8 rooms, 1 suite | $125–$160, $185 suite | AE, D, DC, MC, V.

Inn at Lewis Bay. This beach house built in the 1920s has large rooms with country decor and antique furnishings. It is in a quiet residential area, one block from the beach. Picnic area, complimentary breakfast. No room phones, no TV. No kids under 11. | 57 Maine Ave., West Yarmouth | 508/771–3433 or 800/962–6679 | fax 508/394–1400 | www.innatlewis-bay.com | 6 rooms (2 with shower only), 1 suite | $98–$128, $180–$200 suite | AE, MC, V.

Lane's End Cottage. Tucked at the end of a little dirt lane, this sweet cottage is filled with English antiques. From the library and common room to the tasteful guest rooms with feather comforters and firm mattresses, this homey place exudes the warm spirit of its innkeeper. Complimentary breakfast. Library. Pets allowed (off-season with prior notice). No smoking. | 268 Main St., Yarmouth Port | 508/362–5298 | 3 rooms | $120–$130 | No credit cards.

Liberty Hill Inn on Cape Cod. This inn, an 1825 Greek Revival mansion and carriage house, is on the National Register of Historic Places. There are antiques and reproductions throughout, and rocking chairs on the front porch; all four rooms in the carriage house have gas fireplaces, and one of those rooms has a hot tub. Your deluxe breakfast may feature stuffed French toast topped with blueberry compote, a specialty. Complimentary breakfast. No room phones. Some hot tubs. No smoking. | 77 Main St., Yarmouth Port | 508/362–3976 or 800/821–3977 | fax 508/362–6485 | libertyh@capecod.net | www.capecod.net/lib-ertyhillinn | 9 rooms | $115–$185 | AE, MC, V.

Mariner Motor Lodge. At 1/4 mi away, the family friendly Mariner is the closest motel to Seagull Beach. Picnic area, complimentary Continental breakfast (off-season). Refrigerators, cable TV. Indoor and outdoor pools. Hot tub, sauna. Miniature golf. Video games. Business services. | 573 Main St., West Yarmouth | 508/771–7887 or 800/445–4050 | fax 508/771–2811 | mariner@mariner-capecod.com | www.mariner-capecod.com | 100 rooms | $75–$110 | AE, D, MC, V.

Motel 6. There's nothing unpredictable about this chain motel, except for its sauna and spa. It's on Rte. 28 in South Yarmouth, making it ideally situated for Cape Cod sight-seeing. Cable TV. Pool. Sauna, spa. | 1314 Rte. 28, South Yarmouth | 508/394–4000 or 800/341–5700 | fax 508/394–8319 | www.vacationinnproperties.com | 89 rooms | $65–$95 | AE, D, DC, MC, V.

Ocean Mist Hotel. This oceanfront hotel has its own private beach, and it's close to restaurants, shops, and whale-watching. Some rooms have water views. Some kitchenettes, refrigerators, cable TV. Indoor pool. Hot tub. Beach. Laundry facilities. Business services. | 97 S. Shore Dr. | 508/398–2633 or 800/248–6478 | fax 508/398–2633 | www.capecod-travel.com/oceanmist | 31 rooms, 32 suites | $169–$279, $219–$259 suites | Closed Jan. | AE, D, MC, V.

One Centre Street Inn. A former parsonage, this friendly B&B has a gracious air, colorful gardens, and elegant rooms. Complimentary breakfast. No cable TV in some rooms. Bicycles. No pets. No kids under 8. No smoking. | 1 Centre St., Yarmouth Port | 508/362–8910 | fax 508/362–0195 | www.sunsol.com/onecentrestreet | 6 rooms (2 with shared bath) | $105–$145 | D, MC, V.

Red Jacket Beach Resort. The cottages at this family-friendly beachfront resort are done in Cape Cod–style. Restaurant, bar, room service. Cable TV. Indoor and outdoor pools. Some hot tubs. Putting green, Tennis. Gym, beach. Video games. Children's programs (ages 4–12). Laundry facilities. Business services. | 1 S. Shore Dr., South Yarmouth | 508/398–6941 or 800/672–0500 | fax 508/398–1214 | www.redjacketinns.com | 150 rooms; 13 cottages | $95–$275; cottages $2700–$4600/wk | Closed late Oct.–mid-Apr. | AE, MC, V.

Red Mill Motel. Although the rooms are plain, with nondescript motel-style furnishings, they are comfortable and some have efficiency kitchens. Complimentary breakfast. Refrigerators, cable TV. Pool. No pets. | 793 Main St., South Yarmouth | 508/398–5583 | fax 508/398–2892 | www.sunsol.com/redmillmotel | 18 rooms | $85–$95 | AE, D, MC, V.

Riviera Beach Motor Inn. You can swim and watch the sun set from this motel's private beach. Restaurant, bar. Refrigerators, cable TV. Indoor and outdoor pools. Some hot tubs. Beach, water sports. Children's programs (ages 5–11). | 327 S. Shore Dr., South Yarmouth | 508/398–2273 or 800/CAPE–COD | fax 508/398–1202 | www.redjacketinns.com/riviera | 125 rooms | $180–$280 | Closed mid-Oct.–mid.-Apr. | AE, MC, V.

Seaside. Built in the 1940s, these studio, one-, and two-bedroom units are individually owned, so the decor varies from one to another. Set on 5 acres fronting Nantucket Sound, some are oceanfront and others are wooded. All have kitchens or kitchenettes and many have a fireplace for the colder seasons. Kitchenettes. Beach. No pets. | 135 S. Shore Dr., South Yarmouth | 508/398–2533 | fax 508/398–2523 | 45 cottages | $125–$175 | Closed mid-Oct.–Apr. | D, MC, V.

Tidewater Motor Lodge. There's a Mill Pond across the street from this motel, and a salt-water inlet borders the back of its landscaped four acres of property. Ferries, restaurants, and shops are a short drive away, and it's 1½ mi to downtown Hyannis. Restaurant (breakfast), picnic area. Refrigerators, cable TV. Indoor pool. Hot tub, sauna. Video games. Playground. | 135 Main St., West Yarmouth | 508/775–6322 or 800/338–6322 | fax 508/778–5105 | www.tidewaterml.com | 101 rooms | $119–$159 | AE, D, MC, V.

Village Inn. This old-fashioned hostelry, built in 1795 for a sea captain, still has the original wide plank floorboards and light fixtures. Rooms and in-room amenities vary considerably, from the tiny Wellfleet Room to the enormous Yarmouth Room with its own library and a fireplace in the bathroom. Pets allowed (fee) by arrangement. No smoking. | 92 Main St., Yarmouth Port | 508/362–3182 | 10 rooms | $75–$109 | MC, V.

★ **Wedgewood Inn.** Elegant, handsome, and welcoming are the apt buzz words at this 1812 Greek Revival and renovated carriage house, both of which are set back from the busy road. Most of the spacious guest rooms have Oriental carpets and fireplaces, and there are plenty of lovely antiques and cherry pencil-post beds to go around. Complimentary breakfast. No pets. No smoking. | 83 Main St., Yarmouth Port | 508/362–5157 | fax 508/362–5851 | www.wedgewoodinn.com | 4 rooms, 5 suites | $135–$155, $165–$195 suites.

Yarmouth Resort. This centrally located and recently renovated motel is great for families and close to restaurants, shops, mini-golf, beaches, and ferries. All the rooms have private balconies. In-room data ports, some refrigerators, cable TV. Indoor and outdoor pools. Hot tub, sauna. Exercise equipment. Playground. Business services. | 343 Main St., West Yarmouth | 508/775–5155 or 888/810–0044 | fax 508/790–8255 | 133 rooms, 5 suites | $79–$159, $109–$139 suites | D, MC, V.

Eating Well is the Best Revenge

Start at the top By all means take in a really good restaurant or two while you're on the road. A trip is a time to kick back and savor the pleasures of the palate. Read up on the culinary scene before you leave home. Check out representative menus on the Web—some chefs have gone electronic. And ask friends who have just come back. For big-city dining, reserve a table as far in advance as you can, remembering that the best establishments book up months ahead. Remember that some good restaurants require you to reconfirm the day before or the day of your meal. Then again, some really good places will call you, so make sure to leave a number where you can be reached.

Adventures in eating A trip is the perfect opportunity to try food you can't get at home. So leave yourself open to try an ethnic food that's not represented where you live or to eat fruits and vegetables you've never heard of.

One of them may become your next favorite food.

Beyond guidebooks You can rely on the restaurants you find in these pages. But also look for restaurants on your own. When you're ready for lunch, ask people you meet where they eat. Look for tiny holes-in-the-wall with a loyal following and the best burgers or crispiest pizza crust. Find out about local chains whose fame rests upon a single memorable dish. There's hardly a food-lover who doesn't relish the chance to share a favorite place. It's fun to come up with your own special find—and asking about food is a great way to start a conversation.

Sample local flavors Do check out the specialties. Is there a special brand of ice cream or a special dish that you simply must try?

Have a picnic Every so often eat al fresco. Grocery shopping gives you a whole different view of a place.

Beyond T-Shirts and Key Chains

Budget for a major purchase If souvenirs are all about keeping the memories alive in the long haul, plan ahead to shop for something really special—a work of art, a rug or something else hand-crafted, or a major accessory for your home. One major purchase will stay with you far longer than a dozen tourist trinkets, and you'll have all the wonderful memories associated with shopping for it besides.

Add to your collection Whether antiques, used books, salt and pepper shakers, or ceramic frogs are your thing, start looking in the first day or two. Chances are you'll want to scout around and then go back to some of the first shops you visited before you hand over your credit card.

Get guarantees in writing Is the vendor making promises? Ask him to put them in writing.

Anticipate a shopping spree If you think you might buy breakables, bring along a length of bubble wrap. Pack a large tote bag in your suitcase in case you need extra space. Don't fill your suitcase to bursting before you leave home. Or include some old clothing that you can leave behind to make room for new acquisitions.

Know before you go Study prices at home on items you might consider buying while you're away. Otherwise you won't recognize a bargain when you see one.

Plastic, please Especially if your purchase is pricey and you're looking for authenticity, it's always smart to pay with a credit card. If a problem arises later on and the merchant can't or won't resolve it, the credit-card company may help you out.

© Artville

Rhode Island

To escape rigid Puritanical strictures, Rhode Island's first European settlers emigrated from the Massachusetts Bay and Plymouth colonies. But Massachusetts communities always cast shadows over the colony that grew up around Narragansett Bay. The Boston metropolitan area continues to strongly affect Rhode Island. In southeastern Rhode Island, nearly a majority of the residents derive their income working in Massachusetts. Yet, despite its many ties to the Bay State, Rhode Island (the Ocean State) long ago developed its own character. "Little Rhody" has a long list of particulars, enough for popular cartoonist Don Bosque to make a living lampooning "the quahog state." (A quahog is a large, hard-shell clam harvested in Rhode Island waters.)

Designated Providence by its faithful settler Roger Williams, the capital city at the northern tip of the Narragansett Bay drives the state economy so profoundly that analysts have suggested that the state do away with its 39 townships and operate Rhode Island as a city-state, something Rhode Islanders know will never happen. The state's towns each have their own flavor, and disputes among them are common. In the past few years, residents of the southerly town of Narragansett has been bickering over the taxing of ferry passengers to Block Island, which receives 50¢ from every person arriving on its shores. Because the boats leave from Narragansett, its officials want some of the action, too. The issue—likely to be decided in state courts—exemplifies the local particulars that make Rhode Island an interesting place to visit.

In addition to local lore, Rhode Island steeps its travelers in history and culture. Many ponds, rivers, and communities retain their Indian names; inns and restaurants are often named for settlers. And the state's wide array of architecture spans 300 years. As varied as the state's complex geography are the people who populate its 200 villages. Colonial Rhode Island granted its inhabitants unprecedented levels of religious and civil liberties. Designated "a lively experiment" in governance by King George II, the colony

CAPITAL: PROVIDENCE	POPULATION: 1,003,464	AREA: 1,049 SQUARE MI
BORDERS: CT AND MA	TIME ZONE: EASTERN STANDARD	POSTAL ABBREVIATION: RI
WEB SITE: WWW.STATE.RI.US		

declared that none of its residents were to be "molested, punished, disquieted, or called into question" on matters of religion. Such plain language made Rhode Island a destination for Baptists, Quakers, and Jews. The state's government also encouraged entrepreneurship, and as a result Rhode Island industries attracted thousands of immigrants in the 19th century. During this period, immigrants arrived from French Canada, Italy, Ireland, England, and Eastern Europe to work growing numbers of cotton mills, textile mills, and foundries all across the state. Descendants of these workers have retained much of their heritage in ethnic enclaves throughout the state.

Diversity from community to community has made the Ocean State a primary test market for new businesses and products. But this focus on entrepreneurship and "getting ahead" has at times resulted in a less than savory history. The state was once commonly referred to as "Rogue Island" for its brutal privateers and shrewd businessmen. Following a severe banking crisis in the 1980s, the state has worked to clean up its image, recently convicting former governor William DiPrete of extortion.

Of late, Providence has received national acclaim for an effective city-rejuvenation program. At the end of the 20th century, the waterways and roads of Providence were revamped, a convention center was built, an outdoor ice rink was constructed at the foot of city hall, and a high-end shopping mall emerged where there were once railroad tracks. More work is planned, but already the upgrades have infused in locals a new confidence—an important element in a state that lost thousands of jobs in the 1970s and '80s to military downsizing and the collapse of numerous industries.

Beginning with its first two settlers—William Blackstone, who at the time was believed to have the largest private collection of books in the New World, and Roger Williams, who authored the first text on Native American languages—Rhode Island has nurtured education and the arts, establishing Rhode Island College (later renamed Brown University) in 1764.

More recently Rhode Islanders have begun protecting their wildlands, making substantial progress after decades of industrial pollution. Waterfowl, migrating birds, and sea life thrive in Rhode Island's many preservation areas. The state's late, long-time senator, John Chafee, sponsored many initiatives to preserve critical habitats and view sheds. His strong position in the Republican party led to the passage of the Clean Air Act, which he authored, and a series of endangered species acts.

Other well-known Rhode Islanders include portraitist Gilbert Stuart, whose rendering of George Washington graces the dollar bill. His birthplace near Wickford is now a museum. Behind George Washington, General Nathaniel Greene of Warwick was second command in the American Revolution. Ted Kennedy's son, Patrick, is currently a Rhode Island representative in Congress.

The State of Rhode Island and Providence Plantations, as it is officially known, is comprised of areas of dense population, industry, marshlands, beaches, woods, rivers, and old villages. On any state road the scenery and the townships change quickly. Outstanding vistas and notable architecture are sometimes a short distance from tasteless sprawl or run-down communities. With 6,000 mi of roadways, the Ocean State

RI Timeline

1633	1636	1638	1640
William Blackstone settles near Pawtucket.	Roger Williams moves to in Providence.	Aquidneck purchased from Narragansett Indians; Portsmouth is settled.	First public school established in Newport.

feels bigger than is connoted by the its most well-known attribute—that it's the smallest state in the union. With proper planning, a traveler can pick apples in the morning in the Blackstone Valley, ice-skate in downtown Providence by noon, walk a South County beach after a delicious lunch, and end the day by sailing on the bay or touring a mansion in Newport, all the while learning a good deal about American history.

History

When Giovanni da Verrazano sailed into the Narragansett Bay in 1524, he termed the region the Garden of the New World and called the native people "the goodest and most content" of all he had encountered. Verrazano also compared the pear-shape island at the region's southern extent to the Isle of Rhodes in the Mediterranean. Verrazano was referring to Block Island (later named for Dutch explorer Adriaen Block). However, Rhode Island founder Roger Williams later mistook the reference for Aquidneck Island (where Newport is located), naming it Rhode Island. The name stuck, at least for the state; the Indian name, Aquidneck, is still used for the Narragansett Bay island.

Williams's influence is so integral to the history of Rhode Island that a national park in Providence is dedicated to his memory. Williams was banished from Salem, in the Plymouth Colony, in 1636. A Puritan minister, Williams's revolutionary notions were not embraced by his church. He believed that no ideas should be forced upon churchgoers. And he argued for the rights of the Indians, asking for fair trades between settlers and natives. Known to the Indians as a fair-minded interpreter, he was taken in by the Narragansett Indians and befriended by Sachem Canonicus, who later bequeathed to Williams the land now known as the east side of Providence.

Prior to the arrival of Williams, the enigmatic William Blackstone settled in what is now Central Falls. In 1628, Blackstone became the first European to live in what is now Boston. Five years later, having grown weary of the ways of Puritan settlers who became his neighbors, this Anglican clergyman migrated to unsettled lands to the south. Called "the sage of the wilderness," Blackstone was known to travel atop a docile white bull. It may never be known, however, if he was a 17th-century Thoreau or Emerson. His cabin (nicknamed Study Hill) and his writings were destroyed in 1675, during the yearlong King Philip's War, a devastating conflict between white settlers and Native Americans.

Williams was not as solitary a man as Blackstone. He established a prosperous settlement on the land he'd been given, naming it Providence, a place where two small rivers, the Moshassuck and Woonasquatucket, meet to form a tidal basin and blend into the Narragansett Bay. Waterplace Park now stands in concrete relief around the site of that pond. Other refugees from Massachusetts colonies arrived after Williams. He helped Anne Hutchins, William Coddington, and Samuel Groton establish Portsmouth, Newport, and Warwick, respectively. Williams sought official recognition of Rhode Island, personally petitioning English parliament and lobbying the Crown. His work was rewarded in 1663, when King Charles II issued the Rhode Island Colonial Charter. The emancipating document—on display at the Rhode Island State House—was

1643	1644	1657	1663	1675-76
Rhode Island refused admission to New England Confederacy.	Parliamentary charter issued to Providence Plantations.	Massachusetts's request that Rhode Island exclude Quakers is denied.	Charter granted by King Charles II.	King Philip's Indian war.

unprecedented because it recognized land ownership by Native Americans, guaranteed freedom of thought and religion, and established a democratic process involving "all or the greater part of the free inhabitants."

The colony flourished economically. Its extensive coastline and the numerous harbors in the Narragansett Bay led Rhode Islanders to maritime trade, fishing, and privateering. Colonial Newport became a primary trading center, producing finely crafted candles, furniture, and clocks to be sold abroad. In 1989 a desk made in Newport by carpenters from the Townsend and Goddard families sold for $12 million. Great fortunes were accumulated by traders like John Brown, whose refinements cannot be discounted after a trip to the John Brown House and the venerable university he funded, Brown.

Duties were not charged on slaves, and Newport became the North's primary slave-trading hub. The adjunct industry of rum-making saw 30 distilleries operating by the mid-1700s. Newport was home to 600 trading vessels, including 50 slave ships, most of which were designed and built in Newport. Into the 1800s the city's slave traders continued to carry human cargo. Parts of the graphic Steven Spielberg film about the slave-trading ship, *Amistad,* were shot in Newport in 1996.

Rhode Island renounced allegiance to English rule with the same vigor it later brought to business matters. Colonists burned many revenue (tax-collecting) ships, the most famous being the *Gaspee* in 1772, an act that is commemorated annually in Barrington. And Providence had its own "tea party," after Boston's, in the downtown square.

Two months before the Declaration of Independence was signed on July 4, 1776, Rhode Island became the first of the 14 colonies to formally renounce the Crown, becoming the first independent state established by Europeans in the New World. Rhode Island was the last of the colonies to join the Union formed in 1787 following the Revolutionary War, signing the Articles of Confederation, in 1790, only after other states threatened tariffs and invasion.

There was another revolution in Rhode Island, begun in 1790, when cotton was spun into yarn in Pawtucket. The state's topography, climate, and social conditions—narrow, swift-running streams; low waterfalls; reliable rainfall; and a great "spirit of industry"— were ideal for textile making. By 1812 there were 38 cotton mills and a variety of other industrial shops. The change brought brutal child-labor problems and devastating pollution. Many of the mills today are offices and warehouses; most are still occupied by small industrial companies (manufacturing still employs 24% of the state's workforce).

Business has always been at the forefront of Rhode Island politics. The two forces recently aligned themselves to increase tourism; and tourism has become the state's top industry. The partnership has been an unlikely boon to the environment. In recent years new parklands have been established. The Blackstone Valley was designated a National Heritage Corridor by the National Park Service. Hundreds of historic buildings have been restored. More than ever before, local government and Rhode Island residents realize the value of the state's environmental history. By recognizing its past, Rhode Island is finding that it can forge its future.

1683	1684	1732	1764	1769
Roger Williams dies.	State passes law protecting Jews in liberty of conscience.	First newspaper in Rhode Island established by James Franklin.	Rhode Island College established (renamed Brown University in 1804).	In first overt act of violence against British authority, British tax ship *Liberty* destroyed in Newport.

Regions

1. BLACKSTONE VALLEY

Encompassing eight towns, numerous rivers and streams, and a few dozen hills, the Blackstone Valley is an intricate and intriguing place to explore. Comprising the northern half of the state, the region's cities include Pawtucket, Central Falls, and Woonsocket. Numerous villages line the state roads that wind through the region and make for enjoyable driving, especially in the fall when the foliage is at its peak. The steep and constant drop of the Blackstone River, which runs through the valley from Worcester, Massachusetts, made the area prime for water-powered mills and factories. The American Industrial Revolution began here, and to this day, hundreds of factories produce a wide assortment of products, including toys, jewelry, silverware, textiles, and forged metals. The region's parks attract campers, horseback riders, and hikers. Shoppers enjoy the factory outlets. Others come to enjoy "chicken family-style," an all-you-can-eat affair offered by dozens of northern Rhode Island restaurants. Historic homes and museums are also big draws.

Towns listed: Cumberland, Glocester, Lincoln, Pawtucket, Woonsocket

2. EAST BAY

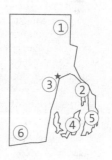

Barrington, Warren, and Bristol are handsome towns chock-full of Colonial and post-Colonial homes. Together they make up Bristol County, also called the East Bay, which serves primarily as a bedroom community for Providence. Through the area's many harbors and marinas, residents maintain a close affinity for the sea. Around 1800, many shipping merchants and ship captains built homes in these towns. Warren was the center of the Rhode Island whaling industry. The towns generally attract visitors who come to spend an afternoon lunching and shopping. Many people stop over in the East Bay en route to Newport from Providence. Businesses in this region tend to be open year-round, unlike their counterparts in the coastal regions. The antiques shops in Warren, many along Water Street, are exceptional. Parks and a few museums, including a sailing museum, are also attractions.

Towns listed: Bristol, Warren

3. GREATER PROVIDENCE

Including Warwick, Cranston, and East and North Providence, this region is one of the most densely populated in the United States. Greater Providence includes many nicely maintained stretches of coastline, suburban sprawl, industry, and the run-down neighborhoods of South Providence. Nearly a million people live in greater Providence, with

1772	1774	1775	1776	1776
British tax ship *Gaspee* burned in Narragansett Bay.	Importation of slaves prohibited.	British frigate *Rose* attacked in first naval engagement of Revolution.	General Assembly renounces allegiance to Great Britain in May.	General Assembly approves Declaration of Independence in July.

just 160,000 living within city limits. Numerous educational facilities and hospitals employ and service thousands of people annually. As the cultural center of the state, the area attracts people seeking varied diversions. There is no shortage of cultural venues and, unlike larger cities, it is rare to be shut out of an event. Dining and sightseeing are the other attractions. Numerous streets in Providence, particularly Thayer, Wickenden, and Atwells, are worth a trip just for an afternoon stroll.

Towns listed: East Greenwich, Providence, Warwick

4. NEWPORT AND JAMESTOWN

Settled in 1639 by religious refugees from the Massachusetts Bay Colony, Newport quickly grew into a bustling seaport. Its deepwater harbor and location at the mouth of Narragansett Bay made it a center for international trade and shipbuilding. As early as the 18th century, wealthy visitors were drawn to the City by the Sea for its mild summer climate and the spectacular promontory upon which it sits.

By the 1880s, New York socialites—with their new fortunes from coal, oil, railroads, and finance—streamed into Newport. They hired the country's finest architects to build extravagant mansions, or as they called them, "summer cottages," which remain a symbol of the Gilded Age's opulence.

Today Newport is famous for recreational sailing, which effectively melds the nautical expertise of the Colonial era and the conspicuous consumption of the Gilded Age. The annual jazz festival in Newport has gained international acclaim and attracts even greater numbers of visitors to the streets of Newport, which can become very crowded during the summer months.

Conanicut Island—also known as Jamestown, the name of its only town—is situated at the mouth of the Narragansett Bay. Once the summer camp of the Narragansett Indians, it was settled in the 1650s, mostly by Quakers who farmed the land. Today Jamestown remains a relatively peaceful and untouristy residential town and summer resort.

Towns listed: Jamestown, Middletown, Newport, Portsmouth

5. SAKONNET REGION

The land east of the salty Sakonnet River and bordered on two sides by Massachusetts includes the towns of Tiverton and Little Compton. Once part of Massachusetts, these charming farmlands, woods, and small villages seem to have been left behind by the rest of the Ocean State. The lack of development now makes properties in Little Compton and Tiverton some of the state's most desirable. Route 77 offers visitors a great day trip. The beaches east of Sakonnet Point are some of the best in the state and offer views of Martha's Vineyard offshore. Though short on accommodations, this region is rich with evocative sights. Traveling here in the fall is especially pleasant.

Towns listed: Little Compton, Tiverton

1776	1778	1779	1780	1787
British Army takes Newport in December.	Battle of Rhode Island.	British evacuate Newport.	Count Rochambeau lands in Newport with 6,000 troops.	First spinning jenny in United States made in Providence.

INTRODUCTION
HISTORY
REGIONS
WHEN TO VISIT
STATE'S GREATS
RULES OF THE ROAD
DRIVING TOURS

6. SOUTH COUNTY

Though it doesn't offer as many historic gems as the northern and eastern portions of the state, Washington County, as it is officially known, is unmatched in its coastal features. Wildlife refuges, management areas, and state parks dot the region's 10 towns. Located in the southern portion of the state, and including Block Island, South County is the largest region in Rhode Island—and the most undeveloped. It is, however, the fastest-growing area in the state; that's one reason Rhode Islanders take such pride in every step made to preserve South County's rural ambience. In addition to whiling away time on the beaches, come here to dine on seafood and to shop. Fishing, hiking, and surfing are also popular. Families from Connecticut, New York, and Massachusetts often spend a week in South County towns each summer. Day trips to Block Island also make for engaging outings. Near the beaches on hot summer days you can expect traffic delays.

Towns listed: Block Island, Charlestown, Galilee, Kingston, Narragansett, North Kingstown, Watch Hill, Westerly

When to Visit

Approximately 400 miles of Rhode Island is bordered by coastline. The salty Narragansett Bay runs 28 mi into the state's interior and is 12 mi across in some areas. The water cools coastal Rhode Island in summer and warms it in winter. On hot summer days, temperatures can be as much as 10 degrees cooler along the coast.

Between the end of July and November, tropical storms and hurricanes can threaten Rhode Island. The state is severely affected by a strong hurricane about once every 10 years. Damage caused by coastal storms—"nor'easters"—is usually limited to coastal areas.

Though extreme temperatures are rare, the thermometer typically dips below freezing 120 days per year. Spring weather is damp and often windy in Rhode Island. Winter weather, though sometimes mild and dry for long stretches, is unpredictable. The average annual snowfall is around 3 ft. Summer and fall are the best times to travel in Rhode Island.

CLIMATE CHART
Average High/Low temperatures and Monthly Precipitation (in inches)

	JAN.	FEB.	MAR.	APR.	MAY	JUNE
BLOCK ISLAND	37/25	37/25	44/32	52/39	61/48	70/57
	3.4	3.2	3.7	3.8	3.5	3.0

	JULY	AUG.	SEPT.	OCT.	NOV.	DEC.
	76/64	76/64	70/58	61/49	52/41	42/30
	2.6	3.2	3.1	3.0	4.1	4.0

1790	1790	1820	1835	1901
Federal Constitution adopted.	Samuel Slater starts cotton factory in Pawtucket.	*Providence Journal* established.	First train runs between Providence and Boston.	General Assembly convenes in new State House in Providence.

	JAN.	FEB.	MAR.	APR.	MAY	JUNE
NEWPORT	38/23	39/24	46/30	55/38	64/47	73/57
	3.8	3.6	4.1	4.1	3.7	3.1
	JULY	AUG.	SEPT.	OCT.	NOV.	DEC.
	78/63	78/63	73/57	63/47	53/38	43/28
	2.9	3.3	3.5	3.5	4.7	4.4
	JAN.	FEB.	MAR.	APR.	MAY	JUNE
PROVIDENCE	37/19	38/21	46/29	57/38	67/47	77/57
	3.8	3.8	4.1	4.2	3.7	3.8
	JULY	AUG.	SEPT.	OCT.	NOV.	DEC.
	82/63	80/62	74/54	64/43	53/35	41/24
	3.2	3.6	3.5	3.7	4.4	4.4

ON THE STATE CALENDAR
SUMMER

June   **Storm Trysail.** This is the largest sailing event on the East Coast, and it's held at Block Island. More than 500 boats participate in a week of competition, the highlight being the around-the-island race. Some of the best racing teams in the world attend. | 914/834–8857 | www.stormstrysail.org.

July   **Bristol 4th of July Parade.** First held in 1785, this is the nation's oldest celebration of U.S. independence. Fire trucks, antique cars, school bands, and military regiments wind through streets that existed during the 1776 American Revolution. | 401/253–0445.

Wickford Art Festival. This art festival on the sidewalks of historic Wickford Village in North Kingstown is one of the country's largest and best. You'll find paintings, photographs, and sculptures, in addition to entertainment, crafts, and food. | 401/294–6840.

Aug.   **JVC Jazz Festival.** Legendary performers and rising stars perform at this world-renowned event. First held in 1954 at the Newport Casino, it grew too large and was canceled for a number of years. It is now held at Fort Adams State Park. In 1998, President Bill Clinton said that when he's out of office, he would like to play saxophone on the stage overlooking Newport Harbor. | 401/847–3700 | www.festivalproductions.net.

1919	1938	1954	1960	1969
Providence College established.	A hurricane, the state's worst natural disaster, struck and took the lives of 311 people.	First Newport Jazz Festival at Newport Casino.	Riot of 12,000 people at Newport Jazz Festival.	The $61 million Newport Bridge opens.

International Quahog Festival. Rhode Islanders gather at the Wickford Festival Grounds to celebrate the state's official shellfish, the quahog. This large clam is used in chowder, fried in clam cakes, or baked after being mixed into a stuffing ("stuffies"). | 401/294–3733.

INTRODUCTION
HISTORY
REGIONS
WHEN TO VISIT
STATE'S GREATS
RULES OF THE ROAD
DRIVING TOURS

FALL

Sept. **Rhythm & Roots Festival.** In a field surrounded by woodlands and old farm buildings, this festival of Cajun, zydeco, and bluegrass music is held each year, attracting about 5,000 people for the three-day event. A wide variety of Cajun foods are sold, and on numerous stages, attendees dance away night and day. Held Labor Day Weekend at Stepping Stone Ranch, Escoheag Hill Road in West Greenwich. | 401/351–6312.

State's Greats

With 78 public libraries, 11 schools of higher learning, and approximately 90,000 college students in Rhode Island, nearly 10 percent of the population takes college courses in any given year. Like education, architecture is no small element of Rhode Island's refinements. Both **Newport** and **Providence,** the state's two premier cities, boast some of the country's outstanding architecture. The state's restaurants are another strong point. Providence, home to **Johnson & Wales Culinary Institute,** has an enormous number of restaurants per capita.

The state's geography includes over 400 mi of coastline, 38 salty islands, and 37 hills over 500 ft high. Conservationists will appreciate the various microcosms in such diverse terrain, including the state's pristine barrier beaches and its offshore reefs.

Though the state is blessed with numerous destinations, **Block Island** is the state's ultimate getaway, 13 mi offshore. Its tropical character in summer makes it relaxing and gratifying, though sometimes crowded; the fall is the island's best season.

Beaches and Parks

Of the approximately 70 saltwater bathing beaches in the state, **Charleston** in Narragansett, **Quonochontaug Beach** in Charlestown, **Mansion** on Block Island, and **Second Beach** in Middletown are at the top of New England's short list. All have deep sand and are extensive enough for a long walk. The Cliff Walk in Newport is a 4-mi path running between a rocky coastline and Bellevue Avenue mansions; it is often called the most beautiful walk in the country, and even the most sedentary can enjoy it. The River Walk that begins at **Waterplace Park** is the pride of the Providence revitalization effort.

Roger Williams State Park in Providence is home to a comprehensive zoo with more than 900 animals of 150 different species. The 430-acre park grounds feature duck ponds, paddleboats, and a carousel.

1994	**1998**	**1998**	**2000**
Convention center and Westin Hotel open in Providence.	Ice rink opens in Providence's Kennedy Plaza.	Former governor Edward DiPrete pleads guilty to charges of extortion.	Ruth J. Simmons is appointed the 18th president of Brown University, becoming the first African-American woman to head an Ivy League school.

Culture, History, and the Arts

Providence is widely considered to be one of New England's leading communities in the arts. Founded in the mid-1960s, the **Trinity Repertory Theatre** is recognized nationally and is an important presence in downtown Providence. On College Hill, east of the business district, is the **Museum of Art at the Rhode Island School of Design;** it has a wide collection of art from around the world and a spectacular collection of textiles.

Just 29 mi south of Providence, the seaside city of Newport is a sophisticated place with an array of attractions for visitors. The **Newport Jazz Festival** is held annually on the lawn fronting the burly 22-acre installation called Fort Adams. Established in 1954, this is one of the oldest traditions in modern music. The **International Tennis Hall of Fame Museum** presents a comprehensive look at the game of tennis. Modern American tennis is said to have been born in Newport.

Newport's mansions served as proving grounds for the country's best young architects. Richard Upjohn, Richard Morris Hunt, and firms like McKim, Mead & White left a legacy of remarkable homes, and many of their ornate creations are open to the public. On the grounds at **The Elms** is an impressive arboretum, and a tour of the home nicely encapsulates the city's vaunted Gilded Age. The **Isaac Bell House** is a classic shingle-style structure that can be toured as a work in progress. **The Breakers** is the city's most opulent home, built for railroad heir Cornelius Vanderbilt II. **Belcourt Castle** is a mansion housing eclectic treasures, including full suits of armor.

In addition to the craftsmanship seen in Newport's mansions, the city is known for its boatbuilding and sailing. Yachts built here have successfully defended the America's Cup many times. Shipwrights, sailors, and sail makers are still a large portion of Newport's population. The state continues to make forays into boating history. The **International Yacht Restoration School** on storied Thames Street houses many of the country's best-known watercraft, and the **America's Cup Museum** is located in nearby Bristol.

Sports

Colt State Park in Bristol has numerous offerings, including a skateboard park and an outdoor hockey rink for rollerbladers. The popular **East Bay Bike Path** runs from Bristol to India Point Park in Providence. For more primitive outdoor activities, the **Trustom Pond National Wildlife Refuge** in South Kingstown features well-marked hiking trails that meander past a coastal pond and to a barrier beach. Finally, the farm team for the Boston Red Sox, the **Pawtucket Red Sox** (known locally as the "Pawsox"), play at McCoy Stadium.

Sportfishing is a popular activity in Rhode Island. Striped bass can be caught from June to December along any of the state beaches. For offshore fishing, cod, striped bass, bluefish are common catch. From the Port of Galilee, the **Frances Fleet** offers charter trips and scheduled fishing trips in the spring, summer, and fall.

Rules of the Road

License Requirements: To drive in Rhode Island you must be at least 16 years old and have a valid driver's license. Residents of Canada and most other countries may drive as long as they have valid licenses from their home countries.

Speed Limit: Maximum legal speed in Rhode Island is 65 mph; 25 mph in business and residential areas; elsewhere, 50 mph in day, 45 mph at night, or as posted.

Right Turn on Red: Permitted after a complete stop, unless prohibited by sign.

Seat Belt and Helmet Laws: Seat belts required for all operators and passengers. All children under age 5 must ride in the backseat. Helmets are not required for operators of motorcycles but are required for passengers. Protective goggles, glasses, or windscreen are required of operators and passengers.

For More Information: Contact Department of Administration, Registry of Motor Vehicles | 401/588–3020, ext. 2039.

INTRODUCTION
HISTORY
REGIONS
WHEN TO VISIT
STATE'S GREATS
RULES OF THE ROAD
DRIVING TOURS

Blackstone Valley Driving Tour

FROM PAWTUCKET TO GLOCESTER

Distance: 46 mi; 74 km   Time: 1 day

Breaks: The tour can easily be completed in one day. Lincoln Woods State Park and Phantom Farms are two places to take a break.

This tour will take you through the heart of northern Rhode Island, an unusual region and an emerging travel destination strewn with historical, cultural, and environmental sites. You will primarily be driving state roads. Most are winding and picturesque, running through communities and businesses that are unique to Rhode Island; a few of the areas that aren't necessarily aesthetically pleasing are intriguing for the architecture, enterprises, and people you'll encounter. Traveling north, then westward, you will pass through industrial cities, small villages, farmlands, and wooded areas. This trip can be taken any time of year, but in the fall the scenery is spectacularly accented by foliage.

❶ ❷ In **Pawtucket** (5 mi north of Providence on U.S. 95, Exit 28), where the harnessing of the Blackstone River in 1793 kicked off the American Industrial Revolution, you'll find

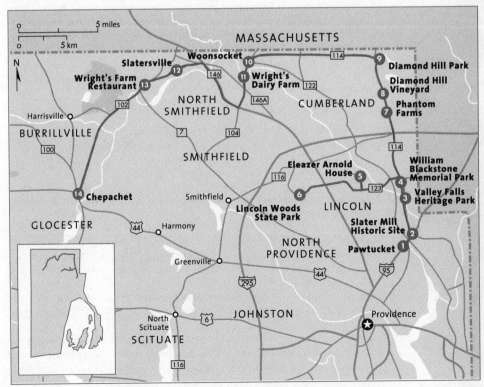

the **Blackstone Valley Visitors Center.** This comprehensive information center in the downtown area features films, kiosks, and a vast assortment of information on northern Rhode Island. Across the street is **Slater Mill Historic Site** (401/725–8638), a functional cotton mill, fully restored with an 8-ton waterwheel, a 19th-century machine shop, and demonstrations of textile production. Slater Mill is perhaps Rhode Island's most recognized historical landmark.

❸ In **Cumberland** (2 mi north of Pawtucket; I–95 N, Exit 28, to Rte. 114 N), you will see many brick row houses that once housed immigrant factory workers; most have been restored and are now popular even with well-to-do families. Just over the Blackstone River on Broad Street is **Valley Falls Heritage Park.** In its course from Worcester, Massachusetts, to the Narragansett Bay, the Blackstone drops in altitude more quickly than any New England river, making it an attractive site for the massive mill complex that was erected here. This small riverside park is part of the newly designated Blackstone Valley National Heritage Corridor. A new type of U.S. park system, heritage corridors encompass towns, cities, and entire regions in an effort to inform the public about the significant historical contributions of these areas.

❹ **William Blackstone Memorial Park** (Broad and Blackstone Sts. in Cumberland) is dedicated to the Reverend William Blackstone, the first European settler in Rhode Island. Also the first settler of Boston, he built his home here in 1635 in an effort to live a quiet life away from the pervasive strictures of the Puritan church. This subtle monument is a tasteful tribute to the man who for many years had the most extensive library in New England.

❺ From Cumberland, a quick westward jaunt to **Lincoln** (Rte. 114 N to Rte. 123 W) will bring you to the **Eleazer Arnold House,** a must-see for architecture enthusiasts. A "stone-ender," the house features a giant stone chimney that comprises the western wall. Built circa 1687, it is open to the public in summer. Small by modern standards, it was considered an expansive home in early Colonial times.

❻ Along this winding, pleasant road is **Lincoln Woods State Park** that has a large pond and a road system by which you can tour the park. With picnic areas, beaches for swimming, and hiking and horseback-riding trails, it's a nice stop for families.

❼ Doubling back to Cumberland, stop by **Phantom Farms,** where hot apple cider, baked goods, and fresh fruit and vegetables are sold year-round. In the fall you can pick your own apples from the small orchard behind the farm stand. Many small farms in Rhode Island welcome visitors and sell baked goods and produce.

❽ **Diamond Hill Vineyard** produces cordial wines made from apples and pears. Its wine is sold only on the premises.

❾ **Diamond Hill Park** is a 427-acre park featuring a stone-faced cliff. The park takes its name from the abundant and glittering quartz deposits. There are numerous unmarked hiking trails, a pond, and a picnic area. Silvy's Brook meanders through the park.

❿ French is commonly spoken in the streets of **Woonsocket** (head west on Rte. 114, then south on Rte. 126). At the **Museum of Work and Culture** you will learn that the city grew to prominence in the 1800s with a flood of immigrants, mostly French Canadians. The museum uses multimedia and traditional exhibits to explore the Industrial Revolution, the genesis of the textile-workers' union, and the events that led to the National Textile Strike of 1934. The *Blackstone Valley Explorer* is a riverboat offering tours of sections

INTRODUCTION
HISTORY
REGIONS
WHEN TO VISIT
STATE'S GREATS
RULES OF THE ROAD
DRIVING TOURS

of the Blackstone River. The 45-minute trips, departing from downtown Woonsocket and other locations along the river, are especially pleasant in fall, when the foliage is at its peak.

⑪ Return to Main Street in Woonsocket, follow it around the rotary, straight over the river, and onto South Main Street. At the end of South Main Street, make a right at the light, then take your second left on Woonsocket Hill Rd. **Wright's Dairy Farm** is a large bakery on a family farm, where the public can see the cows being milked and sample a variety of pastries and dairy products.

⑫ Slatersville (from Rte. 146 N, take the Forestdale/Slatersville exit, follow 1½ mi west to the village of Slatersville), the nation's first "company town," is a magical village that transports visitors back in time. The Slatersville Mill was built in 1807. The village's homes, church, and common area were built around the same time for the plant's operators. Picturesque Slatersville, in the township of North Smithfield, is a great place for a stroll.

⑬ Head southwest on Route 102 to Burrillville. **Wright's Farm Restaurant,** not affiliated with the above dairy farm, is a massive eatery that serves over 300 tons of chicken every year, served family-style. A traditional northern Rhode Island dinner, chicken family-style, includes all you can eat of bread, salad, chicken, pasta, and potatoes. At $8 per person, this meal is hard to beat in value.

⑭ Continue south on Route 102 to Chepachet, a village in **Glocester.** This quaint village is popular with travelers for its unpretentious shopping and dining offerings. The **Brown & Hopkins Country Store** is the nation's oldest continually operated country store. It dates from 1809 and sells antiques, penny candy, and gourmet food. There is also a deli that serves lunch.

Rhode Island Coast Driving Tour

FROM WESTERLY TO NEWPORT

Distance: 59 mi; 94 km   Time: Driving time is 2½ hours.

This tour will take you to many of Rhode Island's best-known spots. You will see a few of the best beaches, massive and notable homes, lighthouses, and nature preserves. Westerly, Narragansett, Jamestown, and Newport are by nature summer places. This tour is therefore best in warm weather; fall is also a nice time to take the tour, though some sights will be closed.

❶ In **Westerly** (I−95 Exit 1, Rte. 3 S, Rte. 78 S, to U.S. 1) the coastal village of **Watch Hill** (Rte. 1A to Watch Hill Rd.) is at Rhode Island's southwestern extreme. This Victorian-era resort village features a harbor and miles of beautiful beaches. The area's many summer homes are renowned for their stylish beauty (look for their trademark foundations of beach stone). Statues commemorating the Native Americans of this region, the Niantics (a branch of the Narragansett tribe), stand on the shores of Watch Hill Cove. Also at the heart of Watch Hill is the **Flying Horse Carousel,** the oldest merry-go-round in America. Built in 1867, its hand-carved horses are suspended from above and swing out when in motion. The 1-mi-long spit of sand known as **Napatree Point** (off Watch Hill Rd.) is

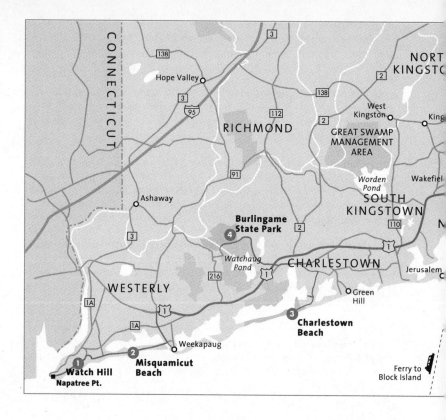

a conservation area teeming with bird life. It is open to the public daily. The **Watch Hill Lighthouse** (Lighthouse Rd., off Watch Hill Rd.) has great views of the ocean and of Fishers Island, New York. It houses a tiny museum that contains exhibits about Rhode Island lighthouses. The small parking lot is for the elderly only; everyone else must walk from the public lot that serves Watch Hill and Napatree Point.

❷ Like Watch Hill, **Misquamicut State Beach** is a village in the town of Westerly. This 2-mi strip of beach homes, hotels, and amusements is considered the Coney Island of Rhode Island. With a water slide, miniature golf, an arcade, and batting cages, Misquamicut is popular with kids. The amusements are open only between Memorial Day and Labor Day. If you prefer quieter beach scenes, visit the next beach on the tour.

❸ Head northeast on Route 1A, which becomes U.S. 1. In **Charlestown, Charlestown Beach** is one of the state's most tranquil and environmentally important areas. A barrier beach, it is bordered by tidal and freshwater marshes. If you have time, walk the beach to the breachway—you can wade across.

❹ North of U.S. 1, **Burlingame State Park** has nature trails and picnic and swimming areas. There are 755 campsites in the 2,100-acre park, located on the banks of Watchaug Pond.

❺ Continue northeast on U.S. 1, then take Route 108 south. In **Galilee** there is a slew of seafood restaurants. For a break, have lunch or dinner upstairs at **George's Restaurant. The Frances Fleet** offers fishing and whale-watching excursions. The **Block Island Ferry** runs to the island daily. Day trips to the island can be planned in the summer

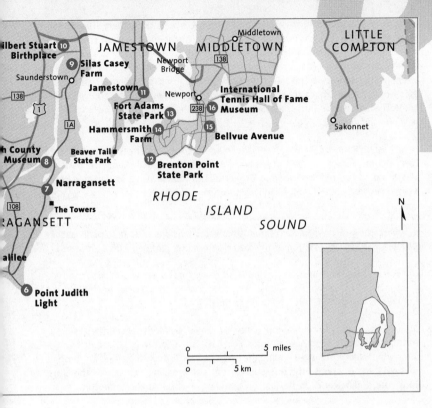

INTRODUCTION
HISTORY
REGIONS
WHEN TO VISIT
STATE'S GREATS
RULES OF THE ROAD
DRIVING TOURS

and fall, when there are numerous ferry trips. **Roger Wheeler State Beach** features a constructed state beach pavilion that won a variety of architectural awards. The calm, protected beach is great for families with small children. A picnic area, playground, showers, and parking are available.

❻ **Point Judith Lighthouse** in Narragansett marks the western mouth of the Narragansett Bay. The lighthouse itself and the active Coast Guard Station are restricted, but the expansive views make this a worthwhile stop.

❼ Farther north in Narragansett are **The Towers.** This is the last remaining section of the once-famous Narragansett Pier Casino, which in its heyday was the center of a comprehensive seaside resort. The ground floor houses the chamber of commerce visitors center. Tours are available in the summer. Nearby is the **Narragansett Town Beach,** which is convenient to many shops and restaurants.

❽ **South County Museum** (off Rte. 1A) houses 20,000 artifacts from 1800 to 1933. Exhibits include a country kitchen, a cobbler's shop, a tack shop, a working printer's shop, and an antique carriage collection.

❾ Return to Route 1A and head north. The **Silas Casey Farm** near **North Kingstown** is a mid-18th-century homestead that still functions as a working farm. The architecturally significant home contains family paintings, prints, china, furniture, and political and military documents from the 18th to the 20th centuries.

⑩ On a country road running along little Mattatuxet River is the **Gilbert Stuart Birthplace.** Built in 1751, this was the first home of America's foremost portraitist of George Washington. The adjacent 18th-century snuff mill was the first in America. From here you'll head east to the islands of Narragansett Bay. The two bridges leading to Newport offer unsurpassed views. The enormous Newport Bridge was designed so that the railings would not obstruct a traveler's line of sight. In summer you'll see countless sailboats. The bay and the Block Island Sound at its mouth are considered the East Coast's best cruising grounds.

⑪ Head east on Route 138 across the bridge to **Jamestown.** Don't miss **Beavertail State Park,** a gorgeous 153-acre park at the southern tip of Conanicut Island. The park has a lighthouse that contains the small **Beavertail Lighthouse Museum,** which features a simple exhibit about Rhode Island lighthouses.

⑫ Continue east on Route 138 across the Newport Bridge, then south to Ocean Drive in **Newport.** The 5-mi drive passes numerous private mansions and a few small beaches with limited parking. In summer, the road is sometimes jammed with sightseers.

⑬ **Fort Adams State Park** presents magnificent panoramas of Newport Harbor and is a great place to take sailing or windsurfing lessons. A massive stone fort built in the early 1800s stands here, but it is closed to the public.

⑮ Ocean Avenue ends at world-famous Bellevue Avenue. The wide street is lit by gas lamps and fronts seven Gilded Age mansions that are open to the public. New signage throughout Newport makes finding the homes easier. To avoid long lines on summer days, go early or choose the less popular but still amazing mansions—**the Elms, Kingscote,** and **Belcourt Castle.** Plan on spending one hour at each mansion.

⑯ The **International Tennis Hall of Fame Museum** at the Newport Casino chronicles the game's greatest moments and players. The Newport Casino is an ideal location for the museum. Considered the birthplace of modern tennis, the magnificent shingle-style club has 13 grass courts and one court-tennis facility (court tennis is the 13th-century precursor to modern tennis). The casino became the social and recreational hot spot of the Gilded Age, a favorite destination for many of the people who summered in the nearby mansions.

BLOCK ISLAND

MAP 3, J7

(Nearby towns also listed: Galilee, Newport; New London, CT)

European explorers gave the island a number of names, but Block (markedly less eloquent than the Native American *Manisses*, pronounced *man*-ih-sees)—after Dutch explorer Adriaen Block—is the one that stuck. In 1661 the island was settled by farmers and fishermen from Massachusetts Bay Colony. They developed their own specialized fishing boats, "double enders," and became part of the colony of Rhode Island in 1672.

Block Island is a laid-back community. Phone numbers are exchanged by the last four digits (466 is the prefix), and you can dine at any of the island's establishments in shorts and a T-shirt. The heaviest tourist activity takes place between May and Columbus Day; at other times most restaurants, inns, stores, and visitor services close down.

Approaching Block Island by boat from New London (Connecticut), Newport, or Point Judith, you'll see Old Harbor and its group of Victorian hotels. (The Old Harbor area is the island's only village.) Three docks, two hotels, and four restaurants huddled in the southeast corner of the Great Salt Pond make up the New Harbor commercial area, the landing point for a ferry running from Long Island. One of the largest harbors on the East Coast, New Harbor is a busy place in summer, sheltering nearly 2,000 boats on busy weekends and hosting sailing regattas.

Information: **Chamber of Commerce** | Water St., Drawer D, Block Island, 02807 | 401/466–2982 or 800/383–2474 | www.blockisland.com.

Attractions

Block Island Farmers Market. Sample Block Island's homegrown produce during summer and fall at the outdoor market, held Wednesday and Saturday mornings at Negus Park. Fresh-baked scones and muffins, and the local honey from the Littlefield Bee Farm, are popular items. | Sat. in Negus Park; Wed. at the intersection of High and Water Sts., in center of town | 401/466–2982 | June–Oct., Sat. and Wed. 9–11.

Block Island Historical Society. This 1850, mansard-roof farmhouse was converted to a hotel in 1871. Today, original furnishings and historical artifacts are displayed. The gift shop has unusual, hand-crafted items. The movie documenting the dramatic move of the Southeast Lighthouse shouldn't be missed. | Old Town Rd. | 401/466–2481 | $3 | Summer, daily 10–5.

★ **Clay Head Nature Trail.** You can access this trail off Corn Neck Road. Walk along towering bluffs to the beach on the north side of the Island. | Corn Neck Rd. | 401/466–2129 | Free.

Ferry Service to and from Block Island. Ferries are Block Island's principal links to the mainland. In summer months ferries depart daily from Providence; Newport; Point Judith; Montauk, New York; and New London, Connecticut. From November to June the only ferry departure point is Point Judith.

Block Island–Montauk Ferry. Viking Ferry Lines operates passenger-only ferry service from Montauk, Long Island, to Block Island. The trip takes 1¾ hours. | Viking Landing in Montauk; on Block Island, the Boat Basin Marina, New Harbor | 631/668–2114 | $20 one-way (bicycles $3) | Mid-May–mid-Oct.

Block Island-New London Ferry. Nelseco Navigation runs daily ferry service from New London, Conn., to Old Harbor, Block Island. Car reservations are recommended for the two-hour trip. | 2 Ferry Rd., New London, CT | 860/442–9553 | $15 one-way (cars $28 one-way, bicycles $3.50) | Mid-June–mid-Sept.

Block Island–Point Judith Ferry. Interstate Navigation operates year-round ferry service daily from Point Judith to Block Island. Call ahead for auto reservations. Foot passengers cannot make reservations, so plan to arrive 45 minutes early in high season. | Galilee State

KODAK'S TIPS FOR USING LIGHTING

Daylight
• Use the changing color of daylight to establish mood
• Use light direction to enhance subjects' properties
• Match light quality to specific subjects

Dramatic Lighting
• Anticipate dramatic lighting events
• Explore before and after storms

Sunrise, Sunset, and Afterglow
• Include a simple foreground
• Exclude the sun when setting your exposure
• After sunset, wait for the afterglow to color the sky

From Kodak Guide to Shooting Great Travel Pictures © 2000 by Fodor's Travel Publications

Pier | 401/783–4613 | www.blockislandferry.com | fax 401/466–3184 | $8.40 one-way (cars $26.30 one-way, bicycles $2.30) | Daily.

Fishing on Block Island. Most of Rhode Island's record-setting fish are caught offshore, but from almost any Block Island beach, skilled anglers can land striped bass. Bonito and fluke are often hooked in the New Harbor Channel. Shellfishing licenses are sold in the Harbormaster's office, at the Boat Basin Marina.

Oceans & Ponds. This outfit sells tackle and fishing gear, operates charter trips, rents canoes and kayaks, and provides guide services. | Ocean and Connecticut Aves | 401/466–5131 | www.blockisland.com/fishbi | Daily 9–6.

Twin Maple. This is the island's only bait shop, and has been in business for 50 years. You'll find a large selection of lures, as well as bait favorites like squid and minnows. | Beach Ave. | 401/466–5547 | Daily 8–5.

Fred Benson Town Beach. On Crescent Beach, 1 mi north of town, this beach has a pavilion with rest rooms and showers. Lifeguards patrol the beach 8–4 daily. The concession stand serves snacks and lunch. Body boards, beach chairs, and beach umbrellas are available for rent, and a masseuse offers massages. | Crescent Beach | 401/466–7717 | Daily 9–6.

Hotel Manisses Animal Farm. Llamas, Sicilian donkeys, and fainting goats are just a few of the animals that roam together on this 3½ acre compound. Behind the turquoise fence look for the Mont Jack, a diminutive deer from Asia. This serene location also has beautiful gardens. | 1 Spring St., | 401/466–2063 | fax 401/466–3162 | www.blockisland.com/biresorts | Free | Daily dawn–dusk.

Lewis Dickins Farm Nature Preserve. Once a working farm, this preserve has the most ecologically significant grassland in Rhode Island. A ½-mi trail along the bluffs offers spectacular wildlife observation, including rare ground-nesting birds, and views of the beaches below. The Nature Conservancy at 352 High Street has trail maps. | Off Cooneymus Rd., | 401/466–2129 | Free | Daily dawn–dusk.

Mansion Beach. The island's most opulent home once stood here. Now the mansion's foundation is a parking lot for this pretty, deep-sand beach. There are no lifeguards or concessions here. | Mansion Beach Rd. | Free | Daily.

Mohegan Bluffs. The 200-ft cliffs along Mohegan Trail—the road running along the south end of the island—are called Mohegan Bluffs after a battle between the local Manisses and a band of marauding Mohegans who met their end on the rocks below. The view from Payne Overlook (of the Atlantic, all the way to Montauk, NY) is spectacular. The wooden staircase descending to the beach is intimidating but well worth the effort. Be careful of the undertow if you choose to swim. | Mohegan Trail | Free | Daily.

New England Airlines. New England Airlines flies from Westerly to Block Island year-round. The company also provides charter flights. | State airports in Westerly (53 Airport Rd.) and Block Island (Center Rd.) | 401/596–2460, 401/466–5881, or 800/243–2460 | fax 401/596–7366 | www.block-island.com/nea | $39 one-way, $69 round-trip | Daily, call for schedule.

New Harbor. Great Salt Pond, where you'll find boats, boats, and more boats docked, anchored, and moored, is the home of New Harbor (at the southeast corner of the Great Salt Pond, where the Long Island ferries dock). Find restaurants, hotels, and marinas here, as well as bike and boat rentals.

North Light. An imposing granite structure at the northern tip of the island, the North Light was built in 1867. The maritime museum in the base of the lighthouse is part of the restoration completed in 1993. The lighthouse is in the Block Island National Wildlife Refuge, an important nesting site for many birds, including the endangered piping plover. | Corn Neck Rd. | 401/466–3200 | $2 | Mid-June–Labor Day, daily 10–4.

★ **Rodman's Hollow.** This unique valley is actually the remnants of a glacial outwash basin. Glacial runoff created this preserved hollow, which is now home to the endangered meadow vole; it is also laced with enjoyable hiking trails. | Cooneymus Rd. | 401/466–2129 | www.asri.org | Free | Daily dawn–dusk.

Settler's Rock. This rock commemorates the landing of the original settlers in 1661. From here, take a sandy walk along the beach to the North Light. | End of Corn Neck Rd., | 401/466–2129 | Free.

Southeast Light. This massive redbrick beacon was moved back from the eroding bluffs in 1993, after a grassroots initiative demanded that the 1873 structure be saved. It has since been designated a National Historic Landmark. | Mohegan Trail | 401/466–5009 | Donation suggested | Memorial Day–Labor Day, daily 10–4.

ON THE CALENDAR
JUNE: *Storm Trysail.* This is the largest sailing event on the East Coast, with more than 500 boats participating in the middle of the month. | 914/834–8857.
SEPT.: *Run around the Block.* A 15-km road race 12 mi offshore, held the first weekend after Labor Day. | Begins at Isaac's Corner on Lakeside Drive | 800/383–2474.
OCT.: *Audubon Birding Weekend.* Bird-watching enthusiasts gather during fall migration. | 401/466–2982 or 800/383–2474.

Dining
Atlantic Inn. Seafood. On the first floor of the Victorian Atlantic Inn is this fine restaurant. The monkfish ramaki has been written up by *Bon Appetit.* | High St. | 401/466–5883 | fax 401/466–5678 | www.atlanticinn.com | Reservations essential | No lunch. Closed Columbus Day–Memorial Day. Closed Mon.–Wed., Memorial Day–Mid-June and Labor Day–Columbus Day | Prix fixe $42 | D, MC, V.

Beachead Tavern. American. Not just seafood, but pastas, burgers, chili, and chowder are on the menu of this year-around place where locals and tourists mix. The nautical theme includes a 21-pound lobster on the wall, hand-carved beams, and tables made from ship's hatches. Look for the carved yellow sea captain outside. | 598 Corn Neck Rd. | 401/466–2249 | $13–$20 | MC, V.

★ **Eli's Restaurant.** Eclectic. Folks say this popular place is not like any place they've ever been. Portions are huge, almost decadent. The menu changes often. It's known for carpetbagger steak, a 12-ounce filet mignon stuffed with lobster, topped with bernaise sauce, and garnished with a claw. | 456 Chapel St. | 401/466–5230 | Closed Nov.–Apr. No lunch | $14–$34 | D, MC, V.

Finn's. Seafood. This classic island establishment boasts a great view of the town and harbor, not to mention terrific seafood dishes—the fisherman's platter is the locals' favorite. There's open-air dining under red patio umbrellas overlooking the harbor. | Water St. | 401/466–2473 | Closed mid-Oct.–mid-May | $10–$50 | AE, MC, V.

Hotel Manisses Dining Room. Continental. The island's finest dining can be found here. It has a constantly changing menu (depending on what's fresh) in the intimate dining room or in the glass-enclosed garden room. Try whatever the chef recommends—most likely it's right off the boat. There's outdoor dining overlooking farming and floral gardens and exotic animals, like peacocks and llamas. Kid's menu. No smoking. | Spring St. | 401/466–2836. | Closed late Oct.–mid-Apr. | $18–$30 | AE, MC, V.

Mohegan Cafe. Seafood. A casual, laid-back spot overlooking the water, this café is a favorite with the locals. Try the seared tuna or surf and turf. Kid's menu. | Water St. | 401/466–5911 | Closed Nov.–Feb. | $12–$20 | AE, D, MC, V.

Stephanie's Airport Diner. American/Casual. Every kind of airplane decoration you can think of festoons the walls at this small restaurant inside the airport. You may sit next to a pilot, a taxi driver, or a passenger waiting for the next flight out. Stephanie's mom makes the chowder, which folks come from the mainland to enjoy. | Block Island Airport, Center Rd. | 401/466–3100 | No dinner | $5–$7 | No credit cards.

Winfield's. Contemporary. This restaurant's light walls are enhanced with local art, linens, candles, and flowers. The wine list has 192 selections, including some rare bottlings, and the fresh Block Island swordfish has to be tasted. Also try mussels islander and beef fillet with saga blue cheese sauce. Menu changes nightly. | Corn Neck Rd. | 401/466–5856 | fax 401/466–7939 | Closed Nov.–May. No lunch | $18–$34 | AE, MC, V.

Lodging

★ **Atlantic Inn.** This classic Victorian hotel, built in 1879, is in New Shoreham. It is at the highest point above Old Harbor and has expansive ocean views from a wraparound veranda. Rooms have views of 6 landscaped acres, with flower and cutting gardens. Restaurant, bar, complimentary Continental breakfast. No TV in rooms. No room phones. Tennis. No smoking. | High St. | 401/466–5883 | fax 401/466–5678 | www.atlanticinn.com | 20 rooms, 1 suite | $130–$210, $230 suite | Closed Nov.–Mar. | D, MC, V.

The Bellevue House. With a variety of accommodations, spectacular ocean views, a big lawn, and a relaxed atmosphere, this hotel makes for an ideal getaway for families or couples. Some rooms—done in comfortable pastels—overlook the rolling landscaped lawn, and down to the ocean. No air-conditioning, some kitchenettes, no room phones, no TV in some rooms. | High St. | 401/466–2912 | www.blockisland.com/bellevue | 8 rooms (5 with shared bath), 4 apartments, 2 cottages | $114–$177 (2–night minimum stay weekends), $875–$1040 apartments (6–night minimum stay), $1560–$1835 cottages (6–night minimum stay) | Closed mid-Oct.–mid-May | MC, V.

Blue Dory Inn. This romantic seaside inn with Victorian charm was built in 1897. A deck in back overlooks the ocean. Rooms have antique furnishings with flowery wallpapers. Complimentary Continental breakfast. Some kitchenettes, some microwaves, some refrigerators. Beach. Pets allowed. | Dodge St. | 401/466–2254 | fax 401/466–9910 | www.bluedoryinn.com | 12 rooms, 3 suites, 4 cottages | $165–$225, $275–$495 suites, $165–$365 cottages | AE, D, MC, V.

Champlin's Hotel, Marina & Resort. This is a family resort on the shores of the Great Salt Pond, Block Island's busy New Harbor. Rooms have country views; one with hot tub. Restaurant, snack bar. Some kitchenettes, microwaves, refrigerators, cable TV. Pool. Tennis. Beach, boating. Bicycles. Baby-sitting, children's programs, playground, laundry facilities. | West Side Rd. | 401/466–2641 or 800/762–4541 | www.blockisland.co/champlins | 30 rooms, 5 suites | $135–$250, $325 suites | Closed Nov.–Apr. | AE, MC, V.

Gables Inn. Rocking chairs on the front porch introduce the old-fashioned charm of this two-building 1860s Victorian inn. The public sitting rooms have lace curtains, flowered wallpaper, and tin ceilings. Breakfast pastries are homemade. The inn is a block from the beach, and provides beach chairs, umbrellas, towels, and coolers. Complimentary Continental breakfast. No air-conditioning, no room phones, TV in common area. Laundry facilities. No pets. No smoking. | Dodge St. | 401/466–2213 | fax 401/466–5739 | gablesinn@aol.com | 19 rooms in 2 buildings (13 with shared bath) | $100–$165 weekends | Closed Dec.–Apr. | MC, V.

Hotel Manisses. Filled with antiques, this 1872 mansion delights with thoughtful touches like a wine nibble hour each afternoon. Complimentary breakfast. No air-conditioning. Laundry facilities. TV in some rooms. TV in common area. No kids under 10. No pets. No smoking. | Spring St. | 401/466–2063 or 800/626–4773 | fax 401/466–3162 | biresorts@riconnect.com | www.blockisland.com/biresorts | 17 rooms | $205–$270 | MC, V.

The National Hotel. This Victorian hotel in the downtown historic district has a front porch that is well known for its view of Old Harbor. Rooms have ocean views. Restaurant, bar. Cable TV. Beach. | Water St. | 401/466–2901 or 800/225–2449 | 45 rooms | $149–$239 | Closed Nov.–Apr. | AE, MC, V.

Rose Farm Inn. A short walk to town and beaches, this historic 20-acre farm has two buildings furnished with antiques; rooms have either country or ocean views. Some rooms have king canopy beds, decks, and double whirlpool tubs. There's complimentary high tea

BLOCK ISLAND VACATION

Over the last decade a small island sometimes termed the "gem of Rhode Island" was discovered by vacationers accustomed to spending summer days on Cape Cod or Long Island. Located 12 mi offshore, 10-square-mi Block Island is one of the most remote islands on the East Coast. Its unassuming name and the difficulty of getting there kept many potential travelers away. But in 1990 the Nature Conservancy deemed the island one of 12 "last great places" in the Western Hemisphere because of the presence of endangered species and the community's bent for conservation. Growing recognition and a strong economy brought an unprecedented number of visitors to Block Island in the 1990s. Many of these smitten travelers purchased a piece of their newfound paradise, building homes and driving up land prices. Fortunately the boom had been anticipated; since 1967, forward-thinking locals have worked to set aside open space lands and preserve the island's moorlike character.

Most of the 870 year-round residents make a living by accommodating visitors and newcomers, making Block Island a remarkably friendly destination. The island is striped with walking paths, and its pretty roads make bicycling a pleasure. Among the coastal brushlands and marshes is a startling variety of birds, making Block Island a destination for bird-watchers during fall migrations. A stunning geographical feature, a glacial wash-out basin called Rodman's Hollow, is a favorite destination for hikers. An effort to save this valley from developers kicked off the island's remarkable conservation movement.

In July and August and into September, the chilly Atlantic waters warm to tolerable levels, making swimming, snorkeling, and surfing enjoyable. The clarity and color of the water along Crescent Beach is sometimes dazzling—one reason the island has in years past been referred to as the Bermuda of the North.

Fishing is another attraction. Block Island is renowned for its striped-bass fishing, and its freshwater ponds hold record-size largemouth bass. Offshore, tuna, shark, and bluefish are commonly hooked.

To meet travelers' increasingly sophisticated demands, the island's modest accommodations have been refurbished. Showcase turn-of-the-century Victorian inns like the Atlantic and the Spring House have been revamped, and cuisine has reached a new level of quality. Aldo's, a family restaurant with a long history on the island, has expanded, while Eli's has developed a unique brand of fusion cooking.

Yet the island retains a laid-back charm. On Block Island a visitor can spend a week without a car and without a worry. There are dozens of beaches to explore. Some are rarely walked; some have deep, white sands; others are strewn with stones for hundreds of yards.

Most visitors come to Block Island for an extended stay; hundreds of homes are offered for rent by the week at rates that beat the cost of hotel rooms. From Block Island, some visitors charter small planes for a day on Nantucket or Martha's Vineyard. For an economical Block Island visit, spend three nights on-island and a few nights in Westerly or Narragansett.

© Artville

in the afternoons. Complimentary Continental breakfast. TV in common area. Laundry facilities. No pets. No kids under 12. No smoking. | 1005 Roslyn Rd. | 401/466–2034 | fax 401/466–2053 | www.blockisland.com/rosefarm | 19 rooms in 2 buildings (2 with shared bath) | $119–$215 | Closed Oct. 23–Mar. 31 | AE, D, MC, V.

Spring House. Sweeping views of the Atlantic from a wraparound porch enhance this Victorian hotel. Rooms are newly renovated and have whitewashed furniture. Some have ocean views. Restaurant, bar, complimentary Continental breakfast. No air-conditioning, no TV. Volleyball, beach. Playground. Business services. Airport shuttle. | Spring St. | 401/466–5844 or 800/234–9263 | www.springhouse.com | 49 rooms (39 with shower only), 19 suites | $175–$275, $275–$375 suites | Closed Nov.–Apr. | AE, MC, V.

The Surf. In downtown Old Harbor, this landmark Victorian hotel sits at the foot of Crescent Beach. It has a giant chessboard and tin ceilings in the lobby. Rooms all have water views—some ocean, some harbor—with period furnishings. Dining room, complimentary Continental breakfast. No air-conditioning, no room phones, TV in common area. Beach. Playground. Airport shuttle. | Dodge St. | 401/466–2241 | 47 rooms (44 with shared bath) | $77–$150 | Closed mid-Oct.–Memorial Day | MC, V.

★ **1661 Inn & Guest House.** Set on a hill above the Atlantic, this gracious inn has spectacular ocean views from its sweeping lawn. There is also a petting farm, which is home to emus, llamas, and Australian swans. Rooms have Victorian-period furnishings and some have fireplaces. Restaurant, bar, complimentary breakfast. No air-conditioning, some kitchenettes, microwaves, refrigerators, some hot tubs, some cable TVs. Baby-sitting, playground. Airport shuttle. | Spring St. | 401/466–2421 or 800/626–4773 | fax 401/466–2858 | www.blockisland.com/biresorts | 60 rooms | $135–$350 | AE, MC, V.

BRISTOL

MAP 3, L4

(Nearby towns also listed: Portsmouth, Tiverton, Warren)

One of the most desirable communities in the state, Bristol is home to many professionals, some of whom moor boats in the town's pretty harbor. With museums, parks, restaurants, biking trails, a few mansions, and a historic main street called Hope, Bristol appears to have materialized from the idyllic pages of a storybook. But the town saw times of trouble in the past; King Philip's War, New England's bloodiest Indian conflict, began here in 1675.

Information: **East Bay Chamber of Commerce** | 654 Metacom Ave., Suite 2, Warren, 02885–0250 | 401/245–0750.

Attractions

Herreshoff Marine Museum/America's Cup Hall of Fame. The Herreshoff Marine Museum celebrates the golden age of yachting with photographs, models, and 46 Herreshoff boats on the site of the Herreshoff Manufacturing Company. The company's founders were John Brown Herreshoff and Nathaniel Greene Herreshoff; John went blind at the age of 18 and had to dictate plans to Nathaniel. Together they were foremost among America's shipbuilders. Eight America's Cup defenders were built here. The America's Cup Hall of Fame is inside the Herreshoff Marine Museum. It features America's Cup memorabilia, including sailboats that competed for the sport's biggest prize. | 1 Burnside St. | 401/253–5000 | fax 401/253–6222 | $5 (Includes admission to both the Herreshoff Marine Museum and America's Cup Hall of Fame) | www.herreshoff.org | May–Oct., Daily 10–5.

Bristol Historical and Preservation Society Museum & Library. Originally built as a county jail in 1828 using ballast stones from Bristol sailing ships, this museum displays 300 years of memorabilia from Bristol's seafaring past. Architectural and walking tours can be arranged by appointment. | 48 Court St. | 401/253–7223 | fax 401/253–7223 | Donation suggested | Wed. and Fri. 1–5, Sun. 1–4, and by appointment.

Blithewold Mansion and Gardens. This charming 45-room, turn-of-the-century mansion overlooks Narragansett Bay and historic Bristol Harbor, and was the former summer home of Pennsylvania coal magnate Augustus Van Winkle. The arboretum was one of the first in America and boasts 50,000 flowering spring bulbs, a Japanese water garden, and the largest giant redwood east of the Rockies. The mansion's interior, gardens, and arboretum were re-created as per original family documents. | 101 Ferry Rd. | 401/253–2707 | $8 | Apr.–Oct., Tues.–Sun. 11–3:30; Grounds open year-round, daily 10–5.

Colt State Park. This park features a picturesque 3-mi road through the bayside property that was formerly the family estate of Colonel Samuel Colt. The area includes picnic areas, playing fields, and a skateboard park. Saltwater fishing is permitted. | Hope St. | 401/253–7482 | www.riparks.com | Free | Daily dawn–dusk.

Coggeshall Farm Museum. Coggeshall Farm Museum offers a trip back to Rhode Island's colonial past. In Colt State Park, the museum is an 18th-century working farm with animals, including a working team of oxen. The staff demonstrates 18th-century farming chores. There's a historical herb and vegetable garden. Call for summer weekend programs. | Colt State Park | 401/253–9062 | $1 | Oct.–Feb., daily 10–5; Mar.–Sept., daily 10–6.

BRISTOL

INTRO
ATTRACTIONS
DINING
LODGING

East Bay Bike Path. Beginning at India Point Park in Providence, this 14½-mi path meanders along Narragansett Bay, over salt meadows and rivers, and through woods in Barrington, Bristol, and Warren. | Independence Park | 401/222–2694, ext. 4034 | Daily.

Haffenreffer Museum of Anthropology. In the 17th century this 50-acre site was a summer camp of the Wampanoag Tribe. Today it is part of Brown University and houses thousands of Native American artifacts from North, Central, and South America. The trails that wind their way through the preserve are open to the public. Overlooks Mt. Hope Bay. | 300 Tower St., off Metacom Ave. (Rte. 136) | 401/253–8388 | fax 401/253–1198 | www.brown.edu/facilities/haffenreffer | $3 | June–Aug., Tues.–Sun. 11–5; Sept.–June, weekends 11–5.

Linden Place. The architectural pride and joy of downtown Bristol, Linden Place is a Federal-style mansion designed by Rhode Island architect Russell Warren. The home is surrounded by rose gardens and 19th-century sculpture. | 500 Hope St. | 401/253–0390 | $5 | May–mid-Oct., Thurs.–Sat. 10–4, Sun. noon–4; mid-Oct.–Apr., by appointment.

Prudence Island. This is the only island in Narragansett Bay that is inhabited year-round but inaccessible by bridge. It is managed by the Rhode Island Department of Environmental Management. A summer naturalist program is offered by the reserve, and there are self-guided hiking trails on the North Prudence Tract of the reserve. Ferry service is available from Bristol year-round. The ferry departs from Bristol's Church St. Wharf. | 401/683–4236 | $5.70 round-trip | July–Sept. 1, leaves Bristol at 6, 8, 10, 3:30, and 5:30.

ON THE CALENDAR

JULY: *Bristol 4th of July Parade.* The nation's oldest celebration of U.S. independence, it has been celebrated continuously since 1785. The center line down Hope Street is painted red, white, and blue for a celebration that begins June 14 (Flag Day) and continues through July 4. Festivities include an orange crate derby and nightly concerts on the green. | Hope St. | 401/245–0750.

SEPT.: *Harvest Fair.* An old-fashioned country fair with music, carriage rides, crafts, and events ranging from an oxen pull to a pumpkin seed–spitting contest at the Coggeshall Farm Museum. | Colt State Park, Hope St. | 401/253–9062.

DEC.: *Christmas at Blithewold.* A Victorian Christmas celebration at a turn-of-the-century mansion complete with 20-ft Christmas tree. | Ferry Rd. | 401/253–2707.

Dining

Aidan's Pub and Grub. Irish. A traditional pub with a great beer selection and lots of comfort food. It's simple and casual, and everybody feels at home here. Known for great beer on tap, bangers and mash, fish and chips. Entertainment. | John St. at Bristol Harbor | 401/254–1940 | $8–$15 | AE, MC, V.

Café La France. Café. Known as the "front porch" of Bristol, locals gather here. Eat-In or take-out the café fare: sandwiches, pastries, ice cream, and espresso. | 483 Hope St. | 401/253–0360 | fax 401/253–3821 | Breakfast also available. No dinner | $3–$5 | No credit cards.

The Lobster Pot. Seafood. One of Rhode Island's oldest restaurants, this casual but upscale eatery offers classically prepared seafood dishes and sits on the shores of Narragansett Bay. The dining room looks out over the bay. Kid's menu. | 119–121 Hope St. | 401/253–9100 | Closed Mon. | $20–$30 | Reservations essential | AE, MC, V.

Redlefsen's Rotisserie & Grill. Eclectic. You can come here for fine, relaxed dining. In summer, eat on the outside patio, right on the water. Known for Wiener schnitzel, pecan-crusted pork tenderloin with a maple cream sauce, and seafood, too. | 444 Thames St. | 401/254–1158 | $7–$22 | D, MC, V.

Lodging

Bradford Dimond Norris House. On beautiful Hope Street, this gracious Federal home, built in 1792 and given a Victorian update in the 1850s, was totally restored in the mid-1990s. Each room has a queen-sized canopy bed and the moldings and dentil work are original. Three of the rooms have nonworking fireplaces. There are also porches and a perennial garden. Complimentary Continental breakfast. No room phones. No pets. No kids under 15. No smoking. | 474 Hope St. | 401/253–6338 or 888/329–6338 | www3.edgenet.net/bdnhouse | 4 rooms (with showers only) | $95–$120 | AE, MC, V.

Joseph Reynolds House Inn. A night at this 1693, red-clapboard inn includes a lesson in Colonial history: George Washington and Thomas Jefferson planned the Revolutionary War Battle of Rhode Island here with the Marquis de Lafayette. The Marquis' room is period-accurate, with a 17th-century marbelized fireplace. Some of the other rooms have four-poster beds. Complimentary breakfast. Some kitchenettes, no room phones, cable TV in some rooms, some in-room VCRs. Business services. Pets allowed. | 956 Hope St. | 401/254–0230 or 800/754–0230 | fax 401/254–2610 | reynoldsbb@aol.com | 3 rooms, 2 suites | $95–$115, rooms; $165–$175 suites | AE, D, DC, MC, V.

King Philip Inn. This inn with banquet and conference facilities is ½-mi from downtown Bristol and Roger Williams University. The rooms have king-size beds. Some kitchenettes, refrigerators. Business services. | 400 Metacom Ave. | 401/253–7600 or 800/253–7610 | fax 401/253–1857 | 30 rooms | $72–$180 | AE, D, DC, MC, V.

Rockwell House. A spacious, four-room inn in the heart of town. The Federal-style house (circa 1809) has fireplaces and hand stenciling in many rooms. Picnic area, complimentary breakfast. No air-conditioning, no room phones, TV in common area. No kids under 12. Business services. | 610 Hope St. | 401/253–0040 or 800/815–0040 | fax 401/253–1811 | www.rockwellhouseinn.com | 4 rooms (1 with shower only) | $110–$150 | AE, D, MC, V.

Swanson House. Enjoy beautiful views of gardens and Narragansett Bay from this three-room suite that can sleep up to five people, in a 1930s colonial-style house. There's a veranda with a wisteria covered pergola in the back, and the property has 1½ landscaped acres, a short walk from downtown. Complimentary Continental breakfast. Pets sometimes allowed. No smoking. | 150 Ferry Rd. | 401/254–5056 | 1 3-room suite | $110–$130 | No credit cards.

William's Grant Inn. This 1808 Federal house is on a quiet street and is furnished with many antiques. There are murals decorating the interior and a sitting area in the back, overlooking a terraced garden and fish pond. Rooms have either Victorian or nautical themes. Complimentary breakfast. No room phones, no TV in rooms, TV in common area. No kids under 12. No smoking. | 154 High St. | 401/253–4222 or 800/596–4222 | fax 401/254–0987 | 5 rooms (2 with shared bath) | $95–$110 | AE, D, DC, MC, V.

CHARLESTOWN

(Nearby town also listed: Westerly)

Of Rhode Island's 39 towns and cities, this coastal town is most favored by local outdoors enthusiasts. Numerous beaches and parks, featuring tidal and freshwater ponds, provide opportunities for fishing, swimming, canoeing, surfing, kayaking, and camping. There are also a few time-worthy antiques and specialty shops clustered around Old Post Rd. (Route 1A) and U.S. 1.

Information: South County Tourism Council | Stedman Government Center, 4808 Tower Hill Rd., Wakefield, 02879 | 401/789–4422 or 800/548–4662.

Attractions

Burlingame State Park. On the banks of Watchaug Pond, Burlingame State Park has nature trails and picnic and swimming areas. There are 755 campsites in the 2,100-acre park, and they are equipped with water, fireplaces, and rest-room facilities. Visitors can go boating and fishing on Watchaug Pond. | U.S. 1 | 401/222–2632 or 401/322–7337 | www.riparks.com | Free | Mid-Apr.–Oct.

Charlestown Beach. One of the state's most tranquil and environmentally important areas, this barrier beach is rarely crowded. Apart from rest rooms and parking, amenities here are essentially nonexistent, so bring whatever you'll be needing. If you have time, walk the beach to the breachway (which you can wade across) that enters into Ninigret Pond. | Charlestown Beach Rd. | 401/364–1222 | Free | Daily.

Kimball Wildlife Refuge. This 29-acre wildlife preserve is maintained by the Audubon Society of Rhode Island. Bordering the second-largest natural pond in the state, the area is especially attractive to waterfowl and migrating birds. It is off U.S. 1 near Watchaug Pond. | Sanctuary Rd. | 401/949–5454 | fax 401/949–5788 | www.asri.org | Free | Daily dawn–dusk.

Ninigret National Wildlife Refuge. About 9 mi of trails weave through 400 acres of beachlands and marshes at this wildlife refuge, which also includes freshwater ponds. | Rte. 1A | 401/364–9124 | Free | Daily dawn–dusk.

Ninigret Park. This 227-acre park has picnic grounds, ball fields, a 10-speed bike course, and tennis and basketball courts. In addition there is a 3-acre, spring-fed swimming pond. On Friday nights an observatory is open for public use of the telescopes. | Rte. 1 A | 401/364–1222 | fax 401/364–1238 | Free | Daily dawn–dusk.

Quonochontaug Beach. This white-sand beach straddles the Westerly town line. Bring all you need, as there are no concessions here. | Spring Ave. | 401/364–7718 | Free, parking fee (Labor Day–Memorial Day) | Daily.

Trustom Pond National Wildlife Refuge. In South Kingstown, 1½ mi east of Charlestown, is this 642-acre haven for waterfowl. The 161-acre coastal pond is a stopover for migrating duck, including canvasback, scaup, goldeneye, and bufflehead, and is one of the best places in the state to observe wild birds. In the upland areas, nesting birds include brown thrasher, bobolink, and red-winged blackbird. One of the more popular parks in the state, Trustom Pond refuge also features a number of walking trails. | Matunuck Schoolhouse Rd., South Kingstown | 401/364–9124 | Free | Daily, dawn to dusk.

ON THE CALENDAR

JUNE–SEPT.: *Theatre-by-the-Sea.* In this theater, 10 mi northeast of Charlestown, is 60 years of the best of Broadway in a historic, weathered theater cooled by breezes off the sea. | Cards Pond Rd. | 401/782–8587.

CHARLESTOWN

INTRO
ATTRACTIONS
DINING
LODGING

AUG.: *Meeting of the Narragansett Tribe.* The Narragansett Indian Church is the site of a tribal gathering featuring music, dance, and storytelling. | Indian Church Rd. | 401/789–4422 or 800/548–4662.

AUG.: *Seafood Festival.* The coastal town of Charlestown hosts this festival where visitors can enjoy chowder, clam cakes, lobster, crabs, and more. Also includes an amateur seafood cook-off, hot-air balloons, antique cars, and BMX bike races. | Ninigret Park | 401/364–4031.

Dining

General Stanton Inn. American. History abounds in the former Stanton Plantation that dates back to 1667. This authentic Colonial Inn has five dining rooms with crooked floors and beamed ceilings. Try the fresh seafood, fresh turkey, and chicken pot pie. A snackbar serves an outside dining area and the weekend flea market next door draws crowds. | 415A Old Post Rd. (Rte. 1A) | 401/364–8888 | fax 401/364–3333 | Breakfast also available. Closed Mon. | $8–$18 | No credit cards.

Lodging

General Stanton Inn. A resting place for travelers since Revolutionary War times, this Colonial inn 3 mi from the beach has been recently refurbished. The rooms have visible hand-hewed ceiling beams, antique oak and cherry beds, and five have fireplaces. There is an antiques flea market here on weekends. Restaurant, bar, dining rooms. | 415 Old Post Rd. (Rte. 1A) | 401/364–8888 | fax 401/364–3333 | $85–$120 | 16 rooms | AE, MC, V.

Hathaway's Guest Cottages. Little rustic cottages, some original to this 1683 property, provide freestanding accommodation in Charlestown's historic area. The efficiencies sleep four, the cottages two. A marina 500 ft away rents boats, and there's good kayaking in the area. Complimentary Continental breakfast weekends only. Some kitchenettes, some refrigerators, no room phones. No pets. No smoking. | 4470 Old Post Rd. (Rte. 1A) | 401/364–6665 | www.myplanet.net/hathaways | 5 cottages, 2 efficiencies | $110–$140 | Closed Columbus Day–Memorial Day | AE, D, MC, V.

Willows Motel-Resort. Rooms, apartments, and cottages set on 20 acres above Ninigret Pond. Clambakes on some weekends. Some rooms have a pond view, others a view of Foster Cove. Restaurant, bar. Some kitchenettes, some microwaves, refrigerators, cable TV. Pool. Tennis. Boating. Fishing. Laundry facilities. | 5310 Old Post Rd. (Rte. 1A) | 401/364–7727 or 800/842–2181 | www.willowsresort.com | 40 rooms, 10 apartments; 4 cottages | $101–$120, $1400 apartments (7–day minimum stay), $950 cottages (7–day minimum stay) | Closed mid-Oct.–mid-May | MC, V.

CUMBERLAND

MAP 3, K2

(Nearby towns also listed: Lincoln, Pawtucket, Woonsocket)

Cumberland is a hilly township with winding roads and a dozen villages. In each of these small communities are charming homes; many once housed the workers, managers, and owners who operated Cumberland's small mills. Factories here still produce a bewildering variety of products. Factory row-housing—now upgraded and generally popular with residents—is a feature of some villages. In the northeast corner of the state, Cumberland has no fewer than 15 roads joining it to Massachusetts.

Information: Northern Rhode Island Chamber of Commerce | 6 Blackstone Valley Pl., Suite 105, Lincoln, 02865 | 401/334–1000.

Attractions

Diamond Hill Park. This 427-acre park with a rocky cliff takes its name from the abundant glittering quartz deposits in the ground. There are numerous unmarked hiking trails, a pond, and a picnic area. Silvy's Brook meanders through the park. | Rte. 114 | 401/334–9996 | www.riparks.com | Free | Daily.

Diamond Hill Vineyard. This small vineyard produces cordial wines made from apples and pears. Its wine is sold only on the premises. | 3145 Diamond Hill Rd. | 401/333–2751 or 800/752–2505 | fax 401/333–8520 | www.favorlabel.com | Tours Apr.–Nov. and at Christmastime.

Phantom Farms. A farm stand in Cumberland that is especially appealing in the fall, Phantom Farms has pumpkins, chrysanthemums, and apples for sale. Inside, visitors can buy homemade pies and muffins. In the summer the farm sells seasonal vegetables. Apple-picking and locally produced honey are two more reasons to stop as you drive through the Blackstone Valley. | Diamond Hill Rd. | 401/333–2240 | Daily.

Valley Falls Heritage Park. The 2-acre riverside park features a picnic area near a historic bridge spanning the Blackstone River. Interpretive signs explain the river's history. The park is a component of the area's recent federal designation as a National Heritage Corridor. | Mill and Broad Sts. | 401/334–9996 | Daily.

William Blackstone Memorial Park. A small park dedicated to the first Rhode Island settler. Blackstone built a small cabin here on what was called Study Hill. At one time he had the largest book collection in the New World and was known to ride a white bull rather than a horse. | Broad and Blackstone Sts. | 800/454–2882 | Free | Daily.

ON THE CALENDAR

AUG.: _Cumberlandfest._ Fireworks, live entertainment, food court, midway rides, rock-climbing wall, arts and crafts, plus special events like tractor pulls make this weekend event at Diamond Hill Park fun for the whole family. Put on by the Cumberland Youth Athletic Council, proceeds benefit town sports programs. | 401/334–9996.

Dining

Davenport's Restaurant. American. Locals enjoy this large, unpretentious place. You'll have a wide range of choices: burgers, roast chicken, stir-fries, prime rib, fisherman's platters, and the like. For dessert find old favorites, like grape nut and tapioca puddings. Both take-out and kid's menus are available. | 1070 Mendon Rd. | 401/334–1017 | fax 401/333–0143 | www.davenportsri.com | $6–$15 | AE, D, MC, V.

EAST GREENWICH

MAP 3, K4

(Nearby town also listed: Warwick)

As the site of the Kent County Courthouse, East Greenwich was once the most important town in this region. Today it is a destination for shoppers and diners. Along the waterfront there are marinas and excellent seafood restaurants. Large yachts juxtaposed with shellfishing skiffs exemplify the range of wealth in this sophisticated, hard-working town.

Information: **Chamber of Commerce** | 5853 Post Rd., Suite 106, East Greenwich, 02818-0514 | 401/885–0020 | www.eastgreenwichri.com.

Attractions

The New England Wireless & Steam Museum. This technical museum illustrates the history of electrical and mechanical engineering, with rare early radio and steam apparatus. Five buildings house the wireless and stationary steam-engine collections, library, and

steam-engine models. A meeting house built in 1822 is also on the site. | 1300 Frenchtown Rd. | 401/885–0545 | fax 401/884–0683 | users.ids.net/~newsm | $10, special rates for kids under 12 | Open year-round by appointment.

Old Kent County Courthouse. This site was the epicenter of Kent County public life in the 18th century. Built in 1750 and recently restored, it is now the East Greenwich Town Hall. The courthouse served briefly as the Rhode Island state capitol. The Declaration of Independence was read to the public here in 1776. | 125 Main St. | 401/886–8606 | fax 401/886–8625 | Free | Daily 8:30–4:30.

Varnum House Museum. General James Mitchell Varnum designed and built this home, which was finished in 1780. The house is filled with period furniture and specimens from the China trade, which Rhode Island shipowners developed. George Washington was once a guest here. | 57 Pierce St. | 401/884–1776 | $4 | June–Labor Day, Thurs.–Sat. 10–2; Sept., Sat. 10–2.

Varnum Memorial Armory and Military Museum. This private museum holds a wide assortment of weaponry used from the late 16th century to World War II. Favorites include a 17th-century crossbow and a Revolutionary War–artillery helmet, of which there are only three in existence. | 6 Main St. | 401/884–4110 | $4 | By appointment only.

ON THE CALENDAR

AUG.: *Waterfront Summer Feast and Fest.* "Feast" on food samplings with entertainment from 11 AM to 10 PM. "Fest" on Main Street 10–6. Arts and crafts, entertainment, and road races. | Norton's Marina | 401/885–0020.

Dining

The Post Office Cafe. Contemporary. This converted post office retains many of its original details, from mailboxes to the hanging lights, updated with touches that make it a restaurant. It's known for beautiful and innovative presentations of classic dishes. Try the shepherd's pie with porcini mushrooms and parmigiana whipped potatoes in a cabernet demi glaze or the diver sea scallops saltimbocca (scallops wrapped in prosciutto over parmigiana whipped potatoes and spinach). | 11 Main St. | 401/885–4444 | fax 401/886–0710 | www.postofficecafe.com | Closed Sun.–Mon. | $13–$29 | AE, D, MC, V.

Lodging

The 1873 House. This 1873 Italianate Victorian house has a three-room suite has period furnishings, modern wall-to-wall carpeting, and a pull-out sofa. Breakfast is self-serve in the fully stocked kitchen, and there's a private entrance. Complimentary Continental breakfast. Kitchenette. No pets. No smoking. | 162 Peirce St. | 401/884–9955 | www.angelfire.com/biz/the1873houseBandB | 1 suite | $95 | No credit cards.

Vincent House. The deck at Vincent House overlooks a former cranberry bog and a picnic area. The reasonably priced rooms are sunny, well-kept, and color coordinated in either rose or blue. There's also a billiards room. Dining room, complimentary Continental breakfast. Cable TV. Laundry service. Business services. | 170 Cedar Ave. | 401/885–2864 | fax 401/886–8919 | www.vincenthouse.com | 2 rooms | $80–$105 | MC, V.

GALILEE

MAP 3, K5

(Nearby towns also listed: Block Island, Narragansett)

A port in the town of Narragansett, Galilee was for years a deteriorating destination. But recently the state, which owns 80% of the land and all the docks in Galilee, refurbished the village. Roads were repaved, and new sidewalks and street lamps were installed. The improvements have made Galilee an even better tourist destination. It is also known for some of the best seafood in the state.

Information: Narragansett Chamber of Commerce | Box 742, Narragansett, 02882 | 401/783–7121 | www.narragensettcoc.com.

Attractions

Block Island Ferry. Interstate Navigation Company operates ferry service from Galilee to Block Island. Make auto reservations well ahead; foot passengers cannot make reservations. Arrive early in the summer; the boats are often filled to capacity. There are eight boats daily in summer, limited service the rest of the year. | Galilee State Pier, Great Island Rd. | 401/783–4613 | fax 401/466–3184 | $8.40 one way (cars $26.30 one-way).

Frances Fleet. With three boats, Frances Fleet offers fishing trips and whale-watching excursions. | 2 State St. | 401/783–4988 or 800/662–2824 | fax 401/782–8520 | Apr.–Nov.

Roger Wheeler State Beach. This beach includes picnic tables, a children's playground and showers, as well as a recently constructed pavilion that has won a number of architectural awards. The calm, protected beach is great for families with kids. Parking is available. | 100 Sand Hill Cove Rd. | 401/789–3563 | www.riparks.com | Free; parking fee | Memorial Day–Labor Day.

Southland Cruises. This mid-size passenger boat offers $1^{3}/_{4}$-hour narrated sightseeing cruises and $2^{1}/_{2}$-hour sunset cruises in the port of Galilee. On these tours you can see the Point Judith Lighthouse, Block Island, and the largest salt pond in Rhode Island. | 304 Great Island Rd., State Pier | 401/783–2954 | www.southlandcruises.com | $7 | May–Oct.

ON THE CALENDAR

JULY: *Blessing of the Fleet.* This weekend festival features the fishing fleet of Galilee, in its finest regalia, and private boats too, touring the harbor for a blessing by the Bishop. A 10 km road race, a carnival, and a seafood festival round out the events. | 401/783–7121.

Dining

George's Restaurant. Seafood. This restaurant at the mouth of the Point Judith harbor has been a "must" for tourists since 1948. The "stuffies" (baked stuffed quahogs) are some of the best in the state. The menu offers a wide variety of fried and broiled seafood, as well as chicken, steak, and pasta. Its proximity to the beach and its large outdoor bar on the second floor make George's a very busy place all summer. | 250 Sand Hill Cove Rd. | 401/783–2306 | Closed Dec. and weekdays in Nov. and Jan. | $15–$20 | AE, D, MC, V.

PACKING IDEAS FOR HOT WEATHER

- ❏ Antifungal foot powder
- ❏ Bandanna
- ❏ Cooler
- ❏ Cotton clothing
- ❏ Day pack
- ❏ Film
- ❏ Hiking boots
- ❏ Insect repellent
- ❏ Rain jacket
- ❏ Sport sandals
- ❏ Sun hat
- ❏ Sunblock
- ❏ Synthetic ice
- ❏ Umbrella
- ❏ Water bottle

*Excerpted from *Fodor's: How to Pack: Experts Share Their Secrets*
© 1997, by Fodor's Travel Publications

Lodging
Lighthouse Inn of Galilee. Across the street from the Block Island ferry dock and 300 yards from sandy Salty Brine Beach lies this very basic, 1970s, two-story motel with outside entrances. Kids love the large indoor pool and huge activity area around it. Restaurant, bar. Some in-room hot tubs, cable TV. Indoor pool. Saunas. Gym. Laundry facilities. Pets allowed (fee). | 307 Great Island Rd. | 401/789–9341 or 800/336–6662 | fax 401/789–1590 | 100 rooms | $105–$150 | Closed Nov.–Apr. | D, MC, V.

GLOCESTER

MAP 3, J2

(Nearby towns also listed: Lincoln, Woonsocket)

Antiques shops and other businesses line Main Street in the village of Chepachet, at the intersection of U.S. 44 and Rte. 102. This 19th-century village is just outside the northeastern end of Glocester, and it is one of the main tourist attractions in the area. Glocester itself is one of the biggest towns in the state. Its country roads are delightful to drive, with farm stands and apple orchards commonplace.

Information: **Northern Rhode Island Chamber of Commerce** | 6 Blackstone Valley Pl., Suite 105, Lincoln, 02865 | 401/334–1000 | www.nrichamber.com.

Attractions
Brown & Hopkins Country Store. In business since 1809, Brown & Hopkins is the nation's oldest continuously operating country store. Antiques, gourmet food, and penny candy are some of the store's offerings. Lunch is served daily in the deli. | 1179 Main St. | 401/568–4830 | Thurs.–Sun.

Buck Hill Management Area. There are great hiking trails at this wildlife area. At one corner of this 2,000-acre preserve you can stand in Connecticut, Massachusetts and Rhode Island simultaneously. At the marsh and impounded water area see great blue herons and beavers. During hunting season, from the third week in October to the end of February, visitors are required to wear 200 square inches of flourescent orange Day-Glo. The entrance to the area is approximately 4 miles north of Glocester. | Buck Hill Rd., Burrillville | 401/789–0281 | Free | Daily, ¹/₂ hr before sunrise–¹/₂ hr after sunset.

George Washington Management Area. This is a 3,500-acre park on the Connecticut border with ponds, wetlands, and stands of oak, maple, and evergreens. There are also 45 campsites with outhouses but no showers. The varied environment attracts different species of birds and wildlife, including warblers during the spring and fall migrations, white-tailed deer, cottontail rabbits, snowshoe hares, foxes, coyotes, and raccoons. During hunting season park visitors must wear flourescent orange Day-Glo. | Putnam Pike (U.S. 44) | 401/568–2013 | fax 401/222–2527 | Free | Daily dawn–dark.

Casimir Pulaski State Park. A beach on the shore of Peck's Pond, a picnic area, a covered bridge, and four ski trails (great for walking in warm weather) are the attractions at this state park in the George Washington Management Area. Bathhouses and lifeguard on site. The park is open year round, but the bathouses are closed from Labor Day through Memorial Day. | Pulaski Rd. | 401/568–2085 | fax 401/222–2527 | Free | Daily dawn–dark.

Snowhurst Farm. This working farm, 2 mi southeast of Glocester, has a farm stand with apples, peaches, and vegetables in season; an old-fashioned garden and hardware store; and farm animals. There are even emus. You can pick your own apples from the third week in August to mid-October. | 462 Chopmist Hill Rd. (Rte. 102), Chepachet, | 401/568–8900 | Free | Mon.–Sat. 8:30–6, Sun. 8:30–noon (open later in apple season).

JULY: *Ancients and Horribles Parade.* Despite the strange name, this July 4 parade means family fun. Starting at the town line of Burrillville and Glocester and continuing through Chepachet, it ends at Acotes Cemetary. Marchers dress up to spoof politicians and Rhode Island foibles from the past year. | 401/568–6206.

Dining

The Purple Cat. American. In Chepachet Village, at the busy intersection where U.S. 44 and Rtes. 102 and 100 meet, sits the Purple Cat. This simple place serves favorites like baked-stuffed shrimp, veal marsala, hot-turkey sandwiches, fresh baked ham, and—on Friday and Saturday nights—Black Angus prime rib. There are three dining rooms with heavy wood tables and booths, and vintage photos of Chepachet on the walls. There's a good kid's menu. | Main St., Chepachet, | 401/568–7161 | fax 401/568–9140 | www.thepurplecat.com | Closed Mon. | $7–$20 | AE, MC, V.

Stagecoach Tavern. American. Feast on prime rib and hand-cut steaks while you dine in the history-imbued site of the Dorr rebellion. This lovingly restored tavern was built in 1760. In summer, dine on the open porch bedecked with flowers. | 1157 Putnam Pike (U.S. 44) | 401/568–2275 | fax 401/567–9155 | www.stagecoachtavern.com | Closed Mon.–Tues. | $7–$20 | AE, D, MC, V.

Lodging

Freeman Farm Bed & Breakfast. A two-room bed-and-breakfast in a 1760 farmhouse with a 3-acre yard and a lake nearby. The large country kitchen houses a pitcher collection, and in the Christmas season, the owners play Santa, setting up "Santa's workshop" in the backyard. Complimentary breakfast. No air-conditioning in some rooms, some room phones, no TV in some rooms. No smoking. | 65 Jackson Schoolhouse Rd. | 401/568–6561 | $50–$70 | 2 rooms | No credit cards.

JAMESTOWN

MAP 3, K5

(Nearby towns also listed: Narragansett, Newport, North Kingstown)

The east and west passages of Narragansett Bay encompass the 9-mi-long, 1-mi-wide island known both as Jamestown and Conanicut. In 1940 the Jamestown Bridge linked Jamestown to western Rhode Island; in 1969 the Newport Bridge completed the cross-bay route, connecting Newport to South County. Summer residents have come to Jamestown since the 1880s, but never to the same extent as in Watch Hill, Narragansett, or Newport. Relatively few tourists visit the charming island, making it a peaceful alternative to the hustle and bustle of nearby Newport and South County.

Information: Newport County Convention & Visitors Bureau | Newport Gateway Center, 23 America's Cup Ave., Newport, 02840 | 401/849–8048 or 800/976–5122 | www.gonewport.com.

Attractions

Beavertail State Park. A 153-acre park at the southern tip of Conanicut Island, Beavertail is a favorite destination for Rhode Island residents. Look for garnet and fool's gold in the outcroppings of slate and granite that line the shore. Hermit crabs, periwinkles, sea anemones, and sea stars can be seen in the tide pools. | Beavertail Rd. | 401/423–9941 or 401/884–2010 | www.riparks.com | Free | Daily dawn–dusk.

The Beavertail Lighthouse Museum. Inside a 1749 lighthouse on the grounds of the state park, this museum features an exhibit on Rhode Island's lighthouses. | 401/423–3270 | Free | Mid-June–Labor Day, daily 10–4; Labor Day–mid-Oct., weekends 10–4.

Fort Wetherill State Park. This park is on a outcropping of cliffs at a peninsula with spectacular views—from the east you can see Newport's Fort Adams and from the south, the ocean. Don't be surprised if you observe a bridal party being photographed, it's that scenic. Most people choose to picnic or scuba dive here. | Ocean St. | 401/884–2010 | fax 401/885–7720 | www.riparks.com | Free | Daily dawn–dusk.

Jamestown Fire Department Memorial Museum. This museum is for everyone who loves fire engines. It has antique fire apparatus, a horse-drawn 1894 operating steam fire engine and a 1859 hand-pump, plus photographs and memorabilia. | 50 Narragansett Ave. | 401/423–0062 | fax 401/423–7278 | Free | Weekdays 7–3, weekends by appointment.

Jamestown Museum. This tiny museum in a former schoolhouse focuses on the history of Jamestown, with various artifacts from the area's past. There is also a special exhibit on the Jamestown ferries, which once provided the only direct connection from Jamestown to the mainland. | 92 Narragansett Ave. | 401/423–0784 | Donation suggested | Mid-June–Labor Day, Wed.–Sun. 1–4.

Old Windmill (Jamestown Windmill). Operated by the Jamestown Historical Society and recently restored, the mill was in use from 1789 to 1896. The gears, the stone for grinding corn, and the granary can all be viewed inside. The windmill will be closed through June 2001, call for more information. | 280 N. Main Rd. | 401/423–1798 | Free.

Sydney L. Wright Museum. Conanicut Island (Jamestown) was used by the Narragansett tribe as a summer camp. Certain areas of the island are being excavated by archaeologists to learn more about the Narragansetts. This small museum, in the Philomenia Library, houses some of the finds. | 26 North Rd. | 401/423–7280 | Free | Mon. 10–9, Tues. and Thurs. noon–5 and 7–9, Wed. 10–5 and 7–9, and Fri.–Sat. 10–5.

Watson Farm. Thomas Carr Watson's family worked the Watson Farm for 190 years before he bequeathed it to the Society for the Preservation of New England Antiquities upon his death in 1979. The 285-acre spread, still partially in use as a working farm, provides the public with the opportunity to learn about agrarian history in the region. The farmhouse itself is not open to the public. The 2 mi of trails along Jamestown's southwest shore have amazing views of Narragansett Bay and North Kingstown. | 455 N. Main Rd. | 401/423–0005 | $3 | June–mid-Oct., Tues., Thurs., and Sun. 1–5.

ON THE CALENDAR
JULY–AUG.: *Summer Music in Jamestown.* Families will enjoy these Sunday evening concerts at Shorby Hill Green or the nearby East Ferry Memorial. Music ranges from a small jazz combo to big bands, and everything in between. | 401/423–7260.

Dining
Bay Voyage. Continental. This gorgeous inn was once on the other side of the bay but was moved across it by ship many years ago. The pleasant, bright dining room now overlooks Newport; it's packed for the inn's fantastic Sunday brunch. Known for lobster, beef Wellington, rack of lamb, baked stuffed shrimp. Kid's menu. | 150 Conanicus Ave. | 401/423–2100 | Reservations essential | $25–$40 | AE, D, DC, MC, V.

East Ferry Deli. Café. This homey café bakes its own muffins, cakes, cookies, and yummy congo bars. While it's known for scrumptious deli sandwiches, quiches and salads are also available. Tables inside and out provide splendid views of Jamestown Harbor and Narragansett Bay. | 47 Conanicus Ave. | 401/423–1592 | fax 401/423–9148 | www.jamestownri.com/efdeli | Breakfast also available. No dinner | $4–$6 | No credit cards.

★ **Jamestown Oyster Bar.** Seafood. Fresh seafood—from oysters and littlenecks to lobster and steamed mussels—is on the menu at this rustic place, popular with locals. The french fries are hand-cut, and the mashed potatoes rise to new heights with roasted garlic and shallots. There's also chicken, steaks, and hefty burgers, ideal if you're not in the mood for the latest catch. | 22 Narragansett Ave. | 401/423–3380 | fax 401/423–3709 | No lunch weekdays | $8–$18 | AE, MC, V.

Trattoria Simpatico. Italian. Folks travel for miles to enjoy specialties like the fried calamari and the cinnamon snap basket stuffed with vanilla bean gelato, fresh berries, and sweet toppings. Fresh seafood comes right from local boats. Outside you sit in the stone-walled garden under a three-century-old beech tree. Inside your choices include the garden room, an enclosed porch, or the charming house itself. Live jazz Thursday evenings. | 13 Narragansett Ave. | 401/423–3731 | fax 401/423–2508 | Closed Tues. No lunch Mon. and Wed. and, Columbus Day–May 31, Thurs.–Sat. | $16–$24 | AE, D, MC, V.

Lodging

Bay Voyage. In 1889 this Victorian, gray-shingled inn with sweeping views of Narragansett Bay was shipped across the water from Newport and named for its historic trip. Blue-green suites have sitting rooms attached and some look out on the inn's rose gardens. Restaurant, dining room, complimentary Continental breakfast. Kitchenettes, cable TV. Pool, hot tub, sauna. Exercise room. Business services, airport shuttle. | 150 Conanicus Ave. | 401/423–2100 or 800/225–3522 | fax 401/423–3209 | 32 suites | $125–$280 | AE, D, DC, MC, V.

East Bay Bed & Breakfast. The rooms in this quiet Victorian home, a block from downtown and the waterfront, offer a mix of contemporary to early 19th-century furnishings. The generously sized rooms are decorated with floral wallpaper and matching curtains. Complimentary Continental breakfast. No air-conditioning, no room phones, no TV. No pets. No smoking. | 14 Union St. | 401/423–2715 | 3 (2 with shared bath, private bath has shower only) | $70–$80 | No credit cards.

KINGSTON

MAP 3, K5

(Nearby towns also listed: Narragansett, North Kingstown)

Confusing to many is the fact that Kingston is a village within the incorporated town of South Kingstown. Kingston is home to the University of Rhode Island. The campus is tucked away just off the main drag, Route 138, and, surprisingly, the 19th-century village lacks the strip malls and fast-food restaurants that plague other college towns. All the roads here are just two lanes wide, making traffic congestion a common problem.

Information: **Chamber of Commerce** | 328 Main St., Wakefield, 02880 | 401/783–2801 | www.skchamber.com.

Attractions

Helme House. One of many historic buildings in Kingston village, this 18th-century home is now the headquarters of the South County Art Association. Shows rotate monthly. | 2587 Kingstown Rd. | 401/783–2195 | fax 401/783–2195 | Free | Wed.–Sun. 1–5.

Kenyon's Grist Mill. Since the 1650s a grist mill has operated on this property. The current building, 6 mi west of Kingston and built in 1886, houses granite millstones 4½ ft in diameter and weighing 2½ tons; they grind cornmeal for that Rhode Island specialty, johnnycakes, as well as wheat, rye, oats, and barley. The store sells baking ingredients, mixes, preserves, chowders, and relishes. It's just off Rte. 138. | 21 Glen Rock Rd., West Kingston | 401/783–4054 or 800/753–6966 | fax 401/782–3564 | www.kenyonsgristmill.com | Free | Shop: weekdays 10–5; Mill tours: by appointment only.

Kingston Balloon Company. There's no better way to see southern Rhode Island than from a hot-air balloon, which affords spectacular aerial views. Perhaps you'll traverse Worden Pond and the Great Swamp Management Area and, if conditions are right, the coastline, Block Island, Boston, and Long Island will be visible. You need to rise early though, because the meeting place for your flight is at sunrise at the Station House Restaurant in West Kingston. | 31 Fortin Rd. | 401/783–9386 | $250 | Daily, at dawn; reservations required.

Kingston Free Library. This stately building, complete with gabled roof and cupola, served as a county courthouse in Rhode Island's colonial days. From 1776 until 1853, it was one of Rhode Island's five rotating statehouses (Providence, Newport, East Greenwich, and Bristol were the sites of the others). The courthouse has been a public library since 1890. Kingston's most notorious criminal, the 18th-century counterfeiter Samuel Casey, escaped from the little jailhouse next door. | 2605 Kingstown Rd. | 401/783–8254 | Free | Mon.–Tues. 10–6, Wed. 10–8, Thurs.–Fri. 10–5 (winter 10–8), Sat. 10–1 (winter 10–5).

Museum of Primitive Art and Culture. This museum in Wakefield's Peace Dale Office Building houses a small collection of Native American artifacts including pipes, beads, and tools from the local tribes, as well as pottery and weavings from other North American tribes. Other exhibits include an Inuit kayak, Australian boomerangs, and South Sea Island headhunters' shields. | 1058 Kingstown Rd., off Rte. 108, Wakefield | 401/783–5711 | By appointment.

Pettaquamscutt Historical Society. The old Washington County Jail is still intact in this gray granite building next to the Kingston Congregational Church. The men's cells are downstairs; the women's, on the second floor, are filled with a collection of quilts, costumes, and toys, as well as such Native American artifacts as arrowheads, hatchets, corn-grinding pestles, and wampum. In addition to these attractions, visitors can see the desk of Julius Booth, the actor-brother of Lincoln's assassin, John Wilkes Booth, who summered in South Kingstown. | 2636 Kingstown Rd. | 401/783–1328 | Free | Mid-May–Oct., Tues., Thurs., and Sat. 1–4.

University of Rhode Island (URI). The University of Rhode Island was founded in 1887 as a state agricultural school. The 1,200-acre campus features Gothic-style buildings made with gray Rhode Island granite. The basketball team, Rhode Island Rams, is perhaps the most popular sports team in the state. | North Rd. | 401/874–1000 | www.uri.edu | Daily.

ON THE CALENDAR

JULY.: *Hot-Air Balloon Festival.* This event features hot-air balloons and ultralights, kites, and radio-controlled model airplanes. Also enjoy bluegrass music, craft and food booths, antique autos, and demonstrations of karate and gymnastics. | URI campus | 401/783–1770.

AUG.: *Washington County Fair.* This authentic country fair at the Washington County Fairgrounds features pulls, country music, carnival midway, livestock, and really good fair food. | 401/782–8139.

Dining

At My Uncles. Pizza. In this eatery about 8 mi south of Kingston both wood-grilled and traditional oven–baked pies will please the most finicky pizza fan. Plus you'll find original salad specials every day, homemade soups, and bread baked twice a day. There's a Mexican menu, too, and dinner specials. | 28 Old Tower Hill Rd., Wakefield | 401/782–8800 | $5–$10 | AE, D, DC, MC, V.

Larchwood Inn. Continental. This pretty, 170-year-old country inn offers a wide variety of dishes, including an especially good prime rib and pan-seared tenderloin with Portobello mushrooms. Each dining room has memorabilia from the Scottish Highlands—one houses family crests, and another features scenes of South County. | 521 Main St., Wakefield | 401/783–5454 | $11–$16 | AE, D, DC, MC, V.

Lodging

Holiday Inn–South Kingstown. This Holiday Inn is 5 mi northeast of the University of Rhode Island campus, and 15 mi west of Newport. Rooms have king-size or double beds and coffeemakers. Restaurant, bar. In-room data ports, cable TV. Pool. Exercise equipment, volleyball. Business services. | 3009 Tower Hill Rd., South Kingstown | 401/789–1051 | fax 401/789–0080 | 105 rooms | $89–$199 | AE, D, DC, MC, V.

The Kings' Rose B&B. On the National Historic Register, this spacious 1933 Colonial Revival house ½ mi east of Kingston Village and URI is on 2¼ acres of gardens with fish and reflecting pools. The large rooms are done in Williamsburg colors and wallpapers, and the furnishings are antiques and family pieces, with a writing table and easy chair in each room. The common area downstairs features an honor bar for guests. You get a menu of breakfast choices. Complimentary breakfast. No air-conditioning in some rooms, some room phones, no TV in some rooms, TV in common area. 1 tennis court. Library. Pets allowed. No kids under 8. No smoking. | 1747 Mooresfield Rd., (Rte. 138), South Kingstown | 401/783–5222 or 888/230–ROSE | fax 401/783–9984 | www.virtualcities.com/ons/ri/s/ris8701.htm | 4 rooms, 1 suite | $120–$150 | No credit cards.

LINCOLN

(Nearby towns also listed: Cumberland, Glocester, Pawtucket, Providence, Woonsocket)

Lincoln is recognized by most Rhode Islanders for its gambling facility, Lincoln Park. However, the small town of Lincoln has a lot to offer beyond gaming. Its old mill villages hold many architectural treasures, and the fall foliage along its twisting, hilly roads is hard to beat.

Information: Northern Rhode Island Chamber of Commerce | 6 Blackstone Valley Pl., Suite 105, Lincoln, 02865 | 401/334–1000 | www.nrichamber.com.

Attractions

Eleazer Arnold House. Colonial travelers on the Great Road that extended from Providence to Mendon, Massachusetts, would have recognized the Eleazer Arnold House by its huge chimney. The late 17th-century stone-ended house was considered a mansion in its day and went on to serve as a tavern. Today it is owned by the Society for the Preservation for New England Antiquities. | 487 Great Rd. | 617/227–3956 | $3 | June–Oct., 2nd Sun. of each month 1–5, or call the Otis House in Boston for an appointment.

Friends Meeting House. This austere meeting house, the oldest in continuous use in New England, dates to 1703, with a 1745 addition. The benches are arranged in a square in the traditional fashion, with room in the middle for congregants to stand and speak. Cushions have been added as a concession to modernization. | 374 Great Rd. | 401/723–2515 | Free | Open Sun. at 10:30 AM for services, or by appointment.

Lincoln Park. The state's premier gambling facility, "the park" features simulcast thoroughbred racing, live and simulcast greyhound racing, video slot machines, and a variety of dining options. | 1600 Louisquisset Pike | 401/723–3200 | fax 401/727–4770 | www.lincolnparkri.com | Daily 10 AM–1 AM.

Lincoln Woods State Park. This 723-acre park consists of woods and rock outcroppings. Its attractions include a pond for fishing and swimming, outdoor skating rink, and cross-country skiing in winter. | 2 Manchester Print Works Rd. | 401/723–7892 | fax 401/724–7951 | www.riparks.com | Free | Daily.

ON THE CALENDAR
DEC.: *Festival of Lights.* One of the seven villages along the Blackstone River that make up the town of Lincoln is highlighted annually for this special weekend event. Friday night has a musical format interspersed with historical readings, caroling and refresh-

ments. Afternoon concerts, tours of historic homes and a closing concert continue this celebration of community. | 401/333–1100.

Dining
The Lodge Pub & Eatery. American. A salad bar with 25 items, all-you-can-eat family-style chicken, plus a full menu draw crowds to this white-shingle, brick-faced restaurant with two dining rooms done in knotty pine and beadboard. There's plenty of parking. Enjoy live entertainment Thursday through Saturday nights in the lounge. | 40 Breakneck Hill Rd. (Rte. 123) | 401/725–8510 | fax 401/724–4842 | $5–$15 | AE, D, DC, MC, V.

Lodging
Whipple-Cullen Farmstead Bed and Breakfast. This 1763 farmhouse has a common room for guests, and a Victorian porch overlooking five acres of fields and woods. Complimentary Continental breakfast. No air-conditioning, no room phones. No smoking. | 99 Old River Rd. | 401/333–1899 | fax 401/334–8842 | 4 rooms (all with shared bath) | $55–$65 | No credit cards.

LITTLE COMPTON

MAP 3, L5

(Nearby town also listed: Tiverton)

The rolling estates, picture-perfect homes, farmlands, woods, and gentle western shoreline make Little Compton one of the Ocean State's most attractive areas. The town's two villages, Adamsville and Little Compton, can be seen in a half-day trip.

Information: Newport County Convention Center and Visitors Bureau | 23 America's Cup Ave., Newport, 02840 | 401/849–8048 or 800/976–5122 | www.gonewport.com.

Attractions
Commons Burial Ground. Of the 3,000 headstones here, 800 date from the 1600s to 1800. The cemetery was divided in half—the south side for freemen, the north for slaves. The attractive commons is unusual in the state; Rhode Islanders did not generally build churches and common grounds in the center of their towns because of a steadfast division of church and state. | Commons Rd.

Gray's Store. Built in the village of Adamsville in 1788, this is one of the oldest continuously operating stores in the country. It is still used primarily as a general goods shop, but there is also a section that sells antiques and gifts. Attractions include an original soda fountain, candy and tobacco cases and an ice chest. | 4 Main St., Adamsville | 401/635–4566 | Mon.–Sat. 9–5, Sun. noon–4.

Rhode Island Red Monument. Many people looking for this sight expect to find a statue of a chicken. Expectation is half the fun, but Rhode Island's monument to its world-famous breed of chicken is a simple plaque mounted flush in the face of a stone wall, directly behind home plate in front of the baseball field in town. | Main St., Adamsville.

Sakonnet Point. Sakonnet Point features an alternately sandy and rocky terrain, which makes for a pleasant walk in this small town. In summer it's best to park near Sakonnet Harbor and walk 100 yards to the entrance to the point area. A family could spend an entire afternoon here hiking and exploring tidal ponds. | Rhode Island Rd. | Daily dawn–dusk.

Sakonnet Vineyards. When they set out to build Sakonnet Vineyards in the 1970s, the owners believed Little Compton's weather to be similar to France's Burgundy region. If success is any measure, they must have been correct: the America's Cup White vintage has won national prizes. Tastings, self-guided vineyard tours, an audiovisual presentation, and sales are available. Summer tours for the general public are Wednesday, Saturday, and Sunday, every hour on the hour. | 162 W. Main Rd. | 401/635–8486 | fax 401/635–2101 | www.sakon-netwine.com | Memorial Day–mid-Oct., daily 10–6; mid-Oct.–Memorial Day, daily 11–5.

Wilbor House. A timepiece of Rhode Island living, the Wilbor House, built in 1680, was occupied by eight generations of Wilbors—the first of which included 11 children born between 1690 and 1712. The common room is 17th-century and the bedrooms are 18th- and 19th-century; the kitchen and the living room are 19th- and 18th-century, respectively. The barn contains historic New England farm tools, utensils, and vehicles. | 548 W. Main Rd. | 401/635–4035 | Free | Mid-June–mid-Sept., Thurs.–Sun. 2–5, or by appointment.

ON THE CALENDAR
JUNE: *Wine and Seafood Festival*. At Sakonnet Vineyards, join about 15 chefs from around the country who showcase their talents with seafood at an afternoon walk-around tasting. A select group of wine producers participate, too, at this popular event that always sells out. It benefits Johnson & Wales University College of Culinary Arts Scholarship programs. | 162 W. Main Rd. | 401/635–8486.

Dining
Abraham Manchester's Restaurant & Tavern. American. This English pub–style restaurant was built in 1800 as the general store. Where the bar now sits, farriers shoed horses years ago. You'll find home cooking with generous portions—the 24 ounce prime rib (smaller portions are available) and mud pie are favorites. Beer-batter fish-and-chips and burgers are also hits. | 16 Main St., Adamsville | 401/635–2700 | fax 401/635–8540 | $7–$15 | MC, V.

Commons Lunch. Seafood. Smack on the Commons, this town institution serves Rhode Island specialties like johnnycakes, clam fritters and fried clams, as well as homemade chowder and lobster rolls, too. Sit at the counter, a booth, or outside by the fish pond. Dinner specials might include meat loaf, but the Commons closes early, at 7 or 8 PM. | The Commons | 401/635–4388 | Breakfast also available | $6–$12 | No credit cards.

Lodging
The Roost. The original early 20th-century farmhouse on the 120-acre Sakonnet Vineyards has delightfully cozy rooms sprinkled with antiques. Rooms are on the second floor and are named for colors. The white room has a double bed with a trundle. Complimentary Continental breakfast. No air-conditioning, no room phones, TV in common area. No pets. No kids under 12. No smoking. | 170 West Main Rd. | 401/635–8486 | fax 401/635–2101 | www.sakonnetwine.com | 3 rooms (2 with shower only) | $85–$100 | AE, MC, V.

MIDDLETOWN

MAP 3, L5

(Nearby towns also listed: Newport, Portsmouth)

Middletown derives its name from its location between Newport and Portsmouth on Aquidneck Island. Once part of Newport, it was incorporated as a separate town in 1743, and later pillaged by British soldiers during the Revolution. Until recently, Middletown was home to many working farms in this once-agricultural state. Today, the farms have mostly disappeared, but the area offers a welcome respite from the crowded streets of Newport, with its wineries, nurseries, and fresh-produce farm stands.

Information: Newport County Convention Center and Visitors Bureau | 23 America's Cup Ave., Newport | 401/849–8048 or 800/976–5122.

Attractions
Butterfly Zoo. A great place to take the kids, the Butterfly Zoo is in a beautiful greenhouse where you can see as many as 30 species of butterflies in flight. Operator Marc Schenck

MIDDLETOWN

INTRO
ATTRACTIONS
DINING
LODGING

also sells plants for attracting butterflies and caterpillars. | 1038 Aquidneck Ave. | 401/849–9519 | fax 401/847–2970 | $6 | Mid-May–mid-Sept., daily 11–4 (unless it rains).

Newport Vineyards and Winery. In a small shopping plaza, visit this winery producing both red and white table and dessert wines from the nearby vineyard. Tours run at 1 and 3 daily. | 909 E. Main Rd. (Rte. 138) | 401/848–5161 | fax 401/848–5162 | www.newportvineyards.com | Free | Mon.–Sat. 10–5, Sun. noon–5.

Norman Bird Sanctuary. This 450-acre bird haven has a barn featuring a natural history museum. Seven miles of hiking trails are highlighted by Hanging Rock, a "pudding stone" formation of fused pebbles. From atop the overhang, you can see all of Middletown's beaches and Sachuest Point. | 583 Third Beach Rd. | 401/846–2577 | fax 401/846–2772 | www.gonewport.com | $4 | Daily 9–5 (winter, Tues.–Sun. 9–5).

Purgatory Chasm. A scenic rock outcropping often depicted in old etchings, you'll see spectacular views of Second Beach, Sachuest Point, and Hanging Rock at the nearby Norman Bird Sanctuary. The 50-ft-deep crevice is an example of "puddingstone" bedrock. Combine a stop here with other nearby area attractions, since parking is for 30 minutes only in the small lot. | Purgatory Rd. | 401/847–2400 | Free | Daily dawn–dusk.

Prescott Farm and Windmill. General George Prescott, commander of the British-occupying forces, became the highest-ranking prisoner of war taken during the Revolutionary War when he was captured in a raid, shortly before midnight on July 9, 1777, by a band of colonists led by Col. William Barton. The house in Middletown has been known as Prescott Farm ever since. The complex includes an 18th-century mill that was moved to the site and a country store that offers cornmeal ground at the mill. | 2009 W. Main Rd. (Rte. 114) | 401/847–6230 | Donation suggested | Mid-April–Oct., daily 10–4.

Sachuest Point National Wildlife Refuge. A 240-acre peninsula extending into the Atlantic. Because it is at the mouth of the Sakonnnet tidal river, this is one of the best places in Rhode Island to observe waterbirds, such as grebes, loons, mergansers, and schoters. Hawks and owls are also common. Well-maintained trails wind through the park, featuring bird-watching stands where visitors can get expansive views of the refuge. | Sachuest Point Rd. | 401/364–9124 | Daily dawn–dusk.

Whitehall Museum House. This fine Colonial farmhouse was built in 1729 for British philosopher and cleric Dean George Berkeley. Berkeley, who eventually became Bishop of Cloyne, Ireland, preached at Trinity Church, helped found the Redwood Library in Newport, and established his home, Whitehall, as a center for religious and philosophical discussion. | Berkeley Ave. | 401/846–3116 | $3 | July–Aug., Tues.–Sun. 10–5; Sept.–June by appointment.

ON THE CALENDAR
OCT.: *The Harvest Fair.* The Norman Bird Sanctuary runs an old-time country fair with children's games, music, petting zoo, crafters and food. It's a terrific family event. | 583 Third Beach Rd. | 401/846–2577.

Dining

Sea Shai. Asian. Not just Japanese fare, but wonderful Korean as well is served at this pleasant place tucked into one side of a small office plaza. If you sit at the sushi bar you can watch chefs perform knife magic on fish and veggies. The menu choices are copious and delicious. | 747 Aquidneck Ave. | 401/849–5180 | No lunch weekends | $8–$20 | AE, MC, V.

Lodging

Courtyard by Marriott. This basic hotel with modern furnishings is 3 mi north of Newport on Route 114. Rooms with king-size beds have pull-out sofas. In-room data ports, some microwaves, some refrigerators. Indoor-outdoor pool. Exercise room. Laundry service, laundry facilities. No pets. | 9 Commerce Dr. | 401/849–8000 or 800/321–2211 | fax 401/849–8313 | www.marriott.com | 138 rooms, 10 suites | $159–$229 | AE, D, DC, MC, V.

Howard Johnson Lodge. This chain option is 2 mi from downtown Newport and within walking distance of shops and restaurants. It offers a free shuttle to Newport on summer evenings. Restaurant, complimentary Continental breakfast. Some microwaves, some refrigerators, cable TV. Indoor pool. Sauna, hot tub, spa. Tennis courts. Business services. Free parking. Pets allowed. | 351 W. Main Rd. | 401/849–2000 | fax 401/849–6047 | 155 rooms | $99–$189 | AE, D, DC, MC, V.

The Inn at Shadowlawn. This 1856 building is thought to be the first Italianate stick-style villa built in the United States. The large rooms are beautifully done in a Victorian style with floral wallpaper, curtains, and shutters. All have working fireplaces. The Inn is on 2½ landscaped acres, ½ mi from Newport, just off Route 138. Complimentary breakfast. In-room data ports. Some kitchenettes, refrigerators, cable TV, in-room VCRs and movies. Laundry service. No smoking. | 120 Miantonomi Ave. | 401/847–0902 or 800/352–3750 | fax 401/848–6529 | 8 suites | $125–$225 | A, D, DC, MC, V.

Newport Ramada Inn. The inn is ½ mi from the naval base and 3 mi north of Newport. Children under 18 stay free. Restaurant, bar. In-room data ports, microwaves, refrigerators, cable TV. Indoor pool. Exercise equipment. Laundry facilities. Business services. Pets allowed (fee). | 936 W. Main Rd. | 401/846–7600 | fax 401/849–6919 | www.ramadainnnewport.com | 134 rooms, 15 suites | $129–205, $179–$239 suites | AE, D, DC, MC, V.

Royal Plaza Hotel. A 115-room hotel catering to vacationers and business travelers that is a five-minute drive from downtown Newport. Complimentary Continental breakfast. Some refrigerators, some in-room hot tubs, cable TV. Laundry service. Business services. | 425 E. Main Rd. | 401/846–3555 or 800/825–7072 | fax 401/846–3666 | www.royalplazahotel.com | 100 rooms, 15 suites | $99–$299, $129–$400 suites | D, DC, MC, V.

West Main Lodge. A hotel that is less than 3 mi from downtown Newport. Some rooms have private balconies. Cable TV. | 1359 W. Main Rd. | 401/849–2718 or 800/537–7704 | fax 401/849–2798 | www.westmainlodge.com | 55 rooms | $75–$145 | Closed mid-Nov.–mid-Mar. | AE, D, DC, MC, V.

NARRAGANSETT

MAP 3, K5

(Nearby towns also listed: Galilee, North Kingstown)

The popular beach town of Narragansett occupies a peninsula east of Point Judith Pond and the Pettaquamscutt River. Its 16 villages include Galilee, Bonnett Shores, and Narragansett Pier. In operation in the late 1800s, Narragansett Pier Casino featured a bowling alley, billiard tables, tennis courts, a rifle gallery, a theater, and a ballroom. The grand and well-known edifice burned to the ground in 1900. This beachside village is now populated by summertime "cottagers," college students, and commuting professionals.

Information: **South County Tourism Council** | Stedman Government Center, 4808 Tower Hill Rd., Wakefield, 02879 | 401/789–4422 or 800/548–4662.

Attractions

Adventureland in Narragansett. Family fun rules here with four activities: state-of-the-art cart track, 18-hole parklike miniature-golf course, bumper boats, and batting cages. | 112 Point Judith Rd. | 401/789–0084 | fax 401/364–8766 | Grounds: free; All-activity pass: $12; prices vary for individual activities | Mid-Apr.–June 15, weekends 10–10; June 15–Labor Day, daily 10–10; Labor Day–mid-October, weekends 10–10.

Narragansett Pier/The Towers. Narragansett Pier is a bustling summer beach community. Once known for its Stanford White–designed Pier Casino, which burned in 1900, what remains are the stone towers and the looming eight-story stone casino entrance that spans Route 1A. You can dance on the wooden floor of the tower bridge Thursday nights from 7 to 10 from June through September. There's a new gift shop and information service on the ocean side of the building. Tours are available by apppointment or from noon to 4 on weekends. | Rte. 1A | 401/782–2597 | Free | Towers open noon–4 weekends or by appointment.

Narragansett Town Beach. There's a pavilion with bathhouse, concessions, and activities for kids here. The south end is great for surfing, while the north end is quieter. | 39 Boston Neck Rd. (Rte. 1A) | 401/782–0658 | $4, parking $5 | Daily.

Point Judith Lighthouse. Visitors can wander the grounds of this important light station; the lighthouse itself and the active Coast Guard Station are restricted. It's a good place to see the area's best surfers in action, when conditions are right. | 1470 Ocean Rd. | 401/789–0444 | fax 401/782–4957 | Parking area, daily dawn–dusk; lighthouse tours by appointment.

South County Museum. The seven buildings on Canochet Farm contain 30,000 artifacts dating from 1800 to 1950. Exhibits include a country kitchen, a living-history farm, carpentry, blacksmith, and letterpress printing exhibits, and an antique carriage collection. | Canochet Farm, Strathmore St. | 401/783–5400 | fax 401/783–0506 | www.southcountymuseum.org | $3.50 | May–Oct., Wed.–Sat. 10–4, Sun. 10–5; Closed Nov.–Apr.

ON THE CALENDAR

FEB.: *Mid-winter Northeastern Surfing Championship.* The best competitive surfers in the Northeast convene annually to test their skills at Narragansett Town Beach. | 39 Boston Neck Rd. (Rte. 1A) | 401/789–3399.

NOV.: *Ocean State Marathon.* This annual event attracts national and international competitors. | Rte. 1A, Narragansett Town Beach | 401/885–4499.

Dining

Aunt Carrie's Restaurant. Seafood. Serving fresh seafood since 1920 on the beach at Point Judith, Aunt Carrie's is revered for clam cakes, and also lobster, lobster rolls, steamers, and steak. You can eat inside or take your seafood out, perhaps to the large, waterside picnic area. | 1240 Ocean Rd. | 401/783–7930 | fax 401/782–6475 | www.auntcarries.baweb.com | Closed Tues. Closed Oct.–Mar. Closed Mon.–Thurs., Apr.–May and Sept. No lunch Fri. in Apr.–May and Sept. | $10–$35 | MC, V.

Basil's. French. Two small, romantic dining rooms serve this Narragansett Pier restaurant where the impeccable service and tasteful appointments are fine introductions to the Continental menu that features selections like duck á l'orange. The wine list has received *Wine Spectator's* Award of Excellence. | 22 Kingstown Rd. | 401/789–3743 | Closed Mon. Closed Tues., Sept.–May. No lunch | $15–30 | AE, D, DC, MC, V.

Coast Guard House. American. Because of its former role—as a late-19th-century Coast Guard house—this restaurant has a terrific location on the ocean and is bustling, popular, and casual. Order grilled seafood or lobster, and eat upstairs on one of the two decks—one shaded by a bright blue awning—for great views of the surfers on Narragansett Town Beach. Kid's menu. Sun. brunch. | 40 Ocean Rd. | 401/789–0700 | $12–$20 | AE, D, DC, MC, V.

Crazy Burger Cafe & Juice Bar. American. An old vegetable market ½ mi from Narragansett Beach has been converted to a funky and fun year-around restaurant that serves an array of burger-shaped patties with funny names and unusual ingredients. Examples include neurotic (tofu, black bean, and couscous) and lunacy (salmon with orange pistacho pesto in puff pastry). The ketchup's homemade, and waffle chips are awesome and they serve great breakfasts, dinner entrées, and wood-grilled pizzas too. There's a garden patio for al fresco dining. BYOB. | 144 Boon St. | 401/783–1810 | Breakfast also available | $12–$18 | D, MC, V.

Ocean View Chinese. Chinese. While the restaurant hasn't had an ocean view since it moved to this tucked-away location at Mariners Square in 1985, its Szechuan and Mandarin fare is some of the best in Rhode Island. The hand-pleated dumplings are standouts on the 200-item menu, which includes 72 chef's specialties | 140 Point Judith Rd. | 401/783–9070 | Closed Tues. No lunch | $6–$18 | No credit cards.

Spain. Spanish. Of course you can find paella here, that complex combination of lobster, clams, mussels, shrimp, sea scallops, and saffron rice, but other Mediterranean specialties are also on the menu. A lovely outside patio with flowers and a waterfall overlooks the ocean, as does the second floor dining room in this modern restaurant about ¼ mi south of Scarborough Beach. | 1144 Ocean Rd. | 401/783–9770 | fax 401/782–2838 | Closed Mon. No lunch | $11–$19 | AE, D, DC, MC, V.

The Spanish Tavern. Spanish. You'll first notice the half-oval windows and large deck of this beautiful yet casual restaurant overlooking Narragansett Beach. While known for Paella Marinera, made with seafood, and Paella Valenciana—which has seafood and chicken, Spanish sausage, and pork—the steak with garlic sauce has a well-deserved reputation. The white and red sangrias are made from scratch, and they're great with shrimp appetizers. Anything gets a lift with the salsa verde, a delicious blend of lemon, white wine, parsley, garlic, and onion. | 1 Beach St. | 401/783–3550 | fax 401/782–8421 | $13–$22 | AE, D, MC, V.

Lodging

Admiral Dewey Inn. The National Historic Register calls this inn, 4 mi west of Narragansett, the "best restoration of a beach boarding house on the Rhode Island shore." Guests say this comfortable, immaculate, and convenient inn is like staying with your favorite aunt. Rooms have interesting decorative wallpaper and pastel curtains covered with cotton lace overcurtains. Beds may be high poster or white iron with brass trim. The town beach is across the street. Complimentary Continental breakfast. No air-conditioning, no room phones, TV in common area. No pets. No kids under 10. No smoking. | 668 Matunuck Beach Rd., South Kingstown | 401/783–2090 or 800/457–2090 | fax 401/783–8298 | www.admiraldeweyinn.com | 10 rooms, (2 with shared bath, 8 with showers only) | $90–$140 | MC, V.

Larchwood Inn. A Colonial and a Victorian house face each other across Wakefield's main street that is less than 1 mi south of Narragansett. The inn offers a range of accommodations. The gardens are beautiful, ancient trees dot the 3 ½ acre property, and antiques are sprinkled throughout. Restaurant, bar. No air-conditioning in some rooms, some room phones, TV in common area. Pets allowed. | 521 Main St., Wakefield, South Kingston | 401/783–5454 or 800/275–5450 | fax 401/783–1800 | www.xpos.com/larchwoodinn | 18 rooms (7 with shared bath) | $65–$140 | AE, D, DC, MC, V.

The Richards. This granite English manor–style house was built in 1884 and is on the National Historic Register. The innkeeper is an avid gardener and the inn has beautiful grounds. Rooms are furnished with chintz fabrics, Oriental rugs, and antiques. All rooms have working fireplaces. Complimentary breakfast. No air-conditioning, no room phones, no TV. No pets. No kids under age 12. No smoking. | 144 Gibson Ave. | 401/789–7746 | fax 401/789–7168 | www.virtualcities.com/ri/richards | 2 rooms, 3 suites (1 2-bedroom suite with shared bath) | $95–$190 | No credit cards.

Village Inn. This newly remodeled hotel with two restaurants and large deck is across from the Narragansett Pier and town beach and is a 10-minute ride from the Block Island ferry and 20 minutes from Newport. Golf, tennis, and parks are nearby. Many rooms have private balconies overlooking Narragansett Bay. 2 restaurants, bar. Cable TV, in-room VCR. Indoor pool. Hot tub. Beach. Baby-sitting. Business services. | 1 Beach St. | 401/783–6767 or 800/843–7437 | fax 401/782–2220 | 63 rooms | $135–$310 | AE, D, DC, MC, V.

NARRAGANSETT

INTRO
ATTRACTIONS
DINING
LODGING

NEWPORT

(Nearby towns also listed: Block Island, Jamestown, Middletown)

The Golden Age of Newport ran from roughly 1720 to the 1770s, when products like cheese, clocks, and furniture, as well as livestock and the slave trade, put the city on a par with Charleston, South Carolina; the two cities trailed only Boston as centers of New World maritime commerce. In the mid-1700s Newport was home to the best shipbuilders in North America. Their small, swift, and reliable slave ships were the stars of the triangle trade (rum to Africa for slaves; slaves to the West Indies for molasses; molasses and slaves back to America, where the molasses was made into rum).

In the 19th century Newport became a summer playground for the wealthiest families in America. These riches were not made in Rhode Island but imported by the titans of the Gilded Age, who built the fabulous "cottages" overlooking the Atlantic. The country's best young architects—Richard Upjohn, Richard Morris Hunt, and firms like McKim, Mead & White—left a legacy of remarkable homes in Newport.

Recreational sailing, a huge industry in Newport, convincingly melds the attributes of two eras: the conspicuous consumption of the Gilded Age and the nautical expertise of the Colonial era. Tan, expensively dressed young sailors often fill Newport bars and restaurants, where they talk of wind, waves, and expensive yachts. For those not arriving by water, a sailboat tour of the harbor is a great way to get your feet wet.

More than 200 pre-Revolutionary buildings (mostly private residences) remain in Newport, more than any other city in the country. Most of these national treasures are in the neighborhood known as the Point. With the exception of Ocean Drive, Newport is a walker's city. In summer, traffic thickens, and the narrow one-way streets can constitute an unbearable maze. Once you're in town, it's worth parking in a pay lot (try one at the Gateway Information Center at 23 America's Cup Avenue) and leaving your car behind while you visit in-town sights.

Information: **Newport County Convention Center and Visitors Bureau** | 23 America's Cup Ave., Newport, 02840 | 401/849-8048 or 800/976-5122 | www.gonewport.com.

Attractions

Artillery Company of Newport Military Museum. This museum has one of the finest collections of foreign and domestic militaria in the United States. Chartered in 1741, the Rhode Island militia is the country's oldest military organization in continuous service. | 23 Clarke St. | 401/846-8488 | fax 401/846-3311 | info@newportartillery.org | www.newportartillery.org | Donation suggested | May–Oct. Sat. 10–4.

Classic Cruises of Newport. You can take a trip around Newport Harbor or Narragansett Bay in either a sailing schooner or a high-powered former rum-running vessel. Charters available. | Bannister's Wharf, America's Cup Ave. | 401/849-3033 or 800/395-1343 | www.cruisenewport.com | May–mid-Oct., daily.

★ **Cliff Walk.** The 3½-mi Cliff Walk began as a footpath in the late 1700s. Today you will find spectacular views of the ocean and backyard glimpses of many of Newport's mansions. It's also a great place to explore tide pools and to bird-watch. | Memorial Blvd., at Eustis Ave. | 401/849-8098 or 800/326-6030 | Free | Daily dawn–dusk.

Easton's Beach. Also known as First Beach, this spot is popular for its carousel. It is also one of the prettiest beaches in Rhode Island. | 175 Memorial Blvd. | 401/846-1398 | Free, parking fee | Daily 8:30–6.

Fort Adams State Park. This 105-acre seaside park presents magnificent panoramas of Newport Harbor and is a great place to take sailing or windsurfing lessons; sailboat rentals are also available. The park is home to the legendary Newport Jazz Festival and Folk Festival. | Harrison Ave. and Ocean Dr. | 401/847–2400 | fax 401/841–9821 | www.riparks.com/for-tadams.htm | Free, parking fee (Memorial Day–Labor Day) | Daily dawn–dusk.

Great Friends Meeting House. In 1657 a ship bearing Quakers arrived in Newport after their attempts to settle in New York and Boston had failed. This Meeting House was erected in 1699, when the Friends made up 60% of Newport's population. It has been called the finest medieval structure in America, and its weathered exterior belies the soaring post-and-beam construction of the interior. | Farewell and Marlborough Sts. | 401/846–0813 | fax 401/846–1853 | www.newporthistorical.com | Donation suggested | Tours by appointment only.

Historic Mansions and Houses. It's best to tour two or three mansions and see the rest from the outside. Signage throughout Newport makes finding the homes easier. To avoid long lines on summer days, go early or choose the less popular but still amazing mansions—The Elms, Kingscote, and Belcourt Castle. Plan on spending one hour at each mansion. The Preservation Society of Newport County (401/847–1000) maintains 12 mansions, some of which are described below. Guided tours are given of each; you can purchase a combination ticket at any of the mansions at a discount.

Astors' Beechwood. Mrs. William Backhouse Astor was the first of the New York *grandes dames* to summer in Newport; many of the 400 (America's first social register) soon followed in her wake. Today your tour of the Vaux and Downing designed Tuscan Revival home is conducted by actors in period costumes playing Mrs. Astor's servants and members of the family itself, circa 1891. | 580 Bellevue Ave. | 401/846–3772 | fax 401/849–6998 | www.astors-beechwood.com | $9 | May–Sept., daily 10–5; Feb.–Apr., Fri.–Sun. 10–4.

Belcourt Castle. Richard Morris Hunt based this 1894 Gothic Revival mansion, built for banking heir Oliver H.P. Belmont (of the Belmont Race Track), on Louis XIII's hunting lodge. The house is so filled with priceless European and Asian treasures that locals have dubbed it the Metropolitan Museum of Newport. Don't miss the Golden Coronation Coach. | 657 Bellevue Ave. | 401/846–0669 or 401/849–1566 | fax 401/847–5345 | $10 | June–mid-Oct., Mon.–Sat. 9–5, Sun. 10–5; mid-Oct.–May Weekends 10–4, closed Jan.

★ **The Breakers.** This most popular of all Newport mansions was built for railroad heir Cornelius Vanderbilt II, amazingly in just two years. Designed by Richard Morris Hunt as a Genoese Renaissance–style palace, the Breakers features, among many other marvels, an acoustically perfect music room complete with gold ceiling, a blue marble fireplace, rose alabaster pillars in the dining room, and a porch with a mosaic ceiling that took Italian workers six months to complete—on their backs. To build the Breakers today would cost more than $400 million. | Ochre Point Ave. | 401/847–6544 | fax 401/847–1361 | www.newportmansions.org | $12; special rates for children | Apr.–Dec., daily 10–5.

Chateau-sur-Mer. Bellevue Avenue's first stone mansion was built in 1852 for William S. Wetmore, a tycoon involved in the China trade. It was enlarged in the 1870s by Richard Morris Hunt. The Gold Room by Leon Marcotte, and the Renaissance Revival–style dining room and library by the Florentine sculptor Luigi Frullini, are sterling examples of the work of leading 19th-century designers. The upstairs bedrooms are decorated in English Aesthetic style with wallpapers by Arts and Crafts designers William Morris and William Burges. | Bellevue Ave. at Shepard Ave. | 401/847–6544 | fax 401/847–1361 | www.newport-mansions.org | $9 | May–Oct., daily 10–5; Jan.–Mar. weekends 10–5.

Chepstow. This Italianate villa with a French-style mansard roof is not as grand as other Newport mansions, but it houses a remarkable collection of 19th-century American paintings and furniture gathered by the members of New York's prominent Morris family. Built in 1860, the home was designed by Newport architect George Champlin Mason and is the latest addition to the list of important homes owned by the Preservation Society of Newport. Reservations required. | 120 Narragansett Ave. | 401/847–1000 | fax 401/847–1361 | www.newportmansions.org | $9 | May–Oct., daily 10–5.

Edward King House. The Kings made a fortune in the China trade and were one of Newport's most generous families. Edward King's Italianate villa was Newport's first grand house in the area. Designed by Richard Upjohn, its monumental exterior contrasts the airy interior. Today the Edward King House serves as Newport's Senior Center. | 35 King St., Aquidneck Park | 401/846–7426 | fax 401/846–5300 | Free | Weekdays 9–4.

The Elms. The Elms was built for Edward Julius Berwind, a coal baron, in 1901 by architect Horace Trumbauer, who paid homage to the French neoclassical style of the Château d'Asnières near Paris. The gardens are the finest in Newport and are labeled, providing an exemplary botany lesson. | Bellevue Ave. | 401/842–1546 | fax 401/847–1361 | www.newportmansions.org | $9 | Daily 10–5.

Hammersmith Farm. This elaborate country estate was the childhood summer home of Jacqueline Bouvier Kennedy Onassis, the site of her wedding to John F. Kennedy, and a summer White House during the Kennedy Administration. Formerly open to the public, the property is now a private home. | Ocean Dr. near Ft. Adams.

★ **Hunter House.** The French admiral Charles Louis d'Arsac de Ternay used this 1748 home on the banks of Narragansett Bay as his Revolutionary War headquarters. The carved pineapple over the door was a symbol of hospitality throughout Colonial America; a fresh pineapple placed out front signaled an invitation to neighbors to visit a returned seaman or to look over a shop's new stock. Pieces made by Newport artisans Townsend and Goddard furnish much of the house. | 54 Washington St. | 401/847–7516 | fax 401/847–1361 | www.newportmansions.org | $9 | May–Oct., daily 10–5.

Isaac Bell House. A fine example of shingle-style architecture, this mansion was completed in 1883 and is currently being restored. The exterior work has been completed and the interior is open to the public as a work in progress. Inside, visitors are shown a short film documenting the effort to revitalize the McKim, Mead & White design and are given a tour of various rooms. Bell was a wealthy cotton broker and the brother-in-law of Gordon Bennett Jr., publisher of the *New York Herald*. | Bellevue Ave. at Perry St. | 401/847–1000 | www.newportmansions.org | $9 | May–Oct., daily 10–5.

Kingscote. The first of the mansions on Bellevue Avenue, Kingscote was built in 1839 for Georgia planter George Noble Jones. The Gothic Revival property was sold to the David Kings of the China trade during the Civil War and expanded under the direction of McKim, Mead & White. Today it is filled with antique furniture, glass, and Asian art, and contains a number of unusual features including a cork ceiling and several Tiffany windows. | Bowery St., off Bellevue Ave. | 401/847–1000 | fax 401/847–1361 | www.newportmansions.org | $9 | May–Oct., daily 10–5.

Marble House. This white marble summer palace was built in 1892 by Richard Morris Hunt for the flamboyant, trendsetting Alva Vanderbilt. Alva propelled the Vanderbilts into the upper crust of American society with the unveiling of Marble House. During the four years the house was being built, the site was hidden and the European workmen sequestered. A trailblazer on the social front (Alva was the first Newport woman to drive an automobile, to bob her hair, and to ride a bicycle), she was also a dynamic leader of the women's suffrage movement. Marble House, with its Gold Ballroom and rare colored marbles, is a testament to her dynamic personality. | Bellevue Ave. near Ruggles St. | 401/847–1000 | fax 401/847–1361 | www.newportmansions.org | $9 | Apr.–Oct., daily 10–6; Nov.–Mar., weekends 10–5.

Rosecliff. Architect Stanford White built Rosecliff for Mrs. Hermann Oelrichs in 1902; he modeled it on the Grand Trianon at Versailles. Considered Newport's most romantic mansion, Rosecliff has 40 rooms, including the Court of Love, and a heart-shape staircase. Its grand ballroom has appeared in several movies, including *True Lies* and *The Great Gatsby*. | Bellevue Ave. at Marine Ave. | 401/847–5793 | fax 401/847–1361 | www.newportmansions.org | $9 | May–Oct., daily 10–5.

Rough Point. You'll have an intimate look at the life of Doris Duke in this mansion, which has remained unchanged since her death in 1992. The 1889 gothic-style mansion has a remarkable collection of art plus breathtaking ocean views. To visit Rough Point, you must take a courtesy shuttle that leaves from the Gateway Visitors Center. You have to purchase tickets the day you want to visit; advance reservations are not available. | Ocean Ave. | 401/849–7300 | $25, includes shuttle transportation | Tues.–Sat., tours only at 10, 12:30, and 3.

Samuel Whitehorne House. One of the few Federal-style mansions in Newport, its owner went bankrupt before construction was completed. Today it has been restored and houses a museum featuring 19th-century period furniture and silver and pewter of Newport origin. | 416 Thames St. | 401/847–2448 or 401/849–7300 | $8 | May–Oct., Fri. 1–4, Sat.–Mon. 10–4; Tues–Thurs., by appointment.

Wanton-Lyman-Hazard House. Newport's oldest residence, this home dates from the mid-17th century. The dark-red building was the site of the city's Stamp Act Riot of 1765—after the British Parliament levied a tax on most printed material, the Sons of Liberty stormed the house, which was occupied by the British stamp master. The house contains period artifacts, and there's a Colonial garden. It is closed until Summer 2001, call for more information. | 17 Broadway | 401/846–0813 | fax 401/846–1853 | www.newporthistorical.com.

International Tennis Hall of Fame Museum. The world's largest tennis museum is housed in the historic Newport Casino. The shingle-style social club was designed by Stanford White and built in 1880 for publisher James Gordon Bennett Jr., who quit the nearby men's club, the Newport Reading Room, after a polo player—at Bennett's behest—rode a horse into the building and was subsequently banned. The museum has displays, artifacts, and memorabilia covering a century of tennis history. There are 13 grass courts, 1 hard court, and 3 indoor courts. | Newport Casino, 194 Bellevue Ave. | 401/849–3990 or 800/457–1144 | fax 401/849–8780 | www.tennisfame.org | $8 | Daily 9:30–5.

Museum of Newport History at the Brick Market. Architecturally and historically one of the most significant buildings in Newport, the Brick Market (1762) is a masterpiece of Palladian design by Peter Harrison. It was originally a market and granary but over the years has been a theater and a city hall. Operated by the Newport Historical Society, it has multimedia exhibits exploring Newport history from Colonial days to Newport's Gilded Age. | Long Wharf and 127 Thames St., at Washington Sq. | 401/846–0813 | fax 401/846–1853 | $5 | Apr.–Dec., Mon., Wed.–Sat. 10–5, Sun. 1–5; Jan.–Mar., call for hours.

Museum of Yatching. The museum brings the visitor back to Newport's heyday as the yachting capital of the world. Its attractions include the America's Cup gallery, the small boat gallery, and the 30-square-meter *Oriole.* The school teaches classes on yacht restoration and shipwright skills. | Fort Adams State Park, Harrison Ave. | 401/847–1018 | fax 401/783–1328 | www.moy.org | $4 | Mid-May–late Oct., daily 9–5; Nov.–mid-May, by appointment.

The New England Aquarium Exploration Center at Newport. With a small collection of local sea creatures, the aquarium is designed for children. It has live exhibits of local animals, educational, interactive exhibits, arts and crafts, and a microscope lab. | At the rotunda in Easton's Beach | 401/849–8430 | www.neaq.com/special/newport | $3 | Memorial Day–Labor Day, Fri.–Wed. 10–4, Thurs. 10–5.

Newport Art Museum and Art Association. Richard Morris Hunt designed this stick-style Victorian building that houses a community-supported center for the arts. The galleries exhibit contemporary works by New England artists. | 76 Bellevue Ave. | 401/848–8200 | fax 401/848–8205 | info@newportartmuseum.com | www.newportartmuseum.com | $4 | Memorial Day–Columbus Day, Mon.–Sat. 10–5, Sun. noon–5; Columbus Day–Memorial Day, Mon.–Sat. 10–4, Sun. noon–4.

Newport Historical Society Archives and Library. This museum serves as a resource for investigating Newport's past through photographs, paintings, furniture, and china. Research facilities include archival manuscript materials and the earliest town records. | 82 Touro St. | 401/846–0813 | www.newporthistorical.com | Free | Tues.–Fri. 9:30–4:30, Sat. 9:30–noon.

Newport Grand Jai Alai. Jai alai matches and video slot machines are the primary draws here, one of the two gambling facilities in Rhode Island. | 150 Admiral Kalbfus Rd. | 401/849–5000 | fax 401/846–0290 | www.newportgrand.com | Free | Daily 10 AM–1 AM.

Naval War College Museum. The history of naval warfare and the naval heritage of the Narragansett Bay region are the focus of this museum, in historic Founders Hall, the original site of the Naval War College and a National Historic Landmark. Permanent exhibits include "Rhode Island and the Navy," featuring a large admiralty model of the *Sloop Providence* and a look back at the evolution of the torpedo in America, and the story of the founding of the Naval War College including a 12-minute video. In addition to the permanent exhibits, there are at least three special exhibits a year. | 686 Cushing Rd. | 401/841–4052

| fax 401/841–7689 | www.visitnewport.com/buspages/navy/exhibits.htm | Free | Weekdays 10–4, weekends noon–4 June–Sept.

Old Colony and Newport Railroad. A meandering rail journey in one of two turn-of-the-century train coaches pulled by a vintage diesel engine lasts 80 minutes and takes you through the Naval Base and along the coast of Narragansett Bay. You'll be told about the historical, cultural, and environmental aspects of the west shore of Aquidneck Island and have views of beaches and boats, including U.S. fleet carriers. | Terminal, 19 America's Cup Ave. | 401/624–6951 or 401/683–4549 | www.ocnrr.com | $5.75 | Call for hours.

Old Stone Mill. One of Newport's oldest standing structures that supposedly was built by Viking voyagers before the time of Columbus. More likely the mill was built by Governor Benedict Arnold (grandfather of the infamous Revolutionary War traitor) sometime in the 17th century. The picturesque ruin is Newport's unofficial trademark. | Touro Park, Mill St. | Free | Daily dawn–dusk.

Providence-Newport Ferry. This ferry service provides an interesting and scenic connection between Newport and Providence. | Perrotti Park Ferry Dock | 401/781–9400 | www.ripta.com | $4 one-way | Daily.

Redwood Library and Athenaeum. The oldest continually operating circulating library in North America, the Redwood Library was established in 1747 by Abraham Redwood. Henry James and Edith Wharton have browsed these stacks. The collection also includes fine Townsend and Goddard furniture and major 18th- and 19th-century portraits by Gilbert Stuart and Robert Feke. | 50 Bellevue Ave. | 401/847–0292 | fax 401/841–5680 | www.redwood1747.org | Free | Mon. and Fri.–Sat. 9:30–5:30, Tues.–Thurs. 9:30–8, Sun. 1–5.

Sachuest Beach. Also known as Second Beach, this mile-long beach is technically in Middletown. The beach features extensive dunes and plenty of parking. | Sachuest Point Rd. | 401/846–1398 | Free; parking fee | Daily 8:30–6.

Seventh Day Baptist Meeting House. Adjacent to the Newport Historical Society Archives and Library, the Seventh Day Baptist Meeting House was built by Richard Munday. | 82 Touro St., | 401/846–0813 | www.newporthistorical.com | Free | Tues.–Fri. 9:30–4:30, Sat. 9:30–12.

Touro Synagogue. This house of worship is the oldest surviving synagogue in the United States—dedicated in 1763—and was designed by Peter Harrison. Although simple on the outside, the synagogue has an elaborate interior and it may have served as an inspiration to Thomas Jefferson in the building of Monticello. One of the oldest torah in North America is on display. Call for group tours (fee). | 85 Touro St. | 401/847–4794 (ext. 11) | fax 401/847–4794 | www.tourosynagogue.org | Free | July–early Sept., Sun.–Fri. 10–5; Sept.–June, call for hours.

Trinity Church. In 1989 a $3 million restoration of this beautiful church, modeled on London churches and designed by Christopher Wren, was completed. Built in 1726, the church features a center aisle and three-tier wineglass pulpit, the only one of its kind in America. George Washington worshipped in pew 81, and the organ was tested by Handel before it was sent from England by Bishop George Berkeley. Queen Elizabeth visited in 1976. Bishop Tutu preached here in 1987. | Queen Anne Sq | 401/846–0660 | fax 401/846–8440 | www.trinitynewport.org | Free | June–Sept., daily 10–4; Oct. and May, daily 10–1.

Viking Boat Tour. A one-hour tour of Narragansett Bay that leaves from Newport Harbor. | Goat Island Marina, off Washington St. | 401/847–6921 | fax 401/847–5773 | $8 | May–Oct., Mon.–Sat., call for hours.

Viking Bus Tour. This company leads year-round, air-conditioned bus tours of Newport. It also has tour packages, which include one or two mansion tours. | Gateway Tourist Center, America's Cup Ave. | 401/847–6921 | fax 401/848–5773 | Mid-June–Oct. daily, call for hours; Nov.–Mar., Sat. at 11:30.

White Horse Tavern. William Mayes, the father of a successful and notorious pirate, received a tavern license in 1687, which makes this building, built in 1673, the oldest pub in the New World. Now home to one of Newport's finest restaurants, the structure features oak-beam ceilings, a cavernous fireplace, and uneven plank floors, and epitomizes Newport's Colonial charm. The restaurant serves reasonably priced lunches. | 26 Marlborough St. | 401/849–3600 | fax 401/849–7317 | whitehorse-tavern@travelbase.com | www.white-horsetavern.com | Daily.

ON THE CALENDAR

JAN.–FEB.: *Newport Winter Festival.* New England's largest winter extravaganza has 150 individual events ranging from sand and ice sculpture contests to a city-wide scavenger hunt. There is also entertainment and special features from many Newport restaurants and attractions. | 23 America's Cup Ave. | 401/849–8048 or 800/326–6030.

MAR.: *St. Patrick's Day Parade.* A citywide celebration of this Irish holiday that takes place at City Hall. | 43 Broadway | 401/849–8048 or 800/976–5122.

JULY: *Black Ships Festival.* Numerous Japanese cultural events are held all across the city in mid-July to commemorate Commander Matthew C. Perry's 1854 expedition, which opened trade with Japan. | 28 Pelham St. | 401/846–2720.

JULY: *Newport Music Festival.* Two weeks of classical music in and around the mansions. There are morning, afternoon, and evening concerts. | 401/849–8048 or 800/326–6030.

AUG.: *JVC Jazz Festival.* Legendary performers and rising stars participate in this world-renowned event. Concerts overlook historic Newport Harbor from Fort Adams State Park. | Harrison Ave. and Ocean Dr. | 401/847–3700.

SEPT.: *Newport International Boat Show.* Hundreds of displays of sail and power boats, and accessories are available here. | 4 Commercial Wharf | 401/846–1115 (ext. 215).

Dining

The Alva. Continental. This elegant restaurant is reminiscent of an English dining room. It serves á la carte or prix-fixe dinners. You can, if you like, relax with drinks and canapés and make your menu selection in a couch-filled room (with blazing fireplace when it's chilly); you'll be escorted to your table in the dining room when dinner is served. The adjoining glass-enclosed Conservatory is less formal and there is a patio for casual outside dining as well. | 41 Mary St. | 401/846–6200 | fax 401/846–0701 | www.vanderbilthall.com | No lunch at The Alva; breakfast also available at the Conservatory | $25–$30; prix–fixe $59 | AE, D, DC, MC, V.

YOUR CAR'S FIRST-AID KIT

- ❏ Bungee cords or rope to tie down trunk if necessary
- ❏ Club soda to remove stains from upholstery
- ❏ Cooler with bottled water
- ❏ Extra coolant
- ❏ Extra windshield-washer fluid
- ❏ Flares and/or reflectors
- ❏ Flashlight and extra batteries
- ❏ Hand wipes to clean hands after roadside repair
- ❏ Hose tape

- ❏ Jack and fully inflated spare
- ❏ Jumper cables
- ❏ Lug wrench
- ❏ Owner's manual
- ❏ Plastic poncho—in case you need to do roadside repairs in the rain
- ❏ Quart of oil and quart of transmission fluid
- ❏ Spare fan belts
- ❏ Spare fuses
- ❏ Tire-pressure gauge

*Excerpted from *Fodor's: How to Pack: Experts Share Their Secrets*
© 1997, by Fodor's Travel Publications

★ **Asterix & Obelix.** Contemporary. What was once a garage has been transformed into a chic restaurant. The walls of the spacious dining room are brightly painted and have paintings and mirrors. Booths and tables with white linens set the tone. Try the crispy salmon with mushrooms and asparagus, orzo risotto with a cabernet sauvignon sauce, or the steak au poivre. There's outside dining in the open front of the building. Entertainment some evenings. | 599 Thames St. | 401/841–8833 | No lunch | $18–$25 | AE, D, DC, MC, V.

The Black Pearl. Continental. Whether you dine in the venerable Commodore's Room, or opt for the casual Tavern or waterside patio, this favorite old Newport restaurant is sure to please. The water-view Commodore's Room is reminiscent of an elegant ship's interior and has black-tie service. It is famous for its creamy clam chowder and the classic menu includes fried Brie, swordfish with tomato-basil buerre blanc, and New England lobster tail stuffed with Maryland jumbo lump crabmeat. | Bannister's Wharf | 401/846–5264 | Reservations essential in the Commodore's Room | Jackets required in Commodore's Room | $20–$30 Commodore's Room, $7–$20 Tavern | AE, MC, V.

Brick Alley Pub. American. The lines start forming early at this midtown favorite. A bar, four dining rooms, plus a brick walled patio offer lots of seating. A real 1938 Red Chevrolet truck divides two rooms, and artifacts and memorabilia of old Newport are everywhere. The diverse menu includes ultimate nachos, which are breathtaking in size. Kids under 9 have a special menu, get crayons, free beverage and dessert, and a selection from a treasure chest. | 140 Thames St. | 401/849–6334 | fax 401/848–5640 | www.brickalley.com | $10–$22 | AE, D, DC, MC, V.

Cafe Zelda. Contemporary. At this restaurant you'll rub elbows with sailors and, possibly, the fisherman who brought in the fresh seafood. The 1895 brick building, once a brewery, is now an elegant restaurant, but you can enjoy lighter fare, too. Menu favorites include striped bass with tomato-basil buerre blanc and balsamic half chicken with spinach-herb gnocchi. The chef has a deft hand with hollandaise, making Sunday brunch inspired. You can eat at the busy mahogany bar too. | 528 Thames St. | 401/849–4002 | fax 401/847–4780 | $15–$22 | AE, MC, V.

Canfield House. American. A unique, old-fashioned-Newport restaurant that is housed in an old casino. The downstairs pub serves good pizza and pasta dishes. Try the pan-seared yellowfin tuna, Thai style. | 5 Memorial Blvd. | 401/847–0416 | fax 401/847–5754 | www.canfieldhouse.com | $12–$30 | AE, DC, MC, V.

Christie's of Newport. American. A classic Newport establishment that has great steaks and seafood overlooking the marina and Newport Harbor. Try the surf and turf. Open-air dining on patio bar overlooking the harbor. Entertainment. Kid's menu. Dock space. | 351 Thames St. | 401/847–5400 | $15–$35 | AE, D, MC, V.

Clarke Cooke House–Skybar. Contemporary. This 1743 sea captain's house in the heart of the waterfront is really three restaurants. First there's the elegant and formal third-floor Skybar with two dining areas; a trellised, protected porch; and the Gilbert Stuart Room, where crystal, silver, lavish floral displays and waiters in white tie set the tone for the superb menu. Favorites are rack of lamb *persillade* with caramelized onion, potato-turnip gratin, and minted tarragon glaze, and the lobster, either sautéed with sauce poivre-rose or in the shell. In winter, fireplaces blaze. | Bannister's Wharf | 401/849–2900 | fax 401/849–8750 | Closed Sun.–Thurs. in Nov.–May. No lunch | $27–$33 | AE, D, DC, MC, V.

Clarke Cooke House–The Candy Store and Grille. Contemporary. The spot for casual waterfront dining that's a favorite of the sailing crowd. You can sit in the first-floor Candy Store or the mezzanine level Grille. Both serve the same menu, but The Candy Store has open-air dining, marble tables, 15-ft ceilings, and boats plying the water a few yards away. In summer there's a raw bar. The Grille has large windows overlooking the the wharf and a fireplace with couches for cozy winter dining. Comfort foods like oven-roasted half chicken with whipped potatoes and roast garlic jus and steak-frites are big hits. When you feel like dancing, there's the Boom Boom Room disco in the basement. | Bannister's Wharf | 401/849–2900 | fax 401/849–8750 | No lunch Jan.–Apr. | $9–$26 | AE, D, DC, MC, V.

Elizabeth's Cafe. Eclectic. This is not a café at all, but a storefront restaurant serving platters of food for two (singles can order a half) in a busy Victorian-style room. There are comfy chairs, and you eat from Elizabeth's unmatched cutlery and china. One large platters (that could serve three) includes your entrée plus pasta, stuffed vegetable breads, sausage, and roasted red and green peppers and onions plus another vegetable. It's BYOB. | 404 Thames St. | 401/846–6862. No lunch. Closed Jan.–Mar. | $25–$32.

La Forge Casino. American. This casual, upscale restaurant is part of the Newport Casino. Built in the 1880's, it overlooks the grass courts of the International Tennis Hall of Fame. Open-air dining on sidewalk cafe. Pianist Fri. and Sat. Sunday brunch. Kid's menu. | 186 Bellevue Ave. | 401/847–0418 | $9–$25 | AE, MC, V.

La Petite Auberge. French. Once a private home, this 18th-century house now caters to those looking for traditional French cooking in a Colonial spot. Known for seafood, chicken. Open-air dining in a bistro-style cafe. | 19 Charles St. | 401/849–6669 | $15–$35 | AE, MC, V.

Le Bistro. French. This intimate establishment, known for the lighter cuisines of the south of France, has been a staple of Newport dining for more than two decades. Choose the fresh local seafood or try the Australian rack of lamb or the sea scallops paella. | 41 Bowen's Wharf | 401/849–7778 | $17–$30 | AE, D, DC, MC, V.

Lucia. Italian. This eatery has two personalities—an Italian restaurant and an even more casual pizzeria next door. The dining room is decorated with yellow and pink tablecloths and curtains; copper and art adorn the walls. Favorites on the northern Italian menu are *Ravioli alla Rucola* (white mushroom ravioli in a fresh tomato and arugula sauce) and *Vitello all'Aceto Balsamico* (veal scallopini sauteed with white wine, balsamic vinegar, black olives, and parsley). | 186B–190B Thames St. | 401/846–4477 | fax 401/848–9009 | Closed Mon. No lunch Tues. | MC, V.

★ **The Mooring.** Seafood. The quintessential Newport dining experience—great seafood, prepared both traditionally or inventively—plus a great view of the Newport "scene"—boats, boats, and more boats. Popular choices include the seafood scampi and lobster. There's open-air dining overlooking the harbor. Kid's menu. | Sayer's Wharf | 401/846–2260 | www.mooringrestaurant.com | Closed Mon.–Tues. in Nov.–Mar. | $15–$35 | AE, D, DC, MC, V.

Ocean Coffee Roasters. Café. As you enter this large, funky coffeehouse with local art and black-and-white tile floor, tables, and tall breakfast counter, you'll see the take-out area where you can buy fresh-roasted coffee by the pound. The bakery makes oversized muffins, muffin tops, scones (yummy raisin and Dutch apple), and desserts like chocolate mousse torte. Full breakfasts include a vegetarian sauté with sour cream and fresh salsa, house-made granola with fresh fruit, and real maple syrup. Lunches include smoked pork and turkey sandwiches. | 22 Washington Sq. | 401/846–6060 | www.oceancoffee.com | Breakfast also available | $3–$6 | MC, V.

The Place. Contemporary. Fantastic food is the draw at this simple, stylish restaurant with white tablecloths, flowers, and candles. The talented chef performs his magic in a range of cuisines: southwestern, Asian, French, and Pacific Rim. Try appetizers such as the roast duck enchilada with mango salsa, or the grilled Thai curried shrimp with lobster-mashed potatoes before moving onto the entrées—Chilean sea bass with a port wine glaze, scallops, wild mushrooms, and a sweet-pepper risotto; and rack of lamb. There's an extensive selection of wines by the glass, flights of wine are available, and the fine wine list has some unusual bottlings. | 28 Washington Sq. | 401/847–0125 | Call for hours | $18–$30 | AE, MC, V.

Pronto. Italian. The warm dining room has chandeliers, paintings, and palm trees. Try the penne with chicken, fresh basil, parmesan cream sauce, and toasted almonds. | 464 Thames St. | 401/847–5251 | www.prontonewport.com | No lunch weekdays Jan.–May | $11–$28 | AE, MC, V.

Puerini's Restaurant. Italian. Four dining rooms in this converted house, two upstairs and two down, can hardly contain the crowds that flock here. Northern and southern specialties include Italian comfort foods like lasagna and eggplant parmesan. A more contemporary spin comes from the swordfish, wood grilled and stuffed with crab, scallops, onions, rosemary, and cream; and linguini marsala, with chicken, mushrooms, marsala wine, pecorino cheese, and garlic. | 24 Memorial Blvd. W. | 401/847–5506 | No lunch | $11–$20 | MC, V.

Restaurant Bouchard. French. A 1785 post-and-beam house is home to classically trained chef Albert Bouchard. His presentations include the no-work (for you) Lobster Cardinal, with a truffled cognac sauce and gruyère cheese topping. A diminutive bar and fireplace add to the style of this lovely restaurant. | 505 Thames St. | 401/846–0123 | fax 401/841–8565 | www.restaurantbouchard.com | Closed Tues. No lunch | $19–$34 | AE, D, MC, V.

Rhumb Line. Contemporary. Just a block from the transportation center of Newport, this colonial restaurant is in a quiet residential neighborhood and is surrounded by 18th- and 19th-century homes. The wide-board floors, beams, and homespun curtains belie the contemporary menu: rosemary-rubbed lamb chops with tomato-mint sauce and Cajun grilled salmon with raspberry-orange sauce are typical. | 62 Bridge St. | 401/849–6950 | No lunch | $13–$20 | MC, V.

Salvation Cafe. Eclectic. Thai, Mexican, Indian, Vegetarian, Japanese, Sushi, and other ethnic cuisines are all deftly prepared at this storefront that has two funky outside patios in a courtyard. Inside there's a stainless steel-horseshoe bar and sectional sofa. The dining room mixes local art with flotsam from flea markets. The pad thai gets raves. | 140 Broadway | 401/847–2620 | No lunch | $8–$18 | AE, MC, V.

Scales & Shells. Seafood. Boisterous and fun describes the open and airy dining room with exposed kitchen at this busy restaurant. It is known for the lobster *fra diavlo*, a 1½ pound lobster, mussels, clams, and calamari, which are served with a spicy marinara sauce over linguini. Another signature dish is the Toro tuna, sushi-grade tuna marinated in soy, lemon, and garlic and wood-grilled. A smaller second-floor dining area called Upscales provides cozier, more intimate dining. | 527 Thames St. | 401/846–3474 | fax 401/848–7706 | Closed Mon. in Jan.–Mar. No lunch | $11–$23 | No credit cards.

White Horse Tavern. Continental. In business since the late 1600s, this is the oldest operating tavern in America. Don't let the simple though gracious setting fool you—the food is also excellent. Try the pan-seared mahimahi or the New Zealand rack of lamb. | 26 Marlborough St. | 401/849–3600 | Reservations essential | Jacket required | No lunch Tues. | $25–$38 | AE, D, DC, MC, V.

Yesterday's. American. In a 1930s building with original tin ceiling, tile floors, tables, and dark-wood booths, you'll discover much more than a place for burgers, chili, and ribs (although they're delicious here). Try the spinach salad with warm andoullie balsamic viniagrette with goat cheese and shrimp, or seasonal seafood like talapia with mango salsa. There are 36 microbrews on tap as well as an extensive wine selection. This is a sister restaurant to the Place, and they share an entrance. | 28 Washington Sq. | 401/847–0125 | $10–$20 | AE, MC, V.

Lodging

Admiral Benbow Inn. In a quiet residential neighborhood between Thames Street and Bellevue Avenue this 1855 Victorian Inn occupies a tree-shaded corner. Antiques decorate the rooms. Complimentary Continental breakfast. No TV in some rooms, TV in commmon area. No pets. No kids under 14. No smoking. | 93 Pelham St. | 401/848–8000 or 800/343–2863 | fax 401/848–8006 | 5star@admiralsinns.com | www.admiralsinns.com/benbow | 15 rooms (13 with showers only) | $85–$180 | AE, D, MC, V.

Admiral Farragut Inn. The meticulous restoration of this colonial-style bed-and-breakfast showcases its hardwood floors and exposed ceiling beams. Complimentary breakfast. TV in common area. | 31 Clarke St. | 401/848–8015 | fax 401/848–8017 | www.admiralsinns.com/farragut.html | 9 rooms (8 with shower only) | $85–$150 | AE, D, MC, V.

Admiral Fitzroy Inn. This European-style inn in the heart of Newport has uniquely decorated rooms with hand-stenciled walls and antiques. A roof deck provides harbor views. Complimentary breakfast. Refrigerators. No pets. No smoking. | 398 Thames St. | 401/848–8000 or 800/343–2863 | fax 401/848–8006 | 5star@admiralsinns.com | www.admiralsinns.com/fitzroy | 17 rooms | $175–$215 | AE, D, MC, V.

Best Western Mainstay Inn. This hotel near the beach has two private function rooms, a full-service restaurant, and entertainment during the summer season. It's just 1 mi from historic downtown Newport. Children under 12 stay free. Restaurant, bar with entertainment, room service. Cable TV. Pool. Business services, airport shuttle. Free parking. | 151 Admiral Kalbfus Rd. | 401/849–9880 | fax 401/849–4391 | www.bestwestern.com | 165 rooms | $119–$169 (2-night minimum stay on weekends) | AE, D, DC, MC, V.

Brinley Victorian Inn. A Victorian inn close to Bellevue Avenue that is actually two connected houses. One of the houses was built in 1850, the other in 1870. The rooms are decorated with a Victorian theme, and many have period antiques. There's also a courtyard with tables. Complimentary Continental breakfast. No room phones, no TV in rooms. Library. No kids under 8. No smoking. | 23 Brinley St. | 401/849–7645 or 800/999–8523 | fax 401/845–9634 | John@brinleyvictorian.com | www.brinleyvictorian.com | 16 rooms (6 with shower only) | $69–$199 | AE, MC, V.

★ **Castle Hill Inn & Resort.** On a 40-acre peninsula overlooking Naragansett Bay and the Atlantic Ocean, this beautifully renovated, turreted 1874 Victorian inn and adjacent beach houses have everything you could want, like marble showers, fireplaces, period furnishings, plus an award-winning chef whose breakfast specials include innovations like lobster hash. A full English tea is served each afternoon. There are hiking trails to the Castle Hill Lighthouse and a private beach. Restaurant, bar, complimentary breakfast. In-room data ports, some kitchenettes, some microwaves, some refrigerators, some in-room VCRs. Spa. Hiking, beach. Laundry service. No pets. No smoking. | 590 Ocean Ave. | 401/849–3800 | fax 401/849–3838 | info@castlehillinn.com | www.castlehillinn.com | 25 rooms | $275–$495 | AE, D, MC, V.

★ **Cliffside Inn.** This grand old home is near the start of the Cliff Walk and on a tree-lined street. It has a two-sided fireplace, antiques, some in-room fireplaces, and private patio gardens. Complimentary, breakfast. Some in-room hot tubs, cable TV. Beach. No kids under 13. No smoking. | 2 Seaview Ave. | 401/847–1811 or 800/845–1811 | fax 401/848–5850 | cliff@wsii.com | www.cliffsideinn.com | 8 rooms, 8 suites | $225–$355, $325–$480 (2-night minimum on weekends) | AE, D, MC, V.

Elm Tree Cottage. There are many personal touches at this amazing, 8,000-square-ft shingle-style Newport "cottage." Owner Priscilla Malone's concern for guests is evident—she accommodates special breakfast requests, provides turn-down service, bubblebath, tub pillows, and other amenities like razors and toothbrushes. Most rooms have fireplaces. Complimentary sherry and a concert grand player piano set the tone. Breakfast seating is at your own private table. Complimentary breakfast. Cable TV. No pets. No kids under 14. No smoking. | 336 Gibbs Ave. | 401/849–1610 or 800/ELMTREE | fax 401/849–2084 | www.elm-tree.com | $225–$295, $450 suite | Closed Dec.–Feb. | AE, MC, V.

Francis Malbone House. Designed by the architect responsible for the Touro Synagogue, this stately restored 18th-century colonial mansion was doubled in size in the mid-1990s to include rooms with hot tubs and fireplaces. Complimentary breakfast. In-room data ports, some in-room hot tubs, some room phones, cable TV. Business services. No smoking. | 392 Thames St. | 401/846–0392 or 800/846–0392 | fax 401/848–5956 | innkeeper@malbone.com | www.malbone.com | 16 rooms (2 with shower only), 2 suites | $205–$295, $345–$395 suites | AE, MC, V.

Harbor Base Pineapple Inn. This basic roadside motel is about 1 mi from downtown Newport. Low prices, a relatively quiet location, 27" TVs and in-room coffeemakers make this a favorite of budget travelers. There's a separate building for smokers. Some kitchenettes,

NEWPORT

INTRO
ATTRACTIONS
DINING
LODGING

some refrigerators. No pets. | 372 Coddington Hwy. | 401/847–2600 | fax 401/847–5230 | 47 rooms (17 with kitchenettes)in 5 buildings | $50–$109 | AE, D, DC, MC, V.

Hammett House Inn. At this five-room bed-and-breakfast with queen-size beds on historic Thames Street your breakfast will be delivered to your room each morning. The Federal Colonial building was built in 1785 and has individually decorated rooms. Restaurant, complimentary breakfast, room service. Cable TV. No smoking. | 505 Thames St. | 401/846–0400 or 800/548–9417 | fax 401/848–2258 | 5 rooms | $165–$185 | AE, D, MC, V.

Hotel Viking. This colonial-style building is on the National Historic Register. It was built in 1926 and has Georgian period furniture. In 1960, the hotel was expanded. Some of the rooms have Queen Anne–style furniture. Restaurant, bar with entertainment, room service. In-room data ports, cable TV. Indoor pool. Hot tub, sauna. Exercise equipment. Business services. | 1 Bellevue Ave. | 401/847–3300 or 800/556–7126 (outside RI) | fax 401/848–4864 | www.hotelviking.com | 226 rooms, 11 suites | $139–$349, $449–$1699 suites | AE, D, DC, MC, V.

Hyatt Regency Newport. This modern 264-room facility on Goat Island has views of the harbor and Newport Bridge. It houses the Newport Spa ($8 a day for guests; additional cost for massages, facials, and other services) and is a brief walk from downtown. It is next to the Marina and there is a heliport for guests. Restaurant, bar with entertainment, room service. In-room data ports. 2 pools (1 indoor). Beauty salon. Spa. Tennis. Exercise equipment. Business services. Free parking. | 1 Goat Island | 401/849–2600 | fax 401/846–7210 | www.hyatt.com | 247 rooms, 17 suites | $250–$310, $395–$675 | AE, D, DC, MC, V.

Inn at Newport Beach. Many rooms in this historic, renovated inn have ocean views. The inn is on the beach and just about 1 mi from downtown Newport. The rooms have either an ocean view or a view of Easton's Pond. Restaurant, bar, dining room, complimentary Continental breakfast, room service. Some refrigerators, cable TV. Beach. Business services. | Memorial Blvd. | 401/846–0310 or 800/786–0310 | fax 401/847–2621 | www.hotelviking.com/innatnewportbeach | 46 rooms, 4 suites | $109–$279, $329–$379 | AE, D, DC, MC, V.

Inn on Long Wharf. This time-share/hotel has suites with kitchenettes, hot tubs, and an outdoor deck overlooking the harbor. Some suites have harbor views with marble whirlpool baths. Beaches are nearby. Restaurant, bar, complimentary Continental breakfast. Kitchenettes, cable TV. Free parking. | 142 Long Wharf | 401/847–7800 or 800/225–3522 (outside RI) | fax 401/845–0217 | www.eastern-resorts.com | 40 suites | $220–$300 | AE, D, DC, MC, V.

Inn on the Harbor. Near a marina and the bustling city pier, this time-share/hotel has suites with kitchenettes and a lively restaurant with a view of the harbor on the ground floor. Restaurant, bar with entertainment. Kitchenettes, cable TV. Hot tub, sauna. Exercise equipment. Free parking. | 359 Thames St. | 401/849–6789 or 800/225–3522 (outside RI) | fax 401/849–2680 | www.eastern-resorts.com | 58 suites | $150–$280 | AE, D, DC, MC, V.

Inntowne. This warm, personal inn just off the hustle-bustle of Thames Street has individually decorated, cozy rooms. The rooms on the upper floors are quieter. Tea is served in the afternoon. Complimentary Continental breakfast. TV in common area. No pets. | 6 Mary St. | 401/846–9200 or 800/457–7803 | fax 401/846–1534 | www.newportri.com/users/inntowne | 17 rooms | $174–$204 | AE, MC, V.

★ **Ivy Lodge.** This bed-and-breakfast in the Mansion District is just two blocks from Cliff Walk. The Victorian inn has large rooms, 11 fireplaces, a wraparound porch, and a three-story Gothic turned baluster staircase. It is ½ mi from the beach. Complimentary breakfast. No room phones, no TV in rooms. No smoking. | 12 Clay St. | 401/849–6865 or 800/834–6865 | fax 401/849–0704 | innkeepers@ivylodge.com | www.ivylodge.com | 7 rooms, 1 suite | $165–$205, $300 suite | AE, MC, V.

Marriott. This luxury hotel on the harbor at Long Wharf has rooms with large decks overlooking the waterfront. The suites have a parlor room separated by French doors, whirlpool baths, and a harbor view. Restaurant, bars, room service. Cable TV, in-room data ports.

Indoor pool. Hot tub, sauna. Exercise equipment, racquetball. Laundry facilities, laundry service. Business services. Parking (fee). | 25 America's Cup Ave. | 401/849–1000 or 800/458–3066 | fax 401/849–3422 | www.marriott.com | 312 rooms, 7 suites | $261–$285, $300–$1000 suites | AE, D, DC, MC, V.

Melville House. This hotel close to Historic Hill and downtown has small but comfortable rooms and a new fireplace suite. The suite is available during the winter months only. Complimentary breakfast. No room phones. No kids under 14. | 39 Clarke St. | 401/847–0640 | fax 401/847–0956 | innkeeper@ids.net | www.melvillehouse.com | 7 rooms (2 with shared bath), 1 suite | $125–$165, $175 suite (winter only) | AE, D, MC, V.

Mill Street Inn. A contemporary inn in a restored turn-of-the-century mill with suites and a spectacular view from the rooftop deck. You'll find complimentary daily newspapers and the Sunday *New York Times*. Two-story town-house suites are also available. Complimentary Continental breakfast. Minibars, some refrigerators, cable TV. Business services. | 75 Mill St. | 401/849–9500 or 888/645–5784 | fax 401/848–5131 | millstreet@travelbase.com | www.millstreetinn.com | 23 suites | $115–$275 | AE, DC, MC, V.

Newport Harbor Hotel & Marina. This hotel is in the heart of downtown Newport and has great views from the sundeck of yachts in the harbor; ask for a room with a balcony and a water view. Restaurant, bar, room service. Cable TV. Indoor pool. Laundry facilities. Business services. Parking (fee, in summer). | 49 America's Cup Ave. | 401/847–9000 or 800/955–2558 | fax 401/849–6380 | www.newporthotel.com | 132 rooms, 1 suite | $269–$289, $699–$999 suite | AE, D, DC, MC, V.

Pilgrim House Inn. A charming bed-and-breakfast in an old home in the heart of historic Newport, close to restaurants, shops, and the harbor. It has a rooftop deck and water views. The rooms are furnished with antiques. Complimentary Continental breakfast. No room phones, no TV in rooms, TV in common area. No kids under 12. No smoking. | 123 Spring St. | 401/846–0040 or 800/525–8373 | fax 401/848–0357 | innkeeper@pilgrimhouseinn.com | www.pilgrimhouseinn.com | 11 rooms (2 with shared bath) | $100–$205 | MC, V.

Sanford-Covell Villa Marina. This impressive waterfront Victorian home with a majestic, 35-ft entrance hall was built in 1869 by architect William Ralph Emerson. A saltwater pool, dock with seating, and wraparound porch adds to the inn's charm, as do original details like parquet floors, walnut wainscoting, and frescoes. The porch swing was featured on *This Old House*. Complimentary Continental breakfast. No air-conditioning, no room phones, no TV. Heated pool. Laundry facilities. Some pets allowed. No smoking. | 72 Washington St. | 401/847–0206 | fax 401/848–5599 | www.sanford-covell.com | 5 rooms (2 with shared bath) | $160–$295 | AE, DC, MC, V.

★ **Vanderbilt Hall.** A 50-room luxury hotel built in 1909 by the Vanderbilt family in the historic downtown section of Newport. It's a short walk from the harbor. The rooms have antique furnishings. Restaurant, dining room, room service. Cable TV. Indoor pool. Hot tub, massage, sauna, steam room. Gym. Laundry service. Airport shuttle. Parking (fee). No kids under 12. | 41 Mary St. | 401/846–6200 or 888/VANHALL | fax 401/846–8701 | www.vanderbilthall.com | 42 rooms, 8 suites | $195–$565, $445–$795 suites | AE, D, DC, MC, V.

Victorian Ladies. A romantic Victorian inn with award-winning gardens close to the beach. Each room is individually decorated with antique or reproduction furniture, and many rooms have four-poster beds. Complimentary breakfast. Some room phones. Library. No kids under 10. No smoking. | 63 Memorial Blvd. | 401/849–9960 | fax 401/849–9960 | info@victorianladies.com | www.victorianladies.com | 11 rooms | $175–$225 | Closed Jan. | MC, V.

Villa Liberte. In this 1910 Italian villa–style building just off renowned Bellevue Avenue rooms have canopy beds or four posters. The buffet breakfast is expansive. Complimentary Continental breakfast. Cable TV. No pets. No smoking. | 22 Liberty St. | 401/846–7444 | fax 401/849–6429 | www.villaliberte.com | 9 rooms,(7 with shower only); 6 suites | $135–$185, $195–$225 suites | AE, DC, MC, V.

The Willows. This charming bed-and-breakfast with a rose-filled garden offers many extras, including breakfast in bed. The canopy beds are also a nice detail. Complimentary Continental breakfast. No room phones. | 8 Willow St. | 401/846–5486 | fax 401/849–8215 | www.newportri.com/users/willows | 6 rooms (3 with shower only) | $158–$278 | No credit cards.

NORTH KINGSTOWN

MAP 3, K4

(Nearby towns also listed: Jamestown, Kingston, Narragansett)

This town on Narragansett Bay is the most varied of Rhode Island towns. The colonial village of Wickford is known for its scenic harbor, dozens of 18th- and 19th-century homes, and antiques and curiosity shops. South of town is a Colonial farmhouse–turned–museum, and rolling seaside farmland. To the north is a massive airfield known as Quonset Point. The state is considering a controversial plan to turn the abandoned facility into an international port for container ships.

Information: South County Tourism Council | Stedman Government Center, 4808 Tower Hill Rd., Wakefield, 02879 | 401/789–4422 or 800/548–4662 | fax 401/789–4437 | sctc@netsense.net | www.southcountyri.com.

Attractions

Gilbert Stuart Birthplace. On a country road running along little Mattatuxet River is the birthplace of Gilbert Stuart, America's foremost portraitist of George Washington. The house was built in 1751 and the adjacent 18th-century snuff mill was the first in America. | 815 Gilbert Stuart Rd., Saunderstown | 401/294–3001 | fax 401/294–3869 | $3 | Apr.–Oct., Thurs.–Mon. 11–4.

Old Narragansett Church. Now called St. Paul's, the Old Naragansett Church was built in 1707. It's one of the oldest Episcopal churches in America. It also houses one of the oldest church organs in North America. | Church La. | 401/294–4357 | Free | July–early Sept., Fri.–Mon. 11–4.

Silas Casey Farm. This mid-18th-century homestead still functions as a working farm. Surrounded by fields, barns, and stone walls, the house overlooks Narragansett Bay and Conanicut Island and contains family paintings, prints, china, furniture, and political and military documents from the 18th to the 20th centuries. | 2325 Boston Neck Rd., Saunderstown | 401/294–1370 | fax 401/295–1030 | $3 | June–Oct., Tues., Thurs., and Sat. 1–5.

Smith's Castle. Smith's Castle was built in 1678 by Richard Smith, Jr., on the site of an early trading post established by Roger Williams, the founder of Rhode Island. Nearby is one of the first military burial sites in the country; 40 colonists who died in the Great Swamp Fight in 1675 are interred here. In the mid-18th century the house was enlarged in the Georgian style seen today. | 55 Richard Smith Dr., Wickford | 401/294–3521 | $3 | May and Sept.–Oct., Fri.–Sun. noon–4; June–Aug., Thurs.–Mon. noon–4, or by appointment.

★ **Wickford Village.** The Colonial village of Wickford—in the town of North Kingstown—has a popular harbor, dozens of 18th- and 19th-century homes, and antiques and curiosity shops. The whitewashed village was the setting for John Updike's novel *The Witches of Eastwick*. | Rte. 1 A, W. Main St., and Main St. | 401/295–5566.

ON THE CALENDAR

JULY: *Wickford Art Festival.* Held on the sidewalks of Wickford, this is one of the country's largest and best arts festivals, featuring paintings, photographs, and sculpture. | Wickford Village | 401/294–6840.

AUG.: *International Quahog Festival.* Rhode Island's state shellfish is celebrated with entertainment and contests, including a baked stuffed quahog cook-off, clam shucking, and bull-raking at the Wickford Festival Grounds. | 401/885–4118.

DEC.: *Festival of Lights.* The festivities include the lighting of the tree, live music, and hayrides through the illuminated village streets. | Wickford Village | 401/295–5566.

Dining

Duffy's Tavern. Seafood. This very casual place seats 300 inside plus 500 on the outside patio. Come for the fresh seafood prepared to order. With a 5,000-pound live-lobster holding system, you can be pretty sure they won't run out of lobsters. The Cajun tuna, sword and catfish, lobster pie, and shore dinners are also popular. You can also purchase seafood packed to go. | 235 Tower Hill Rd., Wickford, | 401/294–3733 | fax 401/295–4441 | www.quahog.com | $6–$27 | AE, MC, V.

Lodging

Best Western Monte Vista Inn. This chain option is just outside Wickford Village on U.S. 1. Children under 12 stay free. Restaurant, complimentary Continental breakfast. Some kitchenettes, cable TV. Pool. Spa. Laundry service. Free parking. | 7075 Post Rd. | 401/884–8000 | fax 401/884–5080 | www.bestwestern.com | 46 rooms | $99–$110 | AE, DC, D, MC, V.

Hamilton Village Inn. This basic motel, about 1½ mi south of Wickford Village, has been renovated with contemporary furnishings. Restaurant. Laundry facilities. No pets. | 642 Boston Neck Rd. (Rte. 1A) | 401/295–0700 or 800/596–0003 | fax 401/294–9044 | 31 rooms (28 with showers only). 3 apartments have full kitchens, 1 room has kitchenette | $70–$100 | Closed Jan.–Apr. | AE, D, MC, V.

PAWTUCKET

MAP 3, K2

(Nearby towns also listed: Cumberland, Lincoln, Providence)

In Algonkian, "petuket" means "waterfalls." A small village was established at the falls in 1670 by Joseph Jenks, Jr., who considered the area a prime spot for an iron forge. Using the ready supply of timber and iron ore, his company manufactured plows, anchors, and scythes. When Samuel Slater arrived 120 years later, he was delighted to find a corps of skilled mechanics ready to assist him in his dream of organizing America's first factory system. Though not an attractive town at first glance, Pawtucket has hidden splendors.

Information: **Blackstone Valley Tourism Council** | 175 Main St., Pawtucket, 02860 | 401/724–2200 or 800/454–2882 (outside RI) | www.tourblackstone.com.

Attractions

Blackstone Valley Explorer. This 34-ft-long, 49-passenger, open riverboat cruises the Blackstone River and Canal. The 45-minute trips departing from various locations along the river are especially pleasant in fall, when the foliage is at its peak. | Blackstone Valley Visitors Center, 175 Main St. | 401/724–1500 or 800/619–2628 | fax 401/724–1342 | $5 | Late Apr.–early Nov., weekends, group tours during weekdays, call for hours.

Blackstone Valley Visitors Center. Stop in here for information on the entire Blackstone Valley. You'll find an information kiosk filled with brochures and a knowledgeable staff. There's also a free 19-minute video on the area. Tours of the Samuel Slater Mill are run from here. | 175 Main St. | 401/724–2200 | Free | Daily 9–5.

Pawtucket Red Sox. The Triple-A farm team of the Boston Red Sox plays at the newly expanded McCoy Stadium. | 1 Columbus Ave. | 401/724–7300 | $5–$7 | info@pawsox.com | www.pawsox.com | Call for schedule.

Slater Memorial Park. Within this stately park that stretches along Ten Mile River are pic-nic tables, tennis courts, playgrounds, a river walk, and two historic sites. | Newport Ave., off Rte. 1A | 401/728–0500 | Free | Daily dawn–dusk.

Daggett House. Eight generations of Daggetts lived in this house, Pawtucket's oldest home, which was built in 1685 to replace an earlier one destroyed in King Philip's War. Among the 17th-century antiques on display are bedspreads owned by Samuel Slater. | Slater Memorial Park | 401/722–2631 | $2 | June–Sept., weekends 2–5.

The Loof Carousel. Built by Charles I. D. Loof, this carousel's 42 horses, three dogs, lion, camel, and giraffe are the earliest examples of the Danish immigrant's work. | Slater Memorial Park | 401/728–0500 (ext. 252) | 25¢ | July–Labor Day, daily 10–5; late Apr.–June and Labor Day–mid-Oct., weekends 10–5.

Slater Mill Historic Site. In 1793 Samuel Slater and two Providence merchants built this, the first factory in America to produce cotton yarn from water-powered machines. The yellow clapboard Slater Mill Historic Site houses classrooms, a theater, and machinery illus-trating the conversion of raw cotton to finished cloth. A 16,000-pound waterwheel pow-ers an operational 19th-century machine shop; it and the adjacent 1758 Sylvanus Brown House, furnished according to an inventory taken in 1824, are open to the public. | 67 Roo-sevelt Ave., at Main St. | 401/725–8638 | fax 401/722–3040 | www.slatermill.org | $6.50 | June–Oct., Tues.–Sat. 10–5, Sun. 1–5; Mar.–May and Nov.–late Dec., weekends 1–5.

ON THE CALENDAR

JUNE: *Arts in the Park Performance Series*. Public art is shown and performed in pub-lic areas throughout the city. | 401/724–2200 or 800/454–2882.

OCT.: *Octoberfest Parade and Craft Fair*. A German beer garden with live entertain-ment, arts and crafts, and ethnic foods are all part of the fun at this festival sponsored by the Pawtucket Jaycees. | 401/726–1100.

Dining

Modern Diner. American. This 1941 diner was the first to be listed on the National Regis-ter of Historic Places. It's a diner with a difference—most don't serve lobster benedict, cus-tard French toast with fresh fruit, or sundried-tomato and caramelized-onion omelets. It's in a working-class neighborhood on the outskirts of Pawtucket | 364 East Ave. | 401/726–8390 | Breakfast also available. No dinner | $2–$8 | No credit cards.

Lodging

Comfort Inn. In the historic Blackstone Valley just north of Providence, this five-story hotel is just 1 mi south of Slater Mill. Restaurant, bar, complimentary Continental breakfast. Some refrigerators, cable TV. Pool. Laundry facilities. Business services. Free parking. | 2 George St. | 401/723–6700 | fax 401/726–6380 | www.comfortinn.com | 131 rooms, 4 suites | $110–$120, $159–$225 suites | AE, D, DC, MC, V.

PORTSMOUTH

MAP 3, L4

(Neaby towns also listed: Bristol, Middletown, Tiverton)

Founded in 1638 by Anne Hutchinson, Portsmouth is the second-oldest settlement in Rhode Island. It was established under the principle of absolute religious freedom for all, as specified in the Portsmouth Compact of 1638. The town is rife with history, yet it features just a few historic sights geared to tourists. Most travelers simply pass through the town on the way to Newport, which is on the same island, Aquidneck.

Information: Newport County Convention and Visitors Bureau | 23 America's Cup Ave., Newport, 02840 | 401/849–8048 or 800/976–5122 | www.gonewport.com.

Attractions

Green Animals Topiary Gardens. The gardens on this Victorian estate are filled with plants sculpted to look like animals, including an elephant, a camel, a giraffe, and even a teddy bear. There is also a remarkable toy collection and plant shop. | 380 Corys La. | 401/683–1267 | fax 401/847–1361 | www.newportmansions.org | $9 | May–Oct., daily 10–5.

Greenvale Vineyards. Take a stroll and enjoy breathtaking views of the Sakonnet River from the acres of vineyards, then visit the tasting room, a faithful restoration of the 1863 Victorian stable. Vineyard tours are at 2 daily. | 582 Wapping Rd. | 401/847–3777 | fax 401/846–0507 | www.greenvale.com | Free | Mon.–Sat. 10–5, Sun. noon–5.

Old Union Church. This church was home to a 19th-century fundamentalist sect that provided a forum for the abolitionist movement and counted Julia Ward Howe and William Ellery Channing among its members. Today it serves as a museum and houses a large collection of artifacts of Portsmouth's coal-mining days, as well as tools and arrowheads from the local Native American tribes, and many possessions from Julia Ward Howe's Union Street house, including her writing desk and a lace cap. | Corner of E. Main St. and Union St. | 401/683–9178 | Sun. 2–4 | Free.

Portsmouth Abbey Chapel. The chapel of this Benedictine Abbey and prestigious private school for boys is open to the public. Officially called the Chapel of St. Gregory, it's an example of contemporary design at its most beautiful. Designed by Pietro Belluschi, it contains a wire sculpture by Richard Lippold. | 285 Corys La. | 401/683–2000 | fax 401/683–5888 | www.portsmouthabbey.com | Free | Daily 8–4:30; tours by appointment.

Sandy Point Beach. This tranquil beach has lifeguards, a snack shack, bath facilities, and a picnic area. | Sandy Point Rd. | 401/683–0449 | $5 per car weekdays; $10 per car weekends | Daily 9–6; no services Sept.–May.

ON THE CALENDAR
JUNE–SEPT.: *Newport International Polo Series.* Polo matches between international teams take place at the Glen Farm Polo Fields. | East Main Rd. | 401/846–0200.

Dining

Flo's Drive-In. Seafood. The quintessential clam shack that has everything except restrooms. You can eat at picnic tables outside or take your selection away. | Park Ave., Island Park | No phone | Closed Nov.–Mar. | $8–$17 | No credit cards.

Sea Fare Inn. American. This Victorian mansion was built in 1887 and has 10 acres with gardens. It's known for great seafood dishes such as baked stuffed lobster tail, and charcoal-grilled swordfish. | 3352 E. Main Rd. | 401/683–0577 | Closed Sun.–Mon. | $18–$27 | AE, MC, V.

Lodging

Best Western Bay Point Inn and Conference Center. Less than 20 minutes from Newport, this hotel is near the beach. Restaurant, bar. Some in-room data ports, satellite TV. Indoor pool. Exercise equipment. Business services. | 144 Anthony Rd. | 401/683–3600 | fax 401/683–6690 | www.bestwestern.com | 84 rooms, 1 suite | $89–$149, $120–$150 suite | AE, D, DC, MC, V.

Bestemor's Hus. The owner of this Scandinavian bed-and-breakfast (the name means grandmother's house) is of Norwegian stock. In a 1931 Colonial-style home on 2 tree-filled acres, the inn's guest rooms have eclectic furnishings with some Scandinavian touches. The Scandinavian room is Danish modern, the English room has a mahogany four-poster, and the Colonial has antiques and a cannonball bed. There is croquet and horseshoes on the property. Complimentary breakfast. No room phones. No pets. No smoking. | 31 W. Main Rd. (Rte. 114) | 401/683–1176 | bestemor31@aol.com | members.aol.com/bestemor31/home/index.htm | 3 rooms with shared baths | $110 | Closed Dec.–Mar. | MC, V.

Founder's Brook Motel. This motel is near the junction of Routes 138 and 24. The suites are separate from the motel, in country-style cabins. Picnic area. Some kitchenettes, some in-room hot tubs, cable TV. Laundry facilities. Pets allowed (fee). | 314 Boyd's La. | 401/683–1244 or 800/334–8765 | fax 401/683–9129 | 8 rooms, 24 suites | $69–$119, $89–$139 suites | AE, D, DC, MC, V.

PROVIDENCE

MAP 3, K2

(Nearby towns also listed: Lincoln, Pawtucket, Warwick, Warren)

The 1998 inauguration of an outdoor ice rink in formerly unremarkable Kennedy Plaza amounted to a debutante ball for Providence, replete with marching bands, fireworks, and speeches. Long considered an awkward stepchild of greater Boston even by its own residents, Providence is beginning to shuck its inferiority complex. In the past five years, rivers have been rerouted, and unsightly railroad tracks have been put underground; dilapidated neighborhoods are being rejuvenated; a convention center and a riverfront park have opened; an upscale shopping mall was constructed, and many travelers now prefer revamped T. F. Green Airport in nearby Warwick to Boston's Logan Airport.

Behind renascent Providence is its personable mayor, elected to his sixth term in 1998, Vincent "Buddy" Cianci, who markets his own pasta sauce and has become a sought-after authority on rejuvenating American cities. Cianci recently forged a cultural exchange program with Florence, Italy (the real Renaissance city), which promises to bring Italian art and artisans to Providence. Time spent courting Hollywood deal makers has resulted in a string of movies being filmed in the city, including *There's Something About Mary* and *Outside Providence,* and the NBC drama *Providence.*

The city is now recognized nationally as a gastronomic hotbed. For a city of less than 200,000 residents, its restaurant offerings at times seem dizzying; increasingly the city attracts diners from Massachusetts and Connecticut.

Roger Williams founded Providence in 1636 as a refuge for freethinkers and religious dissenters escaping the Puritanical dictates of the Massachusetts Bay Colony, and it remains a community willing to embrace independent thinking. Providence is striving to have its once-abandoned downtown (euphemistically called Downcity) populated by artists and art studios. A state referendum has exempted such artists from income taxes. Such statewide support is not surprising; improvements in Providence are typically a boon to the rest of the state. Because it's so integral to the rest of Rhode Island, Providence is sometimes called the city-state of Rhode Island.

Information: Providence Warwick Convention and Visitors Bureau | 1 W. Exchange St., 3rd floor, Providence, 02903 | 401/274–1636 or 800/233–1636 | fax 401/351–2090 | information@providencecvb.com | www.providencecvb.com.

NEIGHBORHOODS

East Side. The architectural heart of Providence's East Side is Benefit Street with its "Mile of History." In 1758 Benefit Street was created "for the common benefit of all" to relieve congestion on Main Street. It was built along a path of existing gardens, orchards, and cemeteries. Today, the majestic merchants' homes of the 18th and 19th century mix with more modest architecture, as well as institutional buildings, courthouses, clubs, and schools. The East Side is home to Brown University and the Rhode Island School of Design, and nearby Thayer Street boasts an amazing array of diverse eating establishments, many catering to students. The Avon Cinema, bookstores, and interesting shops dot the neighborhood as well.

Federal Hill. No visit to Providence would be complete without a visit to Federal Hill. Known as Providence's Italian section, this unique neighborhood welcomes you with a tall arch and Italian pine cone, *La Pigna,* a bronze symbol of fine food. You'll hear Italian and accented English being spoken, reinforcing the feeling that you're in another country, as you wander through the many wonderful and fascinating Italian markets, shops, restaurants, bakeries, and cafés. But The Hill isn't entirely Italian; there is significant ethnic diversity, particularly with a recent Hispanic influx. You'll find a mix of restaurants that represent cultures other than Italy. Steps away from Atwells Avenue, the main street, you'll discover mixed architecture, with early 18th-century and Victorian buildings. A walk on the nearby streets—Bond, Jones, and Mountain—reveals some sweet little houses, in various states of renovation, and the scale of buildings and streets is noteworthy. When you're done walking, stop at a café at the fountained square called DePasquale Plaza for espresso and that favorite Italian dessert, tirimisu.

Fox Point. One of the first settled sections of Rhode Island, this neighborhood is on a peninsula originally known as Foxes Hill; it borders College Hill to the north, I–195 to the south, and the Providence and Seekonk rivers to the west and east. It was once a major seaport for Providence. The Portuguese, who came here in the second half of the 19th century to work on the Fox Point waterfront, continue to dominate the ethnic makeup of the area. Students from nearby Brown and the Rhode Island School of Design live here as well. Wickenden Street—vibrant with ethnic restaurants, galleries, and antiques shops—is one of the liveliest areas of Providence. The construction of I–195 eliminated much of the southern section of Fox Point, and the waterfront area is no longer a commercial harbor, having been replaced by India Point Park.

TRANSPORTATION INFORMATION

Airports: Providence and the surrounding area is served by the T. F. Green Airport in Warwick, a southern suburb off I–95, about 15 minutes from downtown. Major commercial airlines offer regularly scheduled flights. | 401/737–8222 or 888/268–7222.

Amtrak serves Providence from its centrally located station at 100 Gaspee St. | 401/727–7382 or 800/USA–RAIL.

Driving Around Town: The center of downtown Providence is bordered on the west side by I–95 and on the south by I–195. There's only a suggestion of a grid system with loops, curves, and many one-way streets, making it confusing to drive.

Your best bet in this relatively small area is to park your car and walk. There are plenty of parking lots. The one at the new Providence Place Mall (take exit 21 from I–95 and follow signs) generally has space, and parking here is validated. From here you can take one of the trolleys that make city touring so convenient, at 50¢ per trip with all day passes available. The trolleys are run by RIPTA (Rhode Island Public Transit Authority). For information call 401/781–9400 or www.ripta.com. They run every 10 to 15 minutes.

Although the trolleys go to Federal Hill, the East Side, and Fox Point as well as downtown, if you decide to drive to these neighborhoods, you can generally find parking on the side streets. Watch out for residential parking prohibitions though, meter checkers are on duty weekdays from 8 to 4. Meters cost 25¢ per quarter hour. Some parking meters limit you to a maximum of two hours, so watch out. Overtime parking can get you a $10 ticket. You might pay $15 if you park near a hydrant, within 50 feet of a corner or in a space for handicapped. Park in a marked tow zone and you risk a $50 ticket and the towing of your vehicle. You must stop for pedestrians in crosswalks.

The lack of adequate signage, which is being addressed, makes attractions hard to find. Your best bet is to go to the Roger Williams National Memorial Park (not to be confused with the Roger Williams Park Zoo, well outside of downtown) at 282 North Main Street, where you can park for free while you get directions on points of interest, current activities, maps of the city, historical information, and brochures on guided and self-directed walking tours. Hours are daily from 9 to 4:30. Another spot for information, within easy walking distance of the mall, is the Providence Visitor Information Center, in the Rhode Island Convention Center Rotunda, on the ground floor, at 1 Sabin Street. It's open Monday through Saturday from 9 to 4, and the phone number is 401/751–1177.

Attractions

ART AND ARCHITECTURE

Governor Henry Lippitt House Museum. Lippitt made his family fortune in the textile industry, and in 1865 he built this aristocratic Victorian mansion. Must-sees are the faux finishes, wood graining, and hand stenciling in the eight rooms open to the public on two floors, and a newly restored cast-iron water fountain in the back garden that stands a spectacular 28 ft tall. | 199 Hope St. | 401/453–0688 | fax 401/453–8221 | $5 | By appointment.

★ **John Brown House.** John Quincy Adams called this house "the most magnificent and elegant private mansion that I have ever seen on this continent." Designed by Joseph Brown for his brother in 1786, the three-story Georgian residence has elaborate woodwork and is filled with decorative art, furniture, silver, and items from the China trade, on which John Brown made his fortune. In addition to opening trade with China, John Brown is famous for his role in the burning of the British customs ship *Gaspee*. | 52 Power St., at Benefit St. | 401/331–8575 | $6 | Mar.–Dec., Tues.–Sat. 10–5, Sun. noon–4; Jan.–Feb., by appointment.

Market House. Built by Joseph Brown in 1773, and now owned by the Rhode Island School of Design, this brick market house was stragecially placed at the edge of the Providence River. Here farmers and tradespeople crossed the bridge to sell their produce and wares. An early tea party, as a protest against taxation, resulted in the burning of precious tea leaves at Market House in 1775. Originally a two-story building, the first floor had open arches for market sales. The building is not open to the public but plaques outside detail its significance to the history of Providence. | Market Sq. at College and S. Main Sts.

Old State House. On May 4, 1776, the Rhode Island Assembly formally renounced allegiance to King George III on this spot. Today the Old State House serves as the offices of the Rhode Island Heritage Commission and the Rhode Island Historical Preservation Commission. | 150 Benefit St. | 401/277–2678 | fax 401/222–2968 | Free | Weekdays 8:30–4:30.

Rhode Island Black Heritage Society. A permanent exhibit, "Creative Survival," takes a comprehensive look at 19th-century black Rhode Island. Documents, photographs, advertisements, bibles, black mason's attire, early tools, cooking utensils and more create this fascinating look at black history. If you have time, take the informative tour that runs about 1½ hours. | 229 Westminster St. | 401/751–3490 | fax 401/751–0040 | $4 (suggested) | Weekdays 10–4, Sat. by appointment.

Rhode Island State Capitol. Rhode Island's awe-inspiring capitol, erected in 1904, has the first unsupported marble dome in the United States (and the fourth largest in the world). It was modeled on St. Peter's Basilica in Rome. The ornate, white, Georgian-style marble exterior is topped by the gilded statue, *Independent Man*. The interior's focal point is a full-length portrait of George Washington by Rhode Islander Gilbert Stuart, the same artist who created the likeness on the dollar bill. You'll also see the original parchment charter granted to the colony in 1663 by King Charles II, as well as military accoutrements of Nathaniel Greene, Washington's second-in-command during the Revolutionary War. Booklets are available for self-guided tours. A gift shop is located on the basement level. | 82 Smith St. | 401/277–2357 | fax 401/222–1404 | www.state.ri.us | Free | Weekdays 8:30–4:30, guided tours by appointment.

BEACHES, PARKS, AND NATURAL SITES

Roger Williams Park. This beautiful 430-acre Victorian park is immensely popular. You can have a picnic, feed the ducks in the lakes, ride a pony, or rent a paddleboat or miniature speedboat. At Carousel Village, kids can ride the vintage carousel or a miniature train. The tennis center has Rhode Island's only public clay courts. | Elmwood Ave. | 401/785–9450 | Free | Daily 7 AM–9 PM.

Museum of Natural History. In addition to the Cormack Planetarium, this museum in Roger Williams Park has exhibits on Narragansett Bay. | Elmwood Ave. | 401/785–9450 | fax 401/461–5146 | www.osfn.org/museum | $2 | Daily 10–5.

Roger Williams Park Zoo. This zoo has polar bear and penguin exhibits, a Tropical Rainforest Pavilion, an open-air aviary, and an African Savannah exhibit with elephants, giraffes, and cheetahs. There are more than 950 animals of 150 different species in all. It's at Exit 17, off I–95. | 1000 Elmwood Ave. | 401/785–3510 | www.rogerwilliamsparkzoo.org | $6 | May–Oct., weekdays 9–5, weekends 9–6; Nov.–Apr. daily 9–4.

Waterplace Park and Riverwalk. This 4-acre park was a key component in Providence's recent revitalization effort. The Venetian-style footbridges, cobblestone walkways, and an amphitheater surrounding a tidal pond have won design awards. The riverwalk passes the junction of three rivers—the Woonasquatucket, Providence, and Moshassock. On sunny summer days the parks attracts pedestrians, boaters, artists, and performers. The amphitheater hosts free concerts and plays. Inquire about upcoming events at the visitor information center. | Visitors Center, 1 Sabin St. | 401/751–1177 or 800/233–1636 | Free | Mon.–Sat. 10–4.

CULTURE, EDUCATION, AND HISTORY

Brown University. The nation's seventh-oldest college was founded in 1764. This Ivy League institution has more than 40 academic departments, including a school of medicine. Gothic and Beaux Arts structures dominate the campus, which has been designated a National Historic Landmark. University tours leave from the admissions office, in the Corliss-Brackett House. Thayer Street is the campus's principal commercial thoroughfare. | 45 Prospect St. | 401/863–2378 or 401/863–2703 | fax 401/863–9300 | www.brown.edu | Daily.

David Winton Bell Gallery. This imposing modern structure in the Albert and Vera List Art Center is designed by Philip Johnson. The gallery has varied exhibitions, including major works of historical and contemporary art on loan from private collections. | 64 College St. | 401/863–2932 | fax 401/863–9323 | Free | www.brown.edu | Sept.–early July, weekdays 11–4, weekends 1–4.

John Carter Brown Library. This independently funded and administered research library is affiliated with Brown University. It is one of the world's outstanding libraries in the field of Americana. Among some 40,000 volumes are numerous books and pamphlets describing the growth of the American colonies and the impact on Europe of the discovery of the New World. An extensive collection of maps dates from 1477 to the mid-19th century. | George and Brown Sts. | 401/863–2725 | fax 401/863–3477 | www.brown.edu | Free | Weekdays 8:30–5, Sat. 9–noon; closed during school breaks.

John Hay Library. Built in 1910 and named for Abraham Lincoln's secretary, "the Hay" houses 11,000 items related to the 16th president. The non-circulating library also stores American drama and poetry collections, 500,000 pieces of American sheet music, the Webster Knight Stamp Collection, the letters of science-fiction and horror writer H. P. Lovecraft, military prints, and a world-class collection of toy soldiers. | 20 Prospect St. | 401/863–2146 | fax 401/863–2093 | www.brown.edu | Free | Weekdays, 9–5.

University Hall. This hall off Prospect Street is the university's oldest building, built in 1770 when the college moved to Providence from Warren. It served as a barracks for colonial troops and their French allies during the Revolution. | Prospect St. | 401/863–2453 | www.brown.edu | Daily.

Governor Stephen Hopkins House. Twice George Washington visited this early clapboard house with an 18th-century parterre garden. Governor Hopkins, one of Rhode Island's two signatories to the Declaration of Independence, lived in the house from 1742 to 1785. Hopkins was governor of Rhode Island 10 times, chief justice of the Superior Court, and Chancellor of Brown University. He is credited with moving the university to Providence from Warren. | Benefit and Hopkins Sts. | 401/751–7067 | Apr.–Dec., Wed. and Sat. 1–4, or by appointment.

Johnson and Wales University. Internationally recognized for its culinary institute, Johnson and Wales is the largest institution of higher learning in the field of hospitality in the United States. It offers two- and four-year degree programs in business, hospitality, food service, and technology. | 8 Abbott Park Pl. | 401/598–1000 or 800/DIAL–JWU | www.jwu.edu | Daily.

Culinary Archives and Museum. This unique museum contains over 200,000 items amassed by Chicago Chef Louis Szathmary and donated to Johnson and Wales University. The collection includes rare presidential autographs; a gallery of chefs through the ages; tools of the trade from the third millennium BC; original artwork; hotel and restaurant silver; and periodicals and documents relating to the culinary arts. Call for tour appointment | 315 Harborside Blvd. | 401/598–2805 | fax 401/598–2807 | $5 | Tues.–Sat. 10–4.

★ **Providence Athenaeum.** This was the center of the intellectual life of old Providence. Established in 1753 and housed in a granite 1838 Greek Revival structure, it is among the oldest lending libraries in the world. Here Edgar Allen Poe, visiting Providence to lecture at Brown, met and courted Sarah Helen Whitman, who was said to have been the inspiration for his poem "Annabel Lee." The library holds Rhode Island art and artifacts, an original set of elephant folio *Birds of America* prints by John James Audubon, and one of the world's best collections of travel literature. | 251 Benefit St. | 401/421–6970 | fax 401/421–2860 | www.providenceathenaeum.org | Free | Labor Day–mid-June, Mon.–Thurs. 10–8, Fri.–Sat. 10–5, Sun. 1–5; mid-June–Labor Day, Mon.–Thurs. 10–8, Fri. 10–5.

Providence College. A private Catholic university that was founded in 1917 and today has an enrollment of 3,600 undergraduates. | 549 River Ave., at Eaton St. | 401/865–1000 | www.providence.edu | Daily.

Rhode Island School of Design (RISD). Founded in 1877, RISD is still one of the nation's foremost schools of art and design. | 62 Prospect St. | 401/454–6100 | fax 401/454–6309 | www.risd.edu | Daily.

★ **Museum of Art, Rhode Island School of Design.** This small college museum is amazingly comprehensive. Many of the exhibitions, which change annually, are of textiles, a longstanding Rhode Island industry. The museum's permanent holdings include the Abby Aldrich Rockefeller collection of Japanese prints, Paul Revere silver, 18th-century porcelain, and French Impressionist paintings. Popular with children are the 10-ft statue of the Buddha and the Egyptian mummy from the Ptolemaic period (circa 300BC). The admission fee includes the adjoining Pendleton House, a replica of an early 19th-century Providence house. | 224 Benefit St. | 401/454–6345 | $5, free Sat. | Tues.–Sun. 10–5.

Woods-Gerry Gallery. The Rhode Island School of Design maintains this mansion as an important example of the city's 19th-century residential architecture. The three-story house was designed in the Renaissance style by Richard Upjohn in 1860 and today serves as a gallery for faculty and student work. | 62 Prospect St. | 401/454–6141 | Call for hours.

Roger Williams National Memorial Park. Roger Williams's contributions to the development of the concepts underlying the Declaration of Independence and the Constitution were so significant that the National Park Service dedicated a 4½-acre park to his memory. Displays offer a quick course in the life and times of Rhode Island's founder, who also wrote the first-ever book on the language of the North American Indians. | 282 N. Main St. | 401/521–7266 | fax 401/521–7239 | www.nps.gov/rowi | Free | Daily 9–4:30.

Trinity Repertory Company. This company presents plays in the renovated Majestic movie house. Its varied season generally includes classics, foreign plays, and new works. | 201 Washington St. | 401/351–4242.

RELIGION AND SPIRITUALITY

Cathedral of St. John. This brown and white cathedral has Gothic Revival towers. Built in 1810, it was designed by Rhode Island architect John Holden Greene. | 271 N. Main St., at Church St. | 401/331–4622 | Free | Weekdays 9–4, Sat. 10–2, Sun. 8:30–11:30.

First Baptist Church in America. A historic house of worship that was built in 1775 for a congregation established in 1638 by Roger Williams and his fellow Puritan dissenters. The church, one of the finest examples of Georgian architecture in the United States, has a carved-wood interior, a Waterford crystal chandelier, and graceful but austere Ionic columns. | 75 N. Main St., at Waterman St. | 401/454–3418 | fax 401/421–4095 | Donation suggested | Guided tours: Mid-May–June and Labor Day–mid-Oct., weekdays 10–12 and 1–3, Sat. 10–1, Sun. 12:15; July–Labor Day, weekdays 10–12 and 1–3, Sat. 10–1, Sun. 11:15; mid-Oct.–mid-May self-guided tours only, weekdays 10–12 and 1–3 and guided tour Sun. 12:15.

First Unitarian Church of America. This Romanesque house of worship made of Rhode Island granite was built in 1816. Its steeple houses a 2,500-pound bell, the largest ever cast in Paul Revere's foundry. | 1 Benevolent St. | 401/421–7970 | fax 401/421–7972 | Free | Self-guided tours only. Sun. service at 10:30.

SHOPPING

The Arcade. America's first shopping mall (1828) is the sole survivor of many such temples of trade constructed during America's Greek Revival period. A National Historic Landmark, the graceful building is now home to three tiers of shops and restaurants. | 65 Weybosset St. | 401/598–1199 | Weekdays 10–8, Sat. 10–6, Sun. noon–5.

Providence Place Mall. This mall is between the capitol and the downtown area and has over 1 million square ft of shopping space. Filene's, Lord & Taylor, and Nordstrom anchor the facility, while 150 other shops and restaurants complete the mix. | Francis and Hayes Sts. | 401/270–1017 | www.providenceplaza.com | Mon.–Sat 10–9:30, Sun. noon–6.

OTHER POINTS OF INTEREST

Fleet Skating Center. A short walk from Waterplace Park, the Fleet Skating Center has ice-skating October–April, and rollerblading spring and summer. Skate rentals are available. | 2 Kennedy Plaza | 401/331–5544 | $4 | Weekdays 10–6.

KODAK'S TIPS FOR PHOTOGRAPHING WEATHER

Rainbows
- Find rainbows by facing away from the sun after a storm
- Use your auto-exposure mode
- With an SLR, use a polarizing filter to deepen colors

Fog and Mist
- Use bold shapes as focal points
- Add extra exposure manually or use exposure compensation
- Choose long lenses to heighten fog and mist effects

In the Rain
- Look for abstract designs in puddles and wet pavement
- Control rain-streaking with shutter speed
- Protect cameras with plastic bags or waterproof housings

Lightning
- Photograph from a safe location
- In daylight, expose for existing light
- At night, leave the shutter open during several flashes

From Kodak Guide to Shooting Great Travel Pictures © 2000 by Fodor's Travel Publications

Providence-Newport Ferry. A ferry service provides an interesting and scenic connection between Newport and Providence. | Point St. Landing Dock | 401/781–9400 | www.ripta.com | $4 one-way | Daily.

ON THE CALENDAR

MAY–OCT.: *WaterFire.* Time your visit to Providence to coincide with this magical night. Crackling, flaming bonfires on about 100 iron braziers in the Providence River are accompanied by dramatic music. Thousands turn out on WaterFire evenings; as well as the fire on water, join in the street festival that includes live music, dancing and vendors. | 401/272–3111.

JUNE: *Spring Festival of Historic Houses.* Tour the houses and gardens of "the largest concentration of original Colonial homes in America" on Providence's east side. | 401/ 831–7440.

SEPT.: *Providence Waterfront Festival.* A variety of historical and cultural happenings at various places along the city's rivers. | 401/621–1992.

NOV.: *Annual Show of Hands/Artisans' Craft Fair.* A show of work by Rhode Island craftspeople at the Jewish Community Center of Rhode Island. | 401 Elmgrove Ave. | 401/ 861–8800.

DEC.: *First Night Providence.* A family-oriented celebration of the new year featuring arts, entertainment, and fireworks. | 401/521–1166.

WALKING TOURS

Historic Providence (approximately 4 hours, depending on stops)

This tour will take you through the historic East Side of Providence and along Benefit Street, which is said to have the richest concentration of 18th- and 19th-century architecture in the country.

Begin your tour at the **Rhode Island State Capitol** on Smith Street. The white marble dome, designed by McKim, Mead & White and completed in 1904, is one of the largest unsupported marble domes in the world. After touring the interior—don't miss the full-length portrait of George Washington by Rhode Islander Gilbert Stuart— proceed to Smith Street and head east to the **Roger Williams National Memorial,** a 4½-acre park on North Main Street. A spring, which ran through the site, is said to have prompted Rhode Island's founding father to establish his settlement of Providence here. Stop by the visitors center at 282 North Main Street to view exhibits and a slide presentation highlighting Williams's life and the history of "Providence Plantations," as the city was first known.

Across from the visitors center, stop by the **Cathedral of St. John,** built in 1810 by Providence architect John Holden Greene. The largely Georgian structure is topped with a Gothic Revival towers and embellished with Gothic decoration. From the cathedral, head south on North Main Street to the **First Baptist Church in America,** which was built in 1775 by Joseph Brown. The congregation was founded by Roger Williams in 1638, making it the oldest Baptist congregation in the nation.

From North Main Street, head one block up the steep hill to **Benefit Street,** with its cobblestones and well-preserved historic houses. Known as the "Mile of History," Benefit Street is a reminder of Providence's prosperous days as a center for maritime commerce. Stop at the Greek Revival granite building at 251 Benefit Street, which is the **Providence Athenaeum.** It was established in 1753 and moved to this building in 1838, making it one of the oldest libraries in the country. Among the treasures in the athenaeum's collection is a magnificent hand-colored elephant folio of John James Audubon's work.

Continue along Benefit Street to the corner of Benevolent Street, where you will see the **First Unitarian Church of America.** Built in 1816 of Rhode Island granite, this church holds in its steeple the largest bell ever struck in the foundry of Paul Revere and Sons. Two blocks south of the Unitarian Church is the splendid **John Brown House.**

At the time of its completion in 1788, the mansion offered uninterrupted views of the harbor below. The interior is furnished with fine antiques, silver, and china.

From the John Brown House, walk one block downhill and turn right on S. Main Street. Cross the Providence River and conclude your tour with a well-deserved stop at one of the restaurants in the elegant Greek Revival **Arcade**. A National Historic Landmark, the Arcade was the first enclosed shopping mall in the country, built in 1828 and embellished with fine ironwork, cantilevered stairs, and granite pillars.

Dining

INEXPENSIVE

Angelo's Civita Farnese. Italian. Generous portions of homemade macaroni with red sauce, friendly staff, friendly customers, and family-style dining draw hordes to this popular Federal Hill institution. | 141 Atwells Ave. | 401/621–8171 | fax 401/273–6943 | Closed Sun., June–Aug. | $4–$9 | No credit cards.

India. Indian. Right downtown, you'll find robust curries, grilled kabobs, and basmati-rice specialties in a pleasant restaurant with art and oriental carpets. | 123 Dorrance St. | 401/278–2000 | www.indiarestaurant.com | $8–$15 | AE, MC, V.

Tokyo. Japanese. Regular tables, tatami room, and sushi bar are your seating choices at this BYOB restaurant in Fox Point. You can choose from more than 100 kinds of sushi, entrées like chicken teriyaki and *ton katsu* (pork cutlets). | 388 Wickenden St. | 401/331–5330 | $9–$15 | AE, D, MC, V.

Union Station Brewery. American/Casual. In the lower level of what was once the Providence train station, this brew pub serves up eclectic cuisine designed to complement the beer brewed on the premises. Penne pasta is a cheese-lover's dream with chicken, sun-dried tomatoes, and a gorgonzola sauce. The ribs are smoked here and the barbecue sauce is homemade. You can enjoy city views from the landscaped patio. Try the cask-conditioned beer or popular Golden Spike Ale. | 36 Exchange Terr. | 401/274–2739 | www.johnhar-vards.com/union | $8–$17 | AE, D, DC, MC, V.

Wes' Rib House. Barbecue. A simple, no-frills place that's always open late for when you're craving down-home barbecue chicken and ribs. Main dishes are served up with hearty portions of beans and corn bread. | 38 Dike St. | 401/421–9090 | $6–$13 | AE, D, MC, V.

MODERATE

Adesso. Italian. A modern, bustling restaurant just off Thayer Street, Brown University's eclectic main drag. Known for great pasta dishes and pizza. | 161 Cushing St. | 401/521–0770 | $12–$25 | AE, MC, V.

Amicus. American/Casual. A trendy restaurant popular for fun, flavorful twists on fish, meat, and pasta. Known for salads (try duck breast with figs), veal, and blackened swordfish. | 345 S. Water St. | 401/521–7722 | $15–$26 | AE, MC, V.

Cafe Nuovo. Contemporary. The dining room of this modern downtown restaurant is dominated by two huge murals in lively colors, an open kitchen, and floor-to-ceiling windows looking out at the city and River Park. There's outside dining as well. Food is a fusion of American regional, European, Asian, and island flavors with dazzling presentations. For dessert order pot of mousse if you love chocolate. | 1 Citizen's Plaza | 401/421–2525 | Closed Sun. No lunch weekends | $11–$24 | AE, D, DC, MC, V.

Camille's Roman Garden. Italian. This Federal Hill restaurant has been called the grande dame of Providence. You can dine in one of eight intimate curtained alcoves, or in the large main dining room, which has been a restaurant since 1914. A favorite is the pistachio-crusted tenderloin with gorgonzola. Valet parking is available. | 71 Bradford St. | 401/751–4812 | www.camilesrest.com | Closed Sun., July–Aug. No lunch Sat. | $13–$28 | AE, DC, MC, V.

PROVIDENCE

INTRO
ATTRACTIONS
DINING
LODGING

L'Epicureo. Italian. Two dining rooms, one with an open kitchen and one with a fireplace, serve this storefront bistro that was once a butcher shop. From pastas to sausage to ice cream, everything's made in-house. Wood-grilled, aged, prime beef and veal chops are standouts. | 238 Atwells Ave. | 401/454–8430 | Closed Sun.–Mon. No lunch | $15–$28 | AE, D, DC, MC, V.

Pot Au Feu. French. Long known in Providence for the best traditional French cuisine, this restaurant is on two floors; one is casual and one not. Both locations are cozy and reminiscent of Paris bistro dining. Known for cassoulet, escargot, and, of course, *pot au feu.* | 44 Custom House St. | 401/273–8953 | Closed June–Aug. and Sun. | $15–$20 bistro; $18–$30 salon | AE, DC, MC, V.

Twin Oaks. Continental. For decades, this old-fashioned place off the beaten path has been one of state's favorite restaurants. On Saturday nights the wait can be hours, but with the hearty portions of simply prepared food at great prices, it's worth it. Try the baked stuffed shrimp, veal parmigiana, or spaghetti and meatballs. | 100 Sabra St., Cranston | 401/781–9693 | Closed Mon. | $14–$25 | AE, D, MC, V.

EXPENSIVE

Capital Grille. Steak. Renowned for dry-aged steaks, this New York–style steak house also serves fresh seafood and wonderful side dishes. Oversized leather banquettes and mahogany-paneled walls fill this converted train station. It's an easy walk from several hotels. | 1 Union Station | 401/521–5600 | www.thecapitalgrille.com | No lunch weekends | $18–$30 | AE, D, DC, MC, V.

The Gatehouse. Contemporary. This restaurant has established itself as one of the finest in the state by consistently offering eclectic, inventive twists on modern classics in an upscale location overlooking the Seekonk River. Entrées include almond-crusted catfish and grilled four pepper ribeye steak. | 4 Richmond Sq. | 401/521–9229 | Closed Mon. | $17–$27 | AE, DC, MC, V.

Napa Valley Grille. Contemporary. After shopping at the Providence Place Mall, stop in here to relax and enjoy a glass of California wine in the lounge. The dining room has roomy booths and is dominated by a mural of Napa Valley. The menu has a modern spin, with favorites like braised lamb shank with Skyhill goat cheese polenta competing with crab cakes with a smoked bacon aïoli. | 111 Providence Pl., | 401/720–6272 | www.calcafe.com | $18–$30 | AE, D, DC, AM, V.

Neath's. Eclectic. Chef Neath Pal combines the flavors of his Cambodian upbringing with his classic French training in this hot restaurant on the Providence scene. The dining room is warm and open, perfect for sampling such dishes as grilled sea bass or yellowfin tuna with a soy-ginger glaze. Known for seafood, meat, Maine crab salad. | 262 S. Water St. | 401/751–3700 | Reservation essential | Closed Mon. | $18–$25 | AE, MC, V.

New Rivers Bistro. Contemporary. This intimate eatery does incredible things with local, regional, and seasonal foods. In summer, enjoy twelve kinds of heirloom tomatoes with fresh mozzarella and basil oil or lobster salad with poblano-lime vinaigrette. In winter, comfort foods like cassoulet are featured. The menu offers small meals as well as appetizers and regular entrées. For dessert, try the lemon tart. | 7 Steeple St. | 401/751–0350 | Closed Sun.–Mon. No lunch | $18–$24 | AE, MC, V.

Rue de l'Espoir. Contemporary. Eat at a table, booth, or at the bar of this cozy East Side favorite where you'll rub elbows with locals. Side dishes move front and center, and entrées like grilled chicken over smoked gouda and spinach-filled ravioli with a creamy pesto sauce win raves. Weekend brunch. | 99 Hope St. | 401/751–8890 | Breakfast also available weekdays. Closed Mon. | $16–$27 | AE, D, DC, MC, V.

VERY EXPENSIVE

★ **Al Forno.** Italian. Two of the country's most celebrated chefs, George Germon and Johanne Killeen, turn out wonderful pastas and their world-famous thin-crust pizzas at this Italian trattoria. No smoking. Free parking. | 577 S. Main St. | 401/273–9760. | Closed Sun.–Mon. | $30–$40. | AE, DC, MC, V.

Empire. Italian. In the heart of downtown Providence, Empire lives up to its regal name and is perfect for before- or after-theater dining. The open, modern, and bright setting is matched by great selections of pasta, fish, chicken, and meat. The grilled pizza is a must. Free parking. | 123 Empire St. | 401/621–7911 | Closed Sun. | $20–$35 | AE, MC, V.

Hemenway's Seafood Grill and Oyster Bar. Seafood. Here you'll find steaks, chops, and seafood in a grand dining room with soaring ceilings and windows that overlook the city's riverwalk. There's open-air dining on the front patio with partial view of the park. | 121 S. Main St. | 401/351–8570 | $35–$40 prix fixe (includes appetizers and drink) | AE, D, DC, MC, V.

Lodging

INEXPENSIVE

Annie Brownell House. A grand stairway with carved banister adorns this lovely 1899 Colonial Revival home, 1 mi from city hall and about 4 blocks from Brown University. Rooms are individually appointed with period furniture and reproductions; one has a majestic four-poster bed. Complimentary breakfast. Some room phones, no TV in some rooms, TV in common area. No pets. No kids under 12. No smoking. | 400 Angell St. | 401/454–2934 | fax 401/454–2934 | members.home.net/satunder | 3 rooms (with showers only) | $95–$105 | AE, MC, V.

C. C. Ledbetter Bed & Breakfast. A downtown location, a most cheerful C. C. herself, and the charm of this 1770 mansard-roof home make this a special place to stay. The garden has two hammocks and blooms with roses, lilies, and peonies. Its proximity to Brown and RISD makes it a favorite for visiting parents. Complimentary Continental breakfast. Cable TV, no room phones. Free parking. Pets allowed. No smoking. | 326 Benefit St. | 401/351–4699 | 4 rooms (2 with shared bath) | $95–$110 | MC, V.

Ramada Inn Seekonk. This full-service hotel catering to business travelers and families is just over the border (5 mi east) from Providence in Seekonk, Mass. It's within walking distance to shops and restaurants. Restaurant, bar with entertainment, room service. Cable TV. Indoor pool. Hot tub, sauna. Tennis, putting green. Business services. | 940 Fall River Ave., Seekonk, MA | 508/336–7300 | fax 508/336–2107 | www.ramada.com | 128 rooms | $77–$135 | AE, D, DC, MC, V.

★ **State House Inn.** This inviting bed-and-breakfast near the capitol has a few rooms with working fireplaces and is furnished with Colonial and Shaker-style pieces. Complimentary breakfast. In-room data ports, some refrigerators, cable TV. Laundry service. Business services. No smoking. | 43 Jewett St. | 401/351–6111 | fax 401/351–4261 | www.providence-inn.com | 10 rooms | $99–$149 | AE, MC, V.

MODERATE

Holiday Inn Downtown. This 14-story Holiday Inn, built in 1969, is undergoing a multi-million dollar renovation. The redone rooms will be as nice as the location, one block from Federal Hill and two blocks from the Convention Center. Restaurant, bar. In-room data ports, Cable TV. Indoor pool. Hot tub. Gym. Laundry facilities, laundry service. Free airport shuttle. Parking (fee). No pets. | 21 Atwells Ave. | 401/831–1717 | fax 401/751–0007 | www.holiday-inn.com | 274 rooms | $129–$200 | AE, D, DC, MC, V.

Johnson and Wales Inn. This professionally managed hotel and restaurant is staffed by future hoteliers and executive chefs from Johnson and Wales, the largest culinary arts institution in the world. It's on the Massachusetts/Rhode Island border and less than 10 minutes from downtown Providence. Restaurant, bar, complimentary Continental breakfast, room service. Some refrigerators, some mini-bars, some in-room hot tubs, cable TV. Business services, airport shuttle. Free parking. | 213 Taunton Ave., Seekonk, MA | 508/336–8700 or 800/232–1772 | fax 508/336–3414 | 86 rooms, 16 suites | $120–$130, $144 suites | AE, D, DC, MC, V.

The Old Court Bed and Breakfast. This 1863 Victorian-style bed-and-breakfast in a redbrick house is near RISD. The rooms are decorated with 19th-century antiques. Complimentary breakfast, cable TV. | 144 Benefit St. | 401/751–2002 | fax 401/272–4830 | www.oldcourt.com | 10 rooms | $135–$155 | AE, D, MC, V.

Providence Marriott. A full-service hotel in downtown Providence with all the modern conveniences. The restaurant, Bluefin Grille, serves local seafood with a French flair. Restaurant, bar with entertainment, room service. In-room data ports, cable TV. Indoor-outdoor pool. Hot tub, sauna. Exercise equipment. Laundry service. Business services, airport shuttle. Pets allowed. Free parking. | 1 Orms St. | 401/272–2400 | fax 401/273–2686 | www.marriott.com | 346 rooms, 5 suites | $159–$199, $375 suites | AE, D, DC, MC, V.

EXPENSIVE

The Biltmore. Built in 1922, this hotel has an art deco facade with an exterior glass elevator that offers sweeping views of Providence. The staff is very attentive, and the rooms are elegant and spacious. Restaurant, bar, room service. In-room data ports, cable TV. Beauty salon. Gym. Laundry service. Business services. Parking (fee). Pets allowed. | 11 Dorrance St., Kennedy Plaza | 401/421–0700 or 800/294–7709 | fax 401/455–3050 | www.providencebiltmore.com | 278 rooms, 21 suites | $130–$260, $160–$375 suites | AE, D, DC, MC, V.

Courtyard by Marriott. Unique architecture designed to harmonize with Union Station sets this Marriott Courtyard apart from the norm. The seven-story brick building has oversized rooms, and it's downtown, close to everything. In-room data ports, some microwaves, some refrigerators, some hot tubs, cable TV. Indoor pool. Gym. Laundry facilities, laundry service. Parking (fee). No pets. | 32 Exchange Terr., at Memorial Blvd. | 401/272–1191 or 888/887–7955 | fax 401/272–1416 | www.courtyard.com | 216 rooms | $189 | AE, D, DC, MC, V.

★ **The Westin Providence.** The 25-story Westin towers over Providence's downtown and features the wine cellar in its Agora Restaurant. There's a skywalk connecting it to the convention center. Restaurants, bars, room service. In-room data ports, minibars, some refrigerators, cable TV. Indoor pool. Hot tub, massage, sauna. Health club. Laundry service. Business center. Parking (fee). Some pets allowed. | 1 W. Exchange St. | 401/598–8000 or 888/625–5411 | fax 401/598–8200 | www.westin.com | 341 rooms, 23 suites | $249–$329, $324–$400 suites | AE, D, DC, MC, V.

TIVERTON

MAP 3, L4

(Nearby towns also listed: Bristol, Little Compton, Portsmouth; Fall River, MA)

Tiverton is a small but busy town. Because it's just a few miles from the Massachusetts city of Fall River, most of the residents of Tiverton travel across the border for major purchases or, for instance, to see movies. In Tiverton Four Corners, a village south of larger Tiverton, such features as coffee shops, antique stores, and a well-known ice-cream stand make for delightful family outings on warm days.

Information: Newport County Convention Center and Visitors Bureau | 23 America's Cup Ave., Newport, 02840 | www.gonewport.com | 401/849–8048 or 800/976–5122.

Attractions

Fogland Beach. This ½-mi beach is often blanketed by fog while the rest of the state basks in the sun, but it's well worth the drive through the lovely rural countryside of Sakonnet.

Although the beach is rocky, the calm waters make it an ideal place for swimming. | Fogland Rd., off Main Rd.

Fort Barton. When the British captured Newport in 1777, Fort Barton (named for Col. William Barton) was hastily erected in response. At 110 ft above the Aquidneck River, the guns of the earthworks and timber fort had a sweeping command of the north end of Aquidneck Island. The Colonial rebels launched an attack on the British from here in 1778; had it been successful, it might have ended the war. There are over 3 mi of hiking trails and a picturesque view of Aquidneck from the partially restored fort. | Highland Ave., across from Town Hall | Daily dawn–dusk.

Sakonnet Boathouse. The boathouse rents kayaks and other outdoor gear, and provides kayak tours and classes. | 169 Riverside Dr. | 401/624–1440 | fax 401/625–1120 | www.sakonnetboathouse.com | Call for hours.

Tiverton Four Corners. A charming village intersection with historic houses, antiques shops, restaurants including Gray's Ice Cream (expect long lines for their homemade icy treats on Sunday afternoons), art galleries, and some unusual garden shops. The history of this rural village goes back to the 17th century, and it's on the National Register of Historic Places. There's also the Tiverton Four Corners Center for Arts and Education that hosts summer concerts and offers classes for adults and kids. From Route 24, drive 6 mi south on Route 77. | | Free | Daily.

Chase-Cory House. This simple gambrel-roof house, built in 1730, was donated to the Tiverton Historical Society by former Navy Secretary J. William Middendorf. Visitors today can tour the five rooms, including the original kitchen with a 7-ft fireplace with beaded chimney. | 3908 Main Rd., Tiverton Four Corners | Free | May–Sept., Sun. 2–4:30, and by appointment | 401/624–2096.

ON THE CALENDAR

MAY: *Garden & Herb Festival.* This annual event has food, entertainment, and purveyors of plants: flowers, herbs, annuals, perennials—as well as tools, garden ornaments, and furniture. Some antiques dealers bring unique outdoor pieces, and the events for children include face painting and flower pot decorating. | 401/624–2600.

JULY: *The Art and Artisans Festival.* A one-day outdoor festival has demonstrations and workshops so you can make art: printmaking, clay, and banner painting. About 60 artisans offer their wares, from fine art to crafts, for sale. Under the tent there are music and dance performances, and food is available too. | 401/635–4801.

Dining

Evelyn's Nannaquaket Drive In. American. At this rustic joint with a small air-conditioned dining room, your best bet is to eat at the picnic tables outside overlooking Nannaquaket Pond. The menu includes hot dogs, hamburgers, the usual range of fried seafood, and a lobster plate. | 2335 Main Rd. | 401/624–3100 | Breakfast also available. Closed Thurs. and Nov.–Mar. | $4–$26 | No credit cards.

Lodging

Bonniebield Cottage. You can rent this small house, built in the 1920s as a summer cottage for the 1740 main property it ajoins, in a beautifully landscaped rural area. Downstairs there's a kitchen, living room, dining room, and bath with shower. Upstairs, the peaked-roof bedroom has maple twin beds plus a cot, wainscoting, and rough plaster walls, and a thick white carpet. You'll find a tennis court, have beach rights to a Sakonnet River Beach, and enjoy the proximity to Tiverton Four Corners. No air-conditioning, kitchenette, refrigerator, no room phone. 1 tennis court. No pets. No smoking. | 531 Neck Rd. | 401/624–6364 | rglundgren@aol.com | 1 cottage | $100 | No credit cards.

WARREN

(Nearby towns also listed: Bristol, Providence)

Travelers often pass through this town on their way to Bristol and Newport without stopping. It's their loss. Just west of the main road are closely huddled Colonial homes and numerous antiques shops. The pace here is slow, making it an ideal place for a stroll. Warren is a destination that Rhode Islanders in the know consider romantic.

Information: **East Bay Chamber of Commerce** | 654 Metacom Ave., Box 250, Warren, 02885–0250 | 401/245–0750 | info@eastbaychamberri.org | www.eastbaychamberri.org.

Attractions

Bay Queen Cruises. This outfit offers tours of Narragansett Bay aboard the *Vista Jubilee*, a 360-person-capacity, air-conditioned ship. Special events include Newport brunch cruises, weekday luncheons, dinner-dance cruises, and many others. Call for a full schedule of events. | 461 Water St., Gate 4 | 401/245–1350 or 800/439–1350 | fax 401/245–6630 | www.bayqueen.com | May–Dec.

Firemen's Museum. The former headquarters of the Narragansett Steam Fire Company Number 3 has been restored and made into a museum displaying memorabilia of early firefighting, such as *Little Hero*, the town's first engine—which dates from 1802. | 42 Baker St. | 401/245–7600 | By appointment.

ON THE CALENDAR

JULY: *Quahog Festival.* Quahogs, those hard-shelled bivalve clams so beloved in Rhode Island, star at this annual festival sponsored by the Warren Rotary Club. Shucking contests and the chance to eat quahogs raw, stuffed and batter-fried, draw crowds to Burr's Hill Park for the festivities. | 401/245–0750.

Dining

Nathaniel Porter Inn. Continental. An intimate, romantic inn built in 1795 provides the perfect setting for creatively prepared seafood, meat, and game dishes. Sun. brunch. | 125 Water St. | 401/245–6622 | $15–$25 | AE, D, MC, V.

Wharf Tavern. Seafood. This bustling place is right on the Warren River, and almost every table has a view; it's been serving seafood and more since 1955. Dividers break up the large dining room, enhanced by linen-covered tables and candles. There's a lounge with entertainment on weekends. You can get lobster baked, stuffed, sautéed, in Newburg sauce, or steamed, as well as prime rib, steaks, and pasta. Try the award-winning chowder. | 215 Water St. | 401/245–5043 | fax 401/247–2185 | $12–$25 | AE, D, MC, V.

Lodging

Barnscape Bed & Breakfast. The hostess of this Greek Revival inn is an artist who uses color effectively on the walls (ask to see her post-and-beam studio out back). Furnishings are new, with some wicker. Old handmade quilts and paintings by the owner adorn the walls. The queen-bedded guest room is on the first floor; the second-floor room with twin beds has a sloped ceiling. Complimentary Continental breakfast. No room phones, no TV. No pets. No smoking. | 825 Main St. | 401/245–1741 | www.barnscape.com | 2 rooms (1 with shower only, 1 with shared bath) | $95 | No credit cards.

Candlewick Inn. A turn-of-the-century bungalow with spacious guest rooms in downtown. It has antique furnishings. Complimentary breakfast. Refrigerators, no TVs. No smoking. | 775 Main St. | 401/247–2425 | cwickinn@earthlink.net | 4 rooms (2 with shared bath) | $70–$125 | No credit cards.

Nathaniel Porter Inn. This inn was built by a sea captain in 1795. Guests share an upstairs sitting room. The guest rooms have been completely restored, and are furnished with antiques. Restaurant, bar, complimentary Continental breakfast. No room phones, no TV in rooms, TV in common area. No smoking. | 125 Water St. | 401/245–6622 | fax 401/247–2277 | npi@usa.com | 3 rooms | $80 | AE, D, MC, V.

WARWICK

(Nearby towns also listed: East Greenwich, Providence)

Part of the Providence metropolitan area, Warwick is home to T.F. Green State Airport and is also stately and historically important town. Its variety of neighborhoods offer homes in almost any price range. Apart from trips to the shopping malls and plazas located west of I–95, locals do not often visit the city of Warwick; but when they do, most are surprised to find gorgeous homes and well kept parks. The city's well sheltered coves made Warwick popular with colonial settlers. The burning of the revenue ship *Gaspee*, Rhode Island's most remembered act of defiance against British rule, happened here in 1772.

Information: Dept. of Economic Development | City Hall, 3275 Post Rd., Warwick, 02886 | 401/738–2000, ext. 6402, or 800/4–WARWICK | info@warwickri.com | www.warwickri.com.

Attractions

Goddard Memorial State Park. This forest along Greenwich Bay was simply a stretch of sand dunes until the 1870s, when Henry Russell began planting acorns. The trees did so well that the U.S. Forest Service in the early 1900s called it "the finest example of private forestry in America." Today the park offers hiking and bridle paths, outdoor concerts in the summer, ocean swimming, a 9-hole golf course, and cross-country skiing in winter. | Ives Rd. | 401/884–2010 | fax 401/885–7720 | www.riparks.com/goddard.htm | Free | Daily, dawn–dusk.

Historic Pontiac Mills. This old mill complex was once the site of the Fruit of the Loom manufacturing company. It now houses a wide variety of shops featuring items such as hand-painted furniture, vintage clothing, and antiques. | 334 Knight St. | 401/737–2700 | fax 401/737–2701 | Daily.

Walking Tour of Historic Apponaug Village. A self-guided walking tour published by the state is available at Warwick City Hall (3275 Post Rd.). The walk details 31 sites in Warwick's Apponaug Village. | Exit 10A, off I–95 | 401/738–2000 | Daily.

Warwick and Rhode Island malls. The Warwick Mall and the Rhode Island Mall are a few miles apart on Route 2. Between them, 200 stores provide a good portion of the retail commodities purchased by Rhode Islanders. | Warwick Mall, Rte. 2 at Rte. 5; Rhode Island Mall, Rte. 2 at Rte. 113 | Warwick Mall, 401/739–7500; Rhode Island Mall, 401/828–7651 | Daily.

ON THE CALENDAR

MAY–JUNE: *Gaspee Days*. Commemoration and reenactment of the June 9, 1772 burning of the British Revenue Schooner HMS *Gaspee* by Rhode Island patriots. Events held in various locations on different days. | 401/781–1772.

SEPT.: *Conimicut Village Festival*. Every year on Labor Day, this fun family day in quaint Conimicut Village draws crowds for clamcakes, chowder, and food-court fare. There's family entertainment, magic, music, and dancing, and local arts and crafts, too. The Warwick Rotary runs the event, with proceeds going to charities in the community. | Conimicut Village | 800/4–WARWICK.

NOV.: *Warwick Heritage Festival.* Attractions include a Colonial militia encampment and battle re-enactment with a wide variety of militia units. Period demonstrations, artifacts, memorabilia, and other special events. | Warwick City Park | 800/4–WARWICK.

Dining

Chelo's Waterfront Bar and Grille. American. This Rhode Island chain's large, modern waterfront restaurant on Greenwich Cove has great views, upper and lower outside decks, music every night, and an extensive menu of favorites. Its award-winning chowder, fish-and-chips, and lobster pie, plus burgers, pastas, and a kid's menu provide something for everyone. | 1 Masthead Dr. | 401/884–3000 | fax 401/725–0009 | www.chelos.com | $7–$16 | AE, D, MC, V.

Chevys Fresh Mex. Mexican. Bald Hill Road has an endless stretch of chain restaurants, including Chili's, Red Lobster, Lone Star Steakhouse, and Olive Garden. One of the latest is this spare, noisy and festive Mexican place with fine fajitas and ribs. There's also a good selection of salads, and a kid's menu. | 1376 Bald Hill Rd. (Rte. 2), | 401/823–4700 | $8–$16 | AE, D, DC, MC, V.

Legal Sea Foods. Seafood. Boston's famous seafood house has come to this busy spot near the state's airport. The food is simple and fresh. Kid's menu. | 2099 Post Rd. | 401/732–3663 | fax 401/739–8727. | $12–$35 | AE, D, DC, MC, V.

Tomato Vine Restaurant. Italian. This family-owned restaurant in the Apex Shopping Plaza turns out wood-oven pizzas, pasta with all-you-can-eat salad, as well as veal, chicken, and seafood. There's a small bar and and the differing levels of seating make the eating spaces, tables, and banquettes more intimate. | 545 Greenwich Ave. | 401/732–2569 | $9–$11 | AE, D, MC, V.

Lodging

Comfort Inn Airport. This chain option caters to business travelers as it is close to downtown Providence and T. F. Green Airport. Complimentary Continental breakfast. In-room data ports, some refrigerators, some in-room hot tubs, cable TV. Hot tub. Business services, airport shuttle. Some pets allowed. | 1940 Post Rd. | 401/732–0470 or 800/228–5150 | fax 401/732–4247 | www.comfortinn.com | 200 rooms | $159–$179 | AE, D, DC, MC, V.

Crowne Plaza at the Crossings. Warwick's largest and most deluxe accommodation is on 88 acres and has attractive gardens. The rooms have marble baths with whirlpool tubs. Restaurant, bar, room service. In-room data ports, some refrigerators, cable TV. Indoor pool. Hot tub. Exercise equipment. Laundry facilities. Business services, airport shuttle. | 801 Greenwich Ave. | 401/732–6000 | fax 401/732–4839 | www.crowneplazari.com | 266 rooms | $199–$229 | AE, D, DC, MC, V.

Hampton Inn and Suites–Warwick. This chain option opened in 2000 and is only ½ mi from the airport. The suites have two rooms with couch and kitchenette. Complimentary Continental breakfast. In-room data ports, some kitchenettes, some microwaves, some refrigerators, cable TV, some in-room VCRs. Indoor swimming pool, hot tub. Gym. Laundry facilities, laundry service. Airport shuttle. No pets. | 2100 Post Rd. | 401/739–8888 or 800/ HAMPTON | fax 401/739–1550 | www.hamptoninn.com | 123 rooms, 50 suites | $139 rooms, $169 suites | AE, D, DC, MC, V.

Mainstay Suites. This all-suite hotel ½ mi from the airport has modern rooms in a variety of configurations. Some have lounges, some pull-out couches, all have queen-sized beds. Complimentary Continental breakfast. In-room data ports, kitchenettes, microwaves, refrigerators, cable TV. Hot tub. Gym. Laundry facilities, laundry service. Pets allowed (fee). | 268 Metro Center Blvd. | 401/732–6667 or 800/660–MAIN | fax 401/732–6668 | www.mainstaysuites.com | 94 suites | $99–$189 | AE, D, DC, M, V.

Motel 6. Frugal travelers favor this price-conscious chain that provides basic motel amenities. It is 2 mi north of the airport and has a 24 hour Bickford's Restaurant. Restaurant, bar.

In-room data ports, cable TV. Outdoor pool. Laundry facilities. Some pets allowed. | 20 Jefferson Blvd. | 401/467–9800 | fax 401/467–6780 | www.motel6.com | 123 rooms in 2 buildings | $69–$85 | AE, D, DC, MC, V.

Radisson Airport Hotel. Operated in conjunction with Johnson and Wales University, this hotel is staffed by university students and is close to downtown Providence and T. F. Green Airport. Suites have whirlpool tubs. Restaurant, bar, complimentary Continental breakfast, room service. Cable TV. Business services, airport shuttle. Free parking. | 2081 Post Rd. | 401/739–3000 | fax 401/732–9309 | www.radisson.com/warwickri | 73 rooms, 38 suites | $129–$149, $169–$209 suites | AE, D, DC, MC, V.

Residence Inn by Marriott. The Marriott, 15 minutes from downtown Providence, caters to business travelers and families, with rooms and kitchen suites at moderate prices. Complimentary Continental breakfast. In-room data ports, cable TV. Indoor pool. Hot tub. Baby-sitting, playground. Laundry service. Business services. Pets allowed. | 500 Kilvert St. | 401/737–7100 | fax 401/739–2909 | www.residenceinn.com | 96 kitchen suites | $119–$189 | AE, D, DC, MC, V.

Sheraton Inn Providence. The Sheraton is next to T. F. Green Airport and offers a shuttle bus service free of charge. Restaurant, bar. In-room data ports, cable TV. Pool. Spa. Gym, exercise equipment. Business services, airport shuttle. Free parking. | 1850 Post Rd. | 401/738–4000 | fax 401/738–8206 | www.sheraton.com | 194 rooms, 12 suites | $179–$199, $229 suites | AE, D, DC, MC, V.

Susse Chalet. Reasonably priced option near downtown Providence and T. F. Green Airport. Complimentary Continental breakfast. Cable TV. Pool. Laundry facilities. Business services, airport shuttle. Free parking. | 36 Jefferson Blvd. | 401/941–6600 | fax 401/785–1260 | www.sussechalet.com | 115 rooms | $79–$89 | AE, D, DC, MC, V.

WATCH HILL

INTRO
ATTRACTIONS
DINING
LODGING

WATCH HILL

MAP 3, I6

(Nearby town also listed: Westerly)

Watch Hill, a Victorian-era resort village, contains miles of beautiful beaches. The area's many summer homes are renowned for their stylish beauty; look for the homes' trademark foundations of beach stone. A statue of Ninigret, Chief of the Niantics (a branch of the powerful Narragansett tribe who inhabited the land), stands watch over Bay Street.

Information: The Greater Westerly–Pawcatuck Chamber of Commerce | 1 Chamber Way, Westerly, 02891 | 401/596–7761 or 800/SEA-7636 | www.westerlychamber.org.

South County Tourism Council | Stedman Government Center, 4808 Tower Hill Rd., Wakefield, 02879 | 401/789–4422 or 800/548–4662 | www.southcountyri.com.

Attractions
Flying Horse Carousel. At the end of Bay Street, this merry-go-round is the oldest in America. It was built by the Charles W. F. Dare Co. of New York in about 1883. The horses, suspended from above, swing out when in motion. Each is hand-carved from a single piece of wood and embellished with real horse hair, a leather saddle, and agate eyes. Adults are not permitted to ride on the carousel. | Watch Hill Rd. | 50¢ | Mid-June–Labor Day, weekdays 1–9, weekends 11–9.

Napatree Point. A long, sandy spit between Watch Hill's Little Narragansett Bay and the ocean, Napatree is a protected conservation area that is great for a hike and teeming with wildlife. Napatree has no admission fee, no phone, and no parking, but there's parking for a fee nearby. | Watch Hill Rd. | Free | Daily.

Watch Hill Lighthouse. The U. S. Coastguard Light Station has great views of the ocean and of Fishers Island, New York. The tiny museum contains exhibits about the lighthouse. Parking is for the elderly and disabled only; everyone else must walk from lots at the beach. | Lighthouse Rd. | Free | Grounds: daily; lighthouse: May–Sept., Tues. and Thurs. 1–3.

Dining
Ocean House Hotel. Seafood. Whether you're enjoying a lobster roll on the deck at lunch, or baked stuffed lobster in the cavernous dining room of this immense Victorian hotel, the ocean views will enthrall you. | 2 Bluff Ave. | 401/348–8161 | Breakfast also available. Closed Sept.–June | $12–$22 | MC, V.

★ **Olympia Tea Room.** Contemporary. A tearoom in name only, this full-service restaurant serves new American food in a casual but upscale venue. The old-fashioned soda fountain's marble top is now a fully stocked bar, serving perhaps the best martinis in South County. Richly colored folk art adorns the pink walls. Sit at a table outside and enjoy beautiful harbor views and spectacular sunsets. | 74 Bay St. | 401/348–8211 | fax 401/596–6201 | Closed Jan.–Feb. | $12–$25 | AE, MC, V.

Lodging
Ocean House Hotel. This impressive clapboard Victorian structure, built in 1868, has a full wraparound porch overlooking 800 ft of private beach and ocean. Complimentary chairs and umbrellas are provided to guests, and the lifeguard is on duty from 10–5. No air-conditioning, no room phones, TV in common area. Exercise equipment. Private beach. No pets. | 2 Bluff Ave. | 401/348–8161 | 59 rooms | $105–$240 | Sept.–June | MAP | MC, V.

WESTERLY

MAP 3, I5

(Nearby towns also listed: Charlestown, Watch Hill)

The village of Westerly is a busy little railway town that grew up in the late 19th century around a major station on what is now the New York–Boston Amtrak corridor. The 30-square-mi community of 15 villages has since sprawled out. Victorian and Greek Revival mansions line many streets off the town center, which borders Connecticut and the Pawcatuck River. During the Industrial Revolution and into the 1950s, Westerly was distinguished for its flawless blue granite, from which monuments throughout the country were made.

Watch Hill and Misquamicut are two summer communities generally recognized without mention of their township, Westerly. Gaming developments just over the state border in Connecticut are slowly changing Westerly's economic climate. Many residents now work in the casinos, and gambling vacationers are discovering that Westerly's bed-and-breakfasts provide pleasant alternatives to casino hotels.

Information: **The Greater Westerly–Pawcatuck Chamber of Commerce** | 1 Chamber Way, Westerly, 02891 | 401/596–7761 or 800/SEA–7636 | www.westerlychamber.org.

South County Tourism Council | Stedman Government Center, 4808 Tower Hill Rd., Wakefield, 02879 | 401/789–4422 or 800/548–4662 | www.southcountyri.com.

Attractions
Babcock-Smith House. This gambrel-roof, early Georgian home was built for Westerly's first physician, Dr. Joshua Babcock, in 1732. Babcock was a close friend to Benjamin Franklin, who was said to have provided the lightning rods atop the house and fished at nearby Weekapaug Pond. A 19th-century resident of the house, Orlando Smith, discovered granite on the property; Westerly later developed into one of the country's leading granite centers. | 124

Granite St. (U.S. 1) | 401/596–4424 or 401/596–5704 | $3 | May–June and Sept., Sun. 2–5; July–Aug., Sun. and Wed. 2–5, or by appointment.

Misquamicut State Beach. Strip motels jostle for attention in Misquamicut, where a giant water slide, a carousel, miniature golf, a game arcade, children's rides, batting cages, and fast-food stands attract visitors by the hundreds to Atlantic Avenue. The mile-long beach is accessible year-round, but the amusements are open only between Memorial Day and Labor Day. | 257 Atlantic Ave. | 401/596–9097 | www.riparks.com/misquamicut.htm | Memorial Day–Labor Day 9–5.

Water Wizz. Just across from Misquamicut Beach you'll hear the screams from the happy sliders at Water Wizz, featuring waterslides—curvey, twisty, and speed slides. | 330 Atlantic Ave. | 401/322–0520 | fax 401/364–8766 | www.visitri.com/waterwizz | $8 | Memorial Day–June 15, weekends 10–10; June 15–Labor Day, daily 10–6.

Wilcox Park. Eighteen glorious acres include specimen trees, shrubs, and perennial gardens. A Dwarf Conifer Garden illustrates creative use of small plots. A Garden of the Senses features plants with taste, texture or fragrance with labels in braille and raised letters. The lily pond hosts abundant waterfowl, exotic koi, and goldfish and doubles as a skating rink in winter. | 44 Broad St. | 401/596–2877 | fax 401/596–5600 | Free | Daily dawn–9.

ON THE CALENDAR

JULY–AUG.: *Shakespeare in the Park.* Evening productions of various plays by William Shakespeare take place at Wilcox Park. | 44 Broad St. | 401/596–0810.

SEPT.: *Rhythm and Roots Festival.* Cajun, zydeco, and bluegrass music headline this three-day festival of music, dance, and food at Stepping Stone Ranch on Labor Day weekend. | Escoheag Hill Rd., West Greenwich | 401/351–6312 or 888/855–6940.

Dining

Mary's Gourmet Italian. Italian. Eighty-year old Mary Aiello is still cooking southern Italian specialties at this family-owned restaurant. The English tudor–style building houses a greenhouse bar and lounge and three dining rooms, one with a central fireplace. Trees and ceilings sparkle with tiny lights; linens, flowers, and Tiffany-style lamps adorn the dining rooms. The menu includes veal and peppers, lasagna, and rack of lamb. Pizza is served in the greenhouse. Kid's menu. | 336 Post Rd. (U.S. 1) | 401/322–0444 | fax 401/322–3010 | Closed Mon.–Tues. No lunch Sun.–Wed. | $12–$25 | AE, MC, V.

Paddy's. Seafood. Eat inside or out at this fun spot on Misquamicut Beach. Shore dinners, pasta dishes and a great kid's menu make this a fine family place. Frozen drinks come with souvenir mugs. The mussels arrive in a sand pail. | 159 Atlantic Ave. | 401/596–2610 | fax 401/596–3323 | www.paddysrestaurant.com | Closed Oct.–Apr. | $8–$24 | AE, D, MC, V.

Shelter Harbor Inn. American. In the Westerly community of Shelter Harbor, a farmhouse built in 1700 is now an inn and restaurant serving traditional colonial fare with some updated surprises. The finnan haddie, haddock smoked on the premises and served in a bechamel sauce with mashed potatoes, competes with hazelnut chicken in a Frangelico and mandarin orange sauce, as featured in *Bon Appetit*. There is outdoor dining on two terraces. | 10 Wagner Rd., off U.S. 1 | 401/322–8883 | fax 401/322–7907 | Breakfast also available | $15–$21 | AE, D, DC, MC, V.

Three Fish. Contemporary. Asian and Mediterranean flavors influence the inventive cuisine at this hip restaurant in a 19th-century brick mill. Don't miss the chowder and try the grilled leg of lamb or the pan-seared sea scallops. | 37 Main St. | 401/348–9700 | Reservations essential | $18–$25 | AE, D, MC, V.

Weekapaug Inn. Contemporary. The open dining room of this charming inn—replete with linens, silver, flowers, and candlelight—has impressive views of the saltwater tidal pond, but it's the food that is the attraction with six to eight nightly specials, like cornbread-stuffed quail, baked sea bass with crispy leeks, or dill-marinated grilled salmon. BYOB.

| Spray Rock Rd. | 401/322–0301 | fax 401/322–1016 | Reservations essential | Jacket required | Breakfast also available. Closed Sept.–June | Prix–fixe $35 | No credit cards.

Lodging

Breezeway. A modern facility three blocks from Misquamicut Beach that has a variety of accommodations: villas with fireplaces and hot tubs, suites, efficiencies, and standard rooms. Bar, picnic area, complimentary Continental breakfast. Some kitchenettes, refrigerators, cable TV. Pool. Playground. Business services. | 70 Winnapaug Rd., Misquamicut | 401/348–8953 or 800/462–8872 | fax 401/596–3207 | www.breezewayresort.com | 52 rooms, 14 suites, 2 villas | $129–$149, $159–$209 suites, $1,740 villas (7–day minimum stay) | AE, D, DC, MC, V.

Cornerstone Inn. A no-frills, two-story motel at the busy Dunn's Corners intersection. It is 15 mi from Foxwoods Casino in Connecticut, 2 mi from Misquamicut Beach, and 4 mi from Westerly. Cable TV, some room phones. No pets. | 326 Post Rd., (U.S. 1) | 401/322–3020 | 24 rooms | $60–$88 | AE, D, MC, V.

Grandview Bed and Breakfast. A relaxed and affordable bed-and-breakfast with front rooms that have views of the ocean. Complimentary Continental breakfast. No room phones, TV in common area. | 212 Shore Rd. | 401/596–6384 or 800/447–6384 | fax 401/596–6384 | www.grandviewbandb.com | 9 rooms (4 with shared bath) | $85–$105 | AE, MC, V.

Pine Lodge. This hotel has a playground and picnic tables, making it a good solution for families in search of modest accommodations close to the shore. It is in a wooded area, hidden from the road. Kitchenettes, refrigerators. | 92 Old Post Rd. | 401/322–0333 or 800/838–0333 | fax 401/322–2010 | 11 rooms; 19 cottages | $90–$105, $120–$150 cottages | AE, D, DC, MC, V.

Sand Dollar Inn. This 1960s motel set well back from the highway on nearly 6 wooded acres is a favorite for families. The common room has books and board games. The rooms have wall-to-wall carpeting and standard furnishings. It's 2 mi from the beach and 4 mi southeast of downtown Westerly. Complimentary Continental breakfast. Some in-room data ports, some kitchenettes, some refrigerators, some microwaves. Laundry service. No pets. | 171 Post Rd., (U.S. 1) | 401/322–2000 or 800/910–SAND | fax 401/322–1590 | www.visitri.com/sanddollarinn | 32 rooms in 2 buildings (27 with shower only); 1 cottage | $115 | Closed Jan.–Feb. | AE, D, MC, V.

Shelter Harbor Inn. This gracious inn is about 5 mi from downtown in a quiet, rural area. The rooms are furnished with Victorian antiques and reproductions. Many also have fireplaces and decks. Restaurant, bar, picnic area, complimentary breakfast. Cable TV. Playground. Business services. | 10 Wagner Rd. | 401/322–8883 or 800/468–8883 | fax 401/322–7907 | 24 rooms (3 with shower only) | $116–$162 | AE, D, DC, MC, V.

The Villa. This Italian-style villa has a beautiful garden and is ideal for a romantic getaway. Some rooms have whirlpools and fireplaces. Picnic area, complimentary Continental breakfast. Refrigerators, some room phones, some in-room hot tubs, cable TV. Pool. Hot tub. Business services. Some pets allowed. No smoking. | 190 Shore Rd., at Rte. 1 A | 401/596–1054 or 800/722–9240 | fax 401/596–6268 | www.thevillaatwesterly.com | 6 suites | $130–$245 | AE, MC, V.

★ **Weekapaug Inn.** In the Westerly beach community of Weekapaug, this family-owned inn has been run by the Buffums since 1899, although the inn itself was completely rebuilt after the hurricane of 1938. Children's programs morning and evening, tennis, a private protected barrier beach with bath house, chairs, umbrellas and towels, bicycles, sailboats, canoes and kayaks, croquet, lawn bowling, and evening activities make this a favorite for every age. Restaurant. No air-conditioning, no room phones, TV in common area. Laundry service. No pets. No smoking. | Spray Rock Rd. | 401/322–0301 | fax 401/322–1016 | www.weeka-pauginn.com | 55 rooms (10 with shared bath) | $390 | Sept.–June | AP | No credit cards.

Winnapaug Inn. A three-story motor inn overlooking the Winnapaug Golf Course and pond and just over 1 mi from the beach. Many rooms have private balconies overlooking the golf course. Restaurant, complimentary Continental breakfast. Refrigerators, some microwaves, some in-room hot tubs, cable TV. Pool. Video games. Playground. | 169 Shore Rd. | 401/348–

8350 or 800/288–9906 | fax 401/596–8654 | www.winnapauginn.com | 51 rooms, 4 suites, 3 villas | $129–$149, $209–$239 | AE, D, DC, MC, V.

WOONSOCKET

(Nearby towns also listed: Cumberland, Glocester, Lincoln)

Settled in the late 17th century, Woonsocket was home to a sawmill and Quaker farmers for its first 100 years. A steep hill on the northern end of the city looks down on the Blackstone River, which makes a dozen turns in its 5-mi course through the city. The river's rapid flow spawned textile mills that made Woonsocket a thriving community in the 19th and early 20th centuries. Manufacturing plants remain the city's leading employers.

Information: **Northern Rhode Island Chamber of Commerce** | 6 Blackstone Valley Pl., Suite 105, Lincoln, 02865 | 401/334–1000 | general@nrichamber.com | www.nrichamber.com.

Attractions

Museum of Work and Culture. Multimedia and traditional exhibits at this new museum examine the lives of French Canadian immigrants during the Industrial Revolution. There are descriptions of the genesis of the textile workers' union and the events that led up to the National Textile Strike of 1934. A model of a triple decker (a three-family tenement building) demonstrates the practicality behind what was once the region's preeminent style of home. | 42 S. Main St. | 401/769–9675 | $5 | Weekdays 9:30–4, Sat. 10–5, Sun. 1–5.

Wright's Dairy Farm. This Rhode Island classic is 1½ mi over the city line, in North Smithfield. It is both a dairy farm with a bakery and a store. The pastries, pies, and dairy products here are delicious and fairly priced, making this a great lunchtime destination. Free tours of the dairy are also offered. | 200 Woonsocket Hill Rd., North Smithfield | 401/767–3014 | Mon.–Sat. 8–7, Sun. 8–4.

ON THE CALENDAR
OCT.: *Autumn Fest.* Held on Columbus Day weekend, you'll find international food booths, craft vendors, and entertainment at the WWII Veteran's Memorial Park. On Monday there's a big parade with marchers from throughout North America. | 401/767–9203.

Dining

Wright's Farm Restaurant. American. This huge, country restaurant serves family-style chicken, all you can eat, including fries, pasta, salad and dinner rolls for $8 per person, with steak available at a higher price. | 84 Inman Rd., Burrillville | 401/769–2856 | www.wrights-farm.com | Closed Mon.–Wed. No lunch weekdays | $8–$18 | No credit cards.

Ye Olde English Fish and Chips. Seafood. Sure you can get chicken or fried shrimp, or even fish cakes, but the fish-and-chips are what everyone comes here for. The kitchen uses a ton of fish and 2 tons of potatoes each week. The fish-and-chips are traditional English-style, with a light, crispy batter. This family-owned (since 1922) downtown place offers friendly service. | 25 S. Main St., at Market Sq. | 401/762–3637 | fax 401/762–1185 | Closed Sun.–Mon. | $5–$7 | MC, V.

Lodging

The Pillsbury House. This majestic 1875 Victorian home is in a north end neighborhood of stately homes, with period furnishings, a fireplaced parlor, and rockers on the front porch. Complimentary breakfast. No room phones, TV in common area. No pets. No kids under 12. No smoking. | 341 Prospect St. | 401/766–7983 or 800/205–4112 | fax 401/763–0442 | www.pillsburyhouse.com | 3 rooms (2 with shower only) | $75–$115 | AE, MC, V.

Index

Farmington Inn (Farmington, CT), 42

Farmington Marriott (Farmington, CT), 42

Farmington River Tubing (Avon, CT), 16

Farmington Valley Arts Center (Avon, CT), 16

Fazio's Trattoria (Hyannis [Cape Cod], MA), 295

Feast of Chilmark (Chilmark [Martha's Vineyard], MA), 232

Federal Hill (Providence, RI), 503

Federal House Inn (Lee, MA), 303

The Federalist (Boston, MA), 193

Felix Neck Wildlife Sanctuary (Edgartown [Martha's Vineyard], MA), 254

Fenway (Boston, MA), 171

Ferry from New London to Block Island, Rhode Island (New London, CT), 83

Ferry from New London to Fishers Island, New York (New London, CT), 83

Ferry from New London to Orient Point, New York (New London, CT), 83

Ferry Service to and from Block Island (Block Island, RI), 461

Ferry to Port Jefferson, L.I. (Bridgeport, CT), 22

Fiddlers (Chester, CT), 27

Field Farm Guest House (Williamstown, MA), 430

Field Gallery (West Tisbury [Martha's Vineyard], MA), 424

Fife 'N Drum Restaurant and Inn (Kent, CT), 58

Fifteen Beacon (Boston, MA), 200

51 Park Street (Lee, MA), 302

Figaro's (Enfield, CT), 37

Figs (Wellesley, MA), 419

Filippo Ristorante (Boston, MA), 191

Financial District (Boston, MA), 171

Fine Arts Center (Amherst, MA), 154

Finely JP's (Wellfleet [Cape Cod], MA), 421

Finian's Pub (Dedham, MA), 241

Finn's (Block Island, RI), 463

Fire Hose-Cart House (Nantucket, MA), 326

Fire Museum (Manchester, CT), 66

Firemen's Museum (Warren, RI), 514

Fireside B&B of Lexington (Lexington, MA), 313

First and Last Tavern (Hartford, CT), 54

First and Last Tavern (Middletown, CT), 69

First Baptist Church in America (Providence, RI), 507

First Church of Christ, Scientist (Boston, MA), 181

First Congregational Church (Nantucket, MA), 325

First Congregational Church (Wellfleet [Cape Cod], MA), 420

First Presbyterian Church (Stamford, CT), 109

First Unitarian Church of America (Providence, RI), 507

The Fisherman (Gloucester, MA), 274

Fish Monger's Café (Woods Hole [Cape Cod], MA), 432

Fish Pier (Chatham [Cape Cod], MA), 225

Fishing on Block Island (Block Island, RI), 462

Five Seasons (Brookline, MA), 212

Flanders Nature Center/Land Trust (Woodbury, CT), 126

Flatbread (Amesbury, MA), 152

Fleet Skating Center (Providence, RI), 507

Flo's Drive-In (Portsmouth, RI), 501

Flood Tide (Mystic, CT), 73

Florence Griswold Museum (Old Lyme, CT), 96

The Flume (Mashpee [Cape Cod], MA), 322

Flying Bridge (Falmouth [Cape Cod], MA), 266

Flying Fish Café (Wellfleet [Cape Cod], MA), 421

Flying Horse Carousel (Watch Hill, RI), 517

Flying Horses Carousel (Oak Bluffs [Martha's Vineyard], MA), 350

Fogg Art Museum (Cambridge, MA), 217

Fogland Beach (Tiverton, RI), 512

Forbes Library (Northampton, MA), 346

Forest Park (Springfield, MA), 395, 396

Fort Adams State Park (Newport, RI), 486

Fort Barton (Tiverton, RI), 513

Fort Griswold Battlefield State Park (Groton, CT), 46

Fort Phoenix State Reservation (New Bedford, MA), 336

Fort Saybrook Monument Park (Old Saybrook, CT), 97

Fort Wetherill State Park (Jamestown, RI), 476

Foulger-Franklin Memorial Fountain, Boulder, and Bench (Nantucket, MA), 326

Founder's Brook Motel (Portsmouth, RI), 502

Four Acres Motel (Williamstown, MA), 430

Four Chimneys Inn (Dennis [Cape Cod], MA), 247

400 East (Harwich [Cape Cod], MA), 287

Four Points Barcelo Hotel (Burlington, MA), 214

Four Points by Sheraton (Norwalk, CT), 93

Four Points Hotel (Leominster, MA), 311

Four Points Sheraton (Hyannis [Cape Cod], MA), 297

Four Points Sheraton (Waltham, MA), 417

Four Points Sheraton Hotel and Conference Center (Sharon, MA), 390

Four Points Sheraton-National Seashore (Eastham [Cape Cod], MA), 252

Four Seasons B&B (Newton, MA), 344

Four Seasons Hotel Boston (Boston, MA), 200

Fox Hunt Farms Gourmet and Café (Woodstock, CT), 128

Fox Navigation (Vineyard Haven [Martha's Vineyard], MA), 413

Fox Point (Providence, RI), 503

Foxglove Cottage (Plymouth, MA), 364

Foxwoods Resort Casino (Ledyard, CT), 61

Frances Fleet (Galilee, RI), 473

Francesco's Italian Restaurant (Brimfield, MA), 210

Francis Malbone House (Newport, RI), 495

Frank Pepe's Pizzeria (New Haven, CT), 81

Franklin Park Zoo (Boston, MA), 183

Fred Benson Town Beach (Block Island, RI), 462

Frederick Law Olmsted National Historic Site (Brookline, MA), 212

Freedom Cruise Line (Nantucket, MA), 323

Freeman Farm B&B (Glocester, RI), 475

Freestone's (New Bedford, MA), 339

French Cable Station Museum (Orleans [Cape Cod], MA), 352

Friends Meeting House (Lincoln, RI), 479

Friendship Valley Inn (Brooklyn, CT), 25

The Frog and the Peach (Avon, CT), 18

Frog Hollow (Hartford, CT), 49

Front Street (Provincetown [Cape Cod], MA), 368

Fruitlands Museum (Leominster, MA), 311

Fuller Museum of Art (Brockton, MA), 211

Fulling Mill Brook (Chilmark [Martha's Vineyard], MA), 232

Funway Café (Foxborough, MA), 270

G.W. Tavern (Washington, CT), 116

Gables Inn (Block Island, RI), 464

Gables Inn (Lenox, MA), 308

Gail's Tours, Inc. (Nantucket, MA), 325

Gannon Golf Course (Lynn, MA), 317

Garde Arts Center (New London, CT), 83

Garden Gables (Lenox, MA), 309

Garden in the Woods (Framingham, MA), 271

Gardner Heritage State Park (Gardner, MA), 272

Gardner-Pingree House (Salem, MA), 379

Gargoyles on the Square (Somerville, MA), 392

The Garlands (Dennis [Cape Cod], MA), 247

Garrison Inn (New Bedford, MA), 342

Gaslight Motel (Dennis [Cape Cod], MA), 247

The Gatehouse (Providence, RI), 510

Gateways Inn (Lenox, MA), 306

Gateways Inn and Restaurant (Lenox, MA), 309

Gelston House (East Haddam, CT), 36

General Hart House (Old Saybrook, CT), 98

General Stanton Inn (Charlestown, RI), 470

George Fuller House (Essex, MA), 261

Notes

Notes

TALK TO US

Fill out this quick survey and receive a free *Fodor's How to Pack* (while supplies last)

1 Which Road Guide did you purchase?
(Check all that apply.)
- ❏ AL/AR/LA/MS/TN
- ❏ AZ/CO/NM
- ❏ CA
- ❏ CT/MA/RI
- ❏ DE/DC/MD/PA/VA
- ❏ FL
- ❏ GA/NC/SC
- ❏ ID/MT/NV/UT/WY
- ❏ IL/IA/MO/WI
- ❏ IN/KY/MI/OH/WV
- ❏ KS/OK/TX
- ❏ ME/NH/VT
- ❏ MN/NE/ND/SD
- ❏ NJ/NY
- ❏ OR/WA

2 How did you learn about the Road Guides?
- ❏ TV ad
- ❏ Radio ad
- ❏ Newspaper or magazine ad
- ❏ Newspaper or magazine article
- ❏ TV or radio feature
- ❏ Bookstore display/clerk recommendation
- ❏ Recommended by family/friend
- ❏ Other:_____

3 Did you use other guides for your trip?
- ❏ AAA
- ❏ Compass American Guide
- ❏ Fodor's
- ❏ Frommer's
- ❏ Insiders' Guide
- ❏ Mobil
- ❏ Moon Handbook
- ❏ Other:_____

4 Did you use any of the following for planning?
- ❏ Tourism offices ❏ Internet ❏ Travel agent

5 Did you buy a Road Guide for (check one):
- ❏ Leisure trip
- ❏ Business trip
- ❏ Mix of business and leisure

6 Where did you buy your Road Guide?
- ❏ Bookstore
- ❏ Other store
- ❏ On-line
- ❏ Borrowed from a friend
- ❏ Borrowed from a library
- ❏ Other:_____

7 Why did you buy a Road Guide? (Check all that apply.)
- ❏ Number of cities/towns listed
- ❏ Comprehensive coverage
- ❏ Number of lodgings ❏ Driving tours
- ❏ Number of restaurants ❏ Maps
- ❏ Number of attractions ❏ Fodor's brand name
- ❏ Other:_____

8 Did you use this guide primarily:
- ❏ For pretrip planning   ❏ While traveling
- ❏ For planning and while traveling

9 What was the duration of your trip?
- ❏ 2-3 days   ❏ 11 or more days
- ❏ 4-6 days   ❏ Taking more than 1 trip
- ❏ 7-10 days

10 Did you use the guide to select
- ❏ Hotels   ❏ Restaurants

11 Did you stay primarily in a
- ❏ Hotel   ❏ Hostel
- ❏ Motel   ❏ Campground
- ❏ Resort   ❏ Dude ranch
- ❏ Bed-and-breakfast ❏ With family or friends
- ❏ RV/camper   ❏ Other:_____

12 What sights and activities did you most enjoy?
- ❏ Historical sights ❏ Shopping
- ❏ Sports   ❏ Theaters
- ❏ National parks ❏ Museums
- ❏ State parks   ❏ Major cities
- ❏ Attractions off the beaten path

13 How much did you spend per adult for this trip?
- ❏ Less than $500   ❏ $751-$1,000
- ❏ $501-$750   ❏ More than $1,000

14 How many traveled in your party?
___ Adults   ___ Children   ___ Pets

15 Did you
- ❏ Fly to destination   ❏ Rent a van or RV
- ❏ Drive your own vehicle ❏ Take a train
- ❏ Rent a car   ❏ Take a bus

16 How many miles did you travel round-trip?
- ❏ Less than 100   ❏ 501-750
- ❏ 101-300   ❏ 751-1,000
- ❏ 301-500   ❏ More than 1,000

17 What items did you take on your vacation?
- ❏ Traveler's checks ❏ Digital camera
- ❏ Credit card   ❏ Cell phone
- ❏ Gasoline card   ❏ Computer
- ❏ Phone card   ❏ PDA
- ❏ Camera   ❏ Other

18 Would you use Fodor's Road Guides again?
- ❏ Yes   ❏ No

19 How would you like to see Road Guides changed?
- ❏ More ❏ Less Dining
- ❏ More ❏ Less Lodging
- ❏ More ❏ Less Sports
- ❏ More ❏ Less Activities
- ❏ More ❏ Less Attractions
- ❏ More ❏ Less Shopping
- ❏ More ❏ Less Driving tours
- ❏ More ❏ Less Maps
- ❏ More ❏ Less Historical information
- ❏ Other:_____

20 Tell us about yourself.

❏ Male   ❏ Female

Age:
- ❏ 18-24   ❏ 35-44   ❏ 55-64
- ❏ 25-34   ❏ 45-54   ❏ Over 65

Income:
- ❏ Less than $25,000   ❏ $50,001-$75,000
- ❏ $25,001-$50,000   ❏ More than $75,000

Name:_____   E-mail: _____

Address:_____ City: _____ State: _____ Zip: _____

Fodor's Travel Publications
Attn: Road Guide Survey
280 Park Avenue
New York, NY 10017

The information herein will be treated in confidence. Names and addresses will not be released to mailing-list houses or other organizations.

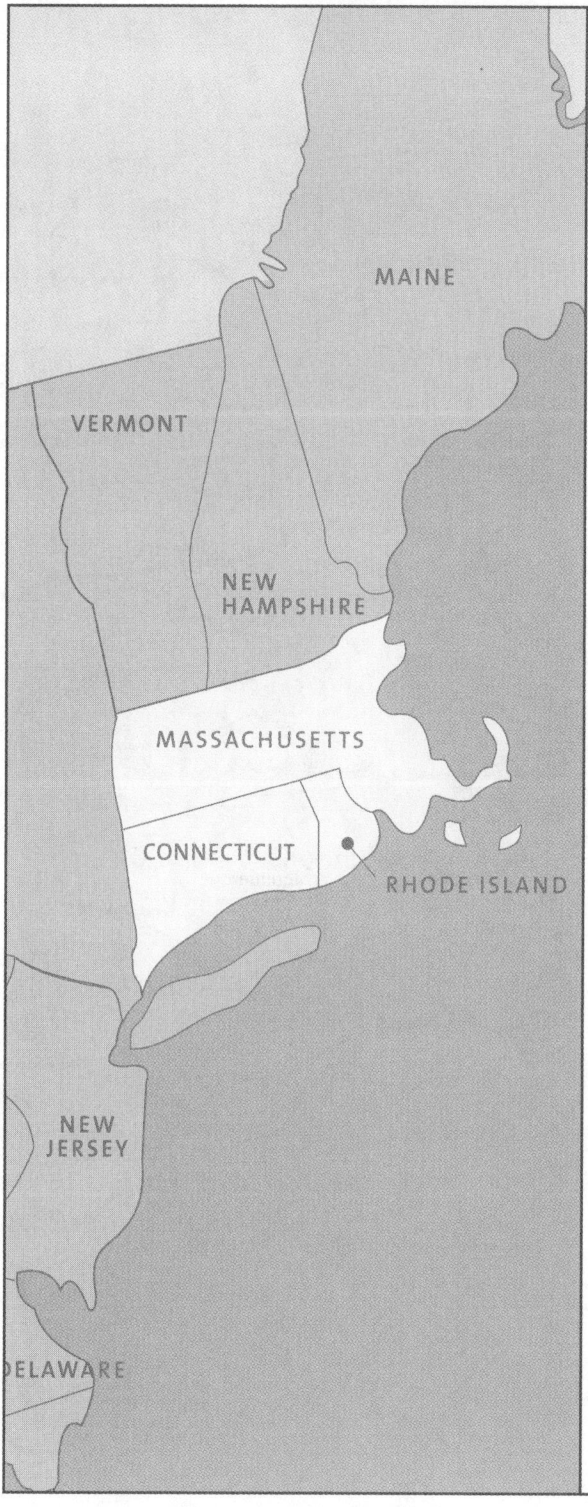
MAINE
VERMONT
NEW HAMPSHIRE
MASSACHUSETTS
CONNECTICUT
RHODE ISLAND
NEW JERSEY
ELAWARE

Atlas

MAP #

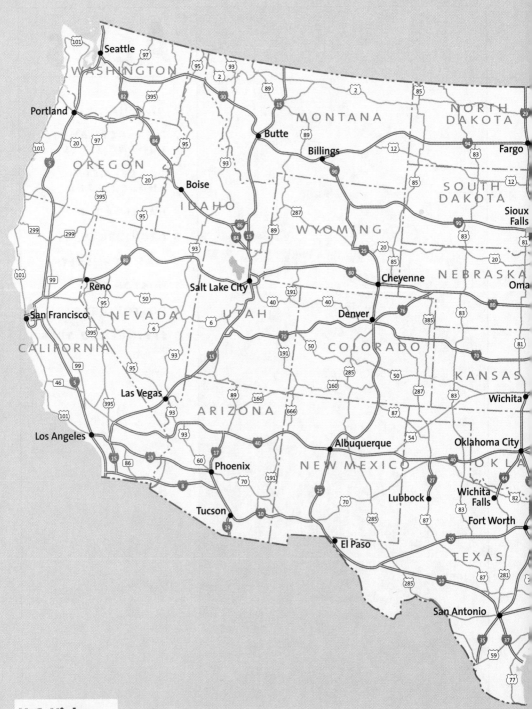

U. S. Highways

Copyright ©2001 by Maps.com and Fodors LLC

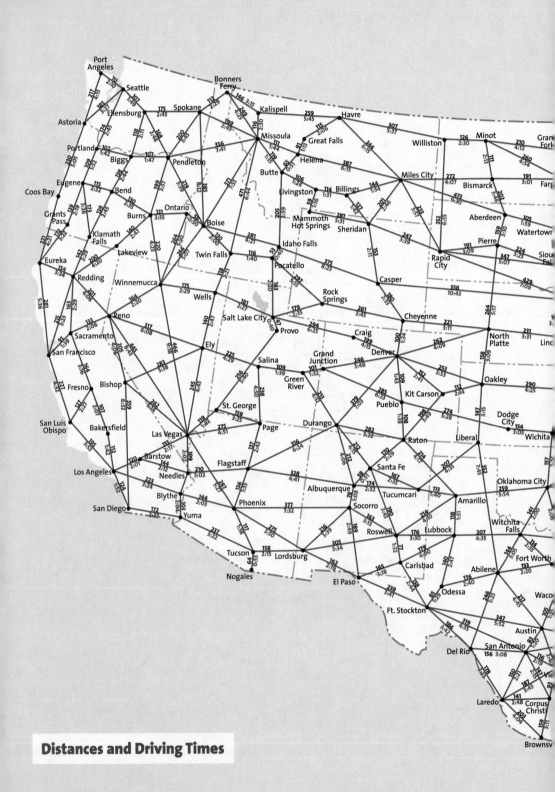

Distances and Driving Times

Copyright ©2001 by Maps.com and Fodors LLC

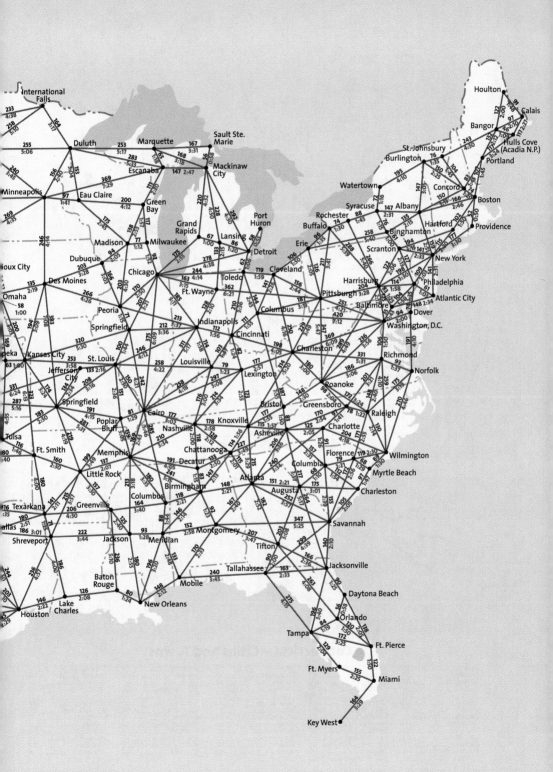

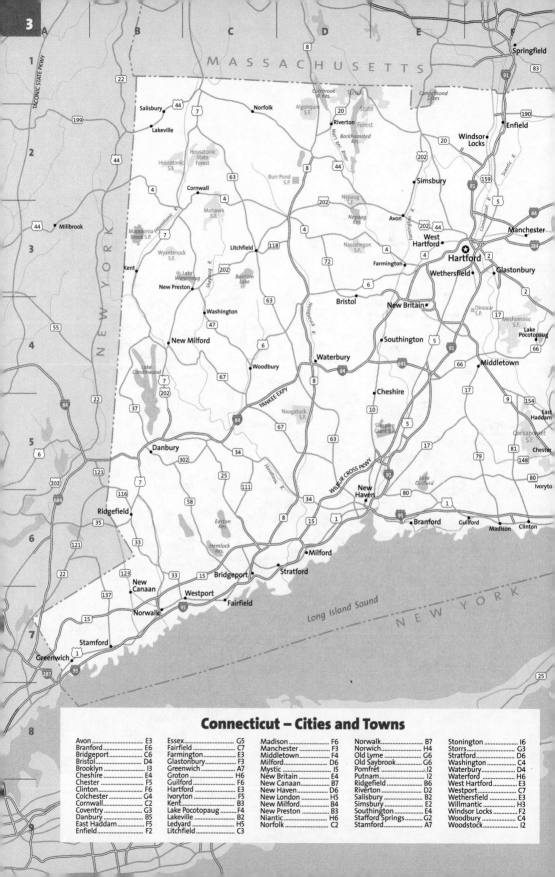

Connecticut – Cities and Towns

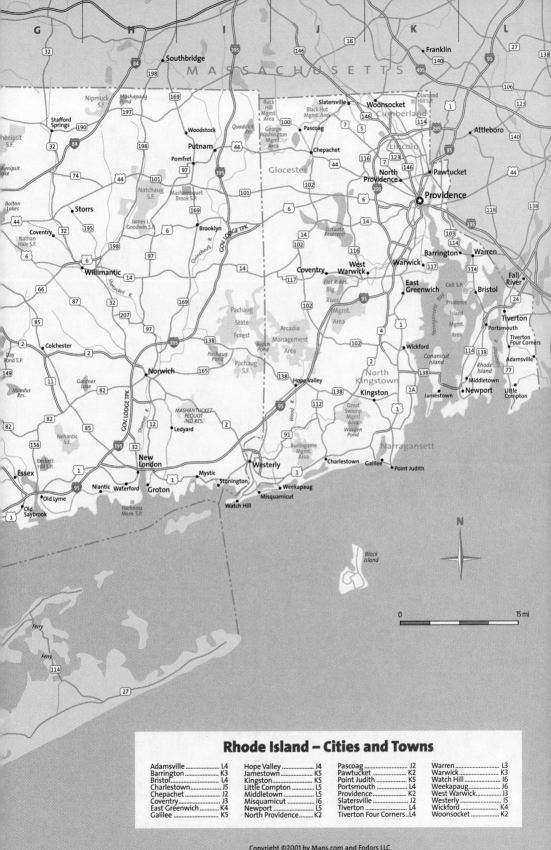

Rhode Island – Cities and Towns

Adamsville L4	Hope Valley J4	Pascoag J2	Warren L3
Barrington K3	Jamestown K5	Pawtucket K2	Warwick K3
Bristol L4	Kingston K5	Point Judith K5	Watch Hill I6
Charlestown J5	Little Compton L5	Portsmouth L4	Weekapaug J6
Chepachet J2	Middletown L5	Providence K2	West Warwick J3
Coventry J3	Misquamicut I6	Slatersville J2	Westerly I5
East Greenwich K4	Newport L5	Tiverton L4	Wickford K4
Galilee K5	North Providence K2	Tiverton Four Corners..L4	Woonsocket K2

Copyright ©2001 by Maps.com and Fodors LLC

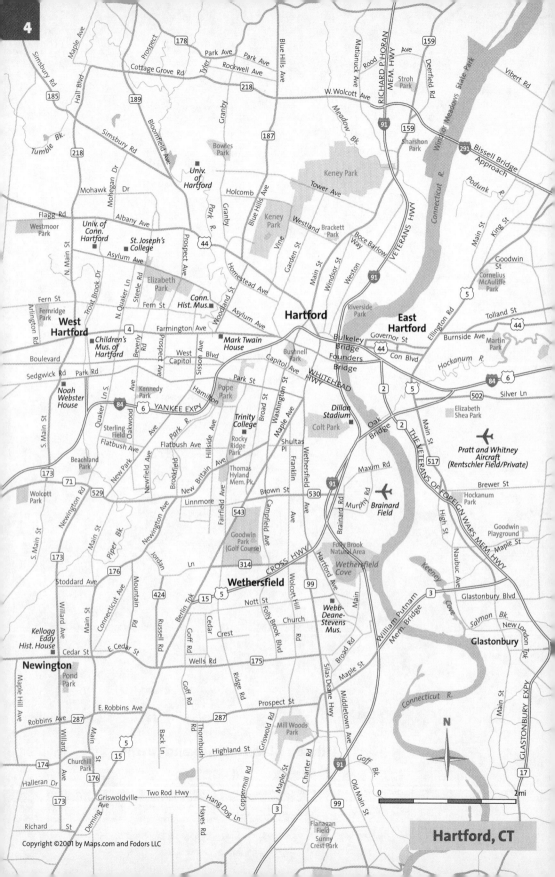

Hartford, CT

Copyright ©2001 by Maps.com and Fodors LLC

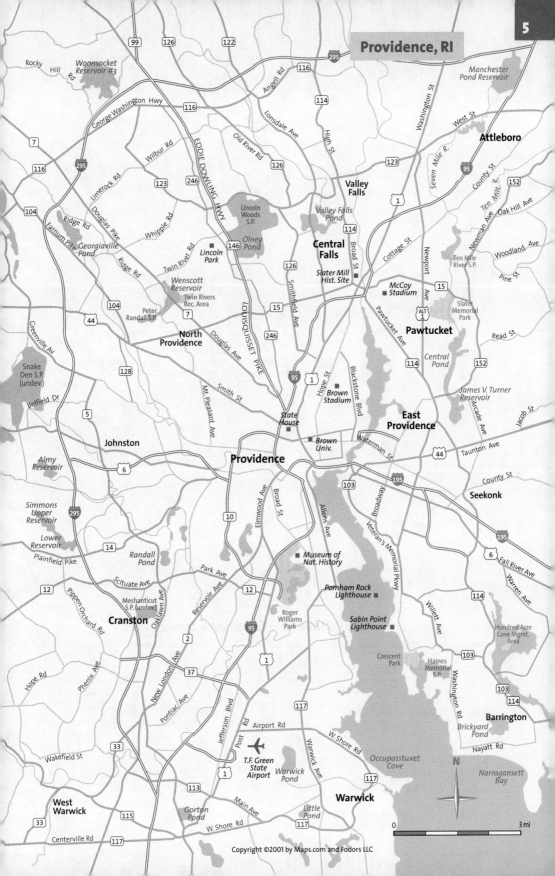

Providence, RI

99 126 122

295

Rocky Hill Rd

Woonsocket Reservoir #3

Angell Rd

116

116

Manchester Pond Reservoir

7

George Washington Hwy

EDDIE DOWLING HWY

116

Lonsdale Ave

Washington St

West St

Attleboro

116

295

Wilbur Rd

Old River Rd

High St

123

Seven Mile R.

95

152

7

116

123

246

Limerock Rd

126

Valley Falls

1

County St

Ten Mile R.

Oak Hill Ave

104

Douglas Pike

Whipple Rd

Lincoln Woods S.P.

Valley Falls Pond

114

Cottage St

Newport Ave

Ten Mile River S.P.

Woodland Ave

Pine St

Ridge Rd

Farnum Pike

Georgiaville Pond

146

Olney Pond

Central Falls

Broad St

McCoy Stadium

15

Slater Memorial Park

Twin River Rd

Lincoln Park

126

Slater Mill Hist. Site

ALT

Read St

Ridge Rd

Wenscott Reservoir

15

Pawtucket Ave

Pawtucket

104

Twin Rivers Rec. Area

7

Smithfield Ave

114

Central Pond

152

44

Peter Randall S.P.

246

LOUISQUISSET PIKE

Douglas Ave

James V. Turner Reservoir

Arcade Ave

Jacob St

North Providence

Smith St

95

1

Hope St

Blackstone Blvd

East Providence

128

Greenville Av

Mt. pleasant Ave

Brown Stadium

44

5

Snake Den S.P. (undev.)

State House

Brown Univ.

Waterman St

Taunton Ave

Belfield Dr

Johnston

6

103

195

County St

Almy Reservoir

Broadway

Veteran's Memorial Pkwy

Seekonk

Simmons Upper Reservoir

295

Elmwood Ave

Broad St

Allens Ave

195

6

Fall River Ave

Lower Reservoir

14

Randall Pond

Museum of Nat. History

Warren Ave

Plainfield Pike

Park Ave

10

Pomham Rock Lighthouse

114

12

Scituate Ave

12

Reservoir Ave

Roger Williams Park

Sabin Point Lighthouse

Willett Ave

Hundred Acre Cove Mgmt. Area

12

Pippin Orchard Rd

Meshanticut S.P. (undev)

Oaklawn Ave

95

Crescent Park

Haines Memorial S.P.

103

Cranston

2

Washington Rd

114

Hope Rd

Phenix Ave

New London Ave

37

Pontiac Ave

1

117

Barrington

33

Jefferson Blvd

Post Rd

Airport Rd

W. Shore Rd

Brickyard Pond

103

Nayatt Rd

Wakefield St

33

1

T.F. Green State Airport

Warwick Pond

Warwick Ave

Occupasstuxet Cove

N

West Warwick

113

Gorton Pond

Main Ave

Little Pond

117

Warwick

Narragansett Bay

33

115

W. Shore Rd

117

117

0   3 mi

Centerville Rd

117

Copyright ©2001 by Maps.com and Fodors LLC

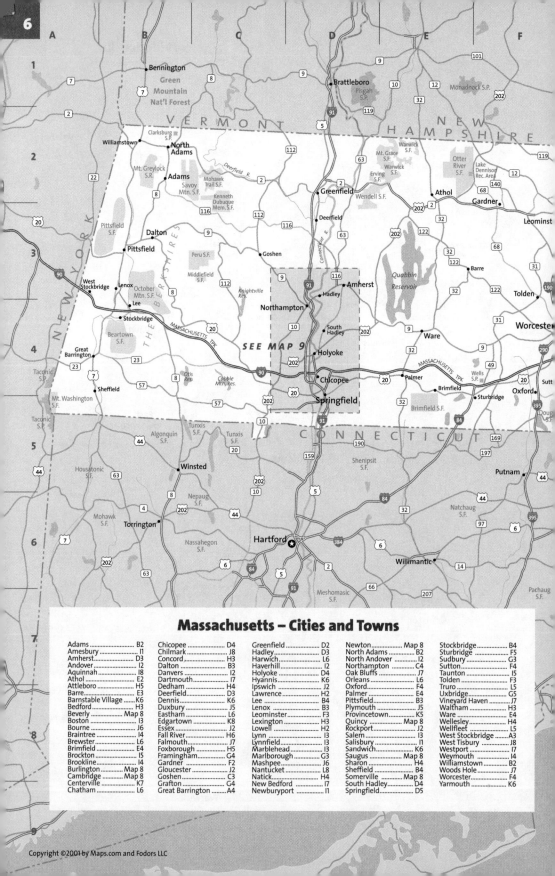

A   B   C   D   E   F

Massachusetts – Cities and Towns

Copyright ©2001 by Maps.com and Fodors LLC

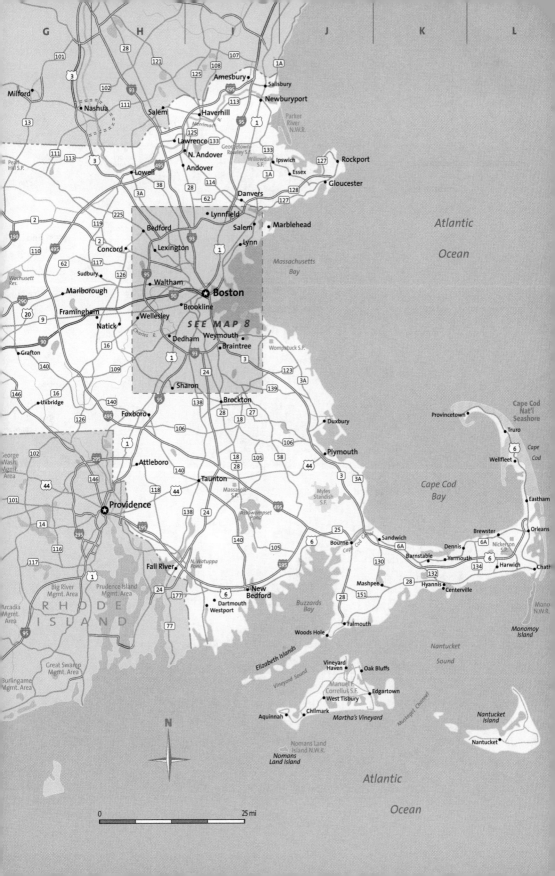

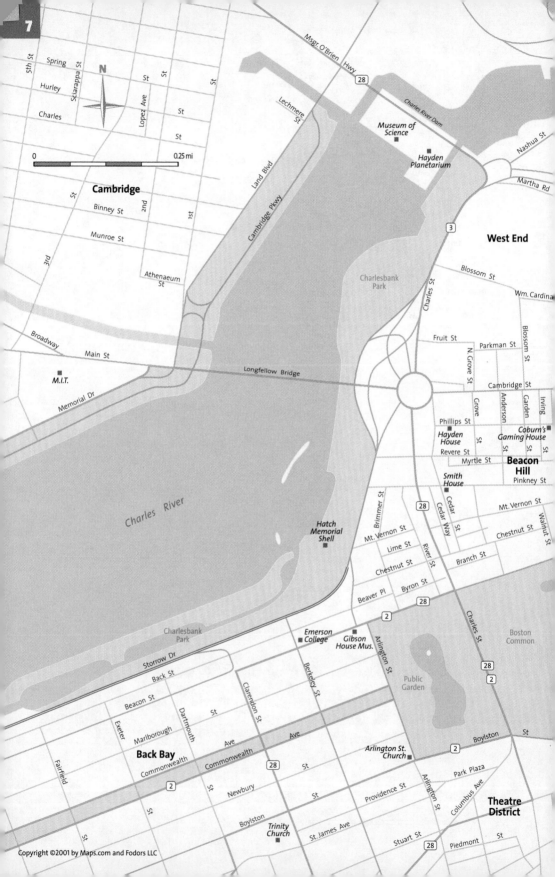

Cambridge

5th St
Spring
Sciarappa St
St
St
St
Hurley
Lopez Ave
St
Charles
St
St

0   0.25 mi

St
Binney St
2nd
1st
St
Munroe St
3rd
Athenaeum St

Broadway
Main St
Memorial Dr

M.I.T.

Msgr. O'Brien Hwy
28
Charles River Dam
Lechmere St
Land Blvd
Cambridge Pkwy

Museum of Science
Hayden Planetarium

Nashua St
Martha Rd

3

West End

Blossom St
Wm. Cardina

Charlesbank Park

Charles St
Fruit St
N. Grove St
Parkman St
Blossom St

Cambridge St

Longfellow Bridge

Phillips St
Grove St
Anderson St
Garden St
Irving St

Coburn's Gaming House

Hayden House
Revere St
Myrtle St

Beacon Hill
Pinkney St

Smith House

Charles River

Brimmer St
28
Cedar St
Cedar Way
Mt. Vernon St

Mt. Vernon St
Lime St
Chestnut St
River St
Branch St
Chestnut St
Walnut St

Hatch Memorial Shell

Chestnut St
Beaver Pl
Byron St
28

2

Charlesbank Park

Storrow Dr
Back St

Emerson College
Gibson House Mus.

Arlington St

Boston Common

Public Garden

28
2

Beacon St
Exeter
Marlborough
Dartmouth
St
Clarendon St
Berkeley St
Ave
Ave
Boylston
St

Fairfield

Back Bay

Commonwealth
Commonwealth
28
St
2
St
Newbury
St
Providence St

Arlington St. Church

2
Boylston

Park Plaza

Arlington St
Columbus Ave

Theatre District

Boylston
Trinity Church
St. James Ave
Stuart St
28
Piedmont
St

Copyright ©2001 by Maps.com and Fodors LLC

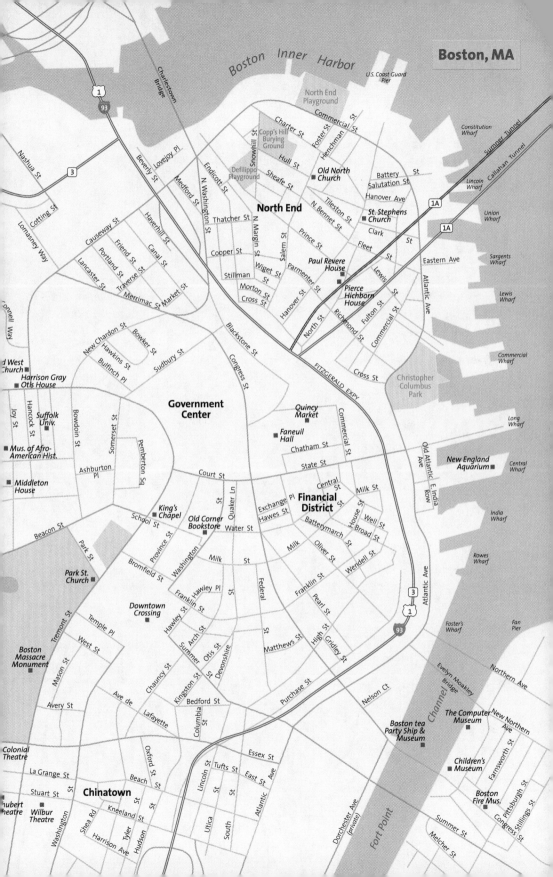

Boston, MA

Boston Inner Harbor

U.S. Coast Guard Pier

Constitution Wharf

North End Playground

Charter St
Commercial St
Foster St
Henchman St
Copp's Hill Burying Ground
Hull St
Sheafe St
Snowhill St
Defilippo Playground
Old North Church
Battery St
Salutation St
Hanover Ave
Lincoln Wharf
Sumner Tunnel
Callahan Tunnel

Charlestown Bridge

Nashua St

Beverly St
Lovejoy Pl
Endicott St
N. Washington St
Medford St
Haverhill St
Thatcher St
N. Margin St
Cooper St
Salem St
Prince St
N. Bennet St
Tileston St
North End
St. Stephens Church
Clark St
Fleet St
1A
Union Wharf
Sargents Wharf

Cotting St
Causeway St
Friend St
Portland St
Canal St
Traverse St
Wiget St
Stillman St
Parmenter St
Morton St
Cross St
Hanover St
Paul Revere House
Pierce Hichborn House
Lewis St
Richmond St
Fulton St
Commercial St
Eastern Ave
Atlantic Ave
Lewis Wharf

Lomasney Way
Lancaster St
Merrimac St
Market St
Blackstone St
North St
Cross St
Commercial Wharf

O'Connell Way

New Chardon St
Hawkins St
Bowker St
Sudbury St
Bulfinch Pl
Congress St
FITZGERALD EXPY
Christopher Columbus Park
Long Wharf

West Church
Harrison Gray Otis House
Government Center
Quincy Market
Faneuil Hall
Chatham St
Commercial St
Old Atlantic Ave
New England Aquarium
Central Wharf

Joy St
Hancock St
Suffolk Univ.
Bowdoin St
Somerset St
Pemberton Sq
State St
India Wharf

Mus. of Afro-American Hist.
Ashburton Pl
Court St
Central St
Milk St
Old Atlantic E. India Row

Middleton House
Quaker Ln
Exchange Pl
Financial District
House St
Well St
Broad St
Rowes Wharf

King's Chapel
Old Corner Bookstore
Water St
Hawes St
Batterymarch St
Oliver St
Wendell St

School St
Province St
Washington St
Milk St
Milk St
Franklin St
Pearl St
Atlantic Ave

Beacon St
Bromfield St
Hawley Pl
Federal St
Franklin St
High St
Gridley St
3
1
93
Foster's Wharf
Fan Pier

Park St
Park St. Church
Franklin St
Hawley St
Arch St

Tremont St
Temple Pl
Downtown Crossing
Summer St
Otis St
Matthews St
Devonshire St

West St
Mason St
Chauncy St
Kingston St
Purchase St
Nelson Ct
Evelyn Moakley Bridge
Northern Ave

Boston Massacre Monument
Avery St
Ave de Lafayette
Bedford St
Columbia St
The Computer Museum
New Northern Ave

Colonial Theatre
Oxford St
Essex St
Boston tea Party Ship & Museum
Children's Museum
Farnsworth St
Stillings St

La Grange St
Beach St
Lincoln St
Tufts St
East St
Atlantic Ave
Boston Fire Mus.
Pittsburgh St
Congress St

Stuart St
Chinatown
Kneeland St
Utica St
South St
Dorchester Ave (private)
Fort Point
Channel
Summer St
Melcher St

Shubert Theatre
Wilbur Theatre
Washington St
Shea Rd
Harrison Ave
Tyler St
Hudson St

Boston Area

Copyright ©2001 by Maps.com and Fodors LLC

Hull

Hull Nat'l Rec. Area
Hull Lifesaving Mus.

Islands

Ft. Warren

Point Allerton
Nantasket Ave
Worlds End
Hingham Harbor

Georges Island
Long Island
Peddocks Island
Bumpkin Island
Grape Island
Moon Island
State Island

Hingham Bay

Quincy Bay

Hingham

Old Ship Church

Union St
Main St

Lincoln St
Beal St

Bare Cove Park

High St

S. Pleasant St
Wompatuck State Park

Pond St

Hingham St

Webster St

Hanover St

Rockland

3 mi

0

Union St

123

139

58

Weymouth

Abington

Brockton

Ames-Nowell State Park

Cleveland Pond

Great Pond

Adams St

Randolph St

Groveland St

Quincy St

D.W. Field Park

Waldo Lake

Brockton Res.

Harrison Blvd

Page St

Turnpike

Stoughton

Randolph

Holbrook

Ponkapoag Pond

Reservoir Pond

Marsapoag Lake

Quincy

Milton

Dedham

Needham

Wellesley

Newton

Norwood

Blue Hills Res.

Neponset River

U.S. Naval Shipbuilding Museum
Abigail Adams Birthplace
John Adams Birthplace
Adams N.H.P.
Quincy Quarries Hist. Site
Robert B. Forbes House
Gen. Sylvanus Thayer Birthplace
Braintree
Blue Hills Trailside Mus.
Fairbanks House
Map & Globe Museum

John F. Kennedy Lib. & Mus.
Univ. of Mass. Boston

Wollaston Beach
Quincy Shore Dr

Franklin Park Zoo
Arnold Arboretum
Stony Brook Res.
Turtle Pond Pkwy
Fowl Meadow Res.

93
1
1A
3
24
27
28
37
93
95
109
135
138
139
203
228
3A
53
16
9

Springfield Area